Fundamentals of Computing

THIRD EDITION

Kamaljeet Sanghera

George Mason University

KENDALL/HUNT PUBLISHING COMPANY
4050 Westmark Drive Dubuque, Iowa 52002

ISBN 978-0-7575-8476-3

Printed in the United States of America

10 9 8 7 6 5 4 3

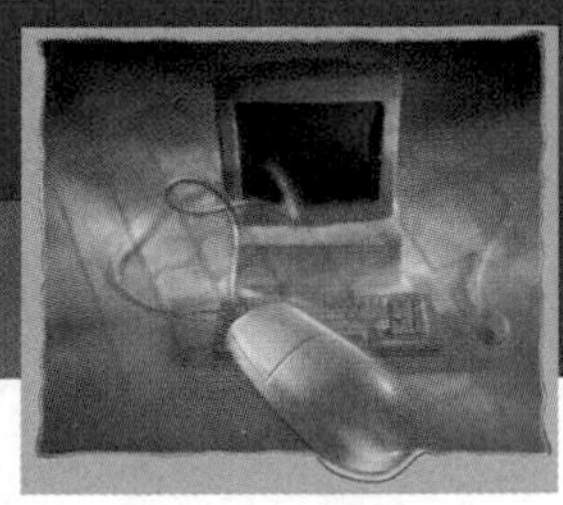

Contents

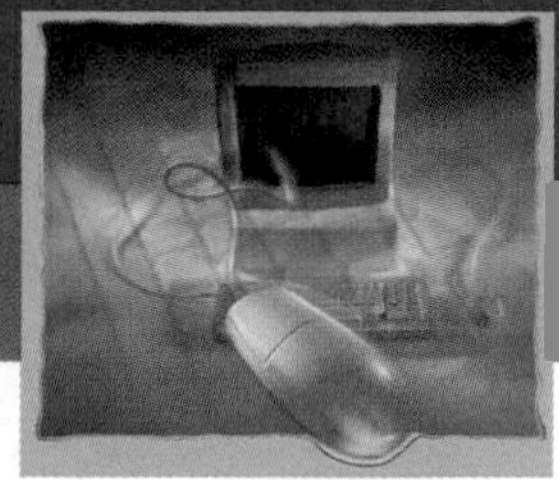

Preface

Welcome to Fundamentals of Computing! This book offers visual, basic to advanced hands-on experiences on Microsoft Operating Systems: Windows Vista, Microsoft Internet Explorer 7, and four applications: Microsoft Word 2007, Microsoft Excel 2007, Microsoft Access 2007, and Microsoft PowerPoint 2007. The chapters are divided into several sections with each section subdivided into several subsections. In each section you will find:

1. A brief introduction to the section concept.
2. Step-by-step "how to" instructions.
3. A hands-on "Let's Try It" exercise which the students perform with the instructor.

Rather than having to sift through blocks of paragraphs of written text, the introductions are brief and easy to understand, illustrated with diagrams, lists, tables and screen shots to aid in comprehension and retention. The step-by-step format of the manual enables for quick scanning during exam preparation time and the ability to pull out the main points quickly without having to filter the desired information from chunks of text.

Course Requirements

This course assumes that the student has a fundamental understanding of the Windows operating system and knows how to maneuver with a keyboard and mouse. It does not require experience with Microsoft Word, Microsoft Excel, Microsoft Access, and Microsoft PowerPoint.

A full installation of Windows Vista, Internet Explorer 7, Microsoft applications 2007—Word, Excel, Access, and PowerPoint should be available on each desktop, with a fresh installation strongly encouraged. In order to try out some of the sections in this book, an active Internet connection is required.

Components of the Manual

This book is written in a tutorial manner. There are ten (10) chapters and an appendix containing some of the new features of Microsoft Word 2007, Microsoft Excel 2007, Microsoft Access 2007, and Microsoft PowerPoint 2007.

Chapter 1—"Introduction to Windows Vista"

Each section of chapter 1 begins with a brief introduction to the section topic and is followed by step-by-step instructions on how the student is to accomplish a particular task. Topics include basics of operating system, opening, closing, minimizing, maximizing, moving, resizing windows, using menus, getting help, working with folders and disks, file and folder management, working with applications, customizing the start menu and desktop, and exploring the control panel.

Chapter 2—"Introduction to Internet Explorer 7"

Chapter 2 begins with a brief introduction to the topic and is followed by step-by-step instructions on how the student is to accomplish a particular task. Topics include basics of Internet Explorer interface, browsing the Web, working with favorites, and customizing Internet Explorer.

Chapter 3—"Microsoft Word 2007—Case Study I"

Chapter 3 introduces students to the basic operations of Microsoft Office Word 2007. The chapter begins with a case study. Students complete the case study by following the steps in "Let's Try It!" exercises. By following steps in these exercises, students will learn how to start, close, save, open Word documents; edit and format text; insert date and time; check spelling and grammar errors; use thesaurus; create columns; create header and footer; set page orientation; insert / modify page numbers; set printer options; and insert watermarks.

Chapter 4—"Microsoft Word 2007—Case Study II"

Chapter 4 introduces students to the intermediate and advanced operations of Microsoft Office Word 2007. The chapter begins with a case study. Students complete the case study by following the steps in "Let's Try It!" exercises. By following steps in these exercises, students will learn how to use existing templates; create and format tables; create and add fields in a form; and use help.

Chapter 5—"Microsoft Excel 2007—Case Study I"

Chapter 5 introduces students to the basic operations of Microsoft Office Excel 2007. The chapter begins with a case study. Students complete the case study by following the steps in "Let's Try It!" exercises. By following steps in these exercises, students will learn how to start, close, save, open Excel documents; edit and format information in cells; enter simple formulas; use Go To commands; insert symbols,; work with ranges; apply cell styles; and spell check the worksheet.

Chapter 6—"Microsoft Excel 2007—Case Study II"

Chapter 6 introduces students to the intermediate and advanced operations of Microsoft Office Excel 2007. The chapter begins with a case study. Students complete the case study by following the steps in "Let's Try It!" exercises. By following steps in these exercises, students will learn how to use relative, absolute, and mixed references; use functions; add clipart; copy, rename, group, add, and delete worksheets; use 3-D formulas and references; use the IF and nested functions; insert and format charts; adjust margins and set page orientations; print documents; and use help.

Chapter 7—"Microsoft PowerPoint 2007—Case Study I"

Chapter 7 introduces students to the basic operations of Microsoft Office PowerPoint 2007. The chapter begins with a case study. Students complete the case study by following the steps in "Let's Try It!" exercises. By following steps in these exercises, students will learn how to start, close, save, open PowerPoint documents; enter, edit, and format information in slides; apply themes to a presentation; create headers and footers; use bulleted lists; use shapes; insert WordArt; and use Help.

Chapter 8—"Microsoft PowerPoint 2007—Case Study II"

Chapter 8 introduces students to the intermediate and advanced operations of Microsoft Office PowerPoint 2007. The chapter begins with a case study. Students complete the case study by following the steps in "Let's Try It!" exercises. By following steps in these exercises, students will learn how to insert a table in a slide; apply quick styles to a table; insert and format a chart; insert and modify an organization chart; modify theme colors, fonts, and effects; rearrange a presentation in slide sorter and in normal view; duplicate slides; apply animation schemes; add slide transitions; preview presentation; page setup; and print slides.

Chapter 9—"Microsoft Access 2007—Case Study I"

Chapter 9 introduces students to the basic operations of Microsoft Office Access 2007. The chapter begins with a case study. Students complete the case study by following the steps in "Let's Try It!" exercises. By following steps in these exercises, students will learn how to start, close, save, open Access database; create tables; set primary key; change field property; enter data into a table; modify table; filter data by selection and form; create, save and run queries in design view; use query, form and report wizards; and use help.

Chapter 10—"Microsoft Access 2007—Case Study II"

Chapter 10 introduces students to the intermediate and advanced operations of Microsoft Office Access 2007. The chapter begins with a case study. Students complete the case study by following the steps in "Let's Try It!" exercises. By following steps in these exercises, students will learn how create relationships; enforce referential integrity; set validation rules; format fields; create an input mask; create a lookup field and a value list; create multi-table queries; create a totals query; create a parameter query; create a find duplicate query; and modify query joins.

Appendix—What's New

Appendix section provides a quick reference to the description of the new features introduced in Windows Vista, Internet Explorer 7, Microsoft Word 2007, Microsoft Excel 2007, Microsoft PowerPoint 2007, and Microsoft Access 2007.

Acknowledgements

The third edition of 'Fundamentals of Computing" would not have been possible without the support of my colleagues in Applied Information Technology department at George Mason University. I am extremely grateful to them. I want to thank my husband, Paramjeet, for his patience and encouragement that has enabled me to accomplish things I never thought were possible, my son Bhavjeet, our little bundle of joy and my constant source of inspiration, and my little princess, Suman who was very accepting of her part-time mother. I would also like to thank my parents-in-law, Gian and Harbhajan Sanghera, for their love and endless support. Finally, I want to thank my parents, Manjit and Surjit Singh, brothers Daljit and Sukhpal, and sister Swarnjit for an upbringing that got me where I am today. Thanks to Curtis Ross and Amanda Smith for their help throughout this project. Thanks to my students and instructors for their suggestions and feedback.

Introduction to Windows Vista

CHAPTER

1

OBJECTIVES

After successfully completing this chapter, you should able to:

- Know Operating System Basics
- Know the Elements of Windows Vista Desktop
- Open, Close, Minimize, Maximize, Move, and Resize Windows
- Switch between Windows
- Use Command Buttons and Menus
- Get Help
- Shut Down Your Computer
- Customize the Navigation Pane
- Use the Folders Tree
- Navigate Using the Address Bar
- Change Window View
- Sort and FilterFolder Contents
- Group Folder Contents
- Set Folder Options
- Create a New Folder
- Create a Shortcut to a Folder
- Rename Files and Folders
- Copy, Move, and Delete Files and Folders
- Restore a Deleted File
- Empty the Recycle Bin
- Search for a File or Folder
- Save Searches
- Select Multiple Files and Folders
- Open Applications from the Start Menu
- Switch between Programs
- Open and Close a Document
- Enter and Edit Text in WordPad
- Select Text
- Cut, Copy and Paste Text
- Format Text
- Save a Document
- Force an Application to Close
- Move the Task Bar
- Work with Taskbar Toolbars
- Set Taskbar Properties
- Customize the Quick Launch Toolbar
- Customize the Start Menu
- Set the Color Scheme
- Change the Desktop Background
- Change the Desktop Theme
- Work with the Sidebar
- Launch Applications at Startup
- Use Windows Aero
- Know the Control Panel
- Modify Date and Time Properties
- Add a Screen Saver
- Set Power Management Options
- Modify the Color Scheme
- Modify the Screen Resolution
- Set Folder Options
- Change or Remove Programs
- Modify Mouse Options
- Use Administrator Access Tools

Operating System Basics

Welcome to Windows Vista! Windows Vista is the latest and most stable Operating System by the Microsoft Corporation and is widely used on computers all over the world. Before we begin working with Windows Vista, it helps to understand what exactly Windows is and what it does.

First of all, Windows Vista is an **Operating System**. An Operating System is a software program that controls just about everything your computer does. For example, it:

- Controls the applications that run on your computer
- Controls the computer's hardware and manages communication between the computer's hardware and the user
- Implements User Management utilities and features
- Organizes the files and folders on your computer

Windows is a **Graphical User Interface or GUI** (pronounced "gooey") which allows the user to direct the computer's operating system by clicking icons (or graphics) rather than typing in commands manually, such as is the case when working with the DOS or UNIX operating system. The GUI makeup of the Operating System allows you to customize the appearance of your computer screen to fit your own individual taste.

If you have worked with previous version of Windows, you will notice many changes—a redesigned Start Menu, easier searching and improved file and folder management, not to mention a newer and slicker interface.

If you are new to computers or to the Windows Operating System, you are about to embark on an exciting new journey—the discovery of Windows Vista.

So let's get started!

A Look at the Desktop

Windows Vista makes working on your computer effortless because everything is accessible from one place—your **Desktop**. The Desktop is the first screen you see after logging on to your computer. The Desktop is the background area of your computer and contains icons that represent applications, folders or individual files.

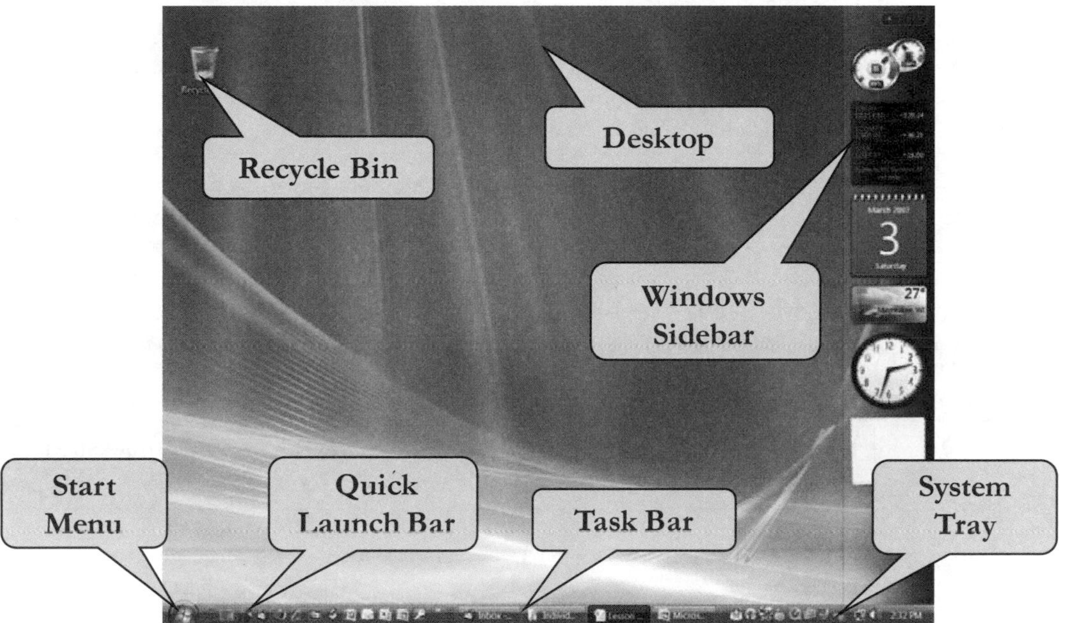

One of icons you will find on your desktop by default is the **Recycle Bin**. The Recycle Bin allows you to recover deleted files or folders. Depending on your setup, another icon you may find is the **Documents** folder (previously named "My Document"). This folder provides a handy location to store any files or folders that you create on your computer. The **Computer** icon lets you see everything on your computer drive, CD-Rom drive, external drive or network drive. You can also search for files and folders and obtain access to the Control Panel to modify your computer's settings. The **Start Menu** provides quick access to your applications. You can also search for files and folders as well as modify your computer's settings from the Start Menu.

New in Windows Vista is the **Windows Sidebar,** which allows you quick access to information via mini-programs called "Gadgets". You can easily add and remove items to the Sidebar as well as hide the Sidebar from view.

Don't worry if the Windows screen appears confusing at first. Each of the Desktop's elements will be discussed in subsequent sections. This section is just to introduce you to the major parts of the Desktop.

The Table below pages summarizes the default elements of the Desktop.

Elements of the Windows Vista Desktop

Element	Description
Desktop	This is the background area of the Windows Vista screen. The desktop is where you will find and add shortcuts to your favorite folders, documents and applications.
Icons	The pictorial representation of applications, files or folders.
Quick Launch Bar	Provides immediate access to your favorite applications, files, folders or Web Sites. You can add additional items to the Quick Launch Bar by dragging them to the Quick Launch Portion of the Taskbar.
Recycle Bin	A receptacle for all deleted files and folders on your computer. You can retrieve deleted items from the Recycle Bin or remove them permanently by emptying the Recycle Bin.
Start Menu	Allows you to quickly launch your applications, search for files or folders and modify your computer's settings.
System Tray	Displays System Icons.
Taskbar	Appears (usually) on the bottom of the screen and contains the Start Button, System Tray, Quick Launch Bar and an icon that displays any currently running programs.

Opening and Closing Windows

When working with the Windows Operating System, you will discover that each file, folder or application resides in its own **Window**. A window is a box that allows you to view and interact with the contents of files, folders and applications. Windows are either square or rectangular and contain buttons, menus and controls that you can use to manage them. Double-clicking an application icon, folder or document will open that item in its own window.

You will most likely find yourself working with several windows as once. The **Active Window** is the window that appears on top of any other of the windows that are open. To close the active window, click the window's **Close Button** or press the **Alt + F4** keystroke combination.

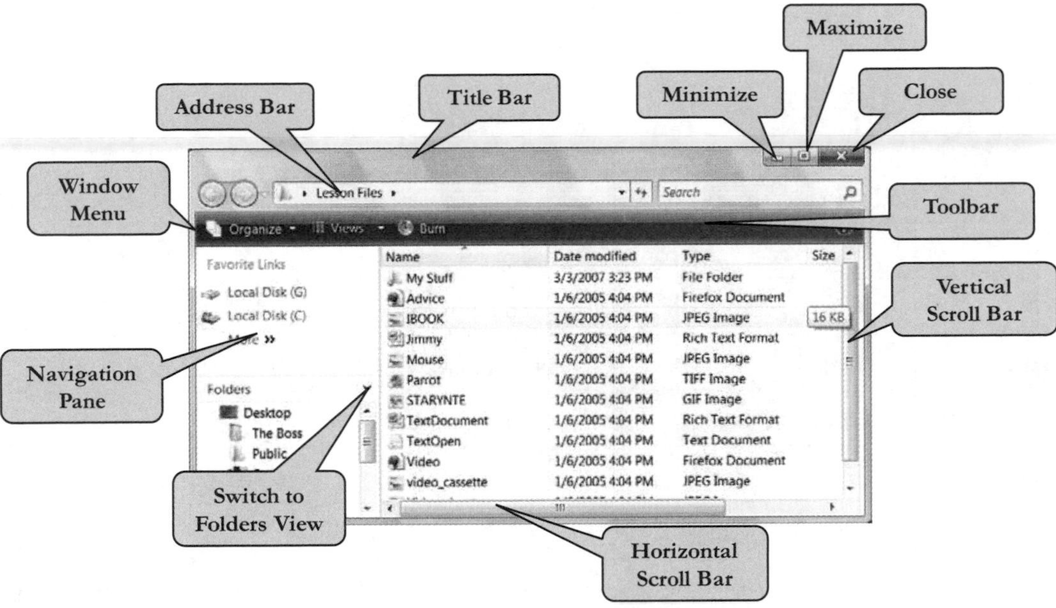

To Open a Window

1. Double-click the icon for the application, file or folder you wish to display.
   Or
   Right-click a folder and choose **Open** from the contextual menu.

To Close a Window

1. Click the window's **Close button**.
   Or
   Press the **Alt + F4** keystroke combination

Let's take a look at the Window controls in more detail:

Control	Description
Address Bar	Displays the address (folder location on your computer) of the current folder. You can also type a Web site address, which will display that particular site in your default Web browser.
Back Button	Moves backward to the last folder you visited.
Burn	Allows you to burn your selected items to a CD or DVD.
Close Button	Closes the window (file, folder or application). The Close button is represented by an **X**.
Explore	Displays the files and subfolders in a selected folder
Forward Button	Brings you back to the current folder after you have clicked the Back button.
Help	Click the blue question mark icon to obtain help at any time.
Main Window	Contains either the document area of the window (list of files and folders) or the working area of a document.
Menu Bar	Displays menus which are used to execute commands in Windows. Clicking on a menu displays a list of commands for that particular menu. By default, the menu bar is hidden in Windows Vista. Press the Alt key to display it.
Minimize Button	Hides the window from your screen and displays the window's icon on the Taskbar. The Minimize button is represented by a minus sign **(−)**.
Organize	Displays a menu with options for managing your folders—create a new folder, delete a folder, specify folder options, etc.
Restore Button	This buttons sizes the window to its previous size. The Restore Button is represented by two miniature windows, one behind the other. **( )**
Scroll Bar	Click and drag the Scroll Bar to bring the contents of another part of the window into view. A window can have a vertical Scroll Bar and a horizontal Scroll Bar.
Scroll Button	Click the Scroll Button (or Scroll Arrow) to move the contents of a window a little at a time. A window has a vertical scroll button and a horizontal scroll button.
Search Box	Allows you to find files and folders on your computer.
Share	Allows you to share your folder with other people on a network.
Title Bar	Displays the name of the folder or document (and its application) you are currently viewing. Click and drag the Title Bar to move the window. Double-click the Title Bar to toggle between Maximize and Restore.
Toolbar	Collection of buttons that execute commands when clicked, such as saving, printing and opening files.
Views	Allows you to display your folders in different ways.

In the rest of this chapter, we will be working with all of these window controls.

Minimizing and Maximizing Windows

On the top right of most windows, you will see three buttons. One of these buttons is the **Close button**, which, as we have already seen, is used to close a window. The furthest button on the left is the **Minimize button**. This button hides the window from your screen and places a miniature copy of the window on the Taskbar. The center button can be either the **Maximize Button** or the **Restore Button** (this button toggles between these two settings). The Maximize button expands the active window so that it fills the entire screen. The Restore button, which is displayed when the window is maximized, changes a maximized window to its previous size. The Minimize and Maximize buttons help you to work more efficiently with multiple windows, which of course, is the beauty of the Windows Operating System.

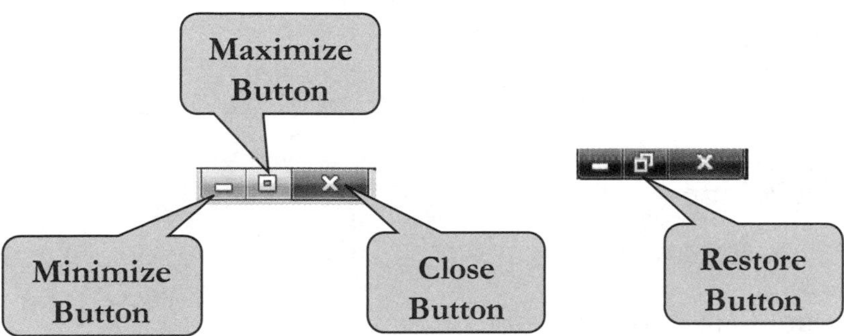

To Minimize, Maximize and Close a Window

1. To minimize a window, click the **Minimize button** (the leftmost button) on the top right side of the window. This will place a miniature replica copy of the window on the Taskbar. Click the replica copy to restore the window.
2. To maximize a window, click the **Maximize button** (the center button) on the top right side of the window. This will expand the window so that it fills the entire screen.
3. After maximizing a window, click the **Restore** button (the center button) on the top right side of the window to restore a window to its original size. The Maximize button changes to the Restore button when a window is in a maximized state.

Moving a Window

When working with several programs, documents or folders, you may find that your **viewing area** becomes cluttered or that one of your windows covers up a portion of another window that you need to see. When this occurs, you can **move a window** to a different area of your screen. To accomplish this, move your mouse pointer over the **Tile Bar** of the window, click and hold down your left mouse button, and then drag the window to its new location.

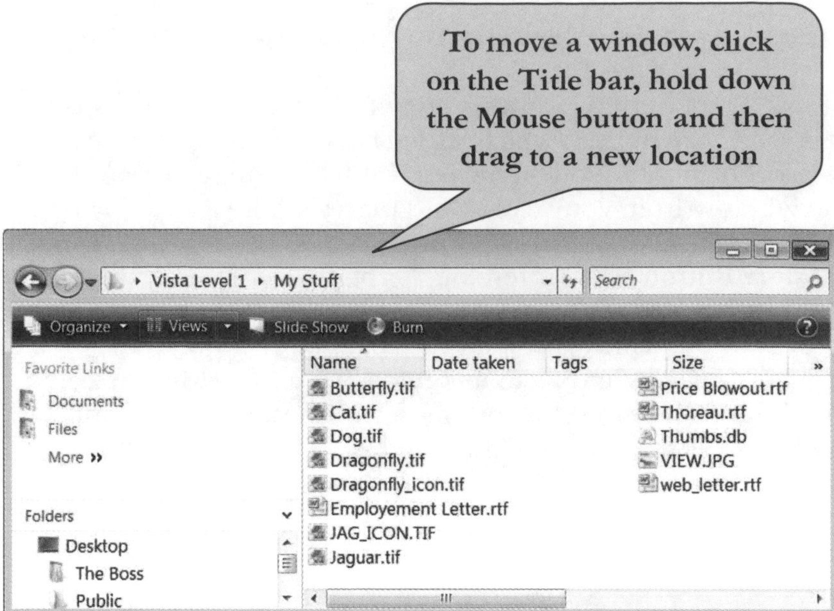

To Move a Window

1. Position your mouse pointer over the **Title Bar** of the window you wish to move.
2. **Press and hold down** the left mouse button.
3. With the mouse button held down, move your mouse **(drag)** until the window is in the desired location in your viewing area.
4. **Release** the mouse button.

NOTE: You cannot move a window when it is in a maximized state.

Resizing a Window

We have already seen that you can increase or decrease the size of a window by clicking the **Maximize** or the **Restore** button. However, you may wish to size your window to a **specific width and height**. To adjust the window size of an open window, move your mouse pointer over the **window border** until your pointer changes into a double-headed arrow. Drag until the window is the desired size.

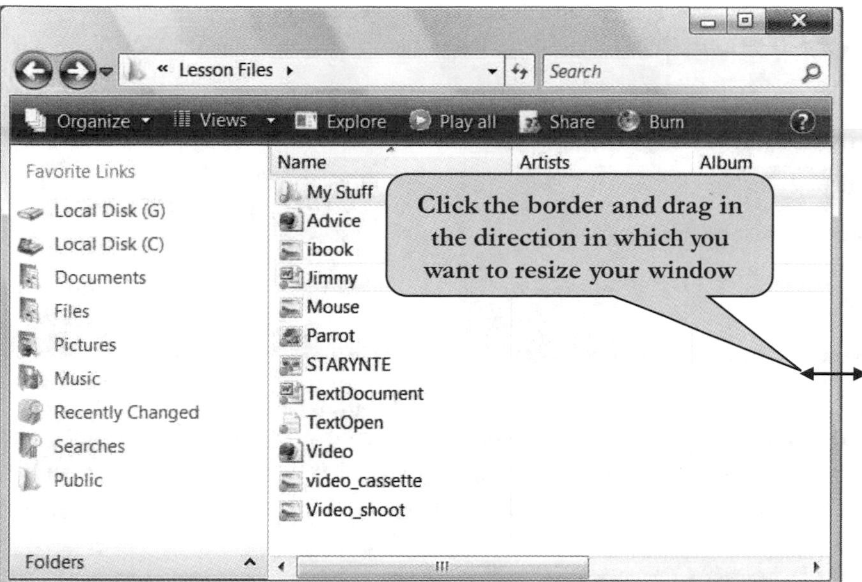

To Resize a Window

1. To **change the width**, position your mouse pointer over the **left or right window border** until the pointer changes into a double-headed arrow. Click and drag to the left or right until the window is the desired size.
2. To change the height, position your mouse pointer over the **top or bottom window border** until the pointer changes into a double-headed arrow. Click and drag upwards or downwards until the window is the desired size.
3. To change the width and height at the same time, position your mouse pointer over any **window corner** until the pointer changes into a double-headed arrow. Drag inwards or outwards until the window is the desired size.

NOTE: You cannot resize a window when it is in a maximized state.

Switching Between Windows

The **active window** is the window that is on top of any of the other open windows. The active window is the window with which you are working—only one window can be active at a time. To switch to any of the inactive windows in the background, either click on any part of the window you want to make active or click on the window's taskbar button on the Taskbar. Taskbar buttons represents open folder or applications.

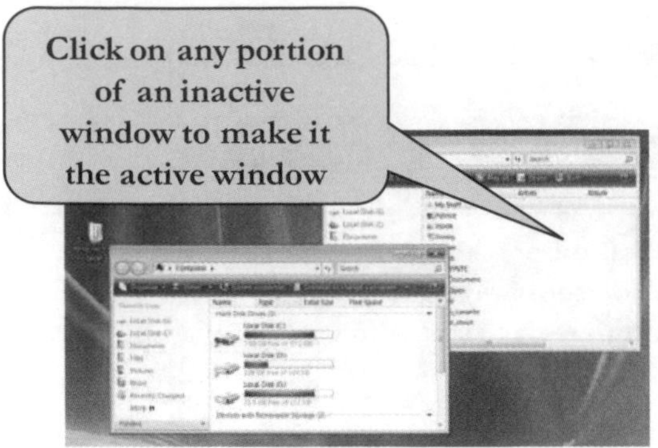

You can also switch to the previously active window by pressing **Alt + Tab**, or you can cycle through open windows by holding down the **Alt** key and repeatedly pressing the **Tab key** until the desired window is highlighted.

To Switch to an Open Window

1. Click any portion of an inactive window to bring it to the front, making it the active window
   Or
   Click the window's icon on the Taskbar to bring it to the front, making it the active window
   Or
   Press **Alt** and then press the **Tab** key.

To Cycle Between Open Windows

1. Press and hold down the **Alt** key.
2. Press the **Tab** key to highlight the previously active window.
3. With the Alt key still held down press **Tab** again. Repeat until the desired window is highlighted.
4. Release the Alt key.

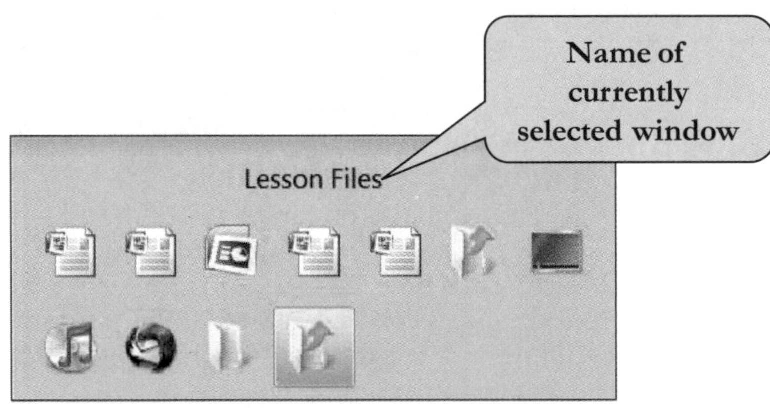

CYCLING THROUGH WINDOW USING ALT + TAB

Using Command Buttons

In Windows Vista, many of the commands that were found on the Menu Bar are now found on **Command Buttons** located on the Windows toolbar, usually located near the top of the window, underneath the Title bar. Clicking on a command button will execute the command associated with that button. For instance, clicking the **Open** button will open the selected file or folder. Many command buttons are contextual. For instance, the Open button will only be displayed if a file or folder is selected.

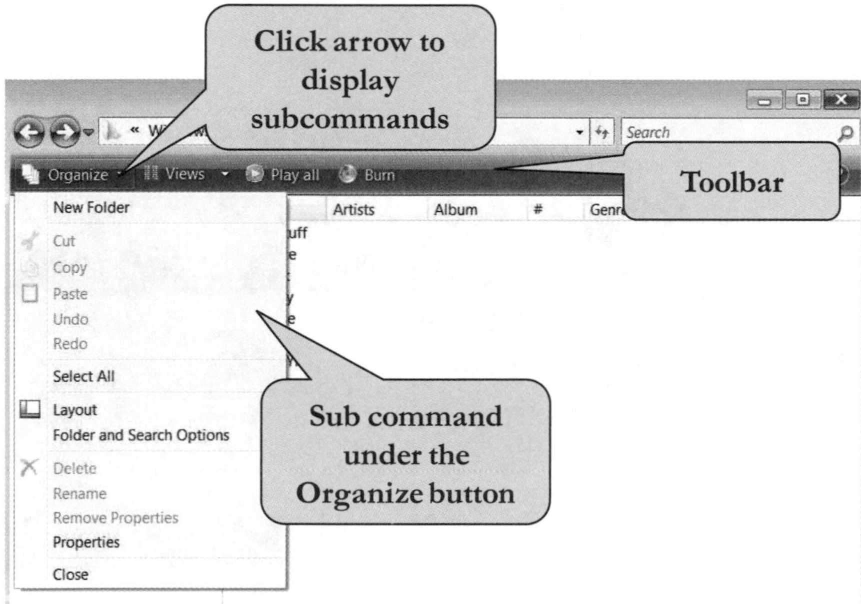

If a command button has an **arrow** on it, this indicates that the command button contains menu items relevant to that particular command button. For instance, clicking the arrow on the **Organize** button will display a list of item relating to organizing a folder—creating a new folder, deleting a file, renaming a file or folder, etc. Clicking an item in the menu list will execute that particular command.

To Use Command Buttons

1. Move your mouse pointer over the desired command button.
2. Click with your left mouse button to execute that command.
3. To display a command's **menu items**, click the submenu **arrow** to display a list of subcommands for that command button.
4. Move your mouse pointer downwards to the desired command to highlight it.
5. Click with your left mouse button
6. If a menu item contains a submenu, click the submenu **arrow** and then trace to the submenu with your mouse pointer.

Using Menus

We have already learned that you can give commands to your PC by using a keystroke combination or by clicking command buttons. Another common way of issuing a command in many applications is by using **menus.** A menu is a categorized list of commands relevant to a particular application. You can most often find menus near the top of the window, underneath the Title Bar, although menus can also be located on the bottom or the side of your screen.

Menu titles are displayed on the **Menu Bar**. However, in order to keep your screen uncluttered, Windows Vista hides the menu bar in every folder window. To display them, click the **Alt** key and they will appear on the top of the window.

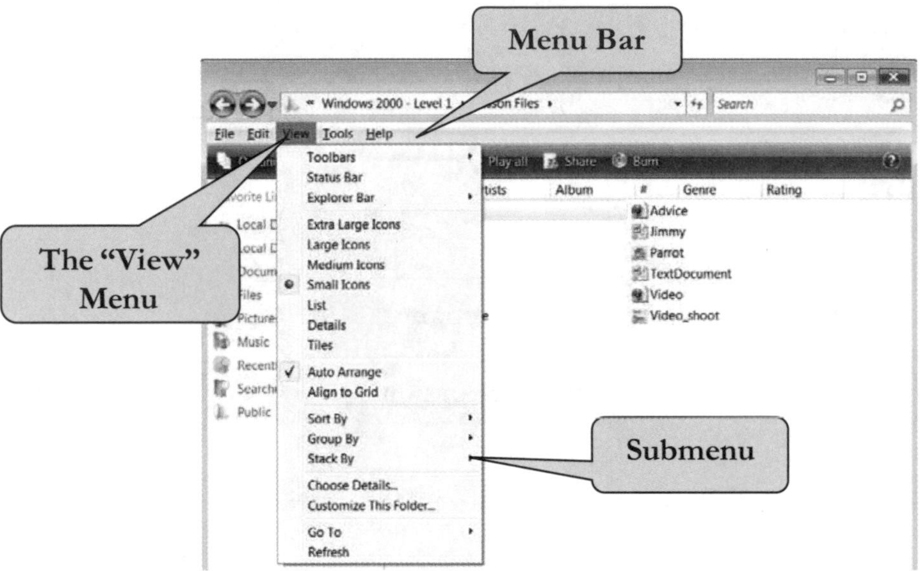

Common menu titles are File, Edit, View and Help. To displays the commands for a menu title, position your mouse pointer over the title and then click with your mouse button. If a menu command item contains a **submenu**, you can trace to the submenu with your mouse pointer to execute any of the submenu's commands.

To Use Menu Commands

1. Press the **Alt** key to temporarily display the Menu Bar.
2. Move your mouse pointer over the desired menu title on the menu bar.
3. Click with your left mouse button to display the menu.
4. Move your mouse pointer downwards to the desired command to highlight it.
5. Click with your left mouse button
6. To display a **submenu**, click the submenu **arrow** and then trace to the submenu with your mouse pointer.

TIP: To permanently display the Menu Bar, click the Organize button, point to Layout and then click Menu Bar.

Using Shortcut Menus

Shortcut menus appear when you move your mouse pointer over an object and then click the **right mouse button**. This is referred to at "**right-clicking**." A shortcut menu is a pop-up menu that contains many useful commands. For example, to view the properties of an object, move your mouse pointer over the object, click your right mouse button and then select Properties from the shortcut menu.

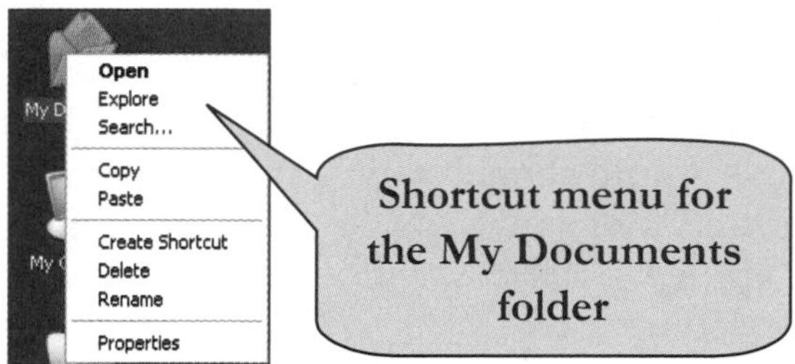

To Use Shortcut Menus

1. Move your mouse pointer over the object whose shortcut menu you want to display.
2. Press your right mouse button.
3. Click the desired menu command on the shortcut menu.

Using the Start Menu

The **Start Menu**, located on the Taskbar, provides access to all of the programs and files on your computer. From the Start Menu, you can perform such tasks as launching applications, opening files, searching for files, obtaining help and customizing your computer. Applications that you have recently opened are displayed on the bottom left side of Start Menu.

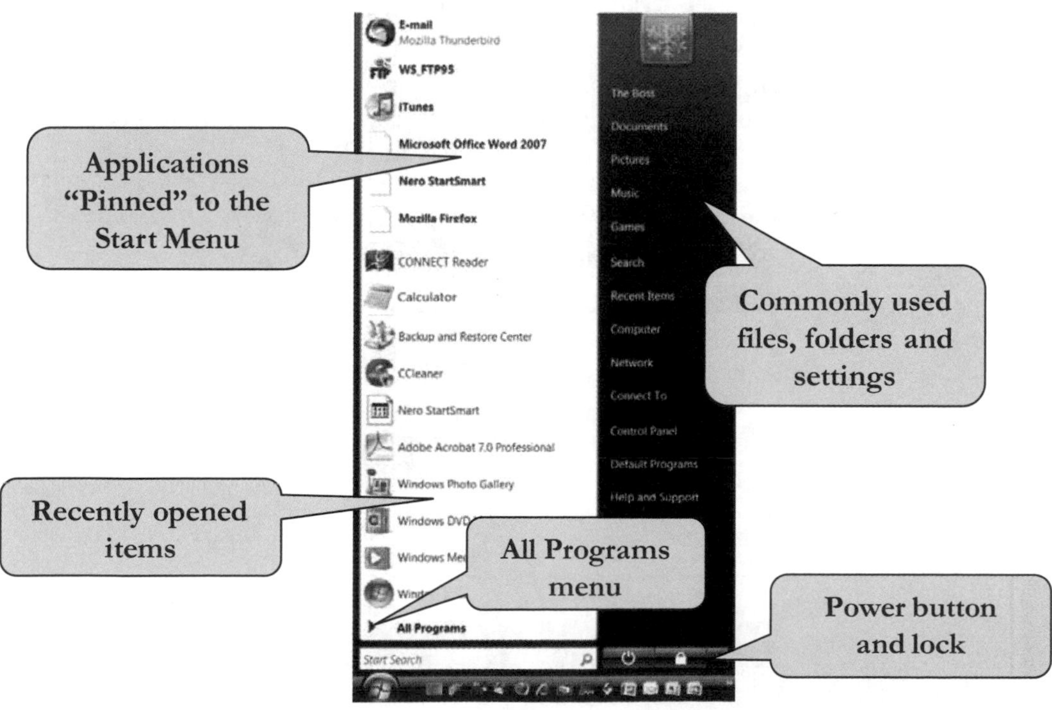

The Start menu is divided into three basic parts:

- The large left pane shows a short list of applications on your computer. The top section contains applications that you have "pinned" to the Start menu. The lower section contains application that you have recently opened. Clicking All Programs displays a complete list of programs (more on this later).
- In the lower left corner is the Search Box, which allows you to look for programs, files and folders on your computer by typing in search terms.
- The right pane provides access to commonly used folders, files, settings, and features. It's also where you go to log off from Windows or turn off your computer.

You can add or **pin** an Application to the Start Menu by selecting the program's icon, right-clicking and then choosing **Pin to Start Menu** from the pop-up menu. The application's icon will then be displayed on the top left portion of the Start Menu.

To open the Start menu, click the Start button in the lower-left corner of your screen. Or, press the Windows logo key on your keyboard. The Start menu will appear on the left side of your screen.

To Use the Start Menu

1. Move your mouse pointer over the **Start** button.
2. Click with your left mouse button.
   Or
   Press the **Windows logo key** on your keyboard.
3. Select an item from the list.
4. To launch an application not pinned to the Start menu, click **All Programs** and then click the application you wish to open.

Using Help

The Windows Help and Support system is the built-in help system for Windows, which allows you to obtain answers to common questions, provide troubleshooting solutions and instructions on how to do things. To display the Windows Help and Support window, click the **Start button** and click **Help and Support** on the Help menu or press the **F1** key.

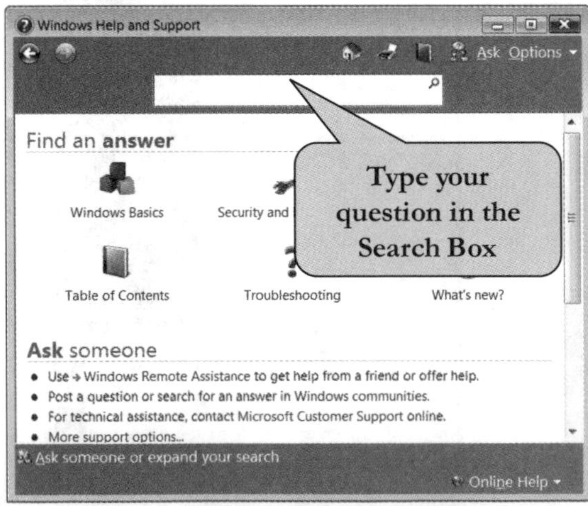

HELP AND SUPPORT WINDOW

The fastest way to obtain help is to type your question in the **Search box** and then press Enter. A list of results appears, with the most useful results shown at the top. Click one of the results to read the topic.

You can browse a list of Help topics by subject. Click the Browse Help button , and then click an item in the Contents list. The Contents list can contain Help topics or other subject headings. Click a Help topic to open it, or click another heading to dig deeper into the subject list.

If you're connected to the Internet, you can include Windows Online Help in your searches. Click the **Options** button on the Help window, choose **Settings** from the menu and then click the radio button next to **Include Windows online Help and Support** when you search for help. This will ensure that you have the most up-to-date contents when searching for help.

To Obtain Help

1. Click the **Start** button and click **Help and Support** from the Start menu.
2. Enter the keyword(s) for which you want to search in the **Search** box.
3. Click the **Search** button
   Or
   Press the **Enter** key.
4. Click the **link** for the help topic you wish to view.
5. To browse Help topics, click the **Browse Help** button.

Shutting Down Your Computer

When you are finished working on your computer, it is important to turn it off properly. Don't just press your computer's OFF button; instead, you should always shut down Windows via one of its official off buttons.

Windows offers several ways to close your session. Rather than shutting your computer off completely, you can put your computer in **Sleep Mode**, which will save your work and put your computer in a low-power state. Your open documents will be there when you awaken your computer just as they were when you left them. Press the power button on your PC to awaken your computer.

The **Lock button** locks access to your computer while you are away. You will be required to enter your password to redisplay your desktop.

Windows also offers several additional methods for closing your session:

- **Switch User**—Allows another user to log in to your computer while still running your session in the background.
- **Log Off**—Closes your session and displays the log on screen, ready for the next user to log on.

- **Lock**—Locks access to your computer while you are away.
- **Restart**—Windows shuts down and reloads itself.
- **Sleep**—Places the computer in Sleep Mode.
- **Hibernate**—Saves your work session and then turns off the computer.
- **Shut Down**—Saves all files and settings and then turns off the computer.

To Close Your Computer Session

1. Click the **Start** button.
2. Click the **Sleep** button to put your computer to sleep.
3. For other shut down options, click the **arrow** to the right of the **Lock** button to display the options menu and click the desired action from the menu.

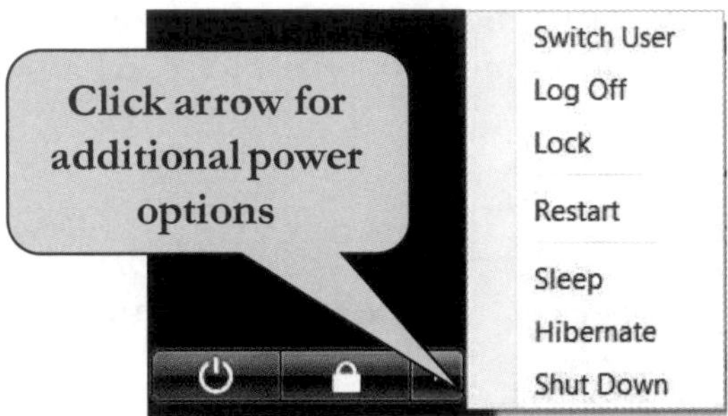

A Look at Windows Disk Organization

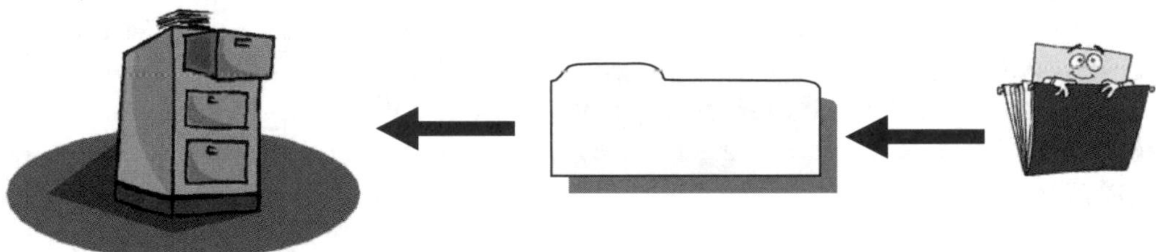

On your desktop, you will see an icon called **My Computer**. This icon represents all of the drives or **storage areas** of your computer. The drives are where all of the information called **files** is stored. Files can contain several types of information, from text, images, and movies to sound files. If all of the files that we use or the computer uses were stored in one area with no separation, it would be very confusing. Imagine if all of your possessions were stored in one room in your house on the floor in a big pile. It would take forever to find anything!

To ensure that files can be easily found when needed, they are grouped and organized into **Folders**. Folders can contain both files and other folders (often referred to as subfolders). The main folder on your computer is the **Local Disk C:** folder. This folder is called the **Root** folder as this is the folder from which all of the other folders and files on your computer branch. This folder represents your computer's **hard drive**, the part of the physical disk on your computer that reads and writes data. Think of your hard drive as one giant file cabinet. The drawers of the file cabinet contain documents that are stored and organized in folders.

In addition to your Local Disk C: drive, there are other types of drives you can use to store and retrieve information. These are:

Floppy Disk—Usually represented by the drive letter A or B. This drive allows you to insert small plastic diskette onto which you can store usually 1.44 megabytes (mb) of data. Most modern computers no longer ship with floppy drives.

CD-Rom or **DVD Drive**—Usually represented by the drive letter D or above. These drives allow you to store data on round discs which resemble a music audio disk. CD's and DVD's store much more data than floppy drives. CD's come in two types: **R** and **RW**. The R CD's allow you to record to them only once, whereas the RW CD's allow you to record multiple sessions on a CD. There are now DVD writers available, allowing you to store data (usually video files) to a DVD disk. Combination CD/DVD drives are called Superdrives.

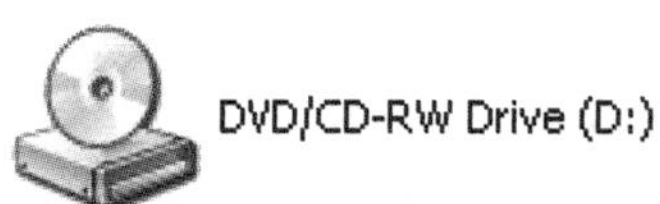

Removable Drive—Usually represented by the drive letter D or above. These drives, which now mostly plug into the USB port of your computer, allow you to save data on a drive external to your computer. There are several different kinds of removable drives with zip drives, jazz drives, compact flash drives and PC Cards being the most popular at the time of this writing. Many of them are comparable in speed to your computer's hard drive.

You can access all of these drives, as well as the Documents folder (the place for you to store all of your personal files) from the **Computer** folder on the Start Menu. Double-click any disk or folder to view its contents. For easier access, you may wish to add the Computer folder to your desktop.

To Browse the Contents of Your Computer

1. Click the **Start button** and then select **Computer** from the Start menu.
2. Double-click the folder or drive whose contents you wish to display.

3. To view the contents of the Documents folder, click the Documents folder in the Favorite Links area of the Computer Window
   Or
   Click the **Start button** and then select **Documents** from the Start menu.

Working with Navigation Pane

The **Navigation Pane**, located on the left side of a folder window, allows you to navigate directly to the folder that you would like to view. The Navigation Pane contains a Favorite Links area as well as an expandable folder tree, which displays the hierarchal structure of the drives, folders and files on your computer.

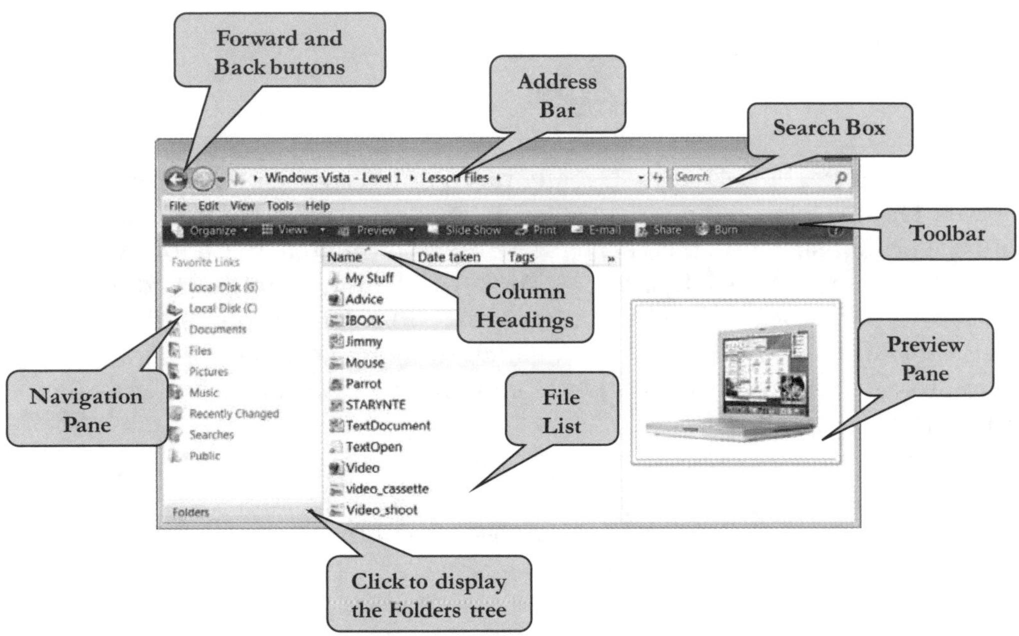

To help you get started, Windows includes several default folders to organize your data in the Favorite Links area. These are:

- **Documents**—Used to store your word processing, spreadsheet, database, presentation or other text files
- **Pictures**—Use this folder to store all of our digital graphic images.
- **Music**—Use this folder to store all of your digital music files.
- **Searches**—Use this folder to store your saved searches.

When you select a folder in the Favorite Links pane, its contents are displayed in the File List pane on the right. To display the contents of a folder in the File List pane, double-click the folder or click the folder and then click the Open button on the Toolbar.

To Browse Using the Navigation Pane

1. Click the **Start button** and then select the folder you wish to browse.
2. To display the contents of a folder in the Favorite Links area, click the desired folder to display its contents in the File List pane.

3. To display the contents of a folder in the File List pane, double-click the folder
   Or
   Select the folder you wish to open and click the **Open** button on the Toolbar.

Using the Folder Tree

The **Folders Pane** (also called Windows Explorer) located on the left side of your document window below the Navigation Pane, displays the hierarchal structure of the files, folders and drives on your computer, allowing you to quickly view the organization of your computer. Click on the word **Folders** to show or hide the Folders Tree. To expand any item in the Folders Tree pane, click on the **right-pointing arrow** next to the item. Click the **downward-pointing arrow** to collapse the item.

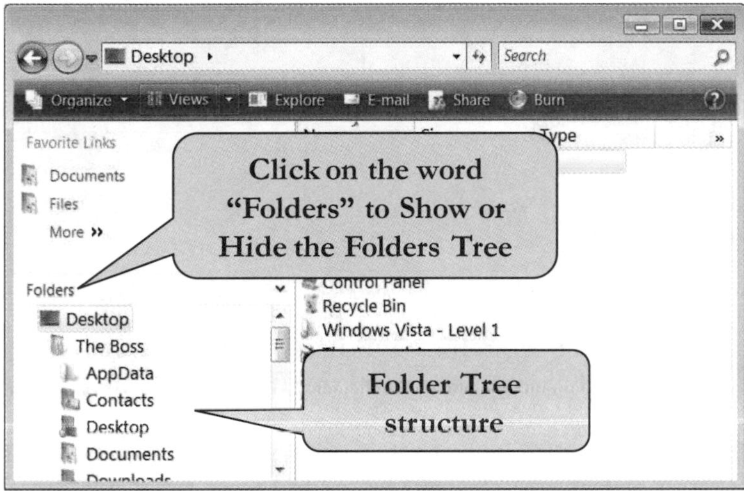

The Folder Tree is especially helpful for copying and moving files from one folder or drive to another. We will discuss moving and copying files later in this chapter.

To Display the Folders Tree

1. Display any document window and click on the word **Folders** in the Navigation Pane
   Or
   Click the **Start button**, click **All Programs**, click **Accessories** and then click **Windows Explorer**.
2. To display the next level subfolder for a folder or drive, click the **right-pointing arrow** to the left of the item's name.
3. To collapse (hide) the subfolder, click the **downward-pointing arrow** to the left of the item's name.

Customizing the Navigation Pane

If you find yourself accessing certain folders regularly, rather than drill down to find them, you can add them to the Favorite Links window on the Navigation Pane. To add a folder, simply **drag** it to the position on the Favorite Links window where you want it to be. A link is then placed on the Navigation Pane and is available from any document window.

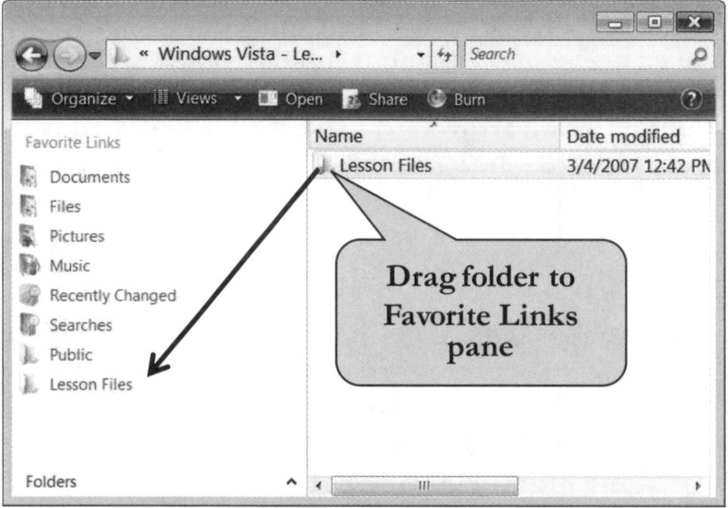

To remove a folder from the Favorite Links pane, right-click the link you want to remove and choose **Remove Link** from the contextual menu. If you wish to restore the default links to the Favorite Links pane (the way they were when Windows Vista was installed), right-click on any blank area of the pane and choose **Restore Default Favorite Links** from the contextual menu.

To Add a Link to the Favorite Areas Pane

1. Display the folder that contains the folder you wish to add.
2. Click the folder with your left mouse button and hold your left mouse button down.
3. Drag it to the position in the Favorite Links pane where you want to the link to be located.
4. Release the mouse button.

To Remove a Link from the Favorite Links Pane

1. **Right-click** the link in the Favorite Links pane that you want to remove.
2. Click **Remove Link** from the contextual menu.

To Restore Default Favorite Links

1. **Right-click** in the blank area of Favorite Links pane.
2. Click **Restore Default Favorite Links** from the contextual menu.

Navigating Using the Address Bar

The **Address Bar** appears at the top of every folder and displays your current location as several links separated by a drop-down arrow. Click on any of the links on the Address Bar to jump to that location. For instance, if you click "Documents" in the address bar, the Documents folder will display in File List pane. If you wanted to jump to a subfolder within the Documents folder, click the **arrow** to the right of the documents folder and select the folder you want.

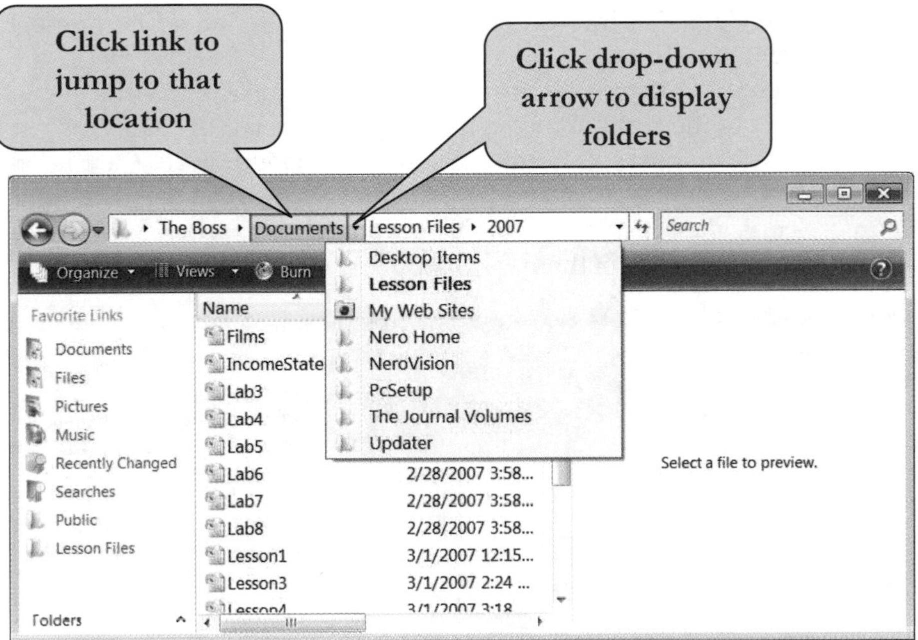

Another way to quickly jump to folders from the Address Bar is the **type in the location**. For common locations, such as Desktop, Computer, Music, Control Panel, Pictures, etc., just type in the word directly into the Address Bar. For other locations, type the complete folder name or path to the new location (such as C:\Users\Public), and then press the **Enter** key.

If you are connected to the Internet, you can display a Web page by typing a web address (URL) into the Address bar, which causes the folder window to switch to your default Web browser.

To Navigate Using the Address Bar

1. To jump directly to a location that's already visible in the Address bar, click the location (link) in the Address Bar.
2. To jump to the subfolder of a location that's visible in the Address bar, click the arrow to the right of the location in the Address bar, and then click the new location in the drop-down list.
3. To type in a new location, click a blank space in the Address bar anywhere to the right of the text that displays the current location and type in the location.

Changing Window View

Folder windows allow you to change the **Window View**. That is to say, you can change how the items in your window are displayed. There are three different view types that you can set:

- **List**—List view displays the contents of a folder as a list of file or folder names preceded by small icons. This view is especially helpful when browsing for a specific file name.
- **Details**—In Details view, Windows lists the contents of the open folder and provides detailed information about your files, including name, type, size, and date modified.
- **Tiles**—Tiles view displays your files and folders as icons with the name of the object to the right of the icon. The icons are larger than those in Icon view, and additional object information is displayed under the file or folder name.
- **Icons**—Icons view displays your files and folders as icons, with the name of the object underneath them.

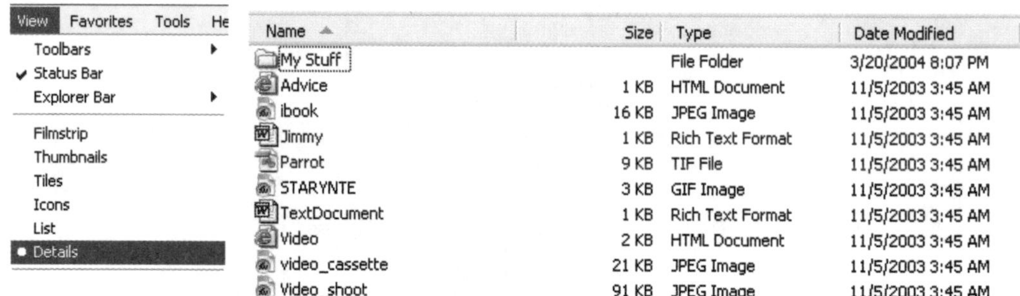

DETAILS VIEW FOR THE LESSON FILES FOLDER

To change the window view, you can cycle through the List, Details and Tiles views until you find the one you like by clicking the **Views button** on the Toolbar. Or click the arrow next to the Views button then select the desired view from the list. To switch to **Icon** view, click the arrow next to the Views button and choose Small Icons, Medium Icons, Large Icons or Extra Large Icons.

To Change Window View

1. Click the **View arrow** on the Toolbar and choose the desired view mode from the list
   Or
   Click the **Views** button on the Toolbar to cycle through the List, Details and Tile views.

Sorting and Filtering the Contents of a Folder

To **sort** the contents of a folder, click on the column heading by which you wish to sort. For example, if you wish to sort by the date the file was changed, click the Date Modified column heading. The tiny **arrow** on top of the column heading lets you know how the column is sorted—if it is pointed downward, the column is sorted in **descending order (Z-A)**. If the triangle is pointed upward, the column is sorted in **ascending order (A-Z)**. Clicking the column heading again reverses the sort order.

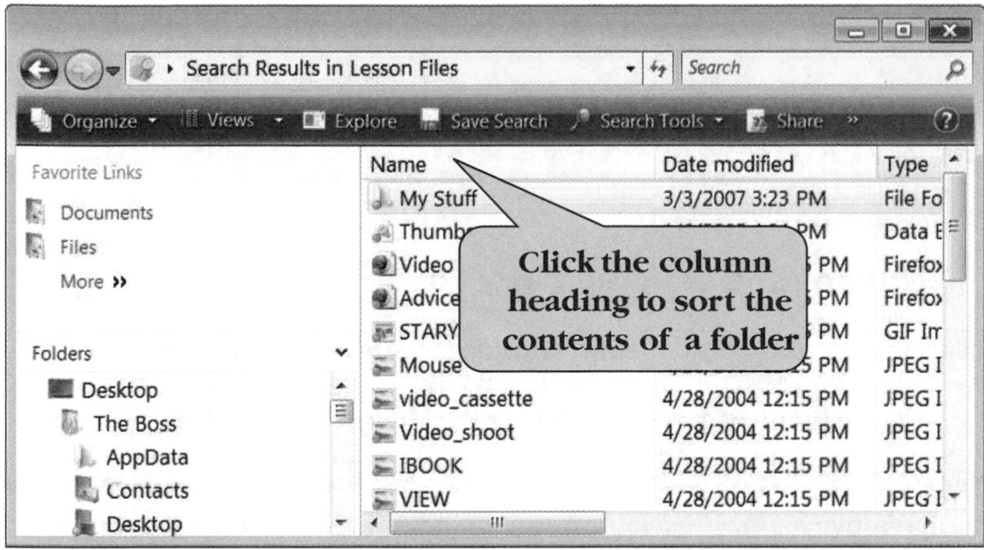

If you wish to **filter** a column, that is to say, only display files that meet a certain criteria, move your mouse pointer over the column heading and click the downward pointing arrow that appears to display the filter list. The contents of the list will vary, depending on the column heading you choose. For instance, the Date Modified column heading allows you to filter by a specific date, whereas the Type column heading displays a list of the different file types in that folder. To display only certain files, click the check box next to the filtering options. For example, if you only wanted to display text files and jpeg files, you would click the arrow next to the Type heading and click the check box next to **Text Document** and **JPEG Image**.

Note that filtering does not delete files; it just changes the view so that you only see the files that you specified in the filtering list.

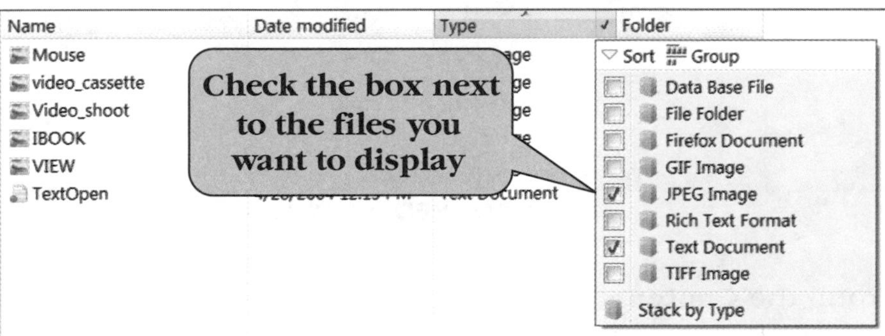

To Sort the Contents of a Folder

1. Click the **column heading** of the column you wish to sort.
2. To **filter files**, move your mouse pointer over the column heading, click the downward pointing arrow that appears and click the box next to the files you want to display.

TIP: If you don't see the column heading you want, right-click on any columns and check the box next to the column heading you want to display. Click **More** to display a list of all available column headings.

Grouping the Contents of a Folder

Grouping allows you to arrange your files by specific file details, such as the file name, file size, file type or the date the file was last modified. To group your files and folders, move your mouse pointer over any column heading, click the downward pointing arrow that appears and click **Group** on top of the list.

To remove a group, click the arrow to the right any column heading and choose **Sort**.

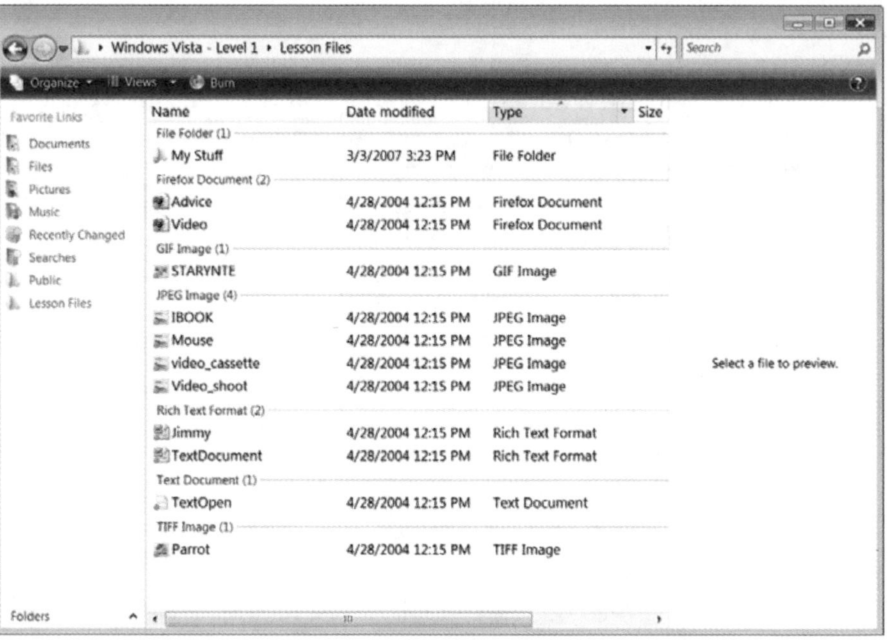

FILES GROUPED BY TYPE

To Group the Contents of a Folder

1. Move your mouse pointer over any column heading.
2. Click the downward pointing arrow that appears.
3. Click **Group** on top of the list.

TIP: You cannot group icons when in **List View**.

Setting Folder Options

Setting **Folder Options** allows you to specify how your folders function and how folder content is to be displayed. For instance, if you do not like the Navigation Pane displayed in your folders window, you can choose **Use Windows Classic folders** from the General Options. You can also choose to hide or display hidden files and folders, specify how folders open, choose to display the last opened folder at login or remember each folder's view settings, just to name a few of the available folder options. You may wish to explore many of the available Folder Options to customize your windows to your own individual taste.

To display Folder Options, click the **Organize button** on the Toolbar and select **Folder and Search Options** from the Tools menu. You can also display Folder Options by double-clicking the Folder Options link in the **Control Panel** (the Control Panel will be introduced later in the chapter).

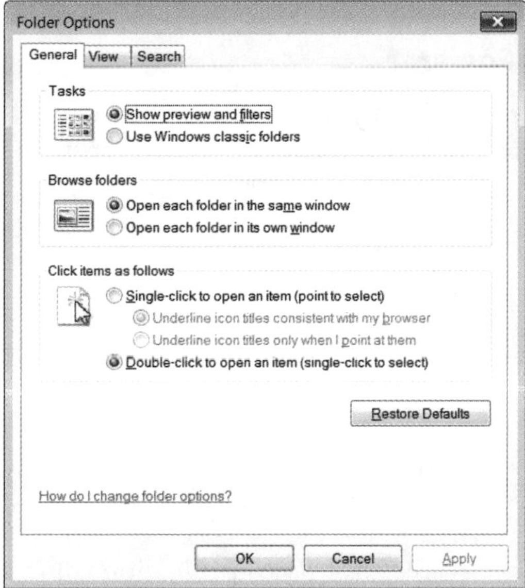

FOLDER OPTIONS WINDOW

To Set Folder Options

1. Click the **Organize** on the Toolbar of any folder window.
2. Click **Folder and Search Options** from the Organize menu.
   Or
   From the Control Panel, double-click the Folder Options link.
3. Click the **General**, **View** or **Search** tab.
4. Set any desired options.

Creating a New Folder

We have seen that when Windows Vista was installed, several folders were created for you (Documents, Pictures, Music, etc). However, in order to manage your files effectively, you will inevitably need to create additional folders. To create a new folder, go to the location (either to another folder or to the Desktop) where you want to create a new folder, right-click, point to **New** and choose **New Folder** from the New submenu. You can also create a new folder by choosing **New Folder** from the **Organize** menu.

When creating a new folder, it is given the generic name of **New Folder**. The text of the folder name is already selected for you so all you have to do is type the name you want for your new folder. Typing over the selected text will replace it with the new text that you type.

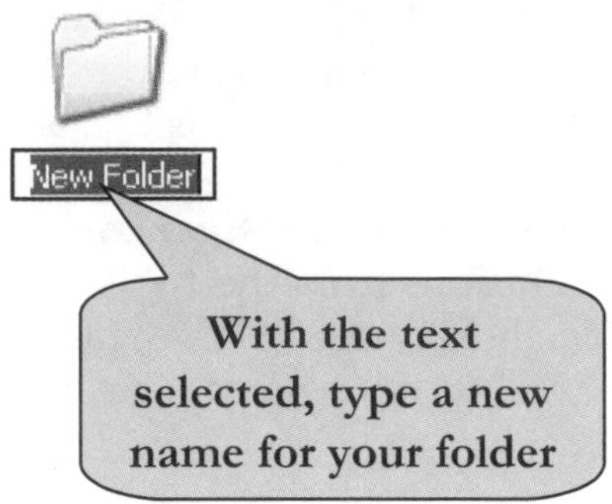
New Folder
With the text selected, type a new name for your folder

To Create a New Folder

1. Display the folder in which you want to create a new folder.
2. Click the **Organize** button and click **New Folder** from the menu.
   Or
   Display the Menu Bar and select **File > New > Folder** from the menu.
   Or
   Right-click in the folder window and then select **New > Folder** from the pop-up menu.
3. With the generic folder name selected, type the name you want for the folder.

Creating a Shortcut to a Folder

To make it easier to access files, folders, applications or even a disk, you can create a **shortcut** to it. A shortcut is a link to the actual file. It's like having a file or folder in two places at once. The icon that represents a shortcut looks just like the original except it has a **small arrow** in the lower left-hand corner. To open the actual item to which a shortcut is linked, **double-click** on the shortcut icon. Keep in mind that a shortcut is not a duplicate of a file; it is just a duplicate of the icon. This means that moving, copying, renaming or deleting the shortcut does not affect the original item. Shortcuts can have the same name as the original objects as long as they both do not reside in the same folder.

The arrow lets you know that the icon is actually a shortcut
Lesson Files

Shortcuts take up almost no disk space, regardless of the size of the original file. They also come in handy for files or folders that you access frequently. Many people like to create a shortcut on their desktop to folders or files that they work with often.

There are a couple of different ways to create a shortcut. You can right-click on the desktop and then choose **New > Shortcut** from the menu. Next, click the **Browse** button and then click the **arrow symbol** next to the folder that contains the object to which you want to create a shortcut. Select the object and then click **Next**. You will then be asked to provide a name for your shortcut.

Another way to create a shortcut is to navigate directly to the object to which you want to create a shortcut and select the object. Then, **right-click** and choose **Create Shortcut** from the contextual menu. To move the shortcut to the Desktop, resize the folder window so that the Desktop is visible, and then drag your shortcut to the Desktop.

To quickly create a shortcut to your Desktop, right-click the item, point to **Send To** and choose **Desktop (create shortcut)** from the contextual menu. A shortcut to the item is then placed on your Desktop.

To Create a Shortcut on Your Desktop from a Folder Window

1. Open the folder that contains the item to which you want to create a shortcut.
2. Right-click the item
3. Point to **Send To**
4. Choose **Desktop (create shortcut)** from the contextual menu.

To Create a Shortcut Directly on Your Desktop

1. Right-click on the Desktop.
2. Select **New > Shortcut** from the menu.
3. Click the **Browse** button.
4. Click the arrow symbol next to a drive or folder to expand its contents.
5. Click the object for which you wish to create a shortcut.
6. Click **Next**.
7. Type a new name in the shortcut box if desired.
8. Click **Finish**.

To Create a Shortcut in a Folder

1. Open the folder that contains the item to which you want to create a shortcut.
2. Right-click the item and choose **Create Shortcut** from the contextual menu.
3. **Resize the folder window** until the Desktop is visible.
4. Click and drag the shortcut to the Desktop (or to another location).

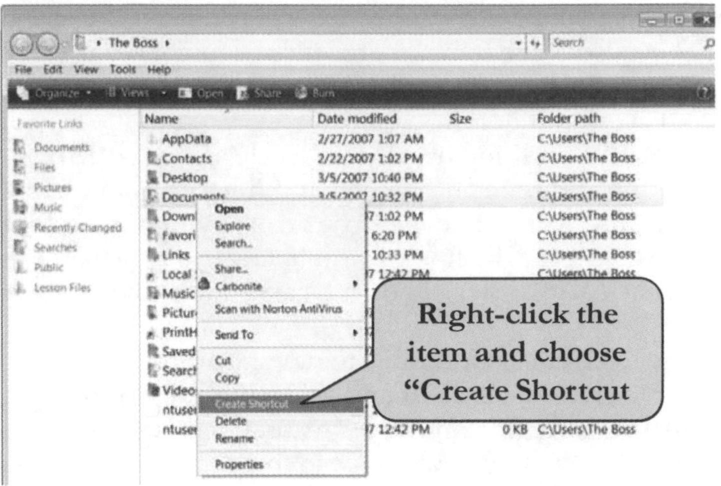
Right-click the
item and choose
“Create Shortcut

Renaming Files and Folders

In order to change the name of a file or folder, you need to select the text of the folder or file whose name you wish to change and then type in the new name. To select the name of a folder or file, right-click on the icon you want to rename, choose **Rename** from the pop-up menu and then type the desired new name..

You can also rename in item by slowly clicking the object's name twice and then typing a new name when the object name is selected.

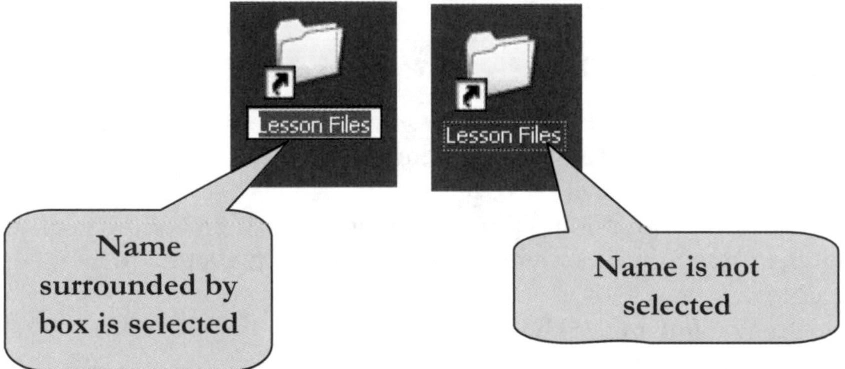
Lesson Files
Lesson Files
Name surrounded by box is selected
Name is not selected

If you want to only change part of a file name, select the part of the item name you wish to replace and then type the new text. To add additional text to a file name, set the insertion point in the area where you wish to add new text and begin typing.

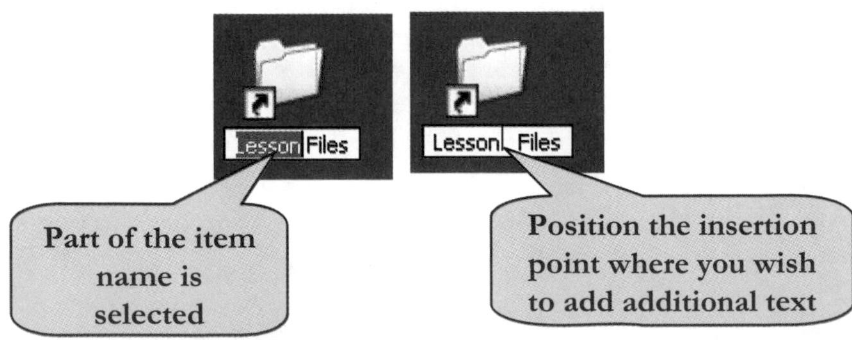
Lesson Files
Lesson Files
Part of the item name is selected
Position the insertion point where you wish to add additional text

To Rename a File or Folder

1. Click the icon to select the object.
2. Right-click and choose **Rename** from the pop-up menu.
3. Type the new file or folder name.
   Or
1. Slowly click the object's name twice until its name is selected
2. Type the new file or folder name.

Copying Files and Folders

At times, you may wish to make a duplicate of a file or folder in another location. The quickest way to do this is to use the **drag and drop** method. Press and hold down your **right mouse button**, drag the item to the new location, release the mouse button and then select **Copy Here** from the contextual menu. Or, if you prefer, hold down the **Ctrl** key and click and drag with your **left mouse button**. As you drag, a light copy of the icon will attach itself to your mouse pointer. If the destination folder already contains an item with the same name as the item you are copying, you will be asked if you wish to replace the item in the destination folder with the item you are copying.

Another way to copy a file or folder is to use the **Copy** and **Paste** commands. Select the item you wish to copy, right-click and select **Copy** from the menu. The item is placed on the Clipboard, a temporary storage area in memory. Next, open the folder where you wish to place a copy of the item. Right-click in the destination folder and select **Paste** from the menu

You can also copy a file or folder using the **Folder Tree**. Select the item in the File List pane that you wish to copy, press and hold down your **right mouse button** and then drag the item to the new location. Release the mouse button and choose **Copy Here** from the contextual menu.

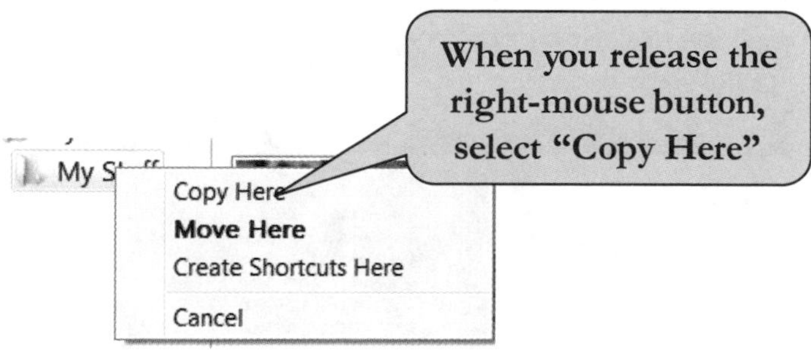

To Copy a File or a Folder

1. To use **Click and Drag**:
   a. Select the item you wish to copy.
   b. Press and hold down your **right mouse button** and drag the item to the new location.
   c. Release the mouse button.
   d. Select **Copy Here** from the contextual menu.
2. To use **Copy** and **Paste**:
   a. Select the item you wish to copy.
   b. Right-click and choose **Copy** from the contextual menu
   Or
   Press the Ctrl + C keystroke combination.
   c. Open the folder into which you want to place a copy of the item.
   d. Right-click and choose **Paste** from the contextual menu.
   Or
   Press the Ctrl + V keystroke combination.

Moving Files and Folders

Moving files and folders consists of deleting the item from its original location and placing it in a new location. Moving items is similar to copying items. To move items using the **Drag and Drop** method, click the item you wish to move with your left mouse button and then drag it to its destination folder. The item will automatically be deleted from its original location and placed in the new location. If you prefer to use your right mouse button, hold down your right mouse button as you drag, release the mouse button and then select Move Here from the contextual menu.

Another way to copy a file or folder is to use the **Cut** and **Paste** commands on the **contextual** menu. Select the item you wish to copy, right-click and select **Cut** from the contextual menu. The item is placed on the Clipboard, a temporary storage area in memory. Next, open the folder where you wish to place a copy of the item right-click in the destination folder and select **Paste** from the menu.

You can also copy a file or folder using the **Folder Tree**. Select the item in the File List pane that you wish to copy, press and hold down your **left mouse button** and then drag the item to the new location. Choose **Copy Here** from the contextual menu.

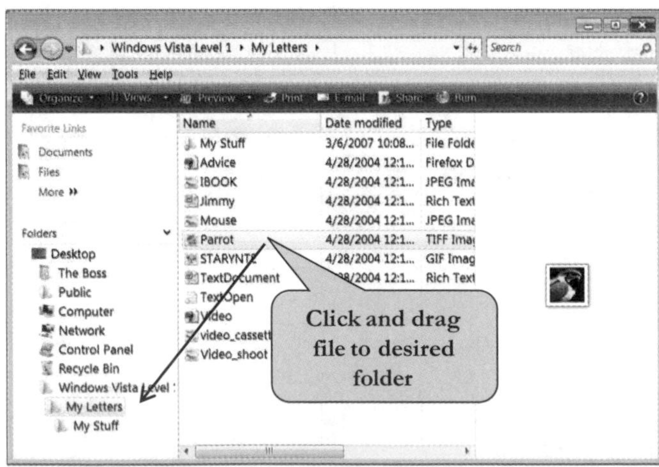

> **NOTE:** If you have accidentally moved the wrong item, you can reverse the action by right-clicking and then selecting **Undo Copy** or **Undo Paste** from the contextual menu or by pressing the keystroke combination **Ctrl + Z**. The undo action is also available in many applications as well.

To Move a File or a Folder

1. To use **Click and Drag**:
   a. Select the item you wish to copy.
   b. Press and hold down your **left mouse button** and drag the item to the new location.
   c. Release the mouse button.
2. To use **Cut** and **Paste**:
   a. Select the item you wish to copy.
   b. Right-click and choose **Cut** from the contextual menu
   Or
   Press the **Ctrl + X** keystroke combination.
   c. Open the folder into which you want to place a copy of the item.
   d. Right-click and choose **Paste** from the contextual menu.
   Or
   Press the Ctrl + V keystroke combination.

Deleting Files and Folders

Deleting files and folders means physically removing those items from your hard disk. When deleting an item, it is placed in the **Recycle Bin**. Items in the Recycle Bin can be retrieved as long as the Recycle Bin has not been emptied since the object was deleted.

To delete a file or folder, select the item to be deleted and then press the **Delete key**. You can also delete a file or folder by **right-clicking** an item, and then choosing **Delete** from the pop-up menu.

> **NOTE:** To **permanently delete** a file or folder, press and hold down the **Shift key** and then drag the object to the Recycle Bin. The deleted item cannot be retrieved from the Recycle Bin later on.

To Delete a File or a Folder

1. Click the item you wish to delete.
2. Press the **Delete key**
   Or
   Right-click the item and then select **Delete** from the pop-up menu
   Or
   Click and drag the item to the **Recycle Bin**

Restoring a Deleted File

As long as you have not emptied the **Recycle Bin**, you can restore a file that you have deleted. Double-clicking on the Recycle Bin icon displays all of the files that reside in the Recycle Bin at the moment. Unlike other folders, you cannot open a file that is in the Recycle Bin. For instance, double-clicking a file usually will open that file in the application with which it is associated. However, if we double-click the Dragonfly file, only the file's property box will display.

Speaking of properties, if you have set the properties of the Recycle Bin to **remove files immediately when deleted**, they cannot be restored once you have deleted them. You also cannot restore items that you delete from **Network drives or removable drives**. Additionally, any items that exceed the maximum size of the recycle bin that you have set in the Recycle Bin's properties box are automatically deleted and cannot be restored. To view the properties for the Recycle Bin, right-click the icon for the Recycle Bin and the choose **Properties** from the pop-up menu.

To Restore a Deleted File or Folder

1. Double-click the **Recycle Bin** icon on the Desktop.
2. **Right-click** the item you want to restore and then choose **Restore** from the contextual menu.
   Or
   Click the **Restore this item** button on the Toolbar
3. To restore all of the items in the Recycle Bin:
   a. Press the Ctrl + A keystroke combination to select all items.
   b. Right-click and select **Restore** from the contextual menu.
      Or
      Click the **Restore this item** button on the toolbar
4. To restore several items at once:
   a. Press and hold down the **Ctrl key**.
   b. Click each item that you want to restore.
   c. Right-click and select **Restore** from the contextual menu.
      Or
      Click the **Restore this item** button on the toolbar

Emptying the Recycle Bin

Deleting an item from your computer is a two-step process. First, you need to move the item to the Recycle Bin and then, you need to **Empty the Recycle Bin**. It is important to note that once you empty the Recycle Bin, that item **can no longer be restored**. It is gone permanently*.

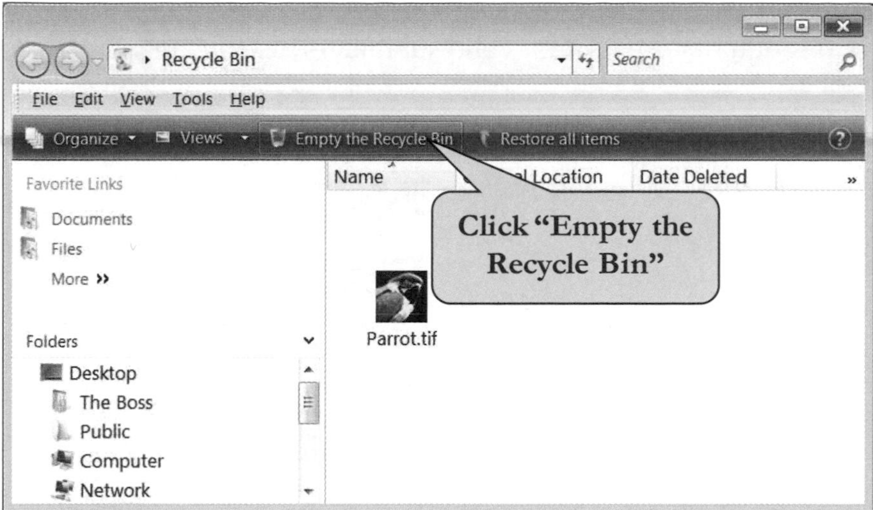

To Empty the Recycle Bin

1. Right-click the Recycle Bin icon on the Desktop and then choose **Empty Recycle Bin** from the pop-up menu.
   Or
1. Double-click the Recycle Bin icon on the Desktop.
2. Click **Empty the Recycle Bin** button on the Toolbar.

***NOTE:** Once a file has been removed from the Recycle Bin, a third-party program such as **Norton Utilities** may be able to restore the deleted file.

Searching for a File or Folder

Inevitably, the day will come when you will forget where you placed a file or folder. Luckily, Windows Vista includes a powerful tool to help you find lost items with ease. Windows Vista creates an index of every file you create, allowing you to find your missing files quickly. If you are unsure of the exact location of a file, the handy **Search Box** at the bottom of the Start Menu will search through all of the files and folders on your computer.

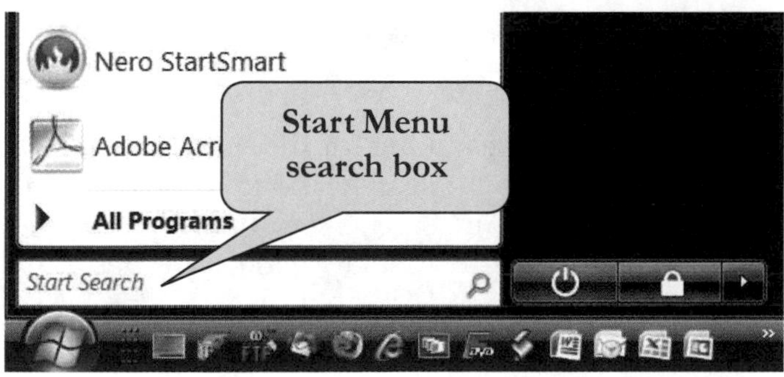

If you know that a file is stored in a particular folder but don't want to browse through hundreds of files and subfolders, use the **Search Box,** located on top of every folder window. Windows will search through all of the files and subfolders in the active folder. For example, if you execute a search from the Search Box of the Documents window, Windows will look through all of the files and subfolders in the Documents folder for your search term.

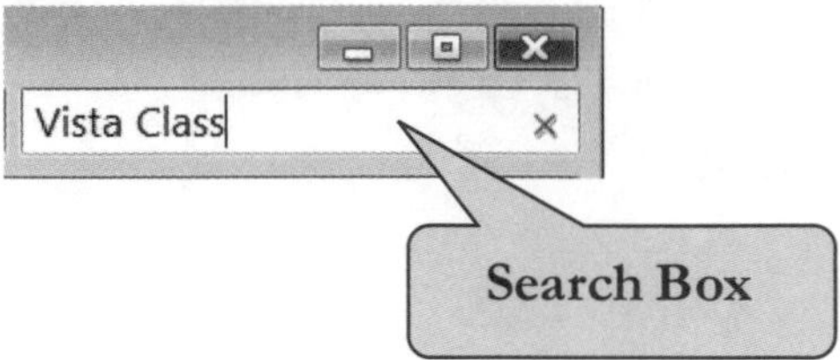

To start a search, type the first few letters of a word, name or phrase that appears somewhere inside of the file. As you type in the Search box, the contents of the folder will be filtered to reflect each successive character you type. When you see the file you want, you can stop typing. You don't need to press Enter, since searching happens automatically. Once you see the file you want, click its name to open it or, to see the folder where the file is located, right-click the file name and choose Open File Location from the contextual menu.

Remember also that you can use the sorting and grouping tools that we discussed in the last chapter to help you quickly find a file in a specific folder.

To Search for a File or Folder

1. Click the **Start button**.
2. Click in **Search Box** on the Start Menu.
3. Type part of all of the file name or type the first few letters of a word, name or phrase that appears somewhere inside of the file.

To Search for a File or Folder in a Specific Folder

1. Display the folder in which you want to search.
2. Click in **Search Box** on top of the folder window.
3. Type part of all of the file name or type the first few letters of a word, name or phrase that appears somewhere inside of the file.

Saving Searches

If you find yourself repeatedly searching for the same group of files, you might want to consider saving your searches. With a saved search, you don't have to manually reconstruct your search every time—just open your saved search. Windows will automatically display all current files that match your search.

Your saved searches are available from the Searches link in the Navigation pane.

To Save a Search

1. Type your search term in the Search Box.
2. Once your search is completed, click the **Save Search** button on the Toolbar.
3. Type in a name for your search in the File Name box.
4. Click **Save**.

To Open a Saved Search

1. Display a folder window.
2. Click the **Searches** link in the Navigation pane.
3. Click the search you wish to execute.

Selecting Multiple Files and Folders

We have already seen that in order to perform an action such as moving, copying or deleting a file or folder, we must first select it. There are times when you may wish to perform such an action on a group of files or folders. To do this, you need to select all of the objects on which you wish to perform the action. To select more than one item, click the first item, hold down the **Ctrl** key and then click any additional items you wish to select.

If the objects are located together, click outside the objects in the window, drag across the items until all of them are enclosed within a rectangle, and then release the mouse button. To select **all of the items in a window**, click the **Organize** button and choose **Select All** from the menu or press the **Ctrl + A** keystroke combination.

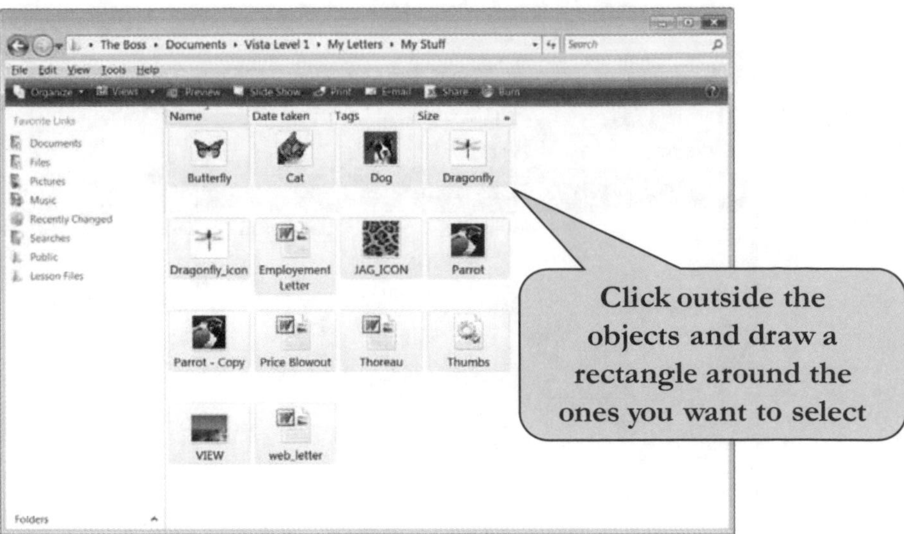

To select objects that are in a **consecutive list**, click the **first** object you wish to select, press down and hold the **Shift key** and then click the **last** item you want included. All items between and including the first and last item will be selected.

To Select Multiple Objects

1. To select non-adjacent objects:
   a. Click the first file or folder you want to select.
   b. Press down and hold the **Ctrl** key.
   c. Select any additional objects.
2. To select several objects that are together:
   a. Click outside of the objects.
   b. Click and hold down your left mouse button.
   c. **Drag across** the items until they are all enclosed within a rectangle.
   d. Release the mouse button.
3. To select a consecutive list of objects:
   a. Click the **first item** you want to select.
   b. Press down and hold the **Shift key**.
   c. Click the **last item** you want to select.

Opening Applications from the Start Menu

Thus far, we have been concentrating on the Windows Vista Operating System. In this section of the chapter, we will be working with applications. Applications provide the tools you need to get your work done. Some typical applications you may work with include word processing programs, spreadsheet programs, presentation programs, image editing programs, Web browsers and HTML editors, just to name a few.

Every application you work with will be a little different, but the method for doing certain tasks is the same in most programs. For instance, the process for opening a document from within an application is usually the same across all applications.

The most common way to launch an application is from the **Start** menu. Click the Start button and then click the icon for the program you want to launch. If you do not see the program on the Start menu, click **All Programs**, and then click the program you want to launch. Sometimes, the program may be in a subfolder so you will need to click on the folder icon to display the application name.

If you have a shortcut to an application on your Desktop or in another folder, double-click the application icon to launch the program.

To Start a Program from the Start Menu

1. Click the **Start** button.
2. Click the icon for the program you wish to open.
3. If the icon for the program is not on the start menu, point to **All Programs** and click on the application you want to open.

Switching Between Programs

The power of Windows lies in its ability to have several program windows open simultaneously. We have already seen that you can have more than one open window. Likewise, you can have more than one application running at a time.

After you launch an application, a button representing the program appears on the **Taskbar**. To switch from one open application to another, click the application's icon on the taskbar.

You can also cycle through all open windows by pressing and holding down the **Alt key**, and then pressing the **Tab** key. Continue pressing the Tab key until the window to which you want to switch is selected. Release the Alt key.

To Switch Between Open Programs

1. Click the icon representing the open program on the **Taskbar**
   Or
1. Press and hold down the **Alt key**.
2. Press the **Tab** key.
3. Press and release the Tab key until the window (application window or file window) is selected.
4. Release the **Alt key**.

Opening and Closing a Document

Application windows contain many of the same components as file windows with which we have been working so far. Most application windows contain three main components: a **menu bar**, a **toolbar** and the **working area**. We have already worked with commands on a menu bar and toolbar. Application windows contain menu bar and toolbar commands relevant to creating and editing documents and files specific to that application. The working area is the component of your application where you enter, modify, and format data.

Many of these commands are standard across most applications. One of these standard commands is the **Open** command, located off of the **File** menu. This command allows you to navigate through your computer's hard drive until you find the document or file you wish to display in the active application. The file will then be displayed in the application's working area.

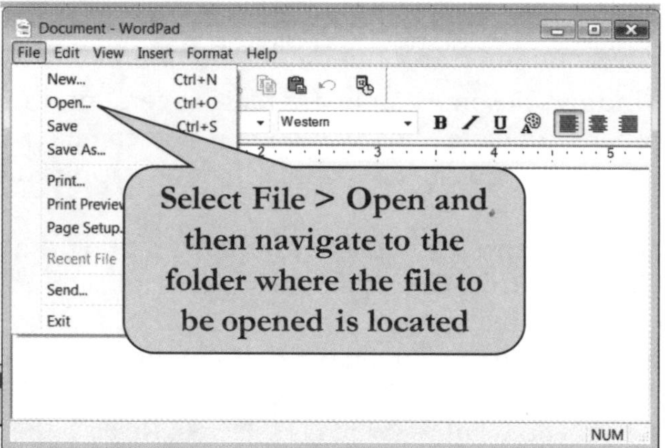

TIP: Double-clicking a document in a file window will open that document in the application with which it is associated.

To **close** a document, select **File > Close** or **File > Exit** from the menu. If the application allows you to open more than one document window, as does Microsoft Word, for example, the File > Close command will close only the active document but leave the application open. WordPad only allows you to open one document window per session. Thus, the File > Exit command closes both the document and the application.

Depending on the application, there may also be an **Open icon** on the Application Toolbar. For instance, in WordPad, the icon to display the Open dialog box is represented by an open file folder, as illustrated below. This is a standard Open icon in many Windows applications.

THE OPEN ICON

NOTE: In the Microsoft Office 2007 applications, the Menu Bar and Toolbar have been replaced by the new Ribbon. Click on a tab on the Ribbon to access application commands.

To Open a Document from within an Application

1. Select **File > Open** from the menu.
   Or
   Click the **Open icon** on the Application Toolbar, if available.
2. Click on either the **My Documents** icon or the **My Computer** icon.
3. Navigate to the folder that contains the file you want to open.
4. Select the file.
5. Click **Open**.

To Close a Document

1. Select **File > Exit** or **File > Close** from the menu.

Entering and Editing Text in WordPad

There are several free programs that come with Window Vista. One of these is the **WordPad** application which is used to create **text documents**. WordPad is a mini word processing program that allows you to enter, edit, delete and format text.

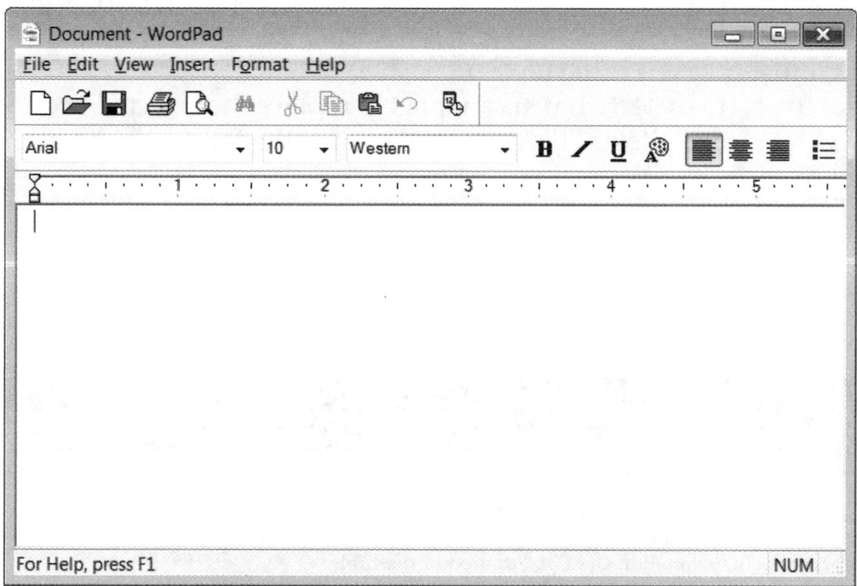

THE WORDPAD APPLICATION

WordPad allows you to save your documents either as a text document (.txt) or as a rich text format document (.rtf), both of which can be opened by a variety of word processing programs.

When WordPad first opens, a new blank document is displayed and the insertion point (the location where you begin entering text) is located at the top left of the document. So you can just begin typing text into your blank document. As you type, the text will automatically wrap to the next line. To insert a new blank line, press the **Enter** key.

To add text to an **existing document**, move your mouse pointer to the location where you wish to begin typing and then click your left mouse button. This will set the insertion point at the new location.

To Enter Text into the WordPad Application

1. Open the WordPad application. A blank new document will automatically be created.
2. Begin typing.
3. To add text to an existing document:
   a. Move your mouse pointer to the location in your document where you wish to add new text.
   b. Click your left mouse button to set the insertion point.
   c. Begin typing.
4. Press **Enter** to insert a new line.

> **TIP:** You can delete text by using either the **Backspace** key or the **Delete** key. Pressing the Backspace key will delete text to the left of the insertion point whereas pressing the Delete key will delete text to the right of the insertion point.

Selecting Text

In the last lesson, we saw how to delete one character at a time from a document. However, often you will want to delete, copy, move or apply formatting changes to an entire word, sentence or paragraph. In order to do this, you must first **select** the text you wish to delete.

Once the text is selected, you can quickly replace the selected text by simply typing in new text. This action automatically deletes the highlighted text and replaces it with what you have typed.

4267 N. Oakland Ave.¶
Columbus, OH ¶
¶
Dear Mr. Frailey:¶
¶
It is a pleasure to extend to you a personal welcome as the proud new owner of a 2002 Ford Acura. We wish you many miles of satisfying and enjoyable motoring in your new automobile. We would also like to take this occasion to thank you for giving us the opportunity to serve you.¶
¶
Please keep in mind that our Ford dealers throughout the co... always happy to serve you and will aid you in making your new automo...
Our personnel is trained in the Ford trained in the high...
excellence... with the sole purpose of keeping your bran...
most pleasurable possessions. Periodic check-ups and oil changes will help ensure that your driving enjoyment will continue for many years to come.¶
¶

Selected Text

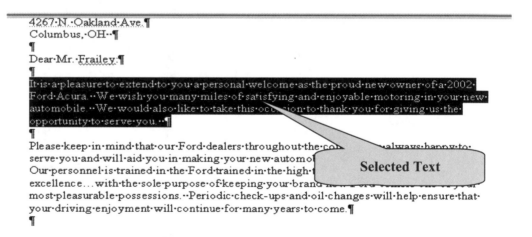

To select a block of text, place the insertion point at the beginning or end of the block that you wish to select. Click and hold the mouse button and drag until the text is highlighted in black.

There are many other ways to select blocks of text. For instance, in many applications you can select a word by **double-clicking** it. The table below outlines several techniques you can use to select text in a document in WordPad.

To Select Text with Your Mouse

To Select This:	Do This:
A word	Double-click on the word.
A line of text	Click to the left of the line in the margin.
Several lines of text	Click to the left of a line in the margin and drag upwards or downwards.
A paragraph	Double-click to the left of the paragraph in the margin or **triple-click** anywhere within the paragraph.
A block of text	Place the insertion point at the beginning of the block to be selected. Hold down the **Shift** key and click at the end of the block you wish to select.
The entire document	Press the **Ctrl + A** keystroke combination or select **Edit > Select All** from the menu.

TIP: You can also select text with your keyboard. Hold down the **Shift** key and press the arrow keys to select the desired text.

Cutting, Copying and Pasting Text

When learning about File Management in Windows Vista, we discussed the concepts of moving and copying files from one location to another. You can also cut copy and paste text from one location to another in a document.

To move or copy text, you must first **select** it. As we learned in the last lesson, to select a block of text, set the insertion point at the beginning of the block of text that you wish to select, click and hold down your left mouse button and then drag until the desired block of text is highlighted.

After you select the text, you can move or copy your selection by choosing **Edit > Copy** or **Edit > Cut** from the menu. Set the insertion point where you want to insert the text and then choose **Edit > Paste** from the menu.

To Copy Text from One Location to Another

1. **Select** the text you wish to copy.
2. Select **Edit > Copy** from the Menu.
   Or
   Click the **Copy icon** on the Application Toolbar.

THE COPY ICON

3. Set the insertion point where you want to insert the copied the text.
4. Select **Edit > Paste** from the Menu.
   Or
   Click the **Paste icon** on the Application Toolbar.

THE PASTE ICON

To Move Text from One Location to Another

1. **Select** the text you wish to move.
2. Select **Edit > Cut** from the Menu.
   Or
   Click the **Cut icon** on the Application Toolbar.

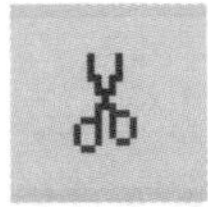

THE CUT ICON

3. Set the insertion point where you want to insert the text.
4. Select **Edit > Paste** from the Menu.
   Or
   Click the **Paste icon** on the Application Toolbar.

Formatting Text

One of the features of a **word processing program** such as WordPad is the ability to apply and modify the **formatting** of your document text, such as selecting the typeface (or font) of your text, selecting the size of your text, or emphasizing text by applying bold, italics, underlining or even changing the font color of the text. The ability to modify text formatting is a feature found in many different types of applications, not just word processing programs.

It is important to note that in order to change the formatting of text in the WordPad program, the text must be in **Rich Text Format (.rtf)**. To convert a text document to Rich Text Format, select **File > Save As** from the menu and then choose Rich Text Format from the **Save as type** drop-down list. Saving documents will be discussed in more detail in the next section.

In WordPad, as in many other programs, font formatting options are found in the **Formatting Toolbar**. In order to apply formatting to text, you must first select the text. Then, choose the desired formatting from the toolbar.

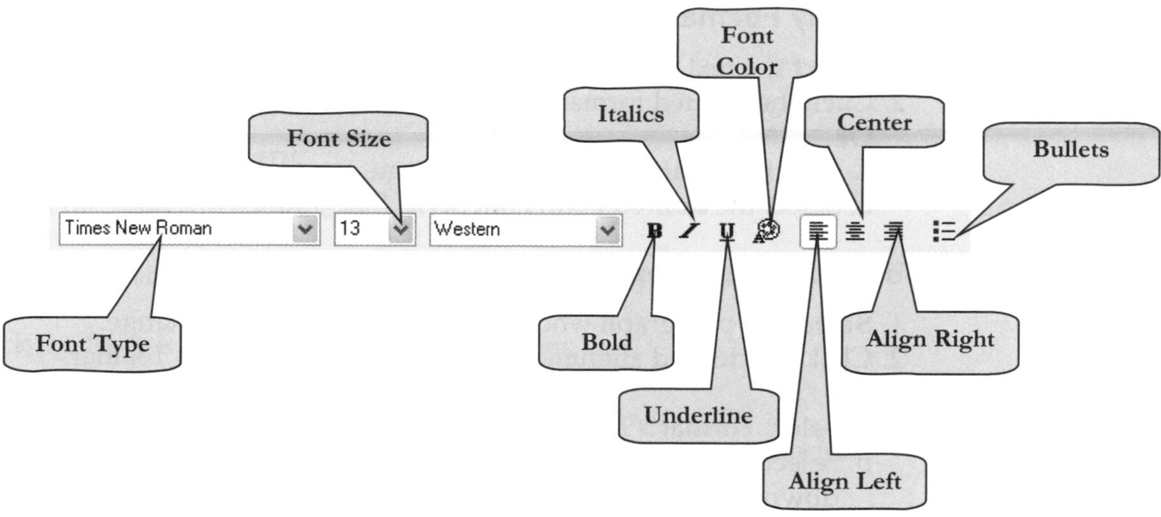

FORMATTING TOOLBAR

You can also use the **Font dialog box** to apply multiple formats (font type, font size, font style and color) to selected text at once. To display the Font dialog box, select **Format > Font** from the menu.

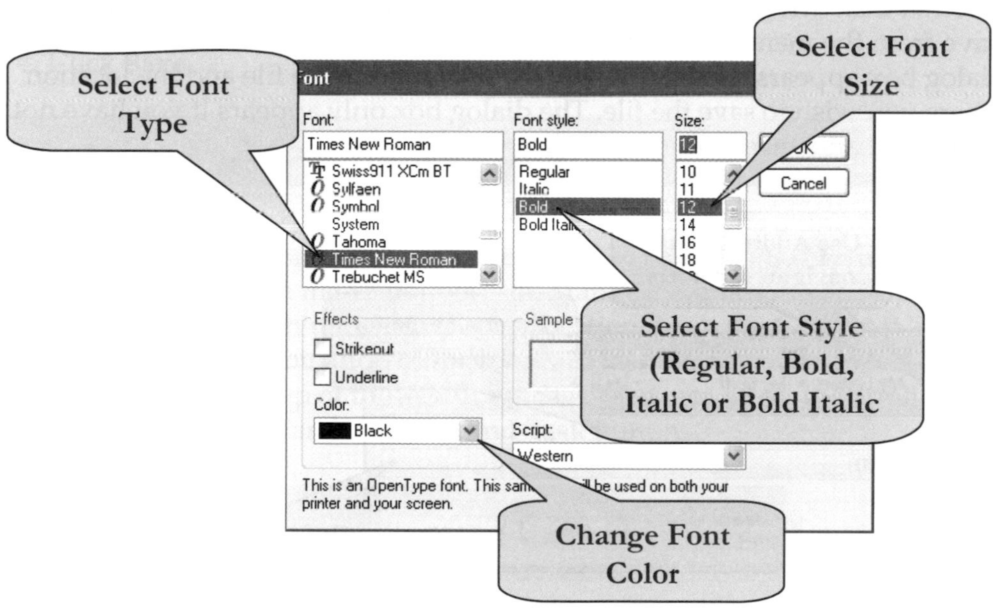

FONT DIALOG BOX

To change the alignment of a paragraph (the arrangement of text in relation to the left and right margins), choose **Format > Paragraph** from the menu and choose the desired alignment type from **Alignment drop-down list**. Or, click the desired alignment button on the Formatting Toolbar. There are three types of alignment that you can apply to a paragraph in WordPad:

- **Align Left**—text is flush with the left margin.
- **Align Right**—text is flush with the right margin.
- **Center**—text is positioned with an even space from the left and right margins.

To Force an Application to Quit

1. Press the **Ctrl + Alt + Delete** keystroke combination.
2. Click **Start Task Manager** from the screen that displays to launch the Windows Task Manager.
3. Click the **Applications** tab.
4. Select the application you wish to close.
5. Click the **End Task** button.
6. Click the **Close** button on the Windows Task Manager window.

NOTE: Using the End Task command is **NOT** a recommended way to close applications. This method should only be used when the application is unresponsive or otherwise out of control and all attempts to otherwise close the application have failed.

Moving the Taskbar

We have already seen the importance of the Taskbar in the Windows Vista multitasking environment. Every open program or window is represented by a **task button** on the Taskbar. Clicking the Taskbar makes that window the active window. However, the Taskbar does not have to be located on the bottom of the screen. You can move the Taskbar to a different location on your screen by clicking and dragging it to the desired location. Before you can change the location of the Taskbar, you will need to **unlock** it first, by right-clicking on the Taskbar and then selecting **Lock the Taskbar** to clear the checkmark designating that the Taskbar should be locked.

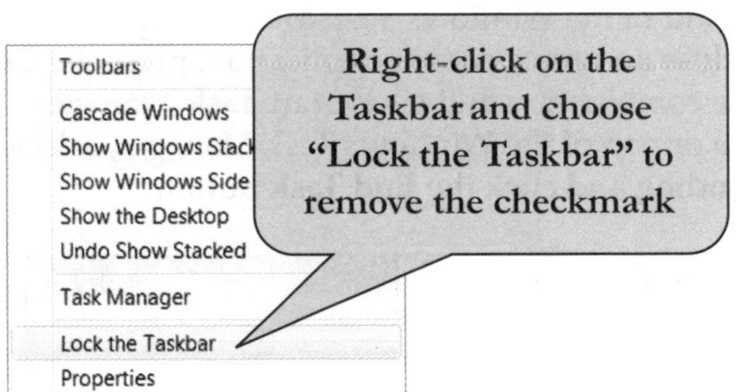

To Move the Taskbar

1. **Right-click** the Taskbar to display the pop-up menu.
2. Click **Lock the Taskbar** to clear the checkmark. The Taskbar is now unlocked.
3. Click and drag the Taskbar to the desired location.

Working with Taskbar Toolbars

You can use the Taskbar to display other **toolbars** that can help you use your computer more efficiently. To display available toolbars, right-click on any empty area of the Taskbar and choose the toolbar you wish to display on the pop-up menu. The toolbar will then appear on the Taskbar. The double-arrows on a toolbar indicate that more toolbar buttons are available.

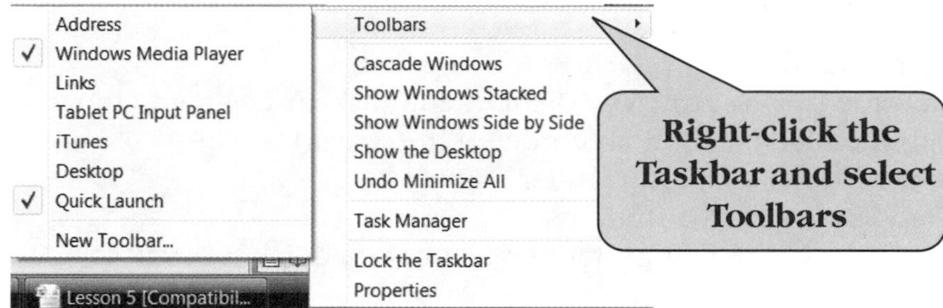

To Display Toolbars on the Taskbar

1. **Right-click** an empty area of Taskbar to display the pop-up menu.
2. Select **Toolbars** from the pop-up menu.
3. Select the desired toolbar from the Toolbars list.
4. Click the toolbar's double-arrow on the Taskbar to display the toolbar's commands.

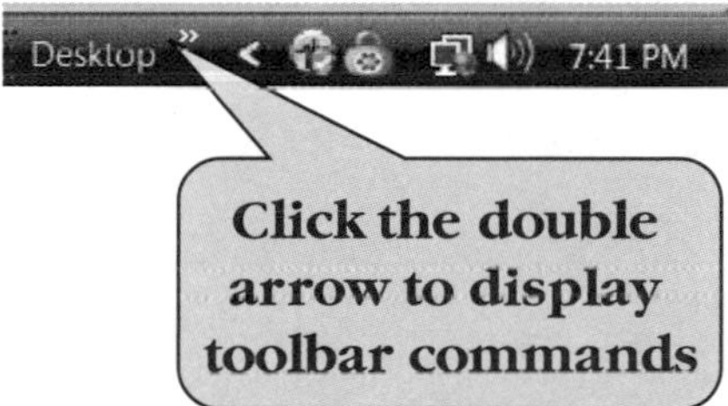

TIP: If you don't see a blank area on your Taskbar you can reduce or increase its size. Click the series of dots next to the leftmost Taskbar application icon and drag to the right to reduce the size of the Taskbar or to the left to increase it.

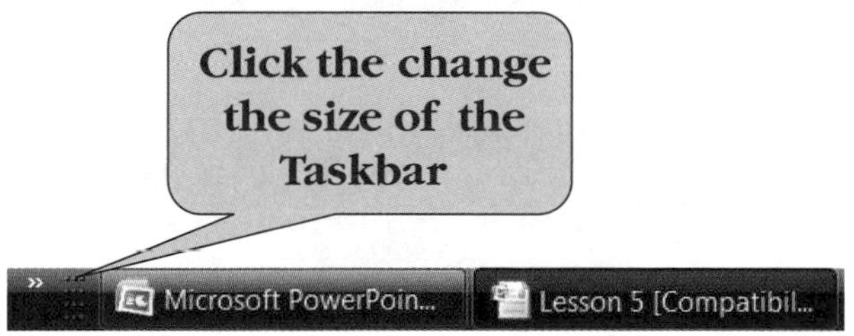

Setting Taskbar Properties

Taskbar Properties allow you to change the appearance of the Taskbar. To display the properties box, right-click on the Taskbar and then chose **Properties** from the pop-up menu. The **Taskbar and Start Menu Properties** dialog box will appear. On top of the box are four tabs—the Taskbar, the Start Menu, the Notification area and the Toolbars tabs. Clicking on the Taskbar tab displays Taskbar properties for that particular tab. From the Taskbar properties box, you can:

- Lock the Taskbar
- Auto-hide the Taskbar (only displays the Taskbar when you move your mouse pointer over bottom border of the screen).
- Keep the Taskbar on top of other windows.
- Group Similar Taskbar buttons.
- Display the Quick Launch toolbar (contains a quick shortcut to applications).

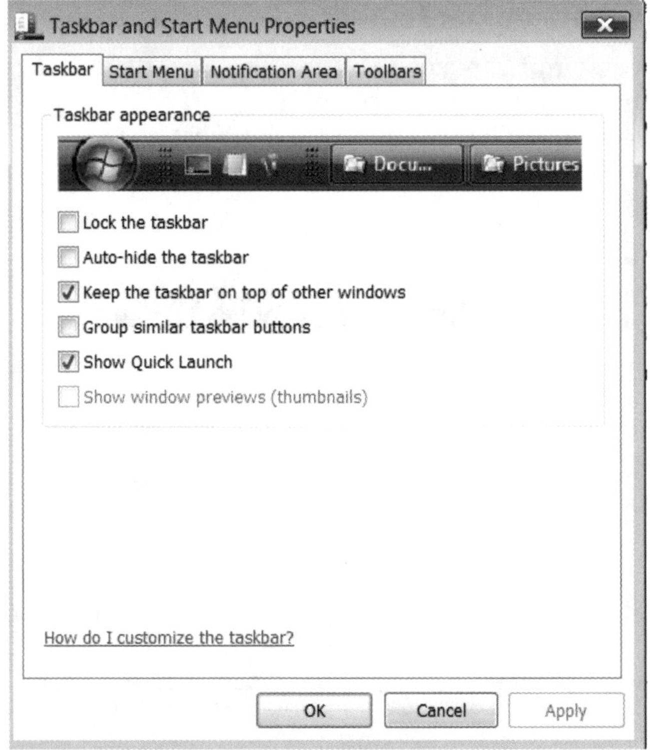

TASKBAR AND START MENU PROPERTIES DIALOG BOX

The Notification Area includes options to hide inactive icons from the system tray, thus making more room on the Taskbar. You can also choose which of the system icons to show from this area.

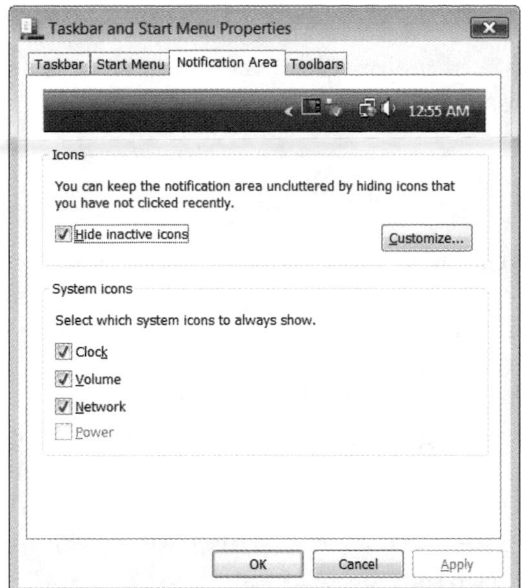

NOTIFICATION AREA TAB

The **Toolbars tab** provides another way to add toolbars to the Taskbar.

To Set Taskbar Properties

1. **Right-click** an empty area of Taskbar to display the pop-up menu.
2. Select **Properties** from the pop-up menu to display the Taskbar and Start Menu Properties dialog box.
3. Click the **Taskbar** tab.
4. Select the desired properties.
5. Click **Apply**.
6. Click **OK**.

Customizing the Quick Launch Toolbar

The **Quick Launch Toolbar**, located on the Taskbar to the right of the Start button, is a convenient way to open applications. You can add applications that you frequently use to the Quick Launch Toolbar by dragging their icon to the desired location on the toolbar.

THE QUICK LAUNCH TOOLBAR

To remove an icon from the Quick Launch toolbar, **right-click** the icon and choose **Delete** from the contextual menu.

To Add a Program to the Quick Launch Toolbar

1. Click the **Start** button and navigate to the program you want to add.
2. Click the icon of the application and **drag** it to the Quick Launch Toolbar
   Or
   Right-click the icon of the application and choose **Add to Quick Launch** from the contextual menu.

To Remove a Program to the Quick Launch Toolbar

1. Right-click the icon of the program you want to remove and chose **Delete** from the contextual menu.

Customizing the Start Menu

Start Menu Properties allow you to change the appearance of the Start Menu. To display the properties box, right-click on the Taskbar and then chose **Properties** from the pop-up menu. Click on the **Start Menu** tab on the **Taskbar and Start Menu Properties** dialog box.

From the Start Menu properties box, you can change the appearance of the Start Menu by choosing between the Windows Vista Start Menu style or the Classic Windows Start Menu Style. For more Start Menu options, click the **Customize button** to display the **Customize Start Menu** dialog box. From here, you can set options, such as icon size or such as choosing which items to display and how to display them.

START MENU TAB

CUSTOMIZE START MENU DIALOG BOX

If you use a program regularly, you can create a shortcut to it by **pinning** it to the Start Menu. This way, you do not have to drill down the All Programs folder to find your application each time you wish to launch it. To pin a program to the Start menu, right-click the desired program icon and then click **Pin to Start Menu** from the contextual menu.

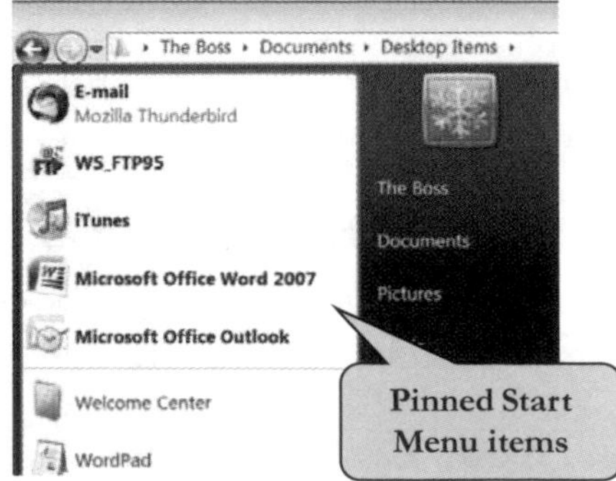

To remove a pinned item from the Start Menu, right-click the item and choose **Unpin from Start Menu**.

To Customize the Start Menu

1. **Right-click** an empty area of Taskbar to display the pop-up menu.
2. Select **Properties** from the pop-up menu to display the Taskbar and Start Menu Properties dialog box.
3. Click the **Start Menu** tab.
4. Click the **Start Menu radio button** to display the new Windows Vista Start Menu style. Click **Classic** to use the Start Menu used in earlier versions on Windows (Windows 95, 98 and 2000).
5. For more Start Menu properties, click the **Customize** button.

To Pin an Application to the Start Menu

1. Right-click the desired program icon and then click **Pin to Start Menu** from the contextual menu.
2. To remove a pinned item from the Start Menu, right-click the item and choose **Unpin from Start Menu**.

Setting the Color Scheme

Should you decide that you want to go "Classic" all the way, you can also change your desktop appearance to the Classic style that you may be used to seeing in earlier versions of Windows. The classic style is noted for square-cornered windows with smaller buttons whereas the XP look had rounded corners, larger buttons and a "crayon-like" appearance to it.

To change your desktop style to Windows Classic or to Windows Standard, right-click on a blank area of the Desktop and then trace to **Personalize** from the pop-up menu. Click the **Windows Color and Appearance** link on the Personalization page and then choose the desired Color scheme from the list box.

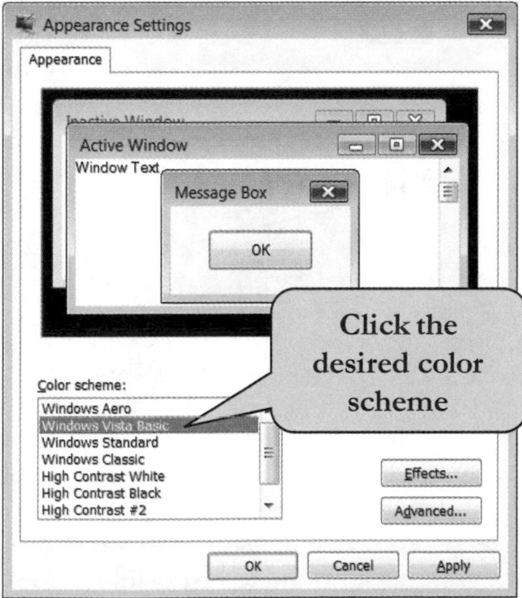

To Set the Windows Color Scheme

1. **Right-click** an empty area of Desktop to display the pop-up menu.
2. Click **Personalize**.
3. Click the **Windows Color and Appearance** link on the Personalization page.
4. Click the arrow on the right side of the **Windows and Buttons** combo box.
5. Choose the desired **Color scheme** from the list box.

> **TIP:** If you wish to use the new Flip 3-D feature, which is part of Windows Aero, you will need to set the Color Scheme to Windows Aero.

Changing the Desktop Background

Many computer users like to customize their Desktop background to suit their own personal tastes and personalities. The easiest way to do this is to change the **Desktop background** (also referred to as Wallpaper). This option is found in the Desktop Properties dialog box from the **Personalization page**.

Several background designs come packaged with Windows Vista with which you can decorate your desktop. A thumbnail preview of each design is displayed in the backgrounds box.

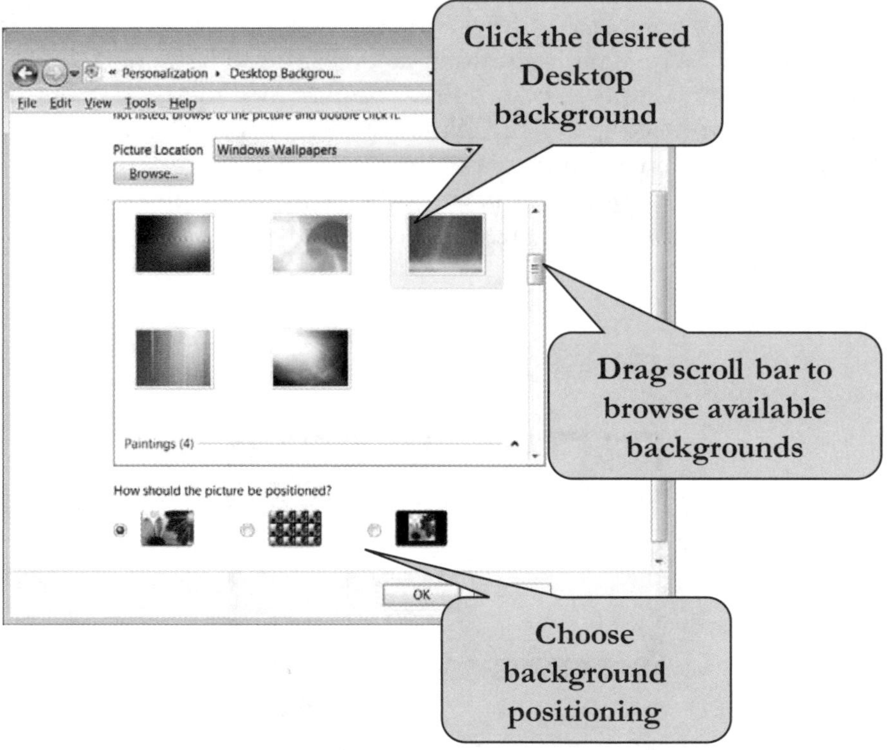

If you prefer to use a picture from a folder on your computer rather than one of the packaged images, click the **Browse** button and then navigate to the folder that contains the image file you wish to use. Once you have chosen your picture, specify how you want your background to be positioned: **Fit to Screen**, **Tile**, or **Center** by choosing the appropriate radio button on the bottom of the window.

To Change the Desktop Background

1. **Right-click** an empty area of Desktop to display the pop-up menu.
2. Select **Personalize**.
3. Click the **Desktop Background** link on the Personalization page.
4. In the Background window, click the image you would like to use as a Desktop background.
5. Drag the scroll bar in the Background window to browse available images.
6. Click the image you would like to use as a Desktop background.
7. To use a picture from a folder as the Desktop background:
   a. Click the **Browse** button.
   b. Navigate to the folder that contains the image you would like to use.
   c. Select the image.
   d. Click **Open**.
8. Click **OK** to close the Desktop Background dialog box and apply the changes.

Changing the Desktop Theme

Another way to customize your desktop is by modifying the desktop **Theme**. A theme is a collection of elements such as icons, fonts, colors, windows and it can include sounds. In addition to the themes that are included with Windows Vista, you can search for additional themes online.

To Change the Desktop Theme

1. **Right-click** an empty area of Desktop to display the pop-up menu.
2. Select **Personalize**.
3. Click the **Theme** link on the Personalization page.
4. Click the **Theme** drop-down list and choose the Theme you want.

TIP: If you wish to use the new Windows Aero features, you will need to set the Theme to Windows Vista.

Working with the Sidebar

New in Windows Vista is the **Windows Sidebar**, which allows you to organize your information quickly. The Sidebar appears on the right-edge of your computer and displays **gadgets**—mini-programs that display such information as weather reports, stock quotes, news headlines, search boxes or even a photo slideshow.

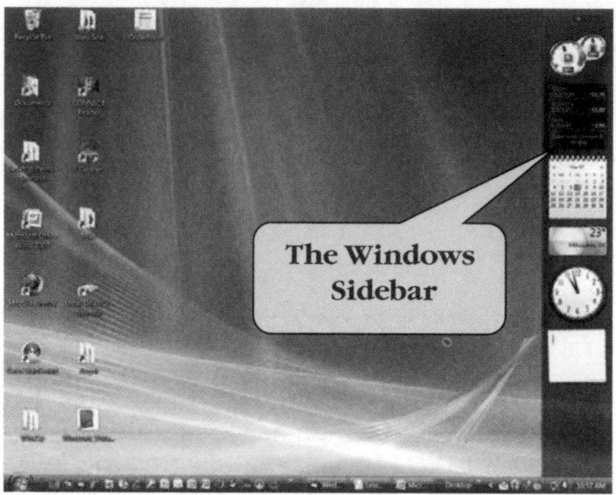

You can customize the Windows Sidebar by hiding it, keeping it on top of other windows, adding gadgets, removing gadgets, detaching gadgets and placing them on the desktop, setting Sidebar to open (or not open) each time you start your computer and more.

To open Windows Sidebar, click the **Windows Sidebar icon** in the Notification area (the System Tray) or type: **Sidebar** in the Search Box on the Start Menu and then press Enter. Once Sidebar is opened, you can modify its properties by right-clicking on the Sidebar strip and selecting **Properties** from the menu. From the properties box, you can set such options as keeping Sidebar on top of other windows and choosing which side of the screen to display the Sidebar.

You can add any installed gadget to Sidebar by right-clicking in the Sidebar strip and selecting **Add Gadget** from the pop-up menu. Double-click the gadget you wish to add from the Gadget Gallery box. Another way is to right-click on a gadget and choose **Add** from the pop-up menu. You can also display the Gadget Gallery by clicking the click the plus (+) symbol on top of the Sidebar.

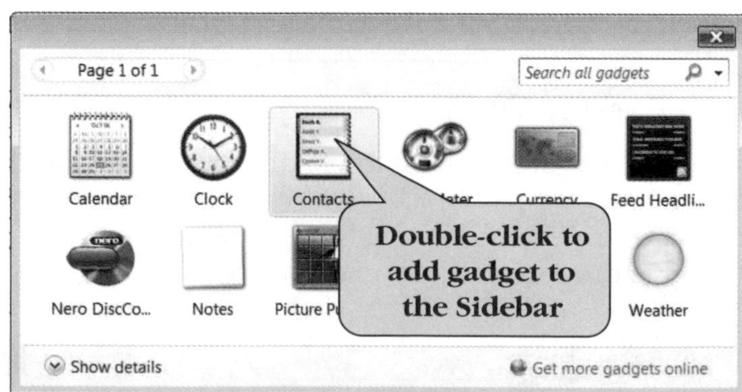

Many gadgets have individual options that you can set. As you move your mouse pointer over a gadget, a tiny toolbar appears. Click the wrench icon to access gadget options. You can also **right-click** a gadget and choose **Options** from the contextual menu. To close a gadget, click the **x** icon on the gadget toolbar.

If you wish, you can detach individual gadgets from the Sidebar and add them to your desktop. Right-click the gadget you want to detach and then choose **Detach from Sidebar** from the contextual menu. To move a gadget back to the Sidebar, right-click the gadget and choose **Attach to Sidebar**. To remove a gadget from the Sidebar, right-click the gadget and select **Close Gadget**.

If you prefer not to display the Sidebar, right-click in the Sidebar strip and choose **Close Sidebar**.

To Use the Sidebar

1. To open Windows Sidebar, click the **Windows Sidebar icon** in the Notification area (the System Tray)
   Or
   Type: **Sidebar** in the Search Box on the Start Menu and then press Enter.
2. To set Sidebar properties, right-click on the Sidebar strip and select **Properties** from the menu. Set your desired properties.
3. To add a gadget, right-click in the Sidebar strip and select **Add Gadget** from the pop-up menu to display the Gadget Gallery. Double-click the gadget you wish to add.
   Or
   Click the click the plus (+) symbol on top of the Sidebar to display the Gadget Gallery.

4. To set individual gadget options, click the wrench icon to the right of the gadget
   Or
   Right-click a gadget and choose **Options** from the contextual menu.
5. To bring the gadgets to the front from another window, press the Windows Logo key + the Spacebar.
6. To close the **Sidebar**, right-click Sidebar, and then click Close Sidebar.

Launching Applications at Startup

You can configure Windows Vista to automatically open applications or documents each time you start Windows. For instance, you may wish your email application and your calendar application to launch every time you log in. To designate which items that are to open, place a shortcut for the item in the **Startup** folder.

To display the Startup folder, **right-click** the Start button and then choose **Open** from the pop-up menu. Then, click the **Startup** folder in the Folder Tree. This will display the actual Startup folder window in the File List pane. Now, right-click and drag any items you want to launch automatically to the Startup folder and select **Copy Here** from the pop-up menu. Clicking and dragging with your **right mouse button** displays the "Copy Here, Move Here, Create Shortcuts Here" pop-up menu.

To remove an item from the Startup folder, display the folder, right-click and then select **Delete** from the pop-up menu.

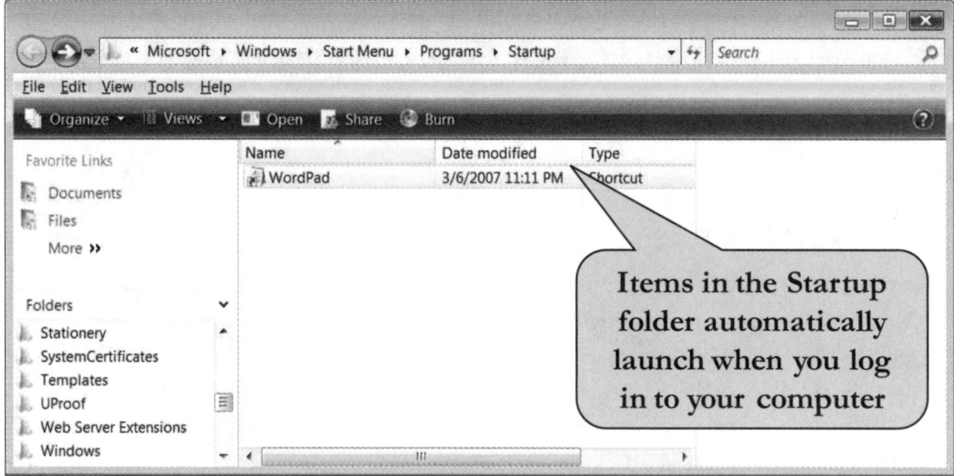

To Launch Applications at Startup

1. Right-click the **Start** button and then choose **Open**.
2. Click the **Startup** folder in the Folder Tree.
3. Click the **Start** button.
4. Click **All Programs** (or Programs if in Classic Mode).
5. Drill down to the folder that contains the application you wish launch at startup.
6. Press and hold down the **right mouse button** on the object you wish to launch at startup.
7. Drag to the Startup window.
8. Release the mouse button.
9. Select **Copy Here** from the pop-up menu.

Using Windows Aero

Windows Vista introduces a new three dimensional look called **Windows Aero**. It features a transparent glass design with window animations, new window colors and a translucent appearance. One of the features of Windows

Aero includes **Flip 3-D**, which displays your open windows in a 3-D stack. The active window is displayed on top of the stack. You can cycle through the stack of open windows by holding down the Microsoft Windows logo key and then pressing the Tab key. If you are not using a Windows keyboard, you can also click the **Switch between Windows** icon on the Taskbar.

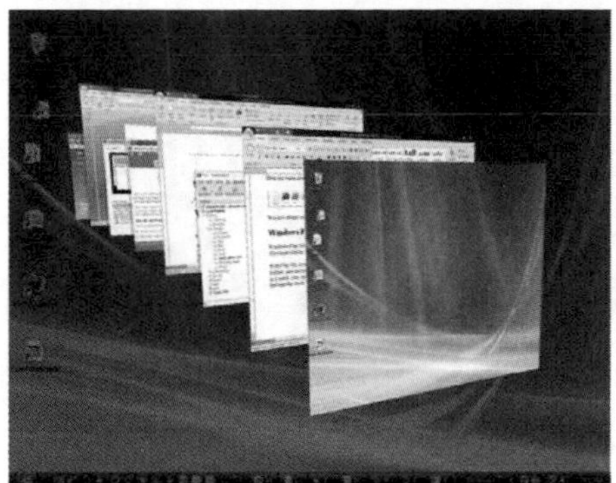

WINDOWS FLIP 3-D

Aero also includes Taskbar previews for your open windows. When you point to an icon on the Taskbar you'll see a thumbnail-sized preview of the window, whether the content of the window is a document, a photo, or a folder.

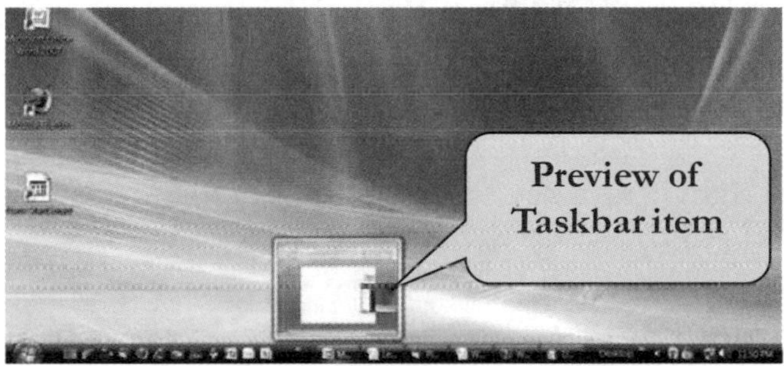

Before running Aero, you may need to make sure your computer meets the minimum requirements:

- 1-gigahertz (GHz) 32-bit (x86) or 64-bit (x64) processor
- 1 gigabyte (GB) of random access memory (RAM)
- 128-megabyte (MB) graphics card

Aero also requires a DirectX 9 class graphics processor that supports a Windows Display Driver Model Driver, Pixel Shader 2.0 in hardware, and 32 bits per pixel.

If you computer meets the requirements, you will then need to modify some settings to enable Aero:

- Color must be set to 32 bit
- Monitor refresh rate must be higher than 10 hertz
- Theme must be set to Windows Vista
- Color Scheme must be set to Windows Aero
- Window Frame Transparency is set to "On"

If your classroom computer does not meet the above requirements, then you will not be able to do the next Let's Try It Exercise—but feel free to experiment at home on your own computer!

To Enable Windows Aero

1. Set the Desktop theme to **Windows Vista**
2. Set the **Color Scheme** to **Windows Aero**
3. Click **Enable Transparency** in the Windows Color and Appearance dialog box.
4. Set the Color to 32 bit (Click Display Settings in the Personalization menu).

To Switch Windows Using Flip 3-D

1. Click the Switch between windows button on the Taskbar to open Flip 3D.
2. Click a window in the stack to activate that window.
3. To cycle through the windows in your stack, rotate the scroll wheel on your mouse
   Or
   Press the **Tab key**
   Or
   Press the **right arrow key** or **left arrow key** to cycle through the stack.
4. To close Flip 3-D, click anywhere outside the stack.

If using a Microsoft Keyboard)

1. Hold down the Windows logo key and then press **Tab**.
2. Continue to press Tab to cycle through the windows in the stack
   Or
   Press the **right arrow key** or **left arrow key** to cycle through the stack.
3. To close Flip 3-D, release the Windows logo key.

About the Control Panel

The **Control Panel** contains specialized tools that allow you to modify various settings of Windows and change the way Windows (and your computer) looks and behaves. Some of these tools allow you to adjust certain settings to make your computer more fun to use. For example, you can use change your mouse pointer to an animated icon, replace standard system sounds with your own, add wallpaper to your desktop, add a screen saver and change your computer's color scheme.

Other tools contain settings that make your computer easier to use. For instance, you can set various accessibility options and modify how your mouse and keyboard behave.

To display the Control Panel, click the **Start** button and then choose **Control Panel** on the right side of the Start Menu. You can also type: **Control Panel** in the Search Box and press Enter. If you are using Classic mode, point to **Start > Settings > Control Panel**.

CONTROL PANEL HOME

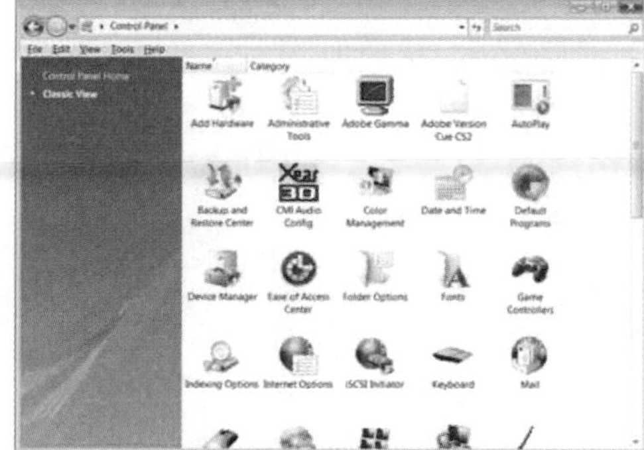

CLASSIC VIEW

The Control Panel Home is the main page for the Control Panel. If you prefer the Classic view in which all Control Panel tools are displayed in one window as icons, click **Switch to Classic View** from the Control Panel Home.

To Display the Control Panel

1. Click the **Start button**.
2. Click **Control Panel** on the Start Menu (if using Classic mode, select **Settings > Control Panel**).
3. Click **Control Panel Home** or **Switch to Classic View** on the left side of your screen to change to the desired view.

Modifying Date and Time Properties

The first Control Panel tool with which we are going to work is the **Date and Time Properties** dialog box, which allows you to change the date and time of your computer, set the time zone where you are located, or synchronize your computer's clock with an Internet Server. When saving or making changes to a file, the current date and time (according to your system's clock) is saved along with the file's information, allowing you to determine when a file was last modified.

The time is usually displayed in the right corner of the Taskbar. To display the date, move your mouse pointer over the clock on the Taskbar. A small box will pop-up displaying the current date (according to your computer).

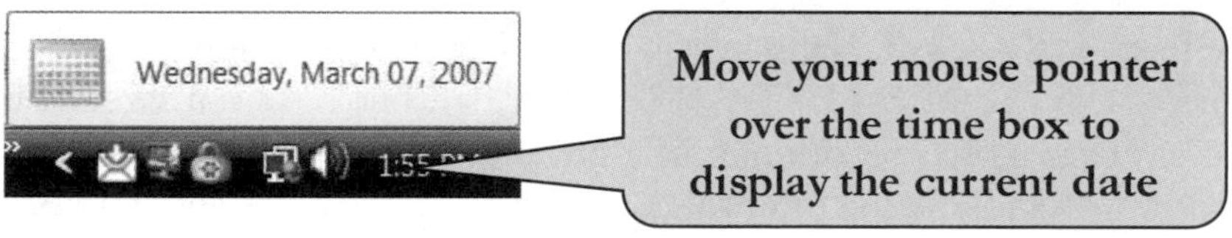
Wednesday, March 07, 2007
Move your mouse pointer over the time box to display the current date

You can open the Date and Time Properties dialog box from the Control Panel or by clicking the clock on the Taskbar and choosing **Change Date and Time Settings** from the pop-up menu.

DATE AND TIME PROPERTIES DIALOG BOX

To Change the Date and Time

1. Display the **Control Panel**.
2. Click **Clock, Language and Region**.
3. Click the **Date and Time** link.
4. Click the **Change Date and Time** button.
5. Click on the **Calendar Date** on top of the small calendar box and select the month you want from the list.
6. To choose a different year, click the **Year** on top of the box and choose the year you want from the list.
7. Click in the **Hour, Minute, Second** or **AM/PM** area of the **Time box** and make the appropriate changes.
8. Click **OK** to close the dialog box and apply the changes.

TIP: To set the **Time Zone**, click the **Change Time Zone** button on the Date and Time tab of the dialog box and select your Time Zone from the drop-down list.

Adding a Screen Saver

A **screen saver** is a picture, often animated, that appears on your computer screen after a specified time interval of inactivity. Screen savers were originally designed to prevent screen burn, a common problem with older computer monitors. Many people still use screen savers as a way to personalize their computer. To view Screen Saver options, click the Screen Saver tab in the **Display Properties** dialog box.

Additionally, you can protect your system while you are away by selecting the **On resume, display logon screen** option. When this option is set, you need to enter your login password in order to terminate the screen saver and gain access to your computer. Note that you must have an established login password to set this option.

Once a screen saver has been launched, you can clear it by moving your mouse or by pressing any key on your keyboard. If the password option is set, you will need to enter your correct login password before the screen saver will clear.

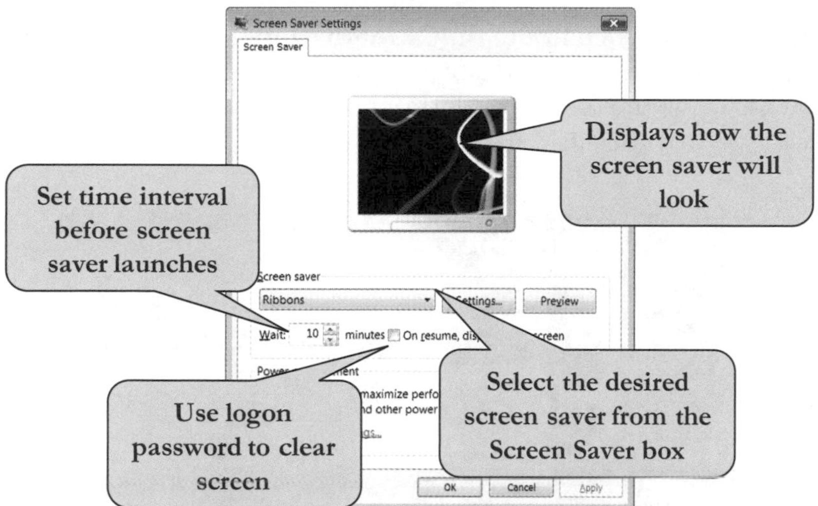

To Set or Change a Screen Saver

1. Display the **Control Panel**.
2. Click **Appearance and Personalization**
3. Under the **Personalization** category, click the **Change Screen Saver** link.
4. Click the **Screen Saver combo box** and select a screen saver to preview.
5. Click **Preview** to see how the selected screen saver will appear.
6. To end the screen saver preview, move your mouse or press any key on your keyboard.
7. Set the time interval that must pass before the screen saver launched in the **Wait** box (the selected screen saver will automatically start when your computer is idle for the time period specified in the Wait box).
8. If desired, click the **On resume, display logon screen** option.
9. Click **Settings** to display additional screen saver settings, if any.

TIP: You can also access the Screen Saver dialog box from the Personalize menu by clicking a blank area of the **Desktop**, selecting **Personalize** from the pop-up menu and then clicking the **Screen Saver** link.

Setting Power Management Options

The **Power Management** feature of Windows allows you to set various options to conserve power and increase the life of your computer. For instance, you can configure your computer to turn off manually or to power off after a specified interval of time. In addition, you can set your own **Power Schemes** to switch between several different power management options. Power management options that you can set include turning off the monitor, turning off the hard disk, putting your system on standby or putting your system into hibernation.

On **standby**, your computer switches to low power mode, and turns off the monitor and hard disk. Pressing a key or moving your mouse will cause your computer to come out of standby. Standby is especially using in conserving battery power in laptop computers.

When you put your computer into **hibernation**, everything in computer memory is saved on your hard drive and your computer is powered off. When you restart your computer, all programs and documents that were open when hibernation was initiated are restored on your desktop.

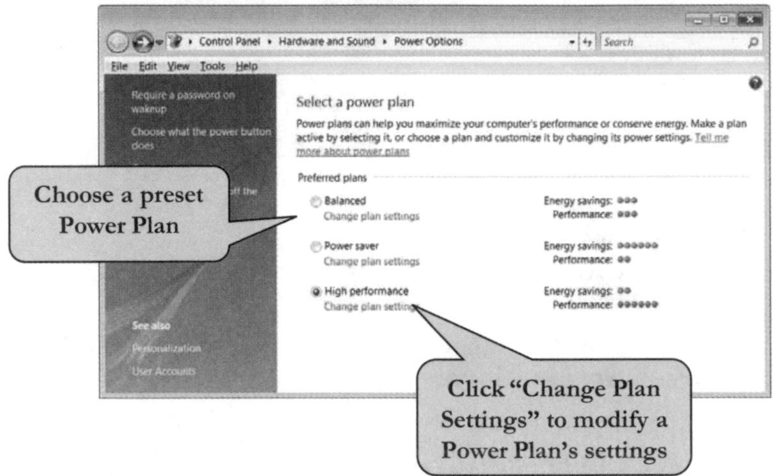

Power Schemes are a set of predefined power options that you can use or you can create you own if desired. The power options that you can set depend on the type of computer you have. For instance, there will be different options for a laptop computer than for a desktop computer. To create your own power plan, click **Create a Power Plan** from the Power Plan menu. You will be prompted for a name for your new power plan and to enter the settings you want.

To Set Power Management Options

1. Display the **Control Panel**.
2. Click **System and Maintenance**.
3. Click **Power Options** to display the **Power Options Properties** dialog box.
4. Click the radio button next to the power plan you want.
5. Click the **Change plan settings** link to display the Edit Plan Settings dialog box from where you can modify the power options for a particular plan.
6. From the Edit Plan Settings dialog box, choose when to turn off the display and/or when to put the computer to sleep.
7. Click **Change advanced power settings** to display additional options.
8. On the Advanced settings tab, expand the category that you want to customize, expand each setting that you want to change. Enter the values you want

Modifying the Window Color Scheme

We have already learned in the last chapter that you can change the appearance of Windows by choosing a color scheme such as Windows Classic, Windows Aero, or Windows Standard. You can also access this option from the Appearance and Personalization category of the Control Panel. In addition to choosing a color scheme, the Advanced button allows you further modify the selected theme by choosing such options as colors and font size

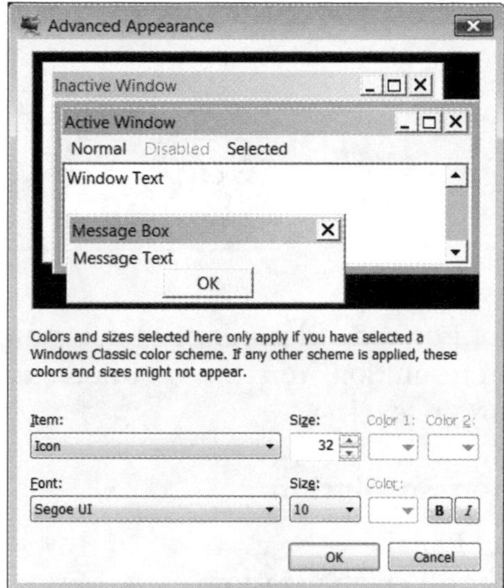

ADVANCED APPEARANCE OPTIONS

To Change the Window Color Scheme

1. Display the **Control Panel**.
2. Click **Appearance and Personalization**
3. Under the **Personalization** category, click the **Change the Color Scheme** link.
4. Click the desired color scheme from the list box.
5. Click the **Advanced** button to set additional options.
6. Click the object whose settings you want to change from the **Item** combo box and enter the settings you want.
7. Click **OK**.

Modifying the Screen Resolution

Screen Resolution refers to the size of the images on your computer screen. A higher screen resolution reduces the size of the items on your screen, thus increasing the relative space on your Desktop. Likewise, a lower screen resolution increases the size of the objects on your screen and reduces your relative Desktop space. The option for changing screen resolution is found under the **Adjust Screen Resolution** link in the **Personalization** category of the Control Panel. Drag the **Screen Resolution Slider** to the left to decrease the resolution or to the right to increase the screen resolution.

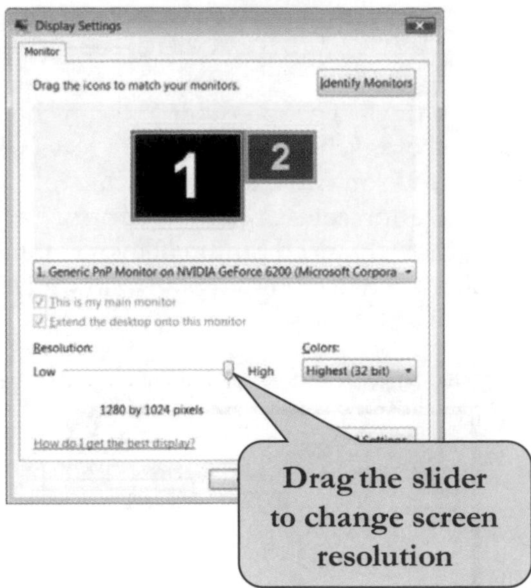

Your hardware (monitor and video adapter) determine how much you can change your screen resolution. You may be unable to adjust the resolution beyond a certain level.

To Change the Screen Resolution

1. Display the **Control Panel**.
2. Click **Appearance and Personalization**
3. Under the **Personalization** category, click the **Adjust Screen Resolution** link.
4. Drag the **Screen Resolution Slider** to the left to decrease screen resolution (objects appear larger) or to the right to increase screen resolution (objects appear smaller).
5. If you wish to use the **Windows Aero** feature, click the **Colors** arrow and choose **32 bit**.
6. Click **OK**.

Setting Folder Options

Folder Options allow you to specify how your folders function and how folder content is displayed. For instance, you can set your folders to display (or hide) system files and folders from view. You can also choose to open folders and files with either a single click or a double click.

To display the **Folder Options dialog box**, click the **Folder Options** link in the Appearance and Personalization category of the Control Panel. Click the desired tab (General, View, or Search) and set any desired folder options.

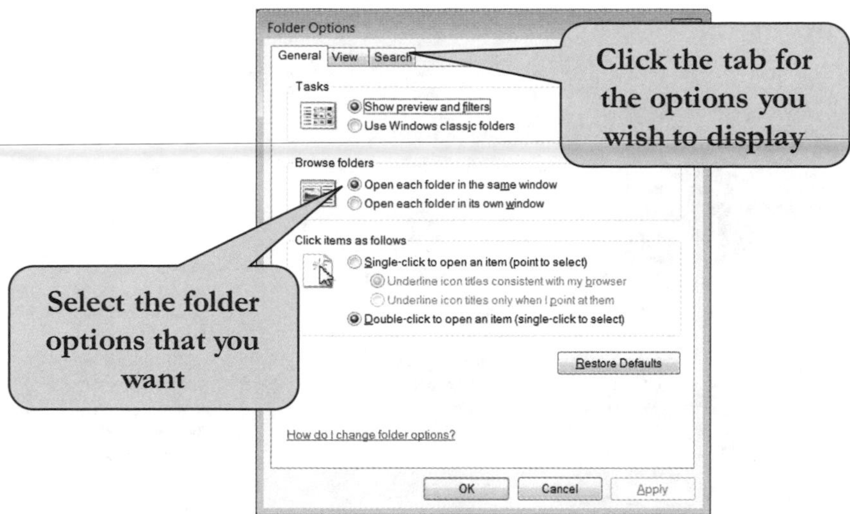

TIP: You can also access folder options by clicking the **Organize button** in any folder window and choosing **Folder and Search Options** from the menu.

To Modify Folder Options

1. Display the **Control Panel**.
2. Click **Appearance and Personalization Link**.
3. Click the **Folder Options** link on the Appearance and Personalization page.
4. Click the **General**, **View** or **Search** tab.
5. Set any desired options.
6. Click **OK**.

Changing or Removing Programs

The Programs and Features tool helps you mange the applications and windows components on your system. With this tool, you can install new windows components, remove existing applications or windows components that you no loner use or need, or install updates, device drivers or program over the internet from Microsoft.

Uninstalling an application should only be accomplished with the Uninstall or Change a Program tool. Simply deleting the program icon or folder will not remove all of the components that were added when the program was initially installed. When installing an application, files often are placed in several different locations on your computer.

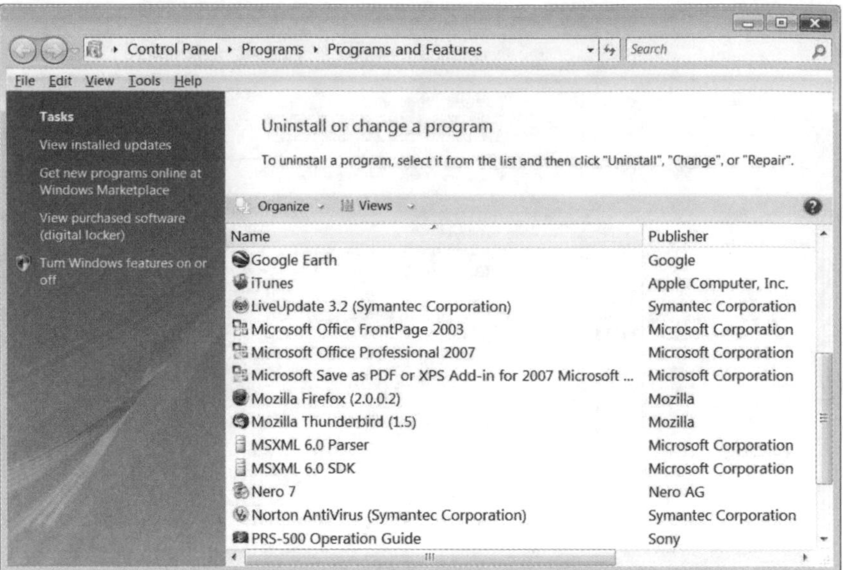

UNINSTALL OR CHANGE A PROGRAM WINDOW

To Remove or Change Programs

1. Display the **Control Panel**.
2. Click the **Programs** link.
3. Click the **Programs and Features** link.
4. To remove a program from your system:
   a. Click the **Uninstall** button on the toolbar.
   b. Follow the instructions (may vary depending on the program).
5. To turn **Windows features** on or off:
   a. Click the **Turn Windows features on or off** link in the left pane.
   b. Check any components you want to turn on.
   c. Uncheck any components you want to turn off.

NOTE: In the **Let's Try It** exercise, we will only look at the various options available. We will not actually add, remove or change any programs on your system.

Modifying Mouse Options

While your mouse should work the first time you start up your computer, many users wish to make changes to its functionality or change the appearance of the mouse pointer. For instance, you can adjust the speed the of "double-click", change the pointer speed, leave a trail of pointers as your move your mouse across the screen or hide your mouse pointer from view when you are typing. You can even personalize your mouse pointer by changing the **Pointer Scheme**.

Mouse options are located under the **Mouse** category in the **Hardware and Sound** area of the Control Panel. Adjusting mouse settings can make it easier for you to work with your computer.

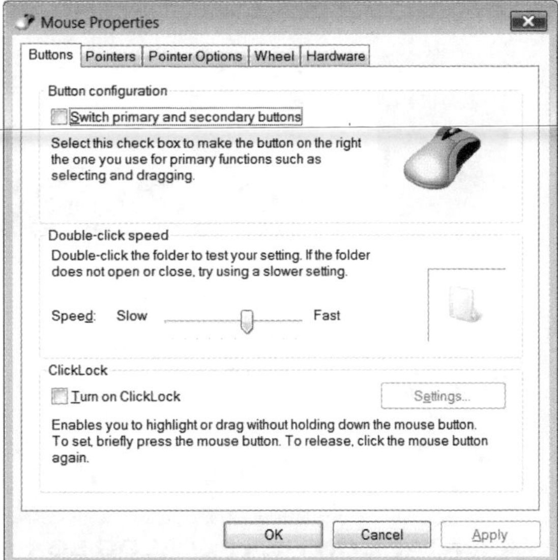

MOUSE PROPERTIES DIALOG BOX

To Adjust Mouse Settings

1. Display the **Control Panel**.
2. Click the **Hardware and Sound** link.
3. Click the **Mouse** link.
4. Click the desired Mouse Properties tab to view its settings.
5. Set any desired mouse properties.
6. Click **OK** when finished.

Administrator Access Tools

There are several additional tools on the Control Panel that can only be used by someone with administrator access. As you may not have such access on your class computer, we will briefly mention some of these tools and will not do any hands-on exercises. Use the Help and Support Center for additional information on using these tools.

Parental Controls

You can use Parental Controls to help manage how your children use the computer. For example, you can set time limits on your children's access to the Web, control the types of Web content your child can view, the hours that they can log on to the computer, and which games they can play and programs they can run based on content rating and more. You can access Parental Controls from the **User Accounts and Family Safety category** of the Control Panel.

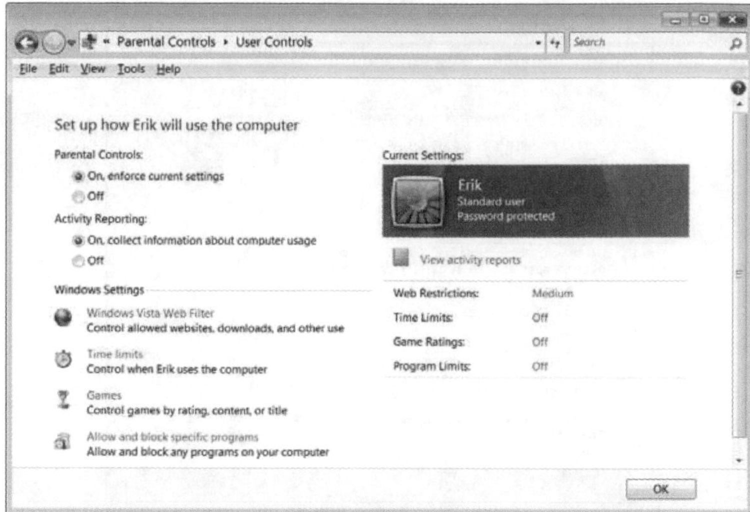

PARENTAL CONTROLS DIALOG BOX

User Accounts

Before you can set up Parental Controls, you will need to set a User Account for each person who has access to the computer. The User Account information tells Windows what files and folders a user can access, what changes a user can make to the computer, as well as a user's personal preferences, such as your desktop background or color theme. Each user will access the computer with their own user name and password. To set up a user account, click the **Add or Remove User Accounts** link under the User Accounts and Family Safety area of the Control Panel.

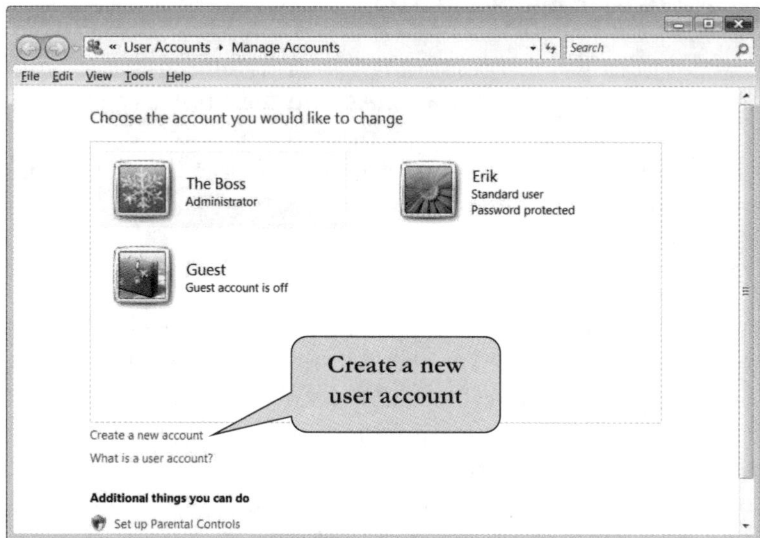

USER ACCOUNTS DIALOG BOX

Security

The **Security area** of the Control Panel contains many options for protecting your computer. Some of these are essential, especially if your computer has always-on Internet Access. The available Security options that you can set are:

- **Windows Firewall**—prevents hackers or malicious software from gaining access to your computer through a network or the Internet.
- **Windows Defender**—New in Vista, Windows Defender scans your system for Spyware, malicious or other unwanted software.
- **Windows Update**—downloads latest Windows security updates and system updates. It is a good idea of turn on automatic updates so that you system has always the latest updates.
- **Internet Security**—Allows you to configure Internet configuration and security options.

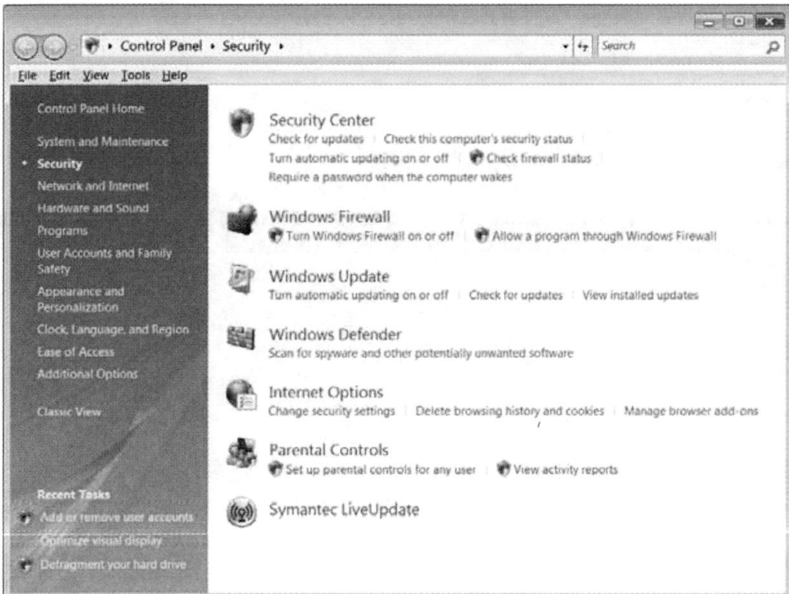

SECURITY PAGE

Disk Defragmenter

The **Disk Defragmentation** tool, located under the **Administrative Tools** category of the **System and Maintenance** area of the Control Panel, consolidates fragmented files on your hard disk to improve system performance. You should defragment your hard drive on a regular basis. You can also access the Disk Defragmentation tool from the Accessories > System Tools subfolder under the All Programs folder of the Start Menu.

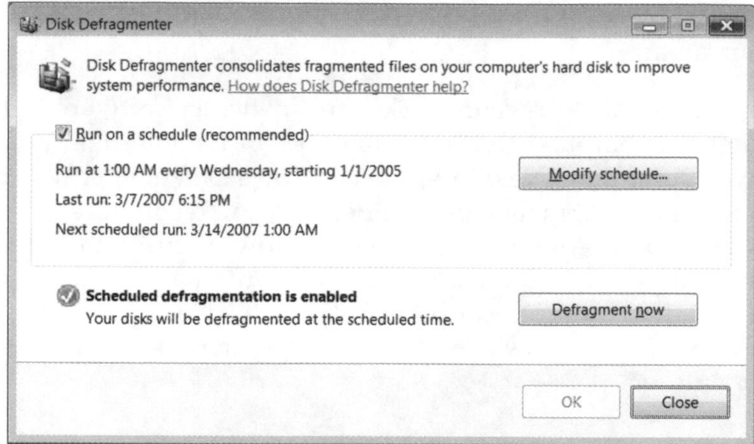

DISK DEFRAGMENTER DIALOG BOX

Conclusion

You have completed Introduction to Windows Vista. You are now ready to use several features of Windows Vista that you have learned in this chapter. You are encouraged to experiment with all you have learned in this chapter. To reinforce your understanding of these techniques, it is recommended that you read and work through it once again.

Introduction to Internet Explorer 7

CHAPTER

2

OBJECTIVES

After successfully completing this chapter, you should able to:

- Understand the Internet
- Launch Internet Explorer 7
- Use the Menu Bar, Address Bar, Links Bar, and Full-Screen Mode
- Use Internet Explorer Buttons
- Stop/Reload a Web Page
- View History
- Use Tabbed Browsing
- Open a Local Web Page
- Save a Web Page
- Save a Picture from a Web Page
- View the Page Source
- Print a Web Page
- Search the Web
- Create, Rearrange, Rename, and Delete Favorites Folders
- Edit Favorites Info
- Import & Export Favorites
- Work with to RSS Feeds
- Save a Tab Group
- Changing the Text Size & Zoom on Web Pages
- Change your Home Page
- Manage Browsing History
- Change Search Settings
- Adjust Tabbed Browsing Settings
- Adjust Security and Privacy Settings
- Block Pop-Ups
- Use the Content Advisor
- Change Program Settings
- Use the Phishing Filter

Understanding the Internet

Welcome to Internet Explorer 7! Before we dive right in and work with Internet Explorer (often referred to as IE), we will first briefly discuss what the **Internet** is. The Internet is an enormous computer network that connects millions of computers across the planet. The Internet is not one single entity but rather a network of different smaller networks. The Internet connects all of these smaller networks together.

Some people mistakenly refer to their electronic mail service as the Internet. In actuality, the Internet consists of several different services. One of these is **Electronic Mail** (e-mail) which allows you to almost instantly send and receive private messages with any other Internet user all over the world. There are many software programs available that you can use to read e-mail. One of these, **Windows Mail**, comes bundled with Windows Vista. Window Mail is a lighter version of Microsoft Outlook, which comes bundled with Microsoft Office. If you are using previous versions of Windows (XP or earlier), Outlook Express was the bundled e-mail program that came with Internet Explorer.

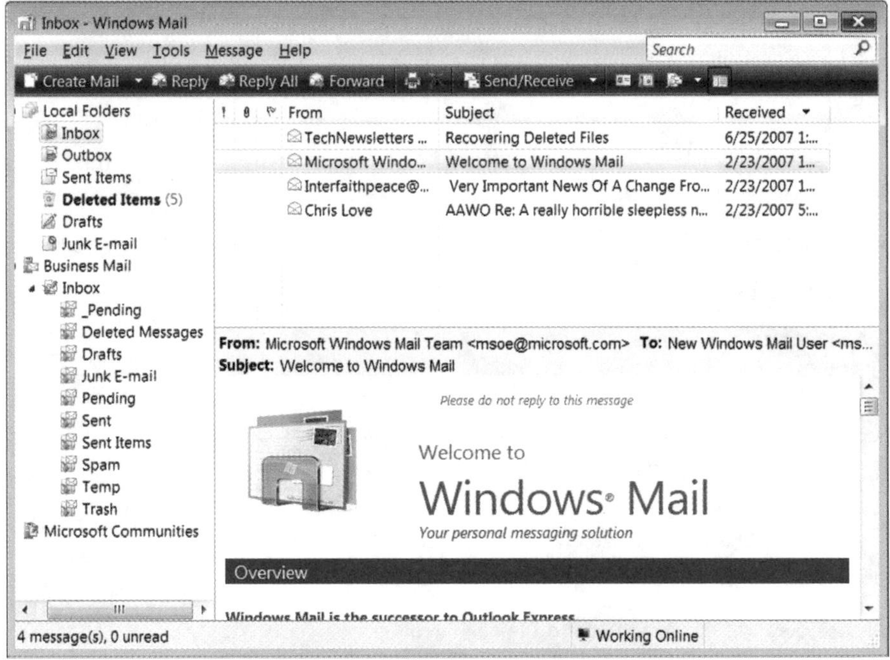

WINDOWS MAIL E-MAIL PROGRAM

Newsgroups are online discussion groups allowing Internet users to share ideas on a wide variety of topics. Most newsgroups are distributed over a network called **Usenet** and a special newsreader software is required to access them. There are, however, many discussion groups that are not part of Usenet, such as Yahoo! Groups or MSN. Newsreader software often comes bundled with a Web Browser or E-mail program. You can access Usenet groups with Outlook Express 6, the software that comes bundled with IE 6.

Another service, **File Transfer Protocol (FTP)**, allows you to upload files to or download files from a network server. There are thousands of FTP sites that make their files available for downloading. Depending on the site, you may have to set up an account and enter a username and password. There are several FTP software programs available, such as WS FTP and Cute FTP. Additionally, Internet Explorer has built-in FTP support.

Internet Relay Chat (IRC) is a service that allows you to chat live with other Internet users. Using IRC requires special chat software programs.

The **World Wide Web (WWW—also referred to as "the Web")**, the most popular Internet service, displays information organized into **Web Pages**. A Web page is a document that can consist of text, graphics, animations, video and sound. In order to access Web, you need to use a program called a **Web browser**. Windows Vista comes bundled with one of the most popular Web Browsers, Internet Explorer 7 (the topic of this course). If you are using a previous version of Windows, you can download Internet Explorer 7 (IE7) from the Microsoft Web site for free.

Before being to use any of the Internet services, you first must be connected to the Internet. If you are at work, your Internet connection has most likely already been set up for you. If you want to access the Internet from home, you will need to establish your connection through an **Internet Service Provider (ISP)**, connecting through either a phone line and modem, or a DSL (Digital Subscriber Line) connection.

Launching Internet Explorer 7

You can launch Internet Explorer from the Start Menu. Click the **Start** button and click **Internet Explorer**. You may also be able to access Internet Explorer from the **Quick Launch Toolbar** if it is displayed. If you have a **default home page** specified in the General tab of the Internet Options dialog box, it will display after the browser has launched.

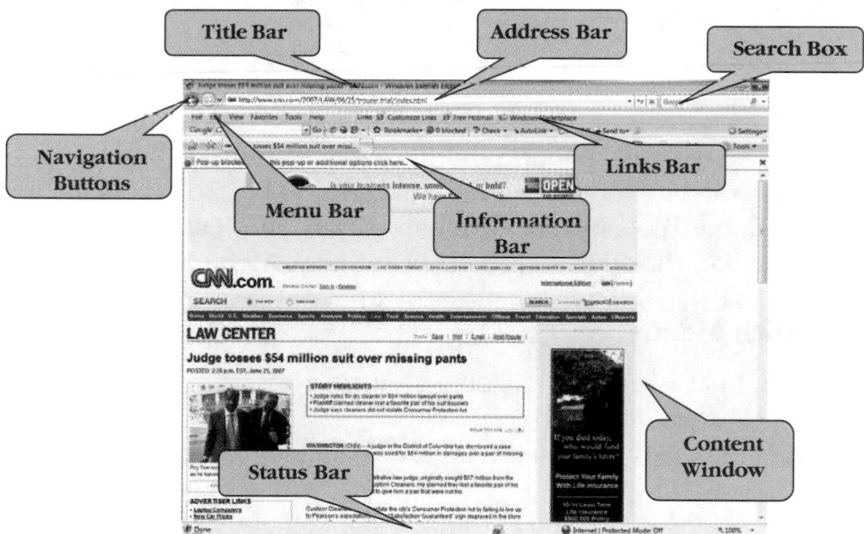

To Launch Internet Explorer

1. Click the **Start** button and then click **Internet Explorer**.
   Or
   Click on the **Internet Explorer** icon on the Quick Launch Toolbar on the bottom of your screen.

The Menu Bar

On top of the Internet Explorer window is the **Title Bar**. The title bar always displays the name of the Web page that you are currently viewing. For instance, if you are viewing Microsoft's Web Page, the title "Microsoft Corporation" will display in the Title Bar.

Directly below the Title Bar is the **Menu Bar**. The Menu Bar contains **menus** which are used to execute commands in Internet Explorer. Clicking on a menu displays a list of commands for that particular menu. You can also press the **Alt key** and the underlined letter of the menu item to display the menu's commands. For instance, press **Alt + T** to display the commands for the Tools menu. To execute a command, click on its name in the menu. Some menus have **submenus**—that is to say, a menu within a menu. Submenus are designated by a right-pointing black arrow. Clicking on the black arrow will display the submenu.

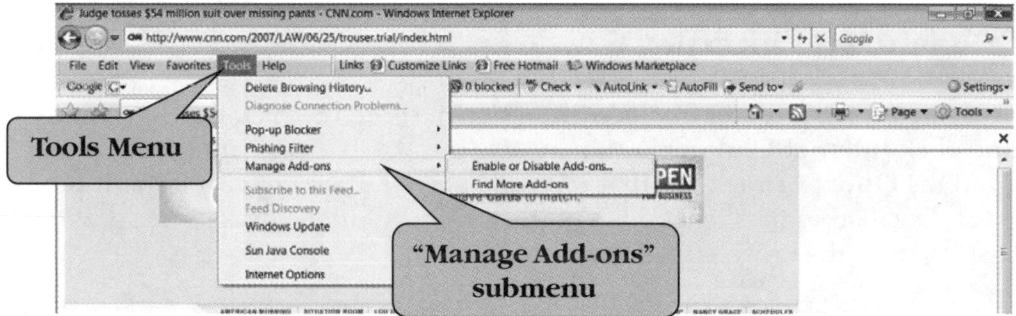

If you have worked with other Windows programs, you may already be familiar with the **File**, **Edit**, **View**, and **Help** menus. The **Favorites** and **Tools** menu are additional menus found in Internet Explorer.

By default, the Menu Bar is hidden when Internet Explorer is installed. To display it, click the **Tools button** and then click **Menu Bar** from the list. To hide the menu bar, click the Tools button and click Menu Bar again.

To Work with Menus

1. If the Menu Bar is hidden, click the **Tools button** on the Command Bar and then click **Menu Bar** to display it.
2. Click the menu name on the Menu Bar to display its commands
   Or
   Hold down the **Alt key** and then press the key of the underlined letter in the menu name.
3. To display a **submenu**, move your mouse cursor over the submenu name. A right-pointing arrow next to the name designates a submenu.
4. Click on a command to execute it.

Using Internet Explorer Buttons

Beneath the Title Bar you will find several clickable buttons that perform common tasks when clicked. Some buttons contain menus that allow you to perform tasks or to navigate to specific locations. Menu buttons have a downwards-pointing arrow on the right side of the button which when clicked, will display a menu. To see what a button does, move your mouse pointer of any button to display an information message as to the purpose of the button.

Some programs will install additional toolbars such as the Google or Yahoo! Toolbar, which will contain their own set of buttons. Each of the standard Internet Explorer buttons is explained in the table below.

Icon	What It Does
Back	Returns to the previous page that you viewed.
Forward	Moves to the next page that you recently viewed.
Stop	Cancels the downloading of a Web page.
Tools Tools	Displays the Tools menu from where you can access the same commands as on the Tools menu on the Menu bar.
Page Page	Displays the Page menu from where you can open a new window, save a Web page as a file, change the text size and zoom level, send a page or link by e-mail, etc.
Print	Prints the current Web page without displaying the Print dialog box. Click the arrow on the icon for additional printing options.
RSS Feeds	Allows you to view the available RSS Feeds on the current Web page.
Refresh	Retrieves a fresh copy of the current Web Page.
Home	Takes you to the page that you designated as your Home page. Click the arrow for additional Home page options.
Favorites Center	Displays/hides the Favorites Center. Favorites contain a list of your saved Internet Locations.
Add to Favorites	Adds the current Web page to the Favorites Center.

To Use the Command Buttons

1. Click on the desired Command Button to execute its command.
2. To display a button's menu, click the drop-down arrow next to the button.

The Address Bar

Beneath the Title Bar is the **Address Bar**. The **Address Bar** displays the current **URL (Uniform Resource Locator)** or **Web address**. Click on the arrow to the far right of the Address Bar to view a list of recently viewed Web Pages. As you visit Web Pages, Internet Explorer adds the URL for each Web Page to the bottom of the Address Bar drop-down list. Click on any of the address in the list to return to back to that Web Page.

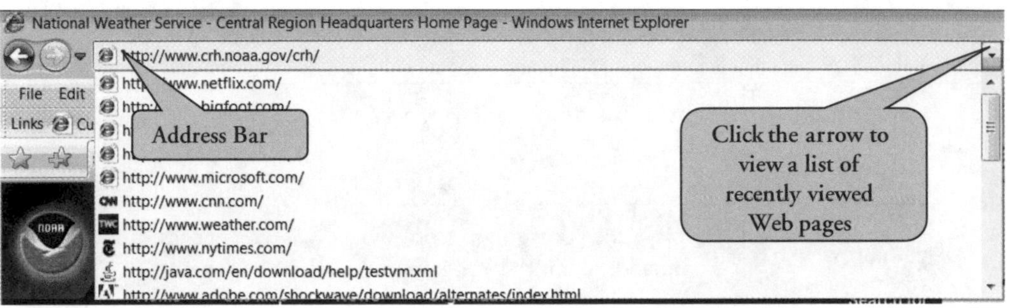

The Address Bar is also used to visit new Web Pages. Type in the Web Address in the Address Bar and then press the **Enter key**. The Web Page will then display in the browser window.

To Use the Address Bar

1. Click in the **Address Bar** to select the current address (if any).
2. Type in the address for the Web Page you wish to visit.
3. To view a list of recently viewed pages, click the **drop-down arrow** located on the far right of the Address Bar.
4. To return to a recently viewed page, click the drop-down arrow on the Address Bar and then **click the desired Web Address** in the list.

The Links Bar

Beneath the Address Bar is the **Links Bar**. The **Links Bar** contains buttons that allow you to jump quickly to a few specific Web Pages. Clicking on the button or **link** will display the Web page associated with that link in the Web browser. When Internet Explorer is first installed, the Links bar contains some default links. To **remove** any of these default links, **right-click** on the link on the Links Bar and select **Delete** from the contextual menu.

You can also add your own links to the Links Bar. First, display the Web page that you want to add to the Links Bar. Then, drag the Web page icon that is located to the left of the URL to the Links Bar. A black **I-beam** will display between the existing buttons as you drag, informing you of where the link will appear. When the link is in the desired position on the Links Bar, release the mouse button.

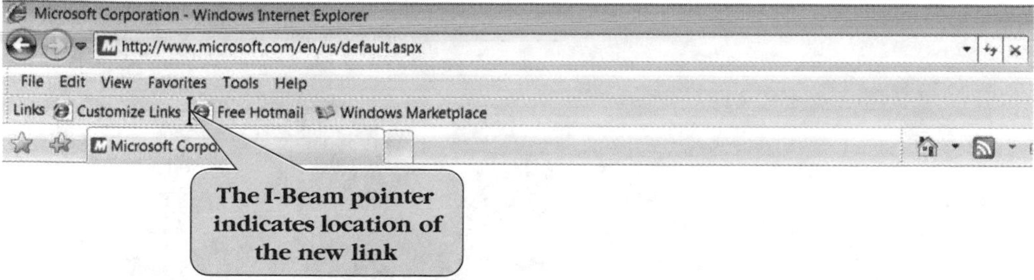

If there is not enough room on the Links Bar for all of the links you've added, a double-arrow will appear on the right-side of the Links Bar. Clicking on the double-arrow displays a menu allowing you access to your links

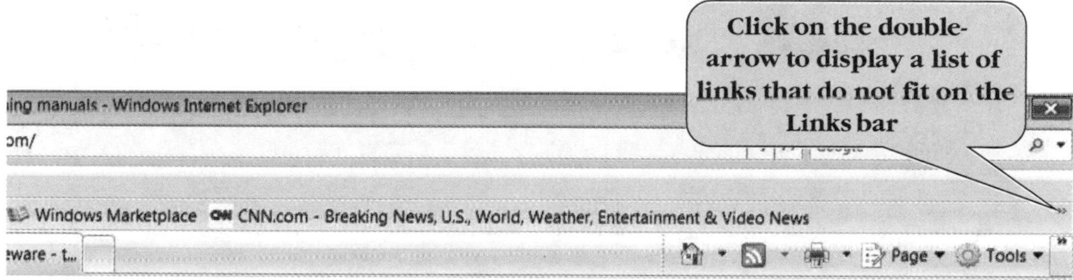

If you only see the word "**Links**" on the right side of your screen but none of the links that you added, you will need to expand the Links Bar. Click on the word "Links" and drag to the left until the links on the Links Bar are visible.

To Use the Links Bar

1. Click on the link on the Links Bar to jump to the Web page associated with the link.
2. To **add a link** to the Links Bar:
   a. Display the Web page whose link you wish to add.
   b. Drag its Web page icon to the location on the Links Bar where you want the link to appear. An I-beam pointer indicates its location.
   c. Release the mouse button.
3. To **delete a link**, right-click the link on the Links Bar and select **Delete** from the contextual menu.

> **TIP:** You can also add links to the Links Bar from the Add to Favorites button menu. We will work with Favorites later in this chapter.

Using Full Screen Mode

When viewing a Web page with a lot of information, you may find it necessary to scroll in order to view all of the contents of the Web page. To minimize the amount of scrolling, you can work in **Full-Screen mode**. When viewing a Web page in Full-Screen mode, the Command Bar, the Menu Bar, the Address Bar and Links Bar are no longer visible. Move your mouse pointer to the top of your screen to temporarily redisplay them.

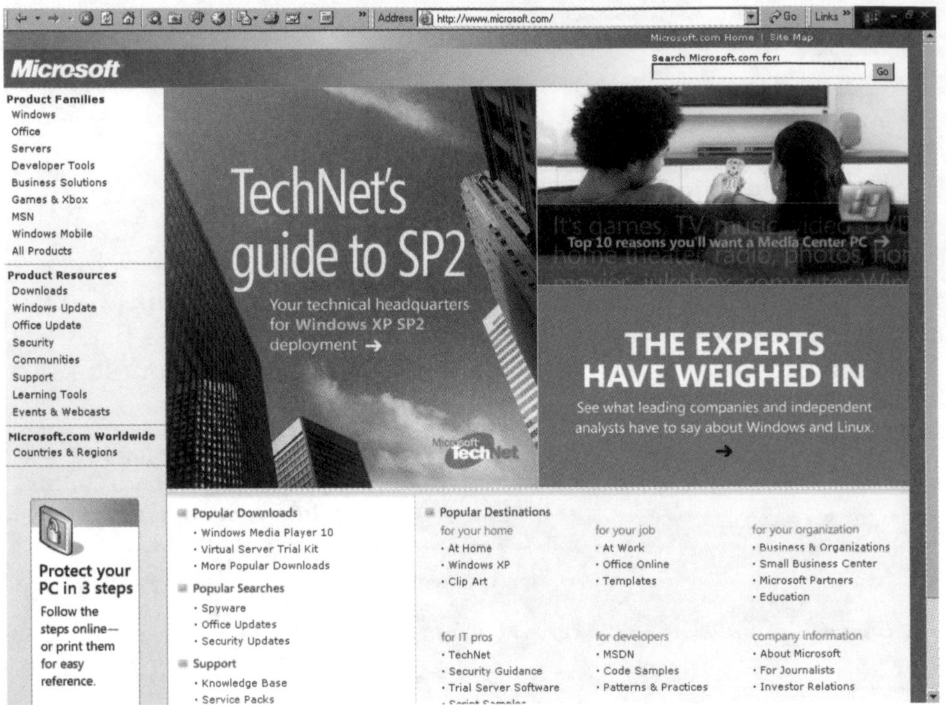

To Use Full Screen Mode

1. Click the **Tools button** on the Command Bar and then click **Full Screen**
   Or
   Press the **F11 key**.
2. To return to normal view, press the **F11 key** again.
   Or
   Click the **Restore button** on the top right corner of the window.

More about Web Pages

Web pages are documents saved in a format called **Hypertext Markup Language (HTML)**. It is the programming language in which Web pages are written. The name of an HTML file usually has either an .html or .htm extension. Luckily, you do not need to know HTML to work with existing Web pages.

We have already seen that in order to view a Web page in your browser, you need to tell the Web browser the **address** or **URL** (Uniform Resource Locator) of the Web page you want to visit. An example of a Web page address is:

http://www.microsoft.com

There are several ways that you can browse (or visit) Web pages. You can visit a Web page by typing the Web Address in the **Address Bar**. You can also jump to another Web page by clicking a **hyperlink** on an existing Web page. Hyperlinks work by assigning a Web address (such as http://www.microsoft.com) to text or to a picture in the Web page. This text or picture then becomes **clickable**. As you move your mouse pointer over the hyperlink, the pointer transforms into an upwards-pointing hand pointer. Clicking the hyperlink brings you to the Web page that is assigned to the hyperlink.

If you visit more than one page, use the **Back** or **Forward** button to move between Web pages. The Back button returns you to the previous Web page that you viewed. The Forward button will bring you forward to the page you were viewing before you clicked the Back button.

To Browse a Web Page

1. Type the **Web page address (URL)** of the Web page you wish to visit in the Address Bar
   Or
   Click on a **hyperlink** in an existing Web page to jump to the Web page address assigned to that link.

Stopping/Reloading Web Pages

Occasionally you may come across a Web page that for one reason or another, is taking an extremely long time to load. Perhaps the Web server is slow or the Web page contains an excessive amount of large graphics. Fortunately, you don't have to sit and wait for the page to load. Click the **Stop icon** located to the right of the Address Bar and Internet Explorer stops loading the Web Page.

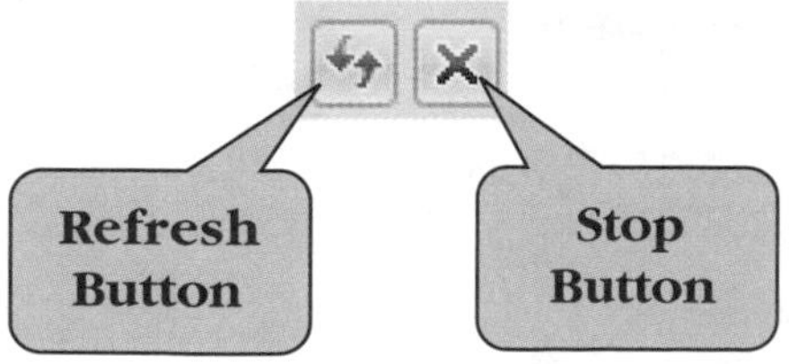

When you view Web pages, the information on that page is saved on your hard drive. This is referred to as a **cache**. The next time you load that page, Internet Explorer uses the cached files instead of downloading the Web page again from the Web site. To make sure that you have the latest version of the Web page, click the **Refresh icon**. This forces Internet Explorer to download a fresh version of the Web page from the Web site.

To Stop/Reload a Web Page

1. Click the **Stop button** on the Navigation Bar to stop a Web page from loading.
2. To ensure you are viewing the latest version of a Web page, click the **Refresh** button.

Viewing History

Internet Explorer keeps track of all of the Web pages that you visit, not only for the current session but for past sessions as well. Depending on your settings, you can view history from several weeks or even several months ago. To display a list of recently visited Web pages and Web sites, click the **History button** located to the right of the forward button. To view the full history list, click the History button and then click History. The **History Pane** will display, listing all recently visited Web pages.

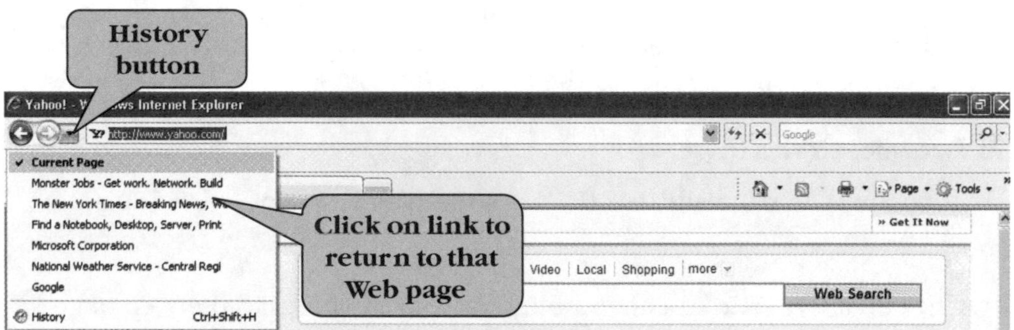

From the History Pane, you can change how the Web sites are listed. Click the **drop down arrow** on the History Pane bar and choose **By Date, By Site, By Most Visited** or **By Order Visited Today** to change the sort order of the list.

To jump to a Web page in the History list, click on the desired site in the History Pane.

To View History

1. Click the **History button** to the right of the forward button.
2. Click on a Web page link in the history list to jump to that particular Web page.
3. To display the History Pane, click the History button and then click **History**
   Or
   Press the **Ctrl + H** keystroke combination.
4. To change how the Web pages are listed, click the **arrow** on the History button (on the History pane) and select the desired sort order.
5. To hide the History Pane, click the History button again and then click **History**
   Or
   Press the **Ctrl + H** keystroke combination.

Using Tabbed Browsing

A new feature in Internet Explorer is the addition of **Tabbed Browsing**, which allows you to open several Web pages in the same browser window. You can then easily switch between open tabs by clicking on the tab associated with the page you wish to view. To open a new tab, press the **Ctrl + T** keystroke combination or click the **blank new tab box** to the right of an existing tab.

To jump to an open tab window, click on any of the tabs on the Tab pane. You can also click the **Tab List arrow** to the left of the leftmost tab to view a list of all open tabs. This comes in especially handy if you have more tabs open than can be displayed on your screen.

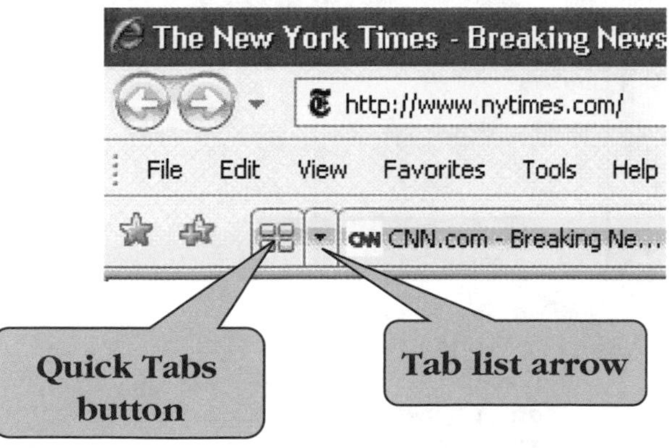

You can also display a miniature thumbnail version of all open tabs by clicking on the **Quick Tabs** button to the left of the tab list arrow. Click on any of the tab thumbnails to display the associated Web page.

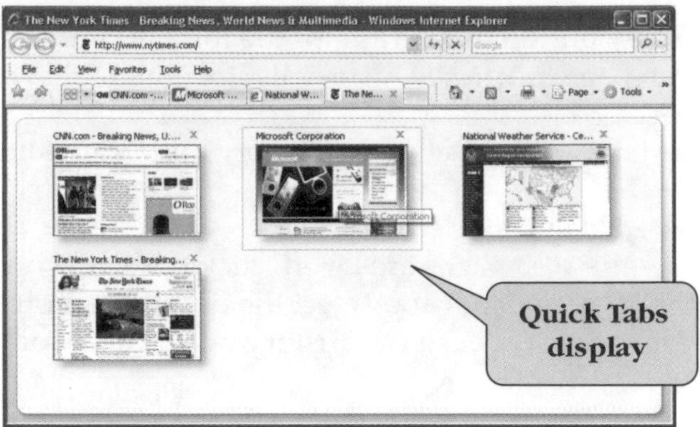

To Use Tabbed Browsing

1. To open a new tab, press the **Ctrl + T** keystroke combination
   Or
   Click the **blank new tab box** to the right of an existing tab.
2. To jump to an open tab, click the tab associated with the Web page you wish to view.
3. To display a list of all open tabs, click the Tab List arrow located to the left of the leftmost tab.
4. To display thumbnails of all open tabs, click the **Quick Tabs** arrow to the left of the Tab List arrow.
5. To close a tab, click the **x** on the right side of the active tab.

Opening a Local Web Page

Internet Explorer can also open Web documents that are stored **locally** on your computer's hard disk or on an external disk drive. For instance, you may be designing a Web page and want to see how it will look in a Web browser. Or you may have downloaded an informational Web page from the Internet.

To open a local Web page, select **File > Open** from the menu or press the **Ctrl + O** keystroke combination, click the **Browse** button and then navigate to the folder that contains the Web page you wish to open in Internet Explorer.

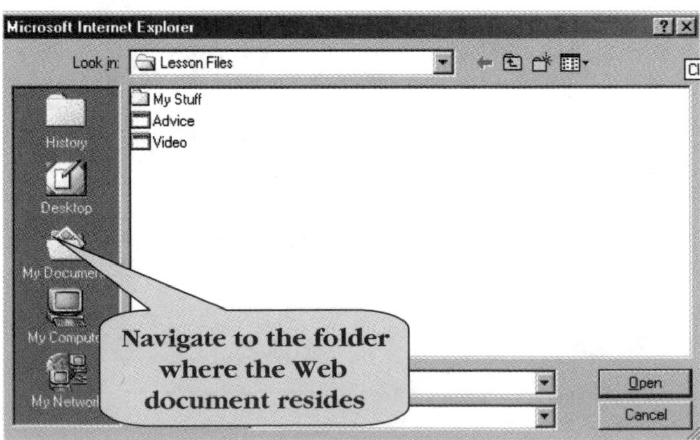

To Open a Local Web Page

1. Select **File > Open** from the menu.
2. Click the **Browse** button.
3. Navigate to the folder that contains the Web file you wish to open.
4. Select the Web page file and then click **Open**.

Saving a Web Page

You can save the contents of any Web page to your computer and then use Internet Explorer to view the Web page offline later on. Use the **File > Save As** command from the menu to display the Save Web Page dialog box.

From the **Save as Type** drop-down list, you will need to choose the format in which you want to save the Web page. Choose from the following options:

- **Webpage, complete**—saves the web page and all supporting files in their original format.
- **Web Archive, single file**—Saves all the Web page information in one singe file. Note that all browsers do not support this format.
- **Webpage, HTML only**—Saves only the HTML file; does not save any supporting files such as graphics, video files or sound files.
- **Text File**—Saves just the text from the active Web page into a text file.

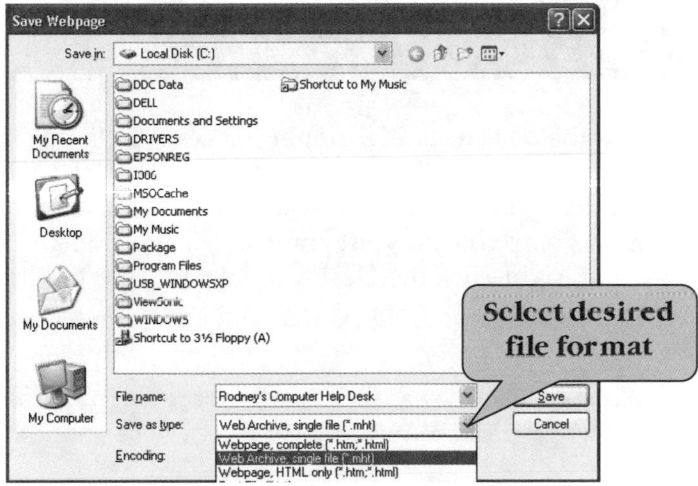

SAVE WEBPAGE DIALOG BOX

After the web page is saved on your disk drive, you can then view it in your Web browser.

To Save a Web Page on Your Computer

1. Display the Web Page in your Web browser that you want to save.
2. Select **File > Open** from the menu.
3. If desired, type a new name for the Web page in the **File name** box.
4. Navigate to the folder where you want to save the Web page.
5. Select the desired file format in the **Save as Type** drop-down list.
6. Click **Save**.

Saving a Picture from a Web Page

You can save most pictures from a Web page to your hard disk. To do this, **right-click** on the picture you want to save and click the **Save Picture As** command from the contextual menu.

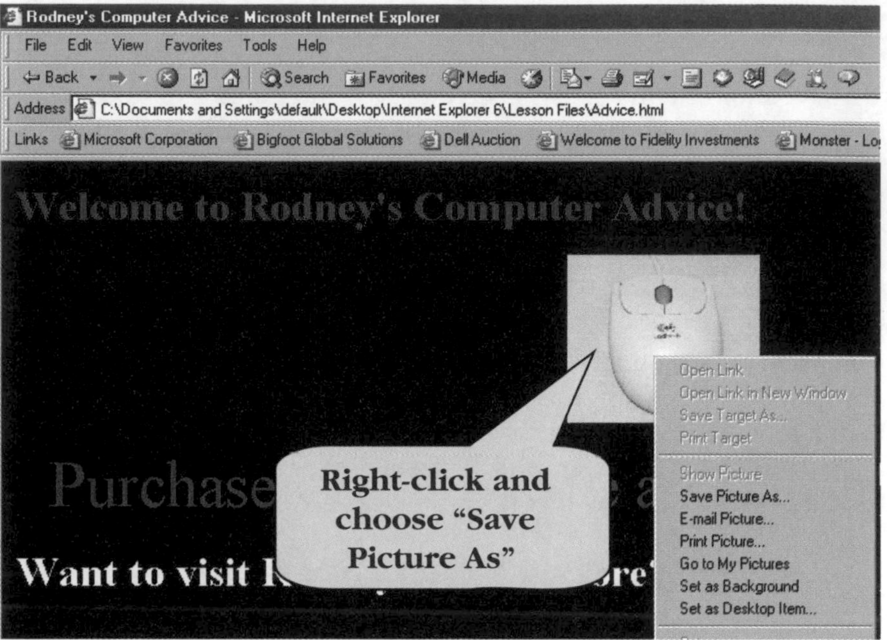

You can also use the picture as **Wallpaper** for your Desktop. Right-click on the picture and choose **Set as Background** from the contextual menu. The picture will automatically be displayed as the Desktop background and will be saved as a bitmap (.bmp) file on your computer's hard disk. To remove or change the wallpaper, right-click the Desktop, select Properties and select a new background.

NOTE: When saving graphics, beware of copyright restrictions as many images on Web sites are copyrighted. Make sure you get the owner's permission before using a graphic.

To Save a Web Page on Your Computer

1. Display the Web Page that contains the picture you want to save.
2. **Right-click** the picture you want to save.
3. Select **Save Picture As** from the contextual menu.
4. Navigate to the folder where you want to save the picture.
5. Enter a new **file name** for the graphic, if desired.
6. Choose the desired file format from the **Save as type** drop-down list.
7. Click **Save**.

Viewing the Page Source

Web pages are basically text documents that use HTML (Hypertext Markup Language) coding. If you are a Web designer or are interested in learning how to design Web pages, you can learn a great deal about HTML by viewing the **source code** behind Web pages.

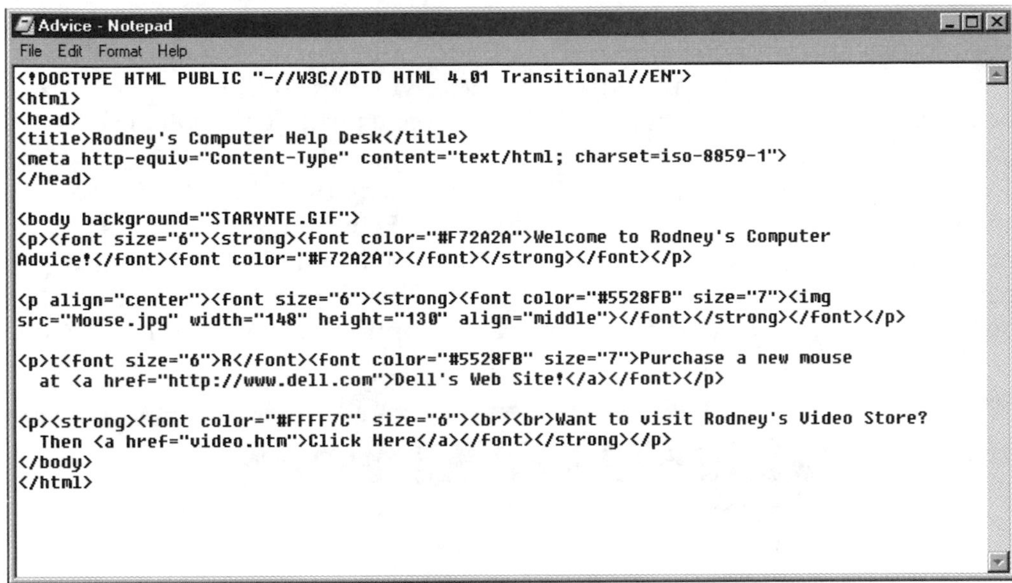

Advice - Notepad

File Edit Format Help

```
<!DOCTYPE HTML PUBLIC "-//W3C//DTD HTML 4.01 Transitional//EN">
<html>
<head>
<title>Rodney's Computer Help Desk</title>
<meta http-equiv="Content-Type" content="text/html; charset=iso-8859-1">
</head>

<body background="STARYNTE.GIF">
<p><font size="6"><strong><font color="#F72A2A">Welcome to Rodney's Computer
Advice!</font><font color="#F72A2A"></font></strong></font></p>

<p align="center"><font size="6"><strong><font color="#5528FB" size="7"><img
src="Mouse.jpg" width="148" height="130" align="middle"></font></strong></font></p>

<p>t<font size="6">R</font><font color="#5528FB" size="7">Purchase a new mouse
  at <a href="http://www.dell.com">Dell's Web Site!</a></font></p>

<p><strong><font color="#FFFF7C" size="6"><br><br>Want to visit Rodney's Video Store?
  Then <a href="video.htm">Click Here</a></font></strong></p>
</body>
</html>
```

VIEWING THE SOURCE CODE OF A WEB PAGE

To view the source code, select **View > Source** from the menu or **Right-click** on the Web page and choose View Source from the contextual menu. The HTML code is then displayed in the **Windows Notepad Utility** application. From this point, you can print the source code or even modify it! Studying the source code of various Web pages is a great way to learn HTML. Again, it is important to be aware of copyright restrictions before using source code from other Web pages in your own Web page design.

To View the HTML Source Code for a Web Page

1. Display the Web Page whose source code you wish to view.
2. Select **View > Source** from the menu. The HTML code is then displayed in **Notepad**.
   Or
   Right-click on the Web Page and choose **View Source** from the contextual menu
   Or
   Click the **Page button** on the Command Bar and click **View Source** from the menu.
3. Close the Notepad application when finished.

Printing a Web Page

If you would like a hard copy of the information on a Web page, you can send the contents of the Web page to your printer. To print a Web page, click the **Print** button on the Command Bar. This automatically sends the entire contents of the Web page to the printer, using the current settings. It is important to note that many Web pages will print on several sheets of paper.

If you wish to set page options before sending the document to the printer, click the arrow next to the Print button and choose **Page Setup** to display the Page Setup dialog box. From here, you can specify the paper size, paper source, page orientation, add/remove page headers or footers and set page margins.

Another method of printing a Web page is using the **File > Print** command from the menu. This will display the **Print dialog box**. From the Print dialog box, you can specify such options as the number and range of pages to print, the number of copies to print, which printer to use, the print quality of the hard copy, and much more. The options available will depend on the printer that you are using.

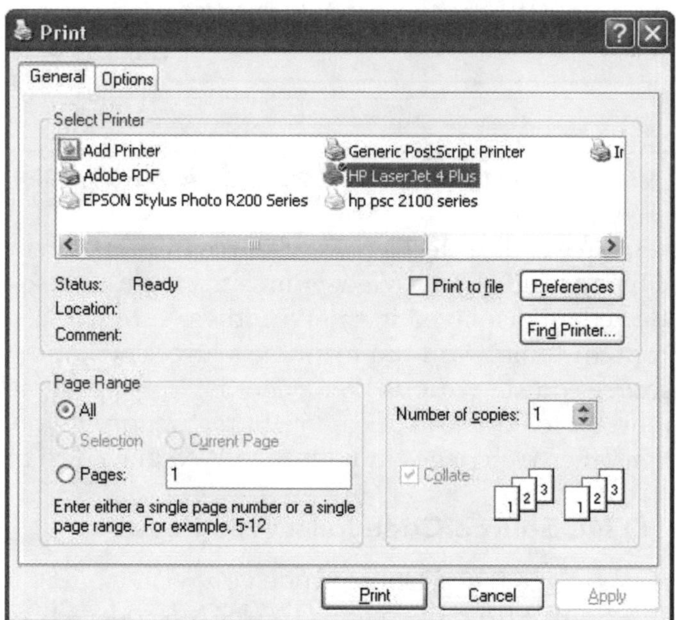

PRINT DIALOG BOX

To Print a Web Page

1. To send the Web page to the printer without displaying the Print dialog box, click the **Print icon** on the Command Bar.
2. To set page options, click the arrow next to the Print button and choose Page Setup. Make your changes in the Page Setup dialog box.
3. To display a preview of your page before printing, click the arrow next to the Print button and choose **Print Preview**.

4. To print a Web page using the Print dialog box:
   a. Select **File > Print** from the menu.
   b. Click the tabs on top of the dialog box to view the various print options.
   c. Select any desired options.
   d. Click **Print**.

Searching the Web

You can search for all manner of information on the Internet: Web pages, businesses, maps, email addresses, music and much, much more. Most browsers have a built-in **Search** feature that allows you to find specific information. In Microsoft Internet Explorer, you can execute a search right from your toolbar using the default search engine. Click in the question box on the right side of your screen (to the right of the Address Bar) and type in your search criteria. Searches are not case sensitive.

The Search tool links to a popular **Search Engine**. A Search Engine is an Internet tool that allows you to search the Internet based upon criteria that you enter. There are many flavors of Search Engines, each with its own look and feel. Most Search Engines, however, serve the same purpose. As of this writing, some highly utilized Search Engines are located at **Google** (www.google.com), **Yahoo** (www.yahoo.com), **AltaVista** (www.AltaVista.com), **MSN** (www.msn.com), **Ask** (www.ask.com), and **Lycos** (www.lycos.com) just to name a few.

Internet Explorer uses Windows Live Search as the default search provider. You can change the default search engine used by clicking on **drop-down arrow** to the right of the search box and then choosing **Find More Providers**. A list of popular search engines will display, allowing you add search engine to your list of providers. To add a provider as the default, click the drop-down arrow next to the Search Box, choose Change Search Defaults, select the search engine you want to set as the default and then click Set Default.

You can change a Search Engine temporarily by clicking the search drop-down arrow and choosing the Search Engine you want from the list. This will be your default Search Engine until you exit from Internet Explorer.

For information about additional search engines, visit **http://searchenginewatch.com**. This Web site also provides helpful tips on searching the Web.

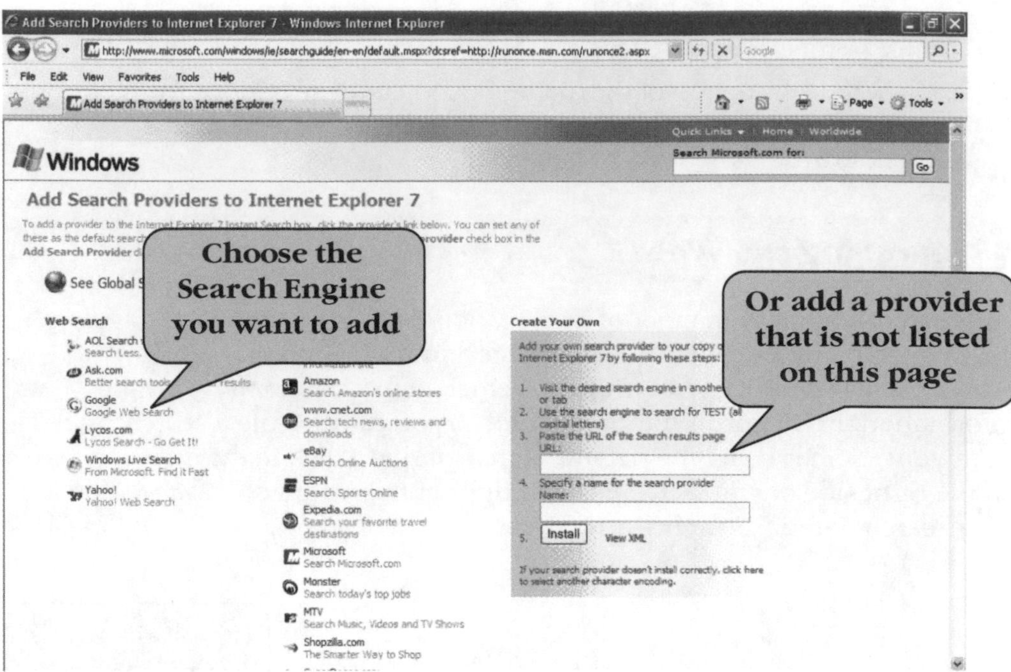

To Search the Internet

1. To use the Search tool in Internet Explorer:
   a. Type your criteria in the **Search box.**
   c. Press **Enter**.
2. To add a new search provider to your list:
   a. Click the drop-down arrow to the right of the Search Box.
   b. Click **Find More Providers**.
   c. Click the Web or Topic Search provider you want to add.
   d. Click **Add Provider** when the Add Search Provider dialog box appears.
   e. To add a provider not in the list, type the URL and a name for your provider in the appropriate boxes under the Create Your Own area.
3. To change the default Search Engine:
   a. Click the drop-down arrow to the right of the Search Box.
   b. Click **Change Search Defaults**.
   c. Select the search provider you want to use as the default in the window.
   d. Click **Set Default**.
   e. Click **OK**.
4. To temporarily change the default Search Engine:
   a. Click the drop-down arrow to the right of the Search Box.
   b. Choose the Search Engine you want to use from the list.
5. To search the Internet from a Search Engine's Web site:
   a. Type the **URL** of the Search Engine in the Address Bar.
   b. Enter the **criteria** for which to search.
   c. Click the Search Engine's search button (this will vary depending on the Search Engine).

Creating Favorites

If you visit specific Web pages often, you can keep track of the pages in Internet Explorer without having to worry about remembering their Web addresses. To do this, you create a **Favorite** for the Web page. A Favorite (also referred to as a Bookmark in some applications) is a shortcut that jumps you to a specific Web page without you having to type in the Web Page address.

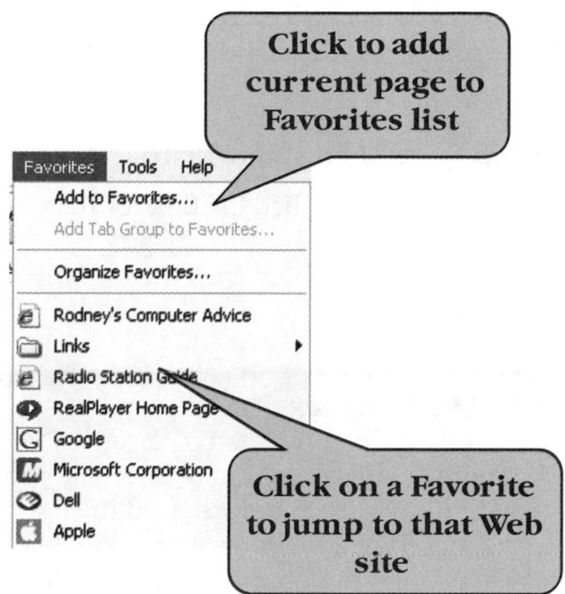

When you create a Favorite, the link is displayed on the **Favorites List**, which provides access to any Web pages that you have saved as Favorites. Any time you want to visit a Web page that you have saved as a Favorite, click its link on the Favorites menu or click the **Favorites Center button** and click the link for the Favorite you want. If there are pages that you visit often, you can add them to the **Links Bar**. The Links Bar is located under the Address Bar and is a convenient place to add links to a few specific Web pages that you visit frequently.

To create a Favorite from a Web page, select **Favorite > Add to Favorites** from the menu or click the **Favorites button** and then click **Add**. You can also press the **Ctrl + D** keystroke combination.

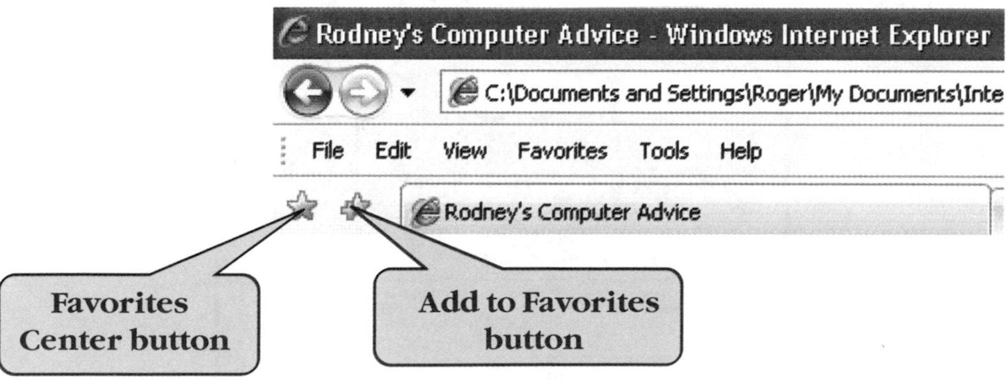

To Create a Favorite

1. Navigate to the Web page for which you want to create a Favorite.
2. Select **Favorites > Add to Favorites** from the Internet Explorer menu
   Or
   Click the **Add to Favorites button** on the Explorer bar and then click **Add**.
   Or
   Press the **Ctrl + D** keystroke combination.
3. Select the folder where you want to place the Favorite.
4. Type in a new name for the Favorite, if desired.
5. Click **OK**.

To Navigate to a Web Page Using a Favorite

1. Click **Favorites** on the menu and click the link for the desired Favorite
   Or
2. Click the **Favorites Center** button and click the link for the desired Favorite from the Favorites list.

Creating Favorites Folders

As you add more and more Favorites, you may find that your Favorites list is becoming long, making it difficult to quickly find the Favorite you are looking for. Luckily, Internet Explorer allows you to create **Folders**, helping you to organize your Favorites. The command to create Favorites folders is located under the **Favorites > Organize Favorites** menu.

When the Organize Favorites dialog box appears, click the **New Folder** button and then type in a new name for your folder. Don't worry about the placement of the folder—you can always move it later.

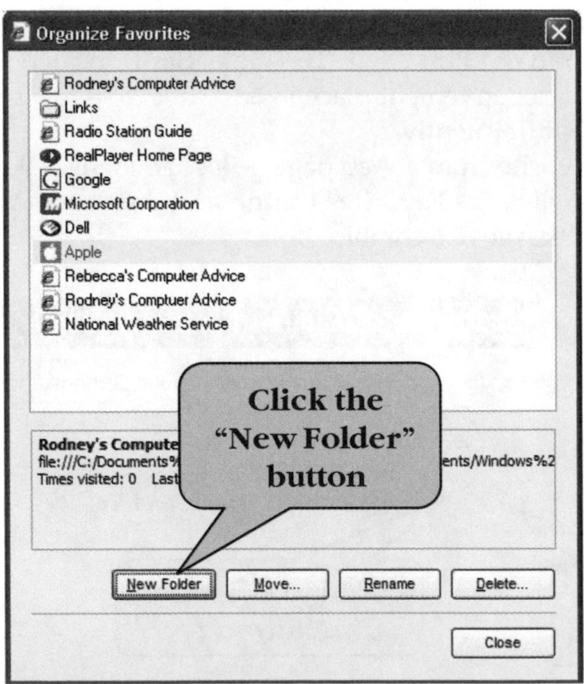

ORGANIZE FAVORITES DIALOG BOX

To create a **subfolder**, that is to say, a folder within a folder, click the folder in which you wish to create a new folder in the window on the right, click the New Folder button and then type in the name for your subfolder.

To Create a Favorites Folder

1. Select **Favorites > Organize Favorites** from the menu
   Or
   Click the **Add to Favorites button** and click **Organize Favorites**
2. If creating a subfolder, click the folder in Favorites window in which you want to place the subfolder.
3. Click the **New Folder** button.
4. Type in a name for your new folder.

Rearranging Favorites

From the Organize Favorites dialog box, you can also **change the position** of your Favorites and folders in the Favorites window. You can move a Favorite or a folder in the Favorites list to another folder by clicking the **Move** button and then selecting the folder in which you want to place the item.

To change the position of a Favorite or a folder in the Favorites window, click the Favorite or folder and then drag it to a new location. As you drag, a black horizontal line appears, letting you know the location of the dragged item.

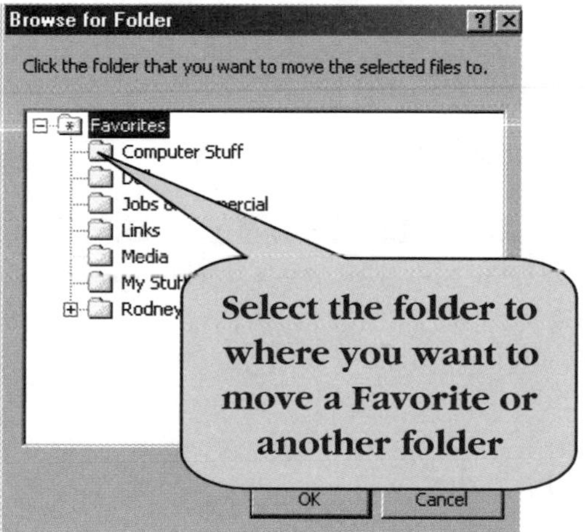

To Rearrange Items in the Favorites Window

1. Select **Favorites > Organize Favorites** from the menu.
   Or
   Click the **Add to Favorites button** and click **Organize Favorites**
2. To move an item to another folder:
   a. Click the item you wish to move.
   b. Click the **Move** button.
   c. Click the destination folder in the **Browse for Folder** window.
   d. Click **OK**.

3. To change the position of an item in the Favorites list:
   a. Click and drag the item to the desired position in the list.
   b. Release the mouse button.

Renaming Favorites

You can **change the name** of your Favorites and Favorites folders from the Organize Favorites dialog box. This will change the display name for that item in the Favorites list. Select the item you wish to rename and click the **Rename** button. The item's name is then highlighted, allowing you to type in a replacement name.

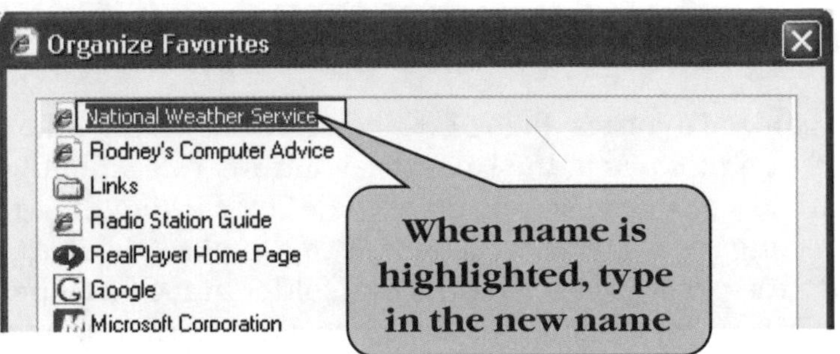

You can also **right-click** on any item to bring up a contextual menu that contains an option for renaming Favorites or folders.

To Rename a Favorite

1. Select **Favorites > Organize Favorites** from the menu.
   Or
   Click the **Add to Favorites button** and click **Organize Favorites**
2. Select the Favorite or folder you wish to rename.
3. Click the **Rename** button.
4. Type in the new name.

Editing Favorites Info

From time to time, you may come across a **broken link**, that is to say, a Web address than no longer works. Often, the Webmaster has simply moved the Web page to a new location on the server. When this happens, you will need to update the Web address for any Favorites that no longer work.

To modify the Web address for a Favorite, right-click on the Favorite and select **Properties** from the contextual menu. Under the **Web Document** tab of the Properties dialog box, type in the new Web address in the **URL** box.

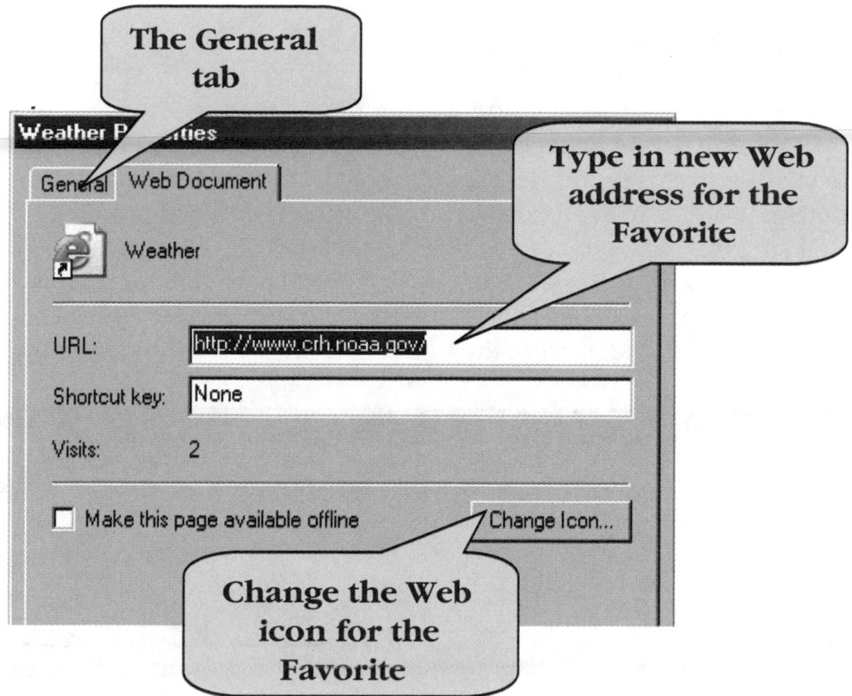

You can also change the **icon** for the favorite. Click the **Change Icon** button and navigate to the folder that contains the icon you wish to use.

The **General** tab contains options that allow you to change the name of the Favorite as well as view various Favorite properties such as the location, size and date created.

To Edit Favorite Info

1. Select **Favorites > Organize Favorites** from the menu.
   Or
   Click the **Add to Favorites button** and click **Organize Favorites**
2. Select the Favorite whose info you wish to edit.
3. **Right-click** and select **Properties** from the menu.
4. To change the **Web address** of a Favorite:
   a. Click the **Web Document** tab.
   b. Type the new Web address in the **URL** box.
5. To change the **icon** of a Favorite:
   a. Click the **Web Document** tab.
   b. Click the **Change Icon** button.
   c. Click the **Browse** button.
   d. Navigate to the folder that contains the icon you want to use.
   e. Select the icon file (often a .dll file)
   f. Click **Open**.
   g. Select the icon you wish to use.
   h. Click **OK**.
6. To change the name of the Favorite:
   a. Click the **General Tab**.
   b. Type in a new name in the first blank text box.

Deleting Favorites

Deleting a **Favorite** involves removing that Favorite from the Favorites list and transferring it to the Recycle Bin. When you empty the Recycle Bin, the Favorite is gone from your system for good.

To delete an item, select the Favorite or folder to be deleted in the Organize Favorites dialog box and click the **Delete** button or press the **Delete** key on your keyboard. A **Yes/No** dialog box will display, asking you if you are sure you want to send the Favorite to the Recycle Bin. It is important to note that when deleting a folder, all of the folder's contents are deleted as well.

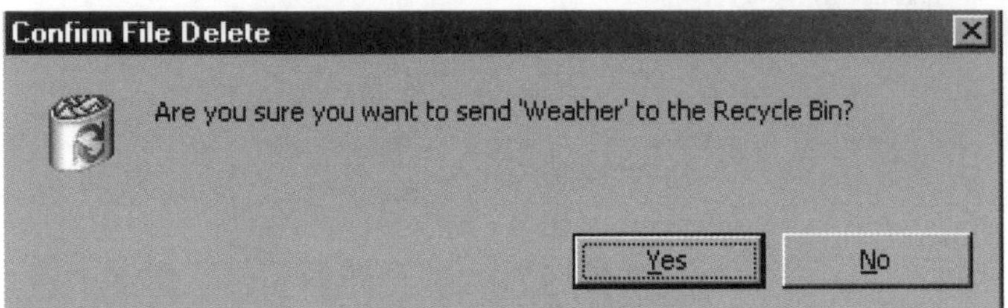

To Delete a Favorite or a Folder

1. Select **Favorites > Organize Favorites** from the menu.
   Or
   Click the **Add to Favorites button** and click **Organize Favorites**
2. Select the **Favorite or Folder** to be deleted.
3. Click the **Delete** button
   Or
   Press the **Delete key**.
4. Click **Yes** when prompted to send the item to the Recycle Bin.

Importing & Exporting Favorites

Internet Explorer allows you to **Import** Favorites from an external file and **Export** Favorites to an external file. If you use several computers, you can share your Favorites between them by importing and exporting them. If you use other browsers such as Netscape Navigator or Firefox in addition to Internet Explorer, importing and exporting Favorites allows you to keep your Favorites (or Bookmarks, as they are called in Netscape) up to date.

To Import and Export files, select **File > Import and Export** or click the Add Favorites button and click Import and Export and follow the instructions of the Import and Export Wizard. Exported Favorites are saved as a regular HTML file, allowing you to import them with both Internet Explorer and Netscape Navigator or Firefox. You can even share your Favorites with others by giving them a copy of the Favorites file, which they can then directly open in their browser.

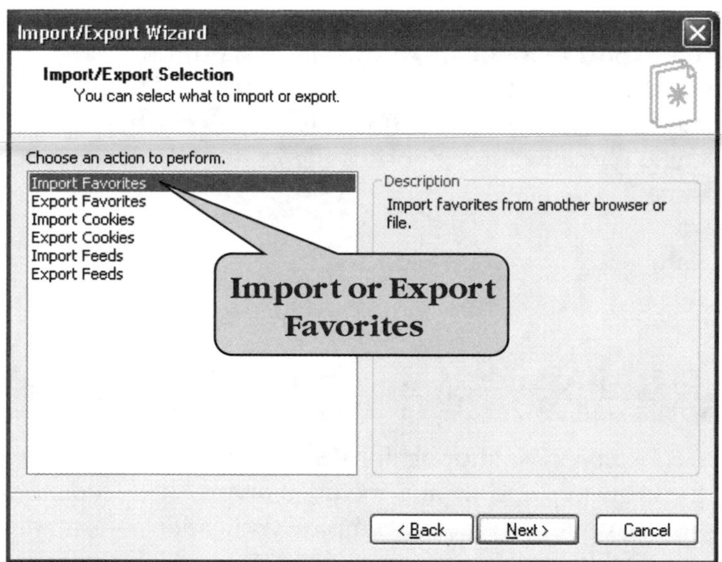

To Import Favorites

1. Select **File > Import and Export** from the menu.
   Or
   Click the **Add to Favorites button** and click **Import and Export** from the menu.
2. Click **Next**.
3. Click **Import Favorites**.
4. Click **Next**.
5. To import Favorites from another Web browser, click the **Import from an Application** radio button and select the application from the drop-down list.
6. To import from an external file:
   a. Click the **Import from a File or Address** radio button.
   b. Click the **Browse** button.
   c. Navigate to the folder that contains the file you want to import.
   d. Click **Save**.
7. Click **Next**.
8. Click the folder where you want the imported Favorites to be placed.
9. Click **Next**.
10. Click **Finish**.
11. Click **OK**.

To Export Favorites

1. Select **File > Import and Export** from the menu
   Or
   Click the **Add to Favorites button** and click **Import and Export** from the menu.
2. Click **Next**.
3. Click **Export Favorites**.
4. Click **Next**.
5. **Select the folder** you want to export from (select the **Favorites** folder to export all Favorites.
6. Click **Next**.
7. To export your Favorites from another Web browser application, click the **Export to an Application** radio button and select the application from the drop-down list.

8. To export to an external file:
   a. Click the **Export to a File or Address** radio button
   b. Click the **Browse** button.
   c. Navigate to the folder in which you want to save the Favorites file.
   d. Type a new name for the Favorites file in the **File name** box, if desired.
   e. Click **Save**.
9. Click **Next**.
10. Click **Finish**.
11. Click **OK**.

Working with RSS Feeds

New in Internet Explorer 7 is support for **RSS**. IE7 now lets you view RSS feeds of articles in the browser window and includes several RSS feeds to get you started. RSS—an acronym for "Really Simple Syndication"—is a new technology that allows you quickly scan large numbers of articles. Many popular websites provide RSS feeds, enabling you to keep up with the latest news and information. Using RSS feeds, you can scan articles from several websites in one window as well as receive notification when new articles are added to a site. An RSS feed displays titles and a brief description of many articles in a simple list, allowing you to decide if you wish to view the entire article.

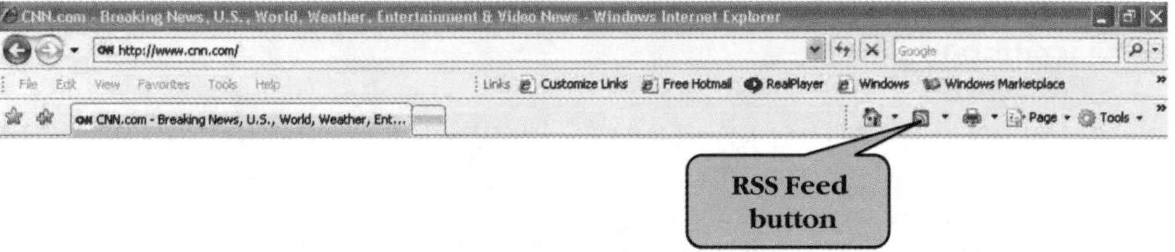

When a Web site has an RSS feed, the orange **RSS button** is lighted. Click on the RSS button to view or subscribe to the feed.

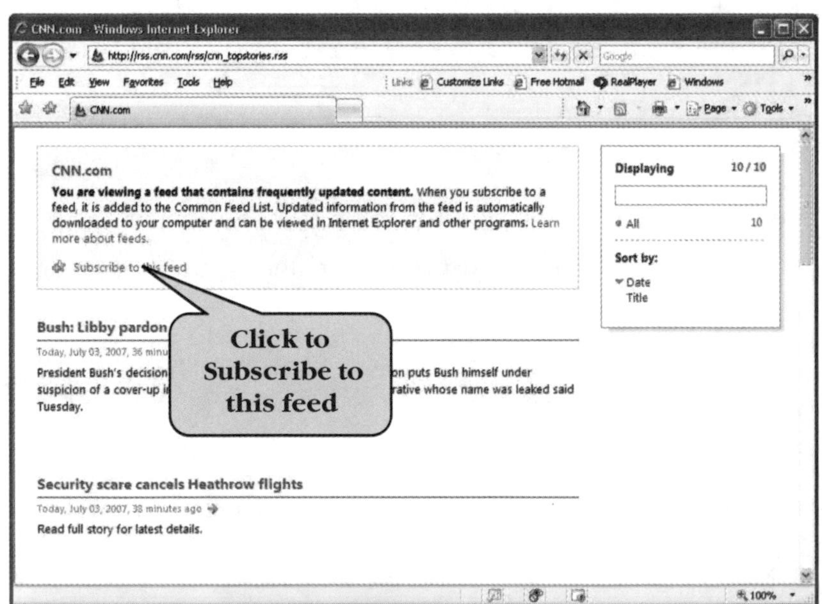

CNN NEWS RSS FEED

To subscribe to a feed, click the **Subscribe to this feed** link on the top of the page. Once you have subscribed to a feed, you can view a summary of your feeds from the **Favorites Center** or choose **View > Explorer Bar > Feeds** to display the Feeds pane. Then, click on the feed you wish to view. You can then search the list for articles on a specific subject, choose the length of their summaries, and sort them by date or title. If you wish to view a full article for a feed, click on the title of the article.

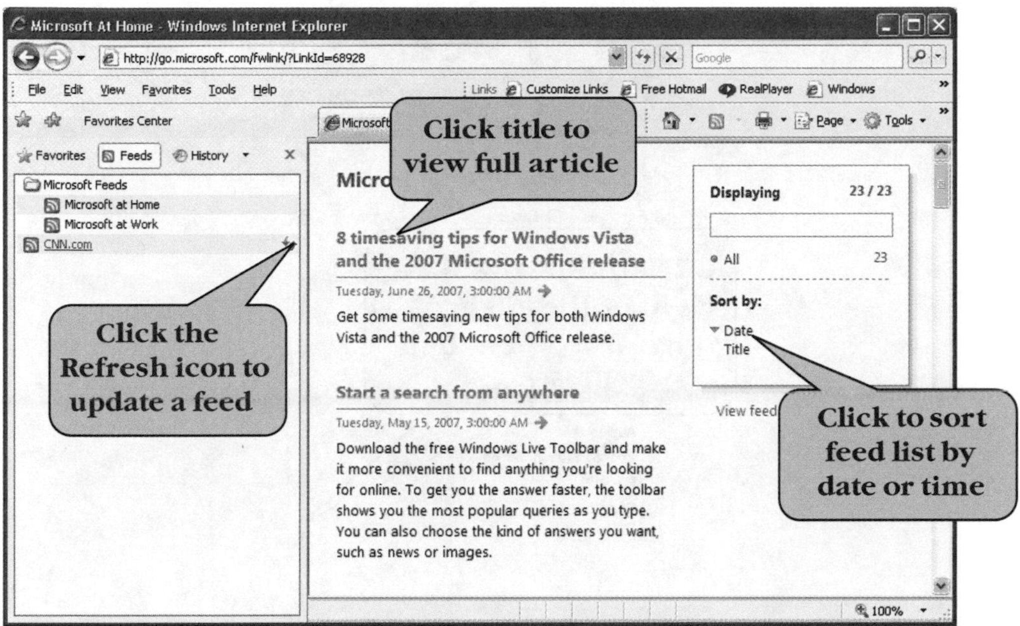

To unsubscribe from a feed, right-click the feed in the feed list and click **Delete** from the contextual menu.

To Use RSS Feeds

1. Navigate to a Web site that contains an RSS feed.
2. Click on the **RSS icon** on the right side of the Home button.
3. To subscribe to a feed, click the **Subscribe to this Feed** link. Enter a desired name for your feed and then click **Subscribe**.
4. To view your feeds list, click the **Favorites Center** icon and then click **Feeds**.
   Or
   Choose **View**, point to **Explorer Bar** and then click **Feeds** to display the Feeds pane.
5. Choose any additional sorting options in the right-hand pane of the RSS window.
6. To refresh a feed, move your mouse pointer over the name of the feed in the feeds list and click the green **refresh icon** to the right of the feed name.
7. To view or modify feed properties, click the **View feed properties** link in the second pane.
8. To view a full article for a feed, click the title of the article you want to view.

Saving a Tab Group

Internet Explorer allows you to save a **set of open tabs**. Perhaps every morning you may wish to view a specific set of Web sites: your stock report, the New York Times headlines and perhaps one or two of your RSS feeds. To save group of open tabs as a Favorite, click the **Add to Favorites button** and then click **Add Tab Group to Favorites**.

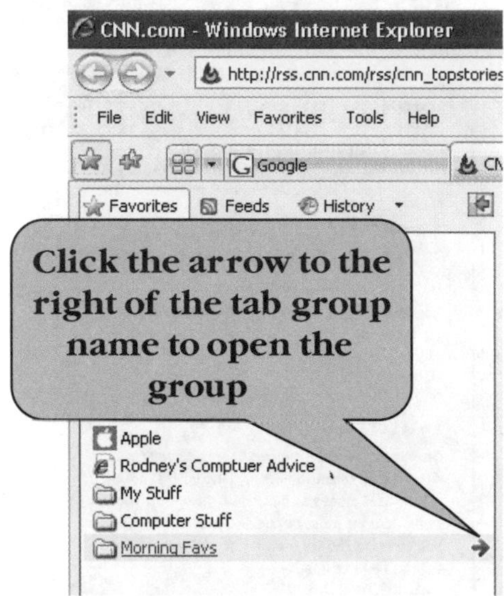

To open a tab group, click the Add to Favorites button, move your mouse pointer over the tab group and click on the arrow on the right side of the tab group name.

To Save a Tab Group as a Favorite

1. Open the tabs that you want to save as a group.
2. Click the **Add to Favorites button**.
3. Click **Add Tab Group to Favorites**.
4. Type a name for the tab group.
5. Specify a folder for the tab group, if desired.
6. Click **Add**.
7. To open a Tab group:
   a. Click the Favorites Center button
   b. Move your mouse pointer over the tab group you wish to open. An arrow will appear to the right side of the tab group name.
   c. Click on the arrow to the right of the tab group name.

Changing the Text Size & Zoom on Web Pages

On some Web pages, you may notice that the text is more difficult to read. This could be because of the font size specified by the Web designer. However, the size of the text is not dependent on the code in the Web page alone but rather a combination of browser settings and Web page settings.

Internet Explorer allows you to **increase** or **decrease the size of the text**. There are five settings from which you can choose:

- **Largest**
- **Larger**
- **Medium**
- **Smaller**
- **Smallest**

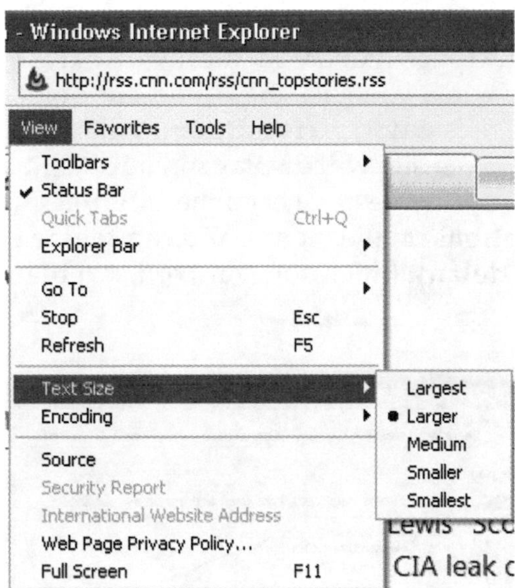

To change the size of the text, select **View > Text Size** from the menu (or click the Page button and point to Text Size) and then select the desired size. Note that if the size of the text remains the same after adjusting the text size setting, the text could very well be part of the graphic file.

You can also increase or decrease the overall size of an entire Web page by using the **Zooming** feature. This is helpful if the Web page was designed for resolution that is different than that of your monitor. To using Zooming, click the Page button, point to Zoom and then click the desired Zoom percentage. If your mouse has a scroll wheel, holding down the Ctrl key as you move the scroll wheel up or down will zoom in or out on a page. You also use the Ctrl plus or Ctrl minus keystroke combinations to zoom in or out on a page respectively.

To Change the Text Size on a Web Page

1. Select **View > Text Size** from the menu.
   Or
   Click the **Page button** on the Explorer bar and point to Text Size
2. Select the desired text size from the list.

To Change the Zoom Percentage

1. Click the **Page button**, point to **Zoom** and then click the desired Zoom percentage
   Or
   Hold down the **Ctrl key** and move the **scroll wheel on your mouse** forward to zoom in and backward to zoom out.

Or
Press the **Ctrl** and the **plus** keystroke combination to zoom in or the **Ctrl** and the **minus** keystroke combination to zoom out
Or
Click the arrow next to the Zoom Level box on the right corner of the Status Bar and select the desired zoom level.

Changing Your Home Page

Your **Home Page** is the page that automatically displays when Internet Explorer launches or when you click the **Home button** on the Command Bar. The default home page is **www.microsoft.com**. Thus, when Internet Explorer launches, Microsoft's Web site will display in your Web browser.

You can change your home page from the **Internet Options** dialog box (**Tools > Internet Options** on the menu). You can set the **current page** as the Home Page, use **the default** (microsoft.com) or use a **blank page** for your home page.

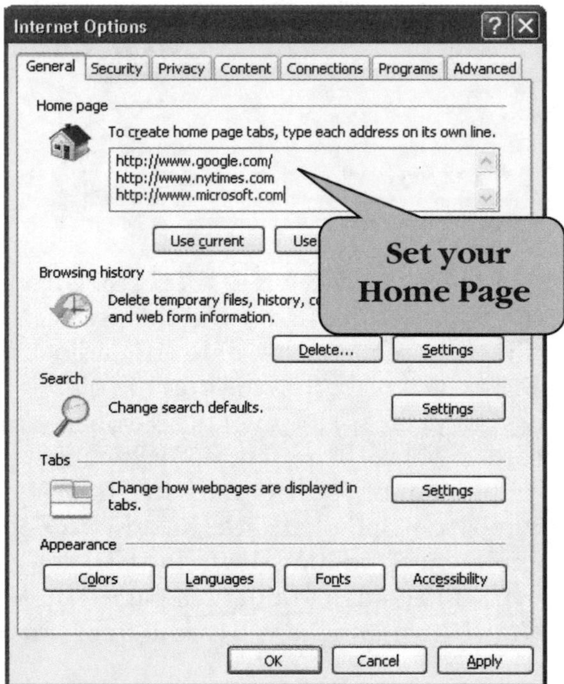

You can also set a tab group as your Home Page by entering a different URL on each line in the Home Page box as shown above. Each Web address will open in a separate tab when you launch your browser or click the Home button.

To Change Your Home Page

1. Browse to the Web page that you want to set as your **Home Page**.
2. Select **View > Internet Options** from the menu.
   Or
   Click the **Tools button** on the Command Bar and click **Internet Options**.
3. Under the **Home Page** area, click the **Use Current** button to replace any other home pages with the active page or type in the Web address in the Home Page box.

4. To add a tab group as your Home Page, enter each Web address (URL) on a separate line in the Home Page box.
5. To reset the Home Page to the Microsoft Web site, click **Use Default**.
6. Click the **Use Blank** button to display a blank web page when the browser launches.
7. Click **OK** when finished.

> **TIP:** You can also change your Home Page by clicking the arrow next to the Home button and making your selections.

Managing Browsing History

When you view an online Web site, the Web pages and other related files are downloaded to your **Temporary Internet Files** folder. These files are referred to as your **cache**. You can increase the amount of space available for these files (the cache size) from the Internet Options dialog box, which causes previously viewed pages to load faster. The downside of this, however, is less available hard drive space.

You may want to periodically purge temporary files, history or tracking cookies. Cookies are small text files that some Web sites place on your computer to store information, such as your preferences for that Web site or other personally identifiable information. Click on the **Delete button** under the Browsing History area on the General tab of the Internet Options dialog box and choose the type of files you wish to delete. The **Settings button** allows you to modify how Internet Explorer treats history and temporary Internet files. For instance, you can change the amount of disk space to allocate to the cache, choose when to check for newer version of stored pages and set how many days browsing history should be kept.

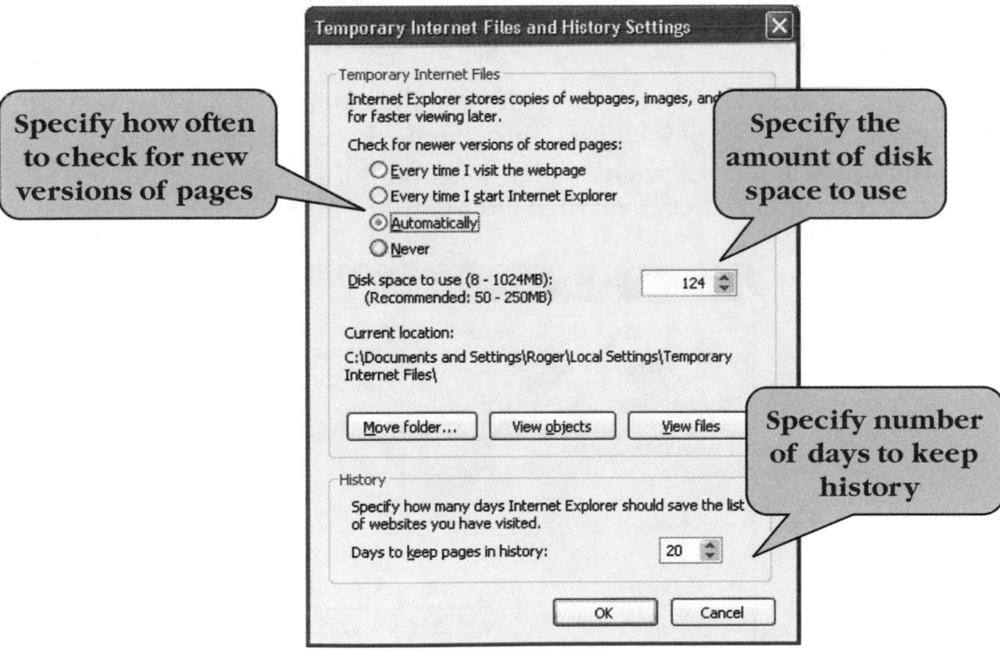

The **History** folder preserves links to the previous pages that you have visited. By clicking on the **History button** in the Favorites Center, you can quickly return to pages that you visited weeks, or even months before. The length of time that Internet Explorer retains a History link is dependent on the value in the **History box** under Internet Options. Here, you can specify the amount of days Internet Explorer is to keep historical track of visited Web pages.

To Manage Temporary Internet Files

1. Select **Tools > Internet Options** to display the **Internet Options dialog box.**
   Or
   Click the **Tools button** on the Explorer Bar and click **Internet Options**.
2. To delete all Temporary Internet Files, click the **Delete** button and then click **Delete Files** next to Temporary Internet Files. Delete any other types of files (history, cookies, Web form data, passwords) if desired. Click **Close** when finished.
3. To change the amount of disk space allocated to Temporary Internet Files:
   a. Click the **Settings** button.
   b. Click the **spinner controls** under the desired value is displayed in the disk space box or type in the desired value in the disk space box.
   c. Click **OK**.
4. To change when Internet Explorer checks for newer versions of Web pages:
   a. Click the **Settings** button.
   b. Click the radio button next to the desired frequency.
   c. Click **OK**.
5. To change how many days browsing history should be kept:
   a. Click the **Settings** button.
   b. Under the **History** are, type the desired value in the **Days to keep pages in history** box.
6. Click **OK** to close the Internet Options dialog box.

Changing Search Settings

The **Search options** allow you to modify which Search Engine providers are available in Internet Explorer. From the Change Search Defaults dialog box, you can remove existing providers, set the default provider and add additional providers by clicking the Find More Providers Link.

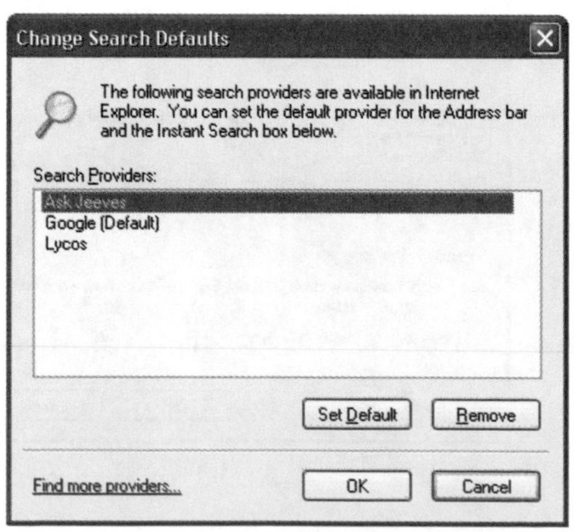

To Change Search Settings

1. Select **Tools > Internet Options** to display the **Internet Options dialog box.**
   Or
   Click the **Tools button** on the Command Bar and click **Internet Options**.
2. Under the **Search area**, click the **Settings button.**
3. To remove a Search Provider, click the provider name in the window and click the **Remove** button.
4. To set the default Search provider, click the provider name in the window and click the **Set Default** button.
5. To add additional providers, click the **Find more providers** and make your selections from the **Add Search Providers to Internet Explorer** page.
6. Click **OK** to close the Internet Options dialog box.

Adjusting Tabbed Browsing Settings

The **Tabs settings** allow you to modify the behavior of tabs in Internet Explorer. For instance, you can turn on or off the warning message when closing multiple tables, enable or disable Quick Tabs, load only the first page of your Home Page group when IE launches and more. You can even disable tabbed browsing completely by clearing the **Enable Tabbed Browsing** checkbox.

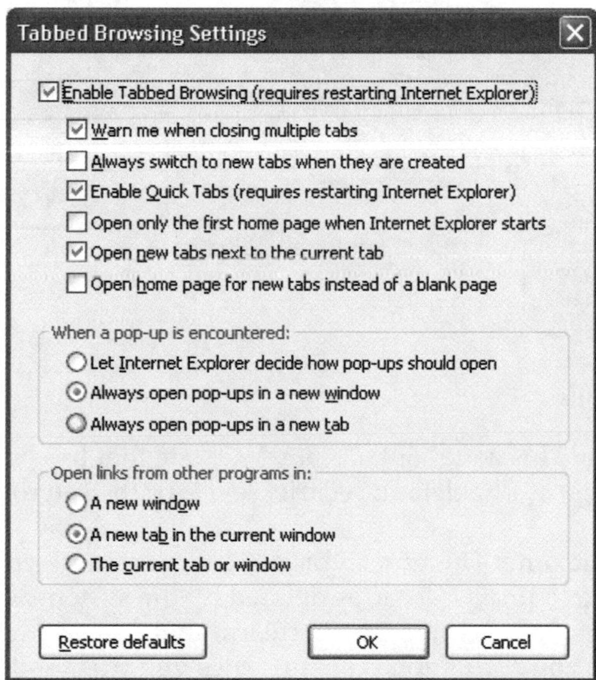

To Adjust Tab Settings

1. Select **Tools > Internet Options** to display the **Internet Options dialog box.**
   Or
   Click the **Tools button** on the Command Bar and click **Internet Options**.

2. Under the **Tabs area**, click the **Settings button**.
3. Make your selections.
4. Click **OK** to close the Internet Options dialog box.

Adjusting Security Settings

Internet Explorer contains a number of **security features** that ensures that any programs that you download or that are added to your system come from a reliable source. One of these features is **Security Zones**. Security Zones divides the Internet into four separate compartments or zones, allowing you to customize the security settings for each zone.

You can tell which zone the current Web page is in by looking at the right side of the Internet Explorer status bar. Whenever you attempt to open or download content from the Web, Internet Explorer checks the security settings for that Web site's zone. To add specific sites to a zone, click the **Sites** button and type in the Web address for the site you wish to add. You cannot add individual sites to the **Internet Zone**.

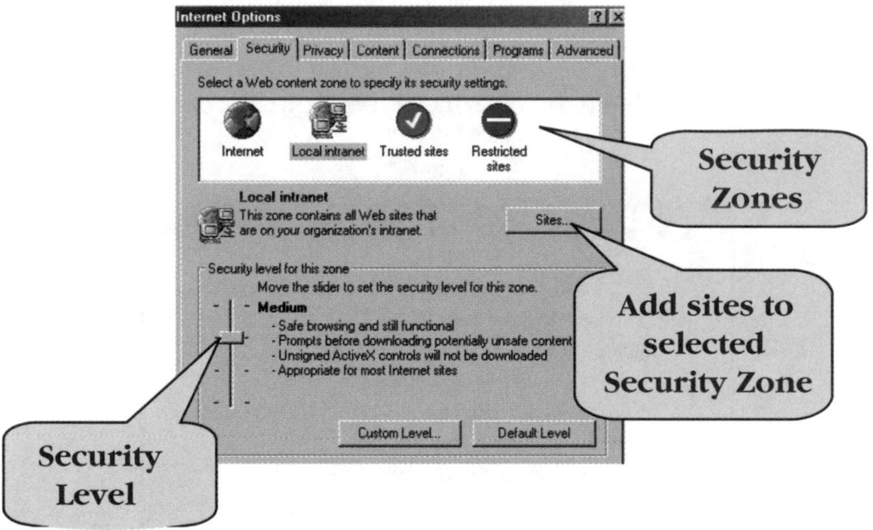

There are four zones:

- **Internet zone:** This zone contains any Web site that has not been assigned to any other zone. The default security level for the Internet Zone is Medium.
- **Local Intranet zone:** This zone typically contains any Web site that does not go through a proxy server, as defined by the system administrator. The default security level for the Local intranet zone is Medium.
- **Trusted Sites zone:** This zone contains sites you trust—sites from where you believe you can download or run files without worrying about damage to your computer or data. The default security level for the Trusted sites zone is Low.
- **Restricted Sites zone:** This zone contains sites that you are not sure whether you can download or run files from without damage to your computer or data. The default security level for the Restricted sites zone is High.

You can change the security level of zone. For example, to ensure maximum protection, you might want to set the Internet Zone to High. Note however, that a setting of High is the least functional of the Security Levels.

To Assign a Web Site to a Security Zone

1. Select **Tools > Internet Options** to display the **Internet Options dialog box.**
   Or
   Click the **Tools button** on the Command Bar and click **Internet Options.**
2. Click the **Security** tab.
3. Click the **Local Intranet, Trusted Sites** or **Restricted Sites** Zone.
4. Click the **Sites** button.
5. If you click **Local Intranet,** click the **Advanced** button.
6. Type the Web site address in the **Add this Web site to the zone** box.
7. Click the **Add** button.
8. Repeat steps 6 and 7 for any additional sites you want to add.
9. Click **OK** when finished.

To Modify Security Levels of a Zone

1. Select **Tools > Internet Options** to display the **Internet Options dialog box.**
   Or
   Click the **Tools button** on the Command Bar and click **Internet Options.**
2. Click the **Security** tab.
3. Click the **Internet, Local Intranet, Trusted Sites** or **Restricted Sites** Zone.
4. To create **custom** settings, click the **Custom Level** button and select the desired settings from the **Security Levels** dialog box. Click **OK** when finished.
5. To change the **default security level** (low, medium-low, medium or high), click the **Custom Level** drop-down arrow and click the security level that you want.
6. Click **OK** when finished.

Adjusting Privacy Settings

Privacy Settings allows you to specify how Internet Explorer is to deal with **cookies,** the small text files which certain Web sites place on your computer that contain personally identifiable information about you. For instance, you can specify that Internet Explorer is to prompt you before placing a cookie on your computer, enabling you to accept or block the cookie. You can even choose to block all cookies if you so choose, although this setting makes for highly restrictive browsing.

To change your privacy settings, drag the **Privacy Settings slider** upwards or downwards until the desired setting is displayed. A description of each setting is displayed to the right of the slider.

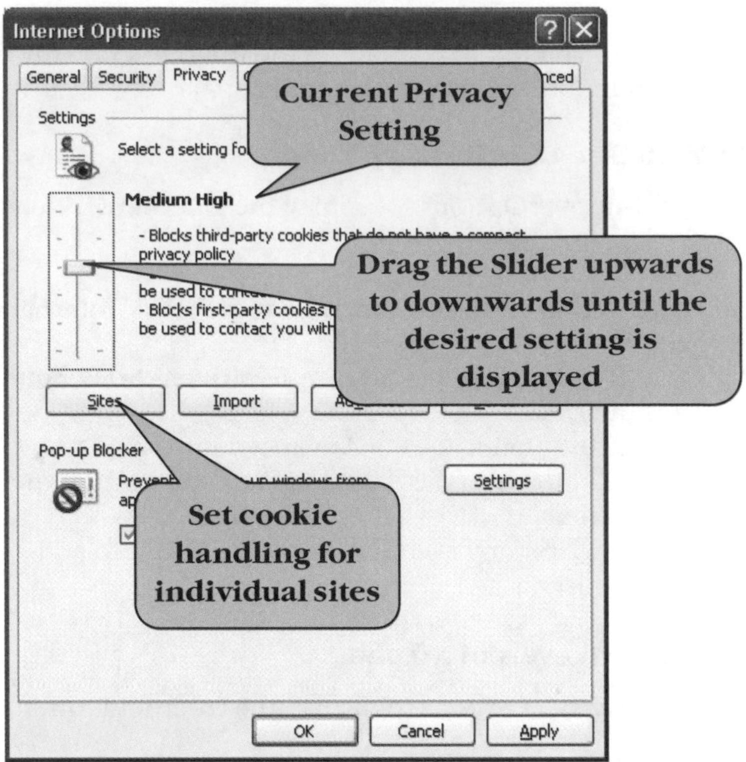

To override your cookie settings for **individual Web sites**, click the **Sites** button to display the Per Site Privacy Actions dialog box. For here, you can add individual sites and choose whether to block or allow cookies from that site.

To Adjust Privacy Settings

1. Select **Tools > Internet Options** to display the **Internet Options dialog box**.
   Or
   Click the **Tools button** on the Command Bar and click **Internet Options**.
2. Click the **Privacy** tab.
3. Drag the **Privacy Settings slider** upwards or downwards until the desired setting is displayed (Block All Cookies, High, Medium High, Medium, Low, or Accept All Cookies).
4. To override cooking handling for individual Web sites:
   a. Click the **Edit** button under the Privacy tab.
   b. Type the site URL in the **Address of Web Site** box.
   c. Click **Block** or **Allow**.
   d. Click **OK** when finished.
5. Click **OK** to close the Internet Options dialog box.

Blocking Pop-ups

Pop-ups are usually advertising that "pop-up" automatically in separate windows when a page from a Web site loads. Most people find the intrusive nature of pop-ups extremely annoying. Luckily, Internet Explorer 7 provides a built-in pop-up blocker that prevents pop-up windows from displaying.

However, some sites use pop-ups to gather necessary information from you or to provide important messages. In such cases, you will want to enable pop-ups for that site.

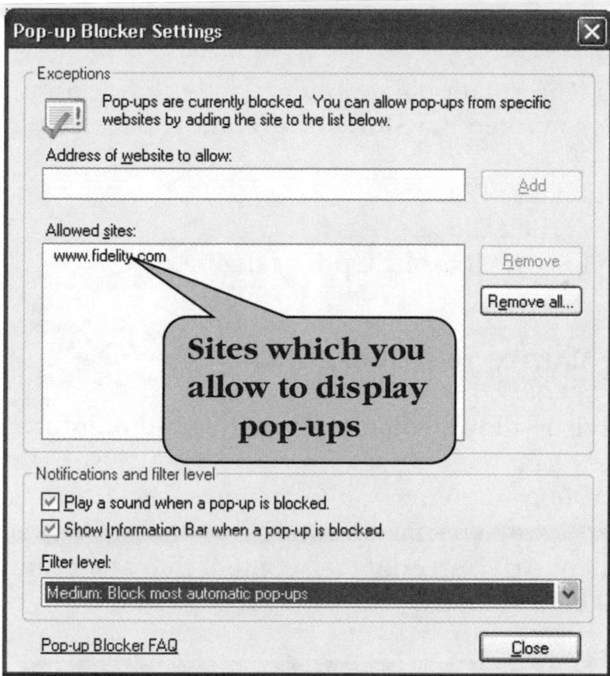

When Internet Explorer blocks a pop-up, a message appears in the **Information Bar** telling you that a pop-up was blocked. If you want to temporarily allow the pop-up for that site or set the option to always allow pop-up from that site, click the Information Bar and make the appropriate choice.

To Modify Pop-up Blocker Settings

1. Select **Tools > Internet Options** to display the **Internet Options dialog box.**
   Or
   Click the **Tools button** on the Command Bar and click **Internet Options**.
2. Click the **Privacy** tab.
3. Check the box next to **Turn on Pop-up Blocker** to enable blocking of pop-ups.

4. Click the **Settings button** under the Pop-up Blocker area to modify pop-up blocker settings.
5. To allow pop-ups from a specific site, type the site URL in the **Address of Web site to allow** box and then click **Add**.
6. To remove a site from your list, click the site name in the window and click **Remove**.
7. To remove the Information Bar notification when a pop-up is blocked, clear the check mark in the **Show Information Bar when a pop-up is blocked**.
8. Set any additional options.
9. When finished, click **Close**.
10. Click **OK** to close the Internet Options dialog box.

Using the Content Advisor

The **Content Advisor** allows you to control the kind of information that your computer can access on the Internet. The Content Advisor works with a national rating system, allowing you to prevent users from accessing Web sites that do not adhere to particular rating standards. Once you have enabled the Content Advisor, only Web content that at a minimum meets your criteria will be displayed.

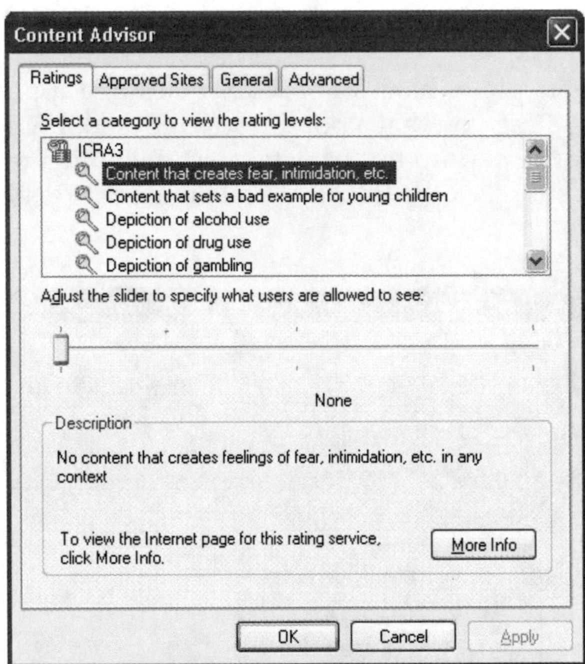

CONTENT ADVISOR DIALOG BOX

With the Content Advisor, you can:

- Establish a **password** in order to change or view Content Advisor settings.
- Specify what users can view in specific categories such as **language, nudity, sex, violence, fear, drug use, etc.**
- Establish a list **of approved sites** that users can always view, regardless of Content Advisor settings.

- Establish a list of **disapproved sites** that users can never view, regardless of Content Advisor settings.
- Decide whether users can view sites that **have no rating**.
- **View and change the rating systems** and the ratings bureaus that you use.

To Activate Content Advisor

1. Select **Tools > Internet Options** to display the **Internet Options dialog box**.
   Or
   Click the **Tools button** on the Command Bar and click **Internet Options**.
2. Click the **Content Tab**.
3. Click the **Enable** button (if a supervisor password already exists, you will be prompted to enter it).
4. Click the **General** tab.
5. Click the **Create Password** button to display the Create Supervisor Password dialog box.
6. Type the password you want to use in the **Password** and **Password Confirm** boxes.
7. Enter a password hint if desired.
8. Click **OK**.

To Control Web Access with Content Advisor

1. Select **Tools > Internet Options** to display the **Internet Options dialog box**.
   Or
   Click the **Tools button** on the Explorer Bar and click **Internet Options**.
2. Click the **Content Advisor** tab.
3. Click the **Settings** button.
4. Click the **Ratings** tab.
5. Click each category (**Language**, **Nudity**, **Sex**, **Violence**, **etc.**) and **drag the slider** until the desired level is displayed.
6. To establish a list of approved or disapproved sites:
   a. Click the **Approved Sites** tab.
   b. Type the Web address in the **Allow this Web site** box.
   c. Click the **Always** button to add the site to your list of approved sites or **Never** button to add the site to your list of disapproved sites.
   d. Click **OK**.
7. To allow access to unrated sites:
   a. Click the **General** tab.
   b. Click the **User can see sites that have no rating** check box.
8. Click **OK**.

Changing Program Settings

The **Programs** tab allows you to specify which programs you want to use to edit HTML documents, read e-mail and newsgroups, make Internet calls, and maintain your calendar and contact list. For example, Windows Live Mail, the e-mail program that is bundled with Windows Vista, is set as the default application for e-mail and newsgroups. The programs available depend on which applications are installed on your computer.

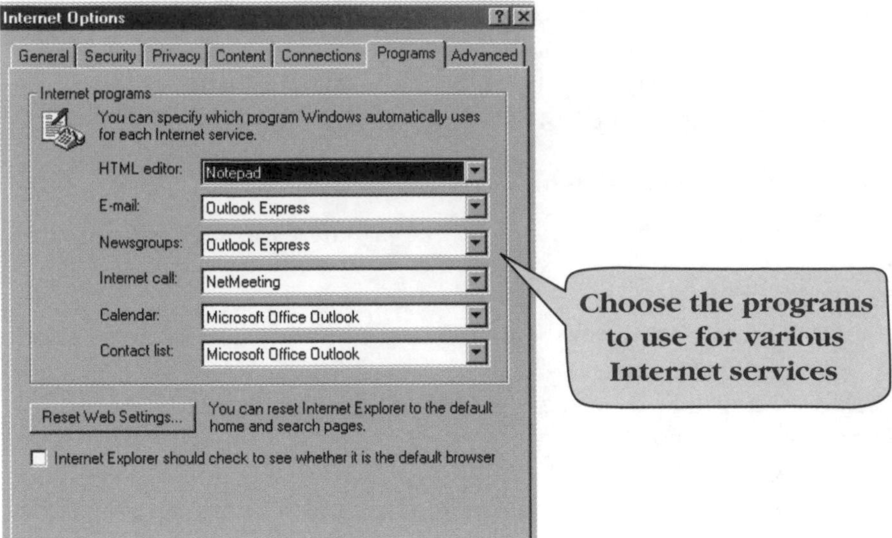

To Change Program Settings

1. Select **Tools > Internet Options** to display the **Internet Options dialog box.**
   Or
   Click the **Tools button** on the Command Bar and click **Internet Options**.
2. Click the **Programs** tab.
3. Click the drop-arrow for the service whose default program you want to change.
4. Select the program to use from the drop-down list.
5. Click **OK**.

Using the Phishing Filter

Online **Phishing** (pronounced like the word "fishing") is a scam used to trick people into revealing personal or financial information through an e-mail message. Very often, the e-mail messages appear as though they are from a legitimate source, such as your bank, credit card company, PayPal, or eBay. In the e-mail message, the recipients are usually asked to click a hyperlink to verify information, which will in actuality take the recipient to a fraudulent Web site where they are then asked to provide account information. The information is then used for identity theft purposes.

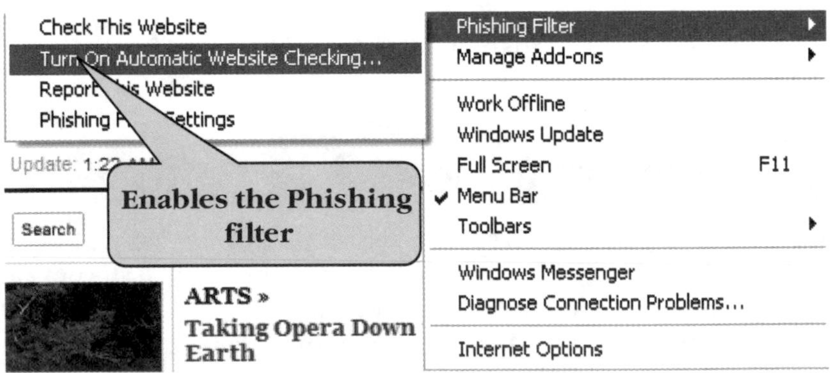

The Phishing Filter in IE7 helps detect phishing Web sites and warn you before you inadvertently provide personal information. The Phishing filter will compare each Web site you visit against a list of known Phishing sites. It will also analyze the sites you visit to see if they contain any characteristics common to a phishing Web site. If you consent, IE will send the Web site addresses you visit to Microsoft to be further checked against a frequently-updated list of phishing sites. If the site you are visiting is on a list of reported phishing Web sites, a warning message will display in the Information Bar.

To Use the Phishing Filter

1. Click **Tools** on the menu, point to **Phishing Filter** and then click **Turn on automatic Website checking** to enable the filter. Click **OK** when the dialog box appears.
2. To check a Web site manually, click **Tools** on the menu, point to **Phishing Filter** and then click **Check this Website**.
3. To turn off the Phishing filter, click **Tools** on the menu, point to **Phishing Filter** and then click **Turn off automatic Website checking**. Click **OK** when the dialog box appears.

Conclusion

You have completed Introduction to Internet Explorer 7. You are now ready to use several features of Internet Explorer that you have learned in this chapter. You are encouraged to experiment with all you have learned in this chapter. To reinforce your understanding of these techniques, it is recommended that you read and work through it once again.

Word Case Study I

CHAPTER

3

OBJECTIVES

After successfully completing this case study, you should able to:

- Start, Create, Close, and Save Word documents
- Set Options
- Enter Text into a Document
- Cut, Copy, and Paste Text
- Use Undo and Redo Buttons
- Insert Date and Time
- Change Document Views
- Check Spelling and Grammar Errors
- Use the Thesaurus
- Use Formatting Tools
- Use the Font Dialog Box
- Use Character Effects
- Add a Drop Cap
- Add Borders to a Paragraph
- Add Shading to a Paragraph
- Align Text
- Adjust Line Spacing
- Adjust Spacing between Paragraphs
- Indent Paragraphs
- Create a Bulleted List
- Create Columns
- Create a Header and Footer
- Set Margins
- Set Page Orientation
- Insert/Modify Page Numbers
- Set Printer Options
- Insert a Watermark

Case Study I—MS Word 2007

This case study is divided into two parts.

Part 1: Assume that you work as a regional sales representative for PCM hosting company. One of your job responsibilities is to update the customer on his web site account activation request. For this, you decided to use MS Word 2007 to compose the letter.

The desired letter looks like the following:

Ms. Kammy Sanghera

1991 Oakton Drive

Fairfax, VA 22030

June 21, 2007

Dear valued customer:

Your web site account has been activated and is ready for you. You may need to wait a couple of days until you can go to http://www.sanghera.com, since your new domain name needs to propagate throughout the world. Meanwhile, you can go to your assigned IP address by going to http://310.143.253.34/. A page has been set-up there to guide you through the basics of our services.

We have also created a control panel that we are currently adding new features to. Your panel is located in your site at http://www.sanghera.com/admin/ or http://310.187.253.34/admin/.

The control panel is used to configure your site and e-mails, password protect pages, view your hit statistics, install scripts, and more. The panel also provides comprehensive help and other web information that might be useful in managing your site. The panel is password protected, and the username and password is supplied below.

If you have any technical questions, please feel free to e-mail us at support@pcmhosting.net. When e-mailing for support, please include your name, domain name, username, and describe your problem in detail (include a URL if applicable). We will respond by e-mail or by phone if necessary to resolve your issues.

Thank you for doing business with PCM Hosting.

Sincerely,

Daniel L. Romney

Regional Sales Representative

PCM Hosting

ACCOUNT ACTIVATION LETTER IN MICROSOFT WORD

Part 2: Assume that you are the newly appointed President of Outdoor Fun group. Your job includes planning events for Outdoor Fun group, coordinate Board meetings and send out the monthly newsletter. For this month's newsletter, you decided to use MS Word 2007. Since you want to revise it one more time before sending it out, you mark it as a DRAFT.

The desired letter looks like the following:

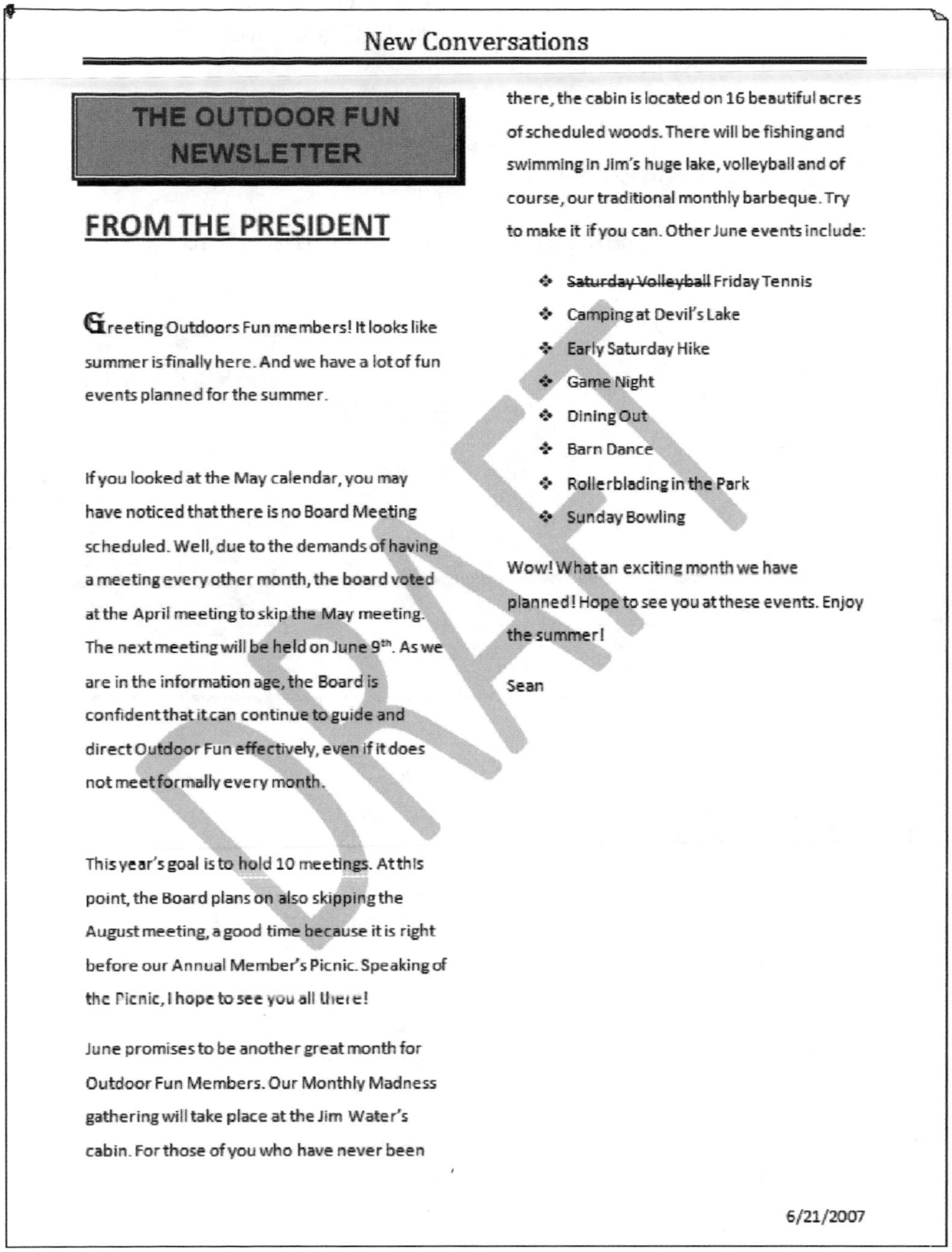

New Conversations

THE OUTDOOR FUN NEWSLETTER

FROM THE PRESIDENT

Greeting Outdoors Fun members! It looks like summer is finally here. And we have a lot of fun events planned for the summer.

If you looked at the May calendar, you may have noticed that there is no Board Meeting scheduled. Well, due to the demands of having a meeting every other month, the board voted at the April meeting to skip the May meeting. The next meeting will be held on June 9th. As we are in the information age, the Board is confident that it can continue to guide and direct Outdoor Fun effectively, even if it does not meet formally every month.

This year's goal is to hold 10 meetings. At this point, the Board plans on also skipping the August meeting, a good time because it is right before our Annual Member's Picnic. Speaking of the Picnic, I hope to see you all there!

June promises to be another great month for Outdoor Fun Members. Our Monthly Madness gathering will take place at the Jim Water's cabin. For those of you who have never been there, the cabin is located on 16 beautiful acres of scheduled woods. There will be fishing and swimming in Jim's huge lake, volleyball and of course, our traditional monthly barbeque. Try to make it if you can. Other June events include:

- ~~Saturday Volleyball~~ Friday Tennis
- Camping at Devil's Lake
- Early Saturday Hike
- Game Night
- Dining Out
- Barn Dance
- Rollerblading in the Park
- Sunday Bowling

Wow! What an exciting month we have planned! Hope to see you at these events. Enjoy the summer!

Sean

6/21/2007

DRAFT

NEWSLETTER IN MICROSOFT WORD

Starting Word

This section will introduce you to Microsoft Word and you will open the Word application.

Welcome to Microsoft Word 2007! Microsoft Word is a powerful and user-friendly word-processing application that allows you to create a variety of professional text-based documents. You can create everything from simple letters to a jazzy newsletters complete with columns, graphics and tables.

Microsoft Word contains many powerful tools to make word-processing more efficient, such as a built-in spell and grammar checker, the ability to autocorrect your document, and much more. In this section, we'll begin by launching the Word Application.

To Open Microsoft Word

1. Click the **Start** button on the lower-left corner of your screen to display the Start menu.
2. **All Programs > Microsoft Office > Microsoft Office Word 2007** from the Start Menu to launch the application.

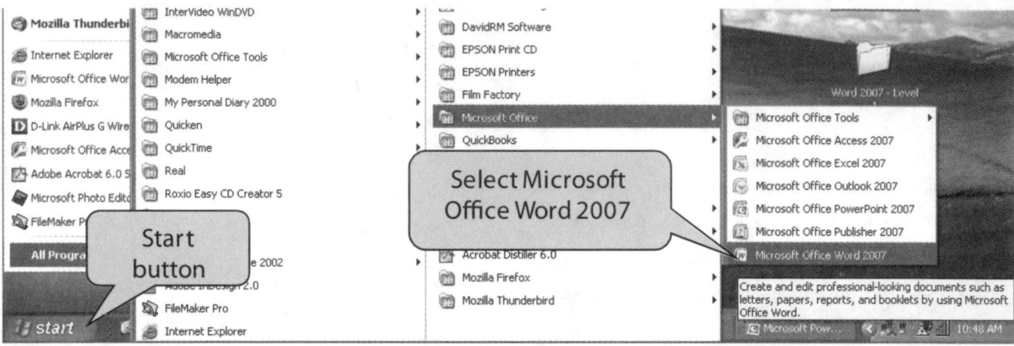

Let's Try It!

- Click the **Start** button on the lower left side of your screen.

Displays the Start Menu, allowing you to select which application to launch.

- Select **All Programs > Microsoft Office > Microsoft Office Word 2007** from the Start Menu.

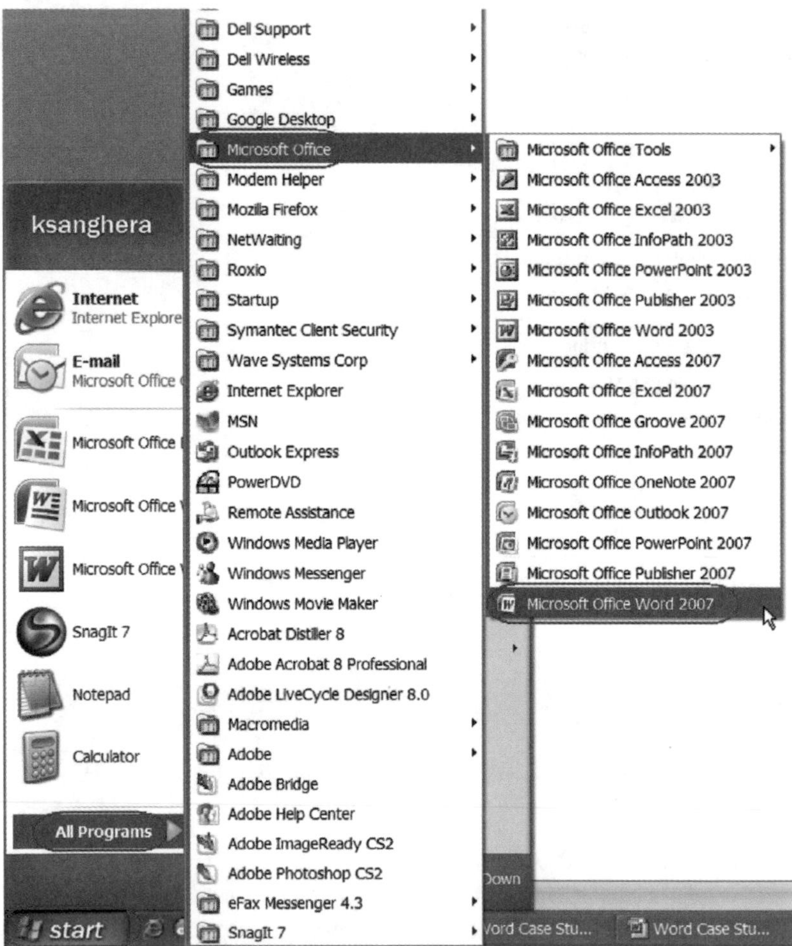

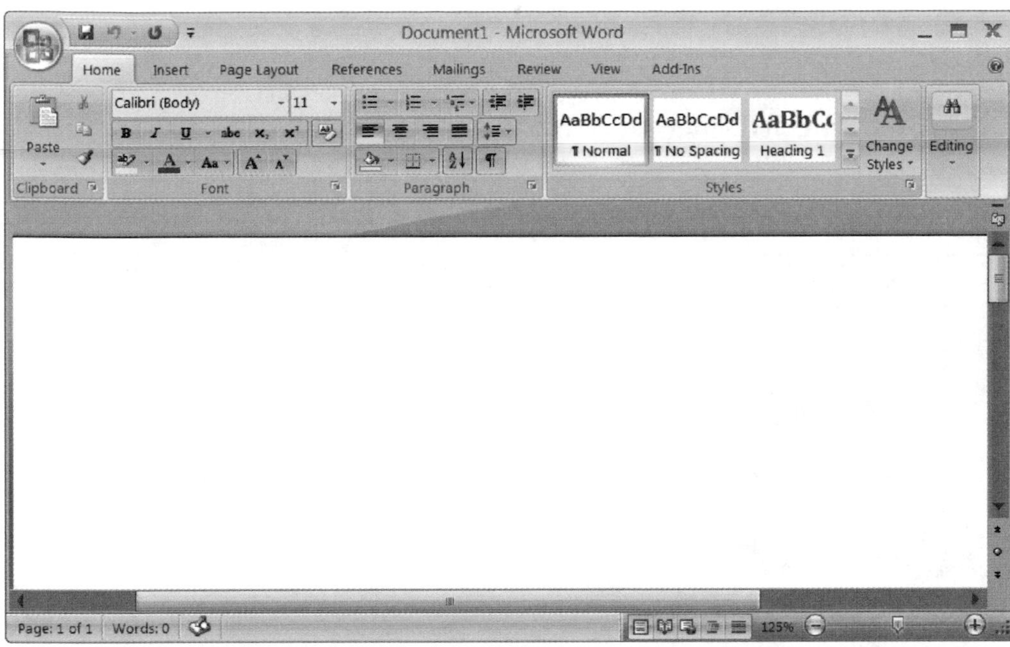

- Launches the Microsoft Word Program and displays a new blank document.

Creating a New Document

In this section, you will learn how to create a new blank document.

We have already seen that when you first launch Microsoft Word, a new blank document is created. You can also create a new document from within another document. The new document command is located under the **File Options** menu. You can also use the keyboard shortcut **Ctrl + N** to bypass the File Options menu.

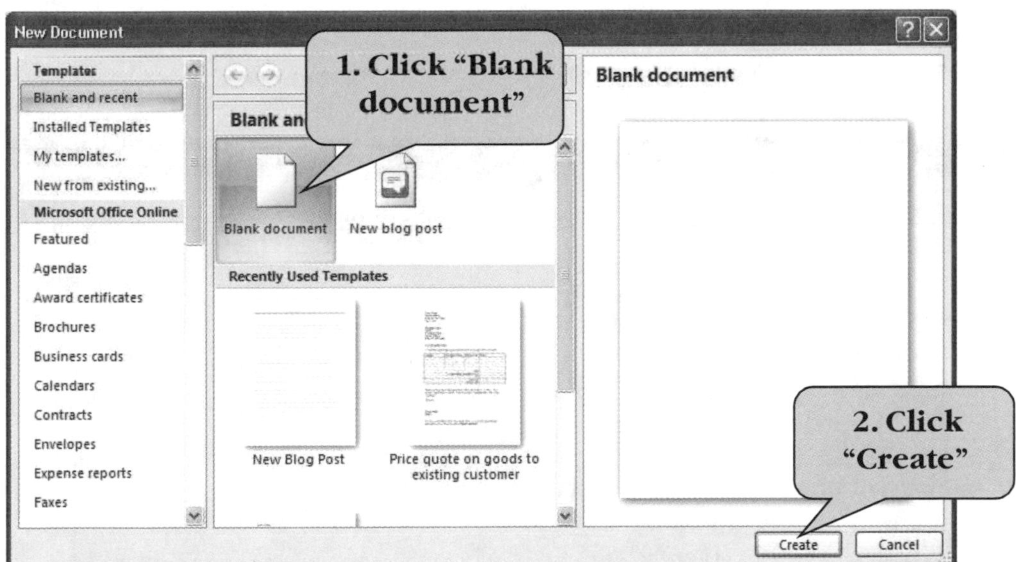

To Create a New Document

1. Click the **Microsoft Office Button** and then click **New** from the menu to display the **New Document** Task Pane.
2. Click **Blank Document** in the center pane.

3. Click **Create**.
   Or
   Hold down the **Ctrl** and **N** keystroke combination (**Ctrl + N**)
4. Begin typing in the new document.

Let's Try It!

- Click the **Microsoft Office Button** and then click **New** from the menu.

Displays the New Document pane.

- In the **Center** Pane, click on **Blank document**.

Specifies that we will create a new blank document.

- Click **Create**.

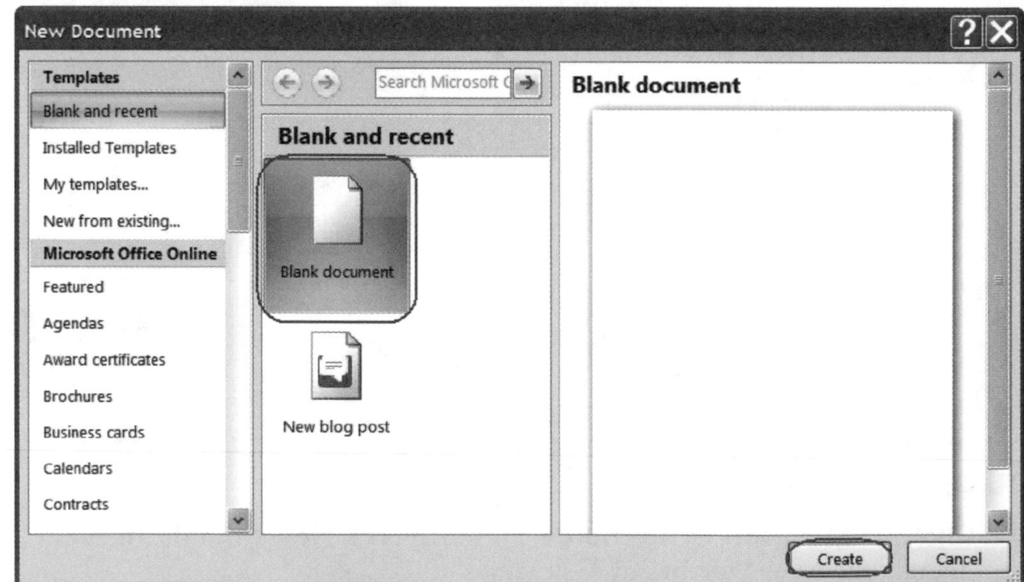

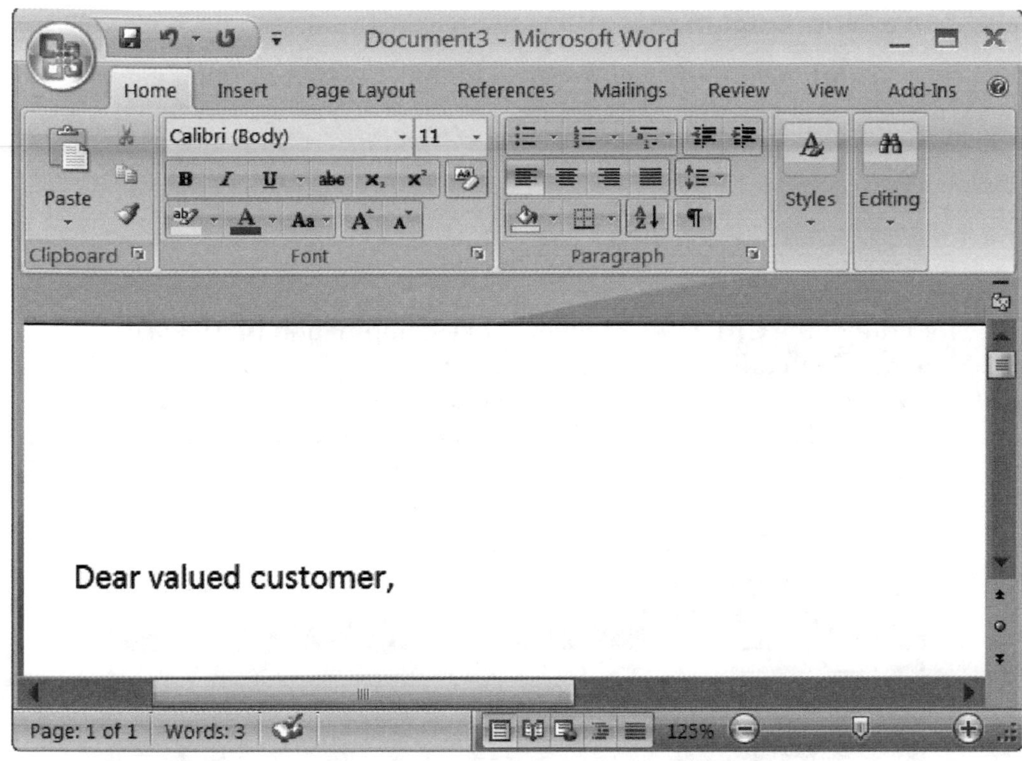

Creates a new blank document.

- Click in the document window and type: **Dear valued customer,**

Enters text into the new document.

Saving a Document

In this section, you will learn how to save a document.

You can **save your document** to a hard disk, to a removable disk such as a zip drive or USB flash drive, or to a network drive. The first time you save a document, the **Save As Dialog Box** will appear, prompting you for the name of the document and the location where you wish to save the document. This box will only appear the first time you save a new document. To save a file, click the **Microsoft Office Button** and then click **Save** or use the keyboard shortcut **Ctrl + S**. You can also click the **Save button** on the Quick Access toolbar, directly to the right of the Microsoft Office button.

To save an exiting document with a different file name, select **Save As** from the File Options menu, and then type the new name for the document in the **file name** text box. The original document will be closed and the document with the new name becomes the active document.

After you save a document, the file remains open so you can continue to work on it. You can save any subsequent changes quickly by clicking on the Save icon. It is a good idea to save your documents often.

To Save a New Document

1. Click the **Microsoft Office Button** and then click **Save** from the menu
   Or
   Click the **Save icon** on the Quick Access Toolbar

SAVE ICON

   Or
   Hold down the **Ctrl key** and **S** keystroke combination (**Ctrl + S**)
2. Type the desired file name in the **File name** box.
3. Navigate to the folder where you wish to save your file in the **Places bar** (many people prefer to save their documents in the **My Documents** folder).
4. Click **Save**.

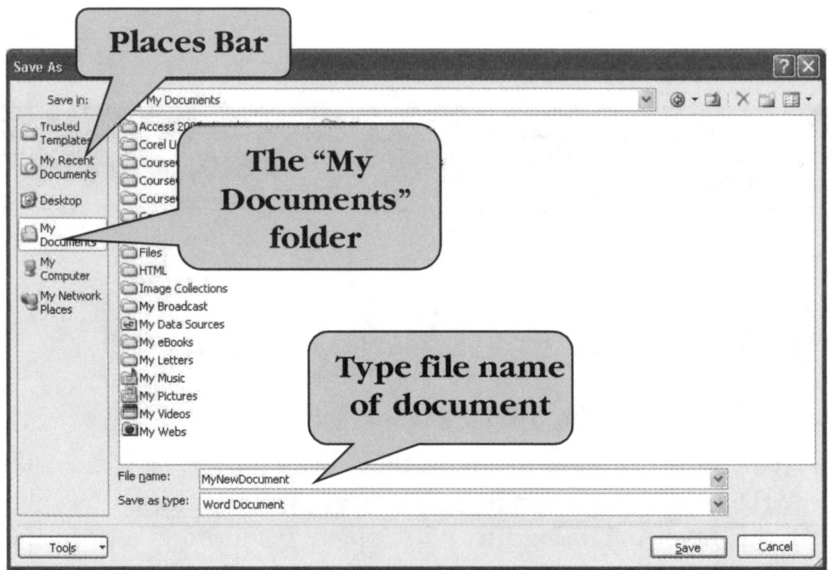

THE SAVE AS DIALOG BOX

Let's Try It!

- Insert **flash drive** in USB port.
- Click the **Save button** on the Quick Access toolbar.

As we have not yet saved our document, the Save As dialog box appears, prompting for the file name and location where we wish to save the file.

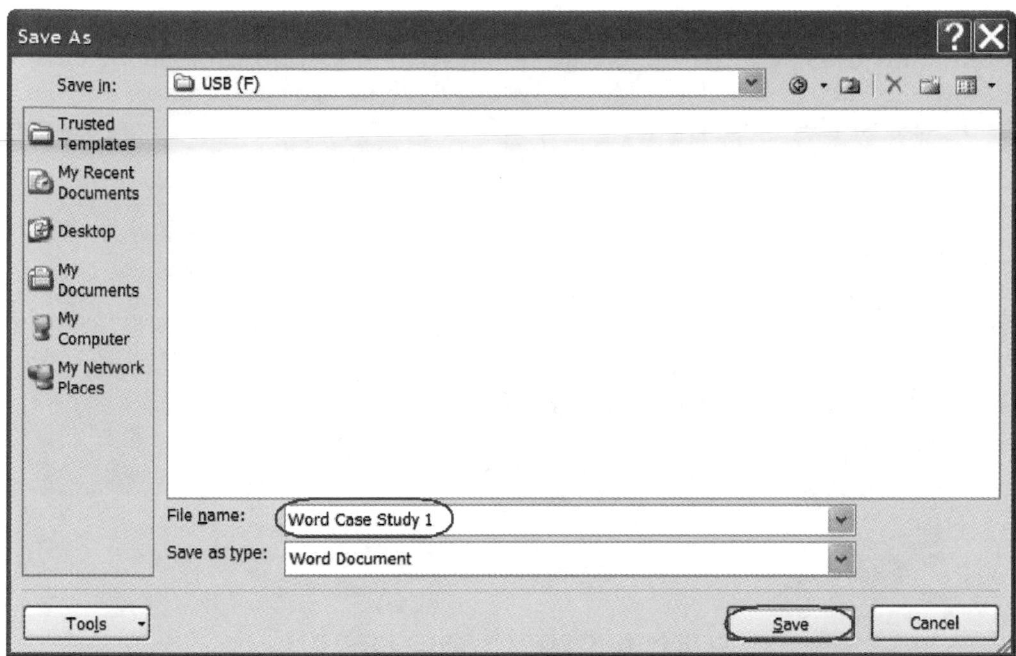

- In the **File name** text box, type: **Word Case Study I** and select **flash drive** in the **Save in** list.

Enters the name of the new workbook.

- Click the **Save** button.

Saves the workbook with the new name.

The Word Environment

In this section, we will look at the different parts of the Word Screen.

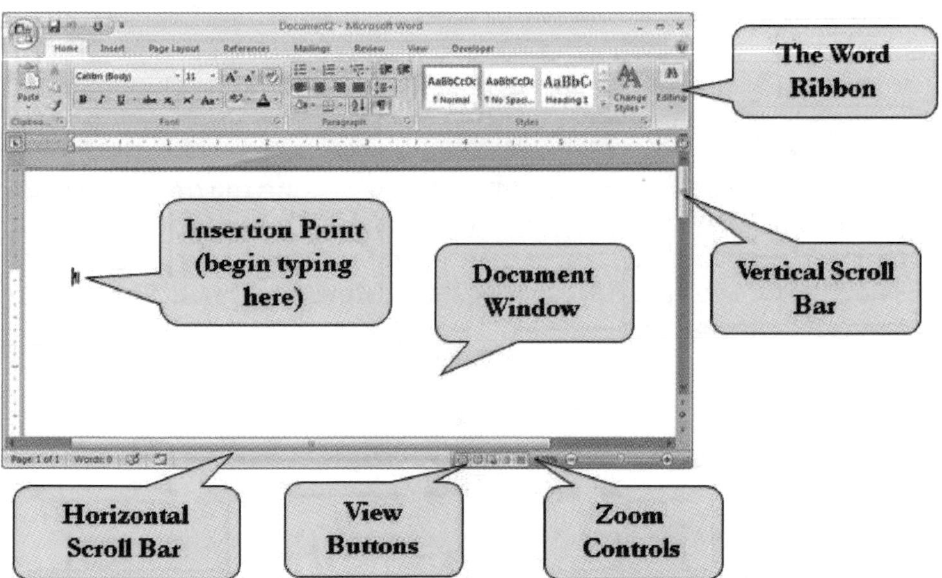

When you first start Microsoft Word, the application opens to a blank document along with the parts of the Microsoft Word screen as shown in the screen shot above. If you have worked with previous versions of Word, you will immediately notice that the user interface has been completely redesigned.

The menu and toolbar system have been replaced by the **Ribbon**. The Ribbon is designed to help you quickly find the commands you need in order to complete a task. On the Ribbon, the menu bar has been replaced by **Command Tabs** that relate to the tasks you wish to accomplish. The default Command Tabs in Word are: **Home, Insert, Page Layout, References, Mailings, Review** and **View**.

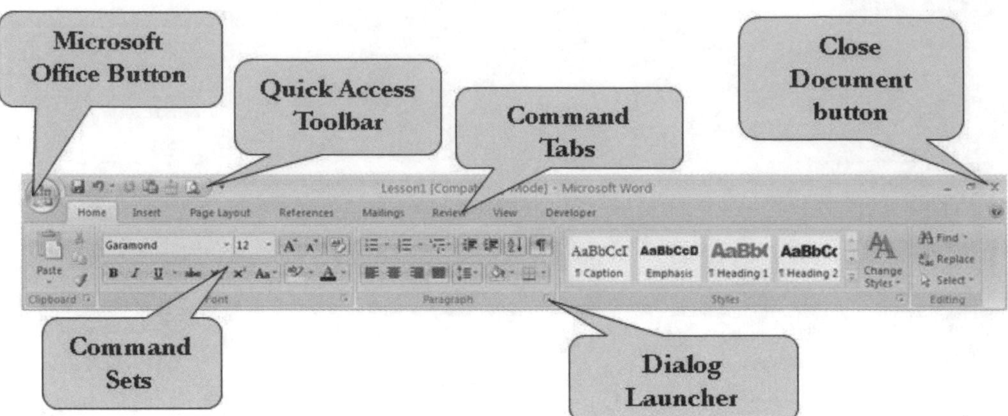

THE MICROSOFT WORD RIBBON

Different command icons, called **Command Sets** appear under each Command Tab. The commands that appear will depend on the Command Tab that is selected. Each command set is grouped by its function. For example, the Insert tab contains commands to add pages, tables, headers, footers, symbols and text objects to your document. **Contextual Commands** only appear when a specific object is selected. This helps in keeping the screen uncluttered.

On the bottom of many of the Command Sets is a **Dialog Launcher**, which when clicked, will launch a dialog box for that set of commands.

To the right of the **Microsoft Office icon** (from where you access file options), is the **Quick Access Toolbar**. This toolbar contains by default the Save, Undo, and Redo commands. In addition, clicking the drop-down arrow to the right allows you to customize the Quick Access Toolbar to add other tools that you use regularly. You can choose from the list which tools to display on the Quick Access Toolbar or select **More Commands** to add commands that are not in the list.

QUICK ACCESS TOOLBAR

We will be working in detail with the various Word tabs and commands in subsequent sections.

Let's take a look at the Word Screen in more detail:

Component	Description
Command Sets	Command icons, grouped by category, under each command tab.
Dialog Launcher	Launches dialog boxes or task panes for a particular set of commands
Document Window	The white area where you type and edit your documents. The document window contains the text, tables, graphics, etc. that you enter into your document.
Horizontal Scroll Bar	Allows you to move horizontally in your document. To navigate horizontally, click the scroll bar with your left mouse button and drag to the left or to the right until the desired portion of the document is in view.
Insertion Point	The small flashing vertical bar which designates the location where you can begin typing or editing text. To change the insertion point, click with your left mouse button in the desired new location of your document.
Office Button	Click to access file commands.
Quick Access Toolbar	Contains frequently used commands. You can customize it to include tools and commands that you frequently use.
Ribbon	Commands and tools organized into command sets.
Status Bar	Displays information about the active document.
Tabs	To access the various command sets and tools.
Title Bar	Displays the name of the application you are currently using and the name of the file (the Microsoft Word document) on which you are working.
Vertical Scroll Bar	Allows you to move vertically in your document. To navigate vertically, click the scroll bar with your left mouse button and drag upward or downwards until the desired portion of the document is in view.
View Buttons	Allows you to display documents in several different document views (Print Layout, Full Screen Reading, Web Layout, Outline and Draft).
Zoom Slider	Allows you to increase or decrease the magnification of your document.

Let's Try It!

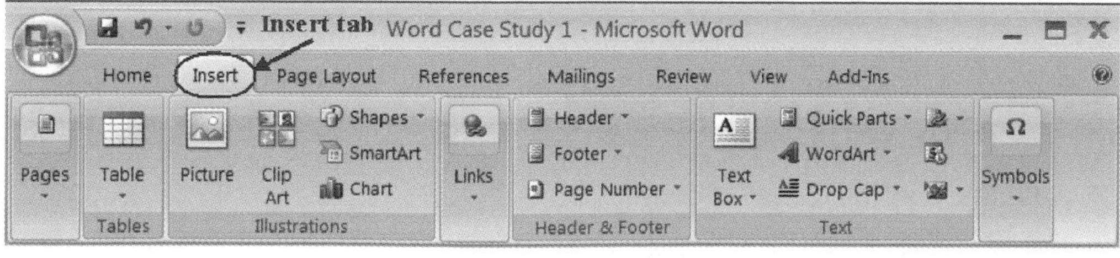

- Click the **Insert tab** on top of your screen.

Displays the commands sets for the Insert command tab.

- Click the **View tab** on top of your screen.

Displays the commands sets for the View command tab.

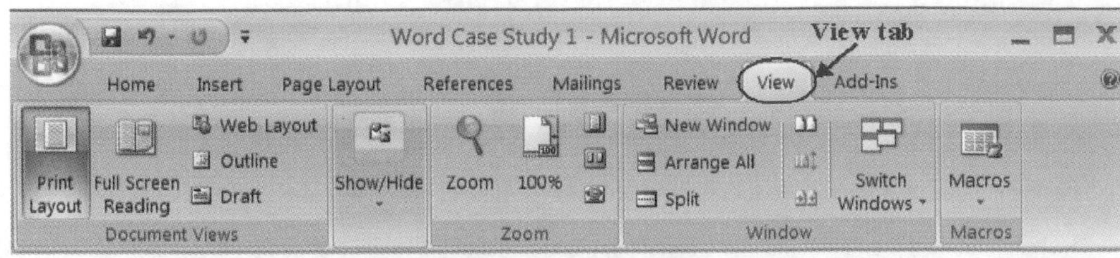

- Click the **Home tab** on top of your screen.

Returns us back to the Home tab.

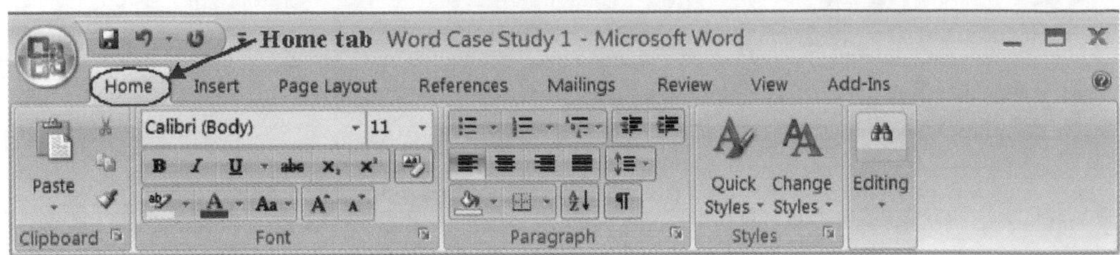

Entering Text into a Document

In this section, you type text into an open document.

When you create a new blank document, the **insertion point (the location where you begin entering text)** automatically begins at the top left of the document. So you can just begin typing text into your blank document. As you type, the text will automatically wrap to the next line. To insert a new blank line, press the **Enter** key.

To add text to an existing document, move your mouse cursor to the location where you wish to begin typing and click your left mouse button. This will move the insertion point to the new location.

Dear·valued·customer,·¶
¶
Your·web·site·account·has·been·activated·and·is·ready·for·you.·You·may·need·t
couple·of·days·until·you·can·go·to·http://www.rodneysvideo.com,
name·needs·to·propagate·throughout·the·world.·Meanwhile,·you
IP·address·by·going·to·http://310.143.253.34/.·A·page·has·been·
through·the·basics·of·our·services.¶
¶
We·have·also·created·a·control·panel·that·we·are·currently·adding·new·features·
panel·is·located·in·your·site·at·http://www.rodneysvideo/admin/·or·
http://310.187.253.34/admin/.¶
¶
The·control·panel·is·used·to·configure·your·site·&·e-mails,·password·protect·pa
your·hit·statistics,·install·scripts·and·more.·The·panel·also·provides·comprehens
and·other·web·information·that·might·be·useful·in·managing·your·site.·The·pane

Click to move insertion point to new location

To Enter Text in Your Document

1. To enter text into a new document:
   a. Open a new document
   b. Begin typing your text.

2. To enter text into an existing document:
   a. Move your mouse pointer to the location where you wish to begin typing.
   b. **Click** with your left mouse button to set insertion point.
   c. Begin typing.
3. Press **Enter** to insert a new blank line.

Let's Try It!

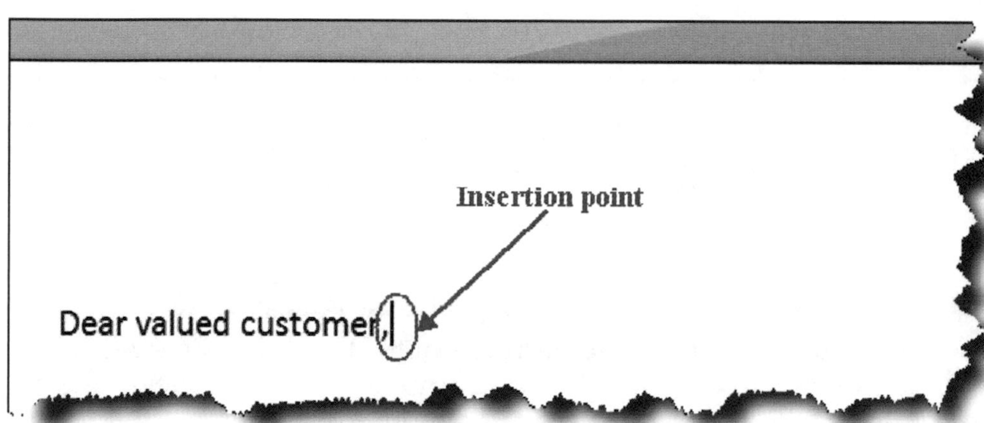

- Click at the end of the **Dear valued customer**,

Moves the insertion point to the end of the first line. We will now enter some more text.

Dear valued customer,

Your web site account has been activated and is ready for you. You may need to wait a couple of days until you go to http://www.sanghera.com, since your new domain name needs to propagate throughout the world. Meanwhile, you can go to your assigned IP address by going to http://310.143.253.34/. A page has been set-up there to guide you through the basics of our services.

We have also created a control panel that we are currently adding new features to. Your panel is located in your site at http://www.sanghera.com/admin/ or http://310.187.253.34/admin/.

The control panel is used to configure your site & e-mails, password protect pages, view your hit statistics, install scripts, and more. The panel also provides complete help and other web information that might be useful in managing your site. The panel is password protected, and the username and password is supplied below.

If you have any technical questions, feel free to e-mail us at support@pcmhosting.net. When e-mailing for support, please include your name, domain name, username, and describe your problem in detail (include a URL if applicable). We will respond by e-mail or by phone if necessary to resolve your issues.

Thank you for doing business with PCM Hosting.

Yours Truly,

Daniel L. Romney

- Press **Enter twice**.

Creates a new paragraph with a blank line between the last paragraph and the new paragraph.

- Type the information shown in the screenshot. Press **Enter twice** to create new paragraph.

Enters the text for the new paragraph.

- Press **Enter** key once and **type: Regional Sales Representative**.

Enters the text in a new paragraph.

- Click the **Save** button.

Saves the changes. As we have already saved this document a first time, the Save As dialog box does not appear.

Yours Truly,

Daniel L. Romney

Regional Sales Representative

Correcting Mistakes

In this section, you will learn how to correct mistakes in your document.

As you type, you may discover that you need to make a change in a document—perhaps correct a misspelled word or remove words from a sentence. You can delete text by using either the **Backspace** key or the **Delete** key. Pressing the Backspace key will delete text to the left of the insertion point whereas pressing the Delete key will delete text to the right of the insertion point.

To Delete Text in a Document

1. Place the insertion point before or after the text you wish to delete.
2. Press the **Backspace** key to delete characters to the left of the insertion point.
3. Press the **Delete** key to delete characters to the right of the insertion point.

Let's Try It!

- Move your mouse cursor after the **comma** in the greeting, after the words: **valued customer**.

Moves our cursor to the location where we wish delete text.

- Click with your **left mouse button**.

Sets the insertion point.

- Press the **Backspace** key.

Deletes the comma from the sentence.

- Hold down the **Shift** key and press the **Colon** (:) key.

Inserts a colon after the salutation.

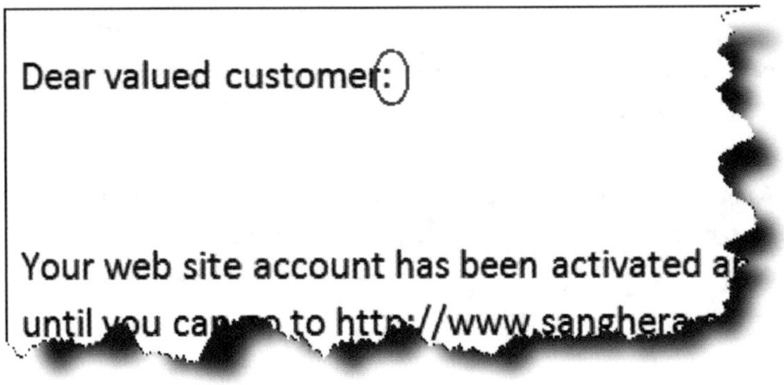

Dear valued customer:

Your web site account has been activated a

until you ca to http://www.sanghera

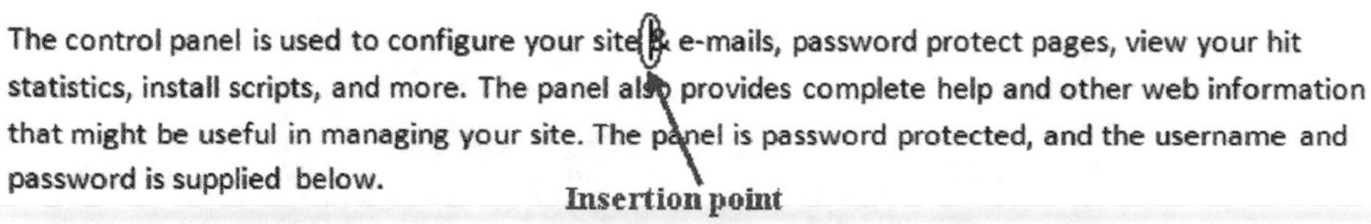

The control panel is used to configure your site & e-mails, password protect pages, view your hit statistics, install scripts, and more. The panel also provides complete help and other web information that might be useful in managing your site. The panel is password protected, and the username and password is supplied below.

Insertion point

- Move your mouse cursor in front of **ampersand (&)** in the first line of the third paragraph, after the word: **site** and click with your left mouse button.

Sets the insertion point at the location where we wish delete text.

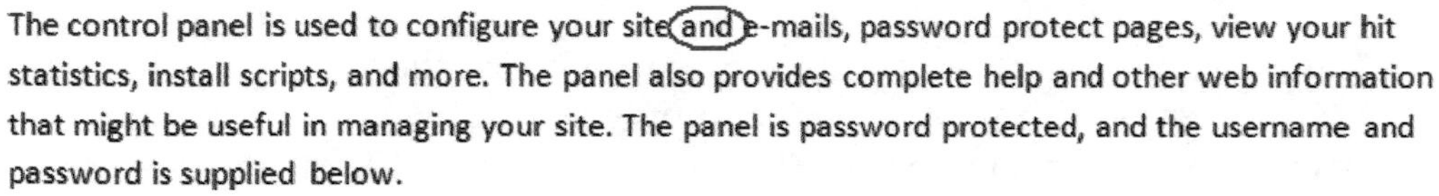

The control panel is used to configure your site and e-mails, password protect pages, view your hit statistics, install scripts, and more. The panel also provides complete help and other web information that might be useful in managing your site. The panel is password protected, and the username and password is supplied below.

- Press the **Delete** key.

Deletes the ampersand.

- Type the word: **and** as shown in the screen shot.

Inserts text into our document.

Navigating a Document

In this section, you will learn how to move around in a document.

You have already learned how to move the insertion point from one location to another in a document. However, moving around in a document becomes more challenging as your document becomes longer. Luckily, Microsoft Word contains many ways to navigate a document.

- **Scroll Bars**—Scroll bars allow you move quickly from one area or page of your document to another. Word contains both **horizontal and vertical scroll bars**. Clicking and dragging the scroll bar moves you to the position or page in the document where you release the scroll bar. As you scroll through a document, a small box appears that displays the page number of the page to which you would be moved if you were to release the mouse button.
- **Scroll Buttons**—Clicking on the **scroll up** and **scroll down** buttons allow you to move upwards or downwards your document one line at a time. Clicking on the page up scroll button or the page down scroll button moves you backward or forward by one page.

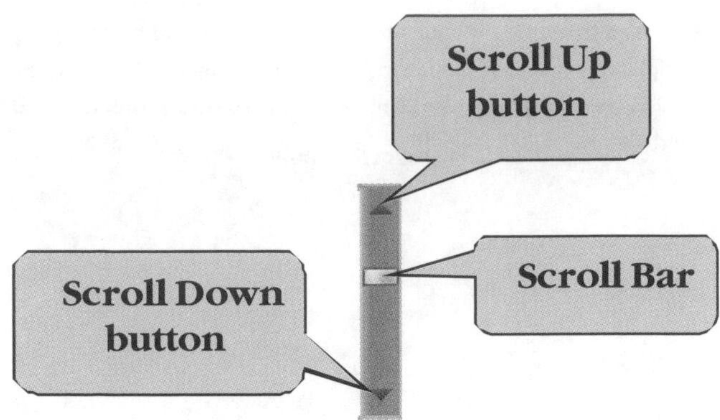

- **Keyboard Shortcuts**—You can also use keyboard shortcuts (pressing one or more keys on your keyboard) to move around in your document. Below are listed some common keyboard navigation shortcuts.

Keyboard Navigation Shortcuts

Method	Action
Move Left one Character at a Time	Left Arrow Key
Move Right one Character at a Time	Right Arrow Key
Move Down one Line at a Time	Down Arrow Key
Move Up one Line at a Time	Up Arrow Key
Move to Beginning of Document	Ctrl + Home keys
Move to End of Document	Ctrl + End keys

Let's Try It!

- Move your mouse pointer before the word **Dear** in the greeting, and then click with your left mouse button.

Places the insertion point at the beginning of the document.

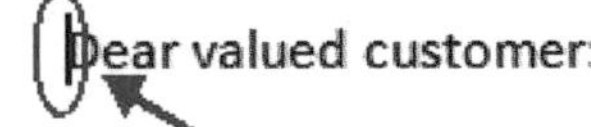

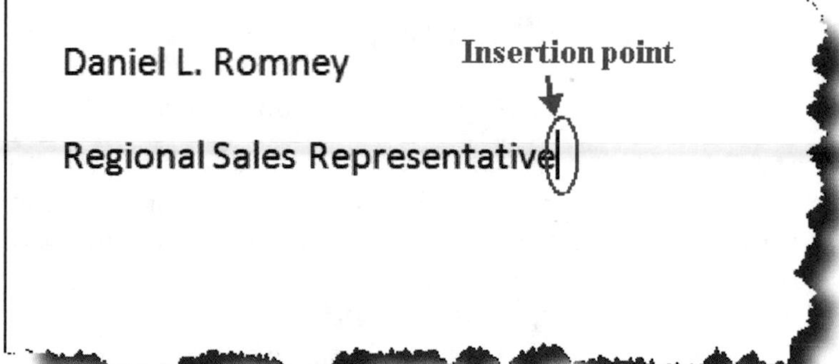

- Press and hold the **Ctrl** key and then press the **End** key (Ctrl + End). Release both keys.

Moves to the end of the document.

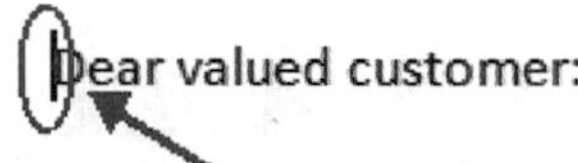

Insertion point

Your web site account has been activated and is ready for you. Yo
until you can go to http://www.sanghera.com, since your new do
throughout the world. Meanwhile, you can go to your assigned IP
http://310.143.253.34/. A page has been set-up there to guide y

- Press and hold the **Ctrl** key then press the **Home** key (Ctrl + Home). Release both keys.

Moves the insertion point to the beginning of the document.

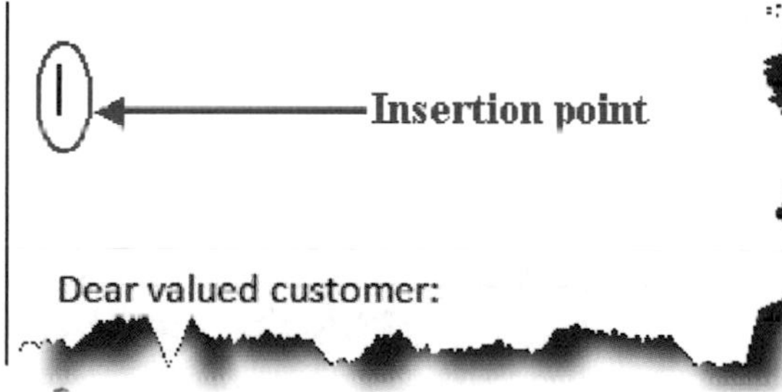

- Press **Enter twice**.

Moves the text two lines from the top.

- Press **Up Arrow** key on your keyboard twice.

Moves up 2 lines in the document to the top of the page.

Ms. Kammy Sanghera

1991 Oakton Drive

Fairfax, VA 22030

Dear valued customer:

- Type the information shown in the screenshot. Press **Enter** key **once** for a new line.

Enters the text in the document.

- Click the **Save** button.

Saves the changes.

Setting Word Options

In this section, we will work with Word Options.

In previous versions of Word, you could set preferences for specific program settings from the Options dialog box. The Options command has been moved to the **Word Options** button on the File Options menu which displays when you click the **Microsoft Office Button**.

From the Word Options dialog box, you can specify such options as setting the color scheme for the Word application, specifying a default location to save files, setting the default file format, and much more.

You may wish to spend some time browsing through the Word Options dialog box and set any preferences that may help you work with less effort.

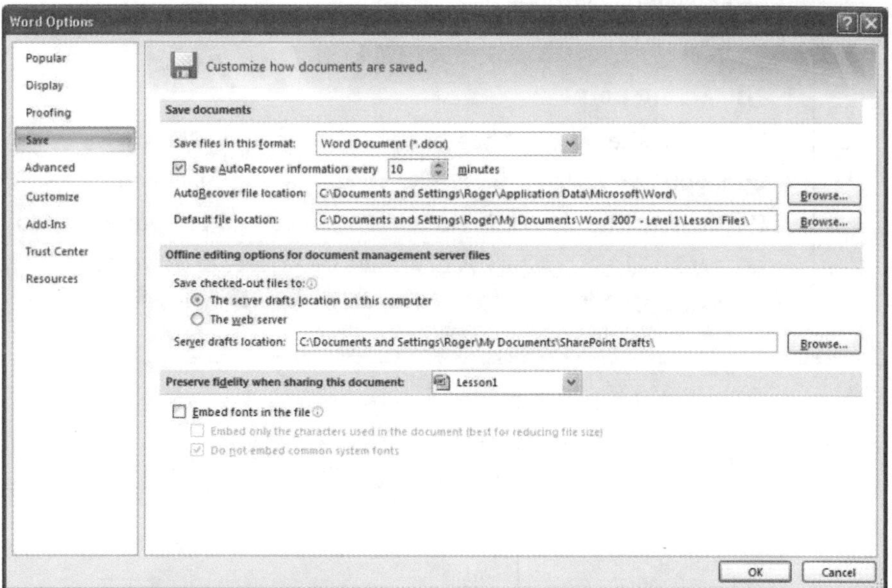

WORD OPTIONS DIALOG BOX

To Set Word Options

1. Click the **Microsoft Office Button** and then click **Word Options** on the bottom of the File Options pane.
2. Click the desired option category in the left pane.
3. Set any options in the right pane.
4. Click **OK**.

Let's Try It!

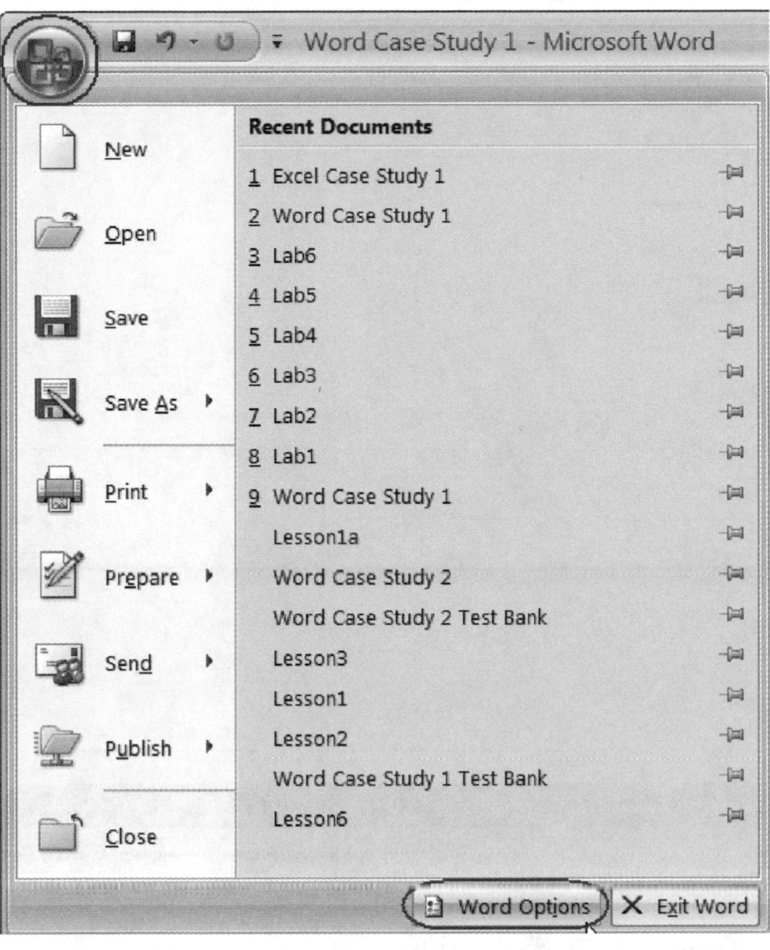

- Click the **Microsoft Office Button**.

Displays the File Options menu.

- Click the **Word Options** button.

Displays the Word Options dialog box.

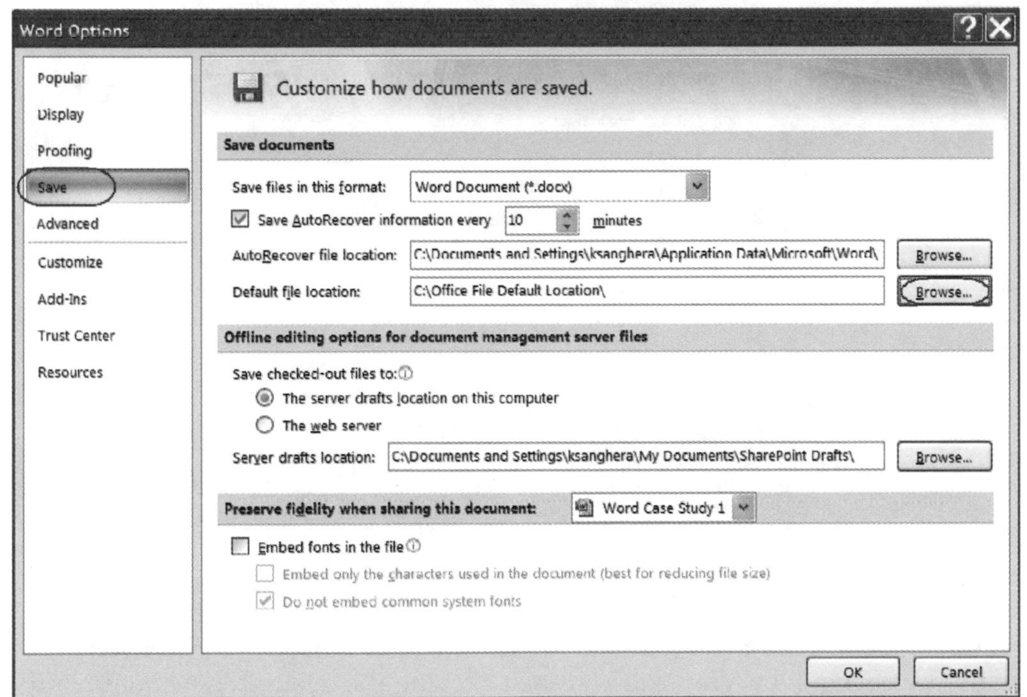

- Click the **Save** category in the left pane.

Displays available Word options for the Save category.

- Click the **Browse** button to the right of the **Default File Location** box.

Displays the Browse window, from where we can browse to the folder that we want to set as the default file location folder—that is to say, the default folder to which Word will save documents.

- In the **Places Bar**, click on **My Computer**.

Opens the My Computer folder.

- **Double-click** on the **USB Flash drive**.

Sets it as the default file location.

- Click **OK**.

Closes the Browse window.

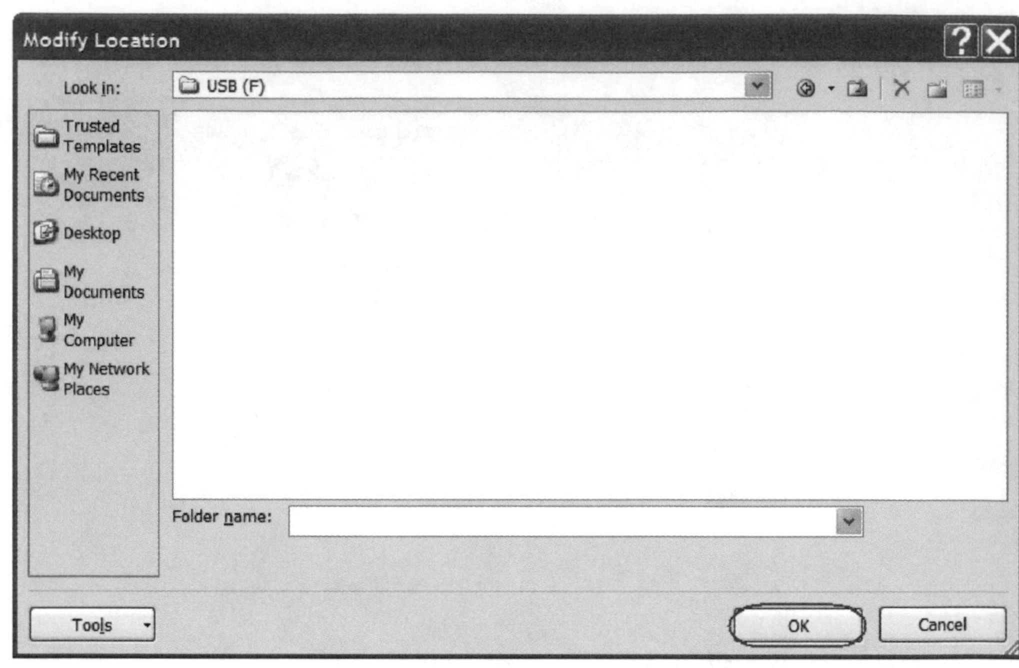

- Click **OK**.

Closes the Word Options window and applies our changes.

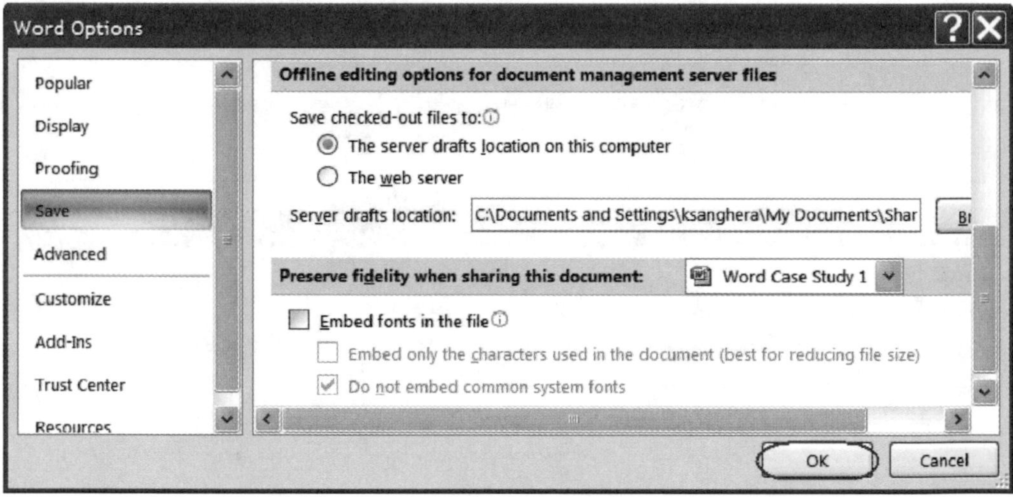

Changing Document Views

In this section, you will learn how to switch between different views.

Views control how your document appears on the screen. You can quickly switch views by clicking on one of the **View Buttons** located on the lower right hand corner of the document window. You can also switch between views by clicking the **View** tab and then clicking the desired View command button on the Ribbon.

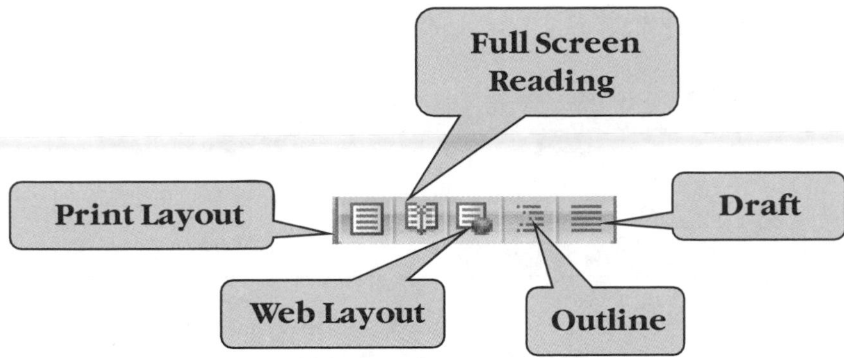

The available views are:

- **Print Layout** Used for entering, editing and formatting text. In Print Layout view, a small gray gap is displayed between each page.
- **Full Screen Reading** Displays the document in full screen and hides the scroll bars and the Ribbon.
- **Web Layout** Allows you to see how your document would display in a Web browser.
- **Outline** Displays your document in outline format with headings and subheadings.
- **Draft** Displays your document without any gaps between pages.

To Switch Between Views

1. Click the appropriate View button on the lower-right corner of your screen
   Or
   Click the **View** tab and then click the desired View command button on the Ribbon

Let's Try It!

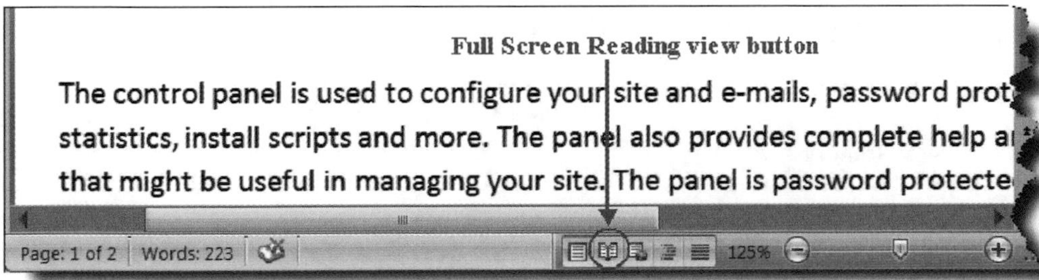

- Click on the **Full Screen Reading** view button (the second view button on the lower-right side of your screen).

Switches to Full Screen Reading view.

- Click the **Close** button on the top-right corner of the screen.

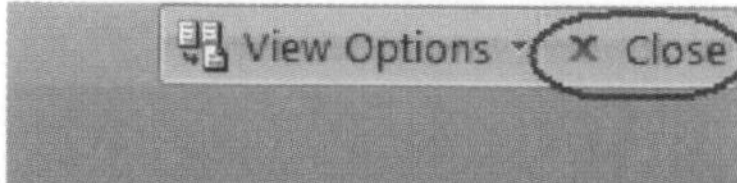

Returns to Print Layout view. You can also press the Esc key to exit Full Screen Reading view.

- Click the **Outline** view button (the fourth button on the lower-left side of your screen).

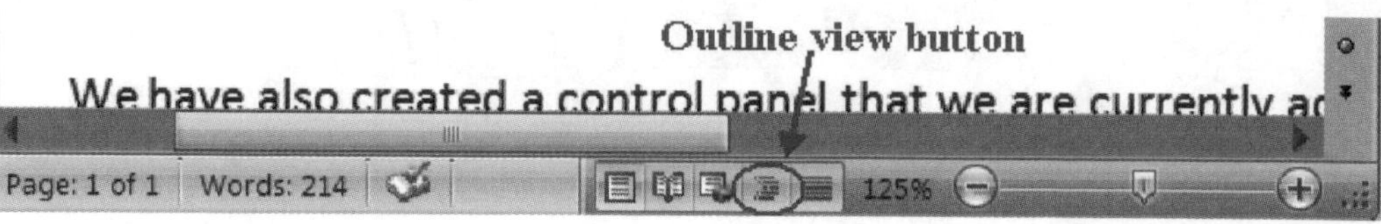

Switches to Outline view.

- Click the **Web Layout** view button (the third button on the lower-left side of your screen).

- Ms. Kammy Sanghera
- 1991 Oakton Drive
- Fairfax, VA 22030
- Dear valued customer:
- Your web site account has been activated and is ready for you. You may need to wait a couple of days until you can go to http://www.sanghera.com, since your new domain name needs to propagate throughout the world. Meanwhile, you can go to your assigned IP address by going to http://310.143.253.34/. A page has been set-up there to guide you through the basics of our services.
- We have also created a control panel that we are currently adding new features to. Your panel is located in your site at http://www.sanghera.com/admin/ or http://310.187.253.34/admin/.
- The control panel is used to configure your site and e-mails, password protect pages, view your hit statistics, install scripts, and more. The panel also provides complete help and other web information that might be useful in managing your site. The panel is password protected, and the username and password is supplied below.
- If you have any technical questions, please feel free to e-mail us at support@pcmhosting.net. When e-mailing for support, please include your name, domain name, username, and describe your problem in detail (include a URL if applicable). We will respond by e-mail or by phone if necessary to resolve your issues.
- Thank you for doing business with PCM Hosting.
- Yours Truly,
- Daniel L. Romney
- Regional Sales Representative

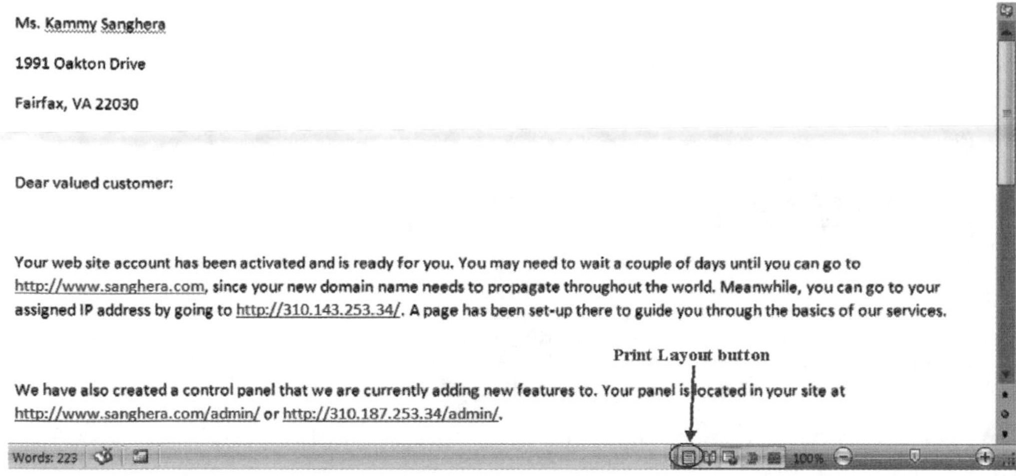
Ms. Kammy Sanghera

1991 Oakton Drive

Fairfax, VA 22030

Dear valued customer:

Your web site account has been activated and is ready for you. You may need to wait a couple of days until you can go to http://www.sanghera.com, since your new domain name needs to propagate throughout the world. Meanwhile, you can go to your assigned IP address by going to http://310.143.253.34/. A page has been set-up there to guide you through the basics of our services.

We have also created a control panel that we are currently adding new features to. Your panel is located in your site at http://www.sanghera.com/admin/ or http://310.187.253.34/admin/.

Switches to Web Layout view.

- Click the **Print Layout** view (the first button on the lower-left side of your screen).

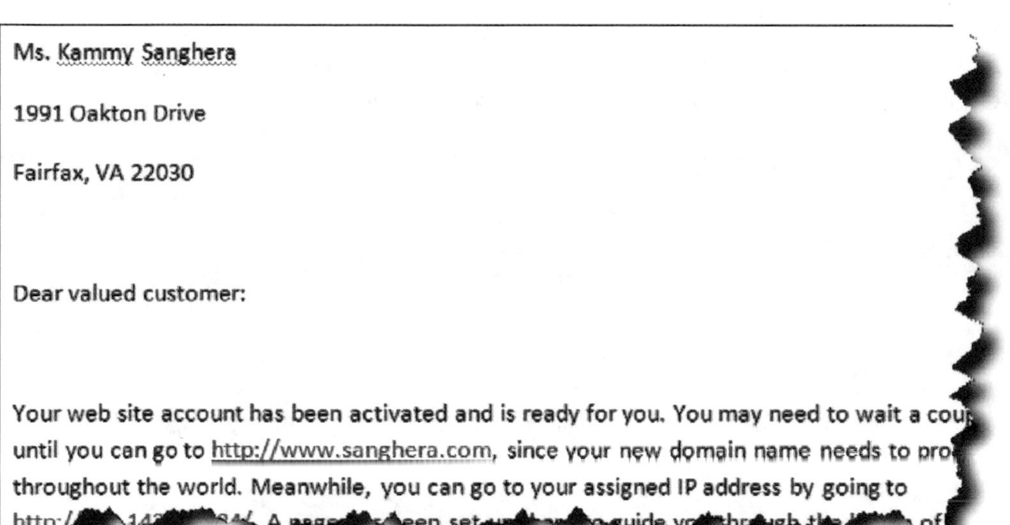
Ms. Kammy Sanghera

1991 Oakton Drive

Fairfax, VA 22030

Dear valued customer:

Your web site account has been activated and is ready for you. You may need to wait a cou
until you can go to http://www.sanghera.com, since your new domain name needs to pro
throughout the world. Meanwhile, you can go to your assigned IP address by going to

Returns us to Print Layout view.

Selecting Text

In this section, you will learn how to select text in a document.

In the last chapter, we saw how to delete one character at a time from a document. However, often you will want to delete, copy, move or apply formatting changes to an entire word, sentence or paragraph. In order to do this, you must first **select** the text you wish to delete.

Once the text is selected, you can replace the selected text by simply typing in new text. This action automatically deletes the highlighted text and replaces it with what you have typed.

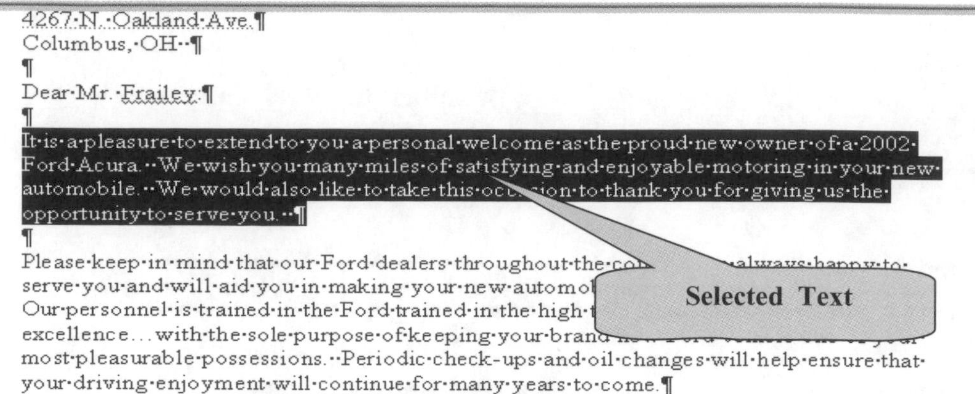
4267 N. Oakland Ave.
Columbus, OH

Dear Mr. Frailey:

It is a pleasure to extend to you a personal welcome as the proud new owner of a 2002 Ford Acura. We wish you many miles of satisfying and enjoyable motoring in your new automobile. We would also like to take this occ[...]ion to thank you for giving us the opportunity to serve you.

Please keep in mind that our Ford dealers throughout the co[...] always happy to serve you and will aid you in making your new automo[...] Our personnel is trained in the Ford trained in the high-t[...] excellence... with the sole purpose of keeping your bran[...] most pleasurable possessions. Periodic check-ups and oil changes will help ensure that your driving enjoyment will continue for many years to come.

To select a block of text, place the insertion point at the beginning or end of the block that you wish to select. Click and hold down the mouse button and drag until the text is highlighted in blue.

There are many other ways to select blocks of text. For instance, you can select a word by **double-clicking** on it. The table below outlines several techniques you can use to select text in a document.

To Select Text with Your Mouse

To Select This:	Do This:
A word	Double-click on the word.
A line of text	Click to the left of the line in the margin.
Several lines of text	Click to the left of a line in the margin and drag upwards or downwards.
A sentence	Hold down the **Ctrl** key and click anywhere in the sentence.
A paragraph	Double-click to the left of the paragraph in the margin or **triple-click** anywhere within the paragraph.
A block of text	Place the insertion point at the beginning of the block to be selected. Hold down the **Shift** key and click at the end of the block you wish to select.
Non-adjacent blocks of text	Hold down the **Ctrl** key and select the desired non-adjacent blocks of text.
The entire document	Press the **Ctrl + A** keystroke combination or click the **Select** button on the Home Ribbon and choose **Select All** from the list.
To the end of a document	Ctrl+Shift+End
To the beginning of a document	Ctrl+Shift+Home

Note

You can also select text with your keyboard. Hold down the **Shift** key and press the arrow keys to select the desired text.

Let's Try It!

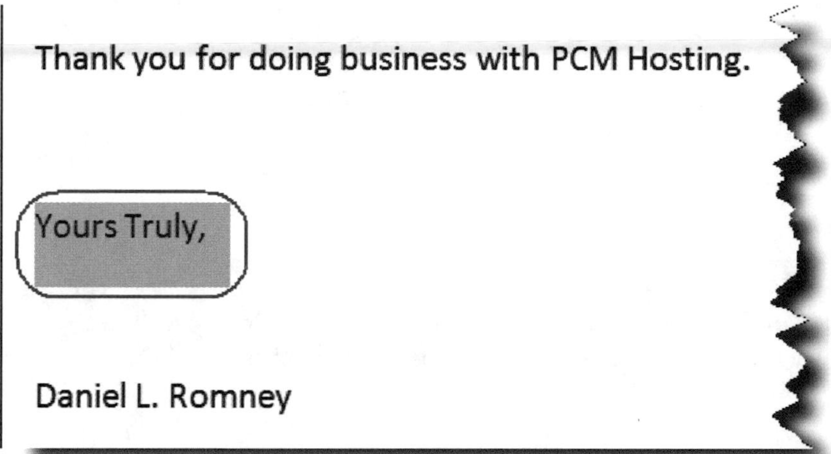

Thank you for doing business with PCM Hosting.
Yours Truly,
Daniel L. Romney

- Move your mouse pointer to the left of the words **Yours Truly** in the margin until the pointer transforms into an arrow. **Click** the left mouse button.

Selects the words "Yours Truly,".

Sincerely,

Daniel L. Romney

- Type: **Sincerely**,

Replaces the words "Yours Truly," with the word "Sincerely,"

- Click the **Save** button.

Saves the active document.

Copying and Pasting Text

In this section, you will learn how to copy text from one location to another.

You can copy any selected text to another location in your document, to another document or even to a document in another application by using the **Copy** and **Paste** commands. When you copy a selection, it is placed on the **Windows Clipboard**, a temporary holding area in memory for your data. You can then insert the selection in another location by using the **Paste** command.

To Copy and Paste Data

1. **Select** the text you wish to copy.
2. Hold down the **Ctrl** and **C** keystroke combination (**Ctrl + C**).
   Or
   Click the **Copy button** on the Home Ribbon.
3. Place the insertion point where you want to insert the copied the text.
4. Hold down the **Ctrl** and **V** keystroke combination (**Ctrl + V**).
   Or
   Click the **Paste button** on the Home Ribbon

TIP: You can also **right-click** on selected text and then choose Copy from the contextual menu. Right-click and choose Paste after you have set the insertion point where you want to insert the copied text.

Cutting and pasting text is similar to the copy and paste text commands that we worked with in the last section, except that rather than making a duplicate of text, the cut and paste command physically removes (deletes) the selected text from its original location and moves it to a new location.

Using the **Cut and Paste commands** allows you to rearrange sentences and paragraphs with ease.

To Cut and Paste Data

1. **Select** the text you wish to move.
2. Hold down the **Ctrl** and **X** keystroke combination (**Ctrl + X**).
   Or
   Click the **Cut button** on the Home Ribbon.
3. Place the insertion point where you want to insert the copied the text.
4. Hold down the **Ctrl** and **V** keystroke combination (**Ctrl + V**).
   Or
   Click the **Paste button** on the Home Ribbon

Let's Try It!

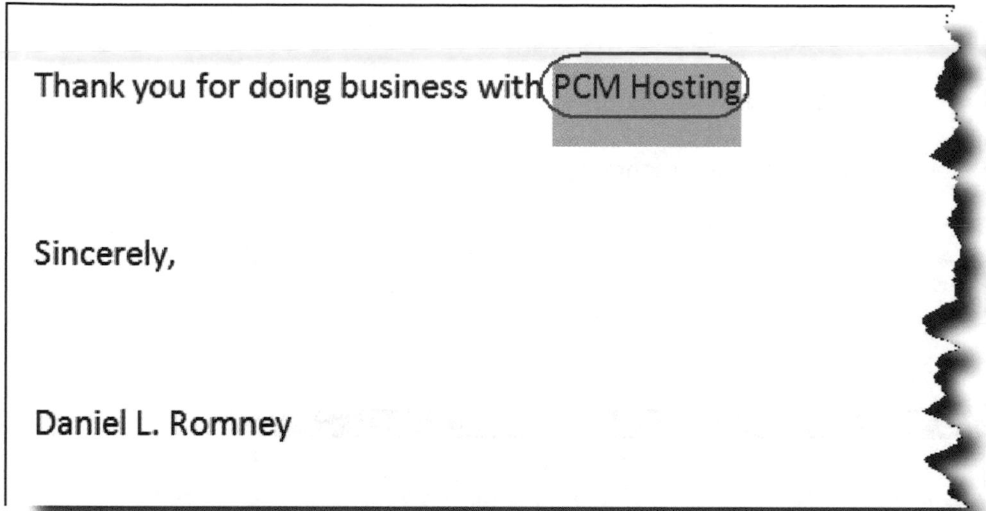

- Select the words **PCM Hosting**.

Selects the text we wish to copy.

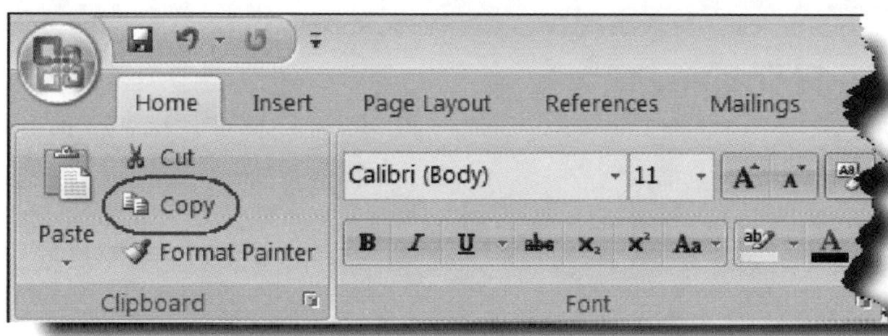

- Click the **Copy icon** in the Clipboard group on the Home Ribbon.

Places a copy of the selection on the Windows clipboard.

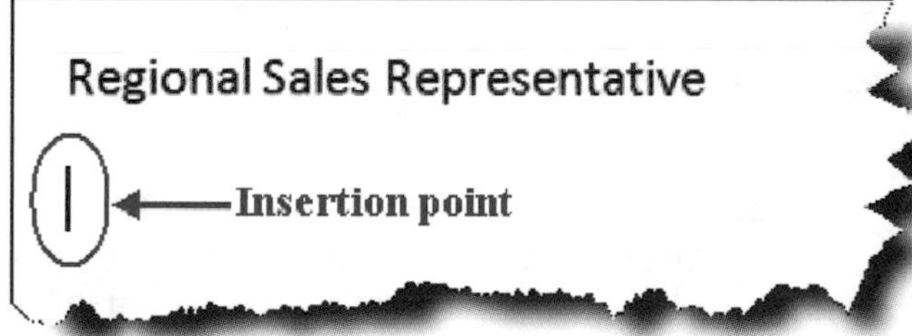

- Place the insertion point after the word **Representative** in the last line.

Sets the insertion point.

- Press the **Enter** key.

Inserts a blank line.

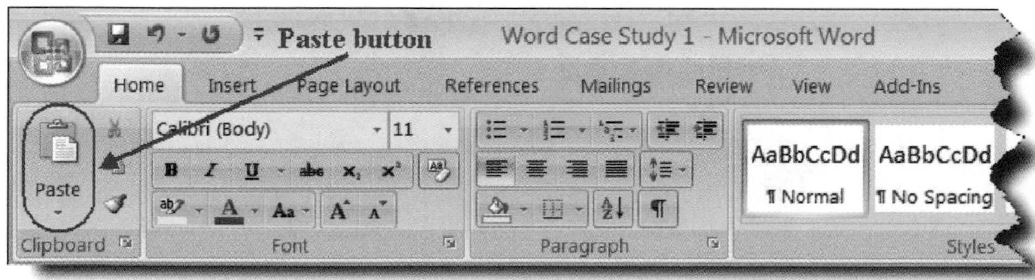

- Click the **Paste icon** on the Home Ribbon.

The new page is created and the copied text is inserted on it.

- Click the **Save** button.

Saves the active document.

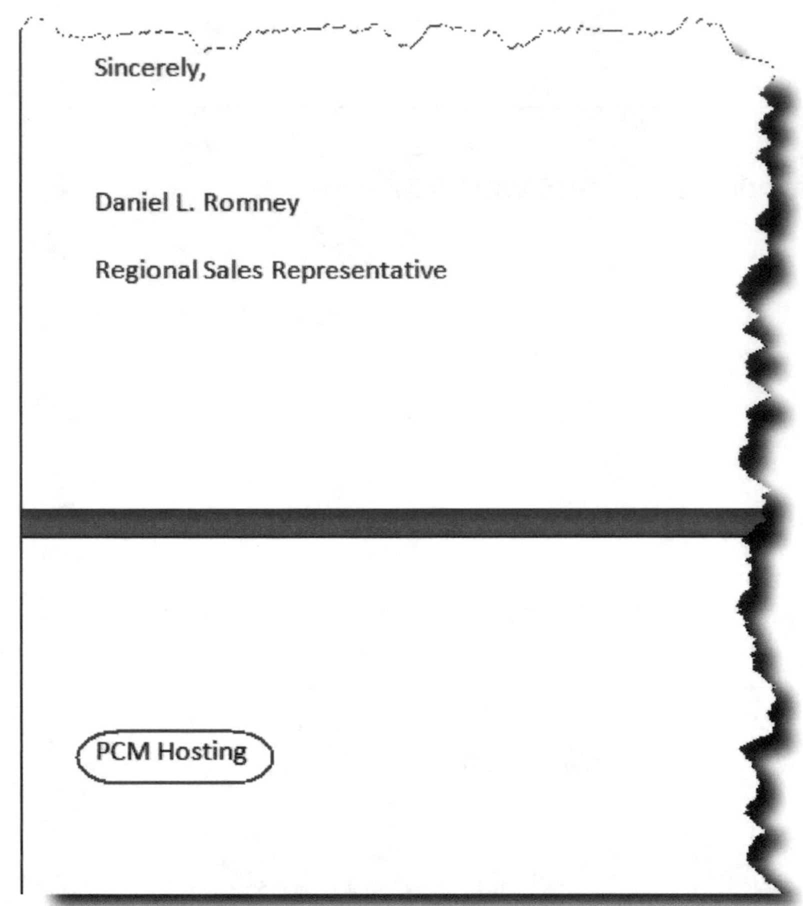

Inserting the Date and Time

In this section, you will learn how to insert the current date and time into a document.

The **Date and Time** dialog box allows you to insert the current date and time into your document and choose from a variety of date and time formats. To have the date and time field update automatically to the current date and/or time every time the document is opened, click the **Update automatically** check box.

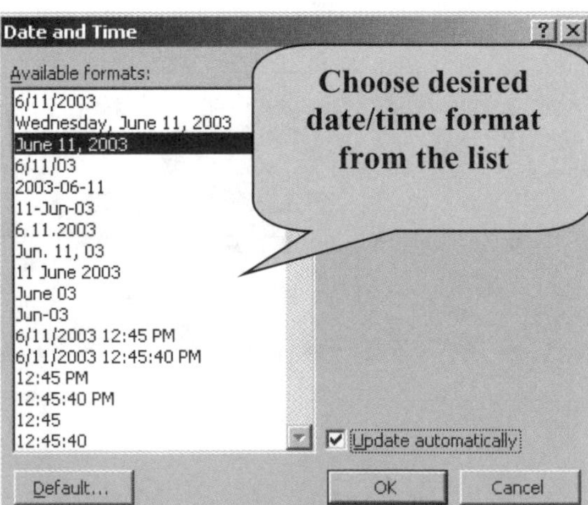

To Insert the Current Date and Time

1. Set the insertion point where you wish to insert the date and time.
2. Click the **Insert** tab on the Ribbon.
3. Click the **Date & Time** button under the Text group to display the Date & Time dialog box.
4. Click the desired date/time **format** from the **Available formats** list.
5. If desired, click the **Update automatically** checkbox to update the date/time field to the current date and time.
6. Click **OK**.

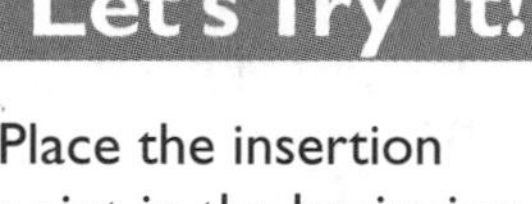

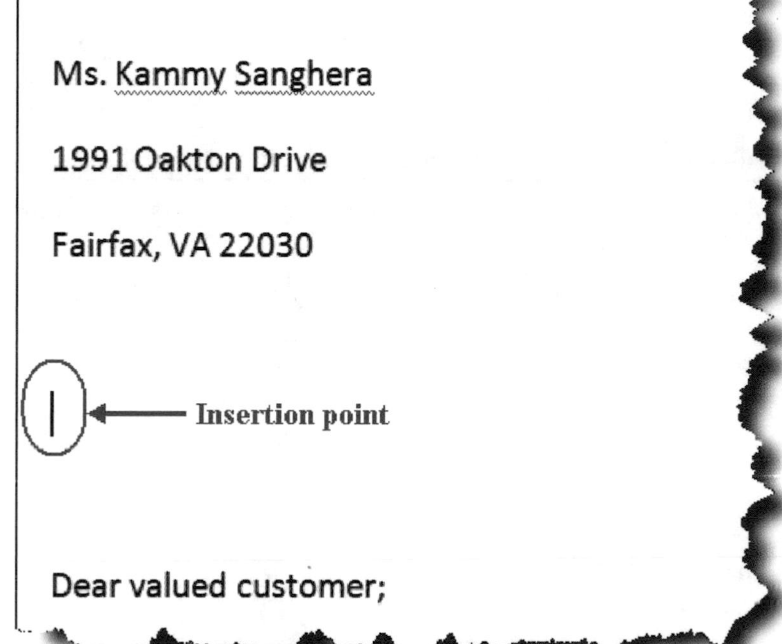

- Place the insertion point in the beginning of the sentence before the words: **Dear valued customer**:

Sets the insertion point.

- Press the **Enter** key **twice**.

Inserts two blank lines above the address.

- Press the **Up Arrow key twice**

Moves the insertion point up two lines to where we want to insert the date.

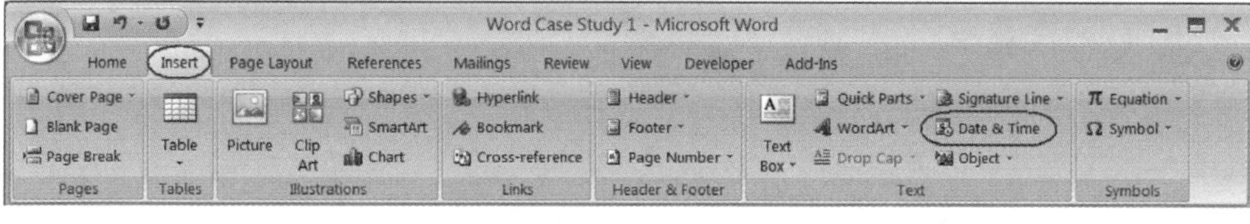

- Click the **Insert** tab on the Ribbon.

Insert tab commands are displayed.

- Click the **Date & Time** button on the Text command set.

Displays the Date and Time dialog box.

- Click on the **third** format from the top in the **Available formats** list.

Selects the date and time format to apply to the current date.

- Click the **Update automatically** checkbox, if it is **unchecked**.

Sets the option to automatically update the date each time the document is opened.

- Click **OK**

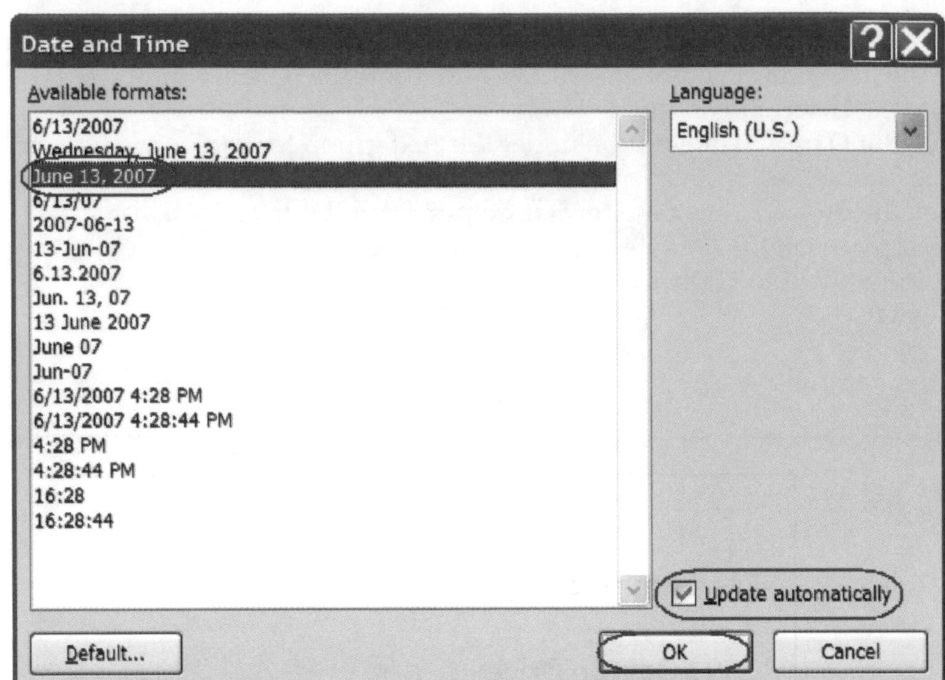

Inserts the current date into the document as a field.

- Click the **Save** button.

Saves the active document.

Checking Spelling and Grammar

In this section, you will learn how to check the spelling and grammar in a Word document.

Microsoft Word has a built-in **spelling and grammar checker** that allows you to automatically check for errors as you type. You can also check an entire document for spelling and grammatical errors by clicking the **Spelling and Grammar** button on the **Review tab**. Microsoft Word will use its built-in dictionary to offer suggestions for any errors it finds. You can then choose the correct spelling of the word from the Suggestions list or add the word to the dictionary so that Microsoft Word will not flag the word in the future.

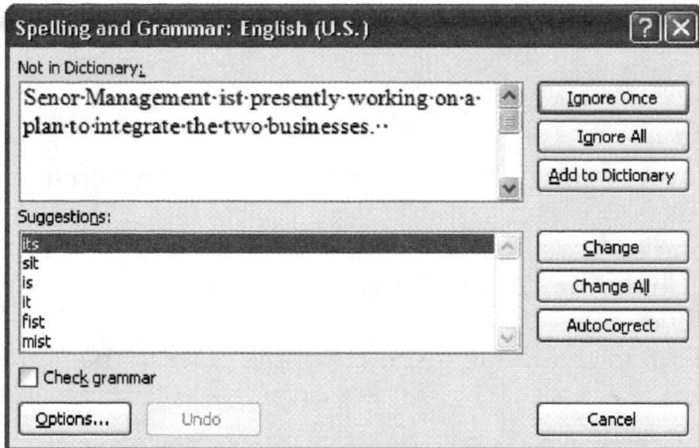

SPELLING AND GRAMMAR DIALOG BOX

When Word finds a questionable spelling error, a dialog box displays, prompting for a suggested action:

- **Change**—Change this instance of the spelling error to the selected suggestion.
- **Change All**—Change all instances of the spelling error in the document to the selected suggestion.
- **Ignore Once**—Ignores this instance of the spelling error and continues to check the rest of the document.
- **Ignore All**—Ignores all instances of the spelling error and continues to check the rest of the document.
- **Add to Dictionary**—Adds the word in question to the built-in dictionary so that it will not be flagged in the future.

When Word finds a questionable grammar error, you can choose to ignore the grammar rule for one instance or for the entire document and continue checking the rest of the document.

Word will also check spelling and grammar as you type and highlight misspelled works by underlining them with red and grammatical errors by underlining them in green. You can then right-click the highlighted word and use on of Word's suggestions from the pop-up list. Or, to display the Spelling and Grammar window, select **Spelling** or **Grammar** from the pop-up shortcut menu.

If you would prefer that Word not display underlining while you are working, display the **Word Options dialog box** (click the Microsoft Office button and click the Word Options button), click the **Proofing** category and uncheck the **Mark Grammar Errors as you type** and/or the **Check Spelling as you type** checkboxes.

To Check Spelling and Grammar in a Document

1. Move to the beginning of the document.
2. Click the **Spelling and Grammar button** on the **Review** Ribbon under the Proofing group

SPELLING AND GRAMMAR BUTTON

Or
Press the **F7 key**.

3. When an error is found, highlight the desired correction from the **Suggestions List**.
4. To change an error:
   a. Choose **Change** to change this particular instance of the error to the highlighted suggestion.
   b. **Change All** to change all instances of the error to the highlighted suggestion.
5. To ignore an error:
   a. Choose **Ignore** to ignore this instance of the error and continue checking the document.
   b. Choose **Ignore All** to ignore all instances of the error and continue checking the document.
6. To add the word to the built-in dictionary so it will not be flagged in the future, click **Add to Dictionary**.
7. If a grammatical error is found:
   a. Click **Ignore Once** to ignore this particular instance of the error.
   b. Click **Ignore Rule** to ignore all instances of the grammatical error.
   c. Click **Change** to change this particular instance of the grammatical error.
   d. Click **Explain** to view a detailed explanation of the grammatical error.
8. Click **OK** when finished.

Let's Try It!

- Hold down the **Ctrl** key then press the **Home** key (Ctrl + Home)

Moves to the beginning of the document.

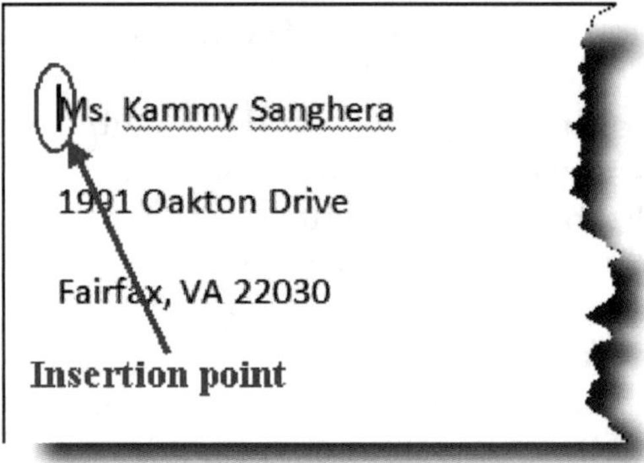

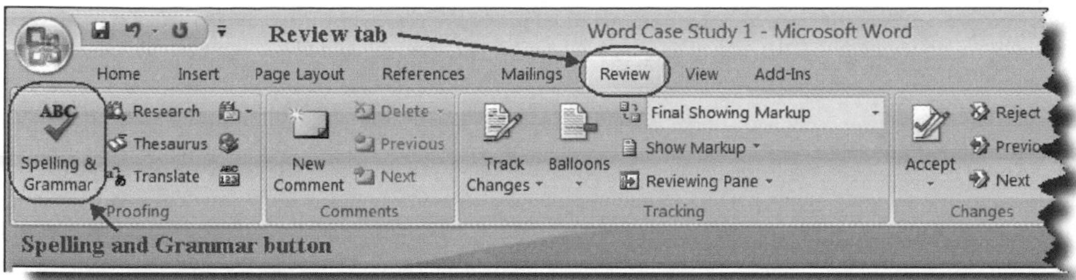

- Click the **Review** tab.

Ensures that the Review tab is active.

- Click the **Spelling and Grammar** button on the Proofing command set.

If an error is found, the Spelling and Grammar dialog box will open with the error highlighted in red.

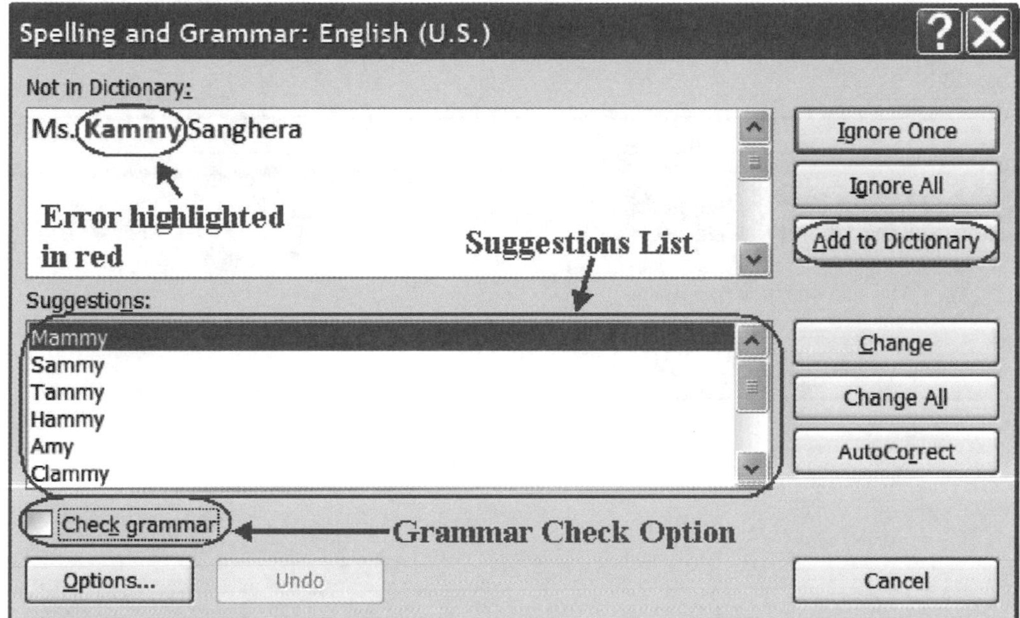

- If Check grammar option is checked, click in the check box next to Check grammar to deselect it.

Deselects the check grammar option. We only want to check spelling in this document.

- Click the **Add to Dictionary** button.

Word cannot find "Kammy" in the dictionary. As that is the name of the customer, we want to add it to the built-in dictionary so that Word will not consider it an error in the future. Word continues checking the document.

- Click the **Add to Dictionary** button for customer's last name—**Sanghera**.

Word Sanghera is added into the built-in dictionary.

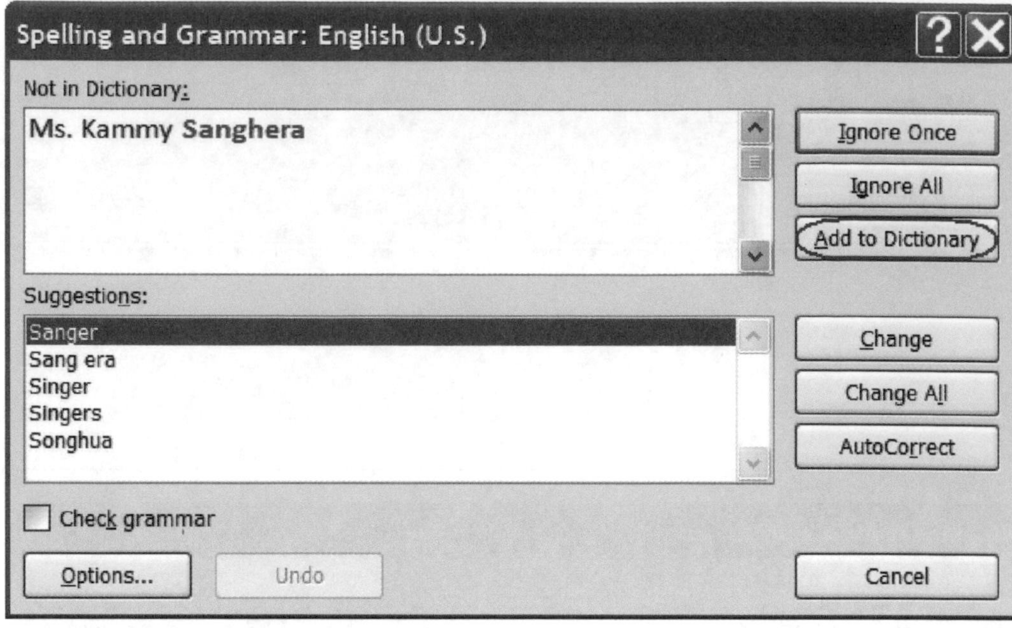

- When the message box appears informing us that the **Spelling check is complete**, click **OK** as shown.

Closes the message box and informs us that Word is finished checking the document.

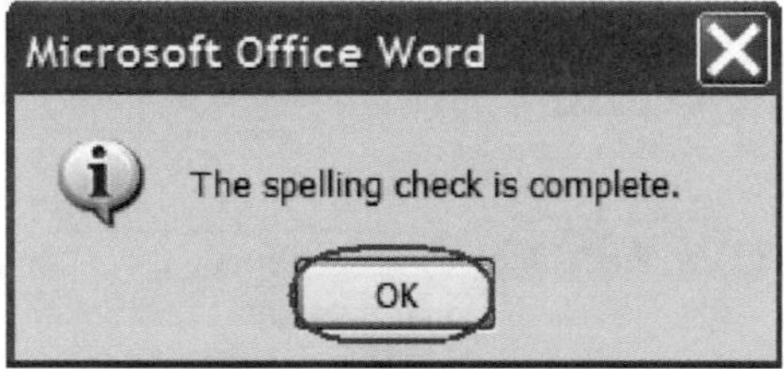

- Click the **Save** button.

Saves the active document.

Use the Thesaurus

In this section, you will learn how to use the built-in Thesaurus.

Under the **Review tab** on the Proofing command set, you will also find the **Thesaurus** button, which will help you quickly find synonyms for selected words. To use the Thesaurus, click the select the word you wish to replace and click the Thesaurus button on the Review Ribbon. The Research task pane will display on the right side of your screen. Click the arrow next to the desired word in the task pane and select **Insert** to replace the selected word in your document with the new word.

Displays the Research task pane and a list of synonyms, from which you can select the word.

- Move your mouse point over the word "**comprehensive**" on the Research task pane.

Displays a list arrow next to the word.

- Click the arrow and choose **Insert** from the list.

Replaces with selected "complete" with the word "comprehensive".

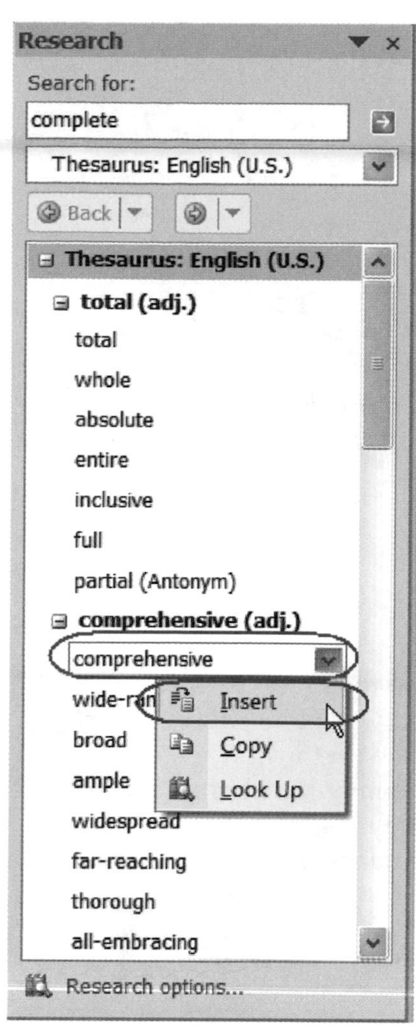

- Click the **Close** button on the Research task pane.

Closes the task pane.

- Click the **Save** button.

Saves the active document.

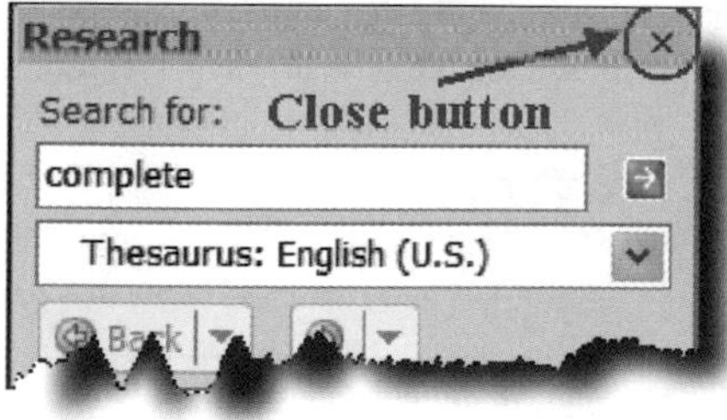

Using Undo and Redo

In this section, you will learn how to undo and redo actions in Microsoft Word.

Word contains a powerful feature called **Undo/Redo** that allows you to reverse any editing action, including formatting. While entering data, you may have made a typo or even accidentally deleted a word or an entire sentence. You can reverse this action with the **Undo** command.

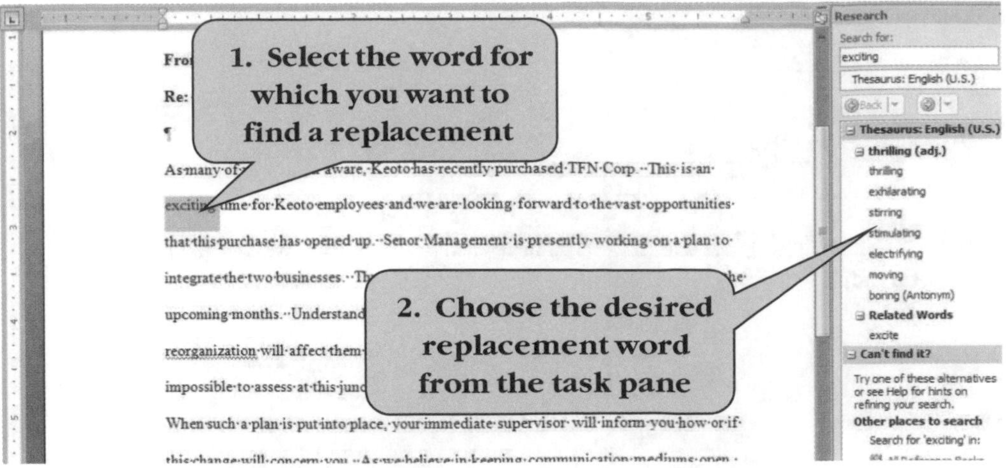

To Use the Thesaurus

1. Select the word that you want to look up.
2. Click the **Review** tab.
3. Click the **Thesaurus** button on the Ribbon on the Proofing group.
4. Click the list arrow to the right of the desired word and choose **Insert** to replace the selected word on your document with the new word.
5. To copy the new word to paste into your document, click the list arrow to the right of the desired word and choose **Copy**.
6. Click the **Close** button on the Research task pane when finished.

Let's T

The control panel is used to configure your site and e-mails, password protect pages, view your hit statistics, install scripts, and more. The panel also provides complete help and other web information that might be useful in managing your site. The panel is password protected, and the username and password is supplied below.

- Double-click "**complete**" second line paragraph.

Selects the wo to look up.

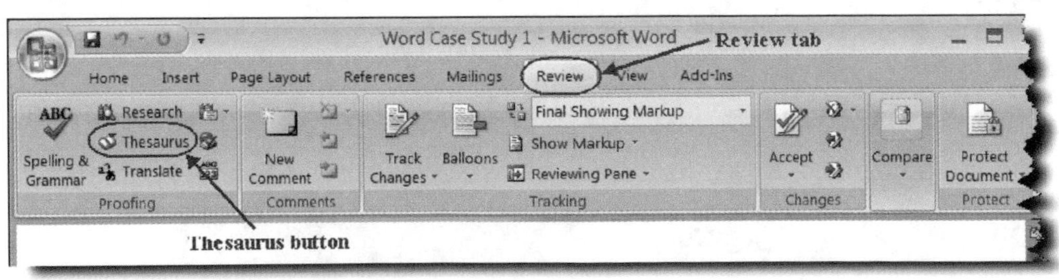

- Click the **R** on the Ribb

Switches to R commands an

- Click the **Th** button on t as shown.

Each time you launch the Undo command, it will reverse the last action you do; thus, clicking the Undo button 20 times will undo the last 20 actions as if they had never happened. Rather than clicking the Undo button 20 times to undo multiple actions, clicking the arrow next to the Undo button allows you to quickly undo multiple past actions by navigating down the history list and selecting the number of actions you wish to undo.

Redo reverses the action of an Undo command.

To Use the Undo Command

1. Click on the **Undo** icon on the Quick Access Toolbar.
   Or
   Press the **Ctrl + Z** keystroke combination
2. To undo multiple actions, click the arrow to the right of the Undo button and scroll down until the desired number of past actions is selected.

To Use the Redo Command

1. Click on the **Redo** icon Quick Access Toolbar.
   Or
   Press the **Ctrl + Y** keystroke combination
2. To Redo multiple actions, click the arrow to the left of the Redo button and scroll down until the desired number of undo past actions is selected.

Let's Try It!

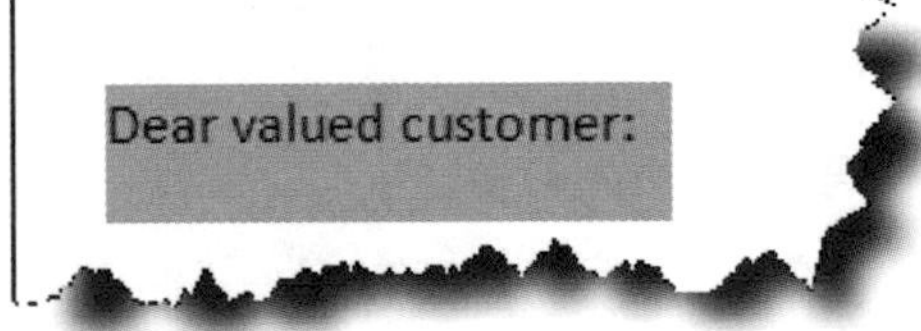

- Move your mouse pointer to the left of the words **Dear valued customer**: in the margin until the pointer transforms into an arrow, and then **Click** with your left mouse button.

Selects the entire sentence beginning with the word "Dear".

• Press the **Delete** key.

Deletes the entire sentence.

• Click **3 times** (triple click) anywhere in the first paragraph.

Selects the entire paragraph.

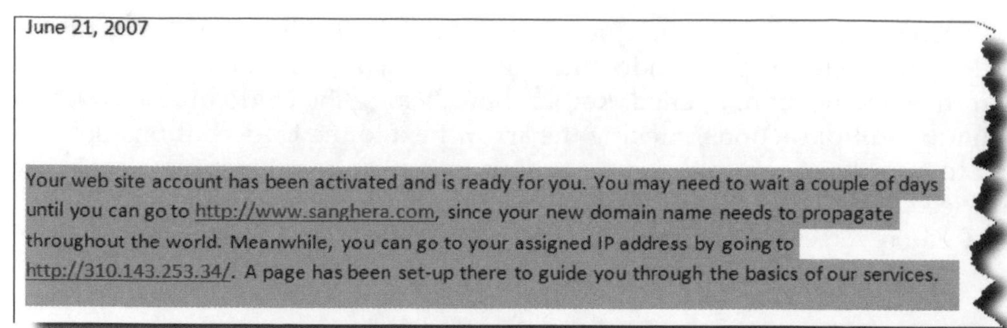

June 21, 2007
Your web site account has been activated and is ready for you. You may need to wait a couple of days until you can go to http://www.sanghera.com, since your new domain name needs to propagate throughout the world. Meanwhile, you can go to your assigned IP address by going to http://310.143.253.34/. A page has been set-up there to guide you through the basics of our services.

• Press **Delete**.

Deletes the entire paragraph.

• Click the **Undo** icon on the Quick Access Toolbar.

Reverses the action of deleting the paragraph.

• Click the **Undo** icon again.

Reverses the action of deleting the "Dear valued customer:" line.

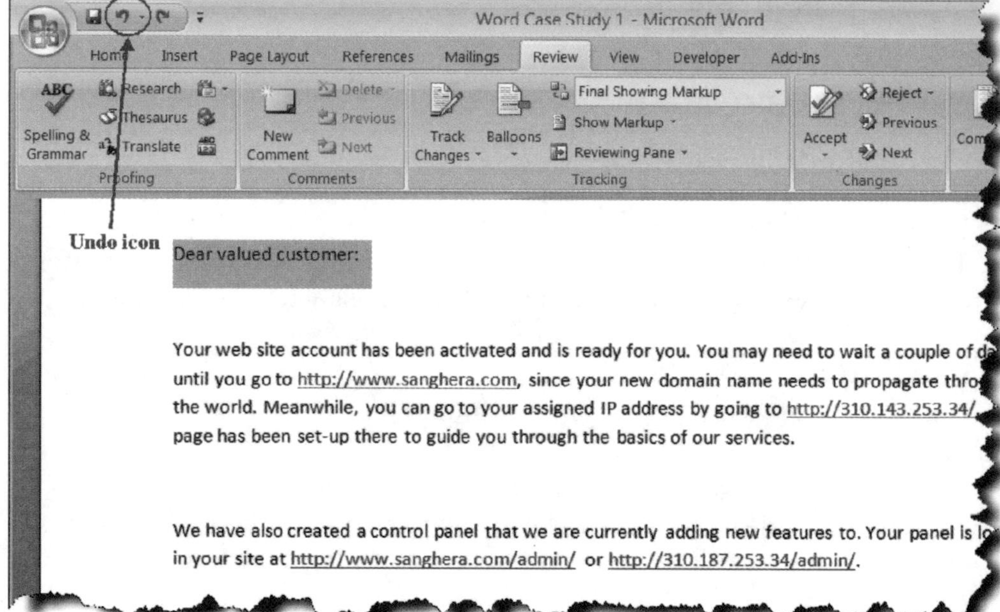

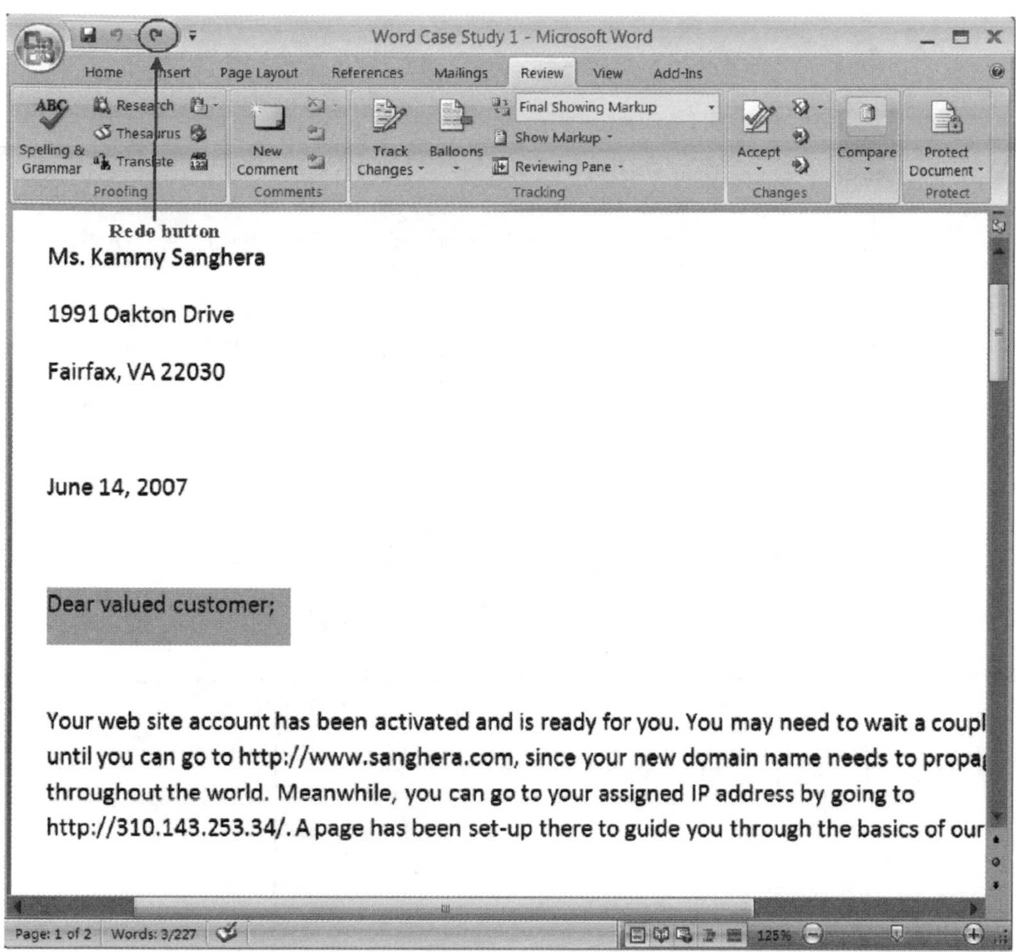

• Click the **Redo** button.

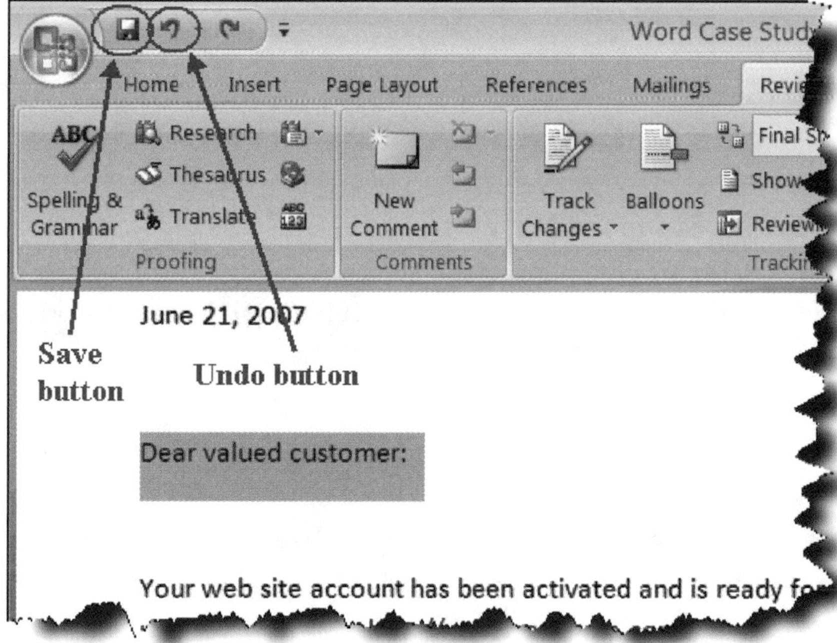

Reverses the action of the last Undo command.

• Click **Undo**.

Reverses the last action and restores the sentence.

• Click the **Save** button.

Saves the active document.

Setting Margins

In this section, you will learn how to change the page margins of your document.

Margins refer to the amount of white space between the text of the document and the left, right, top and bottom edges of the page. Margins can also be thought of as page boundaries—once the text reaches the boundary of the margin, it wraps to the next line or the next page.

Keep in mind that changing the margins of your document affects every page in your document—not just the active paragraph or page. To modify margins, click the **Margins** button on the Page Layout tab and make your selections.

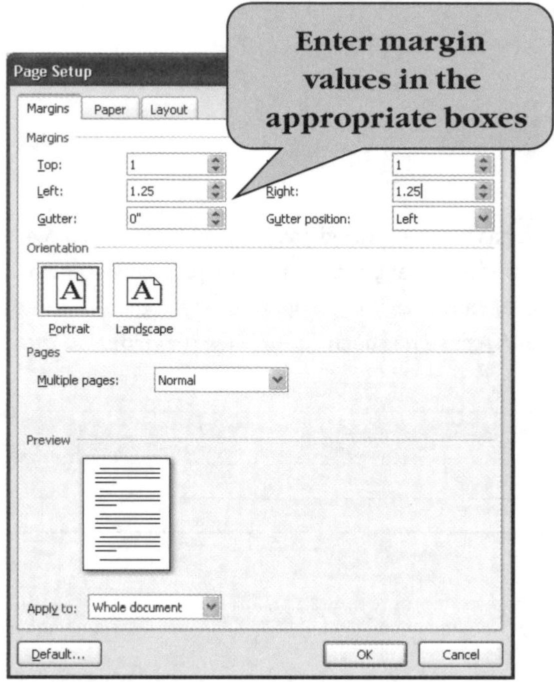

To Select Standard Margins

1. Click the **Page Layout** tab on the Ribbon.
2. Click the **Margins** button and select Normal, Narrow, Moderate, Wide, Mirrored or Office 2003 default.

To Create Custom Margins

1. Click the **Page Layout** tab on the Ribbon.
2. Click the **Margins** button.
3. Click **Custom Margins** on the list to display the Page Setup dialog box.
4. Enter the margin values (in inches) in the **Top, Left, Bottom and Right** boxes in the Margins area.
5. To make your margin settings the default for any new Word documents you create, click the **Default** button and then click **Yes**.
6. Click **OK** when finished

Let's Try It!

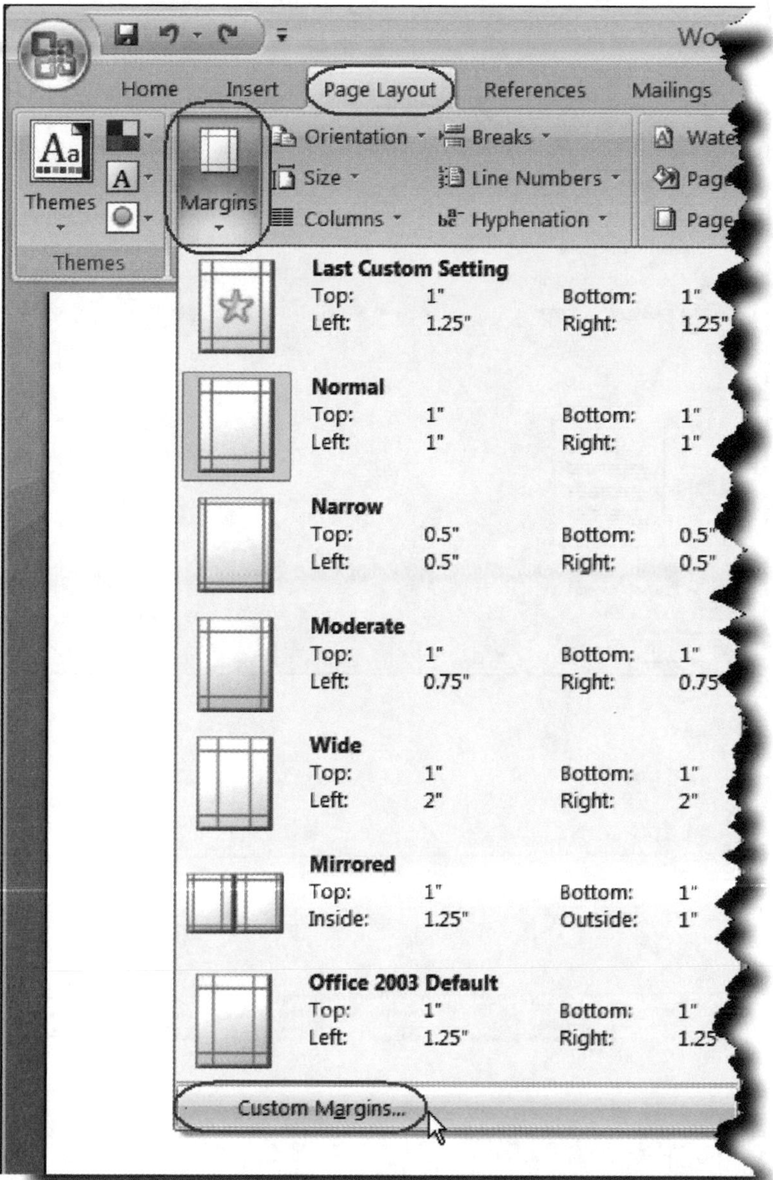

- Click the **Page Layout** tab on the Ribbon.

Switches to Page Layout commands and tools.

- Click the **Margins** button.

Displays the margins options.

- Click **Custom Margins** from the list.

Displays the Page Setup dialog box.

- In the **Top** margin box, type: **1** as shown and then press **Tab**.

Sets top margin at 1 inch and moves to the bottom margin box.

- In the **Bottom** margin box, type: **1** and then press **Tab**.

Sets the bottom margin at 1 inch and then moves to the left margin box.

- In the **Left** margin box, type: **1.25** and then press **Tab**.

Sets the left margin at 1.25 inches and then moves to the right margin box.

- In the **Right** margin box, type: **1.25**.

Sets the right margin at 1.25 inches.

- Click **OK**.

Closes the Page Setup dialog box.

Setting Page Orientation

In this section, you will learn how to change the page orientation to either Portrait or Landscape.

Microsoft Word allows you to change the **Page Orientation**; that is to say, the orientation of text—either wide or long—on the page. There are two choices of orienation—**Portrait** which prints across the shortest width (taller than longer) of the paper and **Landscape** which prints across the longest width (longer than taller) of the paper.

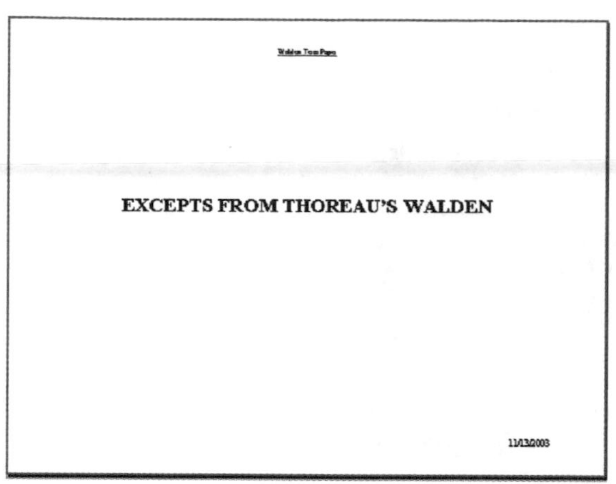

EXCEPTS FROM THOREAU'S WALDEN

LANDSCAPE

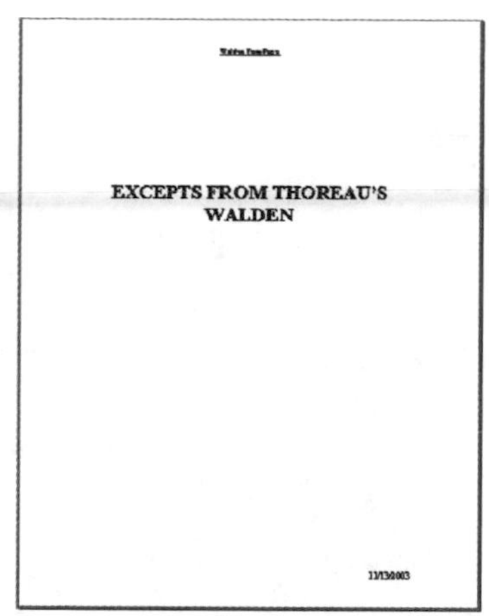

EXCEPTS FROM THOREAU'S WALDEN

LANDSCAPE

To Set Page Orientation

1. Click the **Page Layout tab** on the Ribbon.
2. Click the **Orientation button** and select either **Portrait** or **Landscape**.
3. Click **OK** when finished

   Or

1. Click Portrait or Landscape from the Margins tab of the **Page Setup dialog box**.

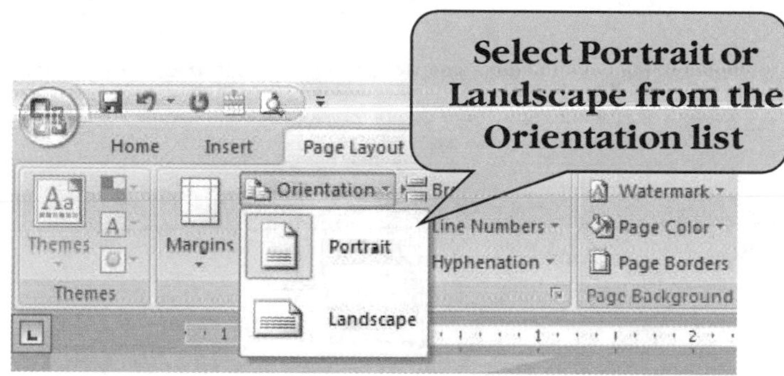

Let's Try It!

- Click the **Orientation** button on the Page Setup group under Page Layout tab.

Displays the Orientation menu.

- Click **Landscape**.

Changes the Page Orientation to landscape.

- Drag the **Zoom slider** on the lower-right and corner of your screen to the left to about **50%**.

Reduces the size of the viewable area to 50% of the normal size. Observe that the page is wider than taller.

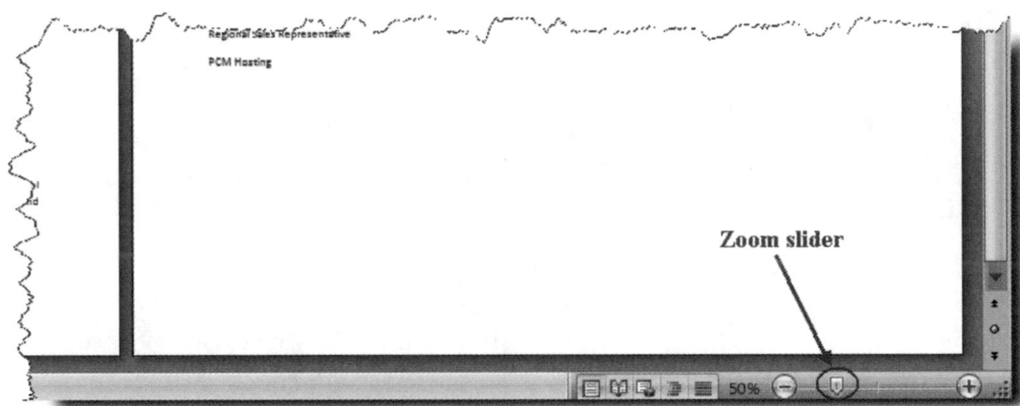

- Click the **Zoom Level box** on the lower-right and corner of your screen.

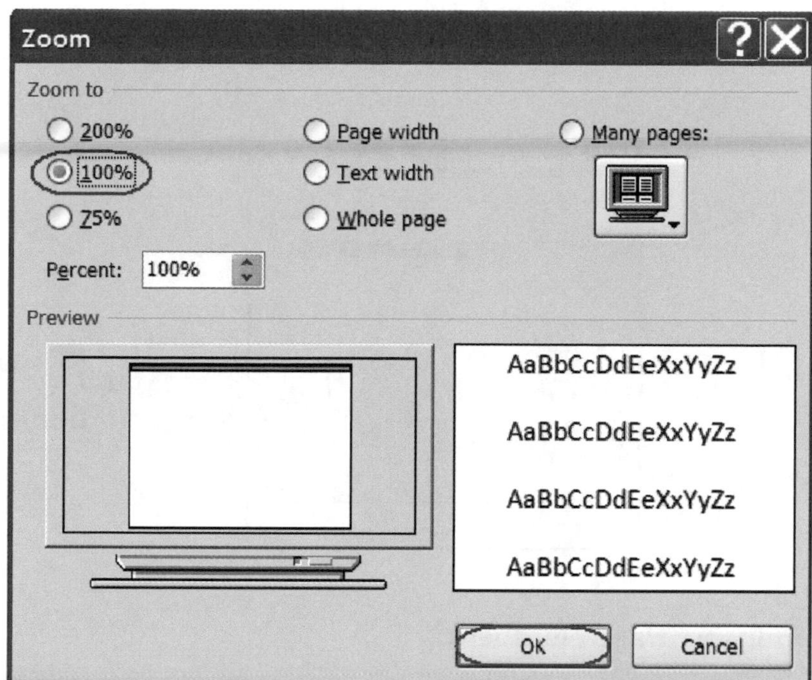

- Choose **100%** from the Zoom dialog box.

Restores the viewable area of the document to 100%.

- Click **Ok**.

Closes the Zoom box.

- Click the **Save** button.

Saves the active document.

Inserting/Modifying Page Numbers

In this section, you will learn how to insert and format page numbers.

We have already learned that you can add page numbers to your document in Header or Footer view. You can also add page numbers to your document by clicking the **Page Numbers** button on the Insert Ribbon, and then choosing the location from the list (top, bottom, page margins or current position) and then choosing the page number style you want from the galelry.

Word also provides numerous page number formatting options:

- Number format
- Include chapter number with page number (i.e. 15-4, 15-5, etc.)
- Set the page number separator
- The number at which to begin page numbering
- Continue numbering from the previous sections (you'll learn more about sections in a later section)

To display the Page Number Format dialog box, click the Page Number button and then choose **Format Page Numbers** from the drop-down list.

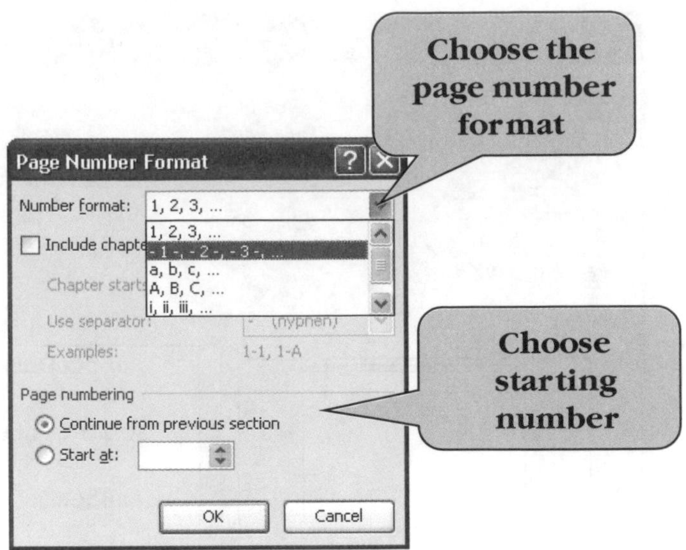

To Insert Page Numbers

1. Click the **Insert** tab.
2. Click the **Page Number** button on the Header & Footer group.
3. **Point to** the position from the list and then **click** the desired page number format from the Page Number Gallery.
4. To format pages numbers, click **Format Page Numbers** from the menu and make your desired choices.
5. Click **OK**.

Let's Try It!

- Click the **Insert tab** on the Ribbon.

Switches to Insert commands and tools.

- Click the **Page Number** button under the Header & Footer command set.

Displays the Page Number menu.

- Point to **Bottom of Page**.

Displays the Bottom of Page gallery.

- Click the **Plain Number 2** from the gallery.

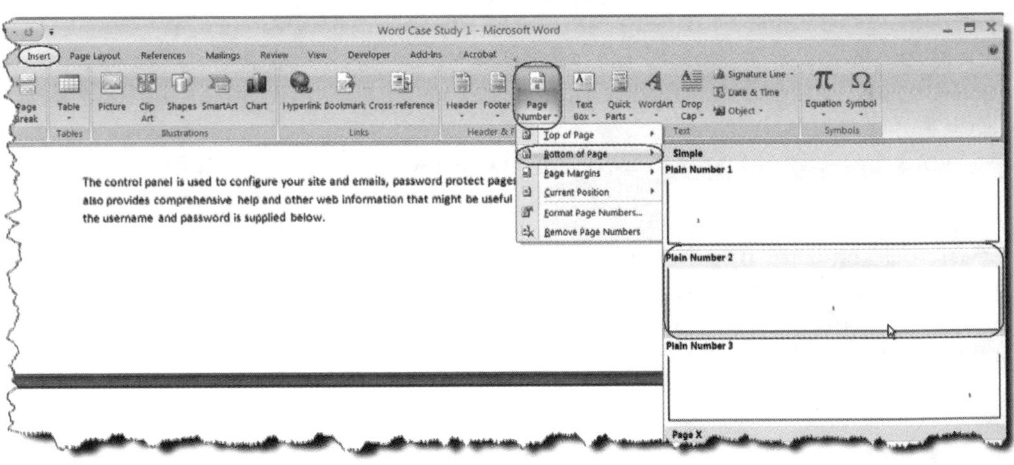

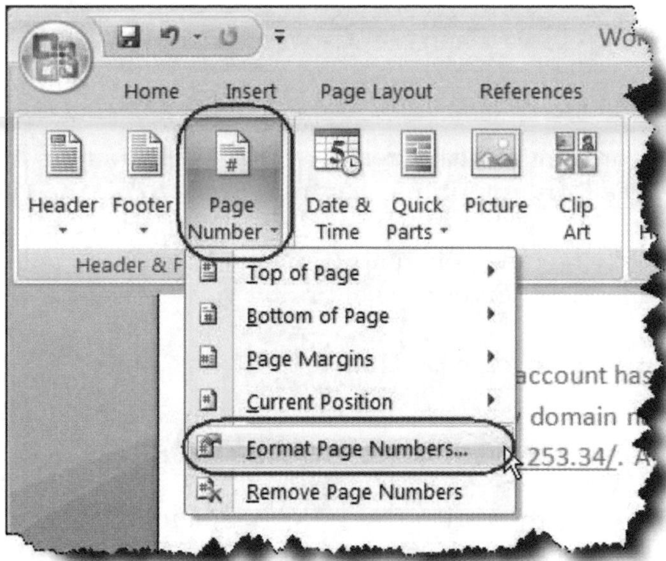

Inserts a plain page number centered on the bottom of the page.

- Click the **Page Number** button and select **Format Page Numbers** from the menu.

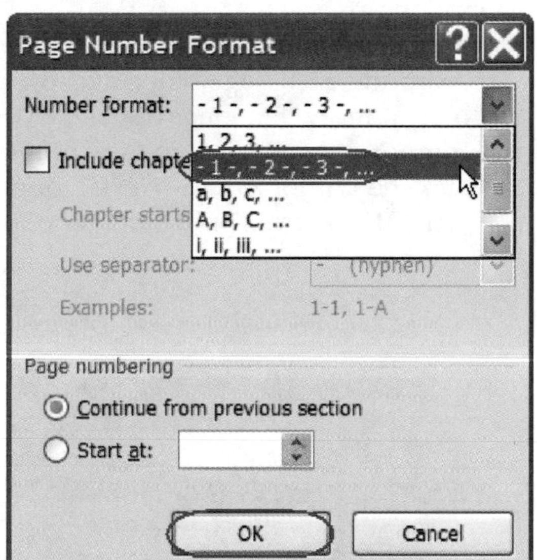

Displays the Page Number Format dialog box for additional page number formatting options.

- Choose the **second option** from the **Number format** drop-down list.
- Click **OK**.

Closes the Page Number Format dialog box.

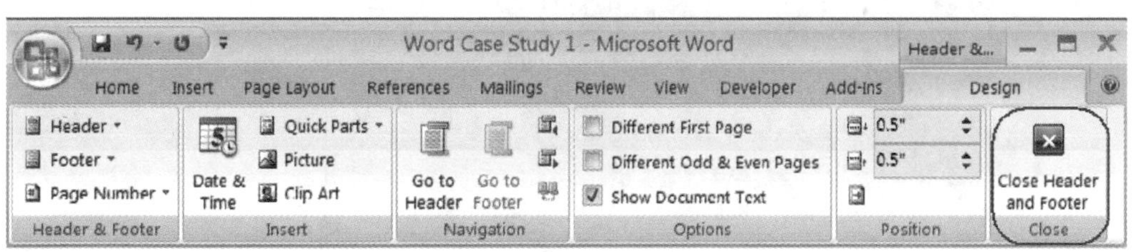

- Click the **Close Header and Footer** button.

Returns us to Print Layout view.

Setting Printer Options

In this section, we will work with printer options.

Before you're finally ready to print your document, you may first want to set some **Printer Options**. For instance, you may need to specify which printer to use, the number of copies to be printed, or even designate Word to print only a specific range of your document. Printer options you can set will vary, depending on the type of printer you are using.

To Set Printer Options

1. Click the **Microsoft Office** button and then click **Print** on the File Options menu to display the Print dialog box.
   Or
   Press the **Ctrl + P** keystroke combination.
2. If necessary, choose which printer to use from the **Name** drop-down list.
3. To print only the current page, select **Current page** under the Page Range Options area.
4. To print a specific range, enter the page numbers in the **Pages** box, separating each page range by a comma (i.e. 1-15, 17, 18, 30-35)
5. To print more than one copy of a document, enter the value in the **Number of copies** box in the **Copies** area.
6. Click the **Options** button for additional printer options.
7. Click **OK** to send the document to the printer.

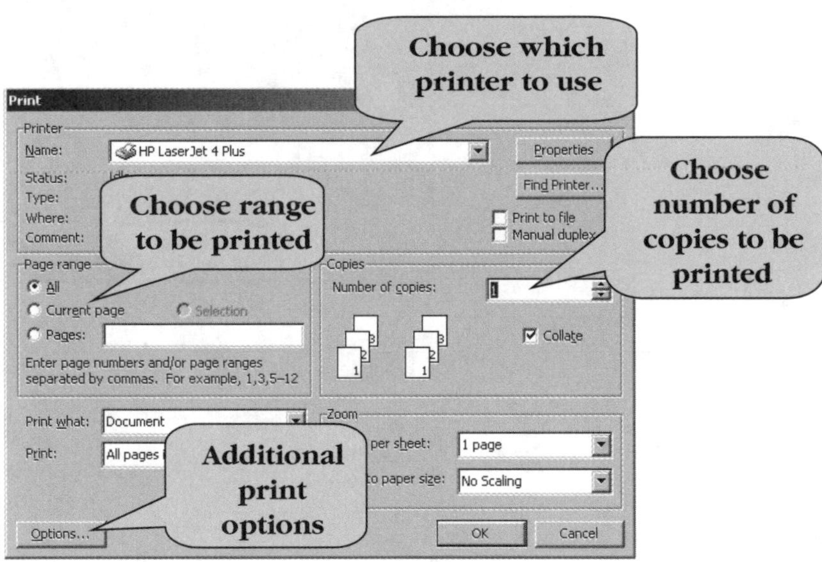

Let's Try It!

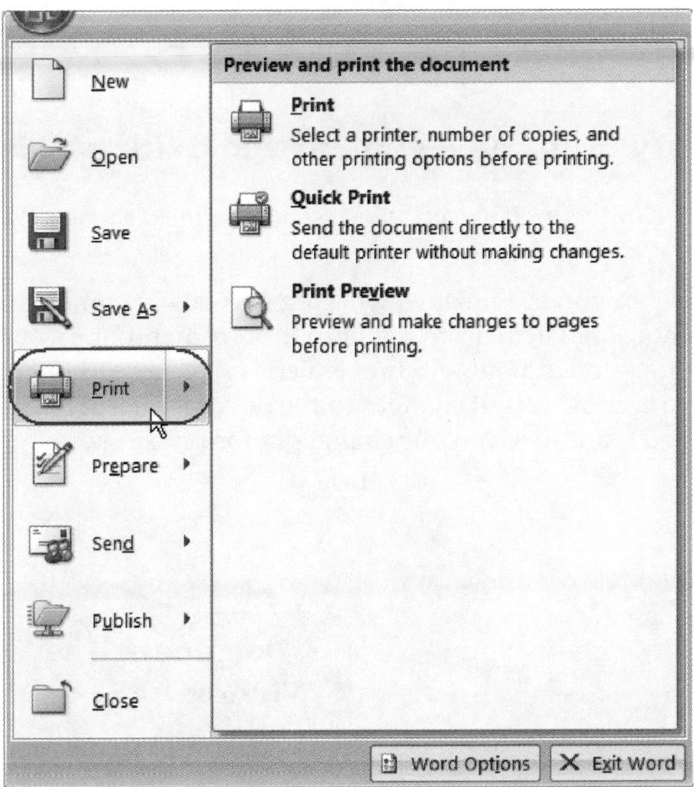

- Click the **Microsoft Office** button and then click **Print**.

Displays the **Print** dialog box.

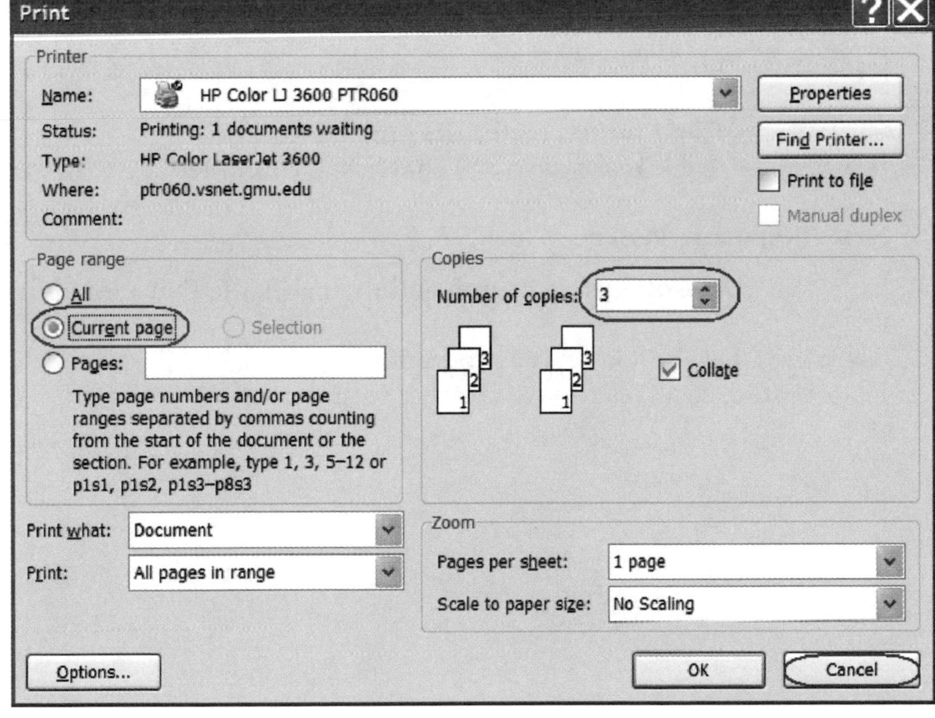

- In the **Copies** box, enter **3**.

Sets the option to print 3 copies of the document.

- In the **Print Range** options, select **Current Page**.

Sets the option to print only the current page (the page where the insertion point is set).

- Click the **Cancel** button.

Closes the Print dialog box without printing

> **TIP:** To send a document directly to the printer, click the Microsoft Office button, point to Print and then click the Quick Print option in the second pane. The Print dialog box will not open.

Closing a Document and Exiting Word

In this section, you will close all existing documents and exit the Microsoft Word Application.

When you are finished working on your document, you can close it by either choosing **Close** from the File Options menu or by clicking the **Close Button** on the document window which is represented by an **x**. If you have not saved your most recent changes to the document, Microsoft Word will ask you if you want to save your changes before closing.

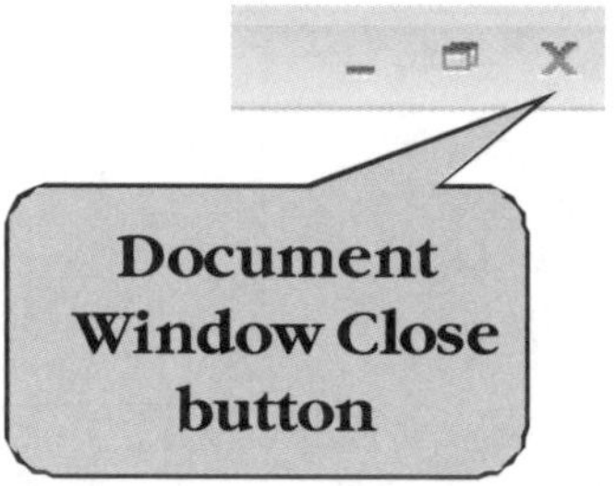

To Close a Document

1. Click the **Microsoft Office Button** and then click **Close** from the File Options menu
   Or
   Click on the **Close** button on the document window.
2. If prompted, click **Yes** to save any changes, if prompted.

To Exit Microsoft Word

1. Click the **Microsoft Office Button** and then click the **Exit Word** button
   Or
   Click the **Close** button on the program window.
2. If prompted, click **Yes** to save changes to any open documents.

Let's Try It!

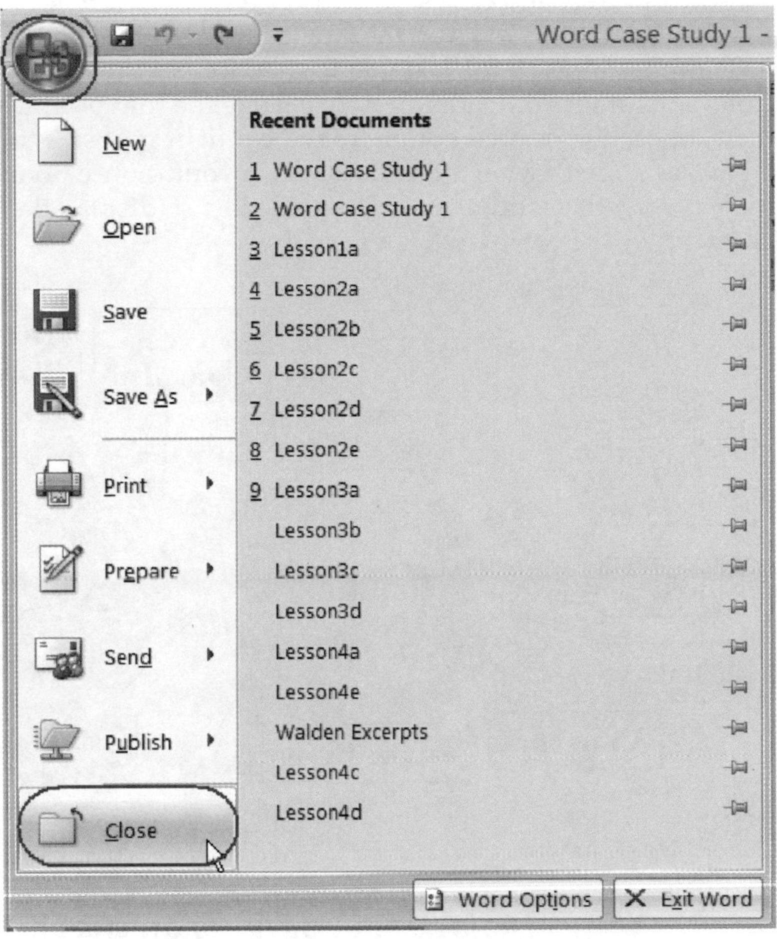

- Click the **Microsoft Office Button** and then click **Close** from the File Options menu.

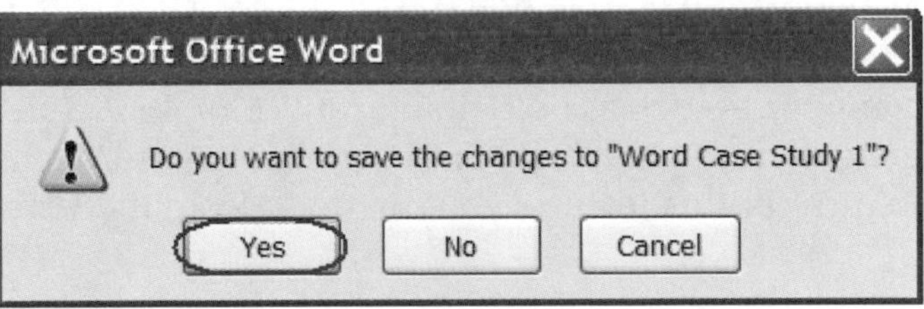

- Click **Yes** if asked to save your changes.

Closes the Word Case Study I document.

Using Formatting Tools

In this section, you will learn how to apply and modify formatting using the Formatting Tools on the Ribbon.

One of the features of a Word Processing program such as Microsoft Word is the ability to apply and modify **text formatting**. For instance, you can modify the typeface (or font) of your text, change the size of your text, or emphasize text by applying bold, italics or underlining. When typing text in your document, each new character you type takes on the formatting of the previous character unless you apply new formatting. When creating a new paragraph (by pressing Enter), the first character takes on the formatting of the paragraph mark.

The quickest and easiest way to apply and modify text formatting is to use the Formatting Tools on the Home tab under the **Font group**. To change text emphasis, select the text you wish to format then click on the appropriate icon (Bold, Italics or Underline). To change the font or font size, select the text then choose the desired option from the font or font size drop-down list. For an explanation of what a tool does, move your mouse pointer over a tool to display an informational box. The box will also display the **keyboard shortcut** for the command, if any.

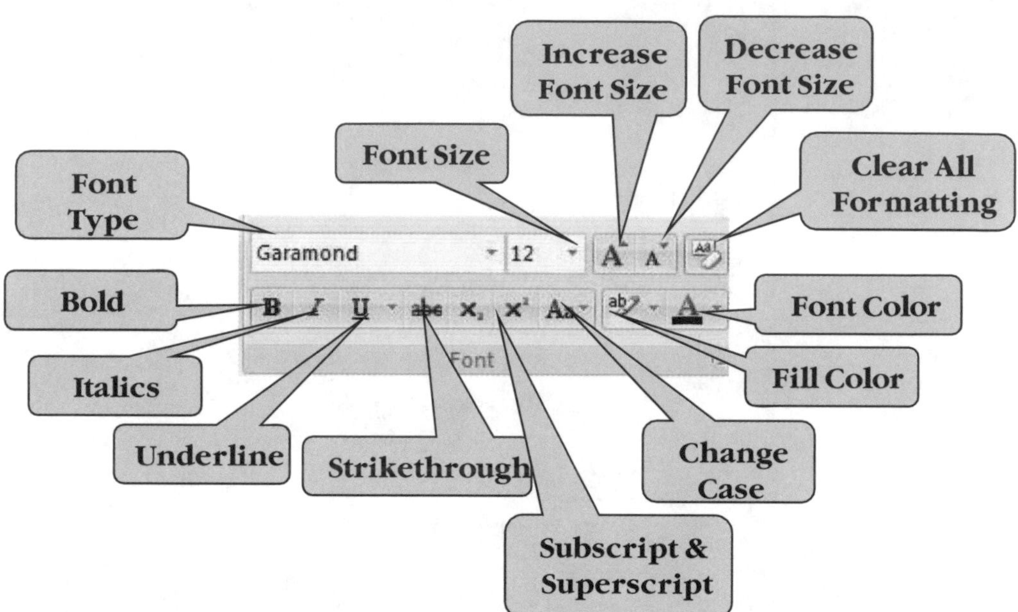

COMMON FORMATTING OPTIONS ON THE FONT GROUP

New in Word 2007 is the **Mini-Toolbar**. The Mini-Toolbar displays whenever you point to selected text and provides quick access to common formatting commands such as bold, italic, font color, font type, font size, fill color, increase indent, decrease indent and increase/decrease font size. If you wish to turn off this feature, you can do so from the Word Options dialog box.

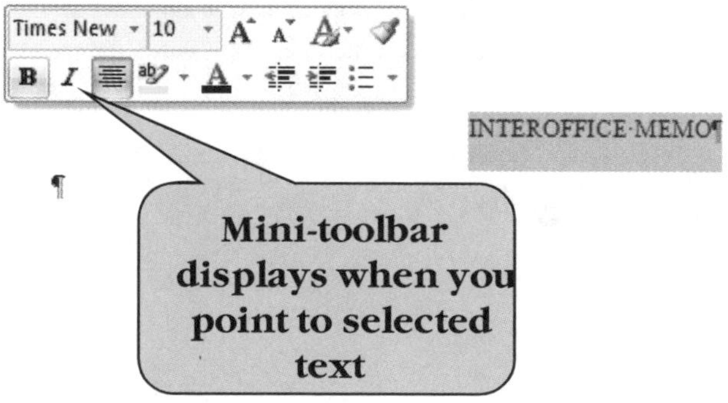

To Use Formatting Tools

1. **Select** the text that you want to modify.
2. Click the **Home** tab on the Ribbon.
3. To emphasize text, click on the **Bold, Italics** or **Underline** icon on the Font group.
4. To change the **font type**, click the arrow on the font drop-down list and select the desired typeface.
5. To change the **font size**, click the arrow on the font size drop-down list and select the desired font size or type the size manually in the font size box.
6. To increase or decrease the size of the selected text (new in Word 2007), click the Increase Font Size button or Decrease Font Size button.
7. To use the **Mini-toolbar**, select the text you want to modify, point to the selected text with your mouse pointer and then choose the desired option from the Mini-toolbar.

Let's Try It!

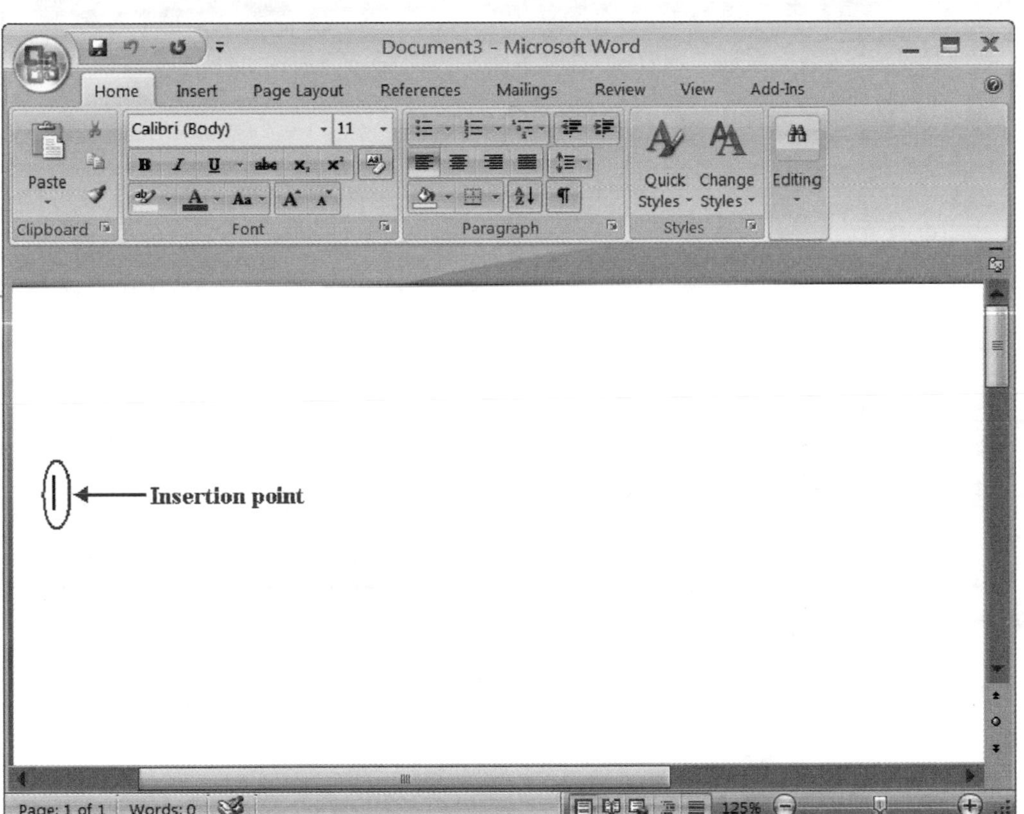

- Click the **Start** button on the lower left side of your screen.

Displays the Start Menu, allowing you to select which application to launch.

- Select **All Programs > Microsoft Office > Microsoft Office Word 2007** from the Start Menu.

Launches the Microsoft Word Program and displays a new blank document.

- Click in the document window and type: **THE OUTDOOR FUN NEWSLETTER**
- Press **Enter key once** and type **FROM THE PRESIDENT**

Enters text into the new document.

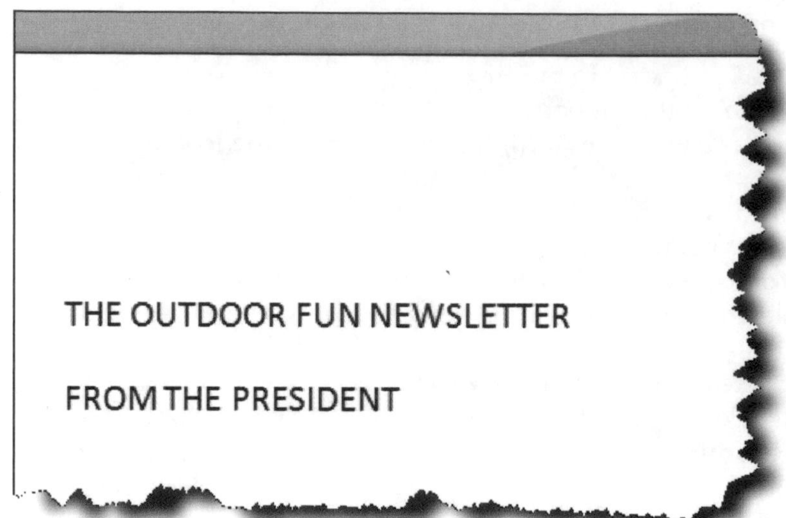

- Click the **Save button** on the Quick Access toolbar and type: **Word Case Study 1b** in the **name** text box and select **flash drive** in the **Save in** list.

Enters the name of the new workbook.

- Click the **Save** button.

Saves the workbook with the new name.

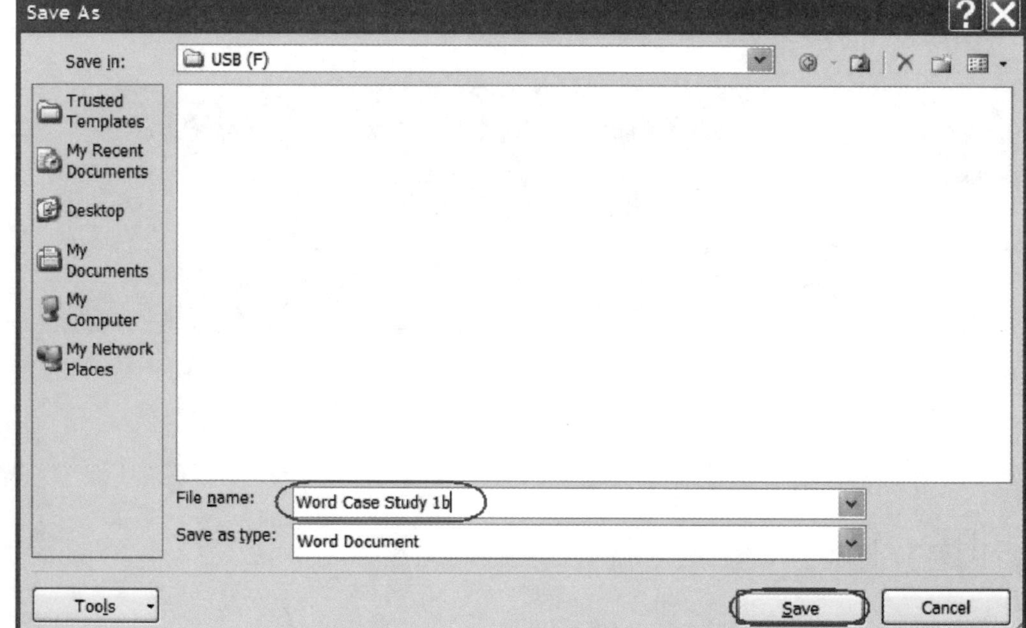

Greeting Outdoor Fun members! It looks like summer is finally here. And we have a lot of fun events planned for the summer.

If you looked at the May calendar, you may have noticed that there is no Board Meeting scheduled. Well, due to the demands of having a meeting every other month, the board voted at the April meeting to skip the May meeting. The next meeting will be held on June 9th. As we are in the information age, the Board is confident that it can continue to guide and direct Outdoor Fun effectively, even if it does not meet formally every month.

This year's goal is to hold 10 meetings. At this point, the Board plans on also skipping the August meeting, a good time because it is right before our Annual Member's Picnic. Speaking of the Picnic, I hope to see you all there!

June promises to be another great month for Outdoor Fun Members. Our Monthly Madness gathering will take place at the Jim Water's cabin. For those of you who have never been there, the cabin is located on 16 beautiful acres of secluded woods. There will be fishing and swimming in Jim's huge lake, volleyball and of course, our traditional monthly barbeque. Try to make it if you can. Other June events include:

- Press **Enter** key **twice** and type the information shown in the screenshot. Press **Enter** key **once** to create each new paragraph.

Enters the text for the new paragraph.

- Click the **Save** button.

Saves the changes.

---

volleyball and of course, our traditional monthly barbeque. Try to make it if you can. Other June events include:

Saturday Volleyball

Camping at Devil's Lake

Early Saturday Hike

Game Night

Dining Out

Barn Dance

Rollerblading in the Park

Sunday Bowling

Wow! What an exciting month we have planned! Hope to see you at these events. Enjoy the summer!

Sean

- Continue typing the information shown in the screenshot. Press **Enter once** to create new paragraph.

Enters the text for the new paragraph.

- Click the **Save** button.

Saves the changes.

- Click the **Home** tab on the Ribbon.

Ensures that the Home tab is active.

- Select the words **Outdoor Fun Newsletter**

Selects the text we wish to format.

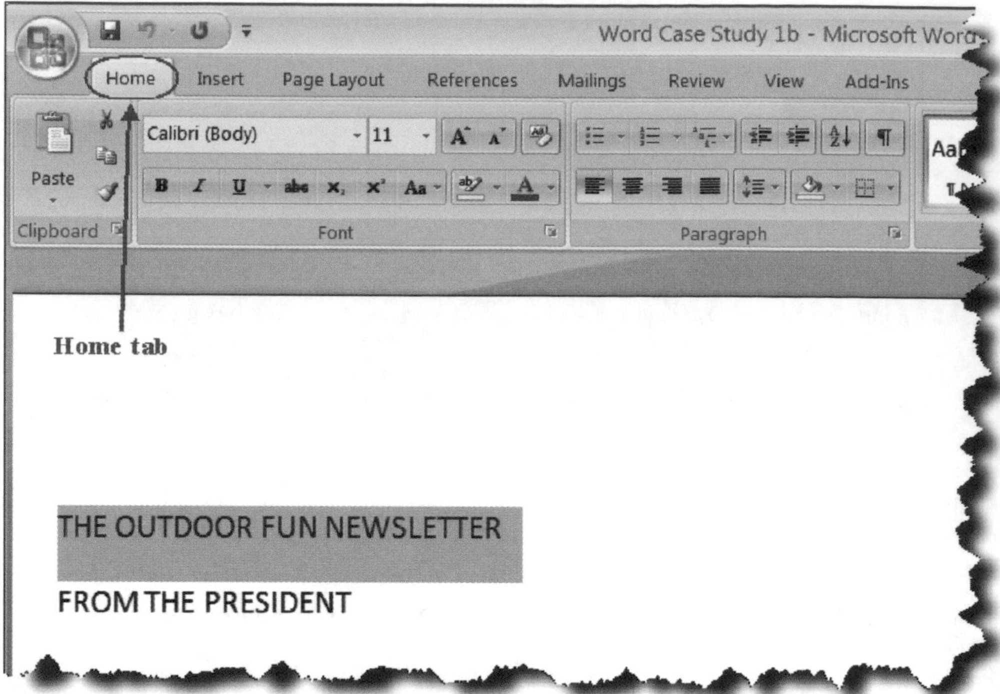

- Click on the arrow next to the **Font** drop-down list on the Ribbon.

Displays a list of available typefaces.

- Scroll down until you see **Arial**, and then **click on Arial** with your left mouse button.

Applies the Arial font to the selected text. Notice that as you scroll through the fonts, the Live Preview feature displays how your text will appear if you apply that font.

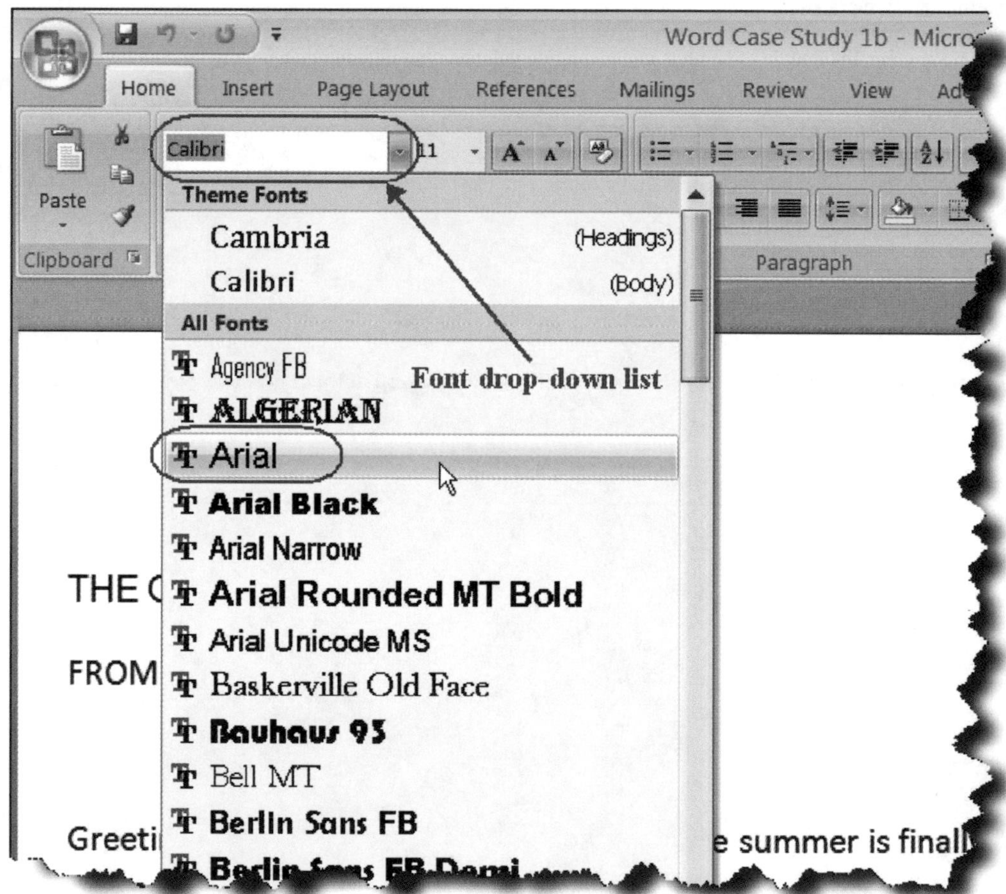

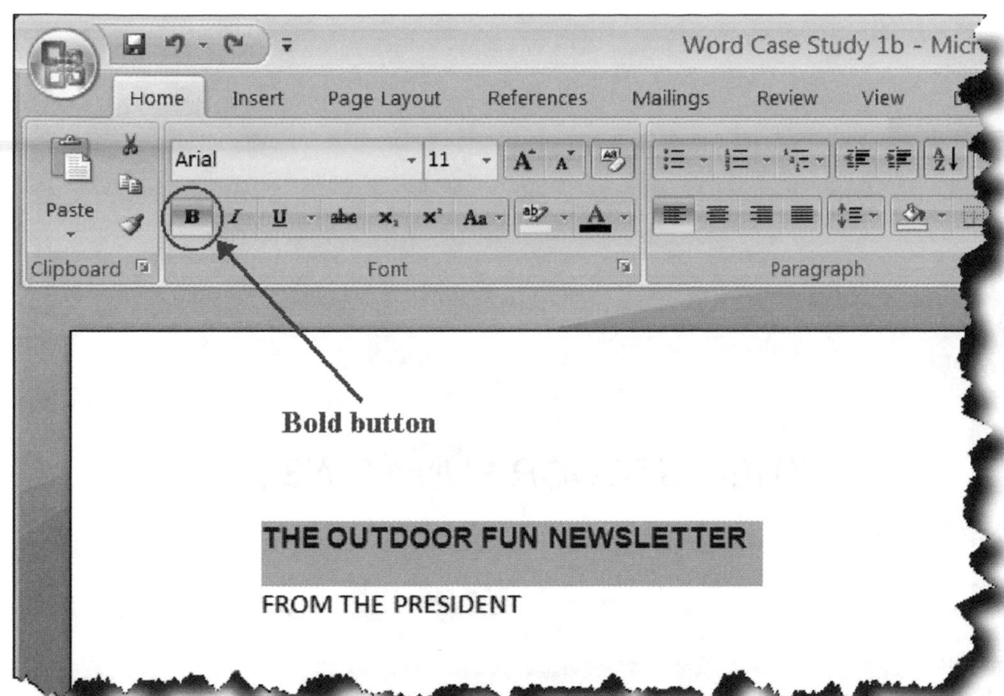

- Click the **Bold** icon on the Ribbon.

Applies bold formatting to the selected text.

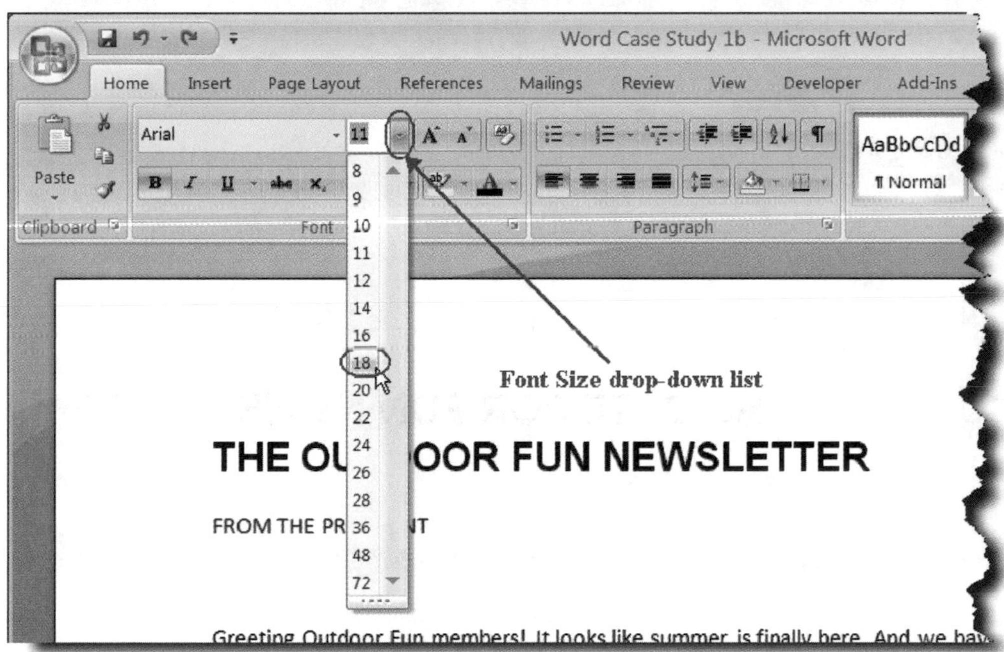

- Click the **Font Size** drop-down list on the Ribbon and select **18**.

Applies a font size of 18 pt to the selected text.

- In the newsletter, highlight the words **FROM THE PRESIDENT**.

Selects the text whose formatting we wish to modify.

- Click the **Italic** button on the Ribbon.

Applies italics formatting to the selected text.

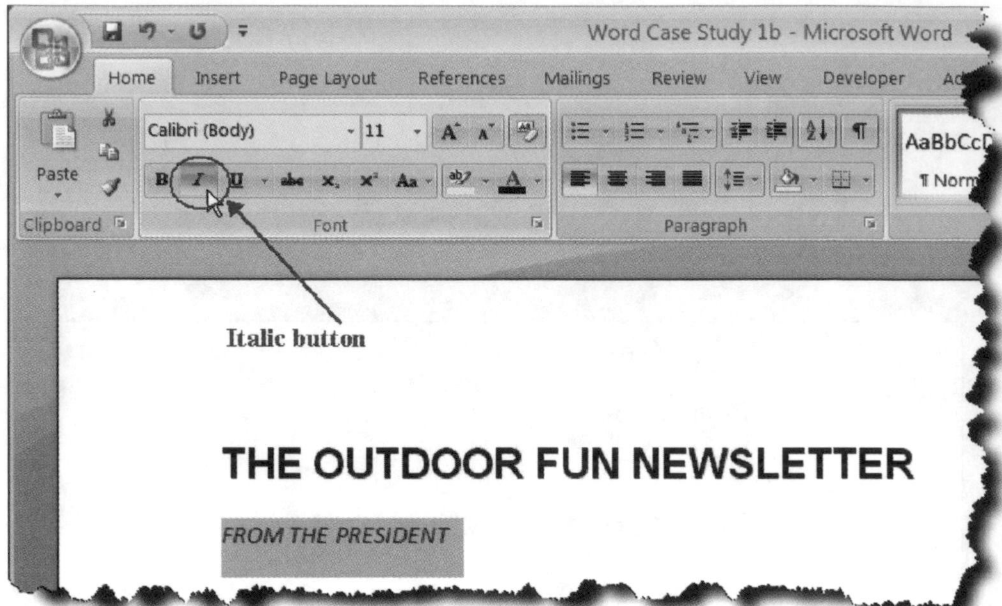

- Click the **Underline** icon on the Ribbon.

Underlines the selected text.

- Press **Ctrl + S**.

Saves the active document.

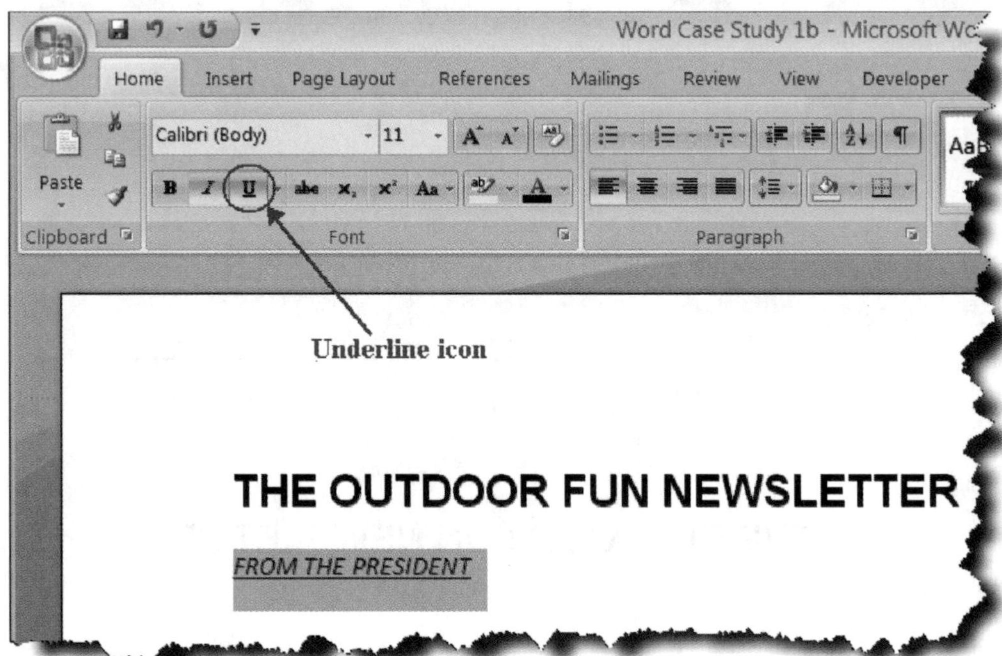

Using the Font Dialog Box

In this section, you will learn how to apply and modify additional formatting using the Font Dialog Box.

The **Font Dialog Box** allows you to apply multiple formats (bold, italics, font size, font type, font color, etc.) to selected text at once. Additionally, you will find formats that are not available on the Formatting Toolbar. To apply multiple formatting to selected text, click the **Font Dialog Box Launcher** on the lower-right corner of the Font command set then make your desired selections.

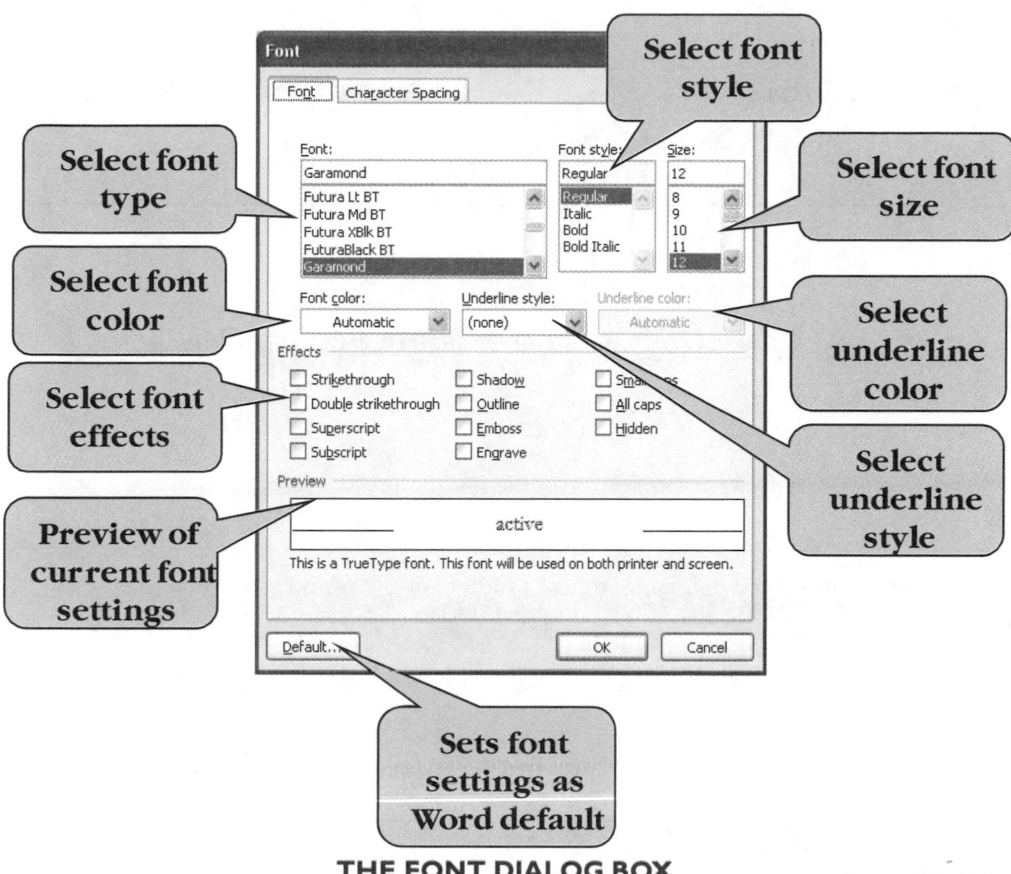

THE FONT DIALOG BOX

If you have worked with previous versions of Word, you may have noticed that the Text Effects tab is missing from the Font Dialog Box. With Word 2007, you can no longer apply text animation effects.

To Use Font Dialog Box

1. Select the text whose formatting you wish to modify.
2. Click the **Font Dialog Box Launcher** on the Ribbon
   Or
   Press the **Ctrl + D** keyboard shortcut.
3. Select the formatting you wish to apply.
4. Click **OK** when finished.

Let's Try It!

- Make sure that the second line of the newsletter: FROM THE PRESIDENT is still selected.

Selects the text whose formatting we wish to modify.

- Click the **Font Dialog Box Launcher**.

Displays the Font Dialog box.

NOTE: Ctrl + D is the keyboard shortcut to display the Font Dialog Box.

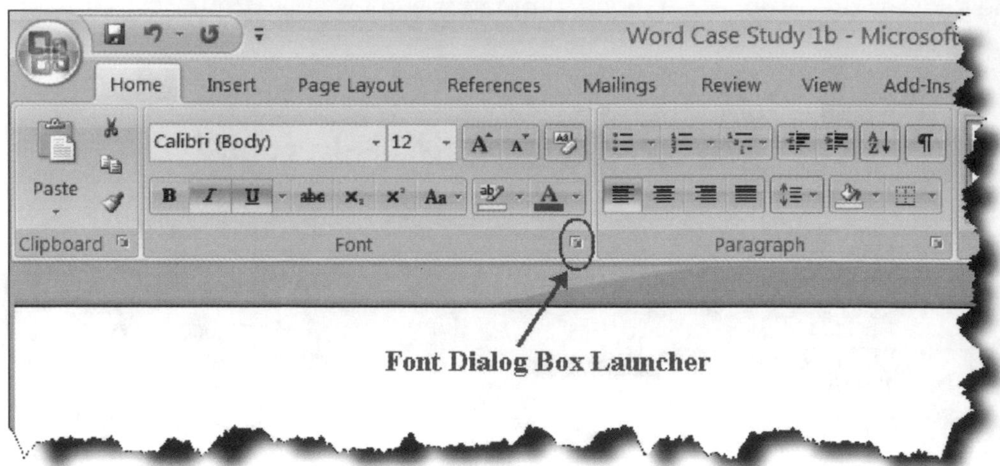

- In the **Font Style** list box, click on **Bold**.

Selects a font style of bold to apply to the selected text.

- In the **Size** list box, scroll down to **22** and click.

Selects a font size of 22 to apply to the selected text.

- Click on the **Font Color** arrow and select **Dark Blue** from the color palette (first row, fourth column) as shown below.

Selects the font color to apply to the selected text.

- Click **OK**.

Closes the font dialog box and applies the changes.

- Click the **Save** button.

Saves the active document.

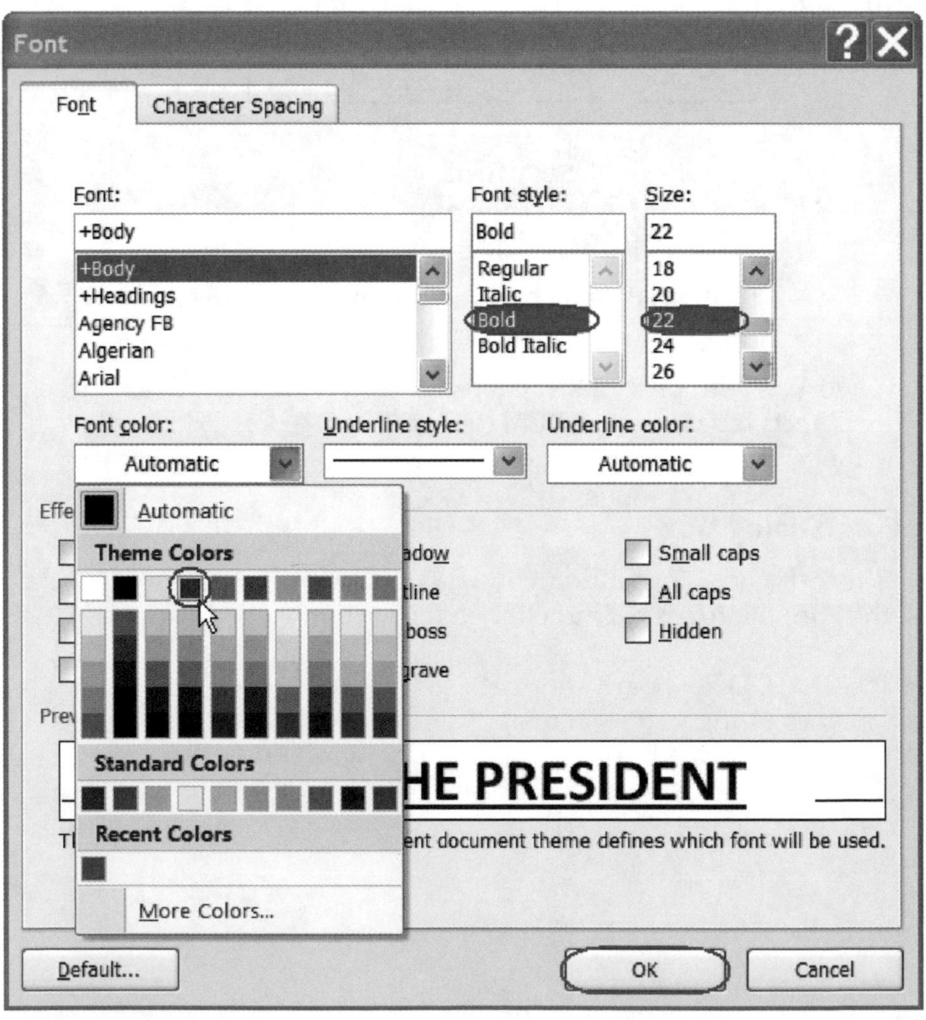

Using Character Effects

In this section, you will learn how to apply Character Effects to selected areas of text.

Character Effects allows you to add special effects to characters, drawing your attention to them and making them stand out from the neighboring text. Character Effects include:

~~Strikethrough~~	**Shadow**	**SMALL CAPS**
~~Double strikethrough~~	Outline	**ALL CAPS**
^{Super}script	**Emboss**	**Hidden (only appears on the screen—not printed)**
$_{\text{Sub}}$script	**Engrave**	

Text effects are found in the Font tab of the **Font** dialog box.

To Use Character Effects

1. Select the text to which you wish to apply a character effect.
2. Click the **Font Dialog Box Launcher** on the Ribbon
   Or
   Press the **Ctrl + D** keyboard shortcut.
3. Click the **Font tab**.
4. Click the check box next to the character effects you wish to apply.
5. Click **OK**.

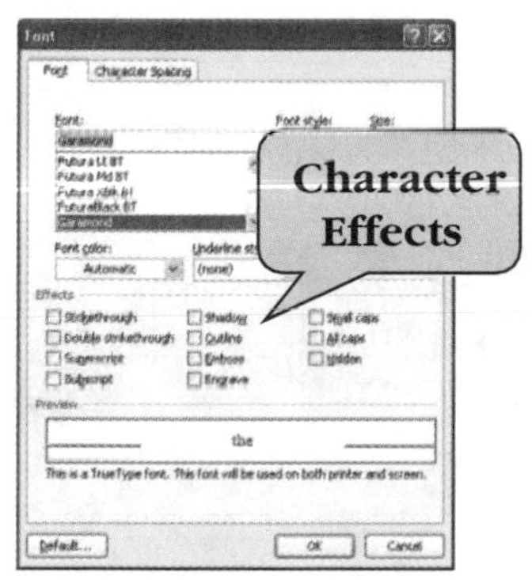

Let's Try It!

- Highlight the text: ***Saturday Volleyball*** in the body of the newsletter.

Selects the text to which we will apply a character effect.

- Click the **Font Dialog Box Launcher**.

Displays the Font dialog box.

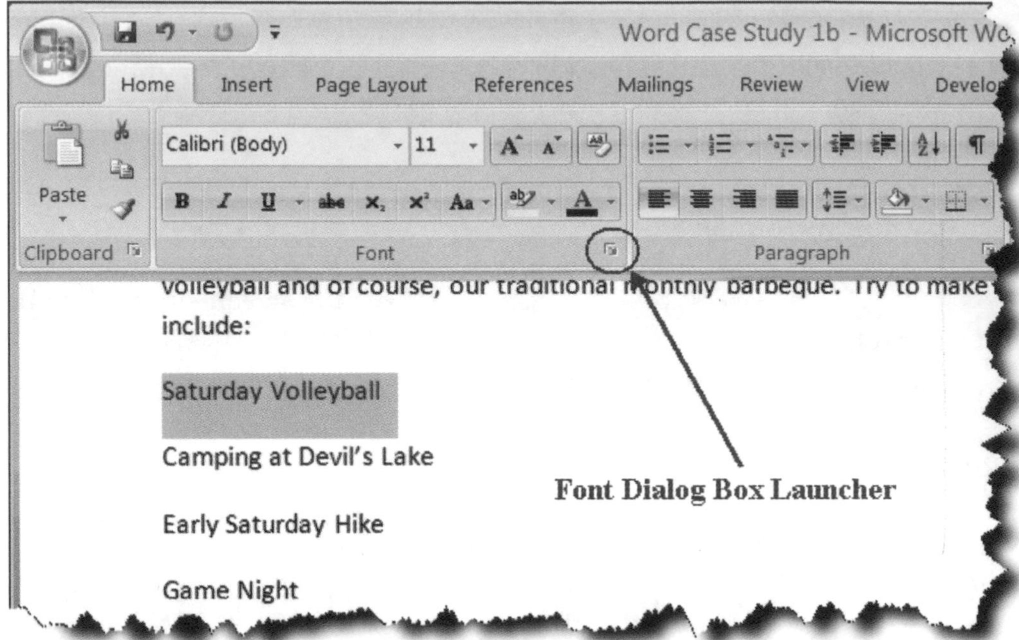

- Click the check box next to **Strikethrough** under Effects category.

Chooses the character effect that we will apply to the selected text.

- Click **OK**.

Applies the character effects and closes the Font dialog box.

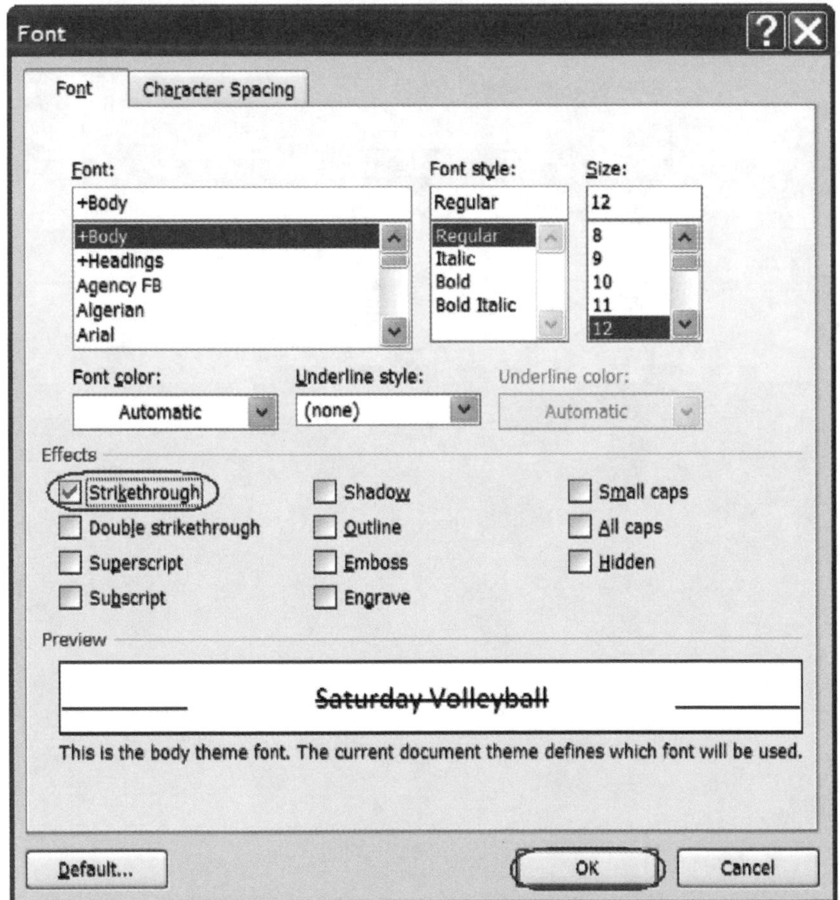

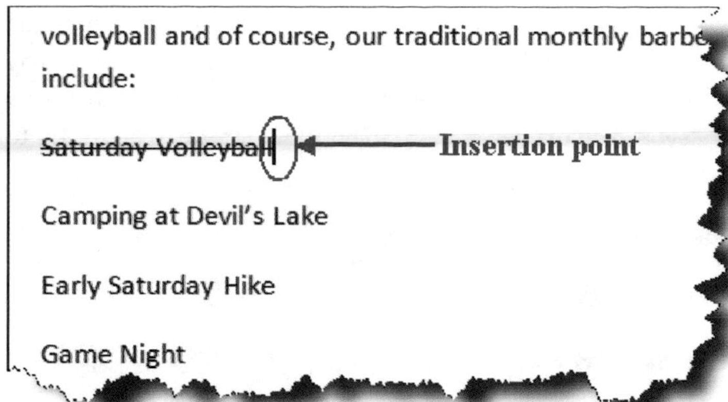

- Set the insertion point at the end of ~~Saturday Volleyball~~.

Sets the insertion point where we will type in the new event.

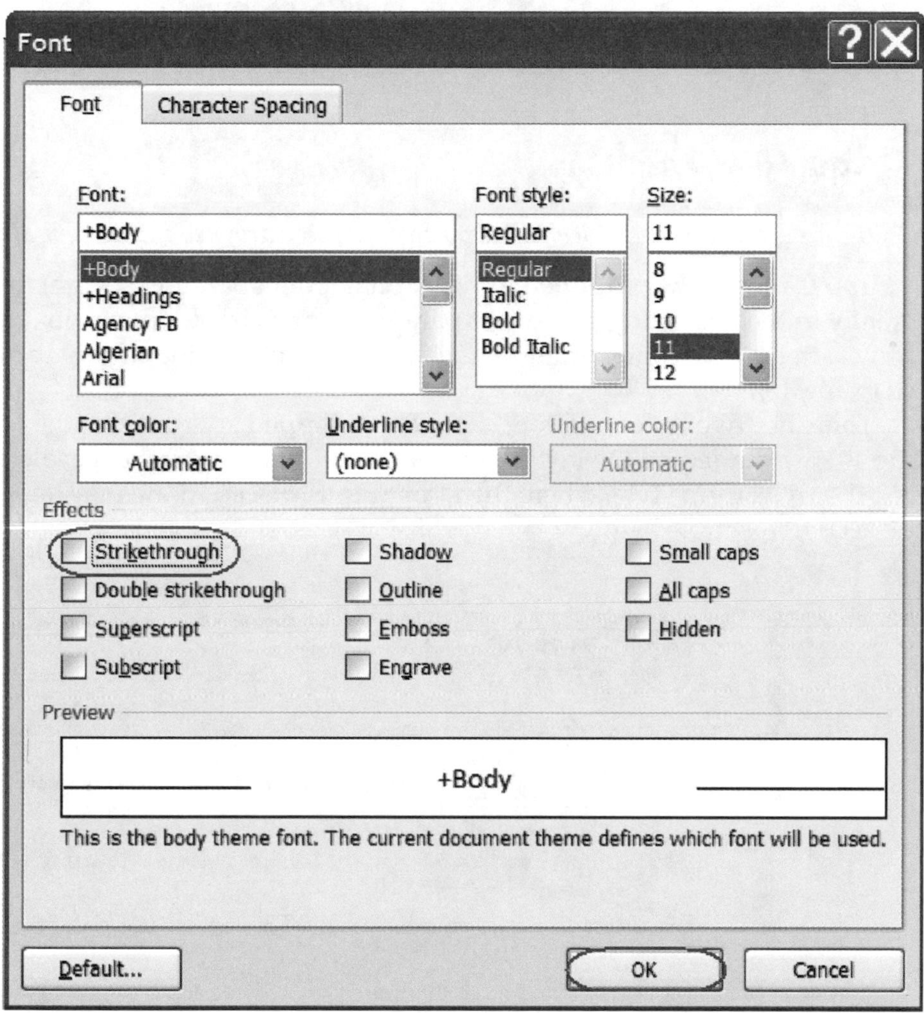

- Press **Ctrl + D**.

Displays the Font dialog box.

- **Uncheck** the box next to Strikethrough.

Turns off the Strikethrough effect so it will not be applied to the new text that we are going to type.

- Click **OK**.

Closes the Font dialog box.

- Press the **spacebar**, and then type: **Friday Tennis**.

Enters new text to the right of the text to which we applied the strikethrough effect.

- Click the **Save** button.

Saves the active document.

June promises to be another great month for Outdoor Fun Members
will take place at the Jim Water's cabin. For those of you who have ne
located on 16 beautiful acres of secluded woods. There will be fishing
volleyball and of course, our traditional monthly barbeque. Try to m
include:

~~Saturday Volleyball~~ Friday Tennis

Camping at Devil's Lake

Early Saturday Hike

Game Night

Adding a Drop Cap

In this section, you will learn how to create a large dropped initial capital letter.

A **Drop Cap** is a large dropped initial capital letter spanning several lines, usually at the beginning of the first paragraph of a chapter or section, that draws attention to that paragraph (such as at the beginning of this paragraph, for example).

There are two types of Drop Caps: The **Dropped** style, where the Drop Cap is surrounded by the text in the paragraph as in the first example below, and the **In Margin** style, where the Drop Cap is placed in the margin, as in the second example below.

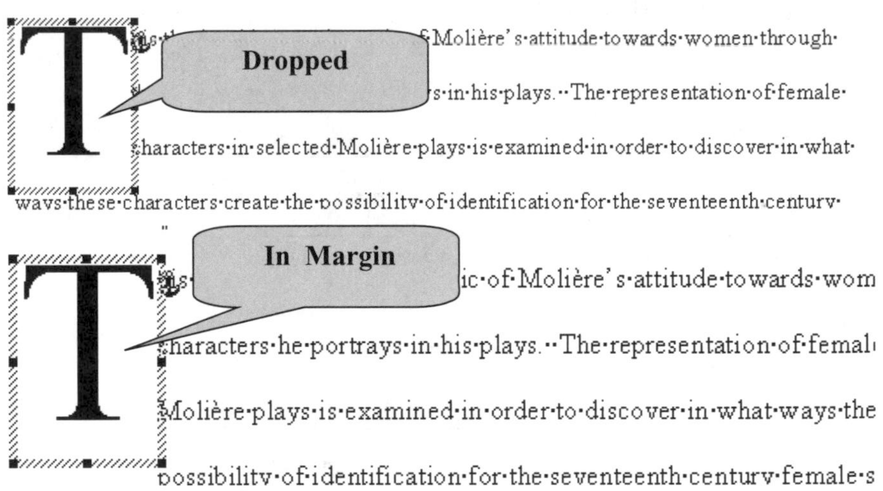

To add a Drop Cap, click anywhere within the paragraph where you want to have a drop cap initial for the first word in the paragraph, click the **Insert tab** and then click the **Drop Cap** button on the Ribbon. A list will display from where you can choose the desired Drop Cap Style. To change Drop Cap options such as the font of the Drop Cap letter, the number of lines across which the drop cap will span or the distance the drop cap is to be placed from the text, select **Drop Cap Options** from the list to display the Drop Cap dialog box.

To Add a Drop Cap

1. Click anywhere within the paragraph to which you want to add a Drop Cap.
2. Click the **Insert** tab.
3. Click the **Drop Cap** button on the Text command set.
4. Select the drop cap style you want from the list.
5. To modify Drop Cap settings:
   a. Click **Drop Cap Options** from the list
   b. Select a font for the Drop Cap from the **Font** drop-down list.
   c. Enter the number of lines across which the Drop Cap should span in the **Lines to Drop** box.
   d. Enter the amount of distance that should be between the Drop Cap and the paragraph text (in inches).
   e. Click **OK** when finished.

Let's Try It!

Greeting Outdoors Fun members! It looks like summer is finally here. And we have a lot of fun events planned for the summer.

- Click anywhere within the paragraph that starts with **Greeting** and ends with summer.

Selects the paragraph to which we will add an initial Drop Cap letter.

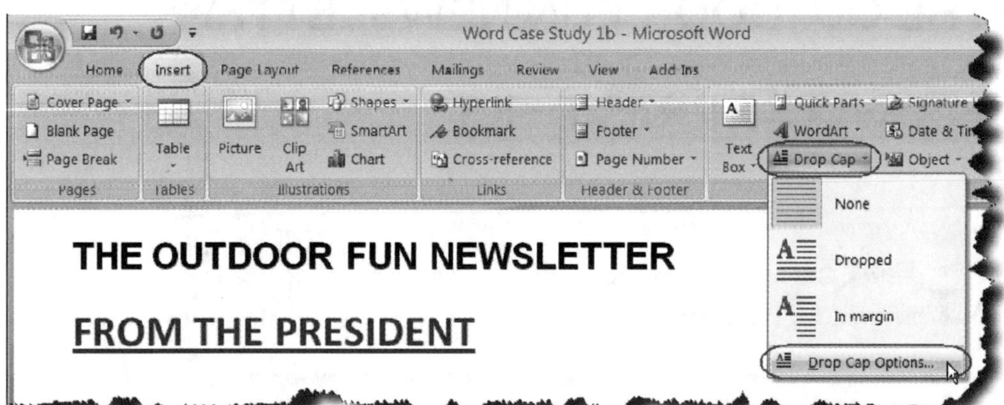

- Click the **Insert tab** on the Ribbon.

Displays Insert commands and tools.

- Click the **Drop Cap Options** button under the **Text command set** and choose **Drop Cap Options** from the list.

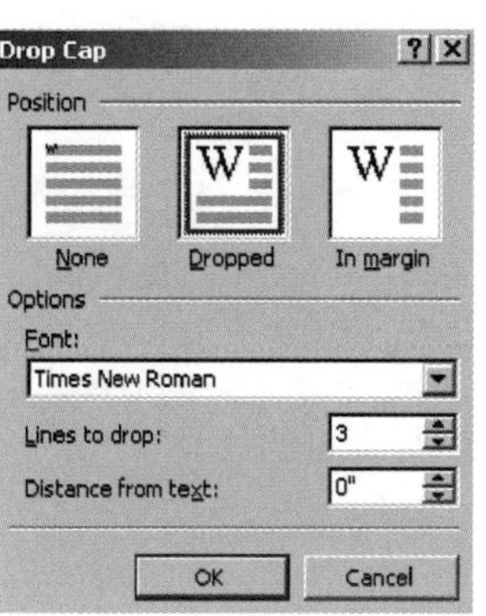

Instead of choosing a default style, we want to adjust some settings.

- In the Position area, click the **Dropped** box as shown.

Selects Dropped as the Drop Cap style.

- Type 2 in **Lines to drop**: box.
- Click the **Font** drop-down list arrow and type "**Alge**" under until **Algerian** appears in the list. Click **Algerian**.

Selects the font for our drop cap letter.

- Click **OK**.

Adds a Dropped style initial drop cap character to the first word of the paragraph.

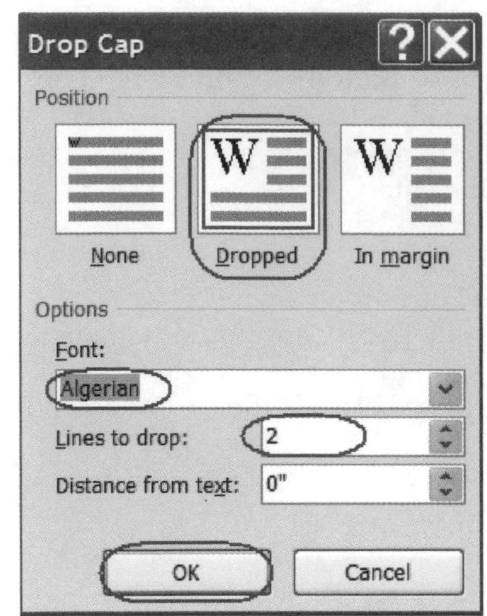

- Click the **Save** button.

Saves the active document.

THE OUTDOOR FUN NEWSLETTE

FROM THE PRESIDENT

Greeting Outdoor Fun members! It looks like summer is finally
planned for the summer.

Adding Borders to a Paragraph

In this section, you will learn how to surround a paragraph with a border

Adding a line or **border** around a paragraph is one way to set the information in a particular paragraph apart from the rest of your document. Microsoft Word offers many different **line styles** to choose from, allowing you to really jazz up a document. You also have the option of changing the color and the width of your borders or adding shadows and 3-D effects.

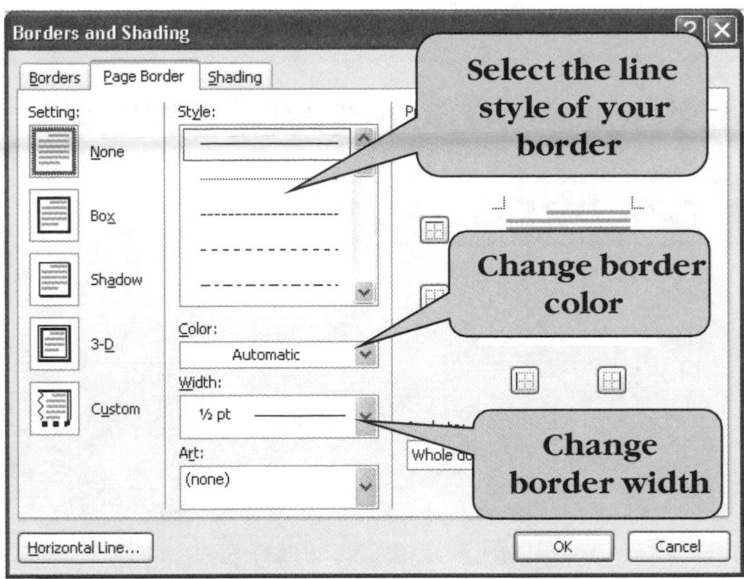

To Add Borders to a Paragraph

1. Select the paragraph that you wish to surround with a border.
2. Click the **Home** tab.
3. Click the arrow next to the **Borders** button on the Paragraph command set and choose the desired border type from the list
   Or
4. Click the arrow next to the Borders button and select **Borders and Shading** from the list to display the Boarders and Shading dialog box.
5. From the **Borders and Shading** dialog box:
   a. Choose the desired line style from the **Style** window to modify all border edges
      Or
      Click in the Preview diagram to modify edges of individual borders.
   b. Choose the desired color from the **Color** drop-down list.
   c. Choose the desired width from the **Width** drop-down list.
   c. Choose the border type (box, shadow, 3-D or Custom) under the **Setting** area.
   d. Click **OK**.

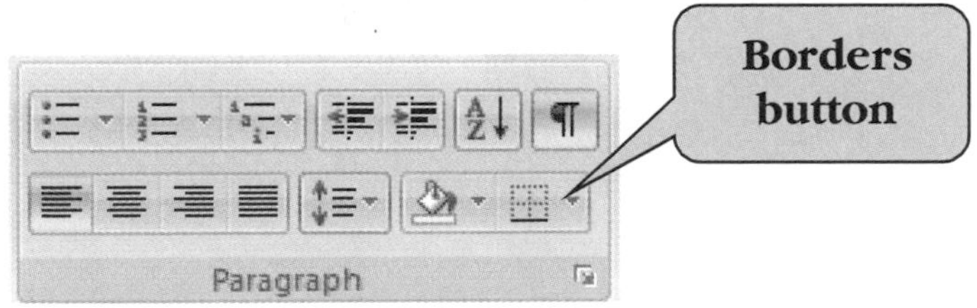

Let's Try It!

- Select the title of the document: **THE OUTDOOR FUN NEWSLETTER**.

Selects the paragraph that we will surround with a border.

THE OUTDOOR FUN NEWSLETTER

FROM THE PRESIDENT

- Click the **Home** tab on the Ribbon.

Switches to Page Layout commands and tools.

- Click the arrow next to the **Borders** button on the Paragraph command set and select **Borders and Shading**.

Displays the Borders and Shading dialog box.

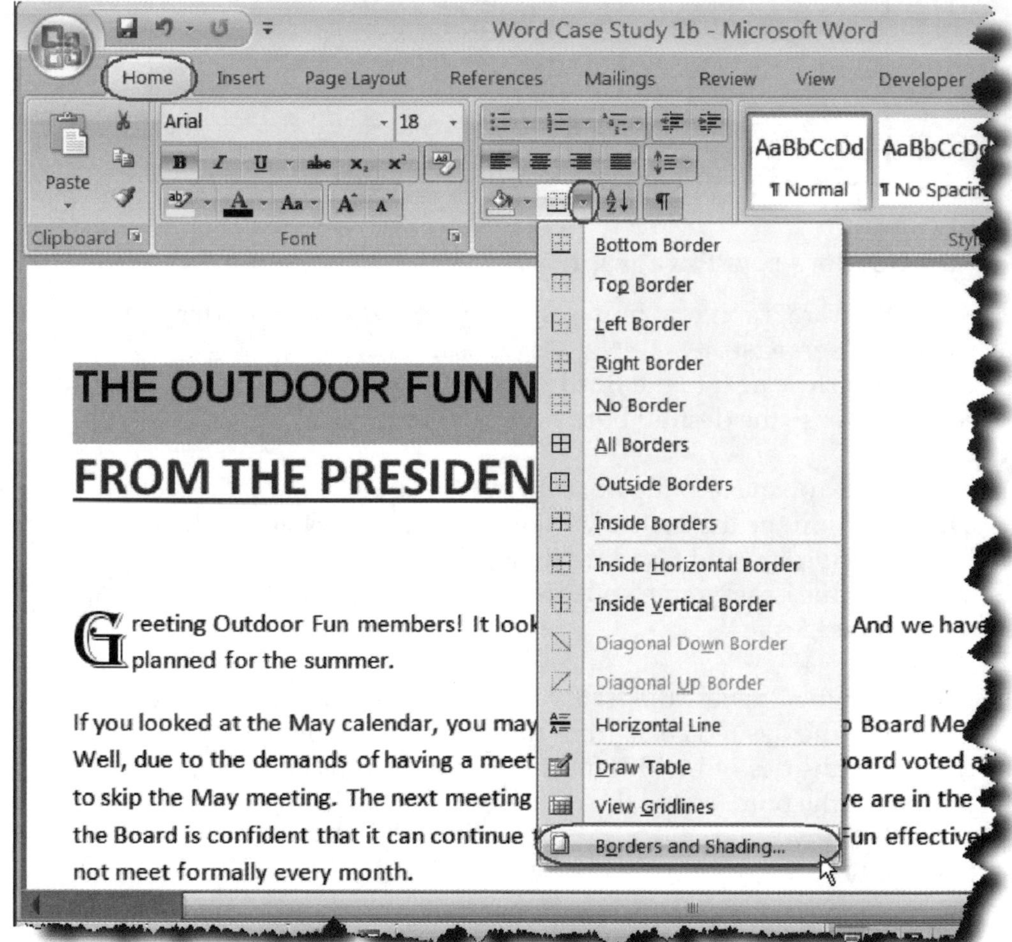

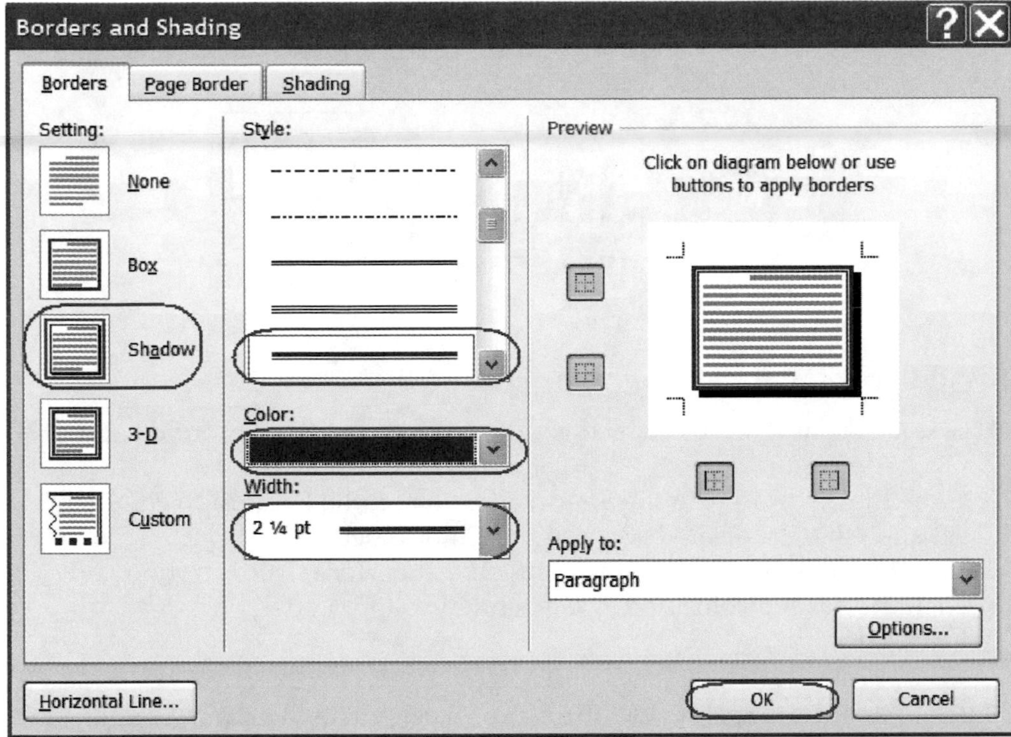

- Choose the **ninth line style** from the top in the **Style list** window, as shown.

Chooses the border line style that we want to apply to our paragraph.

- Under the **Setting** area, click the **Shadow** style.

Chooses Shadow as the border type.

- Click the **Width** drop-down list, and then choose **2¼ pt**.

Chooses the line width of our border.

- Click the **Color** drop-down list, and choose **Dark Blue** (1st row, 4th column).

Selects the line color of our border.

- Click **OK**.

Closes the Borders and Shading dialog box and applies the settings.

- Click the **Save** button.

Saves the changes.

Adding Shading to a Paragraph

In this section, you will learn how to add background shading to a paragraph.

Another way to set one paragraph apart from others is to apply a background color to the paragraph. Click the **Shading** button on the Home Ribbon and choose the desired color from the **Color** palette. To choose colors from a more extensive color palette, click the **More Colors** button.

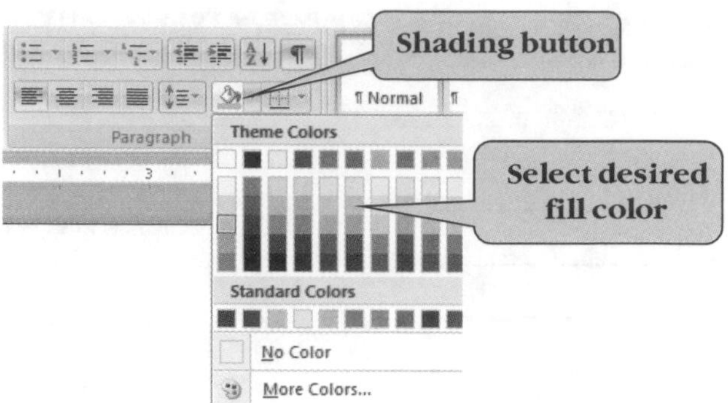

To Add Shading to a Paragraph

1. Select the paragraph to which you want to apply a background color.
2. Click the **Home** tab.
3. Click the arrow next to the **Shading** button on the Paragraph command set and click the desired color on the **Color** palette.
4. If you don't see the color you want, click the **More Colors** option and click the desired color from the extended color palette.
5. Click **OK**.

> **TIP:** You can also apply shading from the Shading tab of the Borders and Shading dialog box.

Let's Try It!

- Select **THE OUTDOOR FUN NEWSLETTER** if it is not already selected.

Selects the text to apply background shading.

- Click the **Shading** button on the Home Ribbon as shown.

Displays the shading Color palette.

- Click on the **fourth color in the third row** as shown.

Chooses the color that we wish to apply as background shading. Notice that as you move your mouse pointer over the various colors, Word temporarily applies the color to the select text allowing you to preview the color.

- Click the **Save** button.

Saves the changes.

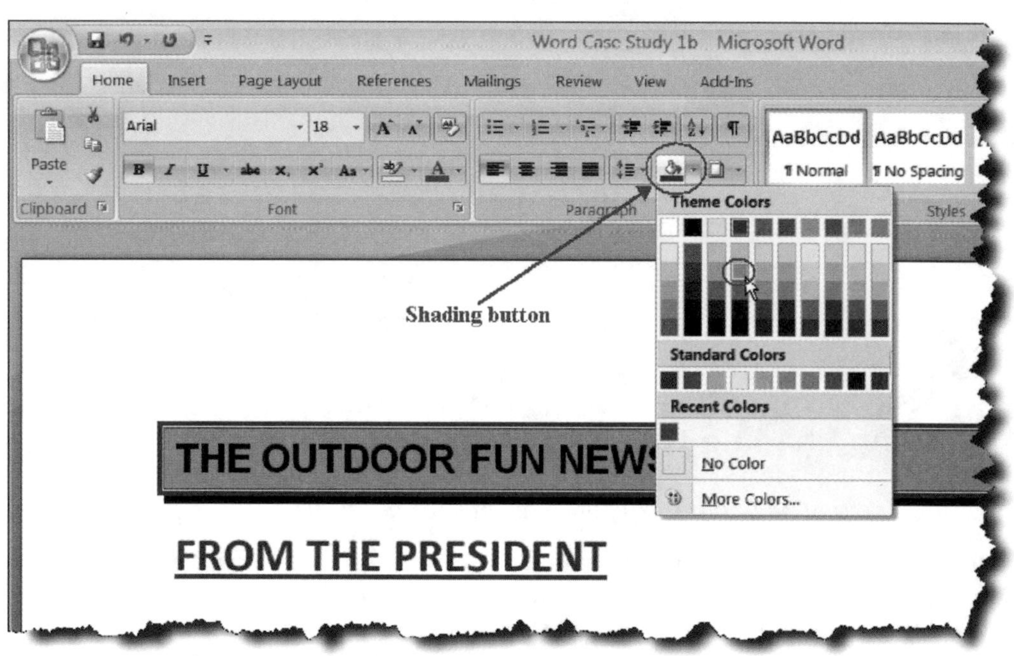

Aligning Text

In this section, you will learn how to align paragraph text to the margins.

Alignment refers to the arrangement of text in relation to the left and right margins. For example, a paragraph that is left-aligned is flush with the left margin. There are four types of alignment that you can apply to a paragraph:

- **Align Left**—text is flush with the left margin
- **Align Right**—text is flush with the right margin
- **Center**—text is positioned with an even space from the left and right margins
- **Justify**—both edges of the paragraph are flush with the left and right margins (extra spaces are added between words to create this effect).

To change the alignment of a paragraph, click anywhere within the paragraph and click the desired alignment button on the Home Ribbon, as shown below. A paragraph is defined by a hard return at the end.

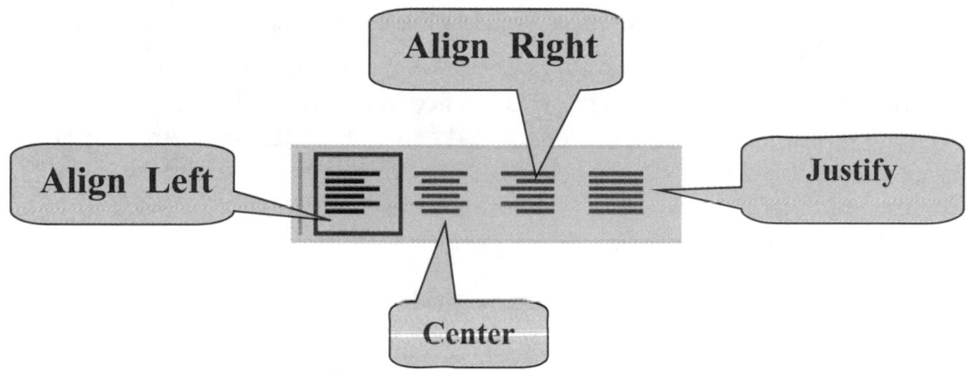

ALIGNMENT BUTTON ON THE STANDARD TOOLBAR

To Change Paragraph Alignment

1. Click anywhere in the paragraph whose alignment you wish to change.
2. Click the desired **alignment button** under the Paragraph command set on the **Home Ribbon**.

Let's Try It!

THE OUTDOOR FUN NEWSLETTER

FROM THE PRESIDENT

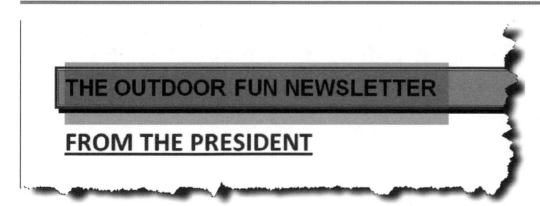

- Highlight **THE OUTDOOR FUN NEWSLETTER** if it is not already highlighted.

Selects the text to apply background shading.

- Click the **Center** button on the formatting toolbar under Home Ribbon.

Centers the line evenly between the left and right margins.

- Click the **Save** button.

Saves the active document.

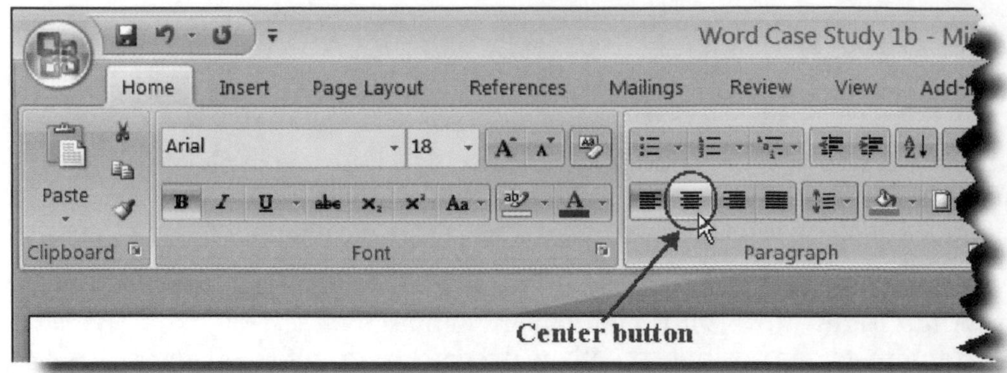

Adjusting Line Spacing

In this section, you will learn how to change the spacing between the lines within your paragraph

Line Spacing refers to the amout of vertical space between each line of text in a paragraph. The default is single-spaced—enough to accommodate a line of text with only a small amount of white space between each line.

To make your document easier to read or to provide extra white space between lines for reader comments, you can change the amount of space between each line in a paragraph. There are several types of line spacing options from which to choose:

- **1.0 lines (Single)**—enough to accommodate a line of text with a small amount of white space between lines
- **1.5 lines**—One and a half times the single space amount.
- **2.0 lines (Double)**—Two times the single space amount
- **2.5 lines**—Two and a half times the single space amount
- **3.0 (Triple)**—Two times the single space amount

From the **Paragraph Dialog box**, you can also specify customized line spacing such as:

- **At Least**—The minimum amount of space (in points) between lines. Enter the point size in the **At** box. Space is increased to accommodate larger characters.
- **Exactly**—The amount of space (in points) between lines. Enter the point size in the **At** box. Space is **not** increased to accommodate larger characters.
- **Multiple**—Enter a multiple of the size of the font. Entering a multiple of 3 when a 10 point font is use results in 30 points between the lines.

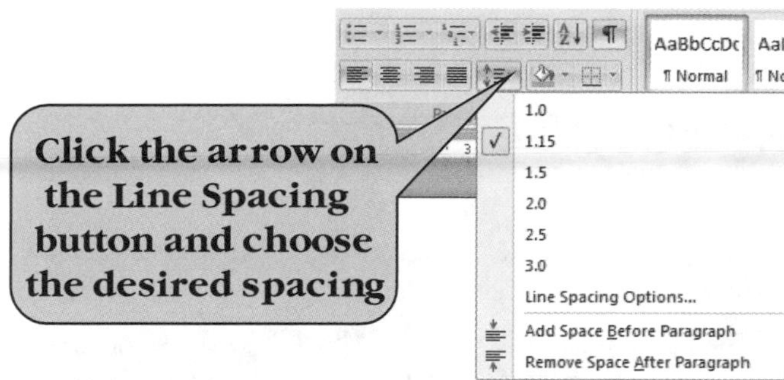

LINE SPACING BUTTON

You can set line spacing by clicking the **Line Spacing button** on the Home Ribbon and selecting the desired line spacing from the list. To set an At Least, Exactly or Multiple line spacing option, click **Line Spacing Options** to display the Paragraph dialog box.

To Change Line Spacing in a Paragraph

1. Click anywhere in the paragraph whose line spacing you wish to change.
2. Click the arrow next to the **Line Spacing** box and select the line spacing you want to apply to your paragraph (1, 1.5, 2, 2.5, 3)
3. To set an At Least, Exactly or Multiple line spacing option, click **Line Spacing Options** from the list to display the Paragraph Dialog box.
4. From the Paragraph Dialog box:
   a. Select the desired line spacing from the **Line spacing** drop-list.
   b. If choosing **At Least**, **Exactly** or **Multiple**, enter the point size amount in the **At** box.
   c. Click **OK**

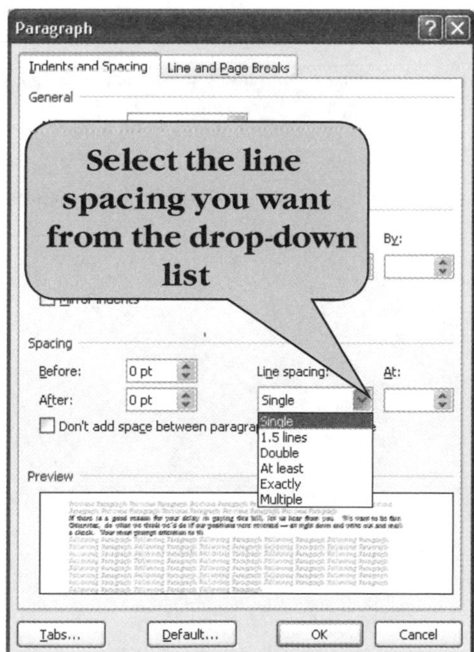

PARAGRAPH DIALOG BOX

Let's Try It!

- Select the body of the newsletter, beginning with the words: **Greeting Outdoors Fun members** to the last word: **Sean**.

Select the body of the newsletter whose line spacing we wish to change. As we wish to change the spacing for multiple paragraphs, we must first select the paragraphs. If we were changing spacing for only one paragraph, we need only click anywhere within the paragraph.

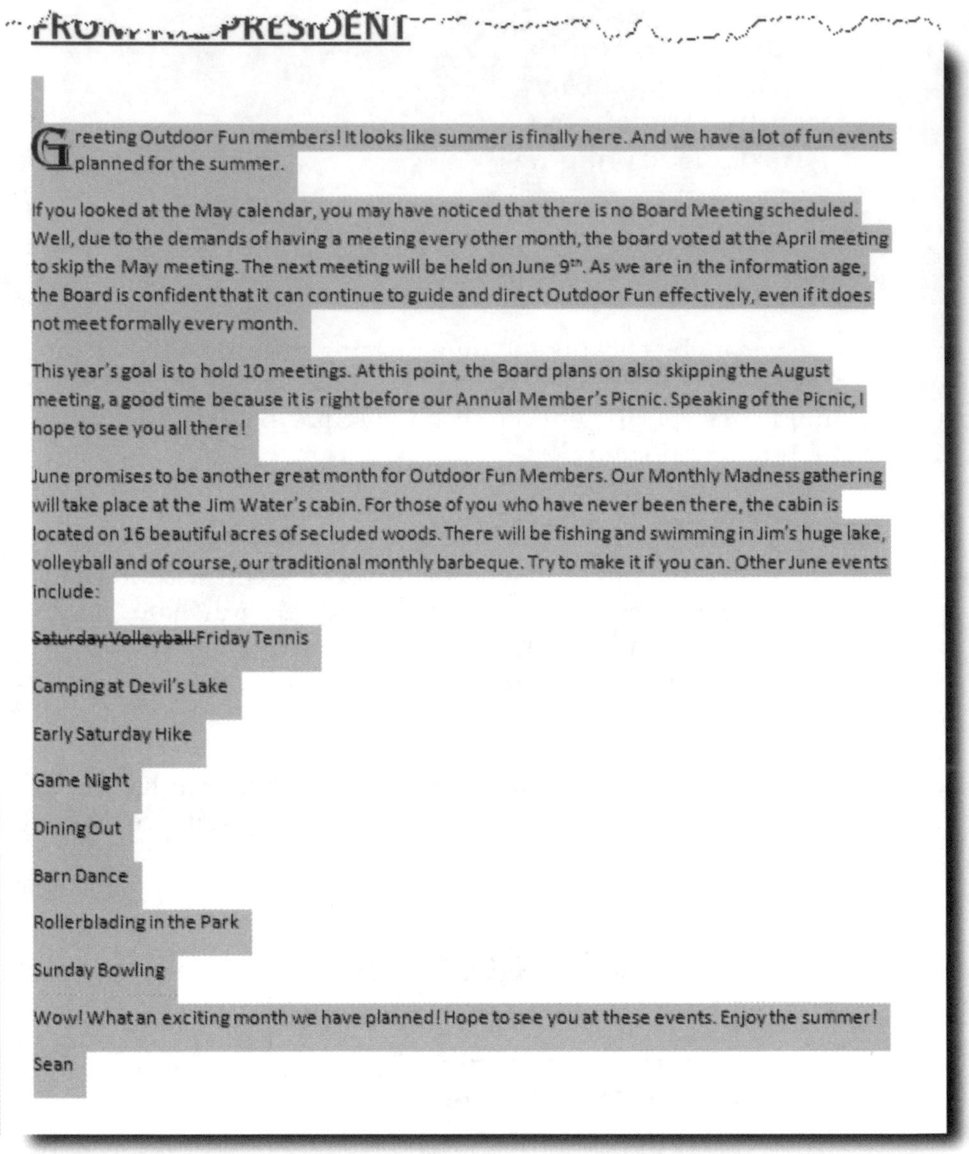

FROM THE PRESIDENT

Greeting Outdoor Fun members! It looks like summer is finally here. And we have a lot of fun events planned for the summer.

If you looked at the May calendar, you may have noticed that there is no Board Meeting scheduled. Well, due to the demands of having a meeting every other month, the board voted at the April meeting to skip the May meeting. The next meeting will be held on June 9th. As we are in the information age, the Board is confident that it can continue to guide and direct Outdoor Fun effectively, even if it does not meet formally every month.

This year's goal is to hold 10 meetings. At this point, the Board plans on also skipping the August meeting, a good time because it is right before our Annual Member's Picnic. Speaking of the Picnic, I hope to see you all there!

June promises to be another great month for Outdoor Fun Members. Our Monthly Madness gathering will take place at the Jim Water's cabin. For those of you who have never been there, the cabin is located on 16 beautiful acres of secluded woods. There will be fishing and swimming in Jim's huge lake, volleyball and of course, our traditional monthly barbeque. Try to make it if you can. Other June events include:

~~Saturday Volleyball~~ Friday Tennis

Camping at Devil's Lake

Early Saturday Hike

Game Night

Dining Out

Barn Dance

Rollerblading in the Park

Sunday Bowling

Wow! What an exciting month we have planned! Hope to see you at these events. Enjoy the summer!

Sean

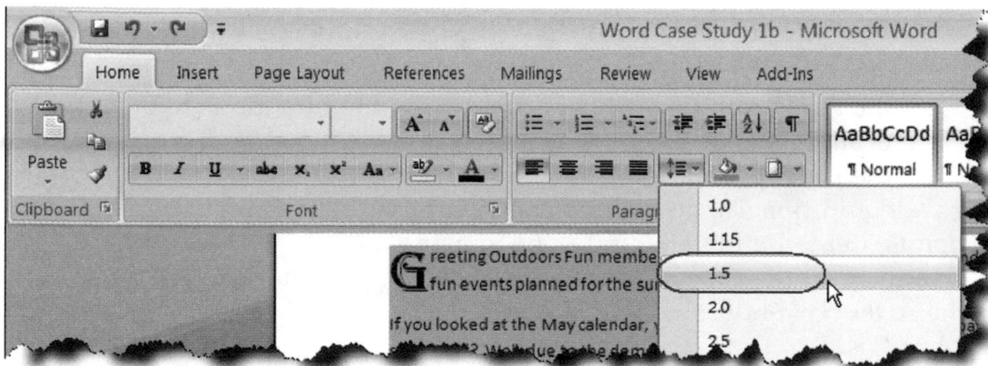

- Click the arrow on the **Line Spacing** button as shown and choose **1.5**.
- Click the **Save** button.

Saves the active document.

Adjust Spacing Between Paragraphs

In this section, you will learn how to change the spacing between paragraphs.

You can tell Microsoft Word to add additional space (in points) before and/or after a paragraph. For instance, you may set your line spacing as single but want additional spacing between your paragraphs. Rather than creating this manually, you can add this setting in the **Before** and/or **After** boxes in the **Paragraph** dialog box, applying it to all paragraphs in your document.

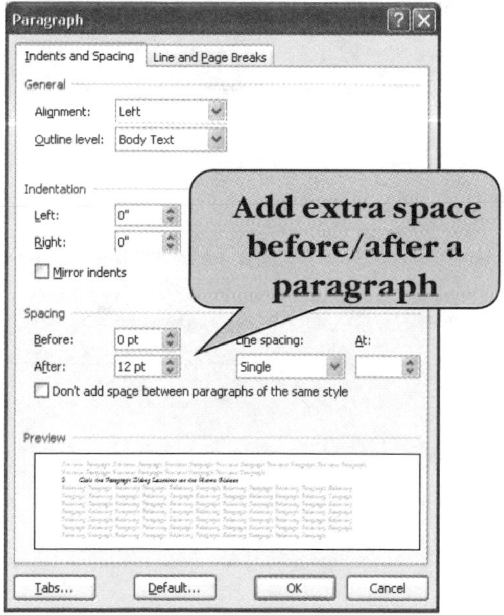

TIP: You can also modify paragraph spacing from the **Page Layout** tab. Enter the before and after values under the Spacing area of the Paragraph command set.

To Change Spacing Before/After Paragraphs

1. Click anywhere in the paragraph whose line spacing you wish to change.
2. Click the **Paragraph Dialog Launcher** on the Home Ribbon to open the Paragraph dialog box.
3. Click the **Indents and Spacing** tab.
4. To add additional space before a new paragraph, type an amount (in points) in the **Before** box under the **Spacing** area.
5. To add additional space after a paragraph, type an amount (in points) in the **After** box under the **Spacing** area.
6. Click **OK**.

Let's Try It!

- Select first two paragraphs within the body of the newsletter, beginning with the words: **Greeting**.

Selects the paragraphs after which we will add additional spacing.

- Click the **Paragraph Launcher**.

Displays the Paragraph dialog box.

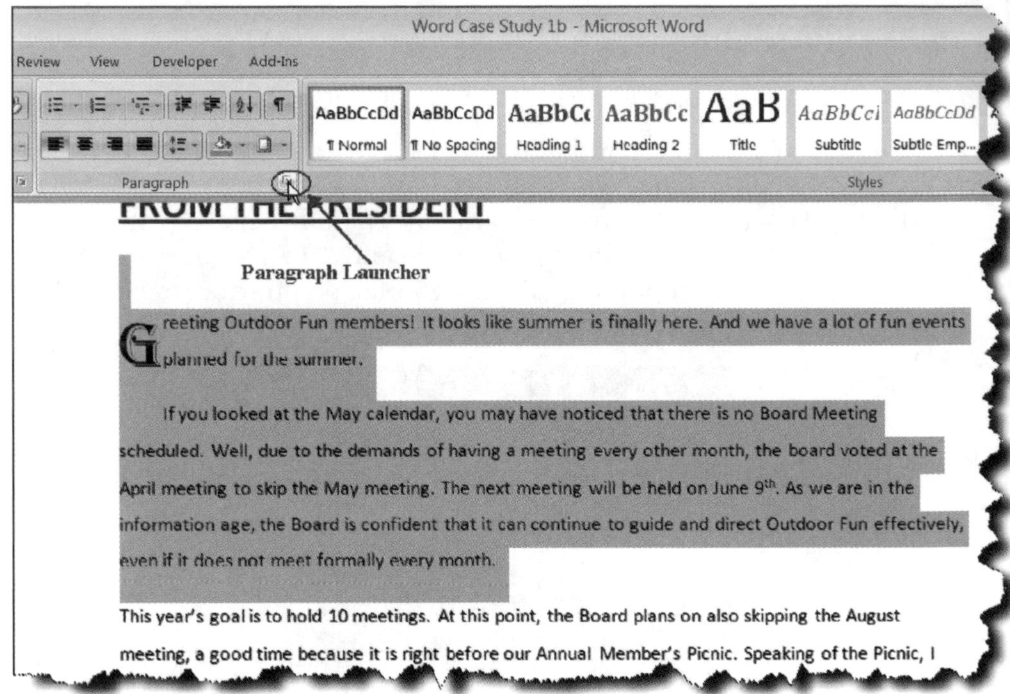

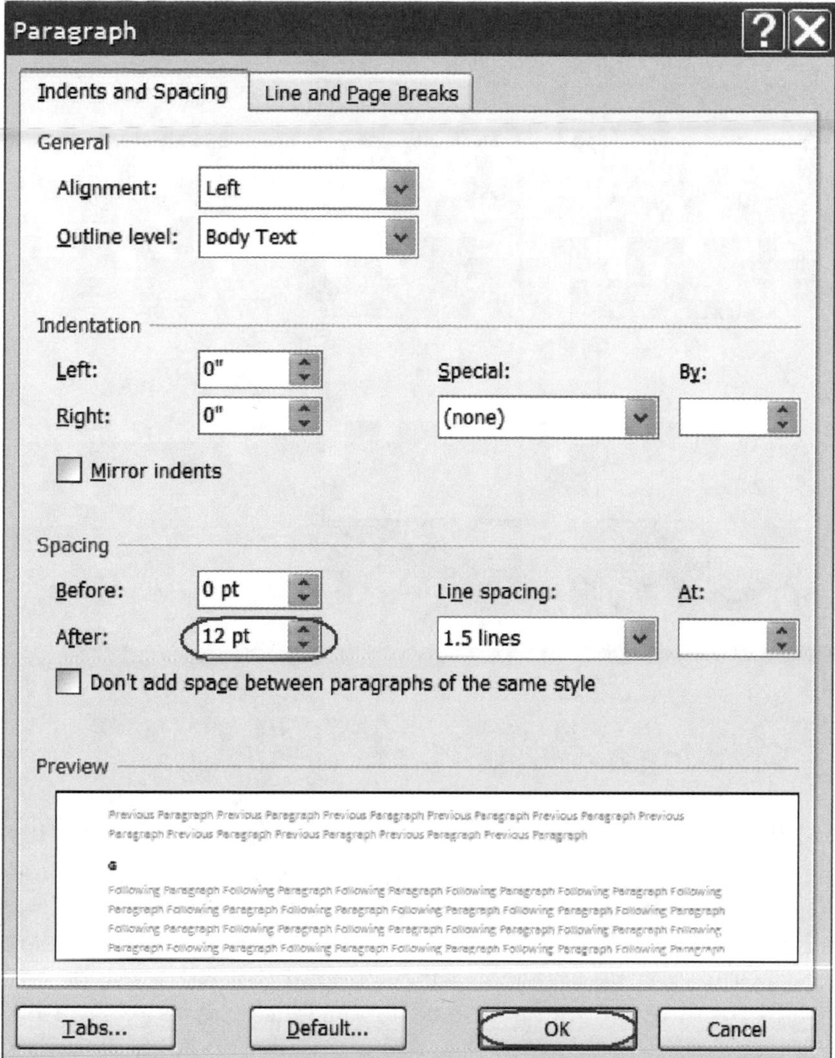

- Under the **Spacing** area, type: **12** in the **After** box as shown.

This will add an extra 12 points of white space after the selected paragraphs.

- Click **OK**.

Closes the Paragraph dialog box.

G eeting Outdoor Fun members! It looks like summer is finally here

lanned for the summer.

f you looked at the May calendar, you may have noticed that th

cheduled. Well, due to the demands of having a meeting every o

the April meeting to skip the May meeting. The next meeting will be he

information age, the Board is confident that it can continue to guide ar

even if it does not meet formally every month.

- Click on letter **G** and then click on the **border** of letter **G**.

- Select font size **20** under Home tab.
- Click the **Save** icon.

Saves the changes.

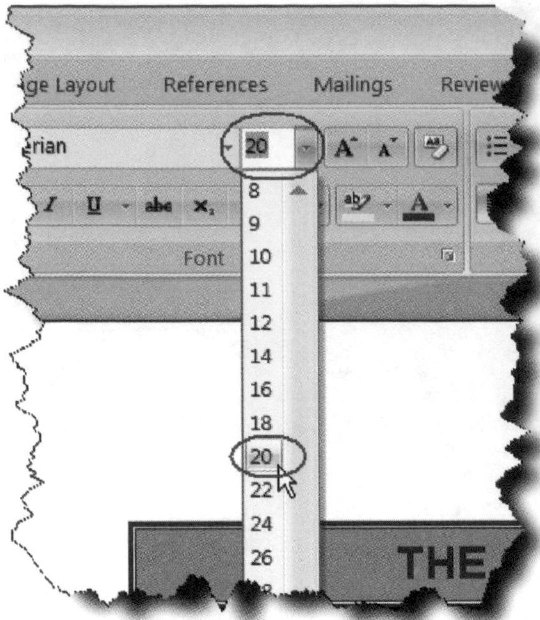

Creating a Bulleted List

In this section, you will learn how to create a list of items preceded by a bullet.

A **Bulleted List** is a list of data that is preceded by a small round dot or bullet. The text is indented from the bullet to the first tab stop (or at .5 inches if no tab stops are set). Bullets make a list of items easier to read and sets the items apart from the other text in your document. To create a bulleted list, click on the **Bullets** button on the Home Ribbon. Click the bullets button again when you are finished with your list. To specify the type of bullet, click the arrow next to the Bullets icon and choose the desired bullet type from the gallery.

For more bullet options, such as setting the type of bullet, indentation, etc., click the arrow next to the Bullets button. Click **Change List Level** to modify bullet indentation or click **Define New Bullet** to create a new bullet type.

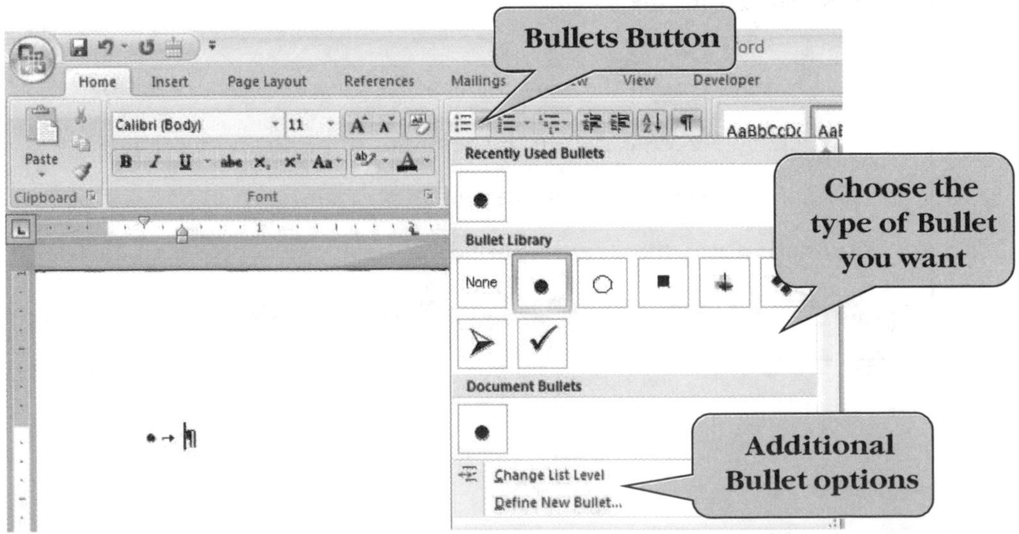

To Create a Bulleted List

1. Select the list to which you want to apply bulleting.
2. To create a default bulleted list, click the **Bullets** button on the Home Ribbon

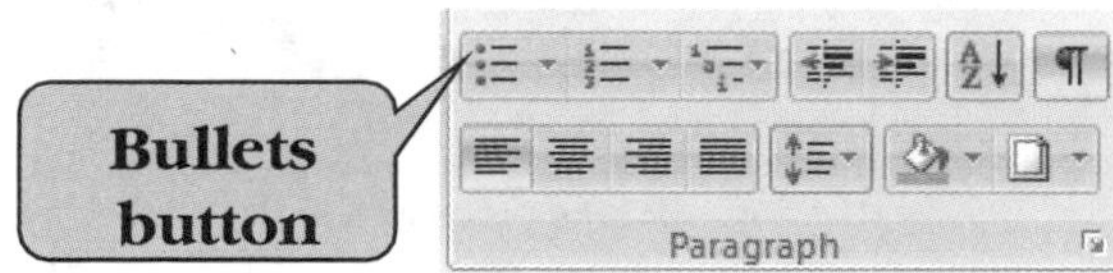

3. For more Bullet options, click the drop-down arrow next to the Bullets button.
4. Click on the desired **Bullet type** in the window.
5. Click **Define a New Bullet** to create a new bullet type. To create a graphic bullet, click the **Symbol, Font** or **Picture** button and then select the new image to be used as the bullet.
6. Click **Change List Level** to modify bullet indentation and choose the level you want from the list.
7. Click **OK**.

Let's Try It!

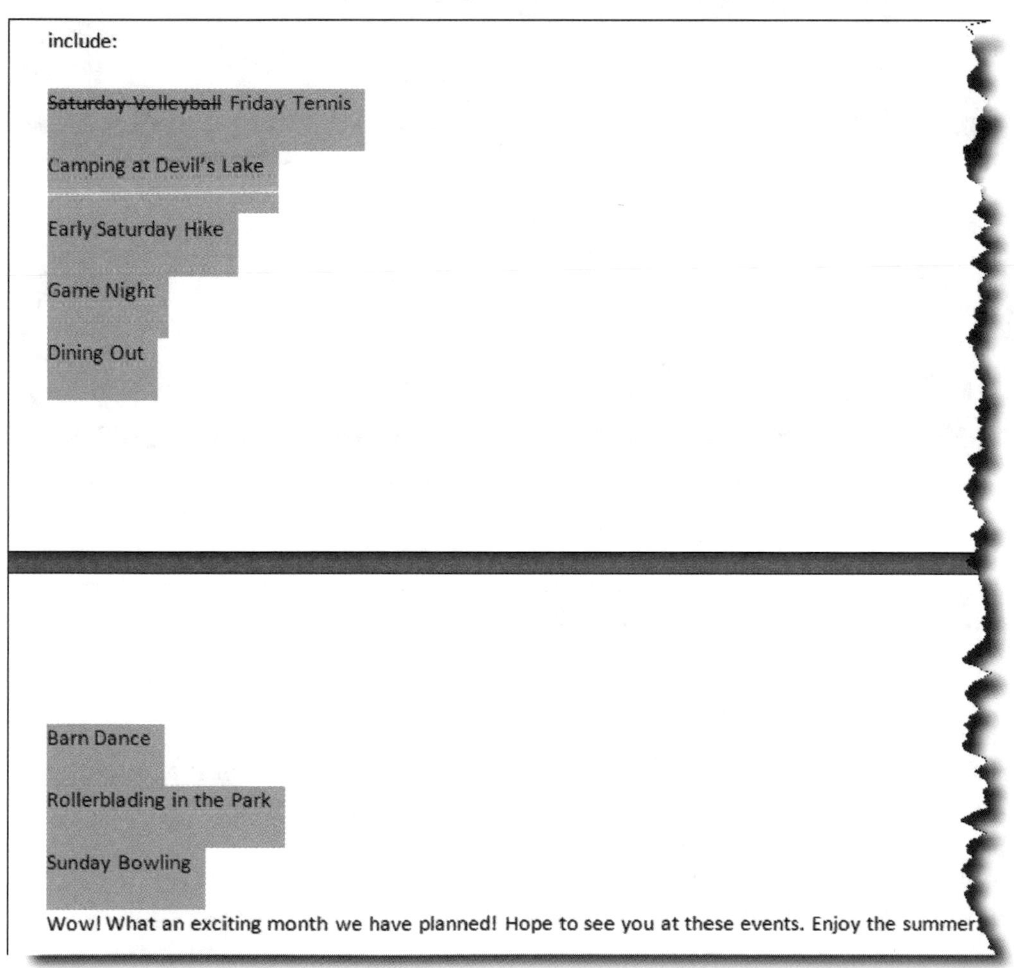

- Select the June events as shown in the screen shot.

Selects June events in the document.

- Click the **Bullets button** on the Ribbon.

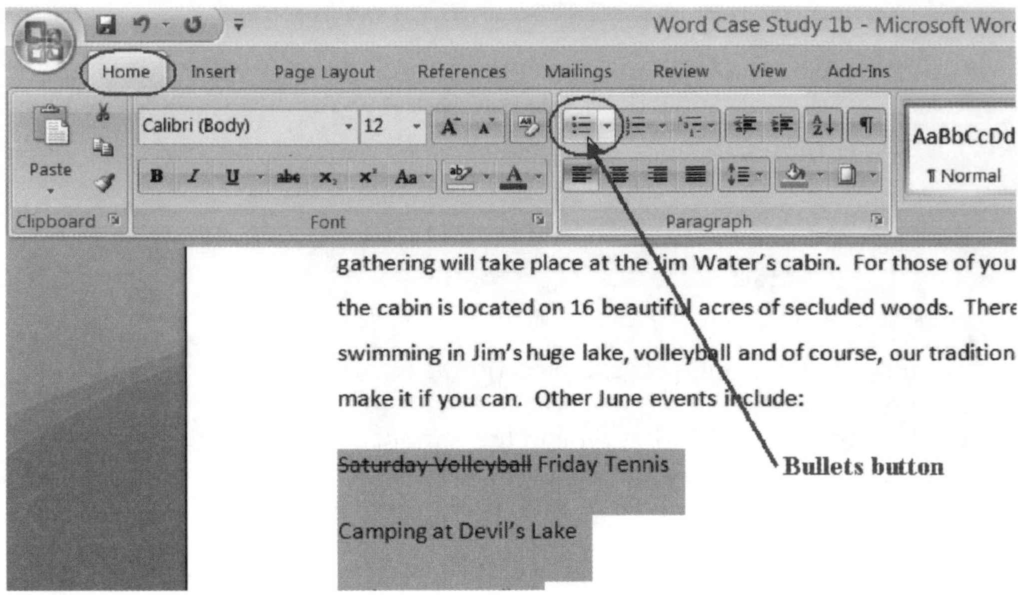

Transforms the list of data into a bulleted list.

- Click the drop-down arrow next to the Bullets icon and choose the sixth bullet in the first row.

Applies a new bullet image to the selected text.

- Click the **Save** button.

Saves the changes.

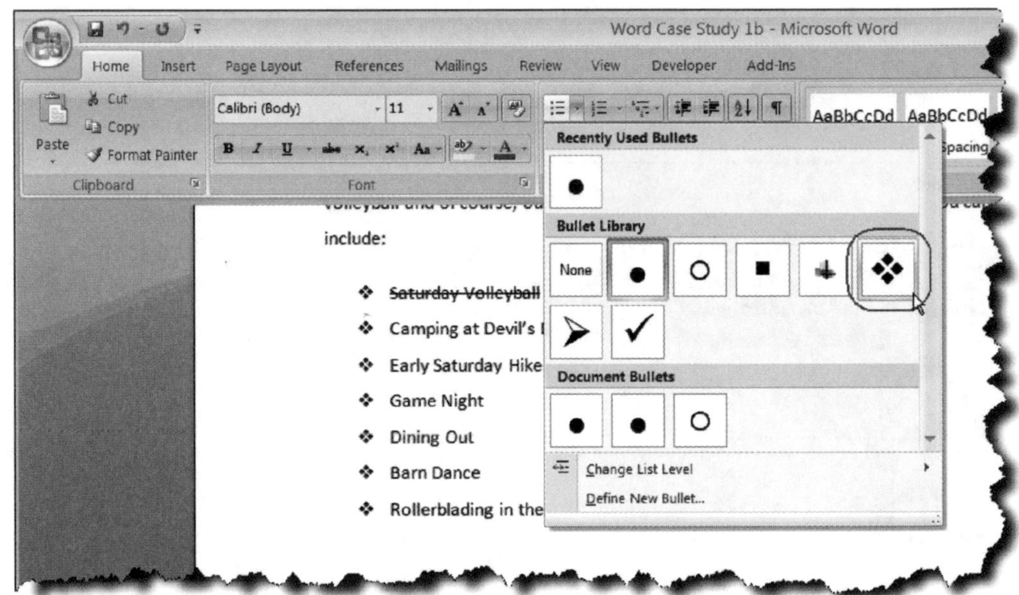

Indenting Paragraphs

In this section, you will learn how to indent a paragraph from the margins.

Paragraph indentation refers to the amount of extra white space from the left and/or right margins which you can add to a paragraph to set it apart from the other paragraphs in your document. Very often, you will see long quotations indented to set them apart from other text.

Paragraph indentation options are located under the **Indents and Spacing** tab of the Paragraph dialog box.

To Add Left and/or Right Paragraph Indentation

1. Click anywhere in the paragraph to which you wish to add indentation
2. Click the **Paragraph Dialog Launcher** on the Home Ribbon to display the Paragraph dialog box.
3. Click the **Indents and Spacing** tab.
4. Type the indentation amount (in inches) from the left margin in the **Left** box.
5. Type the indentation amount (in inches) from the right margin in the **Right** box.
6. Click **OK**.

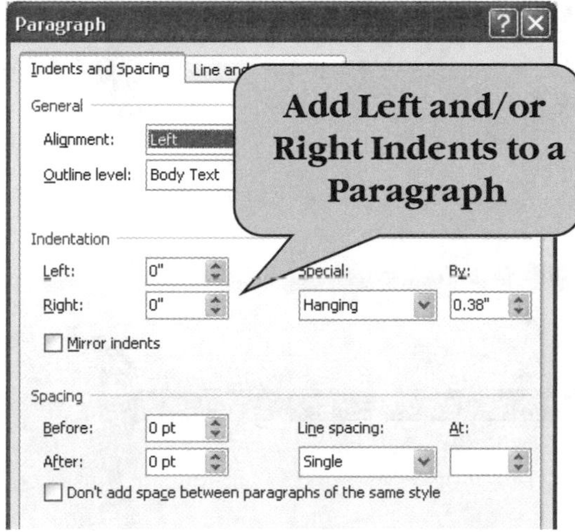

> **TIP:** You can also modify paragraph indentation from the **Page Layout** tab. Enter the Left and Right values under the Indent area of the Paragraph command set.

Let's Try It!

- Select June **events** if they are not already selected.

Selects the bullets to which we will apply indentation.

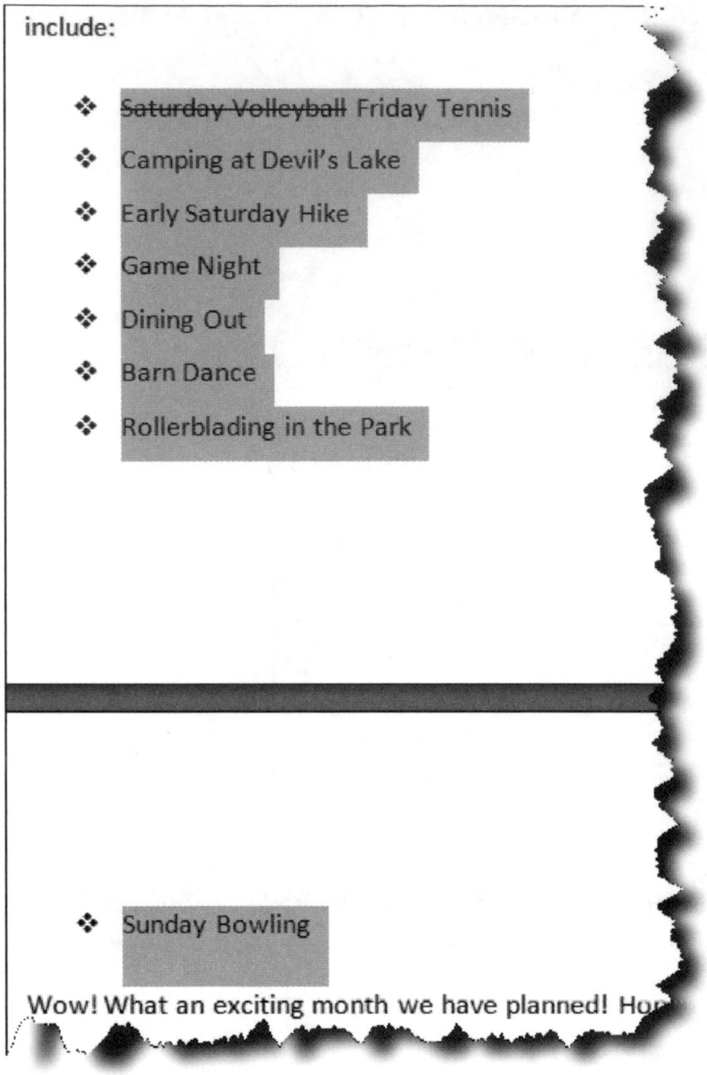

include:

- ~~Saturday Volleyball~~ Friday Tennis
- Camping at Devil's Lake
- Early Saturday Hike
- Game Night
- Dining Out
- Barn Dance
- Rollerblading in the Park

- Sunday Bowling

Wow! What an exciting month we have planned! Ho

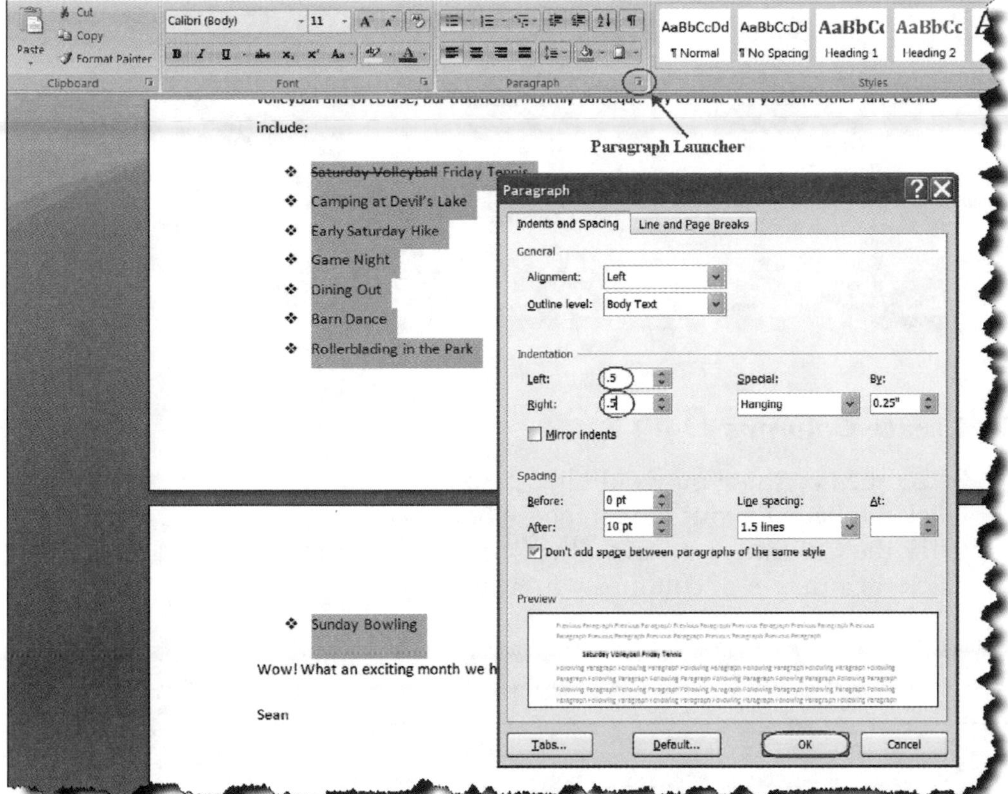

- Click the **Paragraph Launcher** on the Ribbon.

Displays the Paragraph dialog box.

- Under the **Indentation** area, type **.5** in the **Left** box as shown.

Sets an indentation of ½ inch from the left margin for the current paragraph.

- Press the **Tab** key and then type **.5** in the **Right** box.

Sets an indentation of ½ inch from the right margin for the current paragraph.

- Click **OK**.

Closes the Paragraph dialog box.

- Click the **Save** button.

Saves the changes.

Creating Columns

This section will guide you through the process of creating columns in your document.

With Microsoft Word, you can create newspaper-like columns in your document. You probably are most familiar with columns from your daily newspaper or even the newsletter that you receive in the mail, in which text flows down one column and continues on top of the second column. Whether creating newsletters or brochures, using columns can really add pizzazz to your documents.

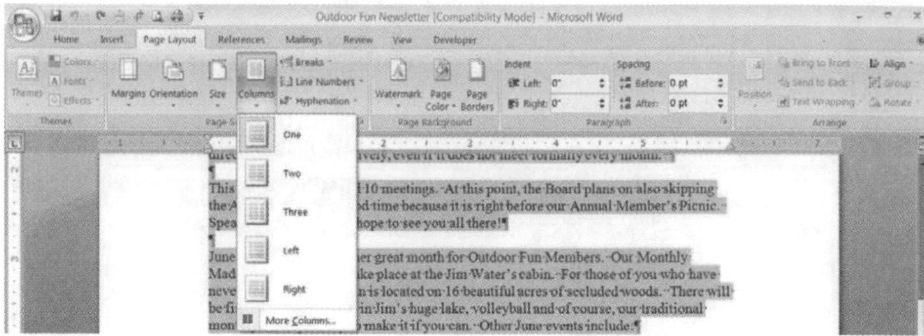

To Create Columns

1. Select the text that you would like placed in columns.
2. Click the **Page Layout tab** on the Ribbon.
3. Click the **Columns button** on the Page Setup group.
4. Click the number of columns you want.

Let's Try It!

- Select the entire document from **From the President** to the **end**.
- Click the **Page Layout tab** on the Ribbon.

Displays Page Layout commands and tools.

- Click the **Columns button** on the Page Setup group and click **Two** from the Columns menu.

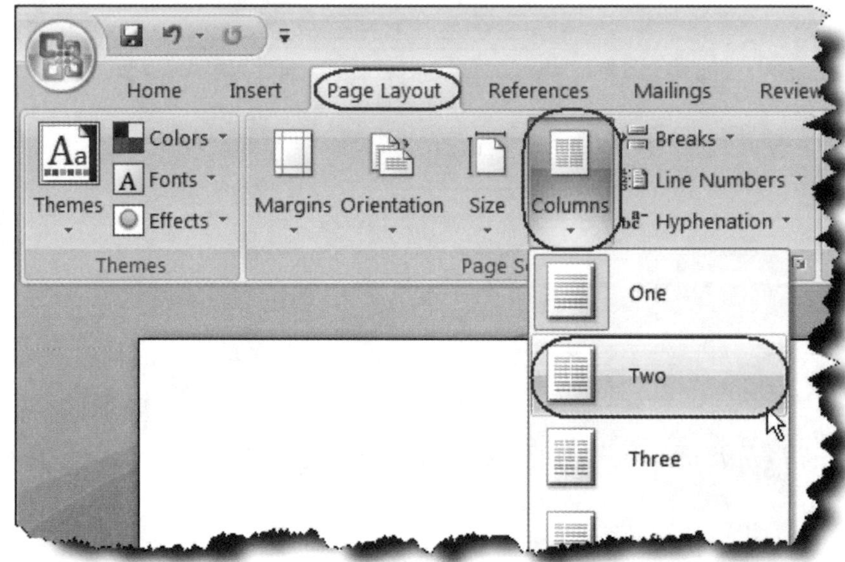

Inserts the selected text into a two-column layout.

- ~~Saturday Volleyball~~ Friday Tennis
- Camping at Devil's Lake
- Early Saturday Hike
- Game Night
- Dining Out
- Barn Dance
- Rollerblading in the Park
- Sunday Bowling
- Freshwater Fishing
- Water Park

Wow! What an exciting month we have planned! Hope to see you at these events. Enjoy the summer!

Sean

- Click after **Sunday Bowling**.
- Press **Enter key** once and add **Freshwater Fishing**.
- Press **Enter Key** again and add **Water Park** as shown in the screen shot.

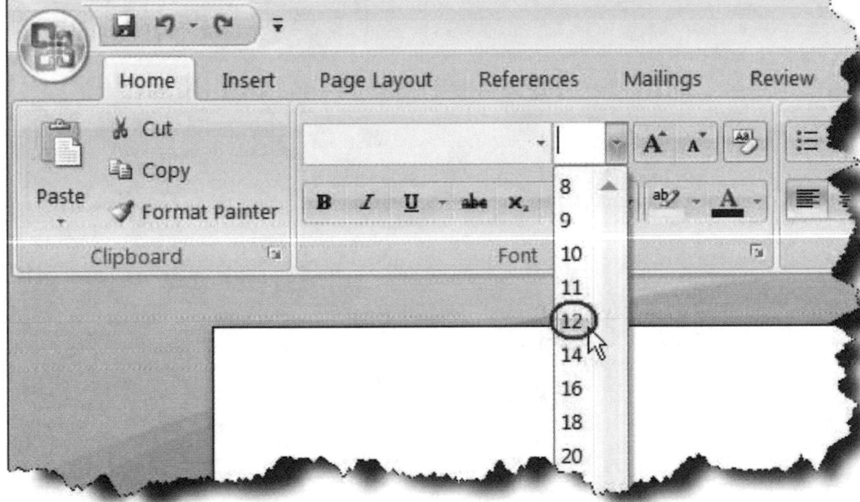

- Highlight the body of the newsletter from the word **reeting (exclude the first letter G)** to the last word: **Sean**.

Selects the text that we wish to modify.

- Select **Home** tab on the ribbon.
- Click the **Font Size** drop-down list on the Ribbon and select **12**.

Applies a font size of 12 pt to the selected text.

- Click the **Save** button.

Saves the changes.

Creating a Header and Footer

In this section, you will learn how to insert a Header and Footer into your document.

Often, you may have information that you want to appear at the top or bottom of every page, such as page numbers, document name, a company name, a company logo, or the document location. **Headers** repeat information at the top of every page and **Footers** repeat information at the bottom of every page. You can add a Header or Footer to your document from the **Insert** tab. Click on the Header or Footer button to display a list of built-in headers or footers from which you can choose. After you insert a header or footer, added your text and closed the Header and Footer window, your document will be displayed in Print Layout view, allowing you to see the header and footer sections of your document.

Once the Header/Footer is activated, you can type your text directly into the Header/Footer window. Additionally, you can access the Ribbo, allowing you to insert a variety of special codes such as page number, current date and time, etc. Clicking on the **Go to Footer** or **Go to Header** button allows you to jump back and forth from Header view to Footer view.

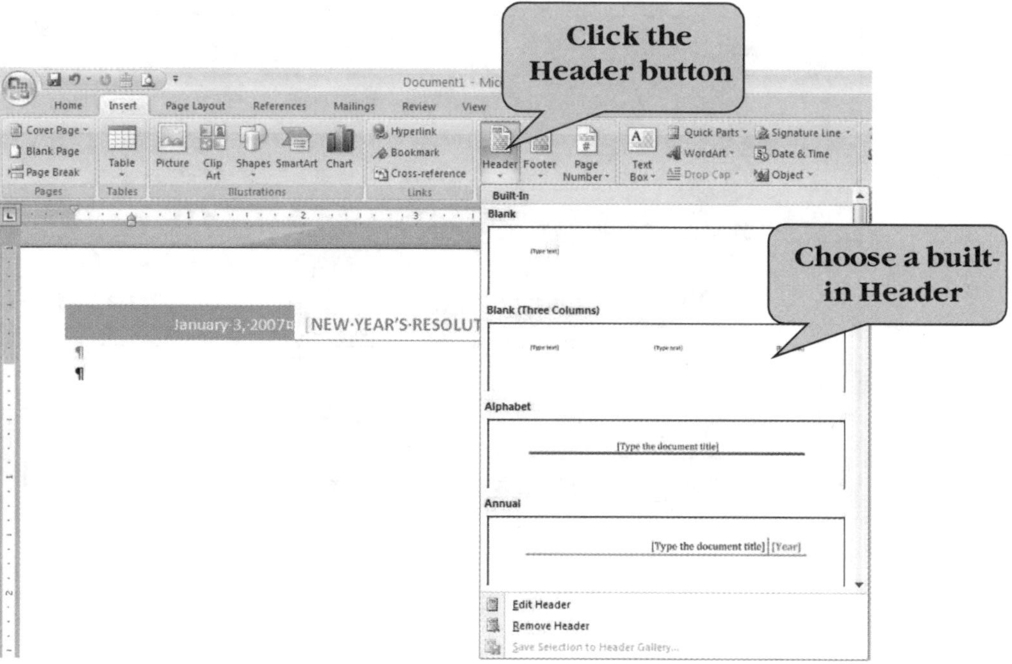

To Create a Header and Footer

1. Click the **Insert** tab.
2. Click the **Header** or **Footer** button on the Ribbon.
3. Click the desired **built-in header or footer** from the gallery.
4. Type your text in the Header or Footer window or choose the appropriate command button (Date & Time, Page Number, etc.) from the Ribbon.

5. To switch between the header and footer, click the **Go to Header** or **Go to Footer** button on the Ribbon.
6. When finished, click the **Close Header and Footer** button on the Ribbon
   Or
   Double-click anywhere outside of the Header or Footer window.

Let's Try It!

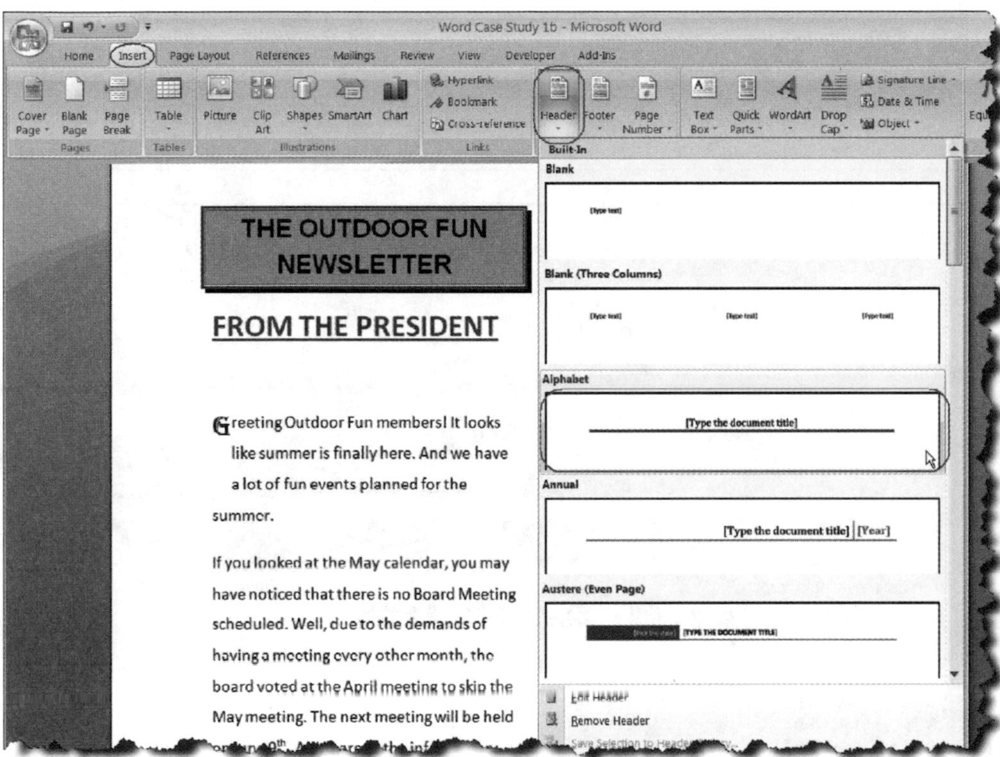

- Click the **Insert** tab on the Ribbon.

Switches to Insert commands and tools.

- Click the **Header** button on the Ribbon.

Displays a gallery of available built-in headers.

- Click the **Alphabet** header style.

Selects the header style we wish to use.

- Press the **Ctrl + A** keystroke combination.

Selects all of the default Header text. We want to replace it with our own.

- Type: **New Conversations**.

Enters text into the Header window.

- Click the **Go To Footer** button as shown.

Switches to the Footer.

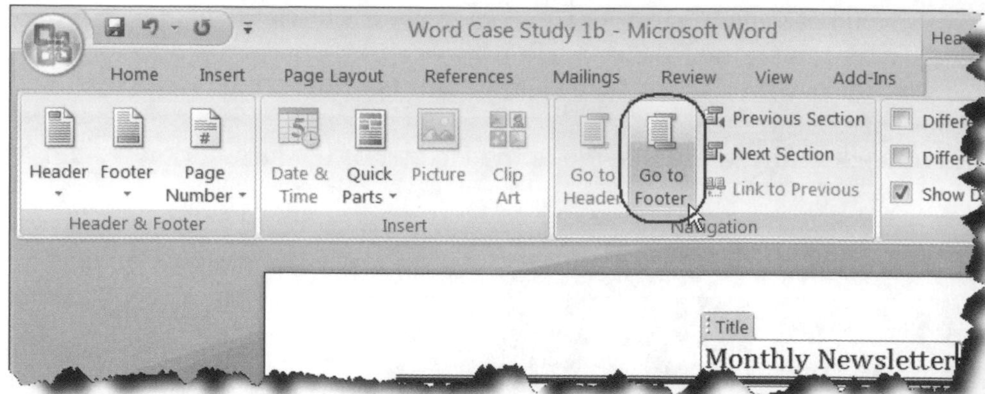

- Click the **Date & Time** button on the Ribbon.

Displays the Date & Time dialog box.

- Click the **first** date format in the list as shown and then click **OK**.

Inserts the current date in the footer.

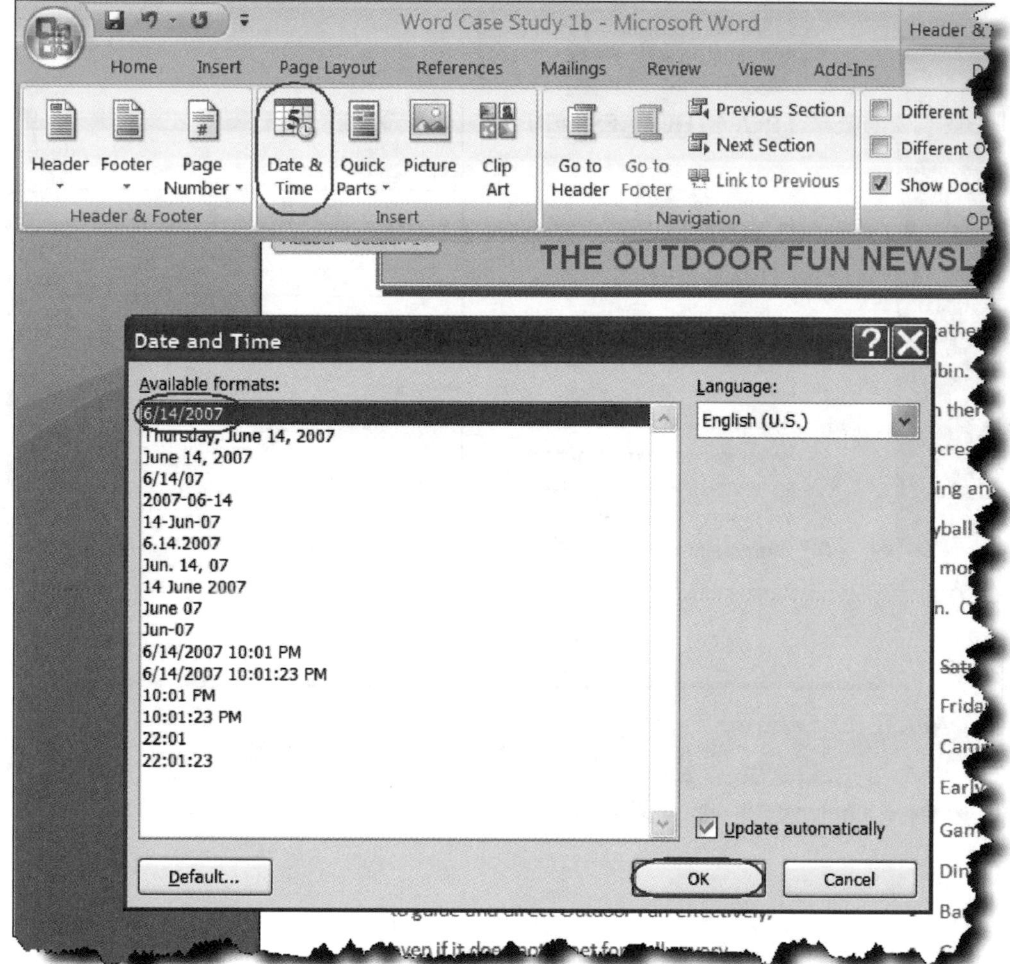

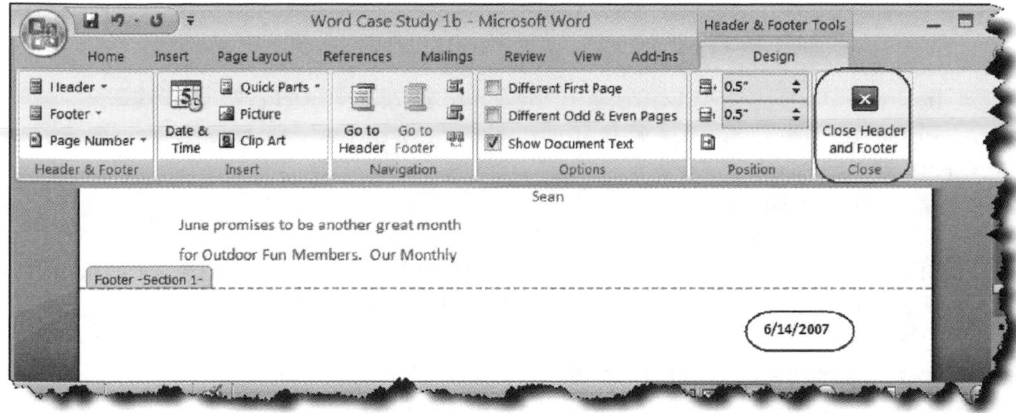

- Press the **Ctrl + R** keystroke combination.

Applies right alignment to the date code. You could also have clicked the right alignment button on the Home Ribbon.

- Click the **Close Header and Footer** button on the Insert Ribbon.

Returns to Print Layout view.

- Scroll up and down to observe the Header and Footer that you created.
- Click the **Save** button.

Saves the changes.

Inserting a Watermark

In this section, you will learn how to insert a Watermark behind the text of your document.

Watermarks are faint text or graphic images that appear behind document text. Watermarks are often used to indentify the type or status of a document, such as "Confidential" or "Draft" or to add a company logo to the background. Watermarks are light enough so that they do not interfere with the reading of the document text and are intended for printed documents. You can choose from a gallery of pre-configured Watermarks or customize your own.

To Insert a Watermark

1. Click the **Page Layout tab**.
2. Click the **Watermark** button on the Page Background command set.
3. To insert a pre-configured watermark, choose the watermark you want from the gallery.
4. To insert a custom watermark:
   a. Click **Custom Watermark**.
   b. To insert a background picture, select **Picture**, click the **Select Picture** button, and then navigate to the location of the picture.
   c. To insert background text, select **Text**, and then either choose preset text option from the **Text** drop down list or type your own in the **Text** box.
   d. Choose any additional watermark options.
   e. Click **OK**.

Let's Try It!

- Click the **Page Layout** tab and then click on **Page Borders** button.

Displays the Page Borders dialog box.

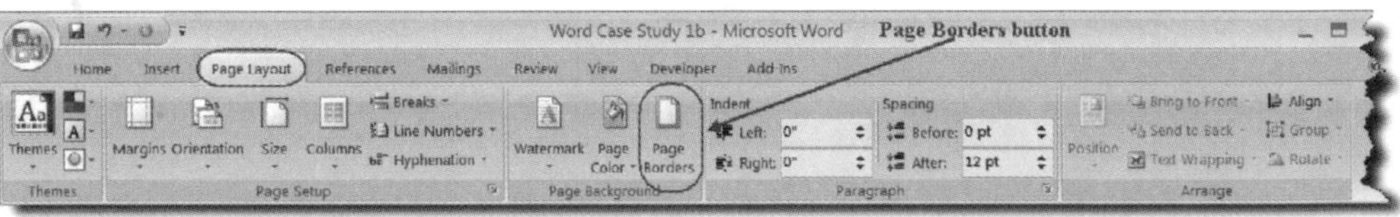

- Scroll down in the Art drop down list and select the shown **Art** for Page Border.
- Click **Ok**.

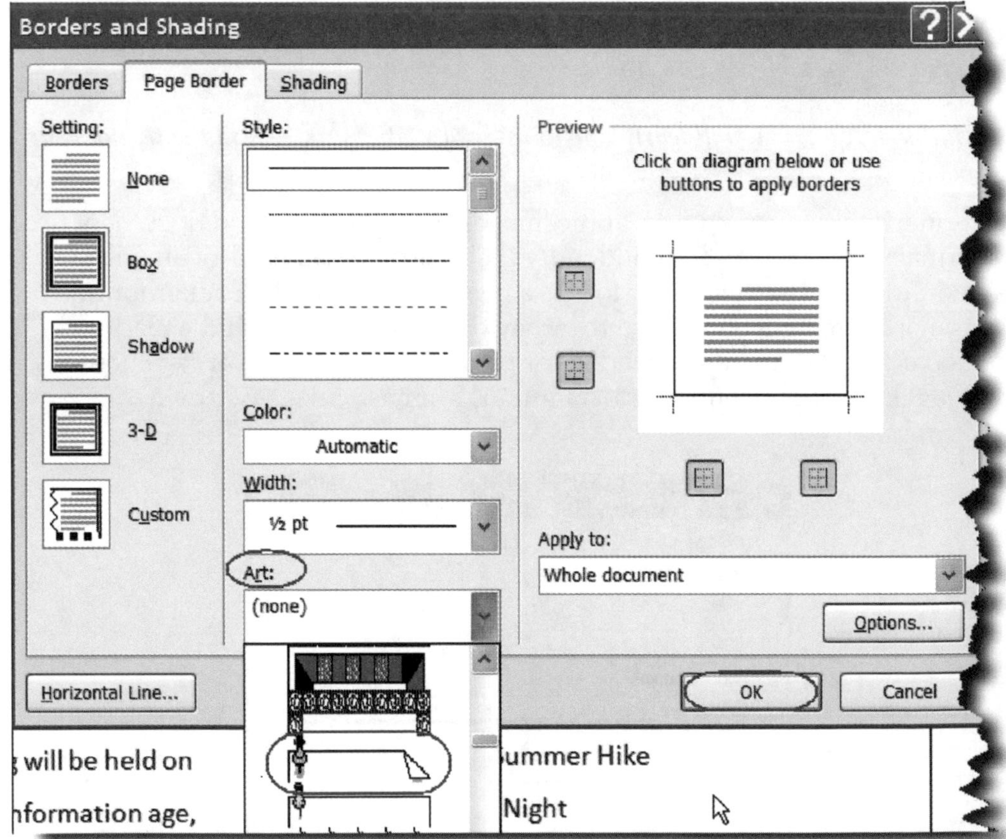

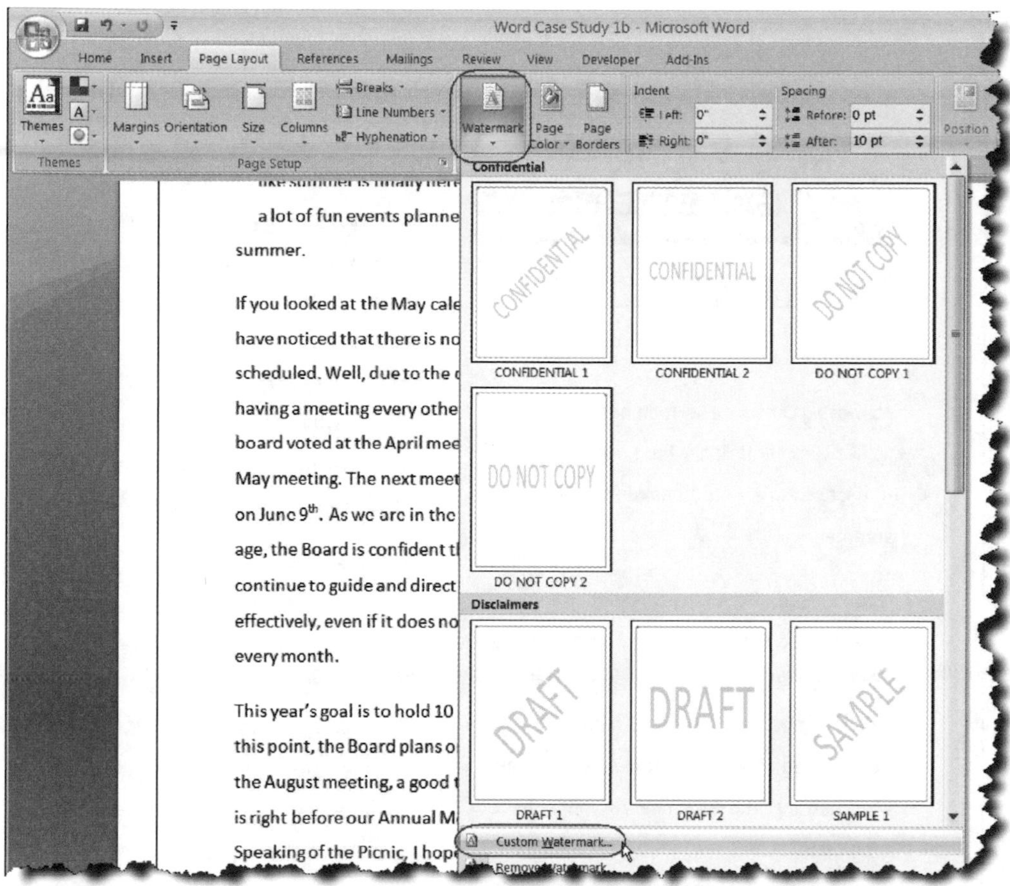

- Click the **Watermark** button on the Page Background group.

Displays a gallery of pre-designed watermarks.

- Click the **Custom Watermark** option on the menu.

Displays the Printed Watermark dialog box, allowing us to create our own custom watermark.

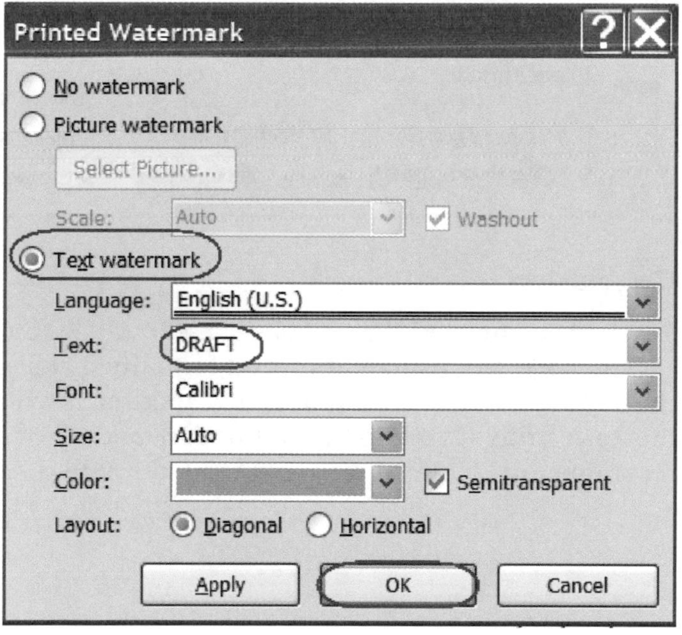

- Click the radio button next to **Text watermark**.

Selects text as the Watermark type.

- In the box next to **Text**:, type: **DRAFT**.

Enters the text for the Watermark.

- Click **OK**.

Closes the Printed Watermark dialog box.

- **Scroll** until you see the Watermark on the page.

Observe the watermark. Notice that the Watermark appears on each page of the document.

- Click the **Save** button.

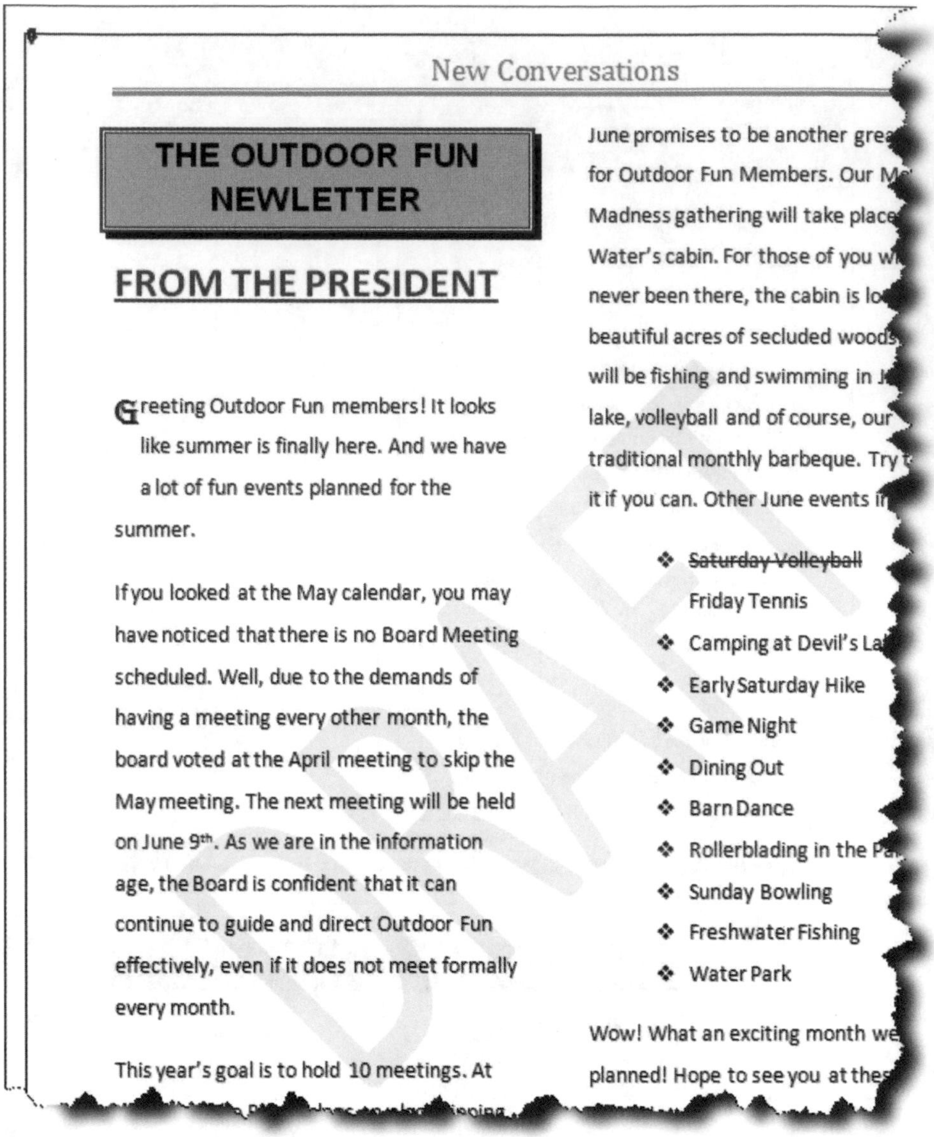

New Conversations

THE OUTDOOR FUN NEWLETTER

FROM THE PRESIDENT

Greeting Outdoor Fun members! It looks like summer is finally here. And we have a lot of fun events planned for the summer.

If you looked at the May calendar, you may have noticed that there is no Board Meeting scheduled. Well, due to the demands of having a meeting every other month, the board voted at the April meeting to skip the May meeting. The next meeting will be held on June 9th. As we are in the information age, the Board is confident that it can continue to guide and direct Outdoor Fun effectively, even if it does not meet formally every month.

This year's goal is to hold 10 meetings. At

June promises to be another grea for Outdoor Fun Members. Our M Madness gathering will take place Water's cabin. For those of you w never been there, the cabin is lo beautiful acres of secluded wood will be fishing and swimming in J lake, volleyball and of course, our traditional monthly barbeque. Try t it if you can. Other June events i

- ~~Saturday Volleyball~~
- Friday Tennis
- Camping at Devil's La
- Early Saturday Hike
- Game Night
- Dining Out
- Barn Dance
- Rollerblading in the Pa
- Sunday Bowling
- Freshwater Fishing
- Water Park

Wow! What an exciting month we planned! Hope to see you at thes

DRAFT

Conclusion

You have completed Word 2007—Case Study I. You are now ready to use several basic MS Word editing and formatting skills that you have learned in this chapter. You are encouraged to experiment with all you have learned in this case study. To reinforce your understanding of these techniques, it is recommended that you read and work through it once again.

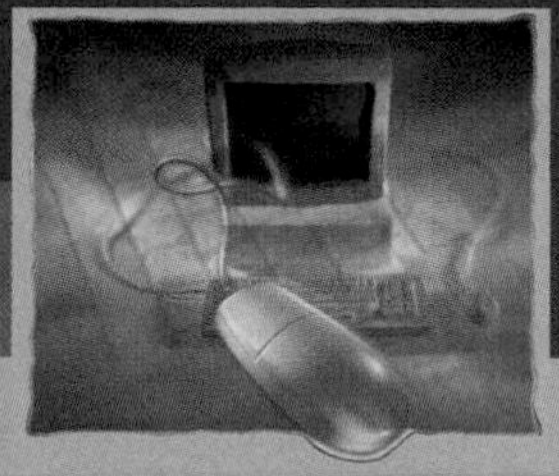

Word Case Study 2

CHAPTER

4

OBJECTIVES

After successfully completing this case study, you should able to:

- Use Existing Templates
- Create and Format a Table
- Insert and Delete Rows and Columns
- Merge Cells
- Create a Form
- Resize a Form
- Add a Text Field to a Form
- Add a Date Picker field to a Form
- Add a Check-Box to a Form
- Add a Drop-down List to a Form
- Add Help to Form Fields
- Protect a Form
- Use a Form Template
- Use Help

Case Study 2—MS Word 2007

This case study is divided into two parts.

Part I: Assume that your company has a Conference Evaluation form that you are asked to fax to all attendees so their comments can help in better planning and executing future conferences. You decided to use MS Word 2007 fax template to create a fax cover page.

The desired fax cover page looks like the following:

FAX

To:	Lisa Wang	**From:**	Kammy Sanghera
Fax:	555-222-6532	**Pages:**	1
Phone:	555-694-7030	**Date:**	8.27.2007
Re:	Conference Evaluation Form	**CC:**	Suman Sanghera

☐ Urgent ☐ For Review ☐ Please Comment ☒ Please Reply ☐ Please Recycle

Comments:

[Type comments]

CONFERENCE EVALUATION FORM FAX IN MICROSOFT WORD

Part II: You are not very impressed with collecting attendees' comments via fax or in a snail mail. You propose to create a MS Word form that can be downloaded from Company's web site or emailed to attendees. Your boss likes your proposal and asks you to create a sample of the form.

The desired sample evaluation form looks like the following:

Conference Evaluation Form

Please help us evaluate the conference by responding to the following questions. Your comments will enable us to better plan and execute future conferences.			
Name of Attendee:			
Date of Conference:	Click here to enter a date.		
How would you rate the Key Note Address?	☐ **Poor**	☐ **Good**	☐ **Excellent**
What is your occupation?	Administration (Administration, Architecture, Education, Engineering, Law, Technical)		

CONFERENCE EVALUATION FORM IN MICROSOFT WORD

Using Existing Templates

In this section, you will learn how to create a new document using an existing Microsoft Word Template.

Microsoft Word has several **pre-designed templates** that you can use to create new documents, saving you the time of creating documents from scratch. Templates are documents that already contain formatting, layout design and commonly used text. Some templates available include letters and faxes, reports, brochures—even web pages. If you find yourself using the same layout, formatting, or wording over and over, using templates can really be a timesaver.

To use a template, create a new document based on a template and fill in the data—the design and formatting process is already done for you. You can use the installed templates that came with Word or download hundreds of additional templates from Microsoft Office Online.

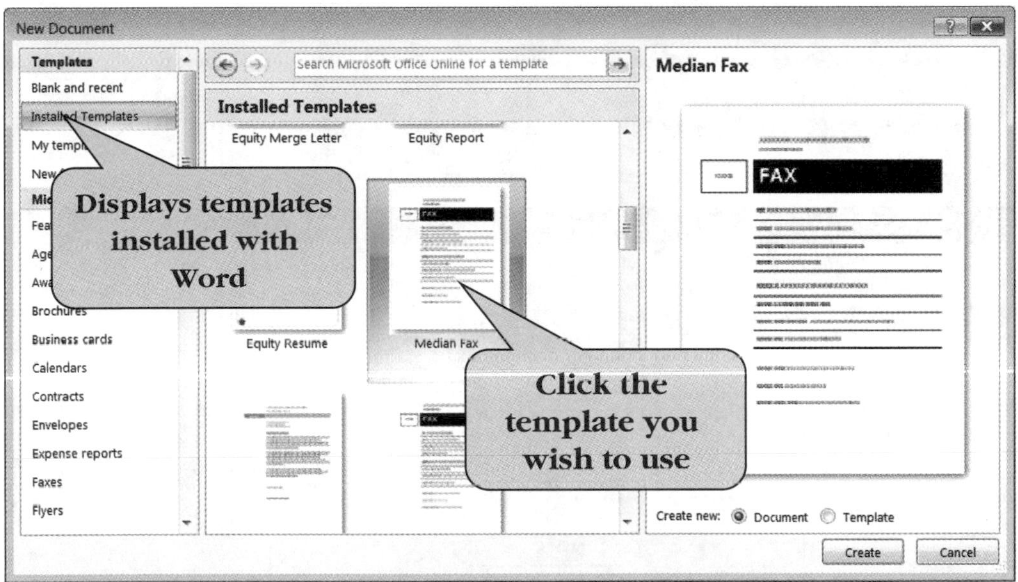

To Create a Document from a Word Template

1. Click the **Microsoft Office Button** and then click **New**.
2. Click **Installed Templates** in the left pane.
3. Click the template you want and then click the **Create button**.
4. To view additional templates from **Microsoft Office Online**:
   a. Under the **Microsoft Office Online** category in the left pane, click the template category.
   b. Select the template you want to use.
   c. Click **Download** to install the template on your computer.

Let's Try It!

- Open **Microsoft Word**

Opens the Microsoft Word application.

- Click the **Microsoft Office Button** and then click **New** from the menu.

Displays New Document Task Pane.

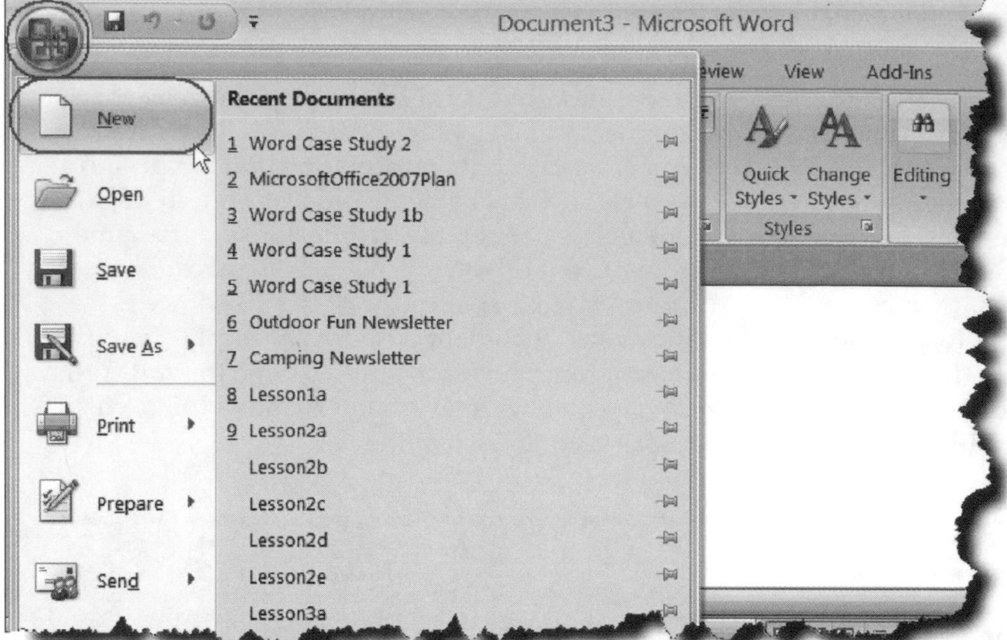

- Under the **Templates** area in the left pane, click **Installed Templates**.

Displays a list of templates that are installed on your computer in the center pane.

- Click the **Equity Fax** template in the center pane.

Selects the template that we will use.

- In the **Create New** area, make sure that the **Document** radio button is selected.

Sets the option to create a new document from the template.

- Click the **Create** button.

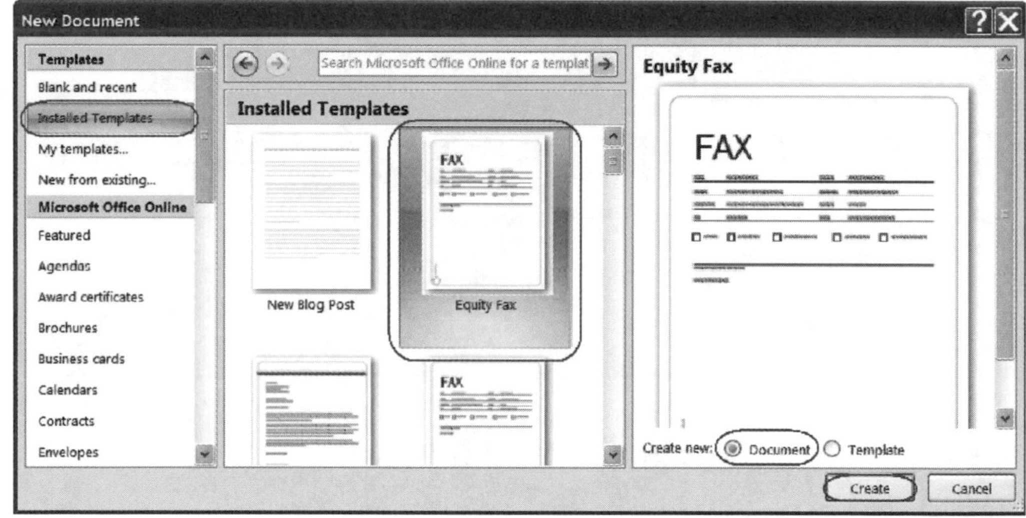

FAX

To:	Lisa Wang	From:	ksanghera
Fax:	[Type the recipient fax number]	Pages:	[Type number of pages]
Phone:	[Type the recipient phone number]	Date:	[Pick the date]
Re:	[Type text]	CC:	[Type text]

Creates a new document based upon the Equity template.

- Click in the **[Type the recipient name]** area after the **To** column, and type: **Lisa Wang**.

Enters information in the "To" area of the fax.

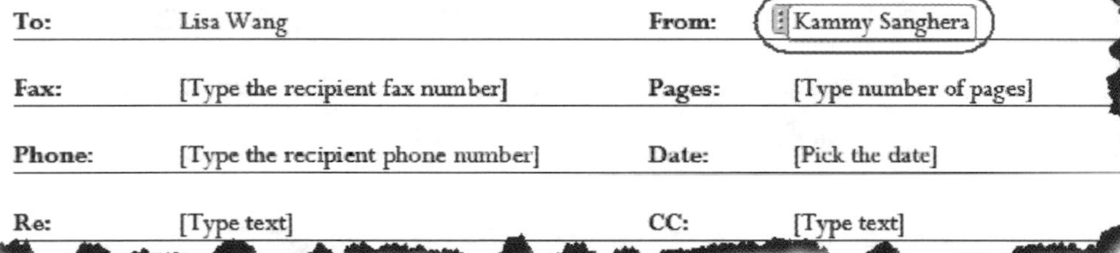

FAX

To:	Lisa Wang	From:	Kammy Sanghera
Fax:	[Type the recipient fax number]	Pages:	[Type number of pages]
Phone:	[Type the recipient phone number]	Date:	[Pick the date]
Re:	[Type text]	CC:	[Type text]

- Press the **Tab** key twice.

Moves to the From field.

- Type: **Kammy Sanghera**

Enters info in the From field.

FAX

To:	Lisa Wang	From:	Kammy Sanghera
Fax:	555-222-6532	Pages:	[Type number of pages]
Phone:	[Type the recipient phone number]	Date:	[Pick the date]
Re:	[Type text]	CC:	[Type text]

- Press the **Tab** key.

Moves to the Fax number field.

- Type: **555-222-6532**

Enters the fax number in the fax field.

- Press the **Tab** key twice.

Moves to the Pages field

- Type: **1**

Enters "1" in the Pages field.

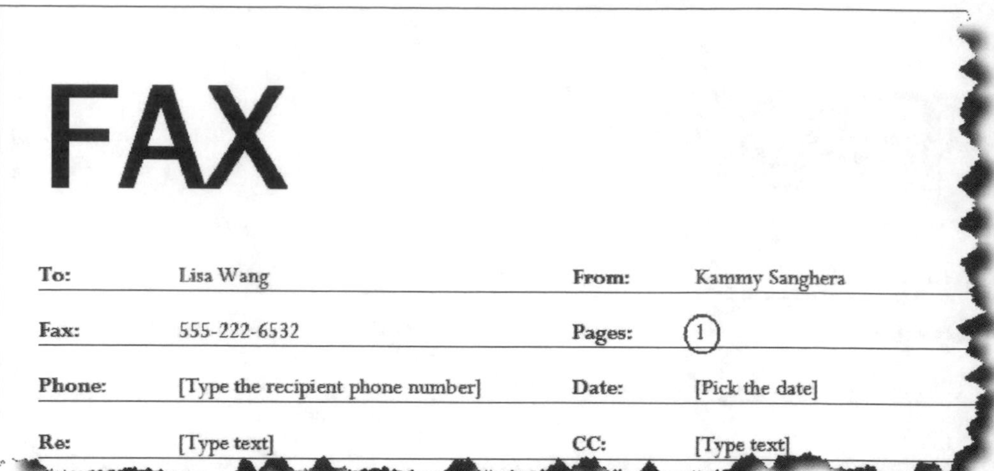

- Press the **Tab** key twice.

Moves to the recipient Phone Number field

- Type: **555-694-7030**

Enters the phone number in the phone field.

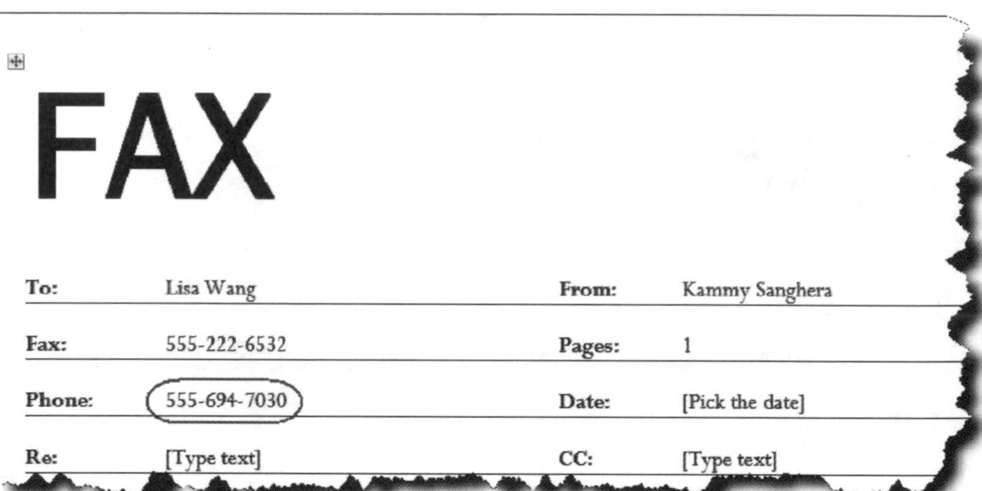

- Press the **Tab** key twice.

Moves to the Date field

- Type: **8/27/2007**

Enters info in the Date field. You could also click the drop-down arrow and choose a date from the calendar.

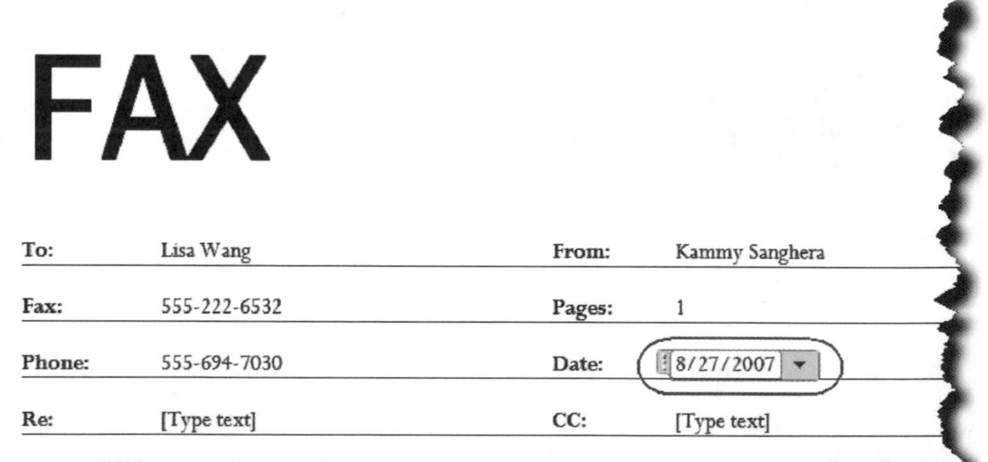

FAX

To:	Lisa Wang	From:	Kammy Sanghera
Fax:	555-222-6532	Pages:	1
Phone:	555-694-7030	Date:	8.27.2007
Re:	Conference Evaluation Form	CC:	[Type text]

☐ Urgent ☐ For Review ☐ Please Comment ☐ Please Reply ☐ Please Recycle

- Press the **Tab** key.

Moves to the Re: field.

- Type: **Conference Evaluation Form**.

Enters info in the Re: field.

FAX

To:	Lisa Wang	From:	Kammy Sanghera
Fax:	555-222-6532	Pages:	1
Phone:	555-694-7030	Date:	8.27.2007
Re:	Conference Evaluation Form	CC:	Suman Sanghera

☐ Urgent ☐ For Review ☐ Please Comment ☐ Please Reply ☐ Please Recycle

- Press the **Tab** key twice.

Moves to the CC: field.

- Type: **Suman Sanghera**.

Enters info in the CC (Carbon Copy) field.

- Click in the **Please Reply** box and type **x**

Enters an "x" in the "Please Reply" box.

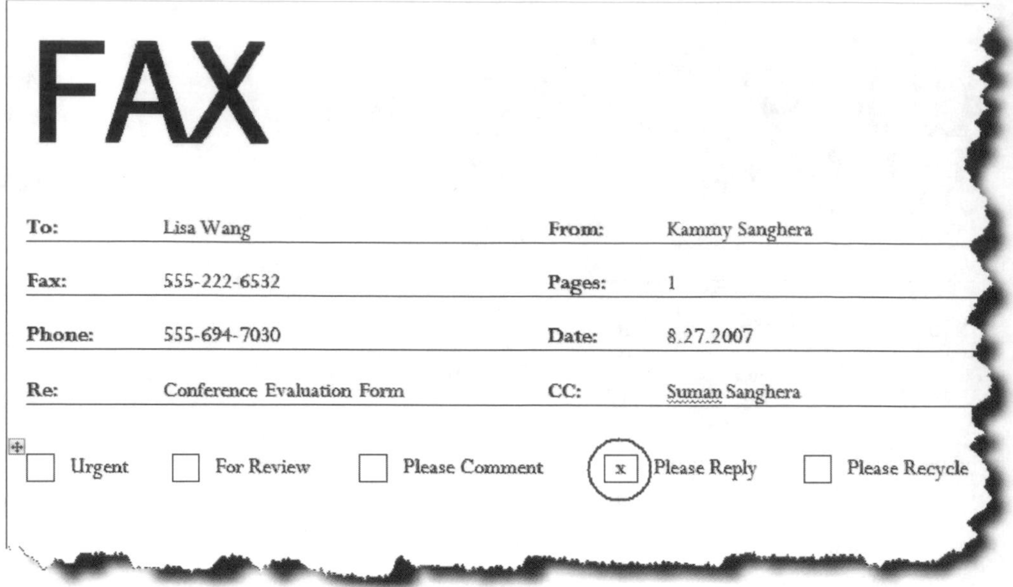

FAX

To:	Lisa Wang	From:	Kammy Sanghera
Fax:	555-222-6532	Pages:	1
Phone:	555-694-7030	Date:	8.27.2007
Re:	Conference Evaluation Form	CC:	Suman Sanghera

☐ Urgent ☐ For Review ☐ Please Comment [x] Please Reply ☐ Please Recycle

---

- Insert **flash drive** in USB port.
- Click the **Save button** on the Quick Access toolbar.

As we have not yet saved our document, the Save As dialog box appears, prompting us for the file name and location where we wish to save the file.

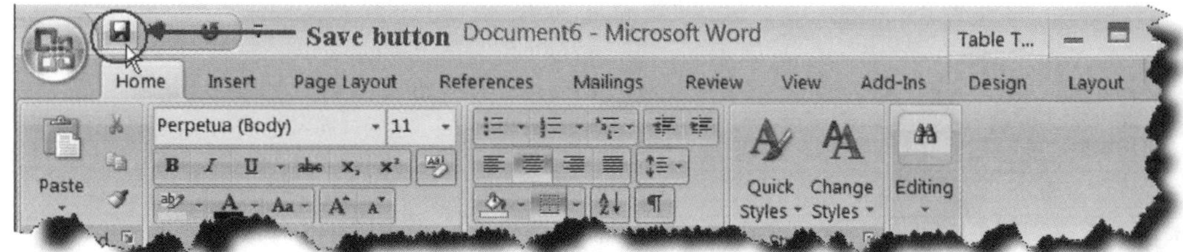

- In the **File name** text box, type: **Evaluation Form Fax** and **select flash drive** in the Save in list.

Enters a file name for the new document.

- Click the **Save** button.

Saves the file with the new name.

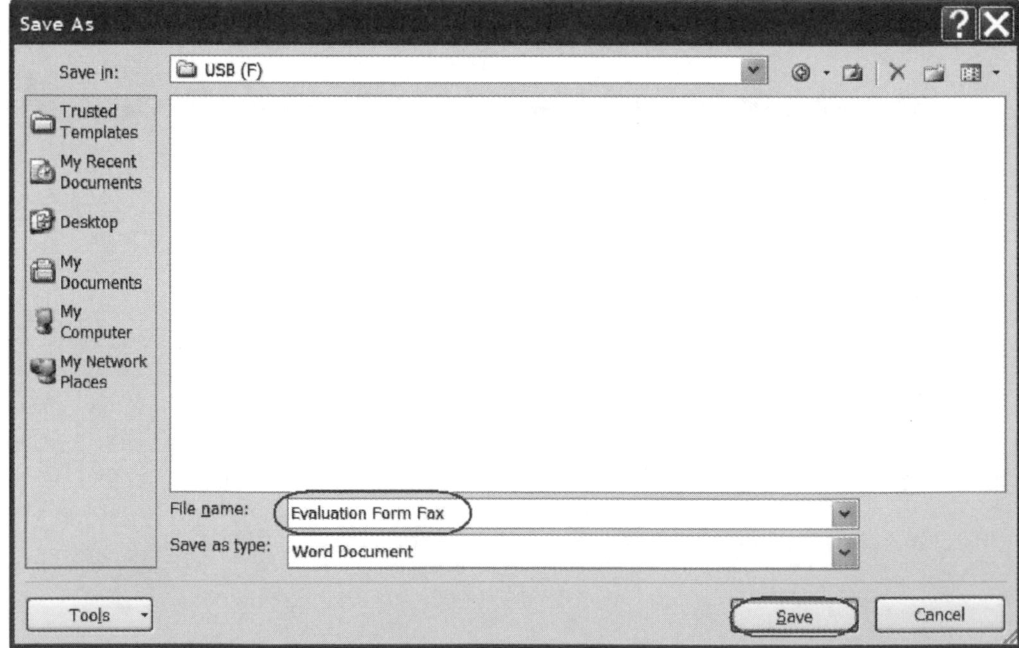

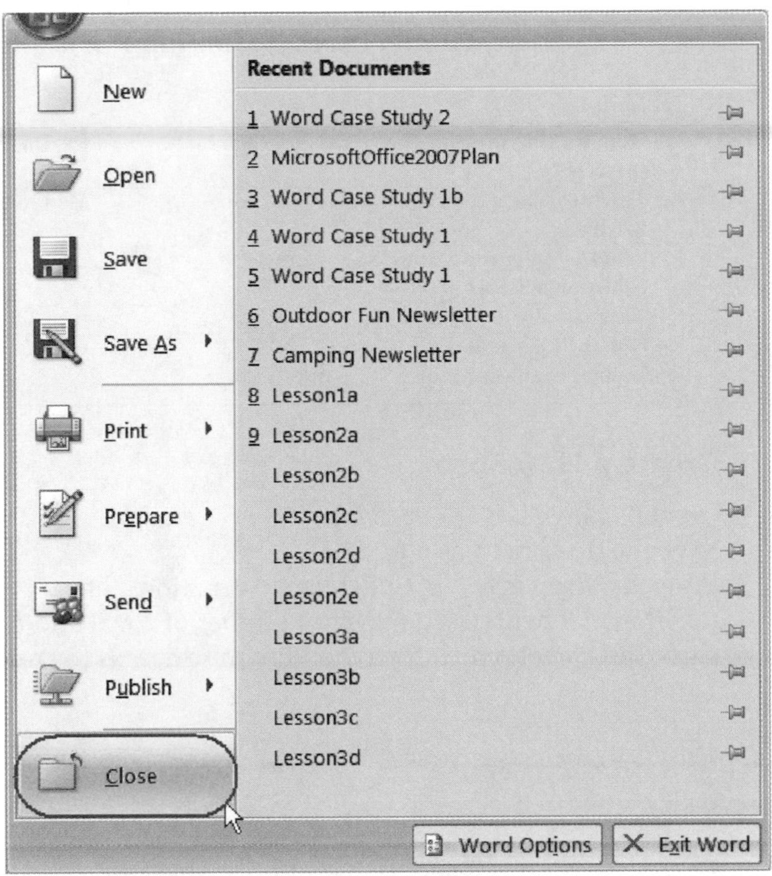

- Click the **Microsoft Office button** and choose **Close** from the File Options menu.

Closes the active document.

Creating a Form

In this section, you will create a new form.

A **form** is a prearranged document with spaces reserved for entering information. It is a means of collecting information. You are most likely already familiar with paper forms, such as customer surveys, employment applications, etc. Microsoft Word allows you to create electronic forms that you can distribute to those from whom you need information. These electronic forms can contain drop-down lists or check-boxes, making the gathering of data more accurate.

Electronic forms are usually based upon templates. This allows the user to enter data into the form, without changing the formatting of the form or the form text. It's a good idea to lay out your form on paper first as this will make designing your form in Word much easier.

When you're ready to create your form, you may wish to consider using a table. Tables allow you to easily align your text and form fields.

Note that the form tools are located on the **Developer Ribbon**. If the Developer tab is not visible, click the Microsoft Office button, click Word Options, click the Popular category and then click the **Show Developer Tab in the Ribbon** checkbox.

Conference·Evaluation·Form¶

¶

Name:··¶

1.→ How·would·you·rate·the·speaker?¤	**··Good¤**	**·Poor¤**	**·Excellent¤**	¤
2.→ The·information·I·received·was:¤	**·Poor¤**	**·Good¤**	**·Excellent¤**	¤
3.→ Would·you·recommend·this·conference·to·others?¤	**Yes¤**	¤	¤	¤
4.→ Name¤	°°°°°¤	¤	¤	¤
5.→ Date·of·Conference¤	°°°°°¤	¤	¤	¤
6.→ Your·Occupation:¤	¤	¤	¤	¤

To Create a New Form

1. Create a new blank document.
2. Save the document as a template.
3. Enter the form text (i.e. title, form instructions, etc.)
4. Insert a table with the necessary number of rows and columns.
5. Click the **Developer tab** on the Ribbon to access form tools.

Let's Try It!

- Open **Microsoft Word** if not already opened.

Opens the Microsoft Word application and creates a new blank document.

- Click the **Microsoft Office button** and then click **Word Options**.

Displays the Word options dialog box. We will add the Developer Tab to the Ribbon if it has not already been done.

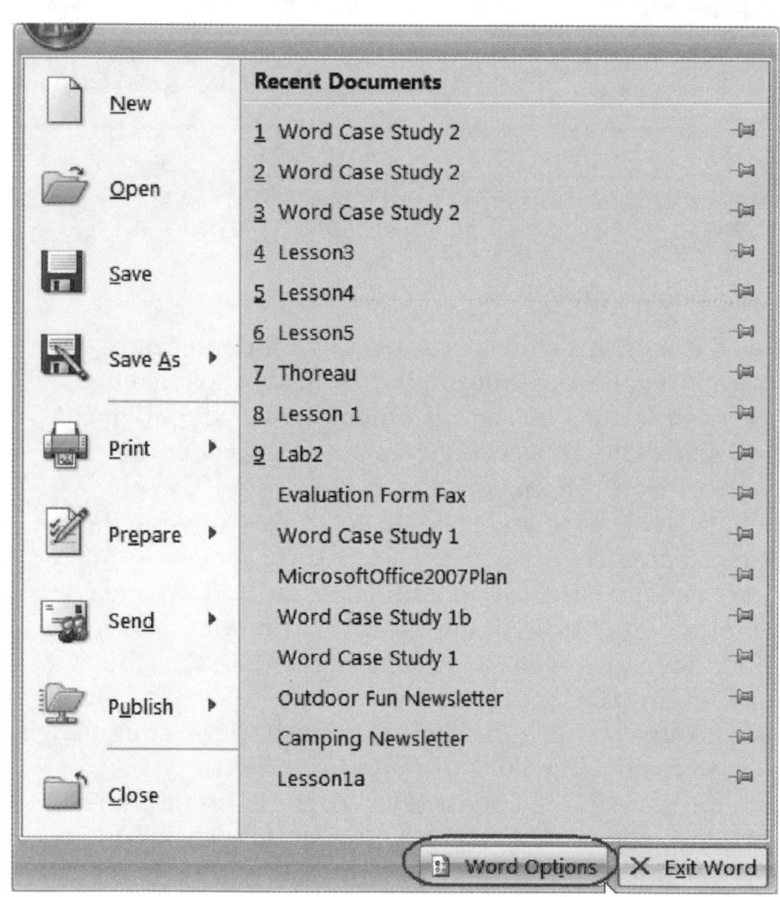

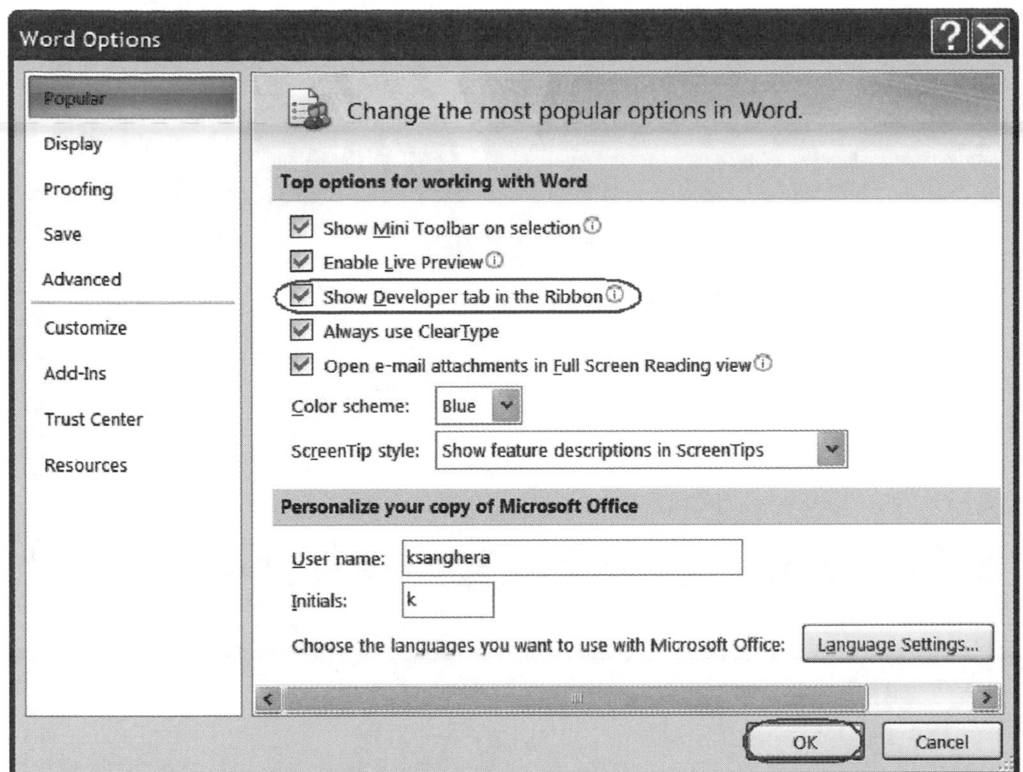

- Ensure that the **Show Developer Tab in the Ribbon** checkbox is checked. If it is not, click the checkbox to check it. Click **OK**.

Adds the Developer Tab to the Ribbon and returns us to our blank document.

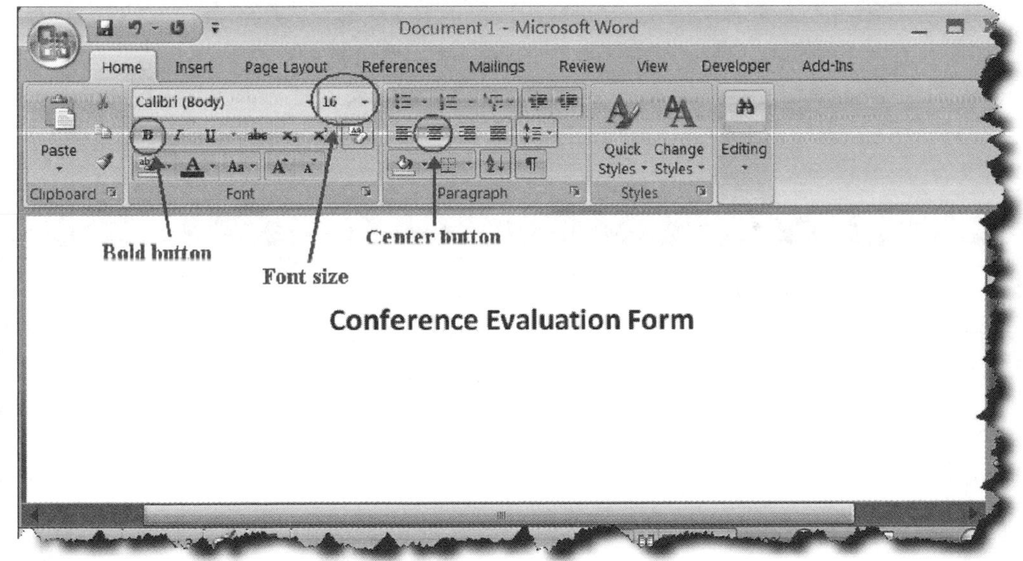

- Click the **Bold** icon on the Ribbon and then change the **font size** to **16 pt**.

Sets the formatting for the form title.

- Click the **Center** alignment button and type: **Conference Evaluation Form**.

- Press **Enter** twice.

Inserts two blank lines after the title.

- Change the **font size** to **12 pt.** and then click the **Align Left** button.

Changes the font size to 12 pt. and left-aligns the text.

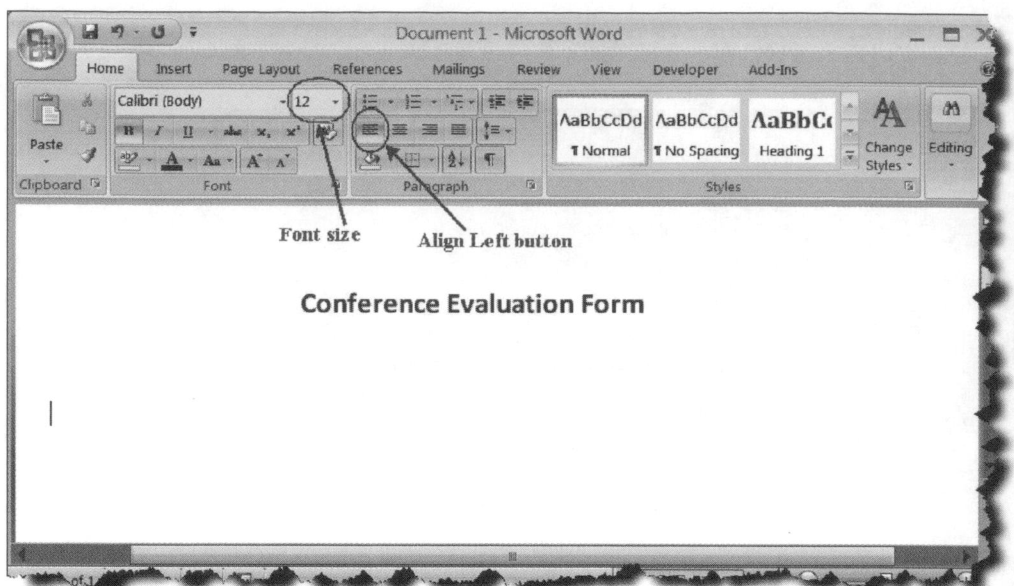

- Click the **Save** button.

Displays the Save As dialog box.

- Select **Word Template** from the **Save as type** drop-down list.

Selects Word Template as the file format.

- In the **File name** box, type: **Word Case Study 2** as shown.

Enters a name for the form.

- Click the **Save** button.

Saves the form as a template with the name "Word Case Study 2".

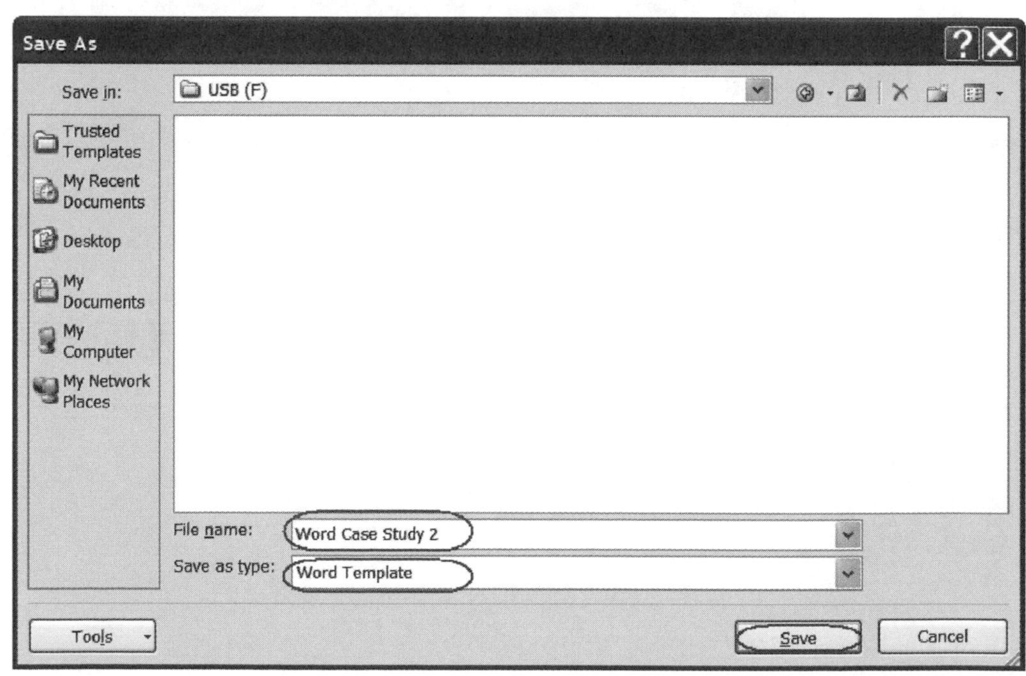

Creating a Table

In this section, you will learn how to insert a table object, organized in columns and rows

Tables are a great way to organize and present columnar data. You can use tables for a variety of tasks such as preparing a budget, tracking inventory, presenting budget and sales data or even creating a monthly calendar. A table is organized in **rows** (the horizontal divisions) and **columns** (the vertical divisions). Data is entered into table **cells**, the intersection of the columns and rows.

You can use tables whenever you need to present columnar data. In fact, some people like tables so much and find them so easy to work with that they often use them instead of tabs.

To enter data into the table, click in the desired cell and begin type. Press the **Tab** key to navigate from one cell to the next.

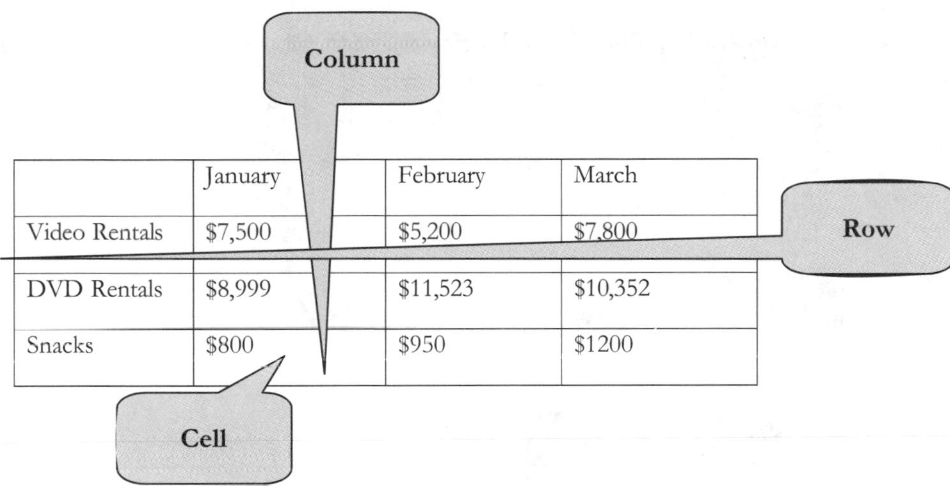

	January	February	March
Video Rentals	$7,500	$5,200	$7,800
DVD Rentals	$8,999	$11,523	$10,352
Snacks	$800	$950	$1200

SAMPLE TABLE IN MICROSOFT WORD

To Create a Table

1. Click the **Insert** tab on the Ribbon.
2. Click the **Table button** on the Tables group.
3. Drag on the grid to select the number of rows and column that you want
   Or
   Click **Insert Table** and type the **Number of columns** for the table in the columns box and the **Number of rows** for the table in the rows box. Click **OK**.

Let's Try It!

- Click the **Insert tab** on the Ribbon.

Switches to Insert commands and tools.

- Click the **Table button** on the Tables group.

Displays the Table menu. You can either drag on the grid to select the number of rows or columns, or click Insert Table to use the dialog box.

- Click **Insert Table**.

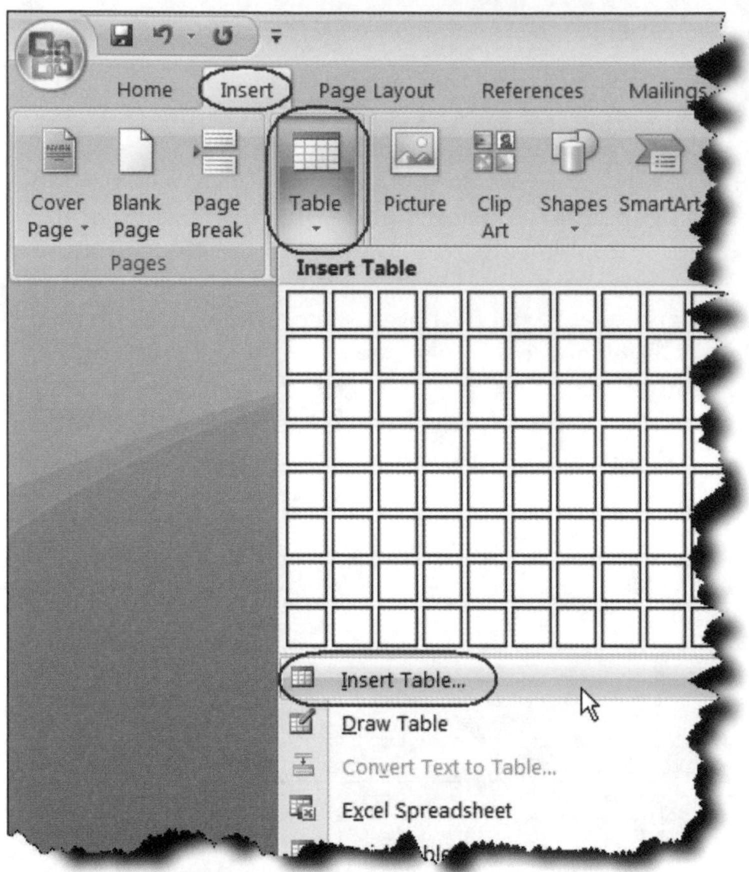

Displays the Insert Table dialog box.

- In the **Number of Columns** box, type: **3** as shown, and then press the **Tab** key.

Designates three for the number of columns for the table and moves the insertion point to the "Number of Rows" box.

- In the **Number of Rows** box, type: **4**.

Designates four for the number of rows for the table.

- Click **OK**.

Closes the Insert Table dialog box and creates our table.

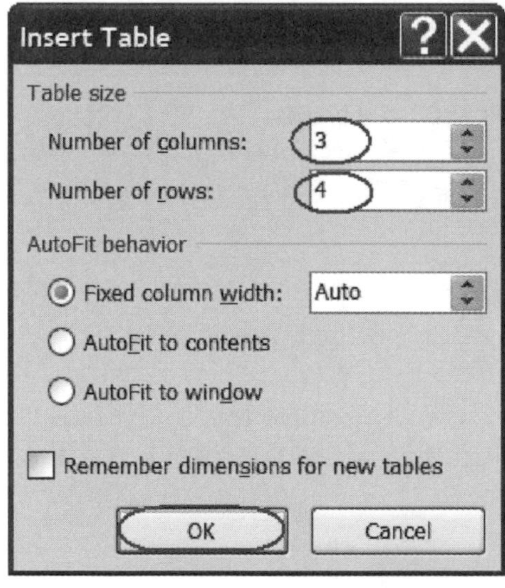

Inserting Rows and Columns

In this section, you will learn how to insert rows and columns into your table.

After creating a table, you may discover that you need another column or row. No problem! You can insert additional rows and columns anywhere in your table by using the **Row and Columns** tools on the contextual **Layout** Ribbon. When adding rows or columns, the table will automatically adjust to accommodate the new arrangement. When you insert a new row, the existing rows shift downward. When entering new columns, the existing columns shift to the right.

You can also quickly insert a new row at the end of a table by clicking in the last cell of the last row of the table, and then pressing the **Tab** key.

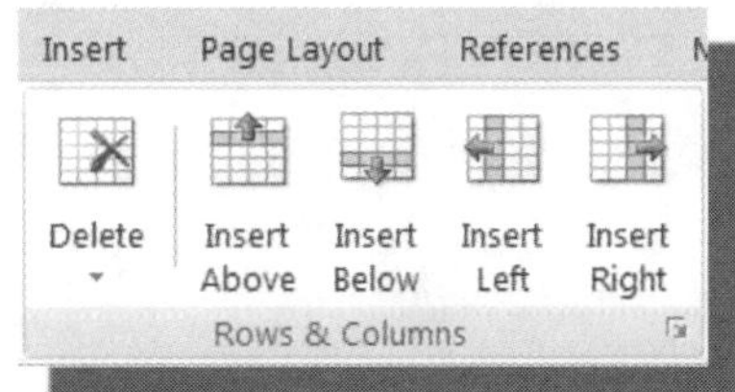

ROWS & COLUMNS GROUP

To add or delete columns and rows, click in the area of the table where you want to add or delete a row or column, and then choose from the following options from the Rows & Columns group:

- Insert Left (inserts columns to the left of the selected column)
- Insert Right (inserts columns to the right of the selected column)
- Insert Above (inserts rows above the selected row)
- Insert Below (inserts rows below the selected row)
- Delete (choose rows or columns)

You can also **right-click** in any table cell, point to insert, and then choose the desired command from the menu. To delete a row or a column, right-click and choose either **Delete Rows** or **Delete Columns**.

To Insert a Row at the End of a Table

1. Set the insertion point in the last cell of the last row of the table.
2. Press the **Tab** key. A new row is automatically inserted at the end of the table.

To Add Columns or Rows

1. Click in the table at the location where you want to insert a row or column.
2. Click the contextual **Layout** tab on the Ribbon.
3. Click the Insert Left, Insert Right, Insert Above or Insert Below to insert a row or a column on the Rows & Columns group on the Ribbon.

Let's Try It!

- Click in any cell of the **first column** of the table.

Sets the insertion point where we wish to insert a new column.

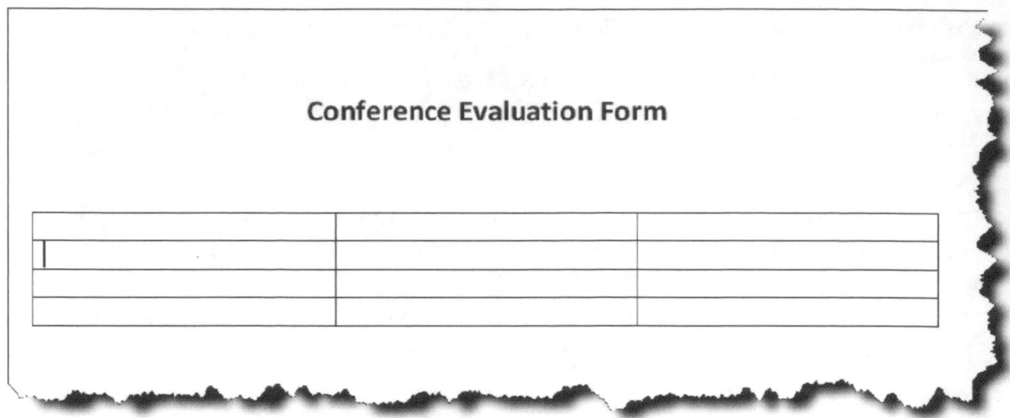

- Click the contextual **Layout tab** on the Ribbon under Table Tools.

Displays table layout commands and tools.

- Click the **Insert Left** button on the Rows & Columns group.

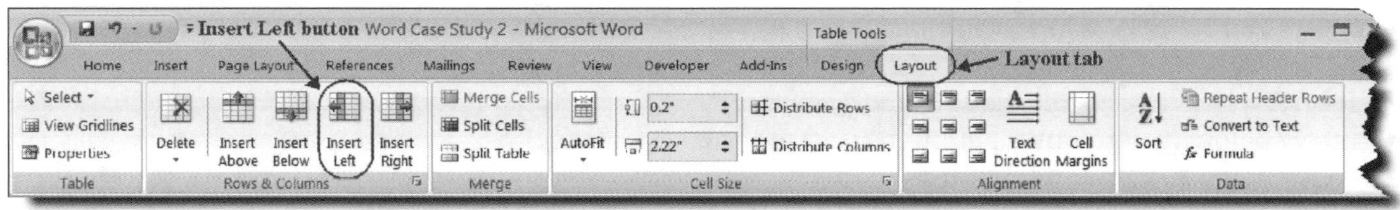

Inserts a blank column to the left of the column that contains the insertion point.

- Set the insertion point in the first row, first column of the table and type **Date of Conference:**

Enters the text in the first cell of the table.

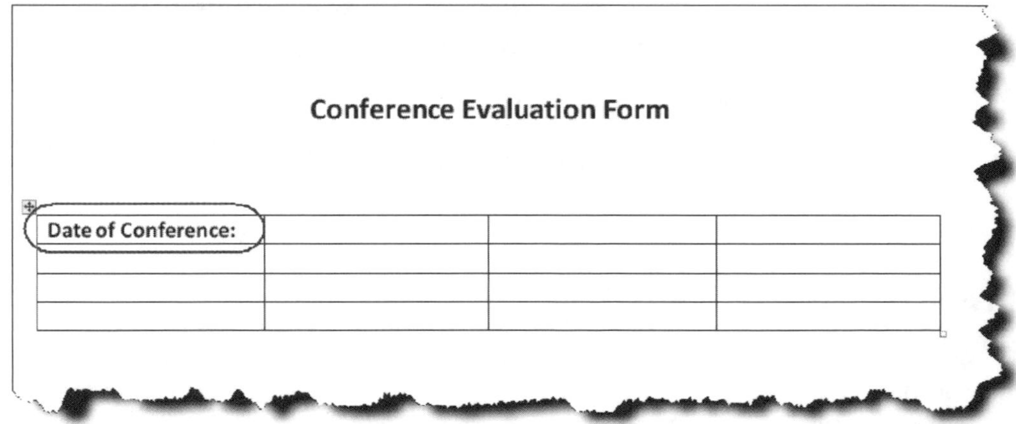

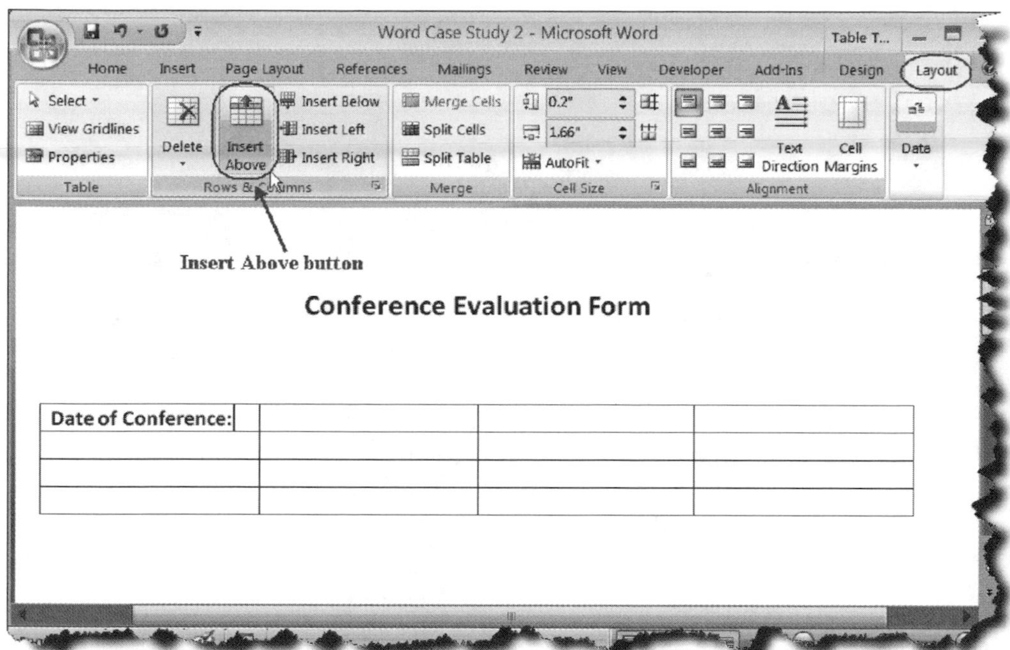

- Click the **Insert Above** button on the Rows & Columns group.

Conference Evaluation Form

Name of Attendee:			
Date of Conference:			

Inserts a new blank row above the current row in the table.

- Select the **first cell** of the table and type **Name of Attendee:**

Enters text in the first cell.

- Click the **Save** button.

Saves our changes.

Deleting Rows and Columns

In this section, you will learn how to remove rows and columns from your table.

Deleting rows and columns from your table is as easy as inserting them. Select the row or column you wish to delete, click the **Delete** button on the Layout Ribbon, and then choose either **Delete Rows** or **Delete Columns**. Other options on the Delete menu include deleting the entire table or deleting individual cells from a table.

To delete more than one column or row, first select the rows or columns you wish to delete. To **select rows**, position your mouse pointer to the left of the table until your mouse pointer transforms to a white, right-pointing arrow. Click and drag upwards or downwards to select the desired rows. To **select columns**, position your mouse pointer above a column until your mouse pointer transforms to a downward pointing black arrow. Drag to the left or right to select desired columns.

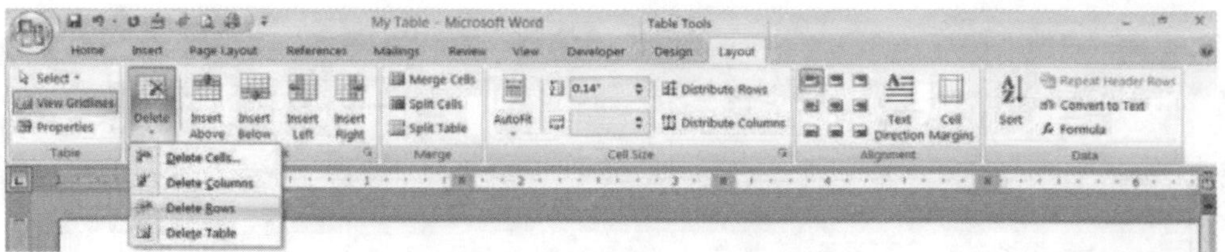

To Delete Rows or Columns

1. Set the insertion point in the row or column you want to delete. To delete more than one column or row, select the columns or rows that you wish to delete.
2. Click the contextual **Layout** tab on the Ribbon.
3. Click the **Delete button** on the Rows & Columns group on the Ribbon.
4. Select **Delete Cells, Delete Columns, Delete Rows or Delete Table** from the Delete button menu.

Let's Try It!

- Click anywhere in **blank row** at the end of the table.

Designates the row that we want to delete.

- Click the **Delete button** on the Rows & Columns group and click **Delete Rows**.

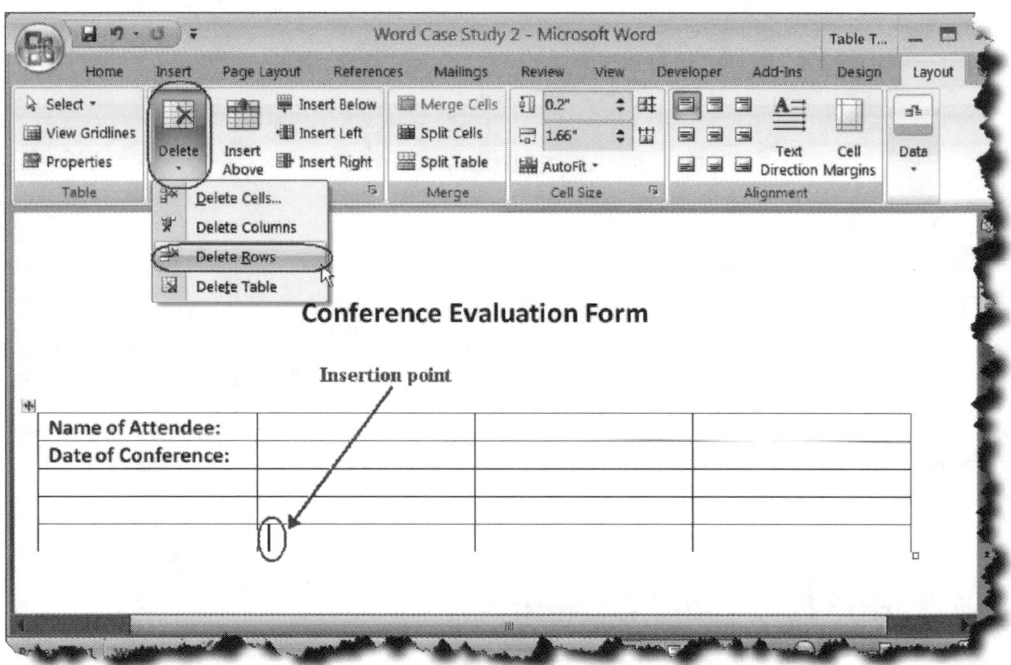

Deletes the row.

- Click the **Undo** icon on the Quick Access Toolbar.

Reverses the delete action and restores the row.

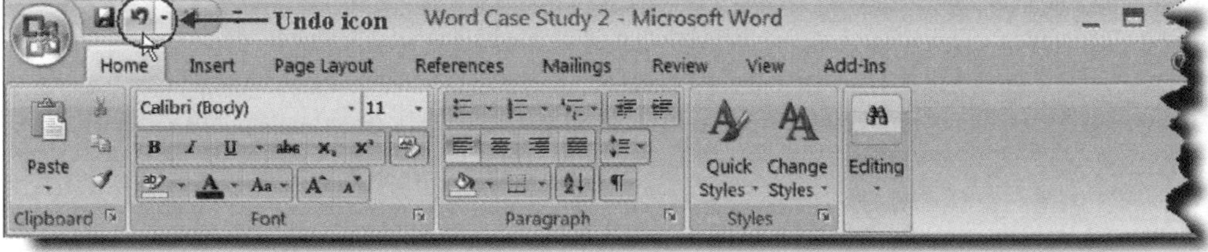

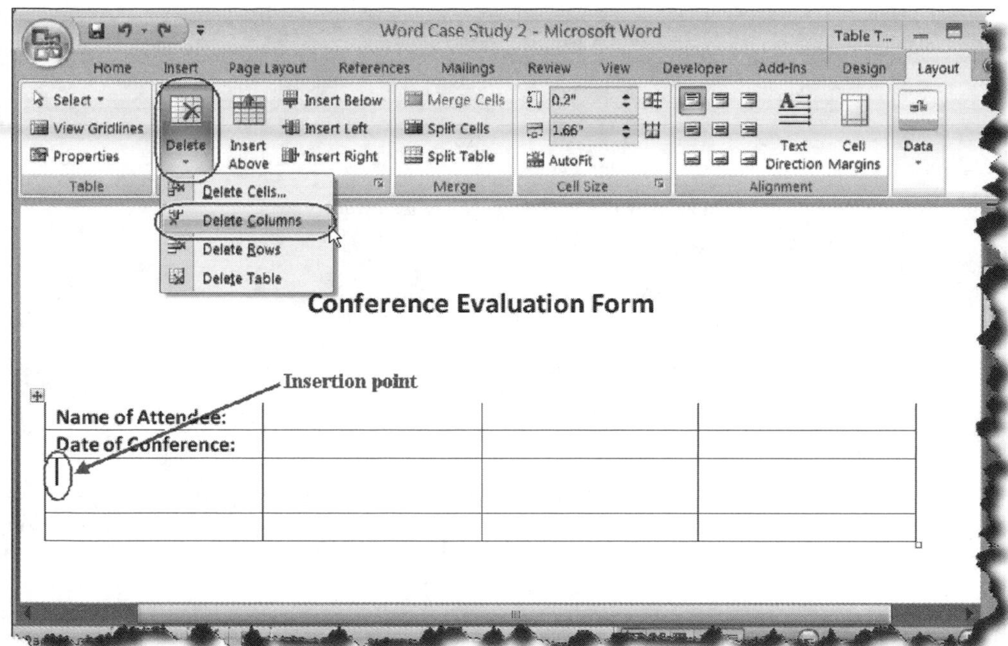

- Click anywhere in the **first** column.

Designates the column that we want to delete.

- Click the **Delete button** on the Rows & Columns group and click **Delete Columns**.

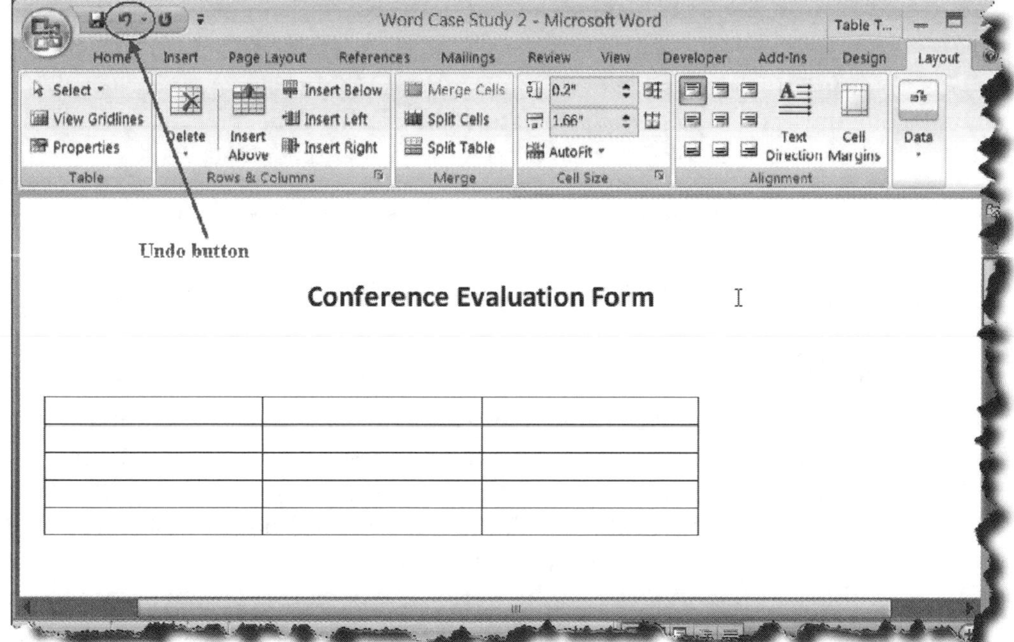

Deletes the first column.

- Click the **Undo** icon on the Quick Access Toolbar.

Reverses the delete action and restores the column.

- Click the **Save** button.

Saves the changes.

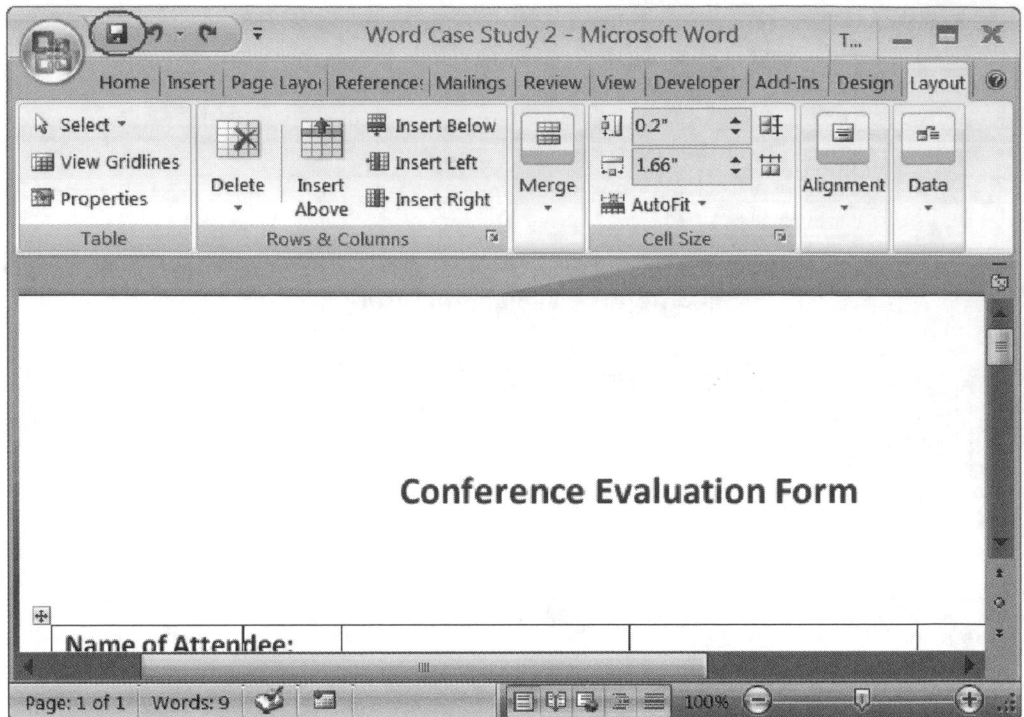

TIP: You can also delete table rows, table columns, table cells or an entire table by selecting the objects you wish to delete, right-clicking your mouse and choosing the object you wish to delete from the contextual menu.

Formatting a Table

In this section, you will learn how to apply a preset formatting style to a table.

Word includes several **quick table styles** that you can add to your table. These table formats include preset colors and borders styles that you can instantly apply to your table. Under the contextual Design tab under the Tables tab, you will see several preset Table Style thumbnails displayed on the Ribbon. Move your mouse pointer over any of these styles to see a preview of the selected style. Click the **Scroll Up** or **Scroll Down arrow** to scroll the style list. To view the entire Table Styles gallery, click the **More Styles** button.

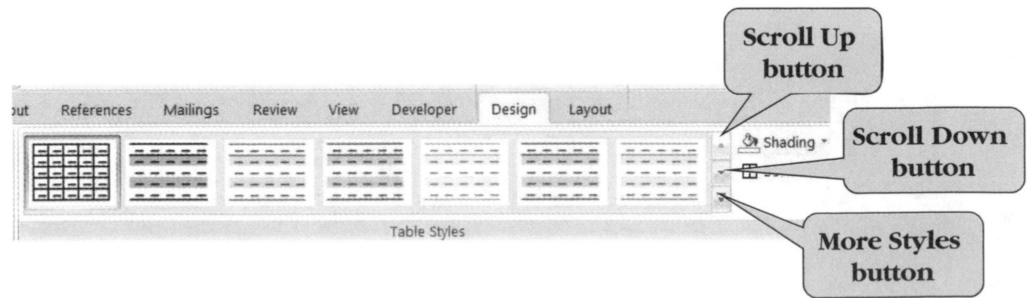

You can further modify the formatting of your table by modifying table style options such as hiding or displaying the header row, adding special formatting to the first or last columns, or displaying banded rows or columns, in which the even rows or columns are formatted differently from the odd rows and columns, much like an accounting greenbar report.

To remove a table style, click the **More button** on the Table Styles group and choose **Clear** from the menu. The table will display in the default table format.

To Apply a Quick Style to a Table

1. Click anywhere within the table to activate it.
2. Click the contextual **Design tab** under Table Tools on the Ribbon.
3. Move your mouse pointer over any of the styles to display a preview of the style.
4. Click the Scroll Up to Scroll Down arrows to display additional table styles.
5. Click the **More button** on the Table Styles group to display the styles gallery.
6. Click the Table Style thumbnail to apply that style to your table.
7. To remove a table style, click the **More button** on the Table Styles group and click **Clear** on the menu.

To Format Table Elements

1. Click anywhere within the table to activate it.
2. Click the contextual **Design tab** under Table Tools on the Ribbon.
3. On the **Table Options group**, do one of the following:
   a. To turn the header row on or off, select or clear the **Header Row** check box. Header rows are repeated at the top of each page if your table extends for more than one page.
   b. To display special formatting for the first or last column of the table, select the **First Column** or **Last Column** check box.
   c. To display odd and even rows with different formatting, select the **Banded Rows** check box.
   d. To display odd and even columns with different formatting, select the **Banded Columns** check box.
   e. To format the bottom row for column totals, select or clear the **Totals**

*To accomplish cell shading to the table, click the **Shading button** on the contextual **Design tab**. You can also right-click the table, choose Borders and Shading to apply colors from the Borders and Shading dialog box.*

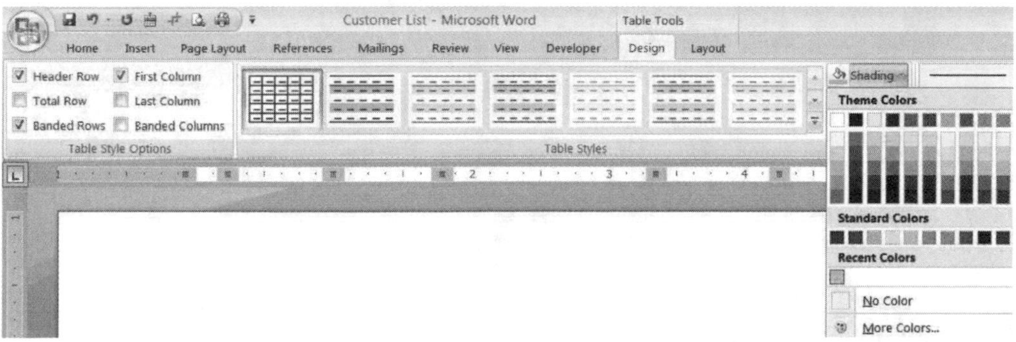

To Apply Shading to Cells

1. Select (click and drag across) the cells to which you want to apply shading.
2. Click the contextual **Design Ribbon**.
3. Click the **Shading** button on the Table Styles group of the Design Ribbon.
4. Click on the desired color in the color palette and then click **OK**.
5. To see additional colors, click on **More Fill Colors** to display the color palette, click on the desired color and then click **OK**.

Let's Try It!

- **Click** anywhere inside of the **table**.

Selects the table.

- Click the contextual **Design tab** on the Ribbon.

Displays table design tools and commands.

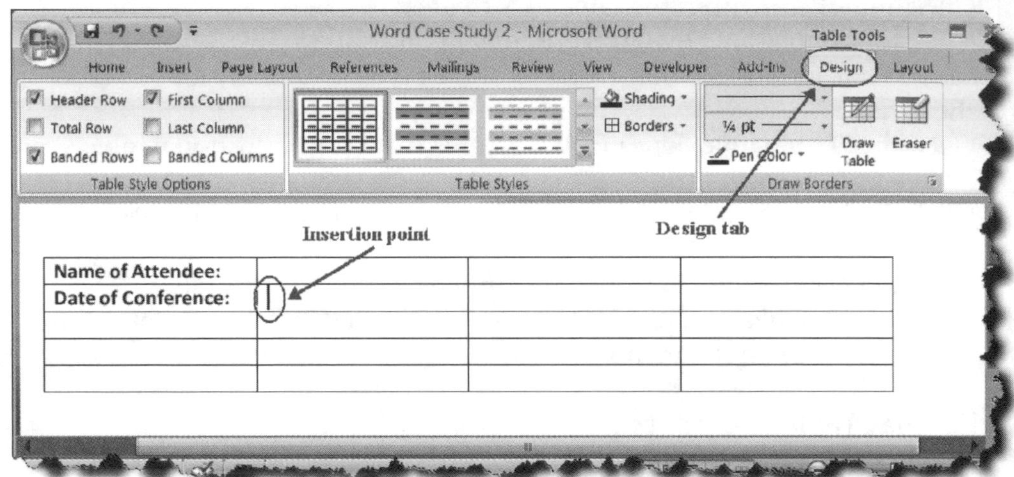

- Click the **More** button on the Table Styles group.

Displays table styles.

- Click the **Light List—Accent 2** Table Style thumbnail in the Table Styles group.

Applies that style to the selected table.

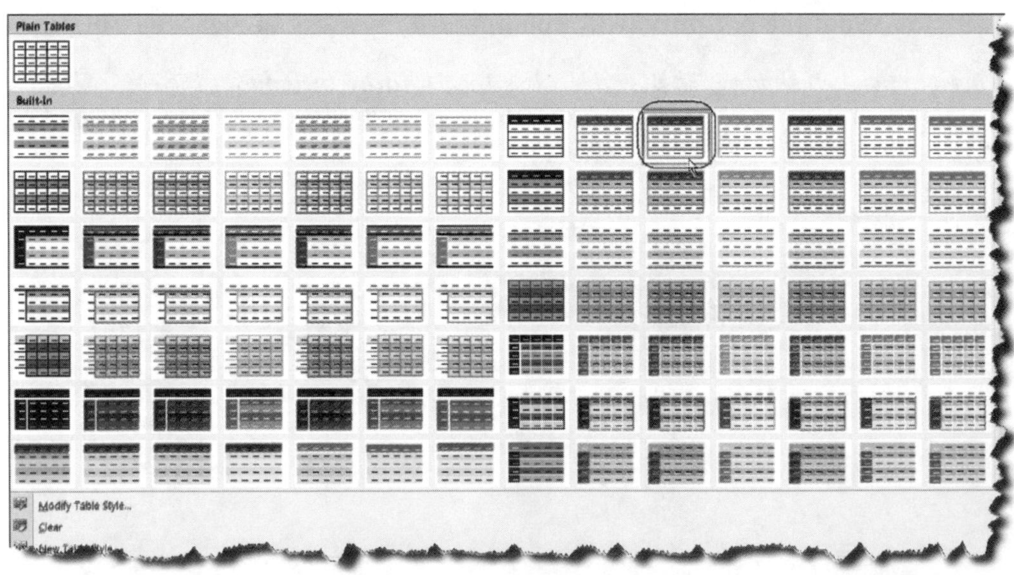

Merging and Splitting Cells

In this section, you will learn how to merge several cells into one longer cell

There are times when you may wish to combine two or more cells into a single larger cell that spans several columns. For example, you may have a title row as the first row of your table and you wish to center the title horizontally over the other cells in your table. To combine several cells into one, select the cells you wish to merge then use the **Merge Cells** command on the contextual Layout Ribbon.

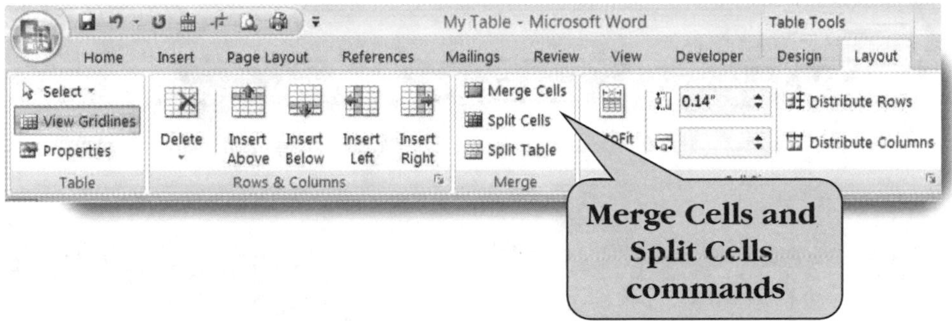

Likewise, individual cells can be split into smaller cells by using the **Split Cells** command from the Table menu.

To Merge Cells in a Table

1. Select the cells you wish to merge into one larger cell.
2. Click the contextual **Layout tab** on the Ribbon.
3. Click the **Merge Cells** button on the Merge group.

To Split Cells in a Table

1. Select the cell you wish to split into smaller cells.
2. Click the contextual **Layout tab** on the Ribbon.
3. Click the **Split Cells** button on the Merge group.
4. Enter the number of cells and rows into which you want to split your cells.
5. Click **OK**.

TIP: You can also right-click and choose **Merge Cells** from the contextual menu to merge the selected cells.

Let's Try It!

- Select the **table** by clicking on the plus (+) sign, upper left corner.

Table is selected.

- Select **All Borders** on the borders button under the Home tab.

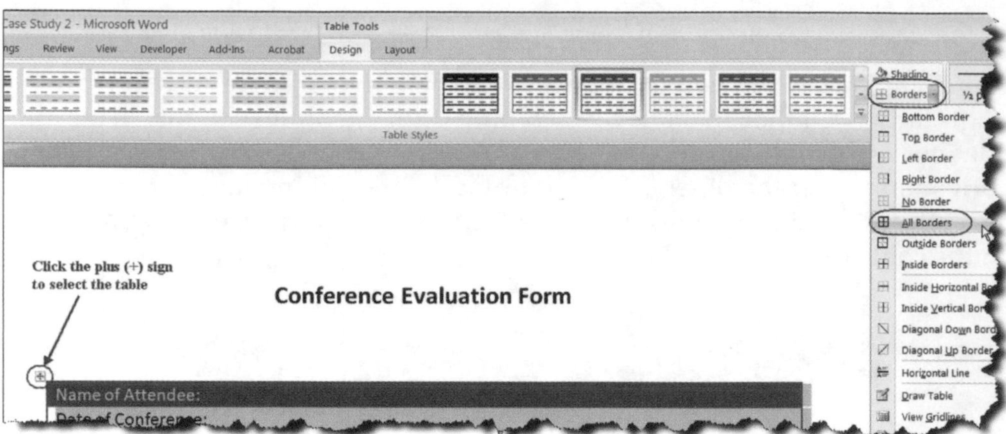

- **Click** anywhere in the **first row** of the table.

Selects the row above which we want to insert a new row. We will use the new row as a Title Row.

- Click the contextual **Layout tab** on the Ribbon.

Switches to table layout commands and tools.

- Click the **Insert Above** button on the Rows & Columns group.

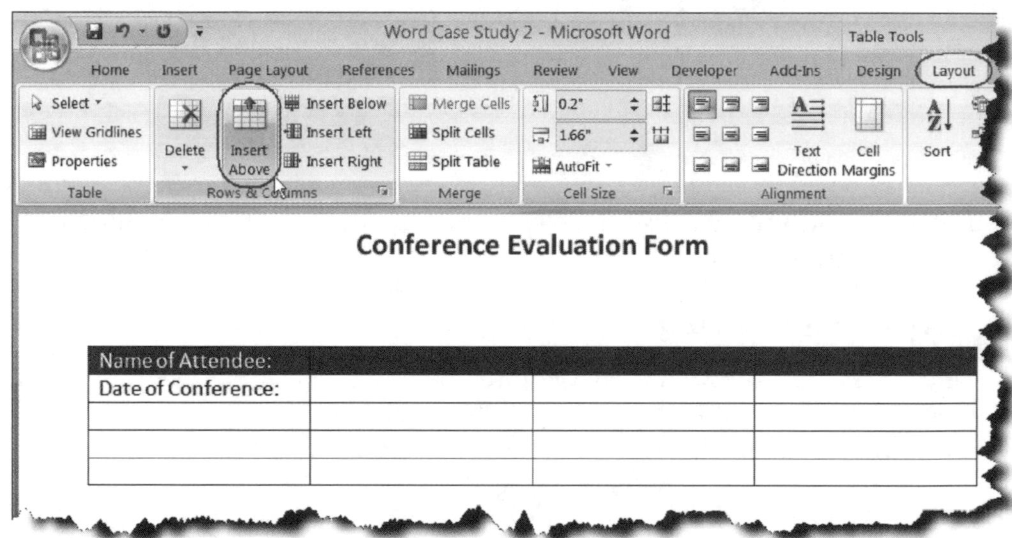

Inserts a new blank row above the selected row in the table.

- Select the first row.
- Click the **Merge Cells** button on the Merge group.

Merges the selected cells into one cell.

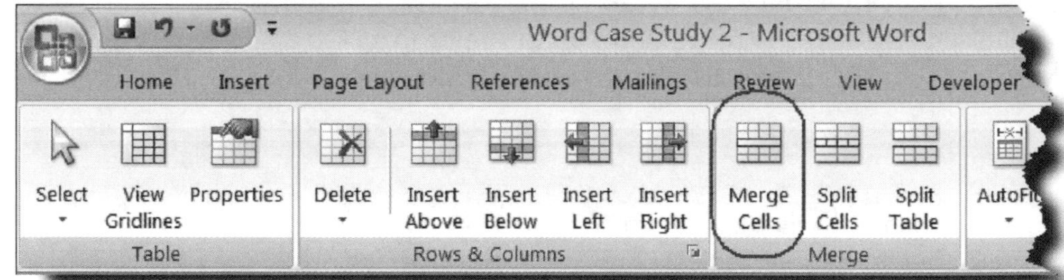

Conference Evaluation Form

Please help us evaluate the conference by responding to the following questions. Your comments will enable us to better plan and execute future conferences.			
Name of Attendee:			
Date of Conference:			

- Type: **Please help us evaluate the conference by responding to the following questions. Your comments will enable us to better plan and execute future conferences.**

Enters the text for first row.

- Click the **Save** button.

Saves the changes.

Resizing a Form

This section will guide you through the process of resizing a form.

Most likely, the size of the columns for your form will not be the size that you want and you will inevitably need to resize the form to accommodate your form labels and form fields. You can adjust the column width by clicking and dragging the column border or the column margin until the column is the desired length. If you wish to use a more precise measurement for your column widths, use the Column Width box on the on the Cell Size group of the contextual Layout Tab (under Table Tools).

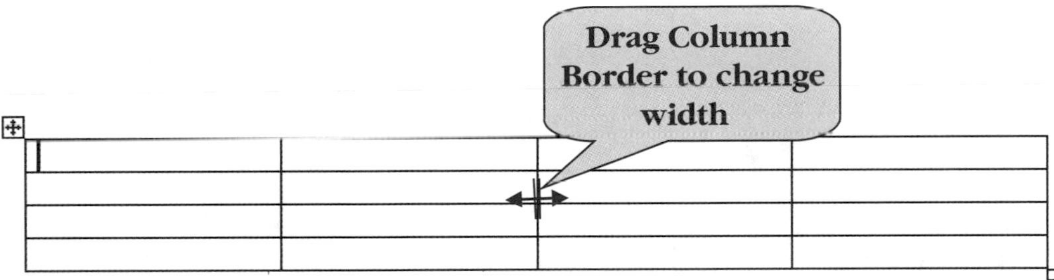
Drag Column Border to change width

To Adjust Column Width

1. Move your mouse pointer over the border you wish to adjust until the pointer transforms into two vertical lines with a horizontal double arrow through it

2. Click and drag to the left or right until border is the desired width.

For a more precise measurement:

1. Click anywhere in the column that you want to adjust.
2. Click the contextual **Layout tab** under Table Tools.
3. Type in the desired width in the Table Column Width box.

Let's Try It!

- Move the mouse pointer over the **left border** of the fourth column, then click and drag to the right until the border is at the **5″** mark on the ruler. The ruler will not appear until you press and hold the mouse button on the border of the column.

Reduces the width of the last column.

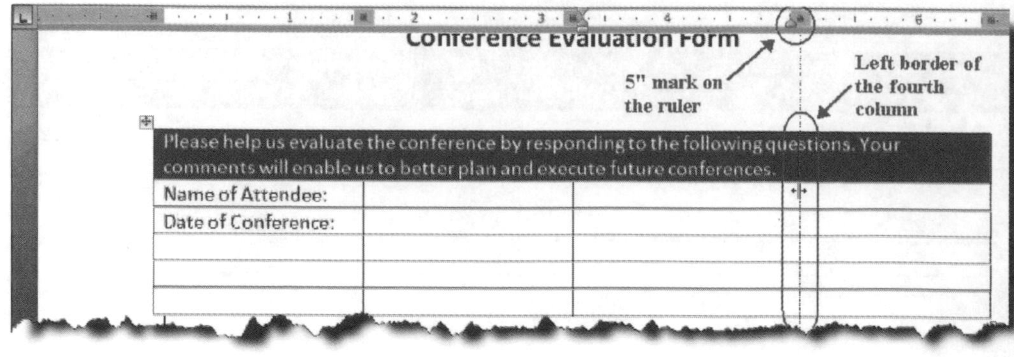

- Move the mouse pointer over the **left border** of the **third** column, then click and then drag to the right until the border is at the **4″** mark on the ruler.

Reduces the width of the third column.

- Click the **Save** button.

Saves the current template.

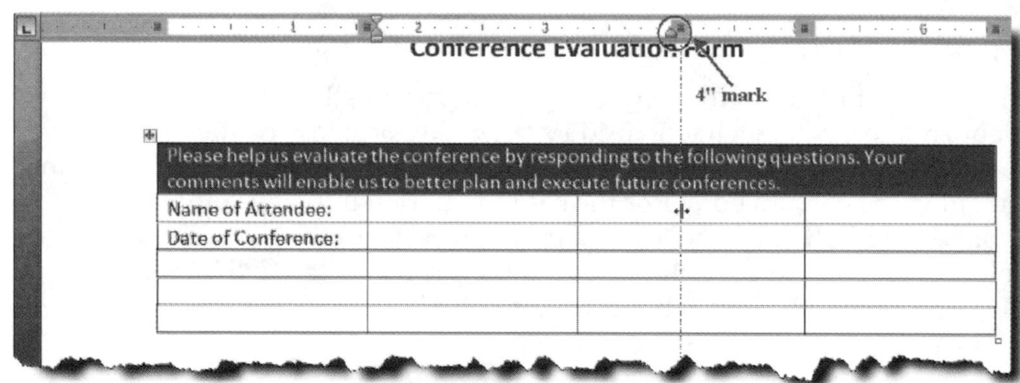

Adding a Text Field to a Form

In this section, you will add a text field to your form.

After you have saved your form as a template and laid out your table, you can begin adding form fields to your form. The form field tools are located on the Controls group of the **Developer** Ribbon. If you are working in Compatability Mode—that is to say, your document is saved in an earlier version of Word—you will only be able to choose from the Legacy Tools.

There are several types of form fields that you can add to a form. Some of the more common ones include:

- **Rich Text or Text box**—a fill-in-the-blank box into which a user enters text.
- **Picture**—Inserts a placeholder where you can click to insert a picture.
- **Check-box**—User selects an option by clicking into a box.

- **Combo Box**—Allows you to choose from a list of choices or to add additional choices.
- **Drop-down list**—Allows you to limit the user's entry to a specific choice. User selects desired choice from a list of valid entries.
- **Date Picker**—Allows you to choose a date from a pop-up calendar.
- **Building Block Gallery**—Allows you to insert a Quick Part control.

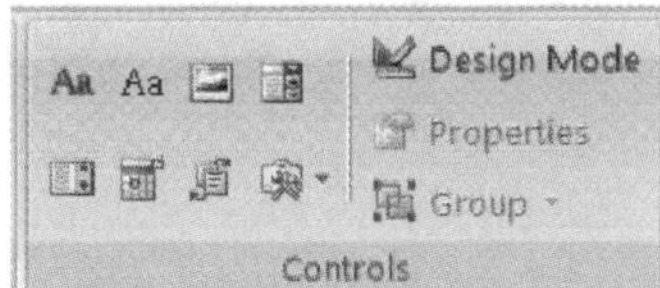

CONTROLS GROUP

Once you have inserted your form field, you can set additional options. For instance, you could set your text field to not allow any more than 4 characters or to allow only valid date entries. To set form field options, click the **Properties** button on the Controls group and the appropriate form field dialog box will display. From there, you can set the desired options. An example of the Text Form Field Dialog box is below.

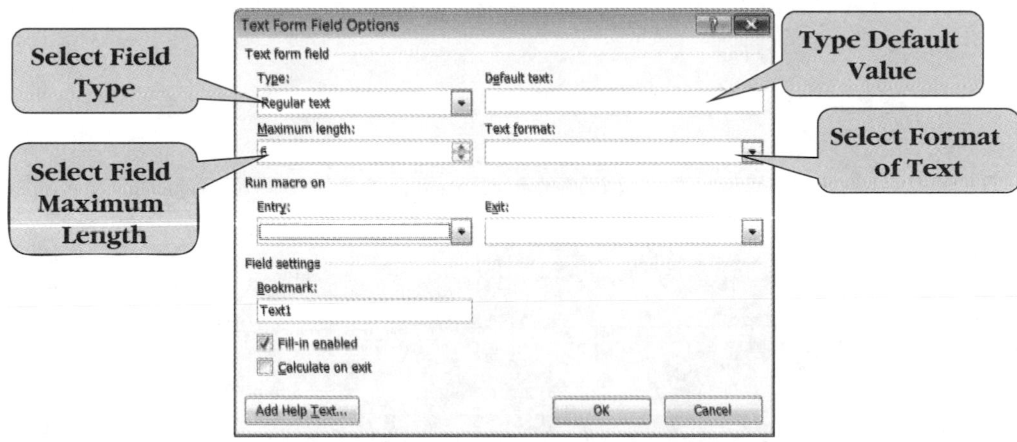

TEXT FORM FIELD OPTIONS

To Add a Text Form Field

1. Set the insertion point where you wish to insert the form field.
2. Click the **Legacy Tools** button on the Controls group and click the **Text Box Tool**.
3. Click the **Properties button** to set additional options.
4. Select any additional options from the Text Form Field Options dialog box.
5. Click **OK**.

Let's Try It!

- Select the **second, third** and **fourth columns** of the **second row** as shown.

As the first field can be somewhat long, we are going to merge the second, third and fourth cells of the first row into one larger cell.

Conference Evaluation Form

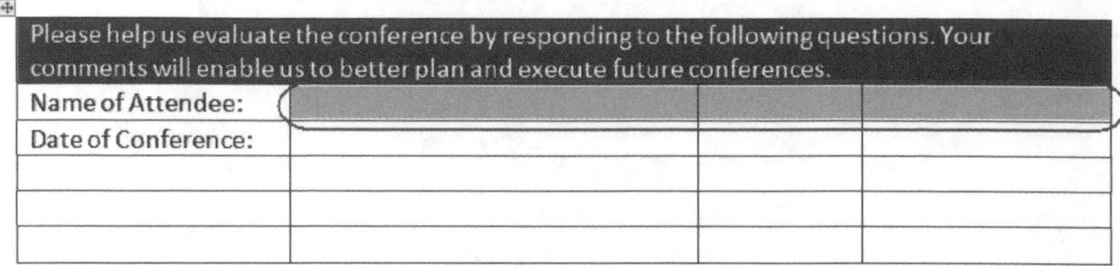

- Click the contextual **Layout tab** on the Ribbon.

Switches to Table Layout tools and commands.

- Click the **Merge Cells** button on the Merge group of the Ribbon as shown.

Merges the selected cells into one larger cell.

- Set the insertion point in the **second column of the second row**.

Sets the insertion point where we want to insert textfield.

- Click the **Developer tab** on the Ribbon.

Switches to Developer commands and tools.

- Click the **Legacy Tools** button on the Controls group and click the **Text Form Field** icon.

Inserts a text form field into the form.

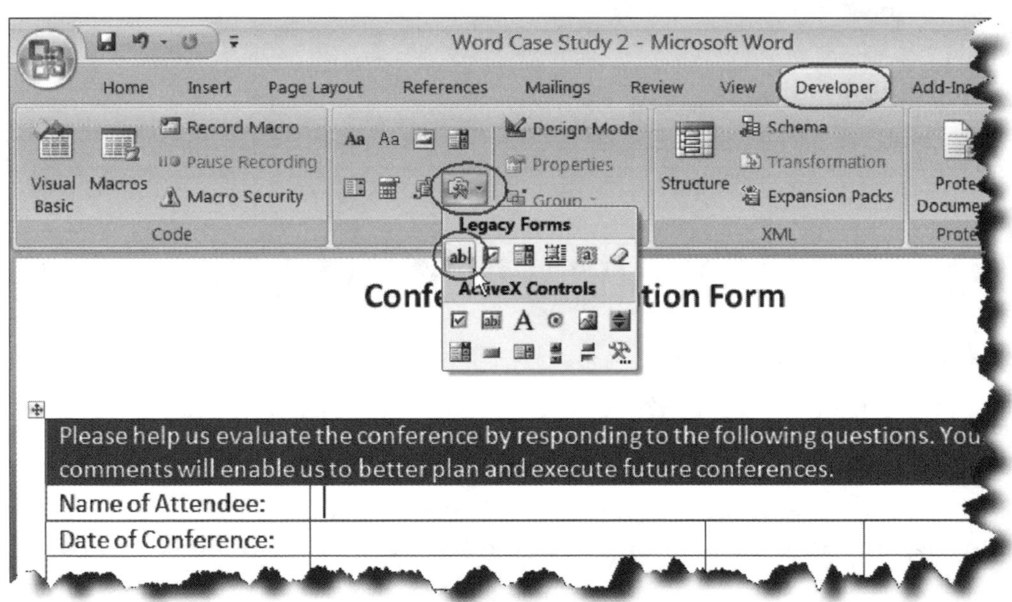

• Press **Tab key twice**.

Moves to the second column of the third row.

Adding a Date Picker Field to a Form

In this section, you will add a date picker field to your form.

The **Date Picker Control** allows the user to select a date from a pop-up calendar. When the user click in the date field a drop-down arrow appears, from which the user can choose the date they want from the mini-calendar. The month is displayed by default. To navigate to a different month, click the **Previous Month** arrow or the **Next Month** arrow.

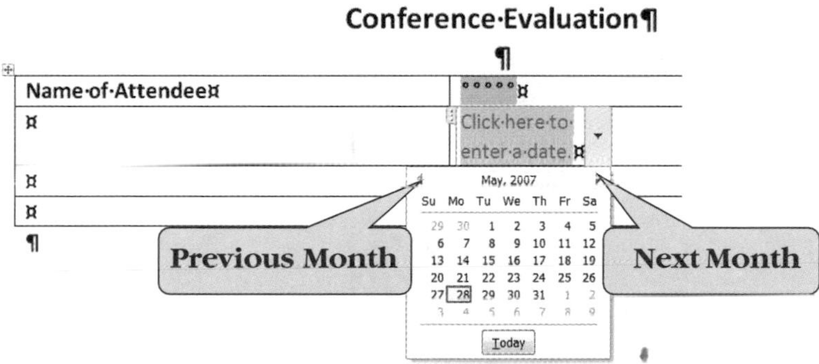

If you are working in Compatibility Mode, you can insert a text field from the Legacy tools and set the form field type to Date from the Text Form Field Options dialog box.

To Add a Date Picker Control to a Form

1. Set the insertion point where you wish to insert the Date Picker field.
2. Click the **Date Picker** icon on the Controls group on the Ribbon.
3. Click the **Properties** button on the Controls group to set additional options.

Let's Try It!

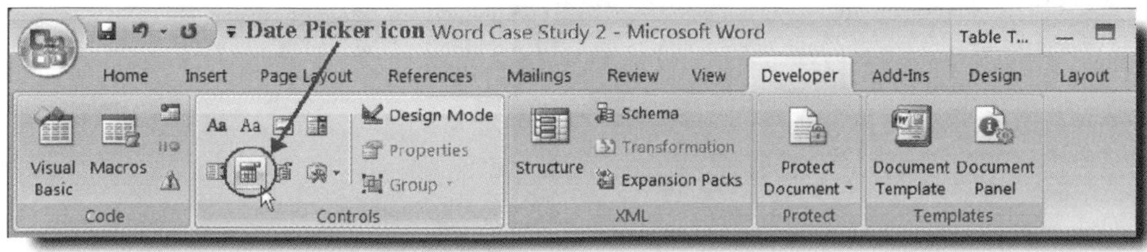

• Click the **Date Picker** icon on the Controls group as shown.

Inserts a date picker field into our form.

- Click the **Properties** button on the Controls group.

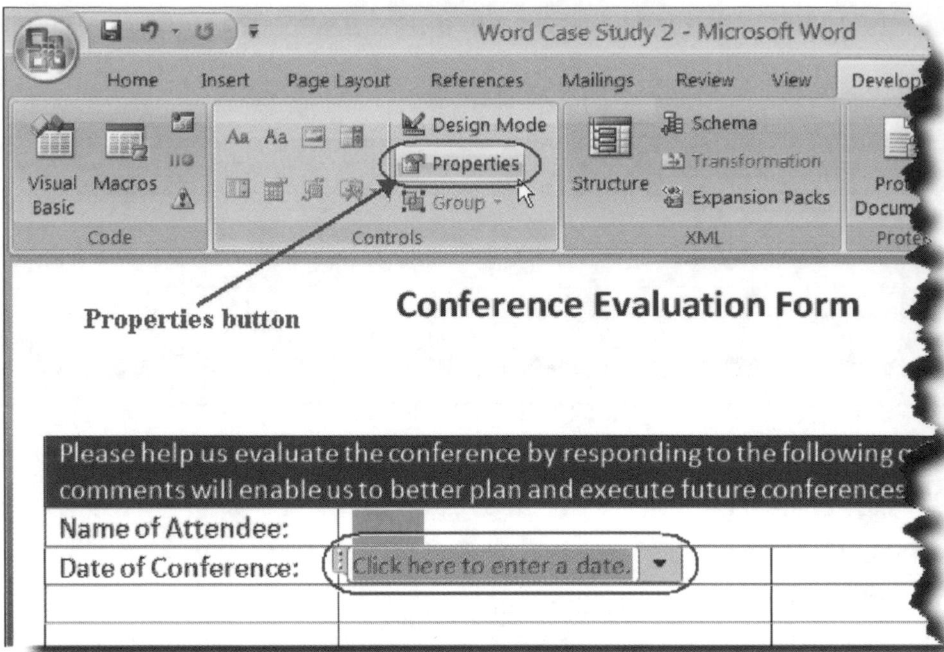

Displays the Content Control Properties dialog box.

- In the **Date Display Box**, click the fourth option from the top as shown.

Specifies that the date will be displayed in mm/dd/yy format.

- Click **OK**.

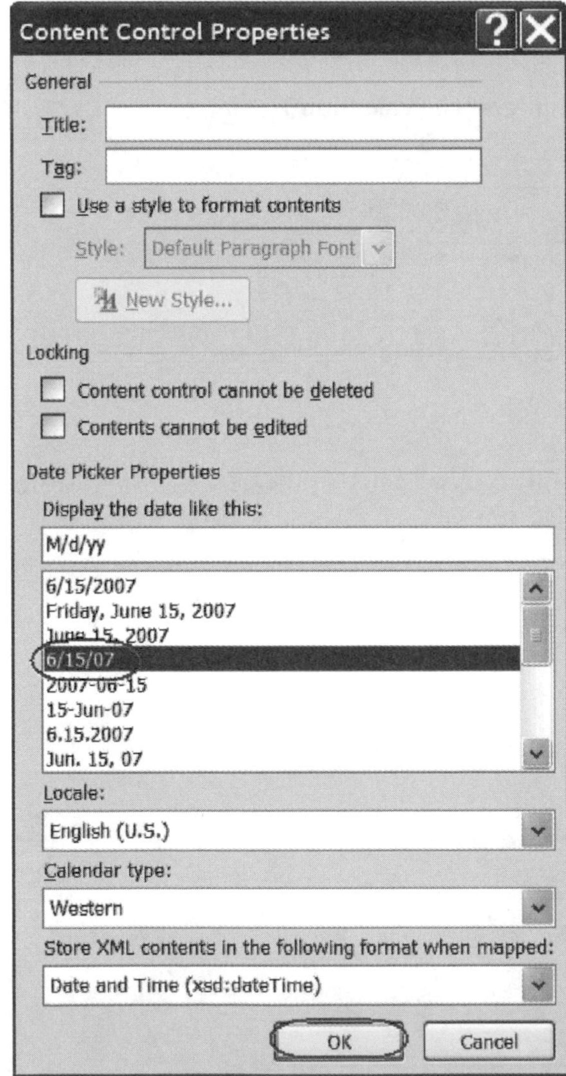

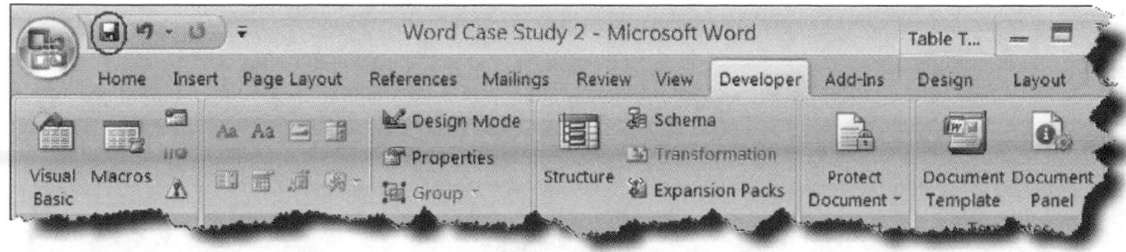

Closes the Content Control Properties dialog box.

- Click the **Save** button.

Saves the changes to the form template.

Adding a Check Box to a Form

In this section, you will add a check field to your form.

Check boxes are controls that a user checks or unchecks to show agreement or diagreement. You might want to use check boxes for items from which the user can make more than once choice. Check boxes are also commonly used for yes/no options. Like the text box, you can set additional check box options from the Check Box Form Field dialog box.

To Add a Check Box Form Field

1. Set the insertion point where you wish to insert the check box field.
2. Click the **Legacy Tools** button on the Controls group and click the **Check Box Tool**.
3. Click the **Properties button** to set additional options.
4. Select any additional options from the Check Box Form Field Options dialog box.
5. Click **OK**.

Let's Try It!

Please help us evaluate the conference by responding to the following questions. Your comments will enable us to better plan and execute future conferences.			
Name of Attendee:			
Date of Conference:	Click here to enter a date.		
How would you rate the Key Note Address?			

- Set the insertion point in the **first column** in the **fourth row**.

Sets the insertion point where we will type our next form field label.

- Type: **How would you rate the Key Note Address**?

Enters the label for the next form field.

- Press **Tab**.

Moves to the next column.

- Click the **Legacy Tools icon** and click the **Check Box Form Field** as shown.

Inserts a check box form field into your form.

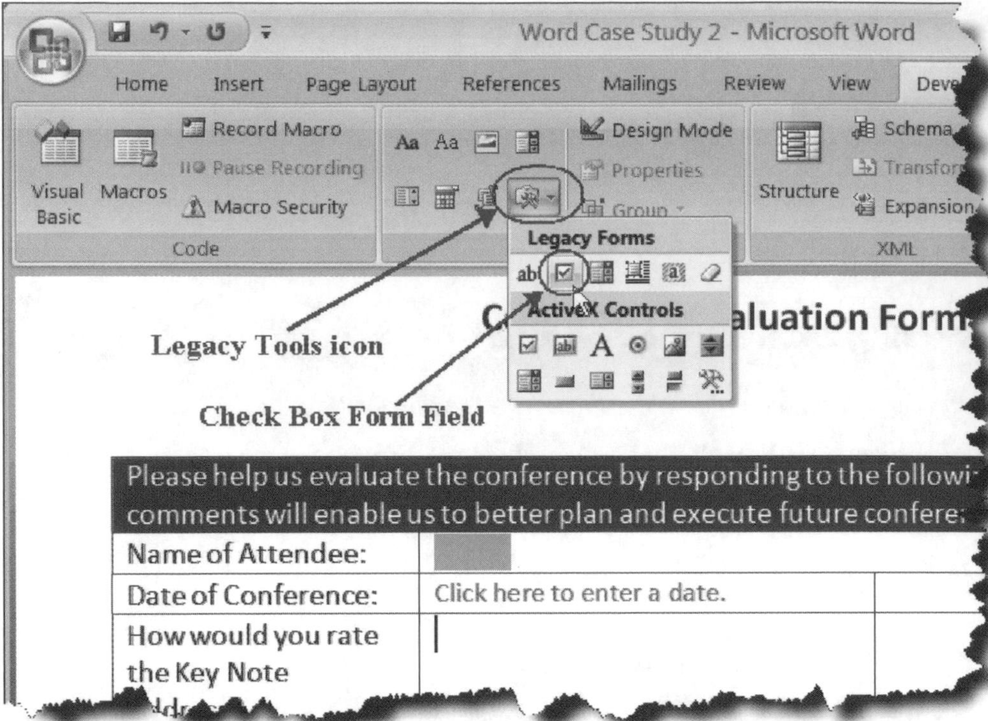

- Press the **Spacebar** and type: **Poor**.

Enters additional descriptive text.

Please help us evaluate the conference by responding to the following questions. Your comments will enable us to better plan and execute future conferences.			
Name of Attendee:			
Date of Conference:	Click here to enter a date.		
How would you rate the Key Note Address?	Poor		

- Press **Tab**.

Moves to the third column.

- Repeat previous step and add another **Check Box Form Field**.

Inserts a check box form field into your form.

- Press the **Spacebar** and type: **Good**.

Enters additional descriptive text.

Please help us evaluate the conference by responding to the following questions. Your comments will enable us to better plan and execute future conferences.			
Name of Attendee:			
Date of Conference:	Click here to enter a date.		
How would you rate the Key Note Address?	Poor	Good	

Please help us evaluate the conference by responding to the following questions. Your comments will enable us to better plan and execute future conferences.			
Name of Attendee:			
Date of Conference:	Click here to enter a date.		
How would you rate the Key Note Address?	Poor	Good	Excellent

- Press **Tab**.

Moves to the fourth column.

- Repeat previous step and add one last **Check Box Form Field**.

Inserts a check box form field into your form.

- Press the **Spacebar** and type: **Excellent** as shown.

Enters additional descriptive text.

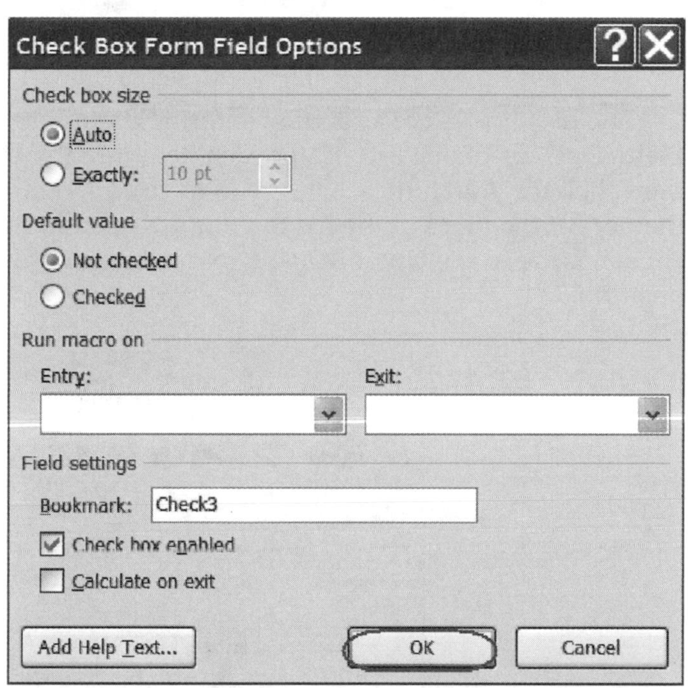

- **Double-click** the Check Box form field for **Excellent** and observe the options.

Opens the Check Box Form Field Options dialog box. Double-clicking a form control is another way of displaying the properties for that control.

- Click **OK**.

Closes the Check Box Form Field Options dialog box.

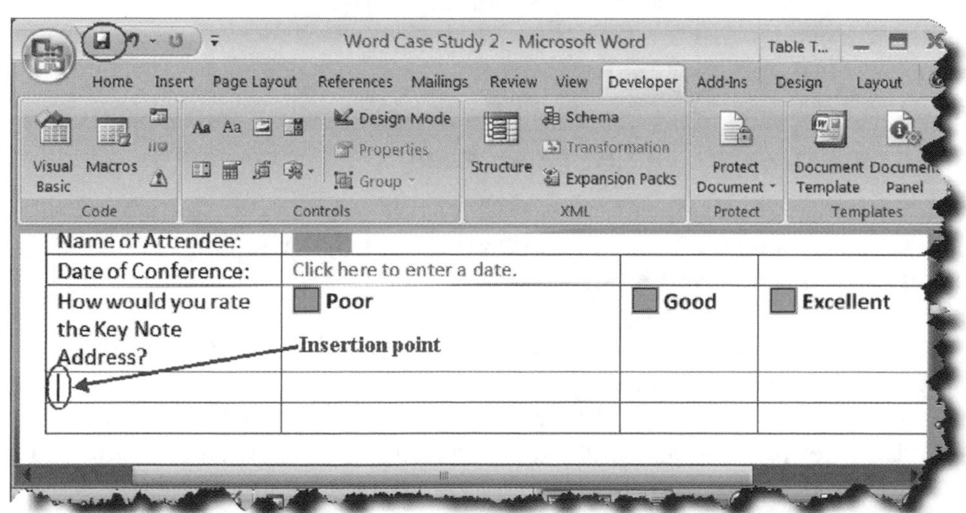

- Press **Tab**.

Moves to the next row.

- Click the **Save** button.

Saves the template changes.

Adding a Drop-Down List to a Form

In this section, you will add a drop-down list to your form.

Drop-down List fields are used when you want to contol the user's entries to a limited choice. When a user enters the drop-down list field, an arrow appears on the right. Clicking the arrow displays the choices from which the user can pick.

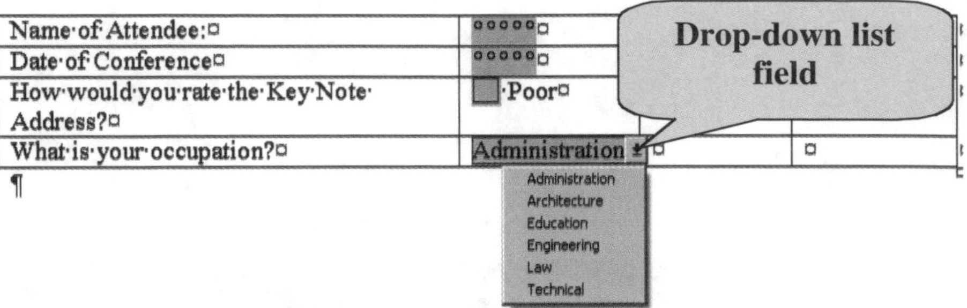

The list choices are added by entering them into the **Drop-Down Form Field Options** dialog box. Enter each item into the **Drop-down** item box, and then click the **Add** button. Once you have added all of the list items, you can then order the items in the list to your satisfaction by selecting the item and choosing the **Move Up** or **Move Down button** until item is in the desired position.

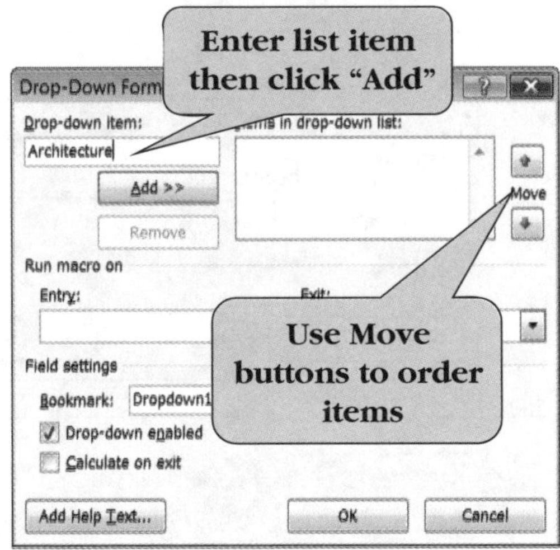

To Add a Drop-Down List Form Field

1. Set the insertion point where you wish to insert the form field.
2. Click the **Legacy Tools** button on the Controls group and click the **Drop-down Form Field icon**.
3. **Double-click** the drop-down form field.
4. In the **drop-down item** box, type the item to be added to the list.
5. Click the **Add** button.
6. Repeat steps 4 and 5 until all items have been added to the list.
7. To order items, select the item to be removed, and then click the **Move Up** or **Move Down** button until the item is in the desired position.
8. Click **OK**.

Let's Try It!

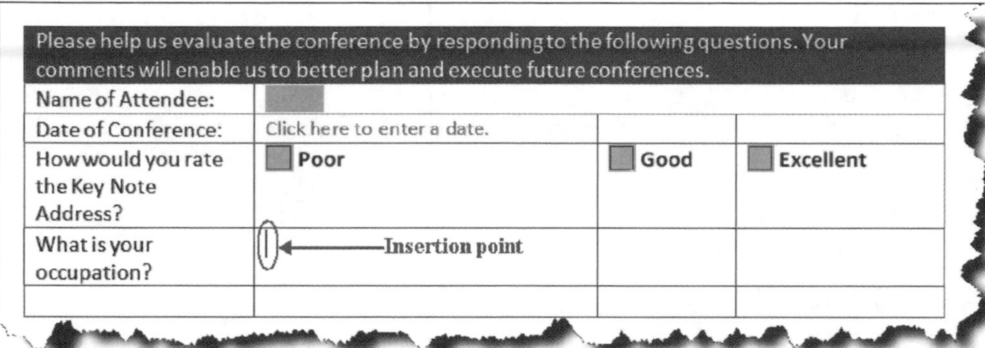

Please help us evaluate the conference by responding to the following questions. Your comments will enable us to better plan and execute future conferences.			
Name of Attendee:			
Date of Conference:	Click here to enter a date.		
How would you rate the Key Note Address?	Poor	Good	Excellent
What is your occupation?			

- Type: **What is your occupation**?

Enters the label for the next form field.

- Press **Tab**.

Moves to the next column.

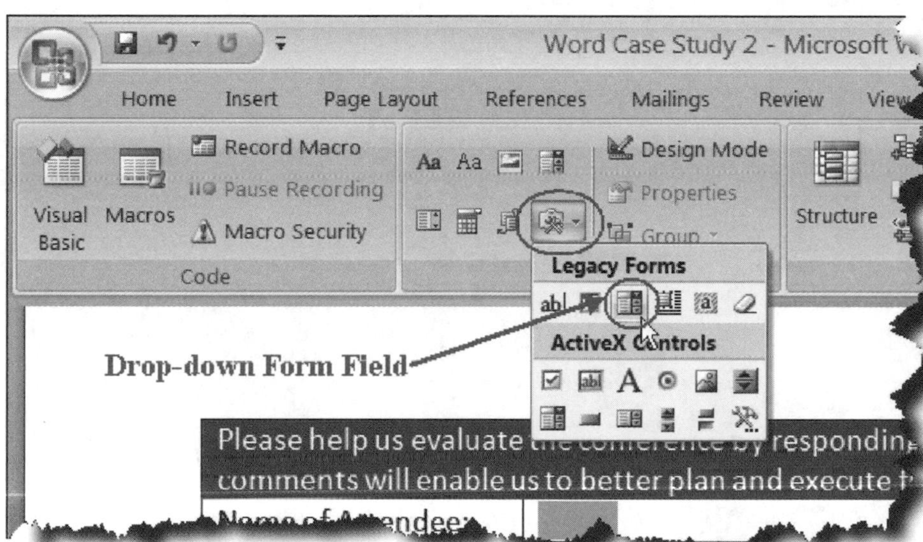

- Click the **Legacy Tools icon** and click the **Drop-down Form Field** icon as shown.

Inserts a drop-down list form field into your form.

Please help us evaluate the conference by responding to the following questions. Your comments will enable us to better plan and execute future conferences.			
Name of Attendee:			
Date of Conference:	Click here to enter a date.		
How would you rate the Key Note Address?	Poor	Good	Excellent
What is your occupation?			

- **Double-click** the drop-down form field you just added.

Opens the Drop-Down Form Field Options dialog box.

- Click in the **Drop-down item:** box and then type: **Architecture**.

Enters the first list item.

- Click **Add**.

Adds the item to the drop-down list.

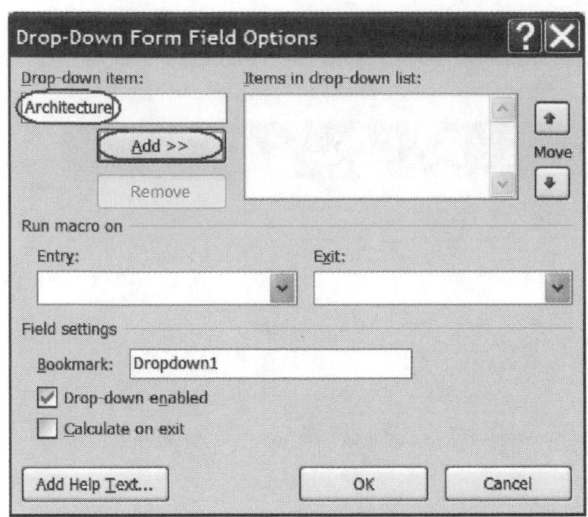

- Continue adding the items below into the Drop-down item box, clicking **Add** after each item.

  Administration
  Education
  Engineering
  Law
  Technical

Enters the rest of the drop-down list items.

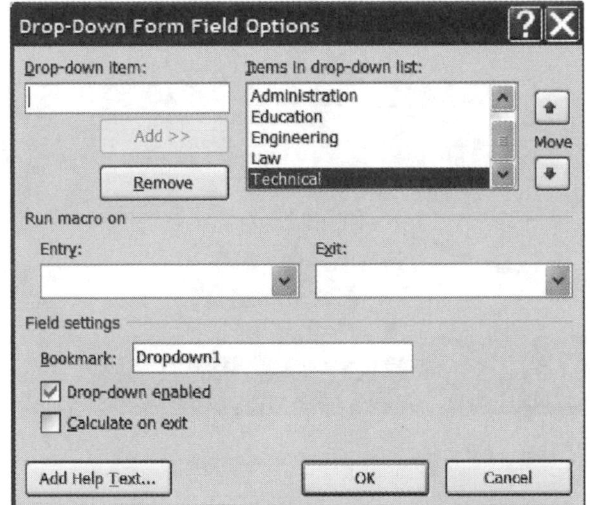

- Click on **Administration** in the **Items in drop-down list** window.

Selects Administration. We are going to move this item to first position.

- Click the **Move Up** button.

Moves the item up one space.

- Click **OK**.

Closes the Drop-Down Form Field Options dialog box and applies the changes.

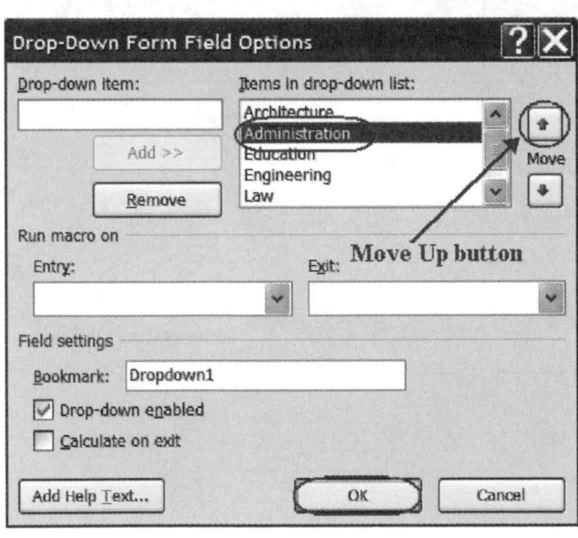

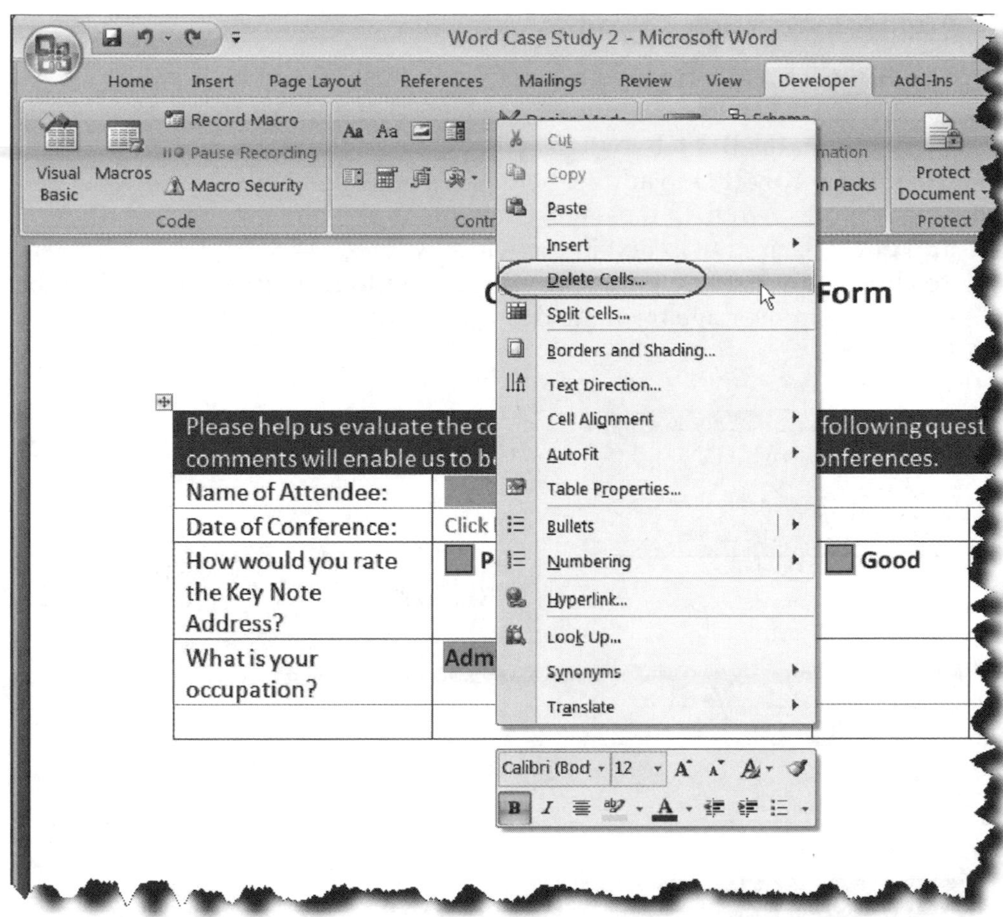

- **Right click** on the last empty row and select **Delete Cells. . .**

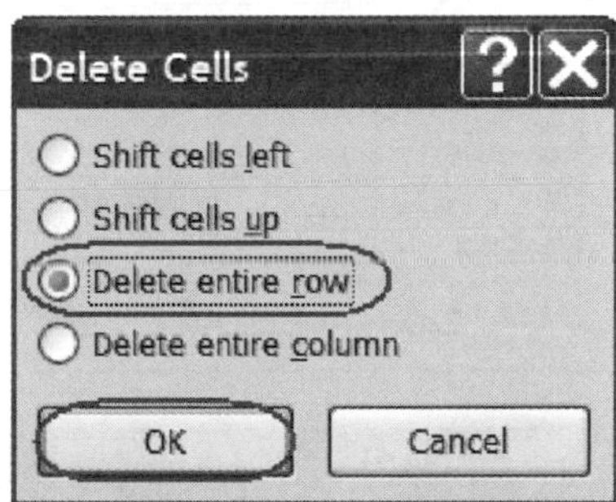

- Select **Delete entire row** and click **OK** button.
- Press **Ctrl+s** to save the changes.

Adding Help to Form Fields

In this section, you will add Status Bar and F1 Key help to your form.

Adding **Help** to your form can make the form easier to fill out for the user. For example, you can inform the user how information is to be entered into a particular field or the type of information that is to be entered. There are two kinds of help that you can add to your form:

- **Status Bar**—Help text is displayed in the status bar when user selects the field.
- **Help Key (F1)**—An information dialog box is displayed when user selects the field and presses the **F1 key**.

To Add Help to a Form Field

1. **Double-click** the form field to which you wish to add help.
2. Click the **Add Help Text** button.
3. Click the **Status Bar** tab to display help text in the status bar.
4. Click **Help Key (F1)** to add F1 help.
5. To add your own help message, click the **Type your own** radio button and enter desired help text in the window.
6. To choose pre-defined help text, click the **AutoText entry** and choose the desired help message from the drop-down list.
7. Click **OK**.

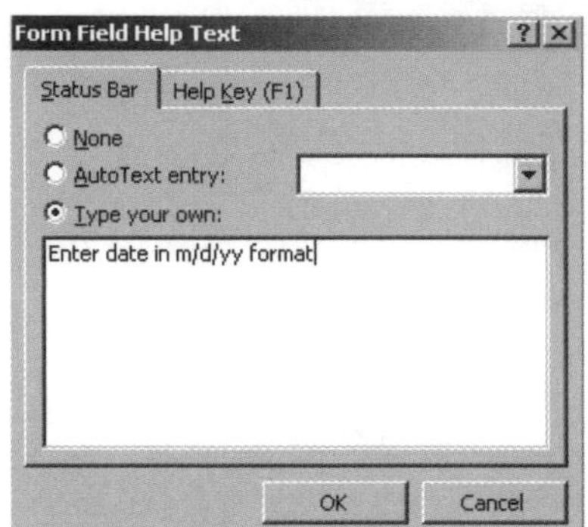

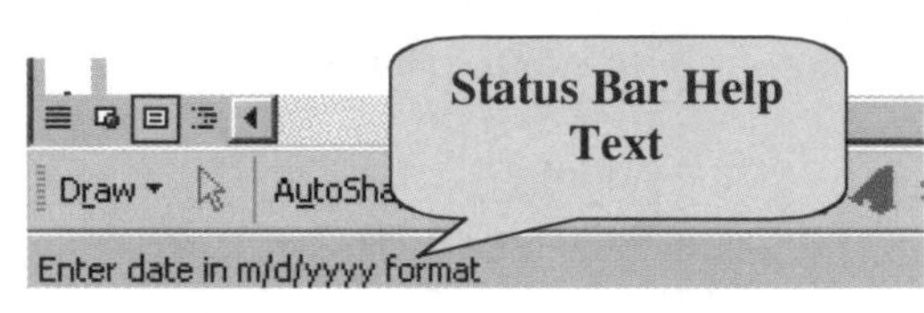

Let's Try It!

- **Double-click** the text form field for **Name of Attendee**.

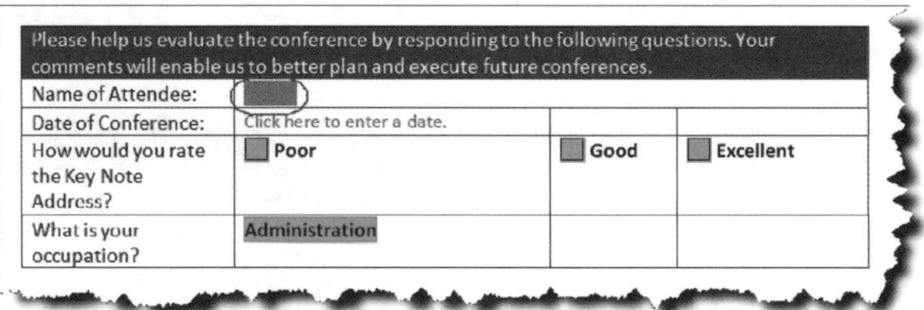

Please help us evaluate the conference by responding to the following questions. Your comments will enable us to better plan and execute future conferences.			
Name of Attendee:			
Date of Conference:	Click here to enter a date.		
How would you rate the Key Note Address?	Poor	Good	Excellent
What is your occupation?	Administration		

Displays the Text Form Field Options dialog box.

- Click the **Add Help Text** button.

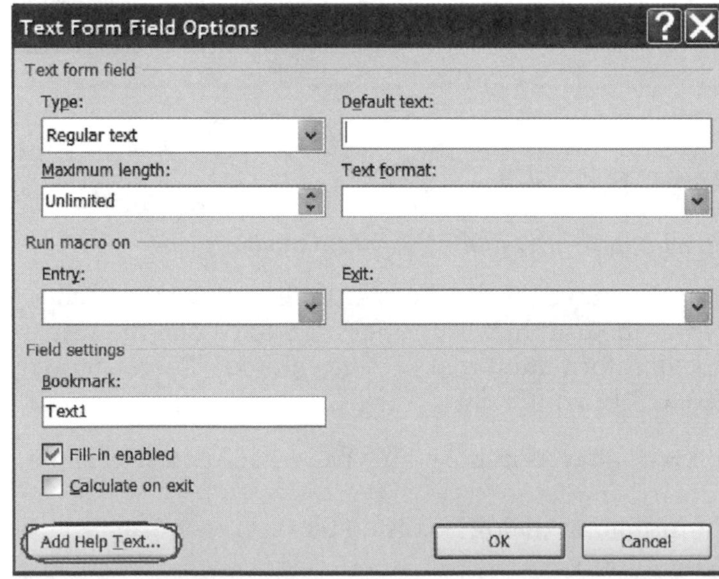

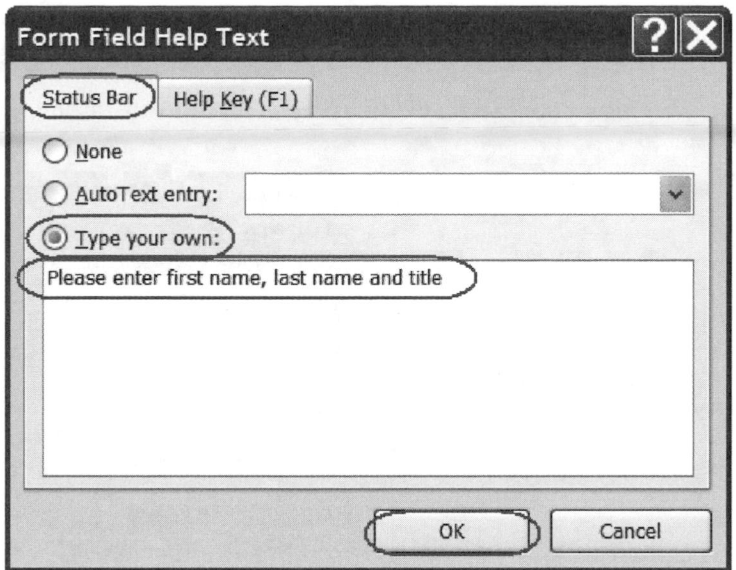

Opens the Form Field Help Text dialog box.

- Click the **Status Bar** tab.

Switches to status bar help options.

- Click the radio button next to **Type your own**.

Sets the option to type our own help message.

- In the **Type your own:** window, type: **Please enter first name, last name and title** as shown.

Enters our status bar help text.

- Click **OK**.

Closes the Form Field Help Text dialog box.

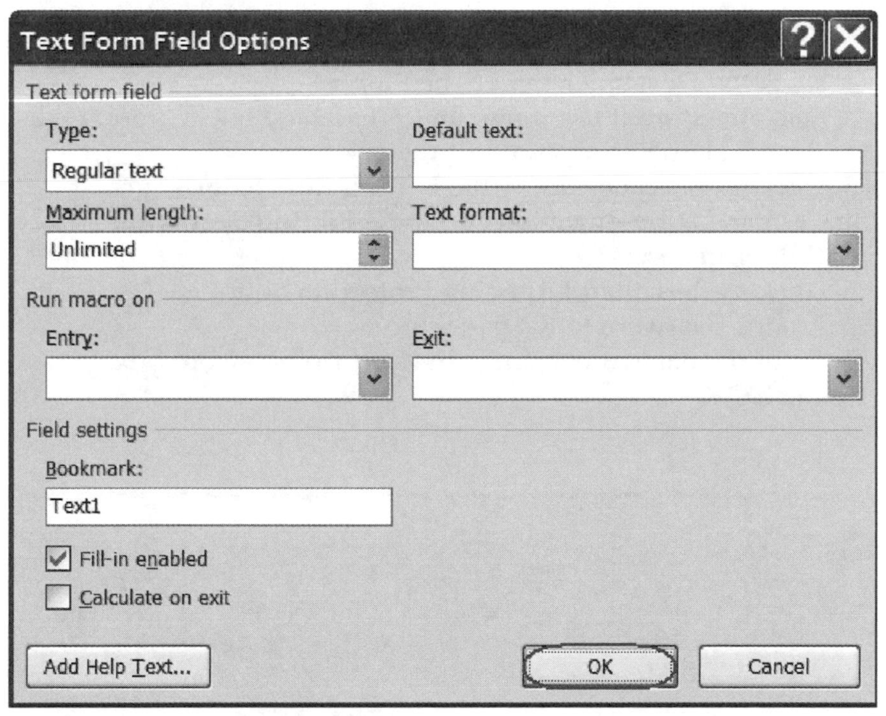

- Click **OK**.

Closes the Text Form Field Options dialog box.

- Click the **Save** button.

Saves the template changes.

Protecting a Form

In this section, you will learn how to protect your form from unauthorized changes.

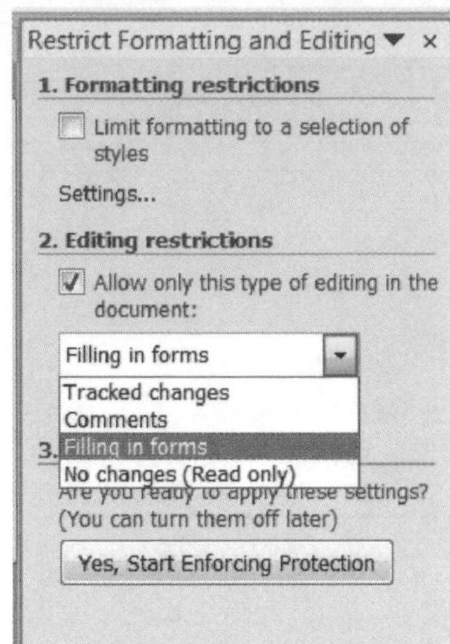

After you create your form, you will want to apply protection to ensure that others will not be able to alter the formatting or text of your form. Additionally, protecting a form turns it into a useable form, that is to say, users can now select check boxes and chose items from drop-down lists.

To Protect a Form

1. Click the **Developer Tab** on the Ribbon.
2. Click the **Protect Document** button on the Protect group to display the **Restrict Formatting and Editing task pane**.
3. Click the checkbox under the **Editing Restrictions** area.
4. Click the **Drop-down list** under the **Editing Restrictions** area and select **Filling in Forms**.
5. Click the **Yes, Start Enforcing Protection** button.
6. Enter a **password** in the password box.
7. Enter the password again in the confirm password box.
8. Click **OK**.

Let's Try It!

- Click the **Protect Document** button on the Developer Ribbon and select **Restrict Formatting and Editing**.

Displays the Restrict Formatting and Editing task pane.

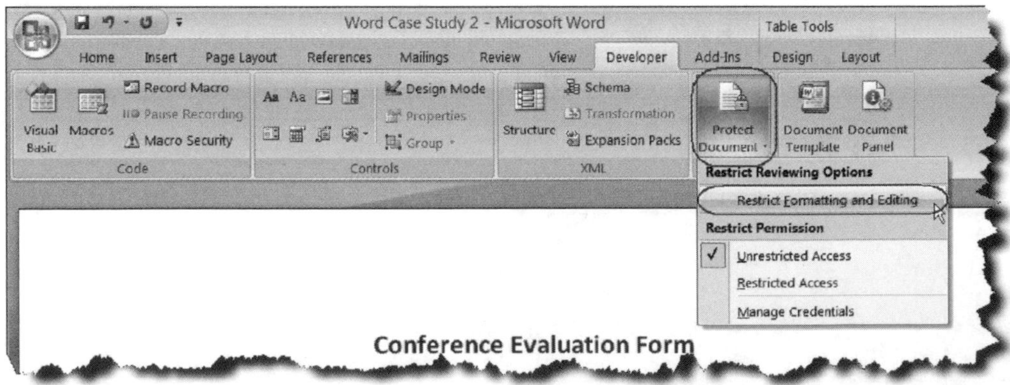

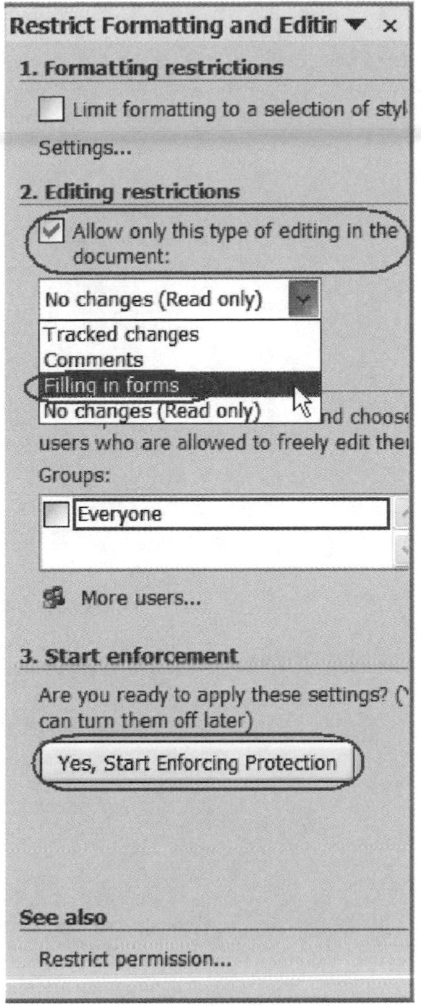

- Click the **checkbox** under the **Editing Restrictions area**.

Enables the Editing Restriction drop-down list from which we will choose the type of protection we wish to apply.

- Click the drop-down list under the Editing Restrictions area and choose **Filling in Forms**.

Selects the type of protection.

- Click the **Yes, Start Enforcing Protection** button.

Displays the Start Enforcing Protection dialog box.

- In the **Password** box, type: **conference**.

Note: Passwords are case-sensitive

Enters the password necessary to make any changes to the form's design.

- Press **Tab** and type **conference** again in the **reenter password box**.

Confirms the password.

- Click **OK**.

Protects the form from changes.

- Click the **Save** button.

Saves the changes to the form.

- Click the **Microsoft Office button** and choose **Close** from the File Options menu.

Closes the template.

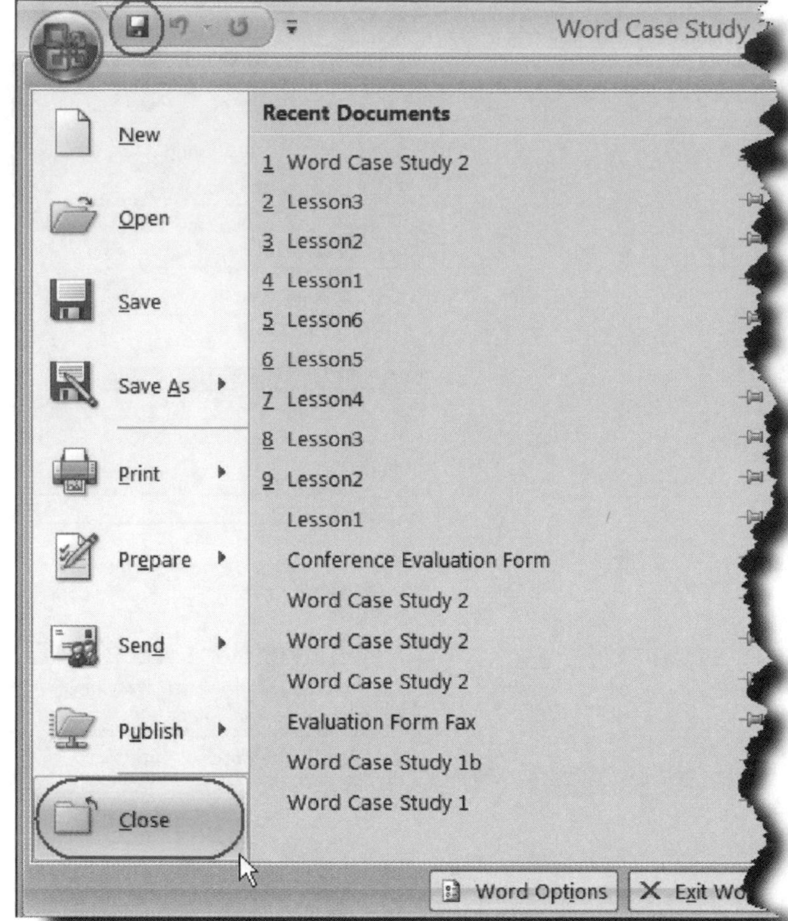

Using a Form Template

In this section, you will learn how to use a form template.

Once you have created your form and protected your template, the form is ready for use. As we saved the form as a template, the form template will appear under the **My Templates** category of the New Document pane. Opening the form as a regular document will enable the user to fill in the required fields, and then save the document with a different name. You can also now distribute your form to others for their use.

To Use a Form Template

1. Click the **Microsoft Office Button** and then click **New**.
2. Click **My Templates** in the left pane.
3. Click the template you want and then click the **OK**.

Let's Try It!

Conference Evaluation Form

Please help us evaluate the conference by responding to the following questions. Your comments will enable us to better plan and execute future conferences.			
Name of Attendee:			
Date of Conference:	Click here to enter a date.		
How would you rate the Key Note Address?	Poor	Good	Excellent
What is your occupation?	Administration		

- Open **Microsoft Office Word 2007**. Locate and open **Word Case Study 2** template.

Opens the form as a regular document.

Conference Evaluation Form

Please help us evaluate the conference by responding to the following questions. Your comments will enable us to better plan and execute future conferences.			
Name of Attendee:	Lisa Wang		
Date of Conference:	Click here to enter a date.		
How would you rate the Key Note Address?	Poor	Good	Excellent
What is your occupation?	Administration		

- Type: **Lisa Wang** and then press the **Tab** key.

Enters information for the first form field then moves to the next field.

Conference Evaluation Form

Please help us evaluate the conference by responding to the following questions. Your comments will enable us to better plan and execute future conferences.			
Name of Attendee:	Lisa Wang		
Date of Conference:	Click here to enter a date.		
How would you rate the Key Note Address?	Po	Good	Excellent
What is your occupation?	Admin		

August, 2007

S	M	T	W	T	F	S
29	30	31	1	2	3	4
5	6	7	8	9	10	11
12	13	14	15	16	17	18
19	20	21	22	23	24	25
26	27	28	29	30	31	1
2	3	4	5	6	7	8

Today

- Click the **drop-down arrow** in the Date of Conference field. Click the **Today** button.

Sets today's date as the conference date field.

- Click the checkbox to the left of the word **Excellent**.

Checks the "Excellent" checkbox.

Conference Evaluation Form

Please help us evaluate the conference by responding to the following questions. Your comments will enable us to better plan and execute future conferences.			
Name of Attendee:	**Lisa Wang**		
Date of Conference:	**6/17/07**		
How would you rate the Key Note Address?	☐ **Poor**	☐ **Good**	☒ **Excellent**
What is your occupation?	**Administration**		

- Click in the **drop-down list** field.

Displays the list items.

- Click on **Technical** from the list.

Selects Technical as the occupation type.

Conference Evaluation Form

Please help us evaluate the conference by responding to the following questions. Your comments will enable us to better plan and execute future conferences.			
Name of Attendee:	**Lisa Wang**		
Date of Conference:	**6/20/07**		
How would you rate the Key Note Address?	☐ **Poor**	☐ **Good**	☒ **Excellent**
What is your occupation?	**Administration**		

Administration
Architecture
Education
Engineering
Law
Technical

Using Help

In this section, you will learn how to use the Help system.

The **Help system** is designed to provide **assistance** to users whether you are online or offline and bring all available resources to you as quickly as possible. To access the Help system, press **F1** or click the **Help icon** on the upper right-hand corner of the Word window.

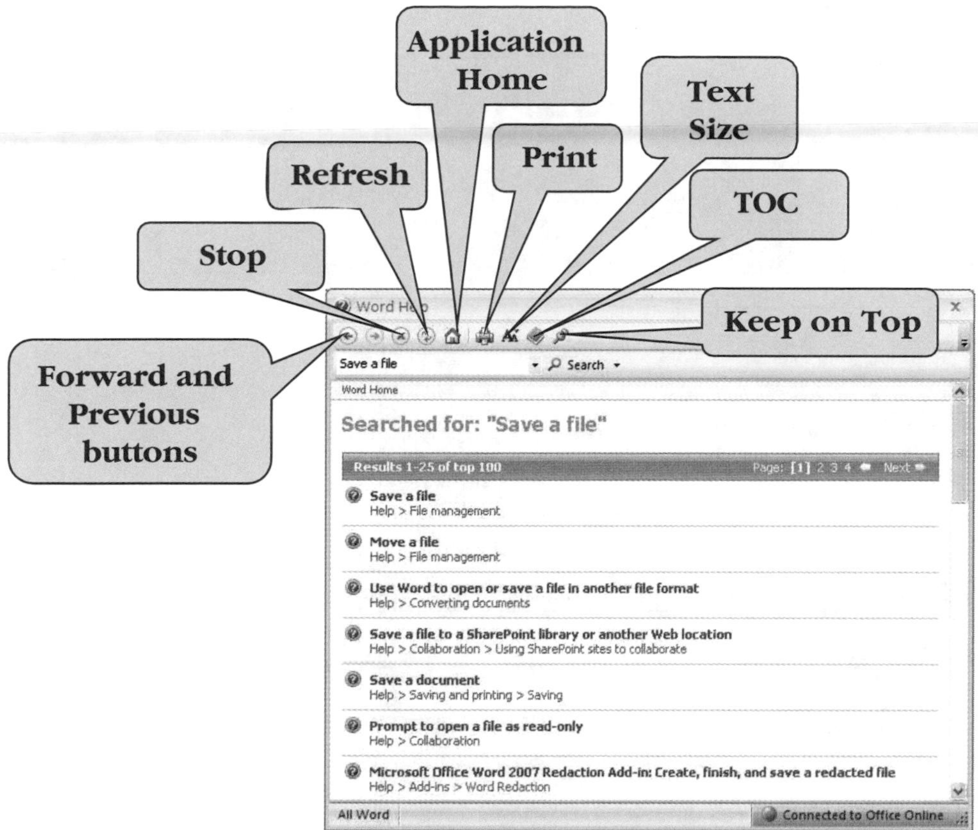

The Help system toolbar includes the familiar Back, Forward and Stop commands. Additionally, you will find the new **Refresh** tool, which allows you to update the content of the Help window. The **Application Home** tool brings you to the Word starting point, where you can browse through information related to the Microsoft Word application. The **TOC** tool displays a listing of available help topics through which you can browse. If you wish to increase or decrease the text size in the Help window, click the **Text Size** tool. Another nice feature on the Help toolbar is the **Keep on Top** tool, which allows you to keep the current Help page open while you work.

To Use the Help System

1. Click the **Microsoft Office Word Help** button on the upper right-hand corner of the Word Window
   Or
   Press **F1**
2. Enter the keyword(s) for which you want to search in the **Search** box.
3. Click the **Search** button
   Or
   Press the **Enter** key.
4. Click the **link** for the help topic you wish to view in the **Search Results pane**.
5. To browse Help topics, click the **TOC** button. Click the TOC button again to hide the Table of Contents.

Let's Try It!

- Click the **Microsoft Office Word Help icon** on the upper right-hand corner of the screen as shown.

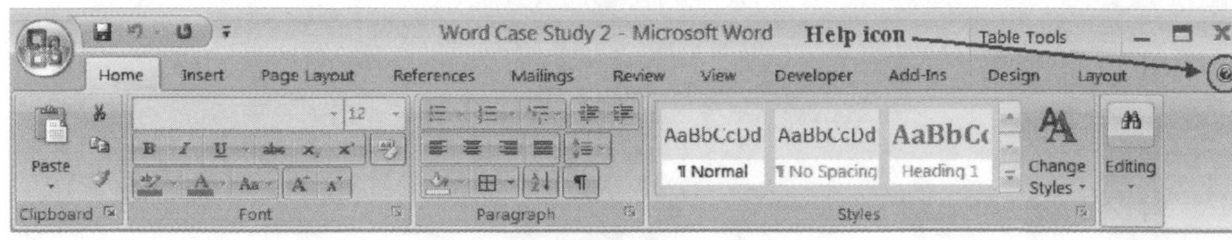

Displays the Word Help System window.

- In the **Search box**, type: **Save a file**.

Enter the keywords for which we want to search.

- Press **Enter**.

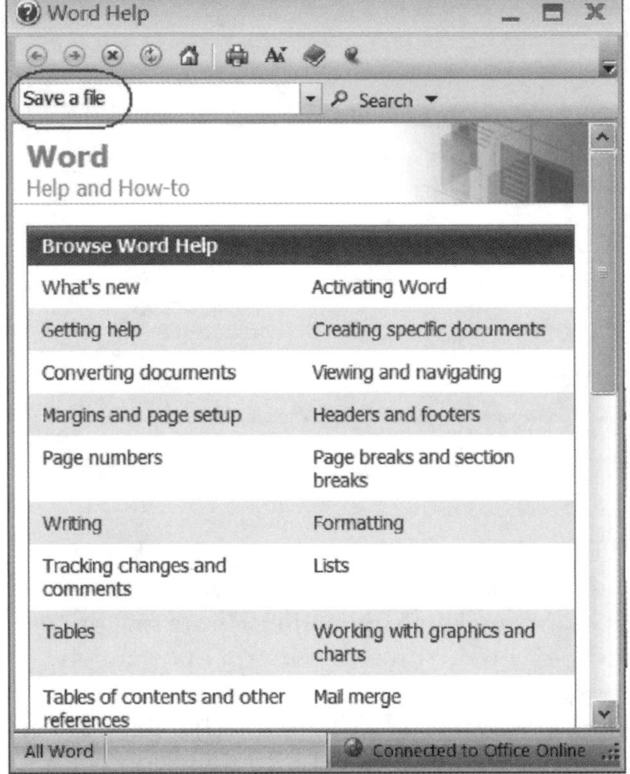

Executes the search. The results are displayed in the Search Results pane.

- Click the **Save a file** link in the Search Results pane.

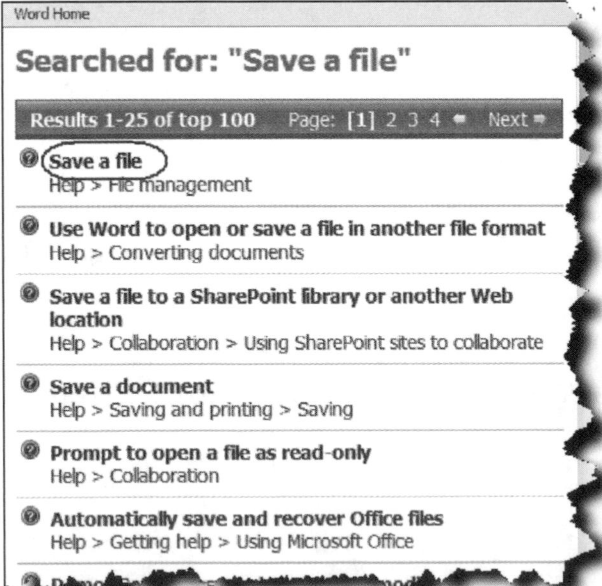

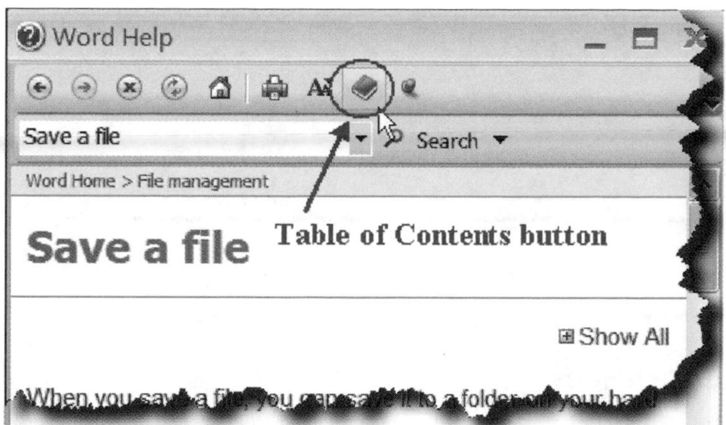

Displays the help topic for that link.

- Click the **Table of Contents** button on the toolbar.

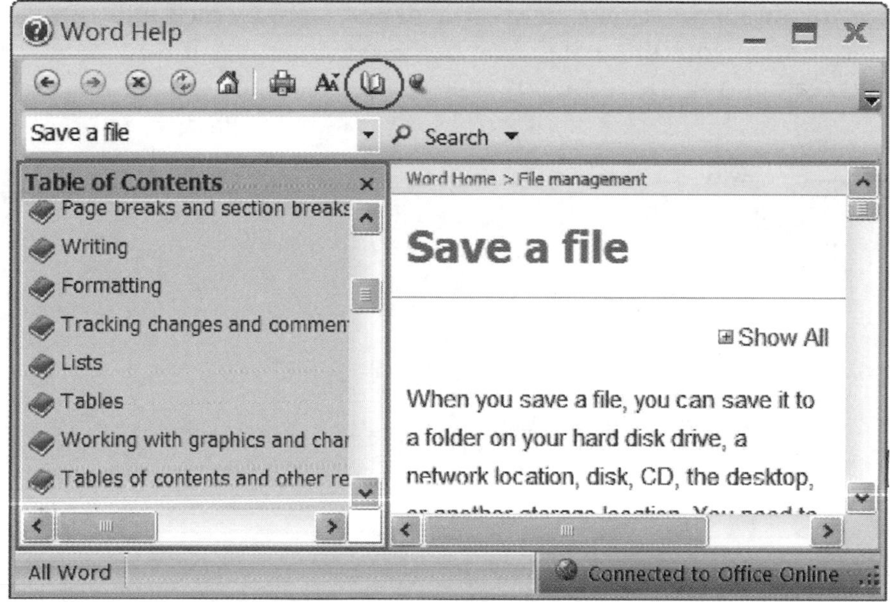

Displays a listing of Microsoft Word help topics.

- Click the **Table of Contents** button again.

Hides the Table of Contents.

- Click the Word Help **Close button** on the upper right-hand corner of the screen.

Closes the Help System window.

- Click the **Microsoft Office button** and choose **Close** from the File Options menu. Click **No** when asked to save your changes.

Closes the form without saving changes.

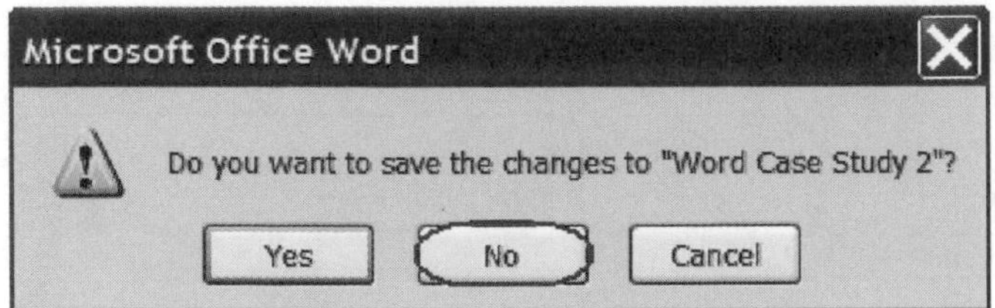

Conclusion

You have completed Word 2007—Case Study II. You are now ready to use several advanced MS Word skills that you have learned in this chapter. You are encouraged to experiment with all you have learned in this case study. To reinforce your understanding of these techniques, it is recommended that you read and work through it once again.

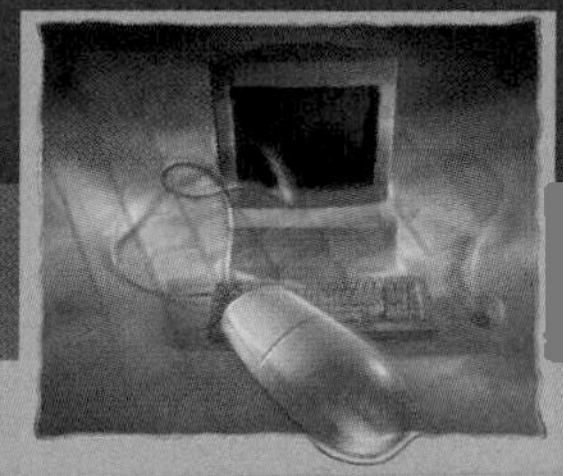

Excel Case Study 1

CHAPTER 5

OBJECTIVES

After successfully completing this case study, you should able to:

- Start, Create, Close, and Save Excel documents
- Set Excel Options
- Enter Text and Numbers
- Enter Simple Formulas
- Choose Formula Cell References Manually
- Use AutoSum
- Use Undo/Redo
- Use Find and Replace
- Use the Go To Command
- Insert Symbols
- Work with Ranges
- Cut and Paste Data
- Copy and Move Cells Using Drag-and-Drop
- Change Column Width and Row Height
- Insert and Remove Rows and Columns
- Copy Data and Formulas with Auto-Fill
- Format Text and Values
- Apply Cell Styles
- Spell Check the Worksheet
- Close the Workbook

Case Study I—MS Excel 2007

Assume that you work in the HR department of Rodney's Video Company. You are asked to prepare the Quarterly Sales report for year 2005 that lists total sales by store for each quarter. In addition, your boss would like to see total sales of each store in year 2005 and the grand total sales in each quarter.

The desired worksheet looks like the following:

	Quarterly Sales for FY 2005					
Store #	Store	Q1	Q2	Q3	Q4	Total
1	New York City	14,391	12,524	16,979	21,075	64,969
2	San Francisco	22,987	25,424	26,552	29,780	104,743
3	Milwaukee	41,224	42,655	38,972	45,268	168,119
4	Dallas	15,344	17,045	19,024	23,242	74,655
	Grand Total	$93,946	$97,648	$101,527	$119,365	$412,486
	©2007 Rodney's Video					

QUARTERLY SALES REPORT OF RODNEY'S VIDEO COMPANY IN MICROSOFT EXCEL

Creating an Excel Workbook

Welcome to **Microsoft Excel 2007**! Microsoft Excel is a powerful and user-friendly spreadsheet application that allows you to enter, calculate, organize and analyze data. You can use Excel for a variety of tasks, such as preparing a budget, creating invoices, tracking inventory, and preparing financial forms, just to name a few. Excel has powerful calculating and charting capabilities as well as formatting features that allow you to really jazz up your documents.

The ***cell*** is the most basic part of Excel—it is in the cell where data is entered. In Excel, data is organized in **rows** (the horizontal divisions) and **columns** (the vertical divisions) which make up an Excel ***Worksheet***. Worksheets are stored in an Excel file called a ***workbook***.

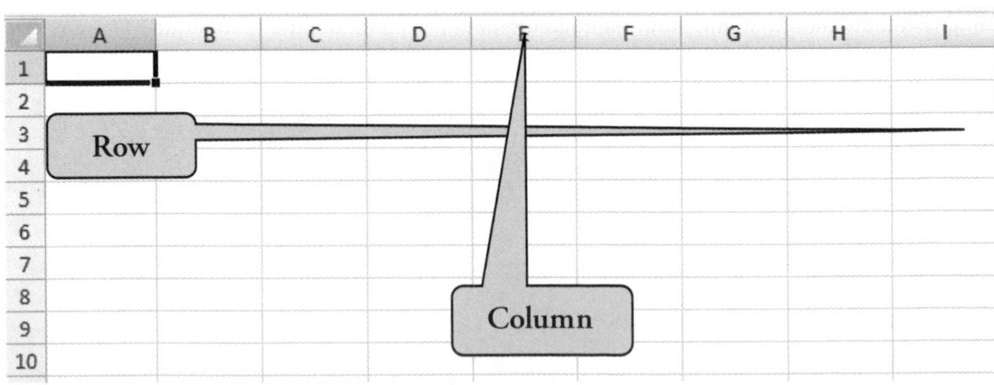

A workbook can consist of several worksheets. When Excel first launches, a blank worksheet appears and you can begin entering your data and formatting the look of your document.

Let's begin by creating a new workbook and examining the Excel environment.

To Start Microsoft Excel

1. Click the **Start** button on the lower-left corner of your screen to display the Start menu.
2. **All Programs > Microsoft Office > Microsoft Office Excel 2007** from the Start Menu to launch the application.

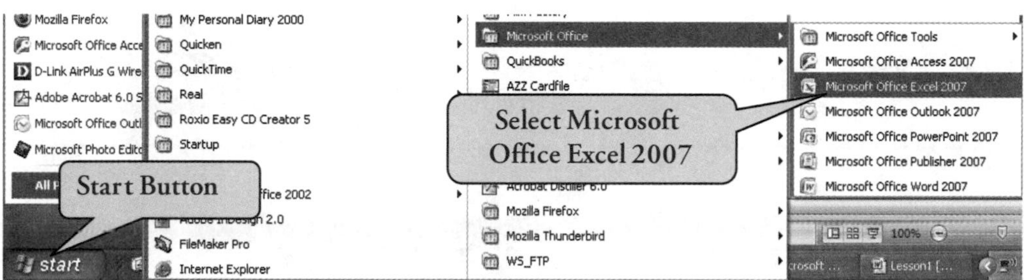

Let's Try It!

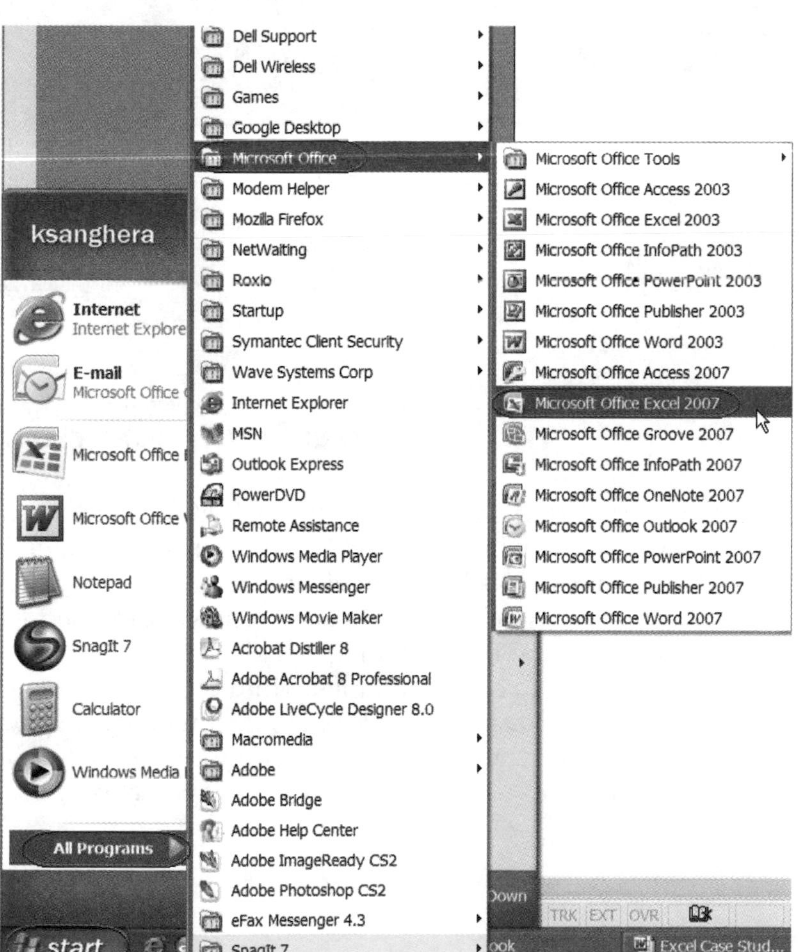

- Click the **Start** button on the lower left side of your screen.

Displays the Start Menu, allowing you to select which application to launch.

- Select **All Programs > Microsoft Office > Microsoft Office Excel 2007** from the Start Menu.

Launches the Microsoft Excel Program and displays a new blank worksheet.

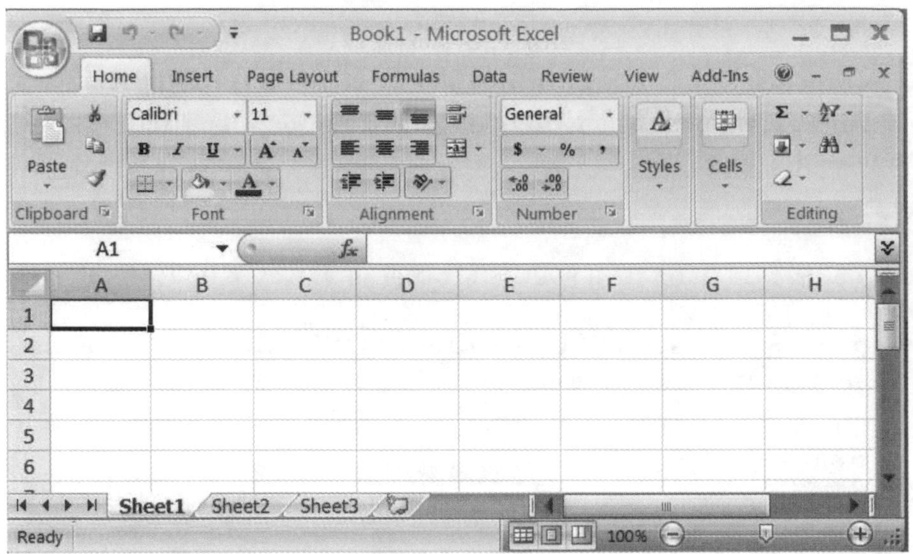

Examining the Excel Environment

In this section, we will look at the parts of an Excel worksheet.

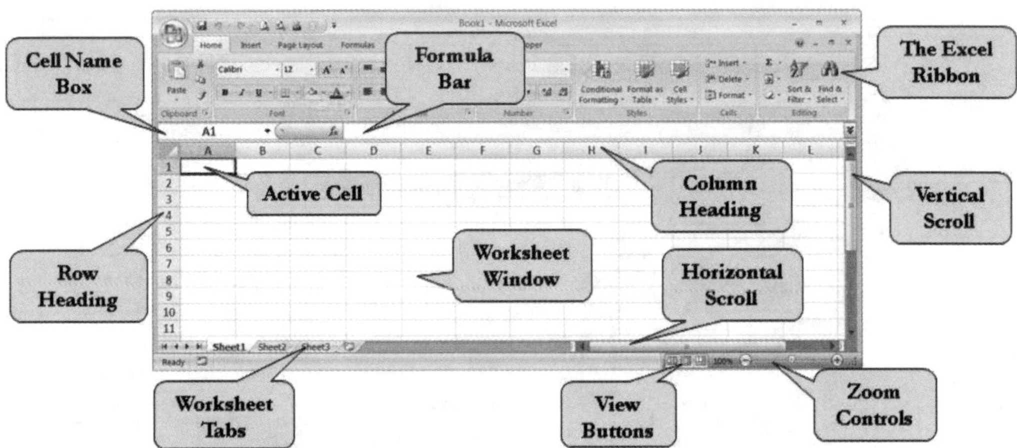

THE EXCEL WORKING ENVIRONMENT

When you first start Microsoft Excel, the application opens to a blank worksheet along with the parts of the Microsoft Excel screen as shown in the screen shot above. If you have worked with previous versions of Excel, you will immediately notice that the user interface has been completely redesigned.

The menu and toolbar system have been replaced by the **Ribbon**. The Ribbon is designed to help you quickly find the commands you need in order to complete a task. On the Ribbon, the menu bar has been replaced by **Command Tabs** that relate to the tasks you wish to accomplish. The default Command Tabs in Excel are: **Home, Insert, Page Layout, Formulas, Data, Review** and **View**.

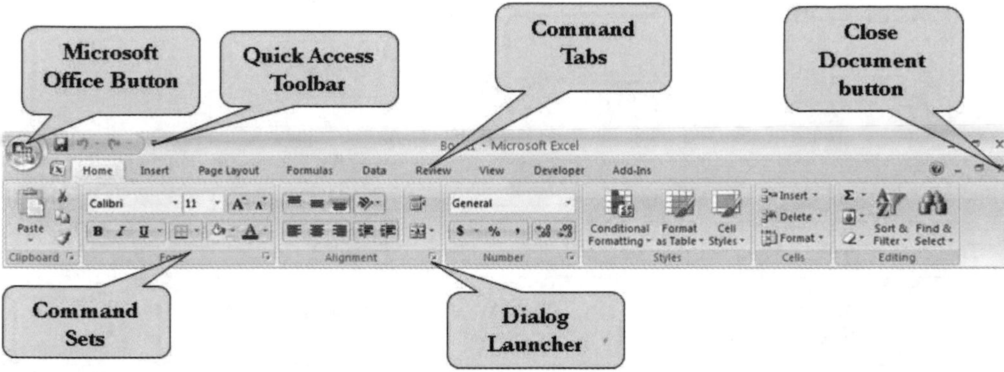

Different command icons, called **Command Sets** appear under each Command Tab. The commands that appear will depend on the Command Tab that is selected. Each command set is grouped by its function. For example, the Insert tab contains commands to add tables, charts, illustrations, links and text objects to your spreadsheet. **Contextual Commands** only appear when a specific object is selected. This helps in keeping the screen uncluttered.

On the bottom of many of the Command Sets is a **Dialog Launcher**, which when clicked, will launch a dialog box for that set of commands.

To the right of the **Microsoft Office icon** (from where you access file options), is the **Quick Access Toolbar**. This toolbar contains by default the Save, Undo, and Redo commands. In addition, clicking the drop-down arrow to the right allows you to customize the Quick Access Toolbar to add other tools that you use regularly. You can choose from the list which tools to display on the Quick Access Toolbar or select **More Commands** to add commands that are not in the list.

As you can see on the **worksheet window**, the columns are labeled with letters of the alphabet while the rows are numbered. These numbers and letters are very important when working with formulas as they provide a means of referring to a particular cell. This is called a ***cell reference***. For example, if you wanted to refer to the cell in the first row and the first column, the cell reference would be **A1**. You will work much more with cell references later.

The Excel Environment

Component	Description
Active Cell	The currently selected cell in which you enter or edit data. The active cell is highlighted by a black box.
Cell Name Box	The cell address of the active cell (i.e. A5 = Column A, Row 5)
Column Headings	Sequential letters in gray boxes at the top of your worksheet. Clicking on the column heading selects the entire column.
Command Sets	Command icons, grouped by category, under each command tab.
Dialog Launcher	Launches dialog boxes or task panes for a particular set of commands
Formula Bar	Displays the contents (labels, values or formula) of the active cell.
Horizontal Scroll Bar	Allows you to move horizontally in your document. To navigate horizontally, click the scroll bar with your left mouse button and drag to the left or to the right until the desired portion of the document is in view.
Office Button	Click to access file commands.
Quick Access Toolbar	Contains frequently used commands. You can customize it to include tools and commands that you frequently use.
Ribbon	Commands and tools organized into command sets.
Row Headings	Sequential numbers in gray boxes on the left side of the worksheet. Clicking on the row heading selects the entire row.
Status Bar	Displays information about the active document.
Tabs	To access the various command sets and tools.
Title Bar	Displays the name of the application you are currently using and the name of the file (the Microsoft Excel worksheet) on which you are working.
Vertical Scroll Bar	Allows you to move vertically in your document. To navigate vertically, click the scroll bar with your left mouse button and drag upward or downwards until the desired portion of the document is in view.
View Buttons	Allows you to display documents in several different document views (Normal, Page Layout, and Page Break Preview).
Worksheet Tabs	Displays the worksheets contained in the current workbook. Clicking on the worksheet tabs allow you to navigate from one worksheet to another.
Worksheet Window	The white working area where you type and edit your worksheet. Consists of columns and rows.
Zoom Slider	Allows you to increase or decrease the magnification of your document.

Let's Try It!

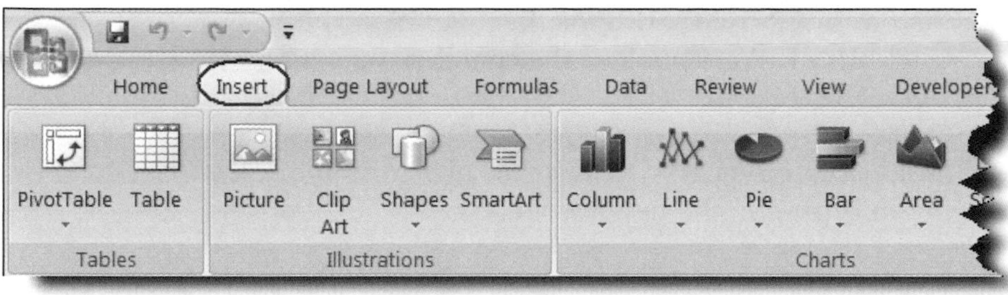

- Click the **Insert tab** on top of your screen.

Displays the commands sets for the Insert command tab.

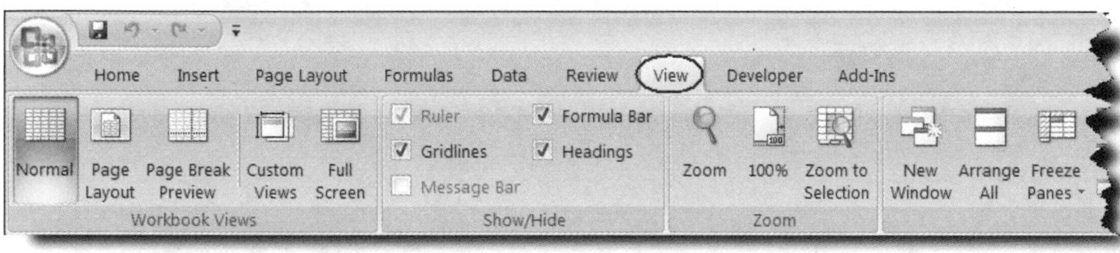

- Click the **View tab** on top of your screen.

Displays the commands sets for the View command tab.

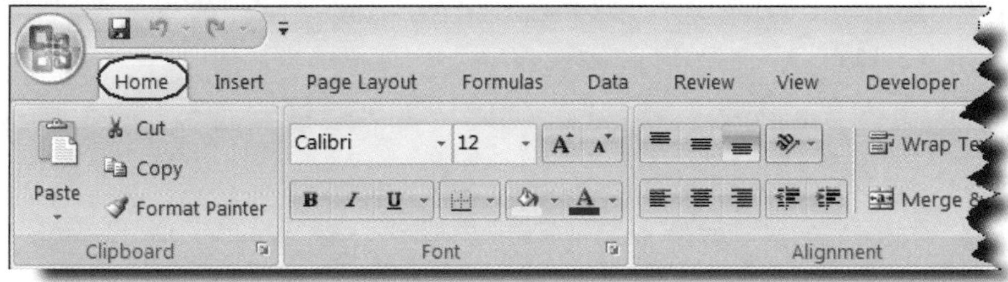

- Click the **Home tab** on top of your screen.

Returns us back to the Home tab.

Creating a New Workbook

In this section, you will learn how to create a new blank document.

We have already seen that when you first launch Microsoft Excel, a new blank workbook is created. You can also create a new workbook from within another workbook. The new document command is located under the **File Options** menu. You can also use the keyboard shortcut **Ctrl + N** to bypass the File Options menu.

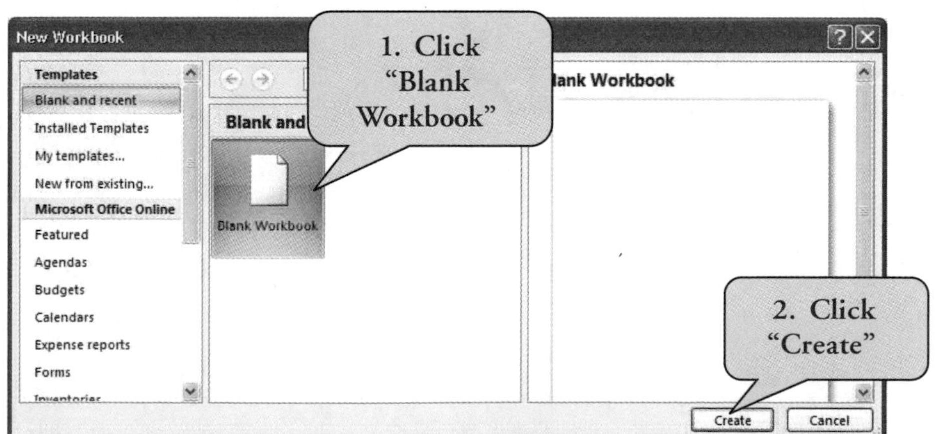

To Create a New Document

1. Click the **Microsoft Office Button** and then click **New** from the menu to display the **New Workbook** Task Pane.
2. Click **Blank Workbook** in the center pane.
3. Click **Create**.
   Or
   Hold down the **Ctrl** and **N** keystroke combination (**Ctrl + N**)
4. Begin typing in the new workbook.

Let's Try It!

- Click the **Microsoft Office Button**.

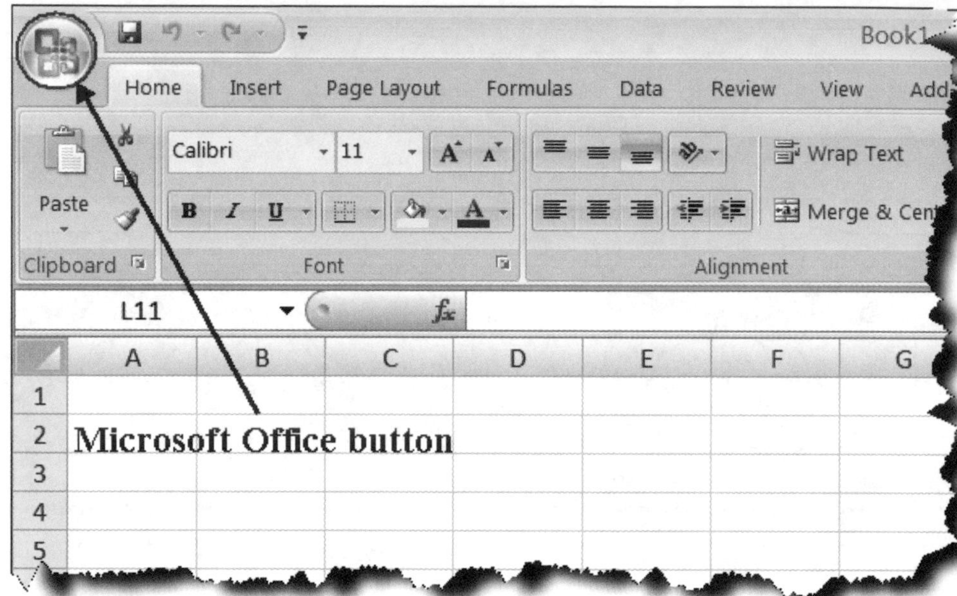

- Click **New** from the menu.

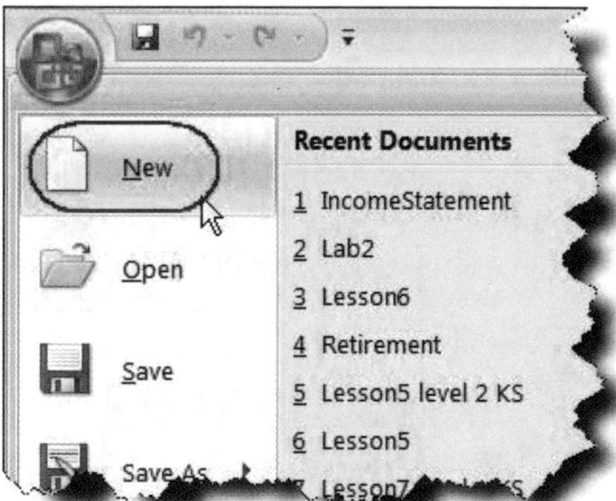

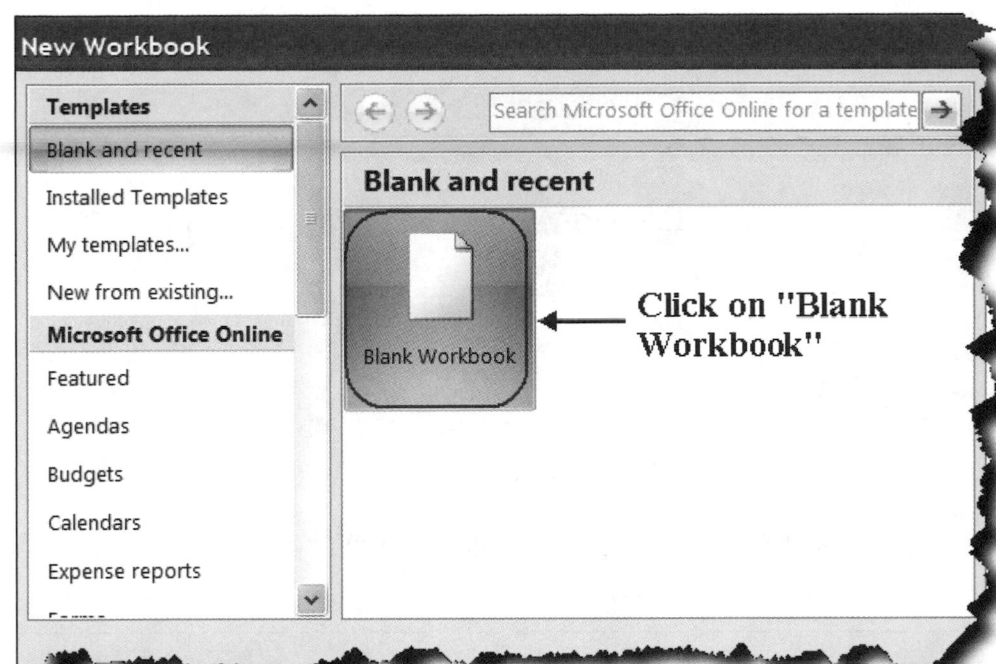

Displays the New Document pane.

- In the **Center** Pane, click on **Blank Workbook**.

Specifies that we will create a new blank workbook.

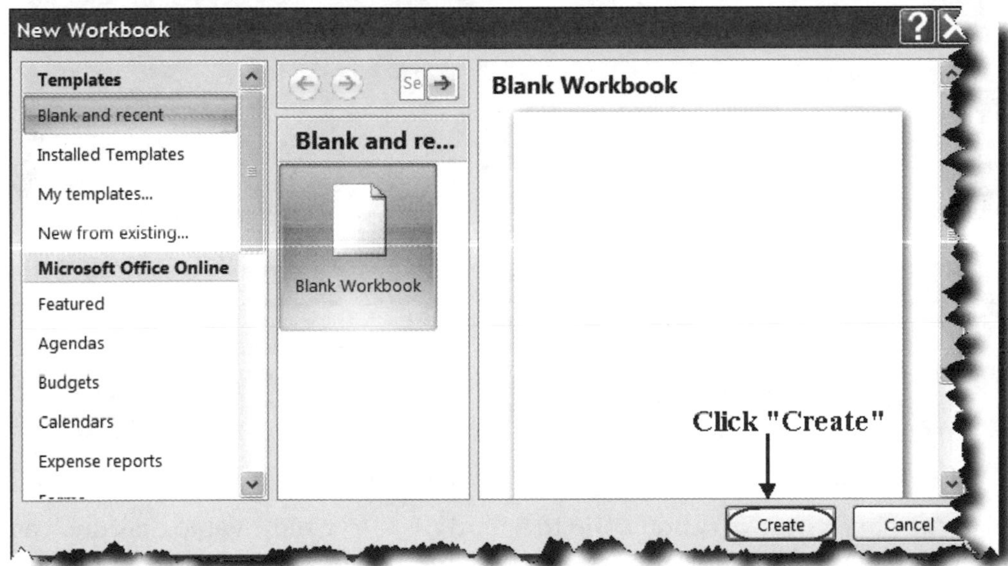

- Click **Create**.

Creates a new blank workbook with three default blank worksheets.

- **Click** in the cell of the first row, first column (**cell A1**).

Activates the cell where we wish to begin typing.

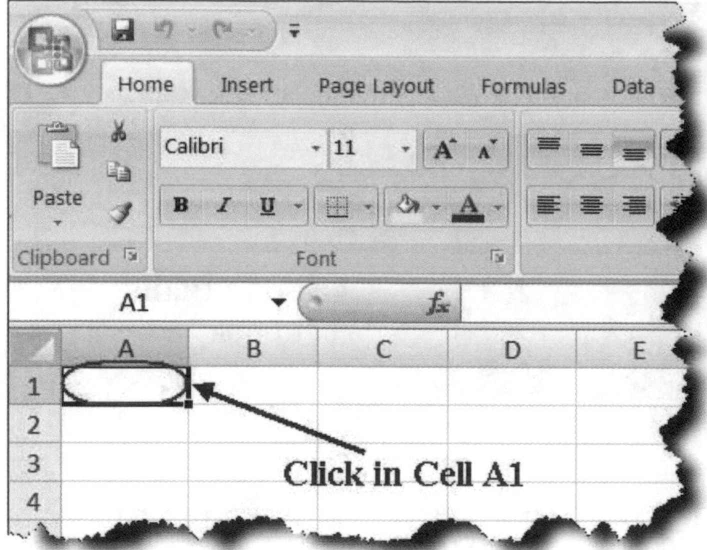

- Type: **Store** and then press **Enter**.

Enters text into the new worksheet.

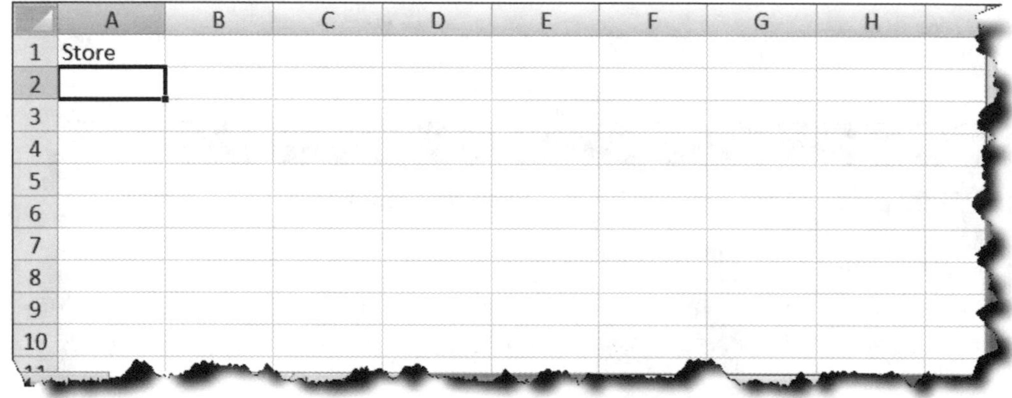

Saving a New Workbook

In this section, you will learn how to save a workbook.

You can **save your workbook file** to a hard disk, to a removable disk such as a zip drive or USB flash drive, or to a network drive. The first time you save a document, the **Save As Dialog Box** will appear, prompting you for the name of the document and the location where you wish to save the document. This box will only appear the first time you save a new workbook. To save a file, click the **Microsoft Office Button** and then click **Save** or use the keyboard shortcut **Ctrl + S**. You can also click the **Save button** on the Quick Access toolbar, directly to the right of the Microsoft Office button. The default file format for new Excel workbooks is XML format, the default format for all Office 2007 documents.

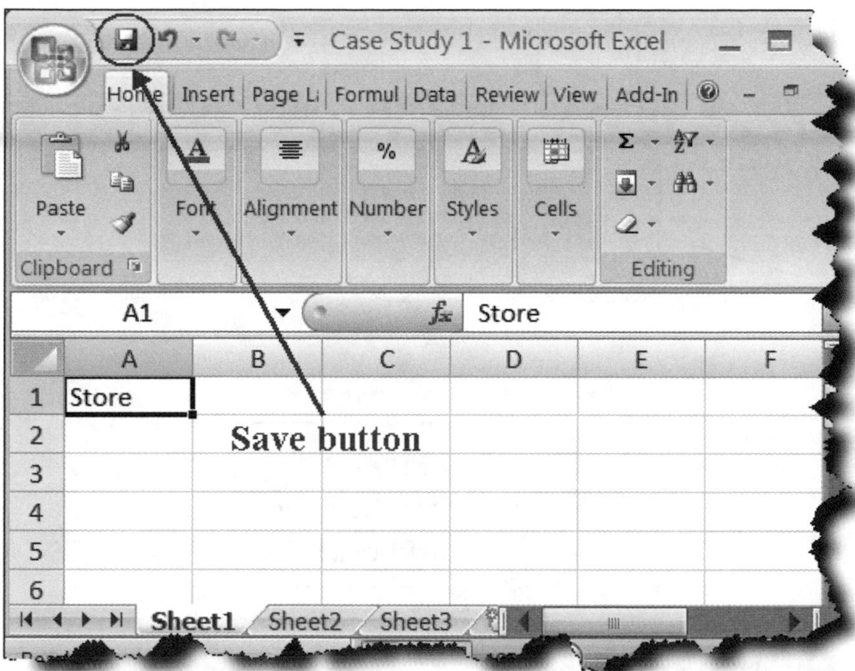

To save an exiting document with a different file name or in a different location, select **Save As** from the File Options menu, and then type the new name for the document in the **file name** text box. The original document will be closed and the document with the new name becomes the active document.

After you save a document, the file remains open so you can continue to work on it. You can save any subsequent changes quickly by clicking on the Save icon. It is a good idea to save your documents often.

To Save a New Workbook

1. Click the **Microsoft Office Button** and then click **Save** from the menu
   Or
   Click the **Save icon** on the Quick Access Toolbar

SAVE ICON

   Or
   Hold down the **Ctrl key** and S keystroke combination **(Ctrl + S)**
2. Type the desired file name in the **File name** box.
3. Navigate to the folder where you wish to save your file in the **Places bar** (many people prefer to save their workbooks in the **My Documents** folder).
4. Click **Save**.

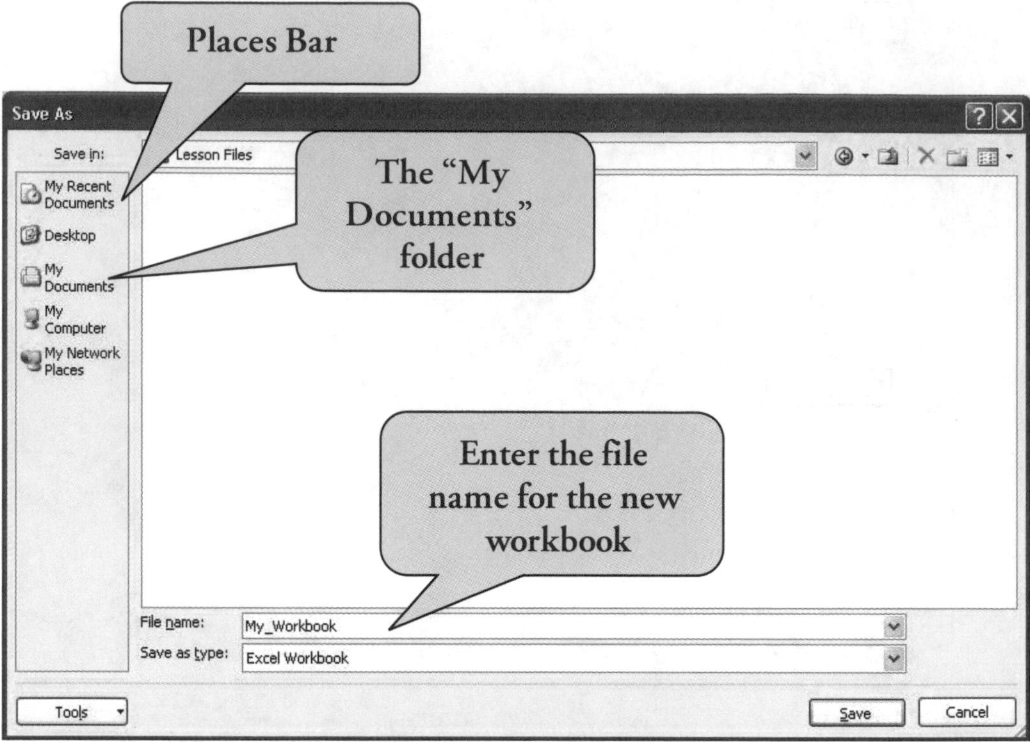

THE SAVE AS DIALOG BOX

To Save a Workbook with a Different Name

1. Click the **Microsoft Office Button** and then click **Save As** from the menu. The Save As dialog box will appear.
2. In the **File name** box, type the new name for your workbook.
3. To save the document in a different file format, click the **Save as Type** drop-down list and choose the desired file format.
4. To save the workbook in a different folder, **navigate to the folder** you want from the Places Bar.

Let's Try It!

- Insert **flash drive** in USB port.
- Click the **Save button** on the Quick Access toolbar.

Since we have not yet saved the document, the Save As dialog box appears, prompting for the file name and location where we wish to save the file.

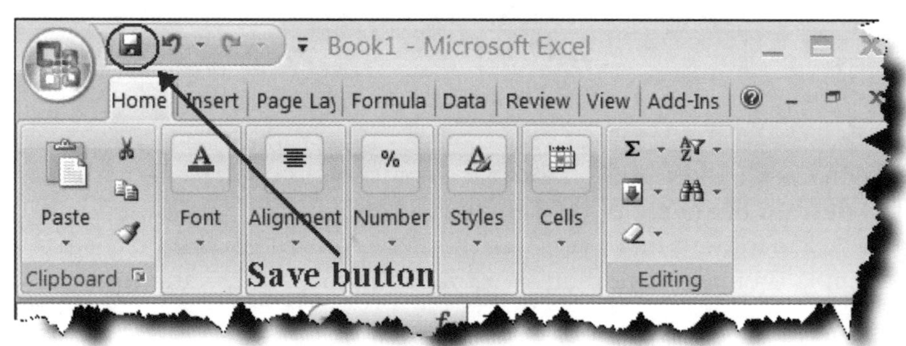

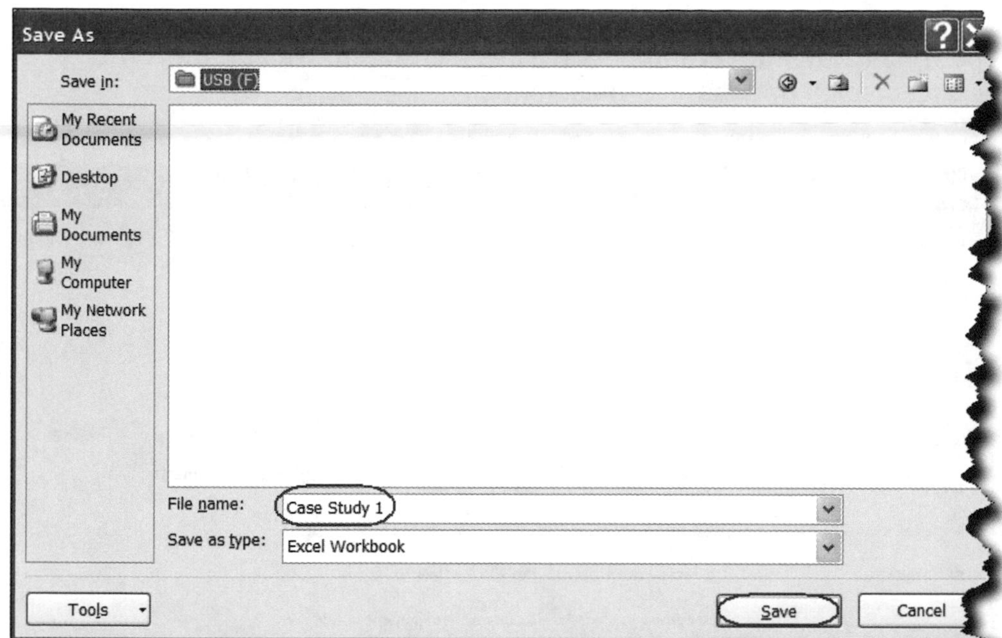

- In the **File name** text box, type: **Case Study 1** and select **flash drive** in the **Save in** list.

Enters the name of the new workbook.

- Click the **Save** button.

Saves the workbook with the new name.

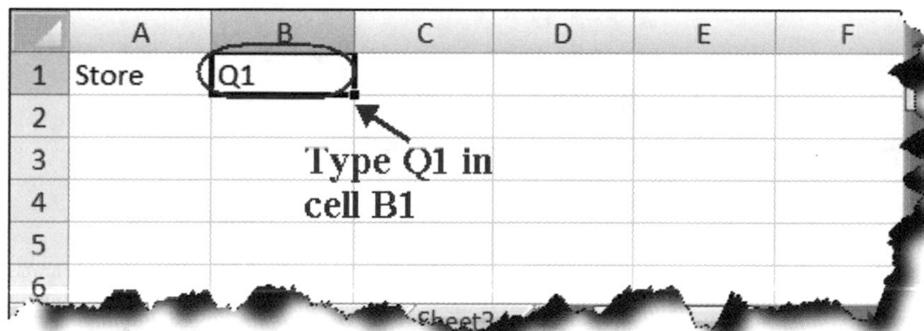

- Click in cell **B1**.

Makes cell B1 the active cell.

- Type: **Q1** in cell B1 and then press the **Enter** key.

Enters text in cell B1 and confirms the entry.

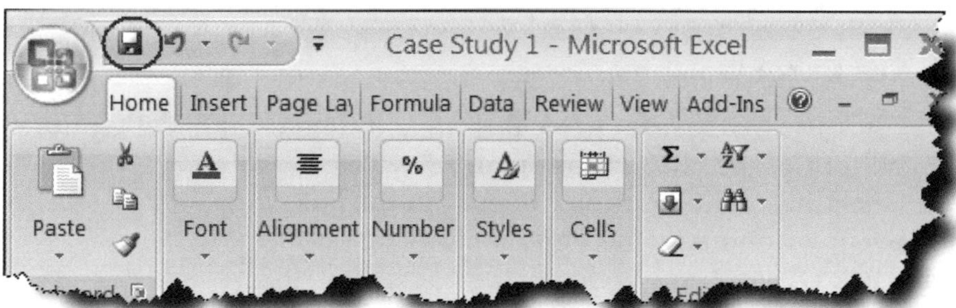

- Click the **Save** icon on the Quick Access toolbar.

Saves the changes. Since we have already saved the workbook, the Save As dialog box does not appear.

Setting Excel Options

In this section, we will work with Excel Options.

In previous versions of Excel, you could set preferences for specific program settings from the Options dialog box. The Options command has been moved to the **Excel Options** button on the File Options menu which displays when you click the **Microsoft Office Button**.

From the Excel Options dialog box, you can specify such options as specifying a default location to save files, setting the default file format, setting display options and much more.

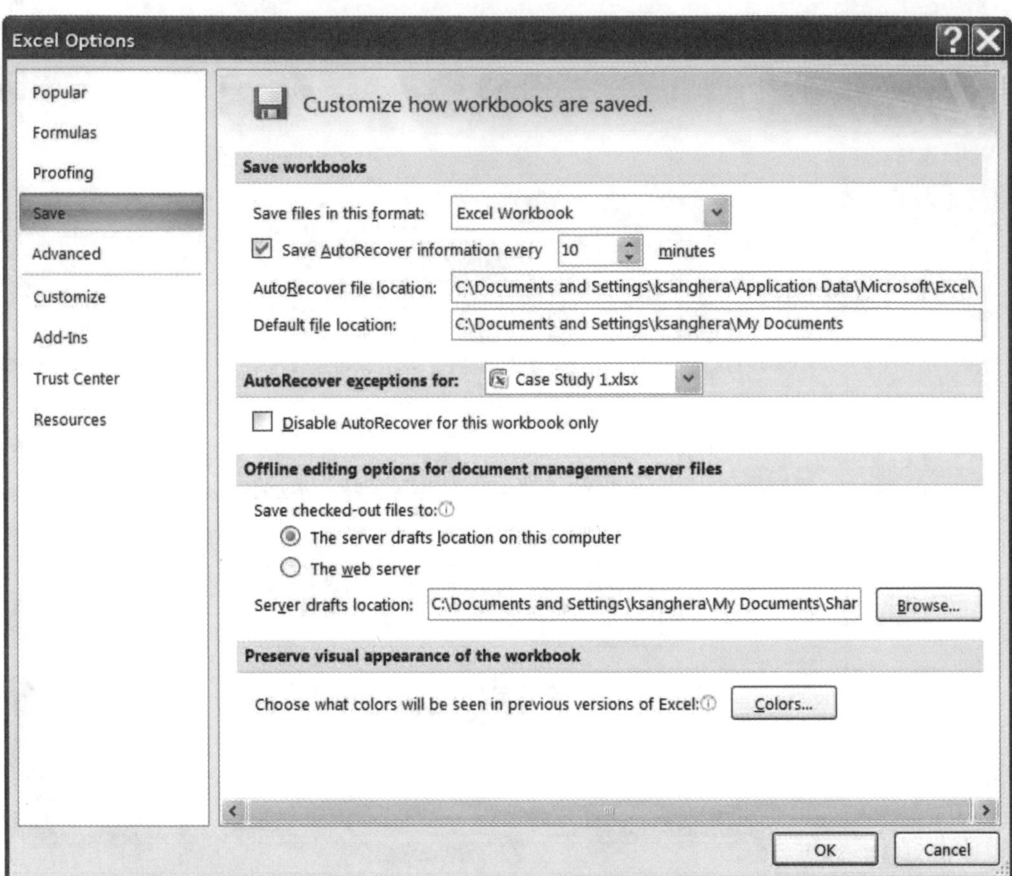

EXCEL OPTIONS DIALOG BOX

To Set Excel Options

1. Click the **Microsoft Office Button** and then click **Excel Options** on the bottom of the File Options pane.
2. Click the desired option category in the left pane.
3. Set any options in the right pane.
4. Click **OK**.

Let's Try It!

- Click the **Microsoft Office Button**.

Displays the File Options menu.

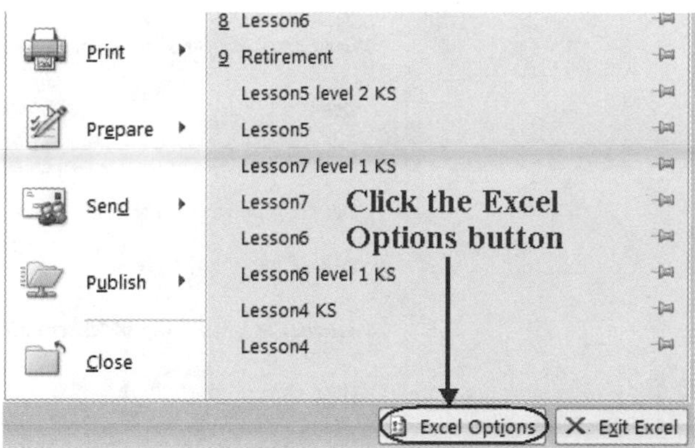

- Click the **Excel Options** button.

Displays the Excel Options dialog box.

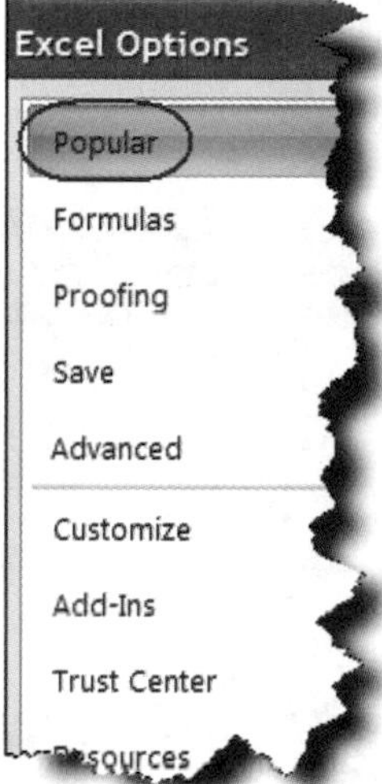

- Click the **Popular** category in the left pane.

Displays available Excel options for the Save category.

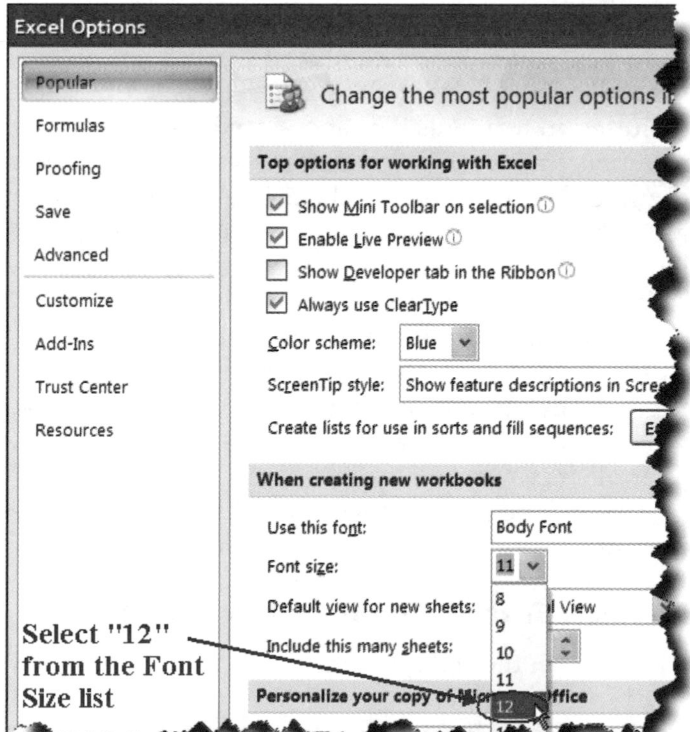

- Under the **Creating New Workbooks** area, click the **Font Size arrow** and choose **12**.

Sets a new default font size for all new Excel workbooks.

• Click **OK**.

Displays a message telling you that your changes will not take effect until you close and restart excel.

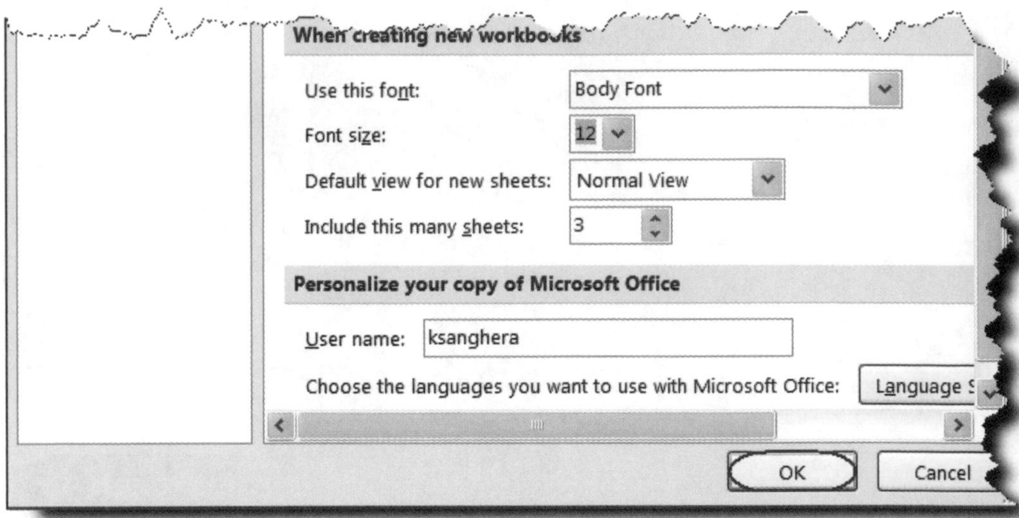

• Click **OK**.

Closes the message box and applies the changes.

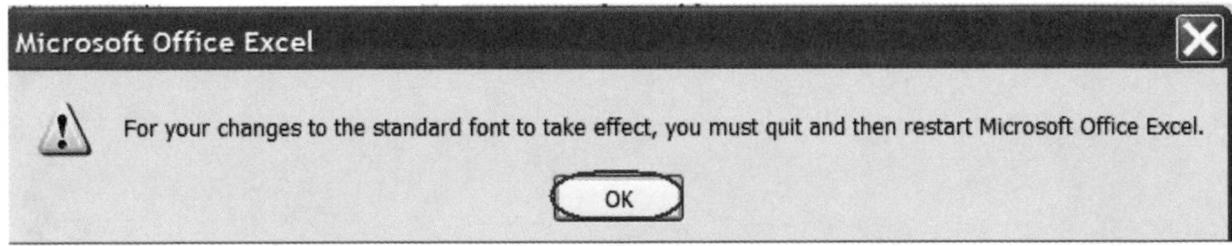

Entering Text and Numbers

This section will guide you through the process of entering text and numbers into cells.

Data that you enter into an Excel worksheet can be either text, numbers or a formula. Text that is entered into cells is referred to as **labels** and is not included in formulas. Numbers can be either labels or **values**. When entering numbers into a cell, Excel automatically treats them as values and aligns them to the right edges of the cell. If you wish a numerical value to be treated as a label—that is to say, to take on the same formatting as labels (which are left-aligned), you can precede the numerical value with an apostrophe ('). Thus, to enter the year as a value, you would type: **'2006**.

To begin entering data, click on the cell into which you wish to enter data (this becomes the **active cell**) and begin typing. Once you are finished, pressing **Enter** confirms your entry. Any time you wish to clear a cell into which you have begun typing, press the **Esc** key **or** the **X** key to the left of the formula bar.

We will begin by creating a blank new worksheet and entering sales information for a video store.

To Enter Text or Numbers into a Cell

1. Click on the cell into which you wish to enter a value.
2. Type your entry.
3. Press **Enter** to confirm your entry and move to the next cell.

Identifying an Active Cell and a Cell Reference

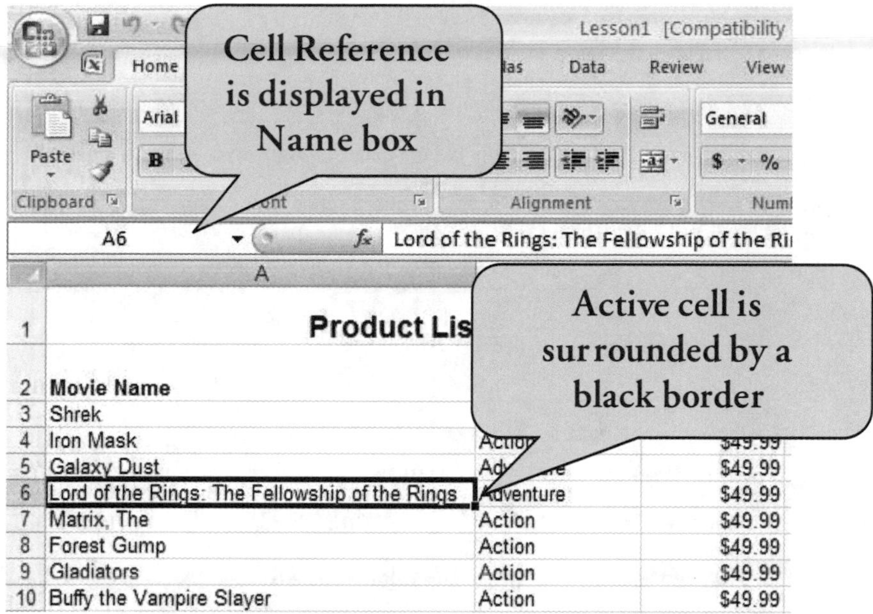

To move from one location to another in Excel, click in the cell that you want to activate. The cell then becomes the **active cell**. Moving around in a worksheet becomes more challenging as the worksheet becomes larger. Luckily, Excel contains **Scroll Bars** to help you move from one area of your worksheet to another. Excel contains both **horizontal and vertical scroll bars**. Clicking and dragging the Scroll Bar moves you to the position in the workbook where you are when you release the mouse button.

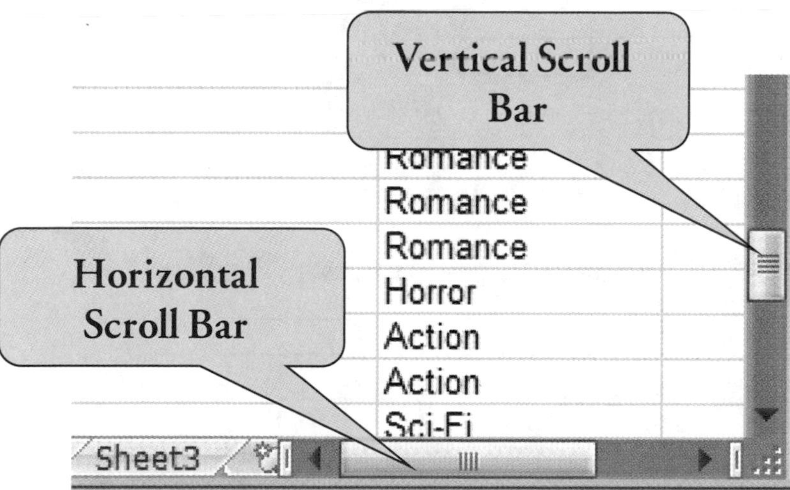

In addition to changing position in the worksheet by clicking with your mouse, there are several methods for navigating a worksheet using your keyboard. Some of these are:

Method	Action
Move Left	Left Arrow Key or Shift + Enter
Move Right	Right Arrow Key, Tab Key or Enter Key
Move Down	Down Arrow Key
Move Up	Up Arrow Key
Move to cell A1	Ctrl + Home keys
Move to last cell containing data in worksheet	Ctrl + End keys
Move to beginning of a row	Home
Move down one screen	Page Down
Move up one screen	Page Up
Move to the next sheet in workbook	Ctrl + Page Down
Move to the previous sheet in workbook	Ctrl + Page Up

Let's Try It!

- Click in cell **C1**.

Makes C1 the active cell.

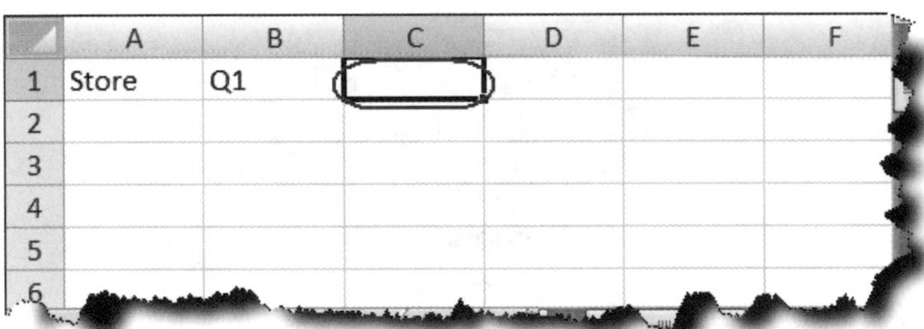

- Type **Q2** and then press **Tab** key.

Enters the third column heading, and then moves to cell D1.

- Type **Q3** and then press **Tab** key.

Enters the fourth column heading, and then moves to cell E1.

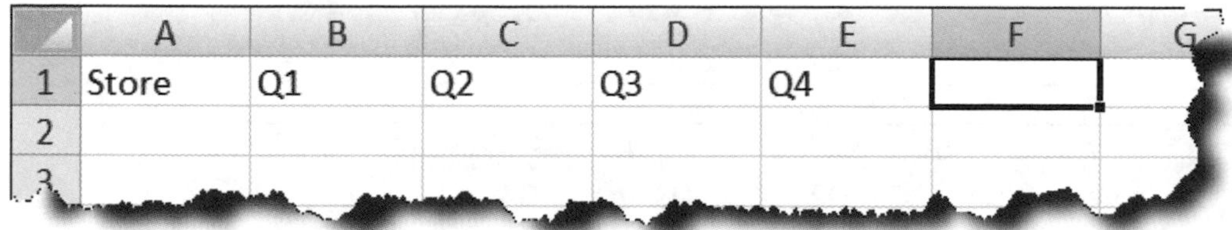

- Type **Q4** and then press **Tab** key.

Enters the fifth column heading, and then moves to cell F1.

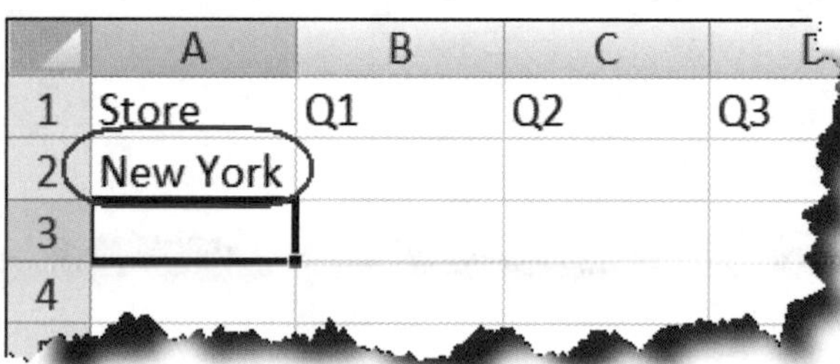

- Click in cell **A2** and type **New York**. Press the **down arrow** key.

Enters the name of the first store in Cell A2 and moves to cell A3.

- Type **San Francisco** and then press the **down arrow** key.

Enters the name of the second store in Cell A3 and moves to cell A4.

- Type **Dallas** and then press **Enter**.

Enters the name of the third store in Cell A4 and confirms the entry.

- Click in cell **B2** and type **14391** and then press **Tab** key.

Enters the value for Q1 and moves to Q2.

	A	B	C	D	E
1	Store	Q1	Q2	Q3	Q4
2	New York	14391			
3	San Francisco				
4	Dallas				
5					

- Continue entering values as shown until your worksheet contains the data as shown in the screen shot. Press **Tab** key to move from one column to the next and **Enter** key to move from one row to the next.

Enters the rest of the quarter sales for the three stores.

	A	B	C	D	E	F
1	Store	Q1	Q2	Q3	Q4	
2	New York	14391	11524	16979	21075	
3	San Franci:	22987	25424	24552	29780	
4	Dallas	15344	17045	19024	23242	
5						
6						
7						

- Press the **Ctrl + Home** keystroke combination.

Returns to cell A1.

	A	B	C	D	E	F
1	Store	Q1	Q2	Q3	Q4	
2	New York	14391	11524	16979	21075	
3	San Franci:	22987	25424	24552	29780	
4	Dallas	15344	17045	19024	23242	
5						
6						
7						

- Press the **Ctrl + End** keystroke combination.

Moves to the last cell containing data in the worksheet.

	A	B	C	D	E	F
1	Store	Q1	Q2	Q3	Q4	
2	New York	14391	11524	16979	21075	
3	San Franci:	22987	25424	24552	29780	
4	Dallas	15344	17045	19024	23242	
5						
6						

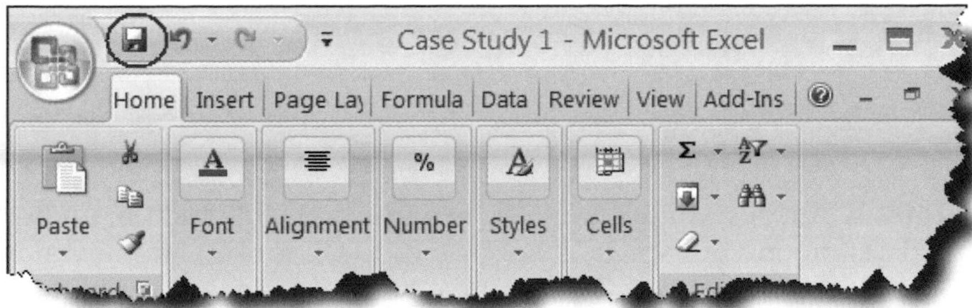

- Click the **Save** button.

Saves the changes.

Changing Column Width

Notice that in **Cell A3**, the end of our store location is cut off as column A is not wide enough to accommodate the text. To widen the column, we must perform the following steps:

1. Move your cursor to the column heading on the right border of the column whose width you wish to change.
2. Your cursor will change into a 4-way black arrow.
3. Click with your left mouse button and drag to the right until the column is the desired width.

Let's Try It!

	A	B	C	D	E	F
1	Store	Q1	Q2	Q3	Q4	
2	New York	14391	11524	16979	21075	
3	San Franci	22987	25424	24552	29780	
4	Dallas	15344	17045	19024	23242	
5						
6						

4-way arrow

- Move your cursor to the column heading between **Column A & B** as until your cursor becomes a 4-way black arrow.

Places you in "drag mode".

	A	B	C	D	E
1	Store	Q1	Q2	Q3	Q4
2	New York	14391	11524	16979	21075
3	San Francisco	22987	25424	24552	29780
4	Dallas	15344	17045	19024	23242
5					
6					

Sheet1 Sheet2 Sheet3

Click and drag until the column is the desired length

- Click on the line between Column A & B and drag to the right until all of the text in Cell A3 is visible.

Widens the column to completely accommodate the text in cell A3.

Entering Simple Formulas

This section will guide you through the process entering basic mathematical formulas into a worksheet.

Formulas perform calculations such as addition, subtraction, multiplication and division on your spreadsheet. You type the formula in the cell where you wish the result to appear. The formula itself does not appear in the cell but rather the result of the formula. The formula will appear in the formula bar.

To tell Excel that you are about to enter a formula, you must begin with an equal sign. For instance, if you wished to find the total for the numbers 8 and 12, we would enter:

=8+12 in the active cell.

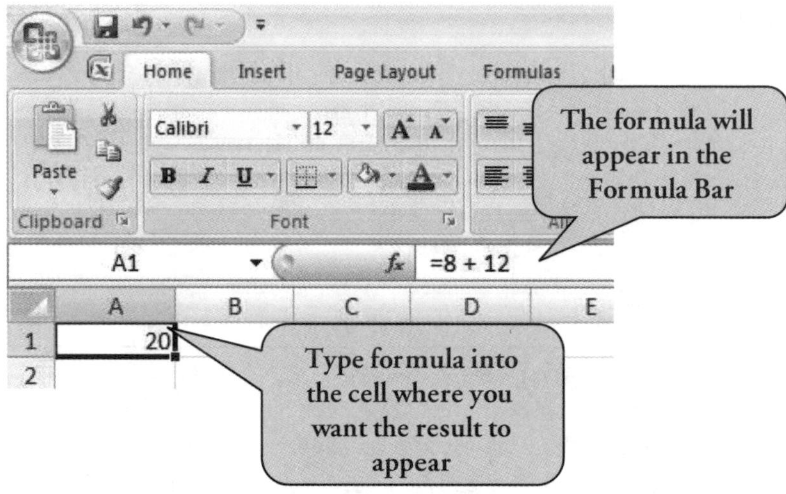

Valid mathematical operators that you can use in your formulas include:

+	Addition
–	Subtraction
*	Multiplication
/	Division

In addition to performing calculations on actual numbers (= 11 + 2 + 5), you can perform calculations on the value of cells by using **Cell References** in your formula. If you wanted to find to total of the cells A3, B6 and C7, you would enter the formula:

=A3 + B6 + C7.

Excel calculates formulas from left to right. If you wished for Excel to perform a particular calculation first, enclose it in parenthesis. For example in the formula = (A1 + A2) / C5 * 6, the A1 + A2 is performed first. The result is then divided by the value in cell C5 and finally, the result of that is multiplied by 6.

In our worksheet, we will create formulas to total the sales values across for each quarter.

To Create a Simple Formula

1. Click in the cell where you want the result of your formula to display.
2. Type: =
3. Type the formula using hard-coded numbers or cell references.
4. Press **Enter** to confirm the formula.

Let's Try It!

	A	B	C	D	E	F	G
1	Store	Q1	Q2	Q3	Q4	Total	
2	New York	14391	11524	16979	21075		
3	San Francisco	22987	25424	24552	29780		
4	Dallas	15344	17045	19024	23242		
5							
6							
7							
8							

- Click in cell **F1** and type the word **Total**.

Creates a new column heading in cell F1.

	A	B	C	D	E	F	G
1	Store	Q1	Q2	Q3	Q4	Total	
2	New York	14391	11524	16979	21075		
3	San Francisco	22987	25424	24552	29780		
4	Dallas	15344	17045	19024	23242		
5							
6							
7							
8							

- Press the **down arrow** key.

Moves to cell F2.

	A	B	C	D	E	F	G
1	Store	Q1	Q2	Q3	Q4	Total	
2	New York	14391	11524	16979	21075	=B2+C2+D2+E2	
3	San Francisco	22987	25424	24552	29780		
4	Dallas	15344	17045	19024	23242		
5							
6							
7							
8							

- Type: **=B2 + C2 + D2 + E2**

Enters a formula that sums the sales values for the New York store.

	A	B	C	D	E	F	G
1	Store	Q1	Q2	Q3	Q4	Total	
2	New York	14391	11524	16979	21075	63969	
3	San Francisco	22987	25424	24552	29780		
4	Dallas	15344	17045	19024	23242		
5							

- Press the **Enter** key.

Confirms your entry and activates cell F3.

- Type: **=B3 + C3 + D3 + E3**

Enters a formula that sums the sales values for the San Francisco store.

	A	B	C	D	E	F	G
1	Store	Q1	Q2	Q3	Q4	Total	
2	New York	14391	11524	16979	21075	63969	
3	San Francisco	22987	25424	24552	29780	=B3+C3+D3+E3	
4	Dallas	15344	17045	19024	23242		
5							

- Press the **Enter** key.

Confirms the entry.

	A	B	C	D	E	F	G
1	Store	Q1	Q2	Q3	Q4	Total	
2	New York	14391	11524	16979	21075	63969	
3	San Francisco	22987	25424	24552	29780	102743	
4	Dallas	15344	17045	19024	23242		
5							

Choosing Formula Cell References Manually

In this section, you will learn how to select cell references manually by using your mouse.

If you have a large worksheet in which you wish to create a formula that uses several different cell references, it might sometimes be easier to select your cells manually, rather than try to remember the cell addresses for each value you want to include in your formula. This can be accomplished by typing the **equal sign (=)**, and then selecting the cells that you want to include in the formula with your mouse.

To Choose Cell References Manually

1. Activate the cell in which you wish to enter the formula.
2. Type = to begin your formula.
3. Click in the first cell you wish to include in your formula.
4. Enter the appropriate mathematical operator (+, −, * or /).
5. Click in the next cell you wish to include in your formula.
6. Enter the appropriate mathematical operator.
7. Continue steps 5 & 6 until you have selected all of the cells to be included in your formula.
8. Press the Enter key to confirm the formula.

Let's Try It!

- Click in cell **F4** and press the = key.

The = begins the formula in F4 cell.

	A	B	C	D	E	F	G
1	Store	Q1	Q2	Q3	Q4	Total	
2	New York	14391	11524	16979	21075	63969	
3	San Francisco	22987	25424	24552	29780	102743	
4	Dallas	15344	17045	19024	23242	=	
5							

	A	B	C	D	E	F	G
1	Store	Q1	Q2	Q3	Q4	Total	
2	New York	14391	11524	16979	21075	63969	
3	San Francisco	22987	25424	24552	29780	102743	
4	Dallas	15344	17045	19024	23242	=B4	
5							

- Click in cell **B4**.

Selects the first cell in the formula.

	A	B	C	D	E	F	G
1	Store	Q1	Q2	Q3	Q4	Total	
2	New York	14391	11524	16979	21075	63969	
3	San Francisco	22987	25424	24552	29780	102743	
4	Dallas	15344	17045	19024	23242	=B4+	
5							

- Type **+**

Enters the addition operator in your formula.

	A	B	C	D	E	F	G
1	Store	Q1	Q2	Q3	Q4	Total	
2	New York	14391	11524	16979	21075	63969	
3	San Francisco	22987	25424	24552	29780	102743	
4	Dallas	15344	17045	19024	23242	=B4+C4	
5							

- Click in cell **C4**.

Selects the next cell in your formula.

	A	B	C	D	E	F	G
1	Store	Q1	Q2	Q3	Q4	Total	
2	New York	14391	11524	16979	21075	63969	
3	San Francisco	22987	25424	24552	29780	102743	
4	Dallas	15344	17045	19024	23242	=B4+C4+	
5							

- Type **+**

Enters the addition operator in your formula.

	A	B	C	D	E	F	G
1	Store	Q1	Q2	Q3	Q4	Total	
2	New York	14391	11524	16979	21075	63969	
3	San Francisco	22987	25424	24552	29780	102743	
4	Dallas	15344	17045	19024	23242	=B4+C4+D4	
5							

- Click in cell **D4**.

Selects the next cell in your formula.

- Type **+**

Enters the addition operator in your formula.

	A	B	C	D	E	F	G
1	Store	Q1	Q2	Q3	Q4	Total	
2	New York	14391	11524	16979	21075	63969	
3	San Francisco	22987	25424	24552	29780	102743	
4	Dallas	15344	17045	19024	23242	=B4+C4+D4+	
5							

- Click in cell **E4**.

Selects the last cell of your formula.

	A	B	C	D	E	F	G
1	Store	Q1	Q2	Q3	Q4	Total	
2	New York	14391	11524	16979	21075	63969	
3	San Francisco	22987	25424	24552	29780	102743	
4	Dallas	15344	17045	19024	23242	=B4+C4+D4+E4	
5							

- Press the **Enter** key.

Confirms your formula entry.

	A	B	C	D	E	F	G
1	Store	Q1	Q2	Q3	Q4	Total	
2	New York	14391	11524	16979	21075	63969	
3	San Francisco	22987	25424	24552	29780	102743	
4	Dallas	15344	17045	19024	23242	74655	
5							
6							

- Click in cell **F4** and observe the formula window.

Allows you to verify the formula you have just entered.

- Click the **Save** button.

Saves the changes.

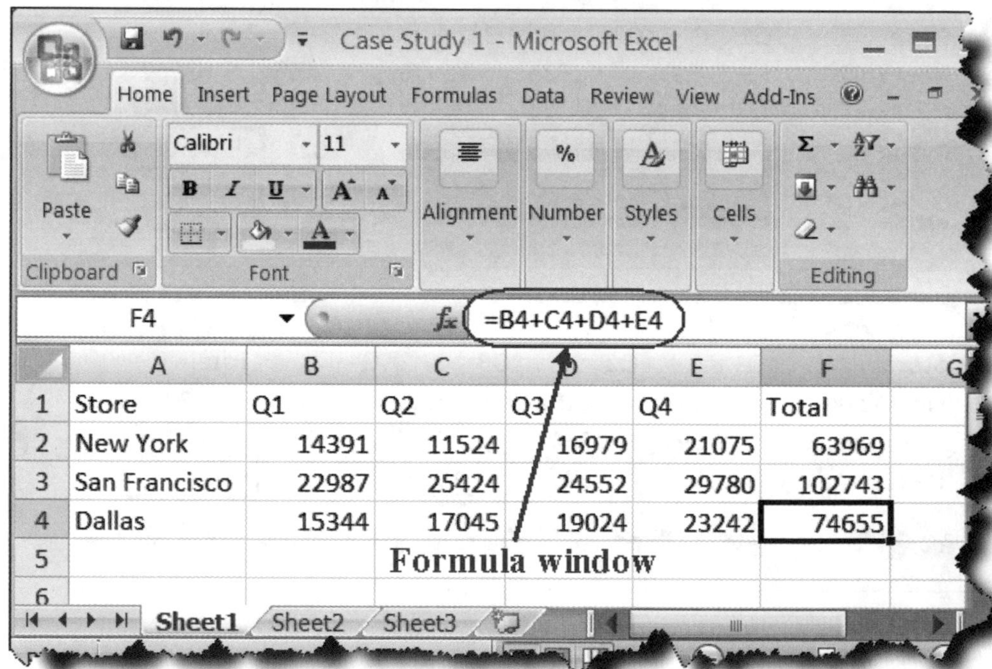

	A	B	C	D	E	F	G
1	Store	Q1	Q2	Q3	Q4	Total	
2	New York	14391	11524	16979	21075	63969	
3	San Francisco	22987	25424	24552	29780	102743	
4	Dallas	15344	17045	19024	23242	74655	
5							
6							

Using AutoSum

This section will show you how to use Excel's AutoSum Feature to perform quick calculations.

If you wish to perform a common calculation such as SUM on a contiguous range of data, you can use the **AutoSum** button (located on the Home Ribbon). Clicking on the AutoSum button automatically selects a range of cells (vertical or horizontal) and calculates the total of all cells in that range. That is to say, when the cell that contains the SUM function is at the end of a row or column, Excel always uses that entire column or row in the calculation. However, if any cell in the range contains a blank row or column, the range to be totaled stops there. If Excel does not choose the range of cells you wish to use, you can choose the range manually by clicking on the first cell of the range and dragging to the last cell of your range.

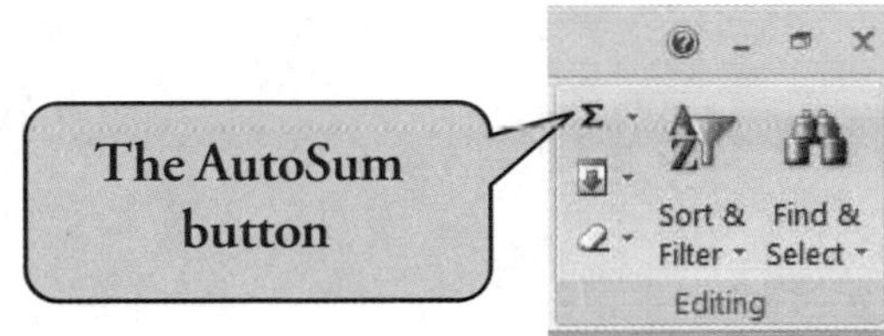

If we wanted to total the values from **B3 to B18**, clicking the AutoSum button while having B19 as the active cell would automatically enter the following formula in cell B19:

=SUM(B3:B18)

This tells Excel to sum the values in the B3 to B18 range.

The AutoSum feature includes other functions in addition to the **SUM** function. By clicking on the arrow to the right of the AutoSum button, you can choose the **AVERAGE**, **COUNT NUMBERS**, **MIN**, or **MAX** functions instead of the **SUM**. These functions will be discussed in more detail in a later chapter.

To Calculate Totals with AutoSum

1 Click in the cell where you want to display the calculation.
2. To sum with only some of the numbers in the range, select the cells to be included in the formula.
3. Click the **AutoSum button** on either the Home Ribbon or the Formulas Ribbon
   Or
   Press the **Alt + =** keystroke combination.
4. To perform another calculation such as Average, Count, Min, or Max, click the arrow next to the AutoSum button and choose the function that you want.
5. Press **Enter**.

Let's Try It!

- Click in cell **A6** and type **Total**.

Enters a heading to identify that we are totaling columns.

	A	B	C	D
1	Store	Q1	Q2	Q3
2	New York	14391	11524	16979
3	San Francisco	22987	25424	24552
4	Dallas	15344	17045	19024
5				
6	Total			
7				
8				

- Click in cell **B6** and click the **AutoSum** button on the Home Ribbon.

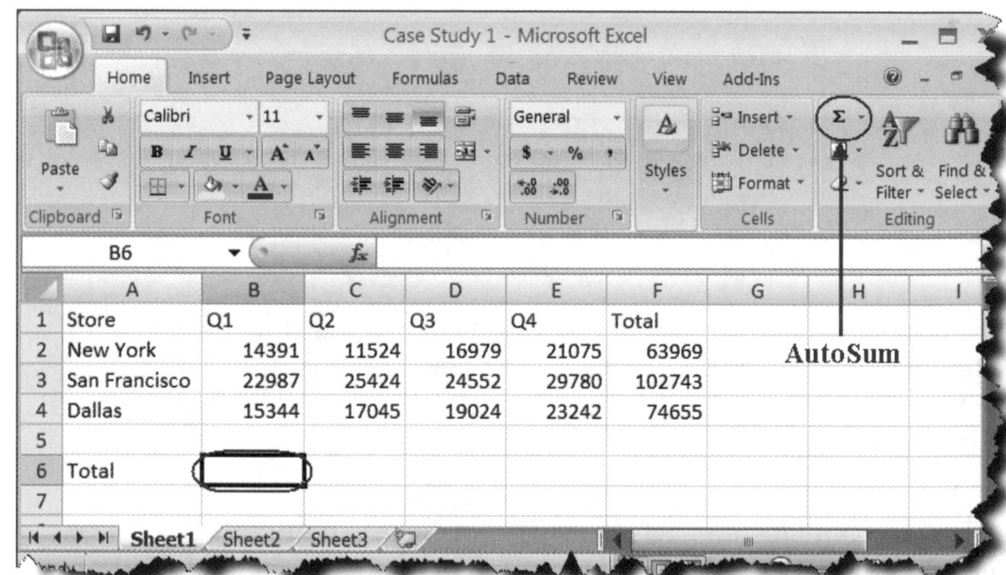

	A	B	C	D	E	F	G	H	I
1	Store	Q1	Q2	Q3	Q4	Total			
2	New York	14391	11524	16979	21075	63969			
3	San Francisco	22987	25424	24552	29780	102743			
4	Dallas	15344	17045	19024	23242	74655			
5									
6	Total								
7									

Selects the range B2 to B5.

To change the range that Excel uses, you can manually select your desired range.

- Press the **Enter** key.

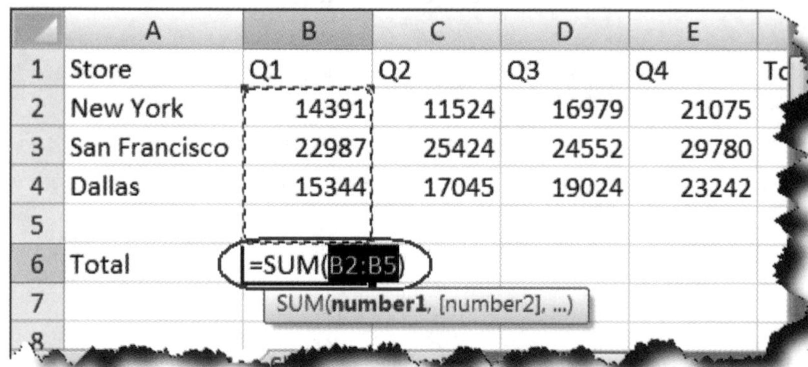

	A	B	C	D	E
1	Store	Q1	Q2	Q3	Q4
2	New York	14391	11524	16979	21075
3	San Francisco	22987	25424	24552	29780
4	Dallas	15344	17045	19024	23242
5					
6	Total	=SUM(B2:B5)			
7		SUM(**number1**, [number2], ...)			
8					

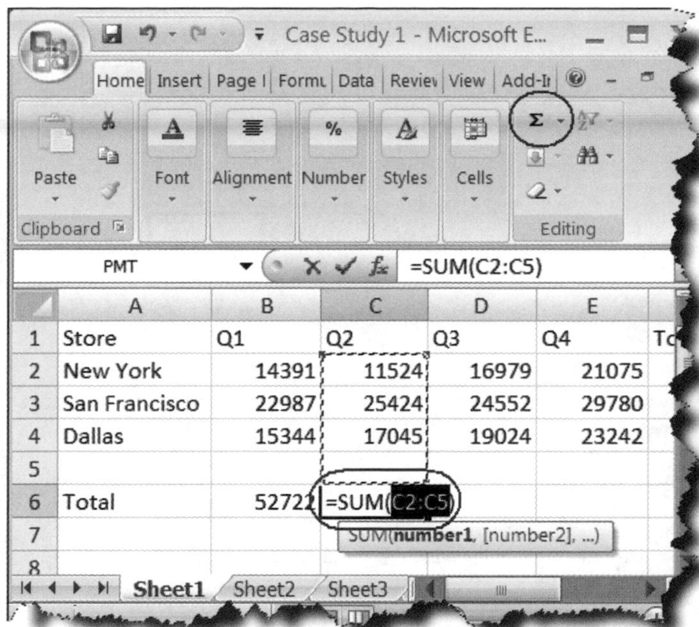

Confirms the formula.

- Click in cell **C6** and then click the **AutoSum** button on the Home Ribbon.

Selects the range C2 to C5.

	A	B	C	D	E
1	Store	Q1	Q2	Q3	Q4
2	New York	14391	11524	16979	21075
3	San Francisco	22987	25424	24552	29780
4	Dallas	15344	17045	19024	23242
5					
6	Total	52722	53993		
7					

- Press the **Enter** key.

Confirms the formula.

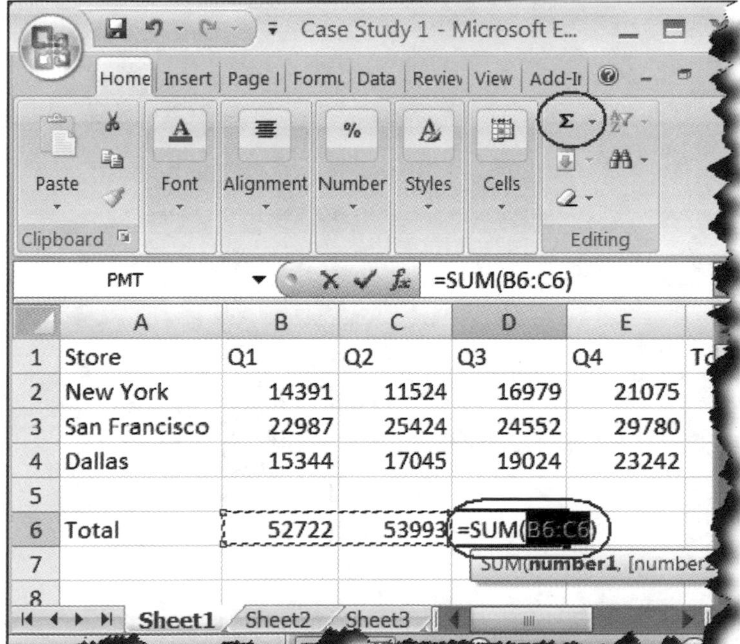

- Click in cell **D6** and then click the **AutoSum** button on the Home Ribbon.

Notice that AutoSum selected cells B6 and C6, which is not what we want. We will need to manually select the cells we want to total.

- Press the **Esc key**.

Cancels the operation.

	A	B	C	D	E
1	Store	Q1	Q2	Q3	Q4
2	New York	14391	11524	16979	21075
3	San Francisco	22987	25424	24552	29780
4	Dallas	15344	17045	19024	23242
5					
6	Total	52722	53993		
7					

- Click in cell **D2**.

Selects the first cell of the range.

	A	B	C	D	E
1	Store	Q1	Q2	Q3	Q4
2	New York	14391	11524	16979	21075
3	San Francisco	22987	25424	24552	29780
4	Dallas	15344	17045	19024	23242
5					
6	Total	52722	53993		
7					

- **Click and hold down** your left mouse button and drag down to cell D6.

Selects the cell range we want to include in the AutoSum Calculation.

	A	B	C	D	E
1	Store	Q1	Q2	Q3	Q4
2	New York	14391	11524	16979	21075
3	San Francisco	22987	25424	24552	29780
4	Dallas	15344	17045	19024	23242
5					
6	Total	52722	53993		
7					

Select the cell range D2 to D6

- Click the **AutoSum** button on the Home Ribbon.

Totals the cell range D2 to D5.

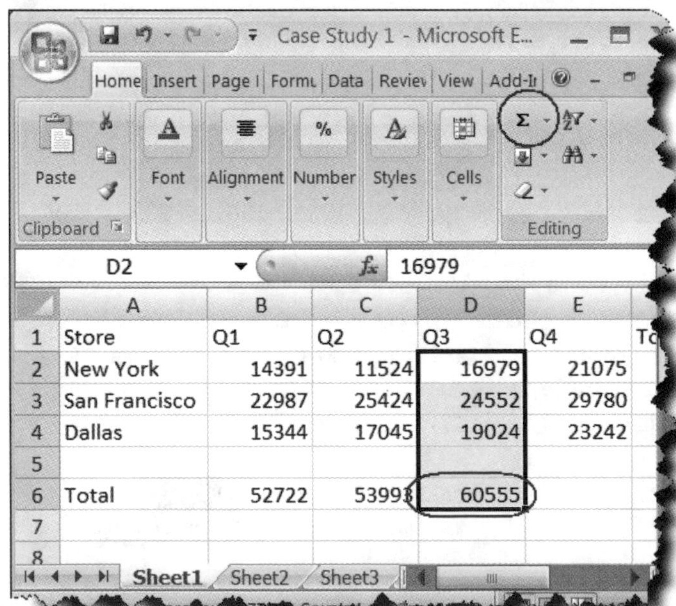

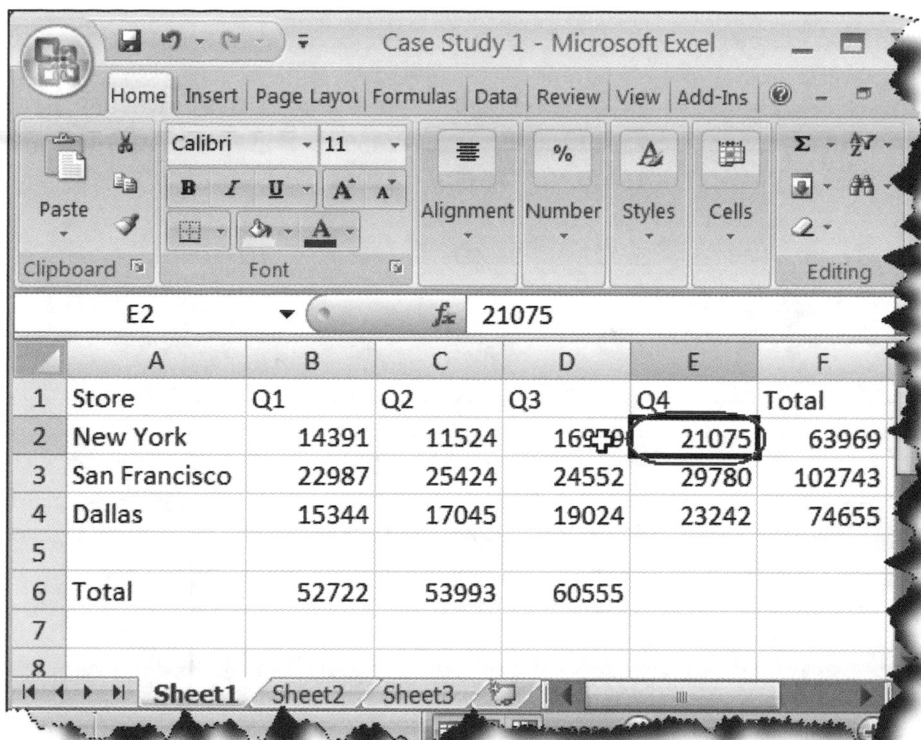

	A	B	C	D	E	F
1	Store	Q1	Q2	Q3	Q4	Total
2	New York	14391	11524	16979	21075	63969
3	San Francisco	22987	25424	24552	29780	102743
4	Dallas	15344	17045	19024	23242	74655
5						
6	Total	52722	53993	60555		
7						

- Click in cell **E2**.

Selects the first cell of the range.

	A	B	C	D	E	F
1	Store	Q1	Q2	Q3	Q4	Total
2	New York	14391	11524	16979	21075	63969
3	San Francisco	22987	25424	24552	29780	102743
4	Dallas	15344	17045	19024	23242	74655
5						
6	Total	52722	53993	60555		
7						

- **Click and hold down** your **left mouse button** and **drag down to cell E6**.

Selects the cell range to include in the AutoSum Calculation.

	A	B	C	D	E	F
1	Store	Q1	Q2	Q3	Q4	Total
2	New York	14391	11524	16979	21075	63969
3	San Francisco	22987	25424	24552	29780	102743
4	Dallas	15344	17045	19024	23242	74655
5						
6	Total	52722	53993	60555	74097	
7						

- Click the **AutoSum** button on the Home Ribbon.

Totals the cell range E2 to E5.

- Click in cell **F2**.

Selects the first cell of our range.

	A	B	C	D	E	F	G
1	Store	Q1	Q2	Q3	Q4	Total	
2	New York	14391	11524	16979	21075	63969	
3	San Francisco	22987	25424	24552	29780	102743	
4	Dallas	15344	17045	19024	23242	74655	
5							
6	Total	52722	53993	60555	74097		
7							

- **Click and hold down** your **left mouse button** and **drag down to cell F6**.

Selects the cell range we want to include in the AutoSum Calculation.

	A	B	C	D	E	F	G
1	Store	Q1	Q2	Q3	Q4	Total	
2	New York	14391	11524	16979	21075	63969	
3	San Francisco	22987	25424	24552	29780	102743	
4	Dallas	15344	17045	19024	23242	74655	
5							
6	Total	52722	53993	60555	74097		
7							

- Click the **AutoSum** button on the Home Ribbon.

Totals the cell range F2 to F5.

- Click the **Save** button.

Saves the changes.

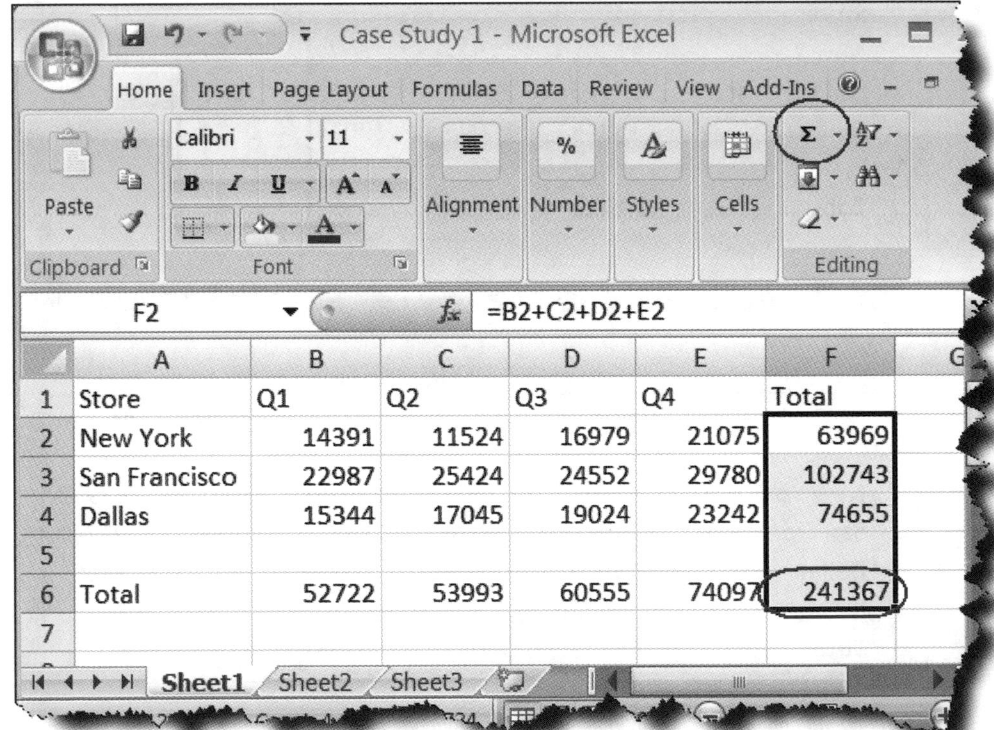

	A	B	C	D	E	F
1	Store	Q1	Q2	Q3	Q4	Total
2	New York	14391	11524	16979	21075	63969
3	San Francisco	22987	25424	24552	29780	102743
4	Dallas	15344	17045	19024	23242	74655
5						
6	Total	52722	53993	60555	74097	241367
7						

Changing & Deleting Data

In this section, you will modify and delete the existing contents of cells.

To delete the contents of a cell, click in the cell to activate it and then press the **Delete** key. This erases the entire contents of that cell. If you wish to simply replace the contents of the cell, you do not need to press the delete key—just begin typing and the contents will be automatically replaced by whatever you type.

There are times, however, when you do not wish to delete the entire contents of a cell but only wish to change part of the cell's contents. For example, you may have discovered an error in a formula you entered and wish to modify it. Rather than retype the entire formula, it would be easier just to edit the existing formula.

To Change the Contents of a Cell

1. Activate the cell you wish to edit and then click in the formula bar.
2. Position the I-beam pointer at the location in the formula bar where you want to change or insert text.
   Or
   Double-click within the cell you wish to edit. This places you in edit mode.
3. Make your changes.

A4 fx Dallas

	A	B	C	D	E	F
1	Stores	Q1	Q2	Q3		
2	New York	14391	11524	16979		
3	San Franci	22987	25424	24552		
4	Dallas	15344	17045	19024		
5						
6	Total	52722	53993	60555	74097	241367

The Formula Bar

Let's Try It!

	A	B	C	D
1	Store	Q1	Q2	Q3
2	New York	14391	11524	1
3	San Francisco	22987	25424	24
4	Dallas	15344	17045	19
5				
6	Total	52722	53993	60
7				

- Click in cell **A6**.

Makes A6 the active cell.

- Type: **Grand Total** and then press **Enter**.

Replaces the contents of cell A6 with the words "Grand Total".

	A	B	C	D
1	Store	Q1	Q2	Q3
2	New York	14391	11524	[illegible]
3	San Francisco	22987	25424	[illegible]
4	Dallas	15344	17045	[illegible]
5				
6	Grand Total	52722	53993	[illegible]
7				
8				

- Click in cell **A2**.

Makes cell A2 the active cell.

	A	B	C	D
1	Store	Q1	Q2	Q3
2	New York	14391	11524	[illegible]
3	San Francisco	22987	25424	[illegible]
4	Dallas	15344	17045	[illegible]
5				
6	Grand Total	52722	53993	[illegible]
7				
8				

- Click in the formula bar after the **k** in New York.

Positions the I-beam pointer after the word New York.

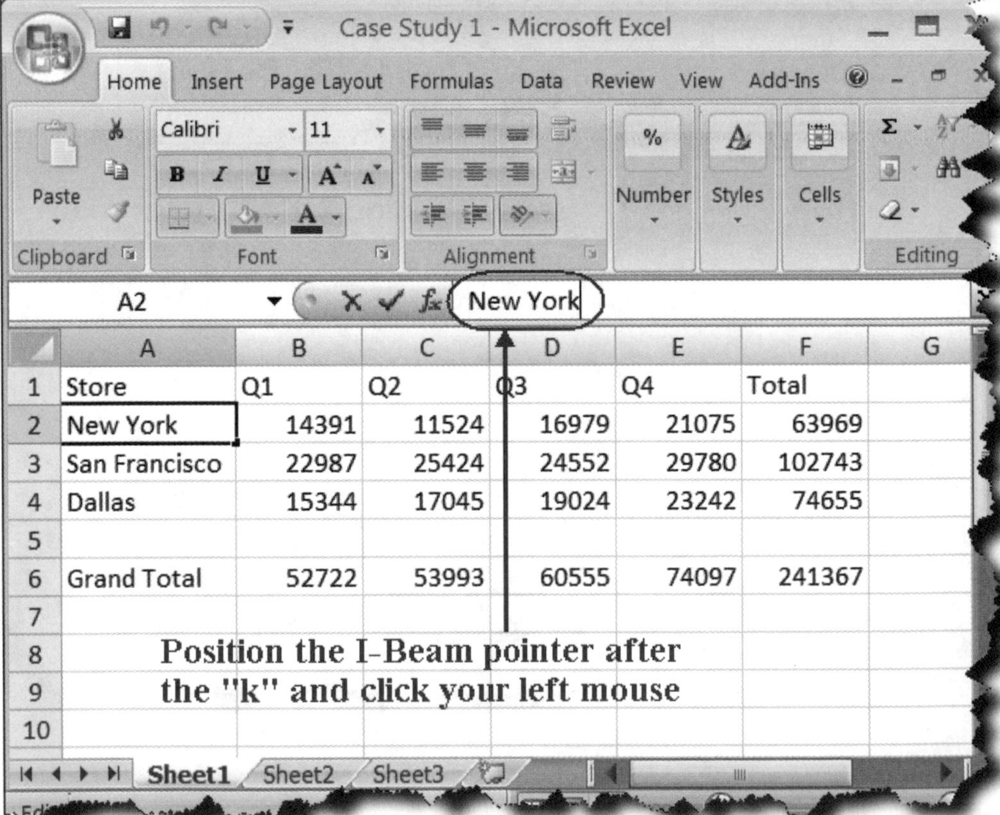

	A	B	C	D	E	F
1	Store	Q1	Q2	Q3	Q4	Total
2	New York	14391	11524	16979	21075	63969
3	San Francisco	22987	25424	24552	29780	102743
4	Dallas	15344	17045	19024	23242	74655
5						
6	Grand Total	52722	53993	60555	74097	241367

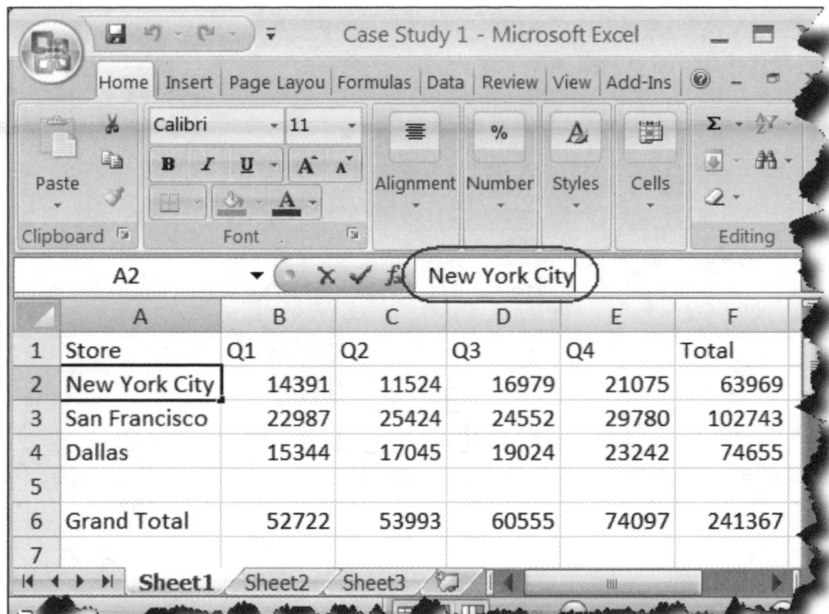

Press the spacebar and then type **City**.

dds the word "city"
ter "New York".

	A	B	C	D	E	F
1	Store	Q1	Q2	Q3	Q4	Total
2	New York City	14391	11524	16979	21075	63969
3	San Francisco	22987	25424	24552	29780	102743
4	Dallas	15344	17045	19024	23242	74655
5						
6	Grand Total	52722	53993	60555	74097	241367
7						

- Press **Enter** to confirm the entry.
- Double-click in cell **C2**.

Enters edit mode in cell C2.

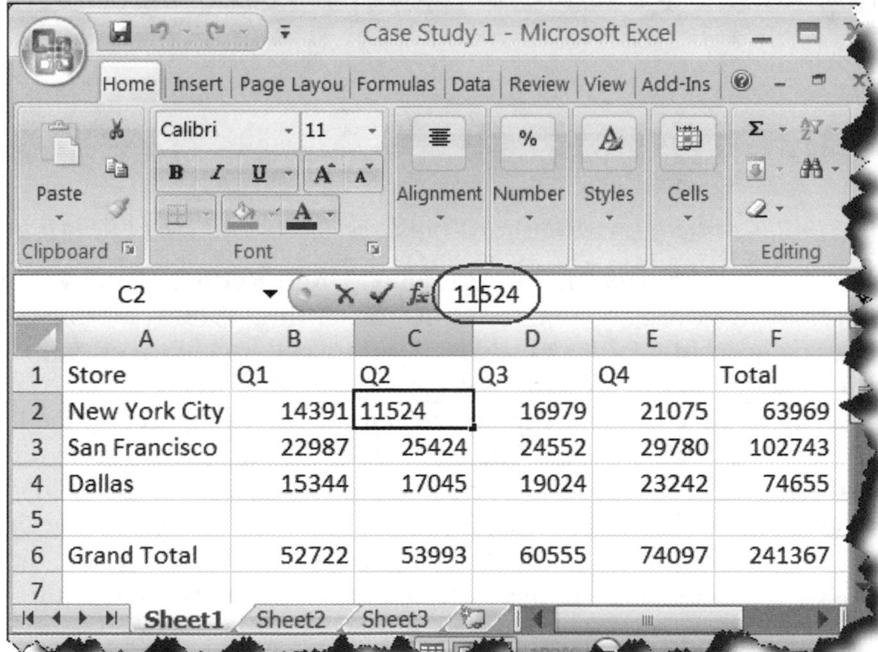

Position the I-beam pointer in front of the **5** and then press the **Backspace key**.

Deletes the I in front of the 5 in cell C2.

- Type **2**

Enters the number 2 between the I and 5 in cell C2.

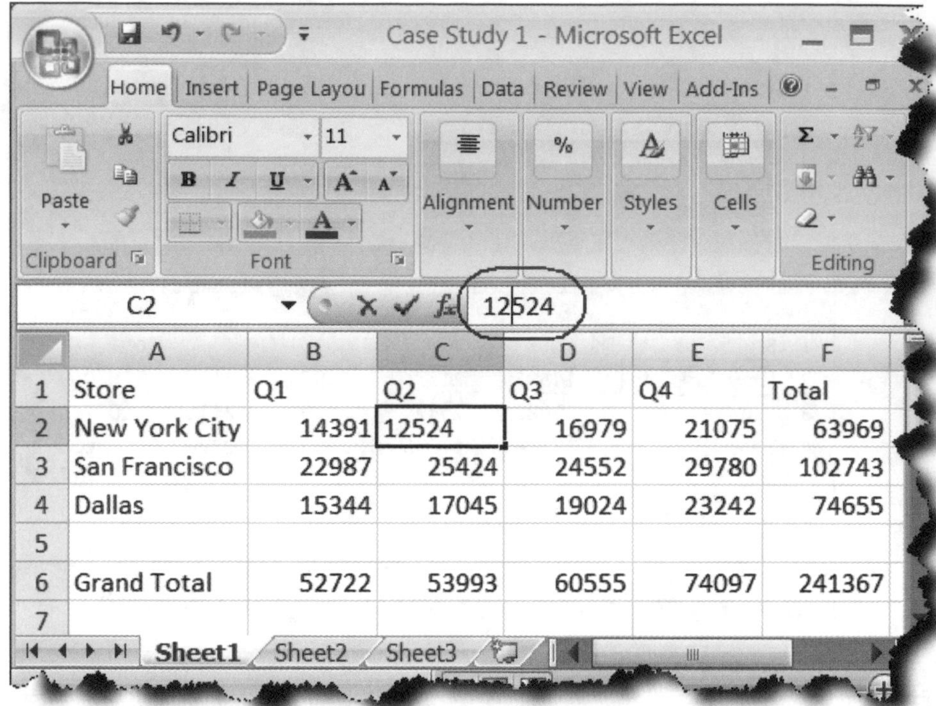

	A	B	C	D	E	F
1	Store	Q1	Q2	Q3	Q4	Total
2	New York City	14391	12524	16979	21075	63969
3	San Francisco	22987	25424	24552	29780	102743
4	Dallas	15344	17045	19024	23242	74655
5						
6	Grand Total	52722	53993	60555	74097	241367
7						

- Press **Enter**.

Confirms the entry.

- Click the **Save** button.

Saves the current workbook.

	A	B	C	D	E	F
1	Store	Q1	Q2	Q3	Q4	Total
2	New York City	14391	12524	16979	21075	64969
3	San Francisco	22987	25424	24552	29780	102743
4	Dallas	15344	17045	19024	23242	74655
5						
6	Grand Total	52722	54993	60555	74097	242367
7						

Using Undo/Redo

In this section, you will learn about Excel's powerful Undo/Redo feature.

Excel contains a powerful feature called **Undo/Redo** that allows you to reverse any editing action, including formatting. While entering data, you may have accidentally activated the wrong cell and inadvertently replaced the data in that cell. You can reverse this action with the **Undo** command.

Each time you initiate the Undo command, it will reverse the last action that you did; thus, clicking the Undo button 20 times will undo the last 20 actions as if they had never occurred. Rather than clicking the Undo button 20 times to undo multiple actions, clicking the arrow next to the Undo button allows you to quickly undo multiple past actions by navigating down the history list and selecting the number of actions you wish to undo.

Redo allows you to reverse the action of an Undo command.

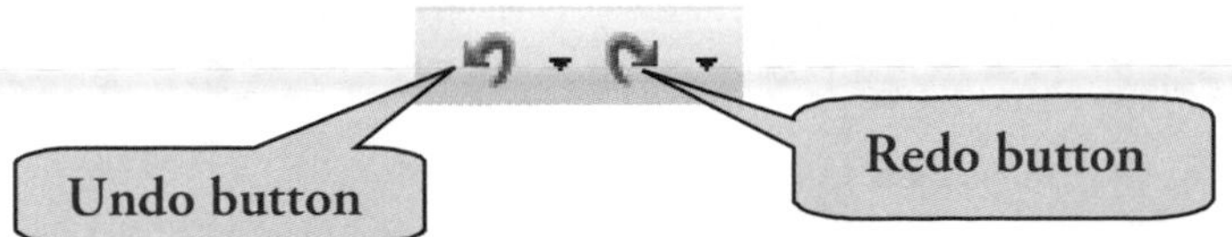

To Use the Undo Command

1. Click the **Undo** icon on the Quick Access Toolbar.
   Or
   Press the **Ctrl + Z** keystroke combination.

To Use the Redo Command

1. Click on the **Redo** icon on the Quick Access Toolbar.
   Or
   Press the **Ctrl + Y** keystroke combination.

Let's Try It!

	A	B	C	D	E	F
1	Store	Q1	Q2	Q3	Q4	Total
2	New York City	14391	12524	16979	21075	64969
3	San Francisco	22987	25424	24552	29780	102743
4		15344	17045	19024	23242	74655
5						
6	Grand Total	52722	54993	60555	74097	242367
7						

- Click in cell **A4** and then press the **Delete** key.

Clears the contents of cell A4.

	A	B	C	D	E	F
1	Store	Q1	Q2	Q3	Q4	Total
2	New York City	14391	12524	16979	21075	64969
3	San Francisco	22987	25424	24552	29780	102743
4	Total	15344	17045	19024	23242	74655
5						
6	Grand Total	52722	54993	60555	74097	242367
7						

- Type the word **Total**

Enters the word Total in cell A4.

- Press **Enter** to confirm the entry.
- Click the **Undo** button on the Quick Access Toolbar.

Reverts to the previous action—an empty cell.

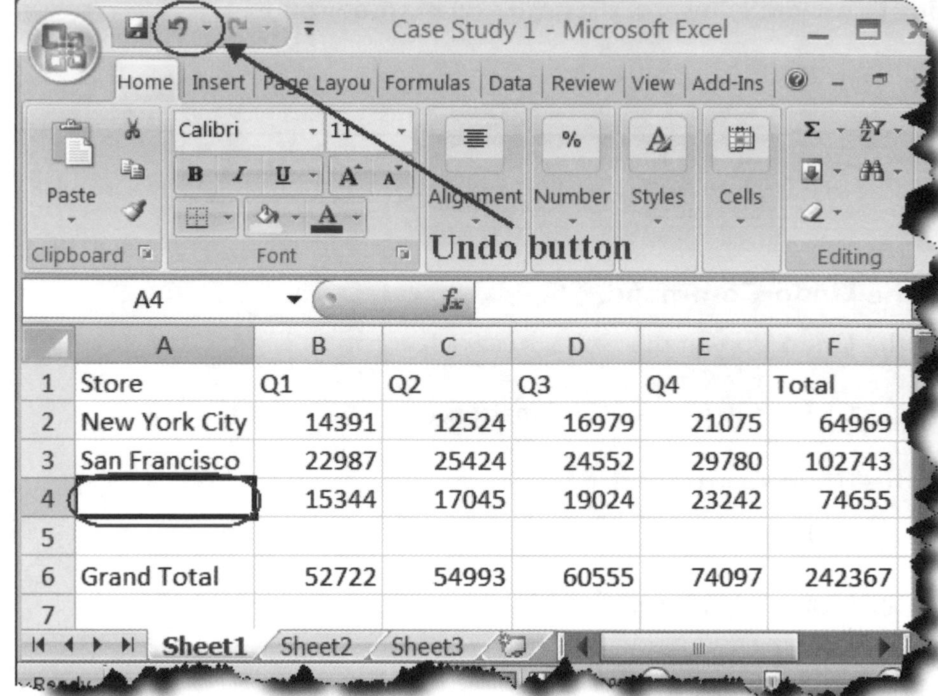

	A	B	C	D	E	F
1	Store	Q1	Q2	Q3	Q4	Total
2	New York City	14391	12524	16979	21075	64969
3	San Francisco	22987	25424	24552	29780	102743
4		15344	17045	19024	23242	74655
5						
6	Grand Total	52722	54993	60555	74097	242367
7						

- Click the **Undo** on the Quick Access Toolbar again.

Restores the cell to its original contents.

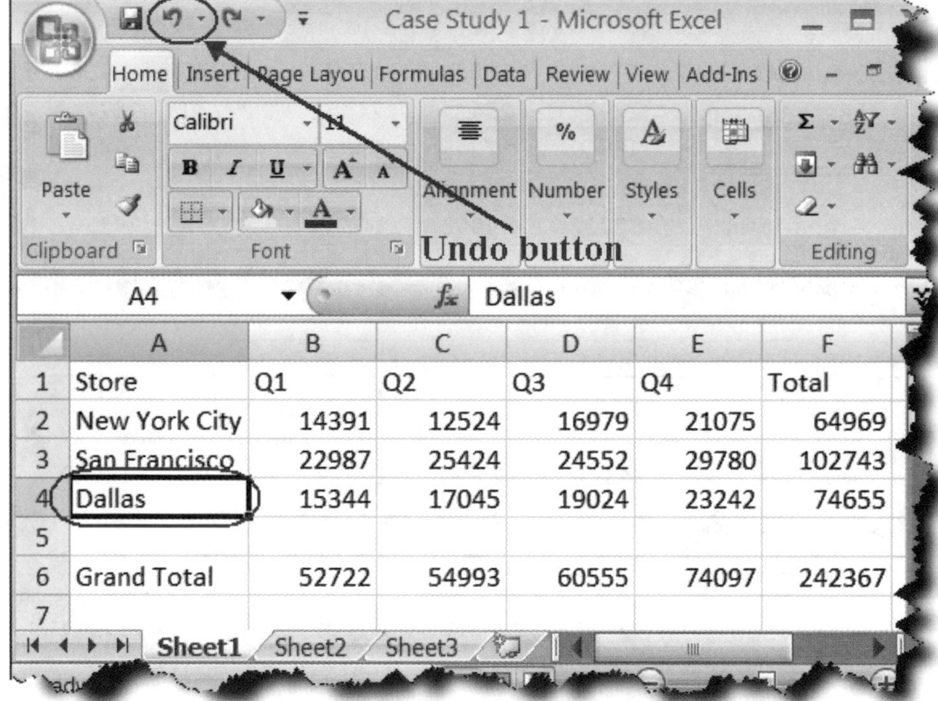

	A	B	C	D	E	F
1	Store	Q1	Q2	Q3	Q4	Total
2	New York City	14391	12524	16979	21075	64969
3	San Francisco	22987	25424	24552	29780	102743
4	Dallas	15344	17045	19024	23242	74655
5						
6	Grand Total	52722	54993	60555	74097	242367
7						

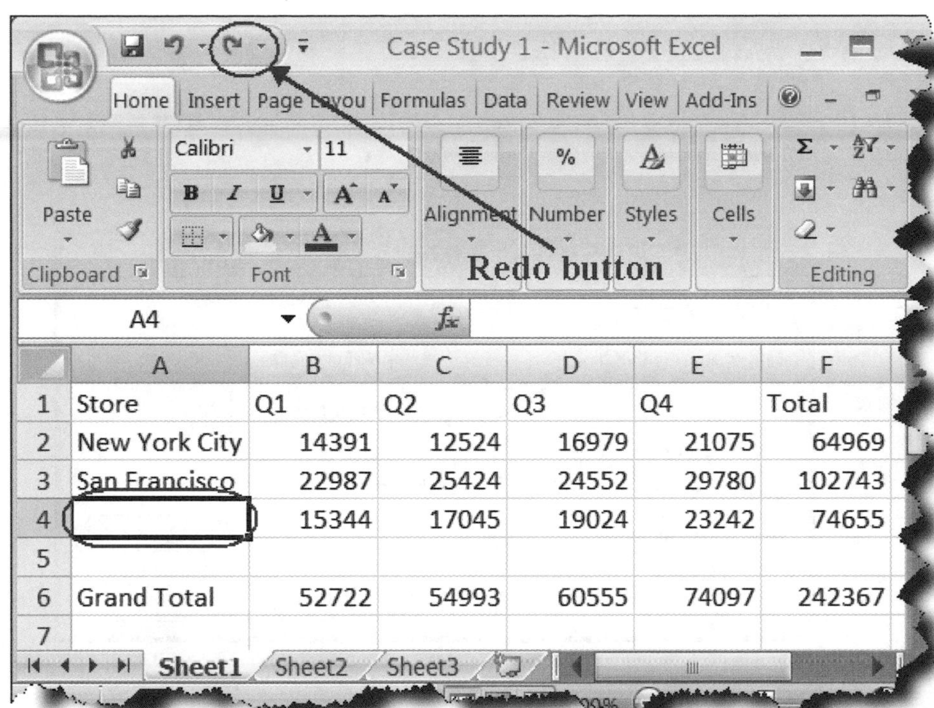

- Click the **Redo** button on the Quick Access Toolbar.

Reverses the last Undo command.

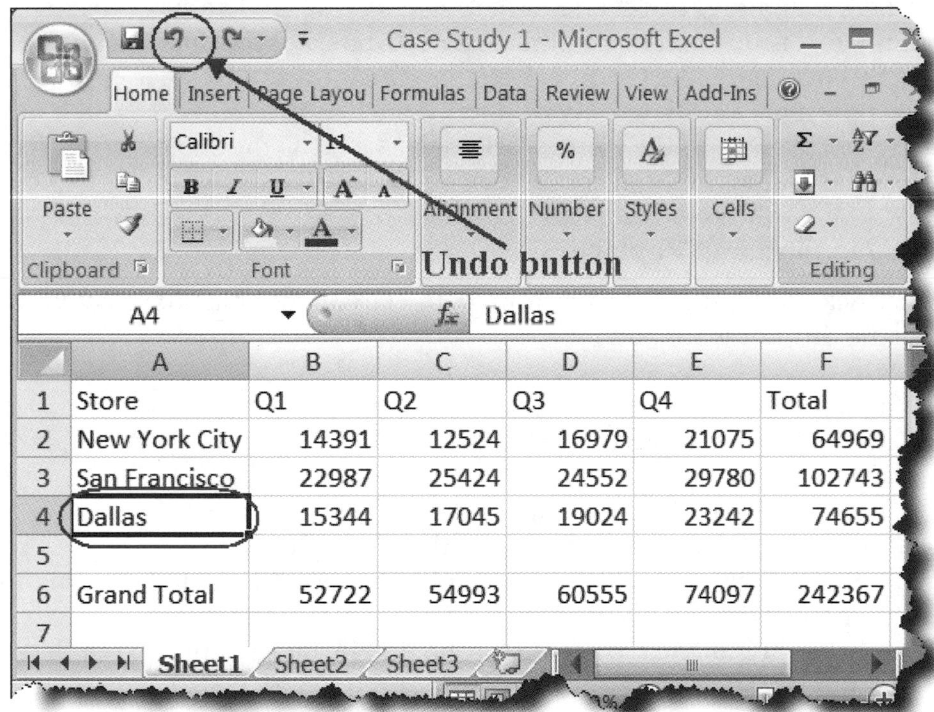

- Click the **Undo** button on the Quick Access Toolbar.

Reverses the Redo command.

- Click the **Save** button.

Saves the current workbook.

Using Find and Replace

In this section, you will learn how to quickly find and replace the contents of cells in a worksheet.

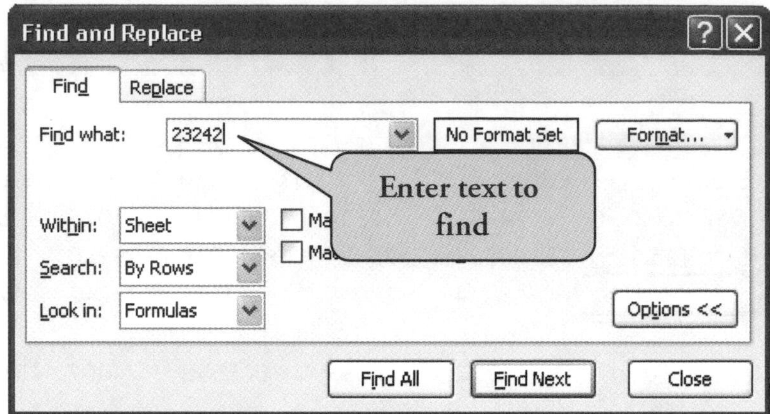

You can find specific information in an Excel worksheet or workbook by using Excel's **Find and Replace** feature. Once you find the entry for which you are searching, you can replace it with any desired value of text or numbers, or move on to find the next occurrence of the data.

By clicking on the **Options** button in the Find and Replace dialog box, Excel presents additional search options such as the ability to search in the active worksheet or the entire workbook as well as the choice to search in formulas, values and cell comments.

To Use Find and Replace

1. Click the **Find & Select** button on the Home Ribbon and select **Find** from the drop-down menu
   Or
   Press the **Ctrl + F** keystroke combination.
2. If you want to replace existing data with new data, click the **Replace** tab
   Or
   Press the **Ctrl + H** keystroke combination.
3. Enter the text you want to find in the **Find what:** box.
4. Enter the text with which you want to replace the existing text in the **Replace with:** text box.
5. Click on **Find Next** to search for the first instance of the text in the Find What box.
6. To search for all instances of the text, click **Find All**. The lower pane of the dialog box will expand to display all instances of the Find All command. You can quickly jump to the desired instance by clicking the data under any of the columns.

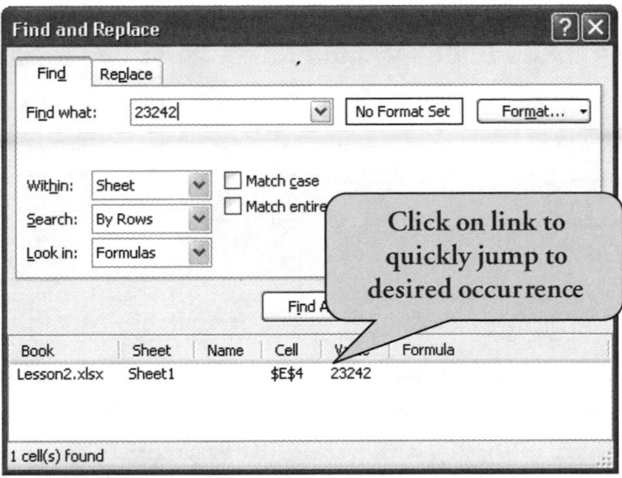

7. Click **Replace** to replace one instance at a time, clicking **Find Next** to move from one instance to another.
8. Click **Replace all** to replace all instances at once.
9. Click **Close** to close the Find and Replace dialog box.

Let's Try It!

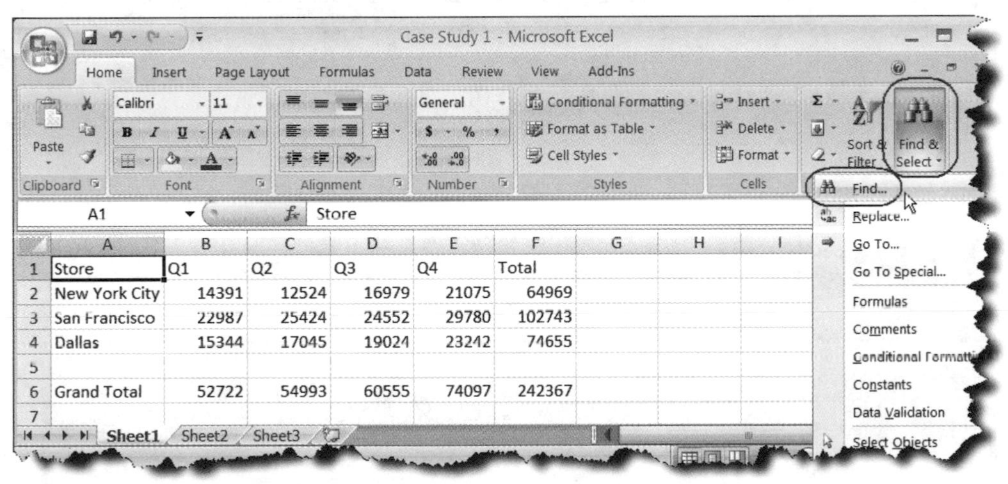

- Click in cell **A1**.

Makes A1 the active cell.

- Click the **Find & Select** button on the Home Ribbon and select **Find** from the list.

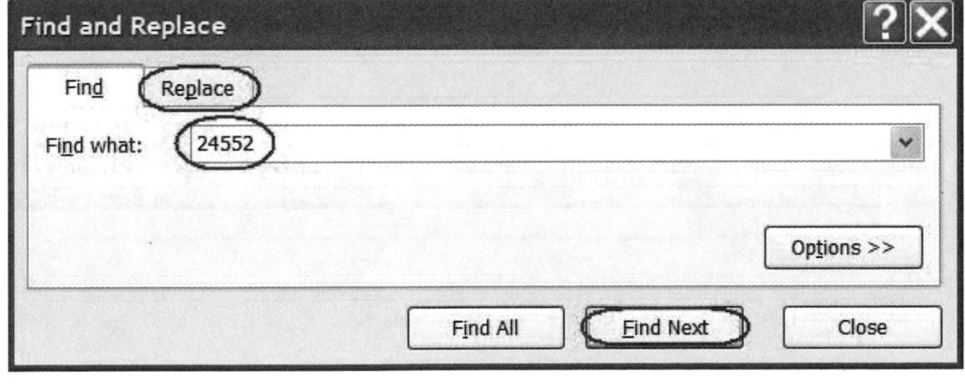

Displays the Find and Replace dialog box.

- Enter **24552** in the **Find what:** text box.

Establishes the value for which we wish to search.

- Click on the **Find Next** button.

Finds the first occurrence of our search value in cell D3.

- Click on the **Replace** tab.

Switches to the Replace screen.

- Enter **26552** in the **Replace with:**

Enters the new value.

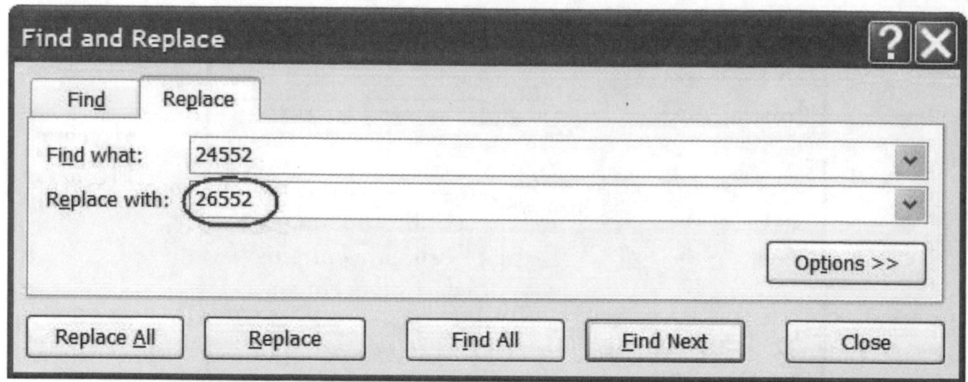

- Click on the **Replace** button.

Replaces the data in cell D3 with 26552.

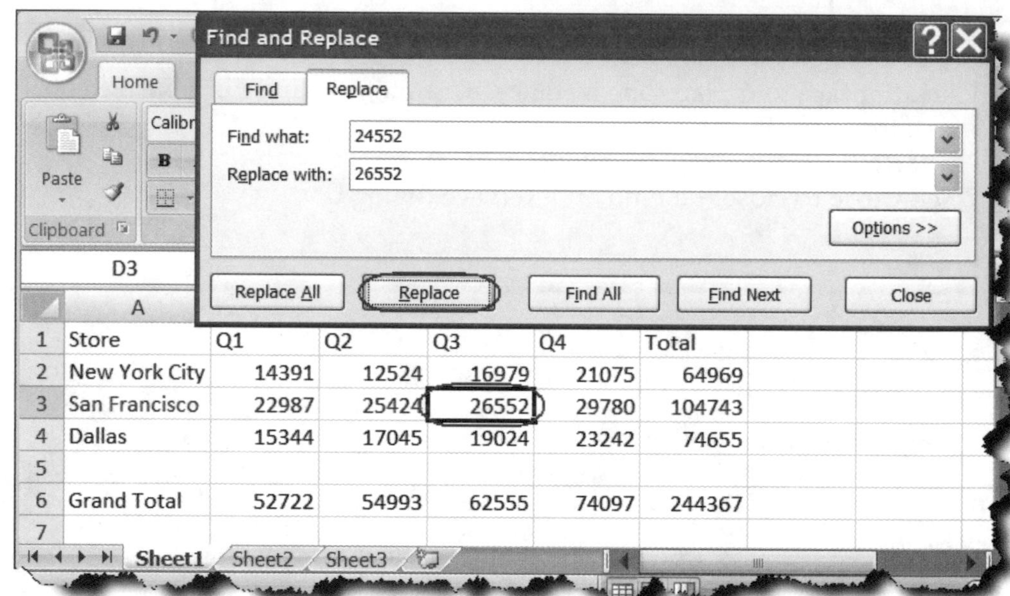

- Click the **Close** button.

Closes the Find and Replace dialog box.

- Click the **Save** button.

Saves the current workbook.

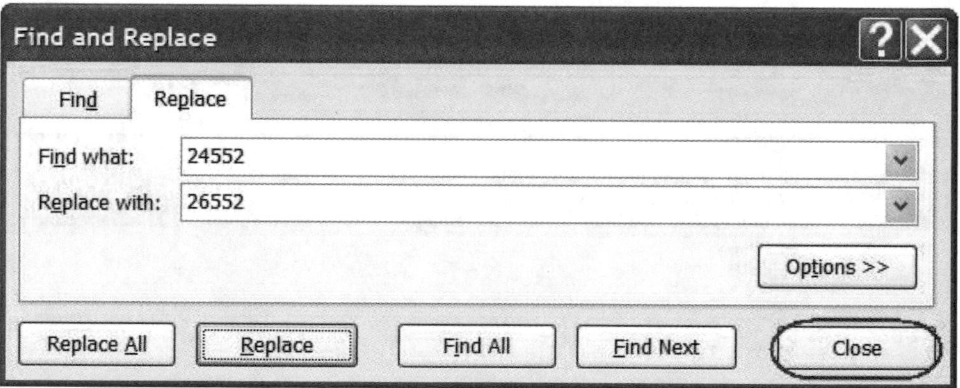

Using the Go To Command

In this section, you will learn how to use Excel's Go To command to navigate to a specific location of your worksheet.

Excel's **Go To** command, located under the Find & Select command button, allows you to quickly jump to and select a specific cell or cell range (including named ranges) in your worksheet. This can come in especially handy if you want to select a long range of cells in a large worksheet.

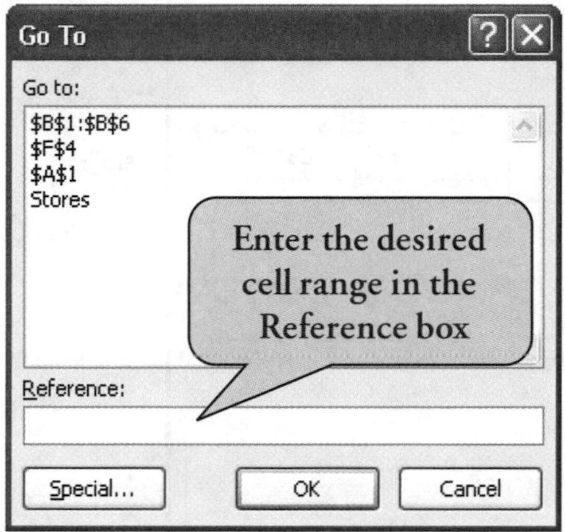

The **Special** button on the Go To dialog box also allows you to select other areas of your worksheet, such as formulas, comments, blank cells within your data range, constants (non-formula entries) and more.

To Use the Go To Command

1. Click the **Find & Select** button on the Home Ribbon and select **Go To** from the list.
   Or
   Press the **Ctrl + G** keystroke combination.
2. Enter the cell, cell range or named range you wish to find and select.
3. Click **OK**.
4. To find other worksheet items such as formulas, comments, blank cells within your data range, constants, etc., click **Special** and make your choices.

Let's Try It!

	A	B	C	D	E	F
1	Store	Q1	Q2	Q3	Q4	Total
2	New York City	14391	12524	16979	21075	64969
3	San Francisco	22987	25424	26552	29780	104743
4	Dallas	15344	17045	19024	23242	74655
5						
6	Grand Total	52722	54993	62555	74097	244367
7						

- Press the **Ctrl + Home** keystroke combination.

Moves to the beginning of the worksheet.

- Press the **Ctrl + G** keystroke combination.

Displays the Go To dialog box.

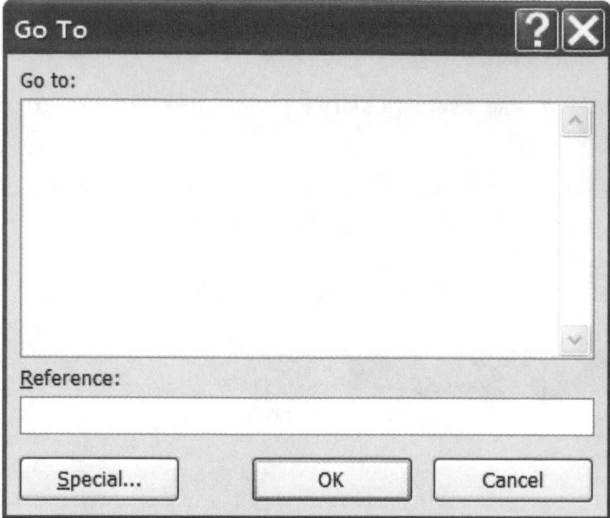

- Type: **C1:C6** in the Reference box and then click **OK**.

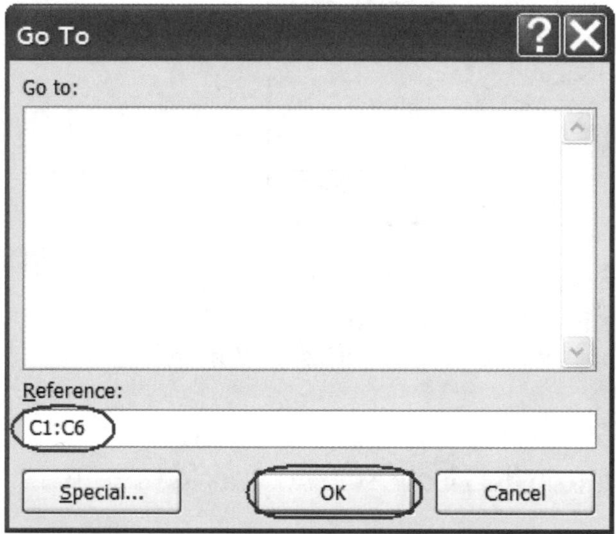

Selects the cell range C1:C6 in your worksheet.

	A	B	C	D	E	F
1	Store	Q1	Q2	Q3	Q4	Total
2	New York City	14391	12524	16979	21075	64969
3	San Francisco	22987	25424	26552	29780	104743
4	Dallas	15344	17045	19024	23242	74655
5						
6	Grand Total	52722	54993	62555	74097	244367

	A	B	C	D	E	F
1	Store	Q1	Q2	Q3	Q4	Total
2	New York City	14391	12524	16979	21075	64969
3	San Francisco	22987	25424	26552	29780	104743
4	Dallas	15344	17045	19024	23242	74655
5						
6	Grand Total	52722	54993	62555	74097	244367

- Press the **Ctrl+Home** keystroke combination.

Moves to the beginning of the worksheet.

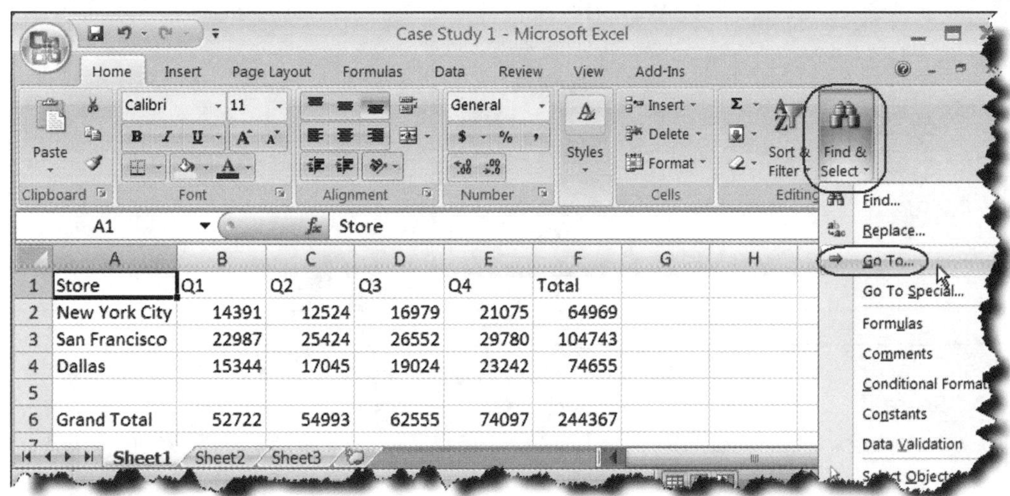

- Click the **Find & Select** button on the Home Ribbon and select **Go To** from the list.

Displays the Go To dialog box.

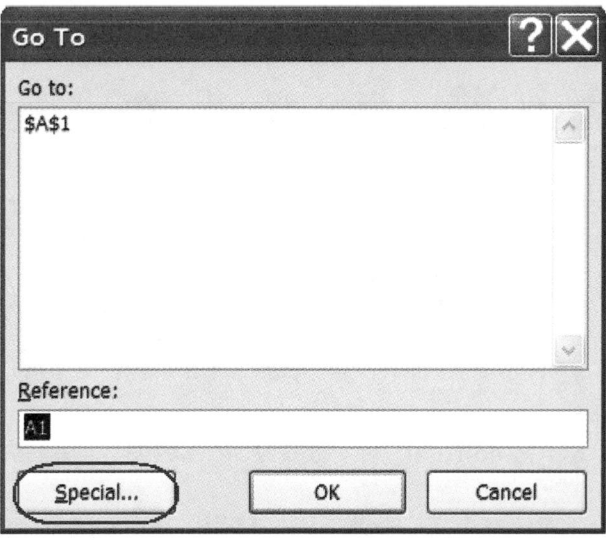

- Click the **Special** button.

Displays the Go To Special dialog box.

- Click the **Formulas** radio button and then click **OK**.

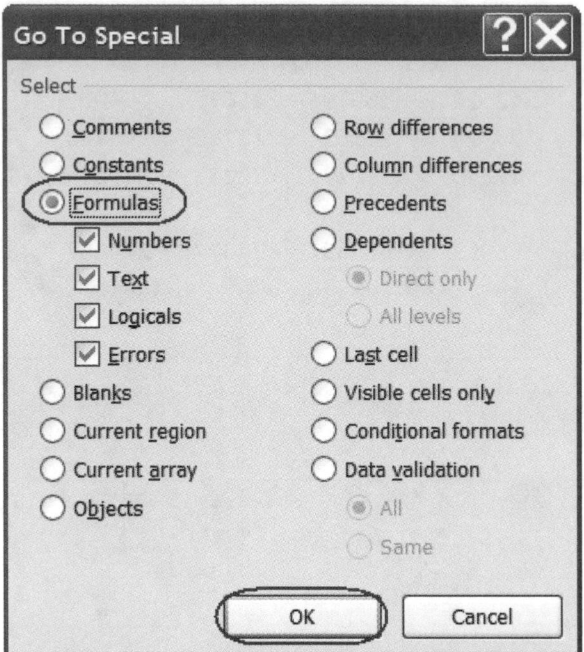

Highlights all cells that contain formulas.

	A	B	C	D	E	F
1	Store	Q1	Q2	Q3	Q4	Total
2	New York City	14391	12524	16979	21075	64969
3	San Francisco	22987	25424	26552	29780	104743
4	Dallas	15344	17045	19024	23242	74655
5						
6	Grand Total	52722	54993	62555	74097	244367
7						

- Click in cell **A1**.

Activates cell A1 and deselects the highlighted cells.

- Click the **Save** button.

Saves the current workbook.

	A	B	C	D	E	F
1	Store	Q1	Q2	Q3	Q4	Total
2	New York City	14391	12524	16979	21075	64969
3	San Francisco	22987	25424	26552	29780	104743
4	Dallas	15344	17045	19024	23242	74655
5						
6	Grand Total	52722	54993	62555	74097	244367
7						

Inserting Symbols

In this section, you will learn how to insert special characters into an Excel worksheet.

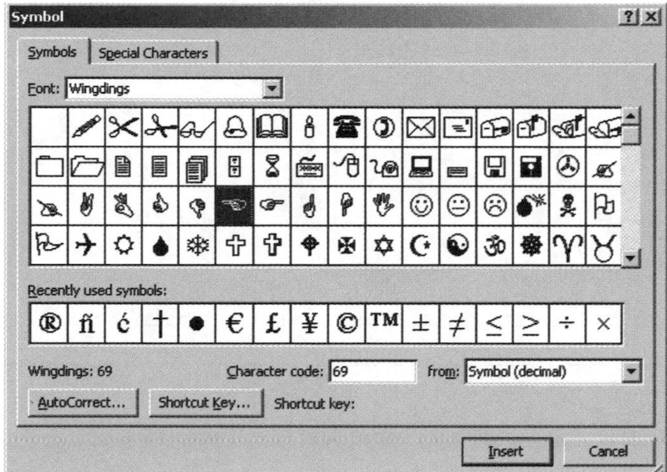

Microsoft Excel supplies hundreds of special characters that do not appear on your keyboard that you can use in your documents. For example, you can insert international symbols such as **ć** or **ñ**, symbols such as a trademark symbol (®), em dash (—), copyright symbol (©) and many more.

Each font set contains its own set of symbols or characters. The **Windings** and **Monotype Sorts** contain a nice variety of useful characters.

You can insert a recently used symbol by clicking the symbol in the **Recently used symbols** list in the **Symbol** dialog box. The **Special Characters** tab displays a list of common symbols such as the em dash, copyright and trademark symbols.

To Insert a Symbol into Your Worksheet

1. Set the insertion point where you wish to insert a symbol.
2. Click the **Insert tab** on the Ribbon.
3. Click the **Symbol** button.
4. Select the font set you wish to use from the drop-down **Font list**.
5. If available, select the font subset from the **Subset** drop-down list.
6. To insert a commonly used symbol, click the **Special Characters** tab.
7. Click the symbol you wish to insert.
8. Click the **Insert** button.
9. Click the **Close** button.

Let's Try It!

- Click in **A8**.

Makes A8 the active cell.

	A	B	C
1	Store	Q1	Q2
2	New York City	14391	12524
3	San Francisco	22987	25424
4	Dallas	15344	17045
5			
6	Grand Total	52722	54993
7			
8			
9			

- Click the **Insert tab** on the Ribbon.

Displays Insert commands and tools.

- Click the **Symbol** button on the Text command set.

Displays the Symbol dialog box.

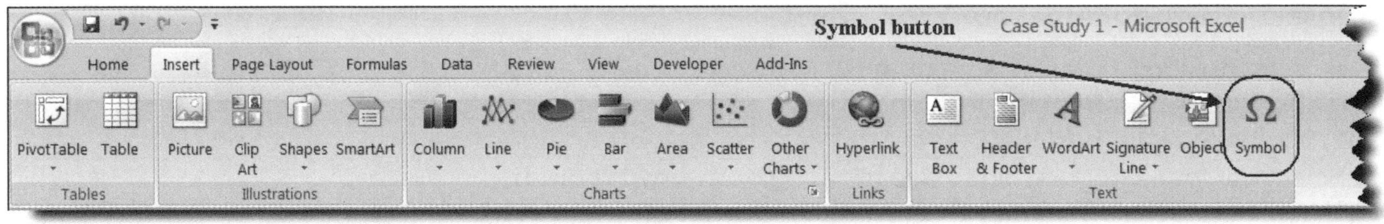

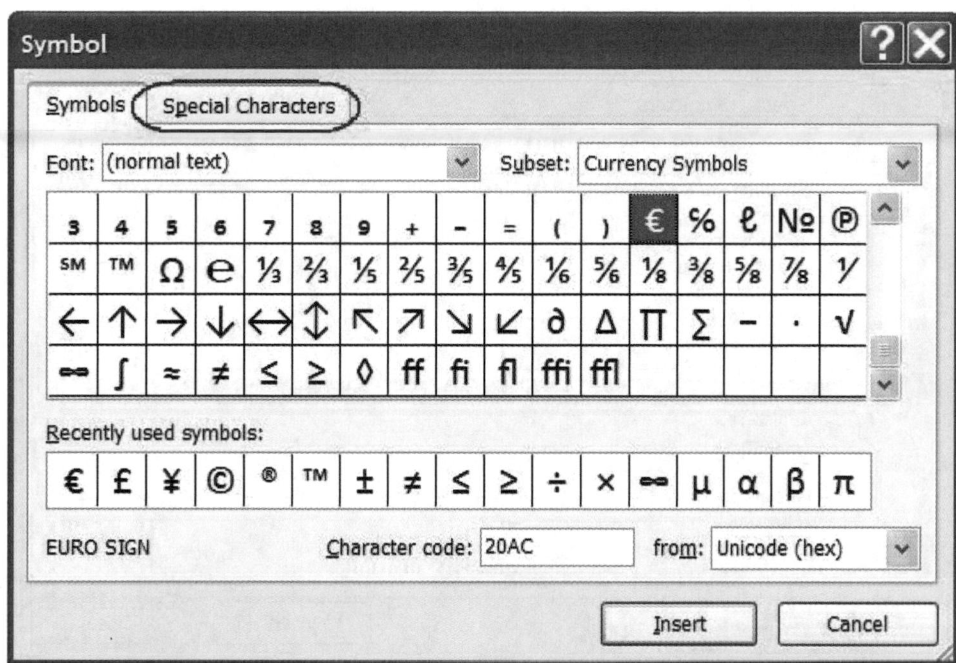

- Click on the **Special Characters** tab.

Displays commonly used symbols.

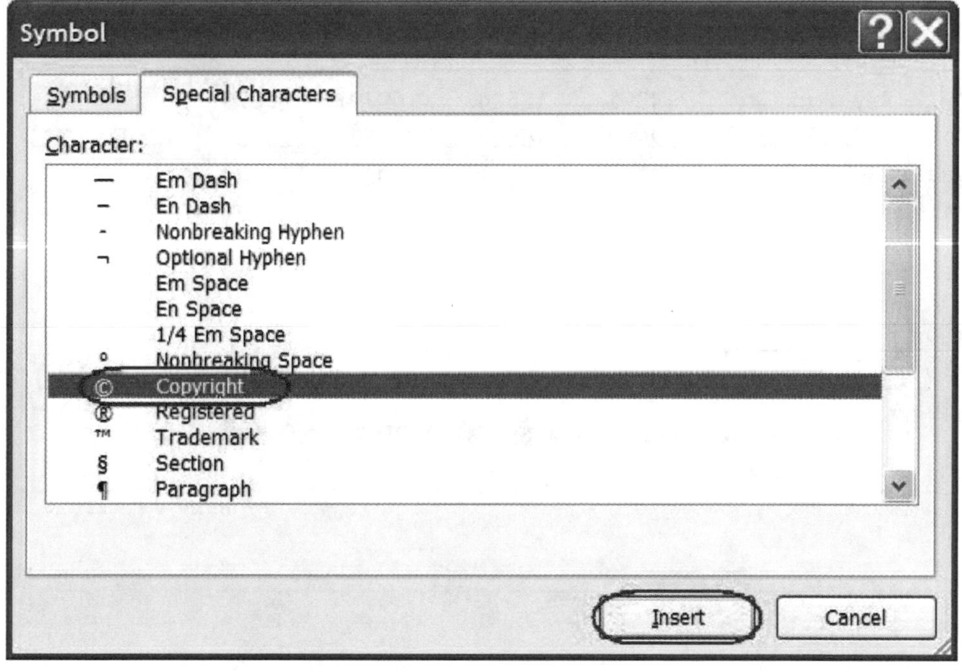

- Select the **Copyright Symbol** as shown and then click **Insert**.

Inserts the copyright symbol at the insertion point.

- Click **Close**.

Closes the Symbol dialog box.

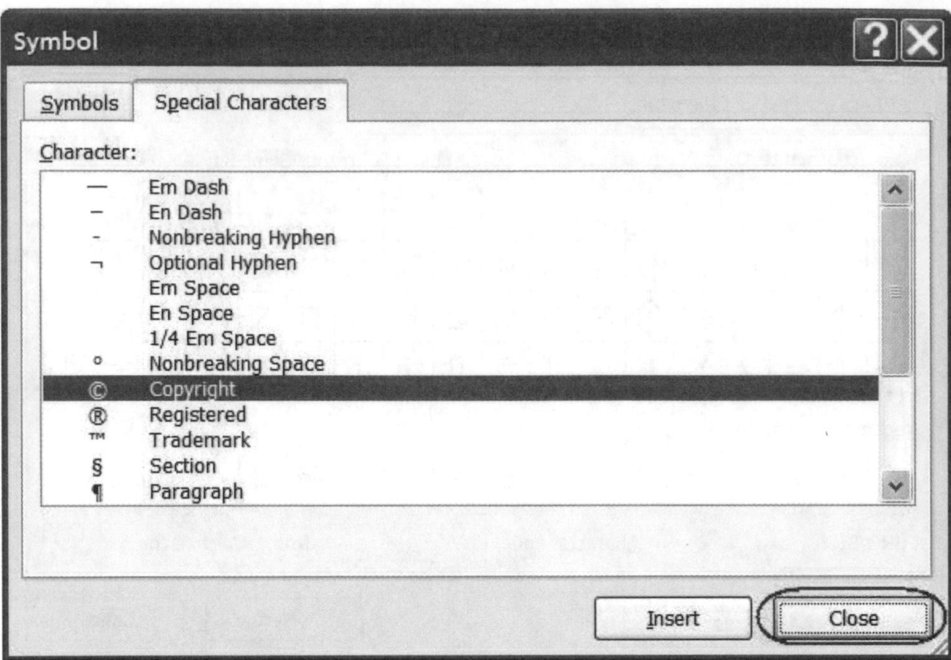

- Type: **2007 Rodney's Video** and then press **Enter**.

Enters the rest of the text into cell A8.

- Press the **Ctrl + S** keystroke combination.

Saves the changes.

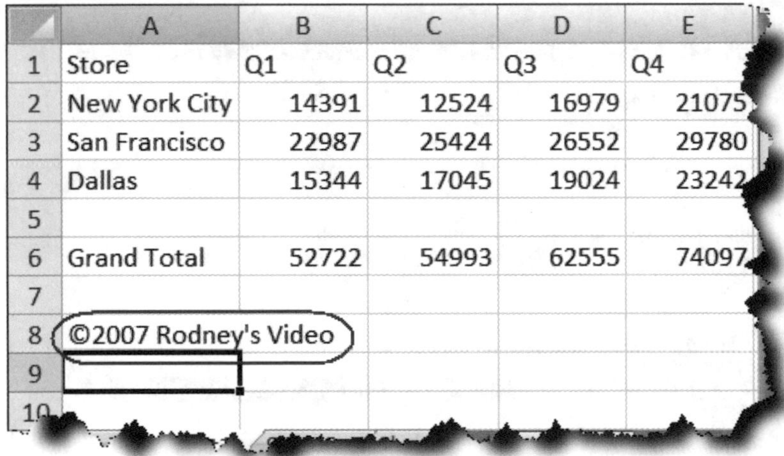

	A	B	C	D	E
1	Store	Q1	Q2	Q3	Q4
2	New York City	14391	12524	16979	21075
3	San Francisco	22987	25424	26552	29780
4	Dallas	15344	17045	19024	23242
5					
6	Grand Total	52722	54993	62555	74097
7					
8	©2007 Rodney's Video				
9					
10					

Working with Ranges

In this section, you will be introduced to working with groups of cells.

A **range** is a related group of cells. We looked at the SUM function where Excel totals a group of cells. If we wanted to retrieve a total for the cells B2 to B15, the formula would be written as:

=SUM(B2:B15)

Here, the formula B2:B15 designates all cells in the **B2 to B15 range**. This is an example of a **contiguous** range, that is to say, a group of cells that are next to each other in the same row or column.

There are several reasons why you might want to select a range in Excel:

- Apply the same formatting quickly to a group of cells
- Use the range in a function such as SUM or AVERAGE

- Apply a function or formula to several columns/rows at once
- Designate a group of cells as a print area
- Designate a group of cells for sorting

	A	B	C
1	Shrek	Adventure	49.99
2	Iron Mask	Action	49.99
3	Galaxy Dust	Adventure	49.99
4	Lord of the Rings: The Fellowship of the Rings	Adventure	[illegible]
5	Matrix, The	Action	[illegible]
6	Forest Gump	Action	[illegible]
7	Gladiators	Action	[illegible]
8	Buffy the Vampire Slayer	Action	[illegible]
9	Saving Private Ryan	Adventure	[illegible]
10	Cool Hand Luke	Action	[illegible]
11	Apollo 13	Action	[illegible]
12	Count of Monte Cristo	Action	[illegible]
13	Fugitive, The	Action	39.99
14	Harry Potter and the Sorcerer's Stone	Adventure	49.99
15	Hunt for Red October	Action	49.99
16	Antz	Comedy	49.99
17	Hair Spray	Comedy	29.99
18	Monty Python's Flying Circus	Comedy	19.99
19	When Harry Met Sally	Comedy	19.99
20	Arsenic & Old Lace	Comedy	29.99
21	Manhattan	Comedy	39.99
22	The Others	Suspense	49.99
23	Vertigo	Suspense	49.99
24	Psycho	Suspense	49.99
25	Airplane!	Comedy	29.99
26	Blazing Saddles	Comedy	49.99
27	Groundhog Day	Comedy	39.99
28	Harold and Maude	Comedy	29.99
29	My Cousin Vinny	Comedy	29.99
30	Dumb and Dumber	Comedy	49.99
31	This is Spinal Tap	Comedy	19.99

Selecting a Range

You can select a range in a variety of ways:

To Select a Contiguous Group of Cells

1. Click in the first cell in the group.
2. With the left mouse button held down, drag in the desired direction to select the range.

To Select an Entire Row or Column

1. Click the column heading or row heading.
2. To select additional rows or columns, hold down the left mouse button and drag in the desired direction.

To Select an Entire Worksheet

1. Click the **Select All** button (above row 1 and to the left of column A).

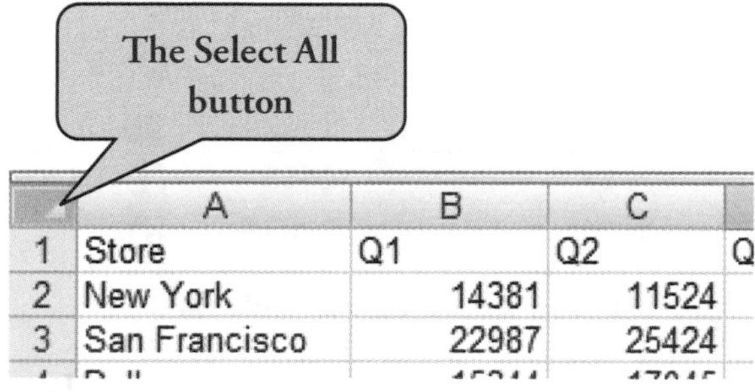

	A	B	C
1	Store	Q1	Q2
2	New York	14381	11524
3	San Francisco	22987	25424

To Select a Non-contiguous Range of Cells

1. Click in the first cell you wish to select.
2. Hold down the **Ctrl** key.
3. With the Ctrl key held down, select any additional non-adjacent cells.

To Select a Large Area of Contiguous Cells

1. Click in the first cell in the upper left of the range.
2. Hold down the **Shift** key.
3. With the Shift key held down, click in the last cell of the lower right of the range.

Let's Try It!

- Click on the **Column Heading** for Column B.

Selects Column B entirely.

	A	B	C	D	E
1	Store	Q1	Q2	Q3	Q4
2	New York City	14391	12524	16979	21075
3	San Francisco	22987	25424	26552	29780
4	Dallas	15344	17045	19024	23242
5					
6	Grand Total	52722	54993	62555	74097
7					
8	©2007 Rodney's Video				

- Click on the **Row Heading** for **Row 3**.

Selects Row 3 entirely.

	A	B	C	D	E
1	Store	Q1	Q2	Q3	Q4
2	New York City	14391	12524	16979	21075
3	San Francisco	22987	25424	26552	29780
4	Dallas	15344	17045	19024	23242
5					
6	Grand Total	52722	54993	62555	74097
7					
8	©2007 Rodney's Video				

- Click in **cell C2**.

Makes C2 the active cell.

	A	B	C	D	
1	Store	Q1	Q2	Q3	Q4
2	New York City	14391	12524	16979	
3	San Francisco	22987	25424	26552	
4	Dallas	15344	17045	19024	
5					

	A	B	C	D	E	F	G
1	Store	Q1	Q2	Q3	Q4	Total	
2	New York City	14391	12524	16979	21075	64969	
3	San Francisco	22987	25424	26552	29780	104743	
4	Dallas	15344	17045	19024	23242	74655	
5							
6	Grand Total	52722	54993	62555	74097	244367	

- Press and hold down the left mouse button and drag to **cell E4**.

Selects the range of cells C2:E4.

	A	B	C	D	E	F	G
1	Store	Q1	Q2	Q3	Q4	Total	
2	New York City	14391	12524	16979	21075	64969	
3	San Francisco	22987	25424	26552	29780	104743	
4	Dallas	15344	17045	19024	23242	74655	
5							
6	Grand Total	52722	54993	62555	74097	244367	

- Select **cell B2**.

Makes B2 the active cell.

	A	B	C	D	E	F
1	Store	Q1	Q2	Q3	Q4	Total
2	New York City	14391	12524	16979	21075	64969
3	San Francisco	22987	25424	26552	29780	104743
4	Dallas	15344	17045	19024	23242	74655
5						
6	Grand Total	52722	54993	62555	74097	244367

- Press and hold down the Ctrl key. Click on **cells C4, D2, E6 and F4**.

Selects a non-contiguous range of cells.

	A	B	C	D	E	F
1	Store	Q1	Q2	Q3	Q4	Total
2	New York City	14391	12524	16979	21075	64969
3	San Francisco	22987	25424	26552	29780	104743
4	Dallas	15344	17045	19024	23242	74655
5	Select All button					
6	Grand Total	52722	54993	62555	74097	244367

- Click on the **Select All** button.

Selects the entire worksheet.

- Click in **cell A1**.

Deselects the selected cells.

- Press the **Ctrl + S** keystroke combination.

Saves the changes.

	A	B	C	D	E	F
1	Store	Q1	Q2	Q3	Q4	Total
2	New York City	14391	12524	16979	21075	64969
3	San Francisco	22987	25424	26552	29780	104743
4	Dallas	15344	17045	19024	23242	74655
5						
6	Grand Total	52722	54993	62555	74097	244367
7						

Cutting and Pasting Data

In this section, you will learn how to move data from one location of your worksheet to another using the Cut and Paste commands.

When you wish to move data from one location to another rather than duplicating data, use Excel's **Cut and Paste** commands. Using the Cut and Paste commands, the data is deleted from its original location and moved to the new location. Like the copy command, the data is stored temporarily on the Windows clipboard.

Using the **Cut and Paste commands** allows you to rearrange worksheet cells, rows and columns with ease.

To Cut and Paste Data

1. Select the cell range you wish to delete.
2. Press the **Ctrl** and **X** keystroke combination (**Ctrl + X**).
   Or
   Click the **Cut button** on the Home Ribbon.
3. Select the cell range to receive the data.
4. Press the **Ctrl** and **V** keystroke combination (**Ctrl + V**).
   Or
   Click the **Paste button** on the Home Ribbon.

TIP: You can also **right-click** on selected text and then choose Cut from the contextual menu. Right-click and choose Paste after you have set the insertion point where you want to insert the copied text.

Let's Try It!

	A	B	C	D	E	F
1	Store	Q1	Q2	Q3	Q4	Total
2	New York City	14391	12524	16979	21075	64969
3	San Francisco	22987	25424	26552	29780	104743
4	Dallas	15344	17045	19024	23242	74655
5						
6	Grand Total	52722	54993	62555	74097	244367
7						
8	©2007 Rodney's Video					

- Select the cell range **A1:F6**.

Selects the entire range of data.

	A	B	C	D	E	F
1	Store	Q1	Q2	Q3	Q4	Total
2	New York City	14391	12524	16979	21075	64969
3	San Francisco	22987	25424	26552	29780	104743
4	Dallas	15344	17045	19024	23242	74655
5						
6	Grand Total	52722	54993	62555	74097	244367
7						
8	©2007 Rodney's Video					

- Press the **Ctrl + X** keystroke combination.

Places a marquee border around the range to be cut.

	A	B	C	D
1	Store	Q1	Q2	Q3
2	New York City	14391	12524	16
3	San Francisco	22987	25424	26
4	Dallas	15344	17045	19
5				
6	Grand Total	52722	54993	625
7				
8	©2007 Rodney's Video			
9				
10				
11				
12				

- Click in cell **B10**.

Activates the cell where we will paste the data.

- Press the **Ctrl + V** keystroke combination.

Removes the data from the original location and places it in the new location.

	A	B	C	D	E	F	G
1							
2							
3							
4							
5							
6							
7							
8	©2007 Rodney's Video						
9							
10		Store	Q1	Q2	Q3	Q4	Total
11		New York	14391	12524	16979	21075	64969
12		San Franci:	22987	25424	26552	29780	104743
13		Dallas	15344	17045	19024	23242	74655
14							
15		Grand Tot:	52722	54993	62555	74097	244367

Copying and Moving Cells Using Drag-And-Drop

In this section, you will learn how to manually move and copy cells using the drag-and-drop method.

Instead of using the Cut/Copy and Paste commands, you can also move and copy cells or ranges of cells using the **drag-and-drop** method. That is to say, you can manually move the contents of cells to another location by first selecting the cell range and then dragging the cells with your mouse to the new location. To copy cells instead of moving, hold down the **Ctrl** key as you drag.

To Copy or Move a Range Using Drag-and-Drop

1. Select the range of cells to be copied or moved.
2. Position your mouse pointer over **the black border** of the selection until it becomes a black 4-way arrow.
3. To move the range, **click** with your left mouse button and **drag** to the new location.
4. To copy the range, press and hold the Ctrl key as you drag.

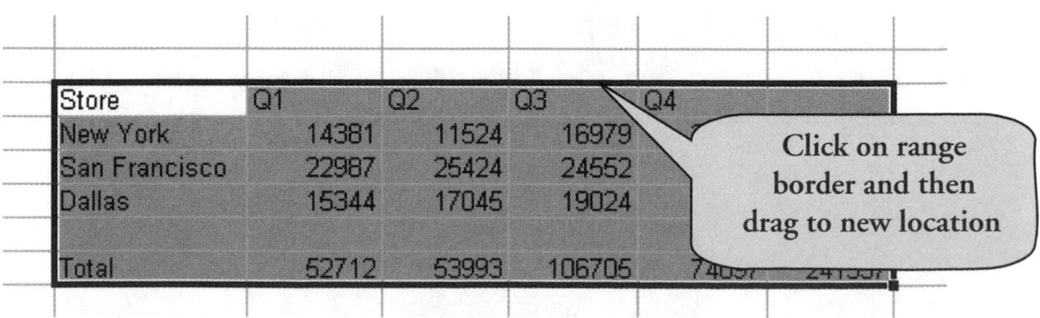

Let's Try It!

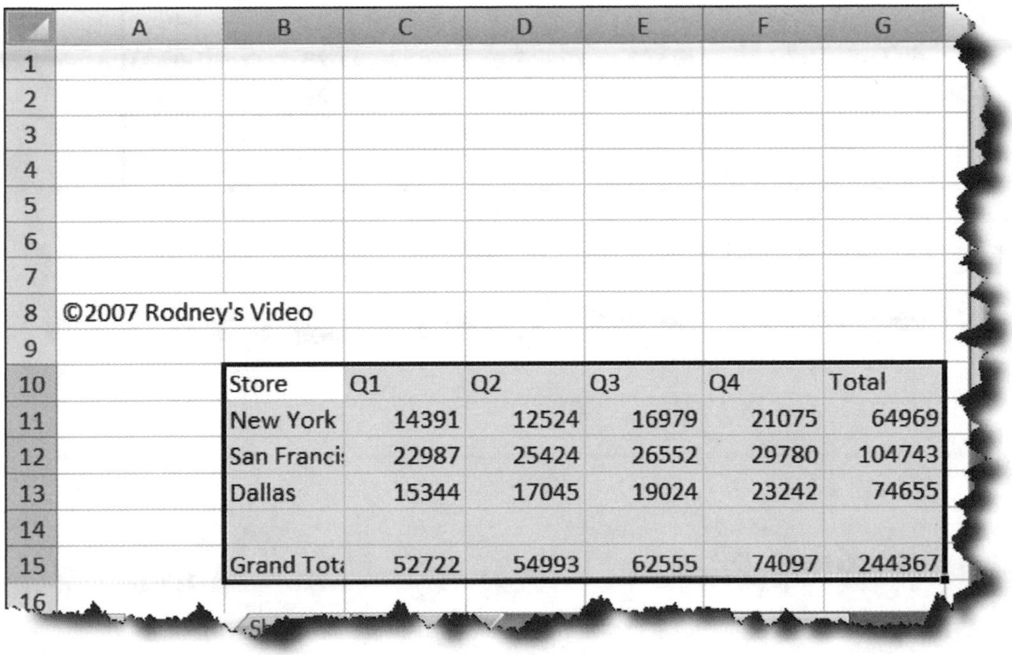

	A	B	C	D	E	F	G
1							
2							
3							
4							
5							
6							
7							
8	©2007 Rodney's Video						
9							
10		Store	Q1	Q2	Q3	Q4	Total
11		New York	14391	12524	16979	21075	64969
12		San Franci:	22987	25424	26552	29780	104743
13		Dallas	15344	17045	19024	23242	74655
14							
15		Grand Tot:	52722	54993	62555	74097	244367
16							

- Select the range **B10:G15** if not already selected.

Selects the entire range of data.

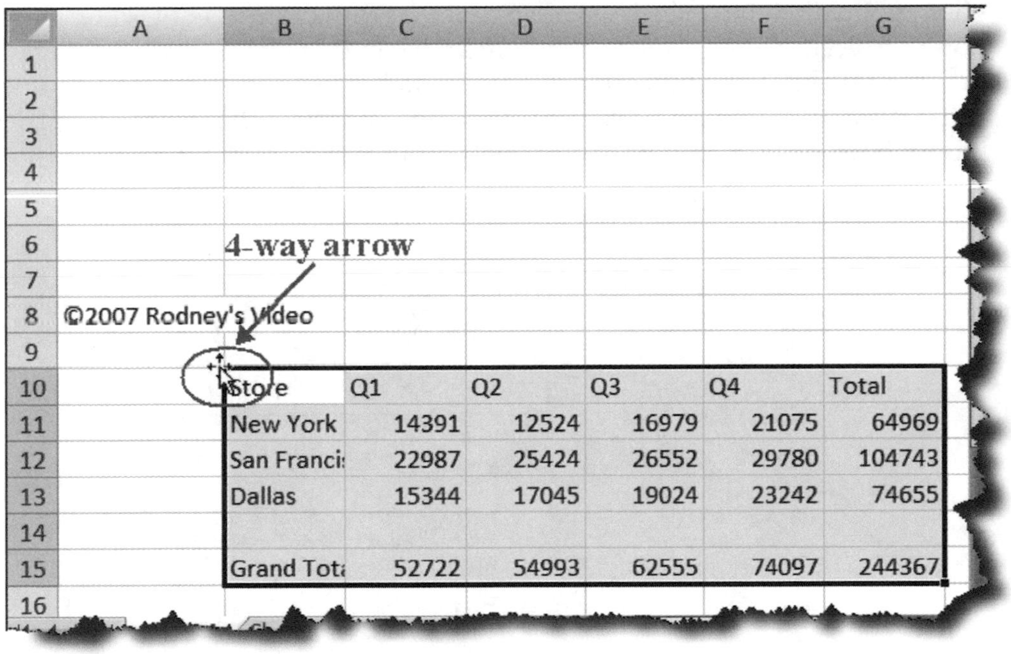

	A	B	C	D	E	F	G
1							
2							
3							
4							
5							
6							
7							
8	©2007 Rodney's Video						
9							
10		Store	Q1	Q2	Q3	Q4	Total
11		New York	14391	12524	16979	21075	64969
12		San Franci:	22987	25424	26552	29780	104743
13		Dallas	15344	17045	19024	23242	74655
14							
15		Grand Tot:	52722	54993	62555	74097	244367
16							

4-way arrow

- Move your mouse pointer over the **top border of the range** until the pointer changes to a 4-way black arrow.

Enters drag mode.

- Click and drag until the top left corner rests in cell **A1**.

Moves the range to its new location, beginning in cell A1.

- Release the mouse button.

Completes the move process.

- Click the **Save** button.

Saves the current workbook.

	A	B	C	D	E	F	G
1	Store	Q1	Q2	Q3	Q4	Total	
2	New York City	14391	12524	16979	21075	64969	
3	San Francisco	22987	25424	26552	29780	104743	
4	Dallas	15344	17045	19024	23242	74655	
5							
6	Grand Total	52722	54993	62555	74097	244367	
7							
8	©2007 Rodney's Video						
9							

Changing Column Width

In this section, you will learn how to modify the width of columns to accommodate text.

When typing data into a cell, we often find that the column is not wide enough to accommodate the text and often, the end of our text will either be cut off or will continue into the next cell. In such a case, we will want to **adjust the column width** by clicking on the boundary of the right side of the column heading and dragging until the column is the desired width.

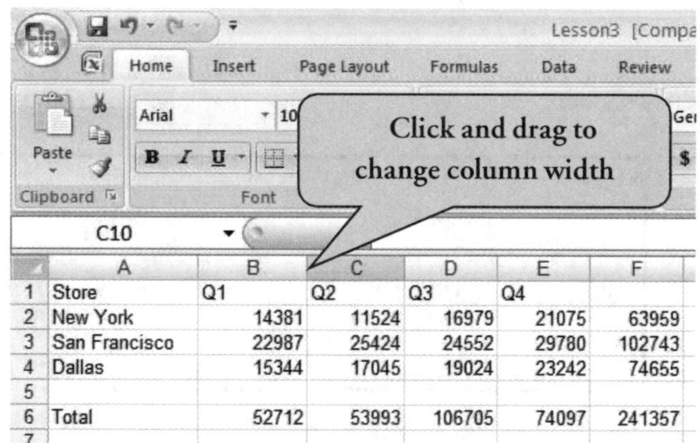

	A	B	C	D	E	F
1	Store	Q1	Q2	Q3	Q4	
2	New York	14381	11524	16979	21075	63959
3	San Francisco	22987	25424	24552	29780	102743
4	Dallas	15344	17045	19024	23242	74655
5						
6	Total	52712	53993	106705	74097	241357
7						

Rather than change the size of a column manually, you can use Excel's **Column Width** commands in which you enter **precise values** for column width.

To Change the Width of a Column

1. Move your mouse pointer over the **boundary** of the right side of the column heading until the mouse pointer changes into a black cross with a double arrow.
2. Click and hold the mouse button down and **drag** until the column is the desired width.

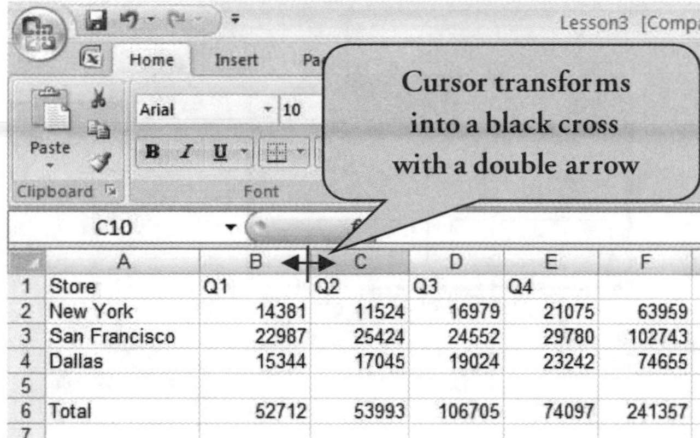

To Change the Width of Multiple Columns

1. Select the columns you wish to change by selecting the column headings.
2. Move your mouse pointer over the **boundary** of the right side of any column heading until the mouse pointer changes into a black cross with a double arrow (To change the columns widths of **All** columns or rows in the worksheet, click the **Select All Button**).
3. Click and hold the mouse button down and **drag** until the columns are the desired width or rows are the desired height.

To Change the Size of a Column Using the Column Width Command

1. Highlight the column(s) you wish to change.
2. **Right-click** and choose **Column Width** from the contextual menu
   Or
   Click the **Format** button on the Cells group on the Home Ribbon and choose **Column Width** from the drop-down menu.

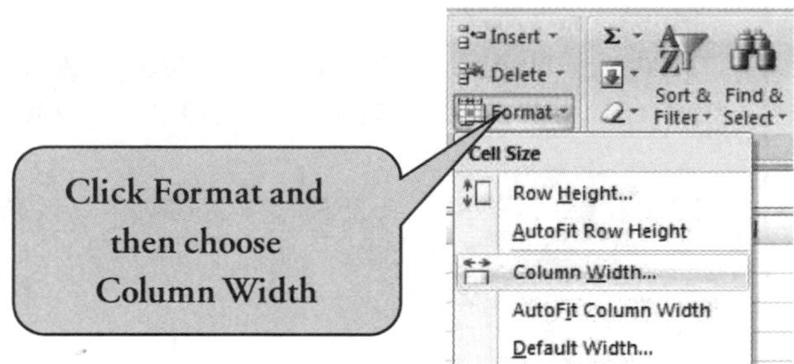

3. Enter the appropriate value in the pop-up dialog box. The value is expressed by average number of digits which the row or cell can accommodate using the default font. For example, a column width of 13 should be able to accommodate 13 digits in that cell.

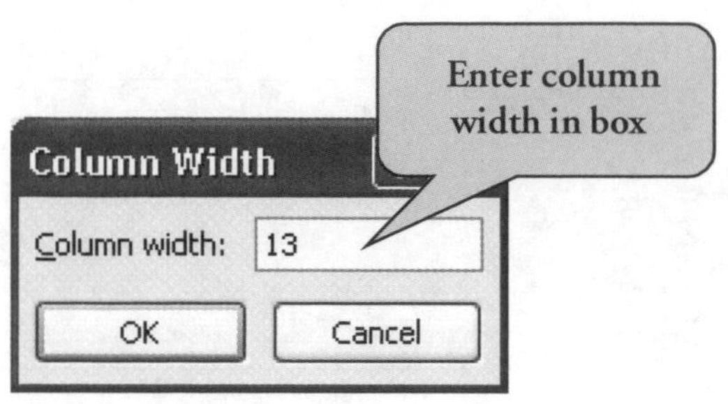

4. Click **OK**.

Let's Try It!

- Click on the column heading for **Column A**.

Selects Column A.

	A	B	C	D	E	F	G
1	Store	Q1	Q2	Q3	Q4	Total	
2	New York City	14391	12524	16979	21075	64969	
3	San Francisco	22987	25424	26552	29780	104743	
4	Dallas	15344	17045	19024	23242	74655	
5							
6	Grand Total	52722	54993	62555	74097	244367	
7							
8	©2007 Rodney's Video						
9							
10							

Sheet1 Sheet2 Sheet3

- Click on the border between **Column A and Column B**.

Enters drag mode.

	A	B	C	D	E	F	G
1	Store	Q1	Q2	Q3	Q4	Total	
2	New York City	14391	12524	16979	21075	64969	
3	San Francisco	22987	25424	26552	29780	104743	
4	Dallas	15344	17045	19024	23242	74655	
5							
6	Grand Total	52722	54993	62555	74097	244367	
7							
8	©2007 Rodney's Video						
9							
10							

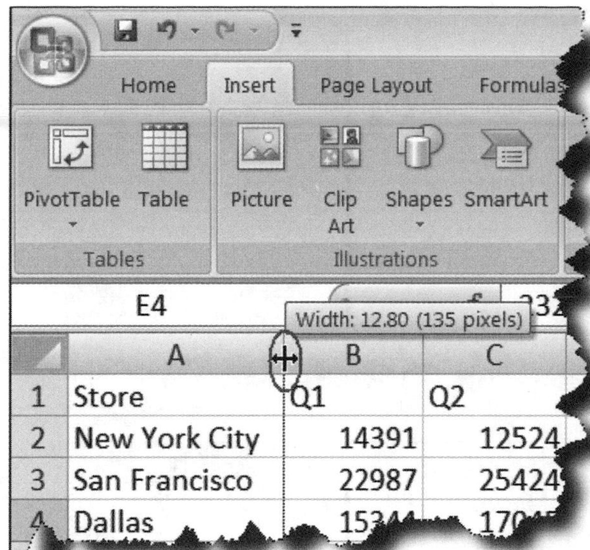

- Click and drag until Column A is about **135 pixels wide**.

Adjusts the width of Column A.

- Click the **Save** button.

Saves the changes.

Autofit

You can also use Excel's **Autofit** feature. This allows you to automatically change the width of a column or height of a row to accommodate the widest or tallest entry.

To Change the Size of a Column or Row Using Autofit

1. For **Columns**, double-click on the **right border** of the column heading. The column width will adjust to accommodate the largest entry in that column.
2. For **Rows**, double-click on the **bottom border** of the row heading. The row height will adjust to accommodate the tallest entry in that row.

Let's Try It!

	A	B	C	D
1	Store	Q1	Q2	Q3
2	New York City	14391	12524	16979
3	San Francisco	22987	25424	26552
4	Dallas	15344	17045	19024
5				
6	Grand Total	52722	54993	62555
7				
8	©2007 Rodney's Video			

- Click on the column heading for **Column B**.

Selects Column B.

- Click and drag over column headings to the right until **Columns B, C, D, E & F** are selected.

Selects columns B through F.

	A	B	C	D	E	F
1	Store	Q1	Q2	Q3	Q4	Total
2	New York City	14391	12524	16979	21075	64969
3	San Francisco	22987	25424	26552	29780	104743
4	Dallas	15344	17045	19024	23242	74655
5						
6	Grand Total	52722	54993	62555	74097	244367
7						
8	©2007 Rodney's Video					

- Double-click on the border between **Columns C & D** in the column heading.

Autofits all selected columns.

- Click the **Save** button.

Saves the active workbook.

	A	B	C	D	E	F	G
1	Store	Q1	Q2	Q3	Q4	Total	
2	New York City	14391	12524	16979	21075	64969	
3	San Francisco	22987	25424	26552	29780	104743	
4	Dallas	15344	17045	19024	23242	74655	
5							
6	Grand Total	52722	54993	62555	74097	244367	
7							
8	©2007 Rodney's Video						

Changing Row Height

In this section, you will learn how to modify the height of rows.

At times, you may wish a particular row to stand out by increasing the font size such as in a worksheet title heading. In this case, you would also need to adjust the row height to accommodate the taller text of the increased font size. The process for changing the width of columns works the same way for changing the height of rows—click on the boundary of the bottom of the row heading and drag until the row is the desired height.

Just as we saw with changing column width, you also change the size of a row or column (rather than dragging manually) by using Excel's **Row Height** command in which you enter **precise values** for row height.

To Change the Height of a Row

1. Move your mouse pointer over the of the bottom border of the row heading until the mouse pointer changes into a black cross with a double arrow.
2. Click and hold down the mouse button and **drag downwards** until the row is the desired height.

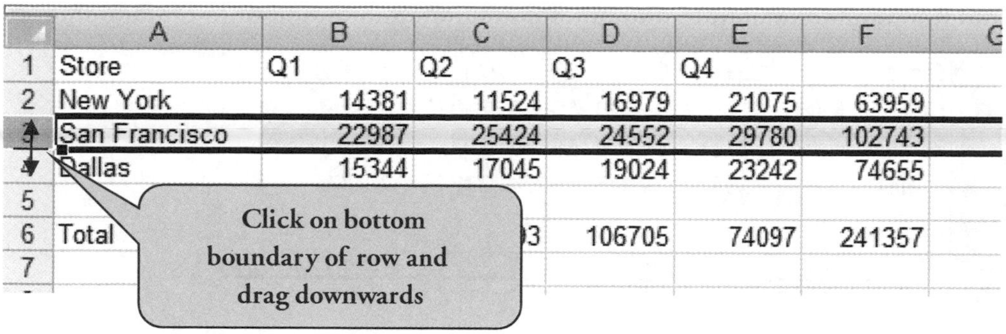

	A	B	C	D	E	F	G
1	Store	Q1	Q2	Q3	Q4		
2	New York	14381	11524	16979	21075	63959	
3	San Francisco	22987	25424	24552	29780	102743	
4	Dallas	15344	17045	19024	23242	74655	
5							
6	Total	[illegible]	[illegible]3	106705	74097	241357	
7							

Click on bottom boundary of row and drag downwards

To Change the Height of Multiple Rows

1. Select rows you wish to change by clicking on the row headings.
2. Move your mouse pointer over the **boundary** of bottom of any row heading until the mouse pointer changes into a black cross with a double arrow (To change the row heights of **All** columns or rows in the worksheet, click the **Select All Button**).
3. Click and hold the mouse button down and **drag** until the rows are the desired height.

To Change the Height of a Row Using the Row Height Commands

1. Highlight the row(s) you wish to change.
2. Right-click and choose **Row Height** from the contextual menu
   Or
   Click the **Format** button on the Cells group on the Home Ribbon and choose **Row Height** from the drop-down menu.
3. Enter the appropriate value in the pop-up dialog box. The value represents height measurements in points (1 point is equal to 1/72 of an inch.

Let's Try It!

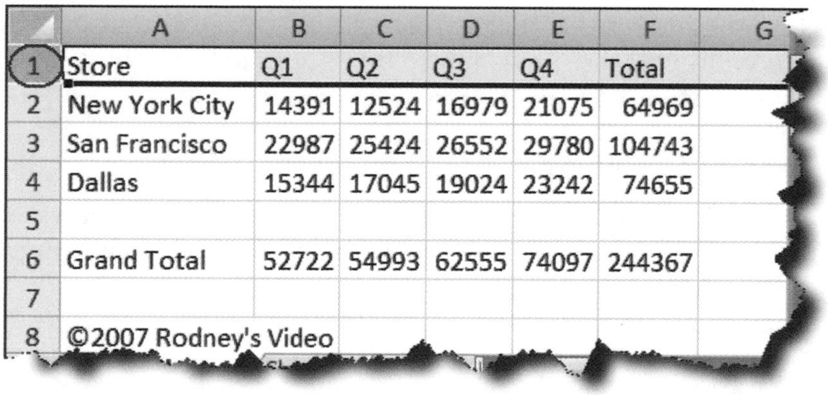

	A	B	C	D	E	F	G
1	Store	Q1	Q2	Q3	Q4	Total	
2	New York City	14391	12524	16979	21075	64969	
3	San Francisco	22987	25424	26552	29780	104743	
4	Dallas	15344	17045	19024	23242	74655	
5							
6	Grand Total	52722	54993	62555	74097	244367	
7							
8	©2007 Rodney's Video						

- Click on the row heading for **Row 1**.

Selects Row 1.

- Click and then drag over the row headings downwards until **Rows 1–6** are selected.

Selects Rows 1–6.

	A	B	C	D	E	F	G
1	Store	Q1	Q2	Q3	Q4	Total	
2	New York City	14391	12524	16979	21075	64969	
3	San Francisco	22987	25424	26552	29780	104743	
4	Dallas	15344	17045	19024	23242	74655	
5							
6	Grand Total	52722	54993	62555	74097	244367	
7							
8	©2007 Rodney's Video						

Sheet1 / Sheet2 / Sheet3

- Click on the border between **Rows 2 and 3** in the row heading and drag downwards about **30 pixels**.

Adjusts all selected rows.

- Click the **Save** button.

Saves the active workbook.

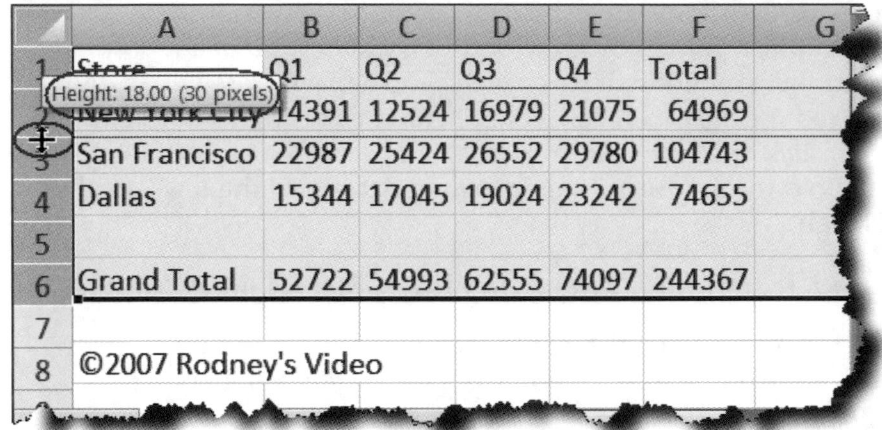

Height: 18.00 (30 pixels)
A B C D E F G
Store Q1 Q2 Q3 Q4 Total
New York City 14391 12524 16979 21075 64969
San Francisco 22987 25424 26552 29780 104743
Dallas 15344 17045 19024 23242 74655
Grand Total 52722 54993 62555 74097 244367
©2007 Rodney's Video

Inserting and Removing Rows and Columns

In this section, you will learn how to insert new rows and columns and delete existing rows and columns in your worksheet.

To change the appearance of your worksheet, you can insert additional columns and rows or delete existing ones. When you insert a new column into your worksheet, existing columns shift to the right. When inserting new rows, existing rows shift down.

To Insert a Column

1. Select the column where you would like to insert a new column. If you wish to insert more than one column, select as many columns as you would like to insert.
2. In the **Home Ribbon**, click the **Insert** button on the **Cells group**.
   Or
   Right Click and choose **Insert** from the contextual menu.

To Insert a Row

1. Select the row where you would like to insert a new row. If you wish to insert more than one row, select as many rows as you would like to insert.
2. In the **Home Ribbon**, click the **Insert** button on the **Cells group.**
   Or
   Right Click and choose **Insert** from the contextual menu.

To Remove a Row or Column

1. Select the column or row that you wish to remove.
2. Click the **Delete** button on the Cells group
   Or
   Right-click and choose **Delete** from the contextual menu.
3. To clear only the **contents** of a row or column, highlight the row or column and press the **Delete** key.

Let's Try It!

	A	B	C	D	E	F	G
1	Store	Q1	Q2	Q3	Q4	Total	
2	New York City	14391	12524	16979	21075	64969	
3	San Francisco	22987	25424	26552	29780	104743	
4	Dallas	15344	17045	19024	23242	74655	
5							
6	Grand Total	52722	54993	62555	74097	244367	

- Click on the Row Heading for **Row 4**.

Selects Row 4.

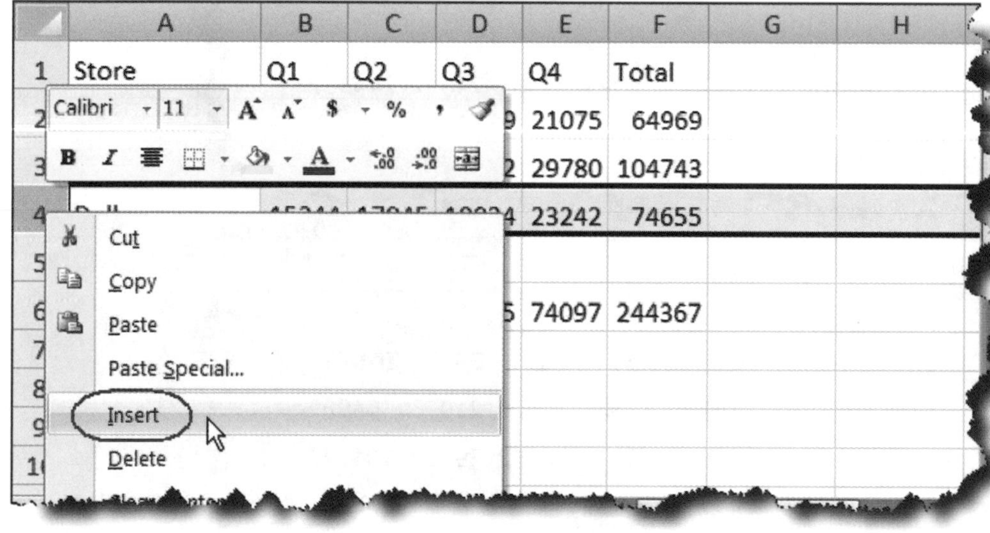

- **Right-click** and then choose **Insert** from the contextual menu.

Inserts a new row above row 4.

- Click in cell **A4** and type: **Milwaukee**.

Enters data into cell A4.

	A	B	C	D	E	F	G
1	Store	Q1	Q2	Q3	Q4	Total	
2	New York City	14391	12524	16979	21075	64969	
3	San Francisco	22987	25424	26552	29780	104743	
4	Milwaukee						
5	Dallas	15344	17045	19024	23242	74655	
6							
7	Grand Total	52722	54993	62555	74097	244367	
8							
9	©2007 Rodney's Video						

- Press the **Tab** key and type: **41224**

Enters Q1 data for Milwaukee.

	A	B	C	D	E	F	G
1	Store	Q1	Q2	Q3	Q4	Total	
2	New York City	14391	12524	16979	21075	64969	
3	San Francisco	22987	25424	26552	29780	104743	
4	Milwaukee	41224					
5	Dallas	15344	17045	19024	23242	74655	
6							
7	Grand Total	52722	54993	62555	74097	244367	
8							
9	©2007 Rodney's Video						

- Press the **Tab** key and type: **42655**

Enters Q2 data for Milwaukee.

	A	B	C	D	E	F	G
1	Store	Q1	Q2	Q3	Q4	Total	
2	New York City	14391	12524	16979	21075	64969	
3	San Francisco	22987	25424	26552	29780	104743	
4	Milwaukee	41224	42655				
5	Dallas	15344	17045	19024	23242	74655	
6							
7	Grand Total	93946	54993	62555	74097	244367	
8							
9	©2007 Rodney's Video						

	A	B	C	D	E	F
1	Store	Q1	Q2	Q3	Q4	Total
2	New York City	14391	12524	16979	21075	64969
3	San Francisco	22987	25424	26552	29780	104743
4	Milwaukee	41224	42655	38972		
5	Dallas	15344	17045	19024	23242	74655
6						
7	Grand Total	93946	97648	62555	74097	244367
8						
9	©2007 Rodney's Video					

- Press the **Tab** key and type: **38972**

Enters Q3 data for Milwaukee.

	A	B	C	D	E	F
1	Store	Q1	Q2	Q3	Q4	Total
2	New York City	14391	12524	16979	21075	64969
3	San Francisco	22987	25424	26552	29780	104743
4	Milwaukee	41224	42655	38972	45268	
5	Dallas	15344	17045	19024	23242	74655
6						
7	Grand Total	93946	97648	1E+05	74097	244367
8						
9	©2007 Rodney's Video					

Sheet1 Sheet2 Sheet3

- Press the **Tab** key and type: **45268**

Enters Q4 data for Milwaukee.

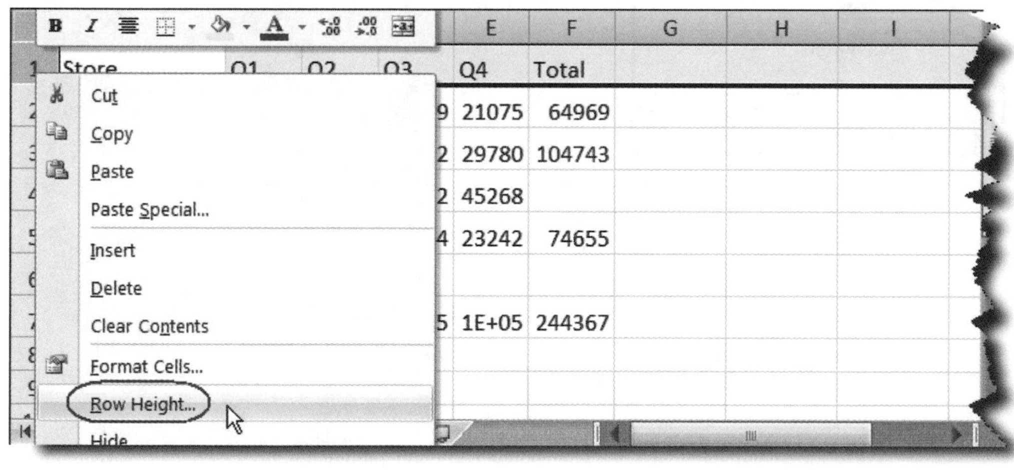

- Click the **Row Heading** for Row 1.

Selects Row 1.

- **Right-Click** and choose **Row Height** from the contextual menu.

Displays the Row Height dialog box.

- Enter **21** in the Row Height dialog box.

Enters a row height of 21 for Row 1.

- Click **OK**.

Closes the Row Height dialog box.

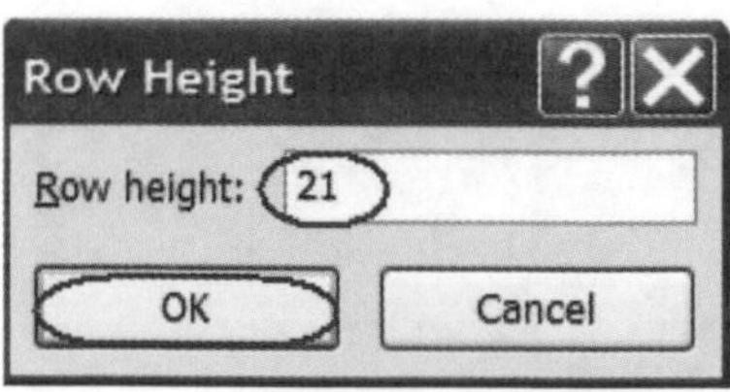

- Click in cell **A1**.

Makes cell A1 the active cell.

- **Right-Click** and choose **Insert** from the contextual menu.

Inserts a new row.

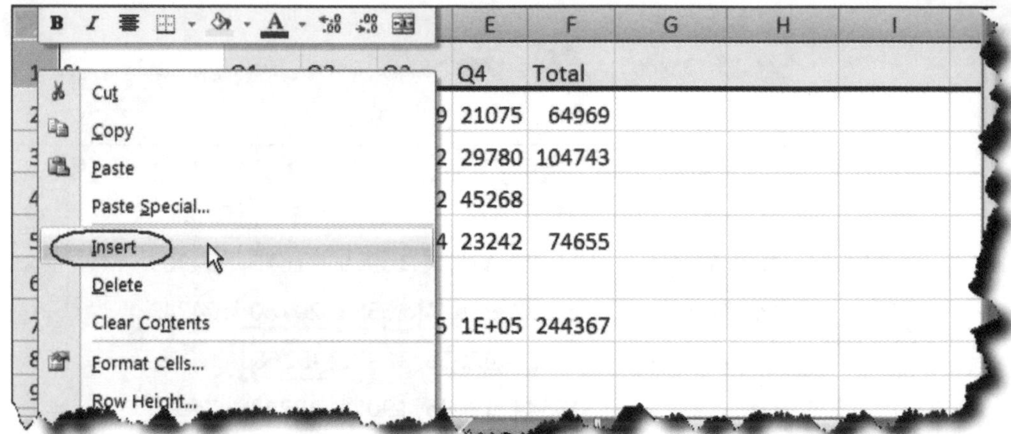

- On the Insert dialog box, select **Entire row** and click **OK**.

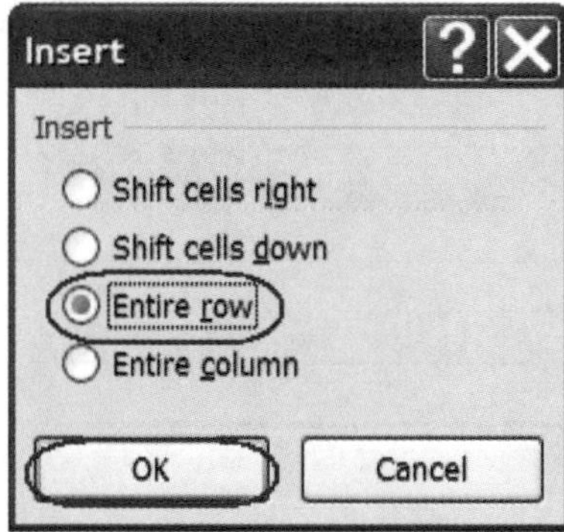

	A	B	C	D	E	F	G
1	Quarterly Sales for FY 2005						
2	Store	Q1	Q2	Q3	Q4	Total	
3	New York City	14391	12524	16979	21075	64969	
4	San Francisco	22987	25424	26552	29780	104743	
5	Milwaukee	41224	42655	38972	45268		
6	Dallas	15344	17045	19024	23242	74655	
7							
8	Grand Total	93946	97648	1E+05	1E+05	244367	
9							
10	©2007 Rodney's Video						
11							

- Click in cell **A1**.

Makes cell A1 the active cell.

- Type: **Quarterly Sales for FY 2005**.

Enters the worksheet title.

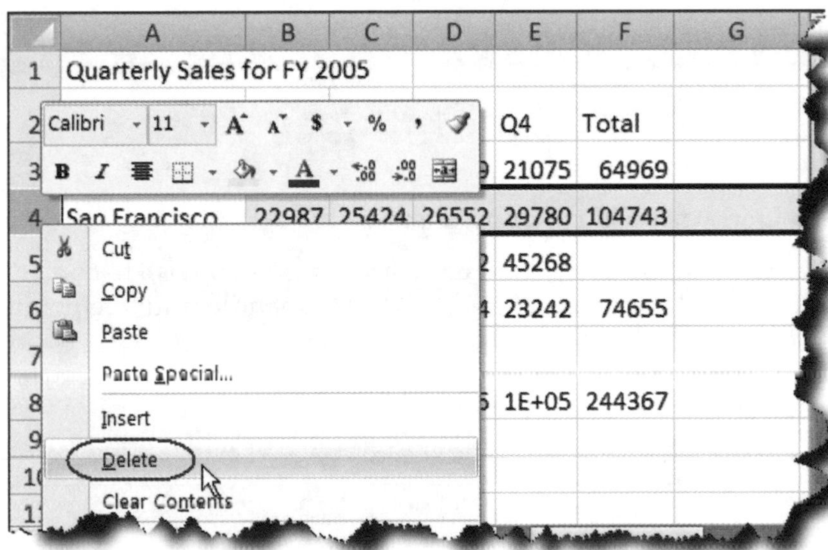

- Press **Enter**.

Confirms the entry.

- Click the Row Heading for **row 4**.

Selects row 4.

- **Right-Click** and choose **Delete** from the contextual menu.

Deletes row 4 from the worksheet.

	A	B	C	D	E	F	G
1	Quarterly Sales for FY 2005						
2	Store	Q1	Q2	Q3	Q4	Total	
3	New York City	14391	12524	16979	21075	64969	
4	San Francisco	22987	25424	26552	29780	104743	
5	Milwaukee	41224	42655	38972	45268		
6	Dallas	15344	17045	19024	23242	74655	
7							
8	Grand Total	93946	97648	1E+05	1E+05	244367	
9							
10	©2007 Rodney's Video						
11							

- Press the **Ctrl + Z** keystroke combination.

Reverses the last action.

- Click the **Save** button.

Saves the current worksheet.

Copying Data and Formulas with AutoFill

In this section, you will learn how to copy data and formulas from one cell to another using Excel's AutoFill feature.

You can copy data and formulas to adjacent cells using the **AutoFill** feature. To use the AutoFill feature, select the cell whose data you wish to copy and then move your mouse pointer over the cell's **fill handle**, the small black box on the lower right corner of the cell. Your mouse pointer will transform into a black cross. Then, click and drag to the adjacent cell(s) where you wish to copy the data. Once the action is completed, the **AutoFill Options** button will appear, allowing you to choose the option of copying just the data, copying the formatting only, or copying the data without the formatting.

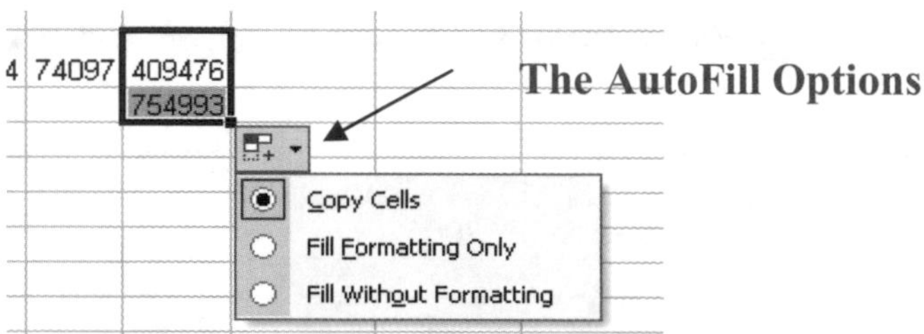

To Use AutoFill to Copy Data or a Formula

1. Activate the cell whose data or formula you wish to copy.
2. Move the mouse pointer over the fill handle until the pointer transforms into a black cross.
3. Click and drag to the cell(s) where you wish to copy the data.
4. Release the mouse button.
5. If desired, choose an option from the AutoFill Option button by clicking the arrow.

	A	B	C	D	E	F
1	Quarterly Sales for FY 2002					
2						
3	Store	Q1	Q2	Q3	Q4	
4	New York	14381	11524	16979	21075	63959
5	San Francisco	22987	25424	24552	29780	102743
6	Milwaukee	41224	42655	38972	45268	
7	Dallas	15344				55
8						
9	Total	93936	96648	190584	74097	241357
10						

Fill Handle

Using AutoFill to Create a Series

You can use AutoFill to create a series or a sequence of values. For instance, you can quickly fill cells that follow a sequence of 5, 10, 15, etc. You need only provide an example of a couple of entries to show Excel the pattern for the series. For a series such as a sequential date, you need only provide one example—Excel will automatically increment the date by one day.

To Use AutoFill to Create a Series

1. Select one or more adjacent cells which contain the series pattern.
2. Move the mouse pointer over the fill handle on the last cell until the pointer transforms into a black cross.
3. Click and drag down or across to the number of cells you wish to contain the series.
4. Release the mouse button.

	A	B	C	D
1		Quarterly Sales for FY 2002		
2	5			
3	10	Store	Q1	Q2
4		New Yo...		
5		San Francisc		
6		Milwaukee		

Click and drag downward to fill in the series

Let's Try It!

	A	B	C	D	E	F	G
1	Quarterly Sales for FY 2005						
2	Store	Q1	Q2	Q3	Q4	Total	
3	New York City	14391	12524	16979	21075	64969	
4	San Francisco	22987	25424	26552	29780	104743	
5	Milwaukee	41224	42655	38972	45268		
6	Dallas	15344	17045	19024	23242	74655	
7							
8	Grand Total	93946	97648	1E+05	1E+05	244367	
9							
10	©2007 Rodney's Video						
11							

- Click in cell **F4**.

Activates cell F4.

- Observe the formula in the formula bar.

The formula sums the values from B4 to E4.

- Move your mouse pointer over **the fill handle** (the box on lower right of cell) until the pointer transforms into a black cross.

Enters drag mode.

- **Click and hold** left mouse button and drag contents down to cell **F5**.

Copies the formula in cell F4 to F5.

	A	B	C	D	E	F	G
1	Quarterly Sales for FY 2005						
2	Store	Q1	Q2	Q3	Q4	Total	
3	New York City	14391	12524	16979	21075	64969	
4	San Francisco	22987	25424	26552	29780	104743	
5	Milwaukee	41224	42655	38972	45268	168119	
6	Dallas	15344	17045	19024	23242	74655	
7							
8	Grand Total	93946	97648	1E+05	1E+05	412486	
9							
10	©2007 Rodney's Video						
11							

- Click in cell **F5**.

Activates cell F5.

- Observe the formula bar.

Formula cell references are automatically updated to our new cell location (formula now sums the values from B5 to E5).

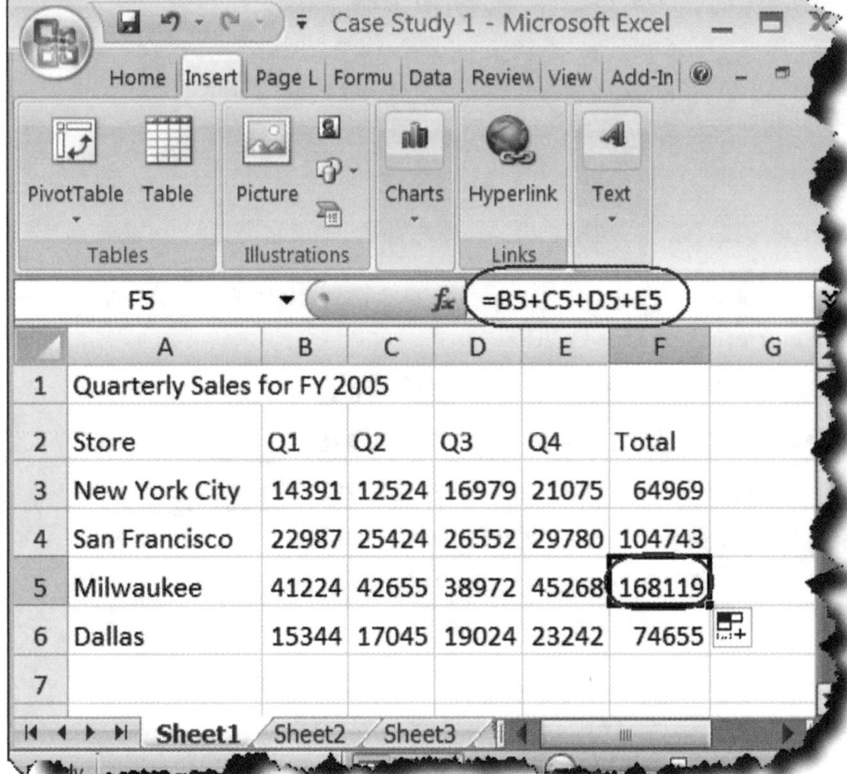

	A	B	C	D	E	F	G
1	Quarterly Sales for FY 2005						
2	Store	Q1	Q2	Q3	Q4	Total	
3	New York City	14391	12524	16979	21075	64969	
4	San Francisco	22987	25424	26552	29780	104743	
5	Milwaukee	41224	42655	38972	45268	168119	
6	Dallas	15344	17045	19024	23242	74655	
7							

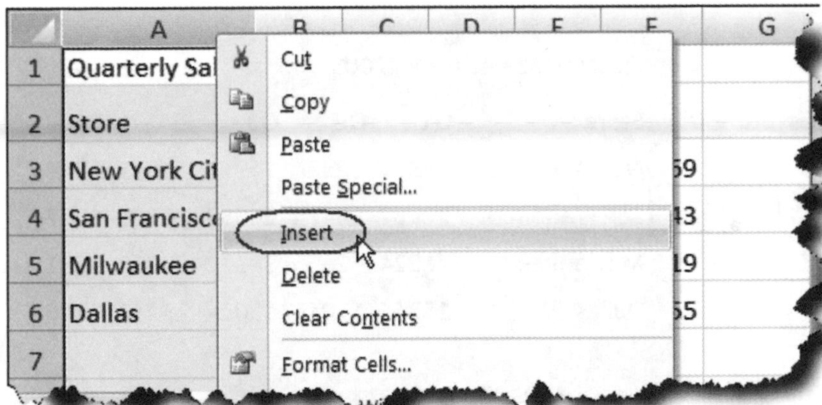

- Click on the column heading for **Column A**.

Selects Column A.

- **Right-click** and choose **Insert** from the contextual menu.

Inserts a new column to the left of Column A.

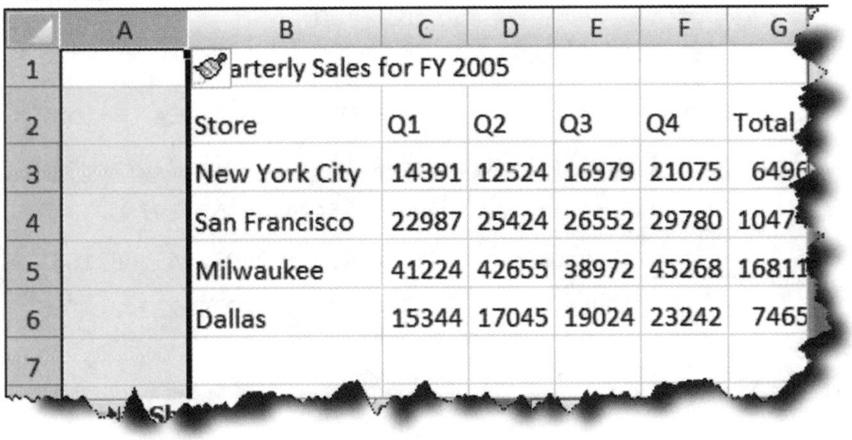

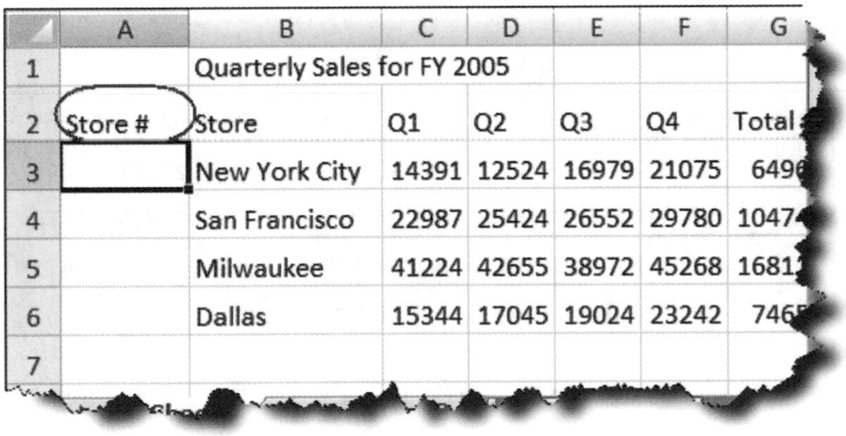

	A	B	C	D	E	F	G
1		Quarterly Sales for FY 2005					
2		Store	Q1	Q2	Q3	Q4	Total
3		New York City	14391	12524	16979	21075	649
4		San Francisco	22987	25424	26552	29780	1047
5		Milwaukee	41224	42655	38972	45268	1681
6		Dallas	15344	17045	19024	23242	7465
7							

	A	B	C	D	E	F	G
1		Quarterly Sales for FY 2005					
2	Store #	Store	Q1	Q2	Q3	Q4	Total
3		New York City	14391	12524	16979	21075	649
4		San Francisco	22987	25424	26552	29780	1047
5		Milwaukee	41224	42655	38972	45268	1681
6		Dallas	15344	17045	19024	23242	746
7							

- Click in cell **A2** and type: **Store #**. Press **Enter**.

Enters text in cell A2 and confirms the entry.

- Type **1** in cell **A3** and then press **Enter**.

	A	B	C	D	E	F	G
1		Quarterly Sales for FY 2005					
2	Store #	Store	Q1	Q2	Q3	Q4	Total
3	1	New York City	14391	12524	16979	21075	6496
4		San Francisco	22987	25424	26552	29780	1047
5		Milwaukee	41224	42655	38972	45268	16811
6		Dallas	15344	17045	19024	23242	7465
7							

- Type **2** in cell **A4** and then press **Enter**.

Enters the second number of our series in cell A4 and confirms the entry.

	A	B	C	D	E	F	G
1		Quarterly Sales for FY 2005					
2	Store #	Store	Q1	Q2	Q3	Q4	Total
3	1	New York City	14391	12524	16979	21075	649
4	2	San Francisco	22987	25424	26552	29780	1047
5		Milwaukee	41224	42655	38972	45268	16811
6		Dallas	15344	17045	19024	23242	746
7							

- Select cells **A3** and **A4**.

Highlights cells A3 and A4.

	A	B	C	D	E	F	G
1		Quarterly Sales for FY 2005					
2	Store #	Store	Q1	Q2	Q3	Q4	Total
3	1	New York City	14391	12524	16979	21075	6496
4	2	San Francisco	22987	25424	26552	29780	10474
5		Milwaukee	41224	42655	38972	45268	1681
6		Dallas	15344	17045	19024	23242	7465
7							

	A	B	C	D	E	F	G
1		Quarterly Sales for FY 2005					
2	Store #	Store	Q1	Q2	Q3	Q4	Total
3	1	New York City	14391	12524	16979	21075	649
4	2	San Francisco	22987	25424	26552	29780	10474
5	3	Milwaukee	41224	42655	38972	45268	16811
6	4	Dallas	15344	17045	19024	23242	7465
7							

- Move your mouse pointer over the **Fill Handle** on the bottom right of cell **A4**.

Enters Drag mode.

- Click and drag down to cell **A6**. **Release** the mouse button.

Completes the series for cells A5 and A6.

- Click the **Save** button.

Saves the current worksheet.

Formatting Text

In this section, you will learn how to change the appearance of text in your worksheet.

One powerful feature in Microsoft Excel is the ability to format the text in your worksheet. For instance, you can modify the typeface (or font) of your text, change the size of your text, or emphasize text by applying bold, italics or underlining.

Some common text formatting options are:

- Changing the font style (typeface)
- Changing the font size
- Adding bold and Italic formatting
- Underlining text
- Adding Borders
- Increasing/Decreasing Font Size

The quickest and easiest way to apply and modify text formatting is to use the Formatting Tools on the Home tab under the **Font group**. To change text emphasis, select the cell or cell range you wish to format then click on the appropriate button (Bold, Italics or Underline). To change the font or font size, select the text then choose the desired option from the font or font size drop-down list. For an explanation of what a tool does, move your mouse pointer over a tool to display an informational box. The box will also display the **keyboard shortcut** for the command, if any.

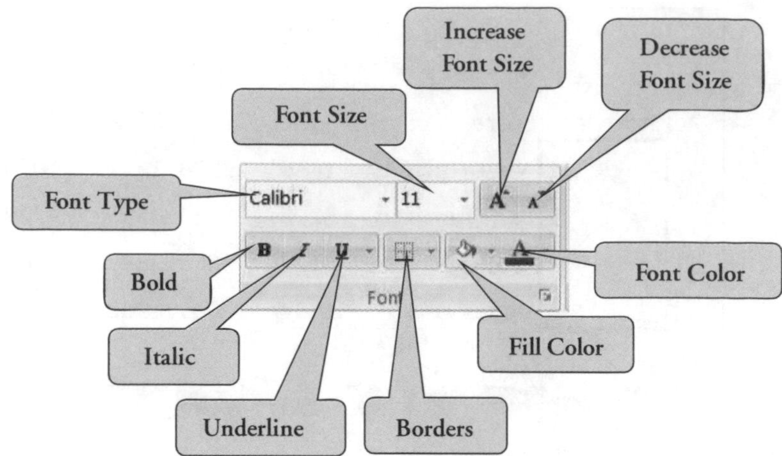

COMMON FORMATTING OPTIONS ON THE FONT GROUP

New in Excel 2007 is the **Mini-Toolbar**. The Mini-Toolbar displays whenever you right-click on selected cells and provides quick access to common formatting commands such as bold, italic, font color, font type, font size, fill color, increase indent, decrease indent and increase/decrease font size. If you wish to turn off this feature, you can do so from the Excel Options dialog box.

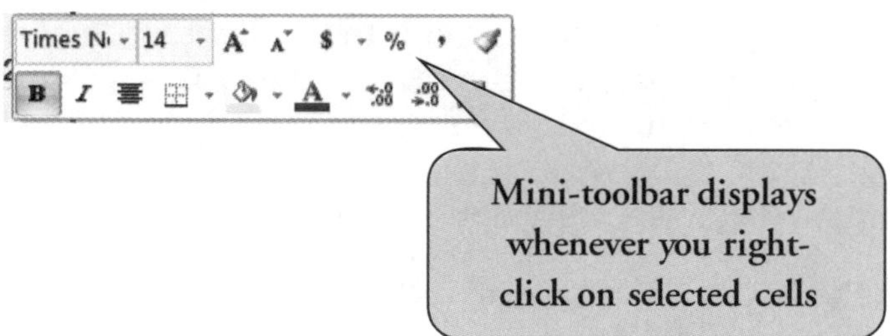

To Use Formatting Tools

1. **Select** the text that you want to modify.
2. Click the **Home** tab on the Ribbon.
3. To emphasize text, click on the **Bold, Italics** or **Underline** icon on the Font group.
4. To change the **font type**, click the arrow on the font drop-down list and select the desired typeface.
5. To change the **font size**, click the arrow on the font size drop-down list and select the desired font size or type the size manually in the font size box.
6. To increase or decrease the size of the selected text (new in Excel 2007), click the Increase Font Size button or Decrease Font Size button.
7. To use the **Mini-toolbar**, select the text you want to modify, right-click and then choose the desired option from the Mini-toolbar.

Let's Try It!

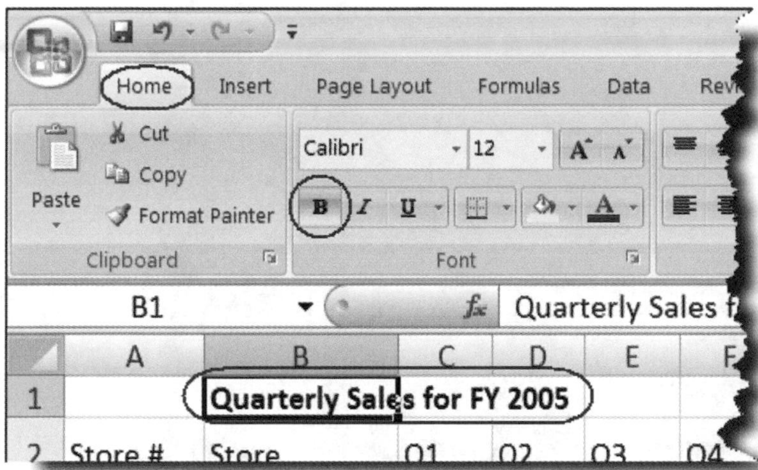

- Click in cell **B1**.

Makes B1 the active cell.

- Select **Home** tab and then click the **Bold** formatting button on the Home Ribbon.

Bolds the title in cell B1.

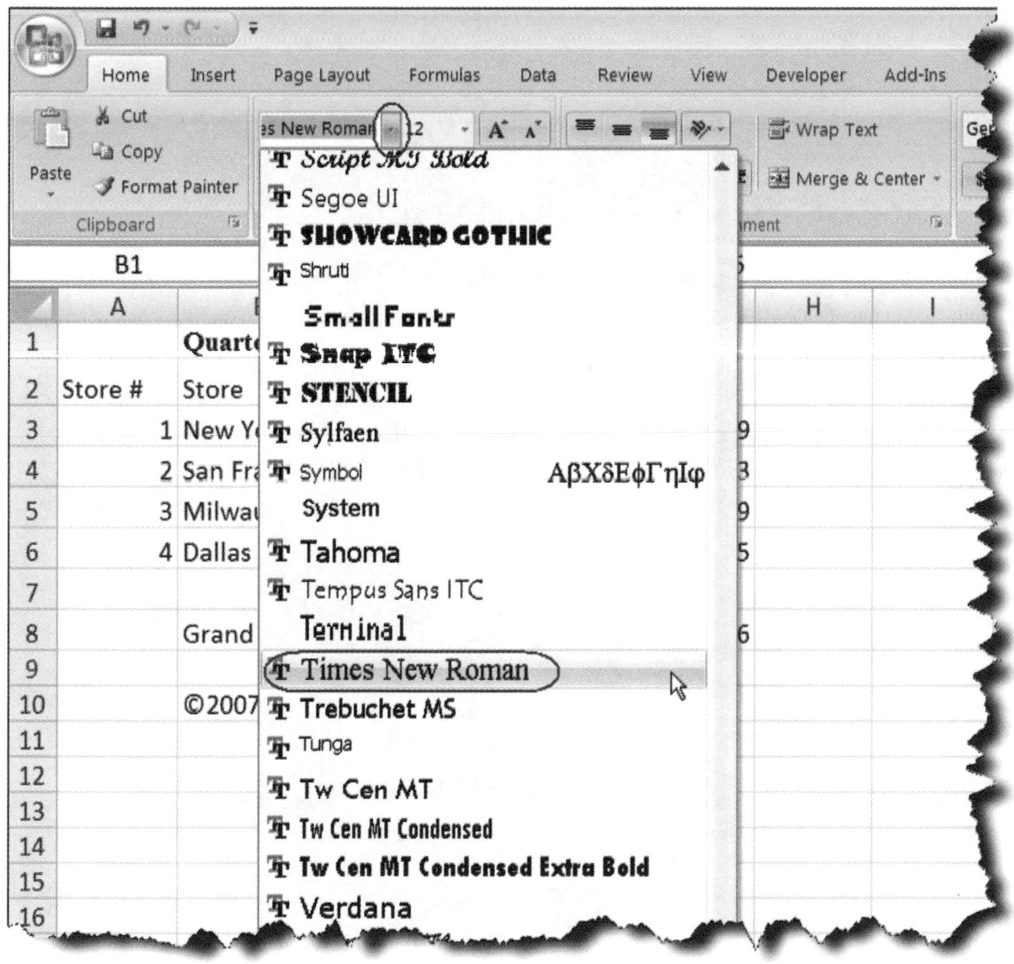

- Click on the **Font** drop down list, scroll down and then choose **Times New Roman**.

Changes the typeface to Times New Roman.

- Click on the **Font Size** drop down list and choose **14**.

Changes the size of the title to 14 pt. Notice that as you move your mouse pointer over the different font sizes and font styles, the data in your worksheet displays a preview of the selected font or font size. This is an example of Excel's new Live Preview feature.

- Press the **Ctrl + S** keystroke combination.

Saves the changes.

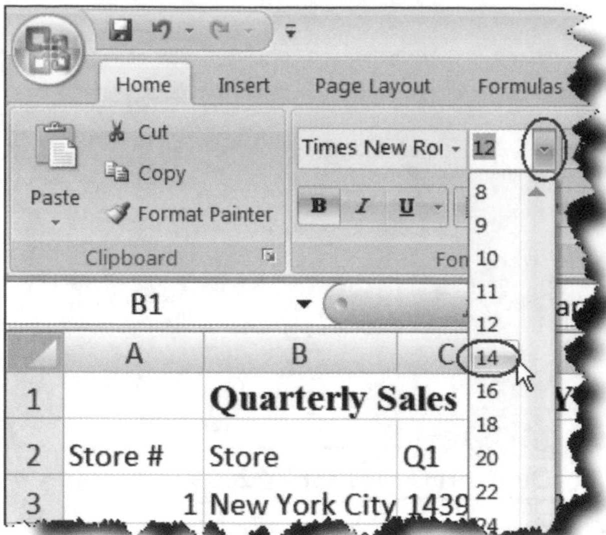

Using the Format Cells Dialog Box

In this section, you will learn how to apply and modify additional formatting using the Format Cells Dialog Box.

The **Format Cells Dialog Box** allows you to apply multiple formats (bold, italics, font size, font type, font color, etc.) to selected text at once. Additionally, you will find formats that are not available on the Ribbon. To apply multiple formatting to selected text, click the **Font Dialog Box Launcher** on the lower-right corner of the Font command set and then make your desired selections.

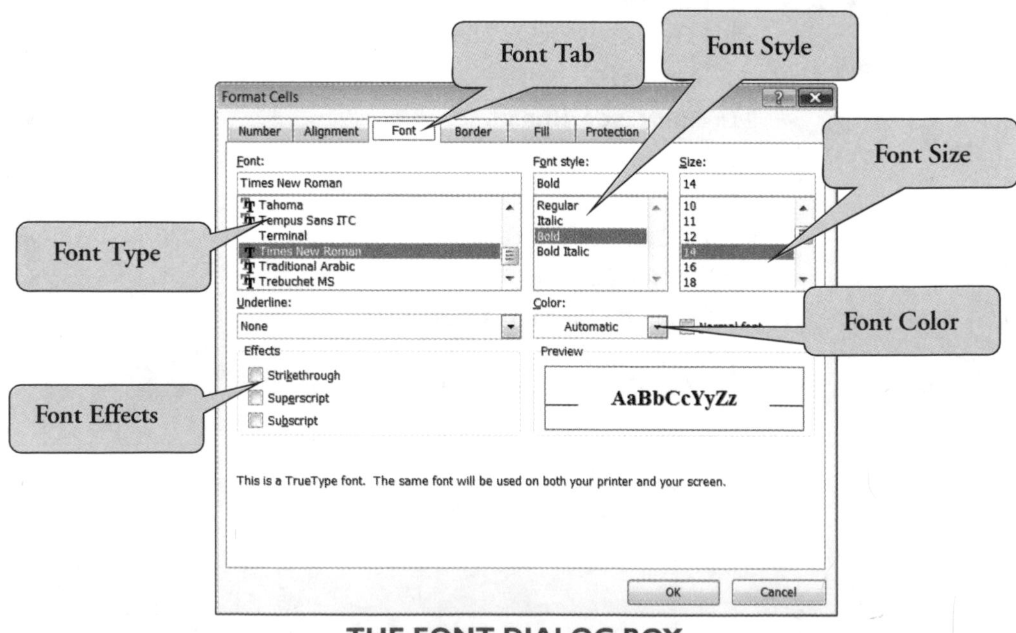

THE FONT DIALOG BOX

To Use the Format Cells Dialog Box

1. Select the text whose formatting you wish to modify.
2. Click the **Font Dialog Box Launcher** on the Ribbon
   Or
   Press the **Ctrl + 1** keyboard shortcut and click the **Font** tab.
3. Select the formatting you wish to apply.
4. Click **OK** when finished.

Let's Try It!

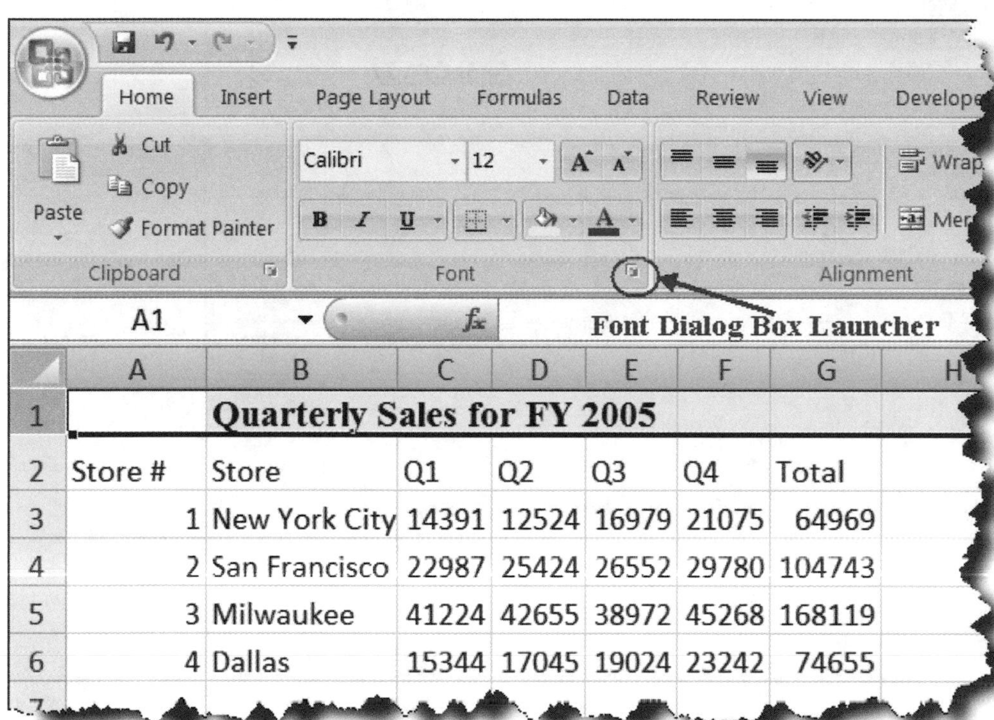

- Select **row 1**.
- Click the **Font Dialog Box Launcher**.

Displays the Font tab of the Format Cells dialog box.

- Select **Font** tab if not already selected.
- In the Font window, select **Calibri (Body)**.
- In the **Size** window, select **12**.
- In the **Font Style** window, select Bold.

Applies Calibri (Body), font 12, and bold formatting to the selection.

- Click the **Underline** drop down list, choose **Single**.

Applies Underline to the selection.

- Click **OK**.

Closes the Format Cells dialog box.

- Click the **Save** button.

Saves the active workbook.

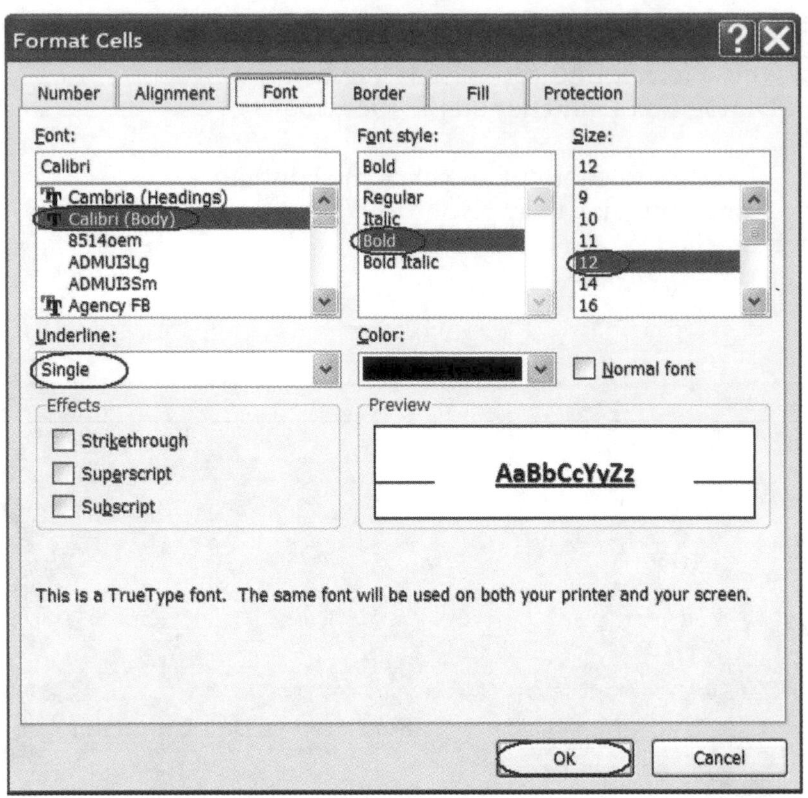

Formatting Values

In this section, you will learn how to change the appearance of numerical values in your worksheet.

The new Ribbon contains many options for applying **number formatting** or, in other words, the way in which numerical values are displayed. Buttons for the three most common number formats—**Currency Style, Percent Style** and **Comma Style** can be found on the Number group on the Home Ribbon. Two additional buttons allow you to increase and decrease the number of decimal places.

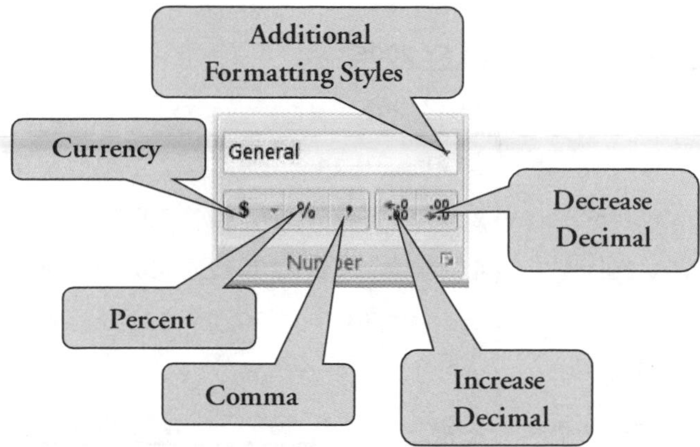

Click the drop-down list on the Number group to choose value formatting options (date, time, text, fraction, etc.). The **Number** tab of the **Format Cells dialog box** contains many additional options for applying **number formatting**.

To Format Values

1. Select the cell or cell range to format.
2. Click the **Home** tab to display the Home ribbon.
3. Choose Currency, Percent or Comma
   Or
   Click the drop-down list on the Number group and choose the desired cell format.
4. To change the number of decimal places, click the Increase Decimal or Decrease Decimal button.
5. For additional formatting options, display the Format Cells dialog box.

Let's Try It!

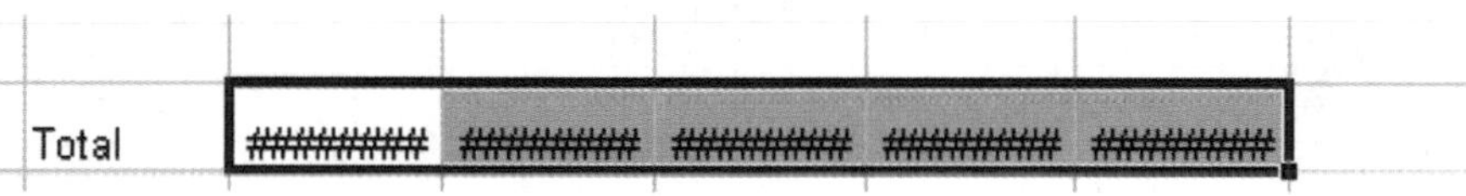

Notice that some of the values are no longer completely displayed. Instead, the cell is populated with the pound sign (or commonly referred to as "the railroad tracks") as shown below or 1E+05. This occurs when a numerical value is longer than the cell can accommodate. To solve this problem, you will increase the width of the columns.

- Adjust the **width of the columns** so all values are visible in the sheet.

- Select the cell range **C3:G8**.

Selects the cell range to be formatted.

	A	B	C	D	E	F	G	H
1		**Quarterly Sales for FY 2005**						
2	Store #	Store	Q1	Q2	Q3	Q4	Total	
3	1	New York City	14391	12524	16979	21075	64969	
4	2	San Francisco	22987	25424	26552	29780	104743	
5	3	Milwaukee	41224	42655	38972	45268	168119	
6	4	Dallas	15344	17045	19024	23242	74655	
7								
8		Grand Total	93946	97648	101527	119365	412486	

- On the **Number group** on the Home Ribbon, click the **Comma Style** button.

Applies a number format with comma and two decimal places.

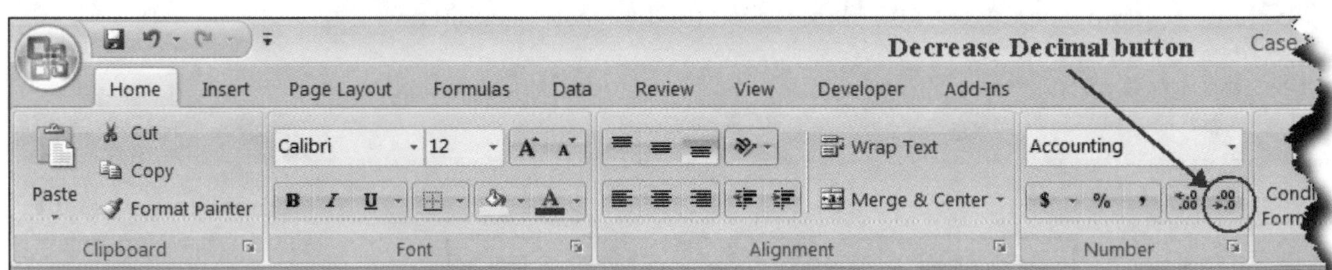

- Adjust the column width if needed.
- Click the **Decrease Decimal** button twice.

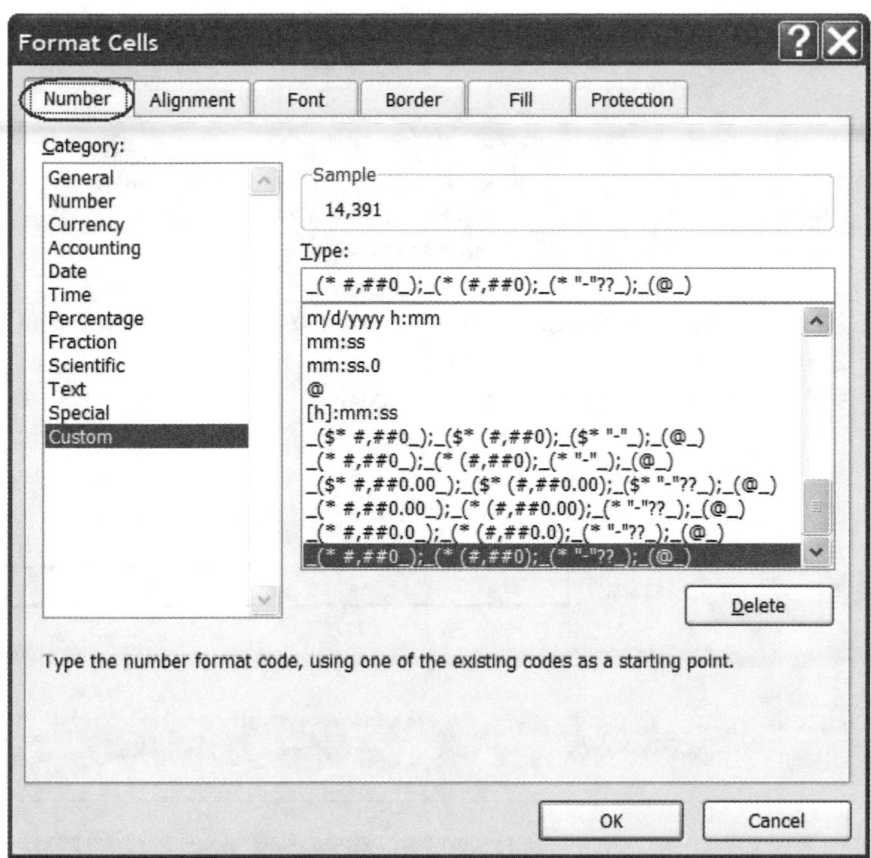

Decimal places will not be displayed.

- Press **Ctrl + 1**.

Displays the Formatting Cells dialog box.

- Click on the **Number** tab.

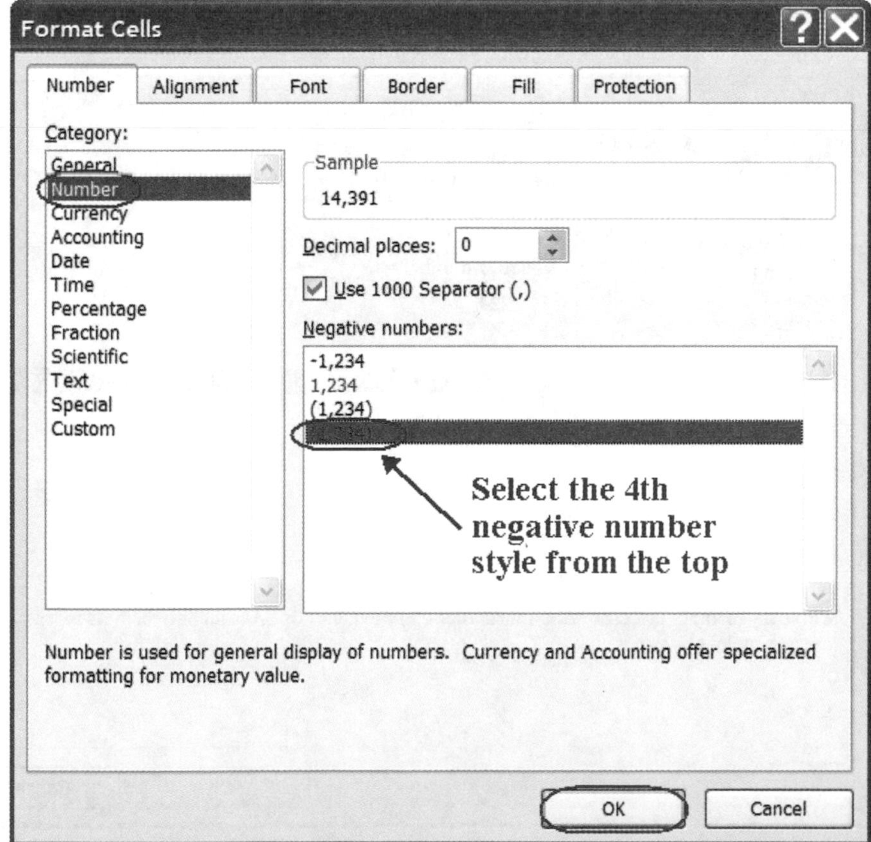
Select the 4th negative number style from the top

- Select **Number** from the **Category** list.

Chooses the Number formatting style. Notice that you can set the number of decimal places and add a comma from here as well.

- In the **Negative Number** list box, choose the fourth style from the top **(1,234)**.

Negative numbers will be displayed in red color and surrounded with parenthesis.

- Click **OK**.

Closes the Format Cells dialog box and applies the changes.

- Select the cell range **C8:G8**.

Selects the cell range to be formatted.

- Click the **Number** Dialog Launch button.

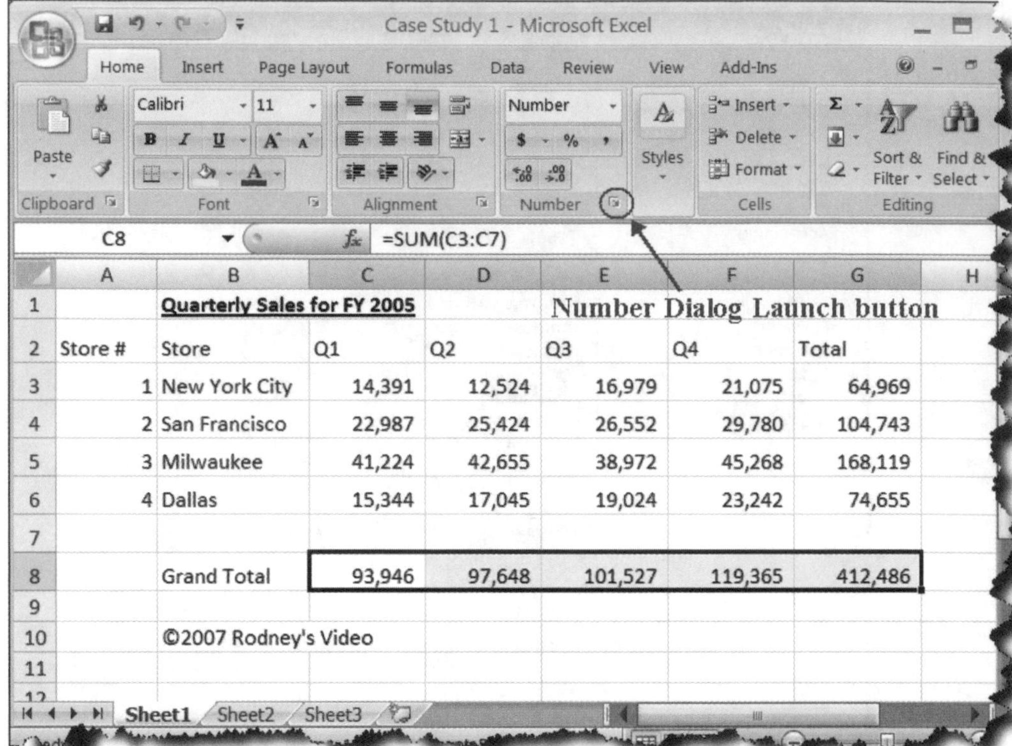

Displays the Number tab of the Format Cells dialog box.

- Select **Currency** from the **Category** list.

Chooses the Currency formatting style.

- In the **Negative Number** list box, choose the fourth style from the top (1,234).

Will display negative number in red color and surround them with parenthesis. If do not need to choose a specific negative number format, you could have clicked the Currency button on the Ribbon as well.

	A	B	C	D	E	F	G
1		**Quarterly Sales for FY 2005**					
2	Store #	Store	Q1	Q2	Q3	Q4	Total
3	1	New York City	14,391	12,524	16,979	21,075	64,969
4	2	San Francisco	22,987	25,424	26,552	29,780	104,743
5	3	Milwaukee	41,224	42,655	38,972	45,268	168,119
6	4	Dallas	15,344	17,045	19,024	23,242	74,655
7							
8		Grand Total	$93,946	$97,648	$101,527	$119,365	$412,486
9							
10		©2007 Rodney's Video					
11							

- Click **OK**.

Closes the Format Cells dialog box.

Applying Cell Styles

In this section, you will learn how to apply pre-defined cell styles to your worksheets.

Another way to format a cell is to use one of Excel 2007's styles from the **Cell Styles Gallery**. A Cell Style is a collection of formats such as a particular font type and size, particular shading, font color, background color, and more. Click the **Cell Styles** button on the styles group on the Home Ribbon to display a variety of pre-defined formats that you can quickly apply to your cells. As you move your mouse pointer over any of the styles in the gallery, the formatting of your worksheet will change to reflect what your cells would look like if you were to apply the style. This is an example of Excel's new **Live Preview** feature.

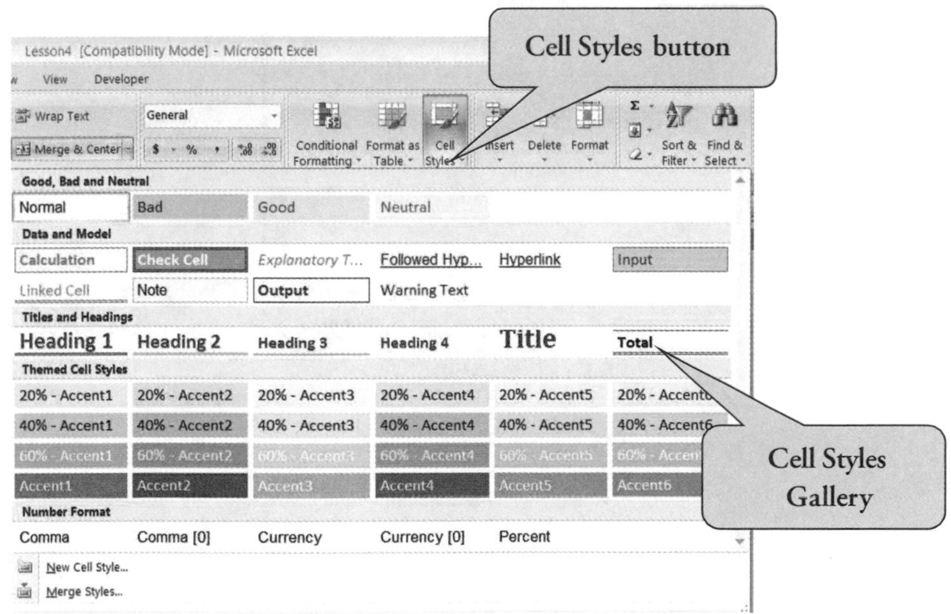

As you work more with Excel, you will most likely develop your own preferred formats for particular worksheets. Rather than setting these formats over and over to worksheets, you can store these formatting options in Excel's **Cell Style Gallery**. You should consider adding any special cell formatting that you plan to use in the future. Cell Styles can be a real time-saver if you find yourself applying the same formatting over and over.

To Apply an Existing Style

1. Select the cell or cell range to which you wish to apply a style.
2. Click the **Cell Styles** button on the Styles Group on the Ribbon.
3. Move your mouse pointer over any of the styles to preview how the formatting will look on our worksheet.
4. Click the Style you wish to use.

To Create a Style

1. Manually apply any formatting to a cell that you wish to include in your style.
2. Click the **Cell Styles** button on the Styles Group on the Ribbon.
3. Click **New Cell Style** on the bottom of the gallery list.
4. Enter a name for your new style in the **Style Name** text box.
5. Uncheck any formatting options underneath the **Style Includes (By Example)** that you do not wish to include in your new style.
6. Click the **Formatting** button to change the formatting options.
7. Click **OK**. Your new style will now display on top of the Cell Styles gallery under the **Custom** category.

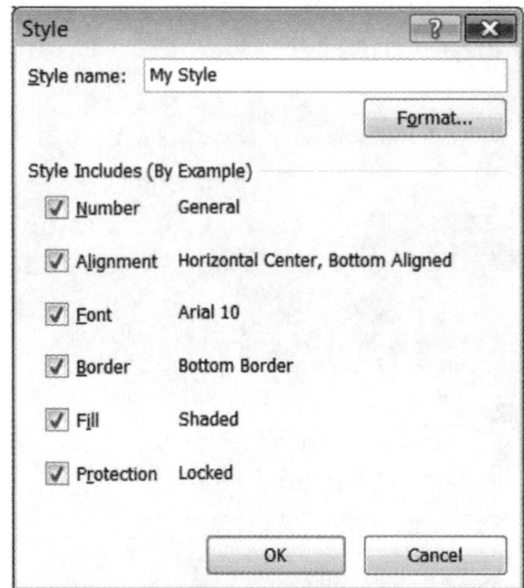

STYLE DIALOG BOX

Let's Try It!

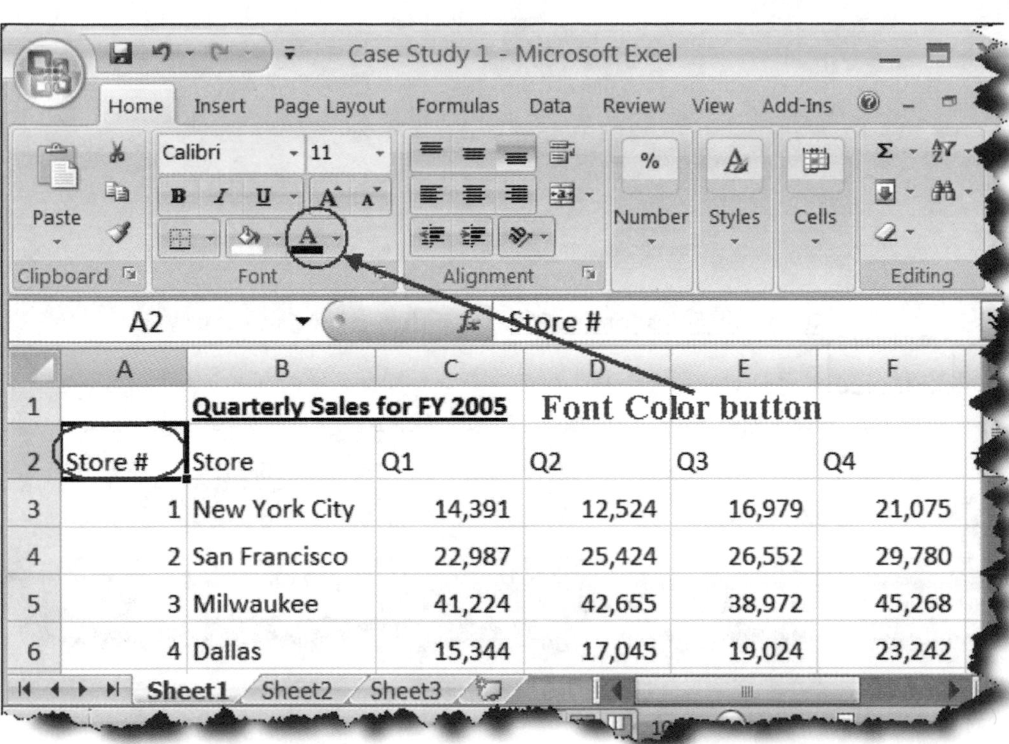

- Select cell **A2**.

Makes A2 the active cell.

- Click the arrow on the **Font Color** button on the Home Ribbon.

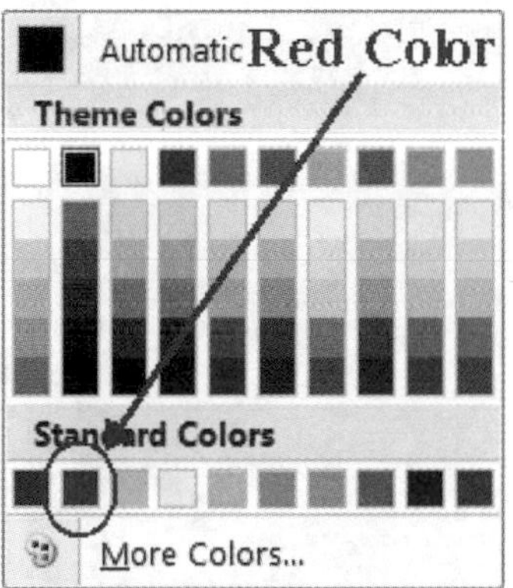

Displays the Font Color Palette.

- Choose **Red** color.

Changes the font color to red.

- Click on **Undo** button.

Font color of Store# is changed back to black.

- Click the arrow on the **Fill Color** button on the Home Ribbon.

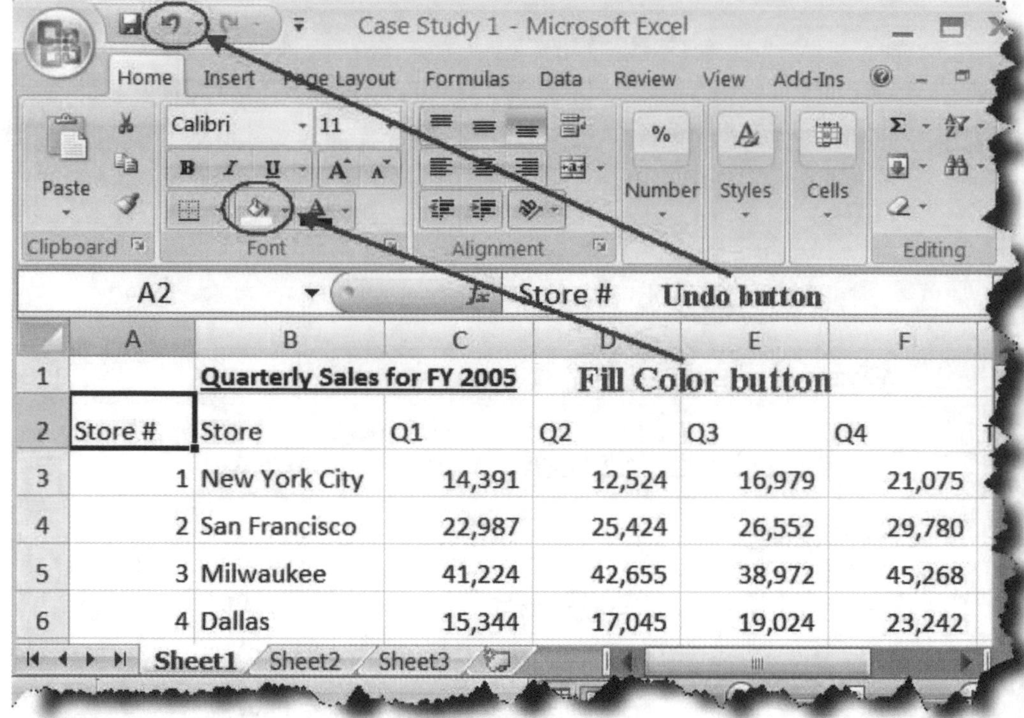

Opens the Fill Color Palette.

- Choose Gray color (**White, Background 1, Darker 25%**) from the color palette.

Applies gray shading to the cell.

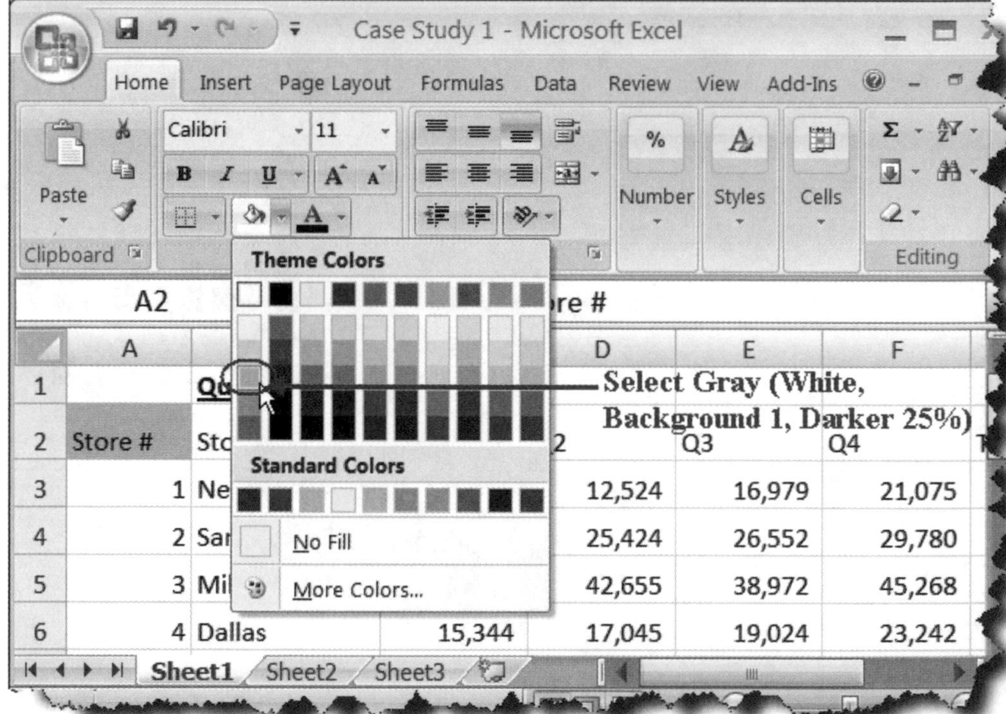

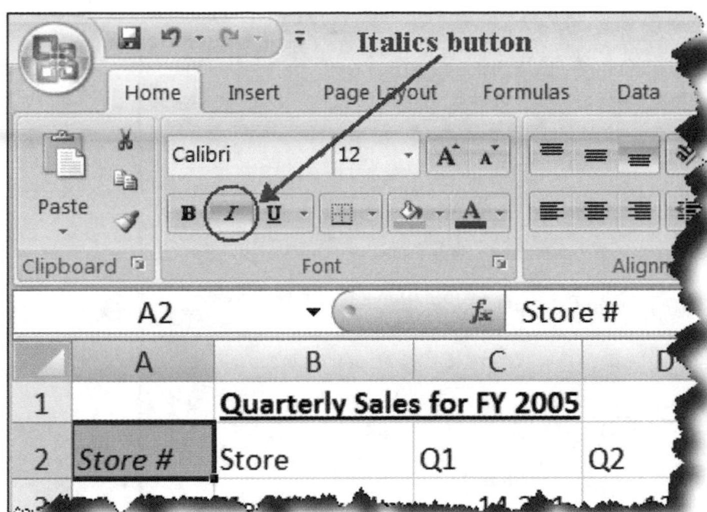

- Click the **Italics** button on the Home Ribbon.

Italicizes the cell value.

- Click the **More** button on the Styles group on the Home Ribbon.

Displays the Cell Styles gallery.

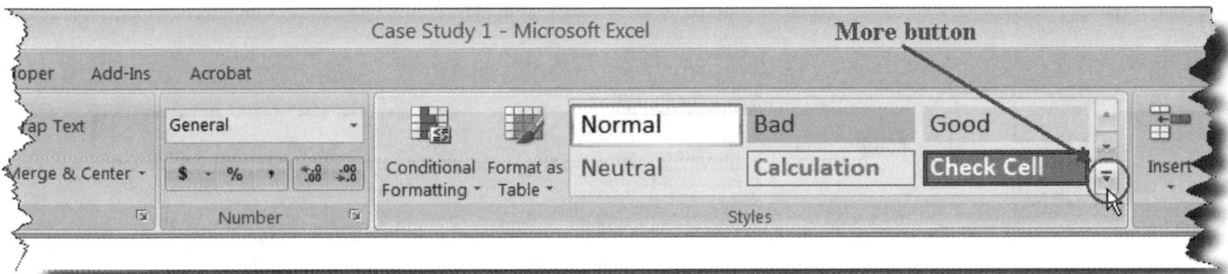

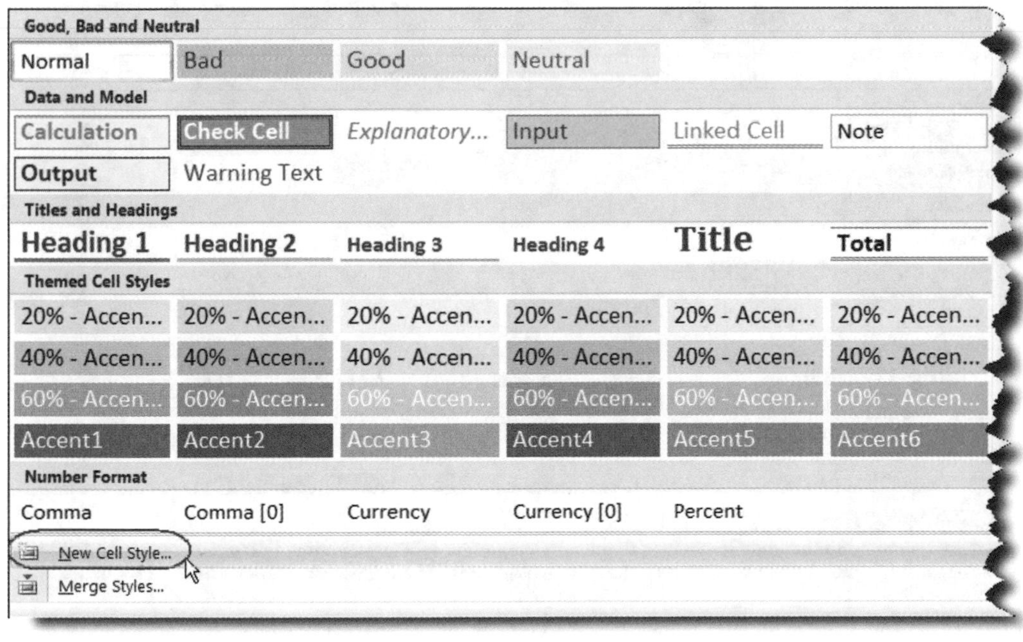

- Click **New Cell Style** on the bottom of the gallery.

Displays the Style dialog box.

- Type **My Heading** in the **Style Name** text box.

Names the new style.

- Click **OK**.

Closes the Style dialog box.

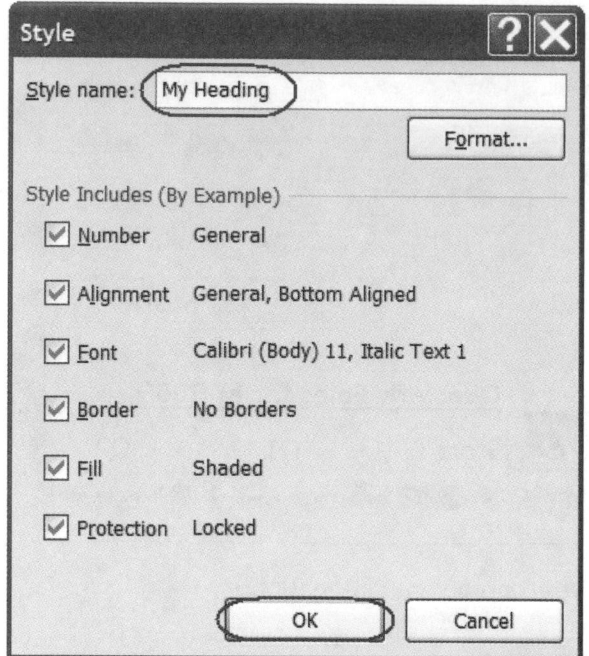

- Select the Cell Range **B2:G2**.

Selects the cell range to which we wish to apply our new style.

	A	B	C	D	E	F	G
1		Quarterly Sales for FY 2005					
2	Store #	Store	Q1	Q2	Q3	Q4	Total
3	1	New York City	14,391	12,524	16,979	21,075	64,969
4	2	San Francisco	22,987	25,424	26,552	29,780	104,743
5	3	Milwaukee	41,224	42,655	38,972	45,268	168,119
6	4	Dallas	15,344	17,045	19,024	23,242	74,655

- Click the **Cell Styles** button on the Ribbon.

Displays the Cell Styles gallery.

- Click on **My Heading** under the **Custom** area.

Applies the style to apply to selected range.

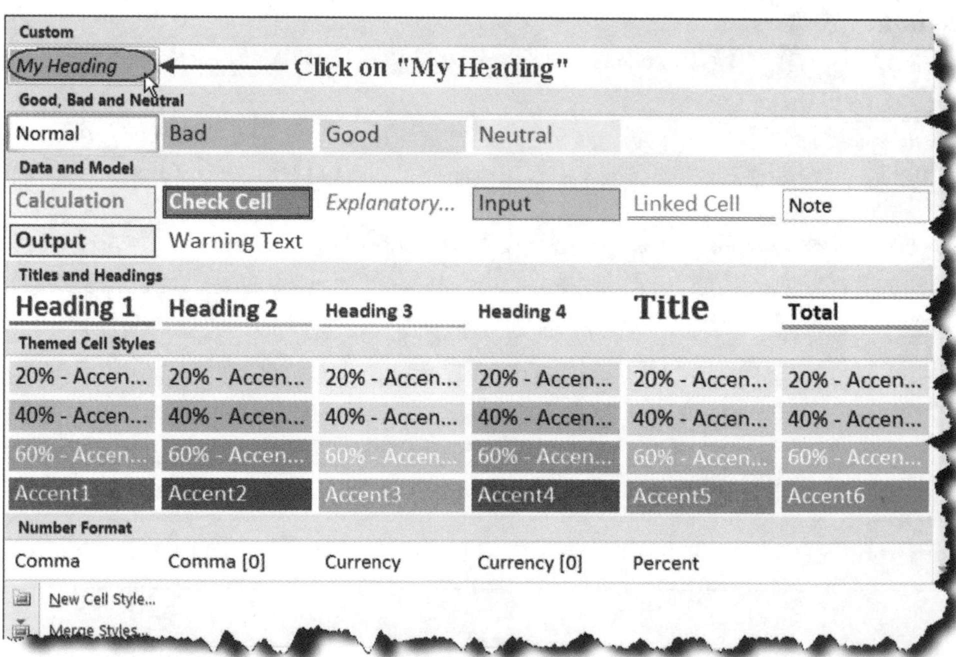

	A	B	C	D	E	F	G
1		**Quarterly Sales for FY 2005**					
2	*Store #*	*Store*	*Q1*	*Q2*	*Q3*	*Q4*	*Total*
3	1	New York City	14,391	12,524	16,979	21,075	64,969
4	2	San Francisco	22,987	25,424	26,552	29,780	104,743
5	3	Milwaukee	41,224	42,655	38,972	45,268	168,119
6	4	Dallas	15,344	17,045	19,024	23,242	74,655
7							
8		Grand Total	$93,946	$97,648	$101,527	$119,365	$412,486
9							
10		©2007 Rodney's Video					

Sheet1 Sheet2 Sheet3

- Click the **Save** button.

Saves the active document.

Spell Checking Your Worksheet

In this section, you will learn how to use Excel's built-in Spell-Checker.

Excel has a built-in **spelling and grammar checker** that allows you to automatically check for errors as you type. Microsoft Excel will use its built-in dictionary to offer suggestions for any errors it finds. You can then choose the correct spelling of the word from the Suggestions list or add the word to the dictionary so that Excel will not flag the word in the future.

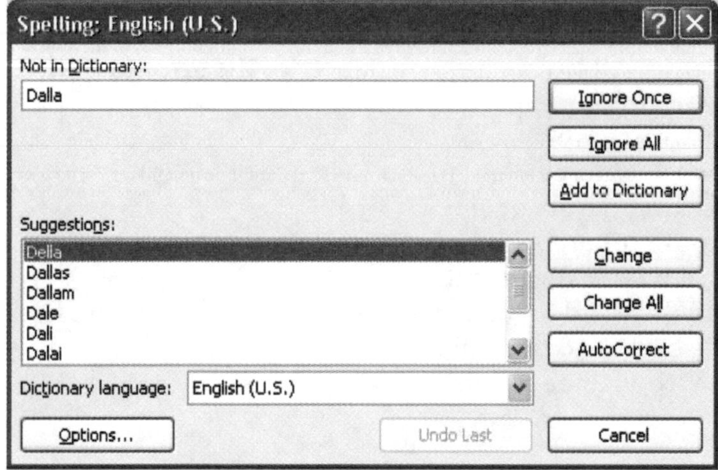

SPELLING DIALOG BOX

When Excel finds a questionable spelling error, a dialog box displays, prompting for a suggested action:

Ignore Once—Ignores this instance of the spelling error and continues to check the rest of the document.

Ignore All—Ignores all instances of the spelling error and continues to check the rest of the document.

Add to Dictionary—Adds the word in question to the built-in dictionary so that it will not be flagged in the future.

Change—Change this instance of the spelling error to the selected suggestion.
Change All—Change all instances of the spelling error in the document to the selected suggestion.
AutoCorrect—Adds the error and the correction to the error to Excel's AutoCorrect list so that Excel will automatically correct the error in the future.

To Check Spelling and Grammar in a Worksheet

1. Move to the beginning of the worksheet.
2. Click the **Spelling button** on the **Review** Ribbon under the Proofing group

SPELLING BUTTON

   Or
   Press the **F7 key**.
3. When an error is found, highlight the desired correction from the **Suggestions List**.
4. To change an error:
   a. Choose **Change** to change this particular instance of the error to the highlighted suggestion.
   b. **Change All** to change all instances of the error to the highlighted suggestion.
5. To ignore an error:
   a. Choose **Ignore** to ignore this instance of the error and continue checking the document.
   b. Choose **Ignore All** to ignore all instances of the error and continue checking the document.
6. To add the word to the built-in dictionary so it will not be flagged in the future, click **Add to Dictionary**.
7. Click **OK** when finished.

Let's Try It!

	A	B	C	D	E
1		Quarterly Sales for FY 2005			
2	Store #	Store	Q1	Q2	Q3
3	1	New York City	14,391	12,524	16,97
4	2	San Francisco	22,987	25,424	26,55
5	3	Milwaukee	41,224	42,655	38,97
6	4	Dallas	15,344	17,045	19,0
7					
8		Grand Total	$93,946	$97,648	$101,52
9					
10		©2007 Rodney's Video			
11					

- **Double-click** in cell **B6**.

Enters edit mode in cell B6.

A	B	C	D
	Quarterly Sales for FY 2005		
Store #	Store	Q1	Q2
1	New York City	14,391	12,524
2	San Francisco	22,987	25,424
3	Milwaukee	41,224	42,655
4	Dalla	15,344	17,045

- Delete the **s** in the word **Dallas** and then press the **Enter** key.

Misspells the word "Dallas" and confirms the entry.

	A	B	C	D	E
1		Quarterly Sales for FY 2005			
2	Store #	Store	Q1	Q2	Q3
3	1	New York City	14,391	12,524	16,979
4	2	San Francisco	22,987	25,424	26,552
5	3	Milwaukee	41,224	42,655	38,972
6	4	Dalla	15,344	17,045	19,024

- Press the **Ctrl+Home** keystroke combination.

Moves to the beginning of the document.

- Click the **Review tab** on the Ribbon.

Switches to Review commands and tools.

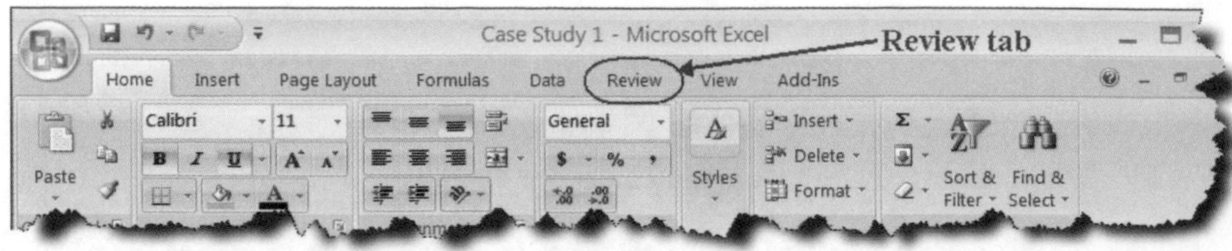

- Click the **Spelling Icon**.

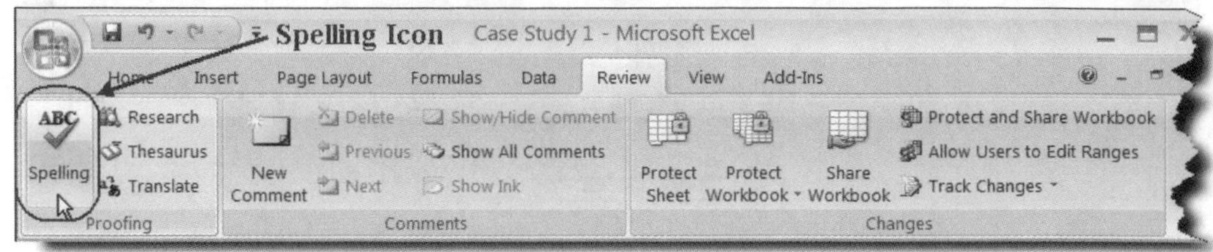

Begins spell checking the worksheet.

- Click **Dallas** in the **Suggestion List Box** and then click the **Change** button.

Changes Dalla to Dallas.

- Click **OK**.

Closes the spell check message box.

- Click the **Save** button

Saves the current workbook.

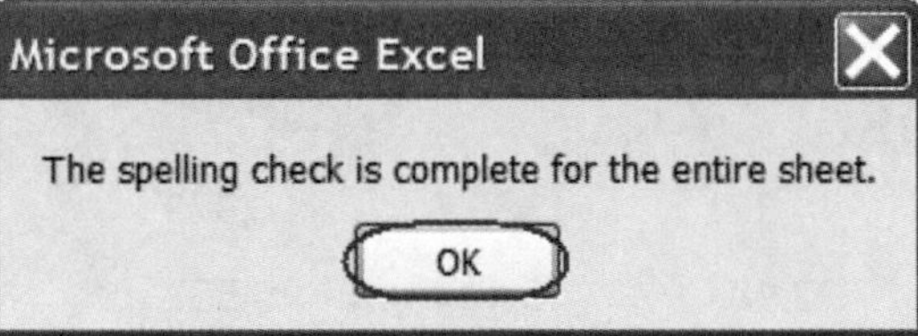

Closing a Workbook and Exiting Excel

In this section, you will learn how to close existing workbooks and exit the Microsoft Excel application.

When you are finished working on your Excel document, you can close it by either choosing **Close** from the File Options menu or by clicking the **Close Window** button, which is represented by an **x** on the top right of your screen.

Notice that there are two **x** buttons. The top one (the **Close button**) closes the Microsoft Excel application. The lower x (the **Close Window button**) closes only the active document window. So if you wish to close the current workbook but wish to continue working in Microsoft Excel, click the lower x. Don't worry if you forget to save your changes—Excel will ask you if you wish to save your recent changes before closing the workbook.

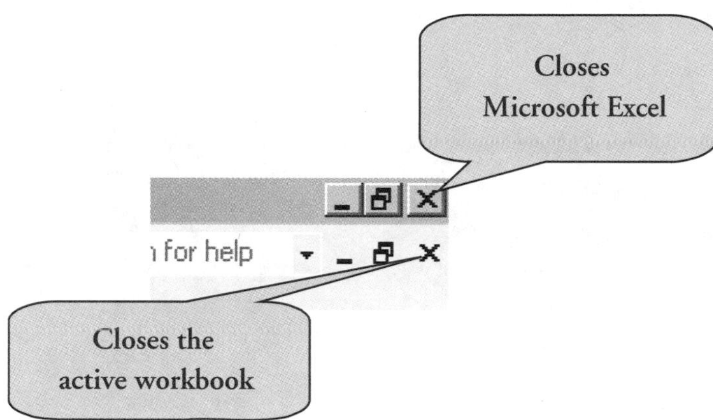

To Close a Workbook

1. Click the **Microsoft Office Button** and then click **Close** from the File Options menu
   Or
   Click on the **Close** button on the document window.
   Or
   Press the Ctrl + **W** keystroke combination.
2. If prompted, click **Yes** to save any changes, if prompted.

To Exit Microsoft Excel

1. Click the **Microsoft Office Button** and then click the **Exit Excel** button
   Or
   Click the **Close** button on the program window.
2. If prompted, click **Yes** to save changes to any open documents.

Let's Try It!

- Click the **Microsoft Office Button** and then click **Close** from the File Options menu. Click **Yes** if asked to save your changes.

Closes the Case Study I document.

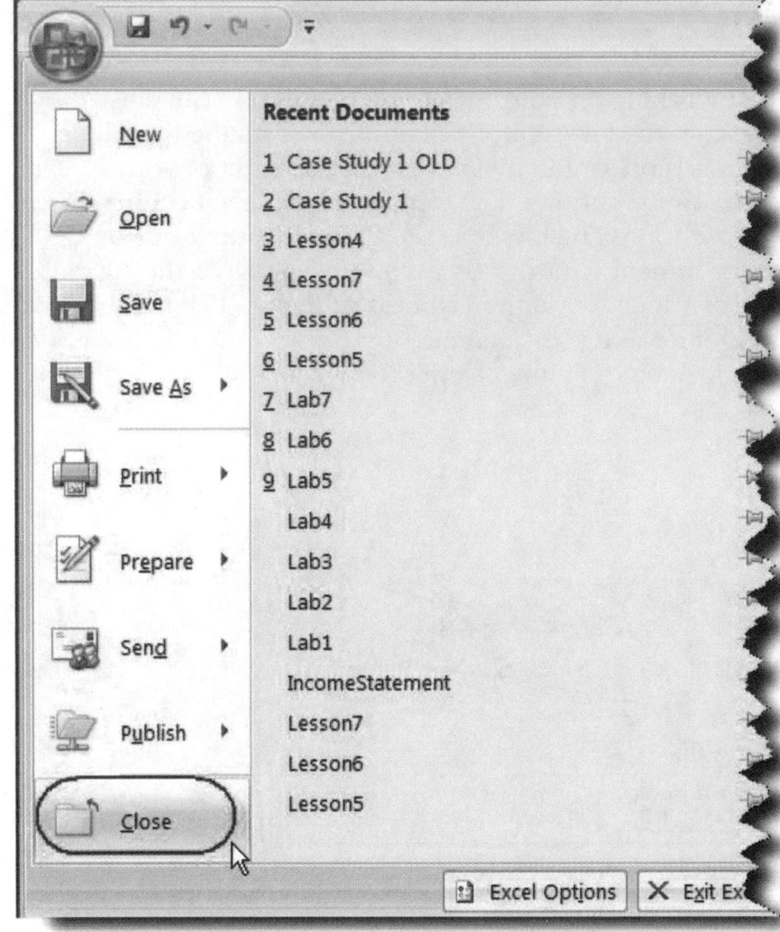

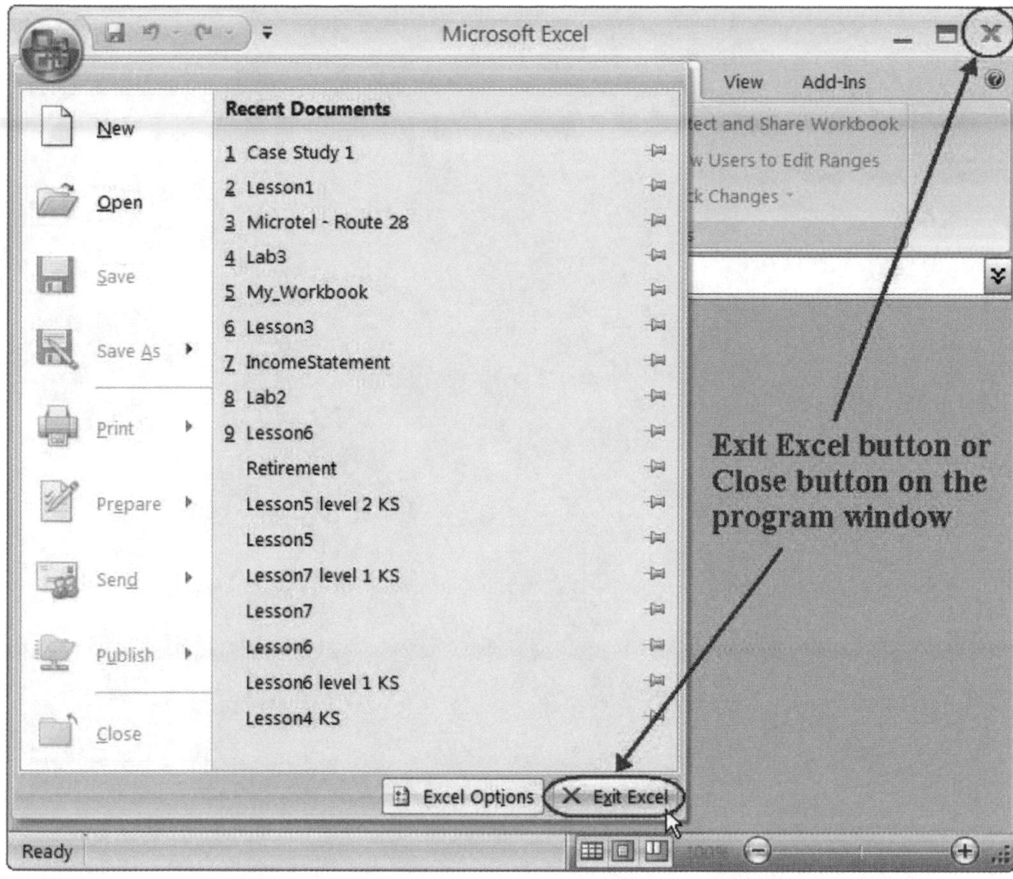

- Click the **Close** button on the Document Window. Or, click the **Microsoft Office Button** and then click the **Exit Excel** button on the lower-right hand corner of the pane.

Closes the Microsoft Excel application.

Conclusion

You have completed Excel 2007—Case Study I. You are now ready to use several basic MS Excel editing and formatting skills that you have learned in this chapter. You are encouraged to experiment with all you have learned in this case study. To reinforce your understanding of these techniques, it is recommended that you read and work through it once again.

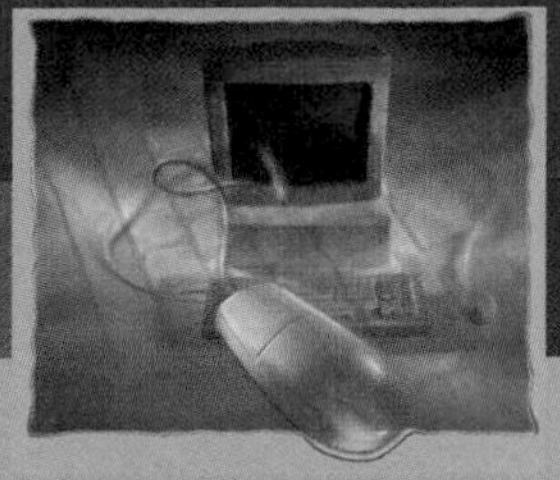

Excel Case Study 2

CHAPTER

6

OBJECTIVES

After successfully completing this case study, you should able to:

- Use Relative, Absolute and Mixed References
- Use MIN, MAX, COUNT and AVERAGE Functions
- Format Labels and Values
- Align and Text Wrap
- Merge Cells and Center Text
- Add Cell Borders
- Apply Colors and Shade to Cells
- Add Clip Art
- Copy, Rename, Group, Add and Delete Worksheets
- Change Worksheet Tab Colors
- Use 3-D Formulas & References
- Use the IF and Nested Function
- Create, Move, and Resize a Chart
- Change the Layout and Style
- Label Chart Elements
- Format Chart Text and Elements
- Customize Axes
- Adjust Margins and Set Page Orientation
- Force a Worksheet to Fit
- Use Help
- Print a Document

Case Study 2—MS Excel 2007

Assume that you are an accountant in Rodney Video Rentals. Your boss asks you to calculate bonuses for store managers who exceed the sales target. The bonus rate is 10% of the exceeded sales. He suggests that you create three worksheets: Actuals, Forecast, and Variance. Actuals worksheet includes actual sales and Forecast worksheet includes projected revenue for each item for each month. The third worksheet, Variance, includes the difference between your projected sales values and your actual sales values. Your boss would also like to see a difference in sales by month on a chart.

The desired worksheet looks like the following:

Rodney Video Rentals
Semi-Annual Sales Report
9/10/2007

	January	February	March	April	May	June	Total	Average	Highest	Lowest
Video Rentals	$12,300	$15,000	$13,995	$15,266	$16,792	$16,094	$89,447	$14,908	$16,792	$12,300
Video Sales	$495	$700	$980	$1,180	$1,358	$1,127	$5,840	$973	$1,358	$495
Investment Interest	$325	$335	$350	$375	$412	$402	$2,199	$367	$412	$325
DVD Player Sales	$400	$525	$605	$495	$544	$675	$3,244	$541	$675	$400
Snack Sales	$200	$150	$225	$315	$346	$258	$1,494	$249	$346	$150
Net Sales	$13,720	$16,710	$16,155	$17,631	$19,452	$18,556	$102,224	$17,037	$19,452	$13,720

ACTUALS WORKSHEET

Rodney Video Rentals
Semi-Annual Sales Report
9/10/2007

January	February	March	April	May	June	Total	Average	Highest	Lowest
$12,275	$14,990	$13,950	$15,200	$16,760	$16,050	$89,225	$14,871	$16,760	$12,275
$450	$650	$990	$1,150	$1,300	$1,100	$5,640	$940	$1,300	$450
$300	$300	$300	$350	$375	$350	$1,975	$329	$375	$300
$380	$500	$590	$500	$530	$640	$3,140	$523	$640	$380
$150	$100	$200	$300	$330	$220	$1,300	$217	$330	$100
$13,555	$16,540	$16,030	$17,500	$19,295	$18,360	$101,280	$16,880	$19,295	$13,555

FORECASTS WORKSHEET

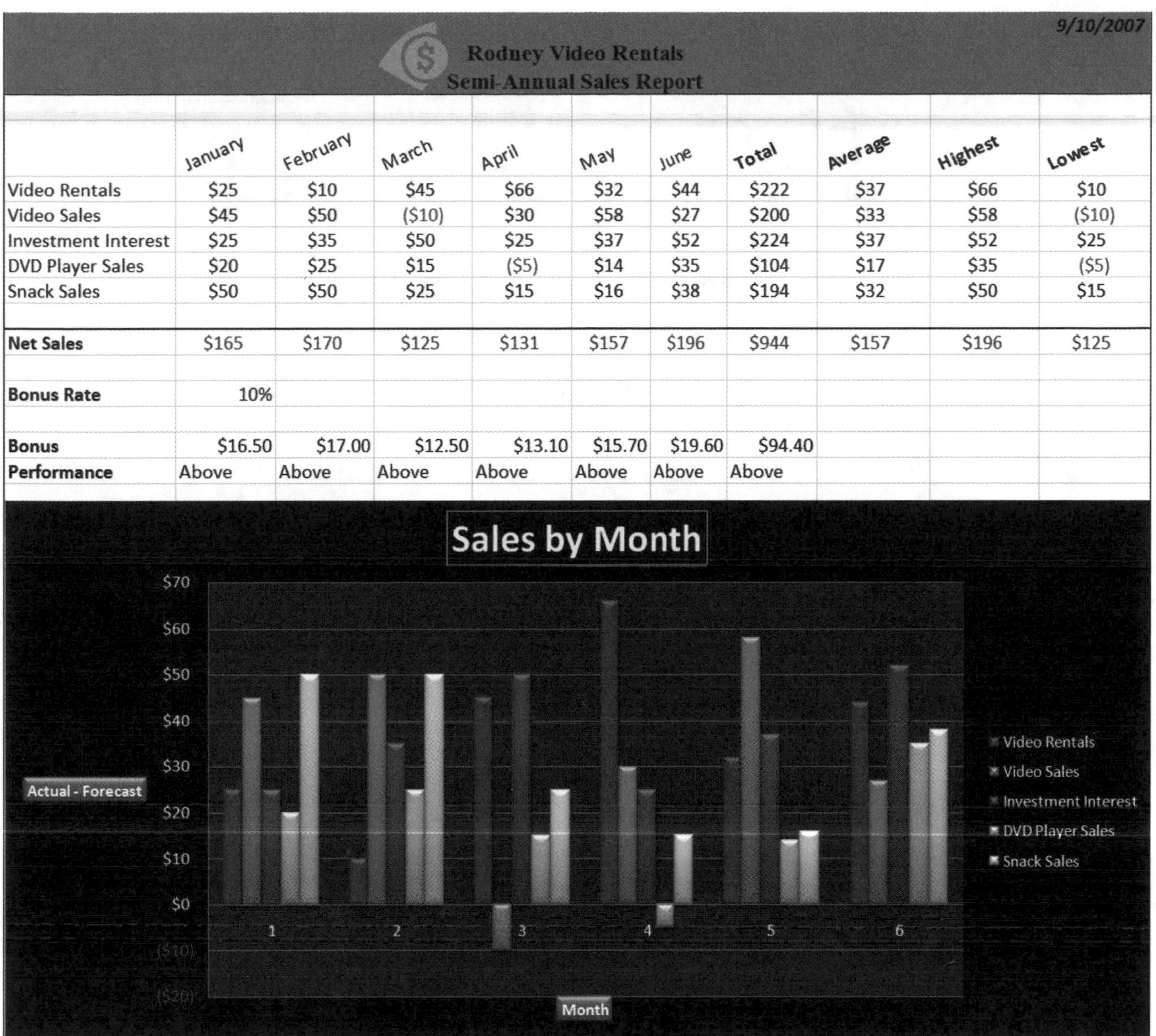

9/10/2007

Rodney Video Rentals
Semi-Annual Sales Report

	January	February	March	April	May	June	Total	Average	Highest	Lowest
Video Rentals	$25	$10	$45	$66	$32	$44	$222	$37	$66	$10
Video Sales	$45	$50	($10)	$30	$58	$27	$200	$33	$58	($10)
Investment Interest	$25	$35	$50	$25	$37	$52	$224	$37	$52	$25
DVD Player Sales	$20	$25	$15	($5)	$14	$35	$104	$17	$35	($5)
Snack Sales	$50	$50	$25	$15	$16	$38	$194	$32	$50	$15
Net Sales	$165	$170	$125	$131	$157	$196	$944	$157	$196	$125
Bonus Rate	10%									
Bonus	$16.50	$17.00	$12.50	$13.10	$15.70	$19.60	$94.40			
Performance	Above	Above	Above	Above	Above	Above	Above			

VARIANCE WORKSHEET

Creating a New Workbook and Entering Text and Numbers into Cells

This section will guide you through the process of opening a new Excel workbook and entering information in it.

To Start Microsoft Excel

1. Click the **Start** button on the lower-left corner of your screen to display the Start menu.
2. **All Programs > Microsoft Office > Microsoft Office Excel 2007** from the Start Menu to launch the application.

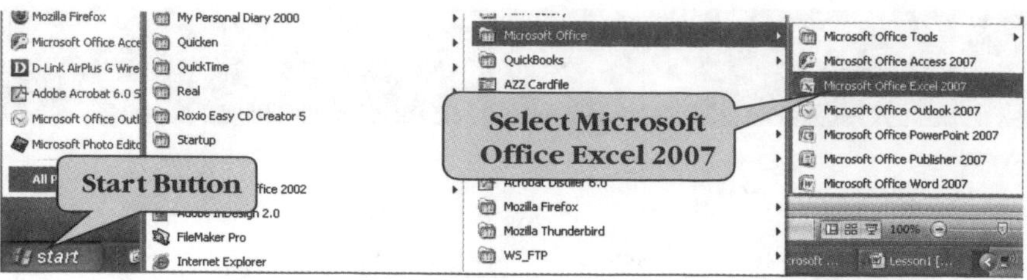

To Enter Text or Numbers into a Cell

1. Click on the cell into which you wish to enter a value.
2. Type your entry.
3. Press **Enter** to confirm your entry and move to the next cell.

Let's Try It!

- Click the **Start** button on the lower left side of your screen.

Displays the Start Menu, allowing you to select which application to launch.

- Select **All Programs > Microsoft Office > Microsoft Office Excel 2007** from the Start Menu.

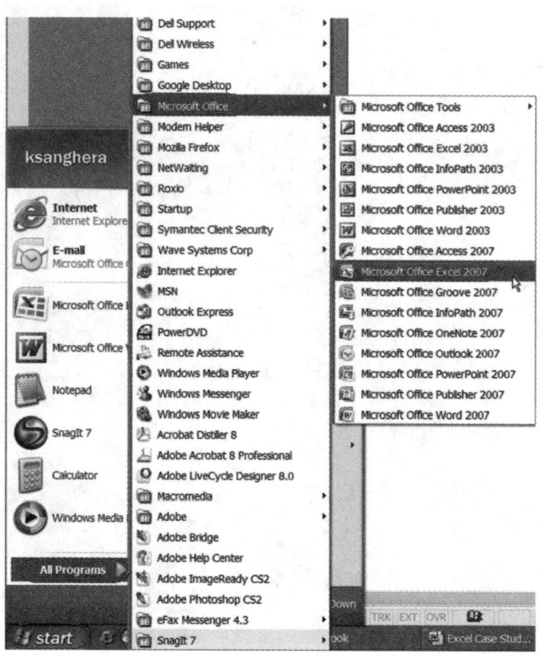

Launches the Microsoft Excel Program and displays a new blank worksheet.

- Enter the information as shown in the screen shot.
- **Increase** the width of **column A** to fit the labels.
- **Save** the work in your **flash drive** as **Case Study 2**.

	A	B	C	D	E	F	G
1							
2	Rodney Video Rentals						
3	Semi-Annual Sales Report						
4							
5		January	February	March	April	May	June
6	Video Rentals	12300	15000	13995	15266	16792	16094
7	Video Sales	495	700	980	1180	1358	1127
8	Investment Interest	325	335	350	375	412	402
9	DVD Player Sales	400	525	605	495	544	675
10	Snack Sales	200	150	225	315	346	258
11							

Sheet1 Sheet2 Sheet3

Relative References, Absolute References, and Mixed References

In this section, you will work with references that can change when the formula is copied from one location to another. Also, you will learn about the references that do not change when the formula is copied from one location to another.

As we have seen previously, when you copy a formula to a new location, the formula automatically adjusts to its new location. For example, suppose you have the following formula in cell D3:

=B3 * C3

If you copy this formula down to cell D4, Excel will automatically change this formula to read:

=B4 * C4

This is called a **Relative Cell Reference**. When a formula is copied to a new location, it will reference the new cells based on their **relative location** to the original cells containing the formula. Relative Cell References are the default type of references in Excel.

There are times when you do not want the cell reference to change when you copy or move cells to a new location. In such a case, you would need to enter the cell reference as an **Absolute Reference**. An absolute reference does not change when it is copied or moved to a new location—it always refers to the same cell address. Absolute cell references are preceded by a **$** (dollar sign) in front of both the column reference and the cell reference.

As an example, suppose we have the following formula in cell D3:

=B3 * C3

If you copy this formula down to cell D4, you would have:

=B4 * C3

The first part of this formula (B4) is a **relative** cell reference, which automatically adjusted to its new location. The second part of the formula (C3) or the **absolute** cell reference did not change after being copied—it still refers to the original cell location of C3.

You can also use a combination of Absolute and Relative cell references in your formulas. This is called a **Mixed Reference**. You have the choice of making either the column or the row absolute, such as $D3 (column is absolute, row is relative) or F$6 (column is relative, row is absolute). The row or column preceded by the $ (the absolute reference) would not change when copied or moved, whereas the row or column reference not preceded by the $ (the relative reference) would automatically adjust to its new location.

As an example, suppose you have the following formula in cell D3:

=$B3 * C3

If you copy this formula down to cell E4 (one column to the right and one row down), you would have:

=$B4 * D4

The $B4 portion of the formula contains a **Mixed Reference**—the row adjusts automatically to the new location (from row 3 to row 4) but the column address will continue to reference column B.

We will try out absolute cell references later in this chapter.

Let's Try It!

- Click in cell **H5**.

Sets cell H5 as the active cell.

- Click the **Bold** button on the Ribbon.

Applies bold formatting to cell H5.

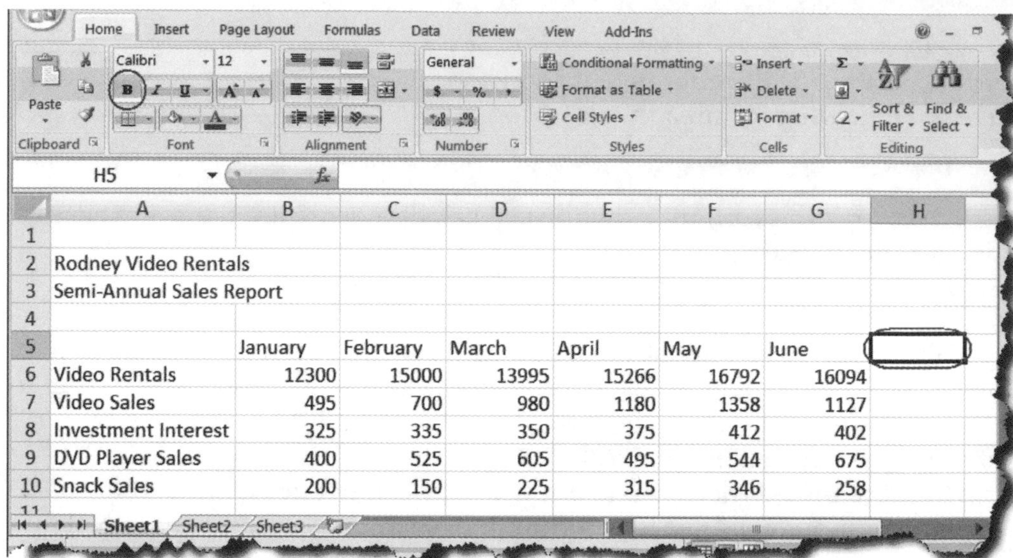

	A	B	C	D	E	F	G	H
1								
2	Rodney Video Rentals							
3	Semi-Annual Sales Report							
4								
5		January	February	March	April	May	June	
6	Video Rentals	12300	15000	13995	15266	16792	16094	
7	Video Sales	495	700	980	1180	1358	1127	
8	Investment Interest	325	335	350	375	412	402	
9	DVD Player Sales	400	525	605	495	544	675	
10	Snack Sales	200	150	225	315	346	258	

- Type: **Total**.

Enters the column title.

	A	B	C	D	E	F	G	H
1								
2	Rodney Video Rentals							
3	Semi-Annual Sales Report							
4								
5		January	February	March	April	May	June	Total
6	Video Rentals	12300	15000	13995	15266	16792	16094	
7	Video Sales	495	700	980	1180	1358	1127	
8	Investment Interest	325	335	350	375	412	402	
9	DVD Player Sales	400	525	605	495	544	675	
10	Snack Sales	200	150	225	315	346	258	

- Click in cell **H6**.

Makes cell H6 the active cell.

- Type in the following formula: **=B6+C6+D6+E6+F6+G6** and then press **Enter**.

	A	B	C	D	E	F	G	H	I
1									
2	Rodney Video Rentals								
3	Semi-Annual Sales Report								
4									
5		January	February	March	April	May	June	Total	
6	Video Rentals	12300	15000	13995	15266	16792	16094	=B6+C6+D6+E6+F6+G6	
7	Video Sales	495	700	980	1180	1358	1127		
8	Investment Interest	325	335	350	375	412	402		
9	DVD Player Sales	400	525	605	495	544	675		
10	Snack Sales	200	150	225	315	346	258		

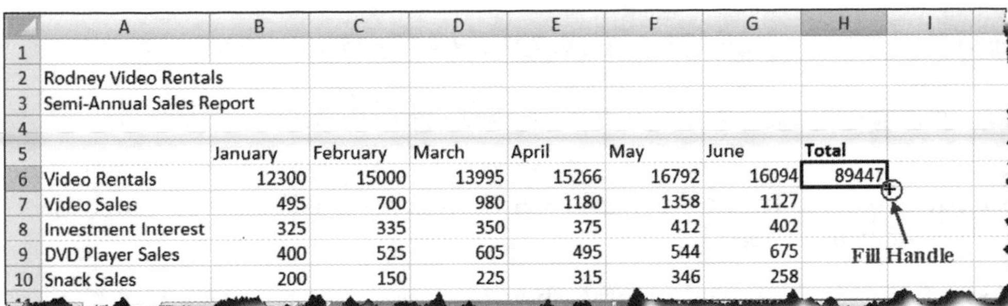

	A	B	C	D	E	F	G	H	I
1									
2	Rodney Video Rentals								
3	Semi-Annual Sales Report								
4									
5		January	February	March	April	May	June	Total	
6	Video Rentals	12300	15000	13995	15266	16792	16094	89447	
7	Video Sales	495	700	980	1180	1358	1127		
8	Investment Interest	325	335	350	375	412	402		
9	DVD Player Sales	400	525	605	495	544	675		
10	Snack Sales	200	150	225	315	346	258		

Sums cells B6 to G6 and verifies the entry.

- Select cell **H6**.

Makes H6 the active cell.

- Click on the lower right **Fill Handle** of cell H6 and drag downwards to cell **H10**. Release the mouse button.

	A	B	C	D	E	F	G	H	I
1									
2	Rodney Video Rentals								
3	Semi-Annual Sales Report								
4									
5		January	February	March	April	May	June	Total	
6	Video Rentals	12300	15000	13995	15266	16792	16094	89447	
7	Video Sales	495	700	980	1180	1358	1127	5840	
8	Investment Interest	325	335	350	375	412	402	2199	
9	DVD Player Sales	400	525	605	495	544	675	3244	
10	Snack Sales	200	150	225	315	346	258	1494	
11									

Copies the formula in H6 to cells H7 to H10.

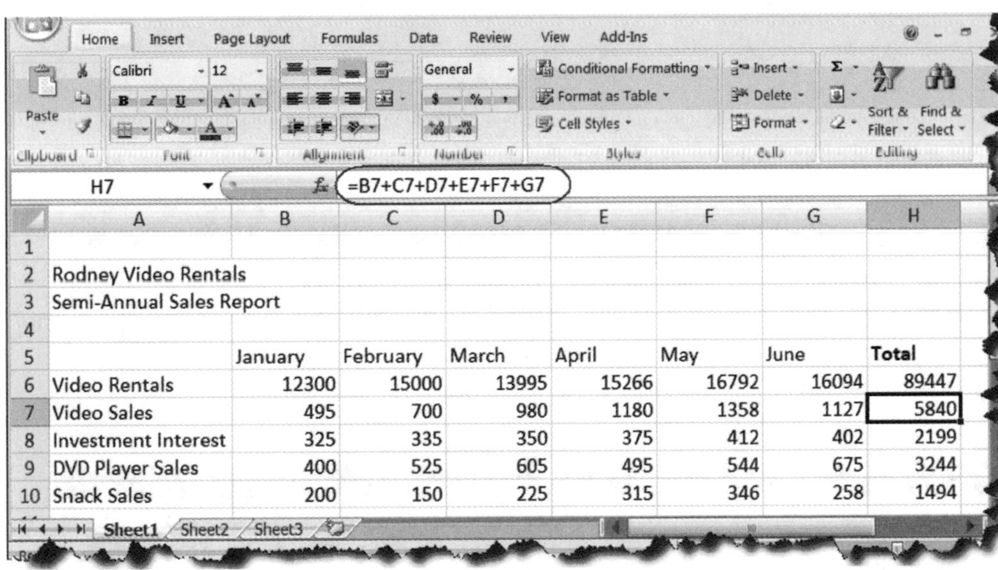

	A	B	C	D	E	F	G	H
1								
2	Rodney Video Rentals							
3	Semi-Annual Sales Report							
4								
5		January	February	March	April	May	June	Total
6	Video Rentals	12300	15000	13995	15266	16792	16094	89447
7	Video Sales	495	700	980	1180	1358	1127	5840
8	Investment Interest	325	335	350	375	412	402	2199
9	DVD Player Sales	400	525	605	495	544	675	3244
10	Snack Sales	200	150	225	315	346	258	1494

- Click in cell **H6** then click in cell **H7**. Observe the formula bar.

Notice the formula is automatically updated to its new location.

MIN, MAX, COUNT and AVERAGE Functions

In this lesson, you will work with some new aggregate functions.

In Excel Case Study 1, you learned how to enter the **SUM** function using the **AutoSum** button. There are also several other functions available using the AutoSum feature. These are:

- **SUM** — Totals the values in a selected range
- **AVERAGE** — Computes the average of the values in a selected range
- **MIN** — Returns the lowest value in a selected range
- **MAX** — Returns the highest value in a selected range
- **COUNT NUMBERS** — Totals the number of cells with values in a selected range

To Enter Additional Functions Using AutoSum

1. Select the cell or range of cells where you want the formula to be inserted.
2. Click the arrow to the right of the **AutoSum** button on the Ribbon.
3. Chose the desired function.

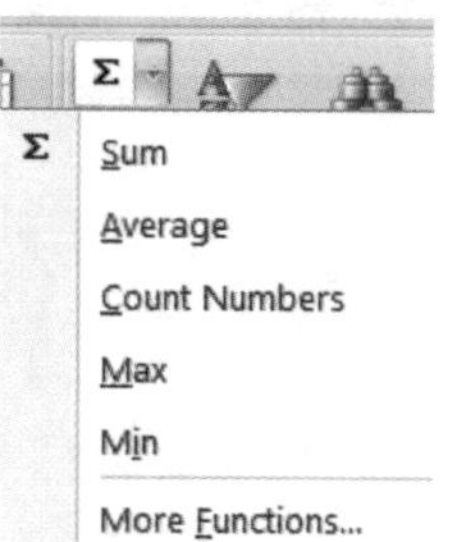

AVAILABLE AUTOSUM AGGREGATE FUNCTIONS

4. If the cell range that Excel chooses is not the desired range, drag over the range to be included in the formula.
5. Press the **Enter** key to verify the formula.

	January	February	March	April	May	June	Total	Average
Video Rentals	$12,300.00	$15,000.00	$13,995.00	$15,266.00	$16,792.60	$16,094.25	$89,447.85	=AVERAGE(B6:G6)
Video Sales	$495.00	$700.00	$980.00	$1,235.00	$1,358.50	$1,127.00	$5	AVERAGE(**number1**, [number2], ...)
Investment Interest	$325.00	$335.00	$350.00	$375.00	$412.50	$402.50	$2,200.00	
DVD Player Sales	$400.00	$525.00	$605.00	$495.00	$544.50	$695.75	$3,265.25	
Snack Sales	$200.00	$150.00	$225.00	$315.00	$346.50	$258.75	$1,495.25	
	$13,720.00	$16,710.00	$16,155.00	$17,686.00	$19,454.60	$18,578.25	$102,303.85	

AVERAGE FUNCTION FOR CELLS B6:G6

In addition to the five functions discussed above, there are many other pre-defined functions available to you in Excel—financial functions, logical functions, date and time functions and statistical functions, just to name a few of the available categories.

To access Excel's pre-defined functions, click the **Insert Function Button**, located to the left of the Formula Bar or on the **Formulas Ribbon**. The Insert

Function dialog box allows you to choose from a wide array of handy functions.

Once you have chosen the desired function, the **Function Arguments** dialog box opens, prompting you for each required (or optional) argument. You can type the cell address directly into the argument boxes or you can click the **Collapse Dialog Box** button and select the cell or cell range to be included in the arguments.

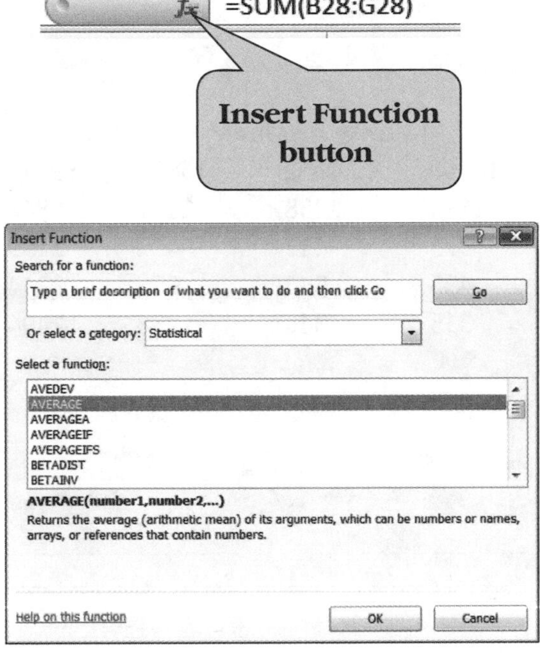

INSERT FUNCTION DIALOG BOX

To Enter a Function Using the Insert Function Feature

1. Click the **Insert Function Button** to the left of the Formula Bar
   Or
   Click the **Insert Function Button** on the **Formulas** Ribbon.
   Or
   Click the arrow on the **AutoSum** button and select **More Functions**.
   Or
   Press the **Shift + F3** keystroke combination.
2. Select a **Function Category** from the **Category** combo box.
3. Select a function from the **Select a Function** list box.
4. Click the **Collapse Dialog Box** button to select the cell or cell range for the arguments (or type the arguments in manually in the argument text boxes).
5. Click the **Display Dialog Box** to return back to the **Function Arguments** dialog box.
6. Click **OK**.

Let's Try It!

- Select **I5** and then press the **Bold** button.

Makes cell I5 the active cell and applies bold formatting.

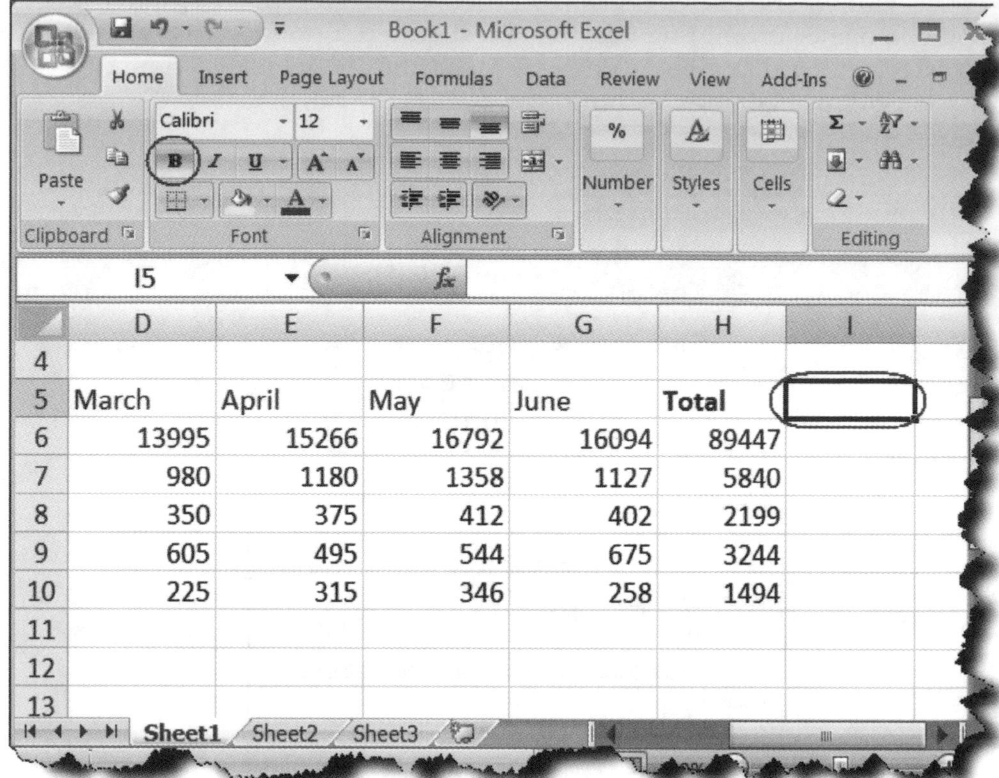

- Type: **Average**.

Enters the column title.

- Press **Enter**.

Confirms the entry.

	D	E	F	G	H	I
4						
5	March	April	May	June	**Total**	**Average**
6	13995	15266	16792	16094	89447	
7	980	1180	1358	1127	5840	
8	350	375	412	402	2199	
9	605	495	544	675	3244	
10	225	315	346	258	1494	
11						

- Select the cell range **B6:G6**.

As we did not want our Totals column to be included in the average, we must manually select the desired range we wish included in the formula.

	A	B	C	D	E	F	G	H	I
4									
5		January	February	March	April	May	June	**Total**	**Average**
6	Video Rentals	12300	15000	13995	15266	16792	16094	89447	
7	Video Sales	495	700	980	1180	1358	1127	5840	
8	Investment Interest	325	335	350	375	412	402	2199	

Sheet1 Sheet2 Sheet3

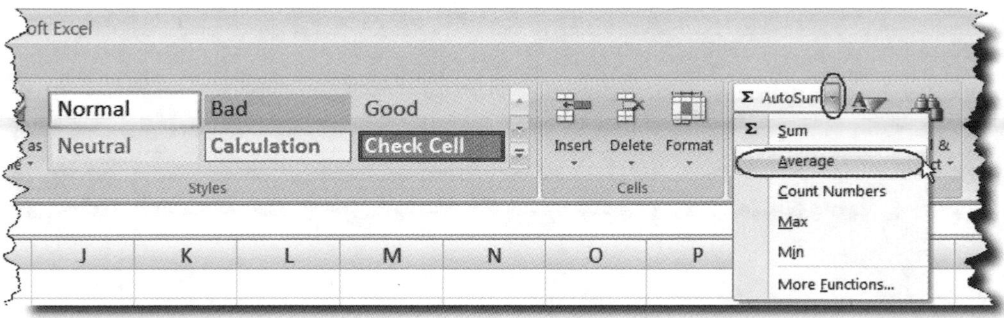

- Click the **arrow to the right of the AutoSum button** on the Home Ribbon.

Presents us with a list of functions we can insert.

- Click on **Average**.

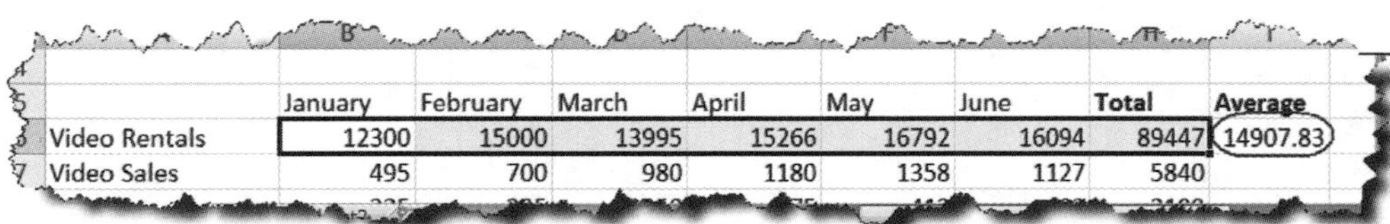

	January	February	March	April	May	June	Total	Average
Video Rentals	12300	15000	13995	15266	16792	16094	89447	14907.83
Video Sales	495	700	980	1180	1358	1127	5840	

Calculates the average for the cell range B6:G6 and displays the result in cell I6.

	D	E	F	G	H	I
4						
5	March	April	May	June	Total	Average
6	13995	15266	16792	16094	89447	14907.83
7	980	1180	1358	1127	5840	973.3333
8	350	375	412	402	2199	366.5
9	605	495	544	675	3244	540.6667
10	225	315	346	258	1494	249
11						

Sheet1 Sheet2 Sheet3

- Select cell **I6**.

Makes I6 the active cell.

- Click the **Fill Handle** on cell I6 and drag downwards to cell I10.

Copies the formula to cell I10.

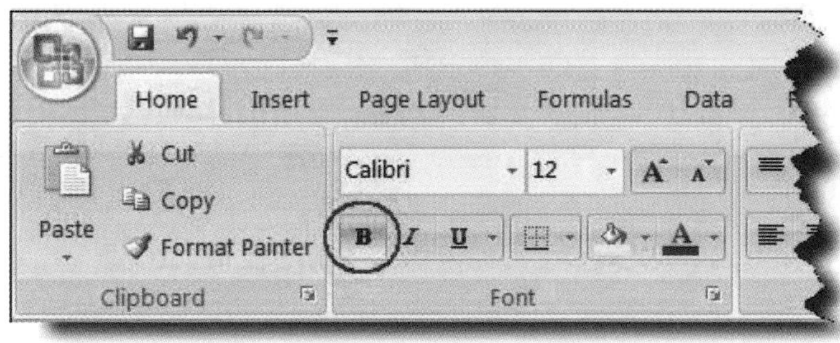

- Select cell **A12** and then press the **Bold** button.

Makes cell A12 the active cell and applies bold formatting.

- Type: **Net Sales**

Enters the row title.

- Press **Enter**.

Confirms the entry.

- Select the cell **B12**.
- Click the **AutoSum button** on the Home Ribbon.

Calculates the sum for the cell range B6:B11 and displays the result in cell B12.

- Press **Enter**.

Confirms the entry.

- Select cell **B12**.

Makes B12 the active cell.

- Click the **Fill Handle** on cell B12 and drag to cell I12.

Copies the formula to cell I12.

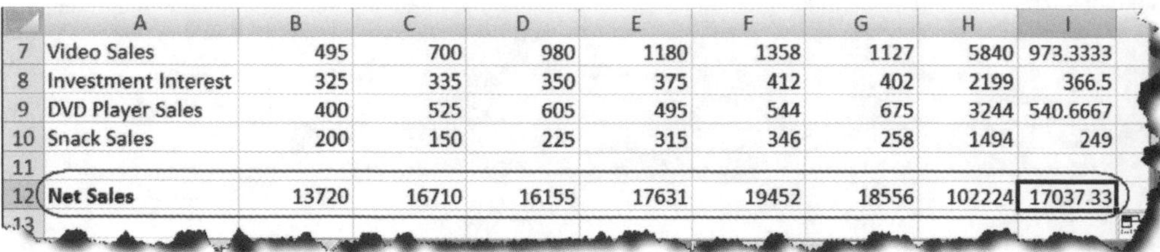

	A	B	C	D	E	F	G	H	I
7	Video Sales	495	700	980	1180	1358	1127	5840	973.3333
8	Investment Interest	325	335	350	375	412	402	2199	366.5
9	DVD Player Sales	400	525	605	495	544	675	3244	540.6667
10	Snack Sales	200	150	225	315	346	258	1494	249
11									
12	**Net Sales**	13720	16710	16155	17631	19452	18556	102224	17037.33
13									

- Select cell **J5** and then press the **Bold** button.

Makes cell J5 the active cell and applies bold formatting.

- Type: **Highest**.

Enters the column title.

- Click in cell **J6**.

Makes J6 the active cell.

- Select the cell range **B6:G6**.

As we did not want Totals and Average columns to be included in the max, we must manually select the desired range we wish included in our formula.

- Click the **arrow to the right of the AutoSum button** on the Home Ribbon

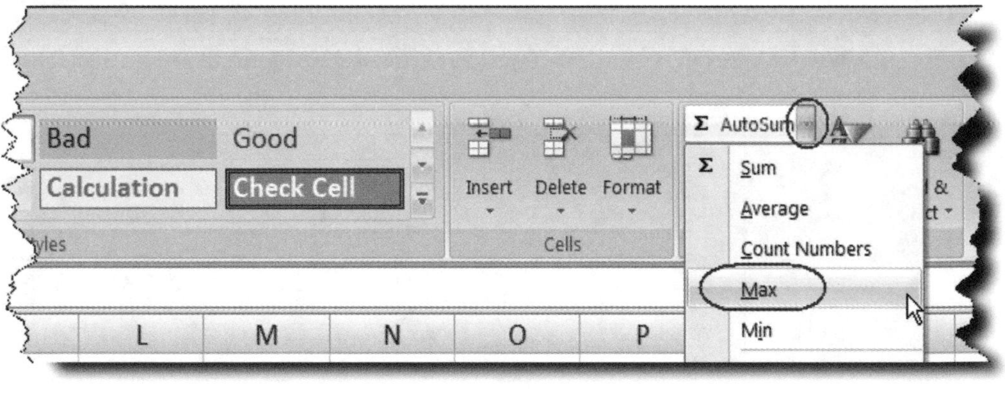

Presents us with a list of functions we can insert.

- Click on **Max**.

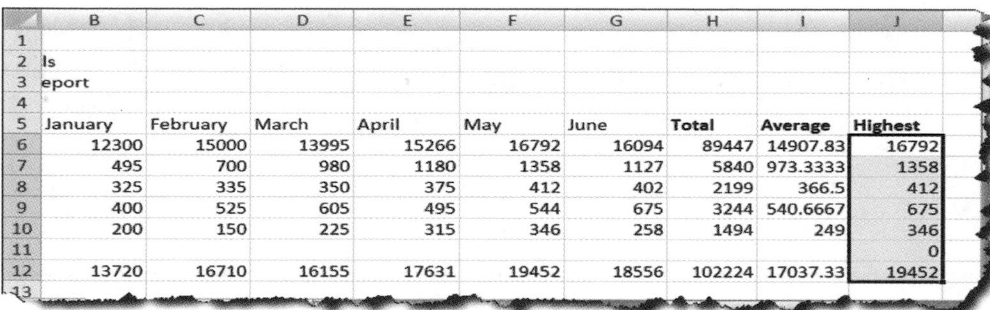

	B	C	D	E	F	G	H	I	J
1									
2	ls								
3	eport								
4									
5	January	February	March	April	May	June	Total	Average	Highest
6	12300	15000	13995	15266	16792	16094	89447	14907.83	16792
7	495	700	980	1180	1358	1127	5840	973.3333	1358
8	325	335	350	375	412	402	2199	366.5	412
9	400	525	605	495	544	675	3244	540.6667	675
10	200	150	225	315	346	258	1494	249	346
11									0
12	13720	16710	16155	17631	19452	18556	102224	17037.33	19452
13									

Calculates the max for the cell range B6:G6 and displays the result in cell J6.

- Select cell **J6**.

Makes J6 the active cell.

- Click the **Fill Handle** on cell J6 and drag to cell J12.

Copies the formula to cell J12.

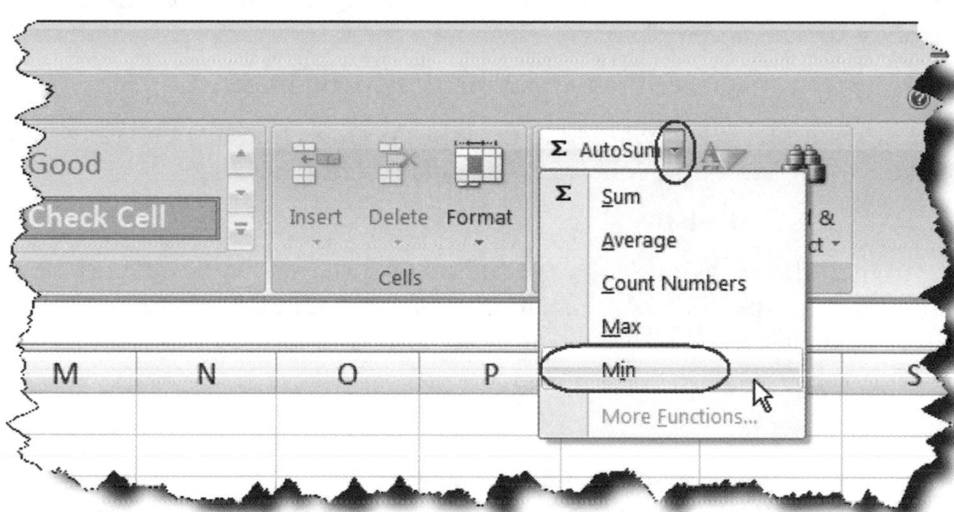

- Select cell **K5** and then press the **Bold** button.

Makes cell K5 the active cell and applies bold formatting.

- Type: **Lowest**.

Enters the column title.

- Press **Enter**.

Confirms the entry and selects K6.

- Select the cell range **B6:G6**.

As we did not want Totals, Average, and Highest columns to be included in the min, we must manually select the desired range we wish included in our formula.

- Click the **arrow to the right of the AutoSum button** on the Home Ribbon.

Presents us with a list of functions we can insert.

- Click on **Min**.

Calculates the minimum for the cell range B6:G6 and displays the result in cell J6.

- Select cell **K6**.

Makes K6 the active cell.

- Click the **Fill Handle** on cell K6 and drag to cell K12.

Copies the formula to cell K12.

- Click the **Save** button.

Saves the active document.

	B	C	D	E	F	G	H	I	J	K
4										
5	January	February	March	April	May	June	Total	Average	Highest	Lowest
6	12300	15000	13995	15266	16792	16094	89447	14907.83	16792	12300
7	495	700	980	1180	1358	1127	5840	973.3333	1358	495
8	325	335	350	375	412	402	2199	366.5	412	325
9	400	525	605	495	544	675	3244	540.6667	675	400
10	200	150	225	315	346	258	1494	249	346	150
11									0	0
12	13720	16710	16155	17631	19452	18556	102224	17037.33	19452	13720
13										

Sheet1 Sheet2 Sheet3

Entering Functions Manually

In addition to using the **AutoSum** button for the above functions, you can also type in these functions manually, directly into the desired cell. The format is:

=Function name, cell range surround by parenthesis.

For example, if you wanted to find the **Average** from the cell range B3 to B8, you would enter the following formula in cell B9:

=AVERAGE(B3:B8)

To include non-contiguous cells in the formula, separate each cell or cell range by a comma. For example, if you wanted to find the **Average** for cells B3:B8, D3:D8 and cell F5, the formula would read:

=AVERAGE(B3:B8, D3:D8, F5)

Formatting Text and Values

In this section, you will practice how to change the appearance of text and values in your worksheet. For more information on formatting, refer back to Excel Case Study 1 where this subject is discussed in detail.

Let's Try It!

- Select **cell A2 and A3**.

Makes A2 and A3 the active cells.

	A	B	C	D
1				
2	Rodney Video Rentals			
3	Semi-Annual Sales Report			
4				
5		January	February	March
6	Video Rentals	12300	15000	13995
7	Video Sales	495	700	98

- Click the **Bold** formatting button on the Home Ribbon.

Bolds the title in cells A2 and A3.

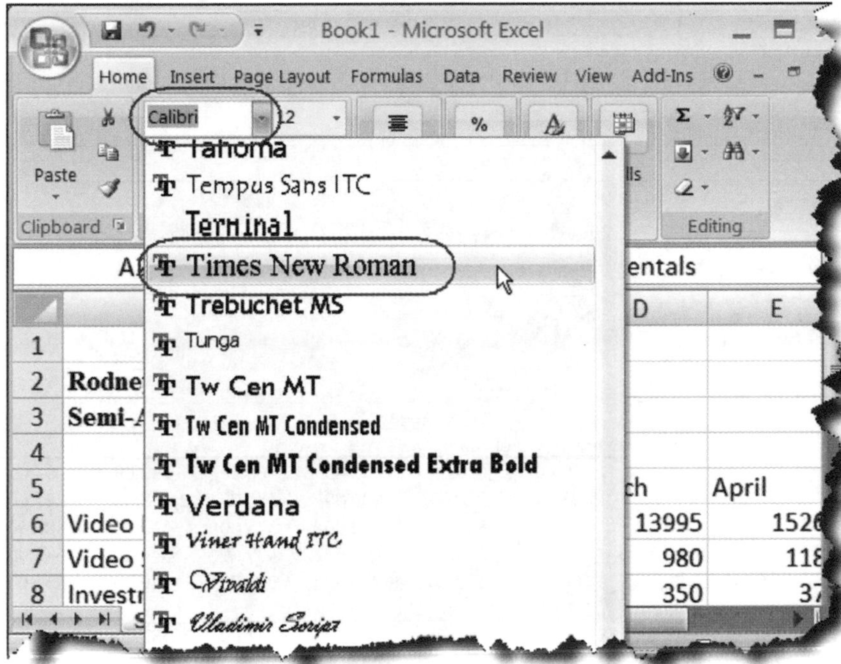

- Click on the **Font** drop down list, scroll down and then choose **Times New Roman**.

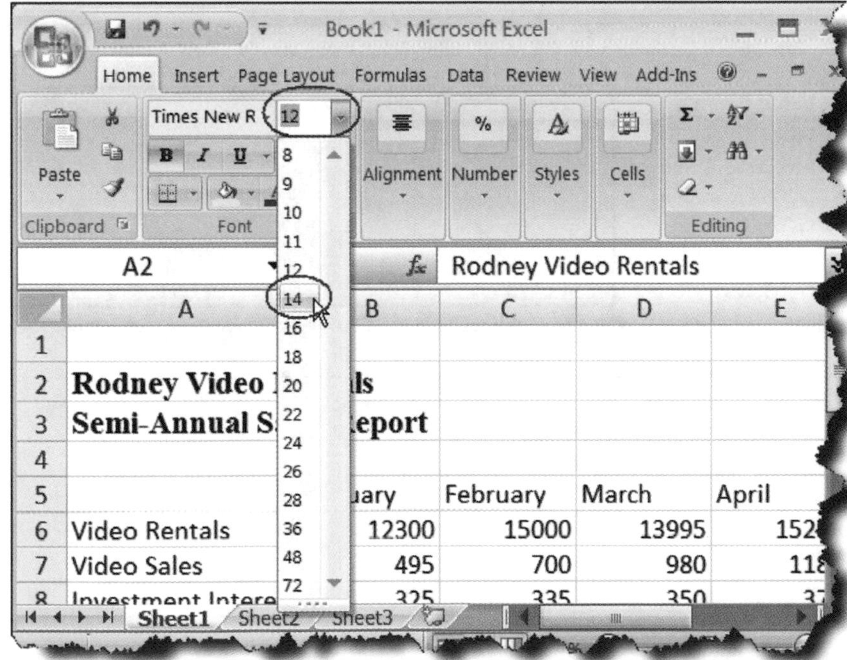

- Click on the **Font Size** drop down list and choose 14.

Changes the size of the title to 14 pt.

- Press the **Ctrl + S** keystroke combination.

Saves our changes.

- Select the cell range **B6:K12**.

Selects the cell range to be formatted.

- On the **Number group** on the Home Ribbon, click the Comma Style button.

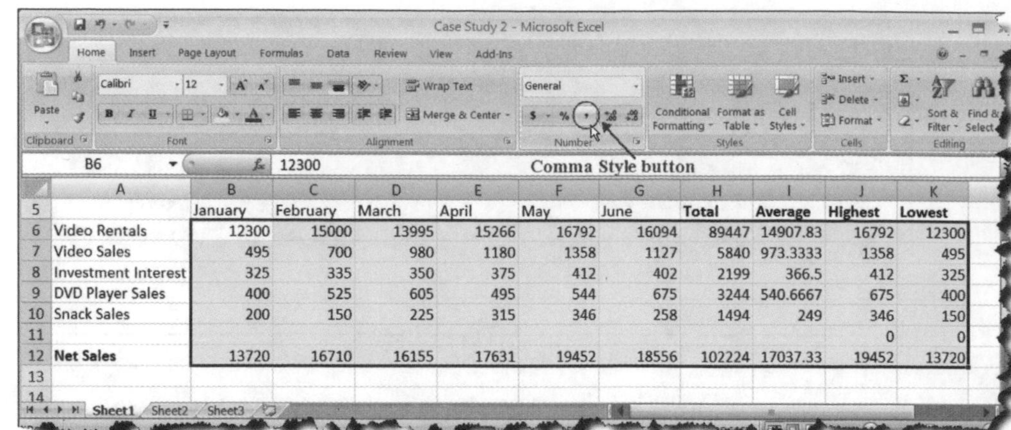

Applies a number format with comma and two decimal places.

- Click the **Decrease Decimal** button twice.

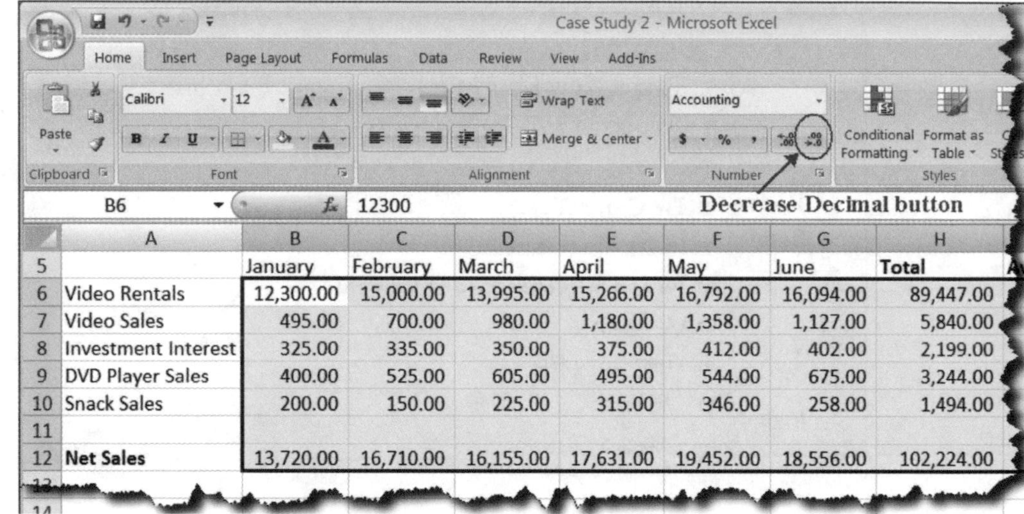

Decimal places will not be displayed.

	A	B	C	D	E	F	G
5		January	February	March	April	May	June
6	Video Rentals	12,300	15,000	13,995	15,266	16,792	16,094
7	Video Sales	495	700	980	1,180	1,358	1,127
8	Investment Interest	325	335	350	375	412	402
9	DVD Player Sales	400	525	605	495	544	675
10	Snack Sales	200	150	225	315	346	258
11							
12	**Net Sales**	13,720	16,710	16,155	17,631	19,452	18,556

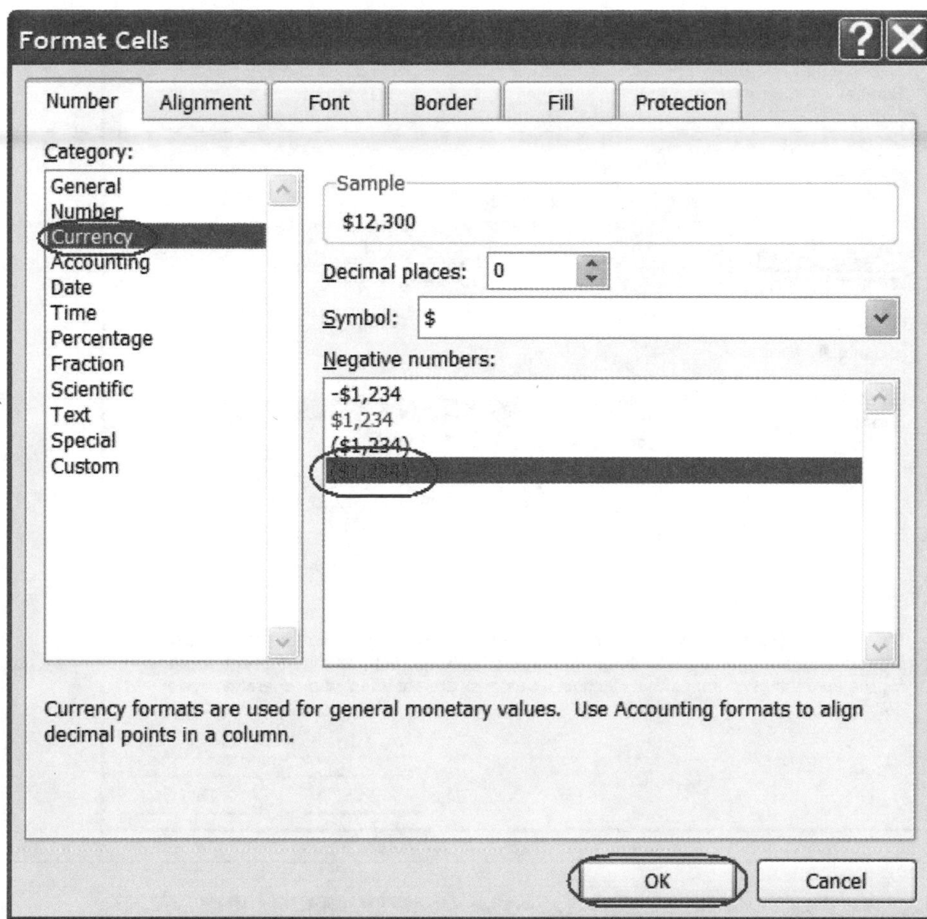

- Make sure cell range **B6:K12** is still selected.
- Press **Ctrl + 1** key.

Displays the Number tab of the Formatting Cells dialog box.

- Select **Currency** from the **Category** list.

Chooses the Currency formatting style.

- In the **Negative Number** list box, choose the fourth style from the top (1,234).

Will display negative number in red color and surround them with parenthesis. If do not need to choose a specific negative number format, you could have clicked the Currency button on the Ribbon as well.

- Click **OK**.

Closes the Format Cells dialog box.

- Select cell **G1** and enter the date **9/10/2007**.

Enters the date in mm/dd/yyyy format.

- Press **Enter**.

Confirms the entry. Excel automatically applied a date format to the cell.

- Select cell **G1**.

Activates cell **G1**.

- Press **Ctrl + 1** key.

Displays the Formatting Cells dialog box.

- Under **Category** click on **Date**.

Chooses the Date formatting style.

- Choose the **March 14, 2001** style.

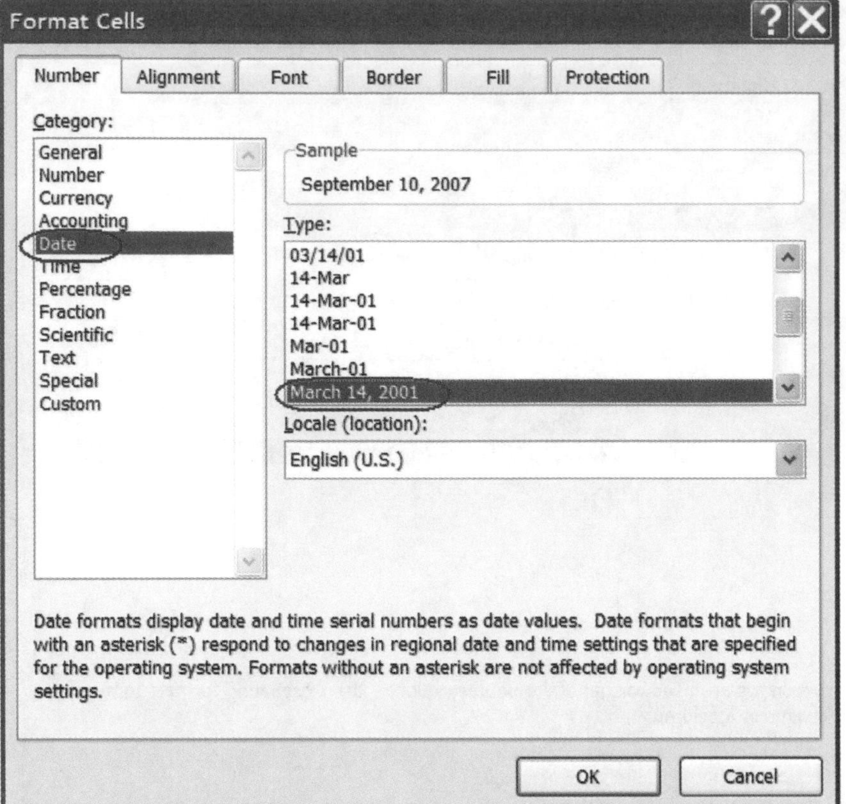

- Click the **Font Tab** on top of the Format Cells dialog box.

Switches to Font options.

- Under the **Font Style** list box, choose **Bold Italic**.

Applies Bold and Italic formatting to the cell.

- Click **OK**.

Closes the Format Cells dialog box.

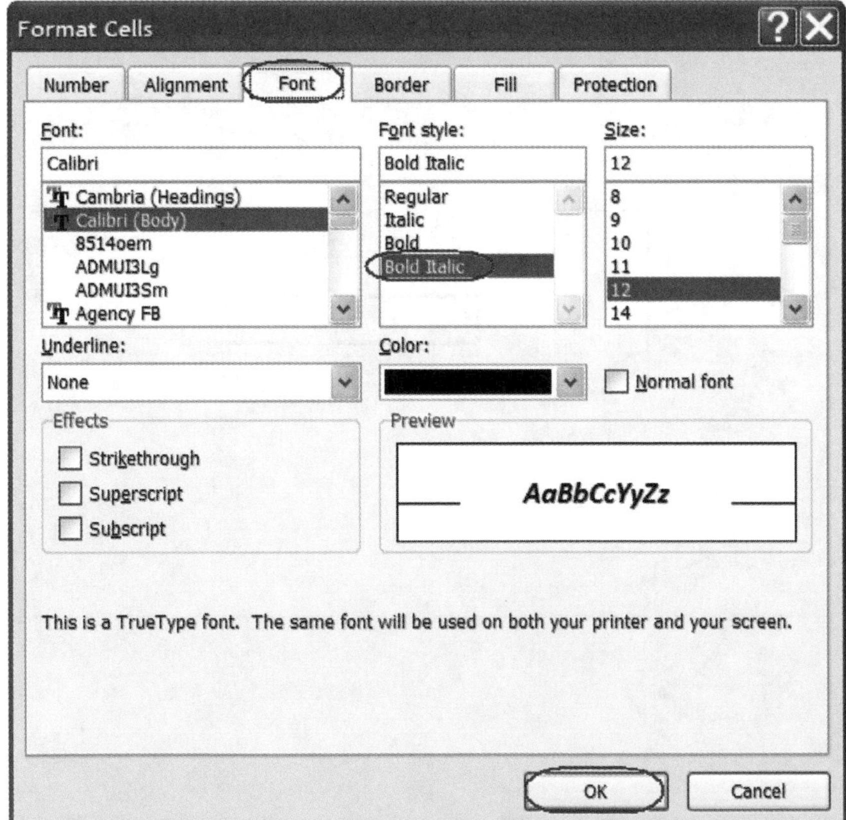

- If you see # signs in G1 instead of a date, select the Column Heading for column **G** and **double-click** on the right border of column G when the mouse pointer transforms into a black cross.

Applies AutoFit which sizes the column to accommodate the longest data value.

- Click the **Save** button.

Saves the active document.

Alignment and Text Wrapping

In this section, you will learn how to align and wrap around text and values within a cell.

When entering data into cells, the default alignment is left-aligned along the bottom for text and right-aligned along the bottom for numbers. Excel supplies many other alignment options from which to choose—left alignment, right alignment, center alignment, as well as horizontal and vertical alignment options.

The alignment options are available on the **Alignment group** on the Home Ribbon:

- **Align Left** Aligns cell contents along the left edge of the cell
- **Align Right** Aligns cell contents along the right edge of the cell
- **Center** Centers the cell contents within the cell
- **Top Align** Aligns text to the top of the cell
- **Middle Align** Aligns text so that it is centered between the top and bottom of the cell
- **Bottom Align** Aligns text to the bottom of the cell
- **Orientation** Allows you to rotate text
- **Decrease Indent** Decrease the margin between the border and the text in the cell
- **Increase Indent** Increase the margin between the border and the text in the cell
- **Wrap Text** Wraps the text within a cell so it does not cross adjoining cells or get cut off

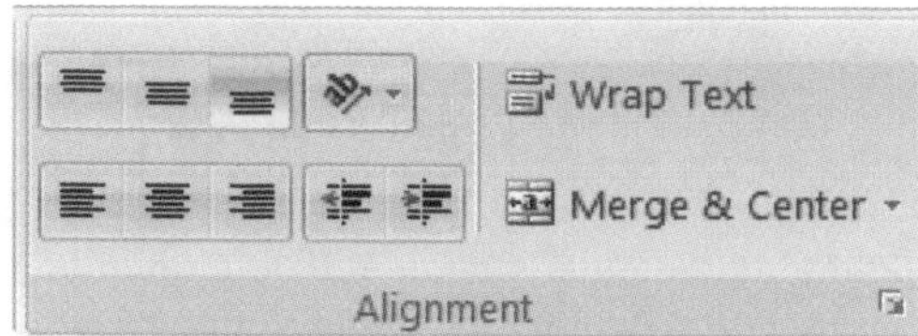

ALIGNMENT COMMANDS

Other alignment options are available from within the **Format Cells** dialog box.

To Change the Alignment of Data within Cells

1. Select the cell or cell range whose data you wish to align.
2. Click the desired alignment button on the Alignment group on the Home ribbon

Or

1. Select the cell or cell range whose data you wish to align.
2. Display the Format Cells dialog box.
3. Click the **Alignment Tab**.
4. Choose options from the **Horizontal** and/or **Vertical** combo box.
5. Select any desired additional options such as **Wrap Text, Orientation** or **Text Direction**.
6. Click **OK**.

Let's Try It!

- Select the cell range **B6:K12**.

Highlights cells B6 to K12.

- Click the **Center** Alignment Button on the Home Ribbon.

Centers the selected data within the cell.

- Select cell **J11** and **K11** and press **Delete** key to remove $0 values.

J	K
Highest	**Lowest**
$16,792	$12,300
$1,358	$495
$412	$325
$675	$400
$346	$150
$19,452	$13,720

- Select the cell range **B5:K5**.

Selects the B5 to K5 cell range.

- Click the **Alignment Dialog Launcher**.

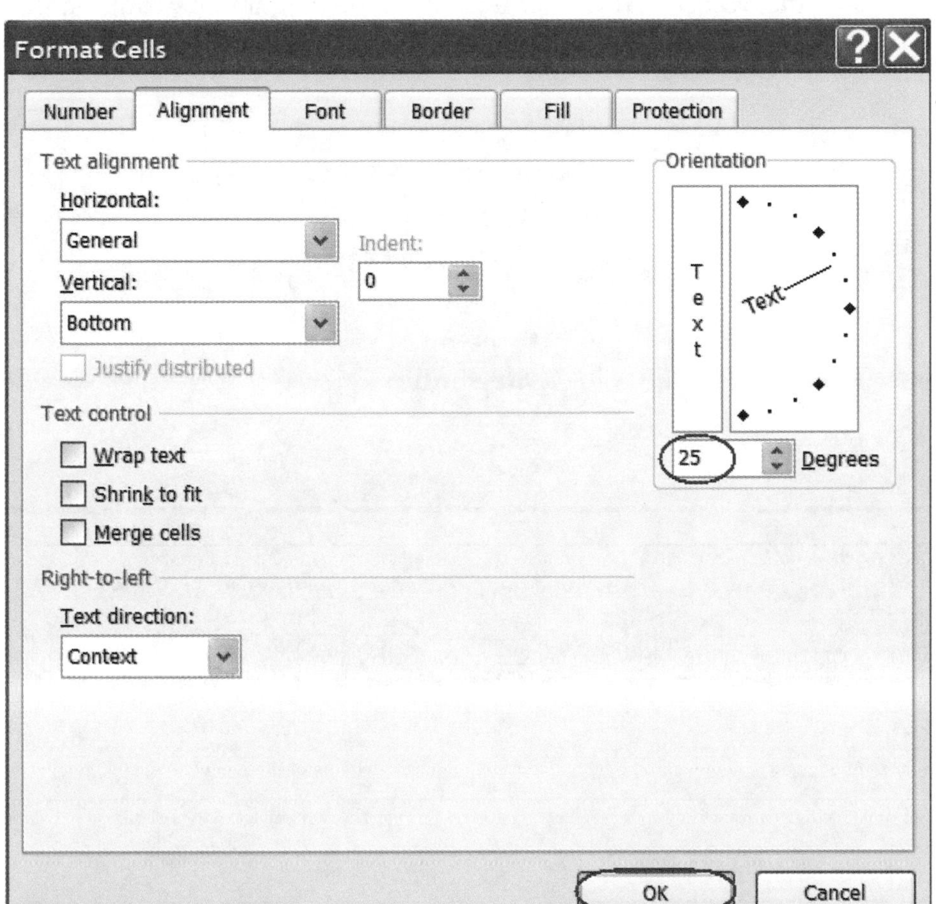

Displays the Alignment tab of the Format Cells dialog box.

- In the **Degrees** text box, type **25**.

Changes the orientation of the text to 25 degrees.

- Click **OK**.

Closes the Format Cells dialog box.

- Click the **Save** button.

Saves the active workbook.

Merging Cells and Centering Text

In this section, you will learn how to merge one or more cells together and center text within the merged cells.

With Excel's **Merge Cells and Center Text** feature, you can spread the contents of several cells into one **merged** cell. A merged cell is created by combining one or more cells into one new larger cell. For instance, you may have a lengthy title that spans several cells. The Merge Cells and Center Text feature will combine the extra cells into one large cell and center the text within the new cell. You can change the text alignment by choosing **Left** or **Right** alignment from the Home Ribbon or by choosing additional options from the Format Cells dialog box.

Once the cells have been merged, they can be returned to their original state by clicking the **Merge and Center** button with the merged cell selected.

To Merge Cells and Center Text

1. Ensure that the data to be merged and centered is located in the leftmost cell.
2. Select the cells you wish to merge.
3. Click the **Merge and Center** button on the Alignment group on the Home Ribbon.

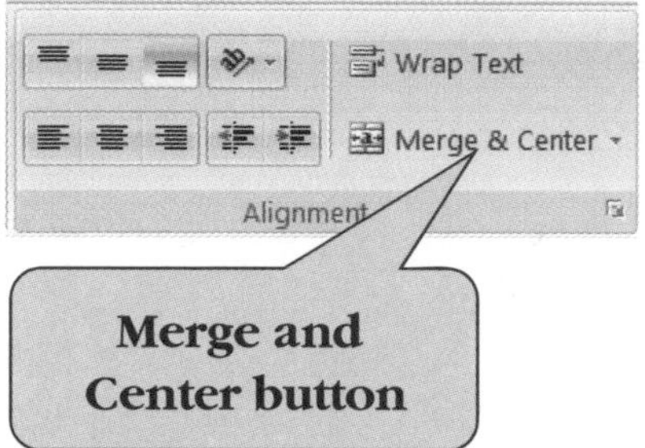

Let's Try It!

- Select the cell range **A2:K2**.

Selects the text and the cells across which we wish to center.

- Click the **Merge and Center** button on the Alignment group on the Ribbon.

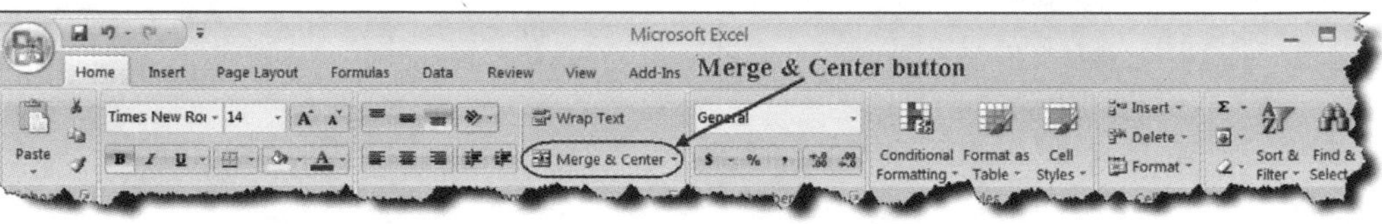

Merges cells A2 to K2 into one cell and centers the text across the range.

- Repeat the same for cell range **A3:K3** and **A1:K1**

- Make sure that cell containing date is selected and then click on **Align Text Right** button.

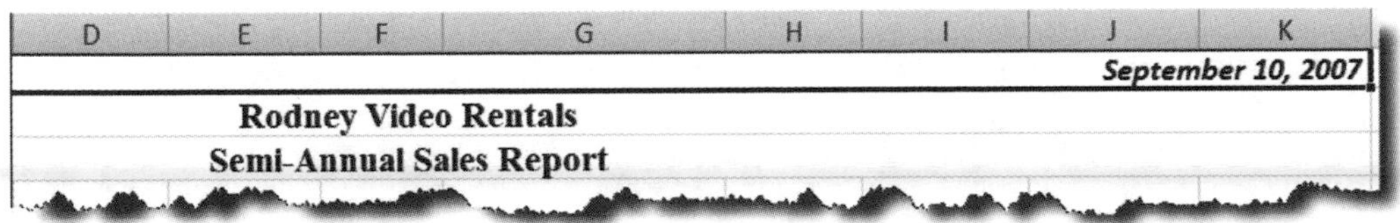

Right aligns the date.

- Click the **Save** button.

Saves the active workbook.

Adding Cell Borders

In this section, you will learn how to make cells stand out by the use of cell borders.

You can separate or outline a cell or group of cells by applying borders (left, right, top or bottom) to the edges of cells. Border options can be found under the **Borders button** on the Font group on the Home Ribbon or under the **Border tab** of the **Format Cells dialog box**. The Format Cells dialog box contains additional border options such as line style and border color.

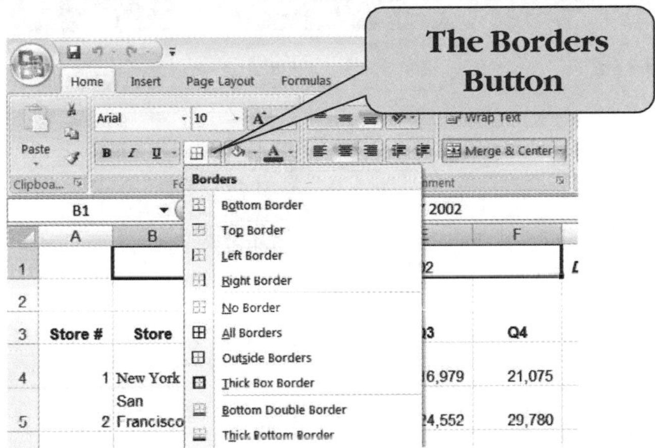

To Apply Cell Borders

1. Select the cell or range of cells to which you want to apply borders.
2. Click the arrow on the **Borders button** on the Home Ribbon.
3. Select a Border from the palette.

Or

1. Select the cell or range of cells to which you want to apply borders.
2. Click the **Font Dialog Launcher**.
3. Click the **Borders tab**.
4. Select **Border Type** from the list surrounding the **Sample Window** (clicking in the Sample Window on the borders will add and remove the border that you have chosen).
5. Select a **Line Style**, if desired.
6. Select a **Border Color** if desired.
7. Click **OK**.

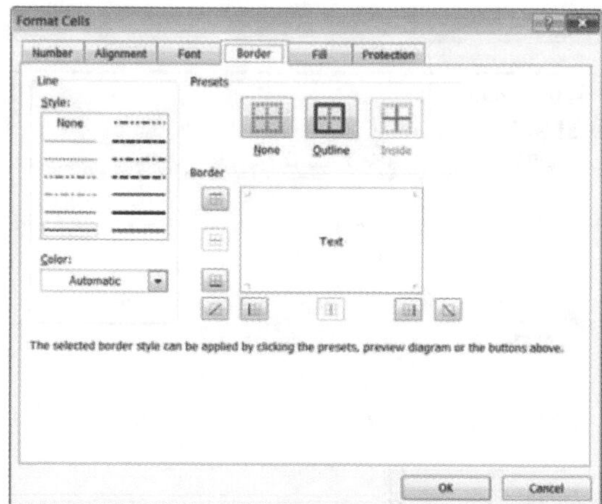

BORDER TAB OF THE FORMAT CELLS DIALOG BOX

Let's Try It!

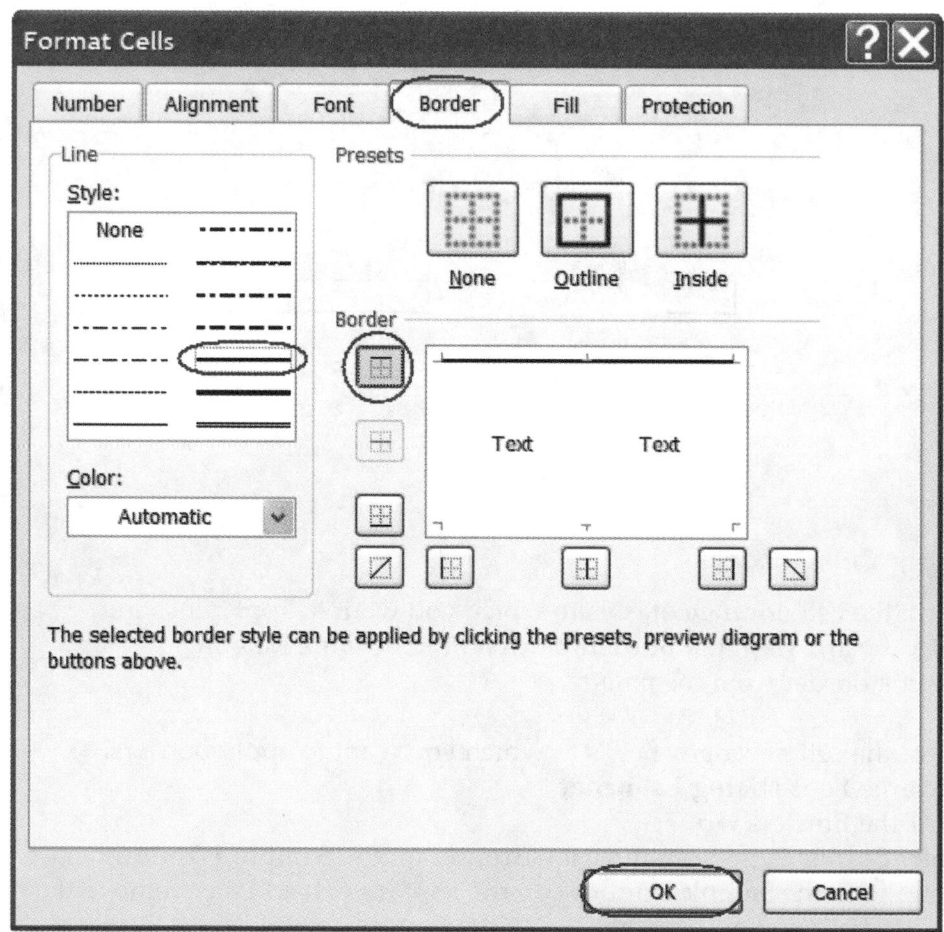

- Select the cell range **A12:K12**.

Selects the cell range to which we wish to apply borders.

- Press the **Ctrl + 1** keystroke combination.

Displays the Format Cells dialog box.

- Click the **Border Tab**.

Switches to borders options.

- Choose the third **Line Style** from the bottom in the second column.

Selects the line style (thickness and type) that we will use.

- Click the Top Border in the **Sample Window**.

Applies the line style to the top border.

- Click **OK** and observe the border.

Closes the Format Cells Dialog box.

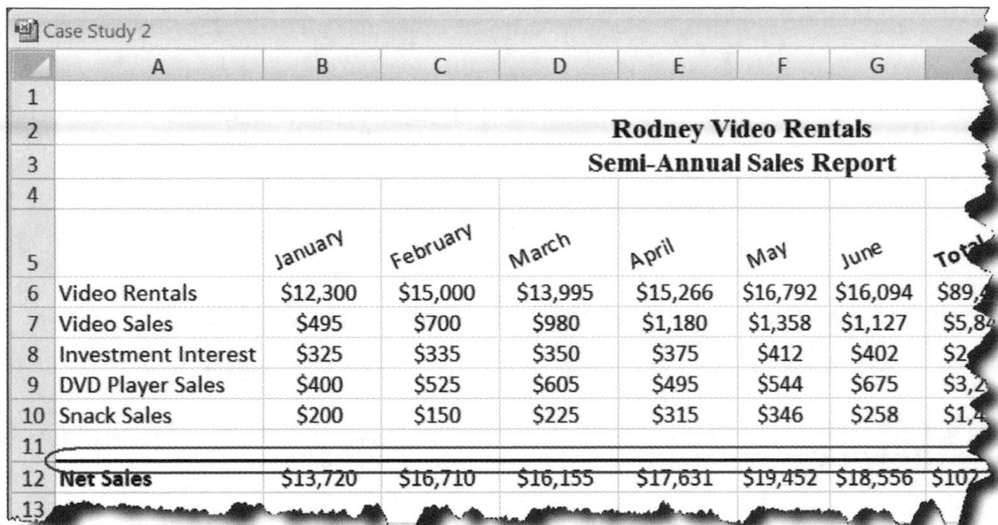

	A	B	C	D	E	F	G
1							
2					Rodney Video Rentals		
3					Semi-Annual Sales Report		
4							
5		January	February	March	April	May	June
6	Video Rentals	$12,300	$15,000	$13,995	$15,266	$16,792	$16,094
7	Video Sales	$495	$700	$980	$1,180	$1,358	$1,127
8	Investment Interest	$325	$335	$350	$375	$412	$402
9	DVD Player Sales	$400	$525	$605	$495	$544	$675
10	Snack Sales	$200	$150	$225	$315	$346	$258
11							
12	**Net Sales**	$13,720	$16,710	$16,155	$17,631	$19,452	$18,556

A top border has been applied to the selected cell range.

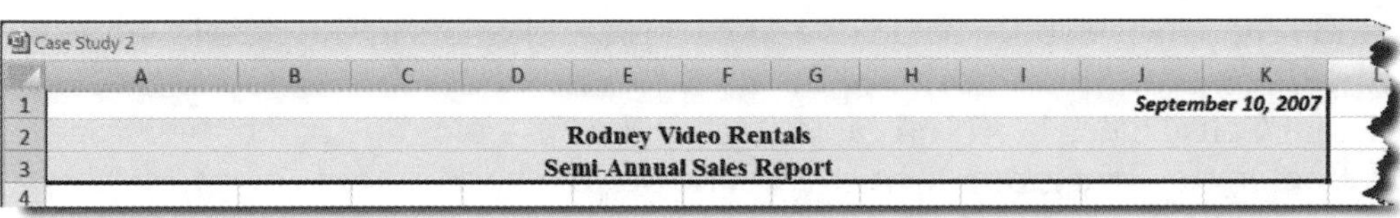

- Select cell range **A1:A3**.

Activates the cells containing title.

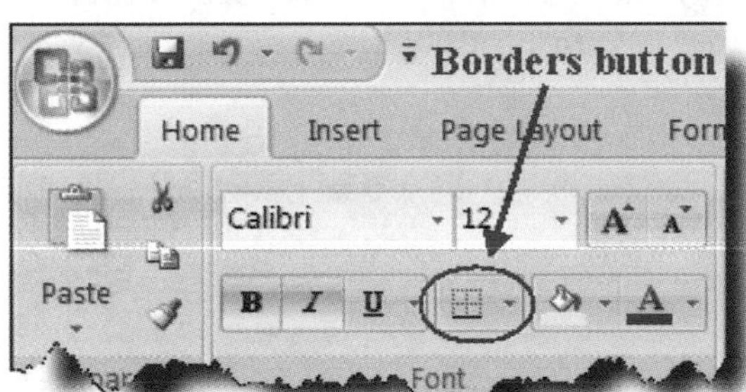

- Click the **Drop Down Arrow** on the **Borders Button**.

Presents us with the border choices.

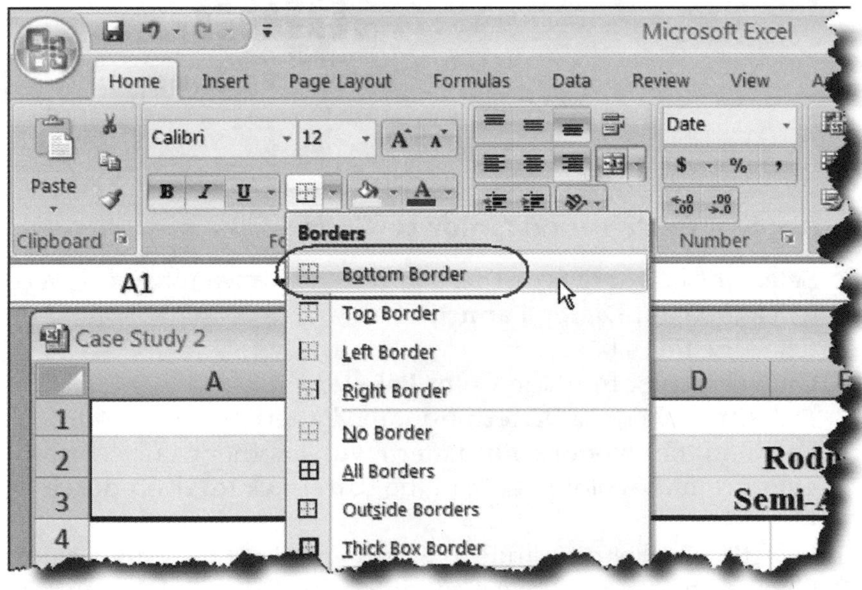

- Select **Bottom Border** (the first option) from the list.

Applies a bottom border to our title.

- Click the **Save** button.

Saves the active workbook.

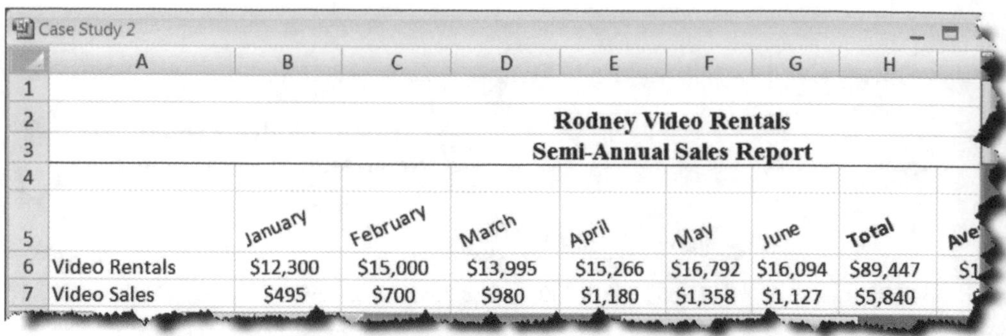

Applying Colors and Shading to Cells

In this section, you will learn how to apply patterns and colors to cells.

To add some pizzazz to your worksheet or to make a particular cell or cell range stand out, you can apply patterns and background colors to the cells in your worksheet. **Background color options** are located under the **Fill tab** of the Format Cells Dialog box (you can also click the Fill Color button on the Home Ribbon on the Font group then choose the desired background color from the color palette). Additionally, you can change the color of the fonts in your worksheet by changing the **foreground color** of a selected cell or cell range. Excel's **Color Palette** provides a wide variety of colors from which to choose.

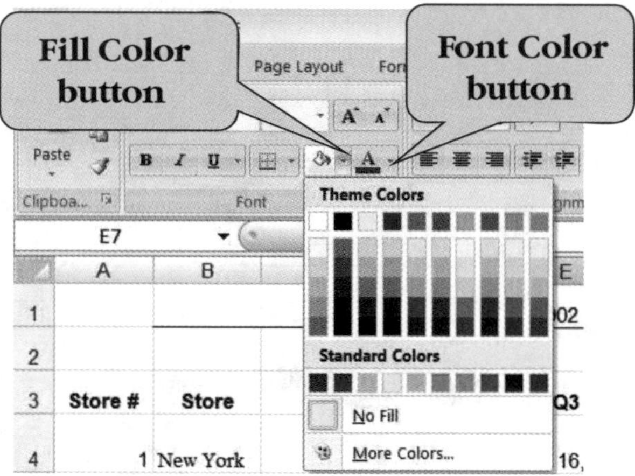

To Apply a Background Color to Cells

1. Select the cell or range of cells to which you want to apply a color.
2. Click the **Font Dialog Launcher**.
3. Click the **Fill** tab.
4. Choose a color from the **Color Palette**.
5. If desired, choose a **Pattern** from the Pattern Style drop-down list.
6. To blend the color of your pattern with another color, select the additional color from the color palette in the **Pattern Color** drop-down list.
   Or
1. Select the cell or cell range to which you want to apply a color.
2. Click on the arrow to the right of the **Fill Color Palette button** from the Home Ribbon.
3. Select the background color from the **Color Palette**.

To Change the Font Color

1. Select the cell or range of cells to which you want to apply a font color.
2. Click the **Font Dialog Launcher**.
3. Click the **Font** tab.
4. From the **Color** list box, choose a color from the **Color Palette**.
5. Click **OK**.

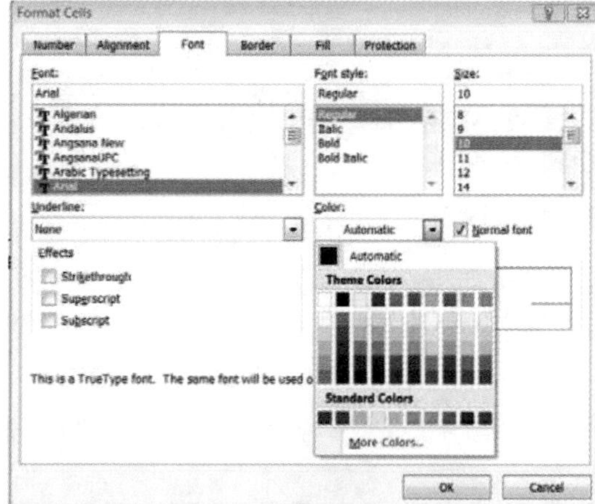

THE FONT TAB OF THE FORMAT CELLS DIALOG BOX

Or

1. Select the cell or range of cells to which you want to apply a font color.
2. Click the arrow to the right of the **Font Color Palette Button** on the Home Ribbon.
3. Click on the desired font color.

Let's Try It!

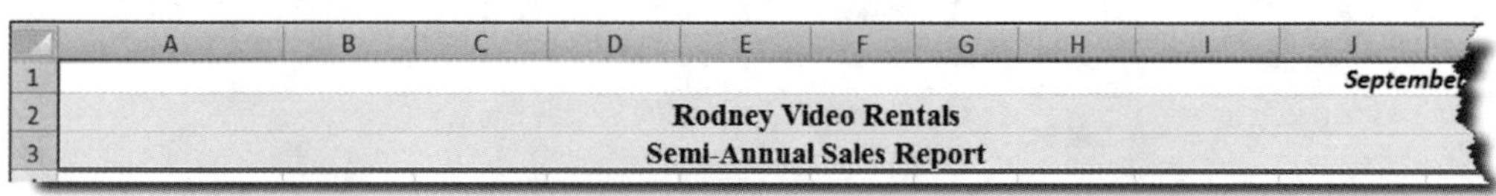

- Select the cell range **A1:A3** if not already selected.

Activates the worksheet title.

- Press the **Ctrl + 1** keystroke combination.

Displays the Format Cells dialog box.

- Click on the **Fill** tab.

Switches to fill color options.

- Click on the **green** color (seventh column, fifth row).

Applies a green background to the cell range.

- Click **OK**.

Closes the Format Cells dialog box.

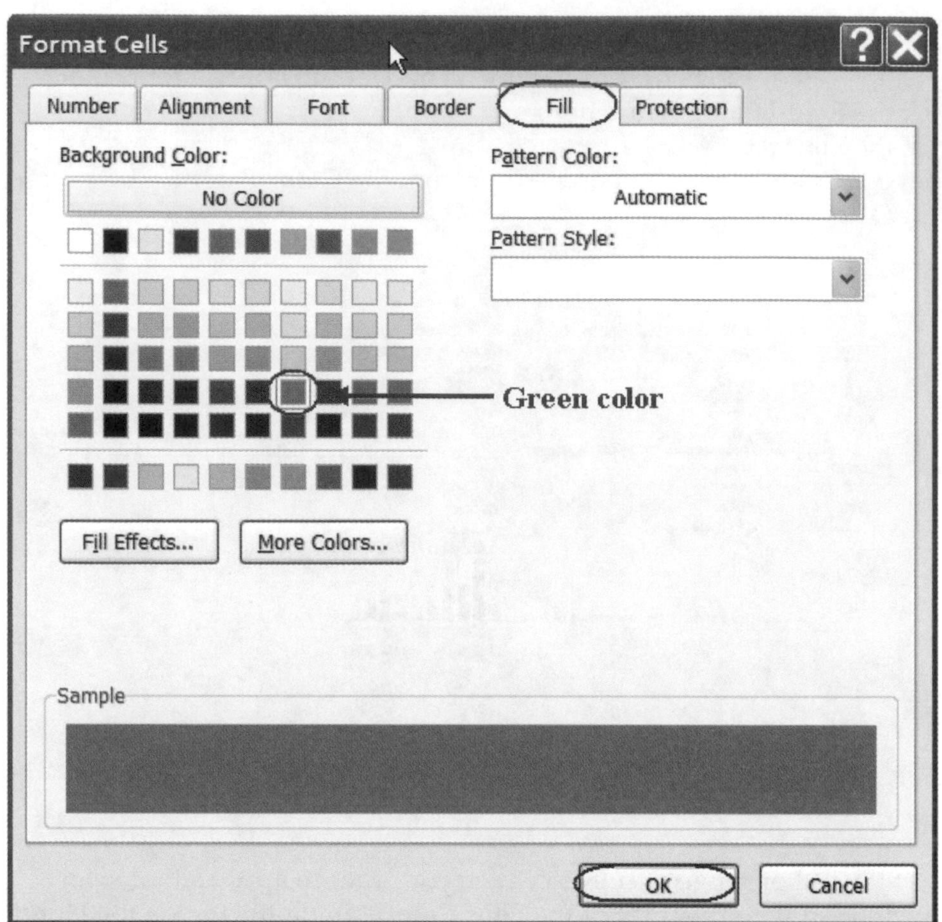

- Select the cell range **B12:K12**.

Selects the cell range from B12 to K12.

- Click on the arrow on the **Font Color Palette** button on the Ribbon.

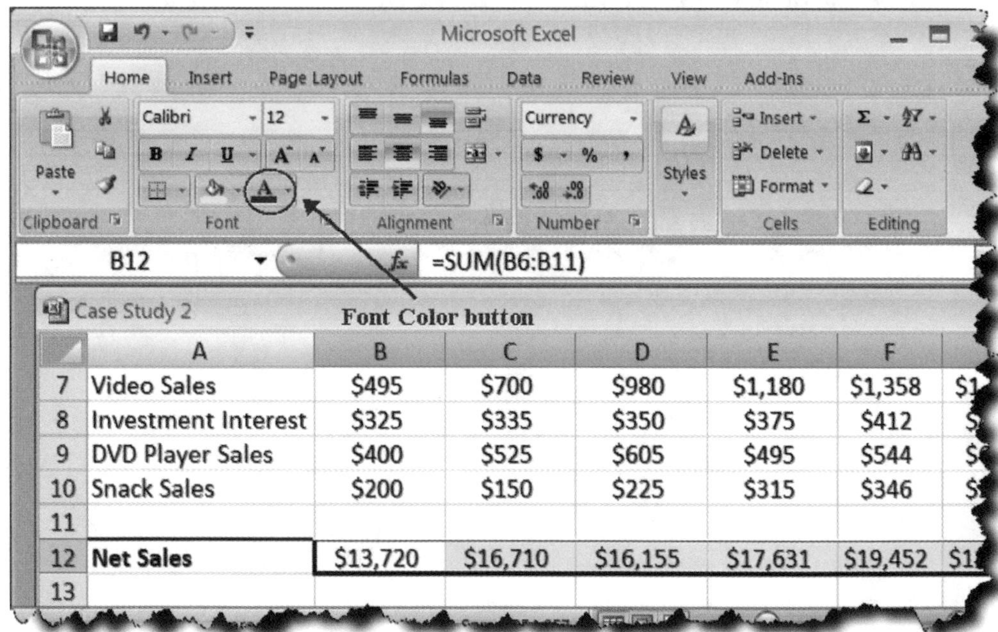

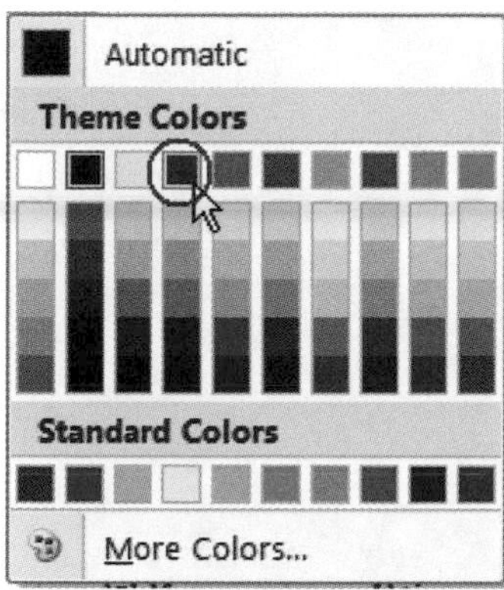

Displays the Font Color Palette.

- Select **dark blue** from the palette (first row, fourth column).

Case Study 2

	A	B	C	D	E	F	
7	Video Sales	$495	$700	$980	$1,180	$1,358	$
8	Investment Interest	$325	$335	$350	$375	$412	$
9	DVD Player Sales	$400	$525	$605	$495	$544	$6
10	Snack Sales	$200	$150	$225	$315	$346	$
11							
12	**Net Sales**	$13,720	$16,710	$16,155	$17,631	$19,452	$1
13							

Changes the font color to dark blue.

- Click the **Save** button.

Saves the current worksheet.

Adding Clip Art

In this section, you will learn how to add Clip Art to your worksheets.

Microsoft Office comes with a collection of images called **Clip Art** that you can add to your Excel worksheets as well as other Microsoft Office documents to make your documents more visually striking. To insert and search for Clip Art, click the **Clip Art** button on the Illustrations group of the **Insert tab** on the Ribbon to display the **Clip Art Task Pane**. To browse Clip Art, enter a **keyword** in the **Search for:** text box, that is to say, a word associated with a particular Clip Art file.

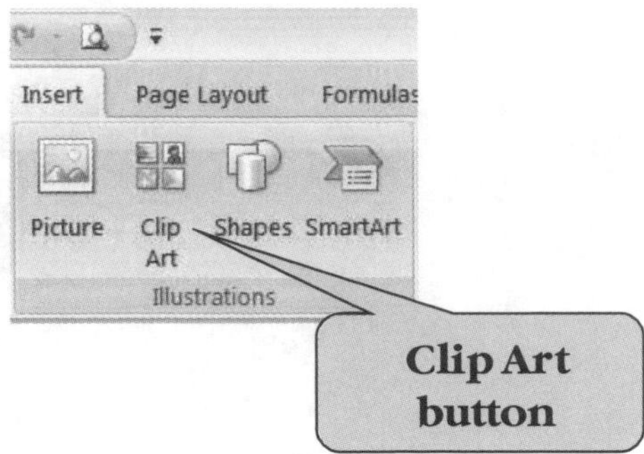

You can also insert Clip Art using the **Microsoft Clip Organizer** (the **"Organize Clips"** link at the bottom of the Clip Art Task Pane). Here, you can browse through clip collections, add Clip Art or catalog your clips.

To Insert Clip Art

1. Activate the worksheet into which you wish to insert Clip Art.
2. Click the **Insert tab** on the Ribbon
3. Click the **Clip Art** button under the Illustrations group to display the Clip Art Task Pane.
4. In the **Search for:** text box, enter a keyword.
5. Click the **Go** button.
6. Click on the desired Clip Art sample in the **Results** list to insert it into your worksheet.

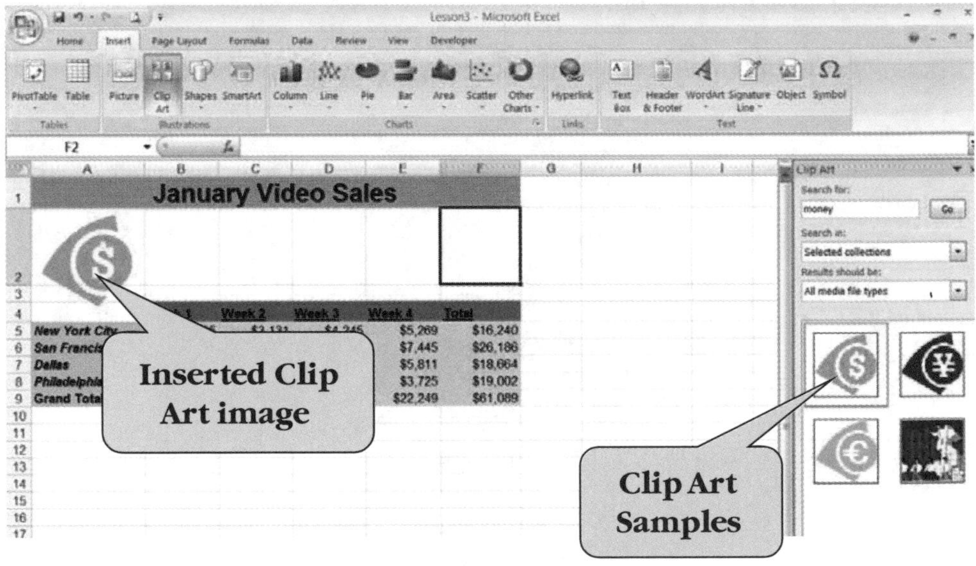

Let's Try It!

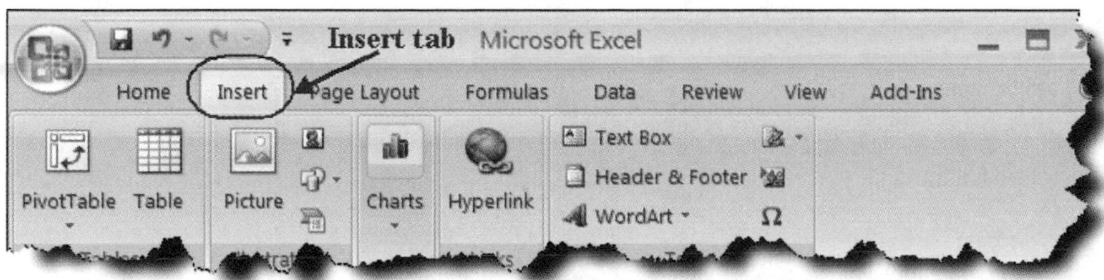

- Click the **Insert tab** on the Ribbon.

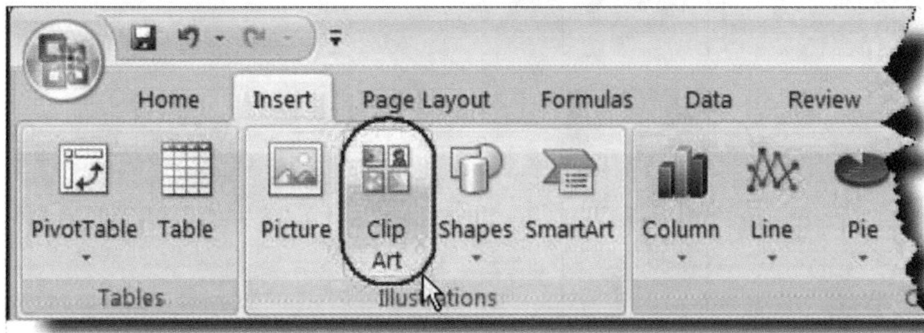

Displays Insert commands and tools.

- Click the **Clip Art button** on the Illustrations group.

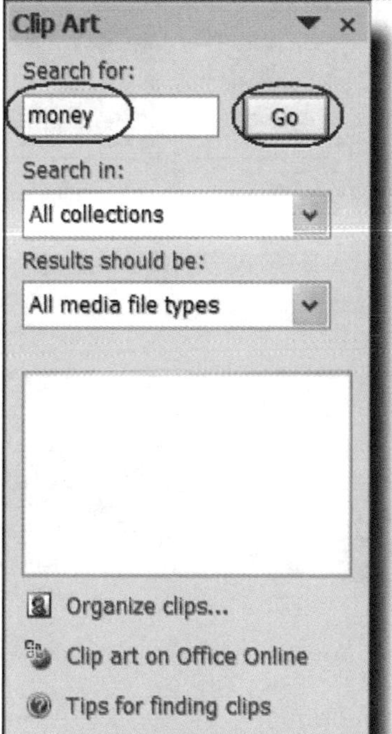

Displays the Clip Art Task Pane.

- In the **Search for:** text box, type in: **money** and then click the **Go** button.

Returns samples of a Clip Art with the keyword money.

- Double-click the sample in the **first row, first column**.

Inserts the Clip Art image into the active worksheet. As the picture came in larger than we would like, we will modify its height.

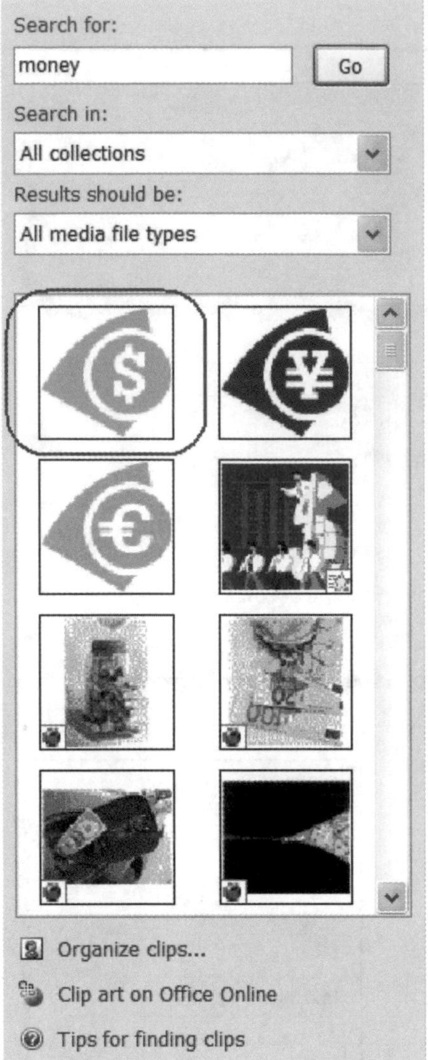

- Click in the **Shape Height** box on the Size group on the Ribbon and type in: **0.6**. Press **Enter**.

Changes the height of the image.

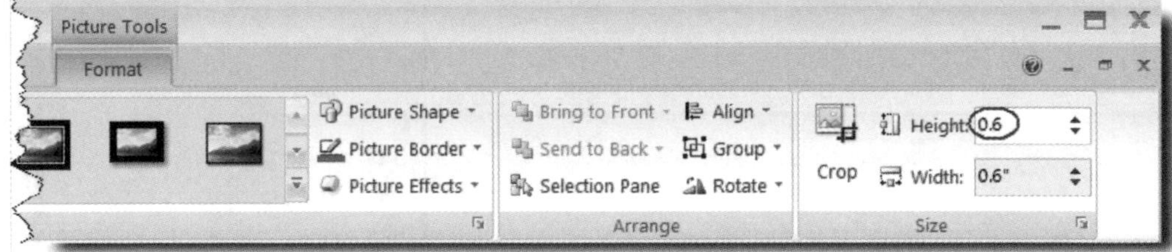

- Click on the image and drag it under column D.

Repositions the image to cell range D1:D3.

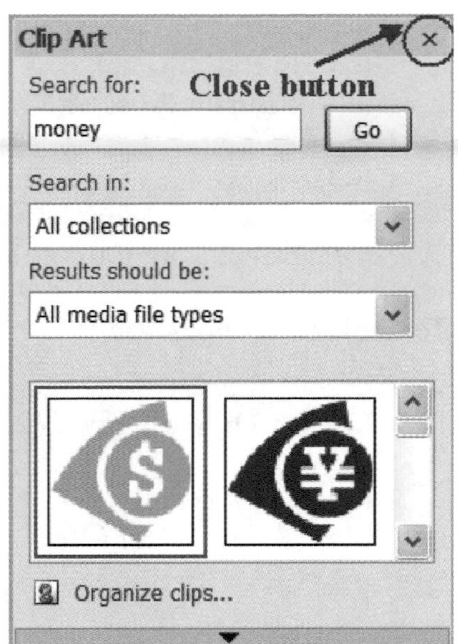

- Click the **Close button** on the Insert Clip Art task pane.

Closes the Clip Art task pane.

- Click the **Save** button.

Saves the current worksheet.

Adding and Deleting Worksheets

In this section, you will learn how to add additional sheets to your workbook and delete existing sheets from your workbook.

When creating a new workbook, Excel provides you with three default worksheets, named Sheet 1, Sheet 2 and Sheet 3. To insert additional worksheets, use the **Insert Worksheet** icon at the end of the sheet tabs. Excel will insert a new worksheet at the very end of the sheet tab. To specify where you want to insert a new sheet, click on the **worksheet tab** of the sheet to the left of which you want to insert a new sheet, **right-click** on the active sheet tab and then choose **Insert** from the contextual menu.

To delete a worksheet, click the **Delete arrow** on the Home Ribbon and choose **Delete Sheet**. Excel will delete the active worksheet.

To Insert a New Worksheet

1. Click the **Insert Worksheet** icon at the end of the sheet tabs
   Or
   Right-click on the sheet tab and to the left of which you want to insert a new sheet and then choose **Insert** from the contextual menu.

Or
Click on the sheet tab and to the left of which you want to insert a new sheet and then **Press Shift + F11**
Or
Click on the sheet tab and to the left of which you want to insert a new sheet, click the **Insert Cells button** on the Home Ribbon and choose **Insert Sheet** from the contextual menu.

To Delete a Worksheet

1. Click on the **tab** of the sheet to be deleted.
2. Click the **Delete arrow** on the Home Ribbon and choose **Delete Sheet**.
   Or
   Right-Click on the tab of the sheet you wish to delete and then choose **Delete** from the contextual menu.

Let's Try It!

- **Right-click** on the **Sheet 1** worksheet tab and select **Insert** from the menu.

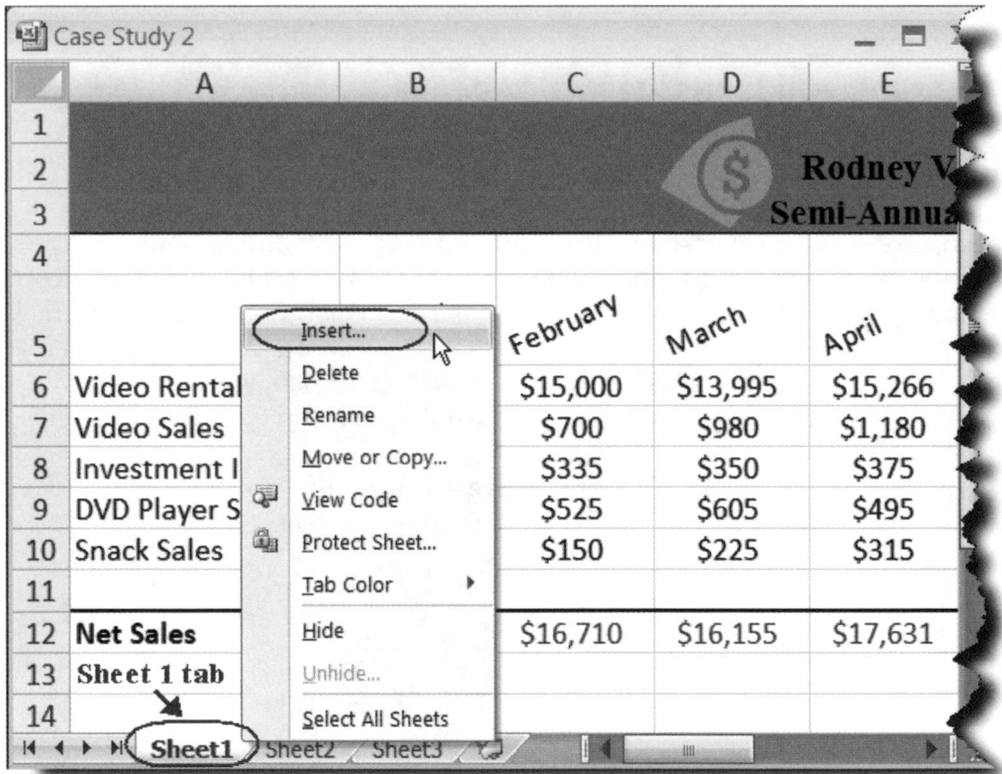

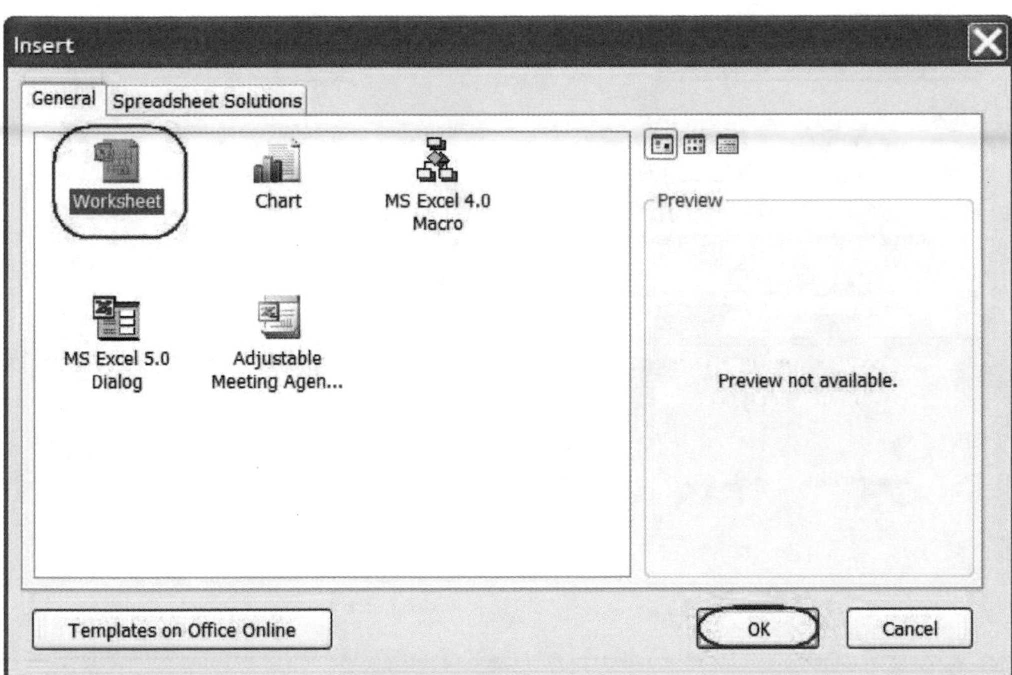

- Select **Worksheet** and click **OK**.

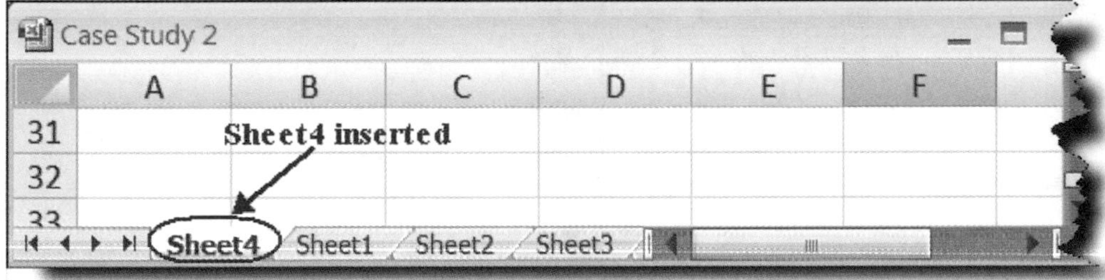

Inserts a new worksheet to the left of the Sheet 1 worksheet.

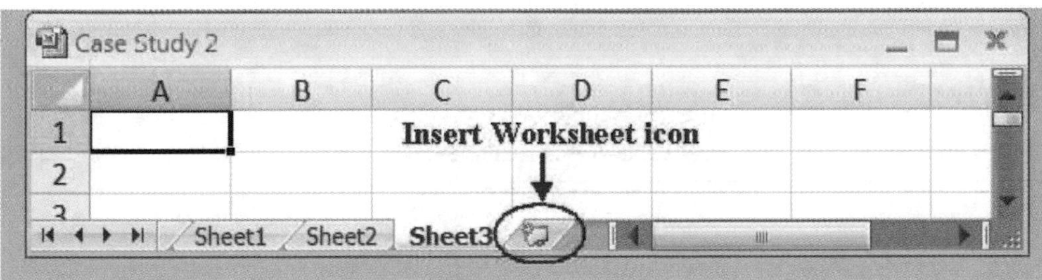

- Click the **Insert Worksheet icon** at the end of the worksheet tabs.

Inserts a new worksheet at the end of the worksheet tabs.

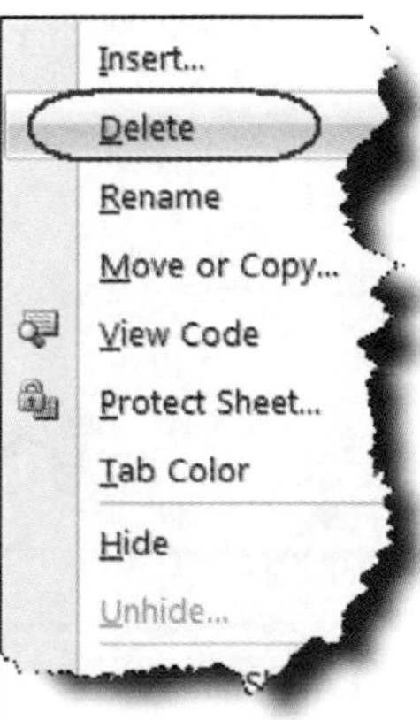

- **Right-click** on the **Sheet 2** worksheet tab and select **Delete** from the menu.

Removes the Sheet 2 worksheet from the workbook.

- Click the **Sheet 5** worksheet tab.

Activates the Sheet 5 worksheet.

- Click the **arrow** on the **Delete button** on the Home Ribbon and choose **Delete Sheet** from the menu.

If there is data in the sheet, it will display a warning box informing that data may exist in the worksheet. You need to press Delete to permanently delete the data from the sheet.

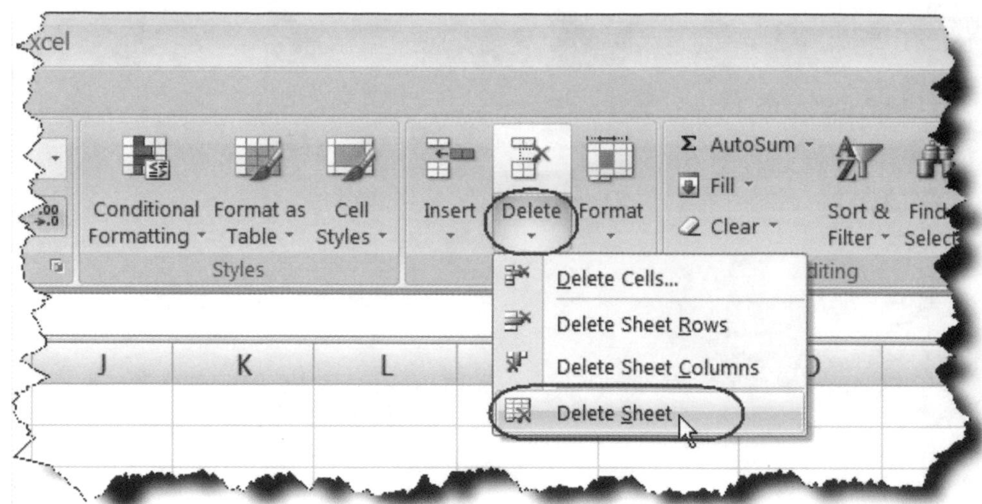

- **Right click** on **Sheet 4** and select **Delete**.

Sheet 4 is deleted.

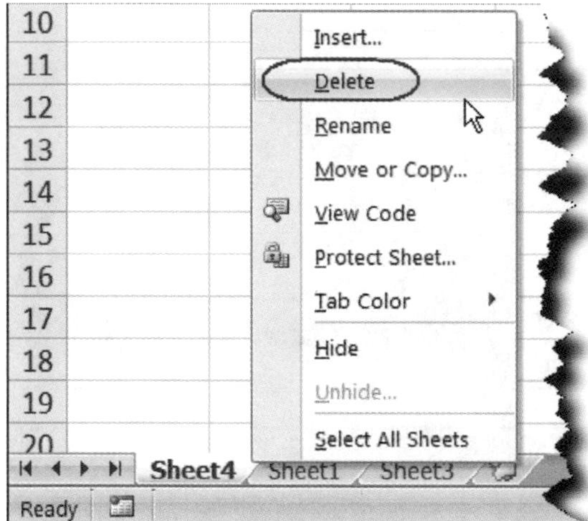

- Repeat the previous step and delete **Sheet 3** as well.
- Click the **Save** button.

Saves the current worksheet.

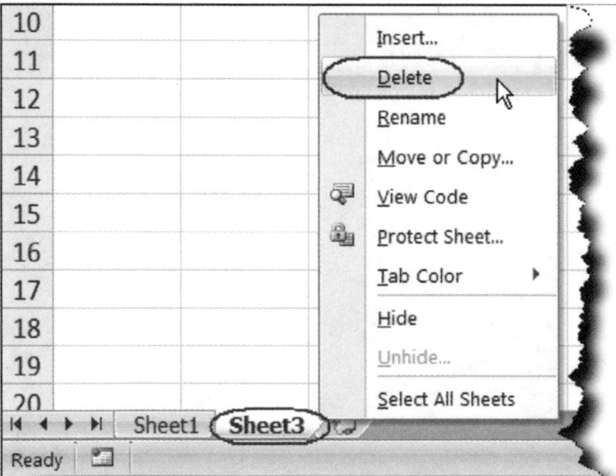

Copying Worksheets

In this section, you will learn how to copy an entire worksheet from one location to another.

You can copy an entire worksheet in Excel, including all of its data and formatting by using the **Move or Copy Sheet** command from the menu. Excel provides a **sequential number** after the worksheet name to allow you to distinguish between the new sheet and the original sheet. For example, if you copied a sheet named June Sales, the new copied sheet would be named June Sales (2). You can copy a worksheet to any workbook that is open, to the current workbook or to a new workbook file. You can also copy a worksheet manually by pressing and holding the **Ctrl** key and then dragging the worksheet tab with your mouse to the new location.

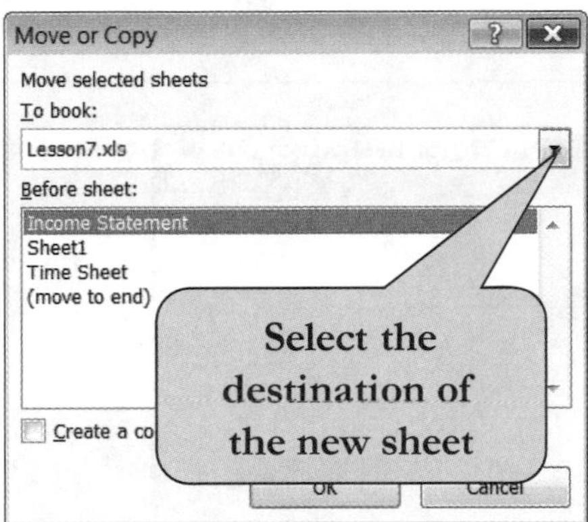

To Copy a Worksheet

1. Click on the **Worksheet tab** of the sheet you wish to copy.
2. Right-click and choose **Move or Copy** from the contextual menu.
   Or
   Click the **Format** button on the Home Ribbon under the Cells group and choose **Move or Copy Sheet** under the Organize Sheets category.
3. Select the **Workbook** into which you wish you copy the worksheet (the default is the current workbook).
4. Select the location of the new sheet in the **Before Sheet** list box.
5. Click the check box next to **Create a Copy** to copy the worksheet rather than move it.
6. Click **OK**.
   Or
1. Press and hold the **Ctrl** key, and then drag with your mouse to the desired location).

Let's Try It!

- Click the **Sheet 1** worksheet tab.

Activates the Sheet 1 worksheet.

- Right-click and choose **Move or Copy Sheet** from the contextual menu.

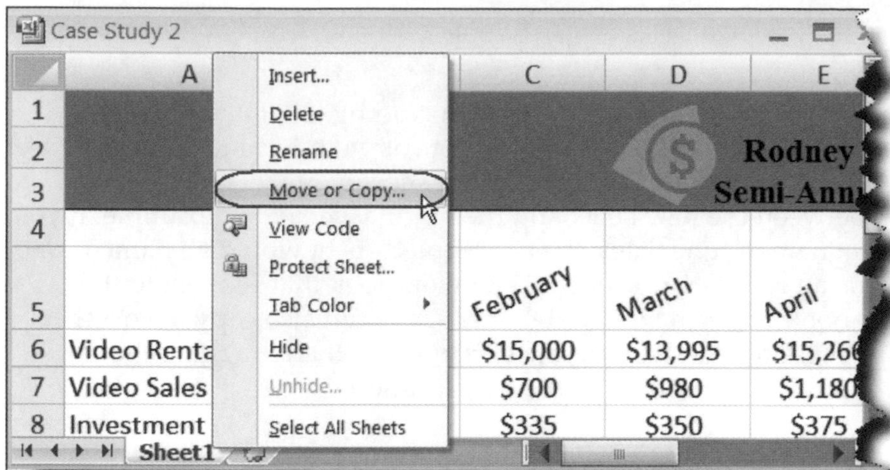

Displays the Move or Copy dialog box.

- Select **Case Study 2.xlsx** under the **To book:** combo box.

Selects the current workbook as the destination for the new sheet.

- Select **(move to end)** from the **Before sheet:** list box.

Sets the position of the new sheet to the right of the Sheet 1 worksheet.

- Click the **Create a copy** checkbox.

Selects the copy option.

- Click **OK**.

Closes the Move or copy dialog box and makes a copy of the Sheet 1 worksheet.

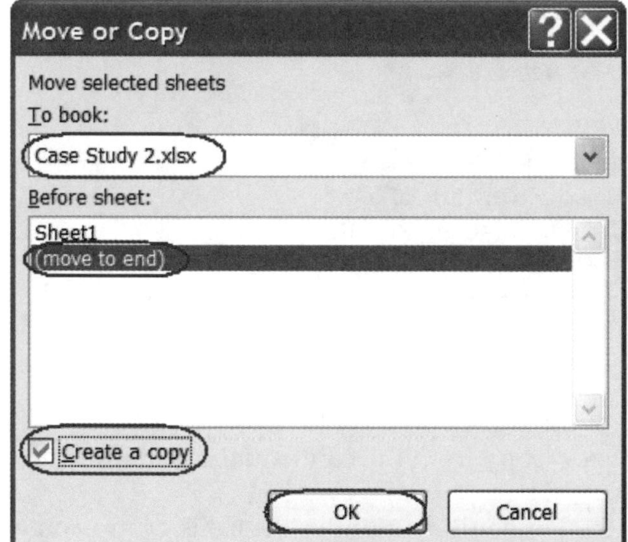

- **Repeat previous steps** and create another copy of Sheet 1.
- Click the **Save** button.

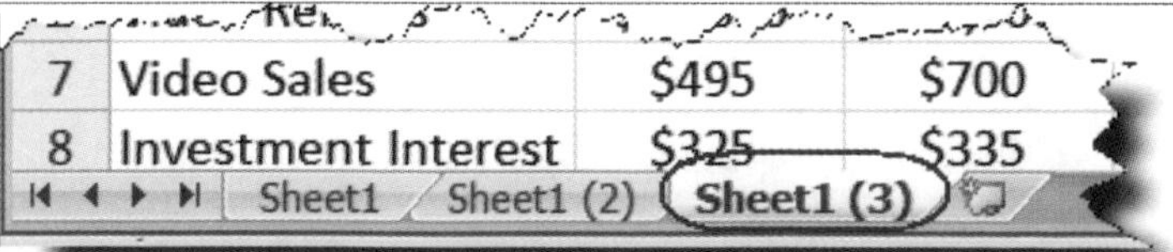

Renaming Worksheets

In this section, you will learn how to rename an existing worksheet in your document.

Excel by default provides the generic names of Sheet 1, Sheet 2 and Sheet 3, etc. to worksheets. To rename a worksheet, **double-click on the tab** of the worksheet to receive the new name and then type the desired name. Another way to rename a worksheet is to **right-click on the worksheet tab**, select **Rename** from the contextual menu, and then type the new name.

To Rename a Worksheet

1. **Double-click** on the worksheet tab of the sheet to be renamed.
   Or
   Right-click on the worksheet tab of the sheet to be renamed and then choose **Rename** from the contextual menu.
   Or
   Click the **Format** button on the Home Ribbon under the Cells group and choose **Rename Sheet** under the Organize Sheets category.
2. Type the new name.
3. Press **Enter**.

TYPE IN NEW NAME WHEN SHEET TAB IS HIGHLIGHTED

Let's Try It!

- Double-click the **Sheet1 (2)** worksheet tab.

Activates the Sheet 1 (2) worksheet tab.

- Type **Forecast**

Enters the new name for the worksheet.

- Press **Enter**.

Confirms the entry.

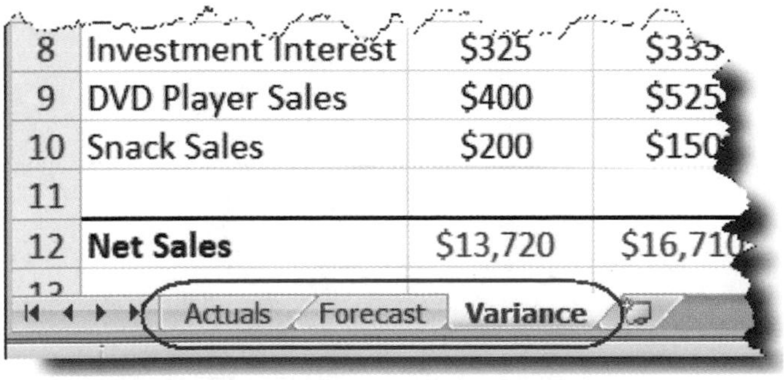

- Repeat previous steps to **rename Sheet1** to **Actuals** and **Sheet1 (3)** to **Variance**.
- Click the **Save** button.

Saves the active workbook.

Grouping Worksheets

In this section, you will learn how to group worksheets together.

Excel allows you to work on several worksheets simultaneously by **grouping** them together. When worksheets are grouped, any formatting, data entry or changes you make to the active sheet are made to every sheet in the group. Grouping sheets is a quick way to apply formatting to or delete several sheets at once. When multiple worksheets are grouped together, [Group] appears in the title bar on top of the worksheet window.

To Group Worksheets

1. Click the tab of the first worksheet in your group.
2. Hold down the **Ctrl** key and then click the tabs of any additional sheets you want to include in your group.
3. To group **all worksheets**, right-click on any worksheet tab and choose **Select All Sheets** from contextual menu.

To Ungroup Worksheets

1. Click the tab of any worksheet **not** in your group
   Or
   Right-click the tab of any grouped worksheet and select **Ungroup Sheets** from the pop-up menu.

Let's Try It!

- Click on the **Actuals** worksheet tab.

Makes Actuals the active worksheet.

- Press and hold the **Ctrl** key and click on the **Forecast** sheet tab and then on **Variance** sheet tab.

Adds the Forecast's and Variance worksheet to the group. Notice that the worksheet tab is highlighted in white and the word [Group] appears in the Title Bar.

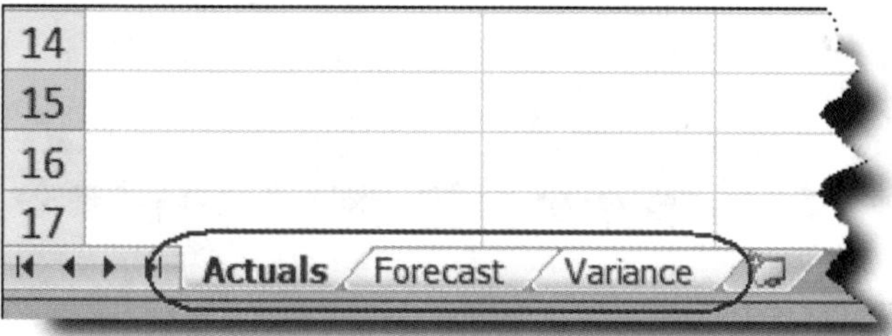

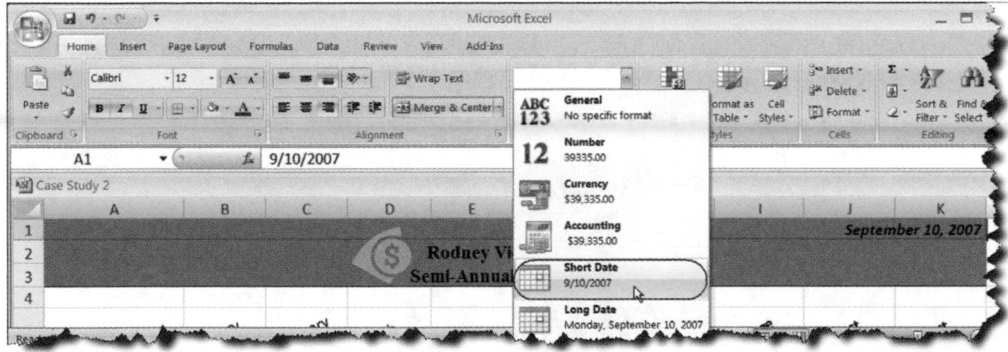

- Click on cell **A1**.

Selects the cell.

- Click the **arrow** on the **Date button** on the Home Ribbon and choose **Short Date** from the menu.

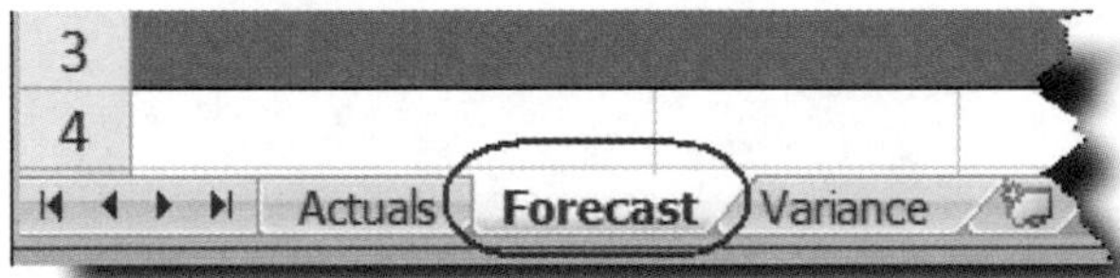

- Click on the **Forecast** worksheet tab and observe the changes.

Ungroups the selected sheets and makes the Forecast worksheet the active sheet.

- Click on the **Variance** worksheet tab and observe the changes.

Switches to the Variance worksheet. The changes that we made in "Actuals" worksheet were also made in "Forecast" and "Variance" worksheet.

- Click the **Save** button.

Saves the active workbook.

Changing Worksheet Tab Colors

In this section, you will learn how to change the tab color of your worksheets to make them stand out.

Excel provides the option of **applying colors** to your worksheet tabs. This can be useful if you have a large workbook comprised of many worksheets. You might want to give each worksheet in a particular group a different color. The tab color only appears when the worksheet is not the active worksheet.

To Change the Worksheet Tab Color

1. Select the tab of the worksheet or worksheets to which you wish to apply a color.
2. Click the **Format** button on the Home Ribbon under the Cells group and choose **Tab Color** under the Organize Sheets category.

Or
Right-click on the tab for the worksheet or worksheet group and then choose **Tab Color** from the contextual menu.

3. Choose a color from the **Format Tab Color Palette**.

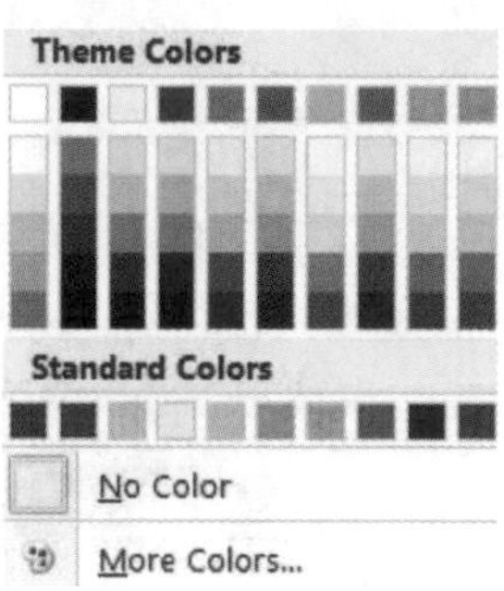

To Remove a Tab Color

1. Select the tab of the worksheet or worksheets whose color you wish to remove.
2. Click the **Format** button on the Home Ribbon under the Cells group and choose **Tab Color** under the Organize Sheets category.
   Or
   Right-click on the tab of the worksheet or worksheet group and then choose **Tab Color** from the pop-up menu.
3. Choose **No Color** from the **Format Tab Color Palette**.

Let's Try It!

- Click on the **Actuals Sheet** worksheet tab.

Makes Actuals the active worksheet.

- Press and hold the **Ctrl** key and click on the **Forecast Sheet** tab and then on **Variance Sheet** tab.

Adds the Forecast and Variance worksheets to the group.

- Click the **Format** button under the **Cells group** and point to **Tab Color**.

Displays the Format Tab Color Palette.

- Choose **Orange** from the color palette (third color in the Standard Colors area).

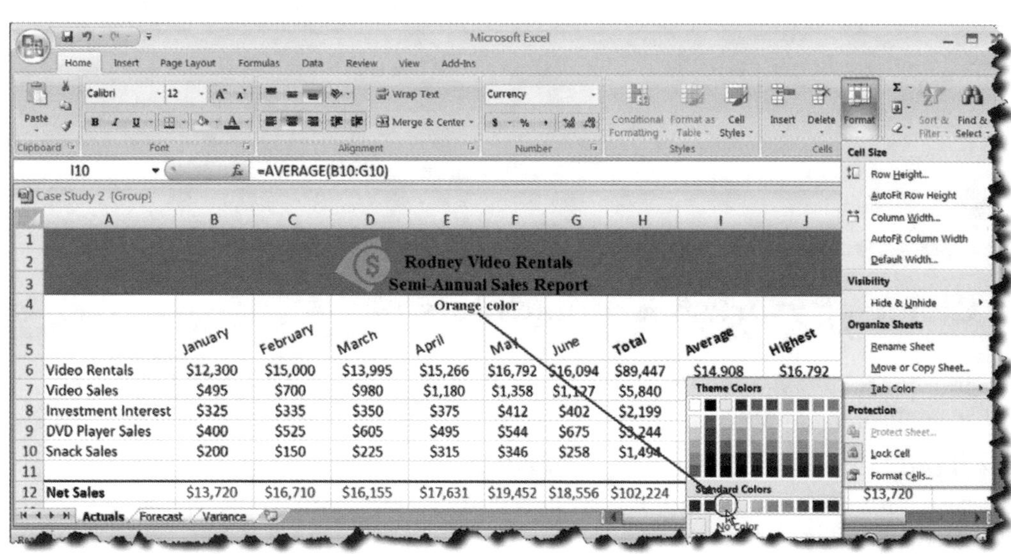

Applies orange to the tab color.

- Click the **Save** button.

Saves the active document.

Using 3-D Formulas & References

In this section, you will learn how to create 3-D References in Excel.

When you want to create a formula which uses data from several worksheets, you create a **3-D Formula**. A 3-D Formula is created using **3-D References**, that is to say, references to cells in a different worksheet. To create a 3-D Reference, the format is:

'Sheet Name'!Cell Name

For example, suppose we have three sheets named **2000, 2001 and Yearly Totals**. In the Yearly Totals sheet, we want to calculate the sum of the values in cell C18 from both the 2000 and 2001 sheets. Thus, our formula in the Yearly Totals worksheet would be:

='2001'!C18 + '2000'!C18

To use a function such as **SUM**, **AVERAGE**, etc. in our 3-D formula, the format is:

=SUM('Sheet1:Sheet2'!C12:C35)

You can create your 3-D formula yourself by typing it into the cell or you can manually select the appropriate worksheets and cells to include in your formula.

To Create a 3-D Formula

1. In the cell where you want your formula to display, type = and the beginning of the formula, such as: **=Sum(**
2. **Group** the worksheets whose data you will include in the formula if the data is in the same cell address in each worksheet.
3. **Select** the cell or cell range to include in the formula.
4. **Type** the remainder of the formula if applicable and press **Enter**.

B7 ='Quarter 1'!E6+'Quarter 2'!E6

	A	B
1	Semi-Annual Income Sta	
2		
3		
4	*Revenue*	
5		
6		
7	Video Rentals	$ 90,909.50
8	Video Sales	$ 6,188.75
9	Investment Interest	$ 2,228.75
10	DVD Player Sales	$ 3,138.75
11	Snack Sales	$ 1,598.75
12	Net Sales	$ 104,064.50

In the Let's Try It exercise, we will first edit the values of the Target sheet and then create a formula using the grouping method and a formula by manually selecting the cell range in each sheet to be included in the formula. Using the Grouping method, we need only select the cell range in one of the grouped sheets.

Let's Try It!

- Click the **Forecast** worksheet tab.

Ungroups the worksheets and makes the Forecast worksheet the active sheet.

- Replace the values of range B6:G10 as shown below. You do not need to include dollar sign ($) while entering these values. Dollar sign will be added by itself.

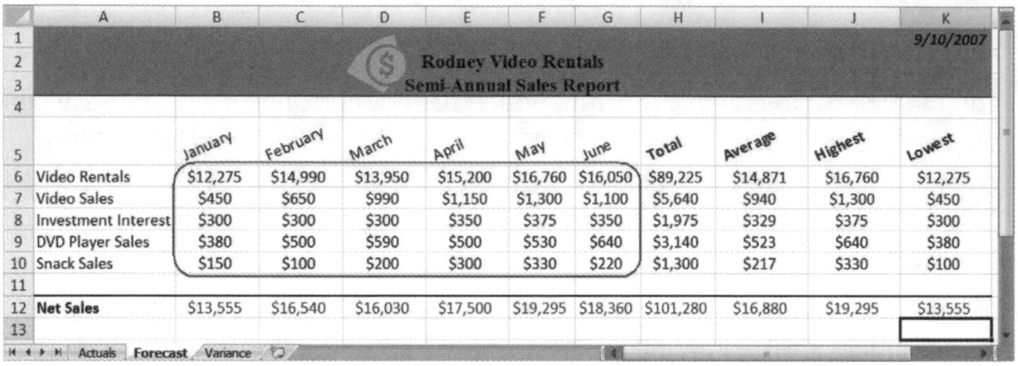

	A	B	C	D	E	F	G	H	I	J	K
1											9/10/2007
2					Rodney Video Rentals						
3					Semi-Annual Sales Report						
4											
5		January	February	March	April	May	June	Total	Average	Highest	Lowest
6	Video Rentals	$12,275	$14,990	$13,950	$15,200	$16,760	$16,050	$89,225	$14,871	$16,760	$12,275
7	Video Sales	$450	$650	$990	$1,150	$1,300	$1,100	$5,640	$940	$1,300	$450
8	Investment Interest	$300	$300	$300	$350	$375	$350	$1,975	$329	$375	$300
9	DVD Player Sales	$380	$500	$590	$500	$530	$640	$3,140	$523	$640	$380
10	Snack Sales	$150	$100	$200	$300	$330	$220	$1,300	$217	$330	$100
11											
12	**Net Sales**	$13,555	$16,540	$16,030	$17,500	$19,295	$18,360	$101,280	$16,880	$19,295	$13,555
13											

Actuals | Forecast | Variance

- Click the tab for the **Variance** worksheet

Makes the Variance worksheet the active worksheet.

- Click in cell **B6** and type: **=**

Begins a new formula in cell B6.

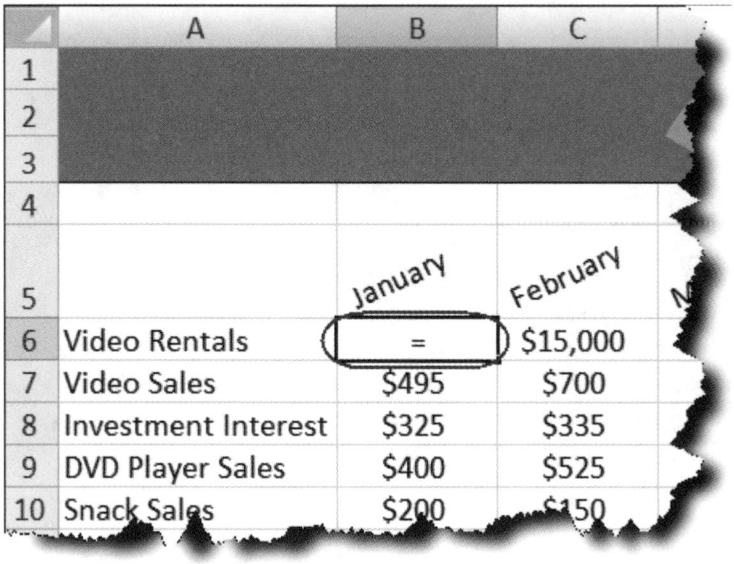

	A	B	C
1			
2			
3			
4			
5		January	February
6	Video Rentals	=	$15,000
7	Video Sales	$495	$700
8	Investment Interest	$325	$335
9	DVD Player Sales	$400	$525
10	Snack Sales	$200	$150

PMT =Actuals!B6

	A	B	C	D
1				
2				
3				
4				
5		January	February	March
6	Video Rentals	$12,300	$15,000	$13,9
7	Video Sales	$495	$700	$98
8	Investment Interest	$325	$335	$35
9	DVD Player Sales	$400	$525	$60
10	Snack Sales	$200	$150	$22
11				
12	**Net Sales**	$13,720	$16,710	$16,
13				

Actuals Forecast Variance

Point

- Click the **Actuals** Tab

Switches to the Actuals Worksheet.

- Click in cell **B6**

Activates cell B6 in the Actuals worksheet.

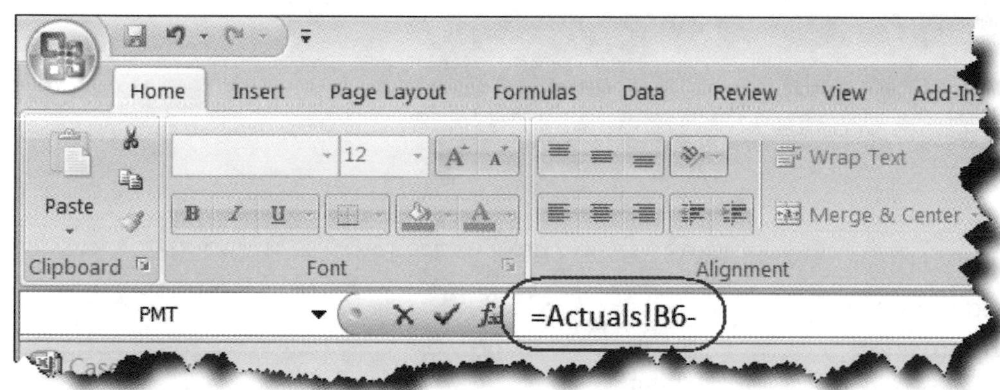

- Click in the **Formula Bar** after **B6** and type: **-**

Adds a minus sign after the first part of the formula.

- Click the **Forecast** sheet Tab.

Switches to the Forecast Worksheet.

- Select cell **B6**.

Activates cell B6 in the Forecast worksheet.

- Click in the **Formula bar** after **B6** and press **Enter**.

PMT | =Actuals!B6-Forecast!B6

	A	B	C	D	E
1					
2					Rodney
3					Semi-Ann
4					
5		January	February	March	April
6	Video Rentals	$12,275	$14,990	$13,950	$15,2
7	Video Sales	$450	$650	$990	$1,1
8	Investment Interest	$300	$300	$300	$35
9	DVD Player Sales	$380	$500	$590	$50
10	Snack Sales	$150	$100	$200	$30
11					
12	**Net Sales**	$13,555	$16,540	$16,030	$17,50
13					

Actuals | Forecast | Variance

Point

- Click on the **Variance** worksheet and verify the formula.
- Select the cell **B6** and then click the **Fill Handle** on the lower right of cell **B6** and drag to cells **B10**

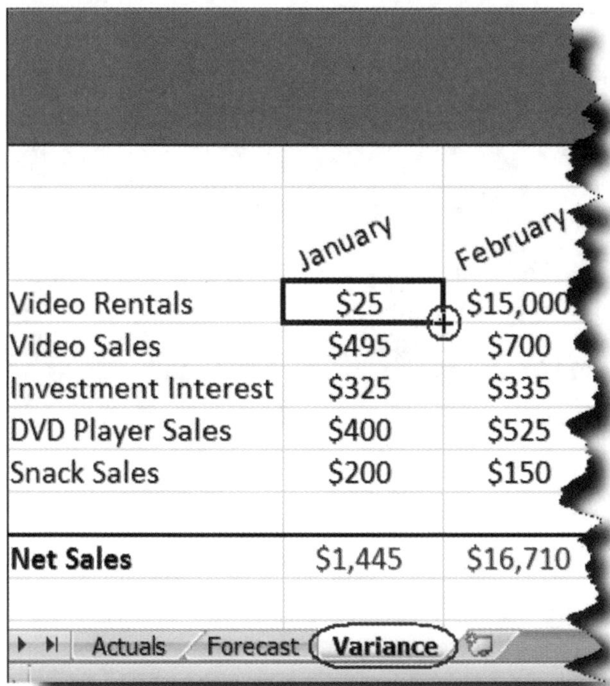

	January	February
Video Rentals	$25	$15,000
Video Sales	$495	$700
Investment Interest	$325	$335
DVD Player Sales	$400	$525
Snack Sales	$200	$150
Net Sales	$1,445	$16,710

Actuals | Forecast | Variance

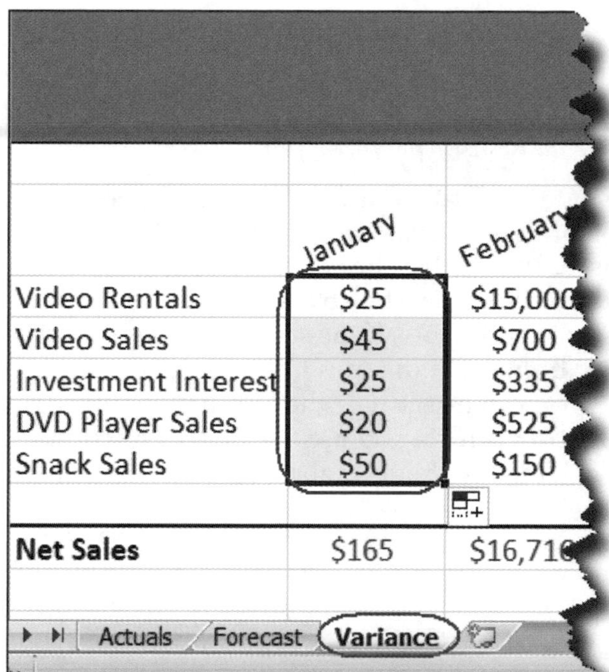

Copies the formula to cells G10.

Rodney Video Rentals
Semi-Annual Sales Report

	January	February	March	April	May	June	Total
Video Rentals	$25	$10	$45	$66	$32	$44	$222
Video Sales	$45	$50	($10)	$30	$58	$27	$200
Investment Interest	$25	$35	$50	$25	$37	$52	$224
DVD Player Sales	$20	$25	$15	($5)	$14	$35	$104
Snack Sales	$50	$50	$25	$15	$16	$38	$194
Net Sales	$165	$170	$125	$131	$157	$196	$944

- While cell range B6:B10 is selected, click the **Fill Handle** on the lower right of cell **B10** and drag to cells **G10**

Copies the formula to cells G10.

Rodney Video Rentals
Semi-Annual Sales Report
9/10/2007

	January	February	March	April	May	June	Total	Average	Highest	Lowest
Video Rentals	$25	$10	$45	$66	$32	$44	$222	$37	$66	$10
Video Sales	$45	$50	($10)	$30	$58	$27	$200	$33	$58	($10)
Investment Interest	$25	$35	$50	$25	$37	$52	$224	$37	$52	$25
DVD Player Sales	$20	$25	$15	($5)	$14	$35	$104	$17	$35	($5)
Snack Sales	$50	$50	$25	$15	$16	$38	$194	$32	$50	$15
Net Sales	$165	$170	$125	$131	$157	$196	$944	$157	$196	$125

Note that formulas in Total, Average, Highest, and Lowest calculate on new values.

- Click the **Save** button.

Saves the Active workbook.

Using the IF Function

In this section, you will learn how to perform a calculation based on given conditions using the IF function.

Using the **IF function**, you can tell Excel to evaluate a condition and perform one of two calculations based on that condition. The two calculations are based on whether the condition is true or false. For example, if the sales of a store was greater than 5000, you could give the manager a $2,000 bonus (condition is true); if the sales were less than $5000, the manger would get a $500 bonus (condition is false).

You can either type the IF function directly into the cell or click the **Insert Function button** and use the **Insert Function dialog box**.

Using the example above, the format of the IF function is:

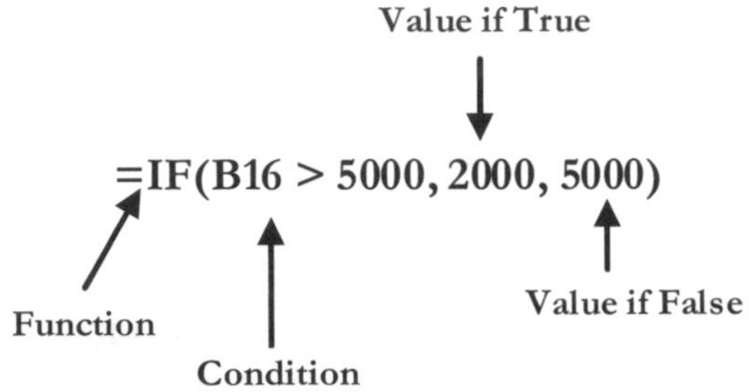

To Use the IF Function

1. Activate the cell in which you want to place the formula.
2. Type: **=IF(**
3. Enter the **condition** for which to test, followed by a **comma.**
4. Enter the **value if the condition is true** followed by a **comma.**
5. Enter the **value if the condition is false.**
6. Type **)** close the formula.
7. Press the **Enter** key to verify the formula.

Let's Try It!

- Click on the **Variance** tab.

Ensures that Variance is the active worksheet.

- Click in cell **A14.**

Activates cell A14.

- Click the **Bold button** on the Home Ribbon and type: **Bonus Rate**

Bolds the text and enters it in cell A14.

- Click in cell **B14.**

Activates cell B14.

- Type: **10%**

Enters 10% in B14 cell.

	A	B	C
10	Snack Sales	$50	$50
11			
12	**Net Sales**	$165	$170
13			
14	**Bonus Rate**	10%	
15			

PMT = IF(B12 > 0, B12*B14, 0)

	A	B	C	D	E
10	Snack Sales	$50	$50	$25	$15
11					
12	**Net Sales**	$165	$170	$125	$131
13					
14	**Bonus Rate**	10%			
15					
16	**Bonus**	= IF(B12 > 0, B12*B14, 0)			
17					

- Click in cell **A16**.

Activates cell A16.

- Click the **Bold button** on the Home Ribbon and type: **Bonus**

Bold the text and enters it in cell A16.

- Click in cell **B16.**
- Type: **= IF(B12 > 0, B12*B14, 0)**

Enters the formula in cell B16.

Note: "If" function includes the absolute cell reference (B14). Refer the relative and absolute reference section for more information on it.

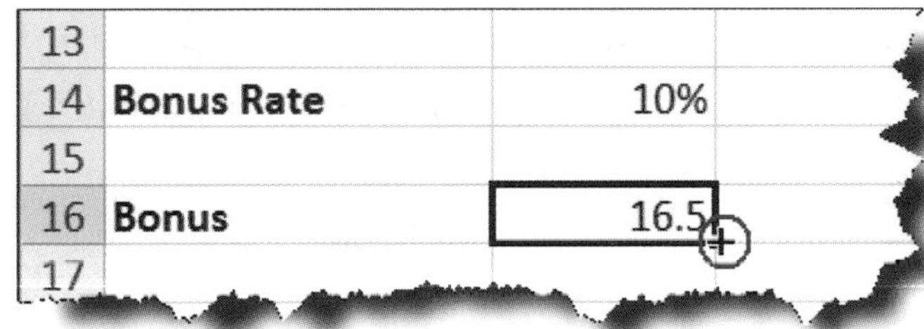

- Press **Enter**.

Verifies the formula.

- Select **B16** and drag and copy it to cell **H16**.

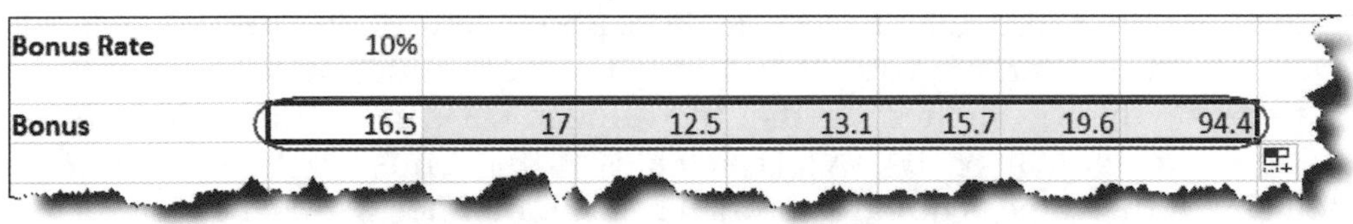

Bonus Rate 10%
Bonus 16.5 17 12.5 13.1 15.7 19.6 94.4

Copies the formula to the cell range C16:H16.

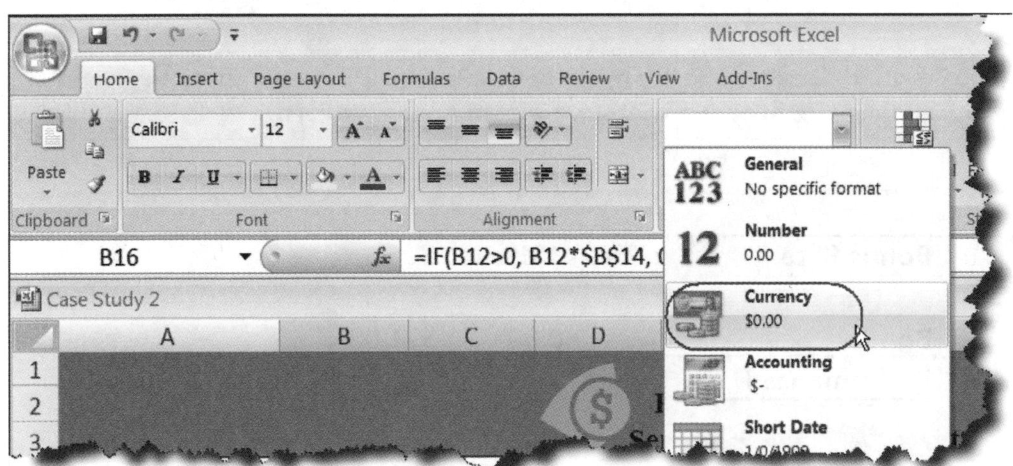

- While cell range B16:H16 is selected, click on the **General** button and select **Currency** from the drop down menu.
- Click the **Save** button.

Saves the active document.

Using Nested Functions

In this section, you will learn how to use Nested functions (functions within functions).

At times, you may want Excel to perform a calculation based on **more than one** condition. For example, if a store has more than $5,000 in sales, the manager receives a 20% bonus. But if a store has more than $7,000 in sales, the manager would receive a 35% bonus. However, if the store has sales less than $5,000, the manager would only receive a 5% bonus. To accomplish this, we need to use a **Nested IF Statement**.

In a nested function, Excel reads the function from left to right. The first part of the formula consists of the first condition and the value if true. If the value does not meet the true condition, Excel continues to the next IF function and evaluates the second condition. The **last part** of the formula will contain the value if all conditions are **false**.

A nested IF function is illustrated below:

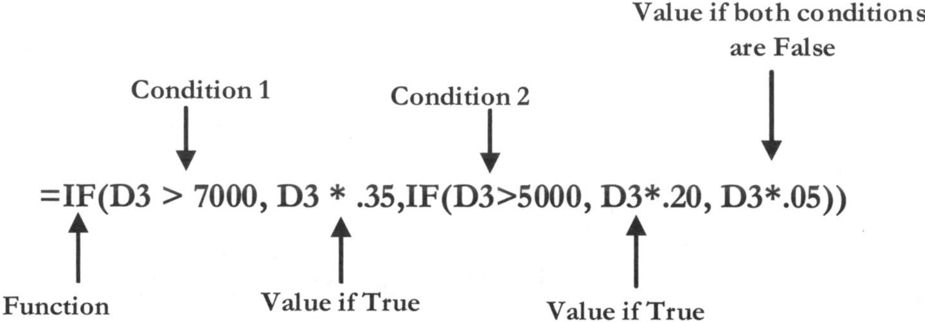

In the above example, we are looking at the value in cell D3. If the value is greater than $7000, then Excel calculates a 35% bonus (.35 * the value of cell D3). If the value is not greater than $7000, Excel continues on to the next IF statement which evaluates whether the value in D3 is greater than 5000. If the value is greater than $5000, Excel calculates a 20% bonus (.20 * the value of cell D3). If the value is not greater than 5000 or, in other words, both of the conditions are false, Excel continues on and instead calculates a 5% bonus.

Note that because the formula contains two IF statements, we need to terminate the formula with two closing parenthesis.

Let's Try It!

- Click in cell **A17**.

Activates cell A17.

- Click the **Bold button** on the Home Ribbon and type: **Performance**

Bolds the text and enters it in cell A17.

14	**Bonus Rate**	10%	
15			
16	**Bonus**	$0.00	$21.00
17	**Performance**		
18			

PMT =IF(B12=0, "Equals", IF(B12<0, "Below", "Above"))

	A	B	C	D	E	F	G	H
10	Snack Sales	$50	$50	$25	$15	$16	$38	$194
11								
12	**Net Sales**	$165	$170	$125	$131	$157	$196	$944
13								
14	**Bonus Rate**	10%						
15								
16	**Bonus**	$16.50	$17.00	$12.50	$13.10	$15.70	$19.60	$94.40
17	**Performance**	=IF(B12=0, "Equals", IF(B12<0, "Below", "Above"))						
18								
19								

- Click in cell **B17**.

Activates cell B17.

- Type: **=IF(B12=0, "Equals", IF(B12<0, "Below", "Above"))**
- Press the **Enter** key.

Verifies the formula.

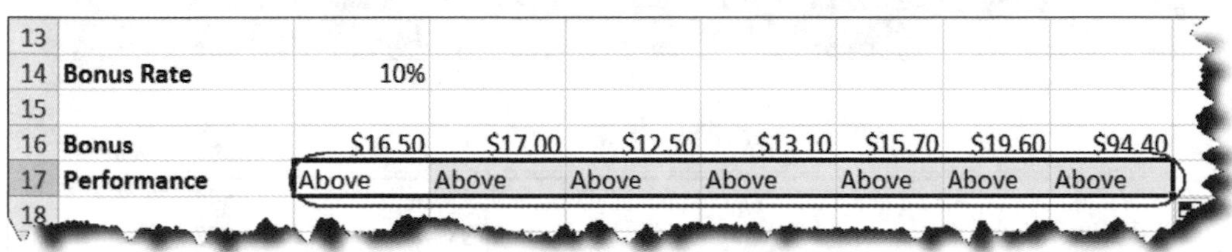

	A	B	C	D	E	F	G	H
13								
14	**Bonus Rate**	10%						
15								
16	**Bonus**	$16.50	$17.00	$12.50	$13.10	$15.70	$19.60	$94.40
17	**Performance**	Above	Above	Above	Above	Above	Above	Above
18								

- Select the cell **B17** and copy the formula down to cell **H17**.

Copies the formula to the cell range C17:H17.

- Click the **Save** button.

Saves the active document.

Creating a Chart

This section will guide you through the process of creating a new chart in Excel

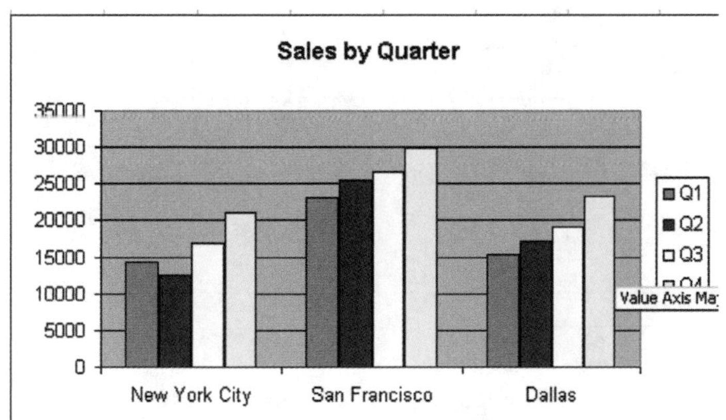

A **chart** is a graphical representation of data and is an effective way to illustrate relationships and/or trends in data. Charts can be a powerful tool when used to provide data analysis and data comparisons. For example, you may wish to illustrate the change in sales trends from one quarter to the next—or the productivity of one store compared to another.

Excel can create a wide variety of charts—bar charts, line charts, pie charts, column charts, etc. and Excel 2007 makes creating charts easy with new charting tools. To insert a chart, select the data you want to include in your chart, click the chart type button on the Insert Ribbon and then choose the chart type you want from the gallery.

To Create a Chart

1. Select the data you wish to include in your chart.
2. Click the **Insert tab** on the Ribbon.
3. Click the button for the chart type you want on the **Chart Types** group on the Ribbon. Click **All Chart Types** to display the entire Chart Types gallery.
4. Click the **Chart Type** you want.

Let's Try It!

- Click on the **Variance** tab.

Ensures that Variance is the active worksheet.

- Select the cell range **A6:G10**.

Selects the cell range to be included in the chart.

	A	B	C	D	E	F	G	H
1								
2					Rodney Video Rentals			
3					Semi-Annual Sales Report			
4								
5		January	February	March	April	May	June	Total
6	Video Rentals	$25	$10	$45	$66	$32	$44	$222
7	Video Sales	$45	$50	($10)	$30	$58	$27	$200
8	Investment Interest	$25	$35	$50	$25	$37	$52	$224
9	DVD Player Sales	$20	$25	$15	($5)	$14	$35	$104
10	Snack Sales	$50	$50	$25	$15	$16	$38	$194
11								
12	**Net Sales**	$165	$170	$125	$131	$157	$196	$944

- Click the **Insert** tab on the Ribbon.

Displays Insert commands and tools.

- Click the **Column button** on the Charts group.

Displays a gallery of all Column Chart types.

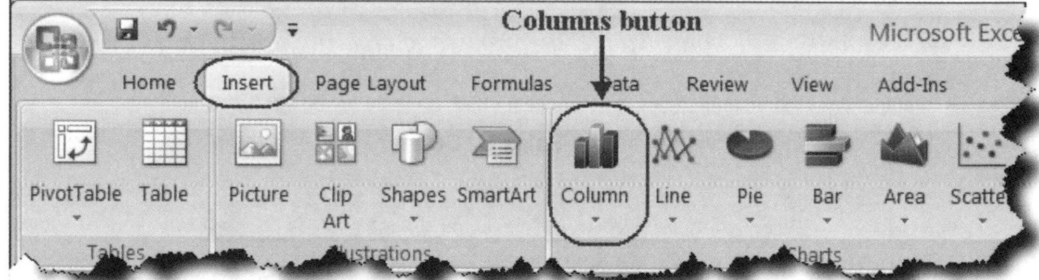

- Click the **Clustered Column** chart type (the first selection under the 2-D Column category).

Inserts an embedded clustered column chart in the active worksheet.

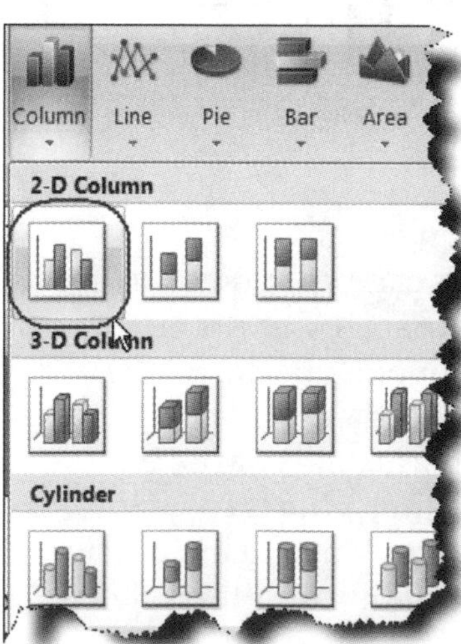

Moving a Chart

In this section, you will learn how to move a chart to different areas of your worksheet.

When you insert a chart in an existing worksheet (instead of its own worksheet), the chart is embedded and can then be moved and resized like a standard graphical object. Most of the time, you will not be satisfied with the placement of the chart in the worksheet and will want to move it to a more desirable location. In order to move a chart, you must first activate it by clicking on the chart's white area or on the border of the chart object. Do not click on an object such as the plot area (the gray section) or a data series as you will select that particular area rather than the entire chart. Once the chart is activated, click inside the chart area, hold down your mouse button and drag the chart to the new location.

Another option for moving a chart is using the **Cut and Paste** method. Select the chart and click the **Cut** button on the Home Ribbon (or press Ctrl + X). Then, select the cell where you wish to paste your chart and click the **Paste** button on the Home Ribbon (or press Ctrl + V).

To Move a Chart by Dragging

1. Click the white **Chart Area** or on the chart's border to select the chart.
2. Click in the chart area and hold down your left mouse button.
3. Drag the chart to the new location on your worksheet.

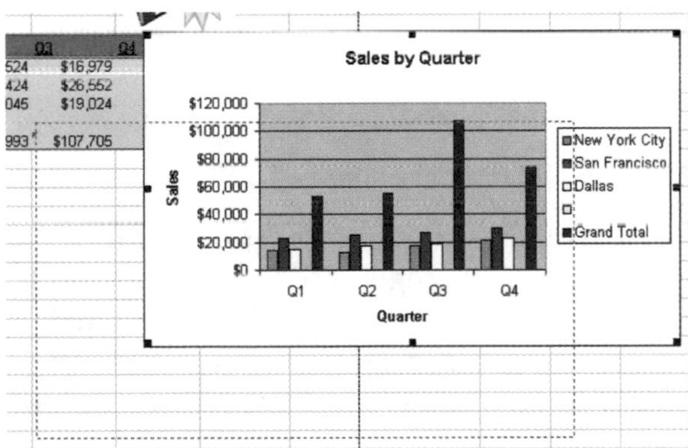

To Move a Chart Using Cut and Paste

1. Click the chart to **select** it.
2. Click the **Cut** button on the Home Ribbon (or press Ctrl + X)
3. Select the cell where you wish to paste the chart.
4. Click the **Paste** button on the Home Ribbon (or press Ctrl + V)

Let's Try It!

- Click anywhere on the **White Chart Area** and hold down your left mouse button.

Activates the chart and enters drag mode.

- Drag the chart until the left corner of the chart's border (which appears as you drag) rests in cell **A20** as shown.

Positions the chart with the left corner in cell A20.

- Release the mouse button.

Drops the chart in the new worksheet area.

- Click the **Save** button.

Saves the current workbook.

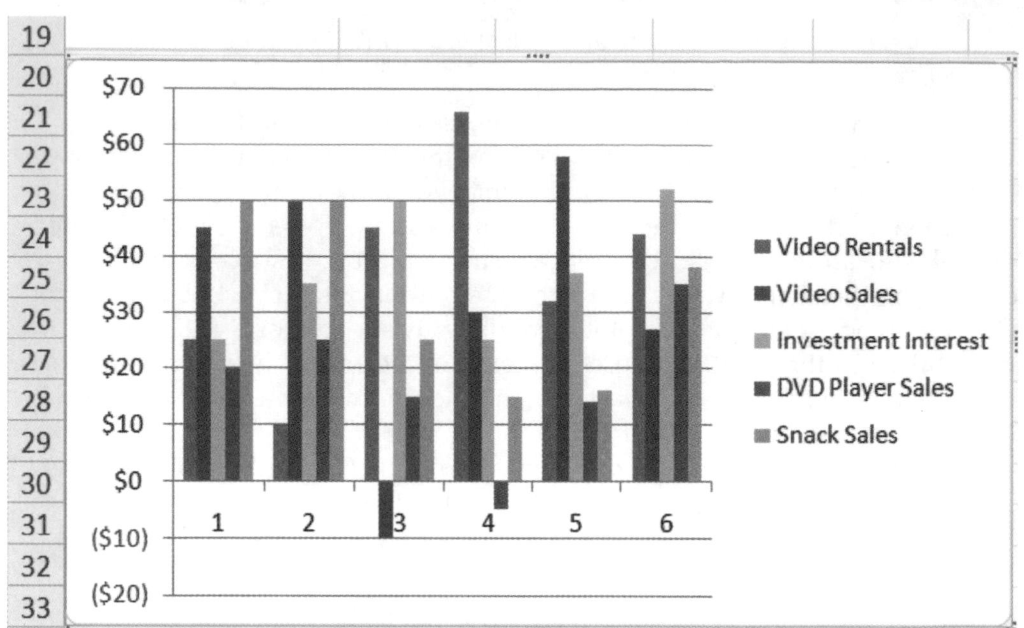

Resizing a Chart

In this section, you will learn how to increase or decrease the size of a chart.

You can change the size of an embedded chart by holding your mouse pointer over any of the chart's sizing handles until the pointer transforms into a double arrow. Then, drag either inwards or outwards, depending on whether you want to decrease or increase the size of the chart. As you drag, you will see a dark bordered outline which represents the size of chart.

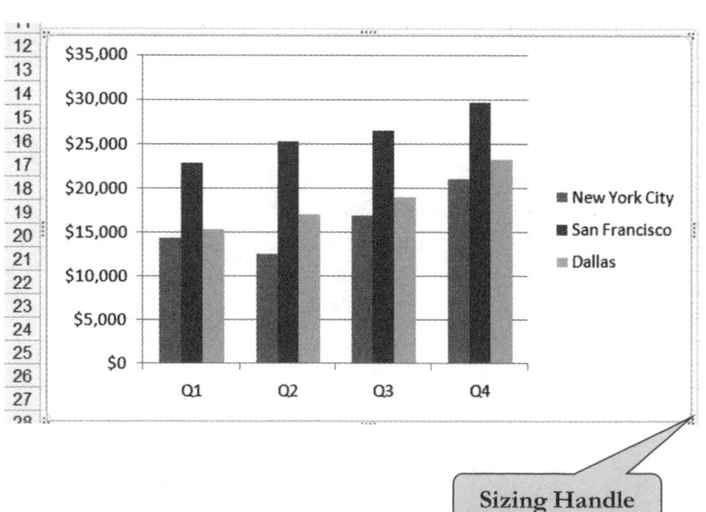

To Resize a Chart

1. Select the chart by clicking on the **white chart area**.
2. Position your mouse pointer over a sizing handle until the pointer transforms into a double arrow.
3. Click the sizing handle and drag it inward to reduce the size of the chart or outward to increase the size of the chart.
4. Release the mouse button when the chart is the desired size.

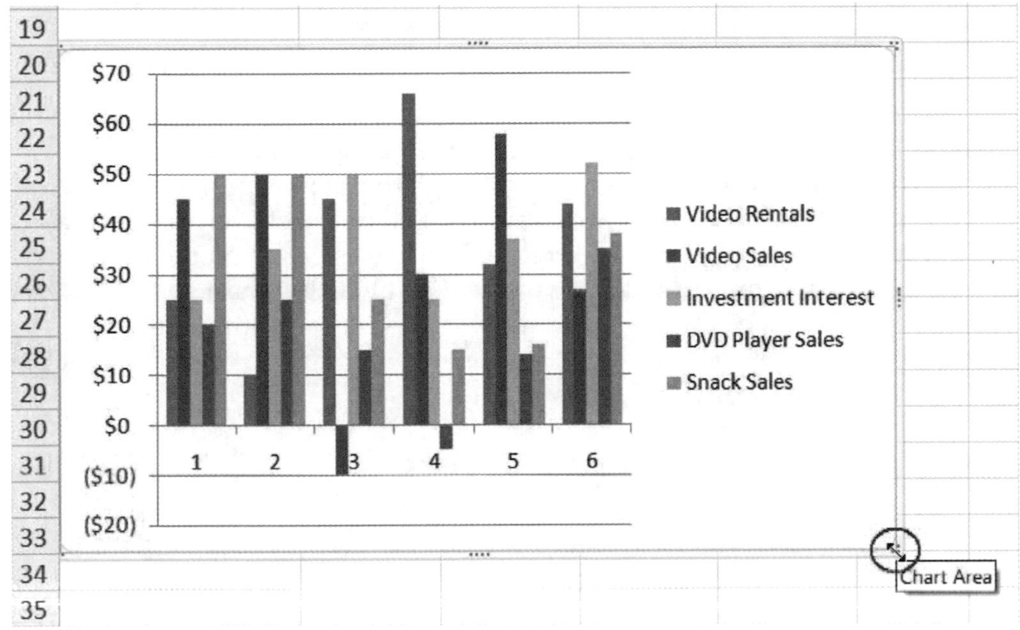

- Click anywhere on the **White Chart Area**.

Activates the chart and enters drag mode.

- Position your mouse pointer over the **lower right sizing handle** until the pointer transforms into a double arrow.

Enters sizing mode.

- **Click and drag** the chart **outward and down** until the lower right edge of the chart is **flush with column K40**.

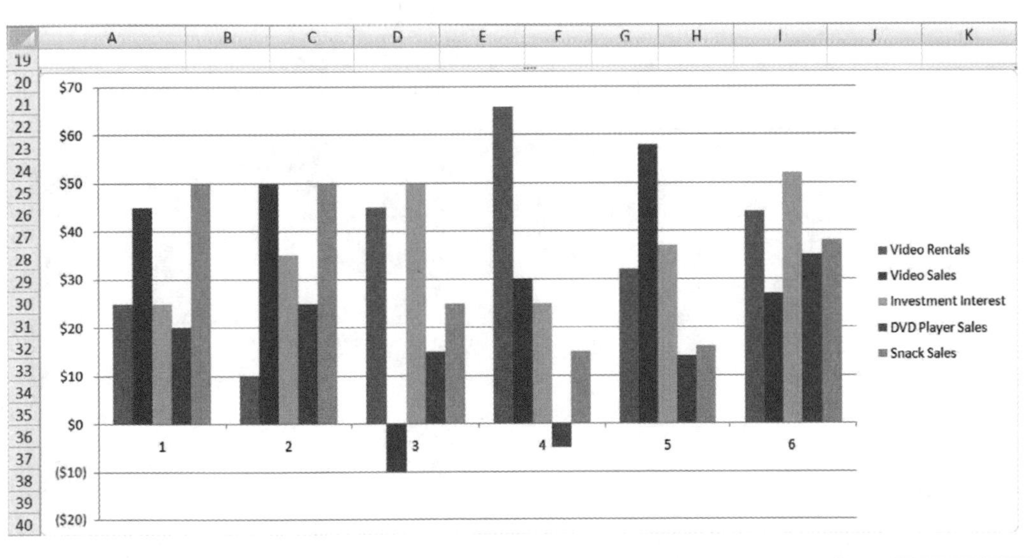

Resizes the chart outward.

- Release the mouse button.

Completes the process of resizing.

Changing the Layout and Style

In this section, you will learn how to change the layout and style of a chart.

After creating your chart, three contextual Ribbons appear under Chart Tools when the chart is selected: **Design, Layout** and **Format**, from where you can format your chart, apply various styles and change the chart layout.

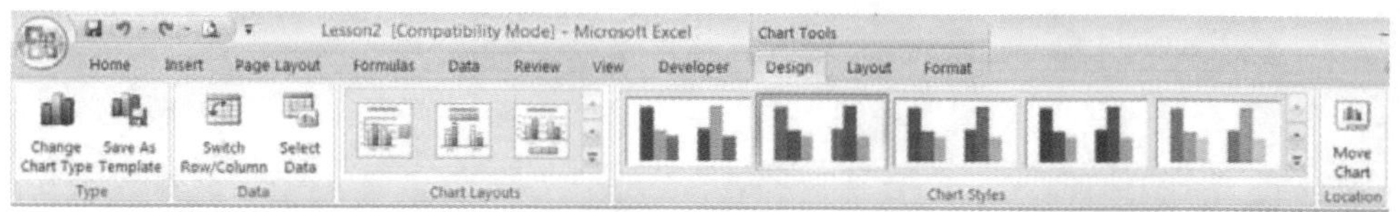

From the contextual **Design Ribbon**, you can apply various predefined chart layouts and chart styles as well as change the chart type and modify the existing chart data. There are a wide variety of chart styles both in 2-D and 3-D formats that you can apply from the Chart Styles group on the Ribbon. Click the **More button** to display a gallery of all available chart styles.

For each chart type, you can also apply a preset layout from the **Chart Layouts** group. Again, clicking the More button on the Chart Layouts group will display a gallery of all available layouts.

Changing the Layout and Style of a Chart

1. Click the chart to select it.
2. To change a chart layout or style, click the contextual **Design tab** under Chart Tools. Make your desired selection from the Chart Layout and/or Chart Style group.
3. Click the More button on the Chart Layout or Chart Style group to display additional layout or style thumbnails.

Let's Try It!

- Click on the border of the chart.

Selects the chart and displays the contextual Design, Layout and Format Ribbons.

- Click the **Design** tab under **Chart Tools** on the Ribbon.

Switches to chart design options.

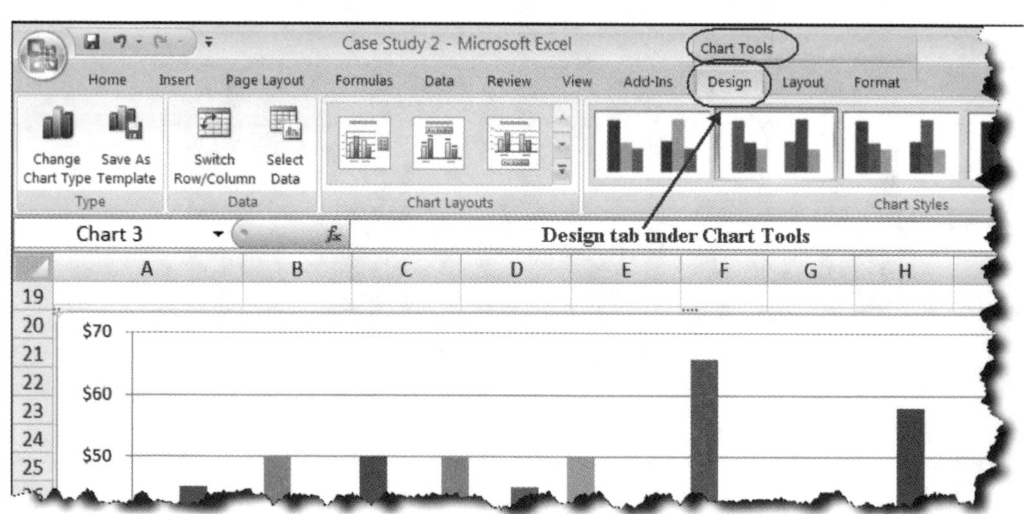

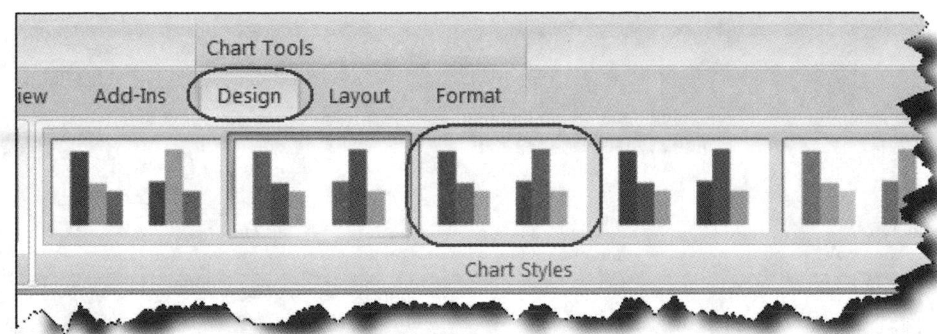

- On the **Chart Layouts** group, click the **third thumbnail** as shown.

Applies the Layout 3 layout to the chart.

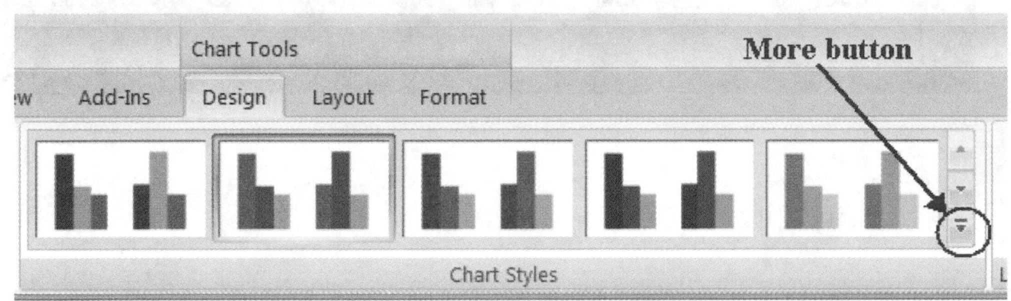

- Click the **More** button on the **Chart Styles** group.

Displays the Chart Styles gallery.

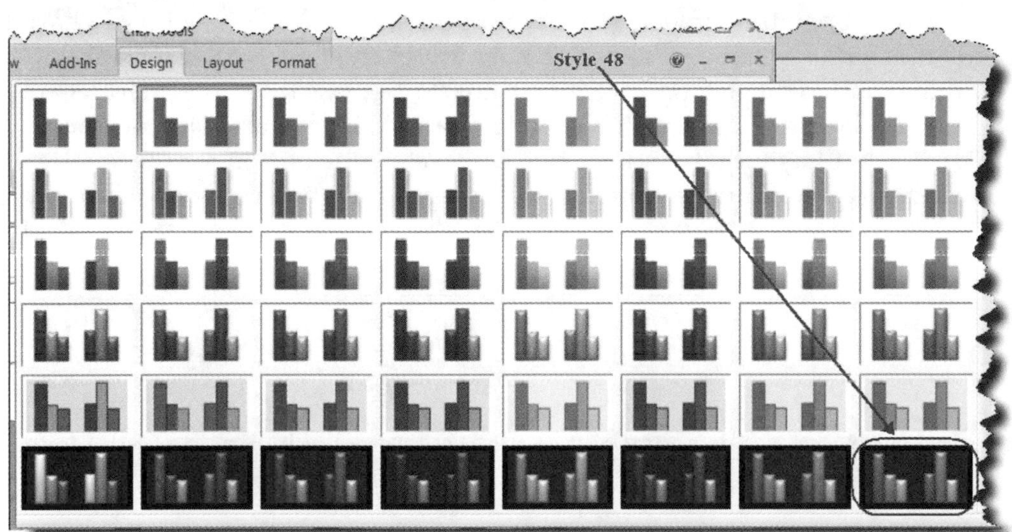

- Click the **last style** in the **last row** (Style 48).

Applies Style 48 to the selected chart.

- On the **Chart Layouts** group, click the **first thumbnail**.

Changes the chart layout back to Layout 1.

• Click the **Save** button.

Saves the active document.

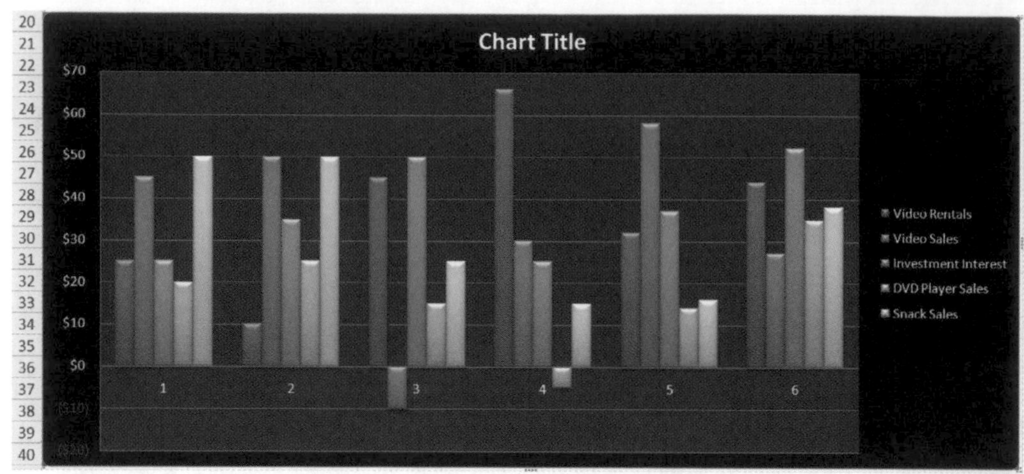

Labeling Chart Elements

In this section, you will learn how to add labels to a chart's elements.

After creating your chart, you may wish to customize the various elements of your chart, depending on the chart layout you have chosen. Labeling a chart element inserts a small text box on or near the chart element. For instance, you may wish to display or reposition a chart title, axis titles, the chart legend or add data labels or the data table. To add or modify a chart element, click the contextual **Layout tab** under Chart Tools, click the button for the label you want to add or modify on the Labels area and then make your selection.

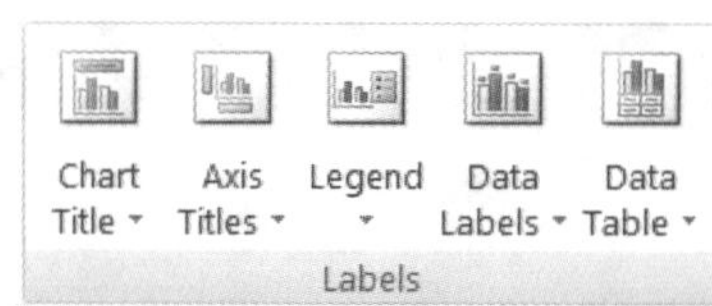

You can then format the actual text of the labels by clicking inside of the text box, drag selecting the existing text and then typing your changes.

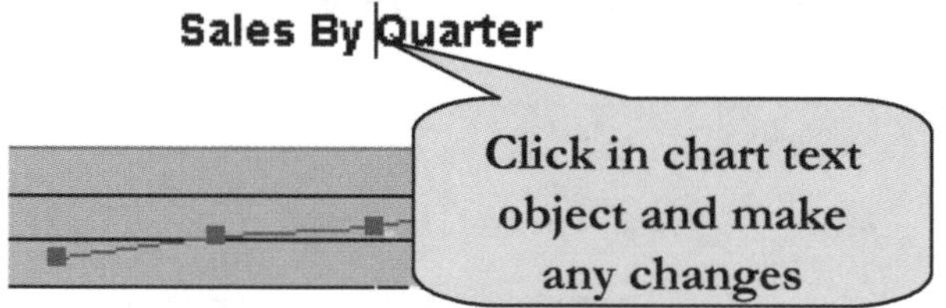

To Add/Modify a Chart's Labels

1. Click the chart to select it.
2. Click the contextual **Layout tab** under Chart Tools.
3. Click the button for the label you want to modify on the Labels group.
4. Select the option you want from the list.

To Change Chart Text

1. Click on the **Text Object** you wish to edit.
2. Click inside of the selected object and begin typing.

Let's Try It!

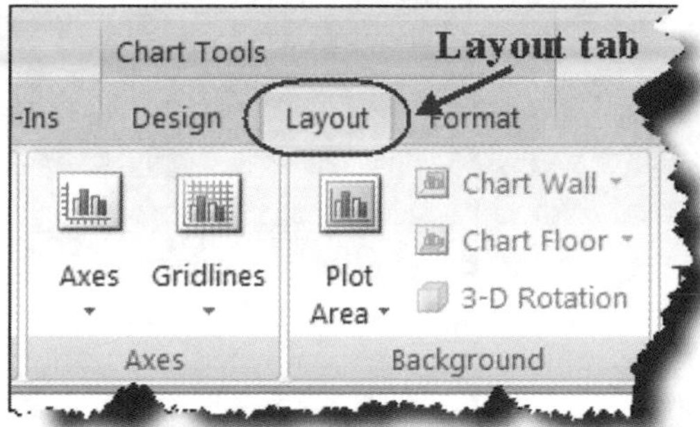

- Click on the border of the chart.

Selects the chart and displays the contextual Design, Layout and Format Ribbons.

- Click the **Layout tab** under Chart Tools.

Displays the Chart Layout Ribbon.

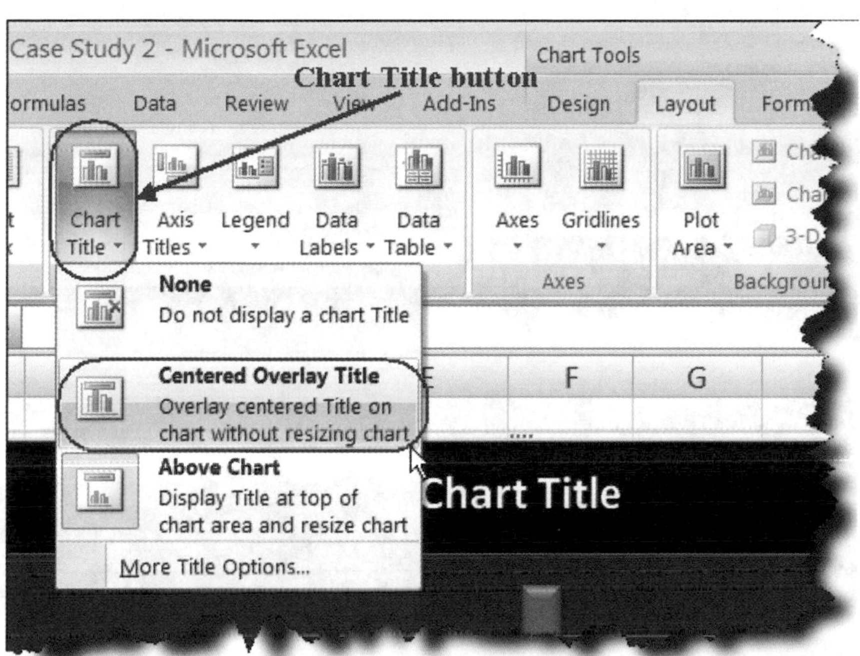

- Click the **Chart Title** button on the Ribbon and choose **Centered Overlay Title** from the menu.

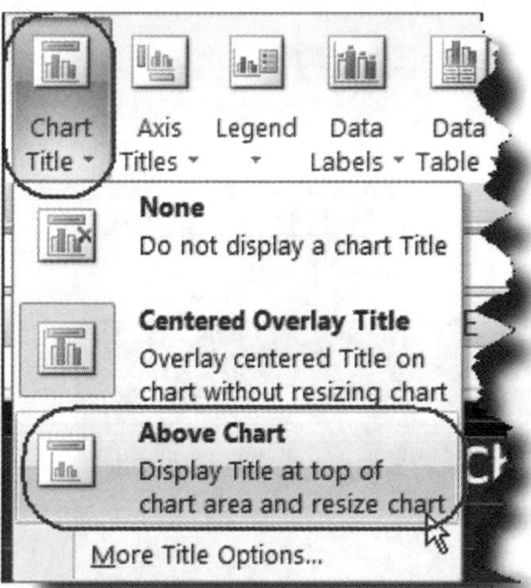

Inserts a Chart Title text box on the chart area.

- Click the **Chart Title** button again on the Ribbon and choose **Above Chart** from the menu.

Inserts a Chart Title text box above the chart and resizes the chart to accommodate it.

- Select the text in the **Chart Title** box, type: **Sales by Month** as shown.

Enters a title for the chart in the chart title box.

- Click the **Axis Titles** button on the Ribbon, point to **Primary Horizontal Axis Title** and choose **Title Below Axis** from the menu.

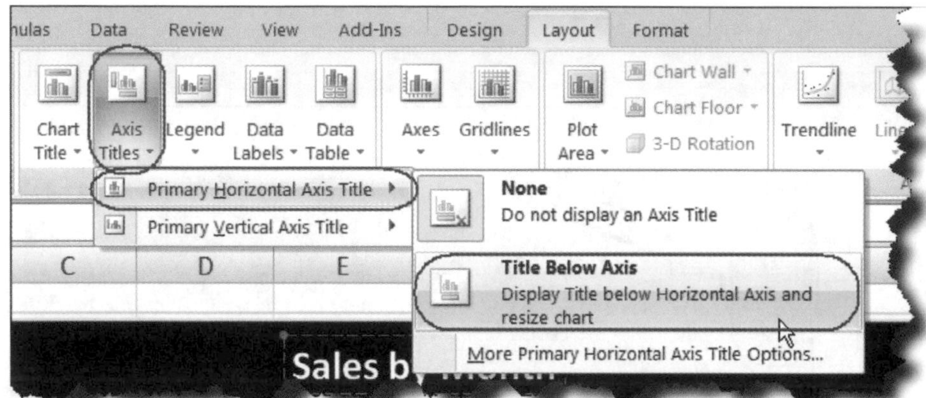

Inserts a text box below the Category X axis.

- Select the text in the **X-Axis Title** box, type: **Month**.

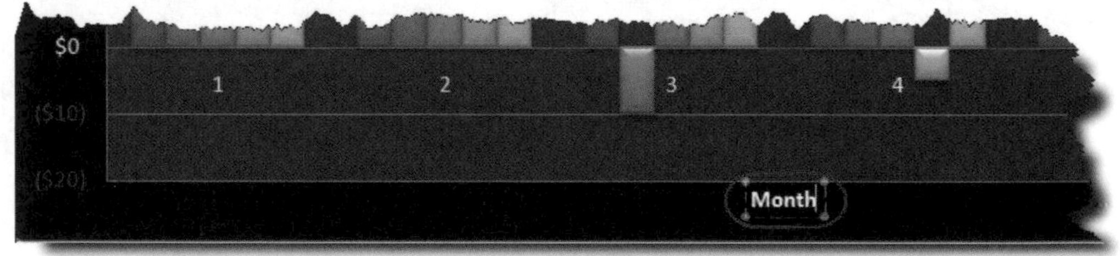

Enters the text for the x-axis box.

- Click the **Axis Titles** button on the Ribbon, point to **Primary Vertical Axis Title** and choose **Horizontal Title** from the menu.

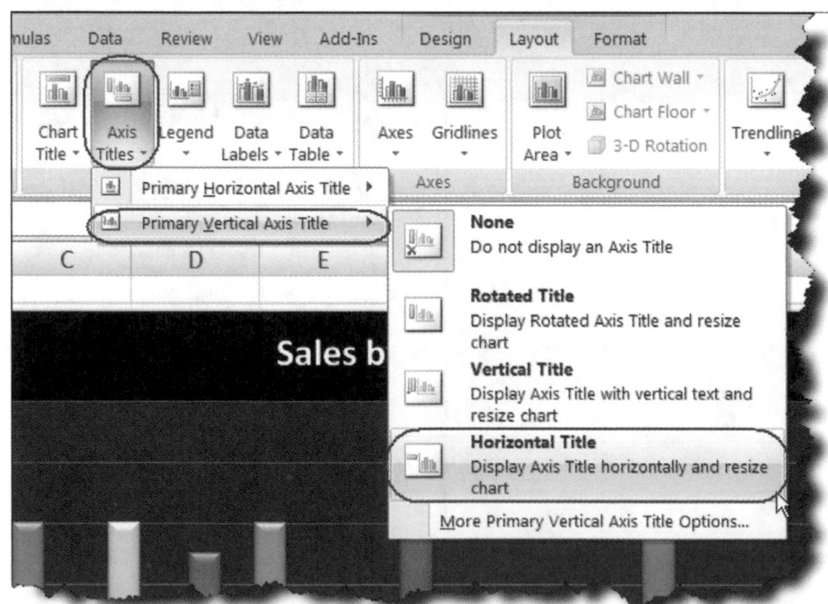

Actual - Forecast

Inserts a horizontal text box to the left of the Value Z axis.

- Select the text in the **Value axis box**, type: **Actual—Forecast**.

Enters the text for the vertical axis title box.

- Click the **Save** button.

Saves the active document.

Formatting Chart Text

In this section, you will learn how to format chart labels.

You can format any text object on your chart, such as the chart title and chart axis labels using the formatting techniques that you have already learned. You can change the text or apply various formatting such as bold, italics, font size, font type, text alignment, and colors and patterns. Use the **Mini-Toolbar** which displays when you right-click on highlighted text or any of the commands on the Font group on the Home Ribbon.

You can use the **Format Object dialog box**, which allows you to apply a wide variety of formatting from one location. Right-click the object and choose Format [Selected Object] from the contextual menu. Click the desired tab in the left pane and make your selections.

To Format Chart Text

1. Click on the border of the **Text Object** you wish to edit.
2. Click the Home tab and make any selections from the Font group on the ribbon
   Or
   Right-click and make any selections from the **Mini-Toolbar**.
   Or
   Right-click and choose Format [Selected Object], click the desired tab and make your changes. Click OK.

Let's Try It!

- Click the **Sales By Month** text object on top of the chart.

Selects the Chart Title.

- Click the **Home tab** on the Ribbon.

Displays Home commands and tools.

- Click the **Font Size** drop-down list and select **24**.

Changes the Font Size of the text to 24 pt.

- Click the **Font Color** button on the Ribbon and click the **Yellow** color swatch under Standard Colors.

Changes the font color to yellow.

- Right-click on the Chart Title (Sales by Month) and click **Format Chart Title** from the menu.

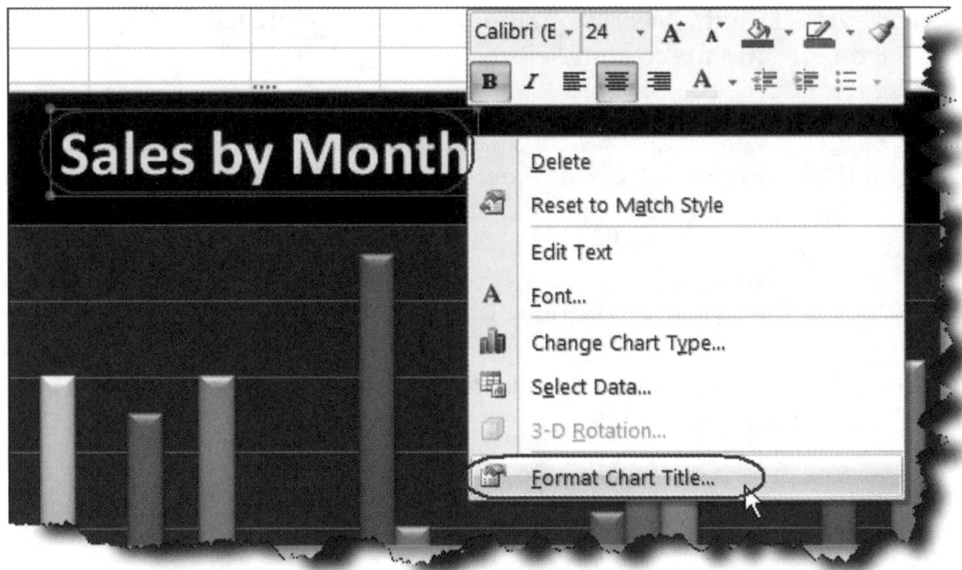

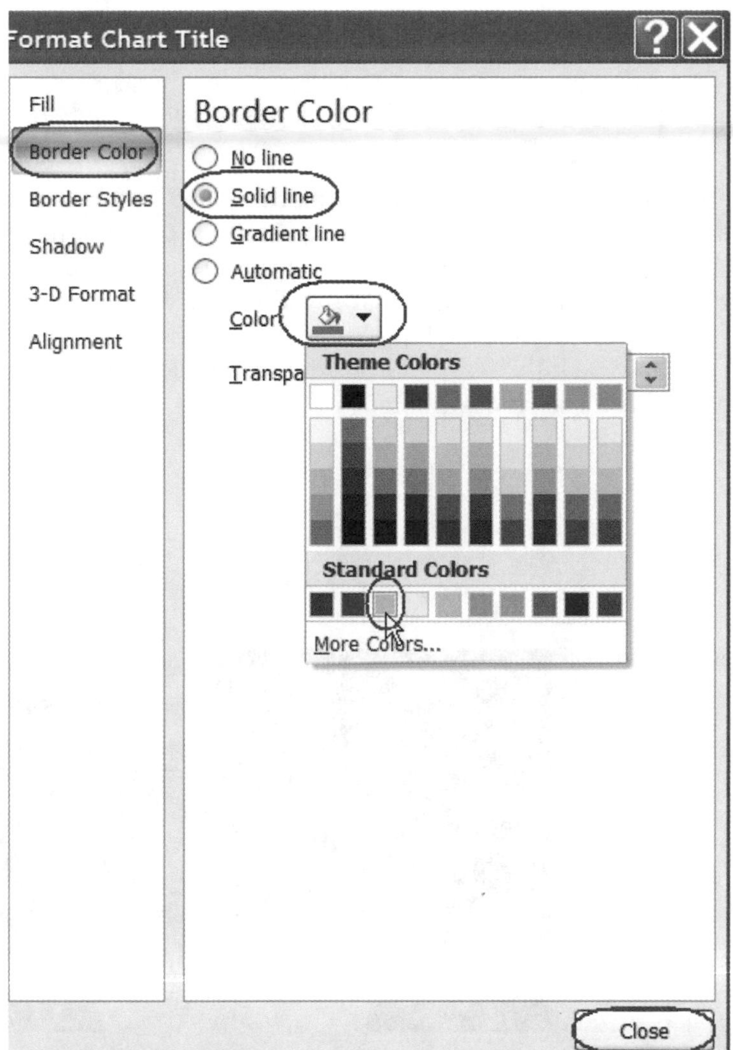

Displays the Format Chart Title dialog box.

- Click on the **Border Color** tab.

Switches to Border Color options.

- Click the **Solid Line** radio button.

Sets the text box to be bordered by a solid line.

- Click the **Color** button and choose **Orange** from the Theme color category.

Sets orange as the border color.

- Click **Close**.

Closes the Format Chart Title dialog box and applies the change.

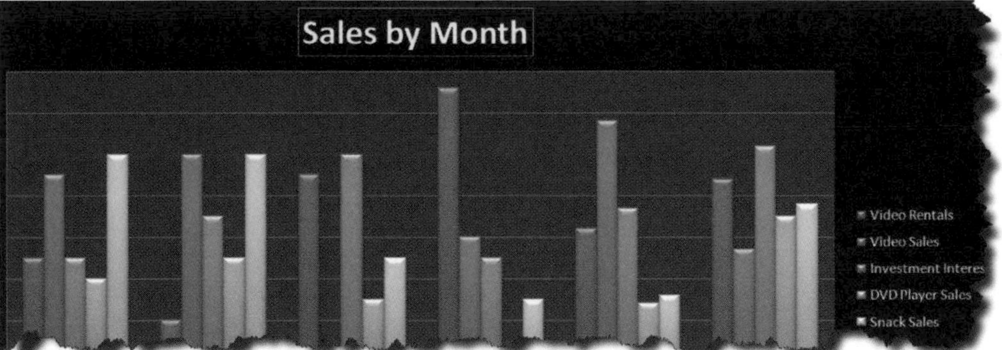

- Click anywhere in the worksheet.

Deactivates the text box.

Formatting Chart Elements

In this section, you will learn how to format individual chart elements.

From the contextual **Format tab**, you can apply formatting such as fill color and (solid, gradient, picture or texture) and borders as well as visual effects such as shadows, reflection, glow, bevel, etc. to the individual elements of your chart. In order to do so, you must first select the object and then choose the formatting you wish to apply. For instance, if you wanted to change the fill color for one of the bars for a specific data series, you would select one of the bars, click the Shape Fill button on the Ribbon and choose the desired color from the color palette.

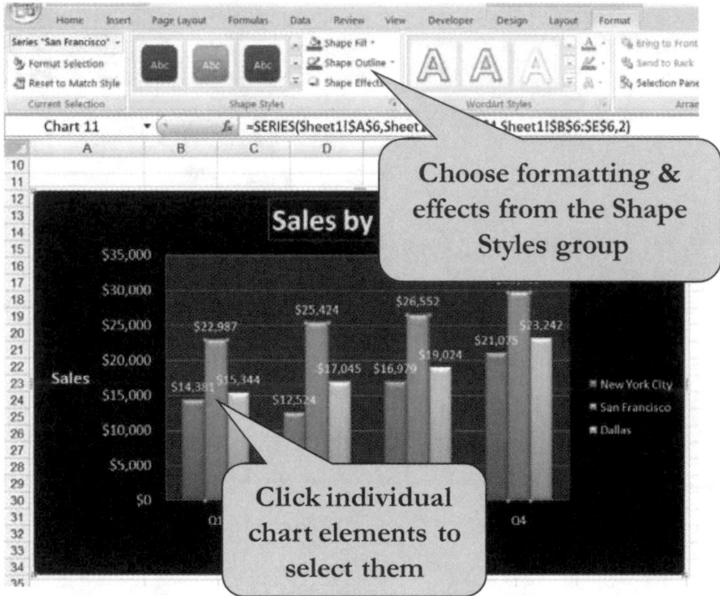

Use the **Shape Fill, Shape Outline or Shape Effects** buttons on the Shape Styles group to apply effects to your chart shapes. The Shape Styles gallery also includes some interesting effects. To add effects to the text on your chart, the **Text Fill, Text Outline or Text Effects** buttons on the WordArt group.

Another handy way to format chart elements is by using the Format Selection button on the Design Ribbon. When clicked, the **Format Object dialog box** appears from where you can apply multiple formatting.

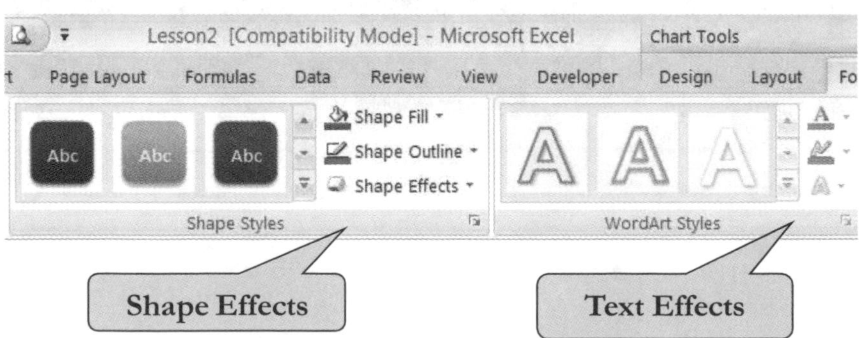

To Apply Formatting to Chart Elements

1. Click the chart object that you want to format.
2. Click the contextual **Format tab** under Chart Tools.
3. To apply a fill color to the object, click the **Shape Fill** arrow on the Shape Styles group and choose the desired color from the color palette. Click Picture, Gradient or Texture to fill the object with any of these items.
4. To apply or modify the lines or border of an object, click the **Shape Outline** arrow on the Shape Styles group and choose the options you want.
5. To apply an effect to an object, click the **Shape Effects** arrow on the Shape Styles group, point to the desired category from the list and then click the effect you want to apply from the gallery.
6. To apply effects to chart text, use the tools on the WordArt Styles group.

- Click on the **Actual—Forecast text box.**

Selects the chart element we want to format.

- Click the **Format tab** under Chart Tools.

Displays the chart Format Ribbon.

- Click the **More button** on the Shape Styles gallery.

Displays available shape styles.

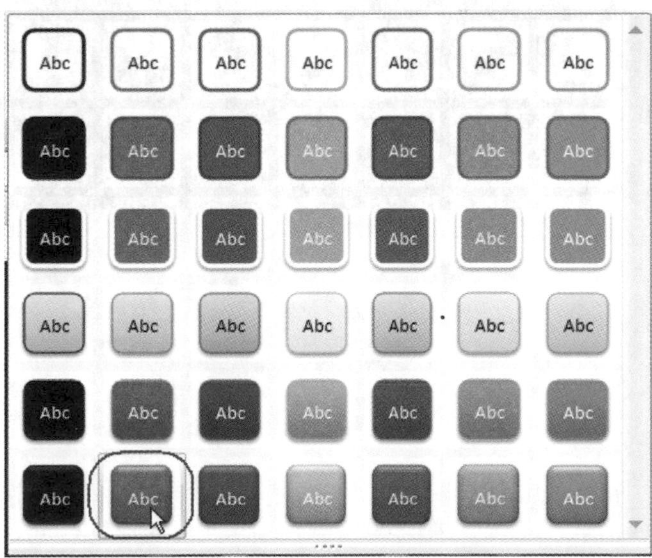

- Click the blue Shape Style in the **last row, second column** (Intense Effect—Accent 1).

Applies the Shape Style to the selected shape.

- Click on the **Month text box**.

Selects the chart element we want to format.

- Click the **blue Shape Style** (Intense Effect—Accent 1) from the Shapes Gallery on the Ribbon.

The most recently used styles are displayed in the Shape Style gallery.

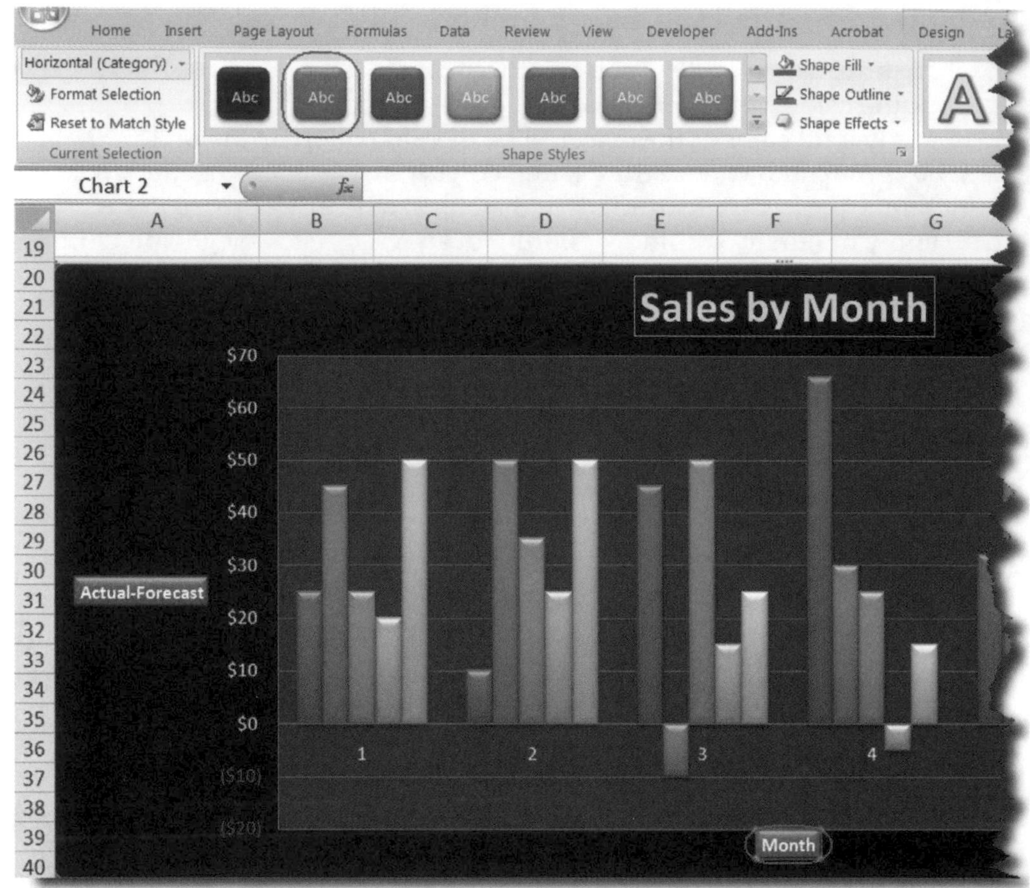

- Click on any of the **orange bars** for **Video Rentals** (the leftmost bar in each group).

Selects the data object we want to format.

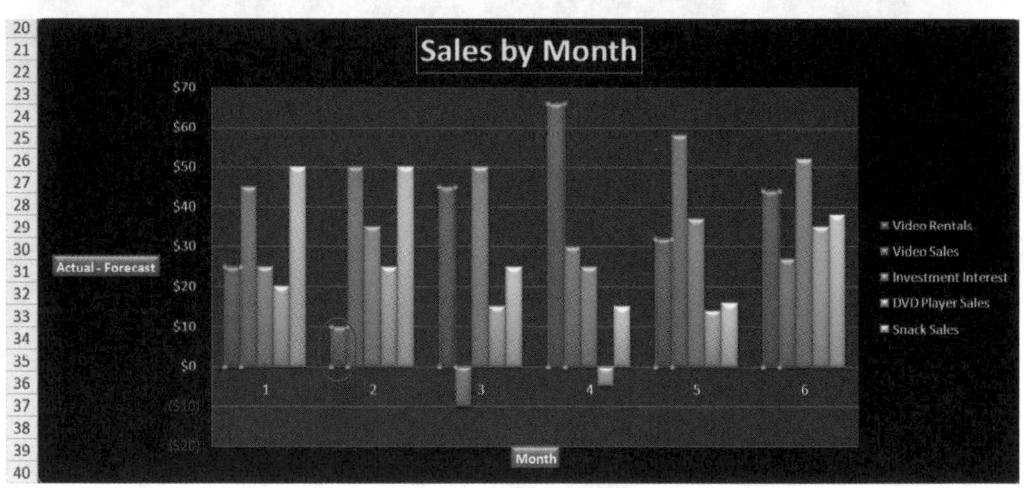

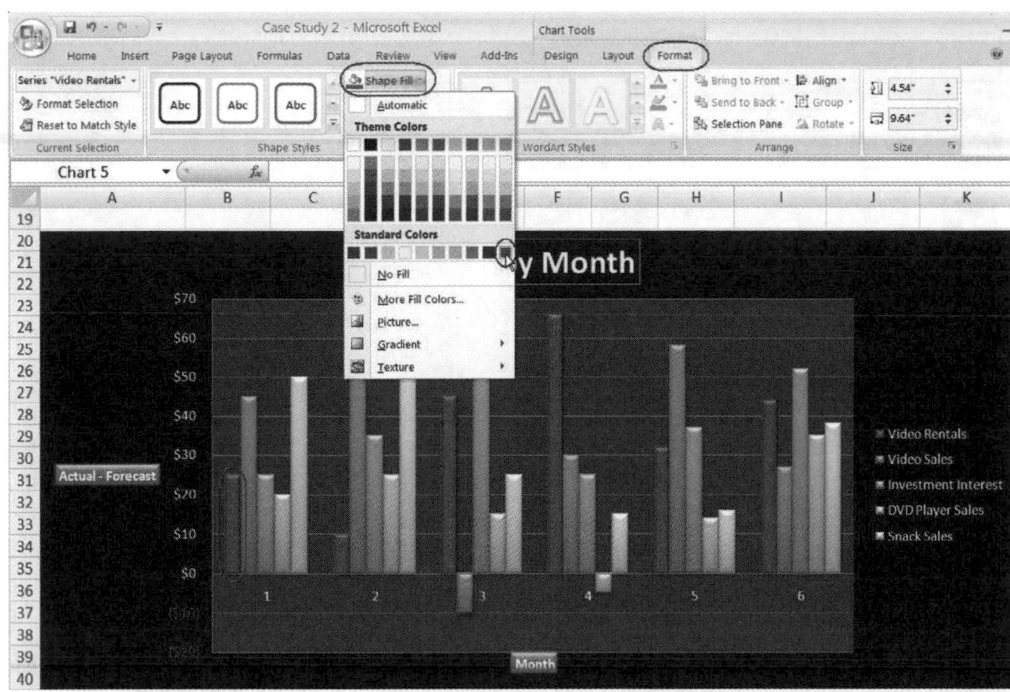

- Click the **Shape Fill** button on the Shape Styles gallery under Format tab and click the **Purple** color swatch under the Standard Colors category.

Changes the bar color for Video Rentals to purple.

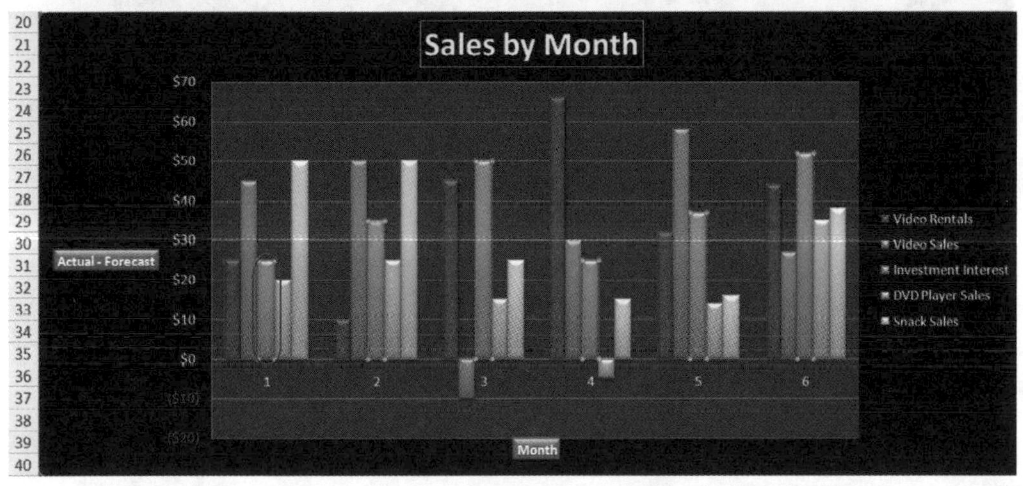

- Click on any of the **orange bars** for **Investment Interest** (the center bar in each group).

Selects the data object we want to format.

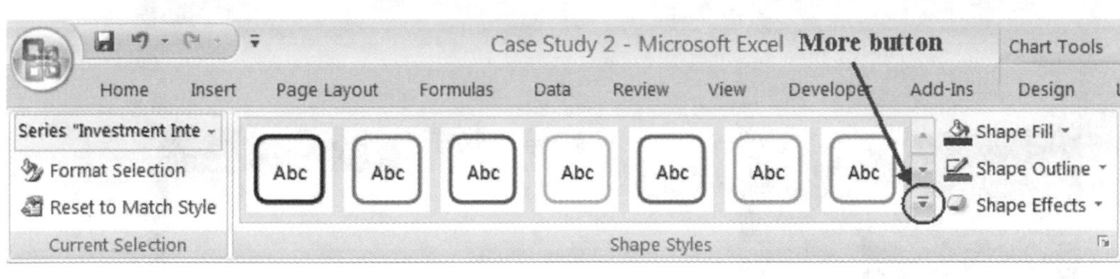

- Click the **More button** on the Shape Styles gallery.

Displays available shape styles.

- Click the red Shape Style in the **last row, third column** (Intense Effect—Accent 2).

Applies the Shape Style to the selected shape.

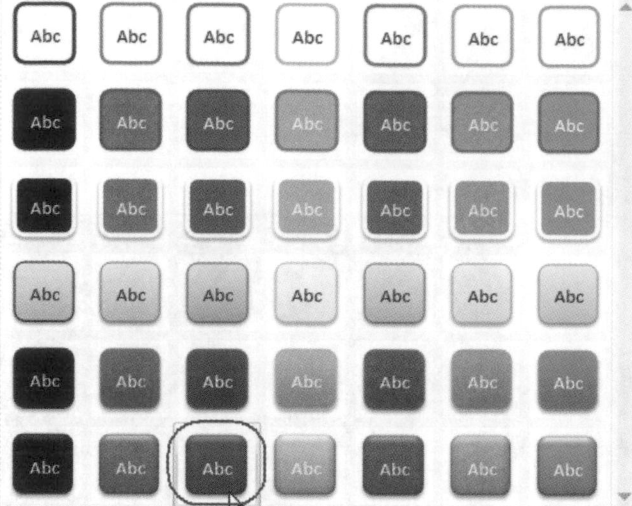

- Click on the **dark gray plot area** of the chart.

Selects the chart element we want to format.

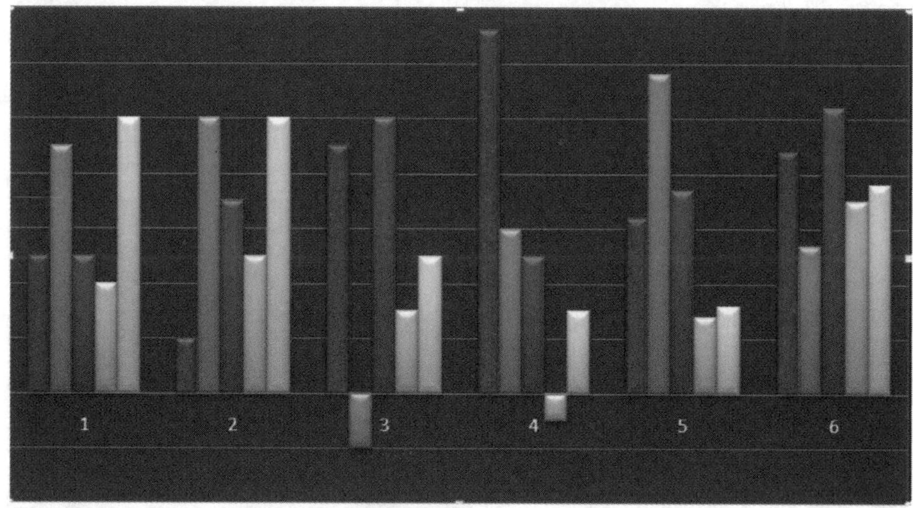

- Click the **Shape Effects** button on the Shape Styles group.

Displays a list of available shape effects.

- Point to **Glow** and click the glow style in the last row, last column as shown below.

Applies a light orange glow to the chart element.

- Click the **Save** button.

Saves the active document.

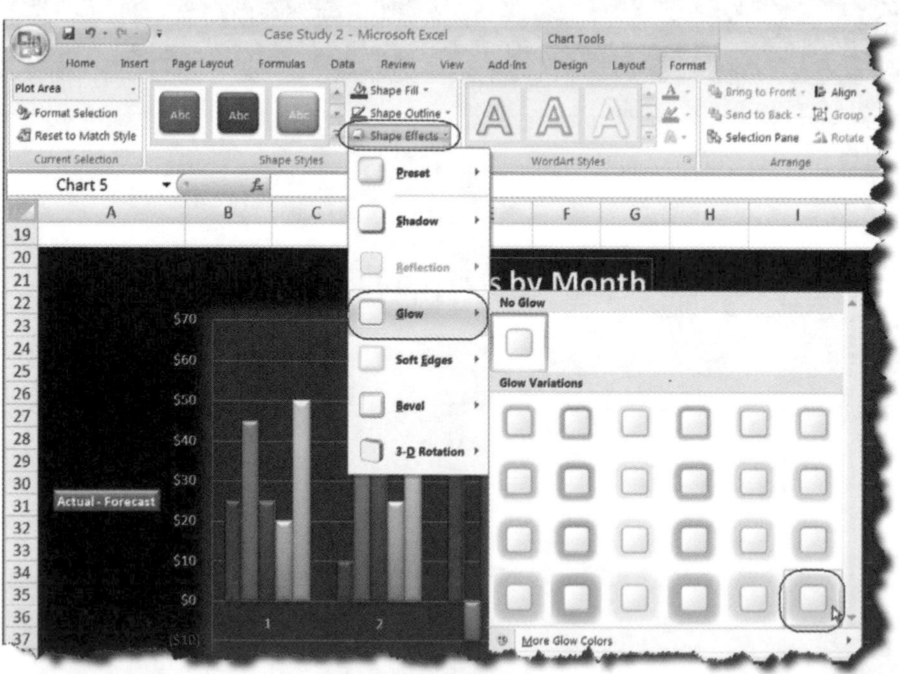

Using Help

In this section, you will learn how to use the Help system.

The **Help system** is designed to provide **assistance** to users whether you are online or offline and bring all available resources to you as quickly as possible. To access the Help system, press **F1** or click the **Help icon** on the upper right-hand corner of the Excel window.

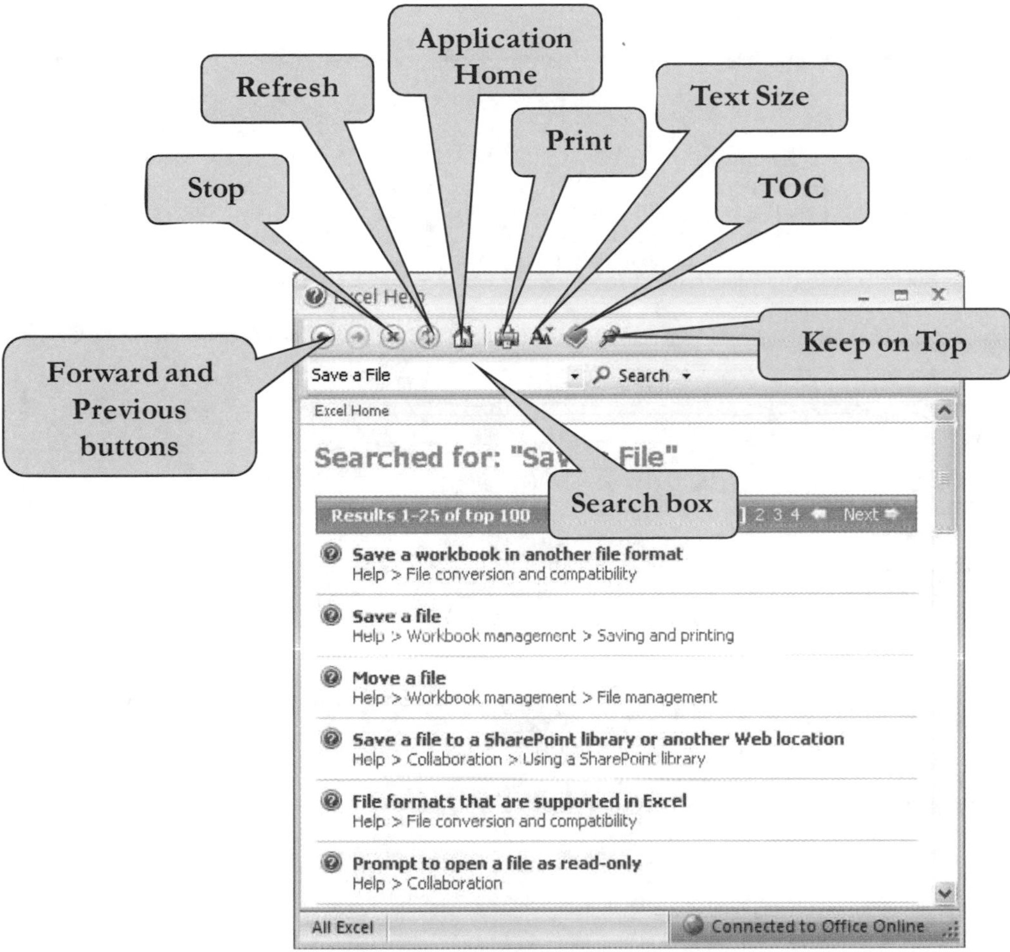

The Help system toolbar includes the familiar Back, Forward and Stop commands. Additionally, you will find the new **Refresh** tool, which allows you to update the content of the Help window. The **Application Home** tool brings you to the Excel starting point, where you can browse through information related to the Microsoft Excel application. The **TOC** tool displays a listing of available help topics through which you can browse. If you wish to increase or decrease the text size in the Help window, click the **Text Size** tool. Another nice feature on the Help toolbar is the **Keep on Top** tool, which allows you to keep the current Help page open while you work.

To Use the Help System

1. Click the **Microsoft Office Excel Help** button on the upper right-hand corner of the Excel Window
   Or
   Press **F1**

2. Enter the keyword(s) for which you want to search in the **Search** box.
3. Click the **Search** button
   Or
   Press the **Enter** key.
4. Click the **link** for the help topic you wish to view in the **Search Results pane**.
5. To browse Help topics, click the **TOC** button. Click the TOC button again to hide the Table of Contents.

Let's Try It!

- Click the **Microsoft Office Excel Help icon** on the upper right-hand corner of the screen as shown.

Displays the Excel Help System window.

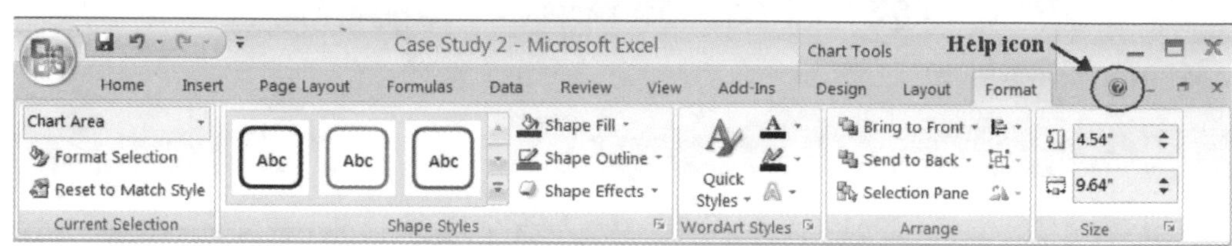

- In the **Search box**, type: **Save a file**.

Enter the keywords for which we want to search.

- Press **Enter**.

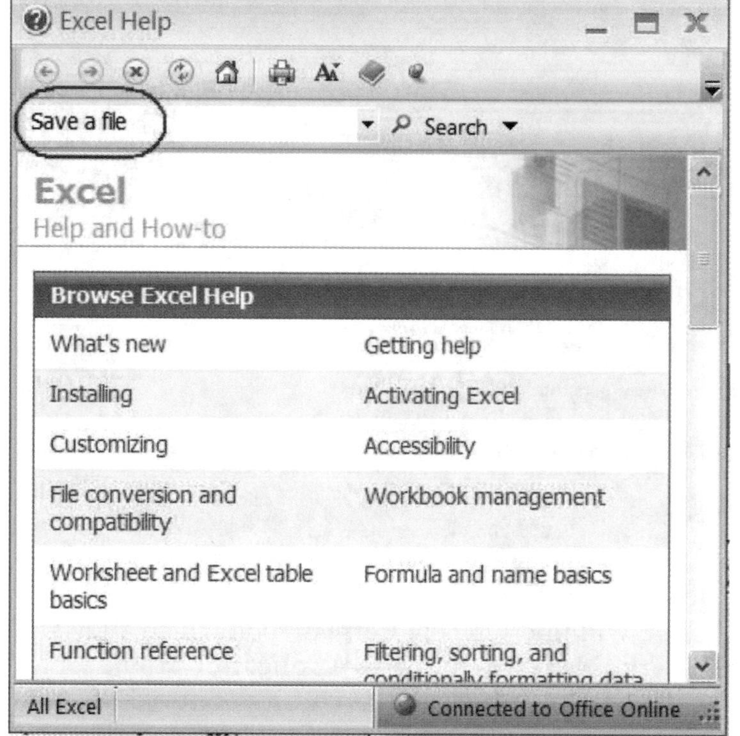

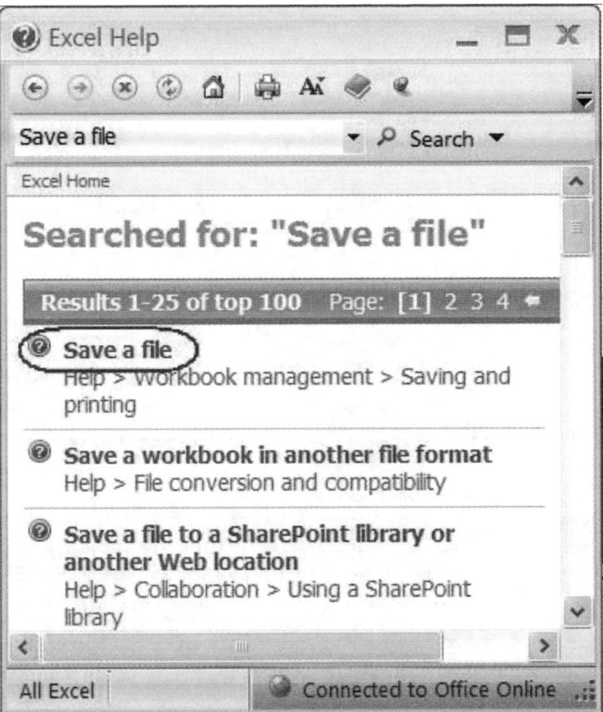

Executes the search. The results are displayed in the Search Results pane.

- Click the **Save a file** link in the Search Results pane.

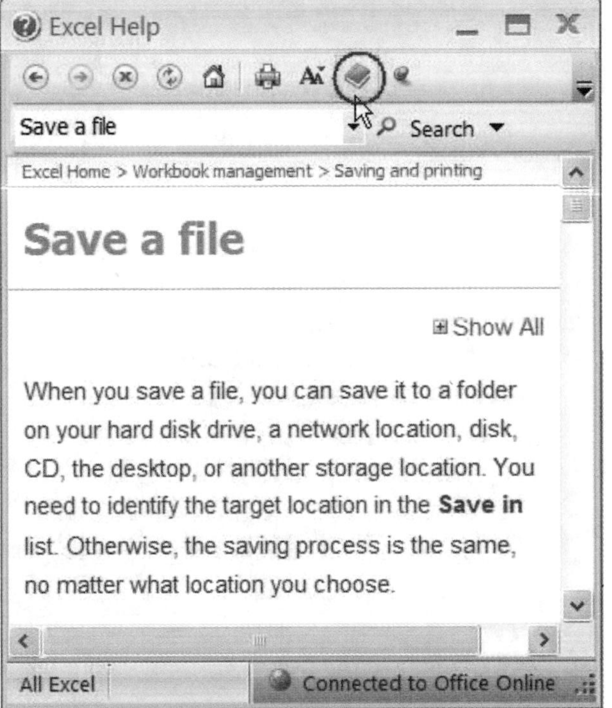

Displays the help topic for that link.

- Click the **Table of Contents** button on the toolbar.

Displays a listing of Microsoft Excel help topics in a new pane.

- Click the **Table of Contents** button again.

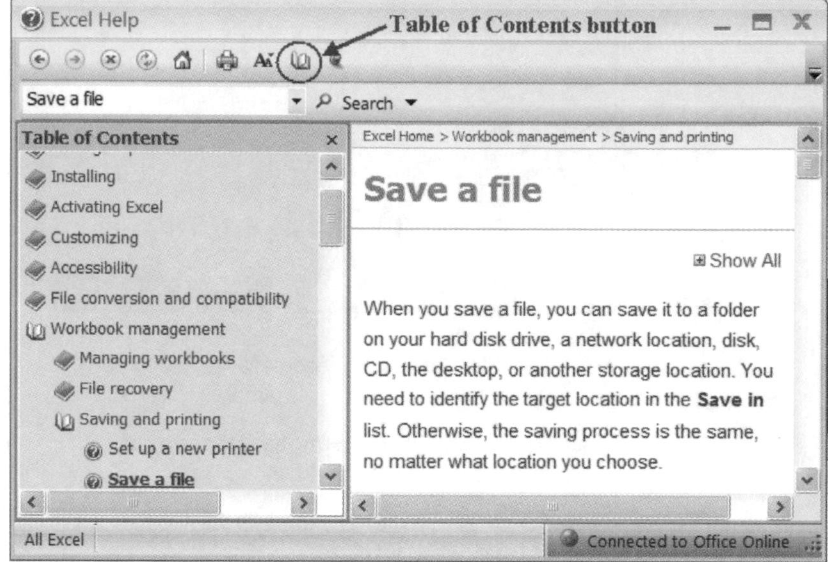

Hides the Table of Contents.

- Click the Excel Help **Close button** on the upper right-hand corner of the Excel Help window.

Closes the Help System window.

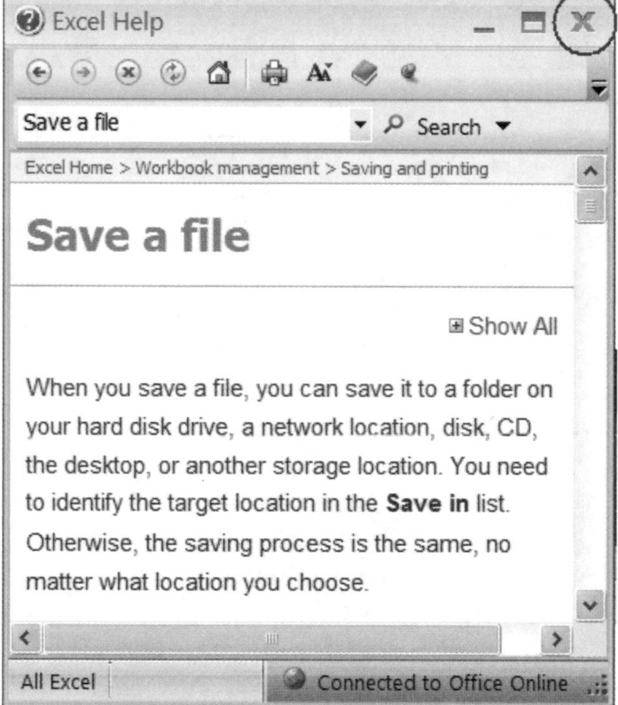

Adjusting Margins

In this section, you will learn how to change the page margins of your worksheet.

Margins refer to the amount of white space between the text of the worksheet and the left, right, top and bottom edges of the page. Margins can also be thought of as page boundaries—once the text reaches the boundary of the margin, it wraps to the next line or the next page.

Keep in mind that changing the margins of your document affects every page in your document—not just the active paragraph or page. To modify margins, click the **Margins** button on the Print Layout tab and make your selections.

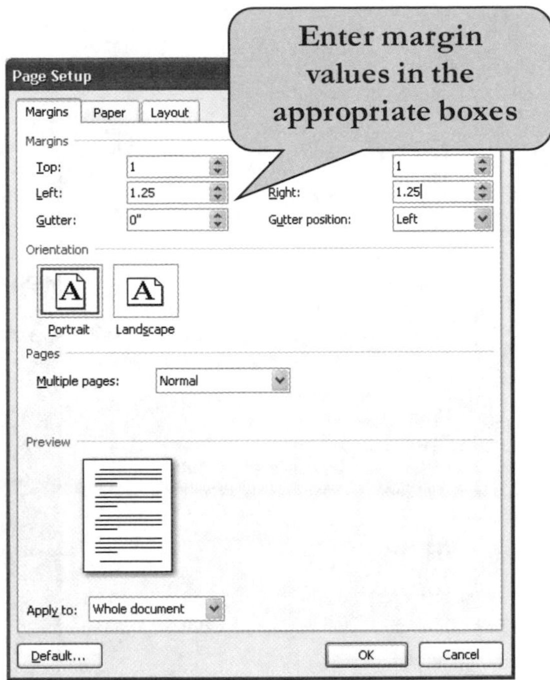

SETTING CUSTOM MARGINS

To Select Standard Margins

1. Click the **Page Layout** tab on the Ribbon.
2. Click the **Margins** button and select Normal, Wide, Top or Narrow.

To Create Custom Margins

1. Click the **Page Layout** tab on the Ribbon.
2. Click the **Margins** button.
3. Click **Custom Margins** on the list to display the **Page Setup dialog box**.
4. Enter the margin values (in inches) in the **Top, Left, Bottom and Right** boxes in the Margins area.
5. If desired, click the checkbox next to **Horizontally** or **Vertically** to center your data on the page.
6. Click **OK** when finished

TIP: You can also display the Page Setup dialog box by clicking on the Page Setup Dialog Launcher. Click on the Margins tab to display margin options.

Let's Try It!

- Click on cell A1.

Selects cell A1.

- Click the **Page Layout** tab on the Ribbon.

Switches to Page Layout commands and tools.

- Click the **Margins** button as shown.

Displays the margins options.

- Click **Custom Margins** from the list.

Displays the Page Setup dialog box.

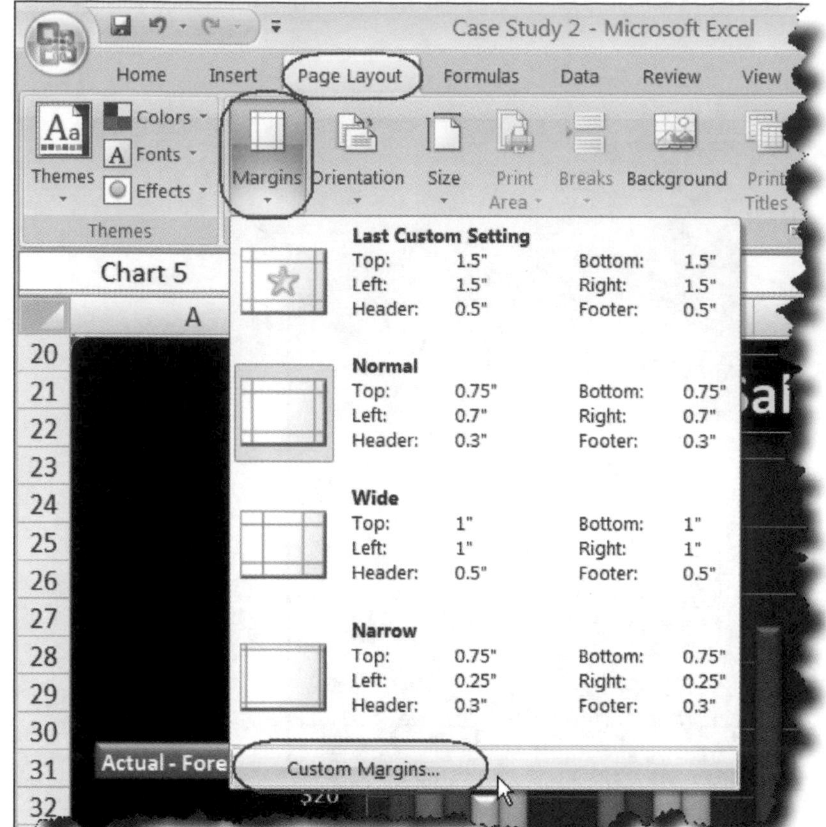

- Double-click in the **Top** margin box, type: **0.25** as shown and then press **Tab**.
- In the **Bottom** margin box, type: **0.25** and then press **Tab**.

Sets the top and bottom margin at 0.25 inches and then moves to the left margin box.

- In the **Left** margin box, type: **0.25** and then press **Tab**.

Sets the left margin at 0.25 inches and then moves to the right margin box.

- In the **Right** margin box, type: **0.25**.

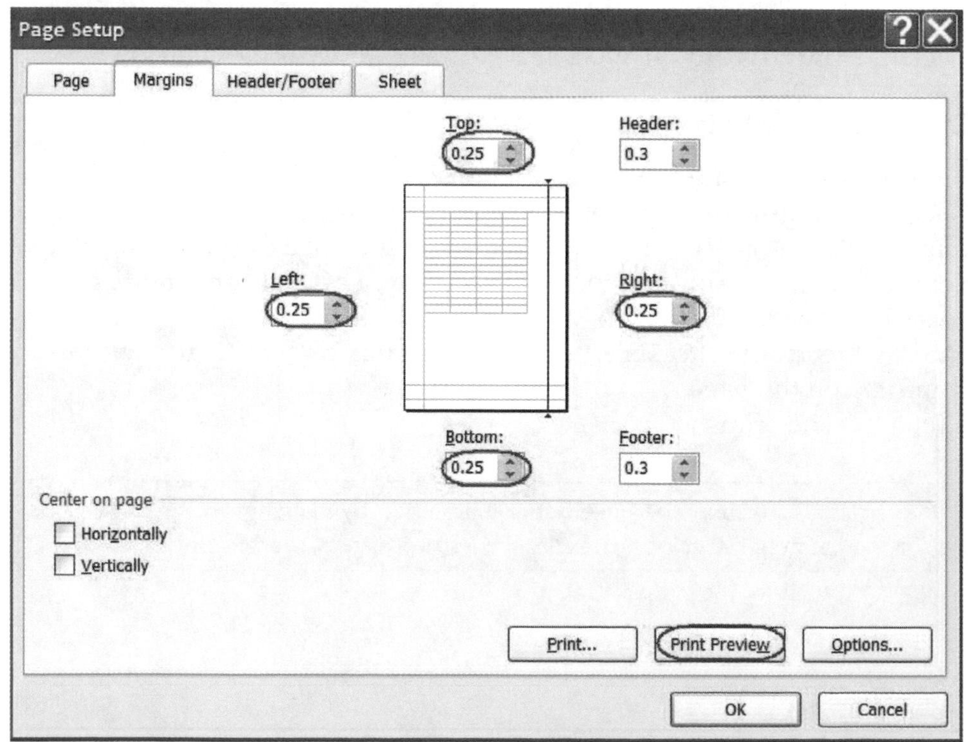

Sets the right margin at 0.25 inches.

- Click the **Print Preview** button.

Displays the document as it will be printed.

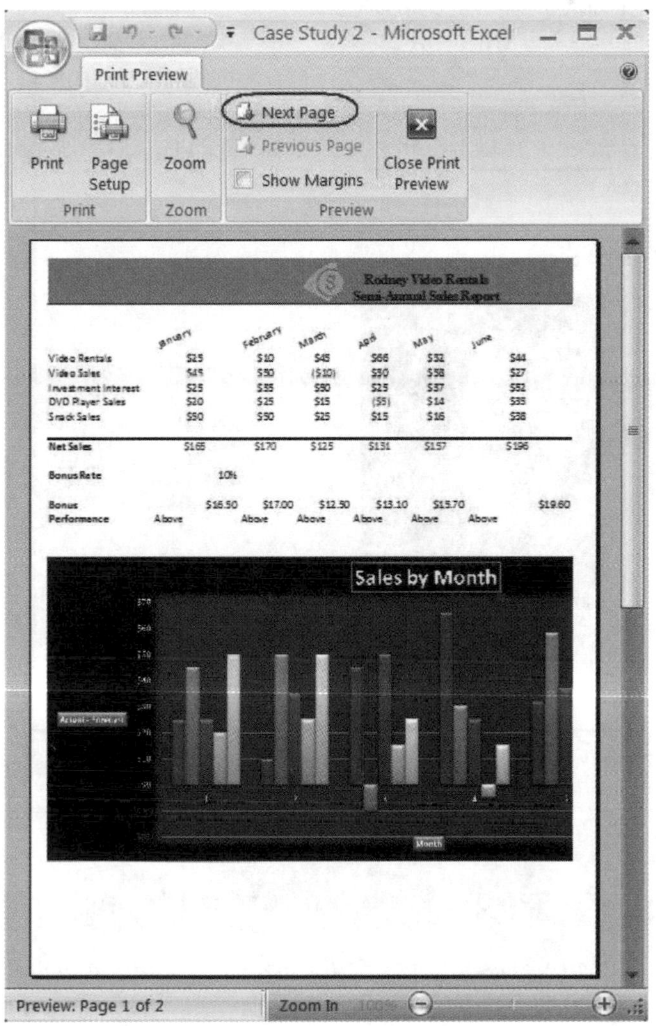

- Click the **Next Page** button on the Ribbon.

Displays the next page of the document.

- Click the **Close Print Preview** button on the Ribbon.

Returns to Normal view.

- Click the **Save** button.

Saves the active document.

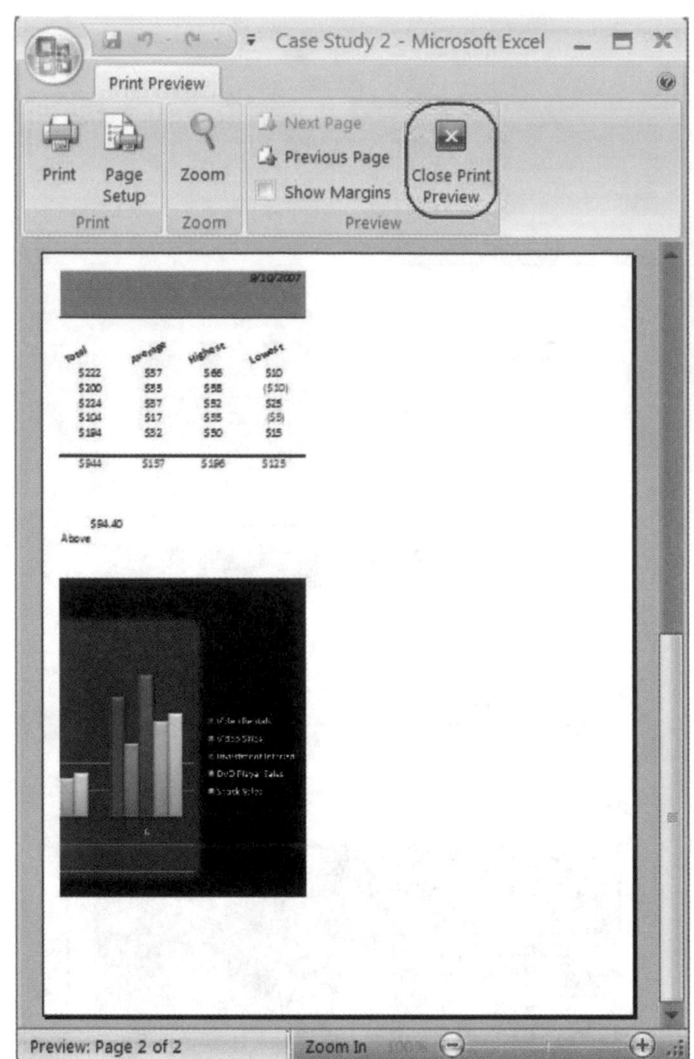

Forcing a Worksheet to Fit

In this section, you will learn how to force a worksheet to fit on a specified number of pages.

If you want to reduce the size of data on a printout, you can use the **Scale to Fit** tools on the Page Layout Ribbon. This is especially helpful if your data spans more than one page in width or height and you wish to shrink it so that it fits on one page. Reducing the scale of your printout allows you to fit more rows and columns on each page. Be careful though—reducing the scaling too much can result in a printout that is unreadable.

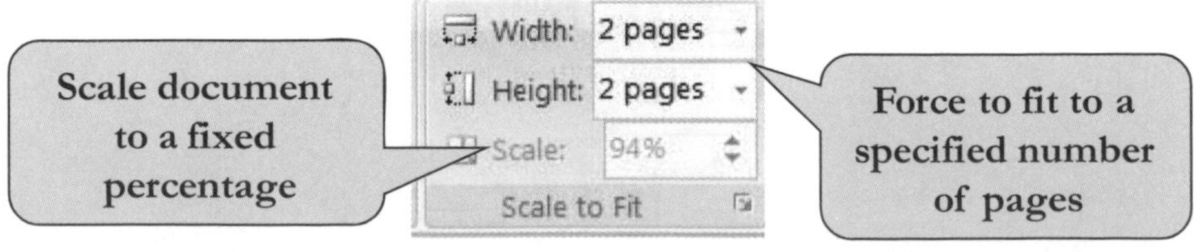

To Force a Worksheet to Fit on a Specified Number of Pages

1. Click the **Page Layout tab** on the Ribbon.
2. To scale the worksheet to fixed percentage, enter a value between 10 and 400 in the **Scale box** under the Scale to Fit group.
3. To adjust the printout to a specific number of pages, click the **Width** and **Height** drop-down arrows and choose the desired number of pages.

> **TIP:** You can also set worksheet scaling from the Page tab of the Page Setup dialog box

Let's Try It!

- Click the **Width** drop-down arrow under the Scale to Fit group and select **1 Page**.

Specifies that the width of the document is to be reduced so that it fits on one page.

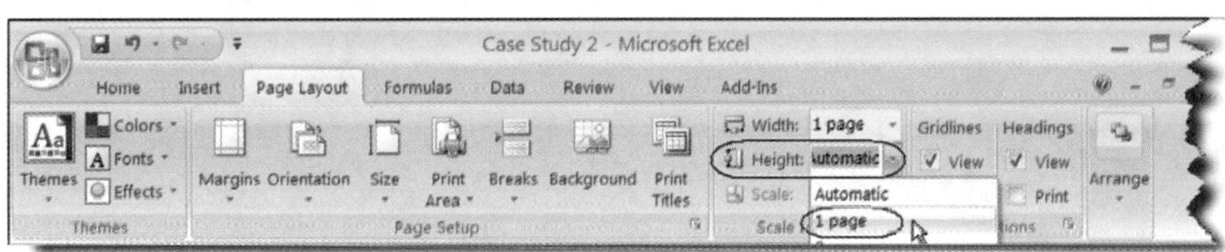

- Click the **Height** drop-down arrow under the Scale to Fit group and select **1 Page**.

Specifies that the height of the document is to be reduced so that it fits on one page.

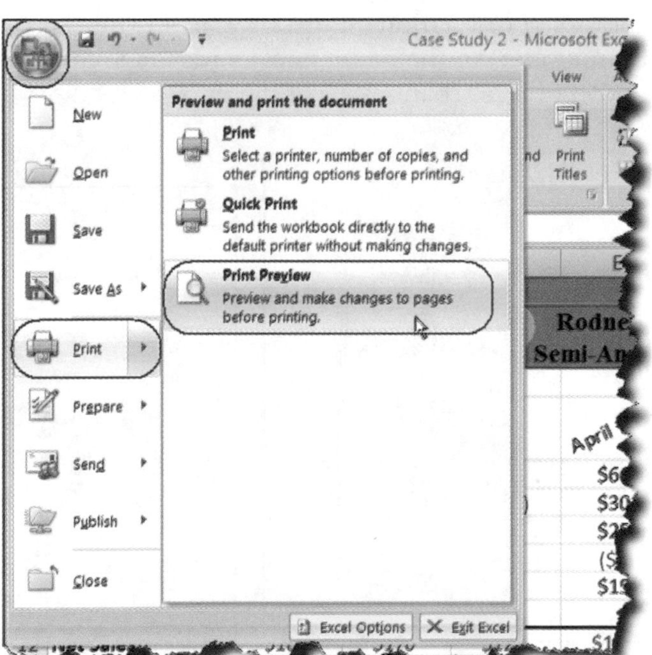

- Click the **Microsoft Office** button.

Displays the file options menu.

- Point to **Print** and select **Print Preview**.

Displays the worksheet in Print Preview view.

- Click the **Close Print Preview** button.

The size of the document has been reduced so that it fits on one page.

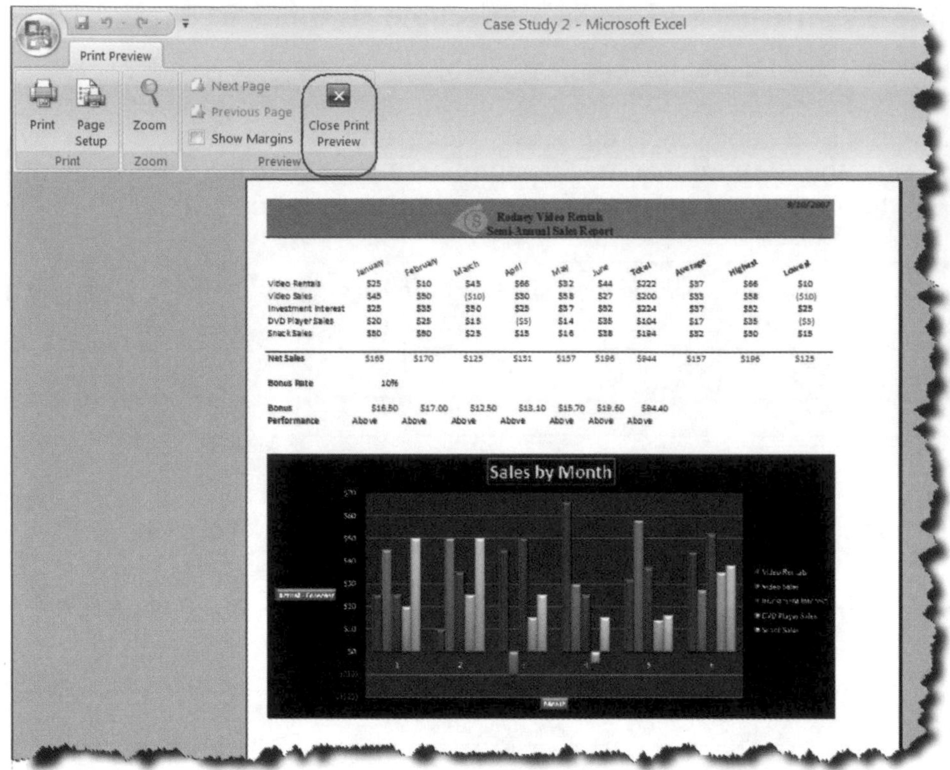

Setting Page Orientation

In this section, you will learn how to change the page orientation to either Portrait or Landscape.

Microsoft Excel allows you to change the **Page Orientation**; that is to say, the orientation of text—either wide or long—on the page. There are two choices of orienation—**Portrait** which prints across the shortest width (taller than longer) of the paper and **Landscape** which prints across the longest width (longer than taller) of the paper.

PORTRAIT

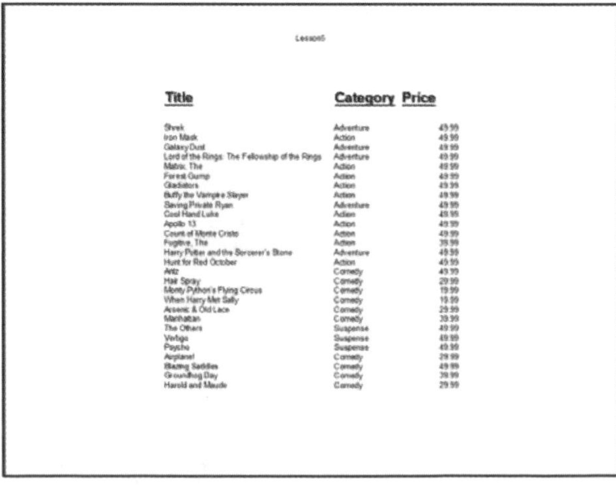

Lesson5

Title	Category	Price
Shrek	Adventure	49.99
Iron Mask	Action	49.99
Galaxy Dust	Adventure	49.99
Lord of the Rings: The Fellowship of the Rings	Adventure	49.99
Matrix, The	Action	49.99
Forest Gump	Action	49.99
Gladiators	Action	49.99
Buffy the Vampire Slayer	Action	49.99
Saving Private Ryan	Adventure	49.99
Cool Hand Luke	Action	49.99
Apollo 13	Action	49.99
Count of Monte Cristo	Action	49.99
Fugitive, The	Action	39.99
Harry Potter and the Sorcerer's Stone	Adventure	49.99
Hunt for Red October	Action	49.99
Antz	Comedy	49.99
Hair Spray	Comedy	29.99
Monty Python's Flying Circus	Comedy	19.99
When Harry Met Sally	Comedy	19.99
Arsenic & Old Lace	Comedy	29.99
Manhattan	Comedy	39.99
The Others	Suspense	49.99
Vertigo	Suspense	49.99
Psycho	Suspense	49.99
Airplane!	Comedy	29.99
Blazing Saddles	Comedy	49.99
Groundhog Day	Comedy	39.99
Harold and Maude	Comedy	29.99

LANDSCAPE

To Set Page Orientation

1. Click the **Page Layout tab** on the Ribbon.
2. Click the **Orientation button** and select either **Portrait** or **Landscape**.
3. Click **OK** when finished

   Or

1. Click Portrait or Landscape from the Margins tab of the **Page Setup dialog box**.

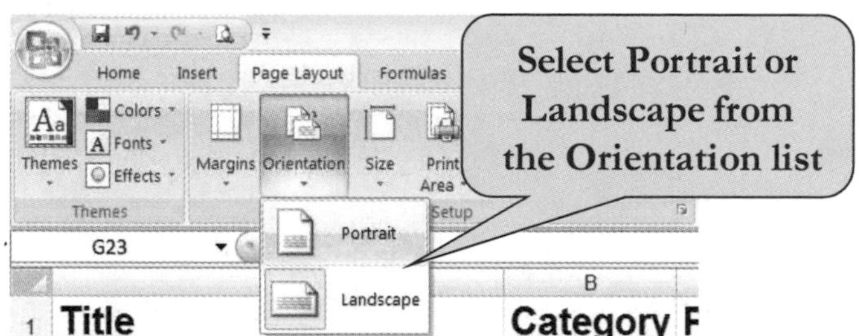

Let's Try It!

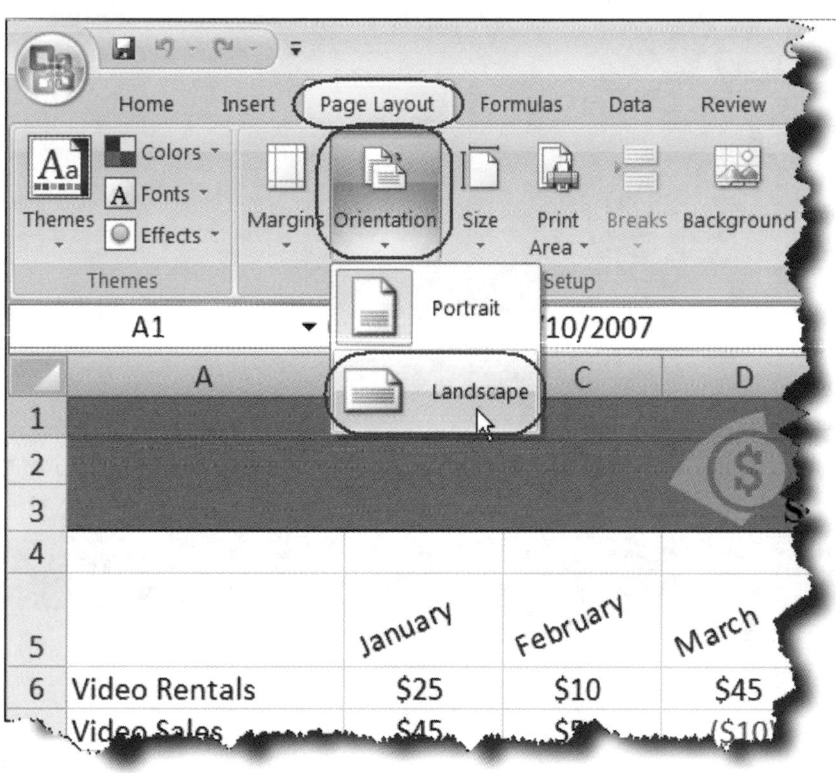

- Click the **Orientation** button on the Page Setup group.

Displays the Orientation menu.

- Click **Landscape**.

Changes the Page Orientation to landscape.

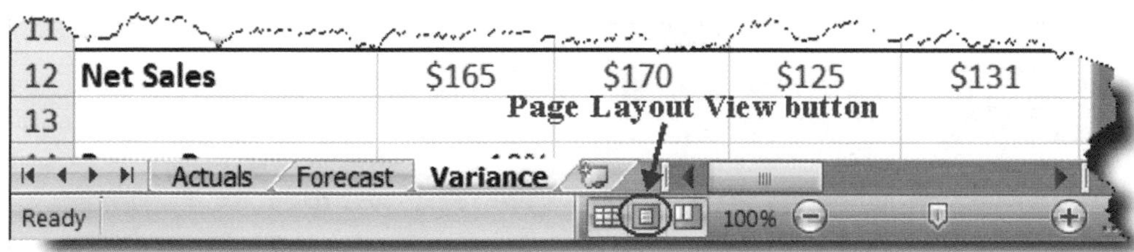

- Click the **Page Layout** view button on the lower-right corner of your screen.

Displays the worksheet in Page Layout view.

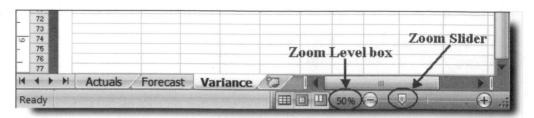

- Drag the **Zoom slider** on the lower-right and corner of your screen to the left to about **50%**.

Reduces the size of the viewable area to 50% of the normal size. Observe that the page is wider than taller.

- Click the **Zoom Level box** on the lower-right and corner of your screen

Zoom Level box
Zoom Slider

- Choose **100%** from the Zoom dialog box.
- Click **OK**.

Restores the viewable area of the document to 100%.

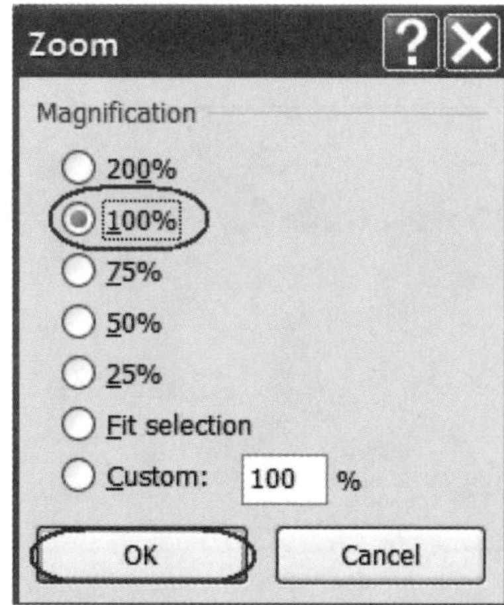

- Click the **Normal** view button on the lower-right corner of your screen.

Displays the worksheet in Normal view.

- Click the **Save** button.

Saves the active document.

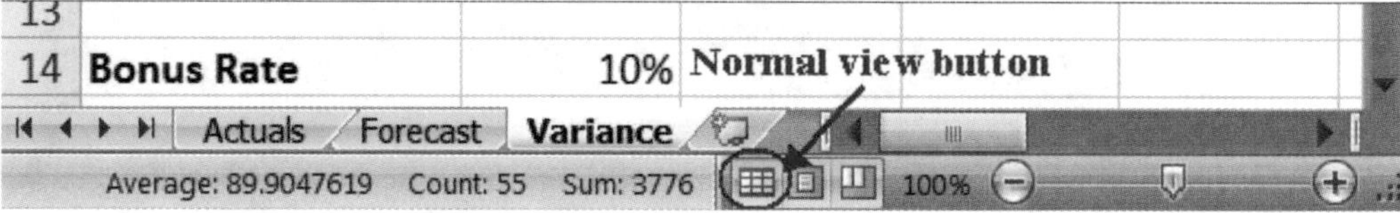

Defining a Print Area

In this section, you will learn how to set a specific print area.

Left to its own devices, Excel will print all the data that is in the currently active worksheet. You can however, force Excel to use a defined print area for the worksheet. Start by selecting the cell range that you want to print. Then, click the **Print Area** button under the Page Set up group on the Page Layout Ribbon and choose **Set Print Area** from the list.

To delete a print area, click the Print Area button and choose **Clear Print Area**.

To Define a Print Area

1. Click the **Page Layout** tab on the Ribbon.
2. Click the **Print Area** button and select **Set Print Area** from the list.
3. To remove a print area, click the **Print Area** button and select **Clear Print Area** from the list.

> **TIP:** You can also add and remove a print area from the Sheet tab of the Page Setup dialog box.

Let's Try It!

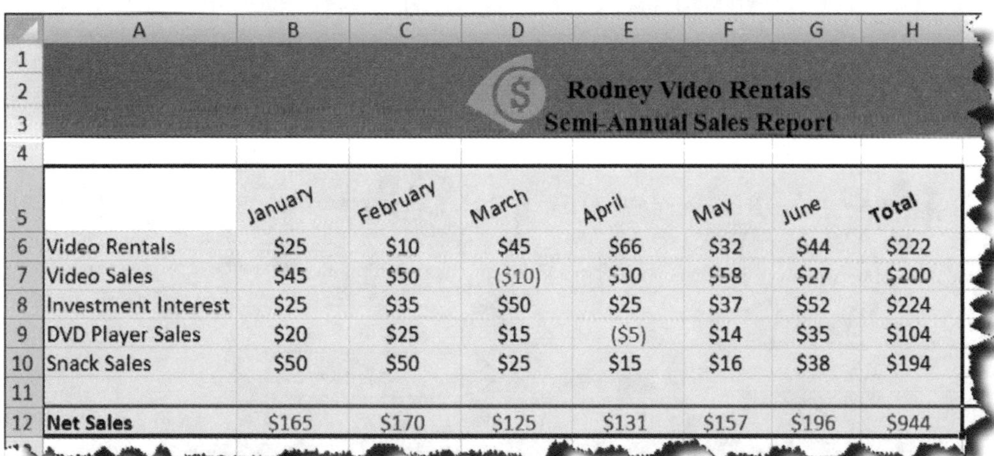

Rodney Video Rentals
Semi-Annual Sales Report

	A	B	C	D	E	F	G	H
5		January	February	March	April	May	June	Total
6	Video Rentals	$25	$10	$45	$66	$32	$44	$222
7	Video Sales	$45	$50	($10)	$30	$58	$27	$200
8	Investment Interest	$25	$35	$50	$25	$37	$52	$224
9	DVD Player Sales	$20	$25	$15	($5)	$14	$35	$104
10	Snack Sales	$50	$50	$25	$15	$16	$38	$194
11								
12	**Net Sales**	$165	$170	$125	$131	$157	$196	$944

- Select the cell range **A5:H12**.

Selects the cell range that we want to set as our print area.

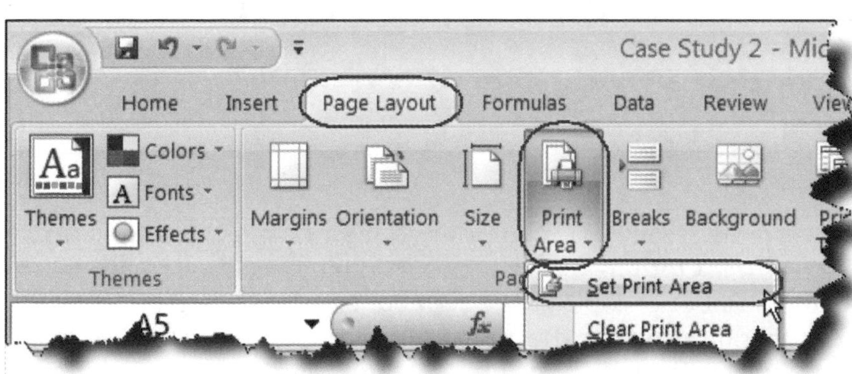

- Click the **Print Area** button on the Page Layout Ribbon and choose **Set Print Area**.

Sets A5:H12 as the range of cells to be printed.

- Press **Ctrl + F2**.

Displays the worksheet in Print Preview view.

- Click the **Close Print Preview** button.

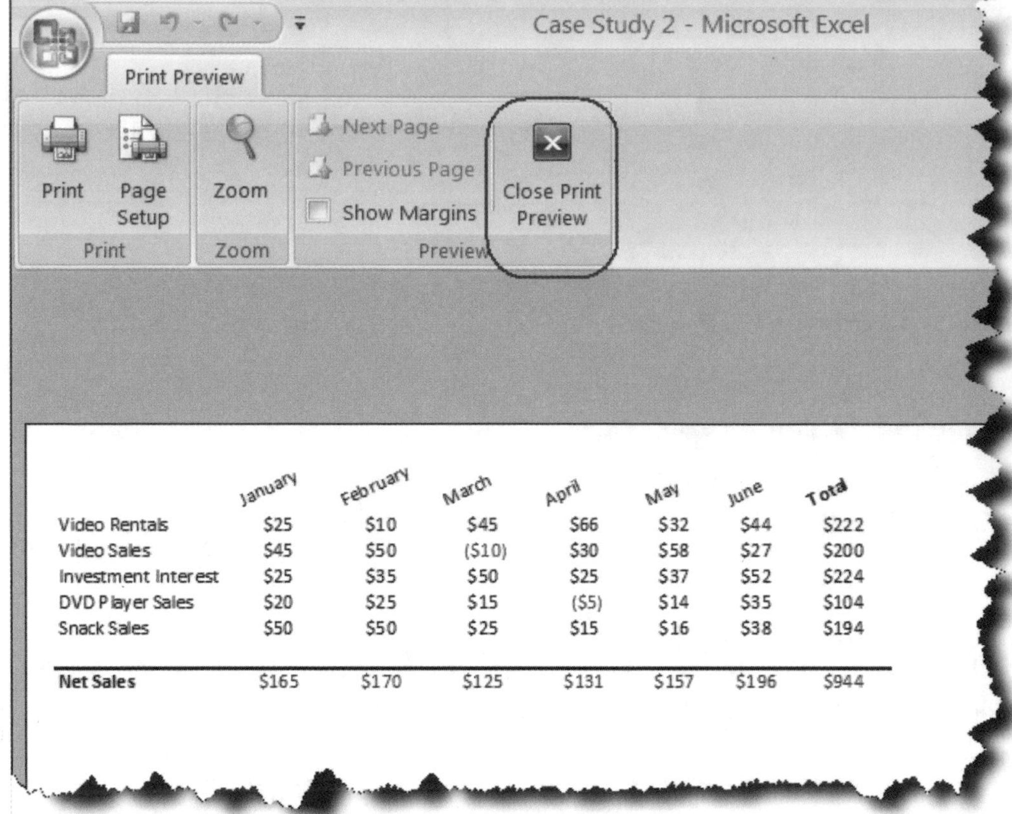

- Click the **Print Area button** and choose **Clear Print Area**.

Deletes the custom print area.

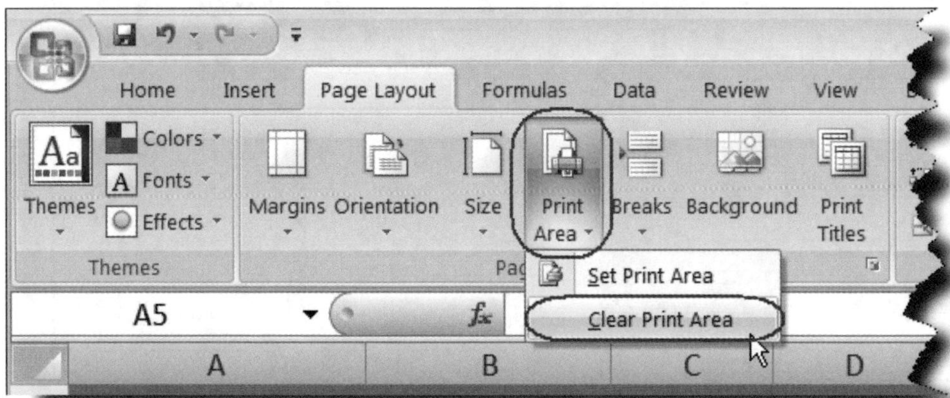

Printing a Worksheet

In this section, we will work with printer options and learn how to print a worksheet.

Before you're finally ready to print your worksheet, you may first want to set some **Printer Options**. For instance, you may need to specify which printer to use, the number of copies to be printed, or even designate Excel to print only a specific range of your document. Printer options you can set will vary, depending on the type of printer you are using.

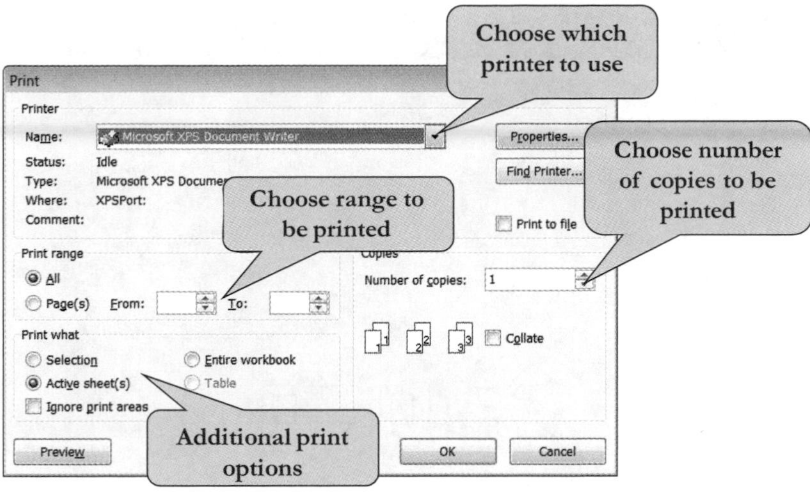

To Set Printer Options & Print a Worksheet

1. Click the **Microsoft Office** button and then click **Print** on the File Options menu to display the Print dialog box.
   Or
   Press the **Ctrl + P** keystroke combination.
2. If necessary, choose which printer to use from the **Name** drop-down list.
3. To print only the current page, select **Current page** under the Page Range Options area.
4. To print a specific range, enter the page numbers in the **Pages** box, separating each page range by a comma (i.e. 1-15, 17, 18, 30-35)
5 To print more than one copy of a document, enter the value in the **Number of copies** box in the **Copies** area.
6. Click **OK** to send the document to the printer.

Let's Try It!

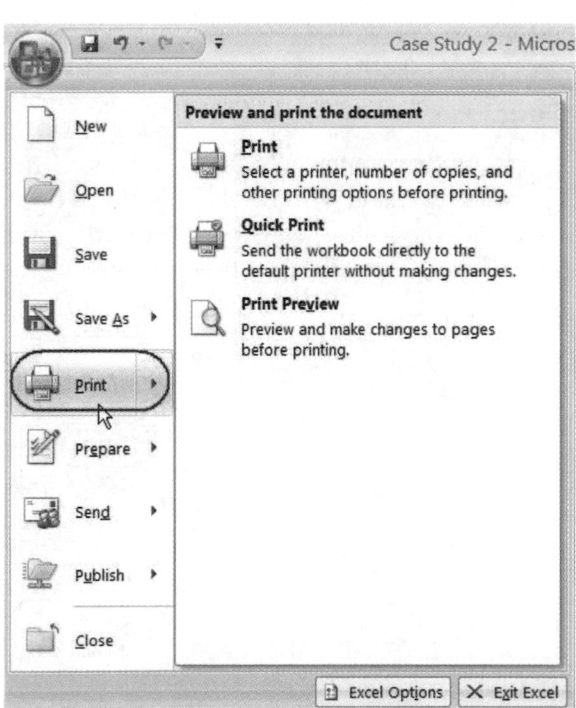

- Click the **Microsoft Office** button and then click **Print**.

Displays the **Print** dialog box. You can also press the **Ctrl + P** keystroke combination to display the Print dialog box.

- In the **Copies** box, enter 3 as shown.

Sets the option to print 3 copies of the document.

- Select **Active sheet(s)** under the Print what category.

Sets the option to print only the active sheet.

- Click the **Cancel** button.

Closes the Print dialog box without printing.

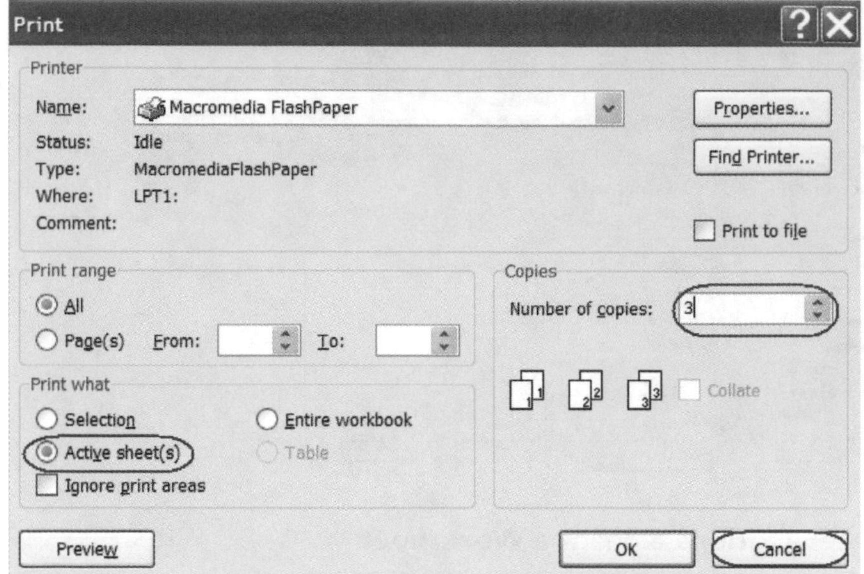

- Press **Ctrl + W**.
- Select **Yes** to save the changes.

Saves and closes the current workbook.

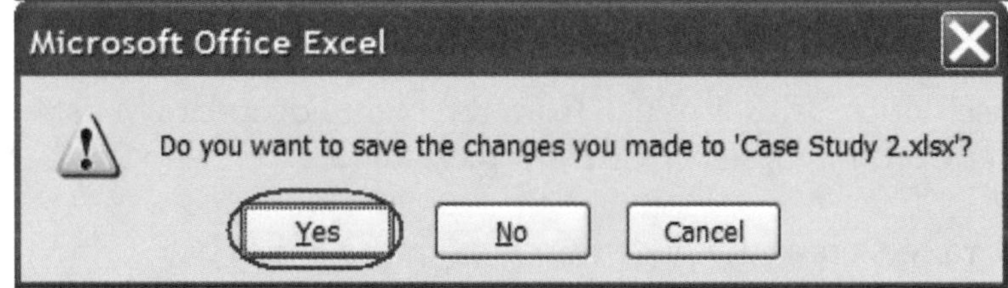

TIP: To send a document directly to the printer, click the Microsoft Office button, point to Print and then click the Quick Print option in the second pane. The Print dialog box will not open. You can also add the Quick Print icon to the Quick Access toolbar from the drop-down list.

Conclusion

You have completed Excel 2007—Case Study II. You are now ready to use several advanced MS Excel skills that you have learned in this chapter. You are encouraged to experiment with all you have learned in this case study. To reinforce your understanding of these techniques, it is recommended that you read and work through it once again.

PowerPoint Case Study I

CHAPTER

7

OBJECTIVES

After successfully completing this case study, you should able to:

- Start, Create, Navigate, Close, and Save PowerPoint Presentations
- Set PowerPoint Options
- Create a Blank Presentation
- Add Slides to a Presentation
- Enter Text on Slides
- Use the Notes Pane
- Apply Themes to a Presentation
- Create Headers and Footers
- Format Text
- Use the Format Painter Button
- Use Bulleted Lists
- Use Shapes
- Insert WordArt
- Use Help

Case Study I—MS PowerPoint 2007

Assume that you work for a ACME Corp. which is publishing the Company Handbook next month. Your task is to produce a presentation that summarizes new additions in the handbook. This presentation includes four slides:

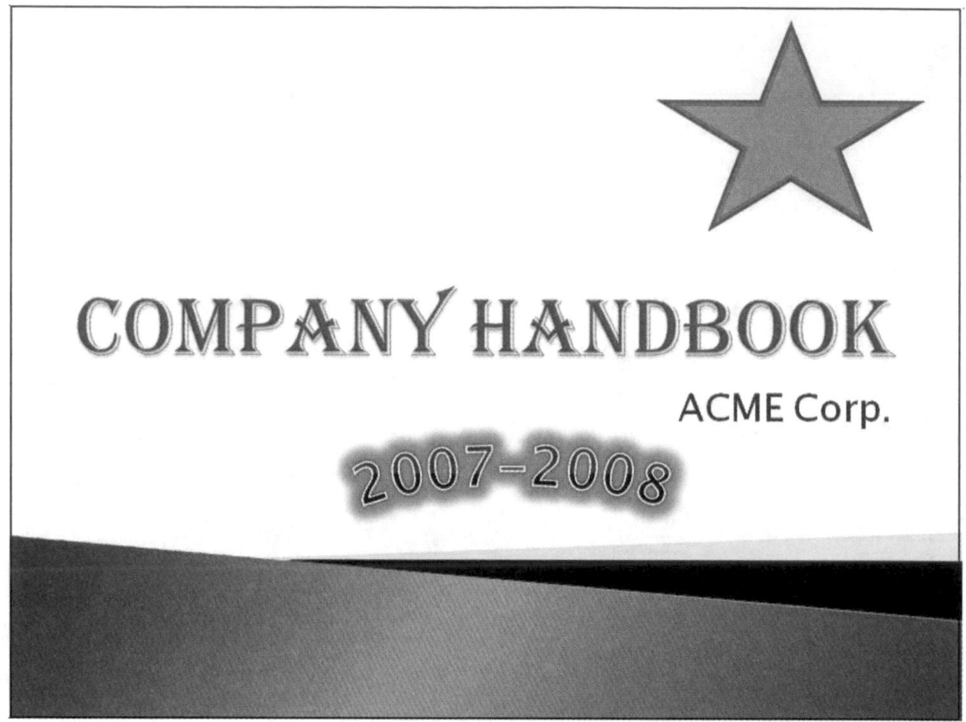

POWERPOINT SLIDE 1

Recruiting

- Campus Recruiting
- Employee Recruiting
- Professional Recruiters

Company Handbook 6/29/2007 2

POWERPOINT SLIDE 2

Leaves & Disability

- Maternity Leave
- Short & Long-Term Disability
- Leave of Absence
- Sabbaticals

Company Handbook 6/29/2007 3

POWERPOINT SLIDE 3

Compensation

- Policies & Levels
- Pay Scales & Bonuses
- Stock Options & Information
- Medical Benefits
- Retirement

Company Handbook 6/29/2007 4

POWERPOINT SLIDE 4

Looking at PowerPoint

In this section, we will take a look at the PowerPoint Program.

Welcome to PowerPoint 2007! PowerPoint is a graphical presentation program which contains easy-to-use tools to help you deliver powerful professional presentations. With PowerPoint, you can create slides that contain tables, charts, text, graphic files, and even sound and video. New and improved tools in PowerPoint make it easier to share and collaborate on presentations over the web. Let's begin by starting the PowerPoint Program and examining the PowerPoint environment.

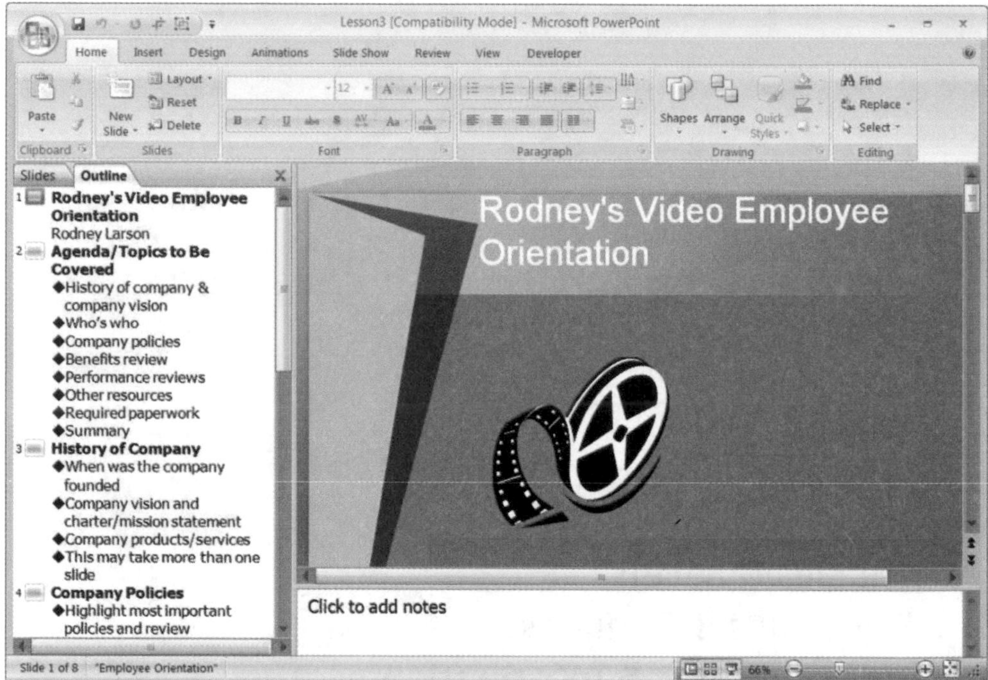

To Start PowerPoint

1. Click the **Start** button on the lower-left corner of your screen to display the Start menu.
2. **All Programs > Microsoft Office > Microsoft Office PowerPoint 2007** from the Start Menu to launch the application.

Let's Try It!

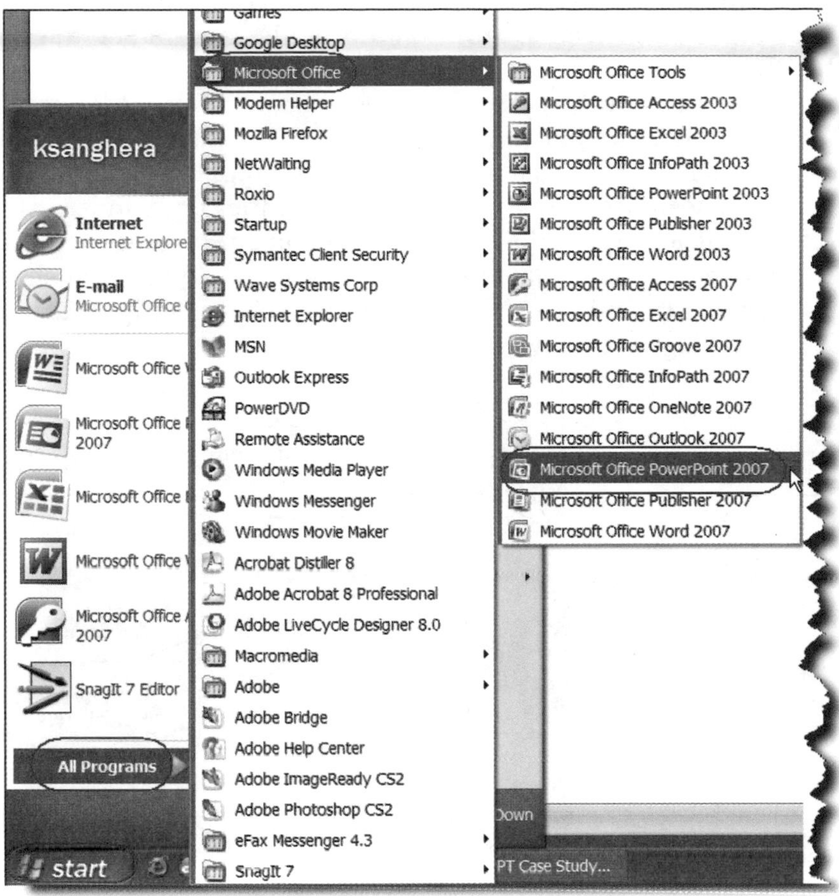

- Click on the **Start** button.

Displays Start menu items.

- Select **All Programs > Microsoft Office > Microsoft Office PowerPoint 2007** from the Start Menu.

Launches the PowerPoint Application.

Examining the PowerPoint Environment

In this section, we will take a look at various elements of the PowerPoint screen.

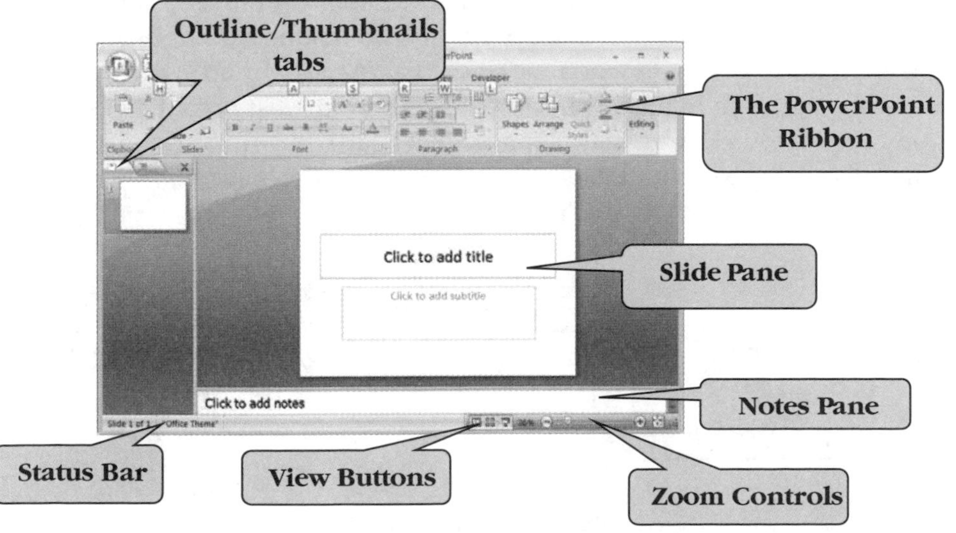

When you first launch PowerPoint, you are presented with a blank presentation consisting of a blank title slide in **Normal** view, which is the main editing view used to write and design your presentation. On the left side of the screen is the **Outline/Thumbnails** pane and on the right side is the **Slide Pane**.

If you have worked with previous versions of PowerPoint, you will immediately notice that the user interface has been completely redesigned.

The menu and toolbar system have been replaced by the **Ribbon**. The Ribbon is designed to help you quickly find the commands you need in order to complete a task. On the Ribbon, the menu bar has been replaced by **Command Tabs** that relate to the tasks you wish to accomplish. The default Command Tabs in PowerPoint are: **Home, Insert, Design, Animations, Slide Show, Review** and **View**.

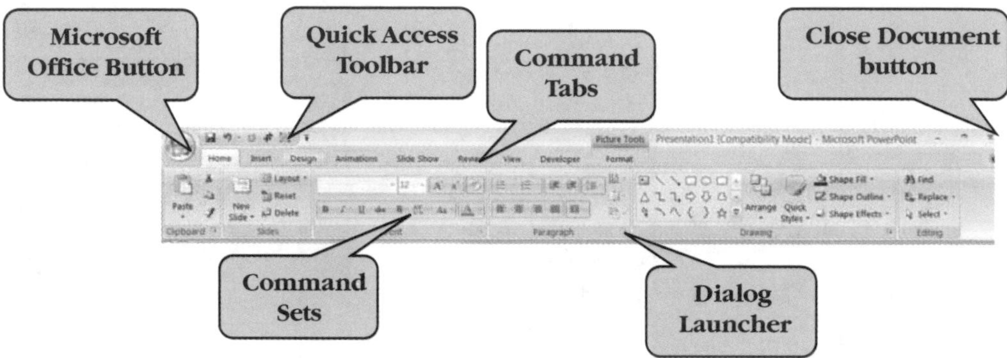

Different command icons, called **Command Sets** appear under each Command Tab. The commands that appear will depend on the Command Tab that is selected. Each command set is grouped by its function. For example, the Insert tab contains commands to add graphics, tables, headers, footers, symbols and text objects to your presentation. **Contextual Commands** only appear when a specific object is selected. This helps in keeping the screen uncluttered.

On the bottom of many of the Command Sets is a **Dialog Launcher**, which when clicked, will launch a dialog box for that set of commands.

To the right of the **Microsoft Office icon** (from where you access file options), is the **Quick Access Toolbar**. This toolbar contains by default the Save, Undo, and Redo commands. In addition, clicking the drop-down arrow to the right allows you to customize the Quick Access Toolbar to add other tools that you use regularly. You can choose from the list which tools to display on the Quick Access Toolbar or select **More Commands** to add commands that are not in the list.

QUICK ACCESS TOOLBAR

We will be working in detail with the various PowerPoint tabs and commands in subsequent sections.

Let's take a look at the PowerPoint Screen in more detail:

Component	Description
Command Sets	Command icons, grouped by category, under each command tab.
Dialog Launcher	Launches dialog boxes or task panes for a particular set of commands
Horizontal Scroll Bar	Allows you to move horizontally in your document. To navigate horizontally, click the scroll bar with your left mouse button and drag to the left or to the right until the desired portion of the document is in view.
Insertion Point	The small flashing vertical bar which designates the location where you can begin typing or editing text. To change the insertion point, click with your left mouse button in the desired new location of your document.
Notes Pane	Here you can add notes that relate to each slide's content, to which you can refer as you give your presentation, or create handouts that you want your audience to see in printed form.
Office Button	Click to access file commands.
Outline Tab	Allows you to display your slide text in outline form.
Quick Access Toolbar	Contains frequently used commands. You can customize it to include tools and commands that you frequently use.
Ribbon	Commands and tools organized into command sets.
Slide Pane	Displays the current slide shown in large view. Here, you can add text, insert pictures tables, charts, drawing objects, text boxes, movies, sounds, hyperlinks, and animations.
Slides Tab	Allows you to see the slides in your presentation as thumbnail-sized images while you edit.
Status Bar	Displays information about the active document.
Tabs	To access the various command sets and tools.
Title Bar	Displays the name of the application you are currently using and the name of the file (the Microsoft PowerPoint document) on which you are working.
Vertical Scroll Bar	Allows you to move vertically in your document. To navigate vertically, click the scroll bar with your left mouse button and drag upward or downwards until the desired portion of the document is in view.
View Buttons	Allows you to quickly switch between the three PowerPoint views: Normal View, Slide Sorter View and Slide Show View.
Zoom Slider	Allows you to increase or decrease the magnification of your document.

Let's Try It!

- Click the **Insert tab** on top of your screen.

Displays the commands sets for the Insert command tab.

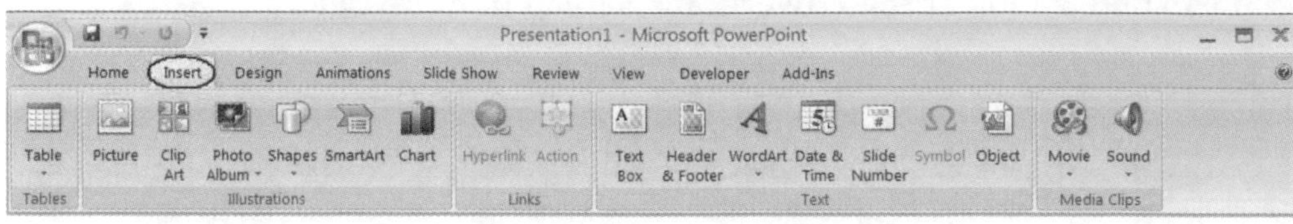

- Click the **Animations tab** on top of your screen.

Displays the commands sets for the Animations command tab.

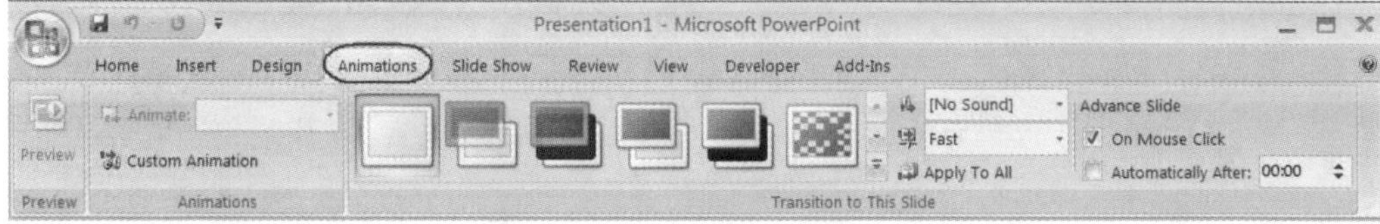

- Click the **Home tab** on top of your screen.

Returns us back to the Home tab.

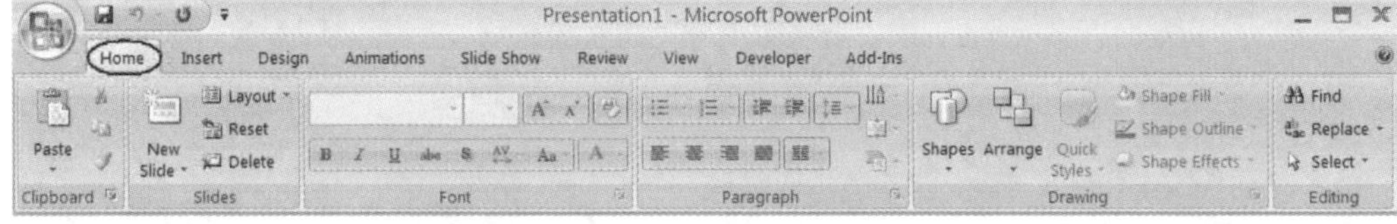

Creating a Blank Presentation

In this section, you will learn how to create a blank presentation.

We have already seen that when you first launch Microsoft PowerPoint, a new blank presentation consisting of a single title slide is created. This blank presentation consists of a simple layout with minimal formatting, no design styles and two text boxes for you to enter a Title and a Subtitle. To change the layout of your blank presentation, click the **Layout button** in the Slides group on the Home Ribbon and choose the layout you want.

You can also create a new presentation from within another presentation. The new document command is located under the **File Options** menu. You can also use the keyboard shortcut **Ctrl + N** to bypass the File Options menu.

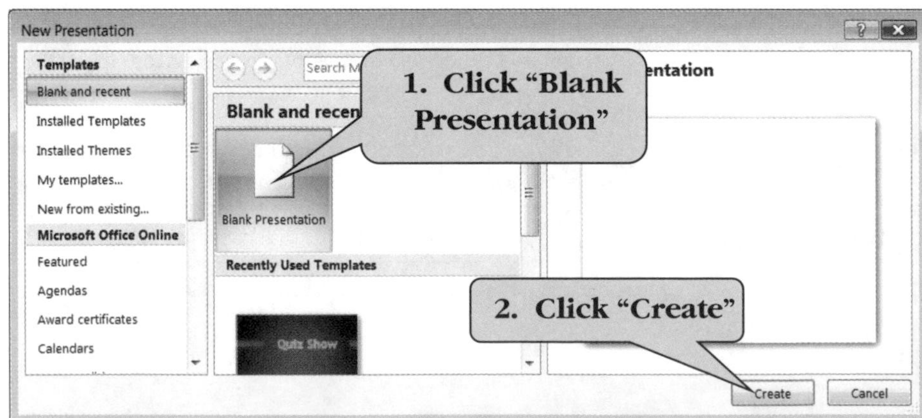

Layouts refer to the way objects are arranged on a slide. Layouts consist of placeholders that contain slide content such as titles, bulleted lists, tables, charts, and pictures. Each time you add a new slide, you can chose a different layout for that slide from the **Layout gallery**. Of course, if you prefer to do things manually, you can choose a blank layout.

To Create a New Presentation

1. Click the **Microsoft Office Button** and then click **New** from the menu to display the **New Presentation** Task Pane.
2. Click **Blank Presentation** in the center pane.
3. Click **Create**.
   Or
   Hold down the **Ctrl** and **N** keystroke combination (**Ctrl + N**).

To Apply a Layout to a Slide

1. Click the **Slides** tab on the left side of your screen.
2. Click the Slide to which you want to apply a layout.
3. Click the **Home tab** on the Ribbon.
4. Click the **Layout button** in the **Slides group**.
5. Click the layout you want from the gallery.

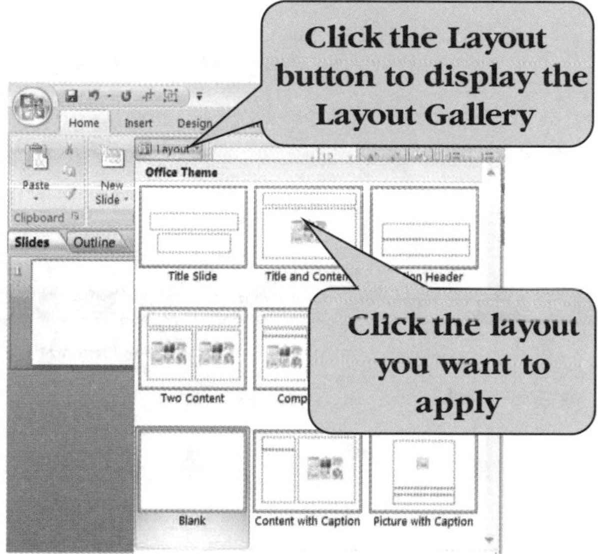

Let's Try It!

- Click the **Microsoft Office Button** and then click **New** from the menu.

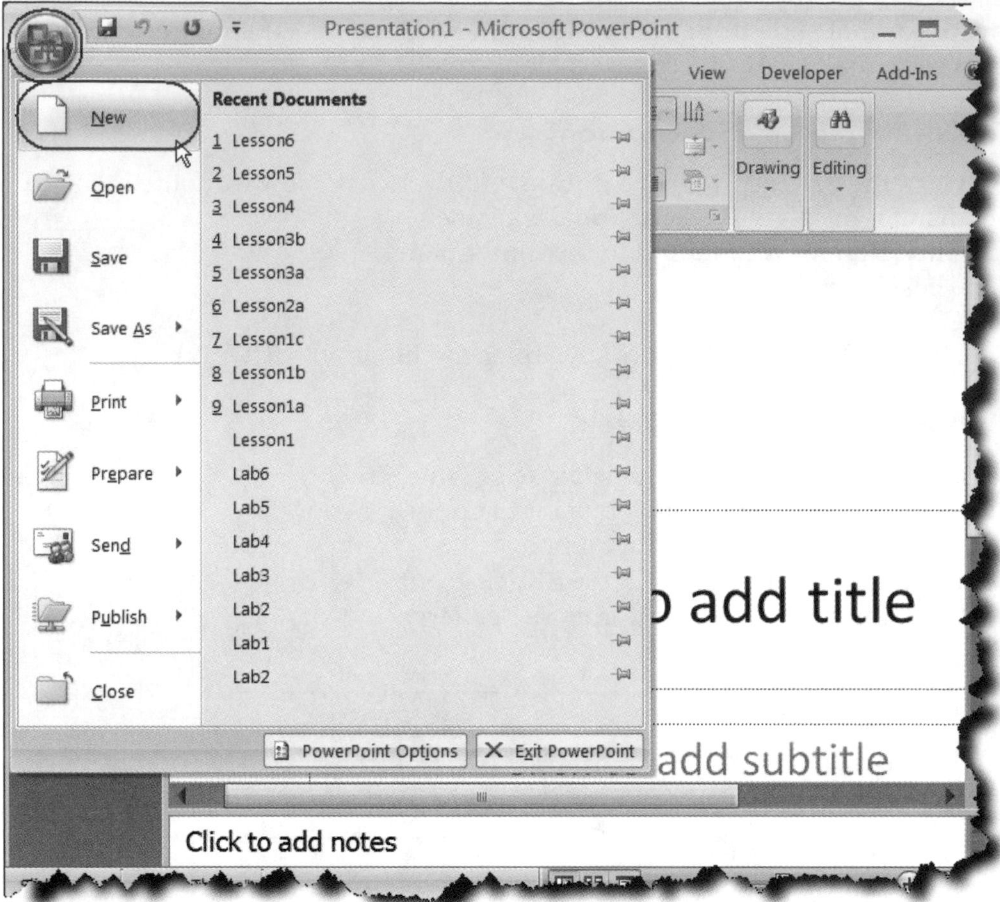

Displays the New Presentation pane.

- In the **Center** Pane, click on **Blank Presentation** as shown.

Specifies that we will create a new blank presentation.

- Click **Create**.

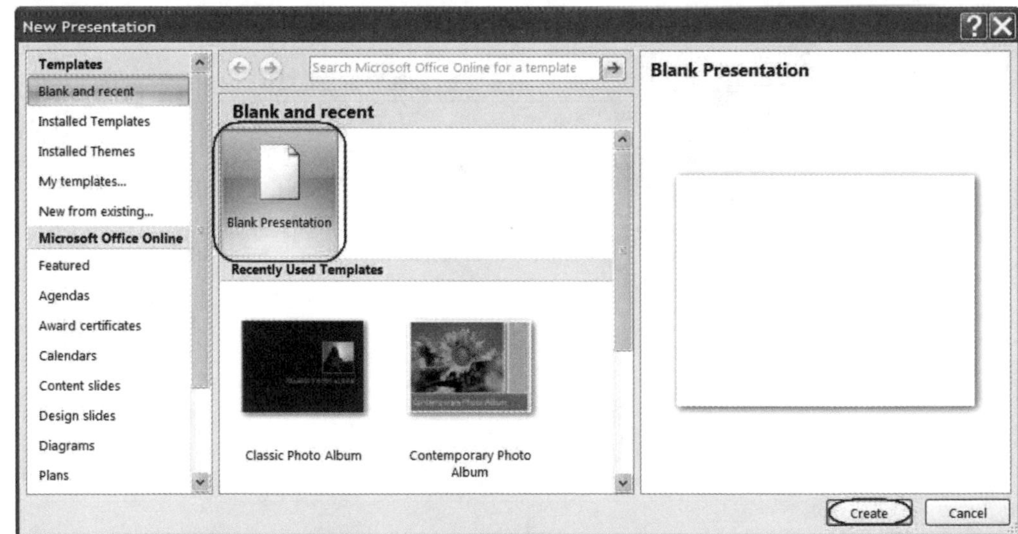

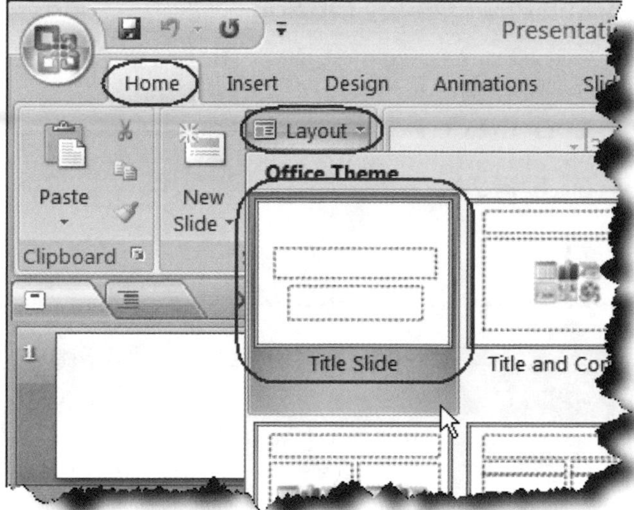

Creates a new blank presentation.

- Click the **Home** tab on the Ribbon.

Ensures that the Home tab is the active tab.

- Click the **Layout button** in the Slides group.

Displays the Slide Layout gallery.

- Click the **Title Slide** layout.

Applies the Title Slide layout to the active slide.

Setting PowerPoint Options

In this section, we will work with PowerPoint Options.

In previous versions of PowerPoint, you could set preferences for specific program settings from the Options dialog box. The Options command has been moved to the **PowerPoint Options** button on the File Options menu which displays when you click the **Microsoft Office Button**.

From the PowerPoint Options dialog box, you can specify such options as setting the color scheme for the PowerPoint application, specifying a default location to save files, setting the default file format, and much more.

You may wish to spend some time browsing through the PowerPoint Options dialog box and set any preferences that may help you work with less effort.

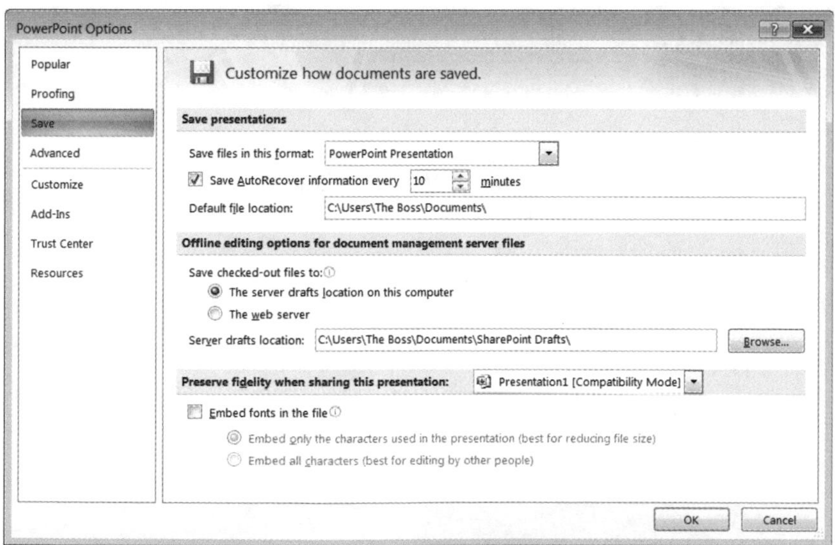

POWERPOINT OPTIONS DIALOG BOX

To Set PowerPoint Options

1. Click the **Microsoft Office Button** and then click **PowerPoint Options** on the bottom of the File Options pane.
2. Click the desired option category in the left pane.
3. Set any options in the right pane.
4. Click **OK**.

Let's Try It!

- Click the **Microsoft Office Button**.

Displays the File Options menu.

- Click the **PowerPoint Options** button.

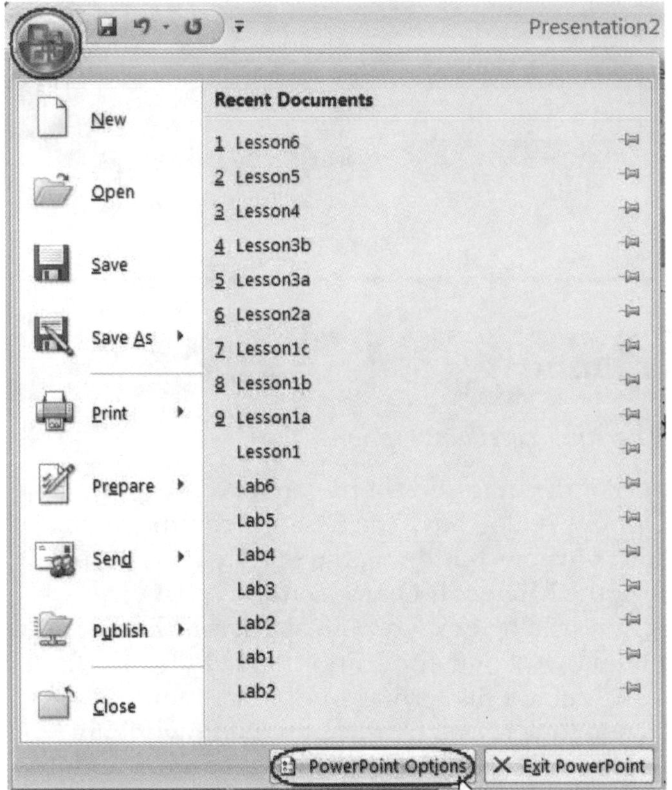

Displays the Word Options dialog box.

- Click the **Save** category in the left pane.

Displays available PowerPoint options for the Save category.

- Click the **Save files in this Format** drop-down arrow and choose **PowerPoint Presentation 97–2003**.

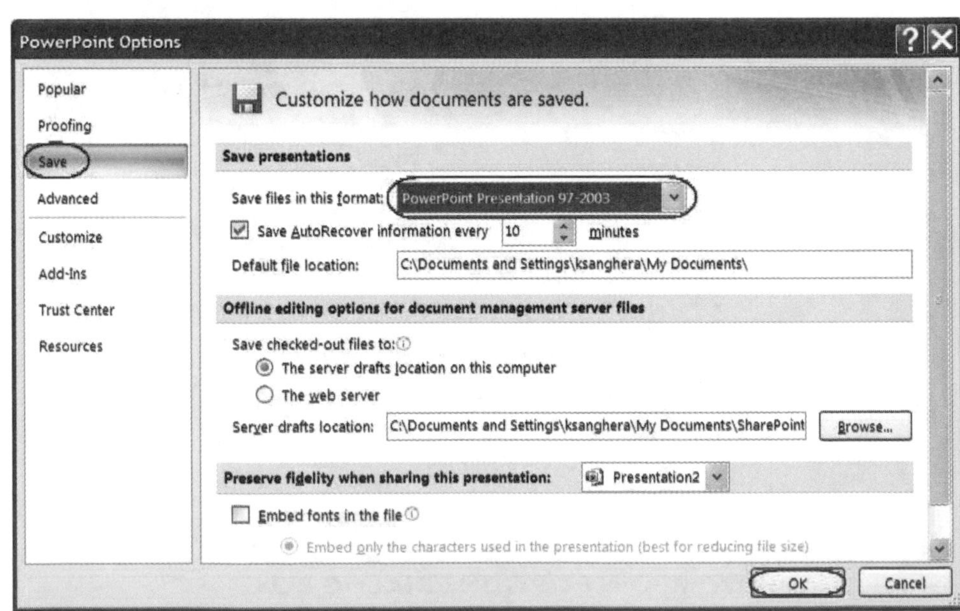

Sets the default file format to PowerPoint 97–2003, allowing users of previous version of PowerPoint to be able to access our files.

- Click **OK**.

Closes the PowerPoint Options window and applies our changes.

Inserting New Slides and Entering Text onto Slides

In this section, you will learn how to enter text onto your slides.

In order to enter text onto your slides, you must enter it into a **placeholder** (the containers with dotted lines that are part of slide layouts). Placeholders can hold text such as title text, bulleted lists, and numbered lists as well as objects such as ClipArt and charts. To enter text into a placeholder, click inside of the placeholder object and then begin typing. When working with bulleted lists, press the **Enter** key to automatically insert a new bullet on the new line. The text you type into placeholders can be edited directly on the slide or from the **Outline Pane**.

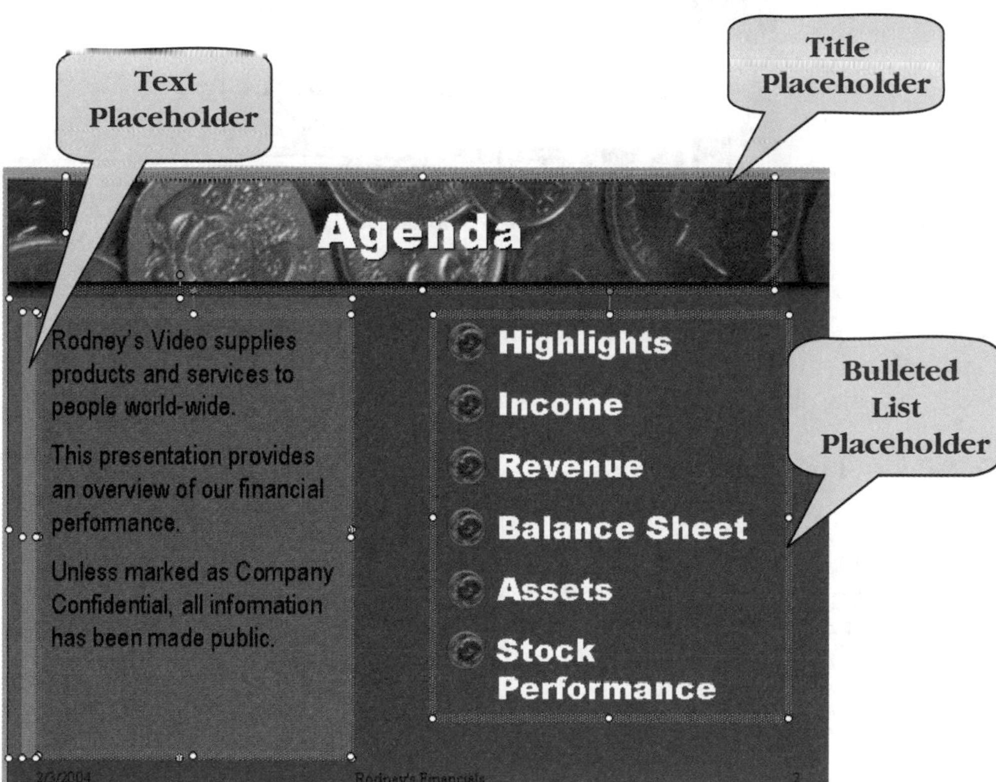

To Enter Text onto Slides

1. Display the slide into which you want to enter text.
2. Click inside the desired placeholder.
3. Move your mouse pointer to the location where you wish to begin typing text.
4. Enter your text.
5. Press the **Enter** key to move to a new line.

In this section, you will learn how to add slides to your presentation.

When inserting a new slide in the presentation, that slide will immediately follow the active slide in the presentation. You can add a new slide to the presentation in either Normal View or Slide Sorter View by clicking the **arrow** on the **New Slide Button** under the **Slides** group on the Home Ribbon and choosing the desired slide layout from the gallery. If you wish to insert a new slide with the same layout as the active slide, click the **New Slide Button** (above the words "New Slide").

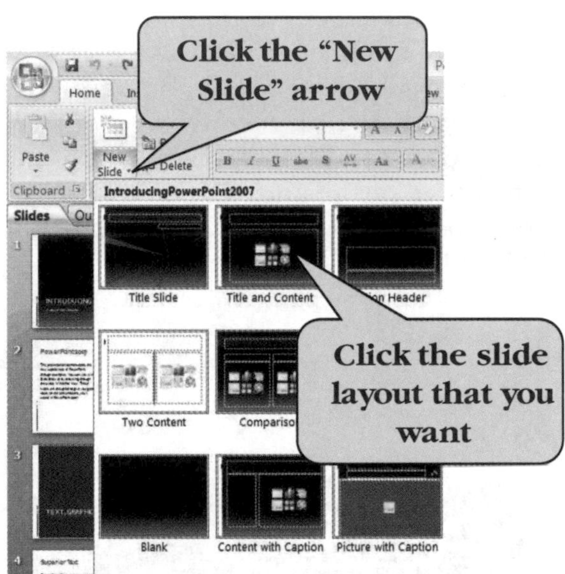

With the exception of the blank layout, all new slides contain **placeholders**. Placeholders are boxes with dotted or hatch-marked borders that hold titles, body text and objects such as charts, tables and graphics.

To Add a New Slide to Your Presentation

1. Select the slide after which you want to new slide to follow.
2. Click the **New Slide arrow** in the Slides group on the Home Ribbon.
3. Select the slide layout you want from the gallery.
4. To insert a new slide with the same layout as the active slide, click the **New Slide** button (above the words "New Slide)
   Or
   Press the **Ctrl + M** keystroke combination.

Let's Try It!

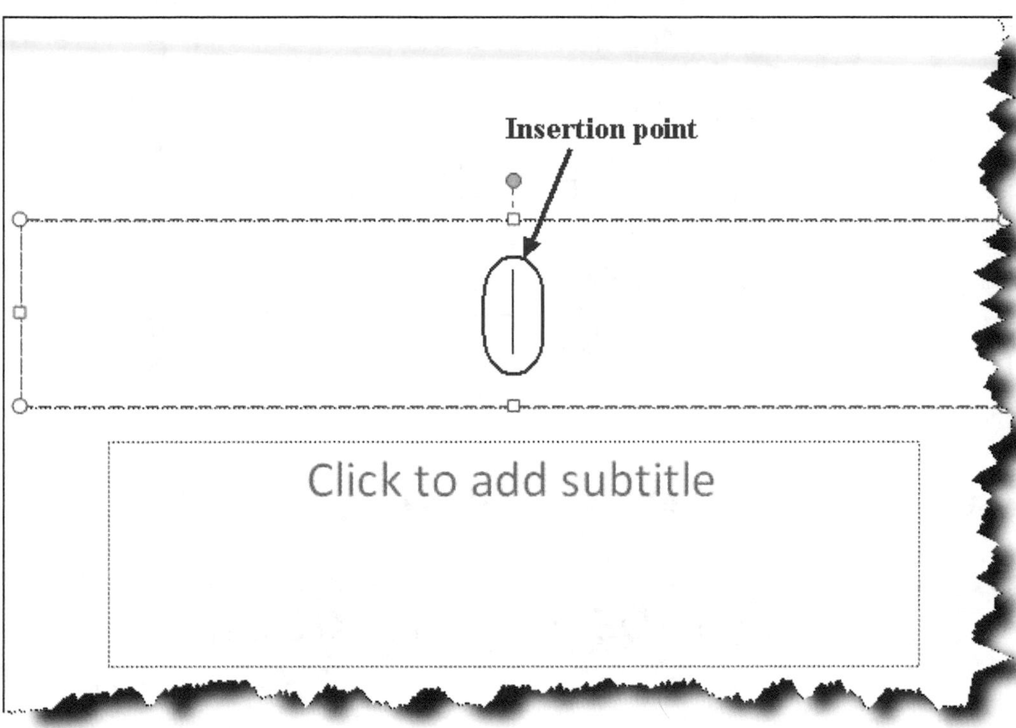

- Click inside the title that contains the text: **Click to add title**.

An insertion point appears inside of the placeholder indicating that you can begin entering text.

- Type: **Company Handbook**

- Click inside the title that contains the text: **Click to add subtitle**.

An insertion point appears inside of the placeholder indicating that you can begin entering subtext.

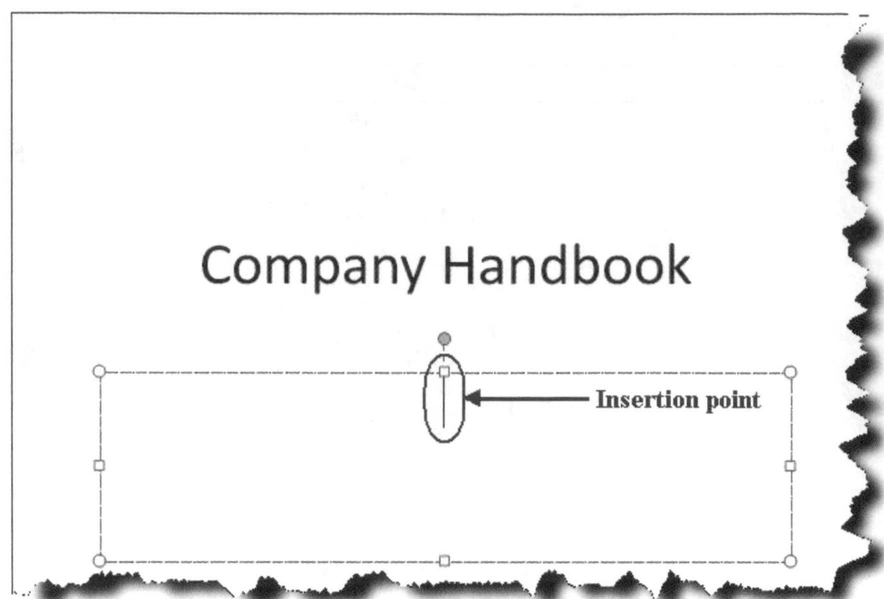

- Type: **ACME Corp.**

- Click anywhere outside of the placeholder.

Deactivates the placeholder.

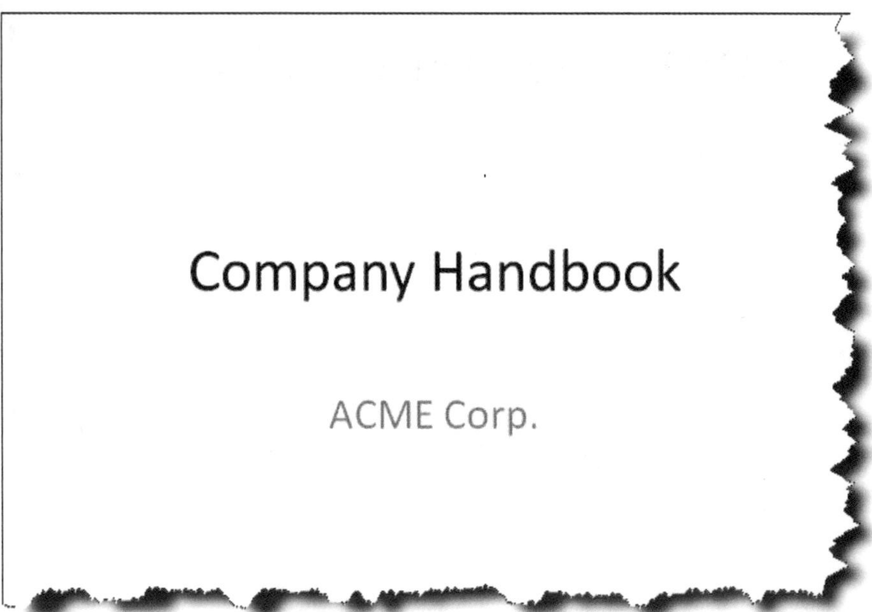

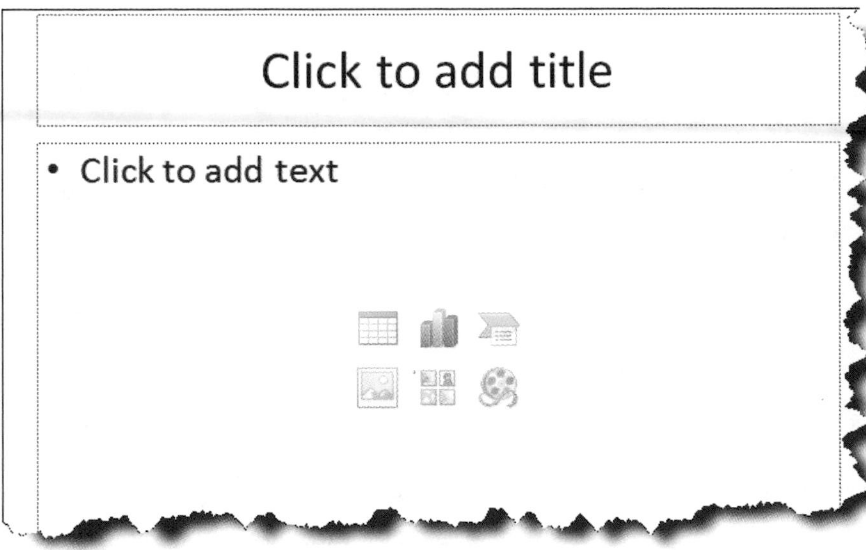

- Press the **Ctrl + M** keystroke combination.

A new slide is inserted with 2 placeholders—a title placeholder and a content placeholder.

- Click in the **Title Placeholder** and type: **Recruiting**.

Enters a slide title in the title placeholder.

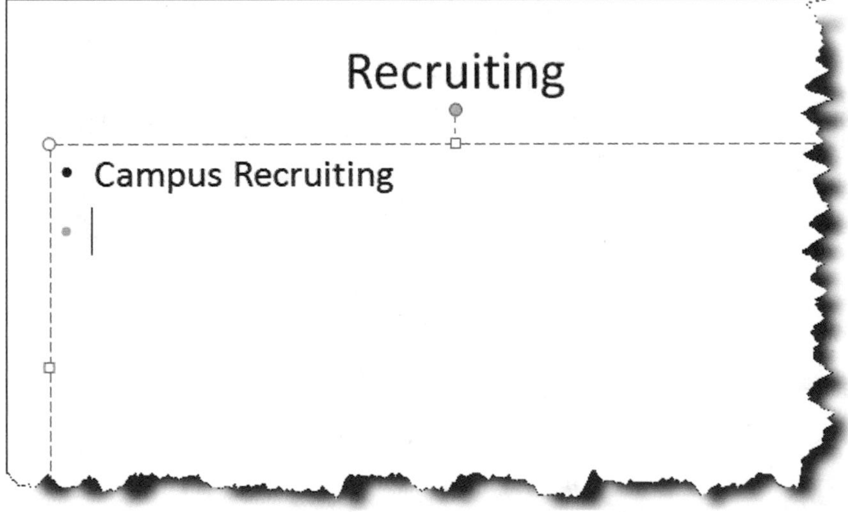

- Click on **Click to add text** in the **Bulleted List Placeholder**.
- Type: **Campus Recruiting**.

Enters the first recruiting event in the bulleted list placeholder.

- Press **Enter**.

Moves to a new line.

- Type **Employee Recruiting**.

Enters the second event in the bulleted list placeholder.

- Press **Enter**.

Inserts a new bulleted line.

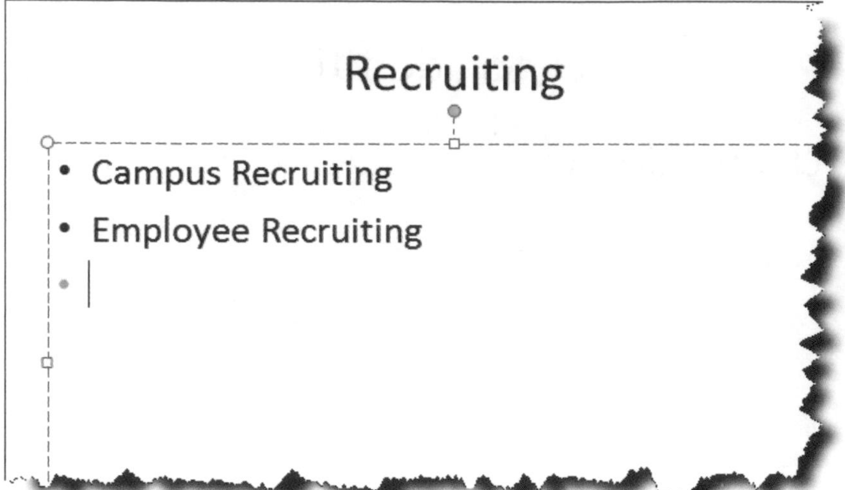

- Type **Professional Recruiters** and then click anywhere outside of the placeholder.

Enters the third recruiting event then deselects the placeholder.

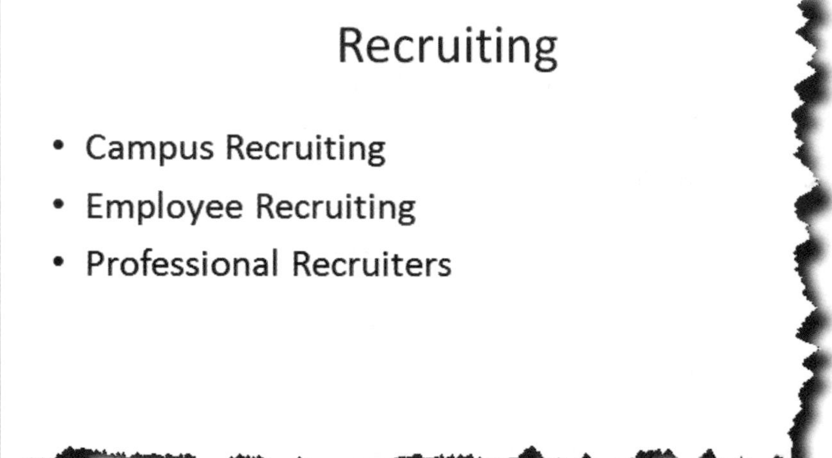

- Click the **New Slide arrow** and click the **Title and Content** layout.

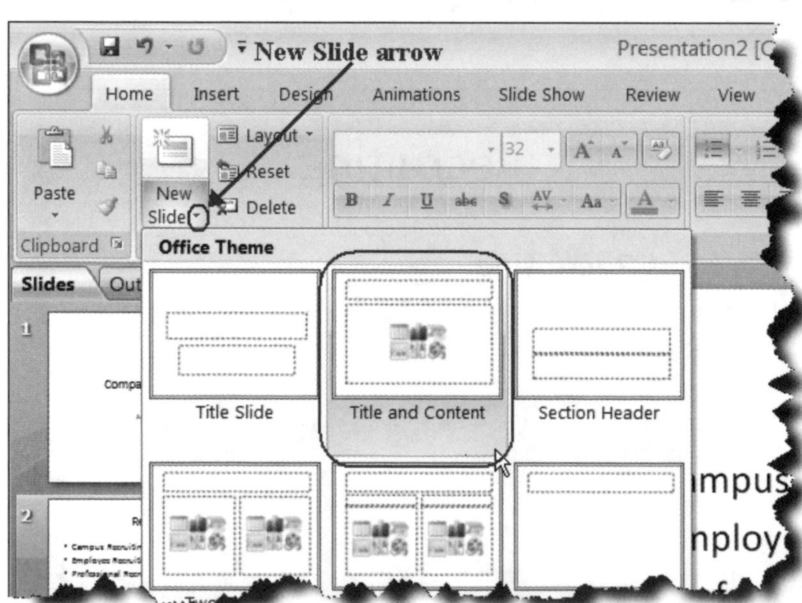

Leaves & Disability

- Maternity Leave
- Short & Long-Term Disability
- Leave of Absence
- Sabbaticals

Inserts a new blank slide after Slide 2.

- Click in the **Title Placeholder** and type: **Leaves & Disability**.

Enters a slide title in the title placeholder.

- Click in the **Bulleted List Placeholder** and type the following while pressing **Enter** key once to go to the next line:

  Maternity Leave

  Short & Long-Term Disability

  Leave of Absence

  Sabbaticals

Enters the information in the bulleted list placeholder.

- Click anywhere **outside** of the placeholder.

Deactivates the placeholder.

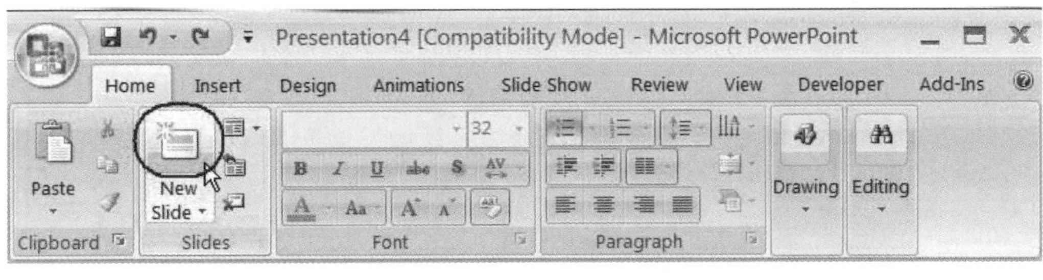

- Click the **New Slide button** (above the words "New Slide).

Inserts a new blank slide after Slide 3.

- Click in the **Title Placeholder** and type: **Compensation**.

Enters a slide title in the title placeholder.

- Click in the **Bulleted List Placeholder** and type the following while pressing **Enter** key once to go to the next line:

  Policies & Levels

  Pay Scales & Bonuses

  Stock Options & Information

  Medical Benefits

  Retirement

Enters the information in the bulleted list placeholder.

- Click anywhere **outside** of the placeholder.

Deactivates the placeholder.

Compensation

- Policies & Levels
- Pay Scales & Bonuses
- Stock Options & Information
- Medical Benefits
- Retirement

Saving a Presentation

In this section, you will learn how to save your presentation file.

Saving a presentation stores it on the hard drive of your computer, a network drive or an external drive for future access. You can save your presentatation to a hard disk, to a removable disk such as a zip drive or USB flash drive, or to a network drive to which you have access. The first time you save a presentation, the **Save As Dialog Box** will appear, prompting you for the name of the presentation and the location where you wish to save the presentation. This box will only appear the first time you save a new presentation. To save a file, click the **Microsoft Office Button** and then click **Save** or use the keyboard shortcut **Ctrl + S**. You can also click the **Save button** on the Quick Access toolbar, directly to the right of the Microsoft Office button.

To save an existing document with a different file name, select **Save As** from the File Options menu, and then type the new name for the document in the **file name** text box. The original document will be closed and the document with the new name becomes the active document.

After you save a document, the file remains open so you can continue to work on it. You can save any subsequent changes quickly by clicking on the Save icon. It is a good idea to save your presentations often.

To Save a Presentation

1. Click the **Microsoft Office Button** and then click **Save** from the menu
   Or
   Click the **Save icon** on the Quick Access Toolbar.

SAVE ICON

   Or
   Hold down the **Ctrl key** and **S** keystroke combination (**Ctrl + S**).
2. Type the desired file name in the **File name** box.
3. Navigate to the folder where you wish to save your file (many people prefer to save their documents in the **My Documents** folder).
4. Click **Save.**

To Save a Presentation with a Different Name

1. Click the **Microsoft Office Button** and then click **Save As** from the menu. The **Save As** dialog box will open.
2. In the **File name** box, type the new name for your presentation.
3. To save the presentation to a different folder, navigate to the folder where you wish to store your file.
4. Click **Save**.

Let's Try It!

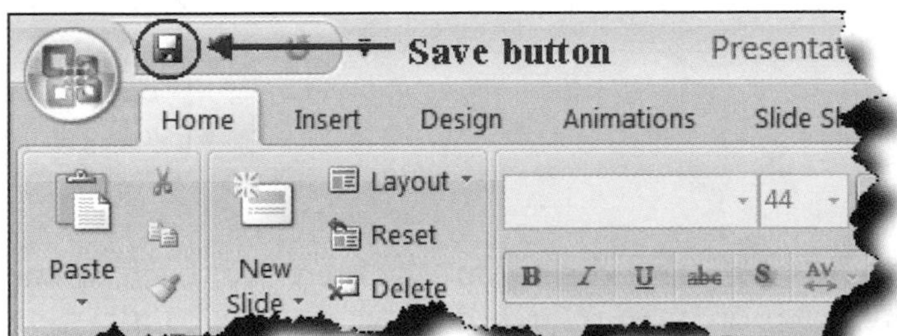

- Insert **flash drive** in USB port.
- Click the **Save button** on the Quick Access toolbar.

As we have not yet saved the document, the Save As dialog box appears, prompting for the file name and location where we wish to save the file.

- In the **File name** text box, type: **PowerPoint Case Study I** and select **flash drive** in the **Save in** list.

Enters the name of the new workbook.

- Select **PowerPoint Presentation** in the Save as type text box.

It will override the default option selected earlier to save presentations in previous versions.

- Click the **Save** button.

Saves the current document.

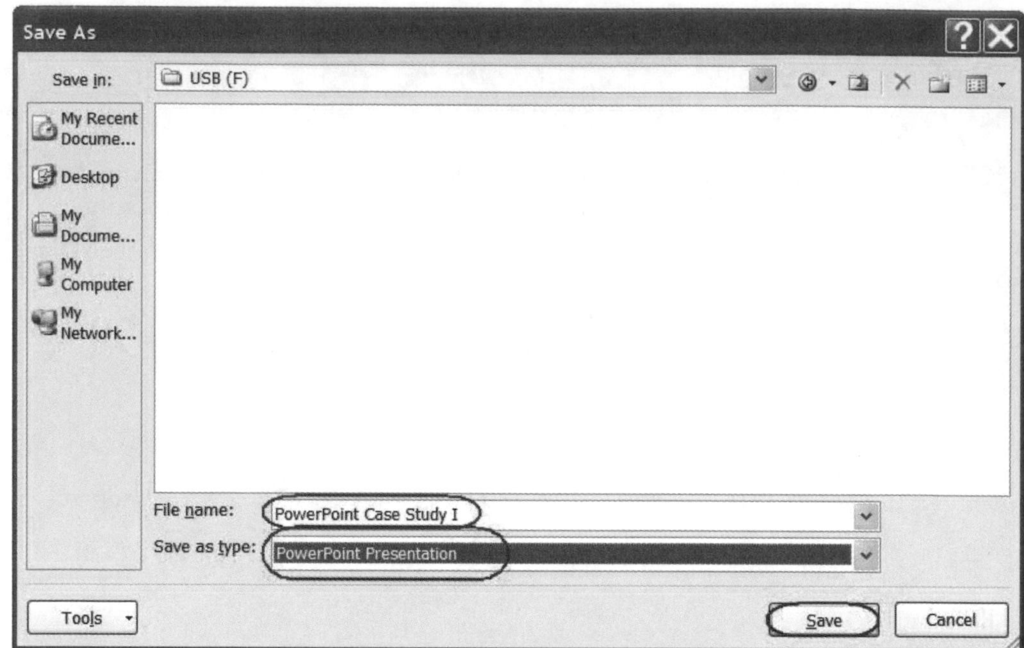

Applying a Theme to a Presentation

In this section, you will learn how to apply a theme to your presentation.

Themes are a quick way to apply preconfigured formatting to your preseentation. Themes consist of theme colors, theme fonts and theme effects that give your presentation a professional and polished look. You can add themes from the **Design tab** on the Ribbon. PowerPoint comes with 20 installed themes that you can use. You can download additional themes from Microsoft Office Online.

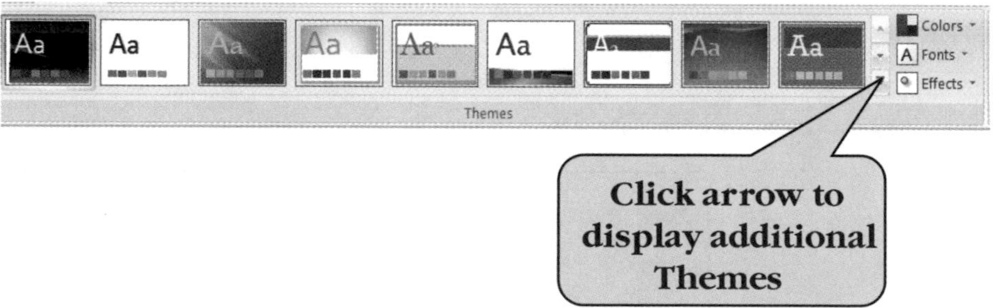

As you move your mouse pointer over each theme in the gallery, your presentation changes to reflect what it would like like if you apply the theme. This is an example of Microsoft Office's new **Live Preview** feature.

You can apply a theme to your entire presentation or to selected slides.

To Apply a Theme to Your Entire Presentation

1. Click the **Design tab** on the Ribbon.
2. Move your mouse pointer over any of the theme thumbnails in the **Themes group** to preview a particular theme.
3. Click the theme thumbnail for the theme you want to apply.

To Apply a Theme to Selected Slides

1. Select the slides to which you want to apply a theme.
2. Click the **Design tab** on the Ribbon.
3. Right-click the theme you want to apply and choose **Apply to Select Slides** from the contextual menu.

> **TIP:** To set a theme as the default theme for all new PowerPoint documents, right-click the theme thumbnail and choose **Set as Default Theme**.

Let's Try It!

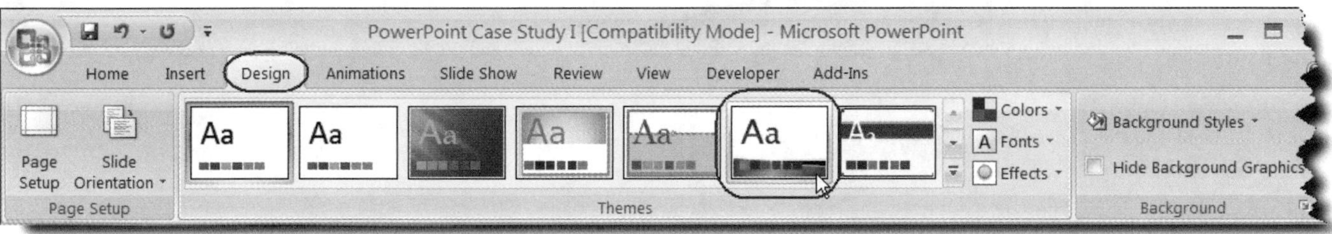

- Click the **Design tab** on the Ribbon.

Switches to Design commands and tools.

- Move your mouse pointer over the **6th theme from the left** (the Concourse theme).

Displays a preview of the Concourse theme.

- Click the **Concourse theme** thumbnail.

- Applies the Concourse theme to the entire presentation.

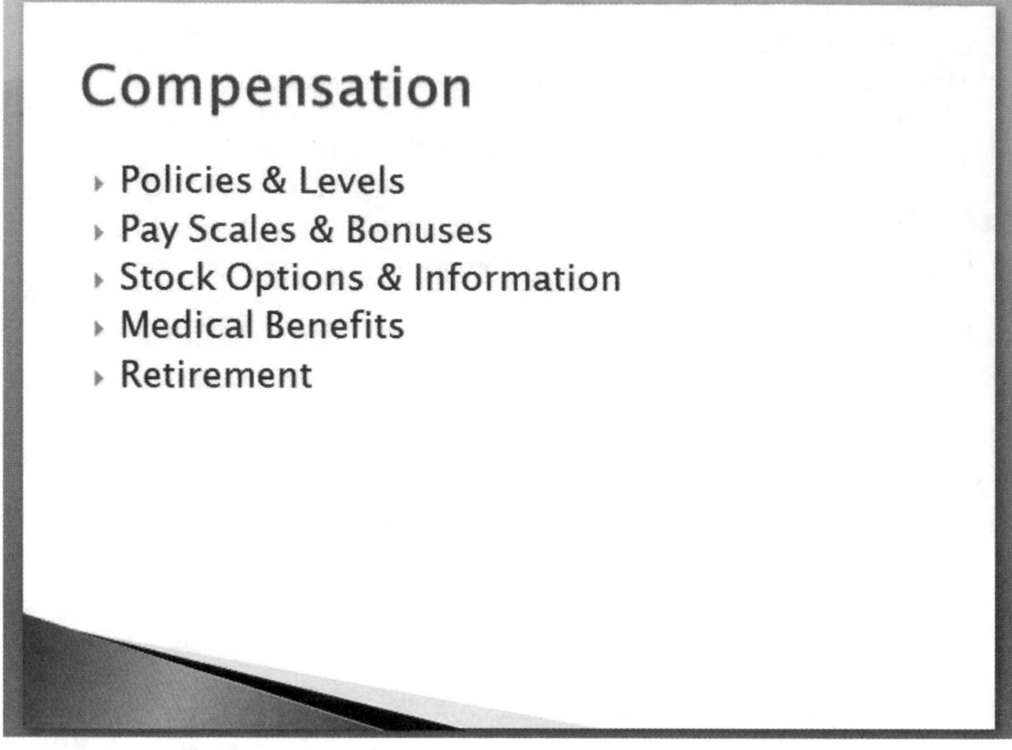

- In the **Slides Pane** select **Slide 2**.

Makes slide 2 the active slide.

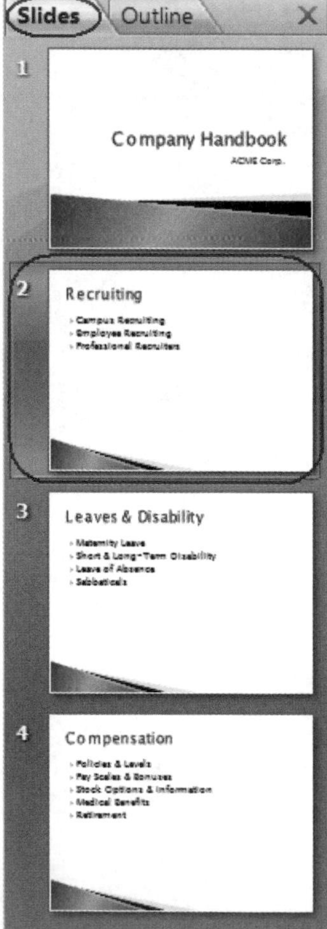

- Hold down the **Ctrl** key and then select **Slide 4**.

Selects slides 2 and 4. Holding down the Ctrl key allows you to select non-adjacent slides.

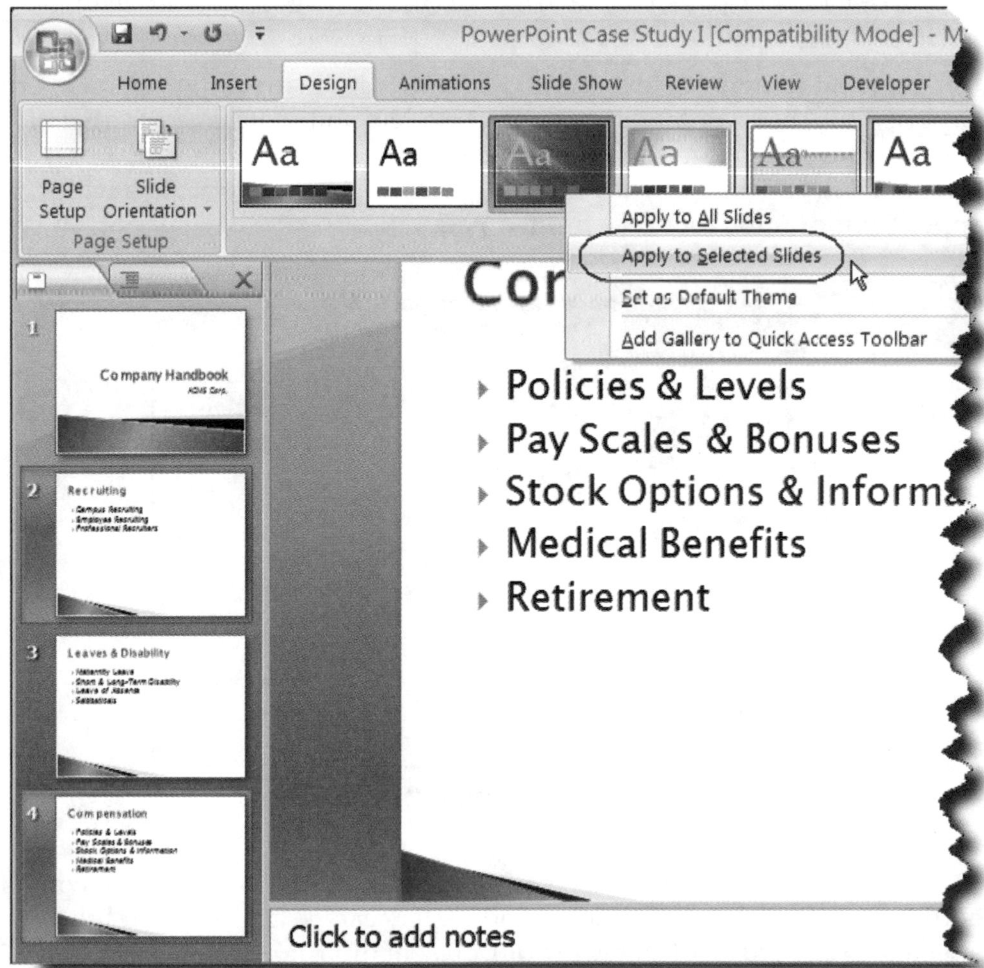

- Right-click on the **third theme from the left** (the Apex theme) and choose **Apply to Selected Slides** from the contextual menu.

Applies the Apex theme to slides 2 and 4.

- Press the **Ctrl + Z** keystroke combination to undo the theme.

Applies the Concourse theme to the entire presentation.

- Click the **Save button** on the Quick Access toolbar.

Saves the current presentation.

- Policies & Levels
- Pay Scales & Bonuses
- Stock Options & Information
- Medical Benefits
- Retirement

Creating Headers and Footers

This section will guide you through the process of creating Headers and Footers in your presentation.

Headers and footers are text that is displayed on the top or bottom of every page of your slides, notes or handouts. Headers and footers can consist of specific text, such as a company logo, the slide or page number, or a date. Headers will appear at the top of every printed page while footers will appear at the bottom of every printed page.

HEADER AND FOOTER DIALOG BOX

Slides can contain only footers whereas Notes and Handouts can contain both headers and footers. Headers and footers can be applied to a single selected slide or to all of slides in your presentation.

By **default**, Notes and Handouts include page numbers, but you have the ability to turn these off. You might choose to include no headers and footers on your slides but instead to reserve them for notes and handouts for that presentation.

To Add a Footer to Slides

1. Click the **Insert tab** on the Ribbon.
2. Click the **Header and Footer button** on the Text group.
3. Click the **Slide tab**.
4. To add an automatically updating date and time, click **Update automatically** under the **Date and time** area, and then select the desired date and time format from the drop-down list. To add a date and time that does not change, click **Fixed**, and type a date and time.
5. To display slide numbers on your slides, click the **Slide Number** check box.
6. To add custom text to your footer, click the **Footer** check box and then type your text in the text box.
7. To omit the footer from the first slide in your presentation, check the **Don't Show on Title Slide** checkbox.
8. To add the information to the selected slide, click **Apply.** To add the information to every slide in the presentation, click **Apply to All**.

To Add a Header to Notes and Handouts

1. Click the **Insert tab** on the Ribbon.
2. Click the **Header and Footer button** on the Text group.
3. Click the **Notes and Handouts** tab.
4. To add an automatically updating date and time, click **Update automatically** under the **Date and time** area, and then select the desired date and time format from the drop-down list. To add a date and time that does not change, click **Fixed**, and type a date and time.
5. To display page numbers on your notes and handouts, click the **Page Number** check box.
6. To add custom text to your footer, click the **Footer** check box and type your text in the text box.
7. To add custom text to your header, click the **Header** check box and type your text in the text box.
8. To add the information to the selected slide note and handout, click **Apply**. To add the information to all notes and handouts in the presentation, click **Apply to All**.

Let's Try It!

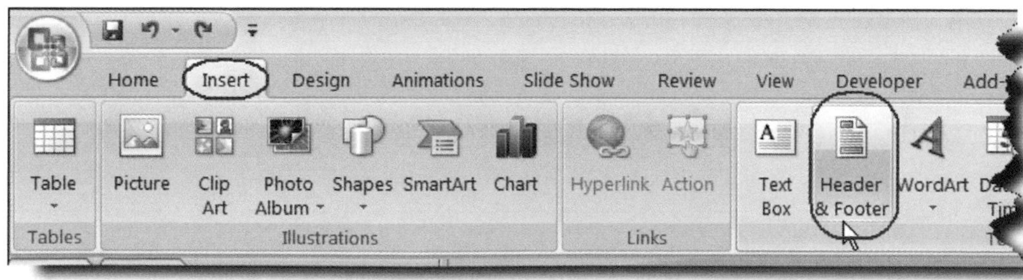

- Click the **Insert** tab on the Ribbon.

Switches to Insert commands and tools.

- Click the **Header and Footer** button in the Text group on the Ribbon.

Displays the Header and Footer dialog box.

- Click the **Date and Time** checkbox.

Includes the Date and Time in the footer.

- Click the **Update Automatically** radio button.

The current date and time will be inserted and updated automatically each time the presentation is opened.

- Click the **Slide Number** check box.

Includes the Slide Number in the footer.

- Click the **Footer** check box and type: **Company Handbook** in the Footer text box.

Enters text to be included in the slide footer.

- Click the **Don't Show on Title Slide** check box.

Omlts the footer information from the first slide in the presentation.

- Click **Apply to All**.

Applies the footer settings to all other slides in the presentation and closes the Header and Footer dialog box.

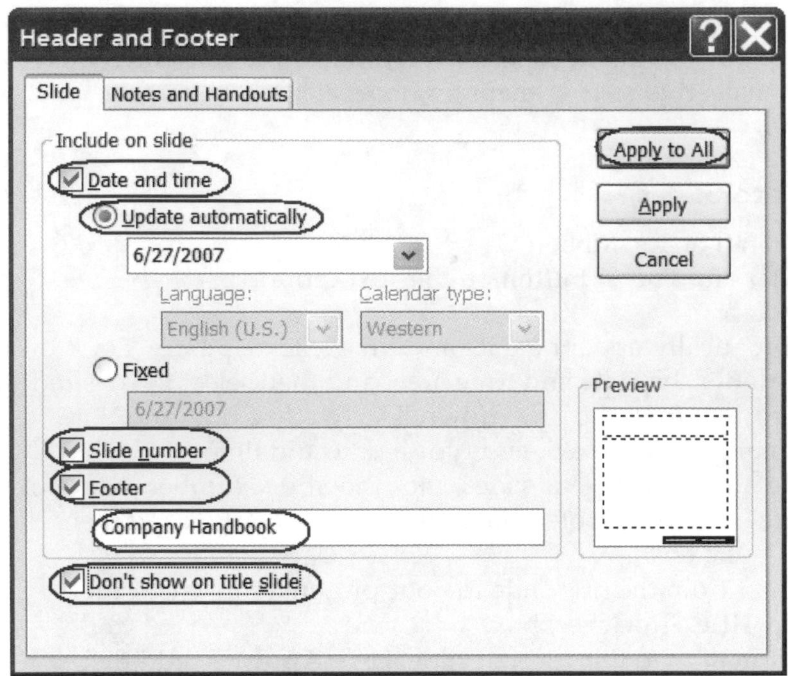

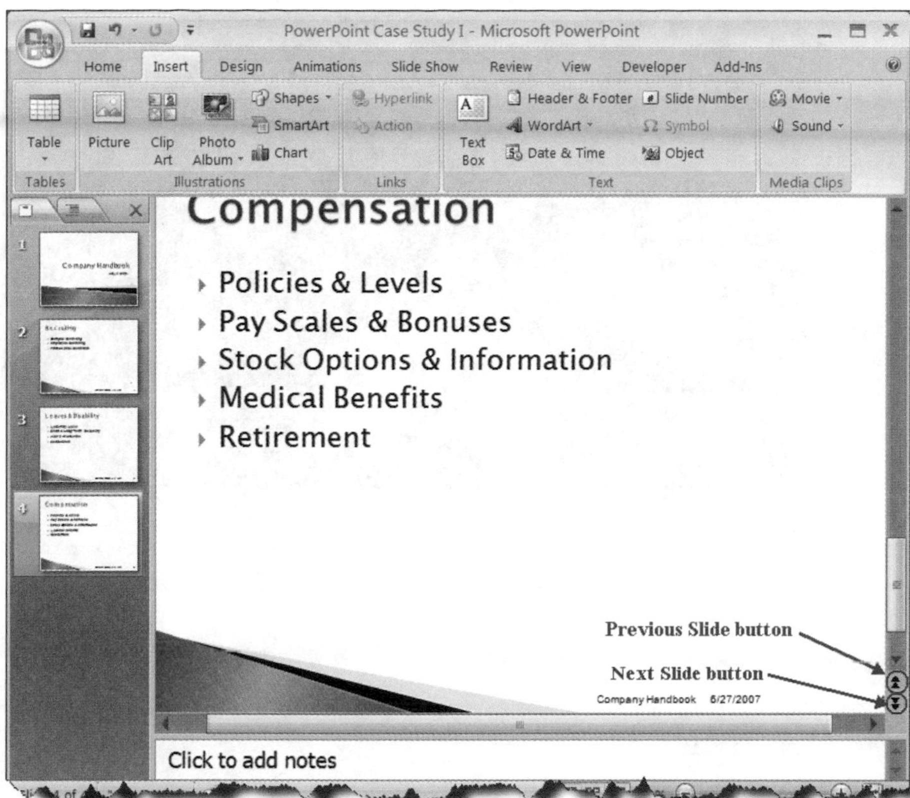

- Click the **Previous Slide** and **Next Slide** buttons and observe the slide footer.

Advances to the previous or next slide in the presentation. The footer information that we specified is inserted on the bottom of each slide except on the title page.

Using the Notes Pane

In this section, you will learn how to enter text into the Notes Pane.

When preparing a presentation, you can use the **Notes Pane** to provide anecdotes, additional details relating to a slide, or any other information that you want to mention in your presentation but do not want to include on your slides. The Notes Pane is displayed in normal view and you type text directly into the notes pane box. Notes are not displayed to the audience when you are running a slide show.

When printing your presentation, you have the option of printing out your **Notes Pages** as well, which include the slide and any notes for that slide underneath. These can serve as handy cue cards or cheat sheets for you when delivering your presentation.

To Enter Text into the Notes Pane

1. Display the slide for which you want add notes in Normal view.
2. Click in the **Notes Pane**.
3. Enter your text.

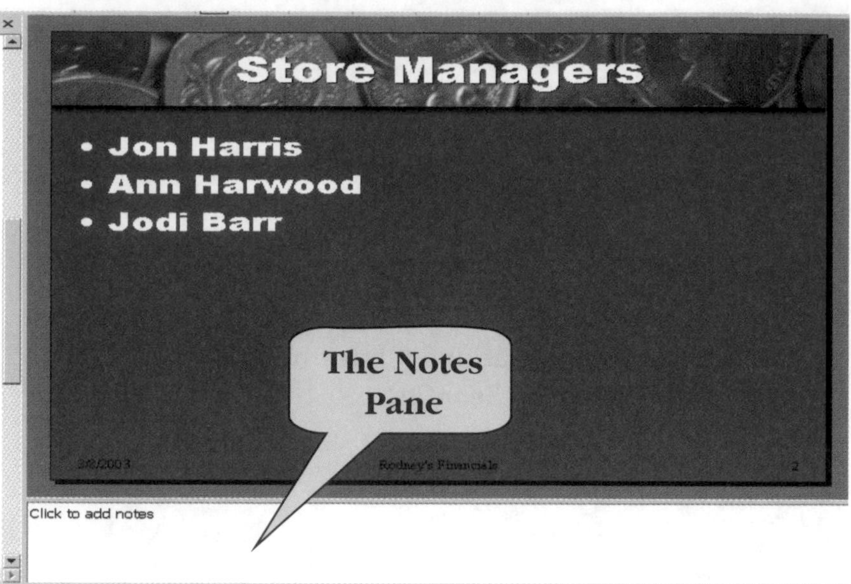

Let's Try It!

- Select **Slide** 2 in the **Slides Pane**.

Makes Slide 2 the active slide.

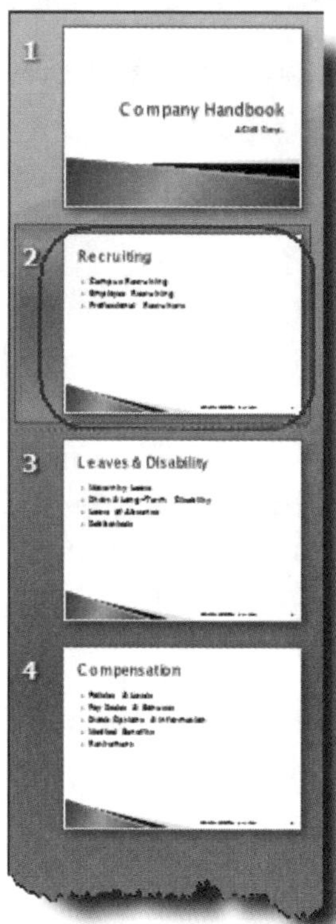

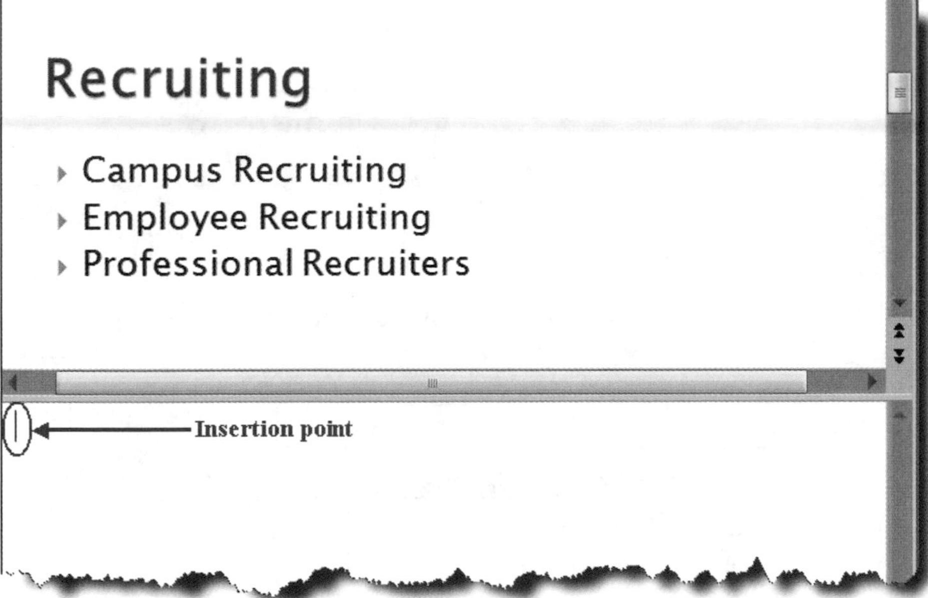

- Click in the **Notes Pane** for Slide 2.

Actives the Notes Pane for Slide 2.

Recruiting

- Campus Recruiting
- Employee Recruiting
- Professional Recruiters

Discuss internal job listings such as finding internal job, contact information needed when applying for internal jobs, and job posting form posted on ACME's web site.

- Type: **Discuss internal job listings such as finding internal job, contact information needed when applying for internal jobs, and job posting form posted on ACME's web site.**

Enters text into the Notes Pane.

- Click the **Save** button on the Quick Access toolbar.

Saves the active presentation.

Formatting Text

In this section, you will learn how to modify the appearance of text in your slides.

You can change the appearance of the text in your slides by applying various types of **formatting**. For instance, you can modify the typeface (or font) of your text, change the size of your text, or emphasize text by applying bold, italics or underlining. When typing text in your document, each new character you type takes on the formatting of the previous character unless you apply new formatting. When creating a new paragraph (by pressing Enter), the first character takes on the formatting of the paragraph mark.

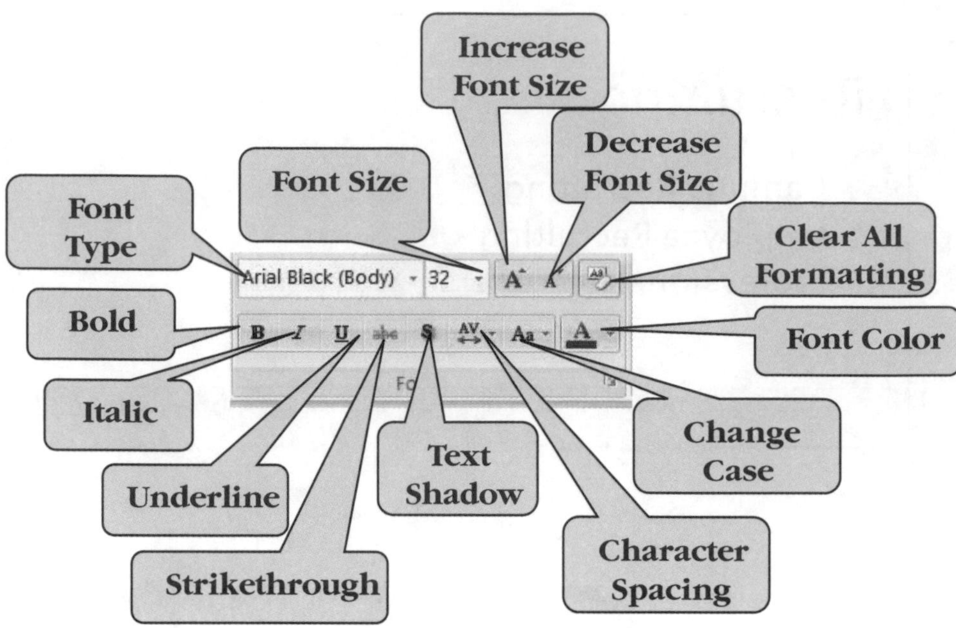

COMMON FORMATTING OPTIONS ON THE FONT GROUP

The quickest and easiest way to apply and modify text formatting is to use the Formatting Tools on the Home tab under the **Font group**. To change text emphasis, select the text you wish to format then click on the appropriate icon (Bold, Italics or Underline). To change the font or font size, select the text then choose the desired option from the font or font size drop-down list. For an explanation of what a tool does, move your mouse pointer over a tool to display an informational box. The box will also display the **keyboard shortcut** for the command, if any.

New in PowerPoint 2007 is the **Mini-Toolbar**. The Mini-Toolbar displays whenever you select text or right-click on selected text and provides quick access to common formatting commands such as bold, italic, font color, font type, font size, fill color, increase indent, decrease indent and increase/decrease font size. If you wish to turn off this feature, you can do so from the PowerPoint Options dialog box.

> **TIP:** You can also apply formatting from the **Font Dialog Box**, which allows you to apply multiple formats (bold, italics, font size, font type, font color, etc.) to selected text at once. To apply multiple formatting to selected text, click the **Font Dialog Box Launcher** on the lower-right corner of the Font command set then make your desired selections.

To Use Formatting Tools

1. **Select** the text that you want to modify.
2. Click the **Home** tab on the Ribbon.
3. To emphasize text, click on the **Bold**, **Italics** or **Underline** icon on the Font group.
4. To change the **font type**, click the arrow on the font drop-down list and select the desired typeface.
5. To change the **font size**, click the arrow on the font size drop-down list and select the desired font size or type the size manually in the font size box.
6. To use the **Mini-toolbar**, select the text you want to modify, point to the mini-toolbar or right-click on the selected text and then choose the desired option from the Mini-toolbar.

Let's Try It!

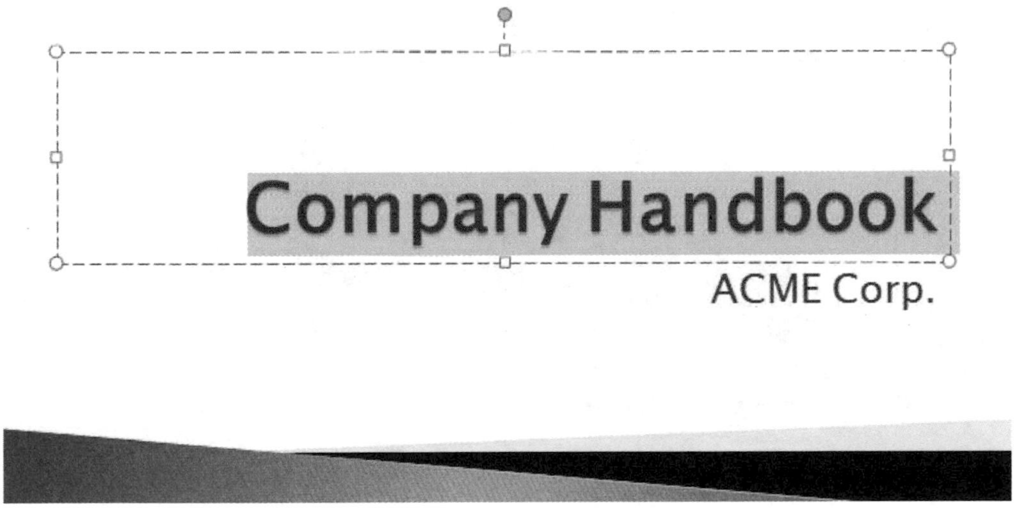

Company Handbook

ACME Corp.

- Select **Slide 1**.

Makes Slide 1 the active slide.

- Click inside the title placeholder and select **Company Handbook**.

Selects all of the text in the placeholder.

- Click on **Home** tab and then click on the arrow next to the **Font** drop-down list.

Displays a list of available typefaces

- Scroll down until you see **Algerian**, and then **click on Algerian** with your left mouse button.

Selects the Font Type (typeface) for the selected text.

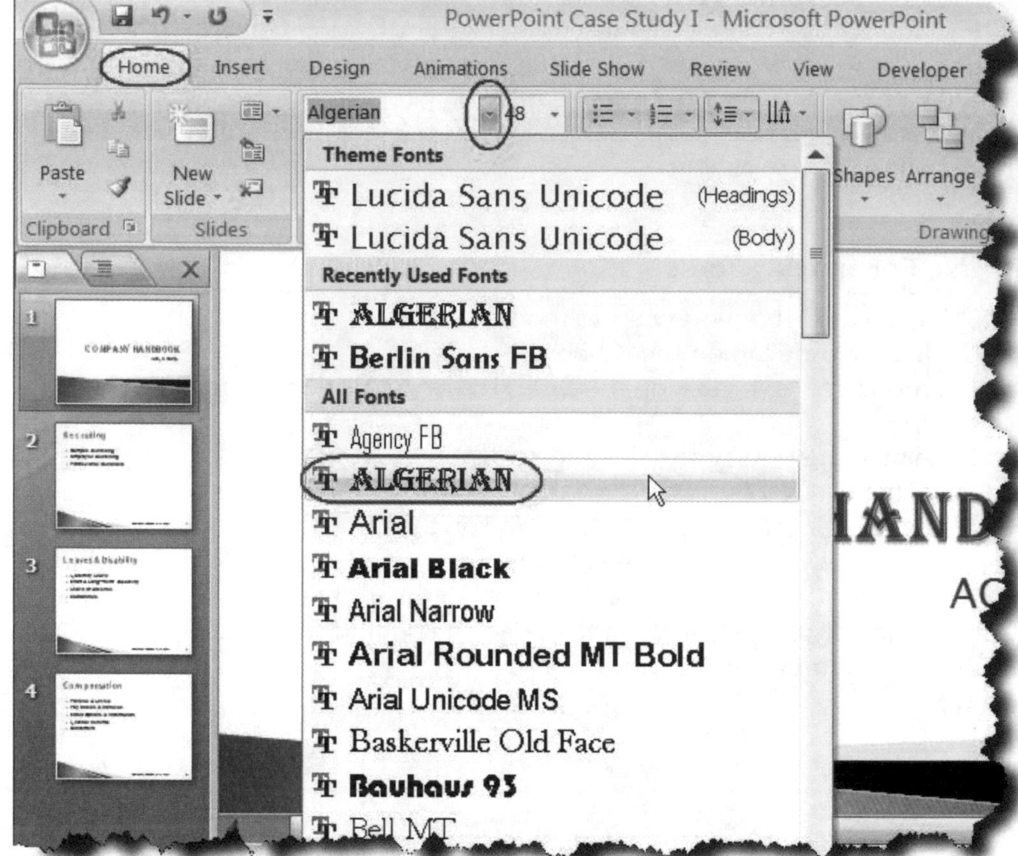

- Click the **Bold** icon on the Ribbon.

Removes the Bold formatting from the selected text.

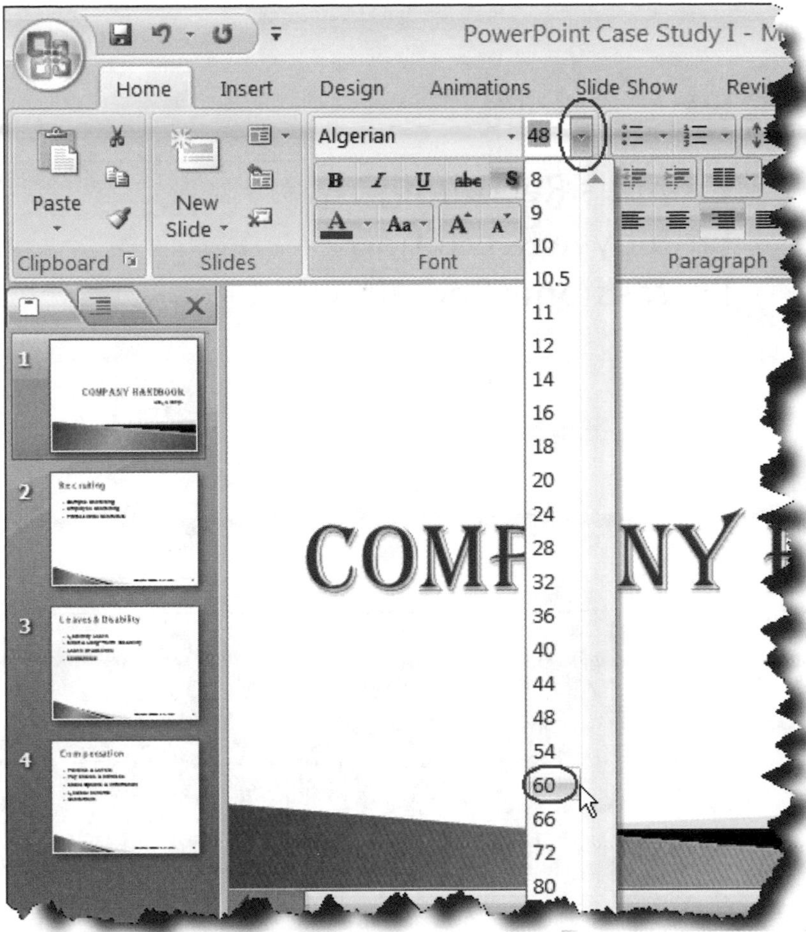

- Click the **Font Size** drop-down list on the Ribbon and select **60**.

Select a font size of 60 pt. for the selected text.

- Click the **arrow** to the right of the **Font Color button** on the Ribbon.

Displays the Color Palette.

- Click on the **fifth row, fifth column** (Turquoise Accent 1, Darker 25%) color button under the Standard Colors category.

Selects Turquoise for the font color of the selected text and closes the Colors Palette.

- Select **Slide 2**.

Makes Slide 2 the active slide.

- Select **Recruiting** inside the title placeholder.

Selects all of the text in the placeholder.

- Click on the arrow next to the **Font** drop-down list and select **Arial Rounded MT Bold** with your left mouse button.
- Click the **Font Size** drop-down list on the Ribbon and select **54**.

Selects the Font Type (typeface) and size for the selected text.

- Click the **Save** button on the Quick Access Toolbar.

Saves the active presentation.

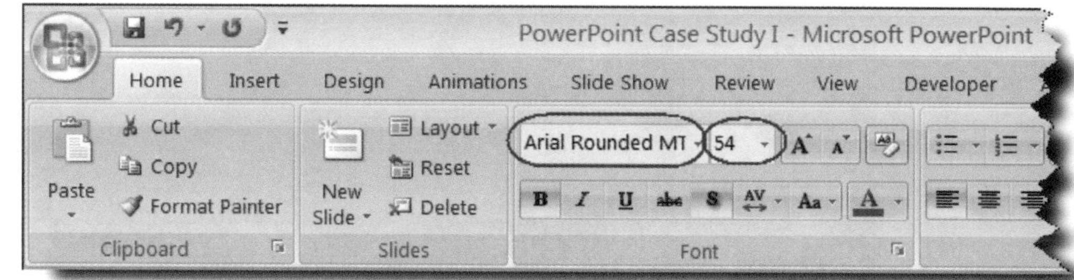

Using the Format Painter Button

In this section, you will learn how to copy formatting from one object to another using the Format Painter button.

The **Format Painter** button on the Home Ribbon allows you to copy the formatting from one object (such as text) and apply it elsewhere in your presentation. This feature copies all formats including font typeface, font color, font size, font style and alignment. to the new object. You can copy all of the attributes of an object to **several** objects by **double-clicking** the Format Painter button and then selecting in succession the objects to which you want to apply the formatting. Click the Format Painter button to deselect it after you have applied the formatting to all desired objects.

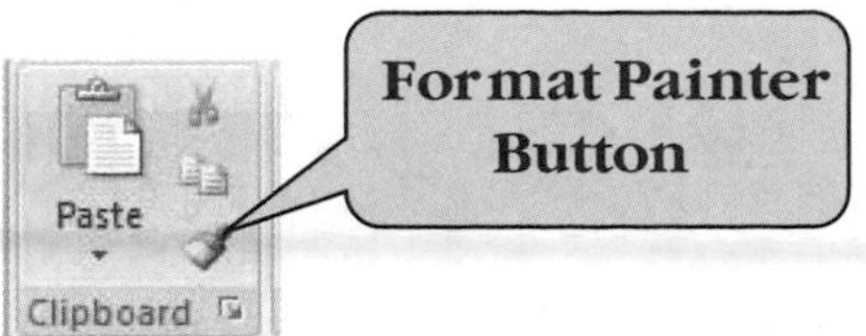

THE FORMAT PAINTER BUTTON

To Copy Formatting from One Location to Another Using the Format Painter Button

1. Select the text whose formatting you wish to copy.
2. Click the **Format Painter** button under the **Clipboard** command set on the Ribbon.
3. Select the object whose formatting you wish to change.

To Copy Formatting from One Location to Several Locations Using the Format Painter Button

1. Select the text whose formatting you wish to copy.
2. **Double-click** the Format Painter button.
3. Click the first object whose formatting you wish to change.
4. Click any additional objects whose formatting you wish to change.
5. When finished, click the Format Painter button to deactivate it.

Let's Try It!

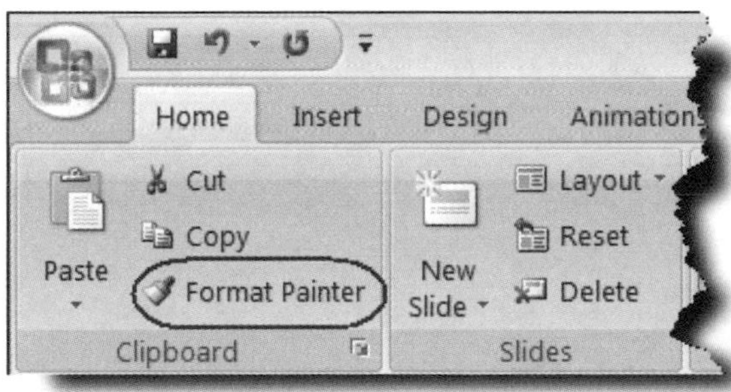

- Make sure **Recruiting** is still selected in slide 2.
- **Double-click** the **Format Painter** button under the Home ribbon.

Activates the Format Painter button to apply formatting to more than one area.

- Select **Slide 3**.

Makes Slide 3 the active slide.

- Select the words: **Leaves & Disability** in the slide title placeholder.

Applies the formatting of the selected text in Slide 2 to the words—Leaves & Disability.

Leaves & Disability
- Maternity Leave
- Short & Long-Term Disability
- Leave of Absence
- Sabbaticals

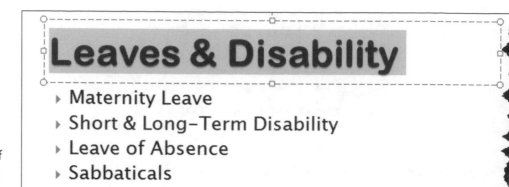

- Select **Slide 4.**

Makes Slide 4 the active slide.

- Click the word: **Compensation** in the slide title placeholder.

Applies the formatting of the selected text in Slide 2 to the word Compensation.

Compensation
- Policies & Levels
- Pay Scales & Bonuses
- Stock Options & Information
- Medical Benefits

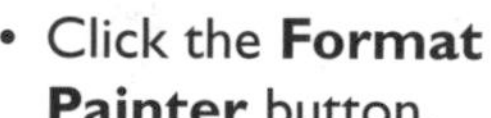

- Click the **Format Painter** button.

Deactivates the Format Painter button.

- Click anywhere outside of the title placeholder.

Deselects the placeholder.

- Click the **Save** button.

Saves the active presentation.

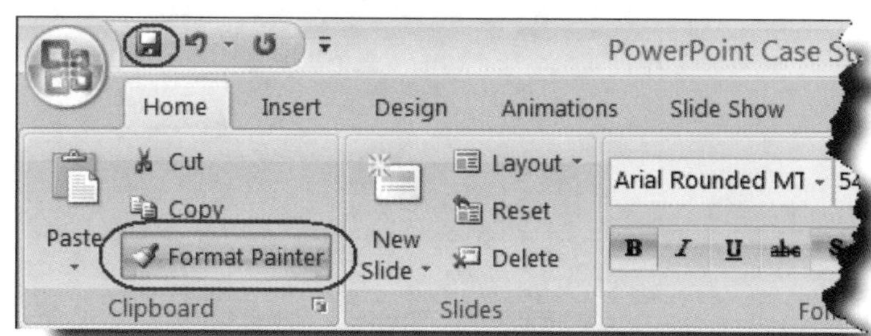

Using Bulleted Lists

In this section, you will work with applying and modifying bulleted lists.

Bulleted Lists are the foundations of conventional presentations. By default, the text placeholder in PowerPoint is formatted to be a bulleted list using the traditoinal • character as the bullet. Bulleted lists present key ideas in a list format but do not necessarily suggest a particular sequence. To create a bulleted list, click on the **Bullets** button on the Home Ribbon. Click the bullets button again when you are finished with your list. To specify the type of bullet, click the arrow next to the Bullets icon and choose the desired bullet type from the gallery.

For more bullet options, such as setting the type of bullet, indentation, etc., click the arrow next to the Bullets button. To Modify bullet indentation or to create a new bullet type, click **Bullets and Numbering** on the menu, click the Bulleted tab and make your selections.

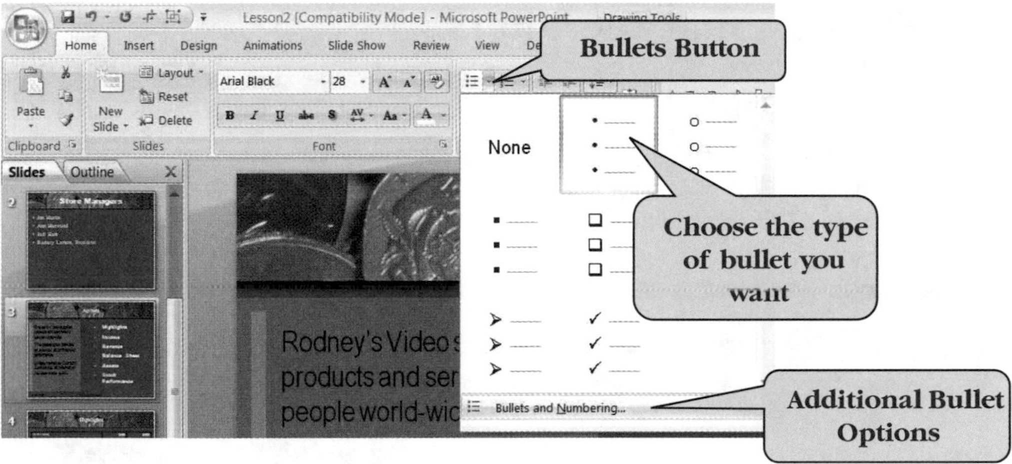

To Create a Bulleted List

1. Select the list to which you want to apply bulleting.
2. To create a default bulleted list, click the **Bullets** button on the Home Ribbon.

To Modify a Bulleted List

1. Click on the placeholder containing the list you want to modify.
2. Click the drop-down arrow next to the Bullets button.
3. Click on the desired **Bullet type** in the window.
4. For additional options, click the drop-down arrow next to the Bullets button, choose **Bullets and Numbering** on the menu, click the **Bulleted** tab and make your desired selections.
5. Click **OK**.

Let's Try It!

- Select **Slide 2**.

Makes Slide 2 the active slide.

- Click anywhere in the **Bulleted List placeholder**.

A dotted border appears around the placeholder.

- Click on the **border** of the placeholder.

Selects the placeholder whose bulleted list we want to modify.

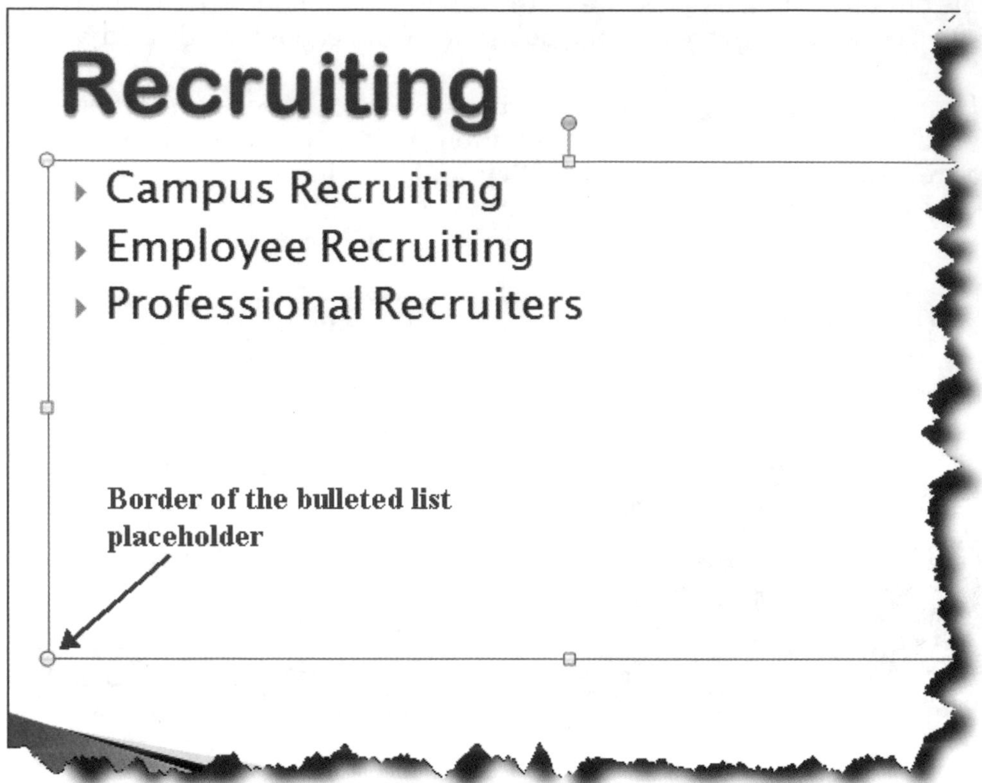

- Click the drop-down arrow next to the **Bullets** icon and click the **second bullet option** in the second row.

Applies the bullet option in row 2, column 2 to our bulleted list.

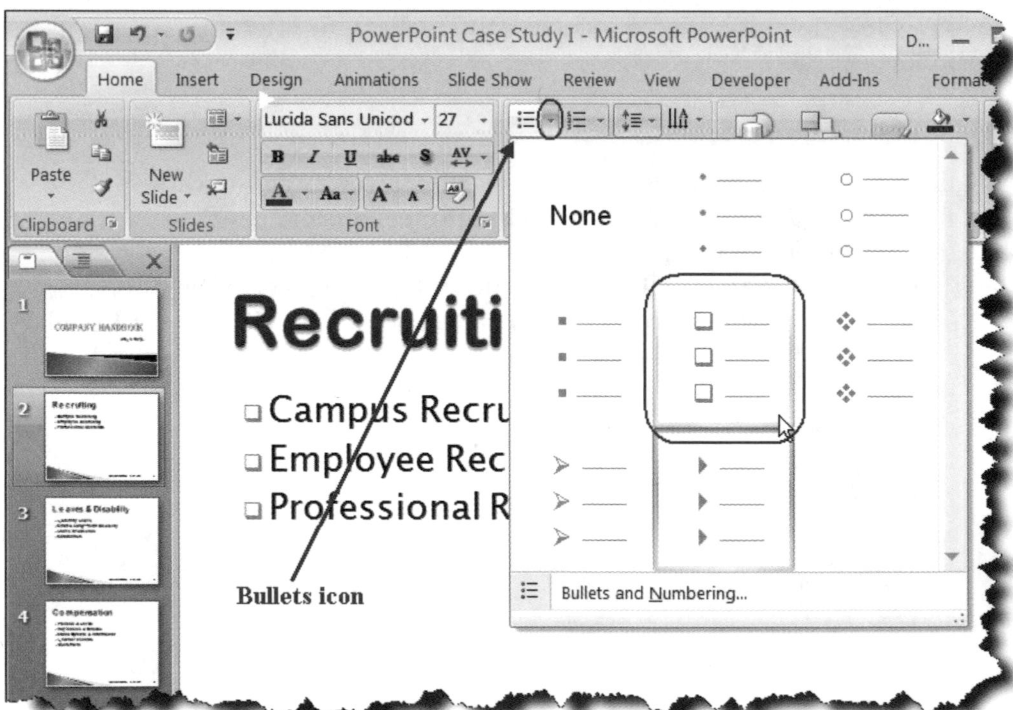

- Click on the **Undo** button on the Quick Access toolbar.

Applies back the custom bullets.

- Click anywhere outside of the placeholder.

Deselects the placeholder.

- Click the **Save** button.

Saves the active presentation.

Using Shapes

In this section, you will learn how to add Shapes to your slides.

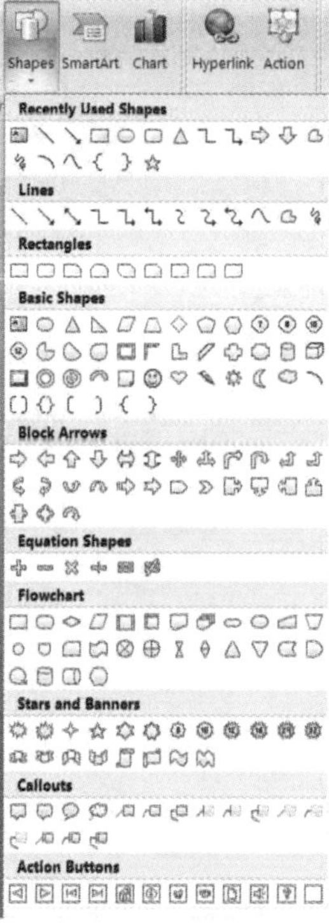

Another nifty feature you can find on the Insert Tab is **Shapes**. Shapes consist of a group of ready-made drawing objects that you can add to your presentation. These include such shapes as rectangles, circles, cubes, lines and connectors, block arrows, callouts, stars and banners and the list goes on. The AutoShapes are grouped for you by the following categories:

- Recently Used Shapes
- Lines

- Rectangles
- Basic Shapes
- Block Arrows
- Equation Shapes
- Flowchart
- Stars and Banners
- Callouts
- Action Buttons

As with other drawing objects, select the AutoShape you want from the Ribbon and then draw the shape on your slide until it is the desired size. You can add text to Shapes which then becomes part of the object. That is to say, if you rotate or move the AutoShape, the text rotates or moves with it.

To Add a Shape

1. Select the slide onto which you want to place an AutoShape.
2. Click the **Insert tab** on the Ribbon.
3. Click the **Shapes** button on the Illustrations group on the Ribbon.
4. Click the Shape that you want to add to your slide from the Shapes gallery.
5. Click on the slide and draw the AutoShape until it is the desired size.

> **TIP:** The Shapes under the Shapes button on the Insert Ribbon and those under the Drawing group of the Home Ribbon are the same.

Let's Try It!

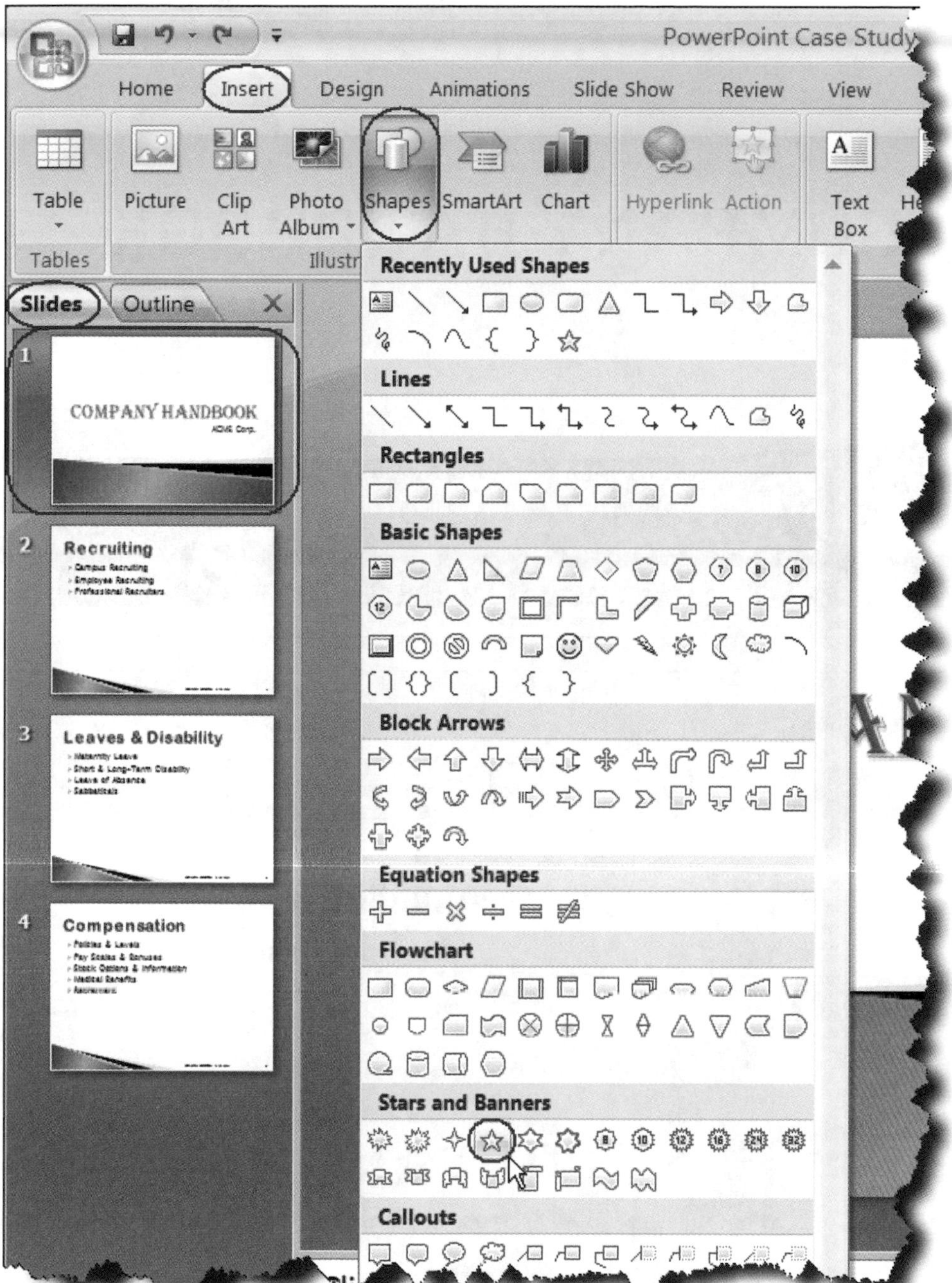

- Select **Slide 1** in the slides pane.

Makes Slide 1 the active slide.

- Click the **Insert tab** on the Ribbon.

Switches to Insert commands and tools.

- Click the **Shapes** button on the Illustrations group.

Displays the Shapes gallery.

- Under the **Star and Banners** category, click on the **5-Point Star Shape** (first row, fourth column) as shown.

- Click on the slide above the title to the right and then draw the AutoShape until it is about 2” in height and 2.5” in width as shown. **Release** the mouse button.

Draws the 5-point star Shape above the slide title.

- Make sure that the **5-Point Star** shape is still selected.

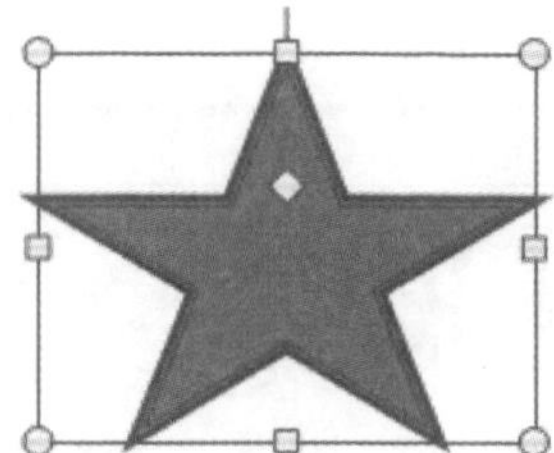

COMPANY HANDBOOK

ACME Corp.

- Click the **Format** tab under the **Drawing Tools** tab on the Ribbon.

Switches to object formatting options.

- Click the **Shape Fill** button on the Shape Styles group and then choose **light blue** (seventh color under the Standard Colors category) from the color palette.

Applies light blue fill color to the Shape and closes the color palette.

- Click anywhere outside the star shape.

Deselects 5-Point Star shape.

- Click the **Save** button.

Saves the active presentation.

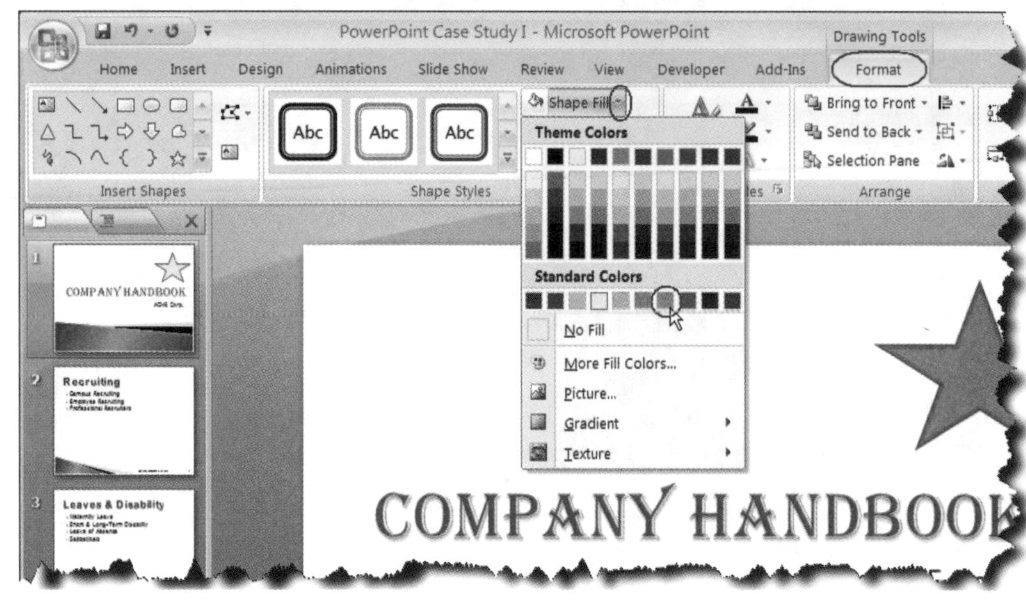

Inserting WordArt

In this section, you will learn how to insert WordArt onto your slides.

WordArt is a gallery of text styles and effects that you can add to your presentations. With WordArt, you can add spectacular effects to the text of your slides—you can shadow it, bevel it, mirror it, and make it glow. In addition, PowerPoint 2007 allows you convert existing text into WordArt format. As with text boxes, you can apply formatting to WordArt shape as well as change the text itself.

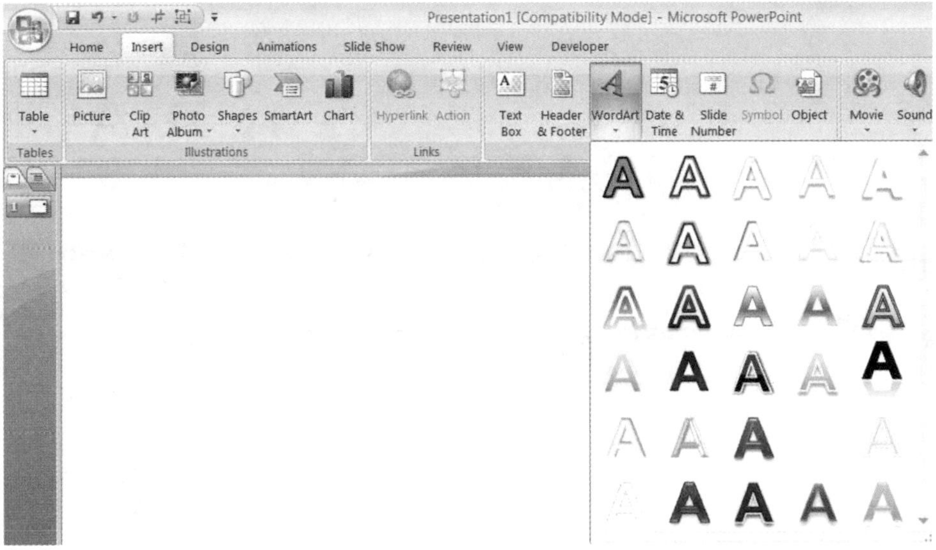

The WordArt button is located on the **Insert Ribbon** on the **Text group** and will launch the **WordArt Gallery** when clicked. From the Gallery, select the **style** of WordArt you wish to add and then type the text for your WordArt object.

From the contextual **Format tab** (which displays when the WordArt object is selected), you can apply a variety of text effects by clicking the **Text Effects** button on the WordArt styles group.

To Insert WordArt

1. Click the **WordArt** button on the Text group of the **Insert tab**.
2. Click on the desired WordArt format in the **WordArt Gallery**.

To Convert Existing Text to WordArt

1. Select the text that you want to convert to WordArt.
2. **WordArt** button on the Text group of the **Insert tab**.
3. Click on the desired WordArt format in the **WordArt Gallery**.

Let's Try It!

- Make sure **Slide 1** is selected.
- Click the **Insert tab** on the Ribbon.

Switches to Insert commands and tools.

- Click the **WordArt** button on the Text group.

Displays the WordArt Gallery.

- Select the WordArt Style in the **third column, fourth row** as shown.

Selects the style for the WordArt object.

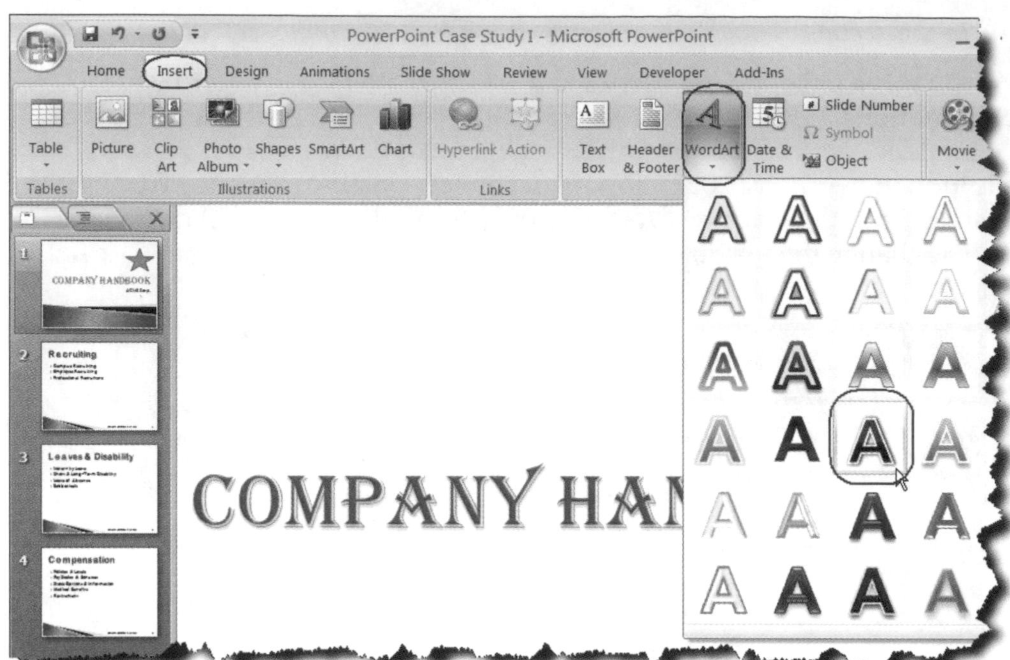

- Type: **2007–2008**.

Enters the text for the WordArt object.

- With the object selected, move your mouse pointer over the object until the pointer transforms into a 4-way arrow.

Enters drag mode.

- Click and drag the WordArt object to the bottom center of the slide and then release the mouse button.

Repositions the object on the bottom of the slide.

- Click the **Home** tab on the **Ribbon**.

Switches to Home commands and options.

- With the WordArt object still selected, click the **Font Size** drop-down list and choose **40**.

Changes the size of the WordArt text to 40 pt.

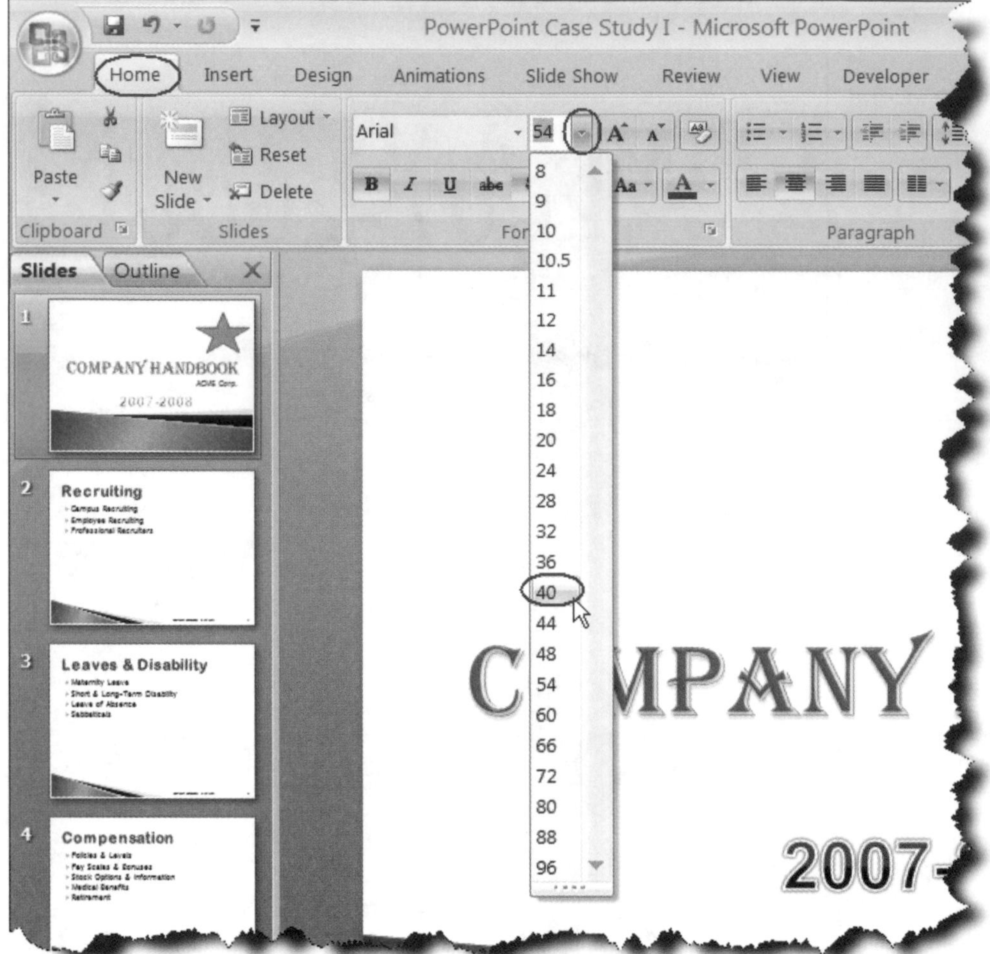

- With the object still selected, click the **Format tab** under the Drawing Tools tab.

Switches to object formatting options.

- Click the **Text Effects** button on the WordArt Styles group.

Displays the Text Effects gallery.

- Point to **Glow** and select the Glow style in the last row, first column.

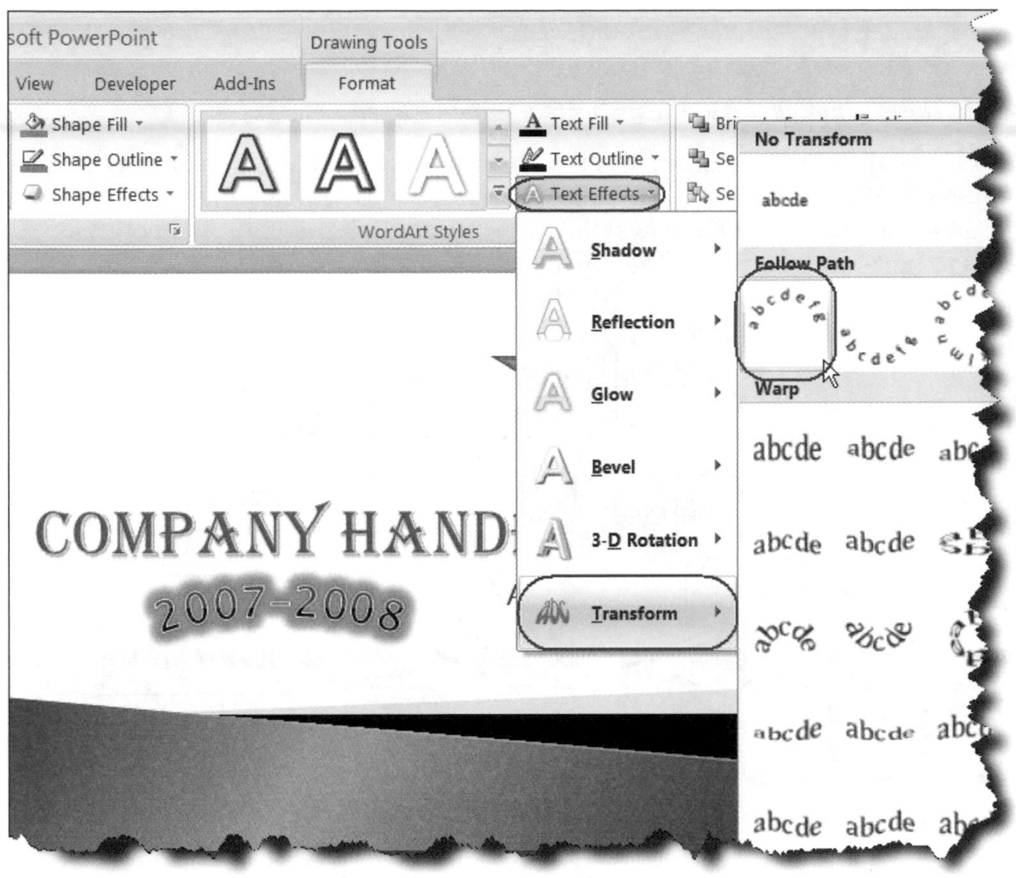

Applies the Accent Color 1, 18 pt. glow style to the WordArt text.

- Click the **Text Effects** button on the WordArt Styles group again and point to **Transform**.

Displays available Transform styles.

- Click the **Arch Up** transform style, the first style under the **Follow Path** category.

Applies Arch Up transform style to the WordArt text.

COMPANY HANDBOOK

ACME Corp.

2007-2008

Click and drag the WordArt to the center of the presentation if needed.

- Click the **Save** button.

Saves the active presentation.

Using Help

In this section, you will learn how to use the Help system.

The **Help system** is designed to provide **assistance** to users whether you are online or offline and bring all available resources to you as quickly as possible. To access the Help system, press **F1** or click the **Help icon** on the upper right-hand corner of the PowerPoint window.

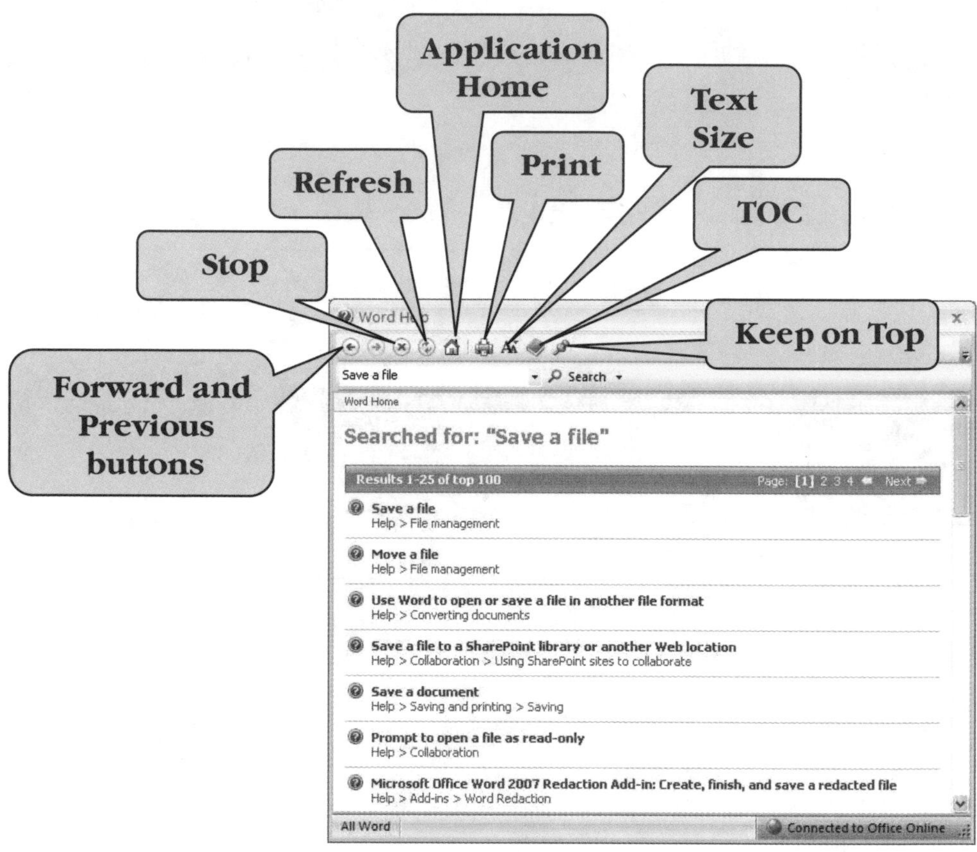

The Help system toolbar includes the familiar Back, Forward and Stop commands. Additionally, you will find the new **Refresh** tool, which allows you to update the content of the Help window. The **Application Home** tool brings you to the Word starting point, where you can browse through information related to the Microsoft Word application. The **TOC** tool displays a listing of available help topics through which you can browse. If you wish to increase or decrease the text size in the Help window, click the **Text Size** tool. Another nice feature on the Help toolbar is the **Keep on Top** tool, which allows you to keep the current Help page open while you work.

To Use the Help System

1. Click the **Microsoft Office PowerPoint Help** button on the upper right-hand corner of the PowerPoint Window
   Or
   Press **F1**
2. Enter the keyword(s) for which you want to search in the **Search** box.

3. Click the **Search** button
   Or
   Press the **Enter** key.
4. Click the **link** for the help topic you wish to view in the **Search Results pane**.
5. To browse Help topics, click the **TOC** button. Click the TOC button again to hide the Table of Contents.

Let's Try It!

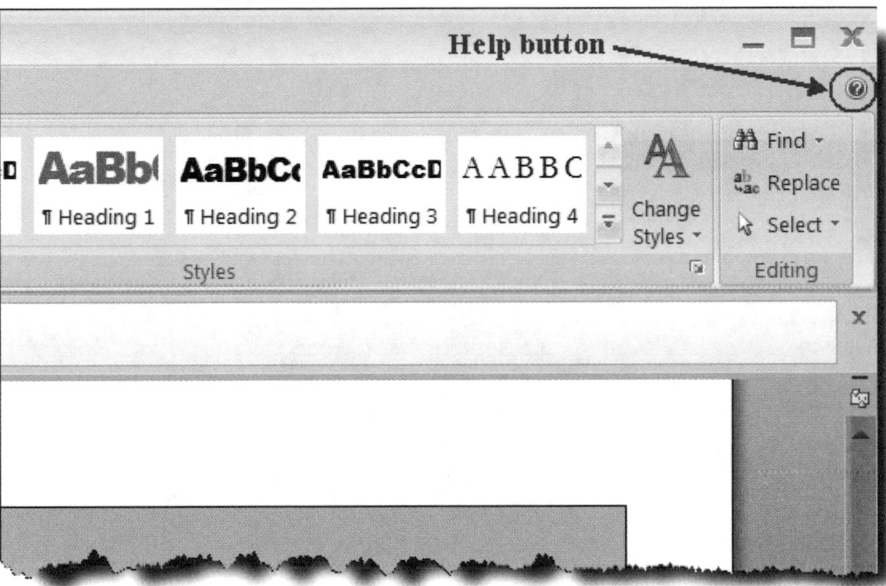

- Click the **Microsoft Office PowerPoint Help icon** on the upper right-hand corner of the screen as shown.

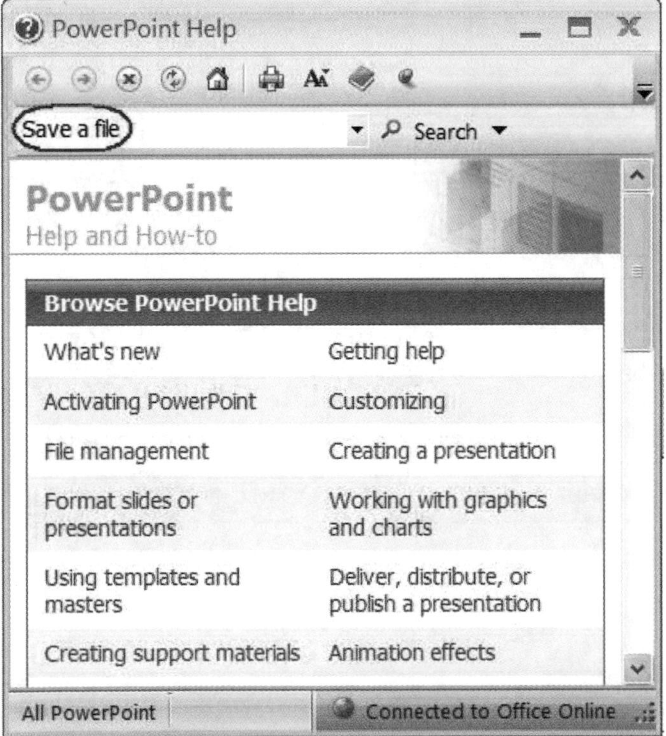

Displays the PowerPoint Help System window.

- In the **Search box**, type: **Save a file**.

Enter the keywords for which we want to search.

- Press **Enter**.

Executes the search. The results are displayed in the Search Results pane.

- Click the **Save a file** link in the Search Results pane.

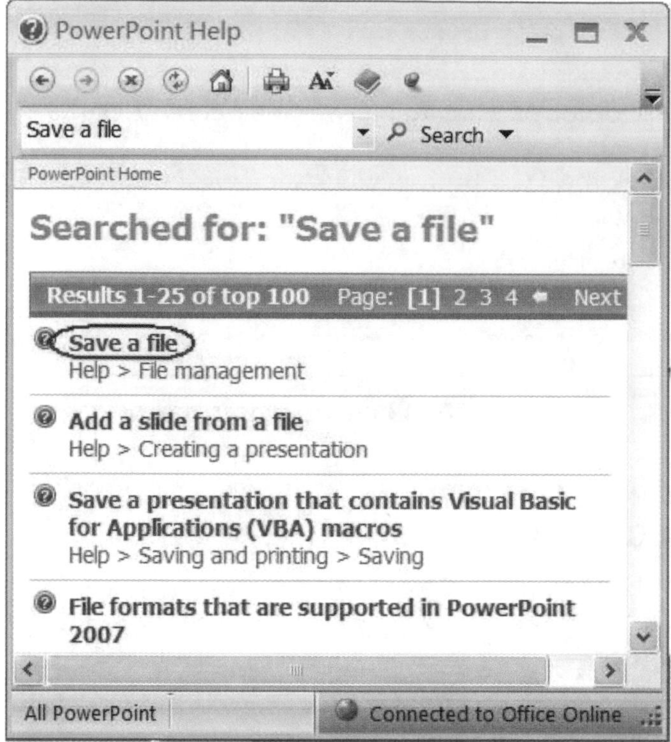

Displays the help topic for that link.

- Click the **Table of Contents** button on the toolbar.

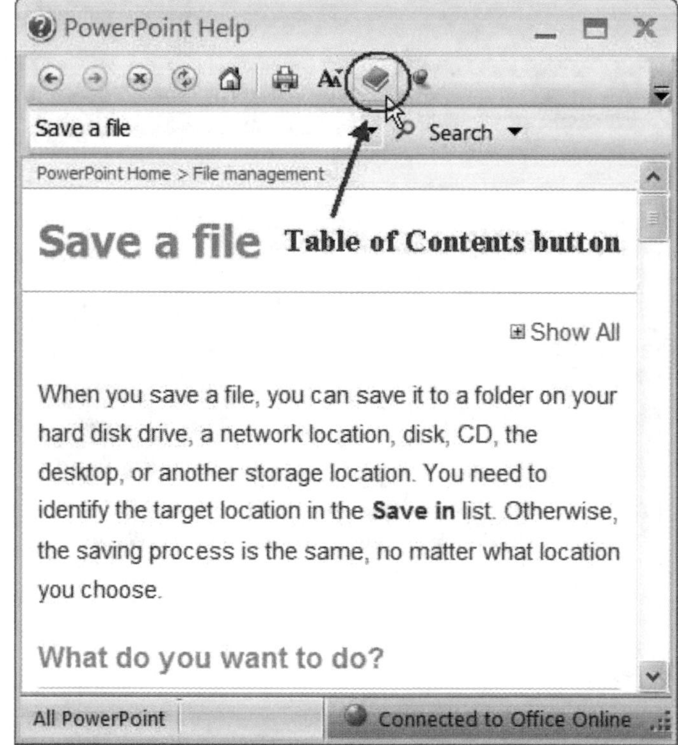

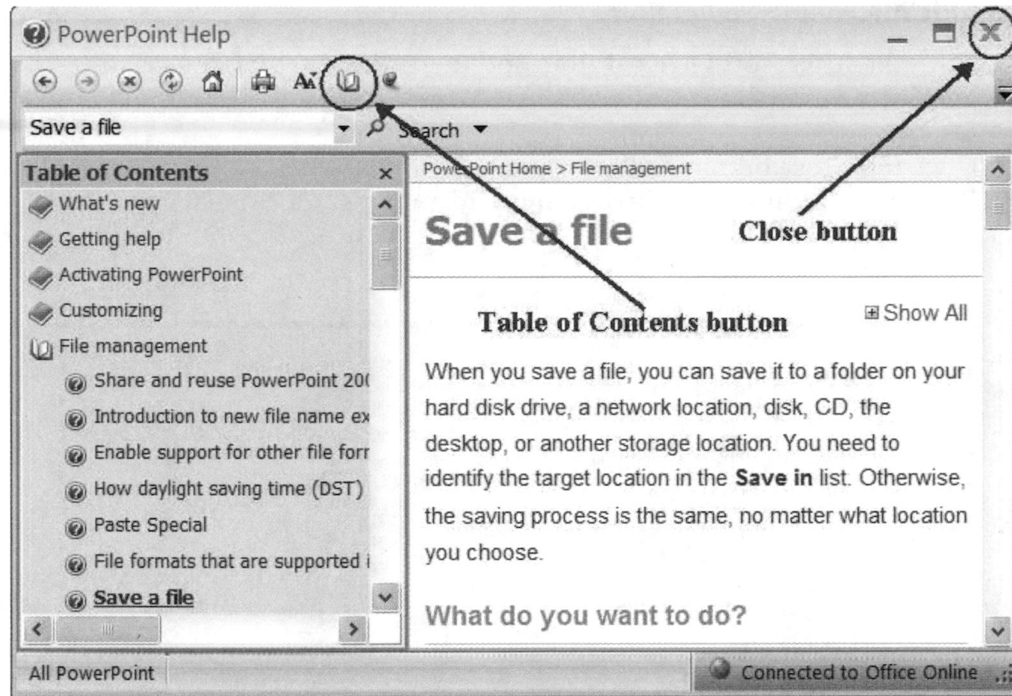

Displays a listing of Microsoft PowerPoint help topics.

- Click the **Table of Contents** button again.

Hides the Table of Contents.

- Click the PowerPoint Help **Close button** on the upper right-hand corner of the screen.

Closes the Help System window.

Closing a Presentation and Exiting PowerPoint

In this section, you will close all existing presentations and exit the Microsoft PowerPoint Application.

When you are finished working on your PowerPoint presentation, you can close it by either choosing **Close** from the File Options menu or by clicking the **Close Button** on the document window which is represented by an **x**. If you have not saved your most recent changes to the presentation, Microsoft PowerPoint will ask you if you want to save your changes before closing.

To Close a Document

1. Click the **Microsoft Office Button** and then click **Close** from the File Options menu
   Or
   Click on the **Close** button on the document window.
2. If prompted, click **Yes** to save any changes, if prompted.

To Exit Microsoft PowerPoint

1. Click the **Microsoft Office Button** and then click the **Exit PowerPoint** button
   Or
   Click the **Close** button on the program window.
2. If prompted, click **Yes** to save changes to any open documents.

Let's Try It!

- Click the **Microsoft Office Button** and then click **Close** from the File Options menu.

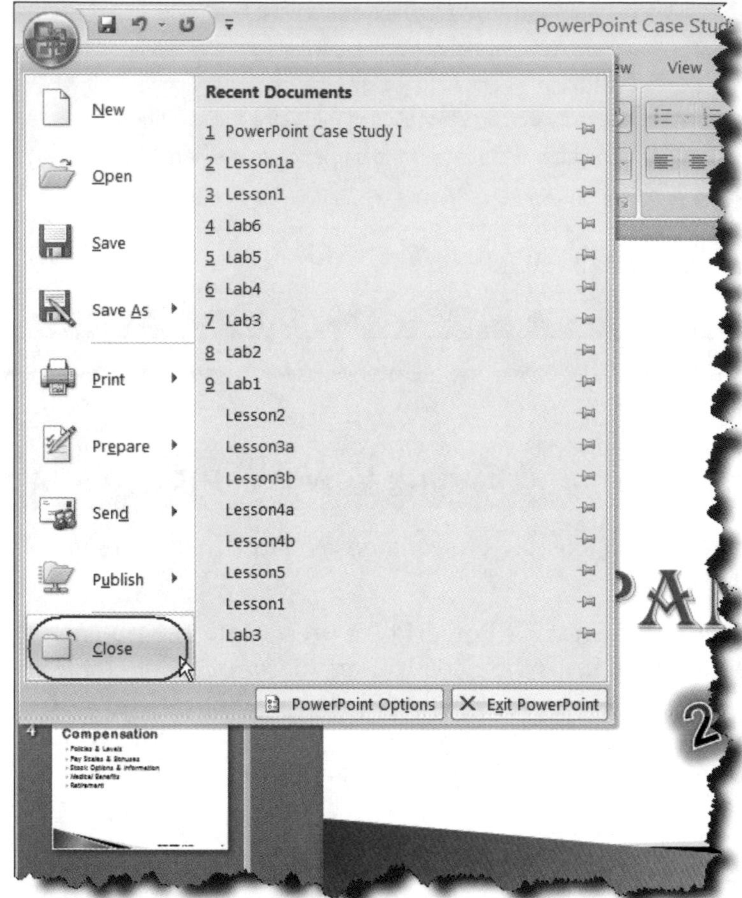

- Click **Yes** if asked to save your changes.
- Closes the **PowerPoint Case Study I** presentation. The blank presentation becomes the active presentation.

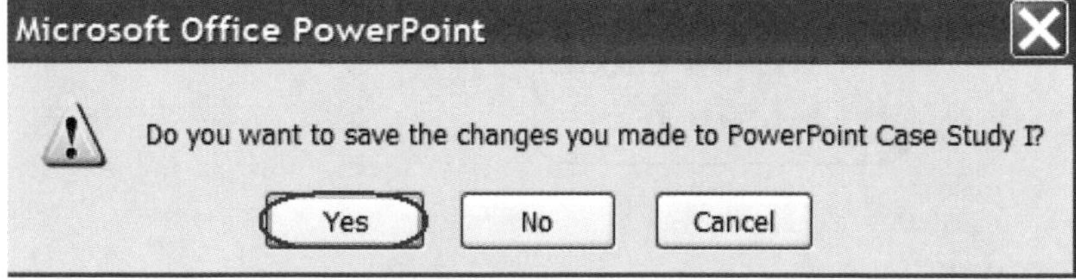

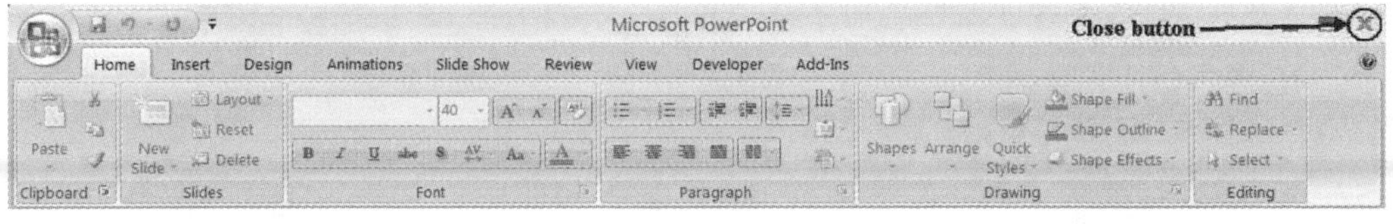

- Click the **Close** button on the Document Window.

Closes the blank presentation.

Conclusion

You have completed PowerPoint 2007—Case Study I. You are now ready to use several basic MS PowerPoint skills that you have learned in this chapter. You are encouraged to experiment with all you have learned in this case study. To reinforce your understanding of these techniques, it is recommended that you read and work through it once again.

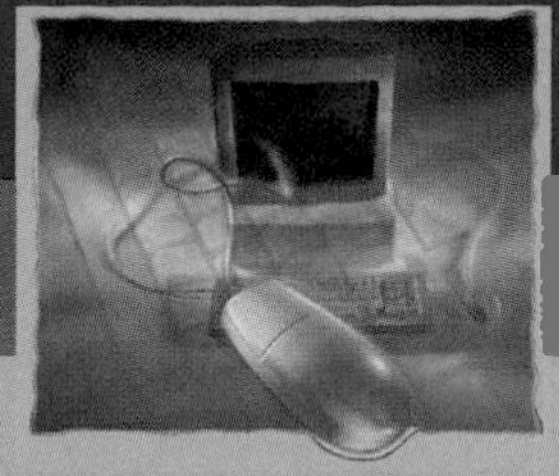

PowerPoint Case Study 2

CHAPTER

8

OBJECTIVES

After successfully completing this case study, you should able to:

- Create a PowerPoint Presenation
- Insert a Table in a Slide
- Apply Quick Styles to a Table
- Format Table Borders
- Apply Cell Shading to a Table
- Insert a Chart
- Format a Chart
- Change the Chart Type
- Insert an Organization Chart
- Modify an Organization Chart
- Apply Themes to a Presentation
- Modify Theme Colors, Fonts & Effects
- Rearrange a Presentation in Slide Sorter View
- Rearrange a Presentation in Normal View
- Duplicate Slides
- Delete Slides
- Apply Animation Schemes
- Add Slide Transitions
- Preview a Presentation
- Page Setup
- Print Slides/Outlines/Handouts

Case Study 2—MS PowerPoint 2007

Your boss is impressed with your work in the Case Study I. He wants you to help him in preparing another company presentation. This presentation includes four slides on the current organization structure and sales by Representatives in last two years. Also, one of the Regional managers is leaving this month so you do not want to list her in the new structure but you want to discuss her performance in the presentation.

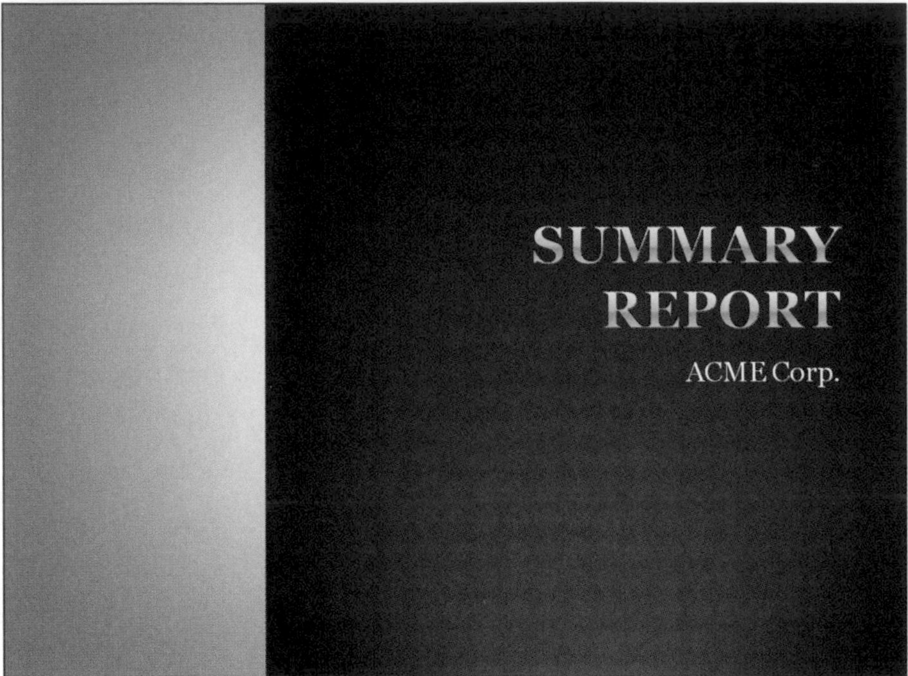

POWERPOINT SLIDE 1

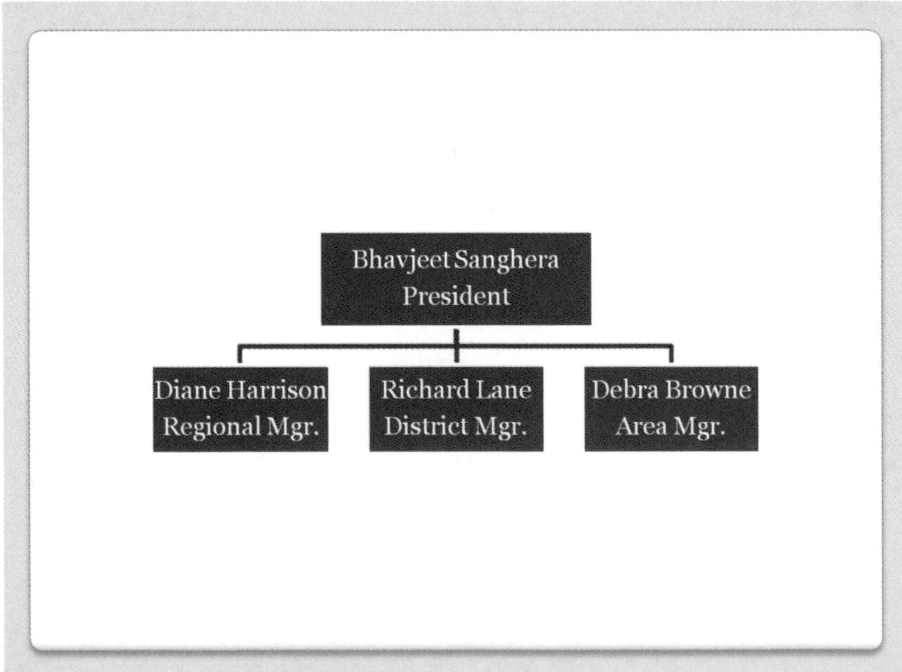

POWERPOINT SLIDE 2

	2006	2007	Variance
Harrison	$35000	$50000	$15000
Lane	$85000	$105000	$20000
Browne	$65000	$50000	($15000)
Hoffman	$90000	$85000	($5000)

Sales by Rep

POWERPOINT SLIDE 3

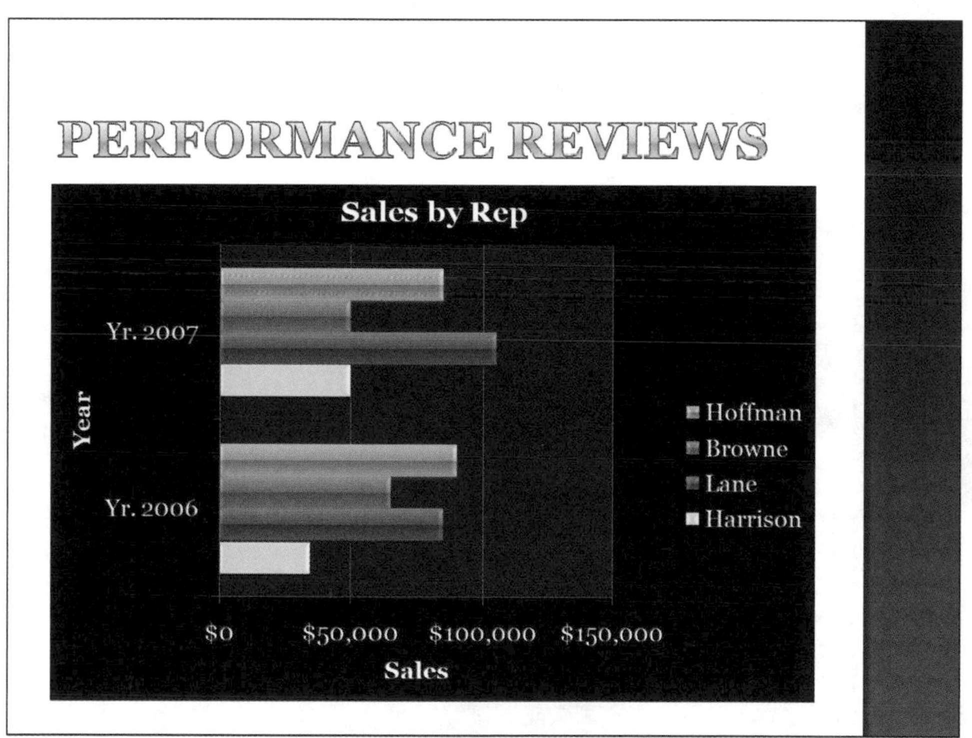

POWERPOINT SLIDE 4

Creating a New Presentation

In this section, you will learn how to create a blank presentation.

To Create a New Presentation

1. Click the **Microsoft Office Button** and then click **New** from the menu to display the **New Presentation** Task Pane.
2. Click **Blank Presentation** in the center pane.
3. Click **Create**.
   Or
   Hold down the **Ctrl** and **N** keystroke combination (**Ctrl + N**)

To Apply a Layout to a Slide

1. Click the **Slides** tab on the left side of your screen.
2. Click the Slide to which you want to apply a layout.
3. Click the **Home tab** on the Ribbon.
4. Click the **Layout button** in the **Slides group**.
5. Click the layout you want from the gallery.

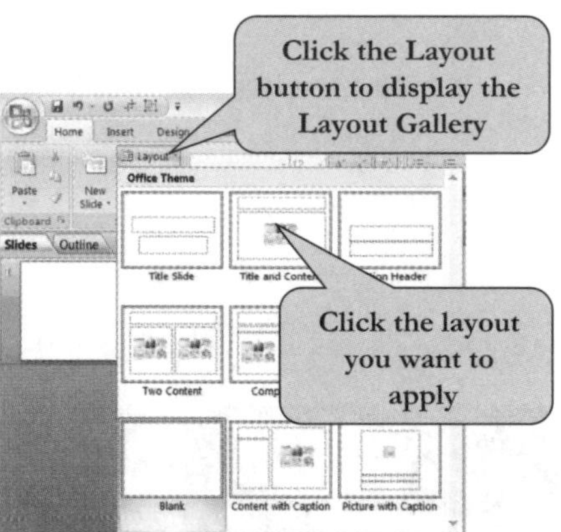

Let's Try It!

- Click on the **Start** button.

Displays Start menu items.

- Select **All Programs > Microsoft Office > Microsoft Office PowerPoint 2007** from the Start Menu.

Launches the PowerPoint Application.

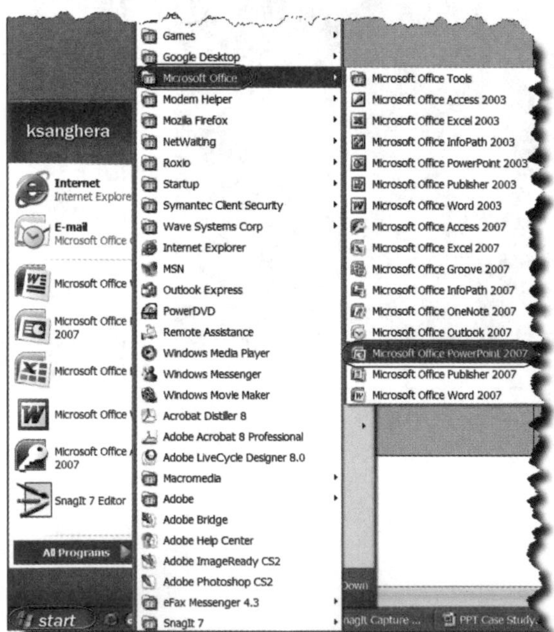

Click to add title

Click to add subtitle

Opens a new blank presentation.

- Click inside the title that contains the text: **Click to add title**.

An insertion point appears inside of the placeholder indicating that you can begin entering text.

- Type: **Summary Report**

Summary Report

ACME Corp.

- Click inside the title that contains the text: **Click to add subtitle**.

An insertion point appears inside of the placeholder indicating that you can begin entering subtext.

- Type: **ACME Corp.**

- Insert flash drive in USB port.
- Click the **Save** button on the Quick Access toolbar.

As we have not yet saved the document, the Save As dialog box appears, prompting for the file name and location where we wish to save the file.

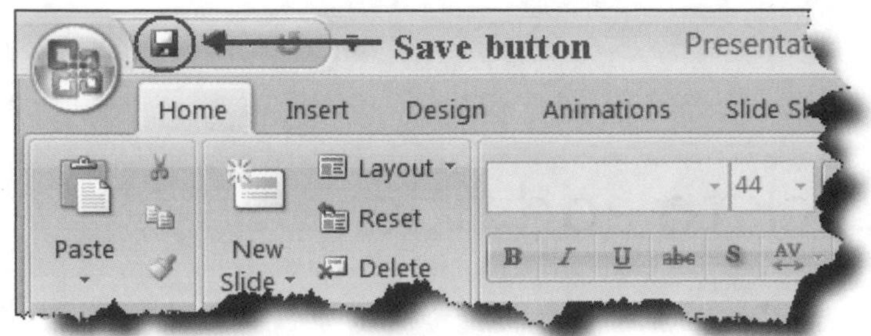

- In the File name text box, type: **PowerPoint Case Study II** and select flash drive in the Save in list.

Enters the name of the new workbook.

- Select **PowerPoint Presentation** in the Save as type text box.
- Click the **Save** button.

Saves the current document.

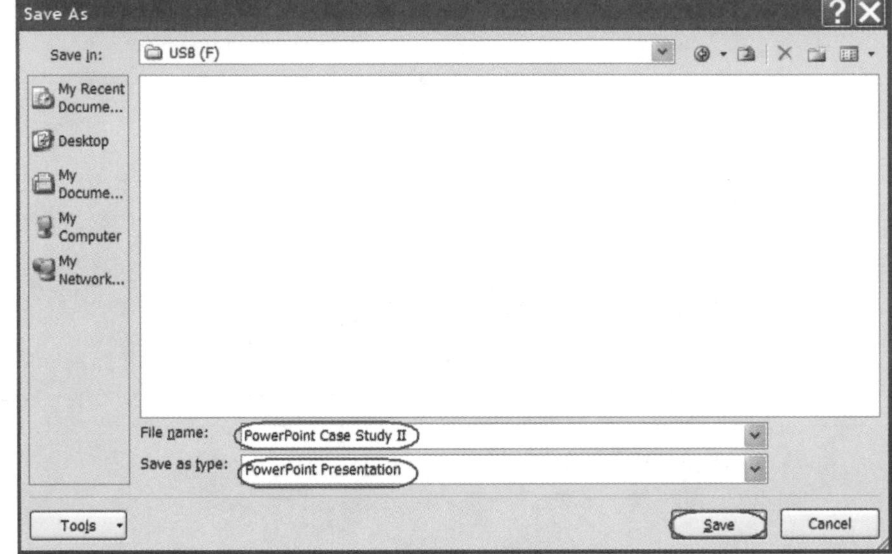

Inserting a Table

In this section, you will learn how to insert a table object on a slide.

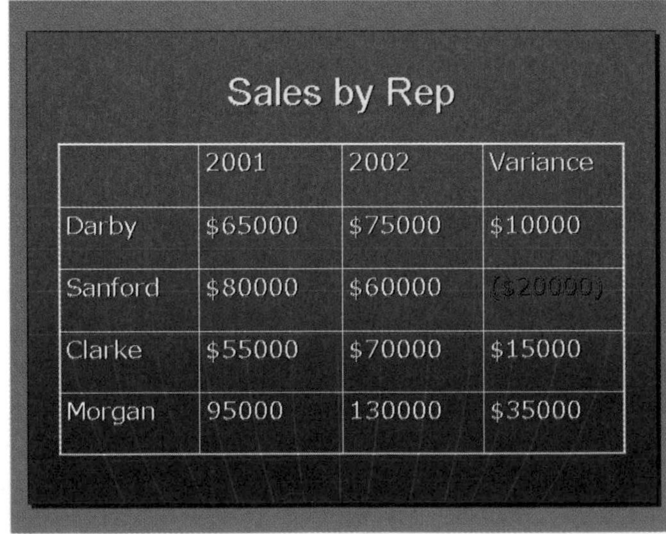

	2001	2002	Variance
Darby	$65000	$75000	$10000
Sanford	$80000	$60000	($20000)
Clarke	$55000	$70000	$15000
Morgan	95000	130000	$35000

Tables are an excellent way to present and organize columns of data. Similar to spreadsheets, tables are organized in rows and columns. The intersection of rows and columns is called a cell. You decide how many rows and columns you want to appear in your table. Pressing the **Tab** key moves your cursor from one cell to another when entering data. Once you insert a table, you can add more rows or columns later if need be. Like other objects in PowerPoint, you can apply a wide array of formats to your table such as borders, cell shading and cell fill.

To Insert a Table on a New Slide

1. Click the **New Slide arrow** on the Home Ribbon.
2. Choose the **Title and Content** layout.
3. Click the **Insert Table icon** on the content area of the slide.
4. Enter the number of **rows and columns** in the insert table dialog box.
5. Click **OK**.

To Insert a Table on an Existing Slide Layout

1. Click the **Table button** on the Insert Ribbon and drag across the grid until the desired number of rows and columns are displayed
   Or
1. Click the **Table button** on the Insert Ribbon.
2. Click **Insert Table** on the menu.
3. Enter the number of **rows and columns** in the insert table dialog box.
4. Click **OK**.

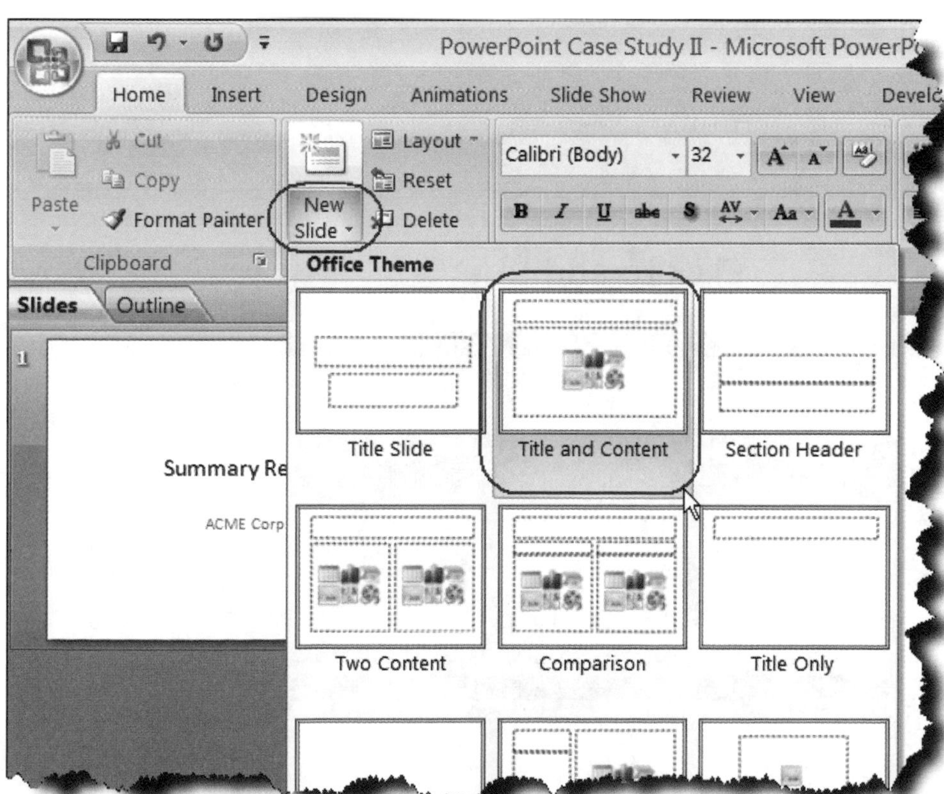

- Click the **New Slide button** on the Slides group of the Home Ribbon and choose **Title and Content** from the gallery.

Inserts a new slide.

- Click the **Insert Table** icon in the Content placeholder.

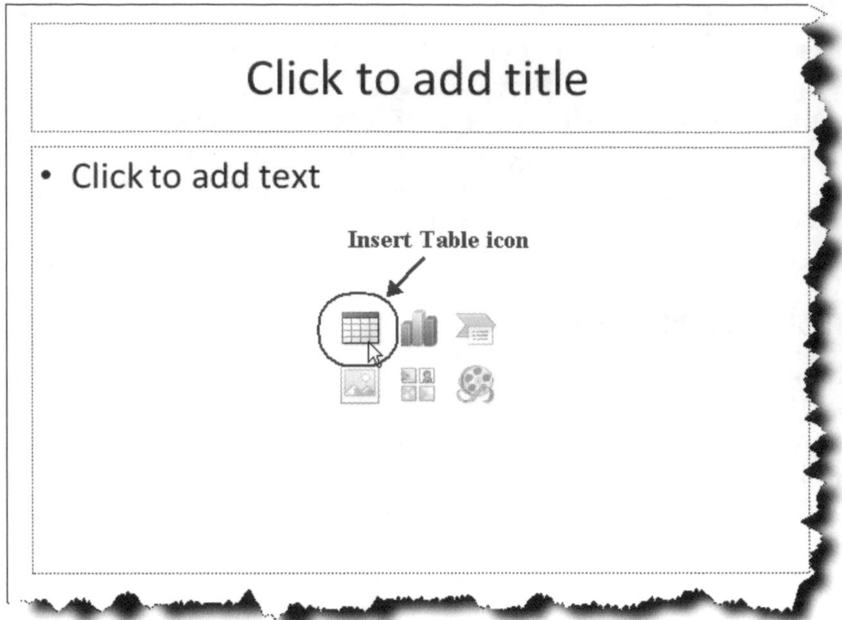

Displays the Insert Table dialog box.

- **Type 4** in the Number of columns box.

Sets the number of columns to 4.

- **Type 5** in the Number of rows box.

Sets the number of rows to 5.

- Click **OK**.

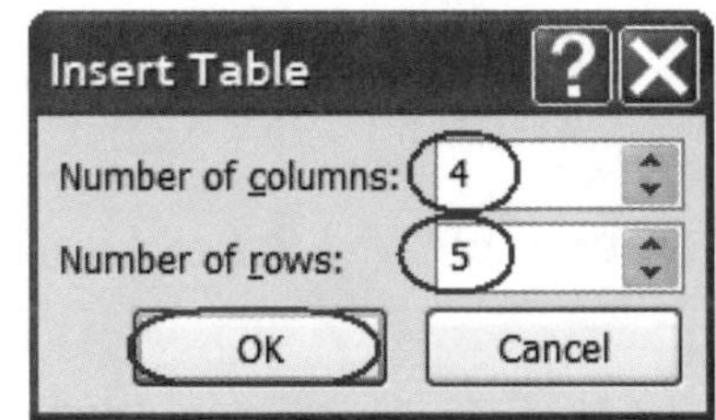

Closes the Insert Table dialog box and creates the table.

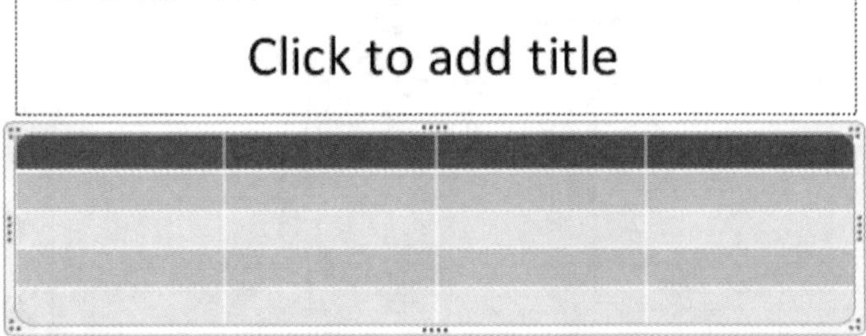

- Click in the **Title Placeholder** and type: **Sales by Rep**

Enters the title for the slide.

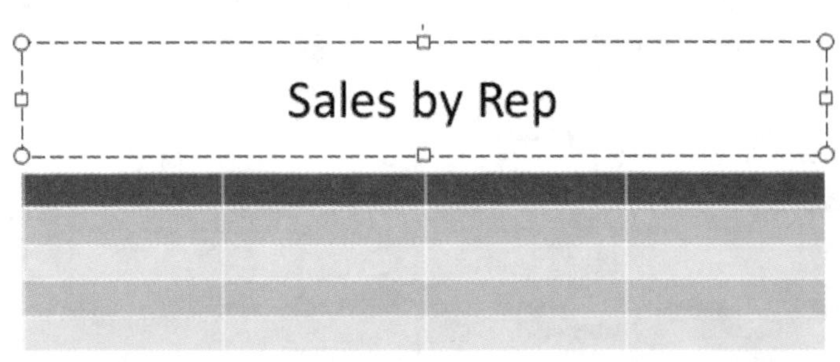

Sales by Rep

	2006	2007	Variance
Harrison	$35000	$50000	$15000
Lane	$85000	$105000	$20000
Browne	$65000	$50000	($15000)
Hoffman	$90000	$85000	($5000)

- Enter the table data as shown in the screenshot (press the tab key to move from one column to the next).

Enters data into the table object.

- Click the **Save** button.

Saves the current presentation.

Applying Quick Styles to a Table

In this section, you will learn how to apply a preset formatting style to a table.

PowerPoint includes several **quick table styles** that you can add to your table. These table formats include preset colors and borders styles that you can instantly apply to your table. Under the contextual Design tab under the Tables tab, you will see several preset Table Style thumbnails displayed on the Ribbon. Move your mouse pointer over any of these styles to see a preview of the selected style. Click the **Scroll Up** or **Scroll Down arrow** to scroll the style list. To view the entire Table Styles gallery, click the **More Styles** button.

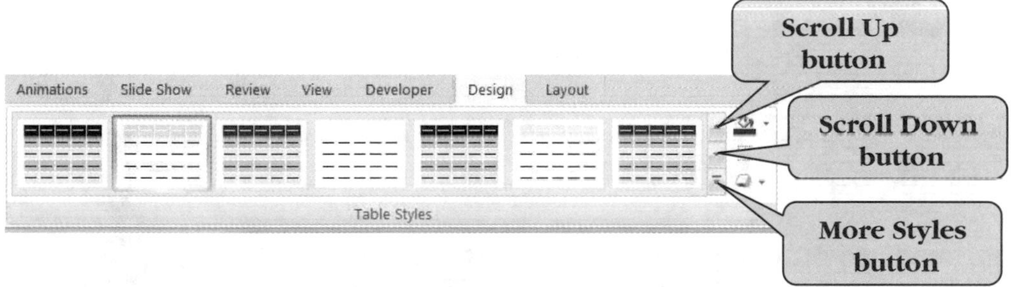

To Apply a Quick Style to a Table

1. Click anywhere in your table to select the table.
2. Click the contextual **Design tab** on the Ribbon.
3. Move mouse pointer over any of the **Table Styles thumbnails** in the Table Styles group.
4. Click the Scroll Up to Scroll Down arrows to display additional table styles.
5. Click the More Styles button to display the entire Table Styles gallery.
6. Click the Table Style thumbnail to apply that style to your table.

Let's Try It!

- Click anywhere inside of the table.

Selects the table.

- Click the contextual **Design tab** on the ribbon.

Displays table design tools and commands.

- Click the **More** button on the **Table Styles** group.

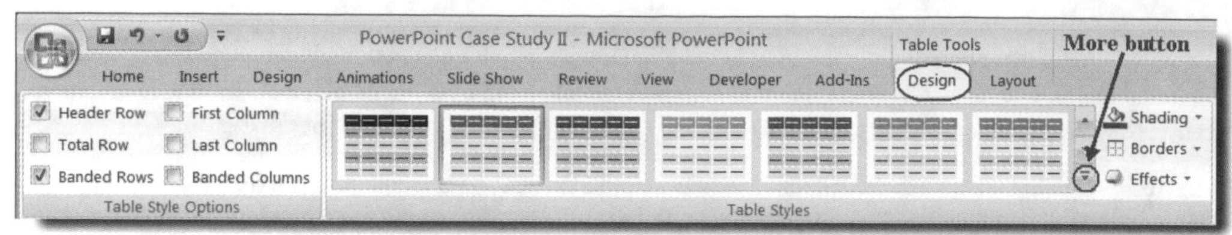

Displays all the table styles.

- Click the **third Table Styles** thumbnail from the left in the Table Styles group under the Best Match for Documents.

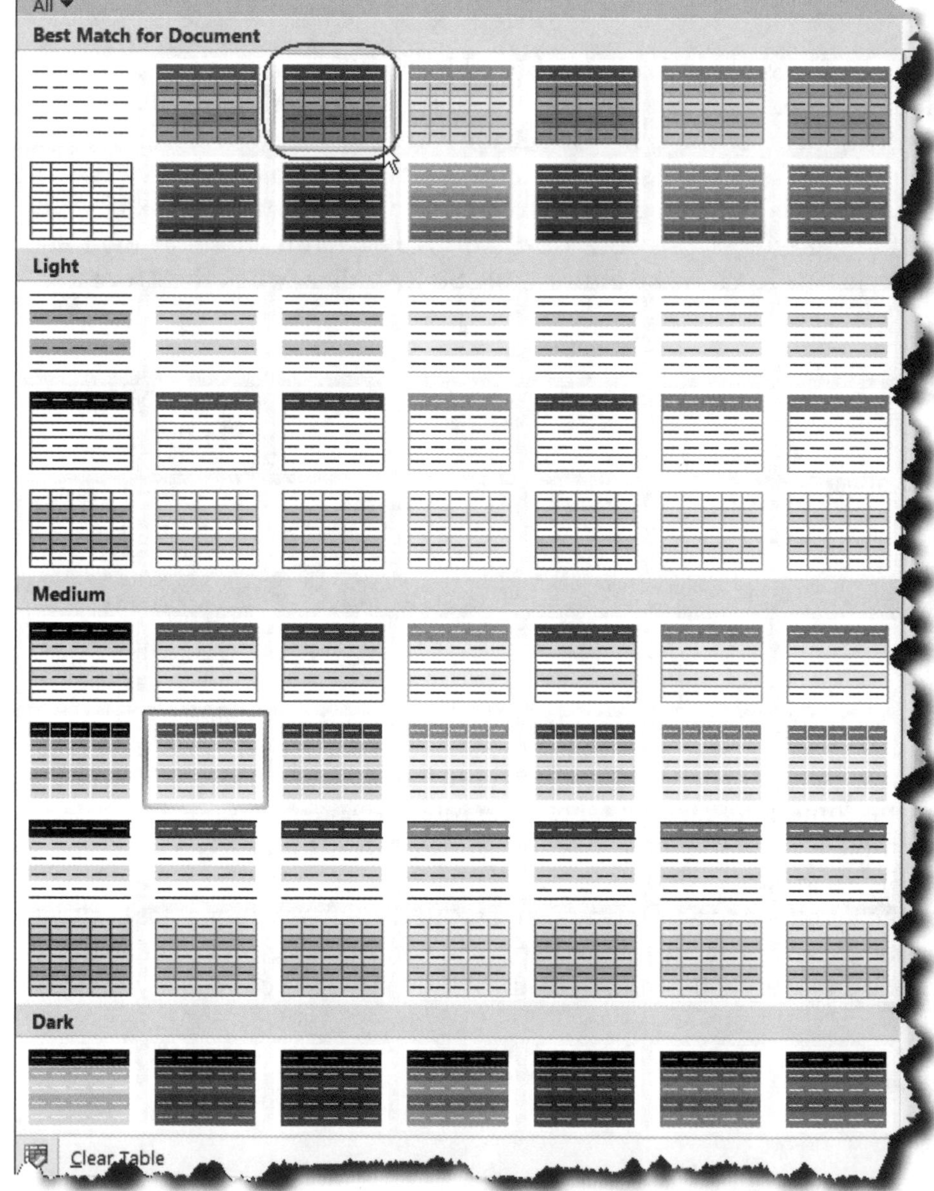

Sales by Rep

	2006	2007	Variance
Harrison	$35000	$50000	$15000
Lane	$85000	$105000	$20000
Browne	$65000	$50000	($15000)
Hoffman	$90000	$85000	($5000)

Applies that style to the selected table.

- Click the **Save** button.

Saves the current presentation.

Formatting Table Borders

In this section, you will learn how to format the style, width, and color of table borders.

The **Draw Borders** group, which can be found under the contextual **Design tab**, allows you to change the borders of both the inside and outside lines of your table or remove the borders completely. Options include the border type, the border thickness (weight) and Pen color.

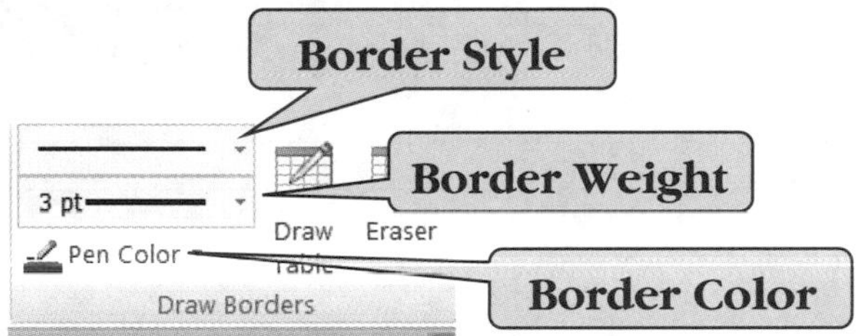

Once you have set the border formatting that you want, click the **Borders button** on the Table Styles group to apply the formatting to your borders.

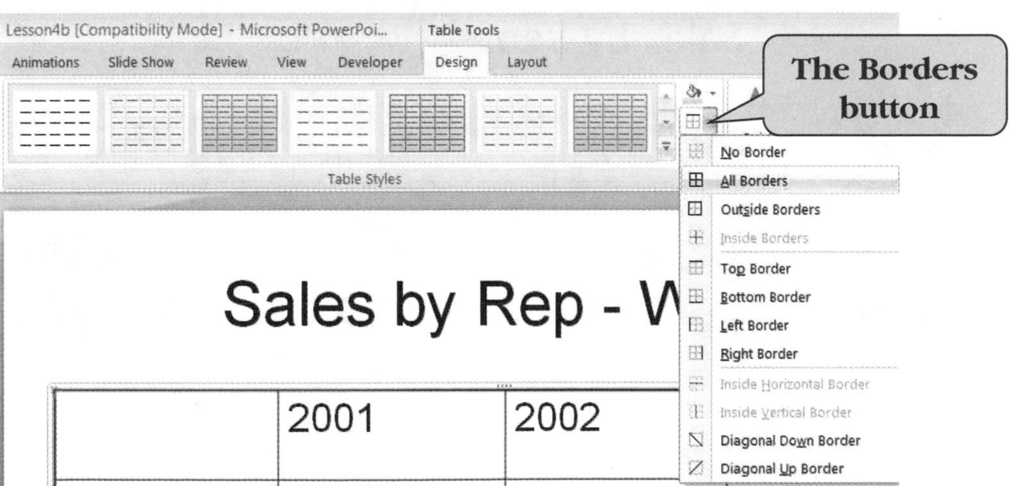

To Format Table Borders

1. Click inside of the table to select a particular cell or select the border of the table placeholder to apply settings to entire table.
2. Click the contextual **Design** tab.
3. To change the weight of the border, click the arrow next to **Pen Weight** on the Draw Borders group and select the weight that you want.
4. To change the style of the border, click the arrow next to **Pen Style** on the Draw Borders group and select the style that you want.
5. To change the color of the border, click the arrow next to **Pen Color** on the Draw Borders group and select the color that you want from the color palette.
6. To apply the formatting, click the **Border button** on the Table Styles group and select the border option that you want to change.

Let's Try It!

- Make sure **Slide 2** is selected.

Click on the placeholder border of the table.

- Select the entire table.

Sales by Rep

	2006	2007	Variance
Harrison	$35000	$50000	$15000
Lane	$85000	$105000	$20000
Browne	$65000	$50000	($15000)
Hoffman	$90000	$85000	($5000)

- Click the contextual **Design tab** on the Ribbon.

Displays table design tools and commands.

- Click the **Pen Weight** drop-down list and then select **3 pt**.

Selects a 3 pt. border width.

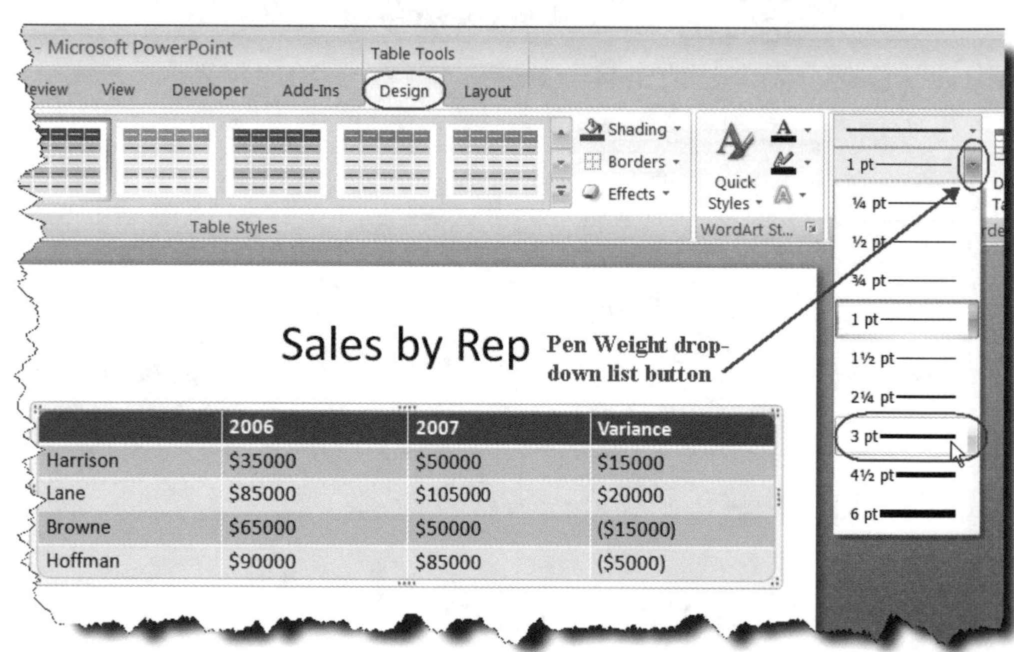

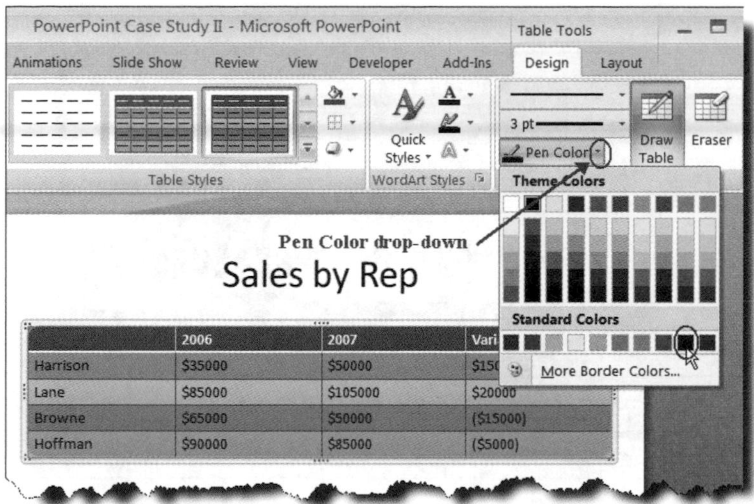

- Click the **Pen Color** drop-down list and then click the **Dark Blue** color swatch under the Standard Colors category (second to the last color).

Sets the border color to a dark blue.

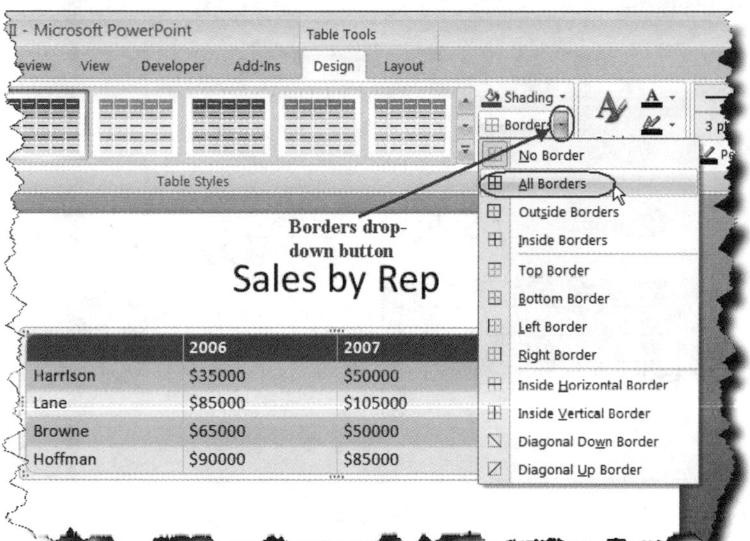

- Click the **Borders button** under the **Table Styles** group as shown below and select **All Borders** from the list.

Applies the changes to all borders in the table.

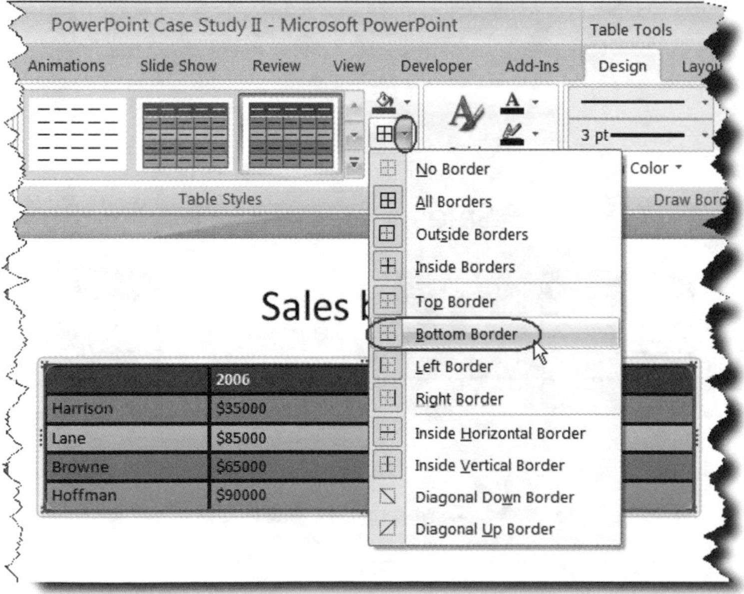

- Click the **Borders button** under the **Table Styles** group and select **Bottom Border** from the list.

Removes the Border Style from the bottom border.

- Click the **Pen Color** drop-down list and then click the **Red** color swatch under the Standard Colors category.

Sets Red as the border color.

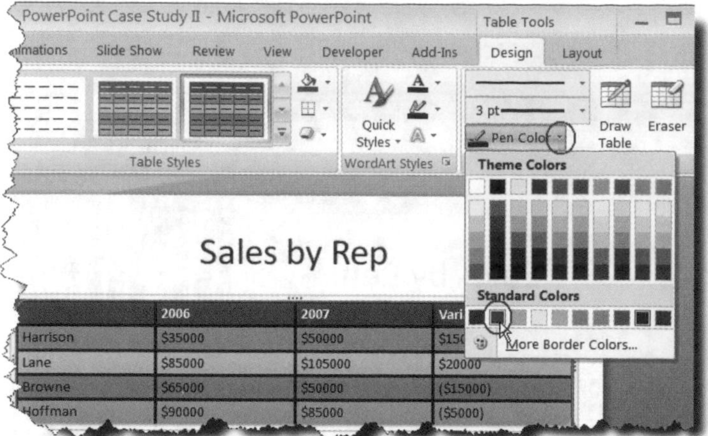

- Click the **Borders button** under the **Table Styles** group and select **Bottom Border** from the list.

Applies a bottom border with the new settings.

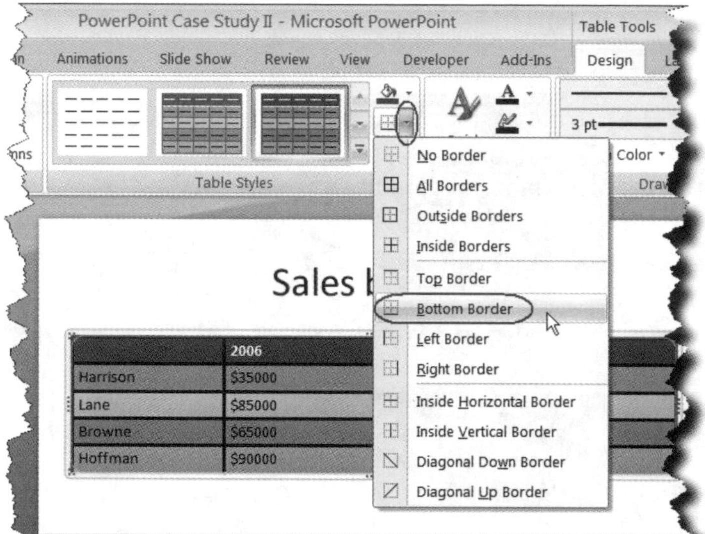

- Click the **Borders button** again and select **Top Border** from the list.

Applies the new formatting to the top border of the table.

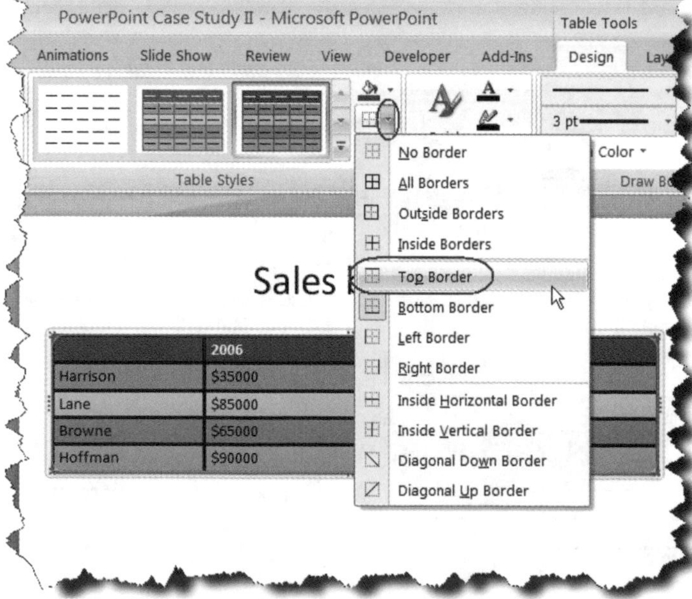

Sales by Rep

	2006	2007	Variance
Harrison	$35000	$50000	$15000
Lane	$85000	$105000	$20000
Browne	$65000	$50000	($15000)
Hoffman	$90000	$85000	($5000)

- Click anywhere **outside** the table.

Deselects the table.

- Click the **Save** button.

Saves the active presentation.

Applying Cell Shading to a Table

In this section, you will learn how to add cell shading to a table

You can apply colors to individual cells or to an entire table. To accomplish this, select the **Shape Fill button** on the Home Ribbon or the **Shading button** on the contextual **Design tab**. You can also right-click the table, choose Format Shape and select any fill color options.

By selecting **Shape Fill** formatting, you can also add such effects as gradient, texture and various patterns to your cells. You could even add a background picture to your cells, if you were so inclined.

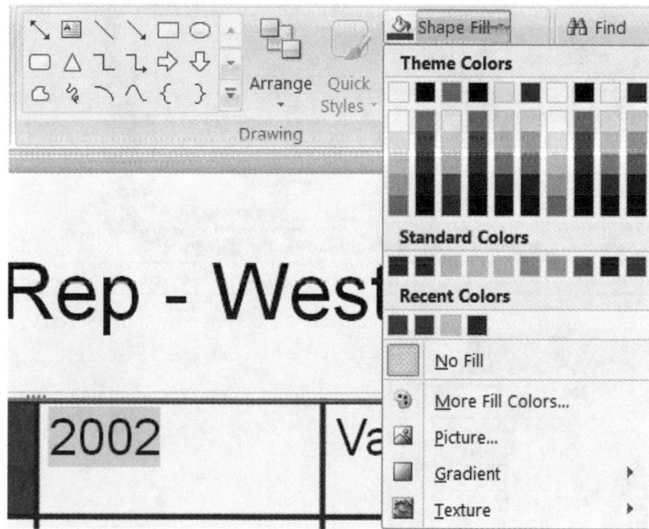

To Apply Shading to Cells

1. Select (click and drag across) the cells to which you want to apply shading. To apply shading to the entire table, select the border of the table placeholder.
2. Click the **Shape Fill button** on the Drawing group of the Home Ribbon
   Or
   Click the **Shading** button on the Table Styles group of the Design Ribbon.
3. Click on the desired color in the color palette and then click **OK**.
4. To see additional colors, click on **More Fill Colors** to display the color palette, click on the desired color and then click **OK**.
5. To add patterns, gradients and textures, select **Picture, Gradient or Texture** from the Fill Color menu and make your selections.

Let's Try It!

- Click in the blank cell in the first row and drag across until the entire first row of the table is selected.

Select the entire first row of the table. This is the range to which we will apply shading.

Sales by Rep

	2006	2007	Variance
Harrison	$35000	$50000	$15000
Lane	$85000	$105000	$20000
Browne	$65000	$50000	($15000)
Hoffman	$90000	$85000	($5000)

- On the **Tables Styles** group under the Design tab, click the arrow next to the **Shading** button.

Displays the Fill Color drop-down list.

- Click **More Fill Colors** from the menu.

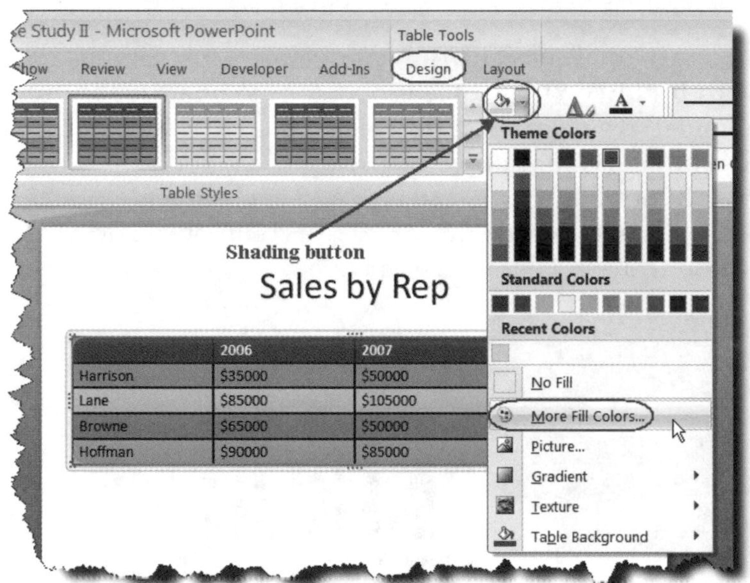

Displays the **Colors** dialog box.

- Click the **Standard** tab.

Switches to the standard colors palette.

- Click a **Dark Blue** color in the Palette as shown.
- Click **OK**.

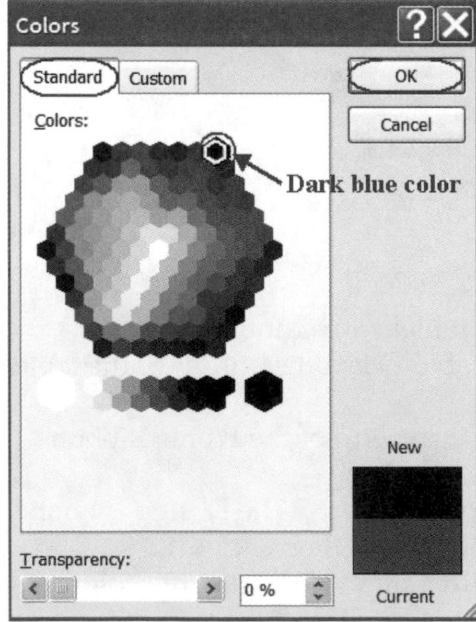

Sales by Rep

	2006	2007	Variance
Harrison	$35000	$50000	$15000
Lane	$85000	$105000	$20000
Browne	$65000	$50000	($15000)
Hoffman	$90000	$85000	($5000)

Applies the shading to the first row of our table.

- Click anywhere in the table.

Deselects the first row.

- Click the **Save** button.

Saves the active presentation.

Inserting a Chart

In this section, you will learn how insert a chart into a slide.

Charts are an ideal way to graphically present your numerical data. If you have Excel 2007 installed on your computer, you can add a chart to your slides to provide a visual element for your numeric data. Click the **Chart** on the **Insert Ribbon**, choose the type of Chart you want and then click OK. An Excel spreadsheet with sample data will then display in a separate pane, into which you replace the sample data with your own data.

Some available chart types are:

- Pie Chart
- Line Chart
- Bar Chart
- Area Chart
- Column Chart
- Doughnut Chart

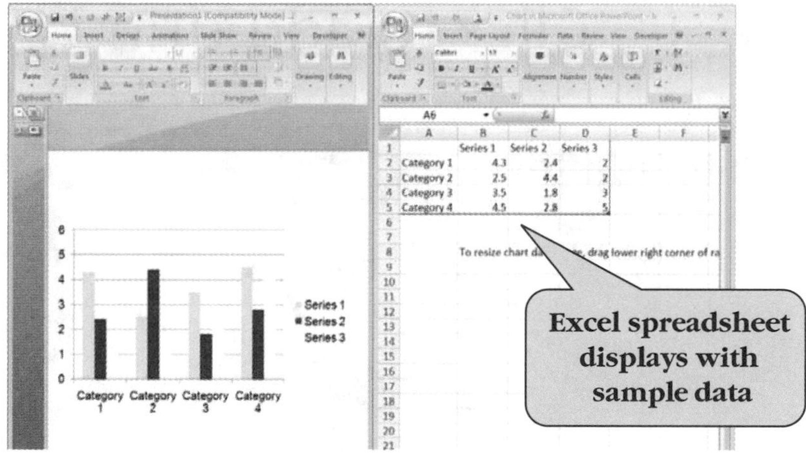
Excel spreadsheet
displays with
sample data

To Insert a Chart on a New Slide

1. Click the **New Slide arrow** on the Home Ribbon.
2. Choose the **Title and Content** layout.
3. Click the **Insert Chart icon** on the content area of the slide.
4. Click the chart type you want from the Insert Chart dialog box.
5. Click **OK** to display an Excel spreadsheet with sample data.
6. Replace the sample data with your own data.
7. Click the Close button on the Excel pane to close the spreadsheet.

To Insert a Chart on an Existing Slide Layout

1. Click the **Chart button** on the Insert Ribbon.
2. Click the chart type you want from the Insert Chart dialog box.
3. Click **OK** to display an Excel spreadsheet with sample data.
4. Replace the sample data with your own data.
5. Click the Close button on the Excel pane to close the spreadsheet.

Let's Try It!

- Click the **Home tab** on the Ribbon.

Switches to Home commands and tools.

- Click the **New Slide arrow** on the Slides group of the Home Ribbon and choose **Title and Content** from the gallery.

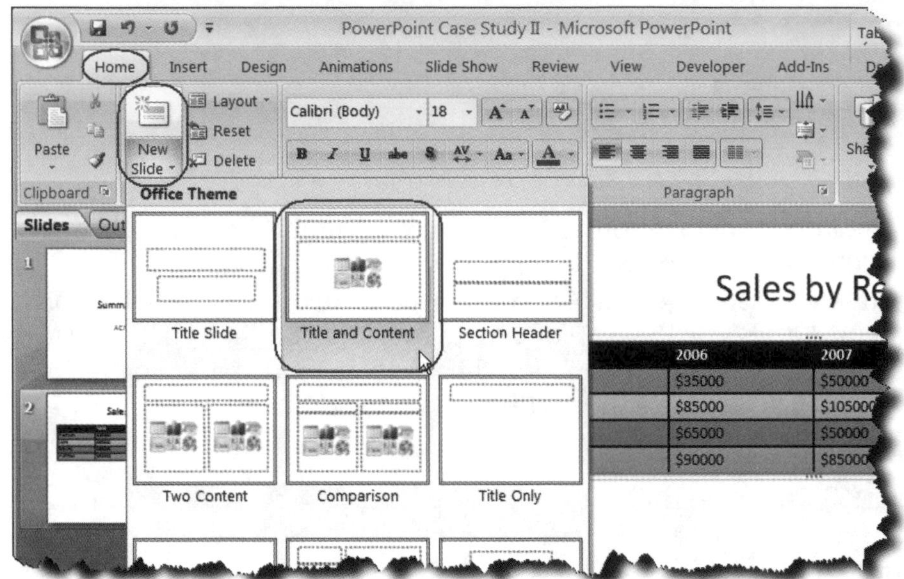

Inserts a new slide with the Title and Content layout.

- Click the **Insert Chart** icon in the Content placeholder.

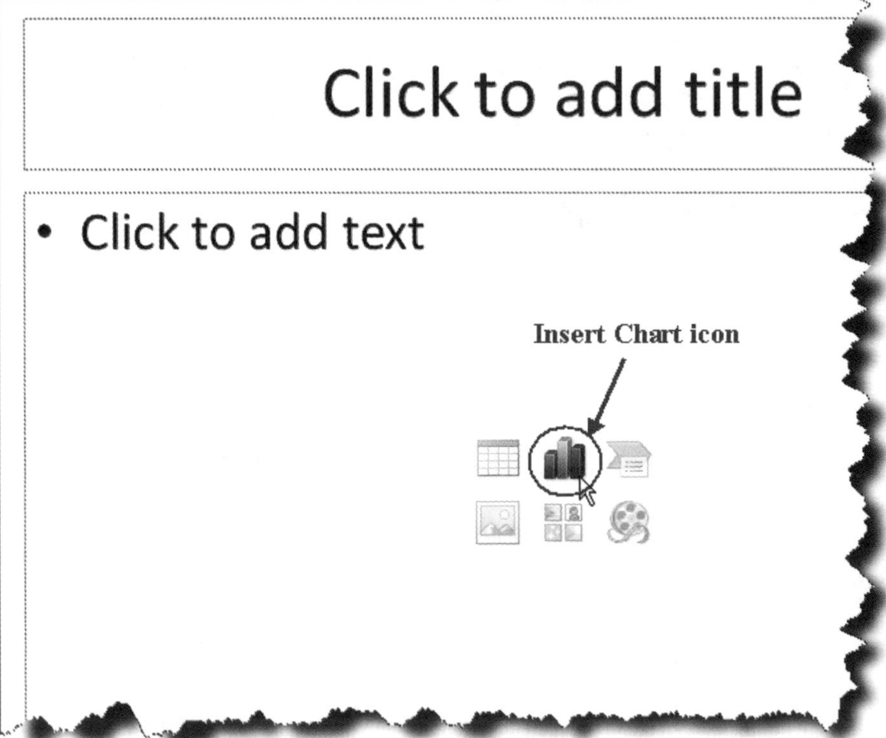

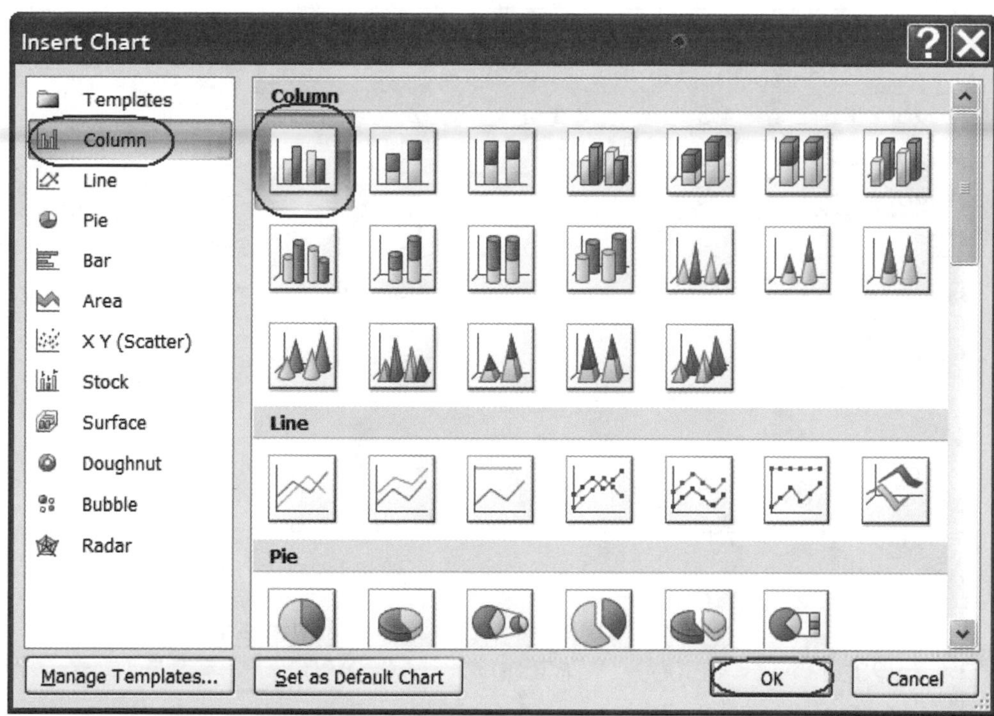

Displays the Insert Chart dialog box.

- Click the **Column category** in the left pane.

Displays available chart types in the Column category.

- Click the **Clustered Bar** Column chart type in the right pane (first row, first column).

Selects the chart type that we want.

- Click **OK**.

	A	B	C	D	E	F	G
1		Series 1	Series 2	Series 3			
2	Category 1	4.3	2.4	2			
3	Category 2	2.5	4.4	2			
4	Category 3	3.5	1.8	3			
5	Category 4	4.5	2.8	5			
6							
7							
8		To resize chart data range, drag lower right corner of range.					
9							
10							

Sheet1

Launches the Excel application and displays a worksheet with Sample Data.

- In the Excel worksheet, click inside of the cell containing the word **Series 1**.

Activates the worksheet and selects the first cell whose data we want to change.

Formula Bar

	A	B	C	D	E	F	G
1		Harrison	Series 2	Series 3			
2	Category 1	4.3	2.4	2			
3	Category 2	2.5	4.4	2			
4	Category 3	3.5	1.8	3			
5	Category 4	4.5	2.8	5			
6							
7							
8		To resize chart data range, drag lower right corner of range.					
9							
10							

Sheet1

- Type: **Harrison** and then press **Tab**.

Enters data into the second cell in the first row and then moves to the cell in C1.

- Type: **Lane**, and then press Tab.

Enters data into the cell.

- Type: **Browne** and then press **Tab**.

Enters data into the cell next to Harrison and moves to cell A2.

- Click in cell **E1**.

Activates cell E1.

- Type: **Hoffman**.

Enters data into the cell.

A	B	C	D	E
	Harrison	Lane	Browne	Hoffman
Category 1	4.3	2.4	2	
Category 2	2.5	4.4	2	
Category 3	3.5	1.8	3	
Category 4	4.5	2.8	5	

- Click in the cell with the words **Category 1** (cell A2) and type: **Yr. 2006**. Press **Tab**.

Enters data into Cell A2 and moves to cell B2.

- Type: **35000** and then press **Tab**.

Enters data into cell B2 and then moves to cell C2.

- Type: **85000** and then press **Tab**

Enters data into cell C2 and then moves to cell D2.

- Type: **65000** and then press **Tab**

Enters data into cell D2 and then moves to cell E2.

- Type: **90000**.

Enters data into cell E2

	A	B	C	D	E
1		Harrison	Lane	Browne	Hoffman
2	Yr. 2006	35000	85000	65000	90000
3	Category 2	2.5	4.4	2	
4	Category 3	3.5	1.8	3	
5	Category 4	4.5	2.8	5	

	A	B	C	D	E
1		Harrison	Lane	Browne	Hoffman
2	Yr. 2006	35000	85000	65000	90000
3	Yr. 2007	50000	105000	50000	85000
4	Category 3	3.5	1.8	3	
5	Category 4	4.5	2.8	5	

- Click in the cell with the words **Category 2** (cell A3) and type: **Yr. 2007**. Press **Tab**.

Enters data into Cell A3 and moves to cell B3.

- Type: **50000** and then press **Tab**.

Enters data into cell B3 and then moves to cell C3.

- Type: **105000** and then press **Tab**.

Enters data into cell C3 and then moves to cell D3.

- Type: **50000** and then press **Tab**.

Enters data into cell D3 and then moves to cell E3.

- Type: **85000**.

Enters data into cell E3.

	A	B	C	D	E
1		Harrison	Lane	Browne	Hoffman
2	Yr. 2006	35000	85000	65000	90000
3	Yr. 2007	50000	105000	50000	85000
4	[illegible]	[illegible]	[illegible]	[illegible]	
5	[illegible]	[illegible]	[illegible]	[illegible]	

- Click on the **Lower-right corner** of the blue border surrounding the data and drag upwards until the last two rows are hidden by a gray band.

Moves the data selection border up, to exclude the last two rows of sample data.

- Click the **Close Button** on the **Excel window**.

Closes the Excel spreadsheet and updates the chart to reflect the new data.

- Click the **Save** button.

Saves the active presentation.

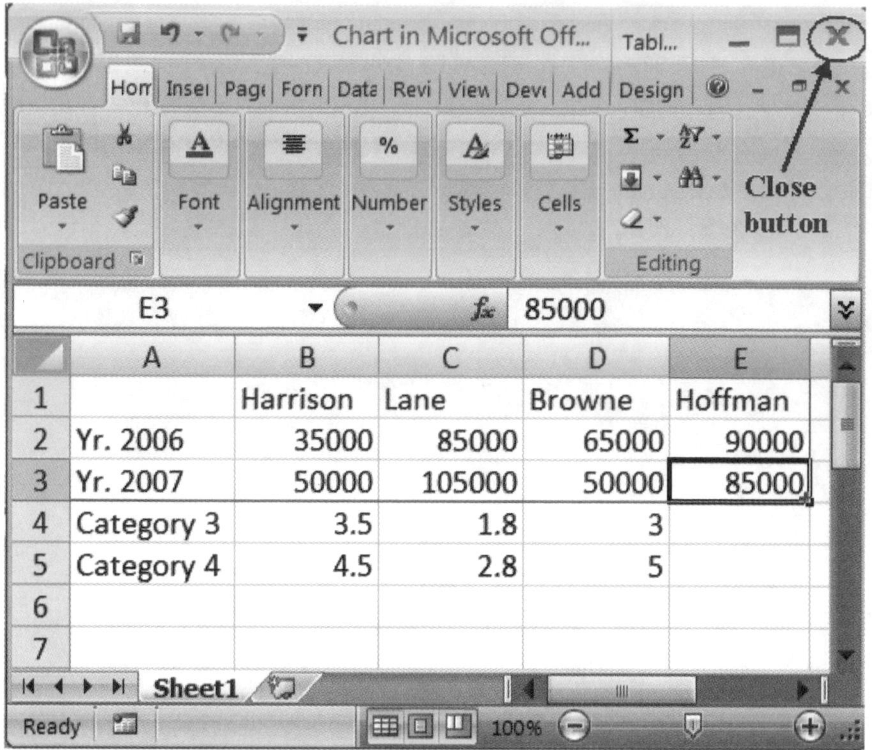

Formatting a Chart

In this section, you will learn how to apply formatting to your chart.

After creating your chart, three contextual Ribbons appear when the chart is selected: **Design**, **Layout** and **Format**, from where you can format your chart, apply various styles and change the chart layout.

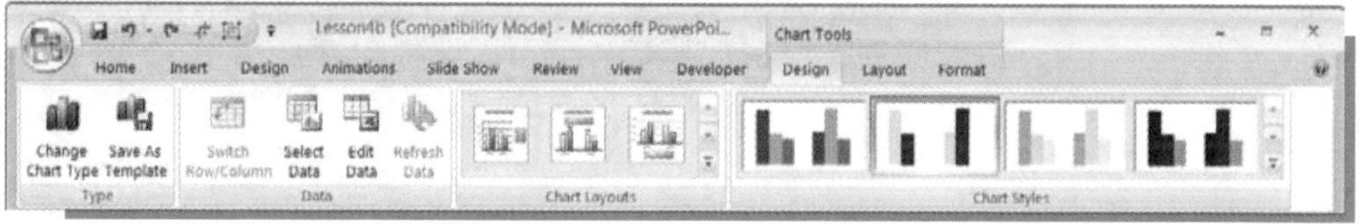

From the contextual **Design Ribbon**, you can apply various chart layouts and chart styles as well as change the chart type and modify the existing chart data. The **Layout Ribbon** allows you to modify and add chart elements such as the chart labels, axes, and plot areas. You are already familiar with many of the features on the **Format Ribbon**. From here, you can change the shape borders, modify the colors and patterns of the graphical data series, and modify Shape Styles. To modify specific chart selections such as a data series or axis options, click the chart element and click the **Format Selection** button on the Format Ribbon to display the appropriate dialog box.

Additionally, you can format the text on your chart (font, color, alignment) just as you would any other text contained in a placeholder from the Home Ribbon.

To Format a Chart

1. Click the chart to select it.
2. To change a chart layout or style, click the **Design tab** under Chart Tools. Make your desired selection from the Chart Layout or Chart Style group.
3. To change chart titles, axis titles, legends, or data labels, click the **Layout tab** under Chart Tools and make the appropriate selection from the Ribbon.
4. To add or modify shape effects, shape fill, border weight, style or color, click the **Format tab** under Chart tools and make your selection.
5. To format a selected object, click the chart object and click the **Format Selection button** on the Format tab to display the Format Object dialog box.

Let's Try It!

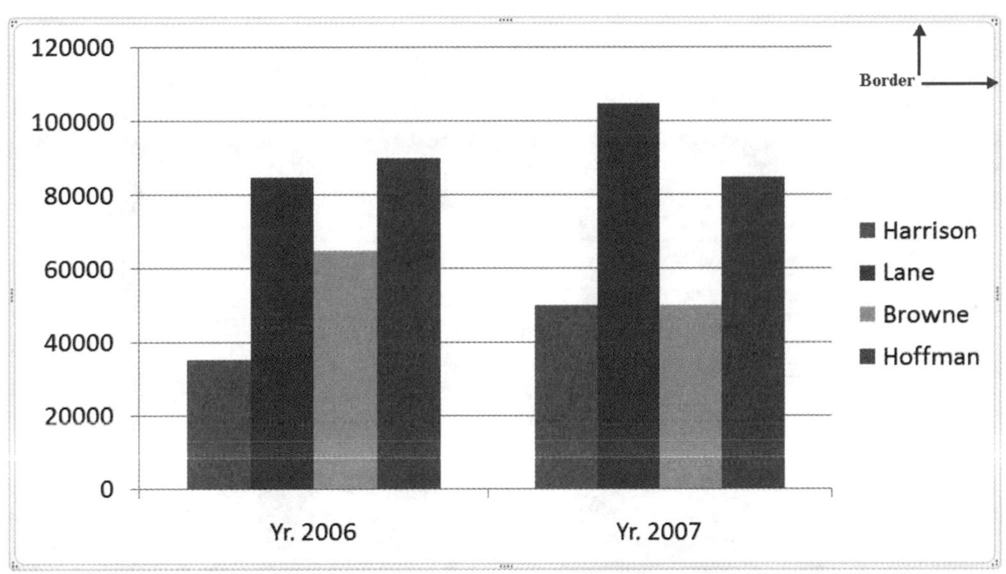

- Click on the border of the chart.

Selects the chart and displays the contextual Design, Layout and Format Ribbons.

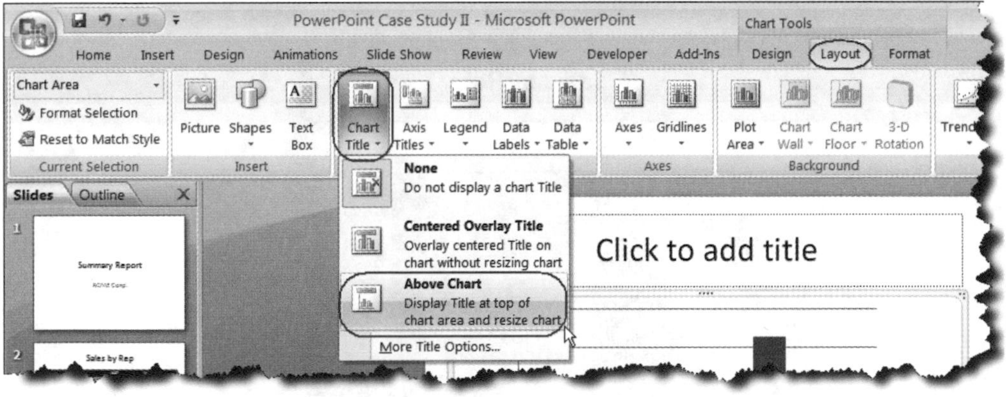

- Click the **Layout tab** under Chart Tools.

Displays the Chart Layout Ribbon.

- Click the **Chart Title** button on the Ribbon and choose **Above Chart** from the menu.

Inserts a Chart Title text box above the chart.

- Select the text in the **Chart Title** box, type: **Sales by Rep** as shown.

Enters a title for the chart in the chart title box.

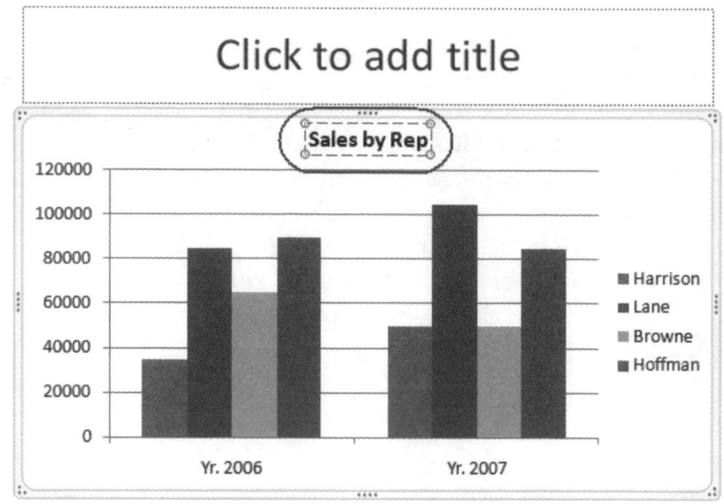

- Click the **Axis Titles** button on the Ribbon, point to **Primary Horizontal Axis Title** and choose **Title Below Axis** from the menu.

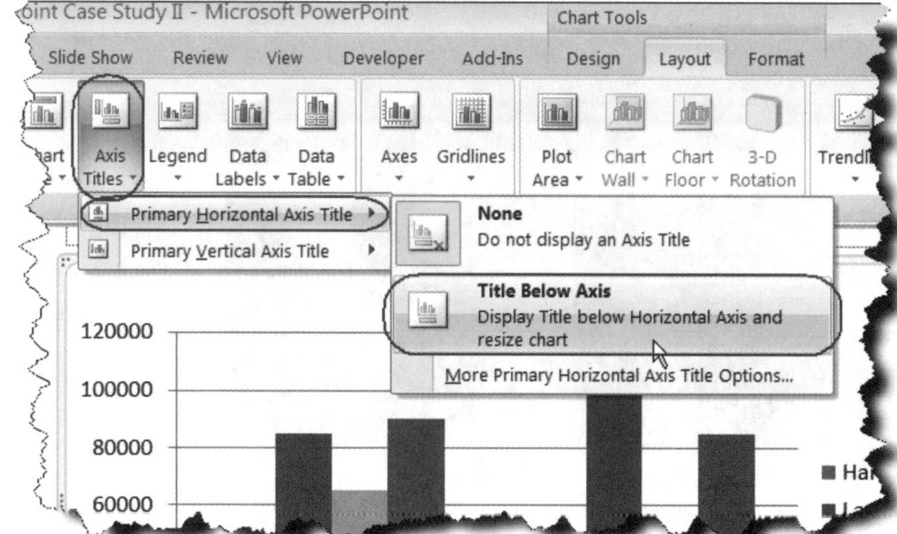

Inserts a text box below the Category X axis.

- Select the text in the **X-Axis Title** box, type: **Year**.

Enters the text for the x-axis box.

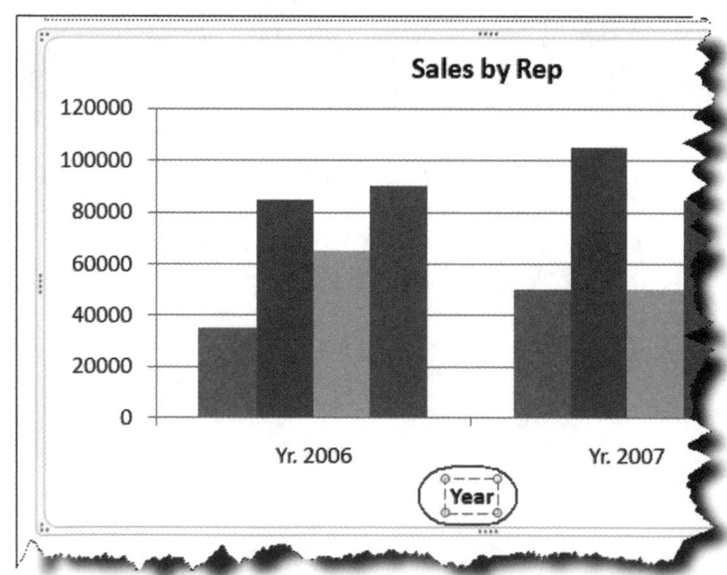

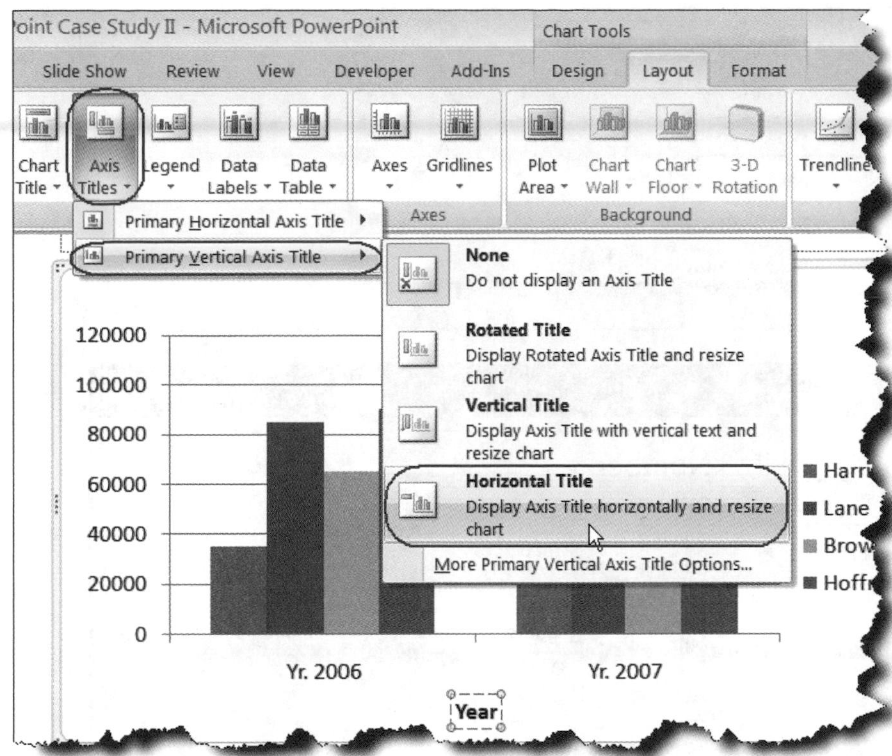

- Click the **Axis Titles** button on the Ribbon, point to **Primary Vertical Axis Title** and choose **Horizontal Title** from the menu.

Inserts a horizontal text box to the left of the Value Z axis.

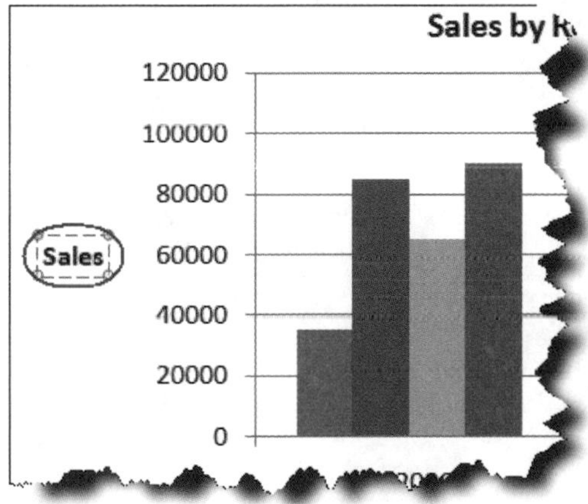

- Select the text in the **Value axis box**, type: **Sales**.

Enters the text for the z-axis box.

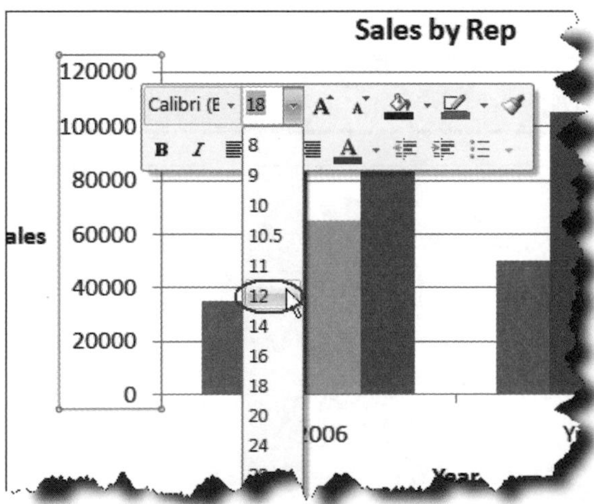

- **Right-click** any of the values on the Value Axis (the vertical axis on the left) and select **12** from the Font Size drop-down list on the Mini-Toolbar.

Right-clicking on a selected object that contains text will display the Mini-toolbar.

- **Click** any of the values on the Value Axis and click the **Format Selection** button under the Current Selection group.

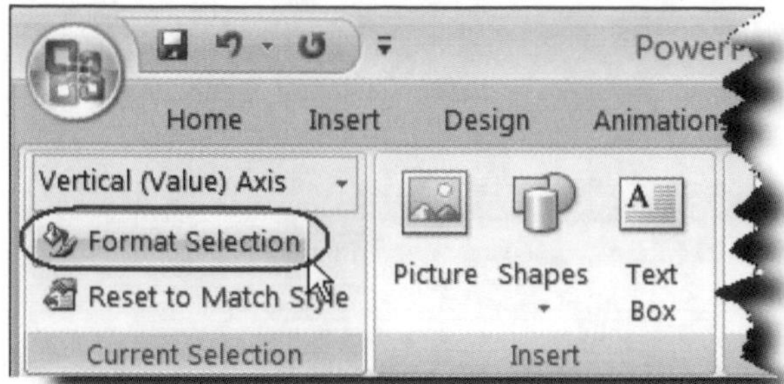

Displays the Format Axis dialog box.

- Click the **Number** category in the left pane.

Displays number formatting options.

- In the **Category** box in the right pane, select **Currency**.

Changes the number formatting of the data series to Currency.

- In the **Decimal places** box, type: **0**.
- Click **Close**.

Set the number formatting to no decimal places.

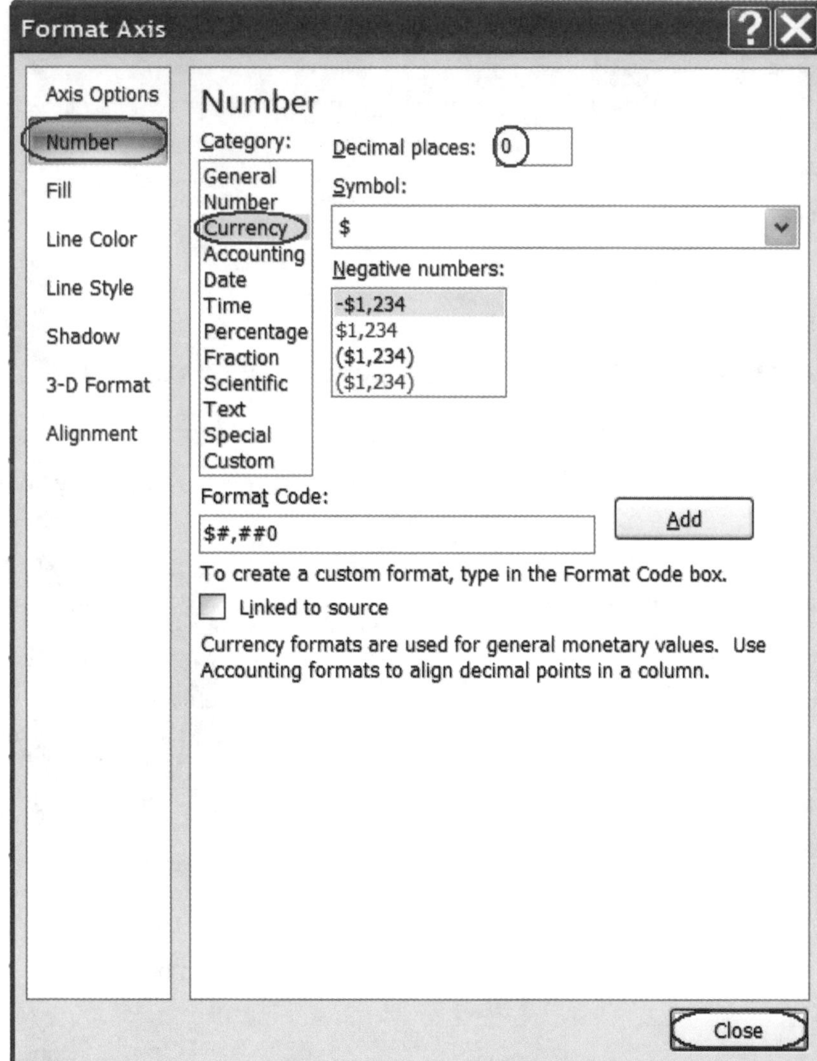

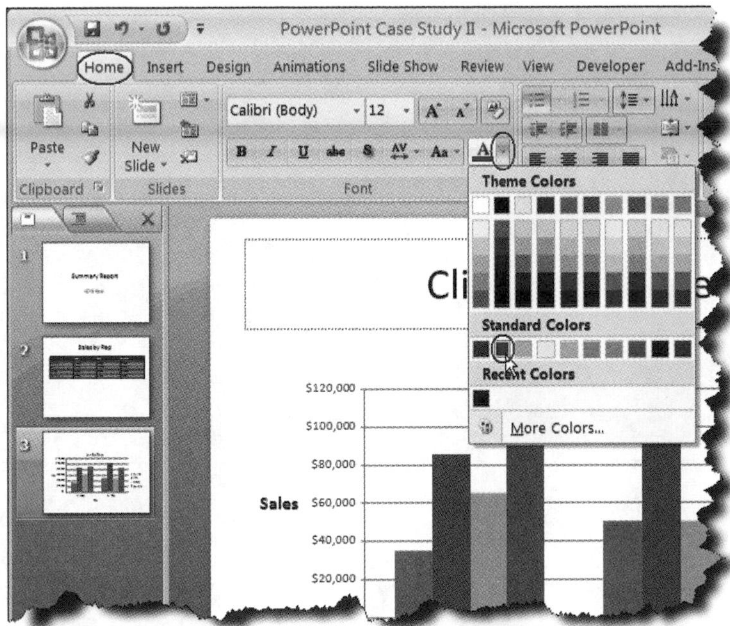

- With the value series still selected, click the **Home tab** on the Ribbon.

Switches to Home tools and commands.

- Click the **Font Color arrow** on the Font group and click the **Red** color swatch in the palette.

Sets the font color of the value axis data to red.

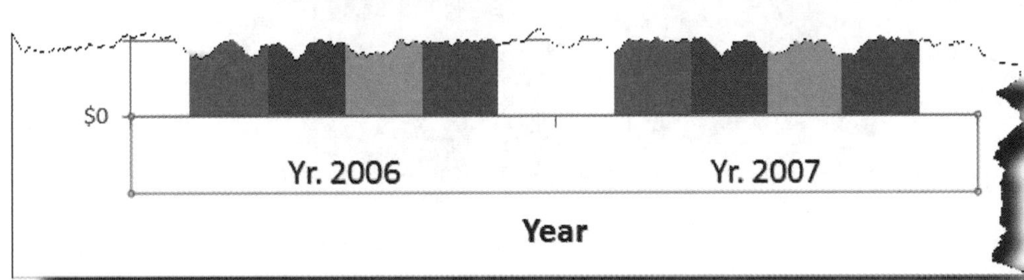

- Click on the either of the values (Yr. 2006 or Yr. 2007) on the Category-X axis.

Selects the values we want to modify.

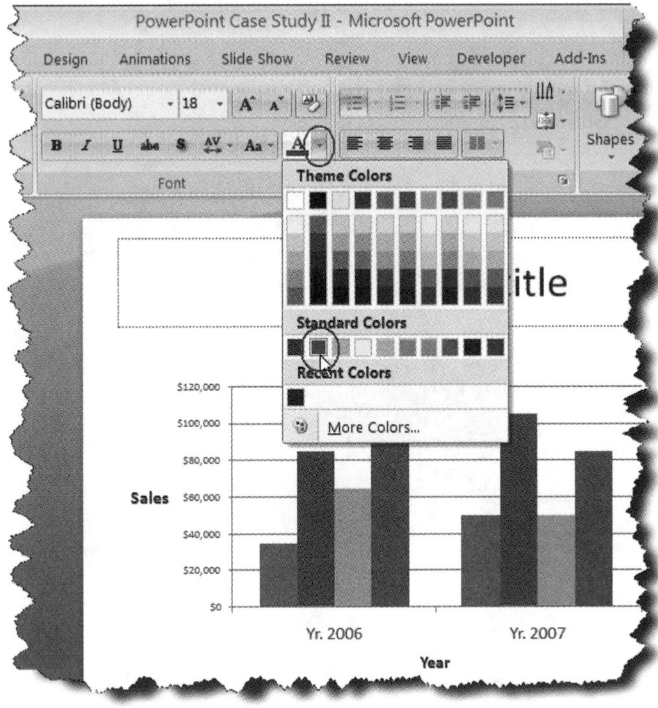

- Click the **Font Color arrow** on the Font group and click the **Red** color swatch in the palette.

Sets the font color of the category axis data to red.

- Click the **Font Size arrow** on the Font group and click **12**.

Sets the font size of the category axis data to 12.

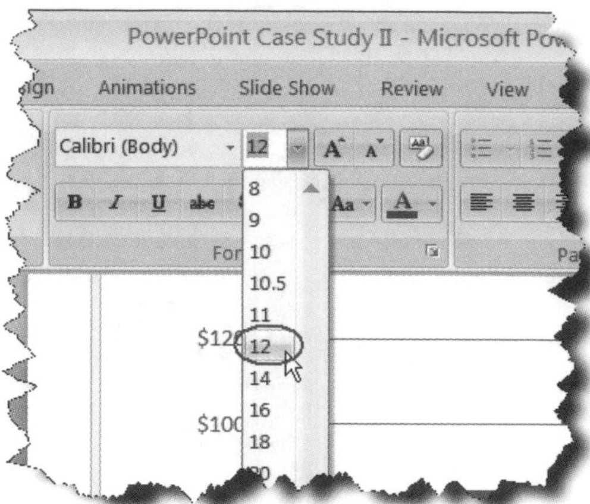

- Click on either of the **purple bars** for **Hoffman**.

Selects the data object we want to format.

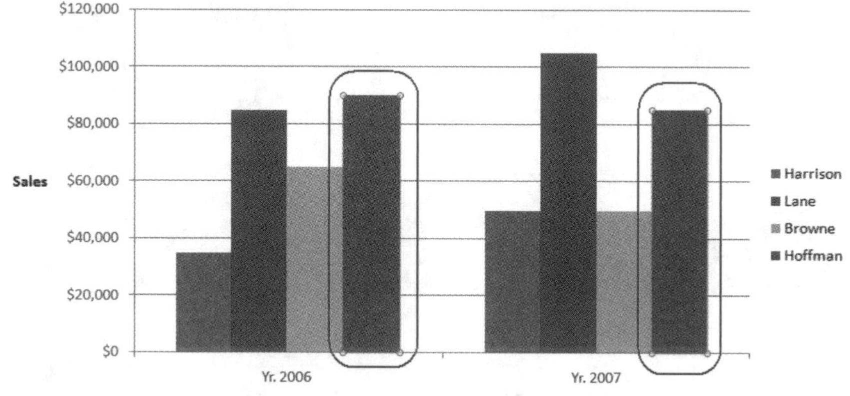

- Click the **Shape Fill** button on the Drawing group and click the **Orange** color swatch under the Standard Colors category.

Changes the bar color for Hoffman to orange.

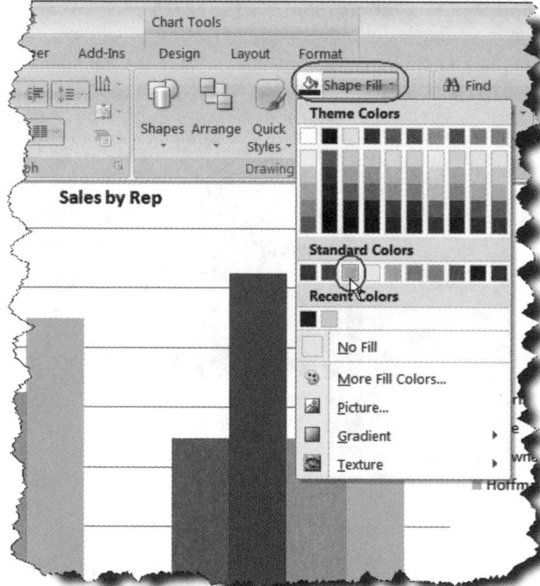

- Click the **Design** tab under **Chart Tools** on the Ribbon.

Switches to chart design options.

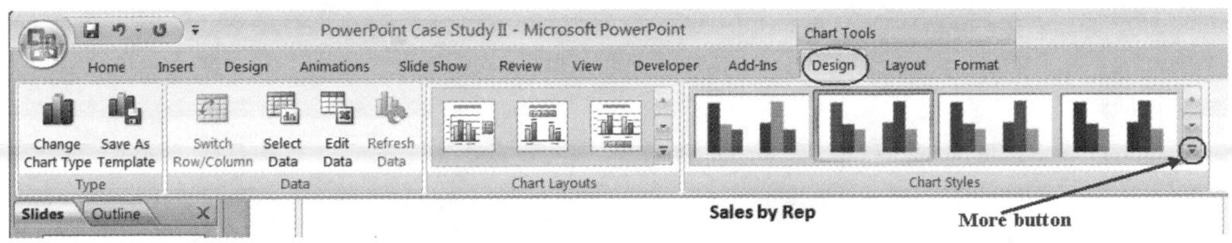

- On the **Chart Styles** group, click the **More** button on the Chart Styles group.

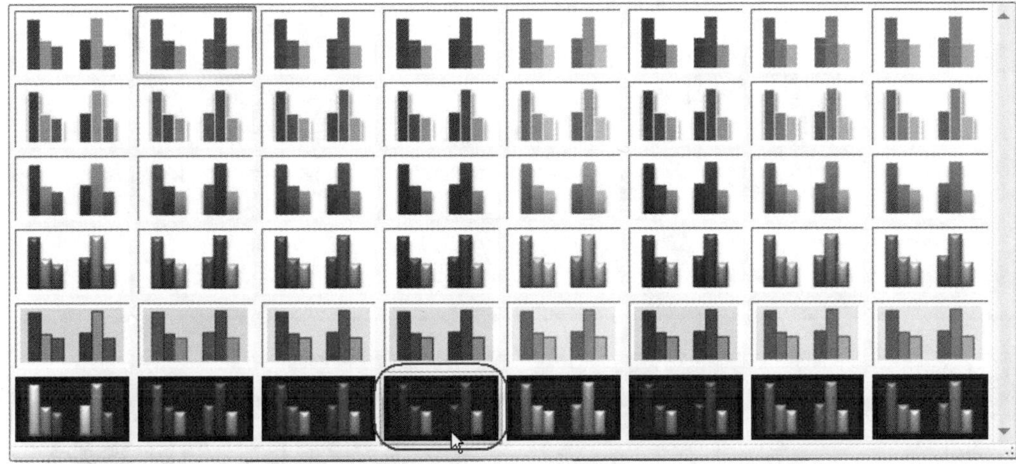

- Click the **fourth column** in the **last row** (Style 44).

Applies Style 44 to the selected chart.

- Click the **Save** button on the Quick Access toolbar.

Saves the active presentation.

Changing the Chart Type

In this section, you will learn how to change the chart type of an existing chart in your presentation.

PowerPoint offers several chart types to aid you in communicating different types of information. To change the chart type, click the **Change Chart Type** button on the Type group under the contextual **Design tab** under Chart Tools to display the Chart Type dialog box. From there, you can choose from a wide array of chart types.

To Change the Chart Type

1. Click the chart to select it.
2. Click the contextual **Design tab** under Chart Tools on the Ribbon.
3. Click the **Change Chart Type** button on the Type group.
4. Click the chart type category that you want in the left pane.
5. Click the chart type that you want in the right pane.
6. Click **OK**.

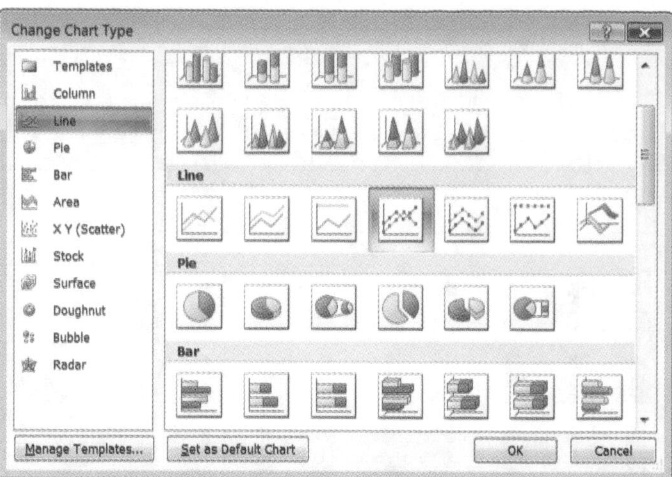

Let's Try It!

- Click anywhere on the chart.

Selects the chart whose type we want to change.

- Click the contextual **Design tab** on the Ribbon.

Switches to chart design tools and commands.

- Click the **Change Chart Type** button on the Type group as shown.

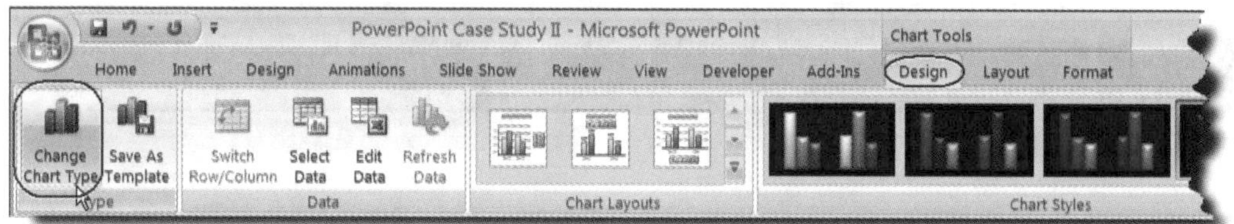

Displays the Chart Type dialog box.

- Click **Line** in the left pane.

Displays chart types in the Line category.

- Click the **fourth** chart type from the left in the right pane in the Line category (**Line with markers**)

Chooses the Line with Markers chart type.

- Click **OK**.

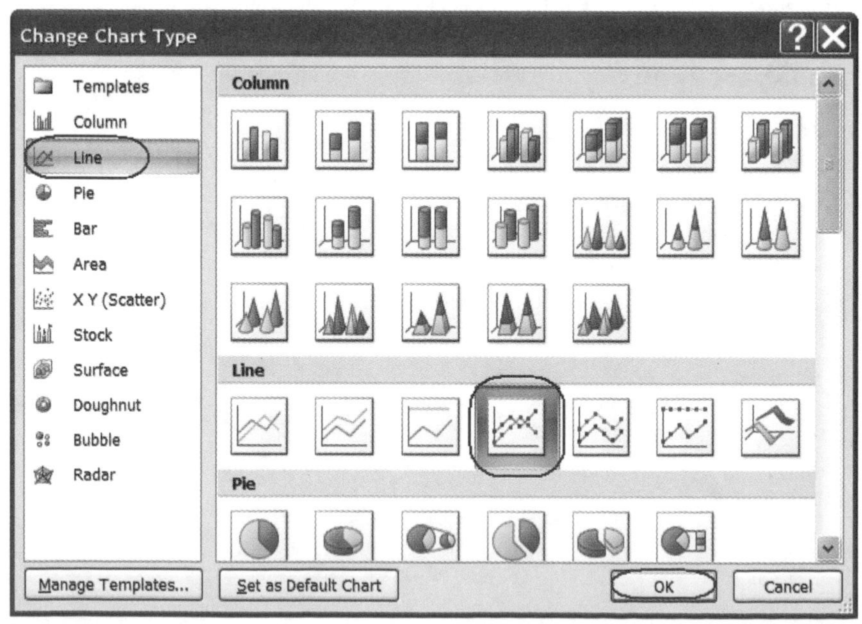

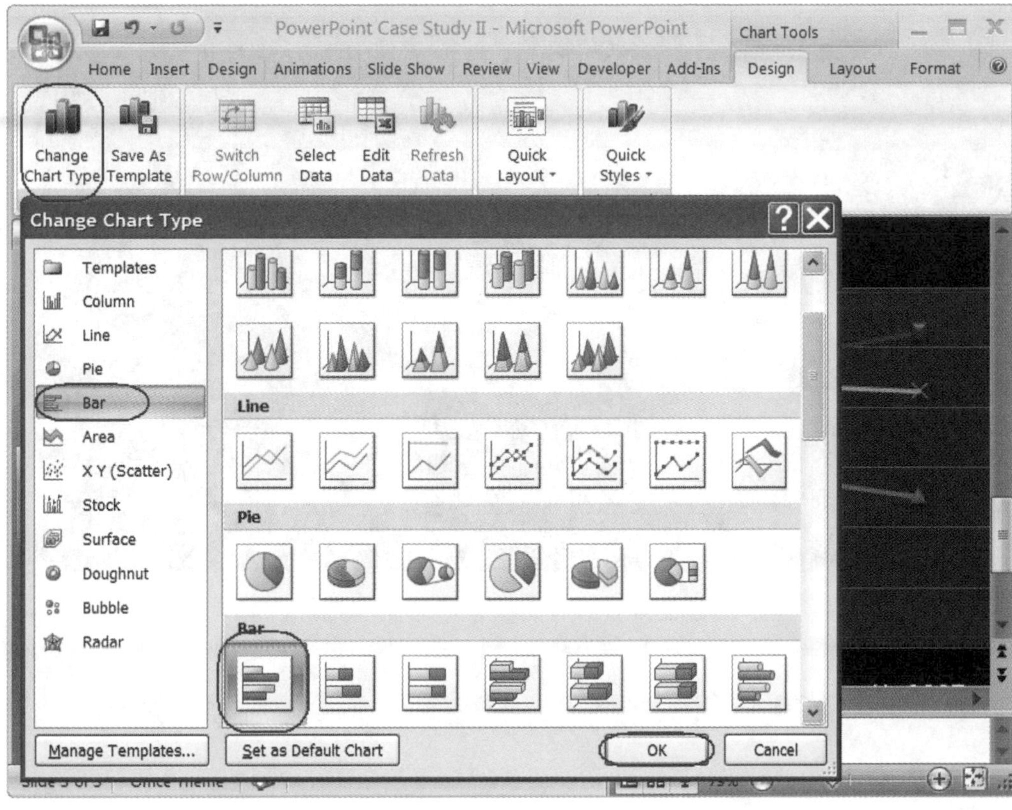

Closes the Chart Type dialog box and applies the new chart type.

- Click the **Change Chart Type** button on the Type group.

Displays the Chart Type dialog box.

- Click **Bar** in the left pane.

Displays chart types in the Bar category.

- Click the **first** chart type from the left in the right pane in the Bar category (**Clustered Bar**)

Chooses the Clustered Bar chart type.

- Click **OK**.

Closes the Chart Type dialog box and applies the new chart type.

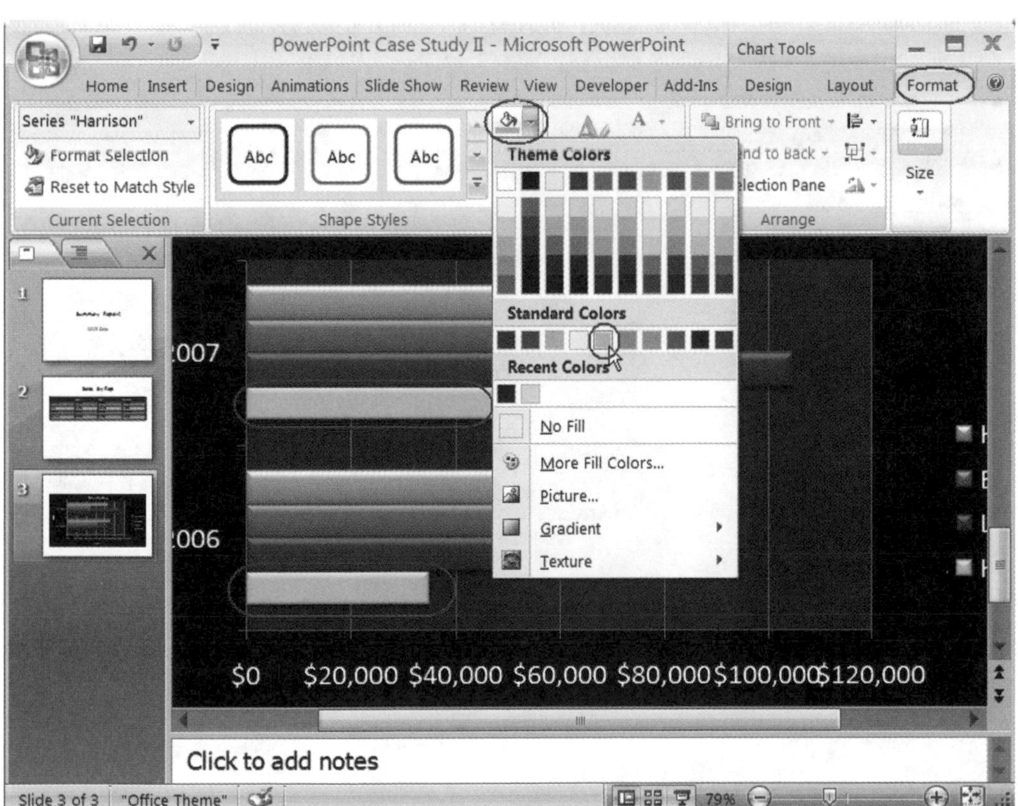

- Click the contextual **Format** tab on the Ribbon.

Switches to chart formatting tools and commands.

- Click the **bottom bar** in the chart area (Harrison) under Yr. 2006.

Selects the bar we want to format.

- Click the **Shape Fill** button and click the **Light Green** (fifth color swatch under the Standard Colors category).

Changes the data series bars for Harrison to light green.

- Click the **Save** button.

Saves the active presentation.

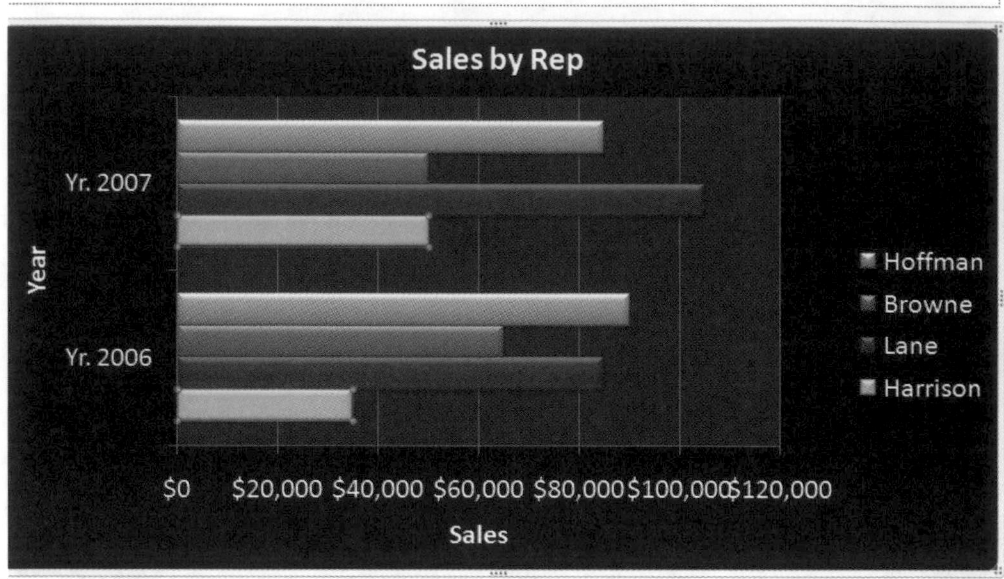

Inserting an Organization Chart

In this section, you will learn how to insert an Organization Chart into your slide.

Microsoft Office provides the ability to insert **diagram objects** into your presentations. One of these diagram objects is the **Organization Chart** which allows you to illustrate hierarchical relationships such as the structure of a business (i.e. names, titles and departments of managers).

The organization chart is the 1st object located in the **Hierarchy category** of the **SmartArt gallery**.

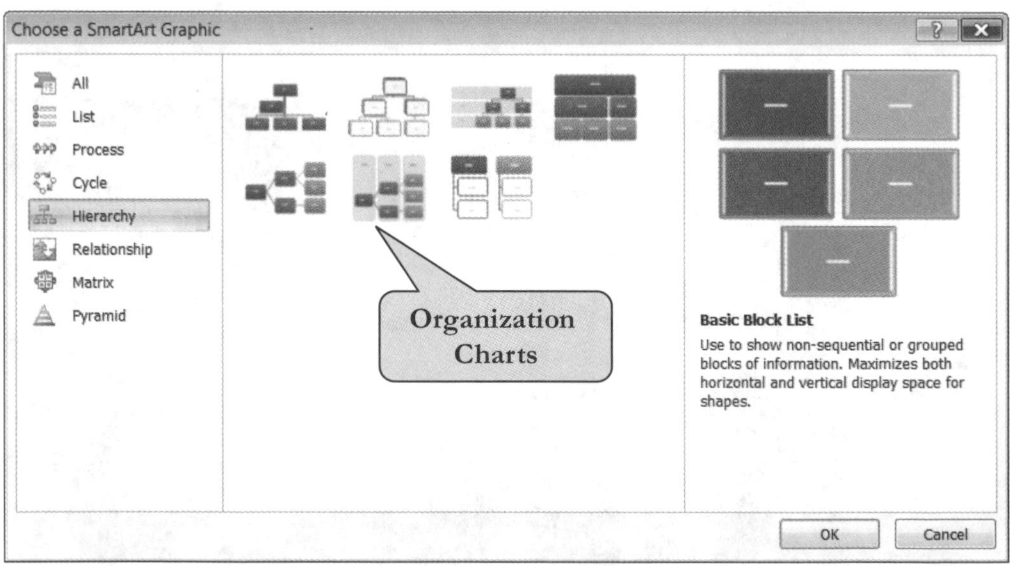

To Insert an Organization Chart

1. Select the slide into which you wish to insert an Organizational Chart.
2. Click the **Insert tab** on the Ribbon.
3. Click the **SmartArt** button on the Illustrations group.
4. In the left pane, click **Hierarchy**.
5. In the middle pane, click the type of Organization chart you wish to insert.
6. Click **OK**.
7. Click inside the text box shape to add text to a shape.
   Or
   Type your text in the Text Pane (click the Text Pane button on the Create Graphic group to display the Text Pane).
8. Click outside of the Organization Chart shape when finished.

Let's Try It!

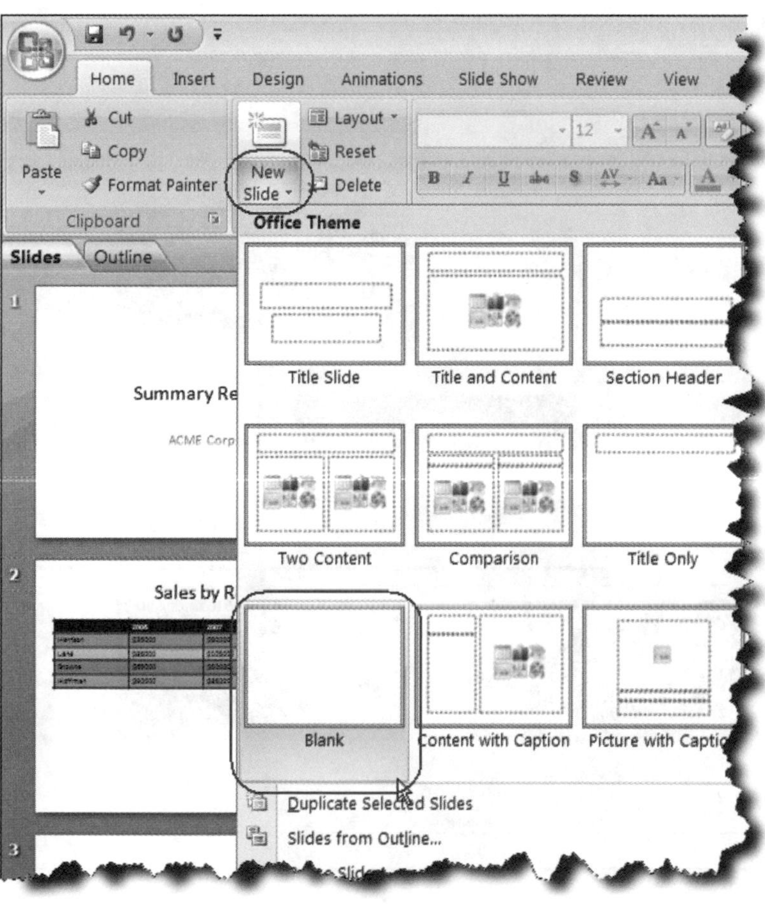

- Click the **Home tab** on the Ribbon.

Displays Home tools and commands.

- Click the **New Slide arrow** and select **Blank** from the layout gallery.

Inserts a new blank slide into our presentation.

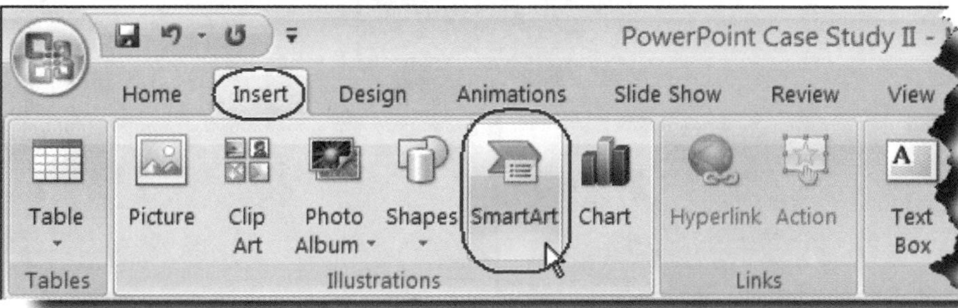

- Click the **Insert tab** on the Ribbon.

Displays Insert commands and tools.

- Click the **SmartArt** button on the Illustrations group.

Displays the SmartArt dialog box.

- In the left pane, click **Hierarchy**.

Displays available Organization Chart shapes.

- Click on the **Organization Chart** diagram object (1st row, 1st column).

Selects the Organization Chart object.

- Click **OK**.

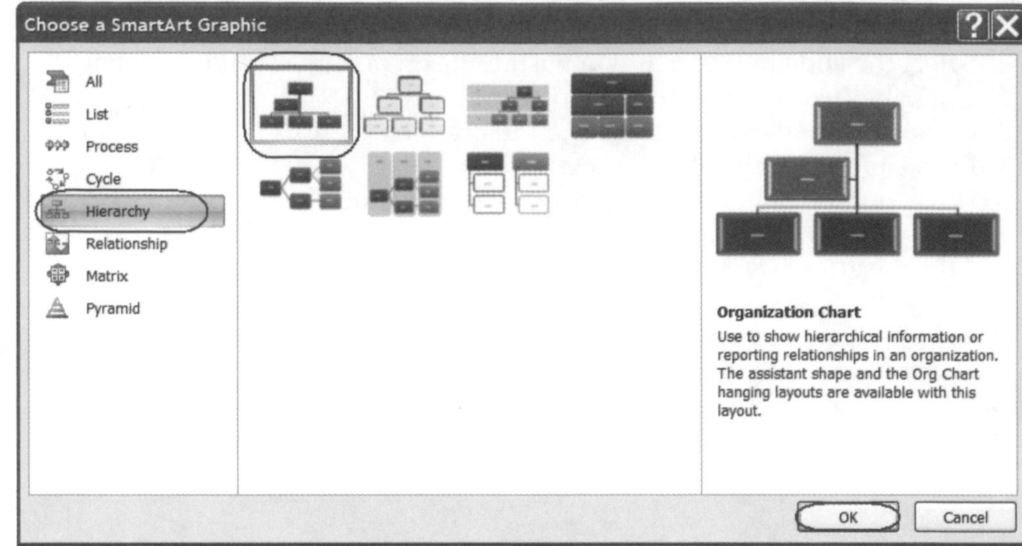

Inserts the Organization Chart onto your slide.

- Click in the topmost box and then type: **Bhavjeet Sanghera**.

Enters the first line of text into the topmost shape.

- Press **Enter**.

Moves to the next line.

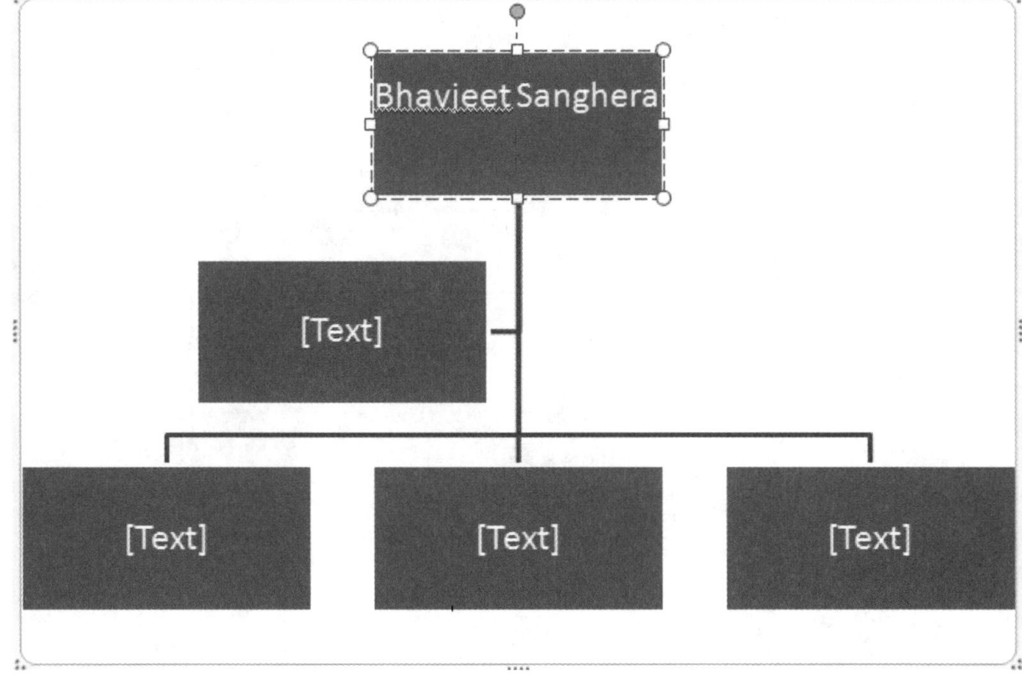

- Type: **President**.

Enters the second line of text in the topmost box.

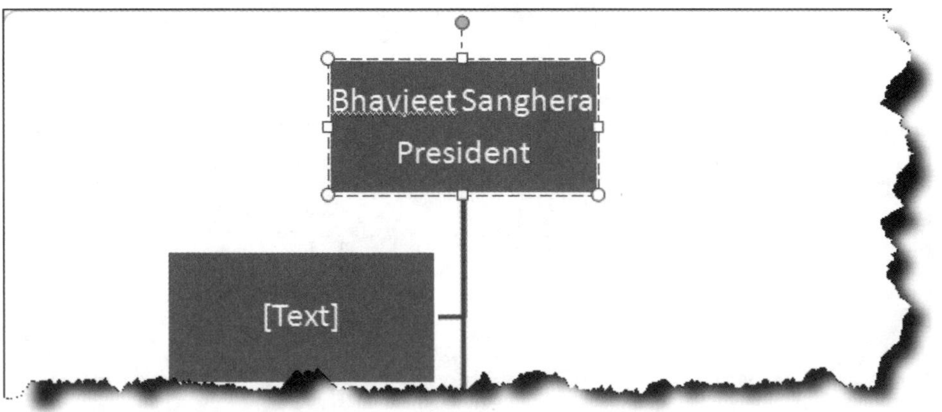

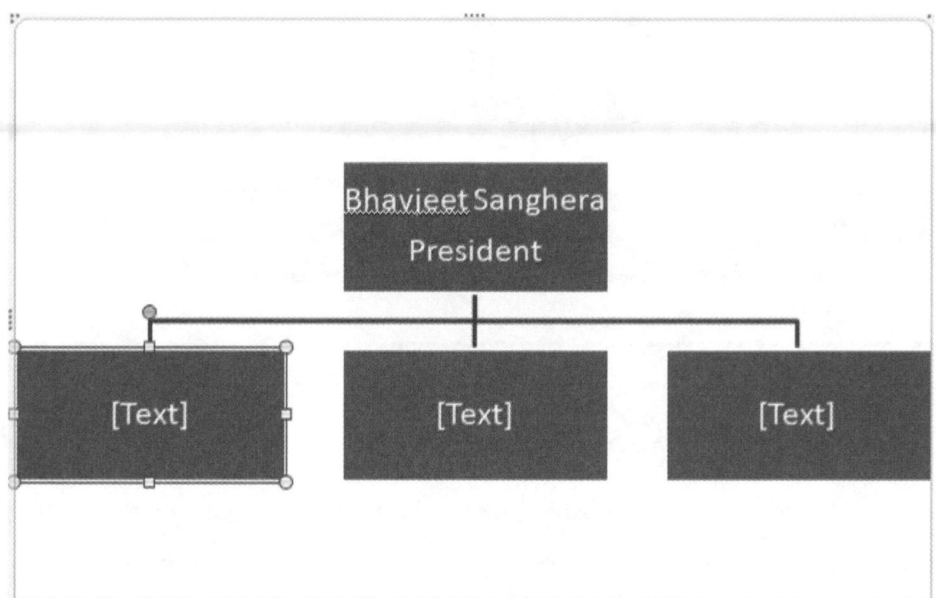

- Click the **border** of the **leftmost shape** on the second row and press the **Delete** key.

Deletes the second level of our Organization chart.

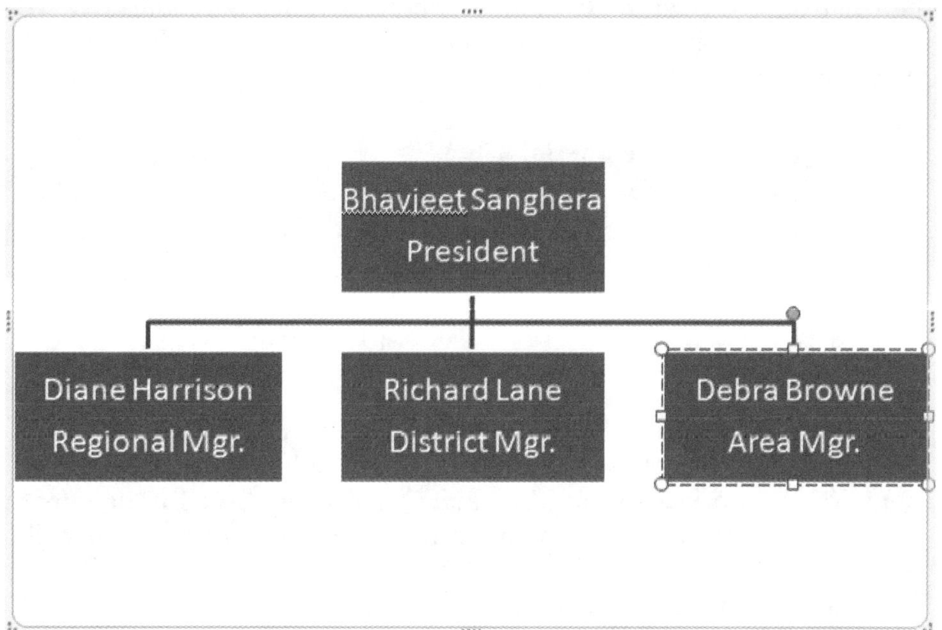

- Click in the **leftmost shape** on the second row and type the following two lines: **Diane Harrison Regional Mgr**.

Enters text into the leftmost box on the second row.

- Click in the **middle shape** on the second row and type the following two lines: **Richard Lane District Mgr**.

Enters text into the middle box on the second row.

- Click in the **rightmost** shape on the second row and type the following two lines: **Debra Browne Area Mgr**.

Enters text into the rightmost box on the second row.

- Click outside the shape anywhere on the active slide.

Deselects the Organization Chart object.

- Click the **Save** button.

Saves the active presentation.

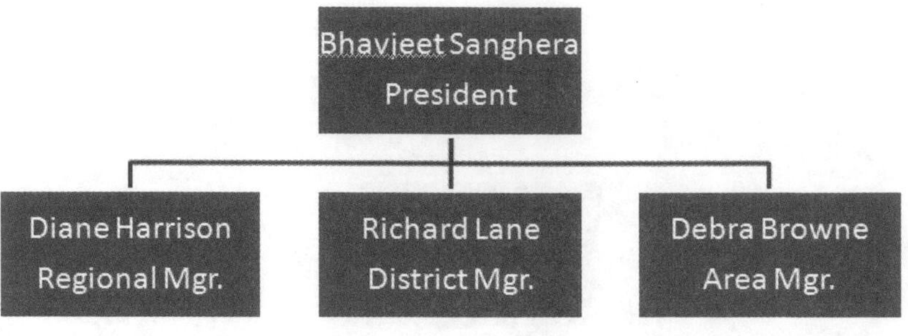

Applying a Theme to a Presentation

In this section, you will learn how to apply a theme to your presentation.

Themes are a quick way to apply preconfigured formatting to your presentation. Themes consist of theme colors, theme fonts and theme effects that give your presentation a professional and polished look. You can add themes from the **Design tab** on the Ribbon. PowerPoint comes with 20 installed themes that you can use. You can download additional themes from Microsoft Office Online.

As you move your mouse pointer over each theme in the gallery, your presentation changes to reflect what it would look like if you apply the theme. This is an example of Microsoft Office's new **Live Preview** feature.

You can apply a theme to your entire presentation or to selected slides.

To Apply a Theme to Your Entire Presentation

1. Click the **Design tab** on the Ribbon.
2. Move your mouse pointer over any of the theme thumbnails in the **Themes group** to preview a particular theme.
3. Click the theme thumbnail for the theme you want to apply.

To Apply a Theme to Selected Slides

1. Select the slides to which you want to apply a theme.
2. Click the **Design tab** on the Ribbon.
3. Right-click the theme you want to apply and choose **Apply to Select Slides** from the contextual menu.

TIP: To set a theme as the default theme for all new PowerPoint documents, right-click the theme thumbnail and choose **Set as Default Theme**.

Let's Try It!

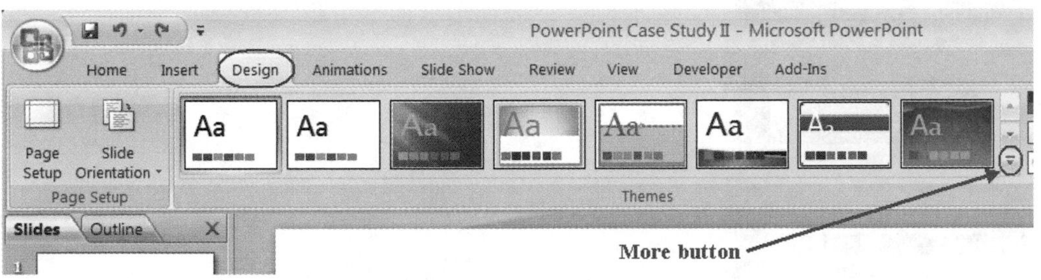

- Click the **Design tab** on the Ribbon.

Switches to Design commands and tools.

- Click the **More button** on the Themes gallery.

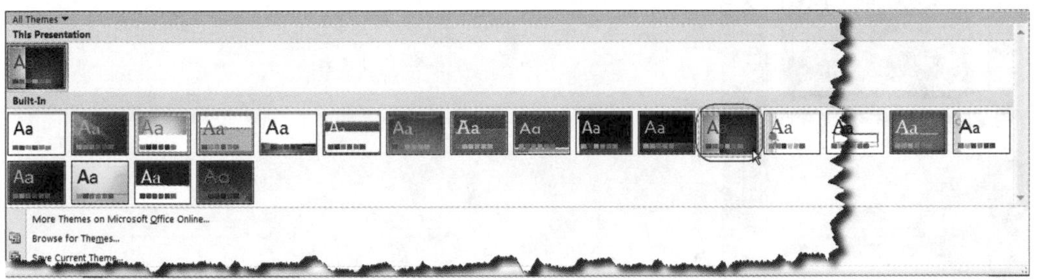

Displays all available themes.

- Click the **Opulent theme** thumbnail.

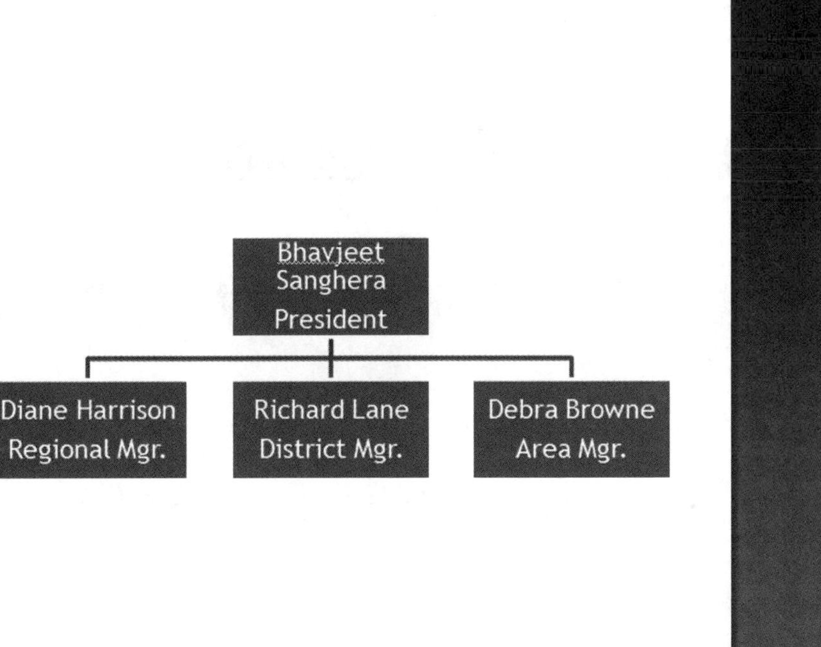

Applies the theme to the entire presentation.

- In the **Slides Pane** select **Slide 2**.

Makes slide 2 the active slide.

- Hold down the **Ctrl** key and then select **Slide 4**

Selects slides 2 and 4. Holding down the Ctrl key allows you to select non-adjacent slides.

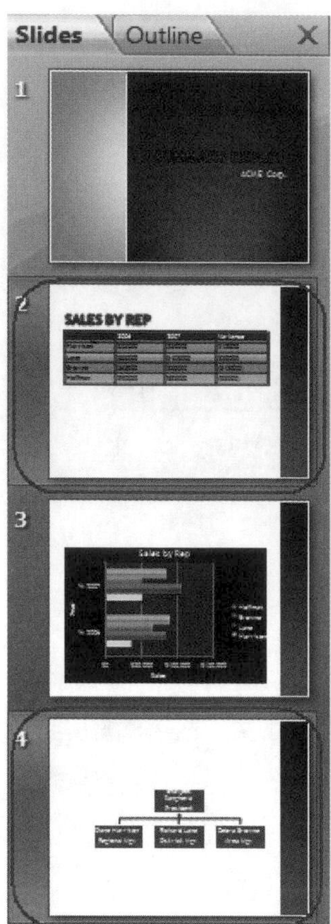

- Click the **More button** on the Themes gallery.

Displays all available themes.

- Right-click on the **third theme from the left** (the Aspect theme) and choose **Apply to Selected Slides** from the contextual menu.

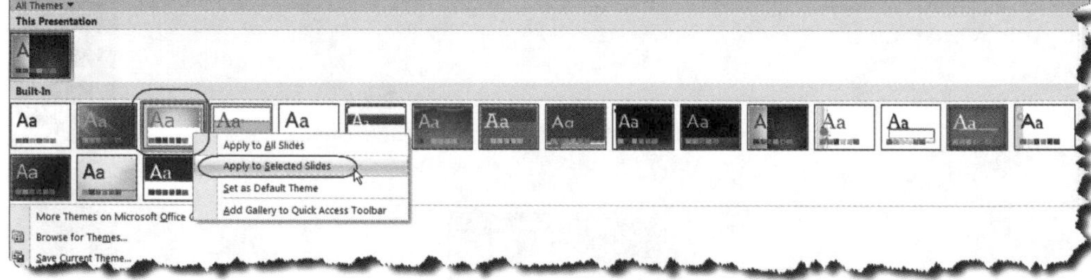

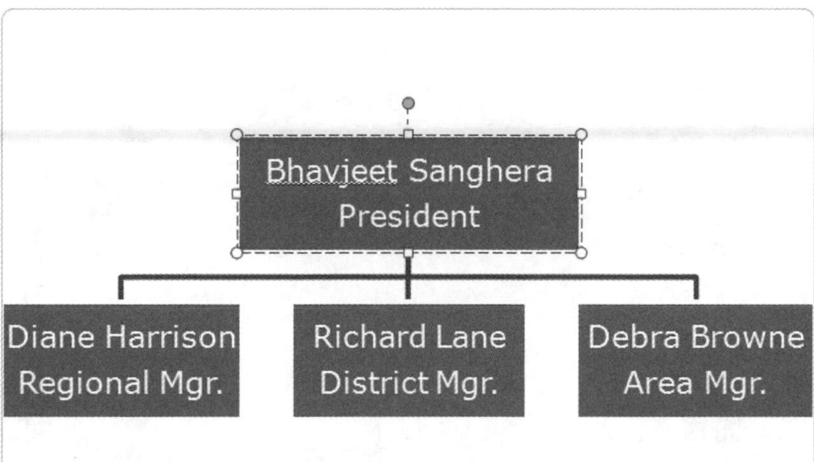

Applies the Aspect theme to slides 2 and 4.

- Select the **topmost** box of slide 4 and widen it so the name "Bhavjeet Sanghera" appears on one line.
- Click the **Save button** on the Quick Access toolbar.

Modifying Theme Colors, Fonts and Effects

In this section, you will learn how to modify the colors, fonts and effects of a theme.

Once you have applied a theme to your presentation, you can customize it further by modifying the theme colors, font or effects from the right side of the Theme group on the Ribbon. The **Colors button** allows you to apply various schemes of colors to the current theme. Click the **Colors** drop-down arrow and move your mouse pointer over any of the color schemes to view a live preview.

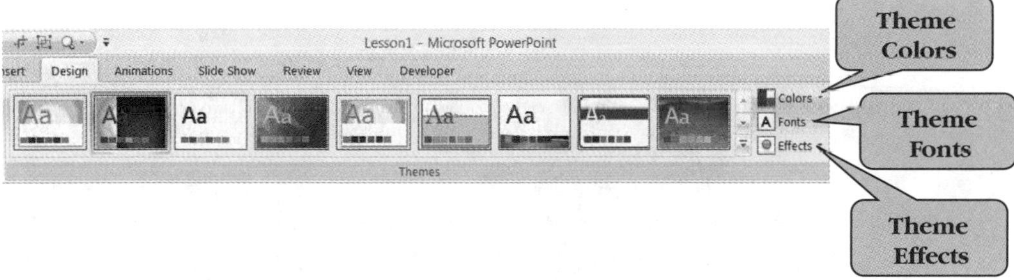

Likewise, the **Fonts** button and the **Effects** button allow you to apply a set of theme font and theme effects to your presentation. To display a Screen Tip that tells you the curent theme colors, fonts or effect, move your mouse pointer over the respective button on the Ribbon.

To Apply a Theme Color Scheme, Font or Effect to a Presentation

1. Select the slides to which you want to apply a theme.
2. Click the **Design tab** on the Ribbon.
3. To apply a color scheme, click the **Color** arrow on the Theme group and click the color scheme you want to apply.
4. To change the theme font, click the **Font** arrow on the Theme group and click the theme font you want to apply.
5. To apply a theme effect, click the **Effects** arrow on the Theme group and click the effect you want to apply.

Let's Try It!

- In the **Slides Pane** select **Slide 2** and **Slide 4**.

Selects the slide whose theme we want to modify.

- Move your mouse pointer over the **Color button** on the Themes group on the Design Ribbon.
- Click the **Opulent** color scheme.

Applies the color scheme to all slides using the current theme—in this case, slides 2 and 4.

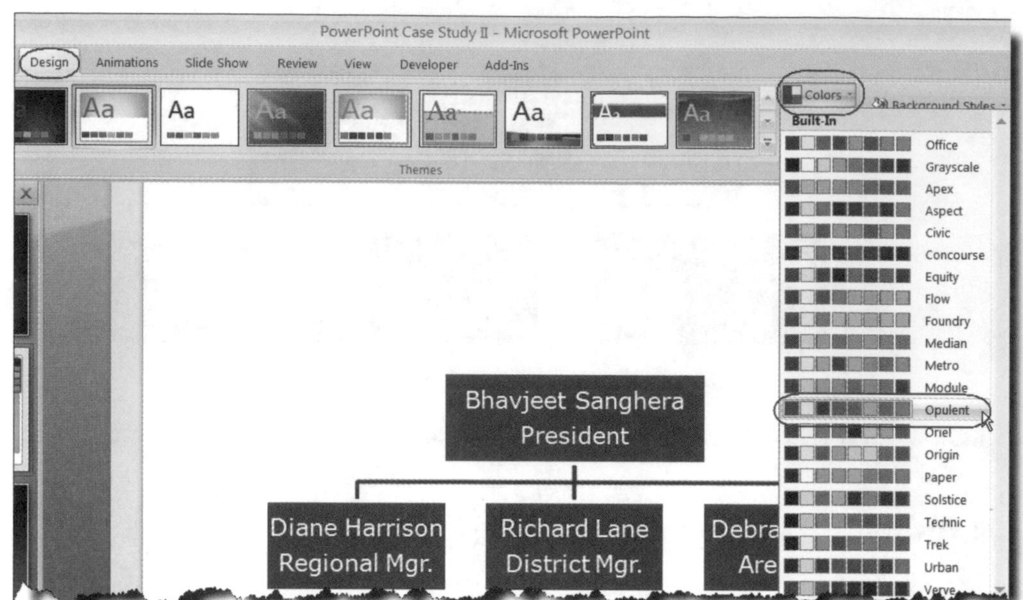

- Make sure slide 2 and 4 are selected.
- Click the **Fonts button** and move your mouse pointer over the **Georgia** font scheme.

Displays a live preview of the Georgia font scheme.

- **Right-click** the Georgia font scheme and click **Apply to All Slides.**

Applies the new font scheme to all slides in the presentation.

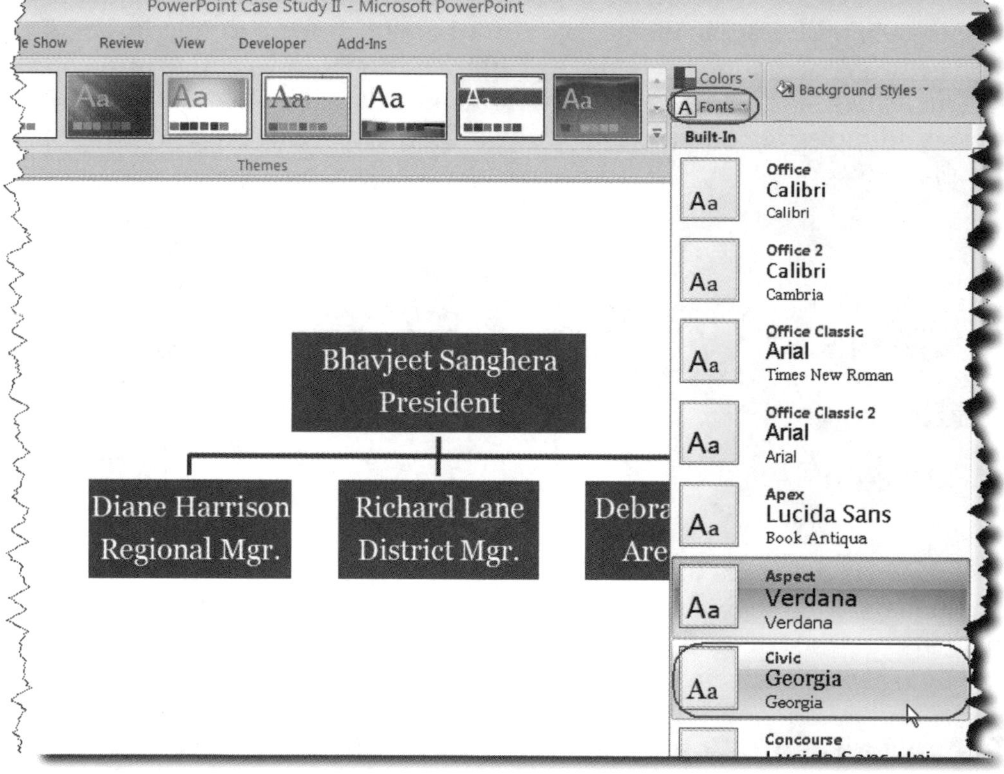

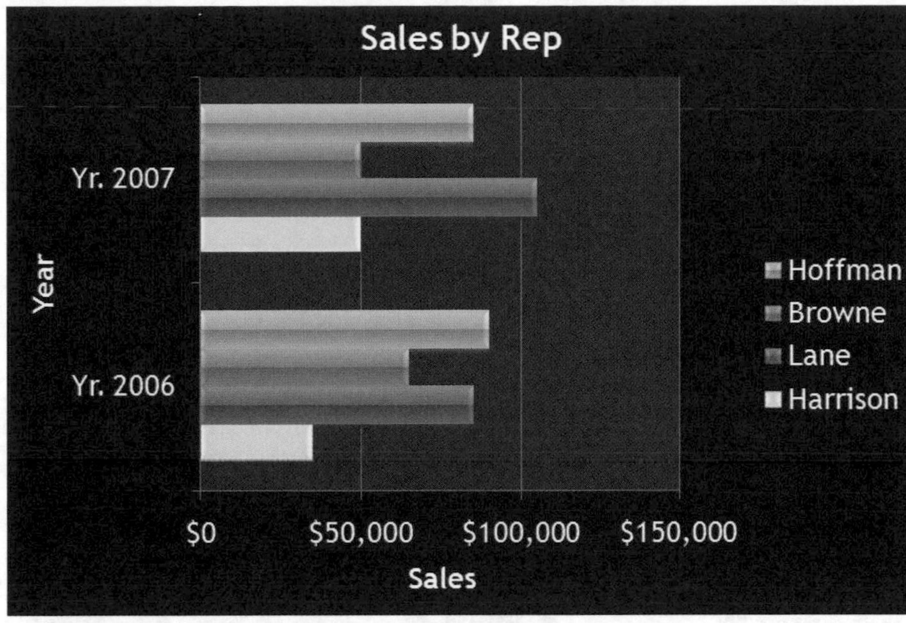

- Select **slide 3** and click on the **title holder**.
- Type: **Performance Reviews**

The title is entered in uppercase.

- Click the **Save button** on the Quick Access Toolbar.

Saves our changes.

Rearranging a Presentation in Slide Sorter View and Normal View

In this section, you will learn how to move slides in your presentation.

You can change the order of the slides in your presentation at any time. While there are several different methods that you can use to accomplish this, the easiest way is to click and drag your slide(s) to the desired new location in **Slide Sorter View**. You can also click and drag slides to a different location in Normal view using either the Outline Pane or the Slides Pane.

To Move a Slide to a New Location in Slide Sorter View

1. Switch to **Slide Sorter View**.
2. Click on the slide that you want to move.
3. Click and hold down your left mouse button.
4. Drag the slide to a new location (as you drag, a vertical line appears indicating where the slide would be placed if you release the mouse button).
5. When the vertical line appears in the desired new location, release the mouse button.

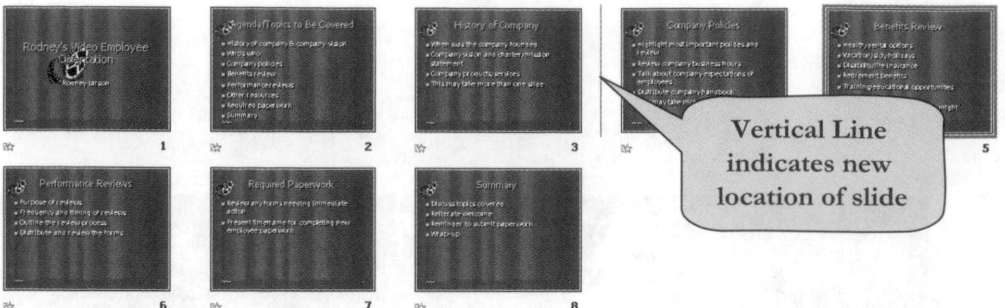

The process for moving slides in Normal View is the same as moving slides in Slide Sorter View. Select the slides you wish to move and then drag them to a new location. You can accomplish this using either the **Slides Pane** or the **Outline Pane**. When moving slides in Normal View, a horizontal line will appear as you drag, indicating the new location.

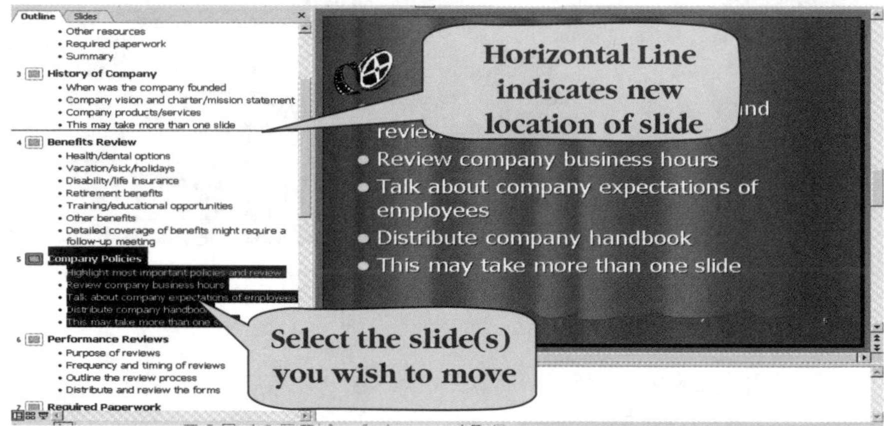

To Move a Slide to a New Location in Normal View

1. Switch to **Normal View**.
2. Click either the **Slides Pane** tab or the **Outline Pane** tab.
3. Click on the slide that you want to move (in outline view, click on the slide icon to the right of the slide number).
4. Click and hold down your left mouse button.
5. Drag the slide up or down to the new location (as you drag, a horizontal line appears indicating where the slide would be placed if you release the mouse button).
6. When the horizontal line appears in the desired new location, release the mouse button.

Let's Try It!

- Click the **Slide Sorter View** button (the middle button on the lower right corner of your screen).

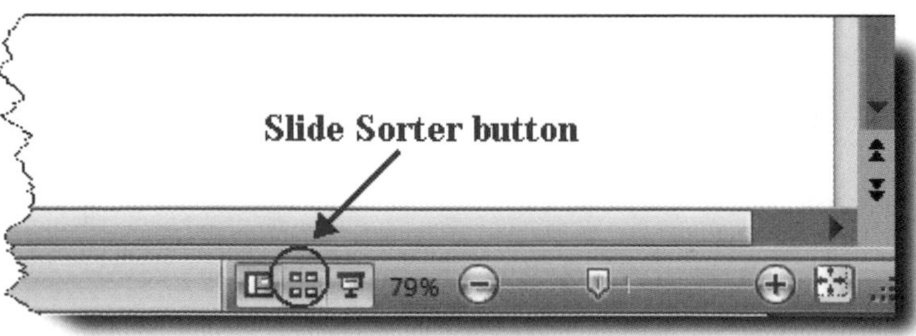

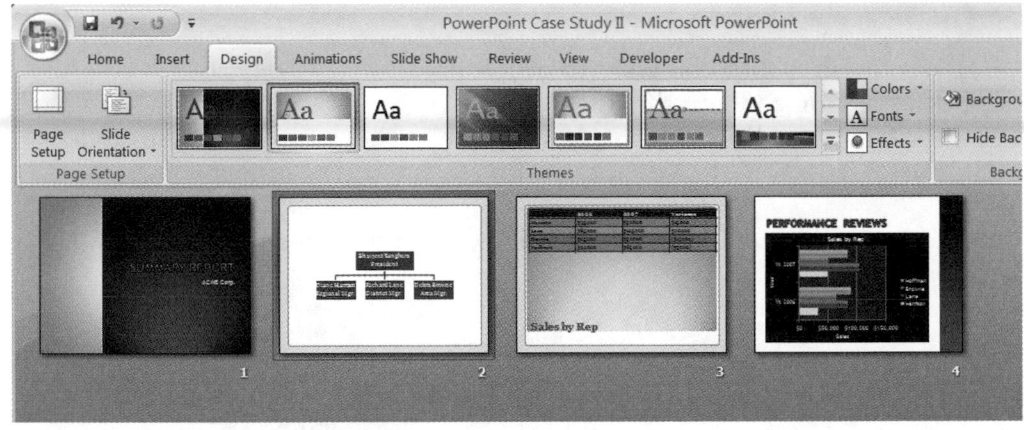

Displays the presentation in Slide Sorter View.

- Click on **Slide 4**.

Makes Slide 4 the active slide.

- Click with your left mouse button and drag to the left until the vertical line is to the left of **Slide 2**.

Positions the insertion point of the new location to the left of Slide 2.

- Release the mouse button.

Completes the move process.

Duplicating Slides

In this section, you will learn how to create a duplicate of an existing slide.

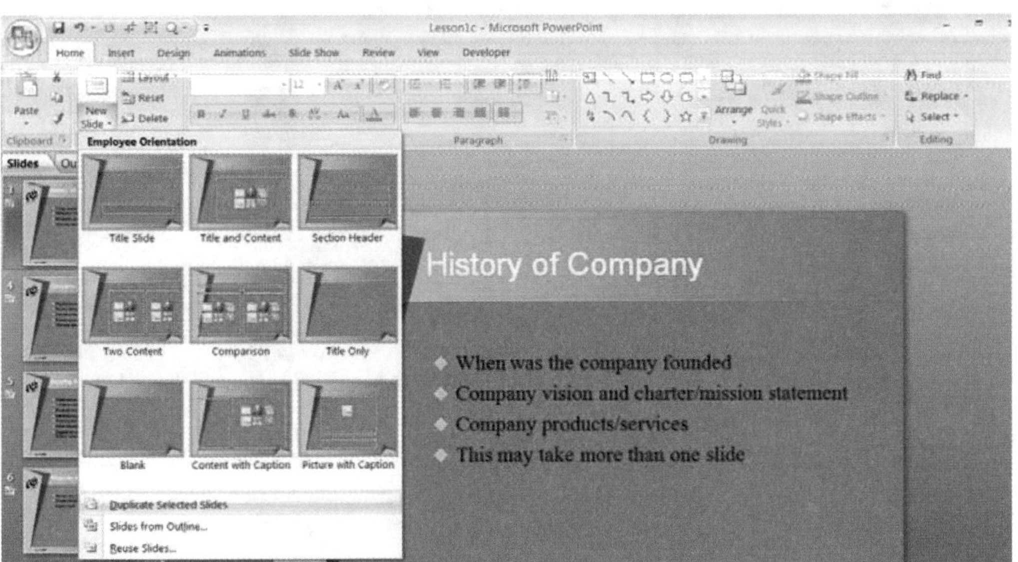

At times, you may wish to create a new slide that is similar to an existing slide. Rather than create the new slide from scratch, it might be easier to create a **copy** of an existing slide and then modify its content. To duplicate slides, use the **Duplicate Slide** command on the New Slide button menu on the Home Ribbon.

Another technique for duplicating slides is using the **drag-and-drop method** in either Normal view (Outline Pane only) or in Slide Sorter View. To make a copy of a slide using drag-and-drop, hold down the **Ctrl** key as you drag. This will make a copy of the selected slide rather than moving the slide. Alternately, you can use the copy and paste commands.

To Duplicate a Slide

1. Select the slide that you want to duplicate.
2. Click the **Home tab** on the Ribbon.
3. Click the **New Slide button arrow** and then click **Duplicate Selected Slides**. The new slide will appear directly below the selected slide.
Or
1. Select the slide, hold down the **Ctrl** key and then drag it to the new location.

Let's Try It!

- Click on **Slide 4** in the Slides Pane.

Selects Slide 4.

- Click the **Home tab** on the Ribbon.

Displays the Home Ribbon.

- Click the **arrow** on the **New Slide button** on the Slides group and click **Duplicate Selected Slides**.

Creates a copy of Slide 4 and inserts it after the selected slide.

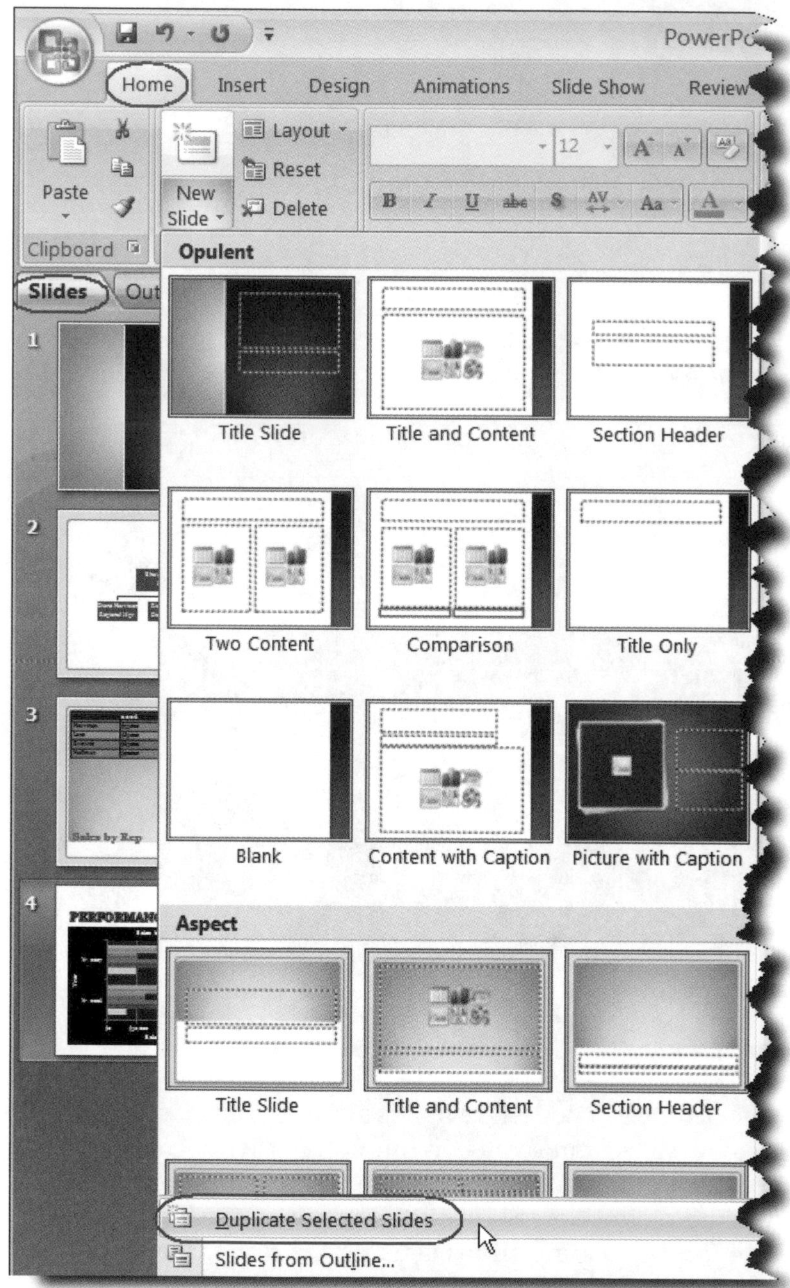

Deleting Slides

In this section, you will learn how to remove an existing slide from your presentation.

Deleting a slide will physically remove that slide from your presentation. Unlike the Cut command, the Delete command does not allow you to Paste the deleted slide in another location—once you delete it, it's gone! To permanently remove a slide from your presentation, select the slide you want to delete and then press the **Delete** key, or click the **Delete button** on the Slides group of the Home Ribbon.

To Delete a Slide

1. Select the slide that you want to delete.
2. Press the **Delete** key.
   Or
   Click the **Delete button** on the Slides group of the Home Ribbon.

Let's Try It!

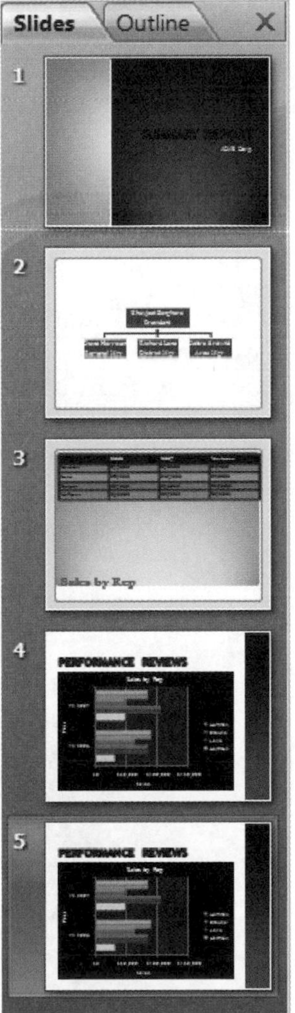

- Click on **Slide 5** in the Slides Pane.

Selects Slide 5.

- Press the **Delete** key.

Removes Slide 5 from the presentation.

- Click the **Save** button on the Quick Access Toolbar.

Saves the active presentation.

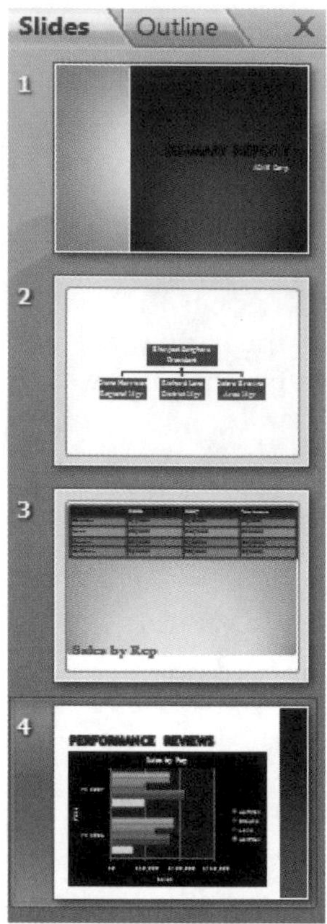

Applying Animation

In this section, you will learn how to apply Animation Schemes to your slides.

An exciting visual effect that you can add to your slides is **Animation**, which allows you to control how your information appears on the slide during a slide show. For instance, you can have your words fly onto the screen one at a time or slowly fade in. With animation, you can control how and when you want an item to appear on your screen. Using animation in your presentation can help you focus on important points and manage the flow of information—as well as add exciting effects to your slide show.

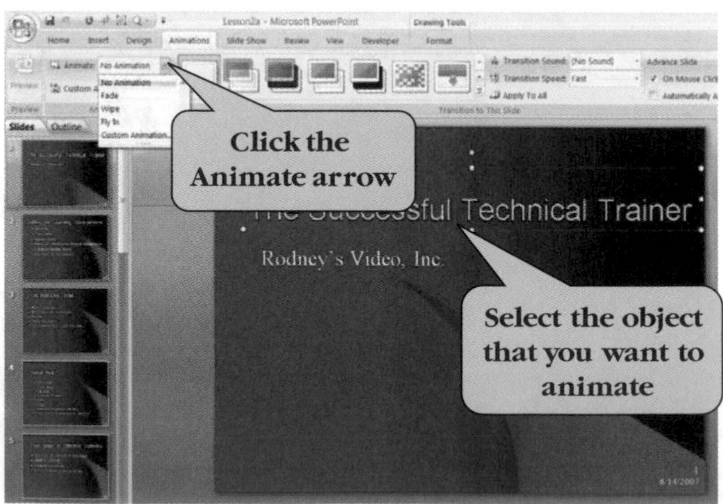

PowerPoint contains several preset visual effects that will help you get started with animation. You can apply an animation scheme to a single object or to a group of selected objects.

To Apply an Animation Scheme

1. Select the object or text placeholder to which you want to apply animation.
2. Click the **Animations tab** on the Ribbon.
3. Click the **Animate** drop-down list arrow.
4. Point to an **Animation Scheme** to display a live preview.
5. Click the Animation Scheme you want to apply.

Let's Try It!

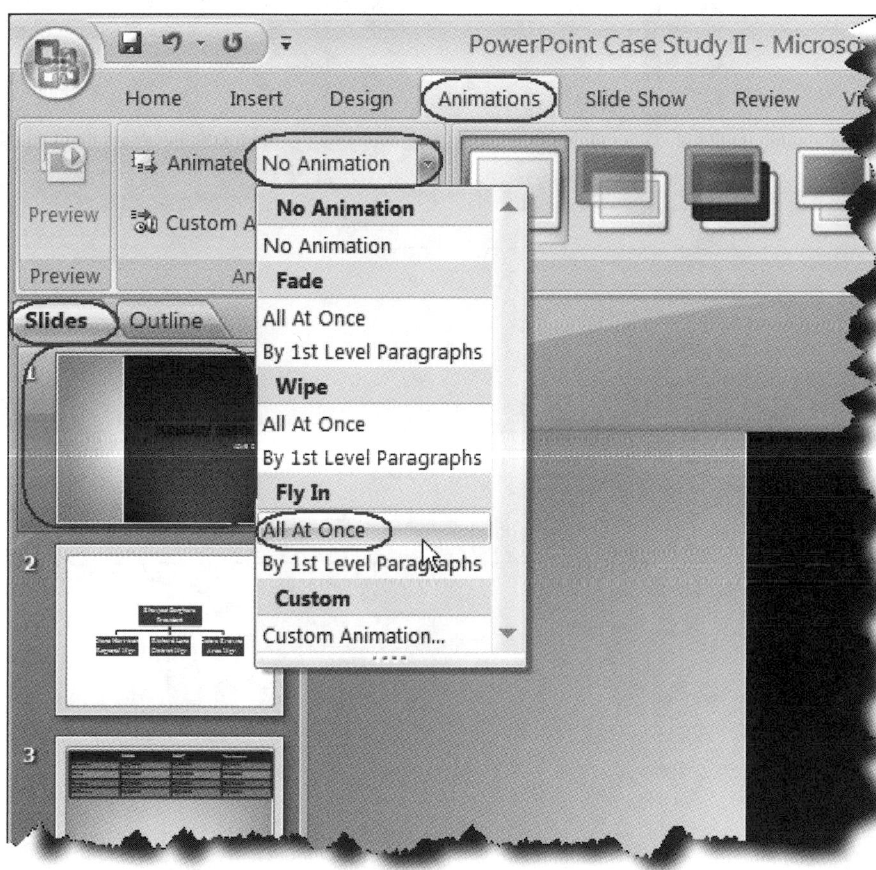

- In the **Slides Pane** select **Slide 1**.

Ensures that the first slide is the active slide.

- Click the **Animations tab** on the Ribbon.

Displays the Animations Ribbon.

- On Slide 1, click the **ACME Corp.** placeholder.

Selects the object to which we want to apply animation.

- Click the **Animate** combo box arrow on the Animations group.

Displays a list of available animation schemes.

- Move your mouse pointer over the **All at once** scheme under the **Fade** category.

Displays a preview of the All at Once scheme under the Fade category.

- Click the **All at once** scheme under the **Fly In** category as shown

Applies the Fly In All at Once animation scheme to the text placeholder.

- In the **Slides Pane** select **Slide 3**.

Activates the third slide in the presentation.

- Click anywhere in the table.
- Click the **Animate** combo box arrow on the Animations group and click **Fade**.

Applies the Fade animation scheme to the table.

- Click the **Save** button on the Quick Access Toolbar.

Saves the active presentation.

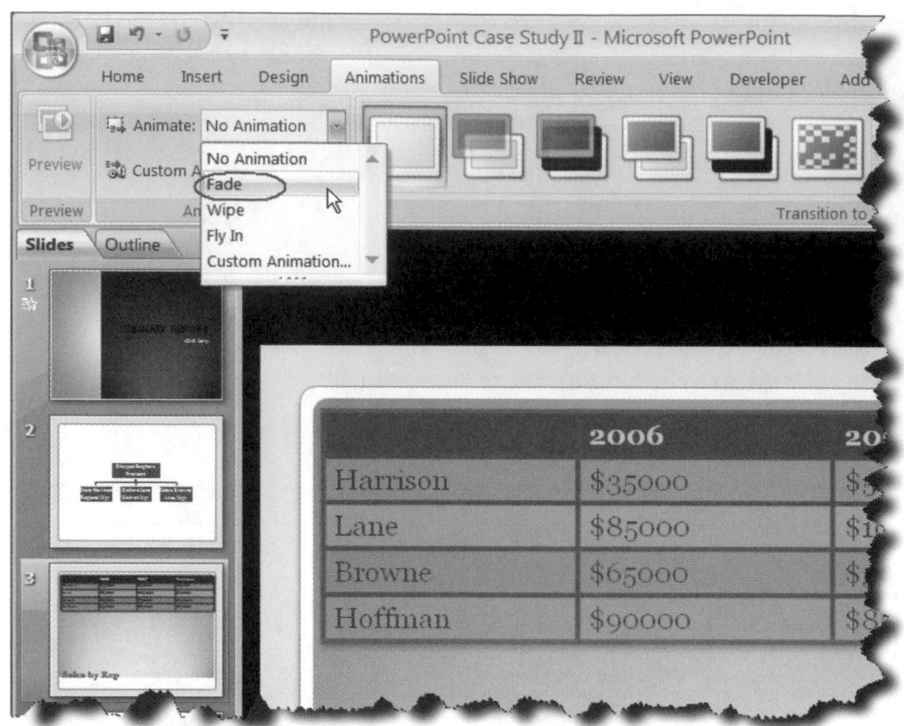

- Select **Slide 1** in the Slides pane.

Actives the first slide in the presentation.

- Press the **F5** key.

Enters Slide Show view.

- Click your left mouse button or press the space bar.

Moves to the next step in the animation.

- Click your left mouse button or press the space bar again.

Moves to the next slide in the presentation.

- Click your left mouse button or press the space bar again **3 more times**.

Moves through each step of the animation.

- Press the **Esc** key.

Returns to normal view.

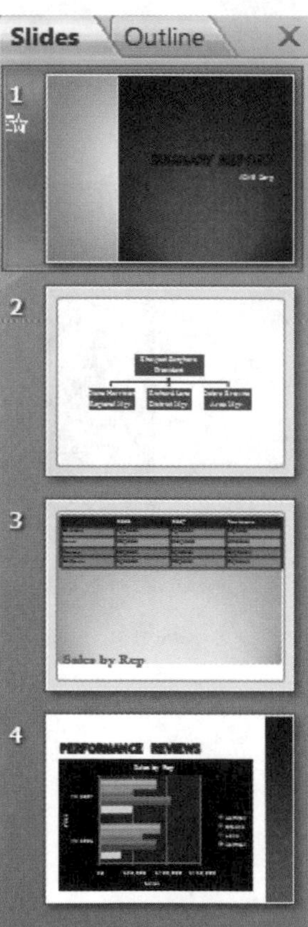

Adding Slide Transitions

In this section, you will learn how to add Slide Transitions as you advance from one slide to the next.

Slide transitions specify how the display changes when you advance from one slide to the next. For example, you can add an animation effect such as Horizontal Blinds or a Checkerboard pattern. You can also add a preset sound effect to the slide transition or use your own sound file.

To apply transitions to specific slides, select the first slide in the **Slide Pane Window**, hold down the **Ctrl** key, and then select any additional slides. The fastest way to apply transitions to multiple slides is to work in slide sorter view. Click the **Apply to All** button on the Ribbon to apply the transition effect to every slide in your presentation.

To Add Slide Transitions

1. Display the slide to which you want to apply **Slide Transitions** or select multiple slides in the Slides Pane window.
2. Click the **Animations tab** on the Ribbon.
3. Click the **More button** on the **Slide Transition gallery** on the Transition To This Slide group.
4. Point to a slide transition in the gallery to view a live preview.
5. Click on the slide transition thumbnail for the effect that you want.
6. Select the desired transition speed (Slow, Medium or Fast) from the **Transition Speed** drop-down list.
7. If desired, select a pre-defined **Sound** from the **Transition Sound** drop-down list.
8. To add a custom sound file, select **Other Sound** from the Transition Sound drop-down list, navigate to the folder that contains the desired sound file, select the file, and then click **Open**.
9. To apply the Slide Transition effect to all slides in your presentation, click the **Apply to All** button on the Transition To This Slide group.

Let's Try It!

- Click the **Slide Sorter button** on the bottom right of your screen.

Switches to Slide Sorter View.

- Click on **Slide 4**.

Selects the slide to which we want to apply a Slide Transition Effect.

- If necessary, click the **Animations tab** on the Ribbon.

Displays the Animations Ribbon.

- Click the **More button** on the Slide Transitions gallery as shown below.

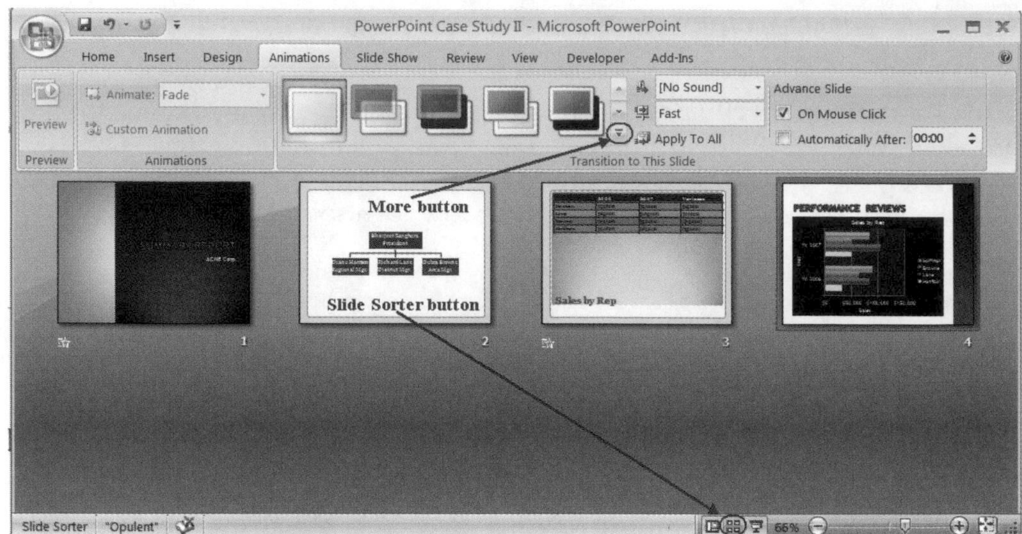

Displays all available slide transitions.

- Scroll down and click the **Checkerboard Across** thumbnail under the **Stripes and Bars** category (3rd thumbnail from the left).

Applies the Checkerboard Across Slide Transition effect to Slide 4.

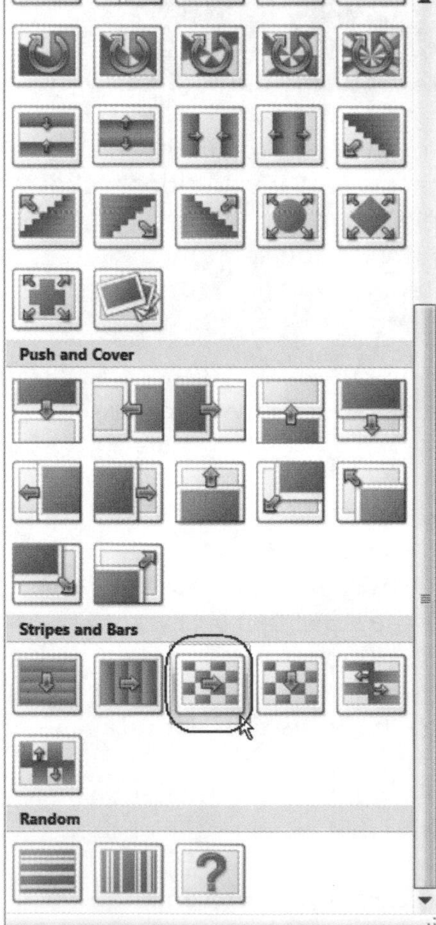

- Click the **Transition Speed** drop-down list on the Ribbon and choose **Medium.**

Applies a medium speed to the transition effect.

- Click the **Transition Sound** drop-down list and choose **Chime**.

Applies the chime sound effect at the end of each transition.

- Click the **Slide Show tab** on the Ribbon.

Displays the Slide Show Ribbon.

- Click the **From Current Slide** button on the Start Slide Show group on the Ribbon.

Switches to Slide Show view beginning with Slide 4. Notice the Checkerboard effect as the slide is presented.

- Press the **Esc** key.

Returns to Normal view.

- Click the **Save** button on the Quick Access Toolbar.

Saves the active presentation.

Setting Up a Slide Show

In this section, you will learn how to modify various Slide Show settings.

Once you are happy with the layout and content of your presentation, you can then set some additional Slide Show options. From the **Set up Show** dialog box, you can set the show type (speaker, individual or kiosk), set the presentation to loop continuously, choose which slides to display, how to advance the slides (manually or using timings) or whether to show them with or without animation or narration.

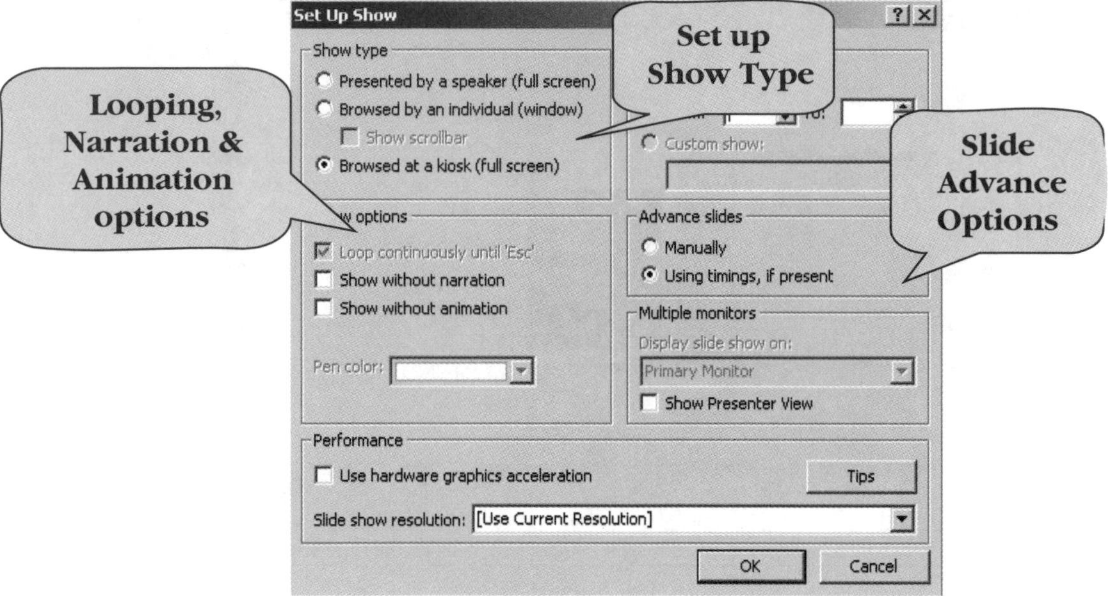

To Set Up a Slide Show

1. Click the **Slide Show tab** on the Ribbon.
2. Click the **Set Up Slide Show** button on the Set Up group on the Ribbon.
3. In the **Show Type** area, choose the desired presentation type (speaker, individual or kiosk).
4. Under **Show Options**, choose desired looping, narration, animation and pen color options.
5. Select the desired options under the **Advance Slides** area. Note: If you want your slides to advance automatically, don't forget to set your timings.
6. Click **OK**.

Let's Try It!

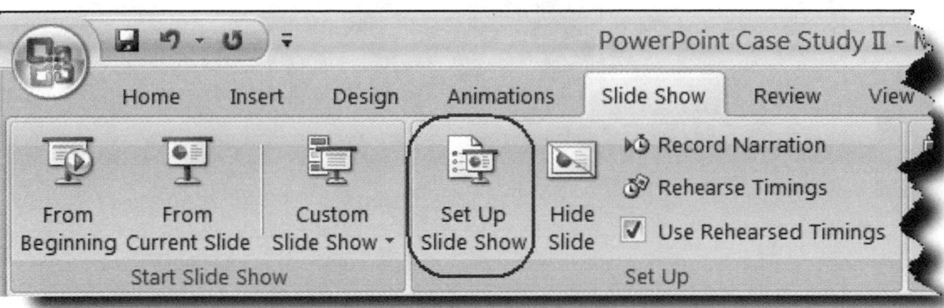

- Click the **Set Up Slide Show** button on the Set Up group of the Ribbon.

Displays the Set Up Show dialog box.

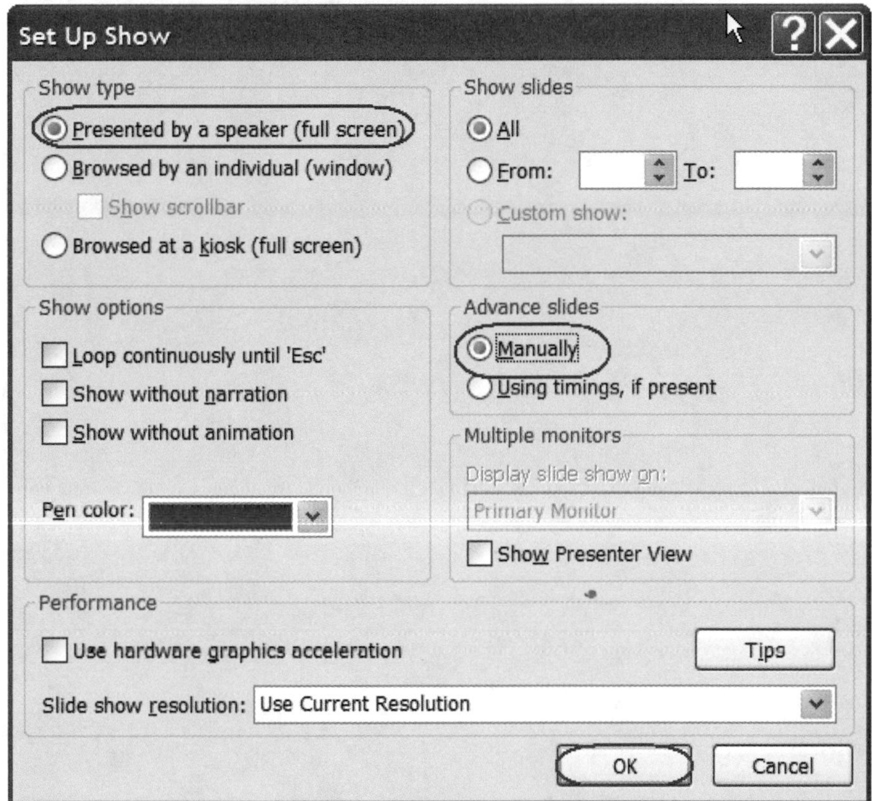

- Under **Show type**, click the **Presented by speaker** radio button.

Sets up the slide show to be presented by the speaker.

- Under **Advance Slides**, select **Manually**.

Slides will be advanced manually by the speaker and any slide timings will be ignored.

- Click **OK**

Closes the Set Up Show dialog box and applies the changes.

- Click the **From Beginning button** on the Start Slide Show group.

Displays the presentation in Slide Show view.

- Press the **Space Bar**

Advances to the next slide.

- Press the **Esc** key.

Terminates the Slide show.

- Click the **Animations tab** on the Ribbon.

Displays the Animations Ribbon. We are now going to add timing to our presentation.

- In the **Advance Slide** area, click the **Automatically After** checkbox and type: 00:03 in the text box as shown.

Sets each slide to advance automatically after 3 seconds.

- Click the **Apply to All** button on the Ribbon.

Applies the above settings to all slides in the presentation.

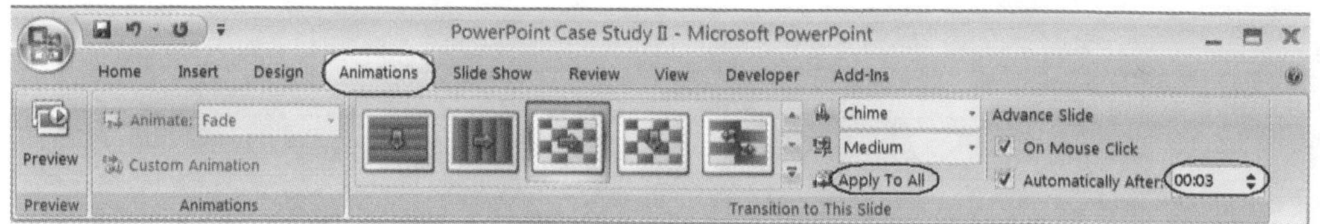

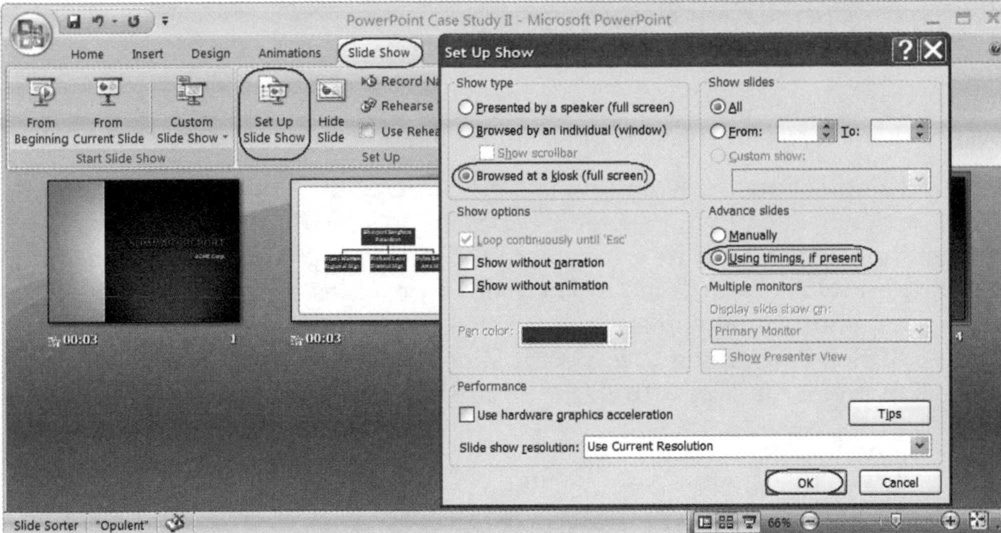

- Click the **Slide Show tab** on the Ribbon.

Displays the Slide Show Ribbon.

- Click the **Set Up Slide Show** button.

Displays the Set Up Show dialog box.

- Under **Show type**, click the **Browsed at Kiosk** radio button.

Sets up the slide show to run automatically and to loop continuously. This setting is best for an unattended presentation.

- Under **Advance Slides**, click the **Use timings, if present** radio button.

Slides will be advanced automatically using the timing settings we set before.

- Click **OK**.

Closes the Set Up Show dialog box.

- Press the **F5** key and observe the slide show.

Displays the presentation in Slide Show View. After 3 seconds, the slides automatically advance.

- Press the **Esc** key.

Terminates the slide show.

- Click the **Save button** on the Quick Access Toolbar.

Saves our changes.

Using Slide Show Navigation Tools

In this section, you will use Navigation Tools to move to other slides in your presentation and learn how to annotate a slide with the pen tool.

During a Slide Show presentation, use the **Slide Show Toolbar** located on the bottom left side of your screen to navigate to specific slides in your presentation. Move your mouse toward the left side of your screen to display the Slide Show Shortcut Toolbar. The toolbar provides easy access to slide show navigation while you are delivering a presentation.

In addition to jumping to a specific slide in your presentation, other options that you can access from the Slide Show Toolbar include:

- Jumping to a particular slide
- Moving to the Next or Previous Slide
- Setting Pointer Options (arrow, pen, etc.)
- Setting Pen Color
- Switching to another application
- Ending the Slide Show

Using the Pen feature allows you to annotate your slides during a presentation. You can highlight information on your slides by circling it, underling it or manually writing in additional information.

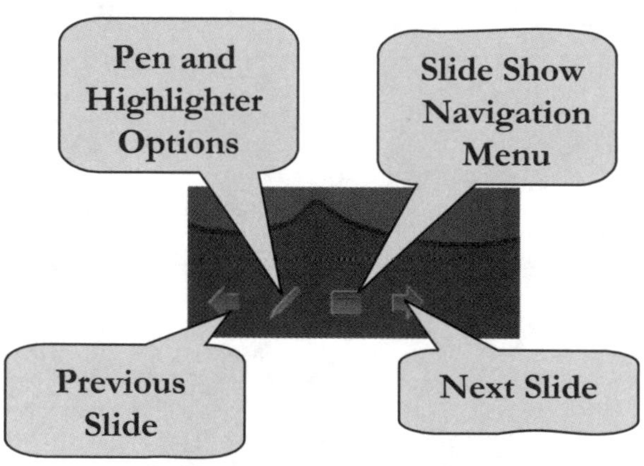

SLIDE SHOW TOOLBAR

You can also right-click anywhere on your slide during the presentation to display the Slide Show Navigation menu.

PowerPoint also provides keyboard shortcuts to quickly access slides in your presentation when in Slide Show View. The table below lists available slide show shortcuts.

Shortcut	Action
Click left mouse button	Advances to next slide
Click right mouse button	Displays the Slide Show Shortcut Menu
Pressing the Enter key	Advances to next slide
Typing in a slide number then pressing the Enter key	Moves to the slide number that you entered before pressing Enter
Pressing the Home key	Moves to first slide in the presentation
Pressing the End key	Moves to the last slide in the presentation
Pressing the Page Up key	Moves to previous slide
Pressing the Page Down key	Moves to next slide
Pressing the B key	Displays a black screen. Press again to redisplay the slide show.
Pressing the W key.	Displays a white screen. Press again to redisplay the slide show.

To Use Slide Show Navigation Tools

1. Press **F5** to enter Slide Show view.
2. Move your mouse pointer to the **bottom left** side of the screen to display the **Slide Show Toolbar**.
3. Click the **Slide Show Menu button** to display the menu.
4. To jump to a specific slide, select **Go To Slide** from the Slide Show menu, and then click on the name of the desired slide.

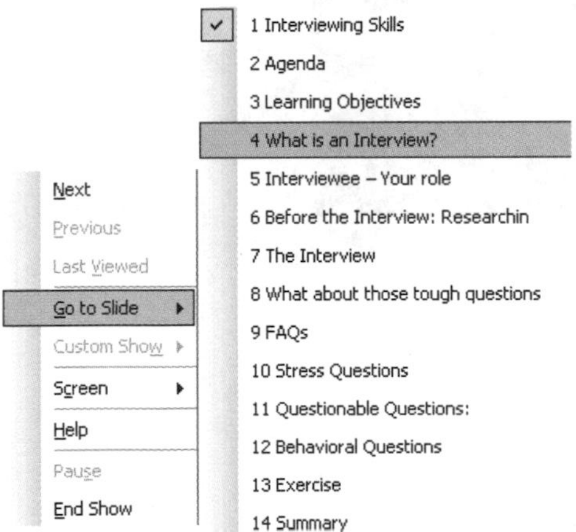

5. To activate the **Pen Tool**, click the **Pen and Highlighter Options button** and select Ballpoint Pen, Felt Tip Pen or Highlighter.

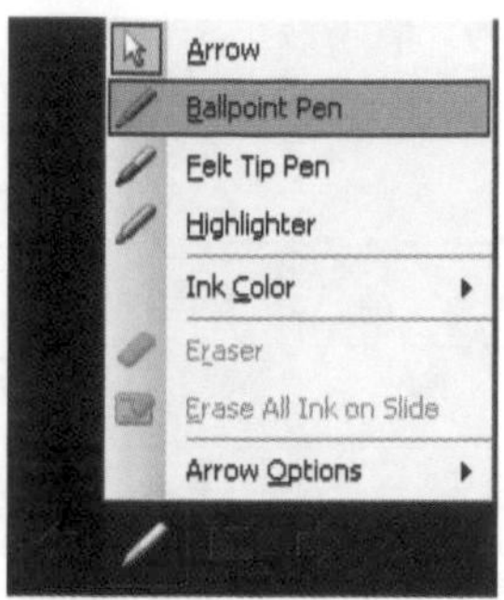

6. To change pen color, select **Ink Color** from the Pen and Highlighter Options menu and then select the desired color from the color palette.
7. Select **Next or Previous button** to move forward or backward one slide at a time.
8. Press the **Esc** key or select **End Show** from the Slide Show menu to terminate the presentation.

NOTE: The slide show type must be set to **"Presented by Speaker"** in order to access the Slide Show Shortcut Menu.

Let's Try It!

- Click the **Set Up Slide Show button** on the Ribbon.

Displays the Set Up Show dialog box. We need to set up our slide show for a speaker presentation in order to access the Slide Show Shortcut Menu.

- Under **Show type**, click the **Presented by speaker** radio button.

Sets up the slide show to be presented by the speaker.

- In the **Advance Slides** area, click the radio button next to **Manually**.

Sets the option to advance the slides manually.

- Click **OK**.

Closes the Set Up Show dialog box.

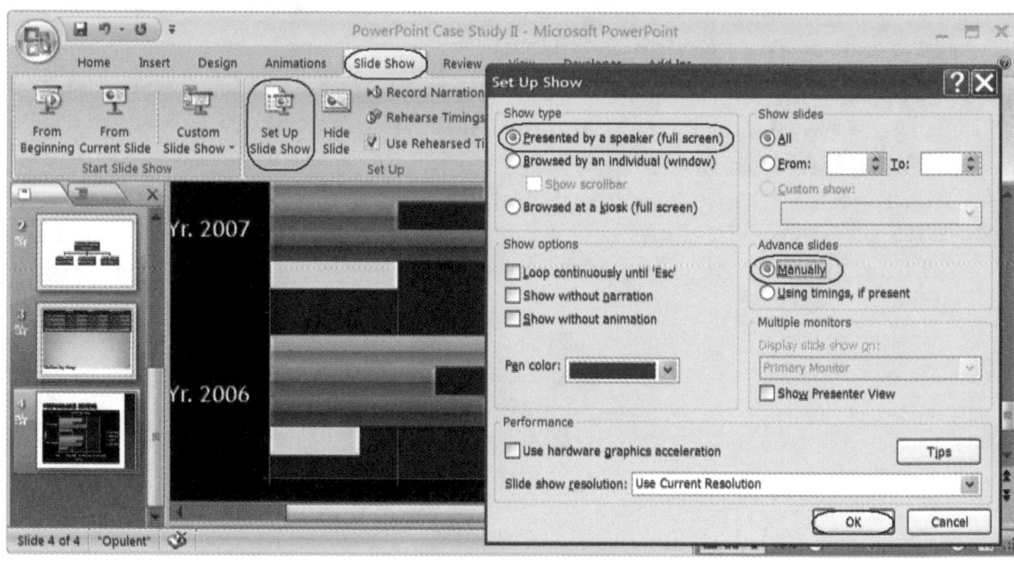

• Press the **F5 key**.

Displays the presentation in Slide Show view.

• Move your mouse pointer to the bottom left side of the screen until the **Slide Show Toolbar** appears as shown.

Displays the Slide Show Shortcut Menu buttons.

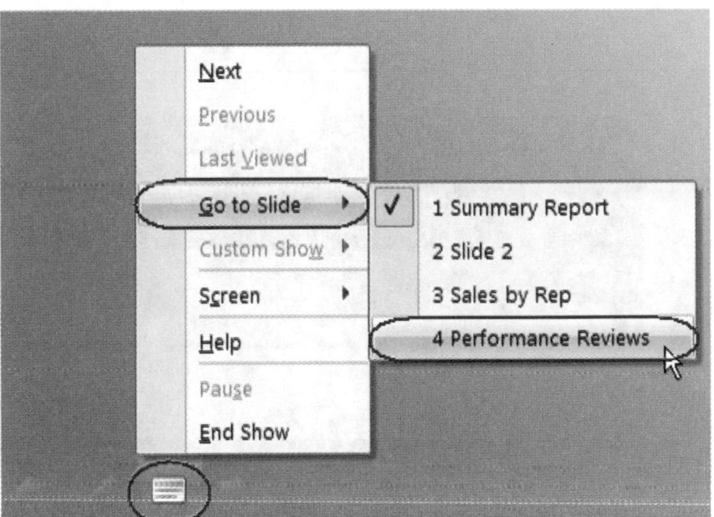

• Click the **Slide Show menu button** and point to **Go to Slide** and then click **Performance Reviews** from the contextual menu shown.

Jumps to Slide 4 in the presentation.

• Click **Previous Slide** button.

Go to the previous slide in the presentation.

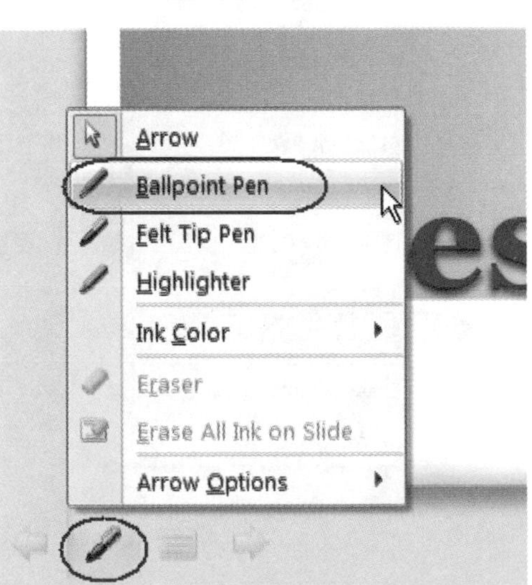

• Press **Space**.

Table shows up.

• Click the **Pen and Highlighter Options** button and select **Ballpoint Pen** from the pop-up menu.

Activates the Pen Tool. Notice that your mouse pointer has transformed into a small rounded pointer.

- Click the **Pen and Highlighter Options** button, select **Ink Color** from the pop-up menu, and then choose **Yellow** under the Standard Colors area.

Changes the pen color to yellow.

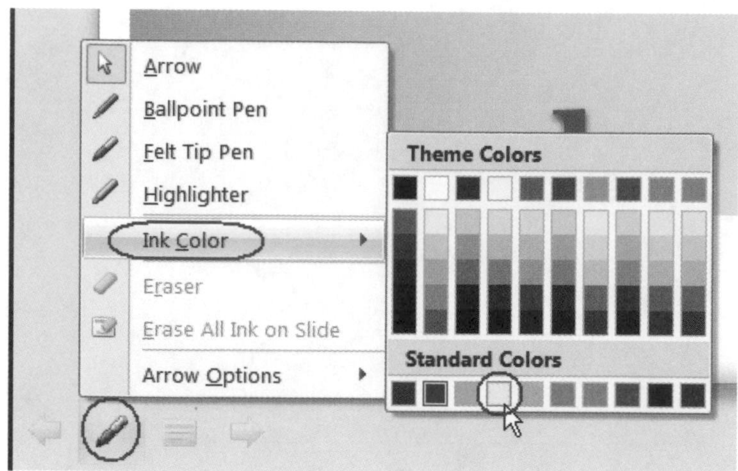

- With the pen tool, **circle** the Rep "**Hoffman**" and then click anywhere on the table.

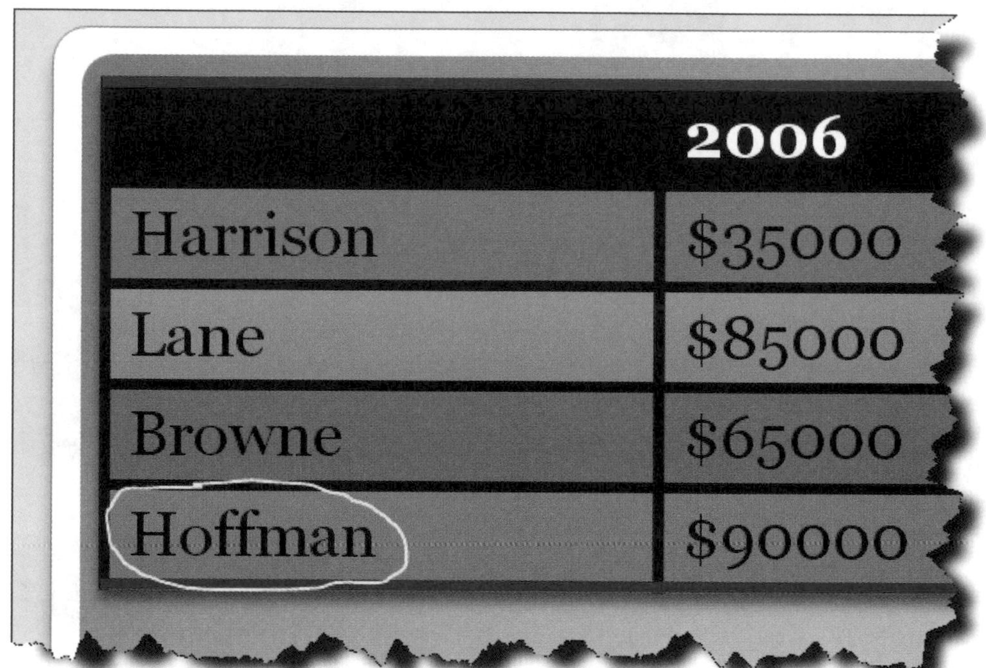

- Click the **Pen and Highlighter Options** button and select **Eraser** from the pop-up menu

Activates the Eraser tool. You now click on any annotation that you made to remove it.

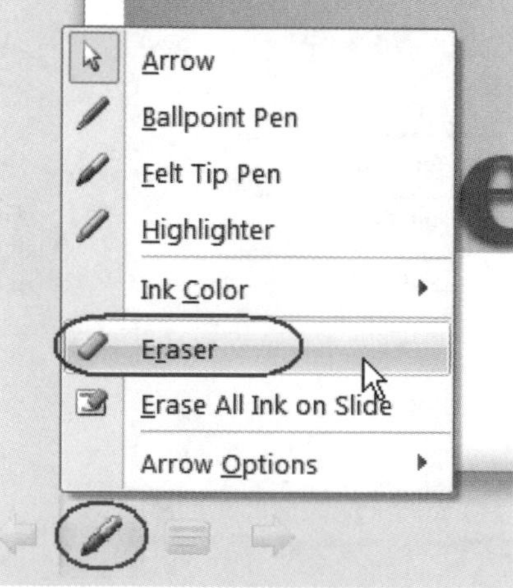

- Click on the circle that you drew around the Rep **"Hoffman"**.

Removes the circle that you drew around the Rep "Hoffman."

- Press the **Esc** key twice.

If a dialog box is displayed, asking you if you wish to keep or discard your ink annotations. Click the **Discard** button.

- Discards the ink annotations that we made during the presentation and returns us to presentation view.

Previewing a Presentation

In this section, you will learn how to view your presentation in Print Preview mode.

Previewing your presentation before printing allows you to get an idea how your presentation output will appear. Additionally, you can change printing options such as setting page orientation (portrait or landscape), including a header or a footer on your output (date, time, page numbers), previewing Notes and Handouts, viewing your output in grayscale, and more. Many additional printing options are found under the **Options** button on the **Print Preview Ribbon**.

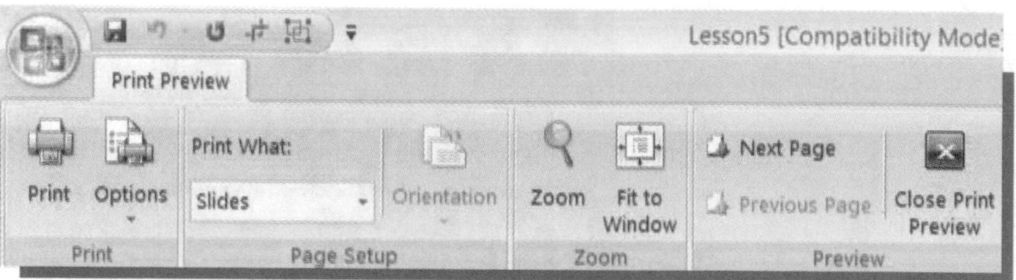

PRINT PREVIEW TOOLBAR

To Preview a Presentation

1. Click the **Microsoft Office Button**, point to **Print** and then click **Print Preview**.
2. Click on the **Previous Page** or **Next Page** buttons to navigate through your presentation.
3. Select **Slides, Handouts** (select the number of slides per page), **Notes Pages, or Outline View** from the **Print What** drop-down arrow to display the desired objects.
4. Click the **Options** button to display additional printing options.
5. Click **Print** to display the Print dialog box.
6. Click the **Close Print Preview** to return to your presentation.

Page Setup

In this section, you will modify the Page Setup of your presentation.

You can change the settings for the printed output of your presentation from the **Page Setup** dialog box. Settings you can modify include:

- Page Orientation for Slides and Notes/Handouts/Outline
- Paper Type (on-screen, letter, ledger, etc.)
- Page Margins (Width & Height)
- Page Numbering

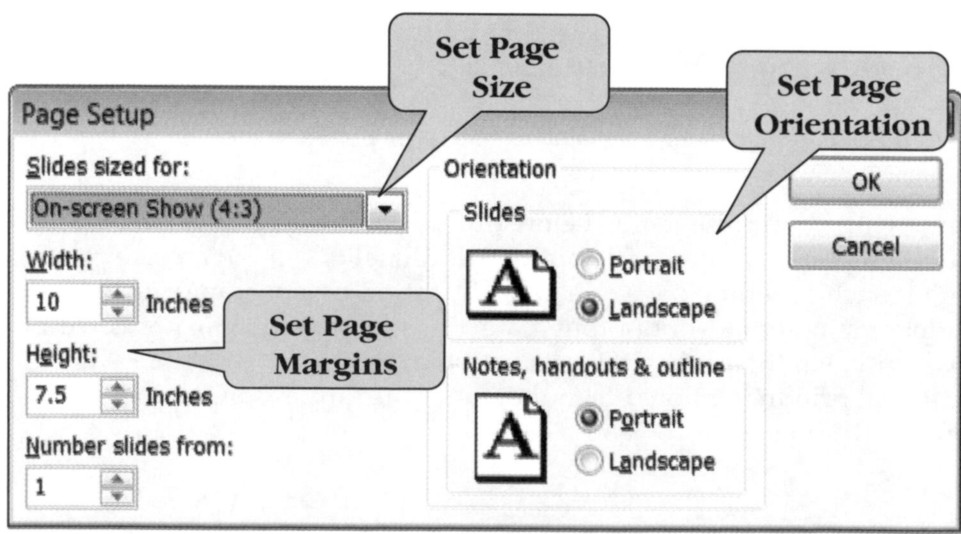

Page Orientation can be set to **Portrait** (taller than wider) or **Landscape** (wider than taller). You can set a different orientation for your slides than for your notes, handouts, and outline. The default orientation for slides is landscape whereas the default orientation for your notes, handouts and outline is portrait.

To Modify Page Setup

1. Click the **Design tab** on the Ribbon.
2. Click the **Page Setup** button on the Page Setup group.
3. Select the drop-down arrow next to **Slides sized for** to select paper type.
4. Type the page width or height (in inches) into **Width** or **Height** margins.
5. Set the **Orientation** for Slides and Notes, Handouts & Outline.
6. Click **OK** when finished.

Let's Try It!

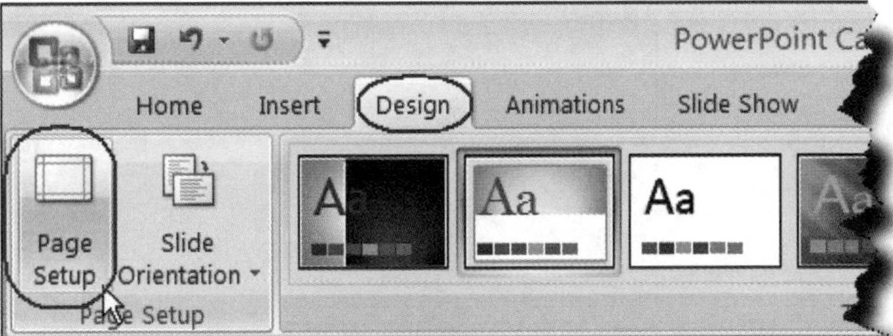

- Click the **Design tab** on the Ribbon.

Displays Design commands and tools.

- Click the **Page Setup** button on the Page Setup group.

Displays the Page Setup dialog box.

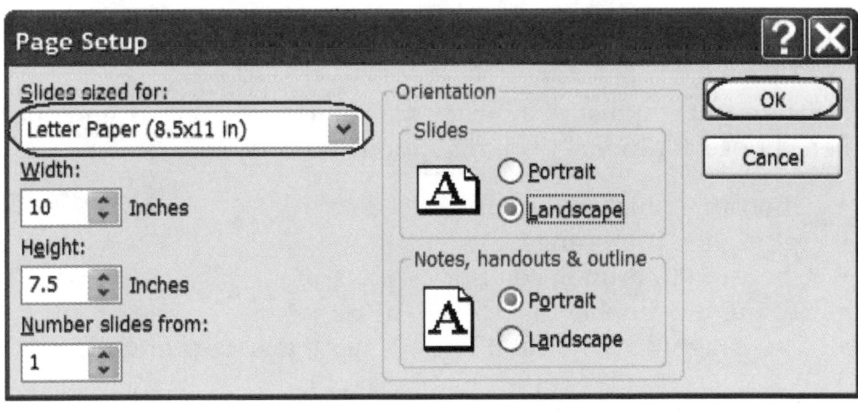

- From the **Slides Sized for** drop-down list, choose **Letter Paper**.

Select 8 ½ x 11 paper for slide output paper type.

- Click **OK**.

Closes the Page Setup dialog box.

Printing Slides

In this section, you will learn how to set print options and send output to the printer.

Before you're finally ready to print your document, you may first want to set some **Printer Options**. For instance, you may need to specify which printer to use, the number of copies to be printed, or even designate PowerPoint to print only a specific range of your document. Printer options you can set will vary, depending on the type of printer you are using.

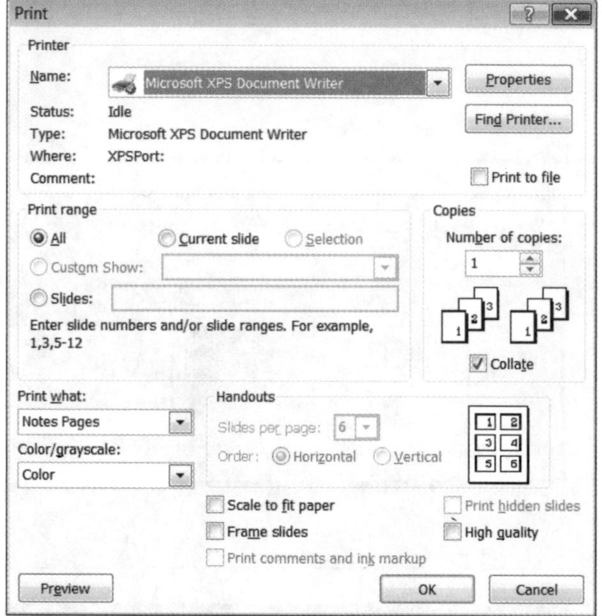

THE PRINT DIALOG BOX

The **Print** command launches the **Print** dialog box, from which you can then choose additional printing options such as:

- Choosing which printer to use
- Setting the print range
- Choosing to Print in color or in grayscale
- Setting the number of copies to print
- Choosing what to print (Slides, Notes, Handouts or Outline)

To Print Slides

1. Click the **Microsoft Office** button and then click **Print** on the File Options menu to display the Print dialog box.
   Or
   Press the **Ctrl + P** keystroke combination.
2. If necessary, choose which printer to use from the **Name** drop-down list.
3. Select the drop-down arrow next to **Print What** and then select **Slides**.
4. Enter the desired number of copies in the **Copies** area.
5. To print only the active slide, click the **Current Slide** under the Page Range Options area.

6. To print a specific range, enter the slide numbers in the **Slides** box, separating each slide range by a comma (i.e. 1-15, 17, 18, 30-35)
7. To print more than one copy of a presentation, enter the value in the **Number of copies** box in the **Copies** area.
8. Click the **Options** button for additional printer options.
9. Click **Preview** to preview the presentation before printing.
10. Click **OK** to send the document to the printer.
11. Click **Cancel** to close the Print dialog box without printing.

> **TIP:** To send a document directly to the printer, click the Microsoft Office button, point to Print and then click the Quick Print option in the second pane. The Print dialog box will not open.

Printing Slide Outlines

In this section, you will learn how to print only the outline portion of your presentation.

From the Print dialog box, you can choose to print only your presentation **Outline**. To select Outline as the object to print, click the **Print What** drop-down arrow and then choose **Outline** from the list. You can additionally choose the slides whose outline you want to print from the Print Range area.

You can manually select the text you wish to print in the **Outline Pane** and then opt to print only what you have selected by choosing **Selection** under the print range area. In this way, you can print outlines for only the slide text that you have selected.

To Print Slide Outlines

1. If you want to print only a selected segment of your presentation, select the slide or manually select the outline to print.

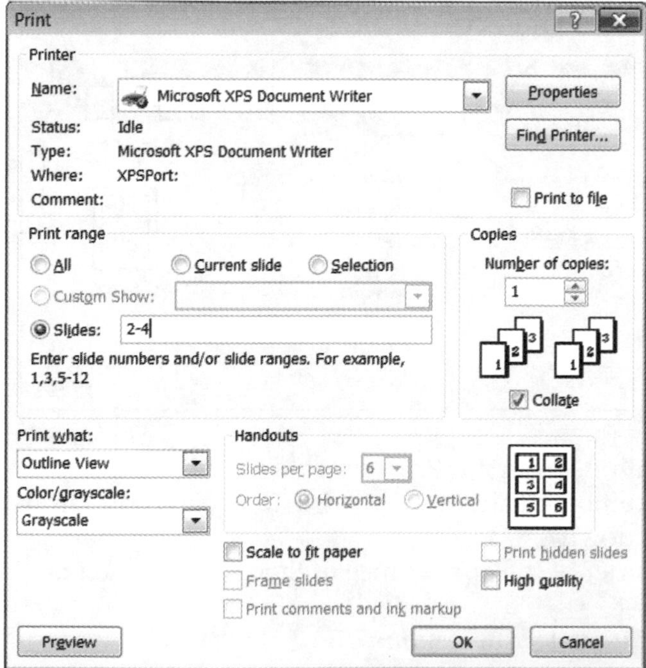

2. Click the **Microsoft Office** button and then click **Print**.
3. Select **Outline View** from the **Print what:** drop-down list.
4. If printing only a selection of the outline, click the **Selection** radio button in the Print Range area.
5. If printing the outline only for specific slides, click the **Slides** radio button and then enter the slide range (i.e. 2-5 or 3, 5, 9, 21)
6. Click **OK**.
7. Click **Cancel** to close the Print dialog box without printing.

Printing Handouts

In this section, you will learn how to print only the Handout pages for your presentation.

Handouts are printed output of your presentation with 1, 2, 3, 4, 6 or 9 slides on each page that your audience can use for future reference. In the Print dialog box, select the number of slides you want to be included in each page and the order of the slides (horizontal or vertical).

You might want to consider passing out the handouts at the end of your presentation so that the audience is not reading your handouts instead of listening to you!

To Print Slide Handouts

1. Click the **Microsoft Office** button and then click **Print** from the menu.

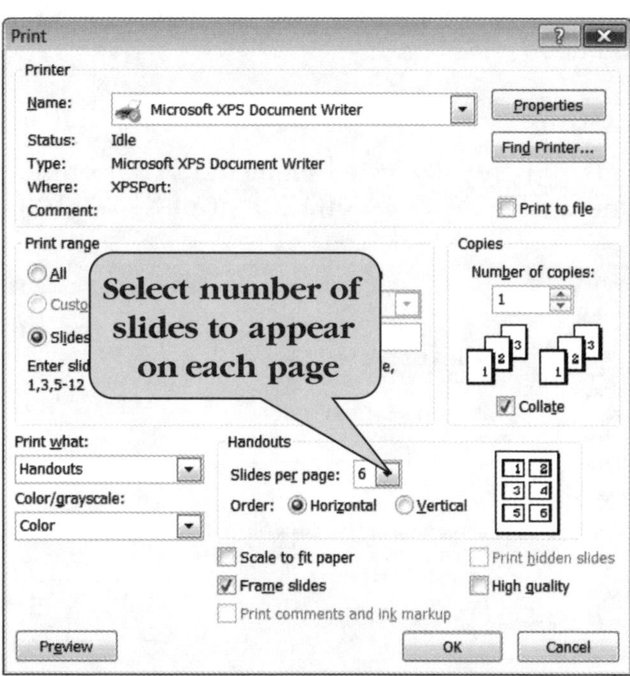

2. Select **Handouts** from the **Print what:** drop-down list.
3. Select the number of slides to be printed on each page from the **Slides per page:** drop down list.
4. Select the order of the appearance of the slides on the page (horizontal or vertical).
5. Set any additional print options.
6. Click **OK**.

Let's Try It!

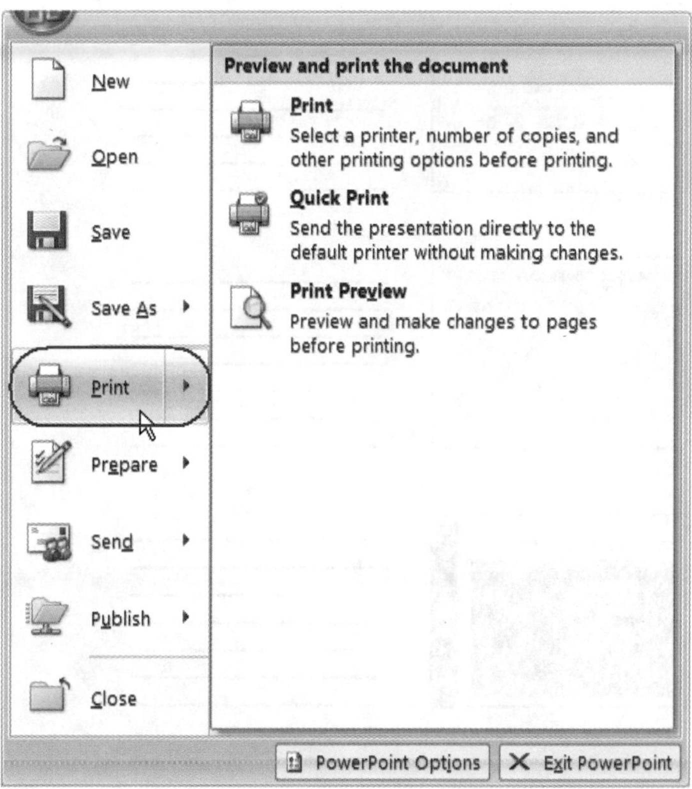

- Click the **Microsoft Office** button and then click **Print**.

Displays the Print Dialog box.

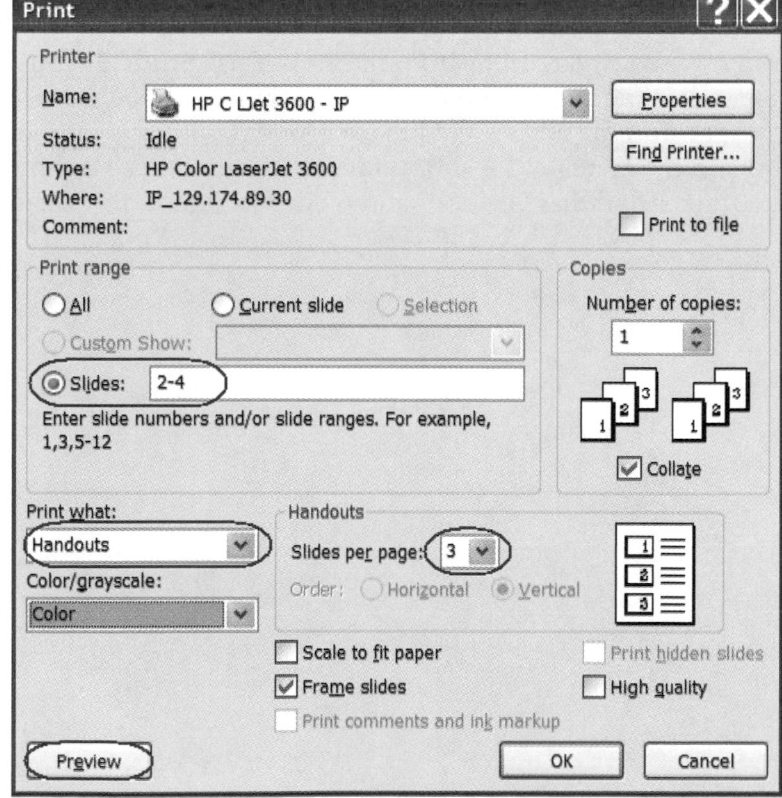

- In the Print Range area, click the radio button next to **Slides**, and then type: **2-4** in the text box.

Sets the option to print only slides 2 through 4.

- Click the **Print What** drop-down arrow and choose **Handouts**.

Chooses Slides as the object to print.

- Click the **Slides per page** drop-down arrow and choose **3**.

Chooses to print 3 slides per page.

- Click the **Preview** button.

Views the Slide Handouts in Print Preview mode

- Click the **Close Print Preview** button.

Returns to presentation view without printing the Handouts Pages.

- Click the **Microsoft Office** button and then click **Close** from the menu. Click **Yes** if asked to save your changes.

Saves and closes the active presentation.

6/28/2007

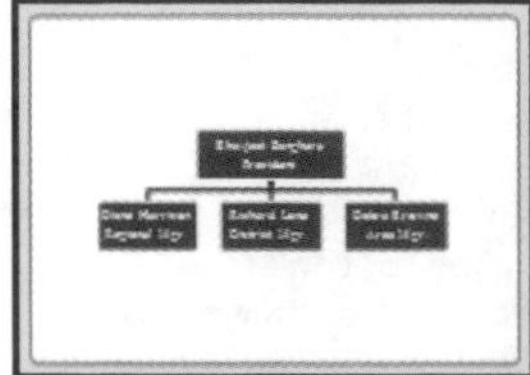

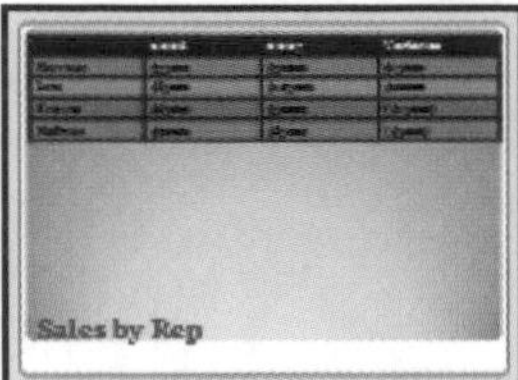

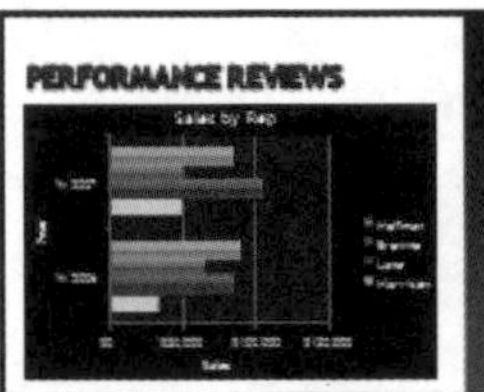

1

Conclusion

You have completed PowerPoint 2007—Case Study 2. You are now ready to use several advanced MS PowerPoint skills that you have learned in this chapter. You are encouraged to experiment with all you have learned in this case study. To reinforce your understanding of these techniques, it is recommended that you read and work through it once again.

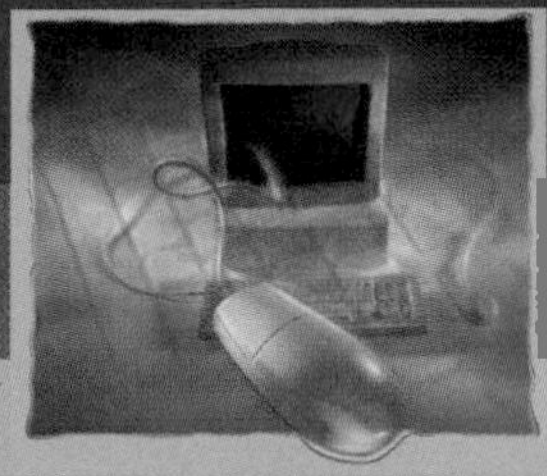

CHAPTER

9

Access Case Study I

OBJECTIVES

After successfully completing this case study, you should able to:

- Understand Databases and the Access Environment
- Create a Blank Database
- Set Access Options
- Create a Table from Scratch
- Set a Primary Key
- Change Field Properties
- Enter Data into a Table
- Select and Delete Records
- Sort Records
- Filter Data by Selection
- Filter Data by Form
- Create a Query in Design View
- Add Fields to a Query
- Save and Run a Query
- Add Multiple Criteria to a Query
- Sort Data in a Query
- Use the Query Wizard
- Use the Form Wizard
- Enter Data into a Form
- Create a Basic Report
- AutoFormat a Report
- Use the Report Wizard
- Report View and Layout View
- Use Help

Case Study I—MS Access 2007

Assume that you work as an intern in the Registrar's office of your University. The head of the Registrar's office has asked you to use Access to maintain and retrieve students' information.

You will store students' information in Access table, create Form to view the information, extract information using Queries, and generate Access report.

StudentID	FirstName	LastName	Major	Address	City	State	Zip	Phone	Add New Field
99416348	Mary	Nolan	IT	4256 N. Oakland Ave.	Fairfax	FL	53211	(414) 555-5242	
99416349	James	Loomis	History	8724 W. Pine St.	Chantilly	VA	21234	(906) 555-3465	
99416351	Nancy	Black	IT	5322 Poodle Lane	Milwaukee	WI	53216	(414) 555-4495	
99416352	Cedrick	Miller	French	612 E. Lyon	Milwaukee	WI	53201	(414) 555-0601	
99416353	Norman	Wyler	Business	6212 Huck St.	Denver	CO	80207	(720) 555-9062	
99416354	David	McBride	Business	802 Patriot's Court	South Range	MI	49950	(414) 555-2702	
99416355	Mona	Fielen	IT	512 N. Hemlock	Alexandria	VA	23123	(906) 555-2308	
99416356	Randy	Andersen	IT	103 N. Riverboat Rd.	Kenosha	WI	53206	(262) 555-9215	
99416362	Lance	Ferrare	Business	10062 Petersburg Dr.	Arlington	VA	82006	(307) 555-4325	
99416363	Daniel	Morris	Education	312 E. Park St.	Dallas	TX	75225	(972) 555-6547	
99416364	Larry	Campbell	Nursing	7323 Sun Dr.	Hollywood	CA	90210	(902) 555-1061	
99416847	Daniel	Harris	French	387 N. Pine St.	Reston	VA	22021	(719) 555-5736	
99416951	Shelly	Turner						(703) 511-6892	
*									

STUDENT INFORMATION IN ACCESS TABLE

FirstName	LastName	State	Phone
Lance	Ferrare	VA	(307) 555-4325
Mona	Fielen	VA	(906) 555-2308
Daniel	Harris	VA	(719) 555-5736
James	Loomis	VA	(906) 555-3465
*			

StudentID	Major
99416348	IT
99416349	History
99416351	IT
99416352	French
99416353	Business
99416354	Business
99416355	IT
99416356	IT
99416362	Business
99416363	Education
99416364	Nursing
99416847	French
99416951	

STUDENT INFORMATION EXTRACTED USING QUERIES

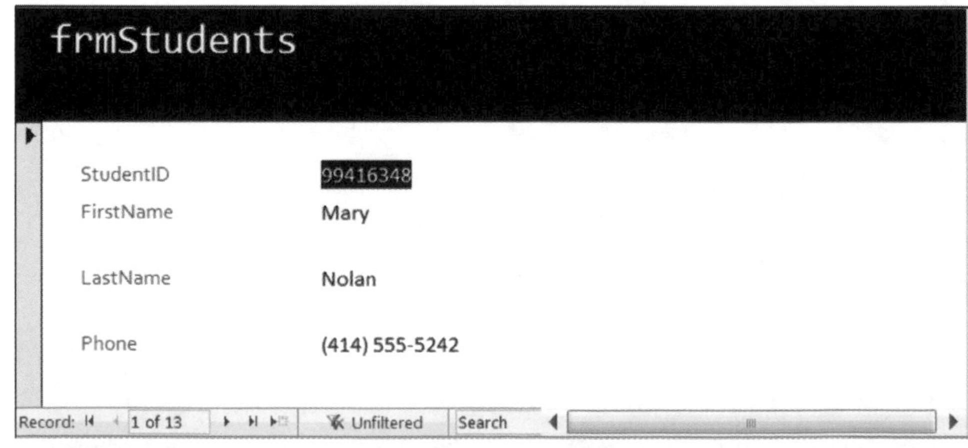

frmStudents

StudentID 99416348
FirstName Mary
LastName Nolan
Phone (414) 555-5242

Record: 1 of 13 Unfiltered Search

STUDENT INFORMATION (ONE RECORD AT A TIME) IN ACCESS FORM

rptStudents

LastName	FirstName	State	Phone
Ferrare	Lance	VA	(307) 555-4325
Fielen	Mona	VA	(906) 555-2308
Harris	Daniel	VA	(719) 555-5736
Loomis	James	VA	(906) 555-3465

Monday, June 25, 2007

STUDENT INFORMATION IN ACCESS REPORT

Understanding Databases

In this section, you will learn about databases.

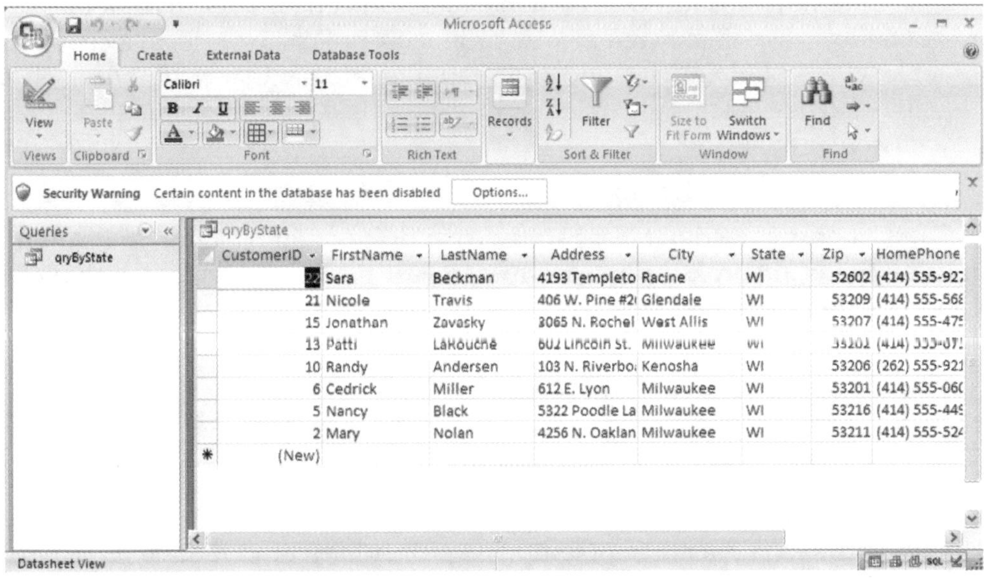

Databases are the core of many business and organization operations. They permit centralized access to information in an efficient and consistent manner and reduce inaccuracies of manual record keeping. A database can be thought of as an information repository pertaining to a specific topic that allows you to manage, store, retrieve and analyze information. An example of a database might be a list of names and addresses of customers or a database of order records.

Information in a database is stored in tables, which are the building blocks of a database. A table consists of rows (all of the information pertaining to one item) for each record and columns for each field.

Microsoft Access is a **relational database management system (RDBMS)**, the most commonly used type of database system in the world today. A relational database:

- Stores data in tables, which consist of tables and rows
- Enables you to retrieve subsets of data from tables
- Allows you to connect tables together for the purpose of retrieving related data stored in different tables

Database Design

The core of good database design is **planning**. Before actually creating a database, you should have a good idea of the kind of data your database will contain and how that data should be broken down. It is recommended to plan your database out on paper before beginning the creation process.

When creating databases, there are rules that most designers follow which help them create consistent, efficient, well thought-out databases. This set of rules is called **normalization**, which dictates that your database tables will eliminate inconsistencies and maximize efficiency. The goal of normalization is to reduce data to its simplest structure with minimum redundancy and maximum data integrity. Some of the important goals of normalization are:

- All fields should be broken down so that data cannot be divided further. For example, the field **Name** could be broken down further to last name, middle name, and first name.
- Each table must have one unique key field called a **primary key**. That is to say, there must be one field that identifies a record and does not allow duplicates. An example of this would be a social security number or customer number. You will learn more about primary keys in a later lesson.
- All fields must directly refer to the primary key. For instance, in a customer table, you would only include information related to that customer, such as name, address, etc. You would not include a field called "Product name" in a customer table.
- A field cannot contain more than one value.

Thus, a normalized database stores each piece of information in its own table, all fields are broken down to their lowest possible level and each piece of information can be referred to by the its primary key.

Creating a Blank Database

In this section, we will create a blank database.

Access 2007 displays the new **Getting Started** window upon launching, which contains a wide range of templates—or fully-featured databases that you can use to get started. Some of the available templates include:

- Asset Tracking
- Contact Management
- Customer Service
- Event Management
- Expenses
- Home Inventory
- Inventory Control
- Issues
- Ledger
- Marketing Projects
- Order Entry
- Resource Scheduling
- Service Call Management
- Time and Billing

To use a template, click the desired template category in the left pane. A selection of template styles for the template category will appear in the center pane. The **Local Templates** category will list templates stored on your computer. The **From Microsoft Office Online** allows you to download templates from the Microsoft Web site.

If instead of using a template you prefer to create a blank database, click the **Blank Database** icon in the center pane.

To Create a Database Based upon a Template

1. Open the Microsoft Access Application. The Getting Started window will automatically display.
2. Click the desired template category in the left pane. Click **Local Templates** to display only those templates available on your computer.
3. Click the desired template in the center pane. The template appears in the right pane.
4. To change the database name, type the new name in the **File Name** box in the right pane.
5. To specify a location where the database is to be saved, click the **file folder icon** and then navigate to the folder where you wish to store your database file.
6. Click **Create**.

If you decide not to use any of the database templates, you can create a blank database by clicking **Blank Database** in the **Getting Started** pane. Once your database is created, you will then need to create all of your tables, queries, forms and reports.

To Create a Blank Database

1. Click the **Microsoft Office Button** and then click **New** from the menu to display the **Getting Started Pane** Task Pane.
2. Click **Blank Database** in the center pane.
3. To specify a name for your database, type the new name in the **File Name** box in the right pane.
4. To specify a location where the database is to be saved, click the **file folder icon** in the right pane and then navigate to the folder where you wish to store your database file.
5. Click **Create**.

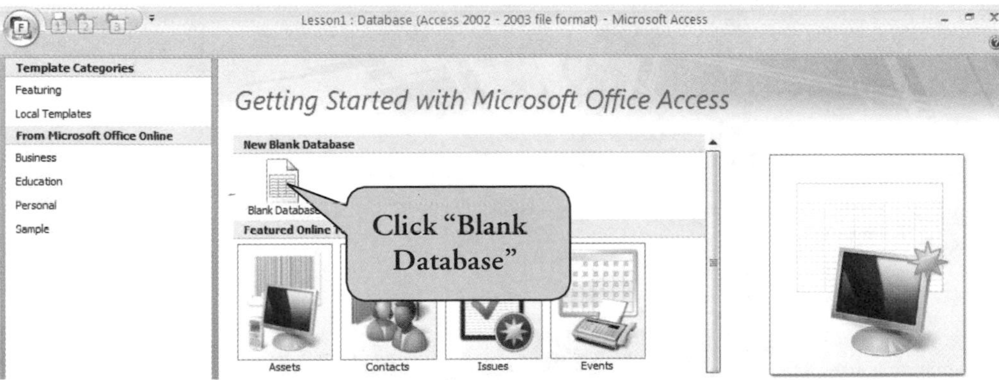

Let's Try It!

- Click on the **Start** button.

Displays Start menu items.

- Select **All Programs > Microsoft Office > Microsoft Office Access 2007** from the Start Menu.

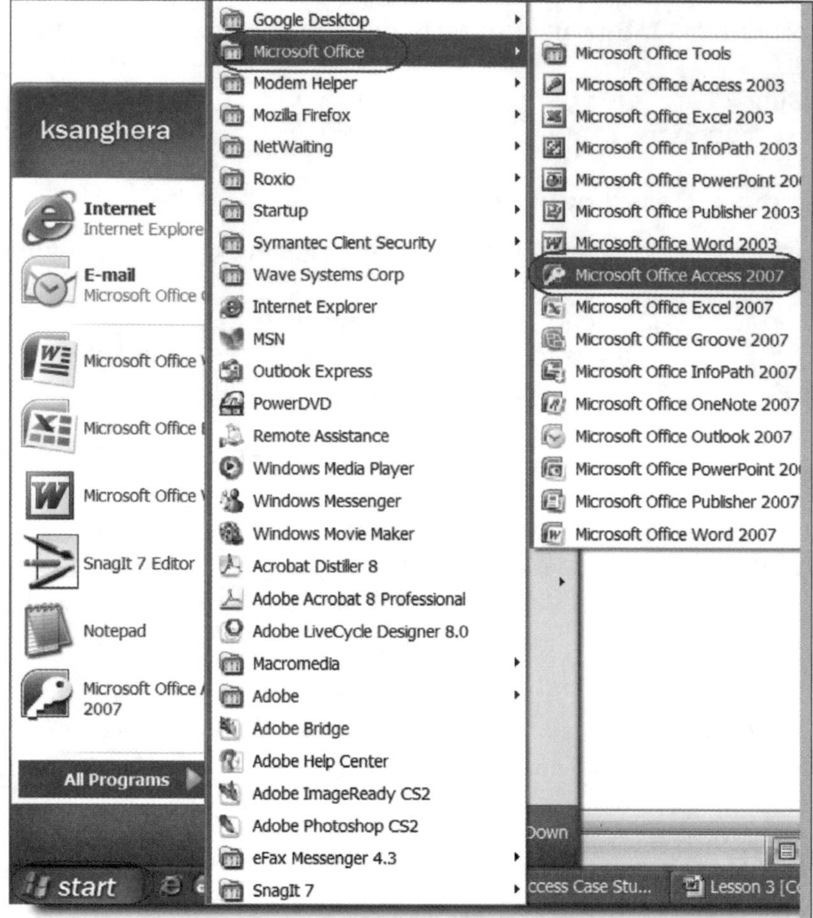

Launches the Microsoft Access Application and displays the Getting Started Task Pane.

- In the **Center** Pane, click on **Blank Database**.

Specifies that we will create a new blank database.

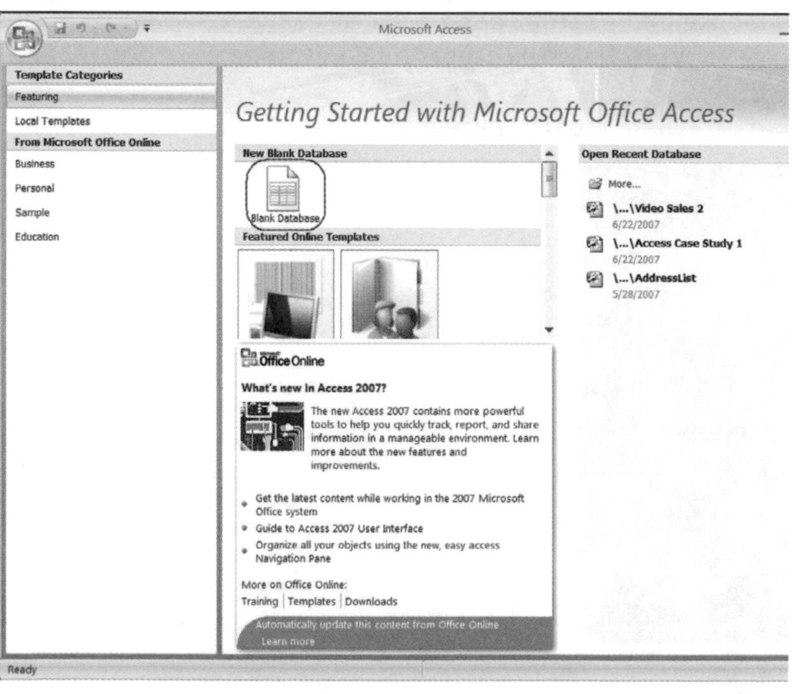

- In the **File name** text box, type: **Access Case Study 1**.

Enters a name for the database.

- Click the **Folder icon** to the right of the File Name box.

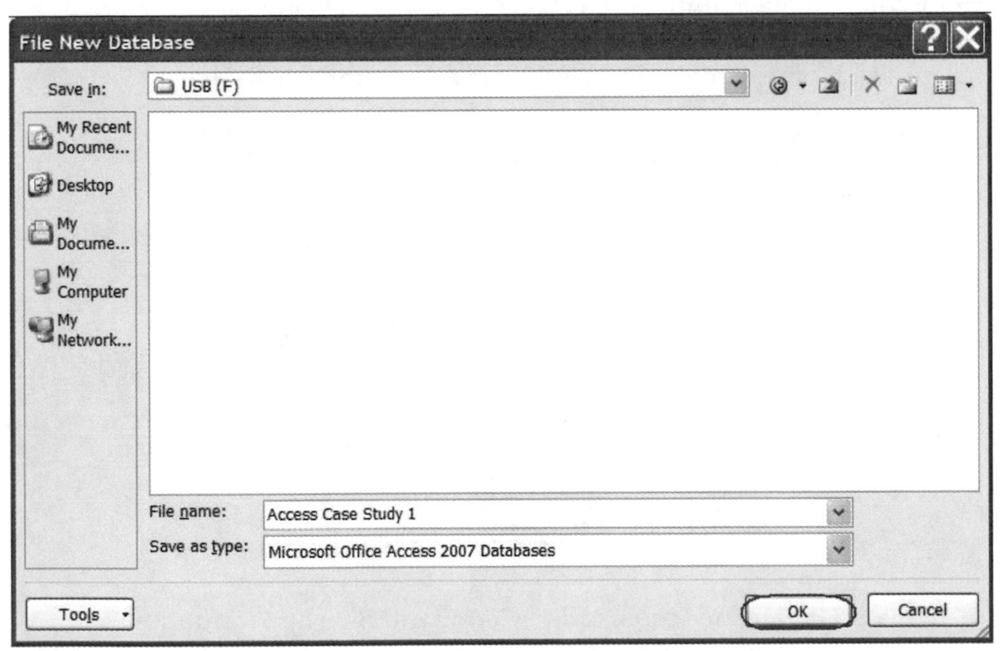

Displays the File New Database dialog box which allows us to browse to the location where we wish to save our database.

- Insert your **USB** drive.
- Browse to **USB** drive and click **OK**.

Closes the File New Database dialog box.

- Click **Create**.

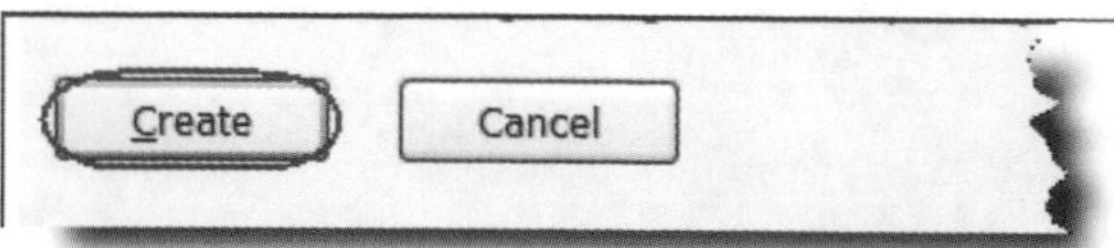

Creates a blank database. A blank new table displays in Datasheet view.

- Click on the **close** button.

Closes Table1.

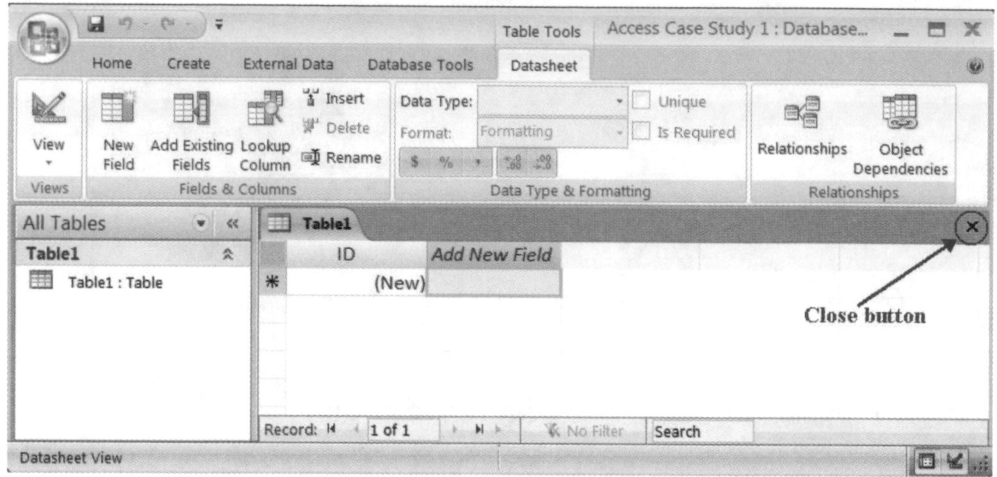

The Access Environment

In this section, we will look at the various components of the Database Window.

If you have worked with previous version of Access, you will immediately notice that the user interface has been completely redesigned. The menu and toolbar system have been replaced by the **Ribbon**. The Ribbon is designed to help you quickly find the commands you need in order to complete a task. On the Ribbon, the menu bar has been replaced by **Command Tabs** that relate to the tasks you wish to accomplish. The default Command Tabs in Access are: **Home, Create, External Data** and **Database Tools**.

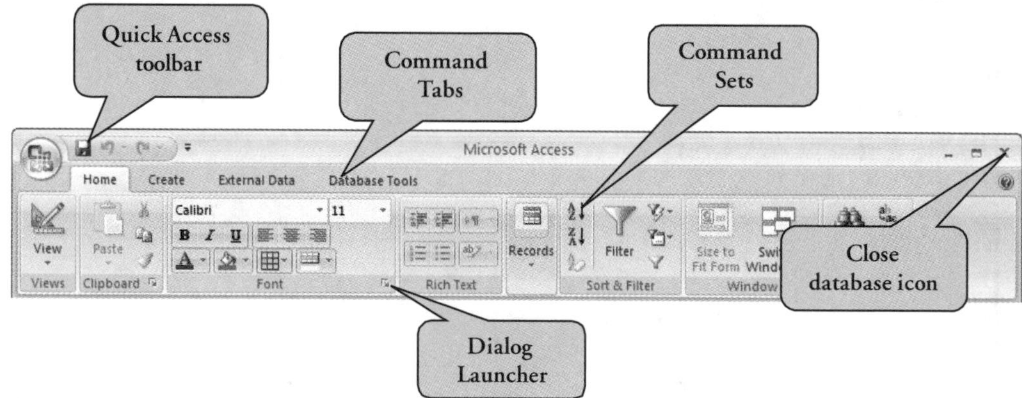

THE MICROSOFT ACCESS RIBBON

Different command icons, called **Command Sets** appear under each Command Tab. The commands that appear will depend on the Command Tab that is selected. Each command set is grouped by its function. For example, the Tables, Forms, Reports and Other are all Command Sets for the Create tab in Access. **Contextual Commands** only appear when a specific object is selected. This helps in keeping the screen uncluttered.

On the bottom of many of the Command Sets is a **Dialog Launcher**, which when clicked, will launch a dialog box for that set of commands.

To the right of the **Microsoft Office icon** is the **Quick Launch Toolbar**. This toolbar contains by default the Save, Undo, and Redo commands. In addition, clicking the drop-down arrow to the right allows you to customize the Quick Access Toolbar to add other tools that you use regularly. You can choose from the list which tools to display on the Quick Access Toolbar or select **More Commands** to add commands that are not in the list.

New in Access 2007 is the **Navigation Pane**. This replaces the Database Window in previous versions of Access. Like the Database Window, you can use the Navigation Pane to work with the various objects in your database (tables, forms, reports, etc.). Whenever you open a database, all of the objects in your dataset appear in the Navigation Pane. You can work on the design of your objects, enter data or run a report or query directly from the Navigation Pane.

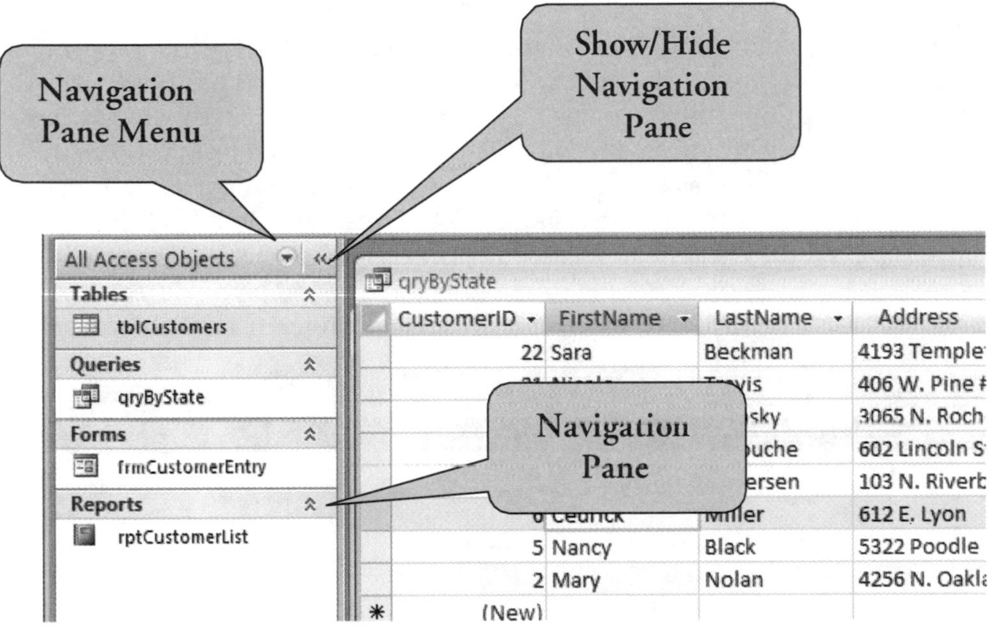

We will be working in detail with the various Access screens and database objects in subsequent lessons.

Let's Try It!

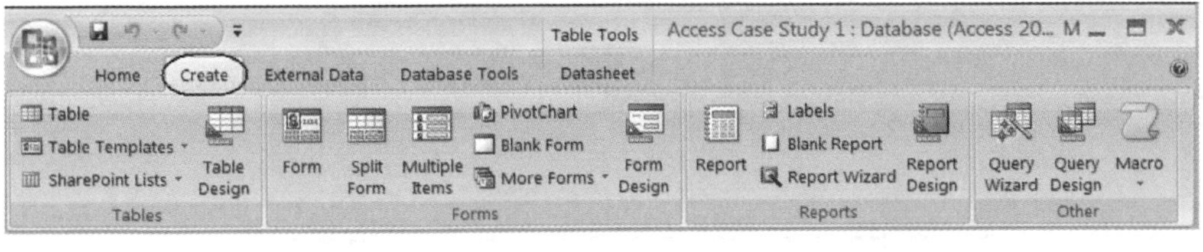

- Click the **Create tab** on top of your screen

Displays the commands sets for the Create command tab.

- Click the **Database Tools tab** on top of your screen.

Displays the commands sets for the Database Tools command tab.

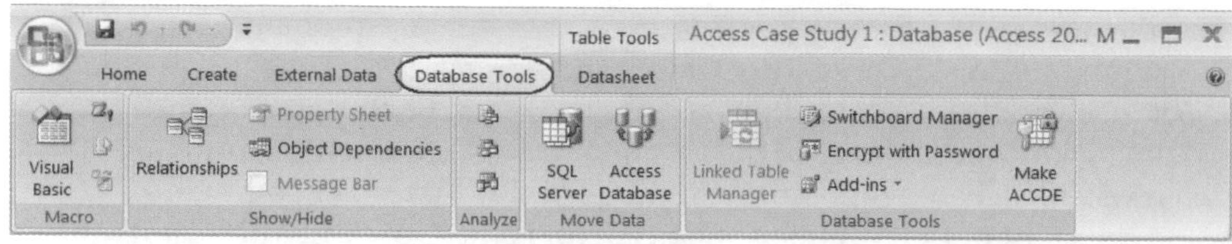

- Click the **Home tab** on top of your screen.

Returns to the Home tab.

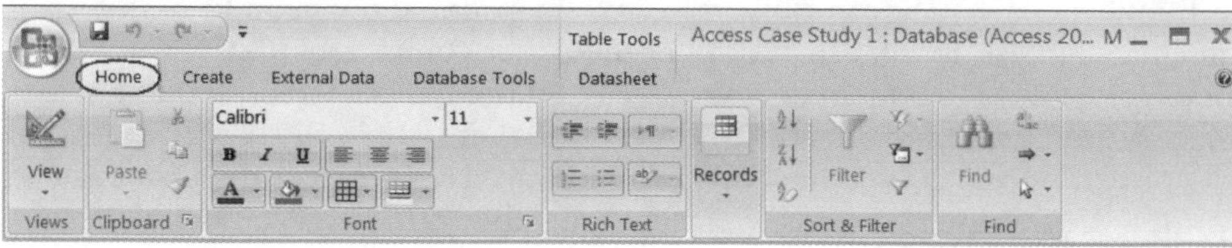

Setting Access Options

In this section, we will work with Access Options.

In previous version of Access, you could set preferences for specific program settings from the Options dialog box. The Options command has been moved to the **Access Options** button on the File Options menu which displays when you click the **Microsoft Office Button**. From the Access Options dialog box, you can specify such options as the default database format and database folder, open Navigation Pane items with a single-click instead of a double-click, have multiple opened objects appear in tabbed windows rather than overalpping windows, and much, much more. You may wish to spend some time browsing through the Access Options dialog box and set any preferences that may help you work with less effort.

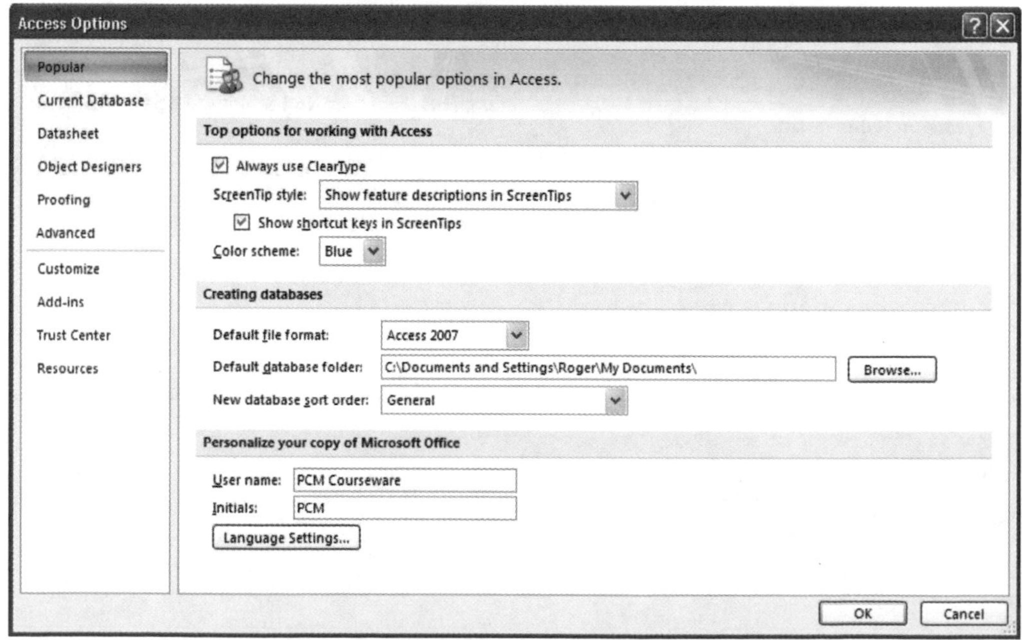

ACCESS OPTIONS DIALOG BOX

To Set Access Options

1. Click the **Microsoft Office Button** and then click **Access Options** on the bottom of the File Options dialog box.
2. Click the desired option category in the left pane.
3. Set any options in the right pane.
4. Click **OK**.

Let's Try It!

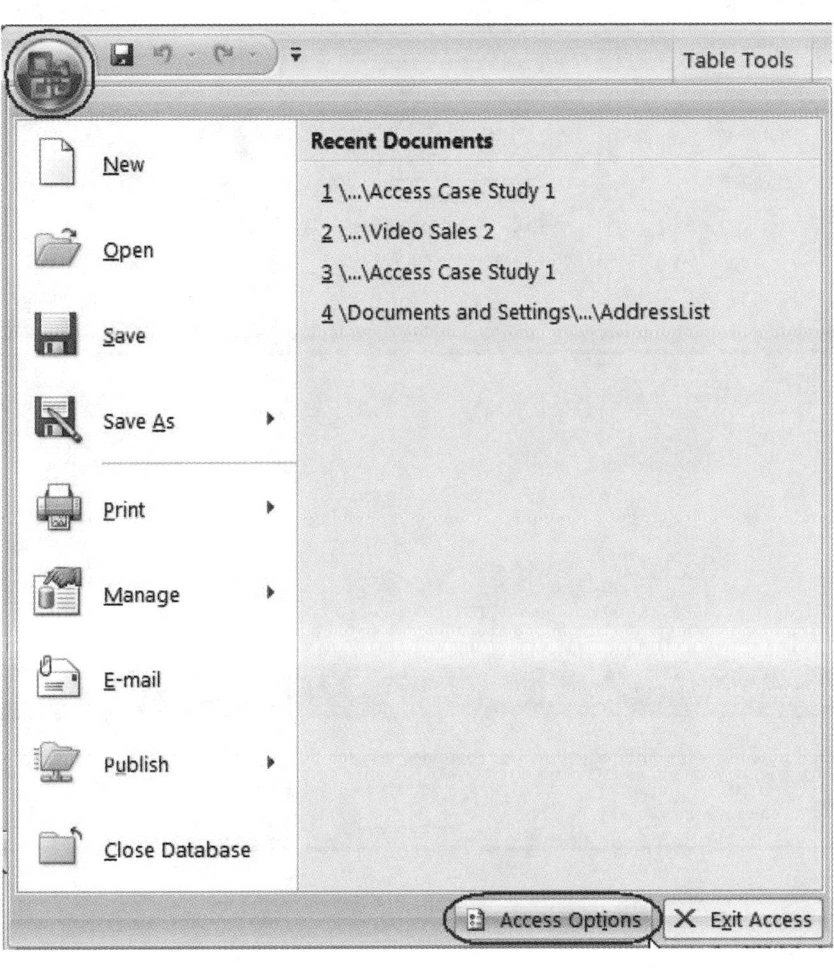

- Click the **Microsoft Office Button**

Displays the File Options menu.

- Click the **Access Options** button.

Displays the Access Options dialog box.

- Click the **Current Database** category in the left pane.

Displays available Access options for the Current Database category.

- Under the Document Window Options, click the **Tabbed Documents** radio button.

New in Access 2007, this option displays multiple opened objects (tables, queries, forms, and reports) in a tabbed window instead of overlapping windows.

- Click **OK**.

Closes the Access Options dialog box and applies the changes.

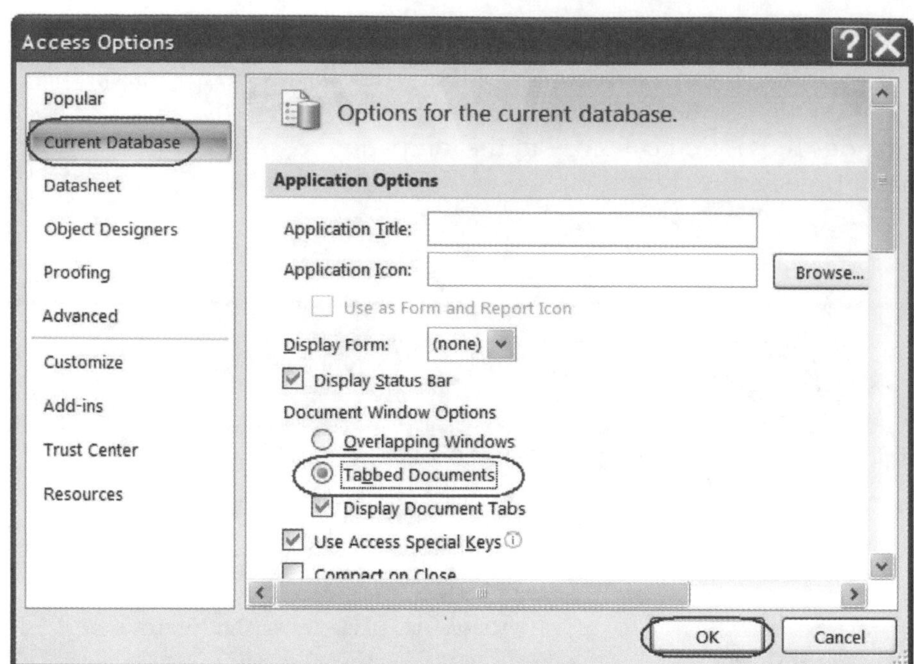

- Click **OK**.

Closes the message box that tells us that we must close and reopen the database for the changes to take effect.

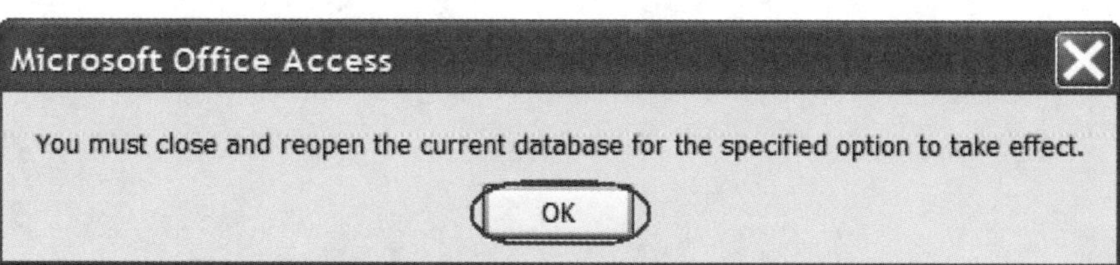

Creating a Table from Scratch

In this section, we will create a new table in Design view.

As you work more with Access, you will most likely want to create your tables from scratch rather than using Table Templates. Creating your tables from scratch allows you maximum flexibility.

When adding fields to a table, you will need to specify a field name and a **data type**. Data types tell Access what type of data to expect in that field. For example, you would be unable to calculate two numbers if their data type was set to Text. Thus, it's important to have a general understanding of data types.

Data Type	Description
Text	Stores text and/or numbers. Set for any field that will not be used for calculation. Entries can be up to 255 characters.
Memo	Allows you to store up to 64,000 characters.
Number	Stores numbers that will be used in calculations. For numbers beginning with 0, use the text data type as 0 will be dropped if data type is set for number.
Date/Time	Used for date and/or times.
Currency	Stores numbers with a fixed number of decimal places and a currency symbol.
AutoNumber	Sequentially numbers the records. AutoNumber is generally used for primary key fields for which unique values are required.
Yes/No	A Boolean value that represents a yes/no or true/false value.
OLE Object	Used for objects created in other applications such as Excel spreadsheets, graphics, and sound files.
Hyperlink	Used for clickable links for files on your computer or to sites on the World Wide Web.
Attachment	New in Access 2007, allows you to attach images, spreadsheet files, documents, and other supported files to records in your database. More flexible than OLE fields.
Lookup Wizard	Used to create a field that allows you to select a value from a list or from a field in another table or query.

NOTE: The **Attachment** data type is only available if your database is saved in Access 2007 format. Click the **Microsoft Office** icon, select **Save As** from the File Options menu and choose **Access 2007 Database** from the second pane. Note that databases saved in 2007 format are inaccessible by previous version of Access.

To Create a Table from Scratch

1. Click the **Create** command tab on the Ribbon.
2. Click the **Table** command icon.
3. Click the **Design View** button to switch to Design view.
4. Enter a Field Name and Data Type for each field.
5. Type in a description for each field if desired.

Let's Try It!

- Click the **Create** command tab on the Ribbon.

Displays commands related to the creation of database objects.

- Click **Table** command icon.

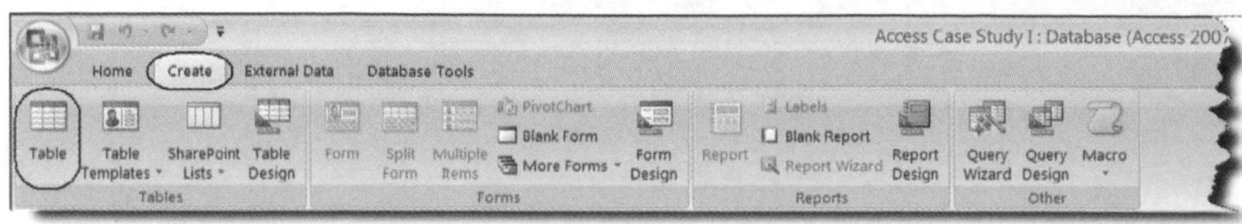

- Click the **View** command icon on the Ribbon.

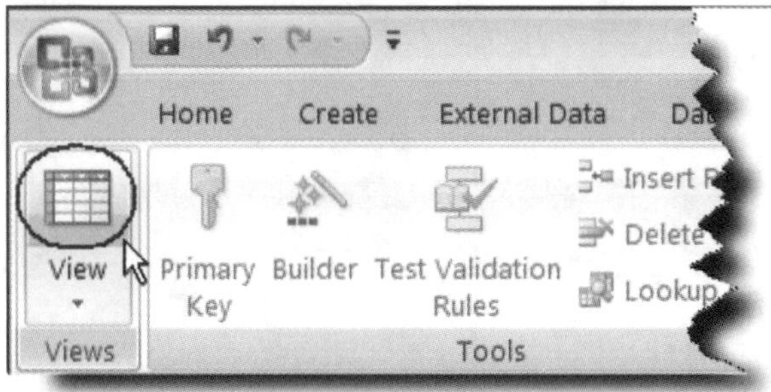

- Type: **tblStudents** in the Table Name box.

Before we can switch to Design view, we must first provide a name our new table.

- Click **OK**.

Saves the table and switches to Design view.

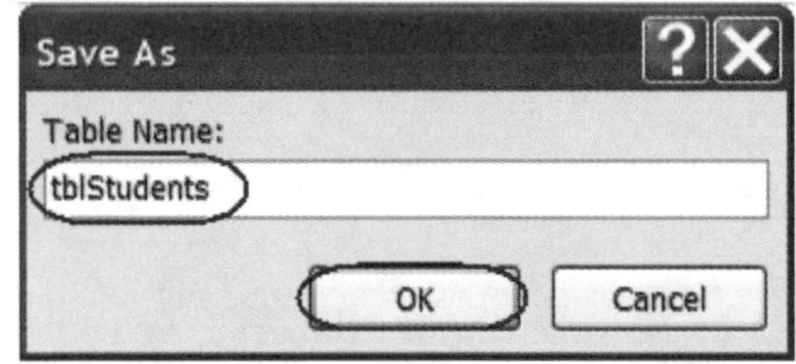

Notice that Access automatically created our first field for us—the ID field.

- Click on the **key** next to the ID field and then press the **Delete** key.

Field Name	Data Type
ID	AutoNumber

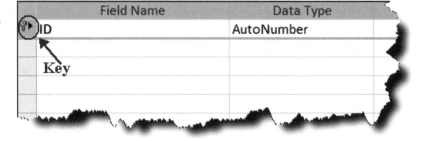

Key

- Click **Yes** when asked if you want to delete the field.

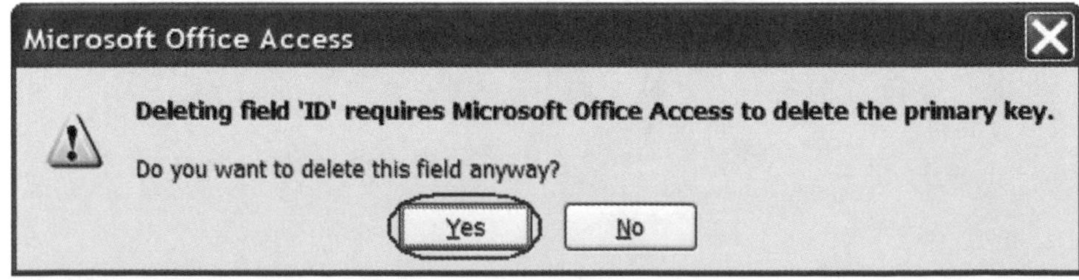

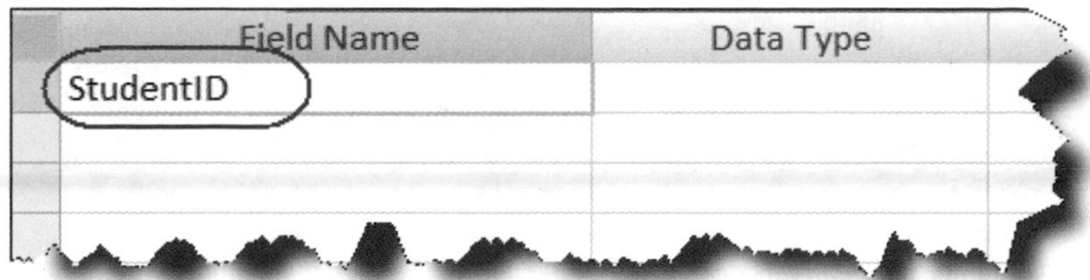

Deletes the default field that Access provided. We are going to create our own ID field.

- Click in the first blank **Field Name** box and type: **StudentID**.

Enters a name for the first field.

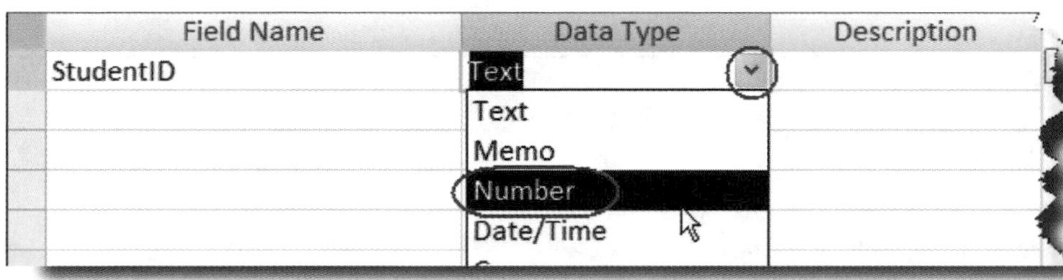

- Click on the **Data Type** arrow and then select **Number** from the list.

Sets the data type for the StudentID field to Number.

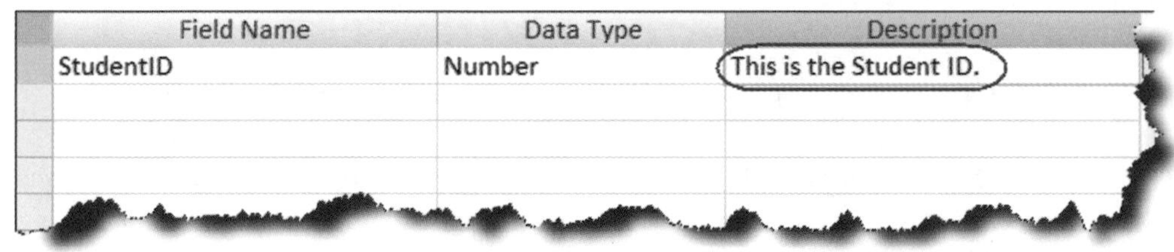

- Press **Tab** to jump to the description field and then type: **This is the Student ID**.

Enters a description for the first field.

Field Name	Data Type	Description
StudentID	Number	This is the Student ID.
FirstName	Text	

- Press **Tab**.

Moves to the next blank Field Name box.

- Type: **FirstName**

Enters the field name for the next field.

- Press **Tab**.

We will accept the default Text data type.

- Press **Tab** again.

We will not give the description for this field.

- **Repeat** the last step and enter information for rest of the fields as shown in the screenshot.

Field Name	Data Type	Description
StudentID	Number	This is the Student ID.
FirstName	Text	
LastName	Text	
Major	Text	
Address	Text	
City	Text	
State	Text	
Zip	Text	
Phone	Text	

- Click the **Save** icon on the Quick Access Toolbar.

Saves our changes.

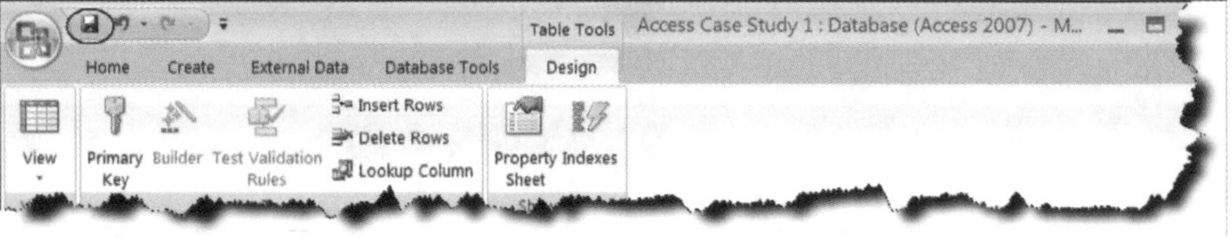

A NOTE ABOUT NAMING CONVENTIONS

Most database developers use some sort of naming conventions to help them organize and quickly identify the database objects in their database. A popular naming convention uses the object type, in lowercase letters, as the first 3 letters of the object name. For example, a Customer's table would be named: ***tblCustomers***, a customer's form would be named ***frmCustomers***, a customer's query would be name **qryCustomers** and a Customer's report would be named ***rptCustomers***.

Naming conventions are optional. However, it is considered good database programming practice to use some sort of naming convention for your objects.

Setting a Primary Key

In this section, you will learn about Primary Keys.

When working with a relational database such as Microsoft Access, you will often need to **link** two or more tables to bring related information together. In order to do this, each table needs to include a field that uniquely identifies each record in the table. This means that the data in that field may not be duplicated in any other of the table records. This unique identifier field is called a **Primary Key**.

A primary key is typically a number, such as an order number, customer number, invoice number or social security number. The most important consideration when adding a primary key to a table is that it must be unique. Some additional rules to keep in mind when setting a primary key field:

- The primary key field can never be blank (or null)
- The primary key field can never be duplicated
- The primary key field should be as short as possible
- The primary key should describe the entity

Another purpose of the primary key is that it **indexes** the information in the record. Indexing helps Access find information quickly, especially when you have a large amount of data.

Designating an **AutoNumber** as the primary key for a table is often the easiest way to create a unique identifier. If you neglect to set a primary key, Microsoft Access will ask if you want it to create a primary key for you. If you answer yes, Access will create an AutoNumber primary key. As we saw in a previous section, Access automatically creates an ID field with a primary key for all new tables.

To Add a Primary Key Field to a Table

1. Click in the **Field Name** box of the field you wish to set as a primary key field.
2. Click the **Primary Key** icon on the Ribbon.
   Or
   Right-click and then select **Primary Key** from the pop-up menu.

PRIMARY KEY ICON

Let's Try It!

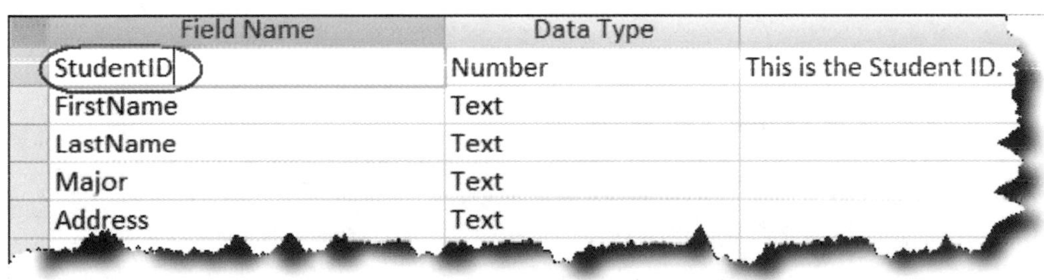

Field Name	Data Type	
StudentID	Number	This is the Student ID.
FirstName	Text	
LastName	Text	
Major	Text	
Address	Text	

- Click in the **Field name** box for **StudentID**

Selects the field that we want to set as a primary key field.

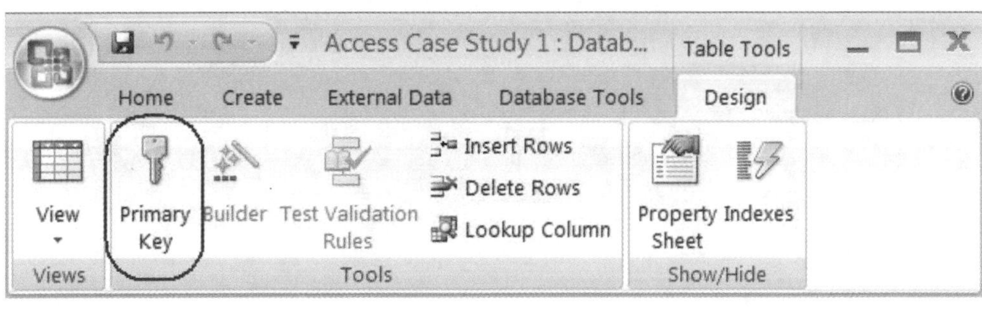

- Click the **Primary Key** command icon on the Ribbon.

Sets the StudentID field as a key field. The key symbol to the left of the StudentID field informs us that this field is set as a primary key field.

- **Save** the changes by clicking on the Save button on the Quick Access Toolbar.

Field Name	Data Type	Description
StudentID	Number	This is the Student ID.
FirstName	Text	
LastName	Text	
Major	Text	

Changing Field Properties

In this section, you will work with the Field Properties of a field.

While data types tell Access what type of data the field will hold, **field properties** govern how the data is displayed or stored. Each data type has its own set of field properties. For example, you can set the field size of the text data type to only allow 3 digits whereas the field size of the number data type is dependent on the size and type of number you choose (integer, long integer, single, double, decimal, etc.).

In this section, we will look at a couple of the more common field properties. The table on the next page summarizes some of the field properties that are most frequently modified.

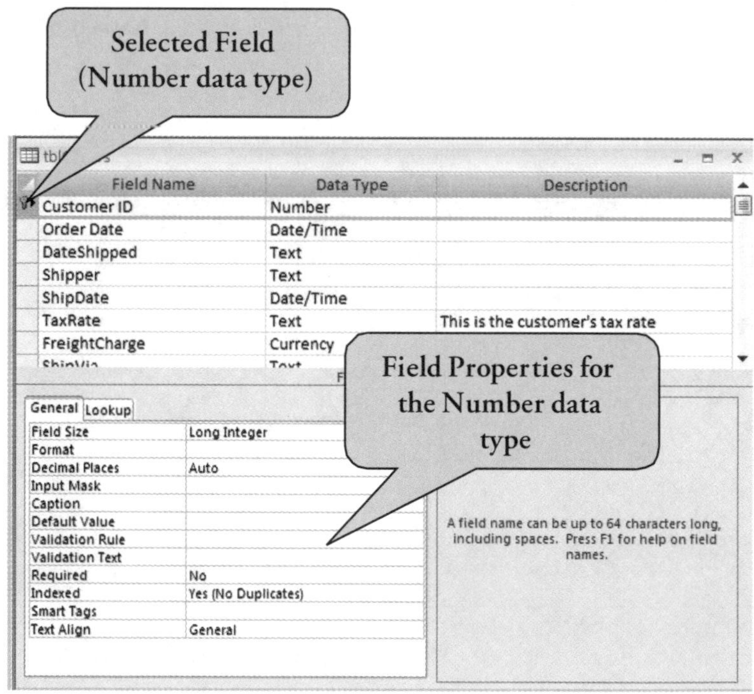

To Modify Field Properties

1. Display the table in **Design view**.
2. Click in the field name box of the field whose field properties you wish to change.
3. Click the General pane in the field properties window.
4. Make any desired changes.

Common Field Properties

Field Property	Description
Field Size	Tells Access the maximum number of characters that can be stored in the field. For text, this is a number up to 255 characters. For numbers, this is a number type (long integer, double, decimal, integer, etc.)
Input Mask	A string of characters on the screen representing how data is to be entered by the user.
Format	How data entered is to be displayed. You can use a pre-defined format or use a custom format.
Decimal Places	The number of decimal places that will be displayed.
Caption	The text (or label) that should appear next to the text box control on a form. If no caption is entered, Access uses the field name.
Default Value	The value that Access automatically enters in the field for new records.
Validation Rule	An expression that controls the value that can be entered into a field.
Validation Text	The message the user receives when the validation rule is violated.
Required	A yes/no property that specifies whether a user must enter a value in the field.
Allow Zero Length	Specifies whether a string containing no characters (a zero-length string) is permissible. You enter a zero-length string by typing two quotation marks with no spaces between them ("").
Indexed	Specifies whether you want to Access to create a data index for the field that can speed up searches and sorts.

Let's Try It!

- Click on the **State** field.
- Under the **Field Properties** area on the bottom of the window, type: **2** in the **Field Size** box.

Selects the Field Size property for the State field.

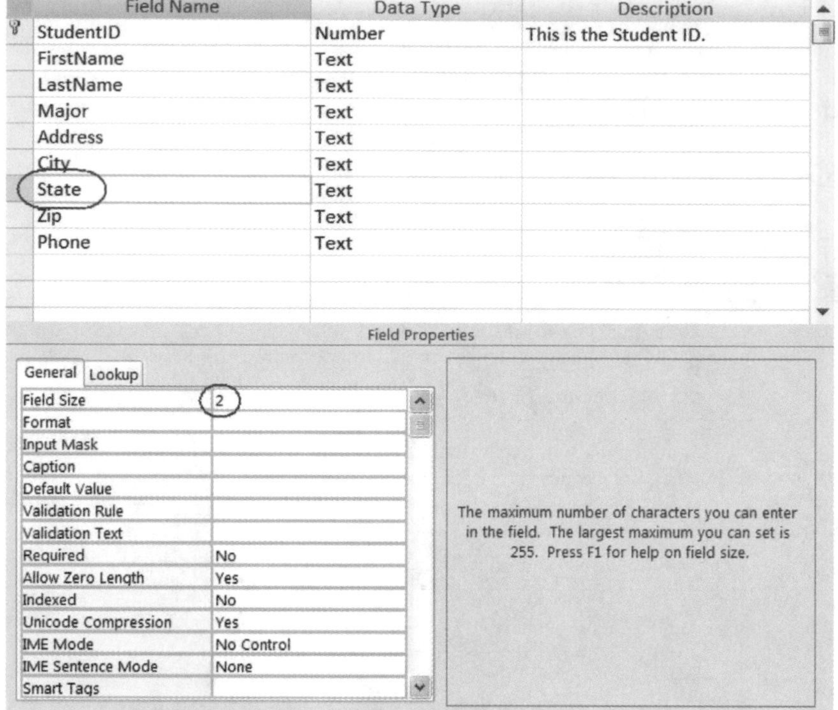

- Click the **View** button on the ribbon.

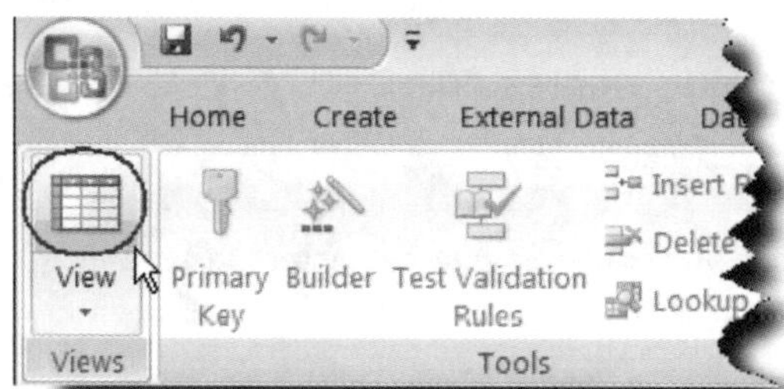

- Click **Yes** when asked if you want to save the table.

Saves the design changes and switches to datasheet view.

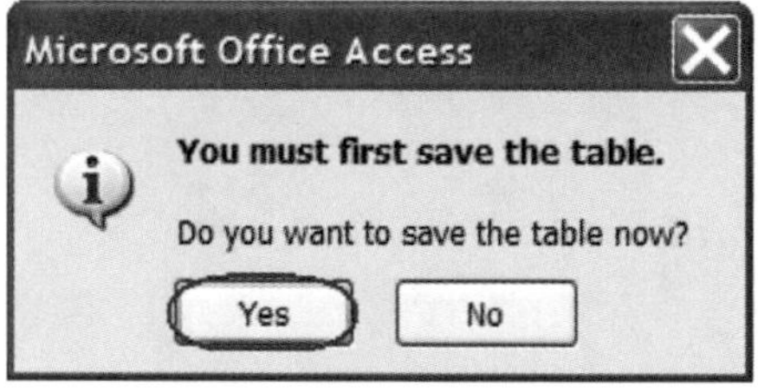

Entering Data into a Table

In this section, you will learn how to enter table data.

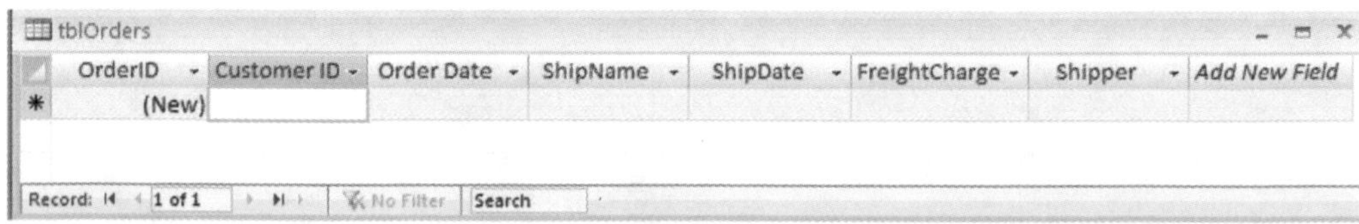

To enter data into a new table, click in the first field into which you wish to begin entering data and then type your information. Pressing the **Tab** key will move you to the next field. Note that you cannot enter data into an **AutoNumber** field.

To enter data into a table with existing data, click the **New Record** button on the Record Navigation Bar and then type your information into the new row.

To Enter Data into a Table

1. Open the table in **Datasheet view**.
2. Click the **New Record** button on the Record Navigation Bar to insert a new record.
3. Click in the first blank field and begin typing.

Let's Try It!

	StudentID	FirstName	LastName	Major	Address	City	State	Zip	Phone	Add New Field
	99416847	Daniel	Harris	French	387 N. Pine St.	Reston	VA	22021	(719) 555-5736	
*										

- Click in the **StudentID** field.
- Type: **99416847** and press **Tab**.

Moves to the next column.

- Type: **Daniel** in the First Name field and then press **Tab**.
- Type: **Harris** in the Last Name field and then press **Tab**.
- Type: **French** in the Major field and then press **Tab**.
- Type: **387 N. Pine St.** in the Address field and then press **Tab**.
- Type: **Reston** in the City field and then press **Tab**.
- Type: **VA** in the State field and then press **Tab**.
- Type: **22021** in the Zip/Postal Code field.
- Type: **(719) 555-5736** in the Home Phone field and then press **Tab**.

- **Repeat** the above steps and enter the rest of the information as shown in the following screenshot.
- **Save** the changes by clicking on the Save icon on the Quick Access Toolbar.

StudentID	FirstName	LastName	Major	Address	City	State	Zip	Phone	Add New Fie
99416847	Daniel	Harris	French	387 N. Pine St.	Reston	VA	22021	(719) 555-5736	
99416348	Mary	Nolan	IT	4256 N. Oakland Ave.	Fairfax	FL	53211	(414) 555-5242	
99416349	James	Loomis	History	8724 W. Pine St.	Chantilly	VA	21234	(906) 555-3465	
99416350	Cathy	Powell	Economics	916 S. Davis	Cheyenne	WY	82005	(307) 555-6254	
99416351	Nancy	Black	IT	5322 Poodle Lane	Milwaukee	WI	53216	(414) 555-4495	
99416352	Cedrick	Miller	French	612 E. Lyon	Milwaukee	WI	53201	(414) 555-0601	
99416353	Norman	Wyler	Business	6212 Huck St.	Denver	CO	80207	(720) 555-9062	
99416354	David	McBride	Business	802 Patriot's Court	South Range	MI	49950	(414) 555-2702	
99416355	Mona	Fielen	IT	512 N. Hemlock	Alexandria	VA	23123	(906) 555-2308	
99416356	Randy	Andersen	IT	103 N. Riverboat Rd.	Kenosha	WI	53206	(262) 555-9215	
99416362	Lance	Ferrare	Business	10062 Petersburg Dr.	Arlington	VA	82006	(307) 555-4325	
99416363	Daniel	Morris	Education	312 E. Park St.	Dallas	TX	75225	(972) 555-6547	
99416364	Larry	Campbell	Nursing	7323 Sun Dr.	Hollywood	CA	90210	(902) 555-1061	
*									

Selecting and Deleting Records

In this section, you will learn how to select and delete records from your table.

Deleting records from a table is straight-forward—click on the row selector to select the record and then press the **Delete** key or right-click and select **Delete Record** from the contextual menu. You can select more than one record by clicking and dragging upwards or downwards over the records you wish to delete. Keep in mind though, that once you delete records, they are gone for good. There is no undo! The only way to get a deleted record back is to retype the information.

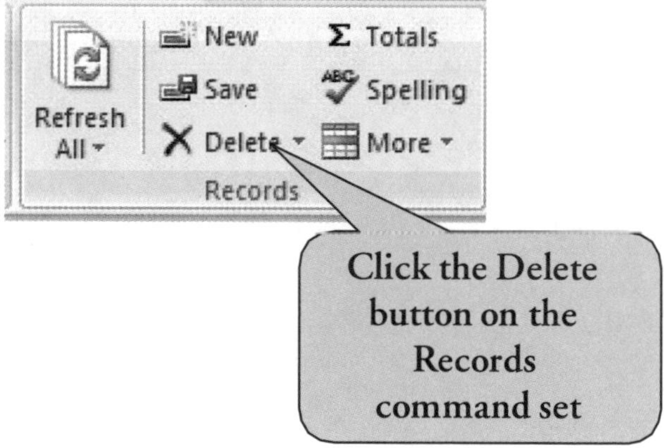

You can also delete records from the **Records** command set under the **Home** tab. Select the row selector and click the **Delete** button. Make sure that you click the Delete button under the Home tab and not the Datasheet tab as clicking the Delete button under the Datasheet tab will delete the entire field, not just an individual records.

To Select and Delete a Record

1. Open the table in Datasheet view.
2. Click the row selector of the record or records you wish to delete.
3. Press the **Delete** key
   Or
   Right-click and select **Delete Record** from the contextual menu.

Or
Click the **Delete** button on the Records command set under the Home tab.

4. Click **Yes** when the message box appears, asking you if you are sure you want to delete the record(s)

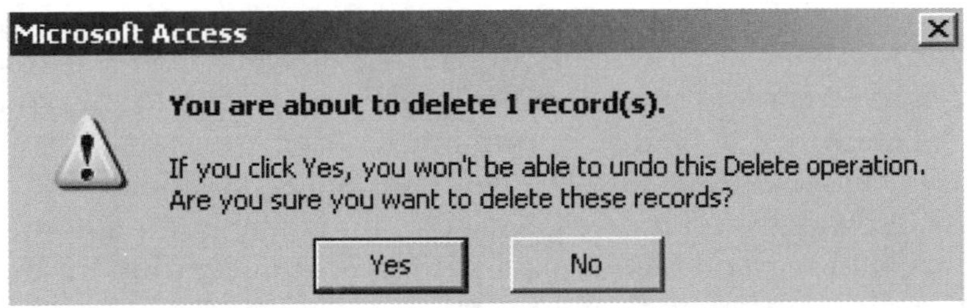
Microsoft Access
You are about to delete 1 record(s).
If you click Yes, you won't be able to undo this Delete operation.
Are you sure you want to delete these records?
Yes
No

> **NOTE:** Clicking **No** will cancel the delete records action and the records will not be deleted from the table.

Let's Try It!

StudentID	FirstName	LastName	Major	Address	City	State	Zip
99416847	Daniel	Harris	French	387 N. Pine St.	Reston	VA	22021
99416348	Mary	Nolan	IT	4256 N. Oakland Ave.	Fairfax	FL	53211
99416349	James	Loomis	History	8724 W. Pine St.	Chantilly	VA	21234
99416350	Cathy	Powell	Economics	916 S. Davis	Cheyenne	WY	82005
99416351	Nancy	Black	IT	5322 Poodle Lane	Milwaukee	WI	53216
99416352	Cedrick	Miller	French	612 E. Lyon	Milwaukee	WI	53201
99416353	Norman	Wyler	Business	6212 Huck St.	Denver	CO	80207
99416354	David	McBride	Business	802 Patriot's Court	South Range	MI	49950
99416355	Mona	Fielen	IT	512 N. Hemlock	Alexandria	VA	23123
[illegible]416356	Randy	Andersen	IT	103 N. Riverb[illegible] Rd.	Kenosha	WI	[illegible]206

- Click on the **Row Selector** for the **Cathy Powell**, the 4th record in the table.

Select the record for the Cathy Powell.

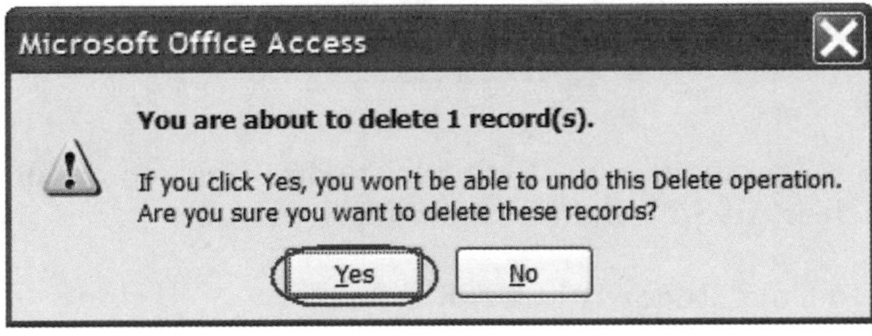
Microsoft Office Access
You are about to delete 1 record(s).
If you click Yes, you won't be able to undo this Delete operation.
Are you sure you want to delete these records?
Yes
No

- Press the **Delete** key.

Displays a message box warning you that you cannot undo the deletion and asking you if you really wish to delete the records.

- Click **Yes**.

Closes the message box and deletes the selected record.

Sorting Records

In this section, you will learn how to sort records a in a table.

Records are automatically sorted alphabetically or numerically by the primary key field if there is one designated. If there is no primary key set, then the records appear in the order in which they were entered. To change the order of the records, you can use **sorting**. Sorting allows you arrange the records in a table in alphabetical or numerical order. You can sort your records in either **ascending** (A–Z) or **descending** (Z–A) order.

The easiest way to sort records is to click anywhere in the column of the field you wish to sort and then click either the **Sort Ascending button** or the **Sort Descending button** on the **Home** tab Ribbon. You can also use right-click on the column you wish to sort and choose Sort A to Z or Sort Z to A from the contextual menu. A new feature in Access 2007 is the ability to sort records by clicking on the drop-down arrow on the column heading and chose the desired sort order.

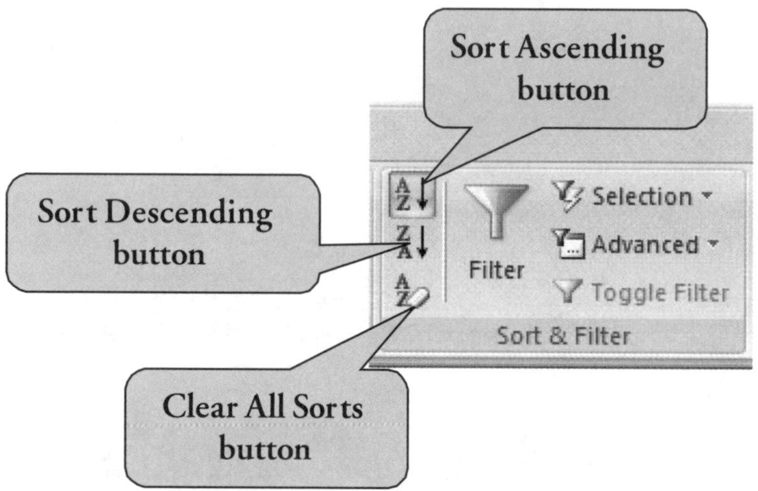

To remove a sort and return to the original order of the records, click the **Clear All Sorts** button under the Home tab.

To Sort Records in a Table

1. Open the table in Datasheet View.
2. Click anywhere in the column of the field you wish to sort.
3. To sort multiple adjacent columns, select the first column, hold down your Shift key and select any other columns you wish to sort.
4. To sort records in ascending order, click the **Sort Ascending Button (A to Z)** under the Home tab.
   Or
   Right-click and choose **Sort A to Z** from the contextual menu.
5. To sort records in descending order, click the **Sort Ascending Button (Z to A)** under the Home tab.
   Or
   Right-click and choose **Sort Z to A** from the contextual menu.
6. To return the table to its original sort order, click the **Clear All Sorts** button under the Home tab.

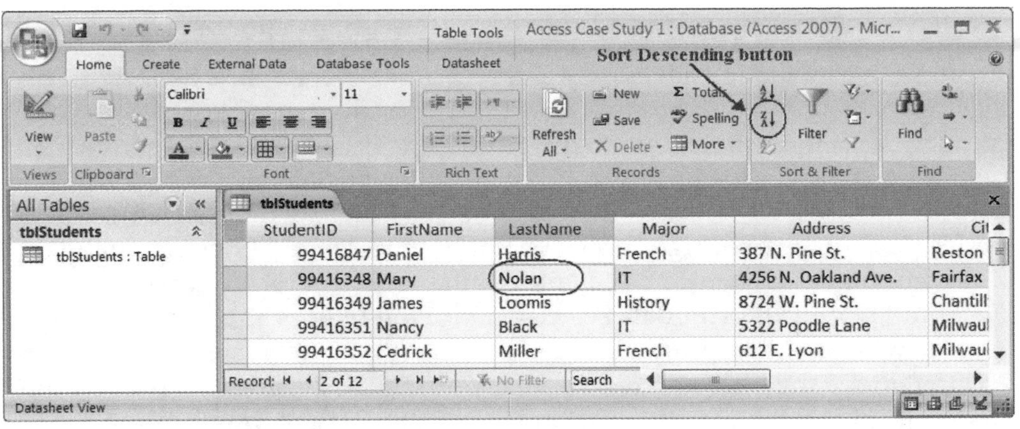

- Click anywhere in the **LastName** column.

Selects the column we wish to sort.

- Click the **Sort Descending** button in the Sort & Filter command set under the Home tab.

StudentID	FirstName	LastName	Major	Address
99416353	Norman	Wyler	Business	6212 Huck St.
99416348	Mary	Nolan	IT	4256 N. Oakland Ave.
99416363	Daniel	Morris	Education	312 E. Park St.
99416352	Cedrick	Miller	French	612 E. Lyon
99416354	David	McBride	Business	802 Patriot's Court
99416349	James	Loomis	History	8724 W. Pine St.
99416847	Daniel	Harris	French	387 N. Pine St.
99416355	Mona	Fielen	IT	512 N. Hemlock

Sorts the data in the LastName field in descending order.

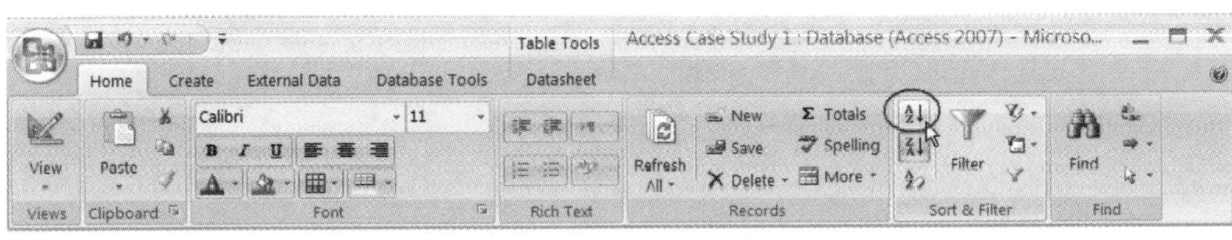

- Click the **Sort Ascending** button on the Sort & Filter command set.

StudentID	FirstName	LastName	Major	Address
99416356	Randy	Andersen	IT	103 N. Riverboat Rd.
99416351	Nancy	Black	IT	5322 Poodle Lane
99416364	Larry	Campbell	Nursing	7323 Sun Dr.
99416362	Lance	Ferrare	Business	10062 Petersburg Dr.
99416355	Mona	Fielen	IT	512 N. Hemlock
99416847	Daniel	Harris	French	387 N. Pine St.
99416349	James	Loomis	History	8724 W. Pine St.
99416354	David	McBride	Business	802 Patriot's Court

Sort the column in the ascending order by LastName.

- Click the **Clear All Sorts** button on the Sort & Filter command set.

Restores the records to their original sort order.

Filtering Data by Selection

In this section, you will learn how to filter data based on selected information.

A **filter** is a tool that retrieves only a subset of the records in a table. For instance, if you only wanted to see customers in the state of Wisconsin, you could apply a filter that hides all the records except those where the state field is equal to Wisconsin. To apply such a filter, click in any field whose contents are "Wisconsin" and then click on the **Filter by Selection** button under the Home tab or right-click and choose the desired filter commands from the contextual menu. The available filter commands will vary depending on the type of data selected. Once the filter is applied, all other records will be hidden from view.

To remove the filter and restore all records, click the **Toggle Filter** button under the Home tab or right-click and select **Clear filter from [Column Name]** from the menu.

To Filter Data for a Selection

1. Open the table in Datasheet View.
2. Click in a field whose information you wish to filter.
3. Click the **Filter by Selection** button and chose the desired filter command.

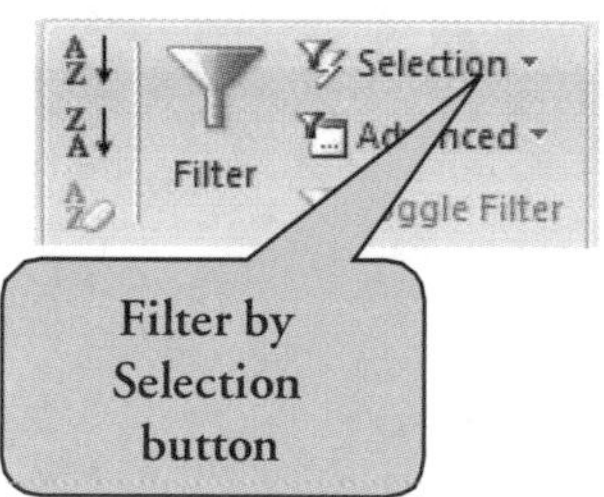

Or
Right-click and choose the desired filter commands from the contextual menu.

To Remove a Filter

1. Click on the **Toggle Filter** button.

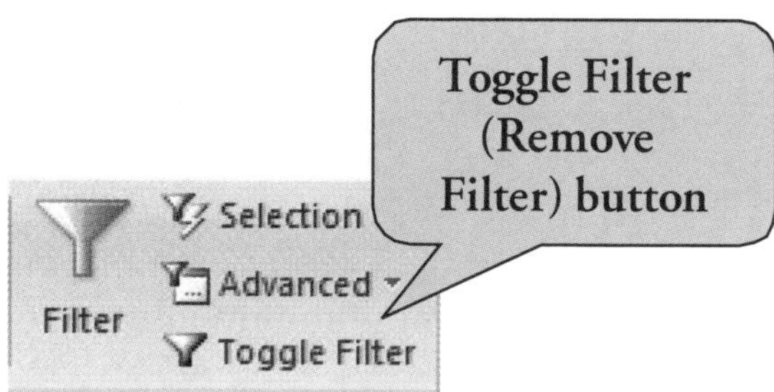

Let's Try It!

StudentID	FirstName	LastName	Major	Address	City
99416348	Mary	Nolan	IT	4256 N. Oakland Ave.	Fairfax
99416349	James	Loomis	History	8724 W. Pine St.	Chantilly
99416351	Nancy	Black	IT	5322 Poodle Lane	Milwaukee
99416352	Cedrick	Miller	French	612 E. Lyon	Milwaukee
99416353	Norman	Wyler	Business	6212 Huck St.	Denver
99416354	David	McBride	Business	802 Patriot's Court	South Range
99416355	Mona	Fielen	IT	512 N. Hemlock	Alexandria
99416356	Randy	Andersen	IT	103 N. Riverboat Rd.	Kenosha
99416362	Lance	Ferrare	Business	10062 Petersburg Dr.	Arlington
99416363	Daniel	Morris	Education	312 E. Park St.	Dallas
99416364	Larry	Campbell	Nursing	7323 Sun Dr.	Hollywood
99416847	Daniel	Harris	French	387 Pine St.	Reston

- **Click** on any instance of the word **Business** in the **Major** column.

Selects the data for which we wish to filter.

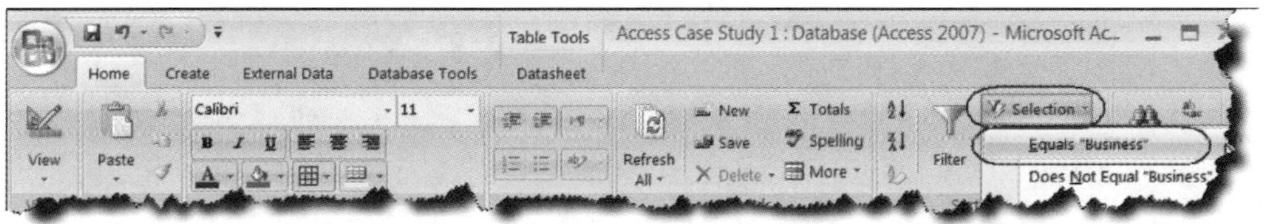

- Click the **Selection** button on the Sort & Filter command set and choose "**Equals Business**" from the command list.

StudentID	FirstName	LastName	Major	Address	City	State
99416353	Norman	Wyler	Business	6212 Huck St.	Denver	CO
99416354	David	McBride	Business	802 Patriot's Court	South Range	MI
99416362	Lance	Ferrare	Business	10062 Petersburg Dr.	Arlington	VA

- Hides all records except those whose category is "Business".

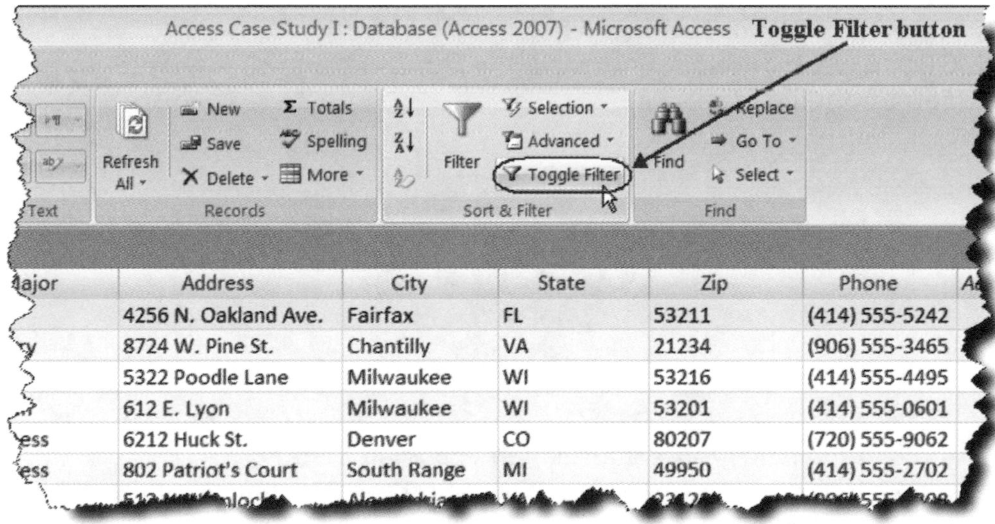

Major	Address	City	State	Zip	Phone
	4256 N. Oakland Ave.	Fairfax	FL	53211	(414) 555-5242
y	8724 W. Pine St.	Chantilly	VA	21234	(906) 555-3465
	5322 Poodle Lane	Milwaukee	WI	53216	(414) 555-4495
	612 E. Lyon	Milwaukee	WI	53201	(414) 555-0601
ess	6212 Huck St.	Denver	CO	80207	(720) 555-9062
ess	802 Patriot's Court	South Range	MI	49950	(414) 555-2702

- Click the **Toggle Filter** button.

Removes the filter and displays all records.

Filtering Data by Form

In this section, you will learn how to filter data based on selected information from a drop-down list.

Filtering by Form allows you to choose the data you want the filtered records to contain from a drop-down list of available data. Clicking the **Filter by Form button** displays a blank record row. Clicking in any of the blank fields displays a drop-down list of available data from which you can choose. This feature is especially helpful if you want to find a specific record or want to filter on several fields in a datasheet.

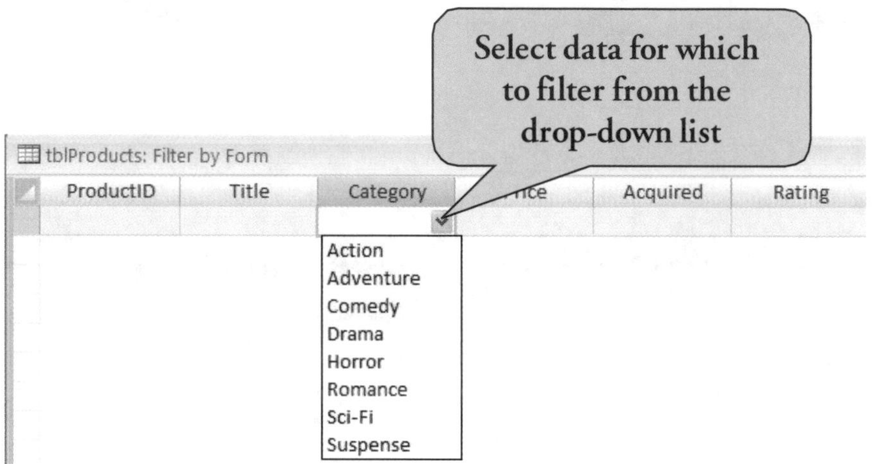

To Filter by Form

1. Open the table in Datasheet View.
2. Click the **Advanced** button under the Home tab and choose **Filter by Form** from the menu.

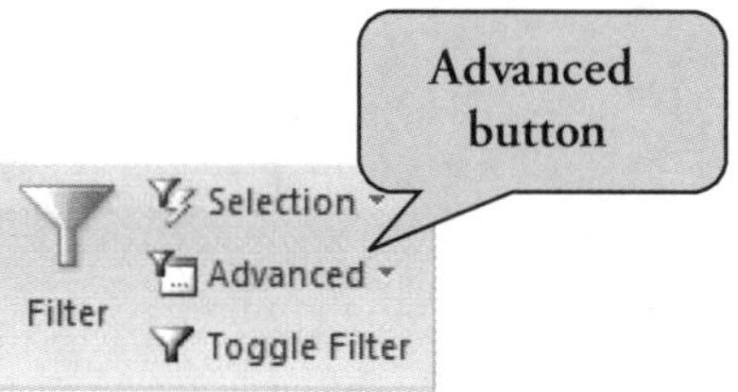

3. Click in the field whose information you wish to filter.
4. Click the drop-down arrow and then select the data you want the filtered records to contain.
5. Repeat step 4 for any additional fields you wish to filter.
6. Click the **Toggle Filter** button (same as Remove Filter button).

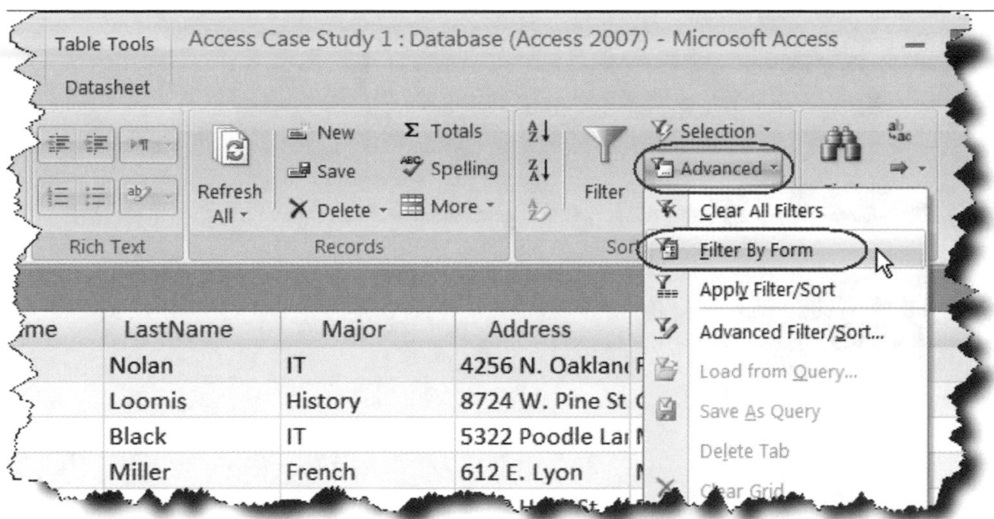

- Click the **Advanced** button on the Sort & Filter command and select **Filter by Form** from the menu.

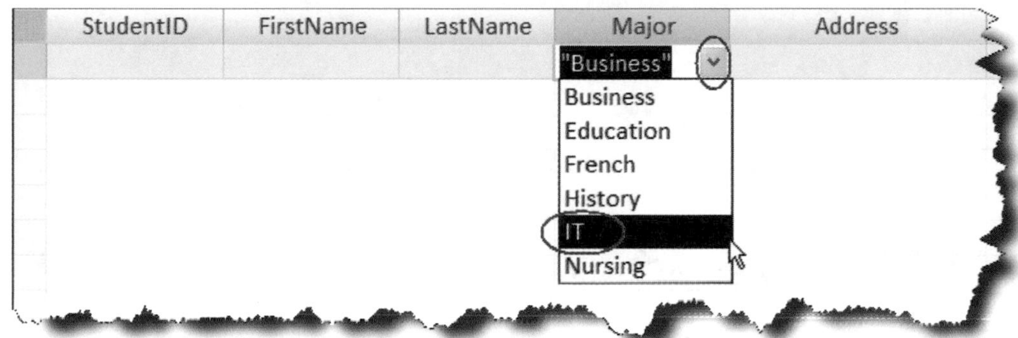

Opens a blank record row with the values automatically inserted from our previous filter.

- Click the Category drop-down arrow and then select **IT**.

Selects the Category by which we want to filter.

- Press **Tab three times**.

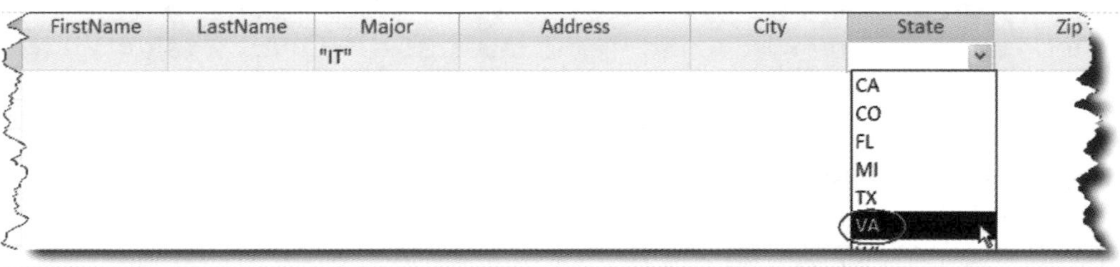

Moves us to the State field and displays the drop-down arrow for the State field.

- Click the State drop-down arrow and then select **VA** from the drop-down list.

Selects the State by which we want to filter.

- Click the **Toggle Filter** button.

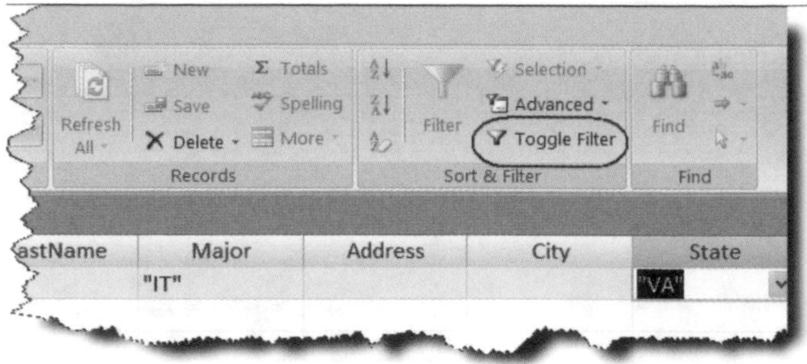

Only displays records with a State of VA AND a Major of IT.

	StudentID	FirstName	LastName	Major	Address	City	Sta
	99416355	Mona	Fielen	IT	512 N. Hemlock	Alexandria	VA
*							

- Click the **Toggle Filter** button again.

Restores the hidden records.

- Click the **Save** button on the Quick Access toolbar.

Saves the changes.

Working in Query Design View

In this section, you will learn about the Query object.

In the last, you learned how to filter data in a table, using the *Filter by Selection* and *Filter by Form* tools. However, for more complex searches, it is often better to create a **query**. Queries are also the fastest and easiest way to retrieve information from a database.

A query allows you to **ask a question** of your data. For instance, you might want to know how many customers in the state of Illinois spent more than $250 in the year 2002. The fields you wish to receive along with the criteria by which you wish to limit your data are set in **Query Design View**.

The parts of a query in Design View are as follows:

Field Lists—the tables along with their fields that are part of the query. This section is the top part of the query.

Design grid—The lower part of the query broken down into rows and columns. This is where you add fields from the field lists that you want to be part of your query.

- **Field**—The table field whose data will be displayed when the query is run.
- **Table**—The table that contains the field.
- **Sort row**—designates how the results of the query are to be sorted.
- **Show row**—designates which fields will be displayed when the query is run.
- **Criteria row**—used to specify the limits placed on the records to be retrieved.

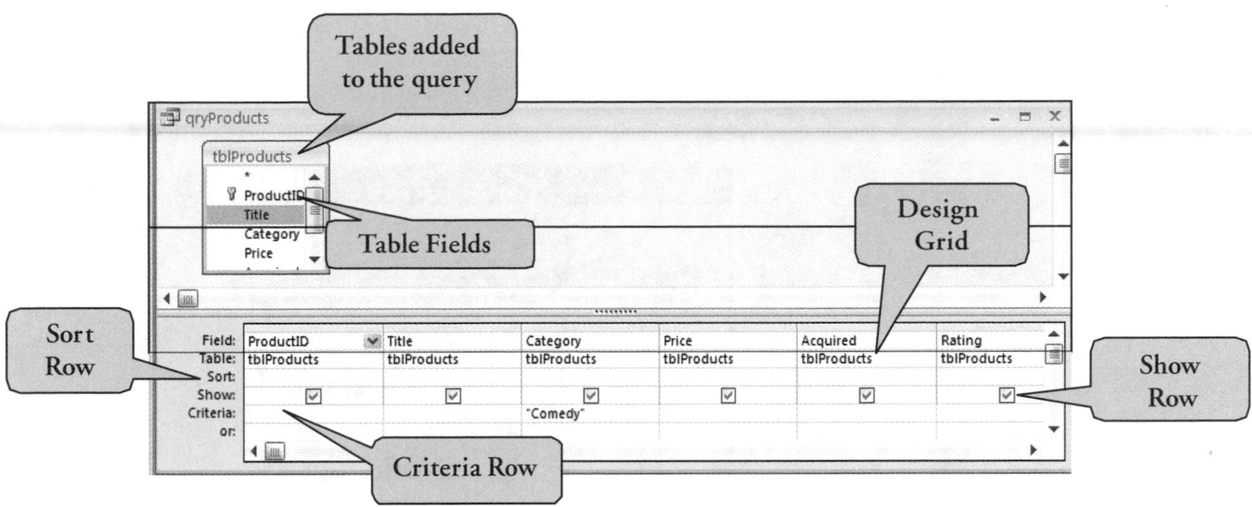

To Open a Query in Design View

1. Select **Queries** in the Navigation Pane.
2. Right-click the query you wish to open and select **Design View** from the contextual menu.
3. Click the **Design** button.
   Or
   From query Datasheet view, click the Design View button on the lower right-hand corner of the Access screen.

4. To close the query, click the query's close button.

There are two ways to create queries: using the query wizard or manually creating a query in Design View. In this section, we will create a query in Design View that returns data from a single table. This is accomplished by clicking **Query Design** button under the Create tab, and then choosing which table you wish to add to the query.

To Create a New Query in Design View

1. Click the **Create** tab on the Ribbon.
2. Click the **Query Design** button in the **Other** command set.

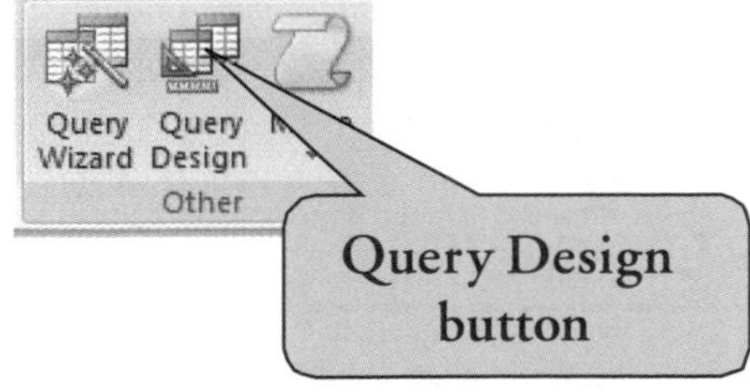

3. Click the **Tables** tab in the Show Table dialog box.
4. Select the table upon which you want to base your query.
5. Click **Add**.

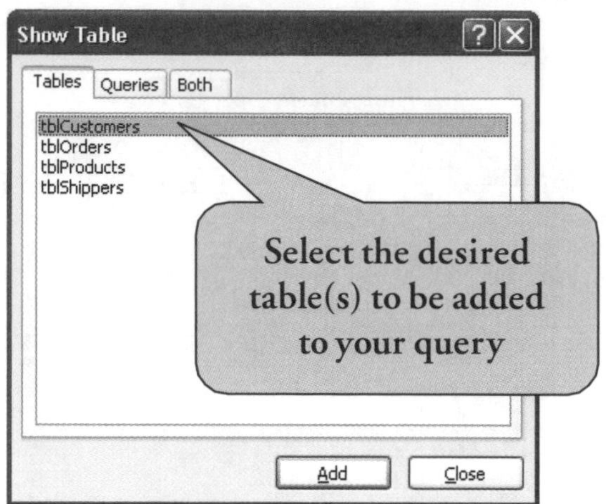

6. Click **Close** when finished.

Let's Try It!

- Click the **Create** tab on the Ribbon.

Displays command for creating Access objects.

- Click the **Query Design** command button.

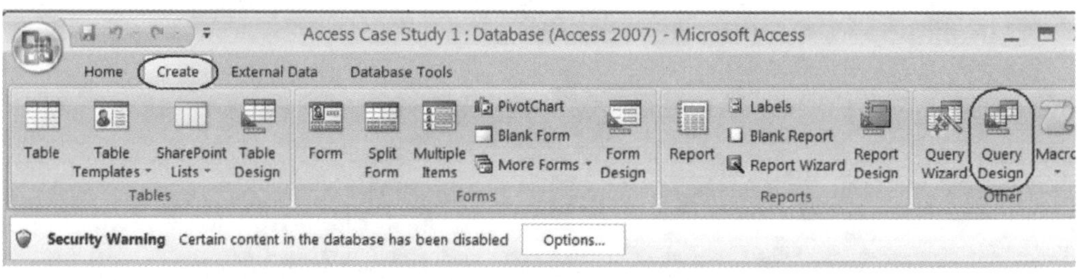

Displays the Show Table dialog box. This lists all tables and queries in your database.

- Click **tblStudents**

Selects the table we wish to add to our query.

- Click **Add**.

Adds **tblStudents** to the Field Lists area (the top portion) of our query.

- Click **Close**.

Closes the Show Table dialog box and displays query Design View.

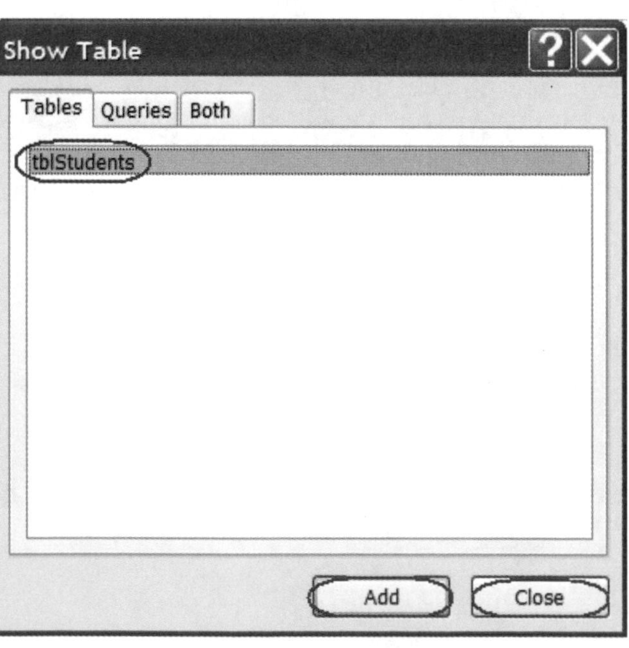

Adding Fields to a Query

In this section, you will manually add fields to your query.

Once you have chosen the table to use in your query, you will next need to add the **fields** to your query that you wish to be included in the query's results. There are several ways to add fields to your query:

- Click and drag the field from the Field Lists area to the design grid.
- Double-click the field in the table list.
- Click in the field row, click the arrow that appears and then select the desired field.
- To add all fields, double-click the **title bar** of the field list box, click anywhere within the field list, and drag to the query grid.
- Click the **asterisk** in the field list box to add all fields to the query results (the individual fields in the query grid are not displayed).

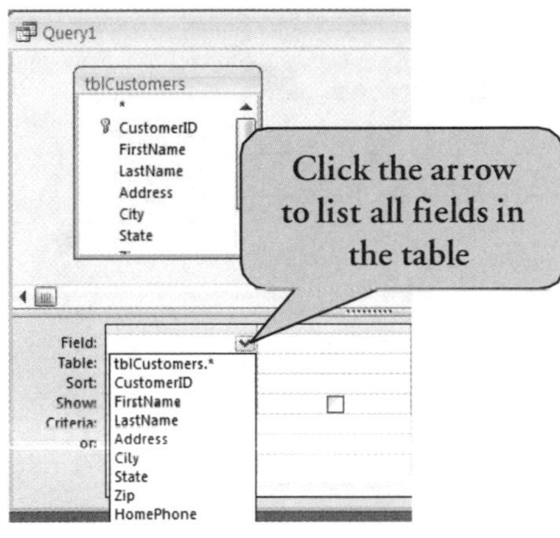

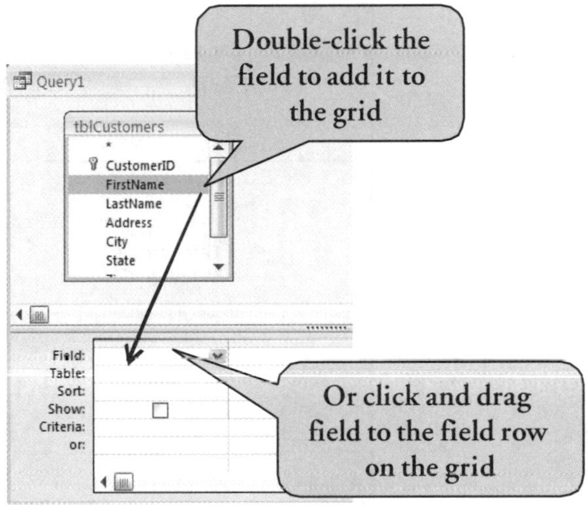

To Add Fields to a Query

1. Double-click the field name in the field list box.
   Or
   Click and drag the field from the field list box to the design grid.
   Or
   Click the field row and then choose the desired field by clicking the drop-down arrow.

To Add All of the Fields in a Table to a Query

1. Double-click the **title bar** of the field list box.
2. Click and hold your left mouse button anywhere within the field list box.
3. Drag to the query grid.

Let's Try It!

- Double-click **FirstName** in the field list box.

Adds the FirstName field to the first column of the query grid.

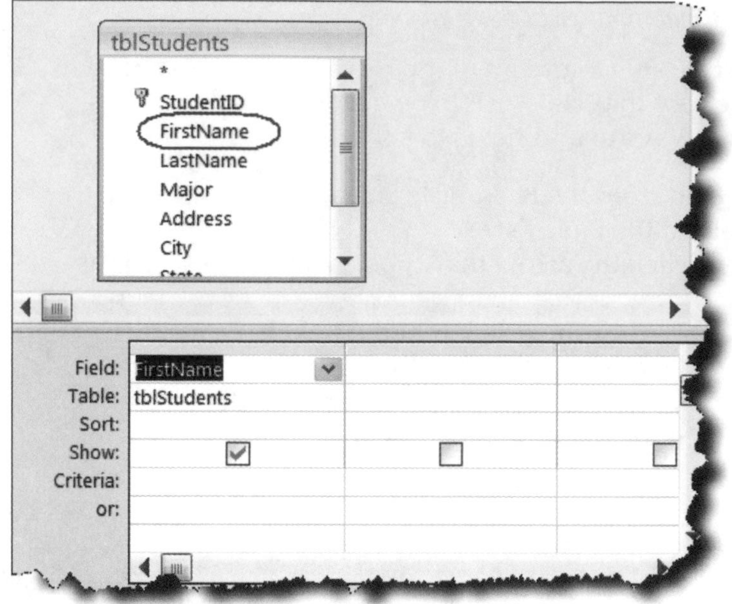

- Click the **LastName** field in the field list box and drag it to the second column of the query grid.

Drags the LastName field to the second column of the query grid.

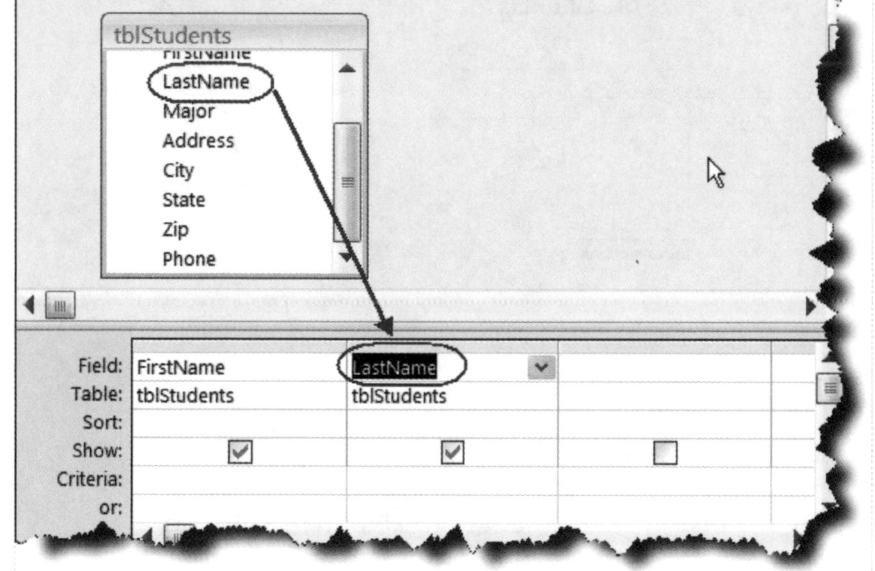

- Press **Tab**.

Moves the insertion point to the field row in the next blank column.

- Click the **arrow** and then choose State from the drop-down list.

Adds the State field to the third column of the query gird.

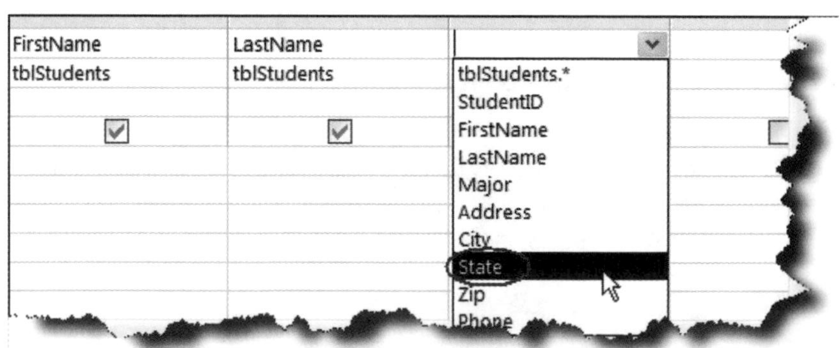

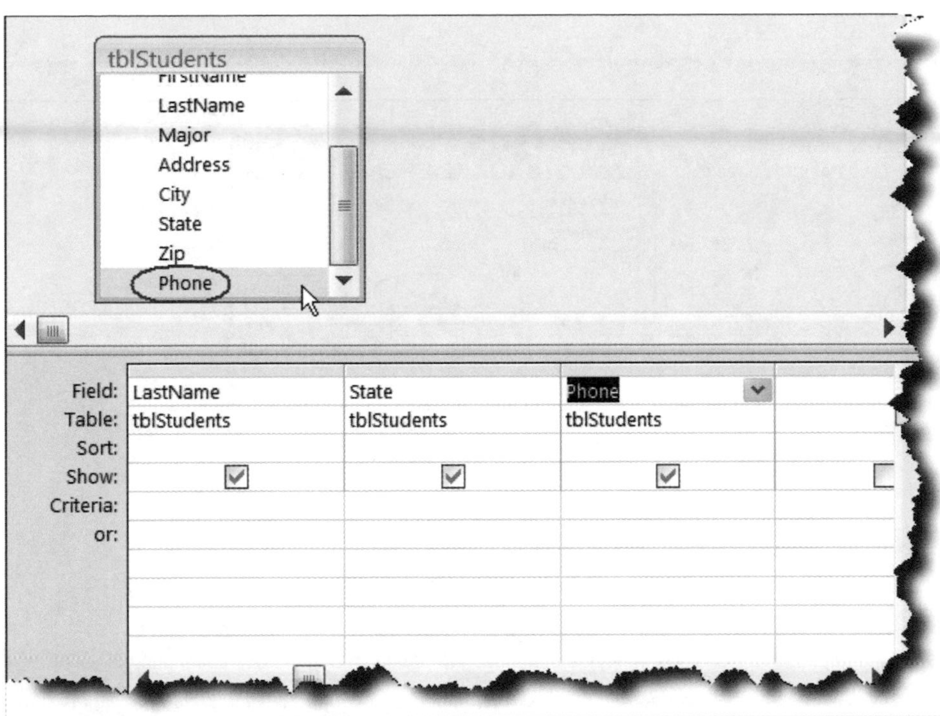

- **Double-click** the **Phone** field.

Adds the Phone field to the query grid.

Saving a Query

In this section, you will learn how to save a query.

If you will need to generate the results for a query more than once, you may wish to **Save** the query, rather than recreating it every time you need it. To save a query, click the **Save button** on the Quick Access Toolbar and then enter the name for your query in the Query Name box. Don't forget about naming conventions!

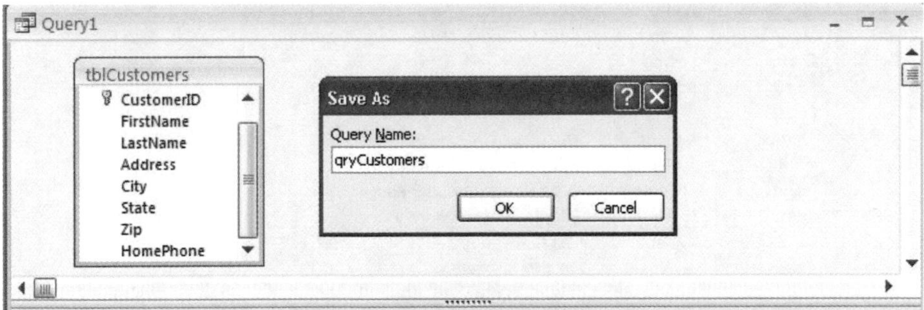

SAVING A QUERY

To Save a Query

1. Click the **Save button** on the Quick Access toolbar.
   Or
   Click the **Microsoft Office button** and click Save.
2. Enter the name for the query in the **Query Name** box.
3. Click **OK**.

Let's Try It!

- Click the **Save** button on the Quick Access toolbar.

Displays the Save As dialog box as we have not yet saved our query.

- Type: **qryStudents** in the Query Name box.

Enters a name for our query.

- Click **OK**.

Saves the query as qryStudents and then closes the Save As dialog box.

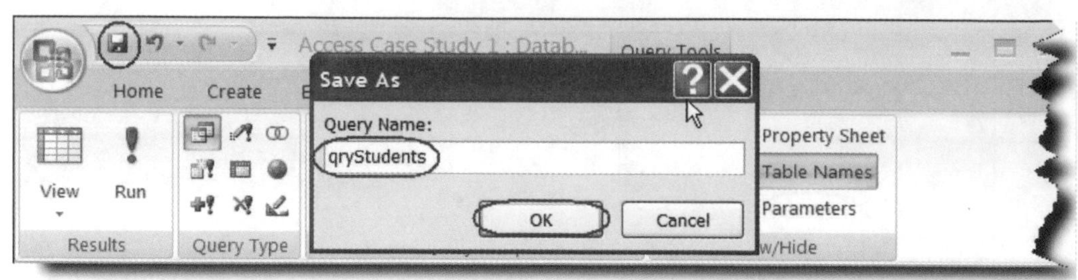

Running a Query

In this section, you will learn how run a query.

We already know that a query is a question that you ask about the data in your database. To receive the answer to your question, you need to run your query. The answer to a query is called a **recordset** or a **result set**. It is also commonly referred to as a **dynaset**. In this class, we will refer to it as a result set.

qryCustomers

FirstName	LastName	Address	City	State	Zip
Daniel	Harris	387 N. Pine St.	Canon City	CO	81212
Mary	Nolan	4256 N. Oaklan	Milwaukee	WI	53211
James	Loomis	8724 W. Pine St	Hancock	MI	49905
Cathy	Powell	916 S. Davis	Cheyenne	WY	82005
Nancy	Black	5322 Poodle La	Milwaukee	WI	53216
Cedrick	Miller	612 E. Lyon	Milwaukee	WI	53201
Norman	Wyler	6212 Huck St.	Denver	CO	80207
David	McBride	802 Patriot's Cc	South Range	MI	49950
Mona	Fielen	512 N. Hemlocl	Hancock	MI	49905
Randy	Andersen	103 N. Riverbo	Kenosha	WI	53206
Alice	Juntinen	2006 W. Center	Denver	CO	80207
Thomas	Henderson	9892 E. Clinton	Orlando	FL	32825
Patti	LaRouche	602 Lincoln St.	Milwaukee	WI	53202
Laura	Prescott	21053 E. Lark	Denver	CO	80207
Jonathan	Zavasky	3065 N. Rochel	West Allis	WI	53207

Record: 1 of 23 No Filter Search

THE QUERY RESULT SET

To run a query if you are in Design View, click the **run icon** on the toolbar or click the **View** button on the Ribbon. To run a query that is not already open, double-click the query name in the Navigation Pane.

To Run a Query from Design View

1. Click the **Run Query button** on the Ribbon.
   Or
   Click the **View button** on the Ribbon.

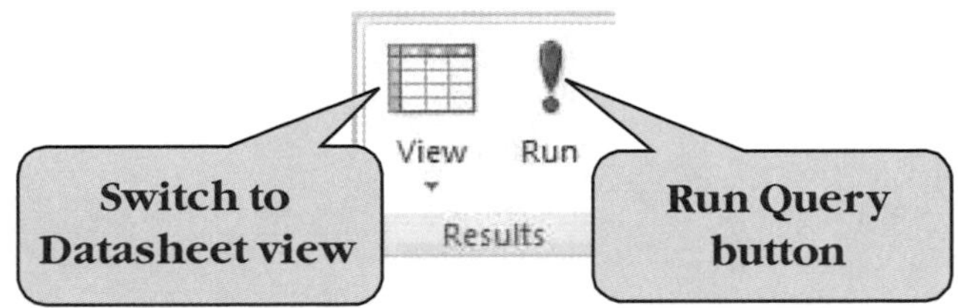

To Run a Query from the Navigation Pane

1. Select **Queries** from the Navigation Pane drop-down menu.
2. **Double-click** the name of the query that you wish to run.

Let's Try It!

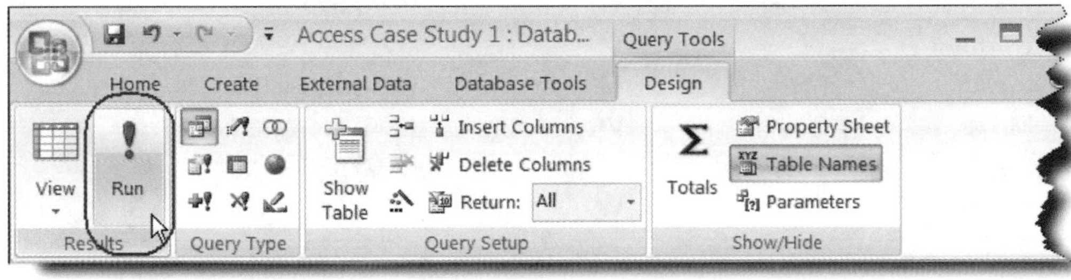

- Click the **Run icon** on the toolbar.

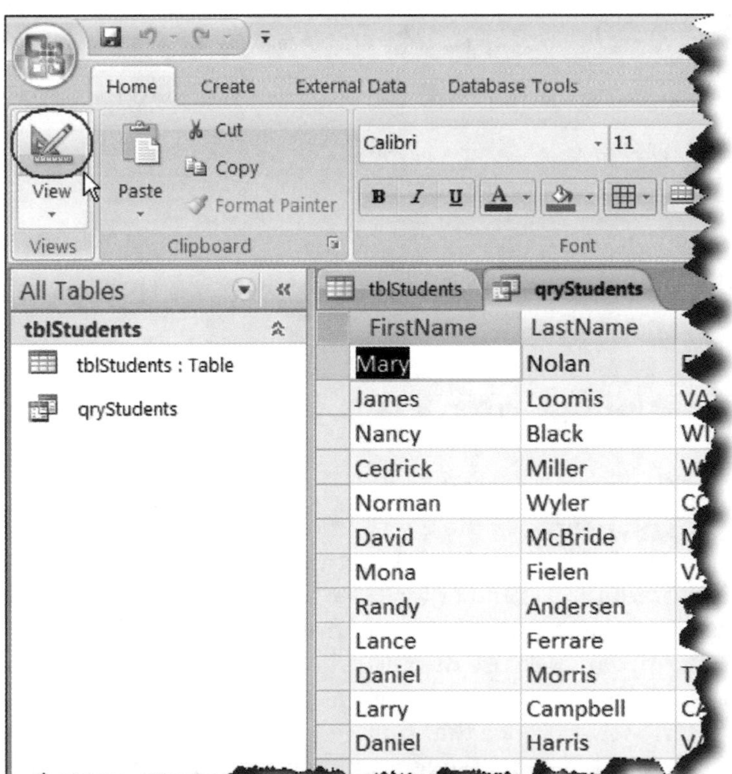

Runs the query and displays the result set.

- Click the **View** button on the Ribbon.

Switches back to Design View.

- Click the **View** icon again on the Ribbon.

Runs the query and displays the result set.

- Click the query's **close button**.

Closes the query.

- Double-click **qryStudents** on Navigation Pane on the left.

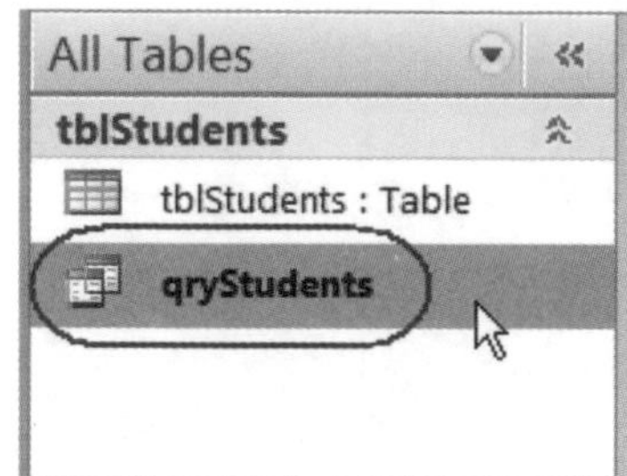

- Opens qryStudents in Datasheet View (in other words, we run the query).

FirstName	LastName	State	Phone
Mary	Nolan	FL	(414) 555-5242
James	Loomis	VA	(906) 555-3465
Nancy	Black	WI	(414) 555-4495
Cedrick	Miller	WI	(414) 555-0601
Norman	Wyler	CO	(720) 555-9062
David	McBride	MI	(414) 555-2702
Mona	Fielen	VA	(906) 555-2308
Randy	Andersen	WI	(262) 555-9215
Lance	Ferrare	VA	(307) 555-4325
Daniel	Morris	TX	(972) 555-6547
Larry	Campbell	CA	(902) 555-1061
Daniel	Harris	VA	(719) 555-5736

- Click the query's **Close** button.

Closes the qryStudents query.

Adding Criteria to a Query

In this section, you will learn how to add criteria to a query.

The **criteria row** of the query grid is where you enter the limits to identify the specific records you wish to return. For example, instead of viewing all of our customers, we could enter "**CA**" in the criteria row for the State field. When we run the query, only customers from the state of California would be returned.

You can also use numerical expressions as your criteria. If you wanted to see all products whose cost was greater than $20, you would enter: **>20** in the criteria row. Notice that numerical expressions are not surrounded in quotes whereas string (text) expessions must be enclosed in quotation marks.

To Specify Criteria for a Query

1. Click in the **Criteria** row of the field whose results you wish to limit.
2. Type in the criteria that must be met.

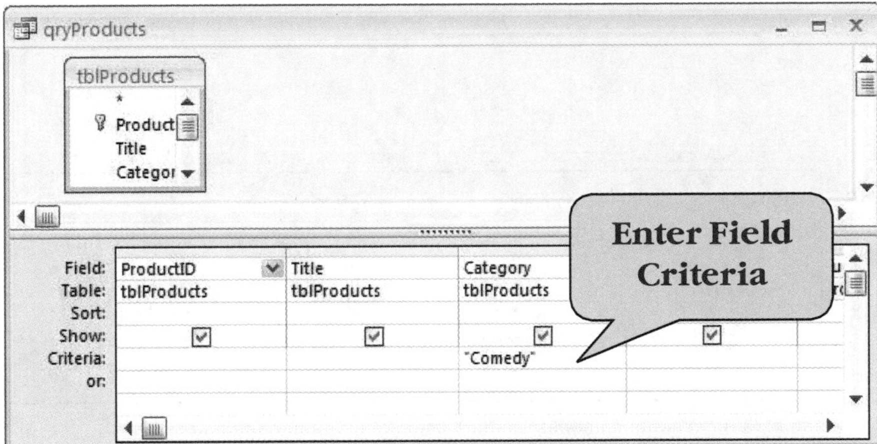

Let's Try It!

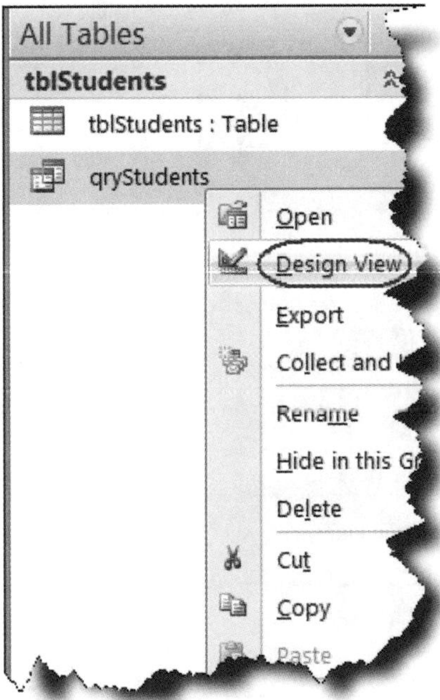

- Right-click on the **qryStudents** query.

Displays the contextual menu.

- Select **Design View** from the contextual menu.

Opens qryStudents in Design View.

- In the **Criteria** row for the **State** field, type: **"VA"**.

Enters the criteria that must be met. In this case, we wish to see only those students who reside in Virginia.

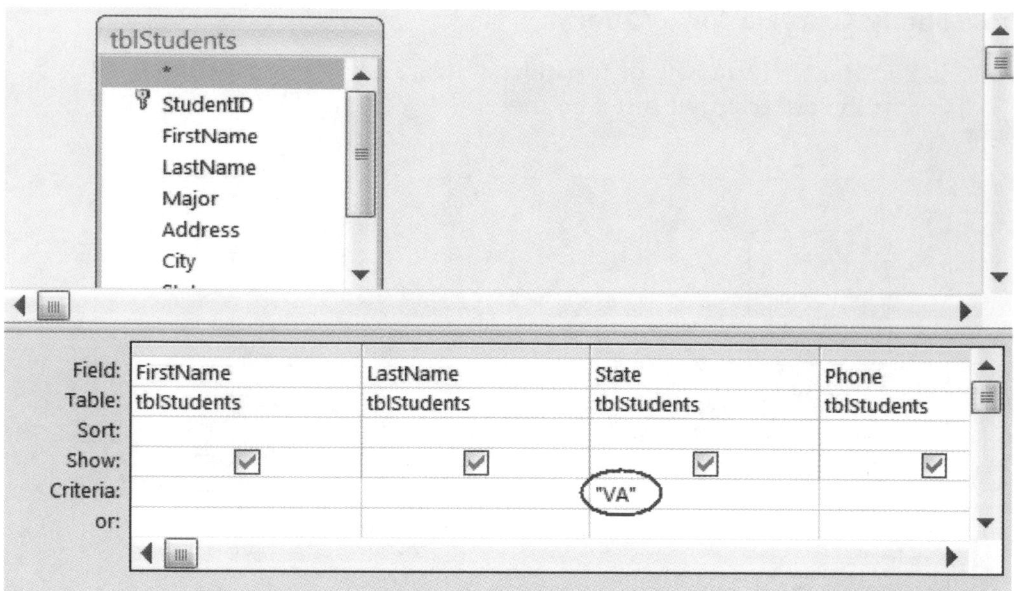

- Click the **Save** button on the Quick Access toolbar.

Saves the design changes that we have made to the query.

- Click the **Run** button.

Displays the results of the query.

FirstName	LastName	State	Phone
Daniel	Harris	VA	(719) 555-5736
James	Loomis	VA	(906) 555-3465
Mona	Fielen	VA	(906) 555-2308
Lance	Ferrare	VA	(307) 555-4325

Specifying Multiple Criteria

In this section, you will learn how to add more than one limit to a query.

As you work more with queries, you will inevitably want to add more than one limit to a query. For instance, you may wish to see a list of all customers who live in the state of Colorado **and** who rented Comedy or Adventure films.

To specify an **OR** condition for the **same field**, separate each limit by the **Or** operator. In the example below, any films with the category of Comedy or Adventure will be returned.

Field:	ProductID	Title	Category
Table:	tblProducts	tblProducts	tblProducts
Sort:		Ascending	
Show:	☑	☑	☑
Criteria:			"Comedy" Or "Adventure"
or:			

Separate each limit in the same field with the "OR" operator

To specify an **OR** condition for **two different fields**, enter each limit on a different row as in the example below.

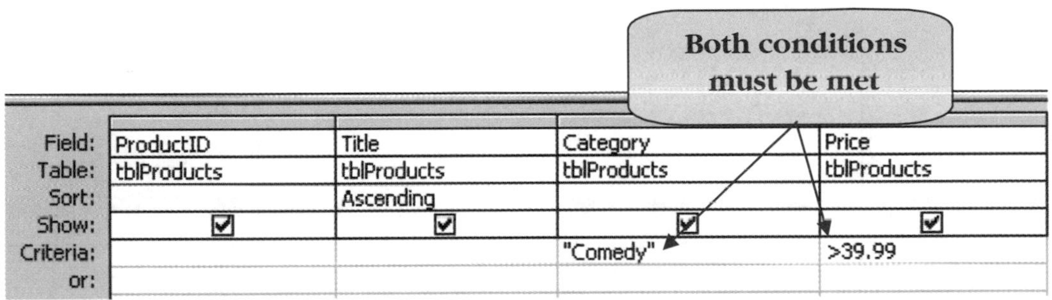

Field:	ProductID	Title	Category	Price
Table:	tblProducts	tblProducts	tblProducts	tblProducts
Sort:		Ascending		
Show:	☑	☑	☑	☑
Criteria:			"Comedy"	
or:				>"$29.99"

To create a query where two or more conditions must be met, enter the criteria on the same row. For instance, you might wish to see all comedy films that cost more than $39.99. You would enter both criteria on the same criteria row, as shown below. This is referred to as an **AND condition**.

Both conditions must be met

Field:	ProductID	Title	Category	Price
Table:	tblProducts	tblProducts	tblProducts	tblProducts
Sort:		Ascending		
Show:	☑	☑	☑	☑
Criteria:			"Comedy"	>39.99
or:				

To Specify Multiple Criteria in a Query

1. For **OR** criteria in the same field, separate each limit by the word OR.
2. For OR criteria in different fields, enter each limit on a separate criteria line.
3. To specify **AND** criteria, enter all limits on the same criteria line.

Let's Try It!

- Click on the **View** button to open qryStudents in the Design View.

Opens qryStudents in Design View so we can enter our criteria.

Notice that we already have a limit of "VA" for the State field.

- Place your cursor after the word "VA" and then type: **OR "WI"**.

Enters a multiple "Or" criteria for the Category field. Students with either a State of "VA" or "WI" will be returned in the results.

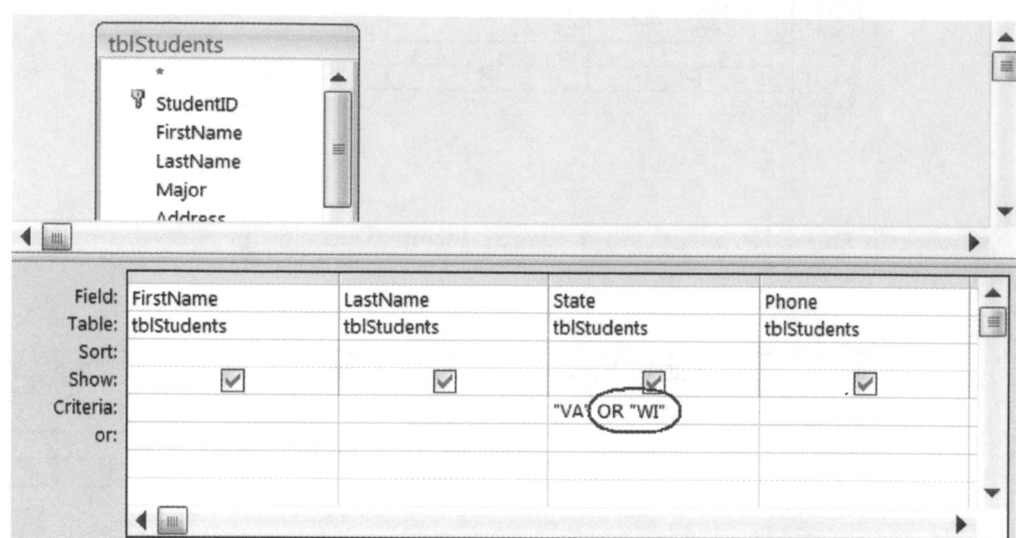

- Click the **Run** button.

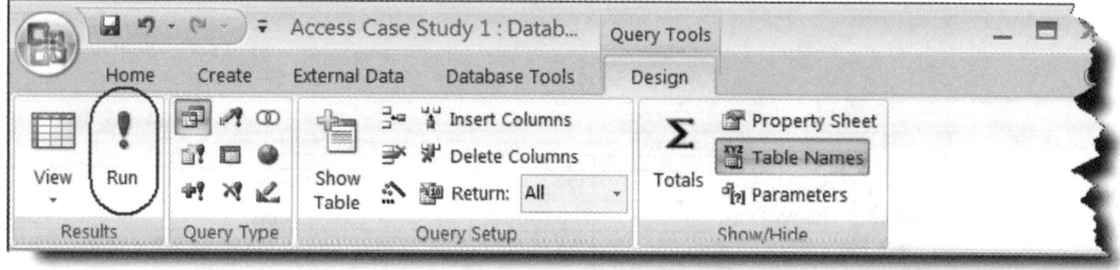

All students from State of VA or WI are returned.

- Click the query's **Close** button.

FirstName	LastName	State	Phone
Daniel	Harris	VA	(719) 555-5736
James	Loomis	VA	(906) 555-3465
Nancy	Black	WI	(414) 555-4495
Cedrick	Miller	WI	(414) 555-0601
Mona	Fielen	VA	(906) 555-2308
Randy	Andersen	WI	(262) 555-9215
Lance	Ferrare	VA	(307) 555-4325
*			

- Click **No** when asked to save your changes.

Closes qryStudents. The criteria changes we made will not be saved.

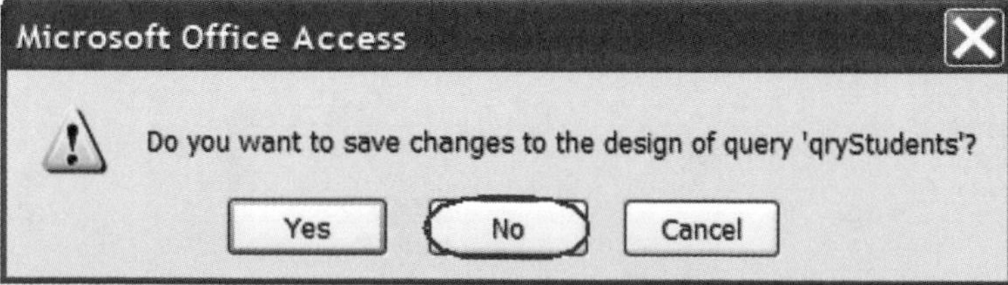

Sorting Data in a Query

In this section, you will learn how to sort the results of a query.

To make the results of your query easier to work with, you will most likely wish to **sort** the query results in some logical order. To sort a query by a particular field, click in the sort field and then choose either **Ascending** (A–Z) or **Descending** (Z–A) from the drop-down list.

You can sort by more than one query field. Access sorts from left to right. In the example below, the data would first be sorted by Category, and then by price within each category.

Field:	ProductID	Title	Category	Price	Acquired
Table:	tblProducts	tblProducts	tblProducts	tblProducts	tblProducts
Sort:			Ascending	Ascending	
Show:	☑	☑	☑	☑	☑
Criteria:					
or:					

ACCESS SORTS FROM LEFT TO RIGHT

To Sort the Results of a Query

1. Click in the **Sort** row for the field you wish to sort.
2. Click the **arrow** and then choose either **Ascending** or **Descending** order.
3. To remove a sort, click in the Sort row and then choose (**not sorted**) from the drop-down list.

Let's Try It!

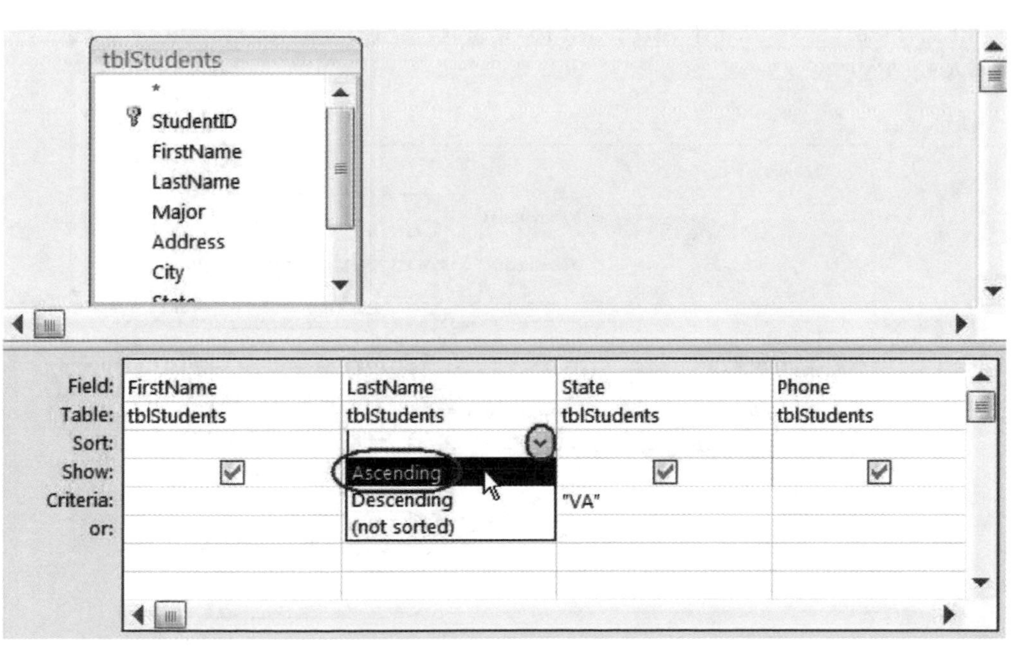

- Open **qryStudents** in **Design View**.

Opens qryStudents In Design View.

- Click in the **Sort** cell for the **LastName** field.

Displays the drop-down arrow for the Category field.

- Click the arrow and then choose **Ascending** from the drop-down list.

Sets the sort order for the LastName field to Ascending.

- Click the **Save** button on the Quick Access toolbar.

Saves the query design changes.

- Click the **Run** button and observe the results.

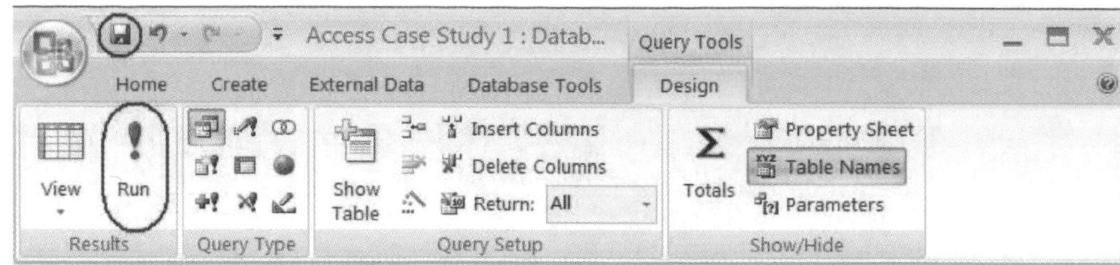

Displays the sorted query results.

FirstName	LastName	State	Phone
Lance	Ferrare	VA	(307) 555-4325
Mona	Fielen	VA	(906) 555-2308
Daniel	Harris	VA	(719) 555-5736
James	Loomis	VA	(906) 555-3465

Using the Query Wizard

In this section, you will learn how to create a query using the Query Wizard.

Rather than create your queries manually, you can use the **Simple Query Wizard** to help you build your query. The Simple Query Wizard steps you through the process of creating a query. You will be first prompted to choose the table and table fields upon which to base your query. Next, you select the desired view (Detail or Summary), and then provide a name for your query. That last step asks you if you want to open your query in Datasheet View or in Design View.

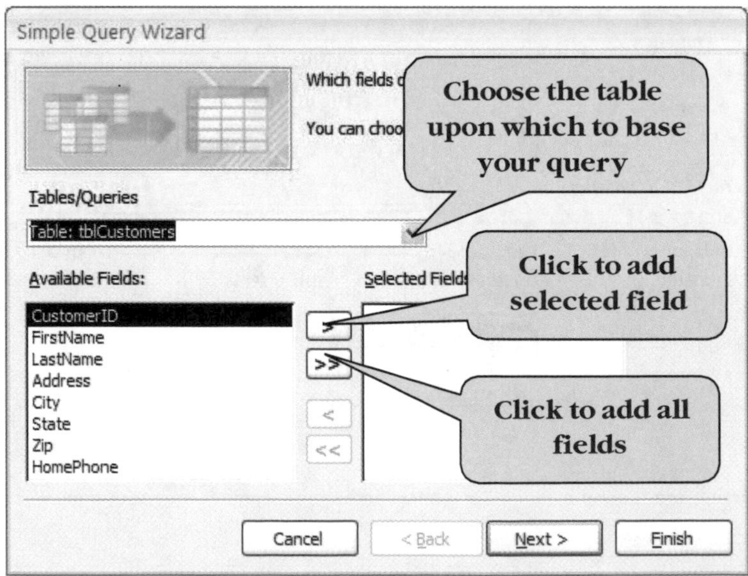

To Create a Query Using the Query Wizard

1. Select **Queries** in the Navigation Pane
2. Click the **Create** tab on the Ribbon.
3. Click the **Query Wizard** button on the Ribbon.

4. Select **Simple Query Wizard** and then click **OK**.
5. From the **Tables/Queries** drop-down list, choose the table or query upon which to base your new query.
6. Choose fields to add to the query by clicking the > button to add the selected field. Repeat for all desired fields.
7. To add all fields to the query, click the >> button.
8. Click **Next**.
9. Enter a name for your query in the "**What title do you want for your query?**" box.
10. Choose whether to view the query's design (Design View) or whether to open the query to view information (Datasheet View).
11. Click **Finish**.

Let's Try It!

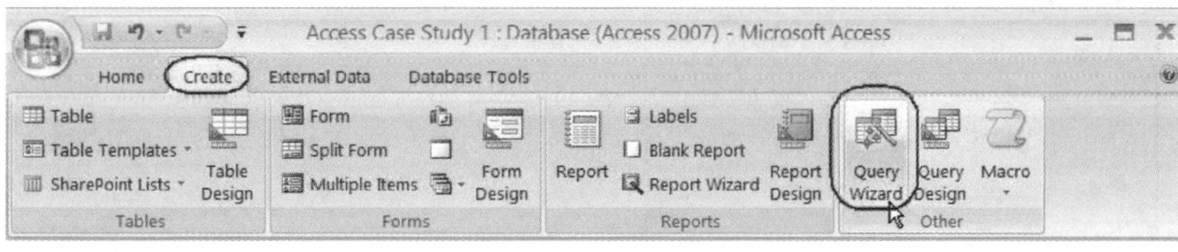

- Click on the **Create** tab.
- Click the **Query Wizard** button on the Ribbon.

Displays the New Query dialog box.

- Ensure that **Simple Query Wizard** is selected and then click **OK**.

Displays the first step of the query wizard.

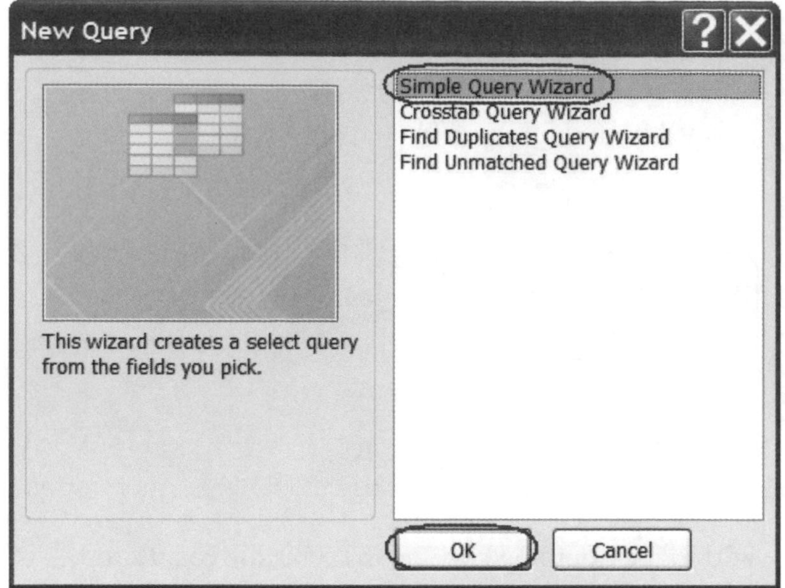

- Click the arrow on the right of the **Tables/Queries** combo box and then select **tblStudents** from the drop-down list.

Selects the table upon which we want to base our new query.

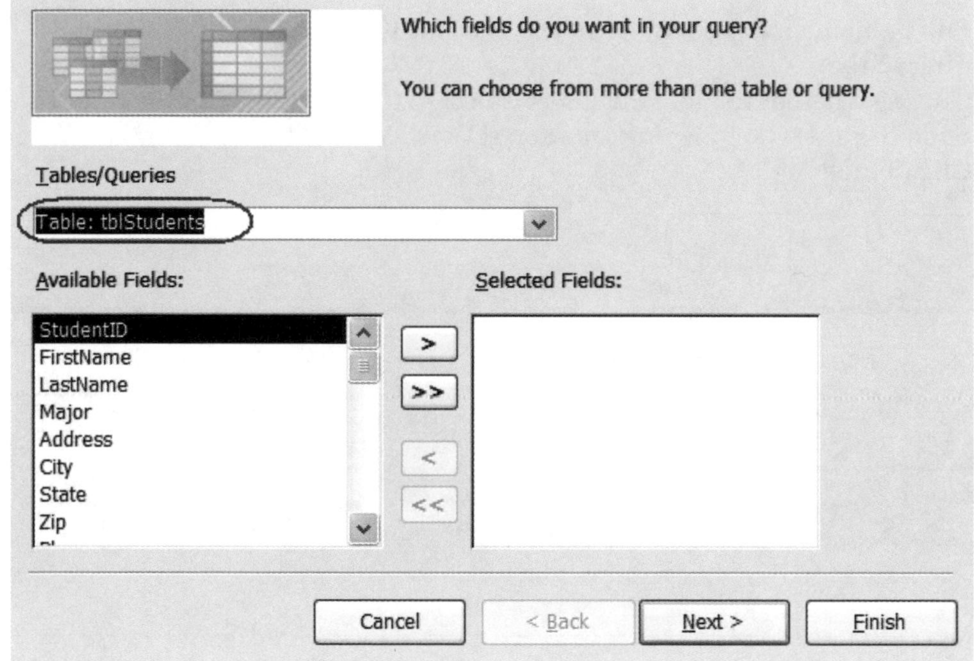

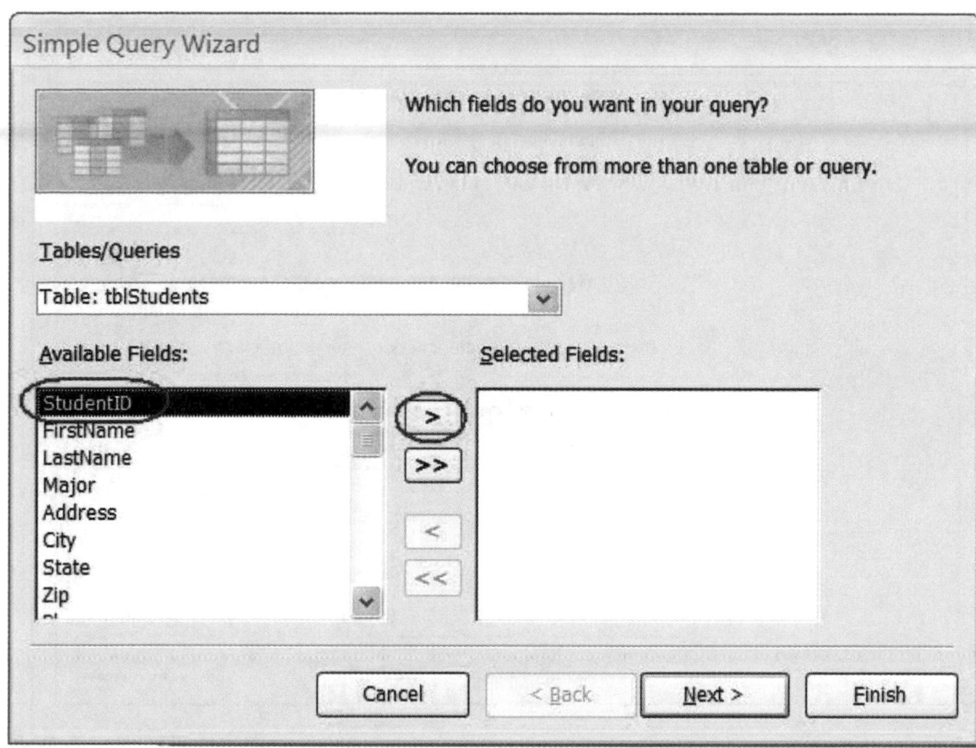

- Select the **StudentID** field in the **Available Fields** window and then click the **>** button.

Selects the StudentID field to be added to our query.

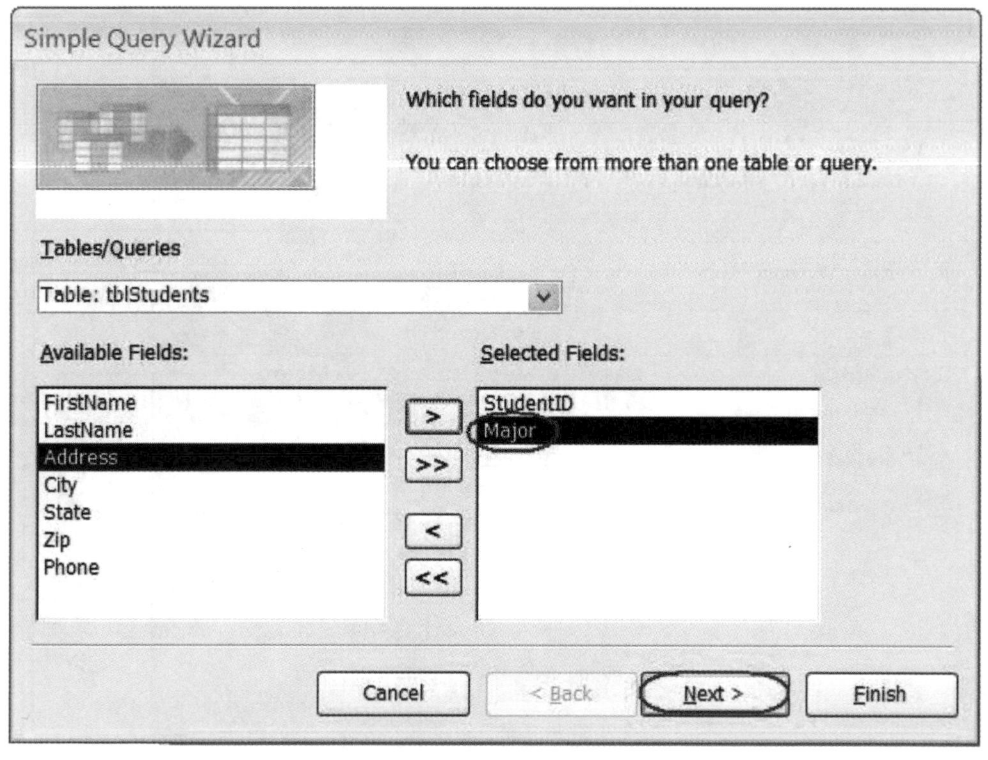

- Select the **Major** field in the **Available Fields** window and then click the **>** button.

Selects the Major field to be added to our query.

- Click **Next**.

Moves to the next step of the wizard.

- In the **Title box**, type: **qryStudentList**.

Enters a name for our query.

- Click the **Open the query to view information** radio button and then click **Finish**.

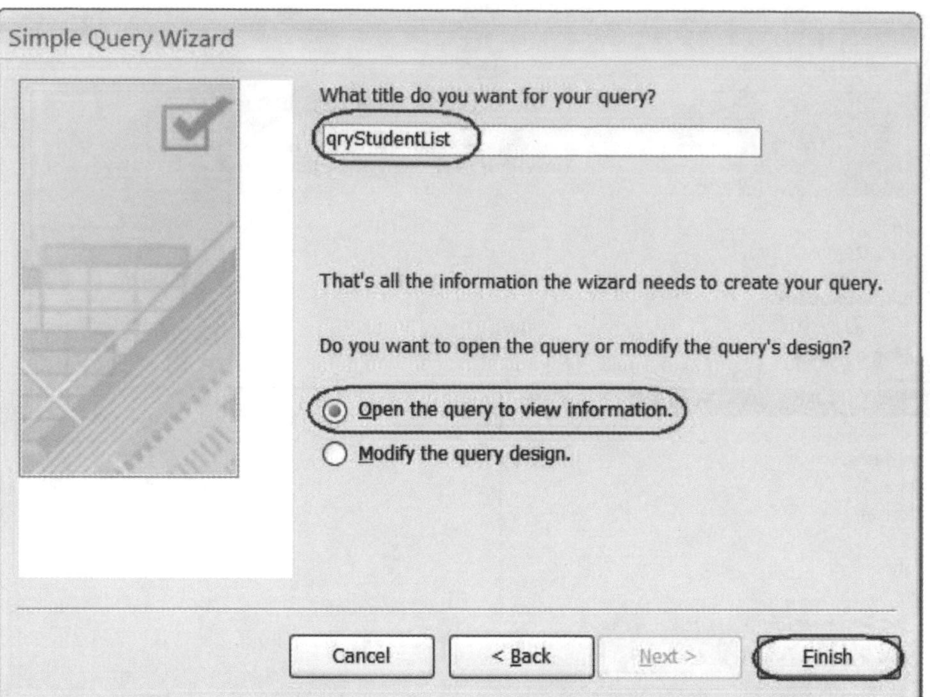

Opens the query in Datasheet View.

- Click the query's **Close** button.

Closes the qryStudentList query.

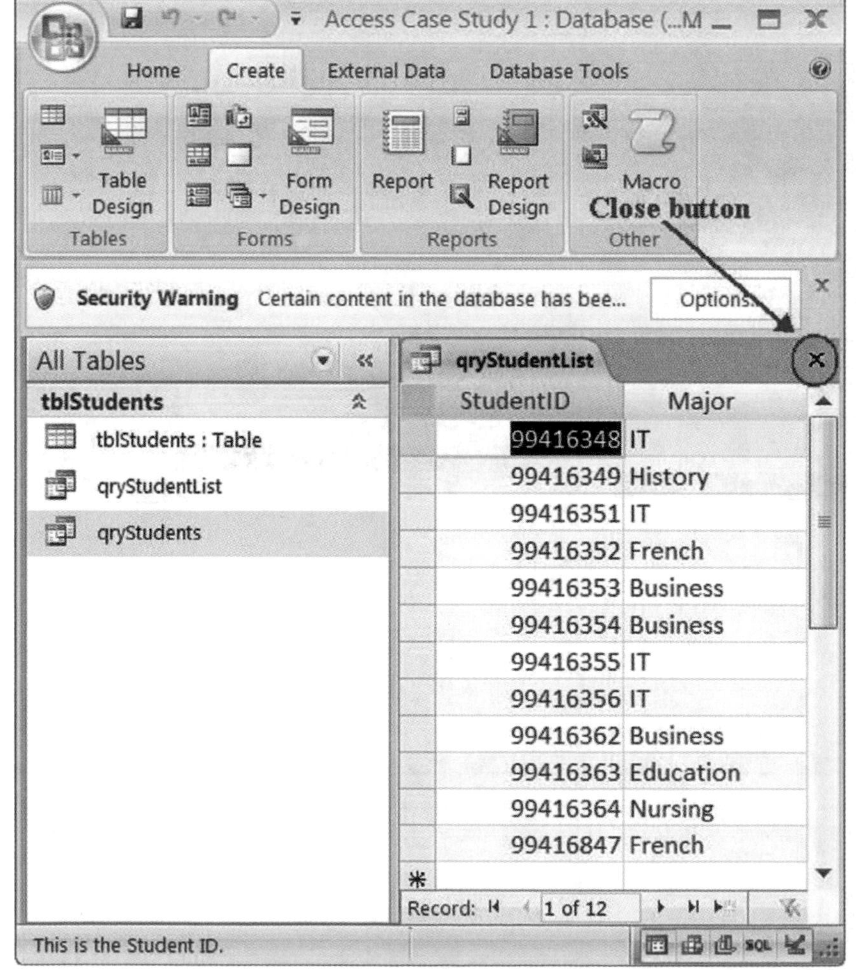

Using the Form Wizard

This section will guide you through the process of creating a form with the Form Wizard.

A **form** is an interface between the user and the data, utilized primarily to enter, edit or display data in a database. The form window contains labels (descriptive text), text boxes, combo boxes, radio buttons etc. that are bound to the data in your table and can help make your database more user-friendly. Entering or changing data in a form automatically enters or changes it in the underlying table.

Using the **Form Wizard** is the easiest way of creating a form. The Form Wizard is similar to the Query Wizard that we worked with in the last chapter—it will step you through the process of creating a form. While you can create a form from scratch, using the Form Wizard is much easier and much quicker.

You may want to consider creating a query upon which to base your form, rather than using a table as the form's data source. Using a query allows you to filter the data that is displayed in the form and provides more flexibility in sorting your data.

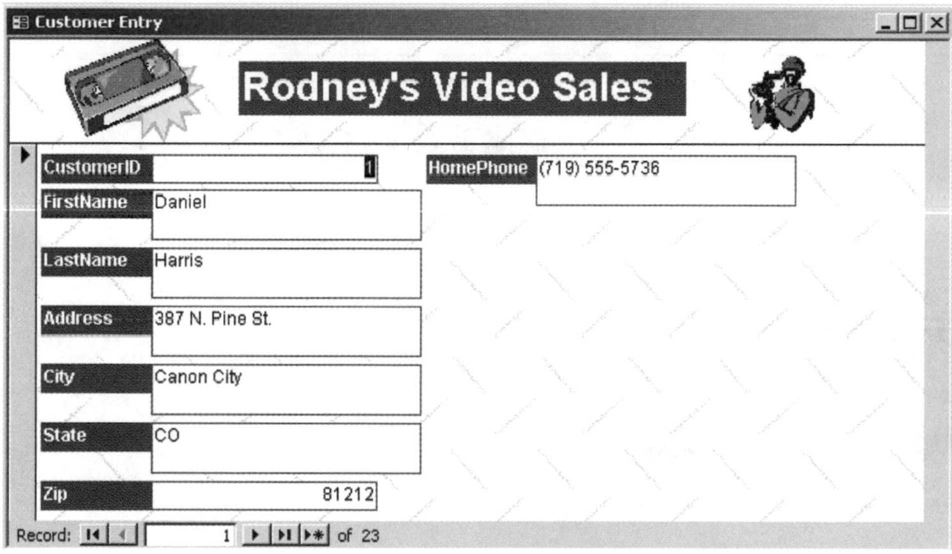

To Create a Form Using the Form Wizard

1. Click the **Create** tab on the Ribbon.
2. Click the **More Forms** button, and select **Form Wizard**.
3. From the **Tables/Queries** drop-down list, choose the table or query upon which to base your new report.
4. Choose fields to add to the report by clicking the > button to add the selected field. Repeat for all desired fields.
5. To add all fields to the form, click the >> button.
6. Click **Next**.
7. Choose the desired layout for your form.
8. Click **Next**.
9. Choose the desired style for your form.

10. Click **Next**.
11. Enter a **name** for your form.
12. Choose whether to view the form's design (Design View) or whether to open the form to view or enter information (Form view).
13. Click **Finish**.

Let's Try It!

- Click the **Create** tab.

Displays commands for creating Access objects.

- Under the **Forms** command set, click the **More Forms button** and the click **Form Wizard**.

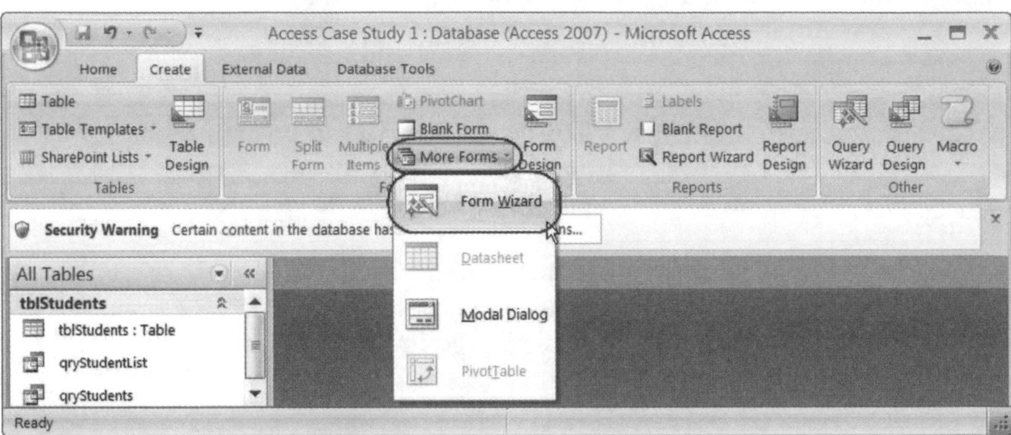

Launches the Form Wizard.

- Click the arrow on the right of the **Tables/Queries** combo box and then select **tblStudents** from the drop-down list.

Selects the query upon which we want to base our new form.

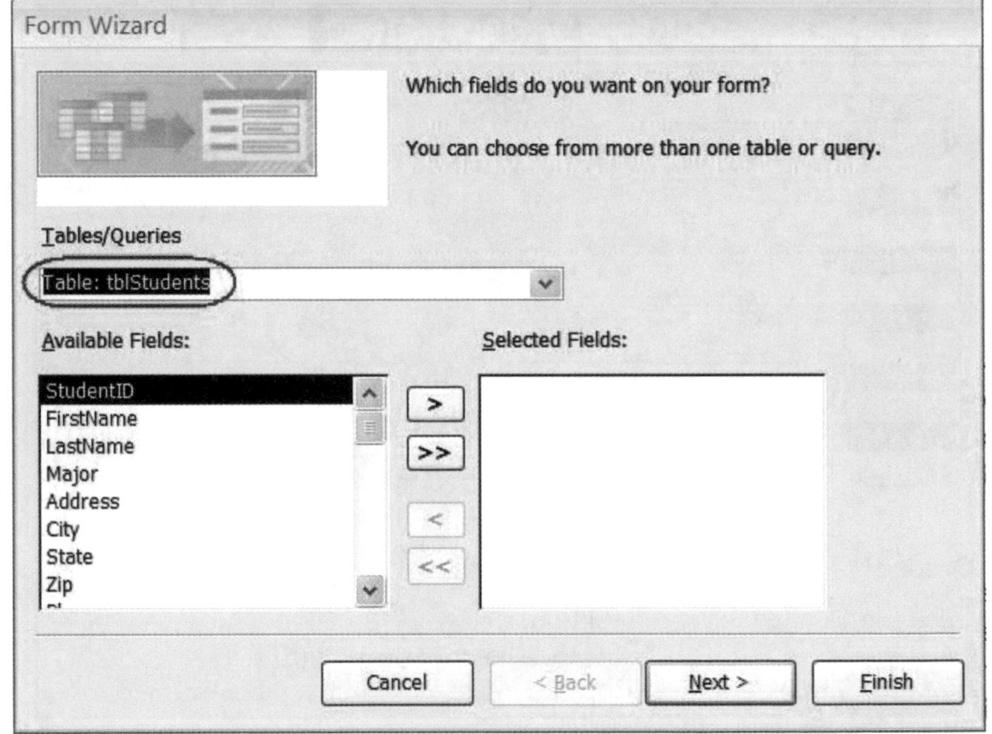

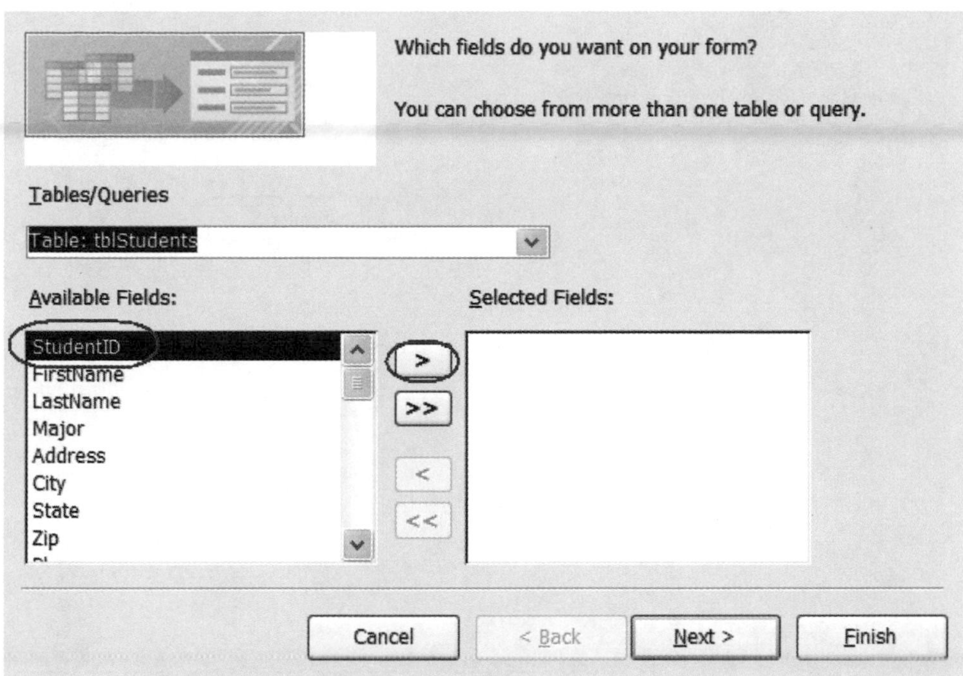

- Select the **StudentID** field in the **Available Fields** window and then click the **>** button.

Selects the StudentID field to be added to our form.

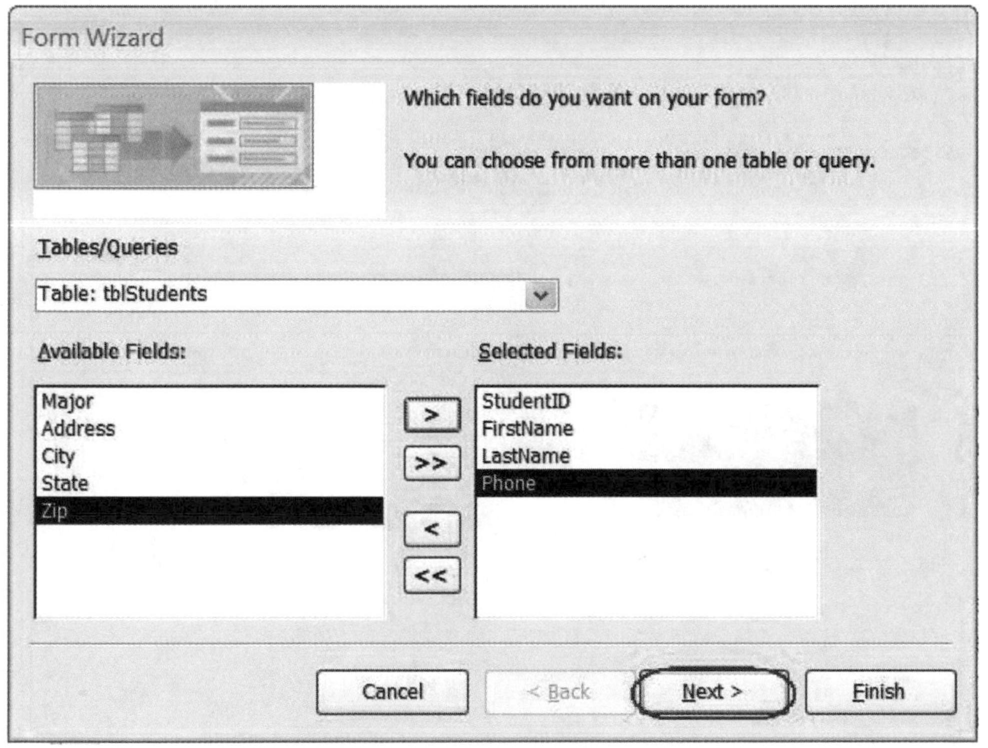

- **Repeat** the last step for the following fields:

FirstName

LastName

Phone

Adds the fields, FirstName, LastName and Phone fields to the form.

- Click **Next**.

Moves to the next step of the Wizard.

- Ensure that **Columnar** is selected as shown and then click **Next**.

Selects Columnar for our form layout and then moves to the next step of the Wizard.

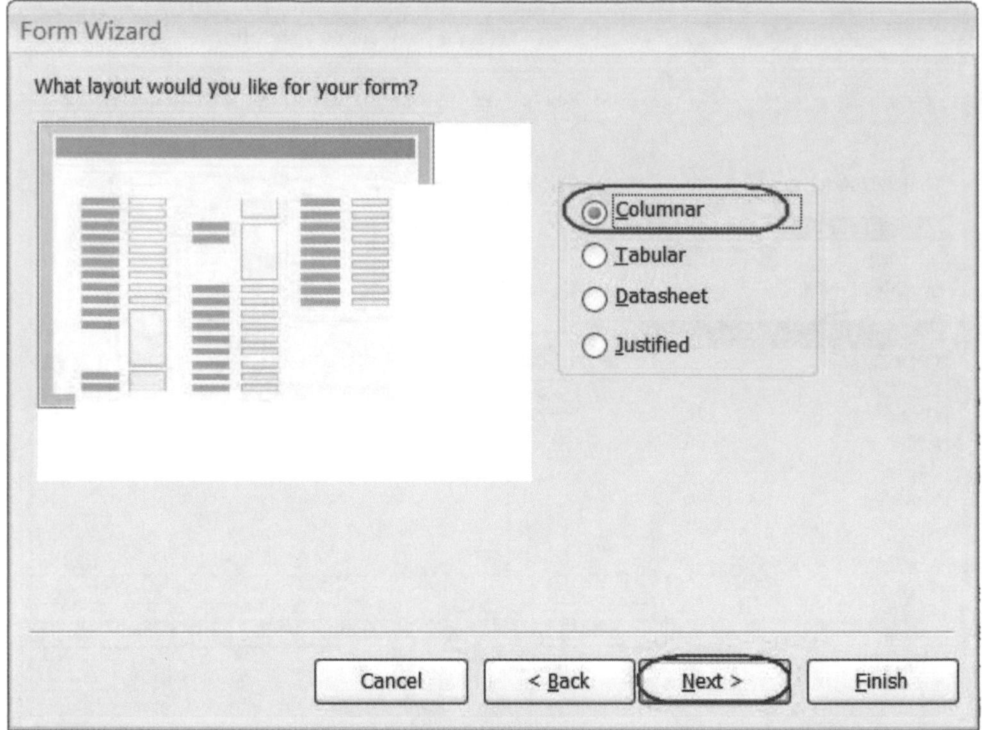

- Select **Metro** for the **Form Style** and then click **Next**.

Selects the form style (or format) for our new form and then moves to the next step of the Wizard.

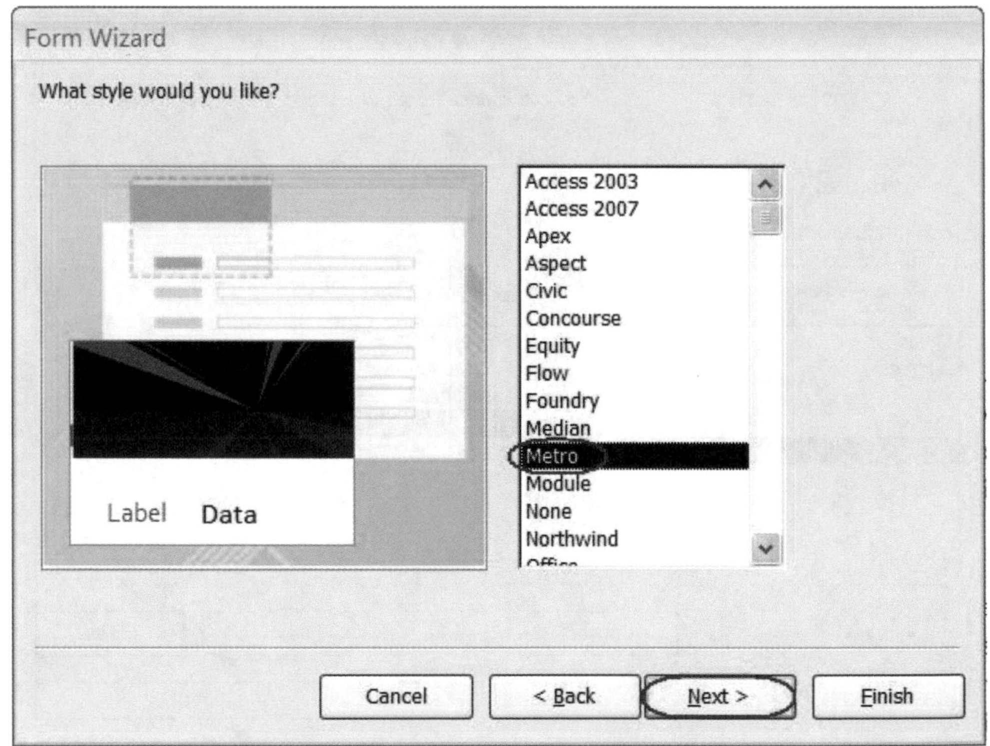

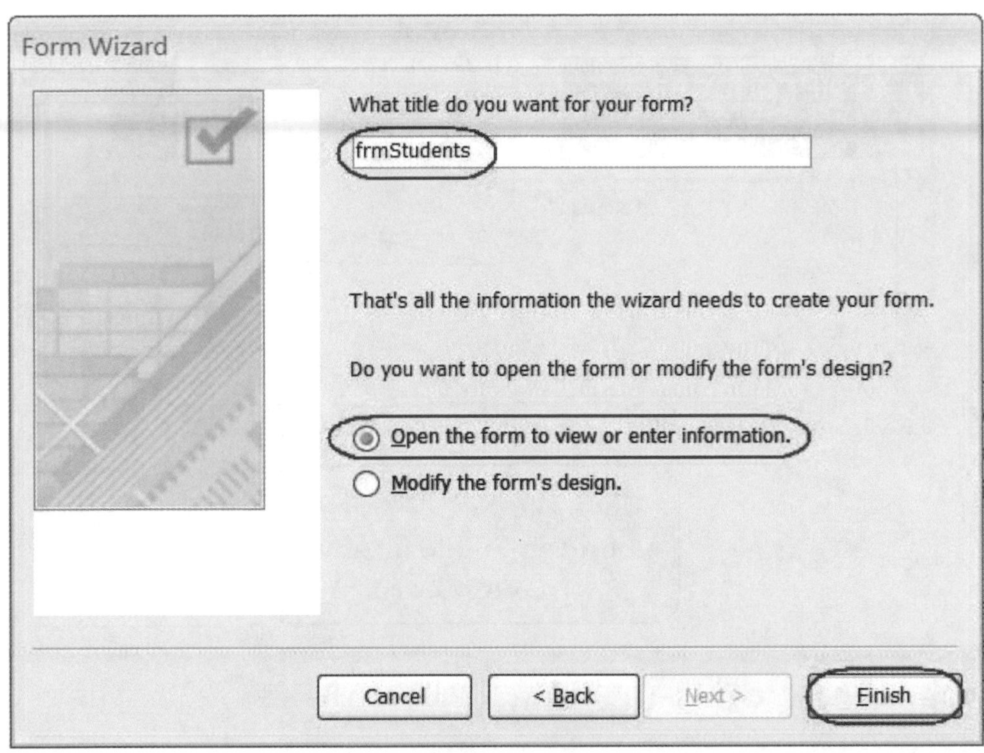

- Type: **frmStudents** in the form title box.

Enters the name for the form.

- Ensure that **Open the form to view or enter information** is selected, and then click **Finish**.

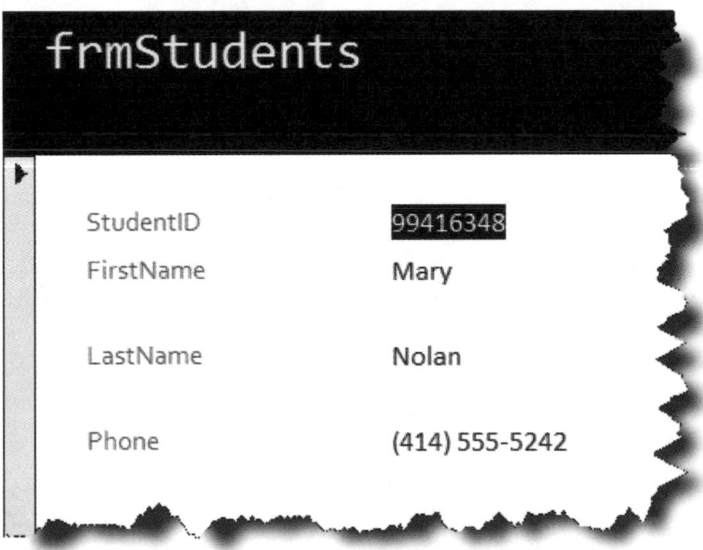

Opens the form in Form View.

Entering Data into a Form

In this section, you will learn how to enter new data into a form.

Similar to tables, the navigation bar on the bottom of the form window allows you to move from one record to another. Clicking the **New Record** button creates a new blank record.

To enter data into a form, click in the first blank text box and begin typing. Pressing the **Tab** key moves you from one field on your form to another. When the cursor is in the last text box of the form, press the Tab key to insert a new blank record.

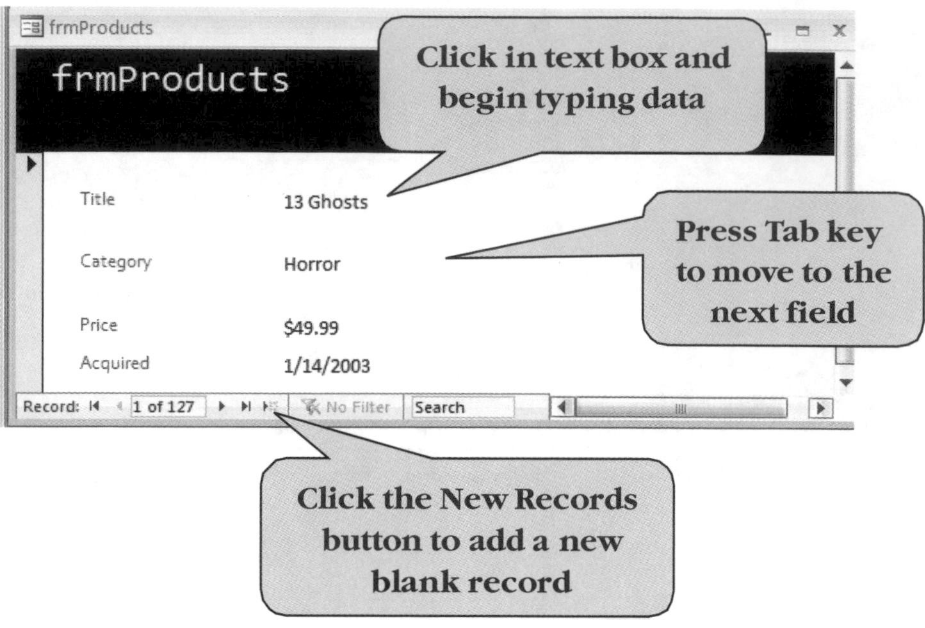

To Enter New Data into a Form

1. In **Form View**, click the **New Record** button.
2. Click in the first text box where you wish to begin entering data.
3. Click **Tab** to move to the next field.
4. To add another new record, click the **New Record button**.
   Or
   Press the **Tab** key when the cursor is in the last field of the form.

Let's Try It!

- Click the **New Record** navigation button.

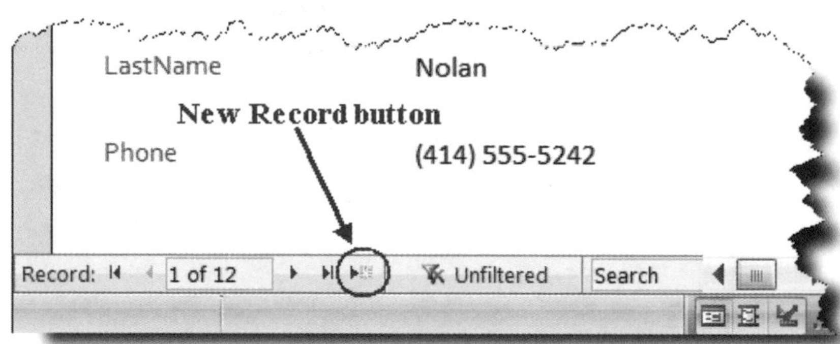

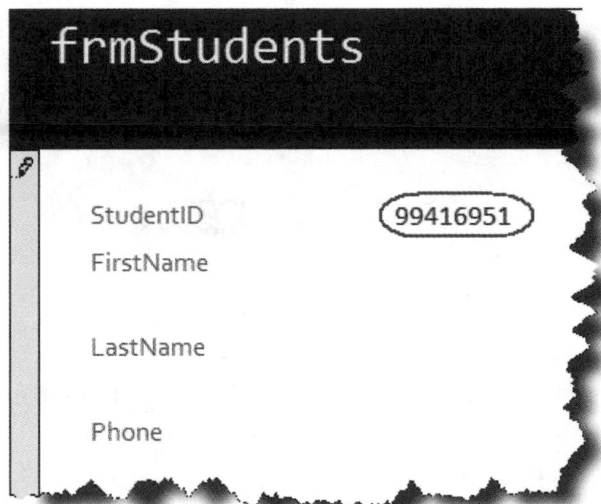

Inserts a new blank record.

- Type: **99416951** for StudentID field.

Enters data for the StudentID field.

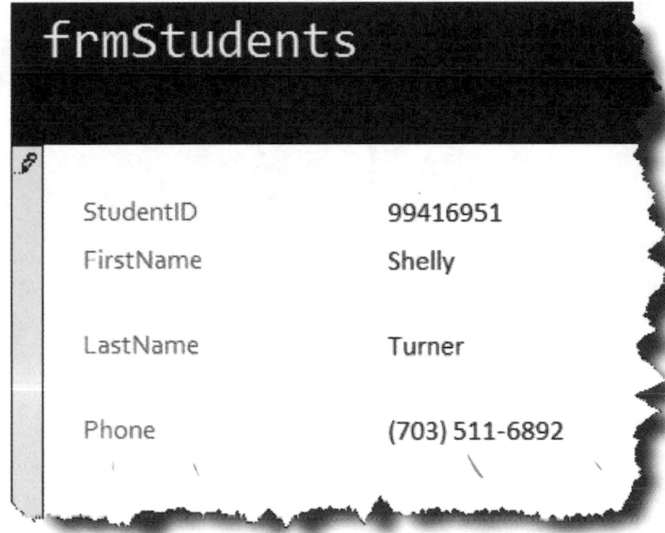

- Press the **Tab** key.

Moves to the FirstName field.

- Type: **Shelly** and then press the **Tab** key.

Enters data for the FirstName field and then moves to the LastName field.

- Type: **Turner** and then press the **Tab** key.

Enters data for the LastName field and then moves to the Phone field.

- Type: **(703) 511-6892** and then press the **Tab** key.

Enters data for the Phone field and then inserts a new blank record.

- Click on the **Previous Record** button.

Shows the previous student record.

- Click on the **First Record** button.

Shows the first student record.

- Click on the **Next Record** button.

Shows the second student record.

- Click on the **Last Record** button.

Shows the last student record.

- Click the form's Close button.

Closes the frmStudents form.

- Click the **Save** button on the Quick Access Toolbar.

Saves our design changes.

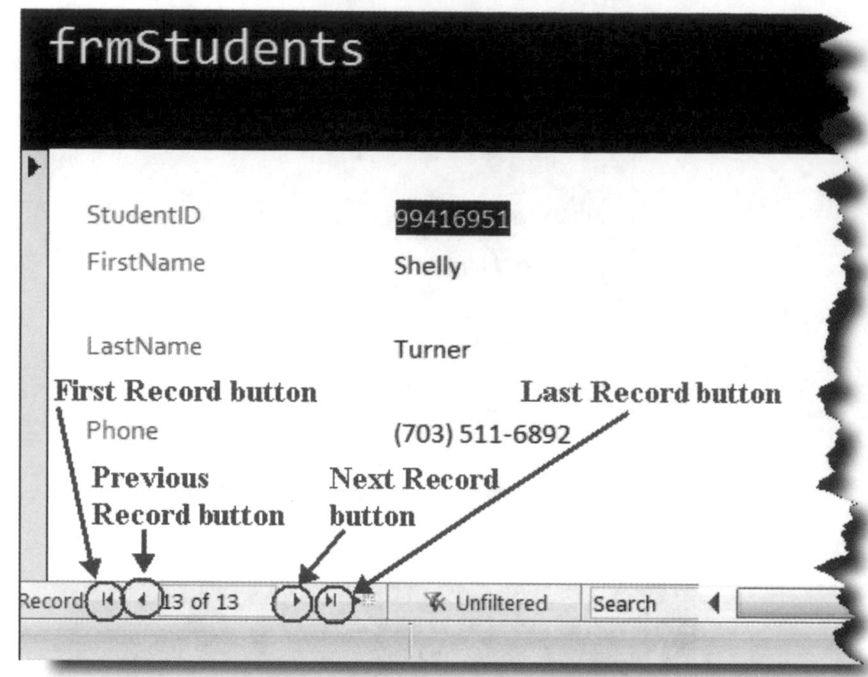

Creating a Basic Report

In this section, you will create a Basic Report.

As with the other objects we have worked with so far, Access also has wizards that help you create reports. If you remember, reports are Access objects that represent your data in printed form. Reports can be based upon either tables or queries, although basing your report upon a query allows you maximum flexibility. Reports, unlike Forms, Queries and Tables do not allow you to make any changes to the data.

The fastest and easiest way to create a report is using a **Basic Report**. A Basic Report creates a "quick-and-dirty" columnar report, based on all fields in the selected table or query. You do not have the option of choosing which fields to include in your report. To only include specific fields in your Basic Report, you may wish to create a query with the fields you want included in your report, and then create a report based on that new query.

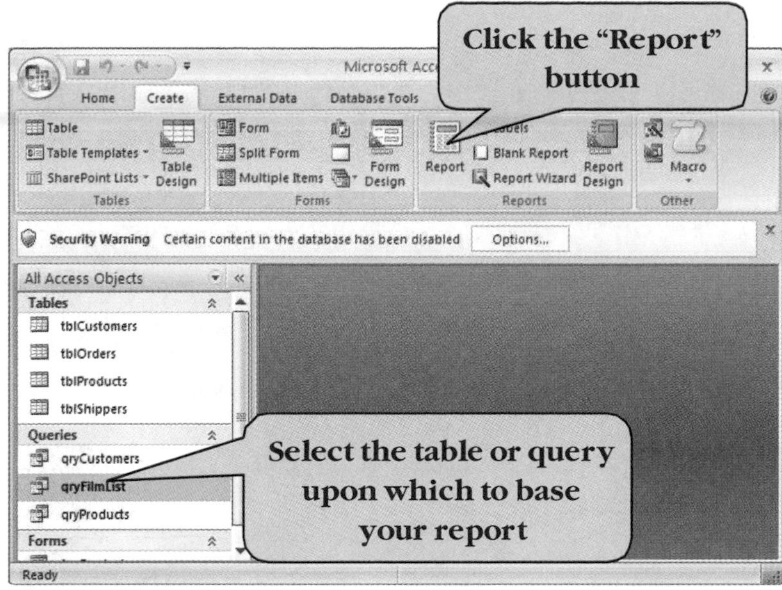

To Create an AutoReport

1. In the Navigation pane, select the query or table upon which to base your report.
2. Click the **Create** tab.
3. Click the **Report** button on the Ribbon.

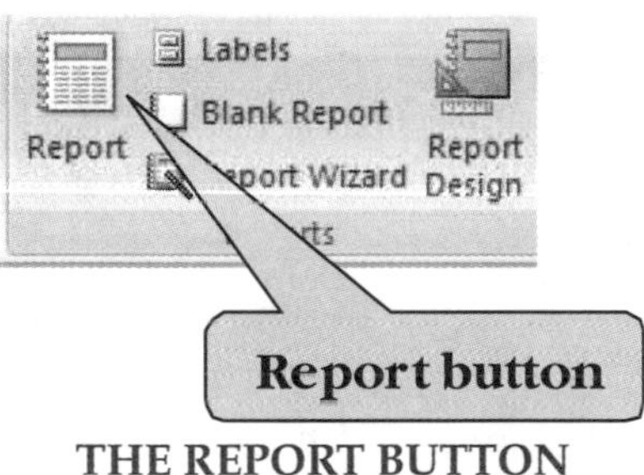

THE REPORT BUTTON

Let's Try It!

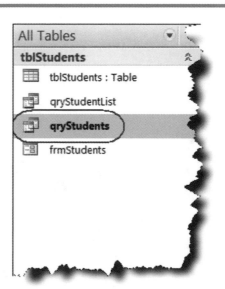

- Click on **qryStudents** in the Navigation Pane.

Selects the query upon which to base our report.

- Click the **Create** tab.

Displays commands for creating Access objects.

- Click the **Report** button on the ribbon on the Reports command set.

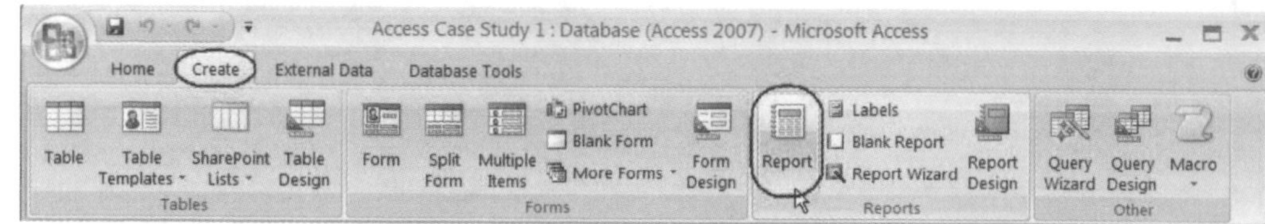

- Create a basic report based upon qryStudents and displays the Report in Layout view.

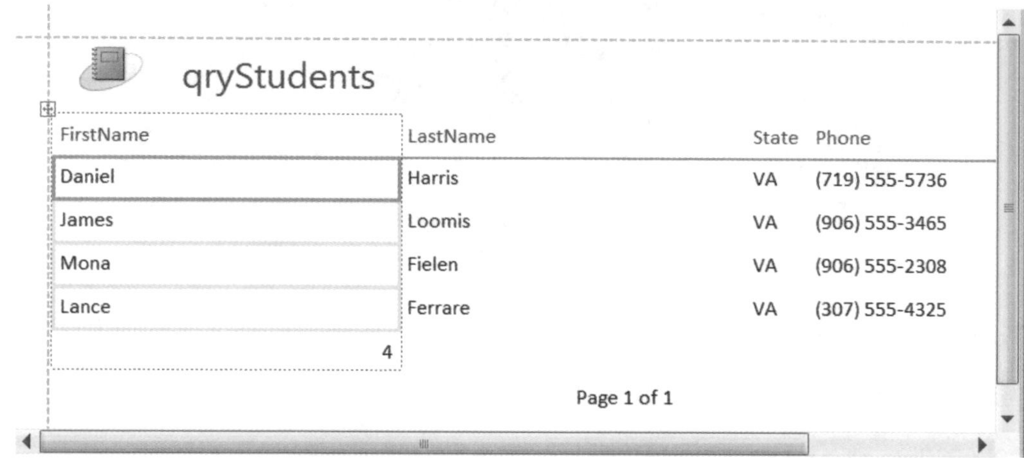

AutoFormatting a Report

In this section, you will learn how to AutoFormat a Report.

Once your report is created, the contextual tab displays three sets of report tools: Format, Arrange and Page Setup. Under the Format tab is the **AutoFormat** command button, which allows you to apply quick formatting by choosing from a gallery of styles. The gallery of styles contains preset formatting that you can quickly apply to your report. Hold your mouse pointer over a style to view the style name.

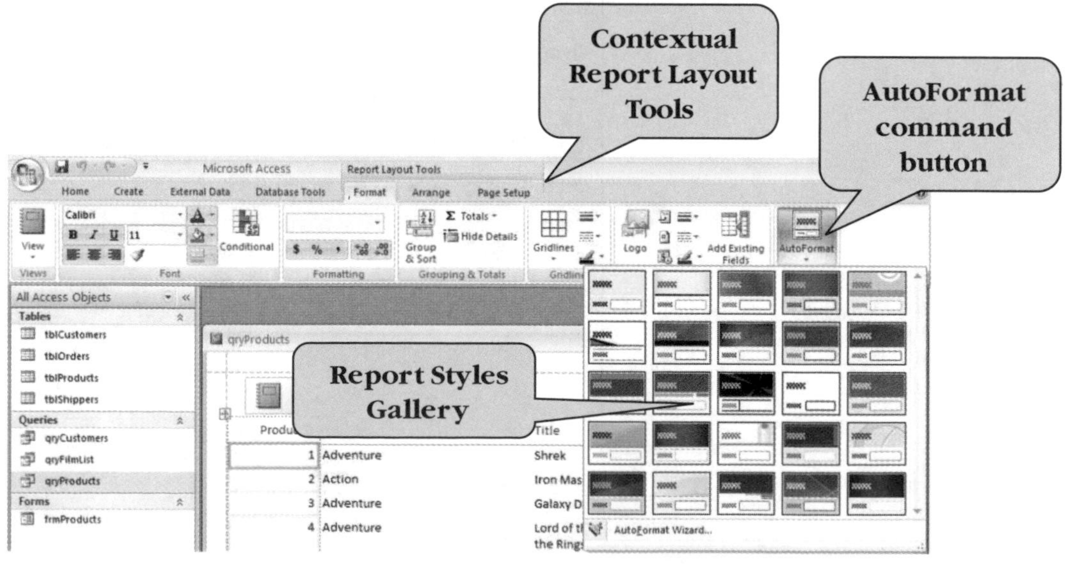

To Apply a Style to a Report

1. Display the Report in Design View or Layout View.
2. Click the **AutoFormat** button under the Format tab under the Report Layout Tools to display the Style Gallery.
3. Click the desired style from the Gallery.

Let's Try It!

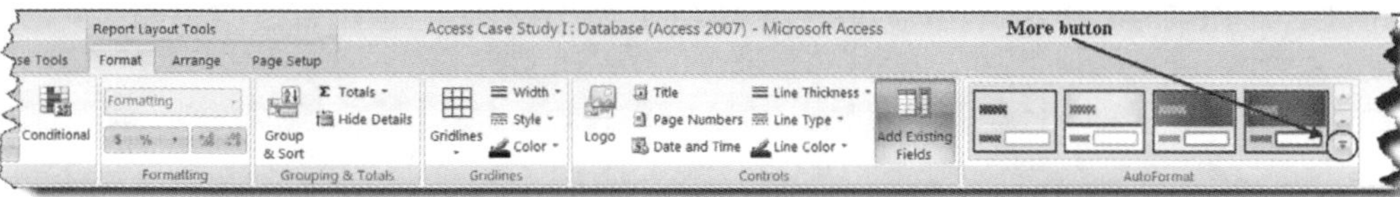

- Click the **More button** on the AutoFormat command group under the Format tab.

Displays the Style Gallery.

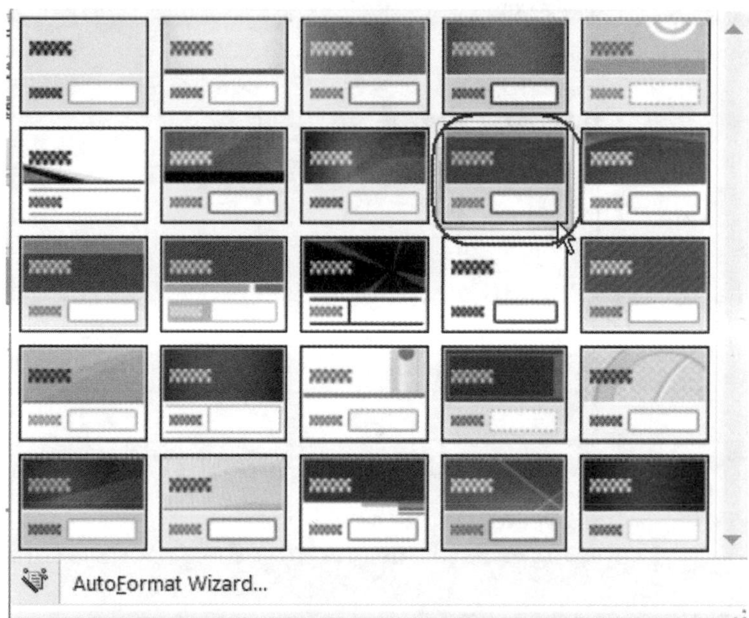

- Click the **Equity** style in the 2nd row, 4th column as shown.

Applies the Equity style to the report.

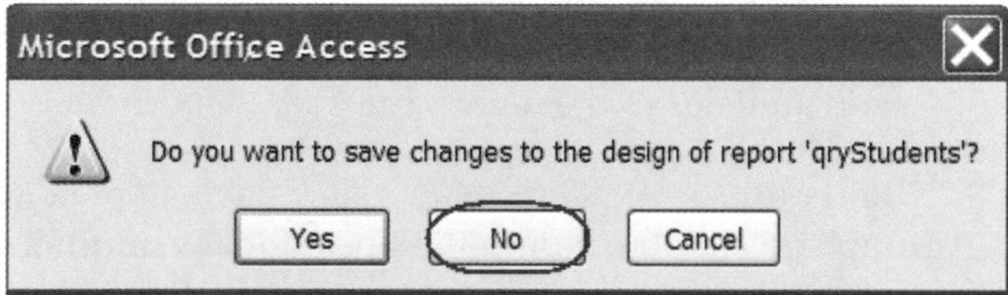

- Click the report's **Close button**. Click **No** when prompted to save your changes.

Closes the Report without saving it.

Using the Report Wizard

In this section, you will create a report using the Report Wizard.

The **Report Wizard** steps you through the process of creating an Access report. Unlike the AutoReport wizard, the Report Wizard allows much more control over the design of your reports. Like the Form Wizard, the Report Wizard allows you select the fields to be included in your report as well as choose various style options. Although you can create a report manually, it can be quite time consuming as reports can be difficult to design. Most people prefer to use the Report Wizard when designing reports.

To Create a Report Using the Report Wizard

1. Click the **Create** tab on the Ribbon.
2. Click **Report Wizard** button under the Reports command set on the Ribbon.
3. From the **Tables/Queries** drop-down list, choose the table or query upon which to base your new report.
4. Choose fields to add to the report by clicking the > button to add the selected field. Repeat for all desired fields.
5. To add all fields to the report, click the >> button.
6. Click **Next**.
7. To add **grouping** to your report, click the field by which you wish to group and click the > button. Repeat for any additional grouping levels.
8. Click **Next**.
9. To add sorting to your report, click the combo box and then choose the desired field by which to sort. Click the **Ascending** button to toggle the sort order to **Descending** (you can sort up to 4 levels).
10. Click **Next**.
11. Choose the desired **layout** and **page orientation**.
12. Click **Next**.
13. Choose the desired **style** for your report.

14. Click **Next**.
15. Enter a **name** for your report.
16. Choose whether to view the report's design (Layout view) or whether to preview the report (Print Preview).
17. Click **Finish**.

Let's Try It!

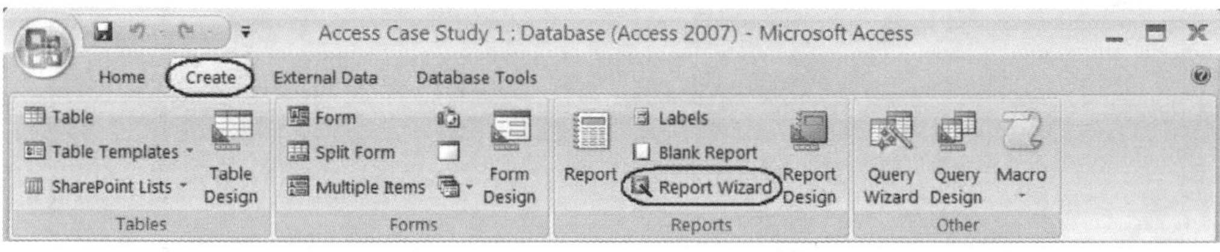

- Click the **Create** tab.

Displays commands for creating Access objects.

- Under the **Reports** command set, click **Report Wizard** button.

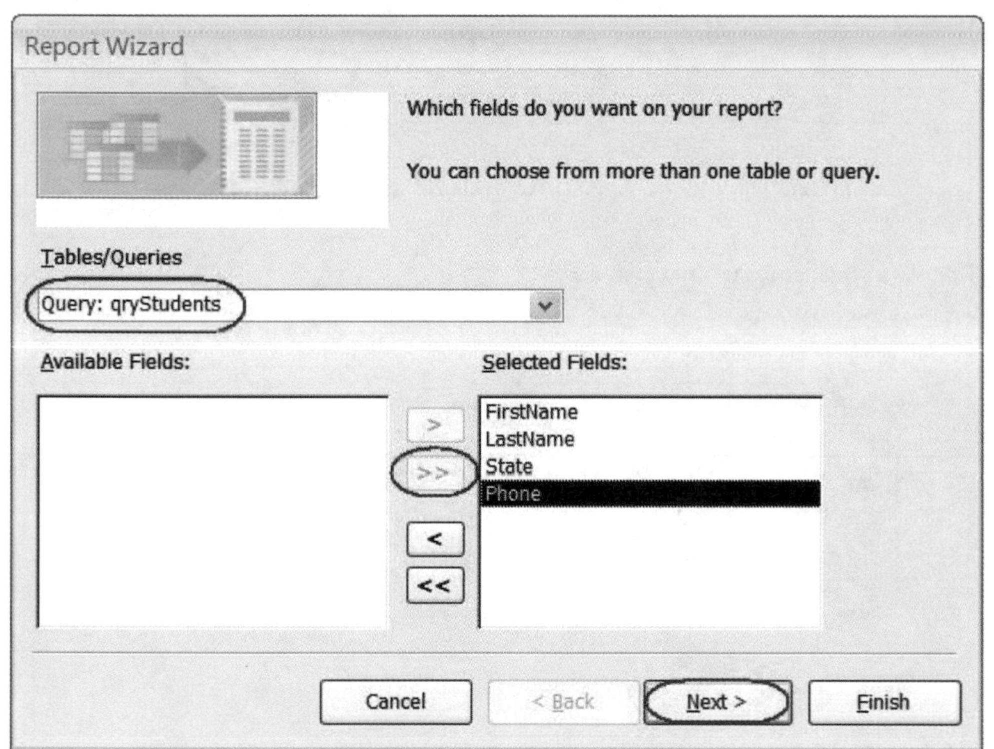

Launches the Report Wizard.

- Click the arrow on the right of the **Tables/Queries** combo box and then select **qryStudents** from the drop-down list.

Selects the query upon which we want to base our new report.

- Click the **>>** button.

All fields in the query will be added to our report.

- Click **Next**.

Moves to the next step of the wizard.

- Click **Next**.

As we do not wish to add any grouping, we will move to the next step of the wizard.

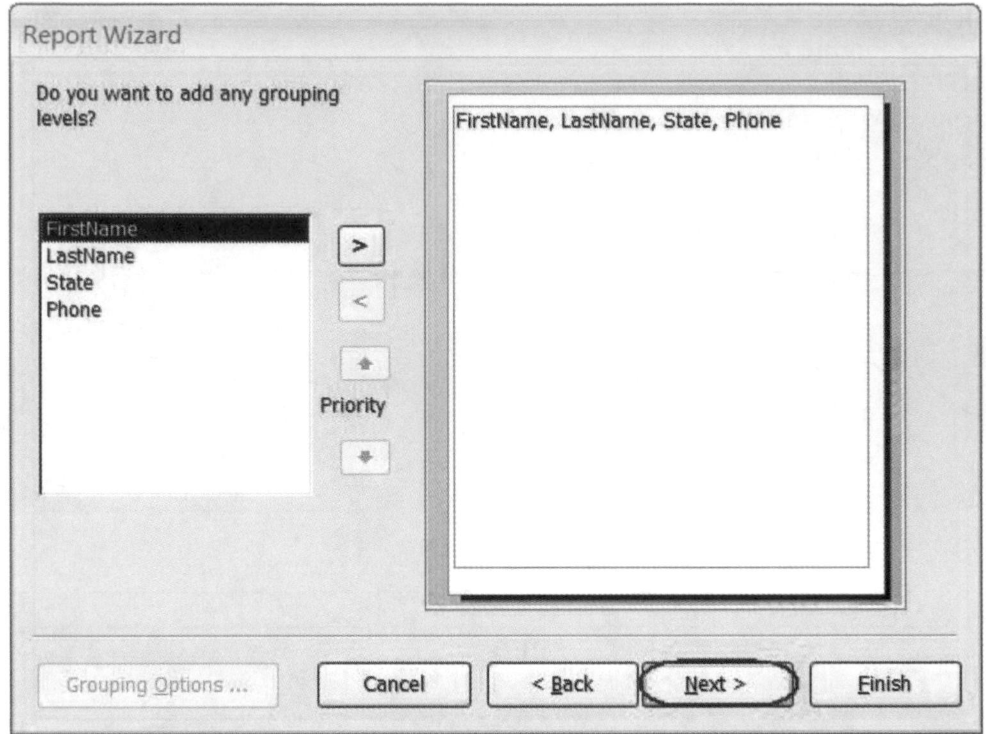

- Click the first **combo** box and then choose **LastName**.

Sets our report to sort ascending by the LastName field.

- Click **Next**.

Moves to the next step of the wizard.

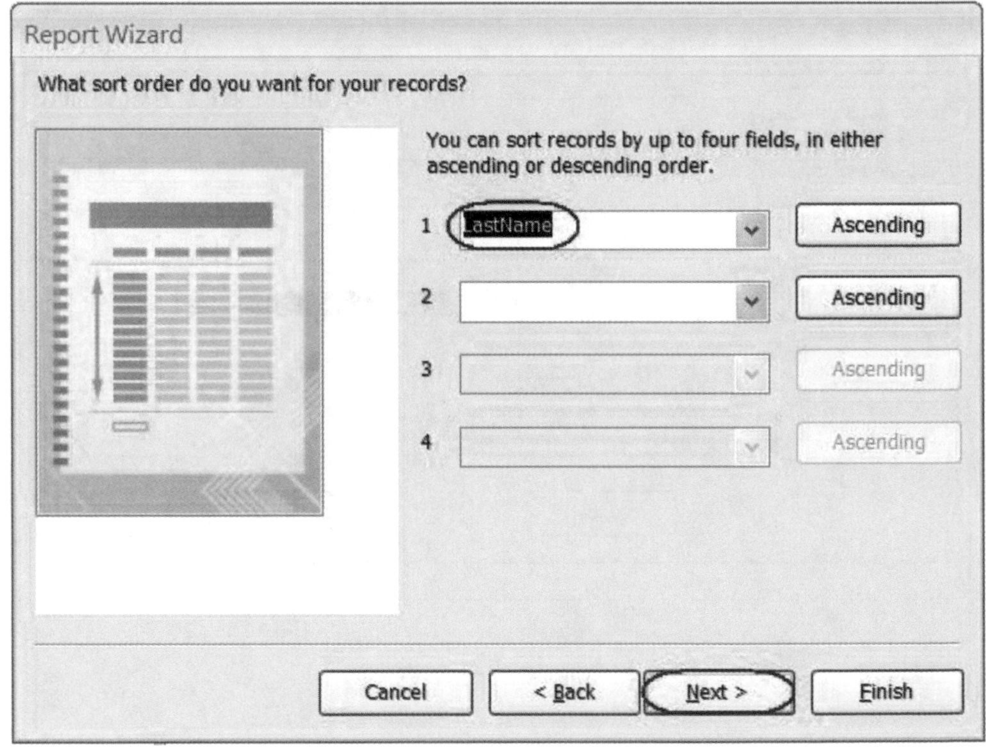

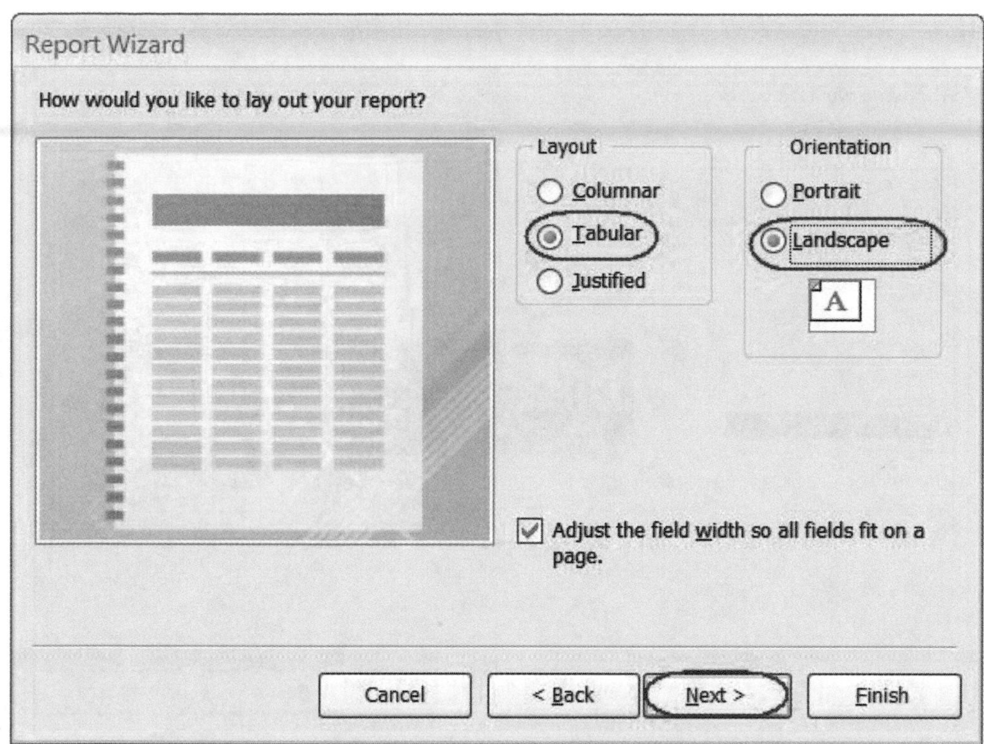

- Click the **Tabular** radio button in the Layout section and then choose **Landscape** in the **Orientation** section.

Chooses Tabular for the report layout and chooses Landscape for the page orientation.

- Click **Next**.

Moves to the next step of the wizard.

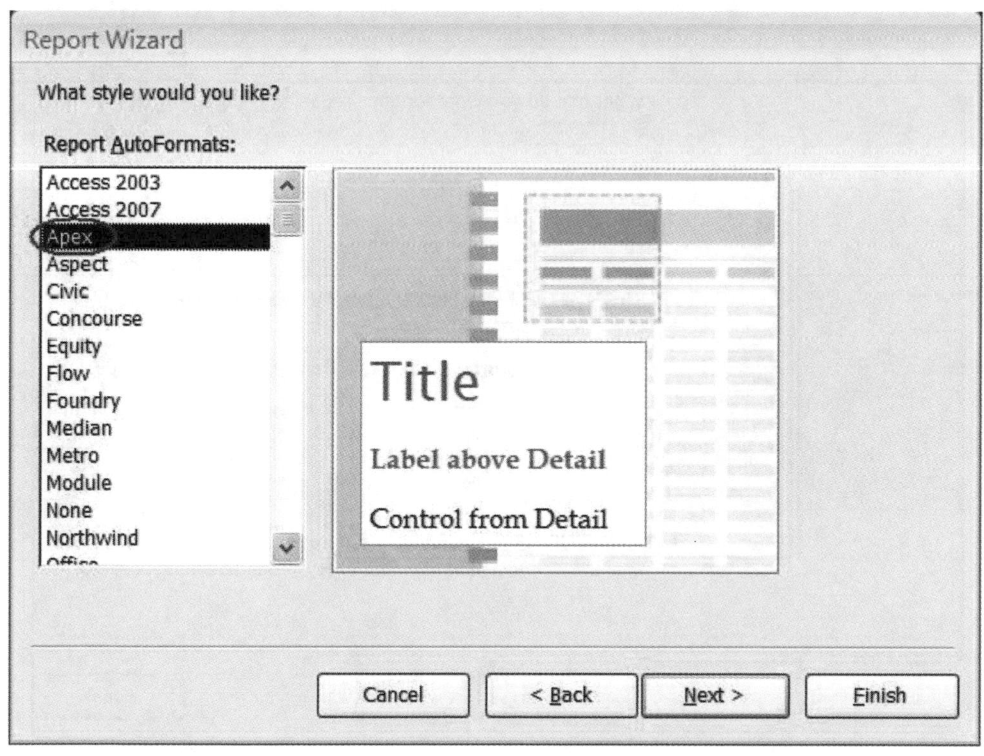

- Click **Apex** in the **Style** window.

Previews the Apex Style.

- Click **Technic** in the Style window.

Chooses Technic as the report style for the report.

- Click **Next**.

Moves to the next step of the wizard.

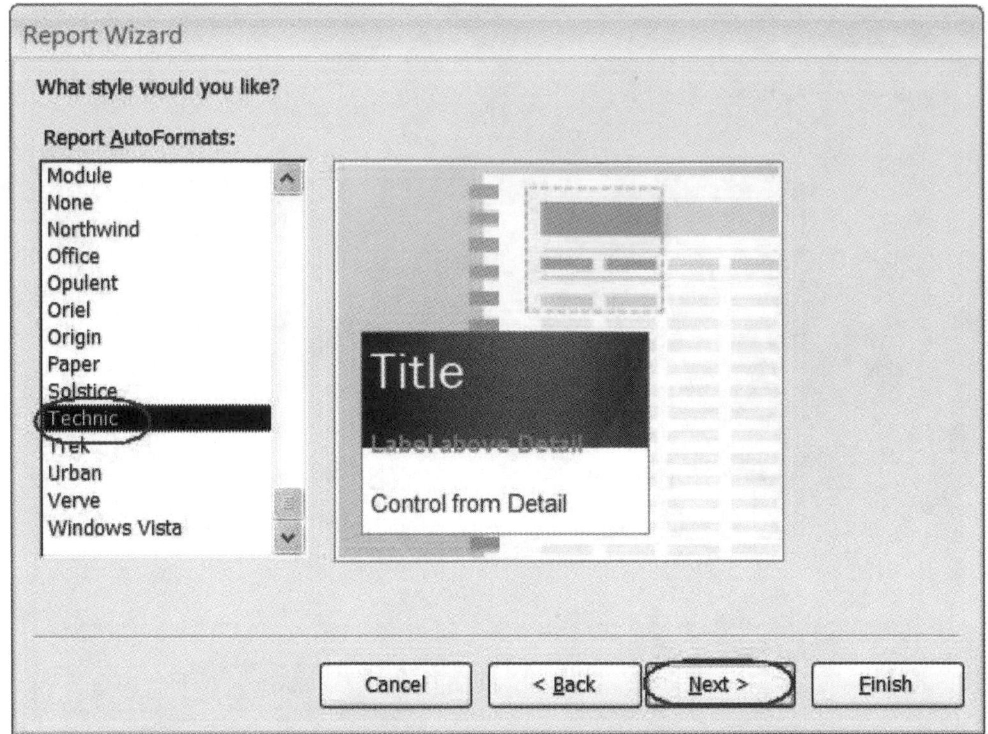

- Type: **rptStudents** in the report title box.

Enters the name for the report.

- Ensure that **Preview the Report** is selected, and then click **Finish**.

Opens the report in Print Preview view.

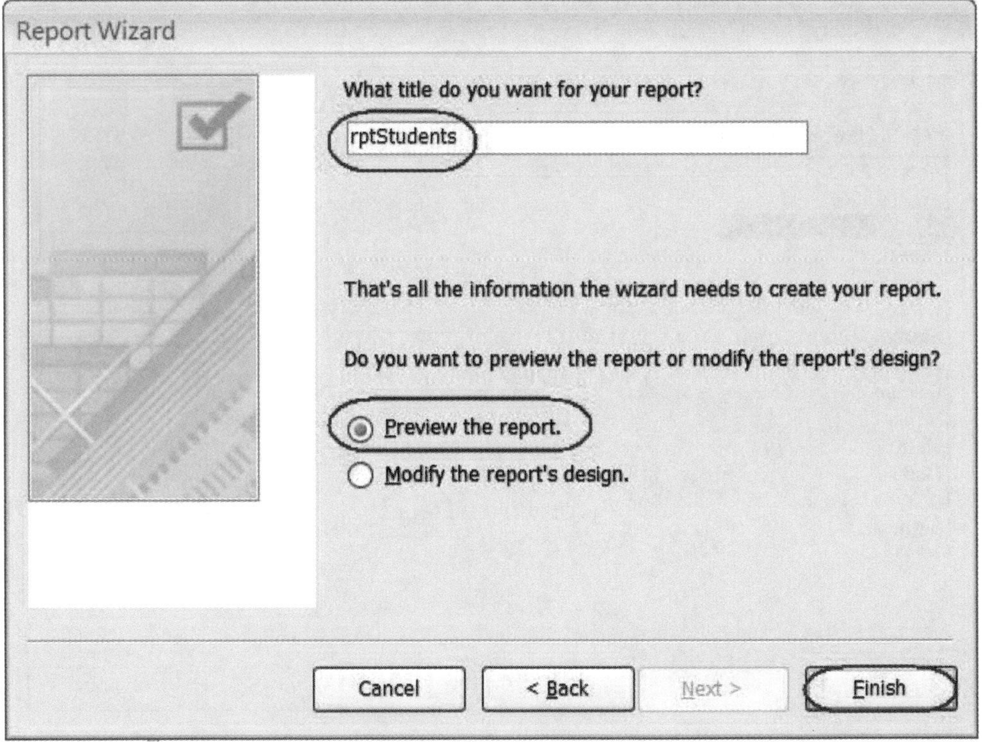

rptStudents

LastName	FirstName	State	Phone
Ferrare	Lance	VA	(307) 555-4325
Fielen	Mona	VA	(906) 555-2308
Harris	Daniel	VA	(719) 555-5736
Loomis	James	VA	(906) 555-3465

- Click the **Close Print Preview** button on the Ribbon.

Displays the report in Design view.

Report View and Layout View

In this section, you will look at two new Access views: Report and Layout Views.

Access 2007 provides two new views for reports—**Layout View** and **Report View**. We have already worked a bit with Layout View when we looked at forms and it works the same way with reports. That is to say, Layout View allows you to change the design of the report while viewing your live data. Like forms, all of your report objects are selectable so you can easily rearrange and resize your fields, columns and rows all while displaying actual report data.

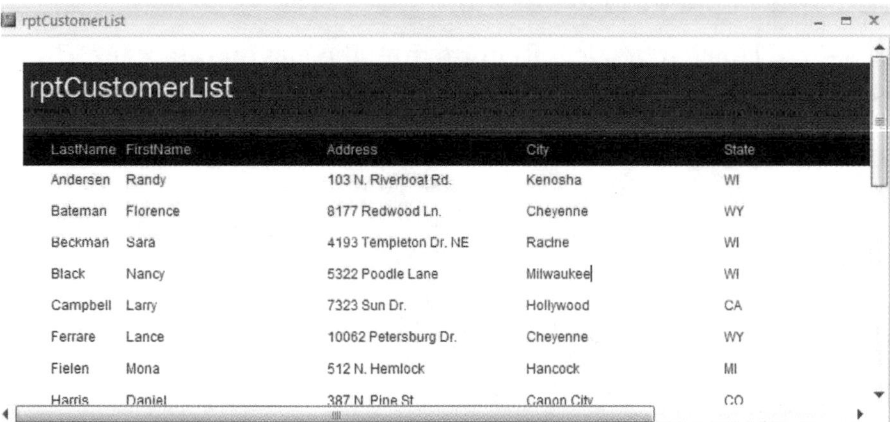

rptCustomerList

rptCustomerList

LastName	FirstName	Address	City	State
Andersen	Randy	103 N. Riverboat Rd.	Kenosha	WI
Bateman	Florence	8177 Redwood Ln.	Cheyenne	WY
Beckman	Sara	4193 Templeton Dr. NE	Racine	WI
Black	Nancy	5322 Poodle Lane	Milwaukee	WI
Campbell	Larry	7323 Sun Dr.	Hollywood	CA
Ferrare	Lance	10062 Petersburg Dr.	Cheyenne	WY
Fielen	Mona	512 N. Hemlock	Hancock	MI
Harris	Daniel	387 N. Pine St	Canon City	CO

REPORT VIEW

Report View allows you to view an accurate rendering of your report and browse your data without the need to display the report in Print Preview view. What's nice about Report View is that you can apply filters to your report data, displaying only specific records, as well as copy and paste fields of report data from one application to another. If you have added hyperlinks to your report, clicking on a hyperlink in Report View will open the link in your default Web browser. Double-clicking a report in the Navigation Pane will automatically display it in Report View.

To Display a Report in Report View

1. Under the Home tab on the **Navigation Pane**, select **Reports** from the drop-down list.
2. **Double-click** the report in the Navigation Pane
   Or
   Right-click the report you want to view and select **Report View** from the contextual menu
   Or
   Click the **View** button arrow on the Ribbon and choose **Design View**.
   Or
   Click the **Report View** button on the lower-right corner of the Access window.

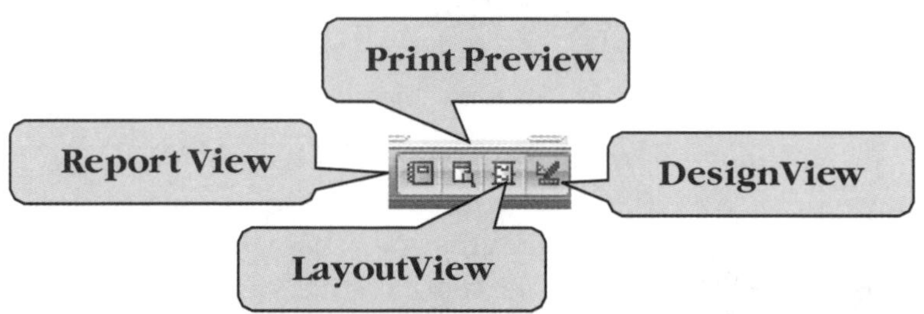

VIEW BUTTONS ON LOWER-RIGHT CORNER OF ACCESS WINDOW

To Display a Report in Layout View

1. Under the Home tab, select **Reports** from the **Navigation Pane**, drop-down list.
2. **Right-click** the report you want to view and select **Layout View** from the contextual menu
   Or
   Double-click the report to open it in Report view, click the **View** button arrow and choose **Layout View**.
   Or
   Click the **Layout View** button on the lower-right corner of the Access window.

Let's Try It!

- Right click on the rptStudents and choose **Layout View** from the list.

Displays the report in Layout view.

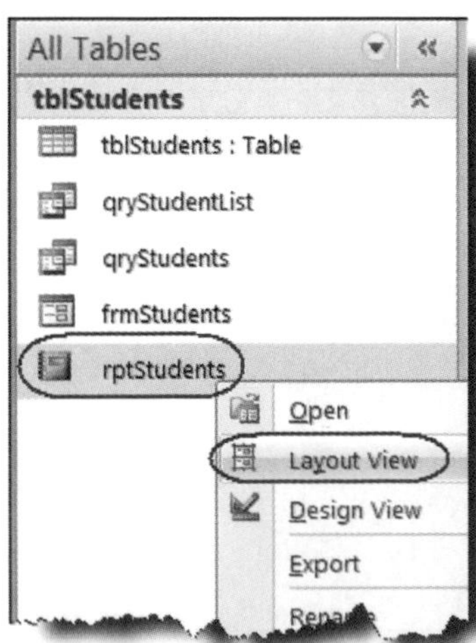

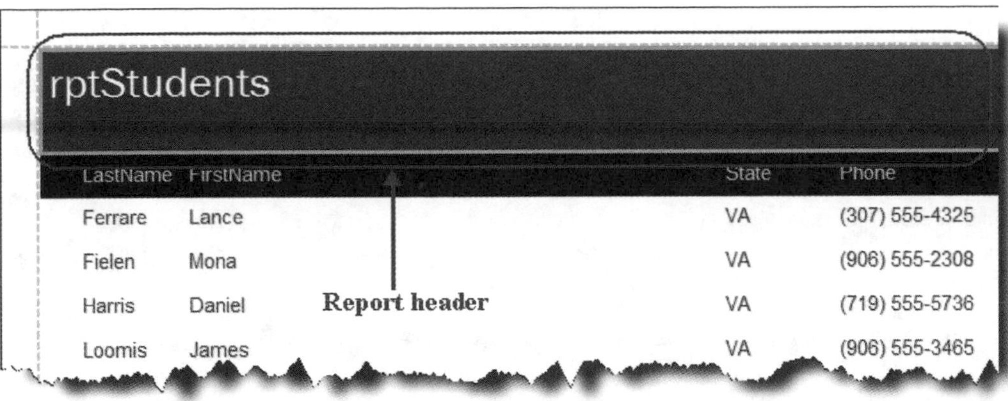

- Click in the **report header** to select the entire header.

Select the report object we wish to modify. In Layout view, report objects are selectable.

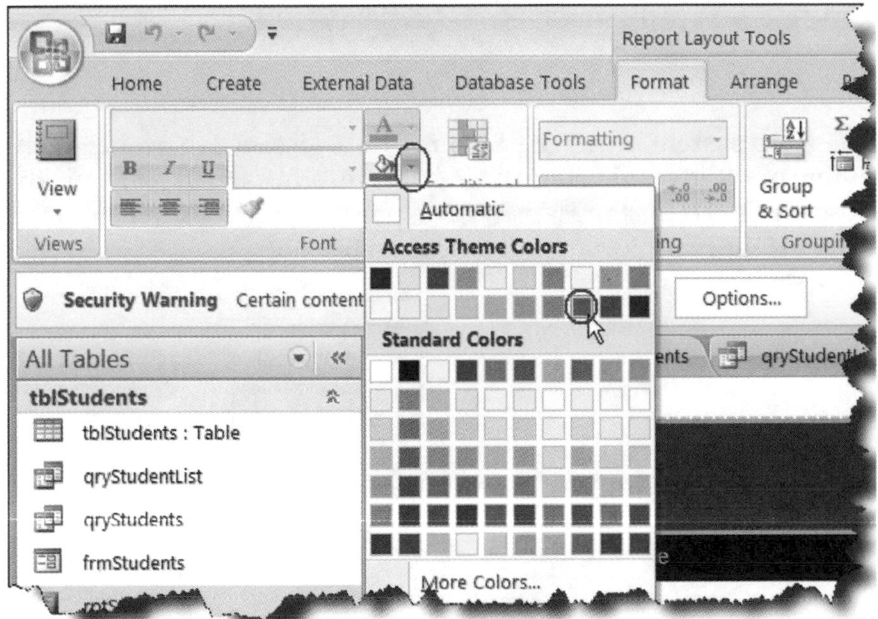

- Click the **Fill/Back Color drop-down arrow** and select Access Theme 8 from the Access Theme Color palette.

Applies Access Theme Color 8 to the report header.

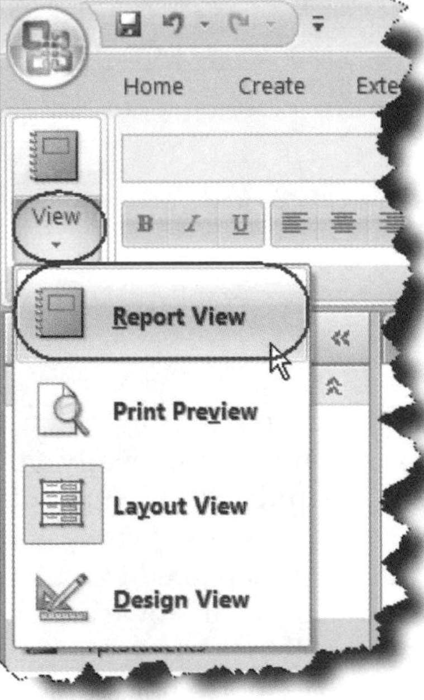

- Click the **View** button arrow on the Ribbon and choose **Report View** from the list.

Displays the report in Report view.

- Click the **Save** button on the Quick Access Toolbar.

Saves our design changes.

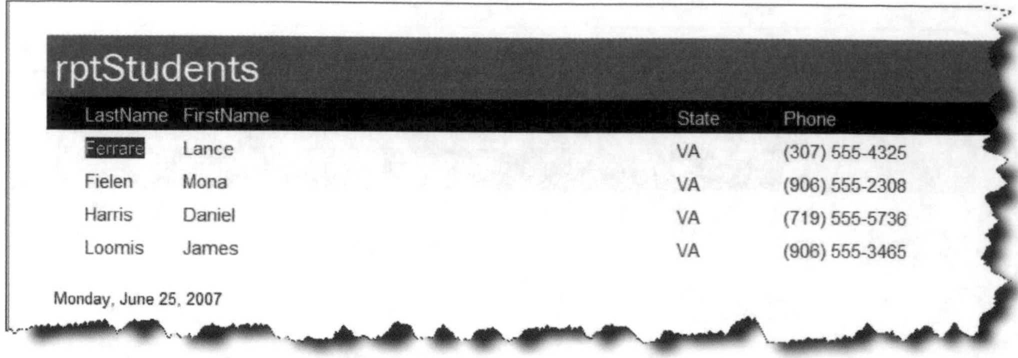

Using Help

In this section, you will learn how to use the Help system.

The **Help system** is designed to provide **assistance** to users whether you are online or offline and bring all available resources to you as quickly as possible. To access the Help system, press **F1** or click the **Help icon** on the upper right-hand corner of the Access window.

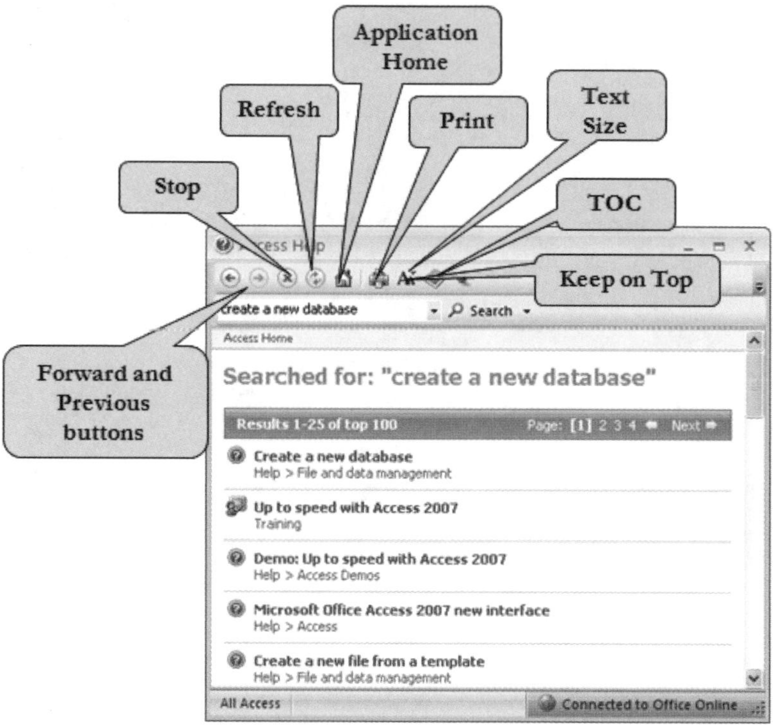

The Help system toolbar includes the familiar Back, Forward and Stop commands. Additionally, you will find the new **Refresh** tool, which allows you to update the content of the Help window. The **Application Home** tool brings you to the Access starting point, where you can browse through information related to the Microsoft Access application. The **TOC** tool displays a listing of available help topics through which you can browse. If you wish to increase or decrease the text size in the Help window, click the **Text Size** tool. Another nice feature on the Help toolbar is the **Keep on Top** tool, which allows you to keep the current Help page open while you work.

To Use the Help System

1. Click the **Microsoft Office Access Help** button on the upper right-hand corner of the Access Window
   Or
   Press **F1**
2. Enter the keyword(s) for which you want to search in the **Search** box.
3. Click the **Search** button
   Or
   Press the **Enter** key.
4. Click the **link** for the help topic you wish to view in the **Search Results pane**.
5. To browse Help topics, click the **TOC** button. Click the TOC button again to hide the Table of Contents.

Let's Try It!

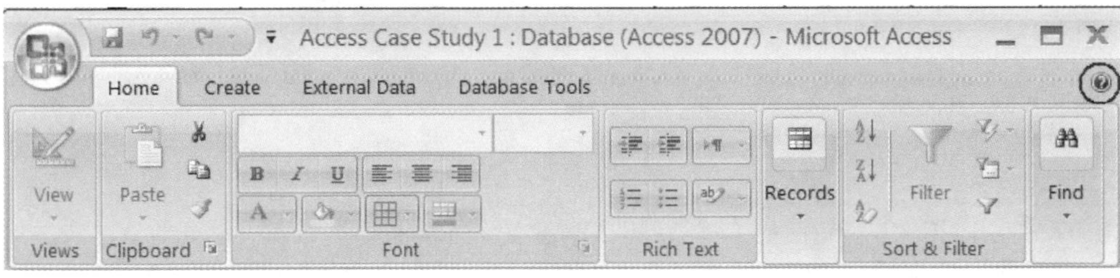

- Click the **Microsoft Office Help icon** on the upper right-hand corner of the screen.

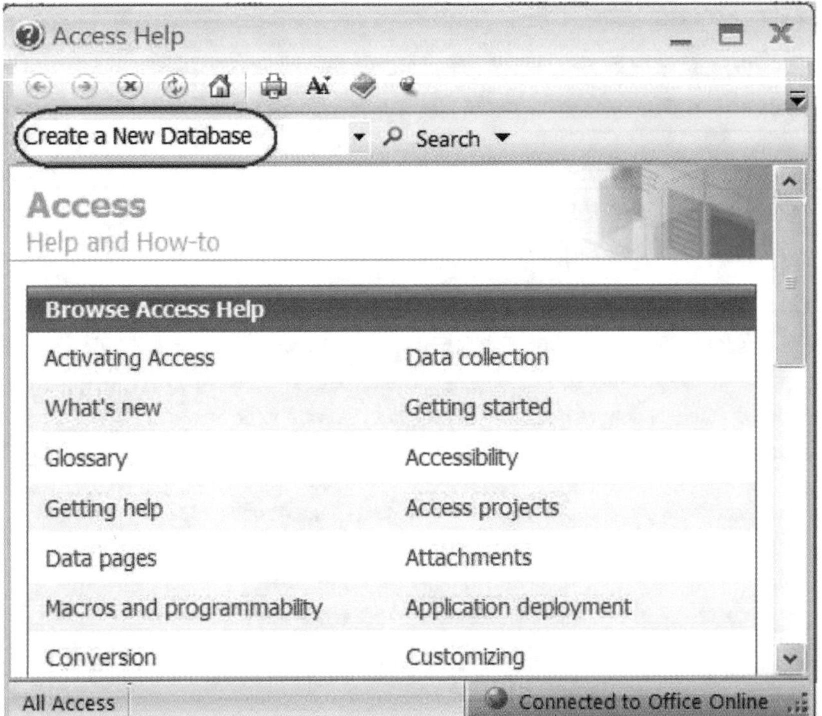

Displays the Access Help System window.

- In the **Search box**, type: **Create a New Database**.

Enter the keywords for which we want to search.

- Press **Enter**.

Executes the search. The results are displayed in the Search Results pane.

- Click the **Create a new database** link in the Search Results pane.

Displays the help topic for that link.

- Click the **Table of Contents** button on the toolbar.

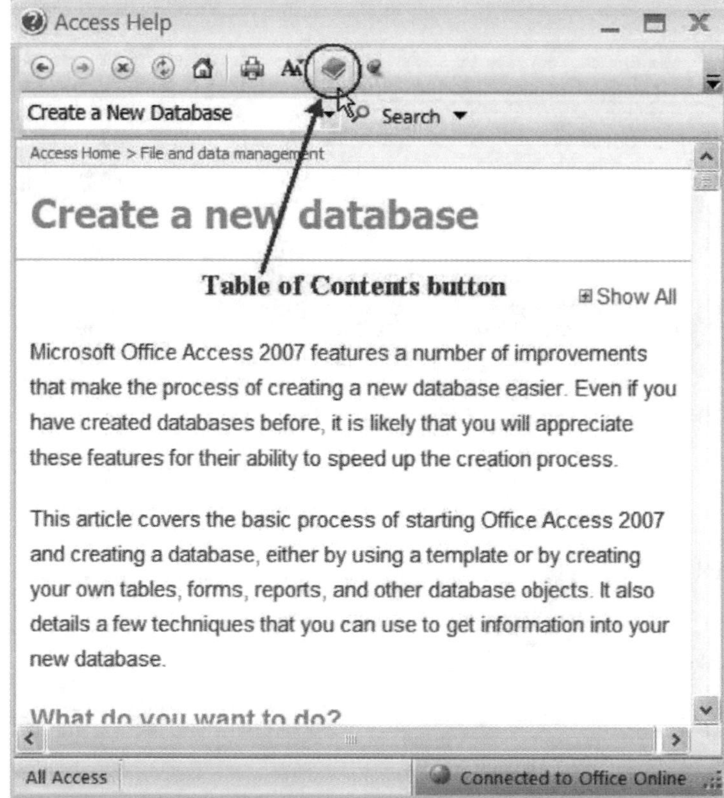

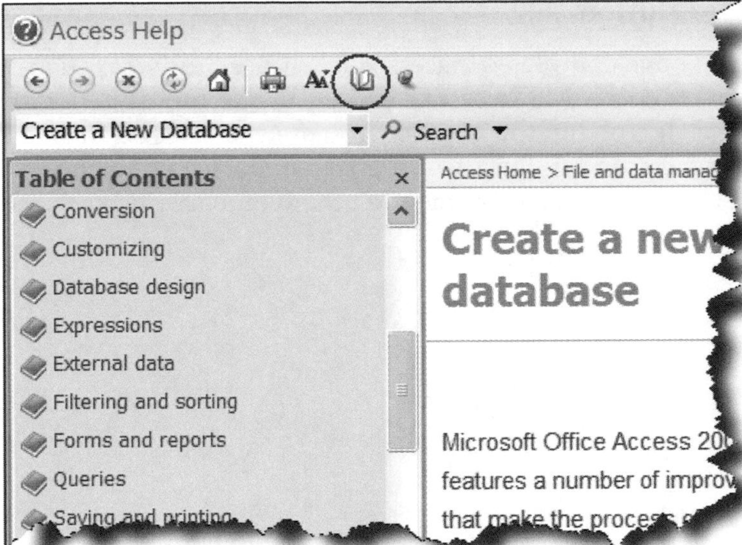

Displays a listing of Microsoft Access help topics.

- Click the **Table of Contents** button again.

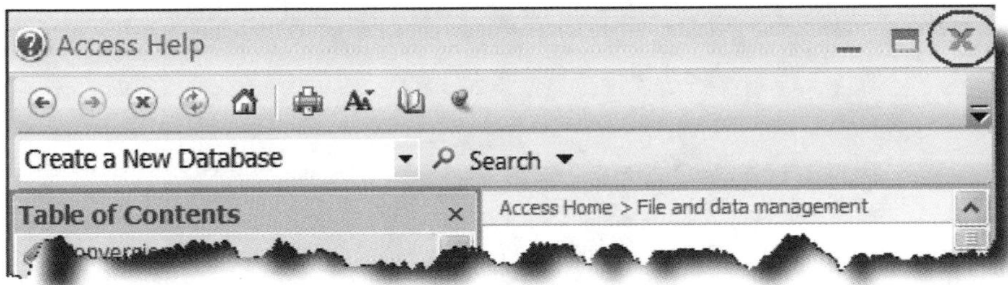

Hides the Table of Contents.

- Click the Access Help **Close button** on the upper right-hand corner of the screen.

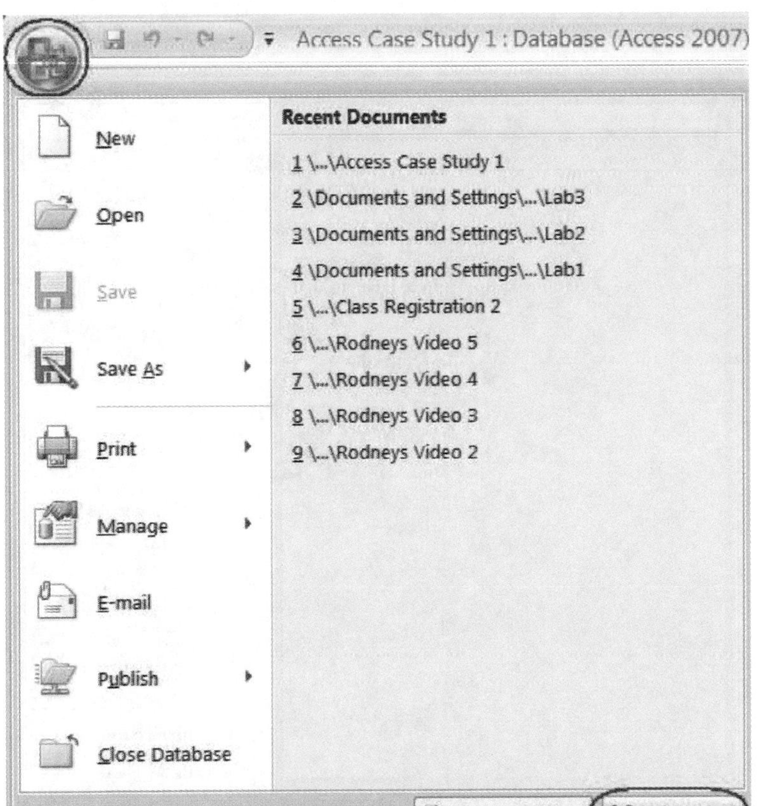

Closes the Help System window.

- Click the **Microsoft Office Button**.

Displays the File Options menu.

- Click the **Exit Access** button on the bottom of the window.

Closes the database and exits the Access application.

Conclusion

You have completed Access 2007—Case Study I. You are now ready to use several basic MS Access query, form, and report generating skills that you have learned in this chapter. You are encouraged to experiment with all you have learned in this case study. To reinforce your understanding of these techniques, it is recommended that you read and work through it once again.

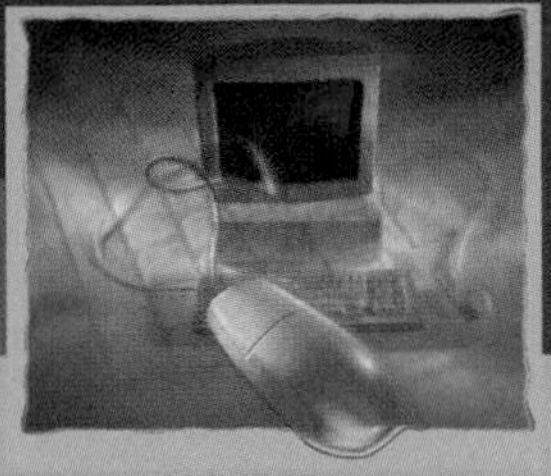

Access Case Study 2

CHAPTER

10

OBJECTIVES

After successfully completing this case study, you should able to:

- Create Relationships (One-to-One, One-to-Many, Many-to-Many)
- Enforce Referential Integrity
- Cascade Update Related Fields and Delete Related Records
- Set Validation Rules
- Format Fields
- Set Rules to Require Data Entry
- Create an Input Mask
- Create a Lookup Field and a Value List
- Create Multi-Table Queries
- Create a Totals Query
- Create a Parameter Query
- Create a Find Duplicates Query
- Create a Find Unmatched Records Query
- Modify Query Joins

Case Study 2—MS Access 2007

Assume that you are the owner of Suman's Teddy Bear store. You want to create a database to keep track of current customers and orders placed by these customers. To do this, you will create multiple tables (Customers and Orders) and relate them through common fields. You will also create several queries that extract information from related tables.

CustomerID	FirstName	LastName	Address	City	State	Zip	HomePhone
123	Florence	Bateman	4133 Redwood Ln.	Atlanta	GA	30303	(414) 234-4456
234	Sara	Beckman	343 Templeton Dr.	Racine	WI	52602	(414) 456-2342
345	Nicole	Travis	406 W. Pine St.	Glendale	VA	20123	(703) 435-5673
456	Jaime	Rickman	704 Clark St.	Fairfax	VA	20330	(703) 555-0922
780	Thomas	Henderson	98 Clinton Dr.	Orlando	FL	32825	(407) 555-8637

Customers Table

OrderID	CustomerID	OrderDate	DateShipped	FreightCharg	PaymentMethod
1	456	Wednesday, May 01, 2002	Tuesday May 07	$5.95	MasterCard
2	234	Wednesday, July 24, 2002	Monday Jul 29	$6.00	Visa
3	780	Thursday, March 23, 2000	Friday Mar 24	$5.50	American Express
4	456	Monday, June 21, 1999	Wednesday Jun 23	$5.50	Visa
5	780	Tuesday, June 24, 2003	Friday Jun 27	$5.50	Discover
6	123	Friday, June 25, 2004	Sunday Jun 27	$4.95	American Express

Orders Table

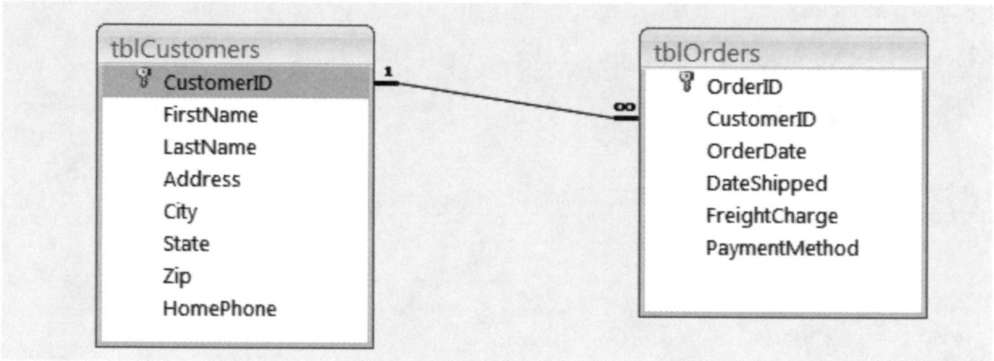

Customers and Orders Tables in One-To-Many Relationship

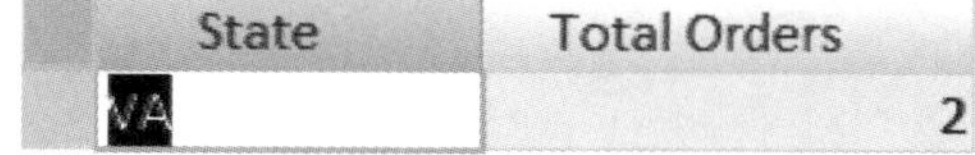

State	Total Orders
VA	2

Query of Information from Single Table (Number of Orders from VA State)

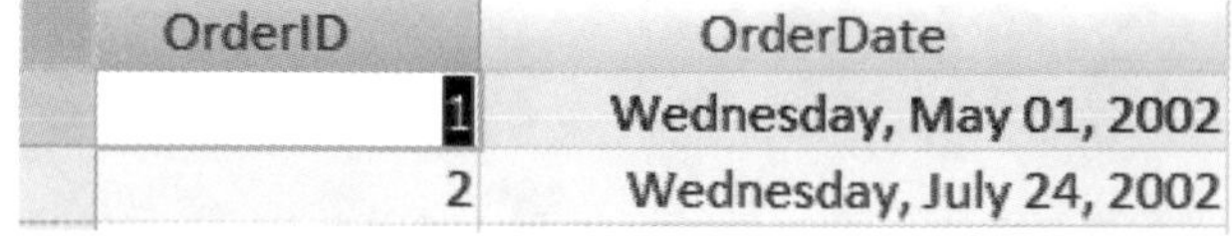

OrderID	OrderDate
1	Wednesday, May 01, 2002
2	Wednesday, July 24, 2002

Query of Information from Single Table (Orders placed in Year 2002)

FirstName	LastName	OrderDate	PaymentMethod
Florence	Bateman	Friday, June 25, 2004	American Express
Sara	Beckman	Wednesday, July 24, 2002	Visa
Jaime	Rickman	Wednesday, May 01, 2002	MasterCard
Jaime	Rickman	Monday, June 21, 1999	Visa
Thomas	Henderson	Thursday, March 23, 2000	American Express
Thomas	Henderson	Tuesday, June 24, 2003	Discover

Query of Information in Multiple Tables (Customers Order Date and Payment Method)

LastName	FirstName	OrderID
Bateman	Florence	6
Beckman	Sara	2
Travis	Nicole	
Rickman	Jaime	1
Rickman	Jaime	4
Henderson	Thomas	3
Henderson	Thomas	5

Query of Information in Multiple Tables (Customers with or without Orders)

CustomerID	FirstName	LastName	Address	City	State
345	Nicole	Travis	406 W. Pine St.	Glendale	VA

Query of Information in Multiple Tables (Customer(s) without Orders)

Creating a New Database

In this section, we will create a new database.

We learned in our last case study that to create a new database, we need to

1. Click the **Microsoft Office Button** and then click **New** from the menu to display the **Getting Started Pane** Task Pane.
2. Click **Blank Database** in the center pane.
3. To specify a name for your database, type the new name in the **File Name** box in the right pane.
4. To specify a location where the database is to be saved, click the **file folder icon** in the right pane and then navigate to the folder where you wish to store your database file.
5. Click **Create**.

Let's Try It!

- Click on the Start button.

Displays Start menu items.

- Select **All Programs < Microsoft Office > Microsoft Office Access 2007** from the Start Menu.

Launches the Microsoft Access Application and displays the Getting Started Task Pane.

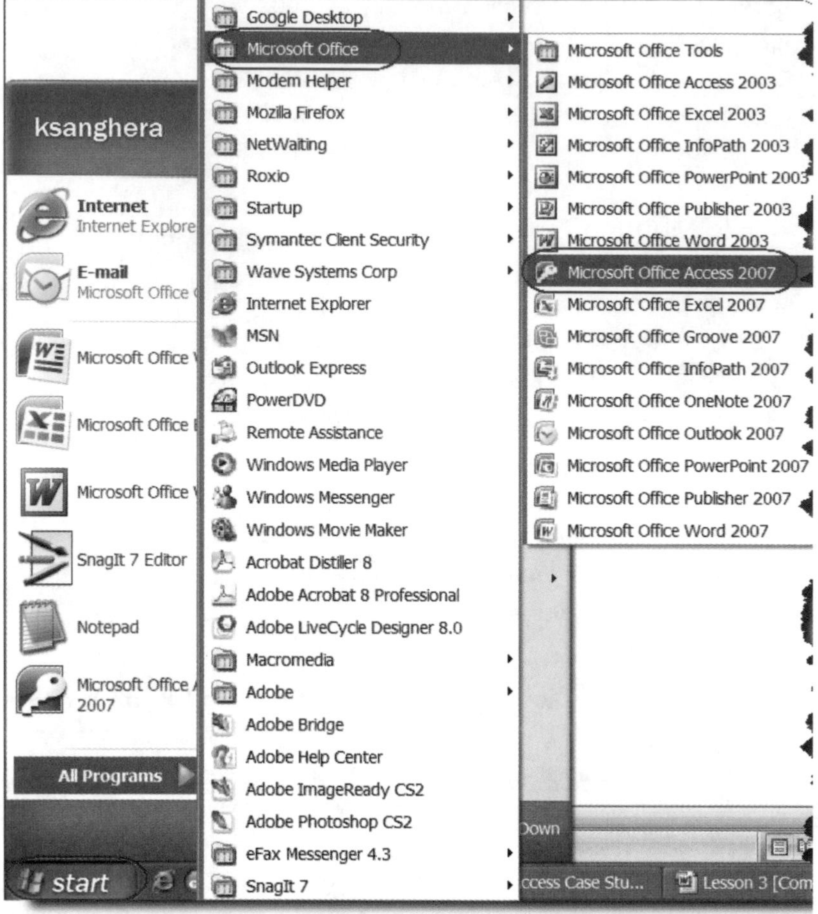

- In the **Center** Pane, click on **Blank Database**.

Specifies that we will create a new blank database.

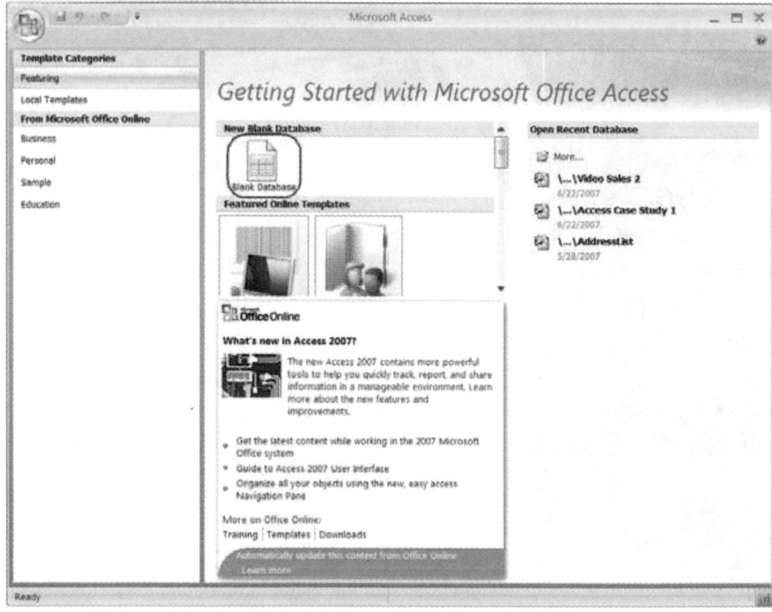

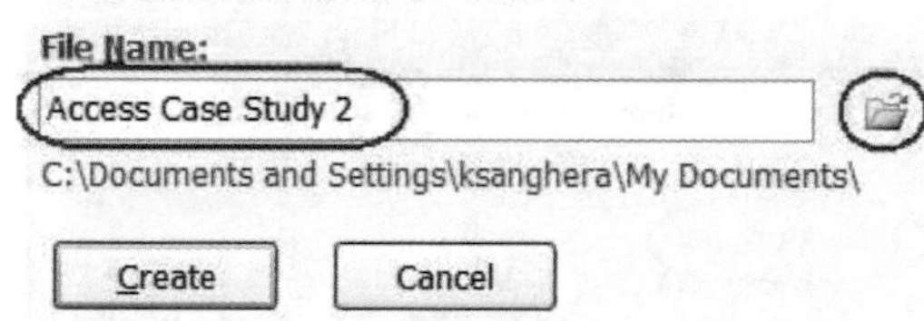

- In the **File name** text box, type: **Access Case Study 2**.

Enters a name for the database.

- Click the **Folder icon** to the right of the File Name box.

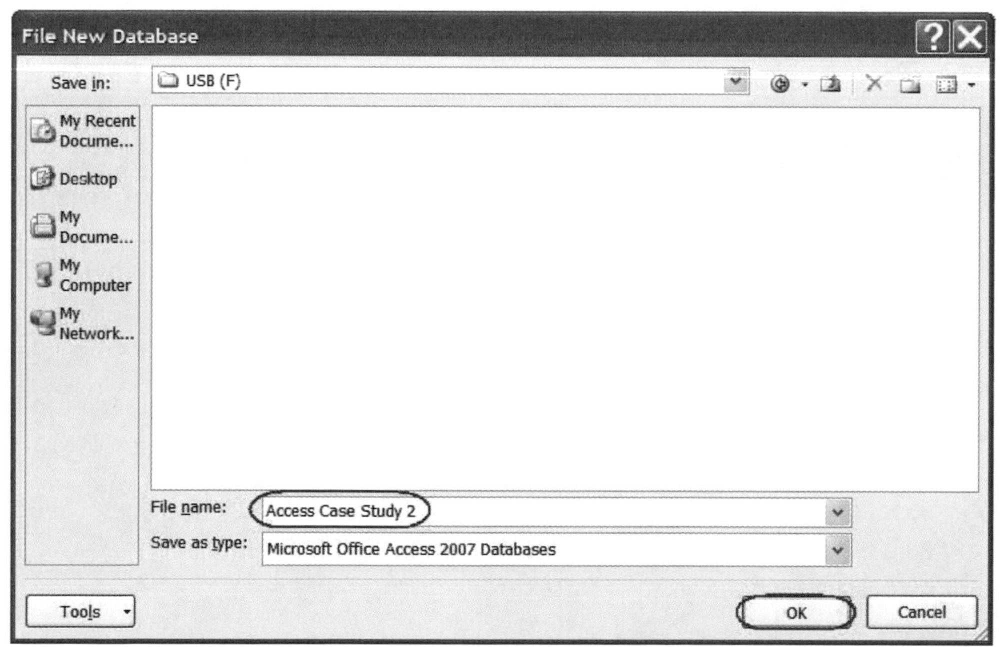

Displays the File New Database dialog box which allows us to browse to the location where we wish to save our database.

- Insert your **USB** drive.
- Browse to **USB** drive and click **OK**.

Closes the File New Database dialog box.

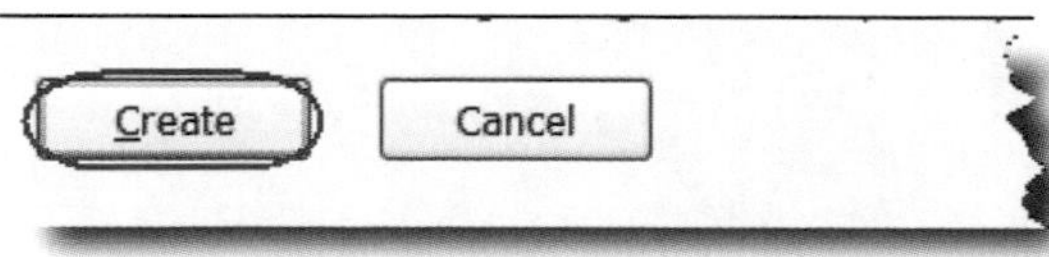

- Click **Create**.

Creates a blank database. A blank new table displays in Datasheet view.

- Right click on the **Table1** button under navigation pane and then click on **Design View**.

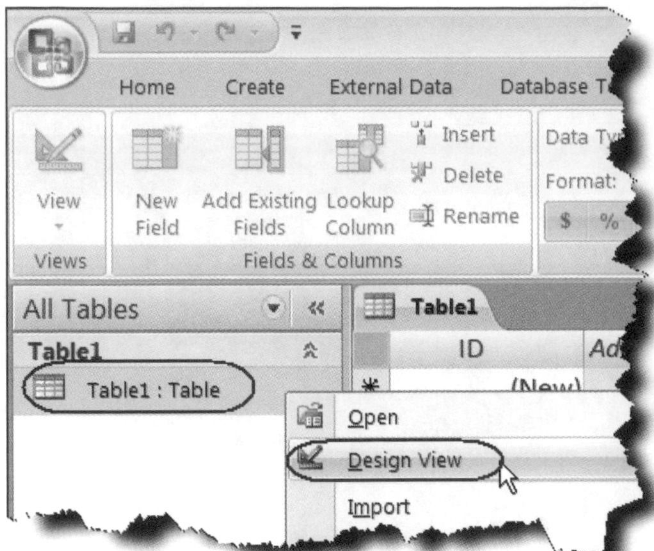

- Type: **tblCustomers** in the Table Name box.

Before we can switch to Design view, we must provide a name to a new table.

- Click **OK**.

Saves the table and switches to Design view.

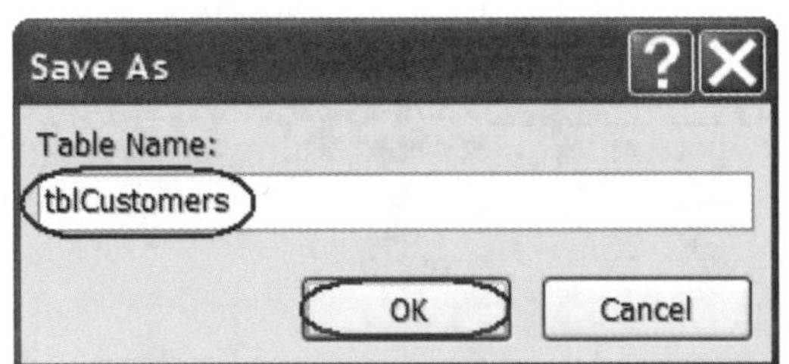

- Select ID in the first **Field Name** box and type: **CustomerID**.

Enters a name for the first field.

Field Name	Data Type	Description
CustomerID	AutoNumber	

- Press **Tab** key and select **Number** for the Data Type field.
- Enter the rest of the information as shown in the screenshot.
- Click the **Save** icon on the Quick Access Toolbar.

Saves our changes.

Field Name	Data Type	Description
CustomerID	Number	
FirstName	Text	
LastName	Text	
Address	Text	
City	Text	
State	Text	
Zip	Number	
HomePhone	Text	

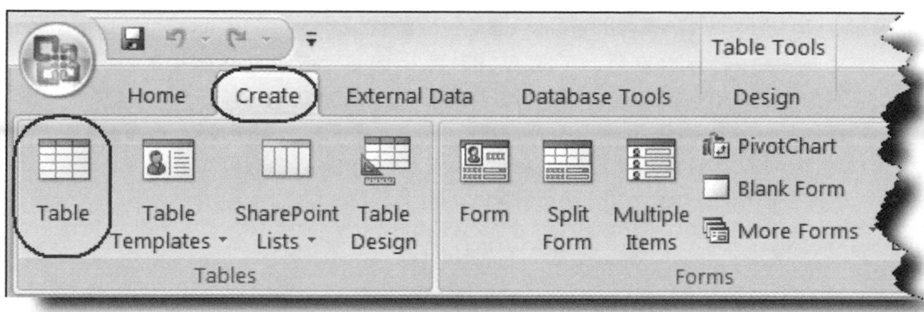

- Click the **Create** command tab on the Ribbon.

Displays commands related to the creation of database objects.

- Click **Table** command icon.

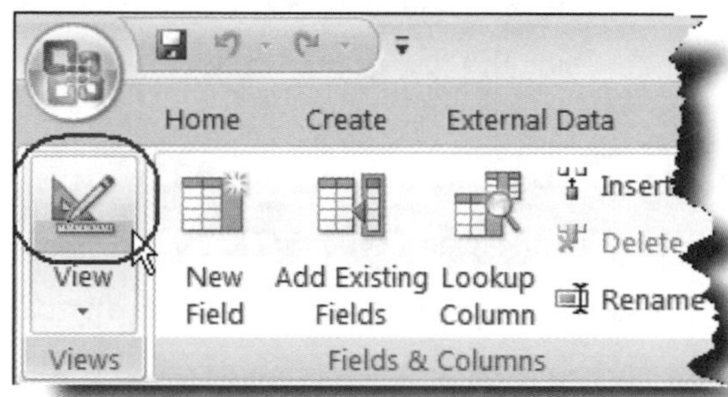

- Click the **View** command icon on the Ribbon.

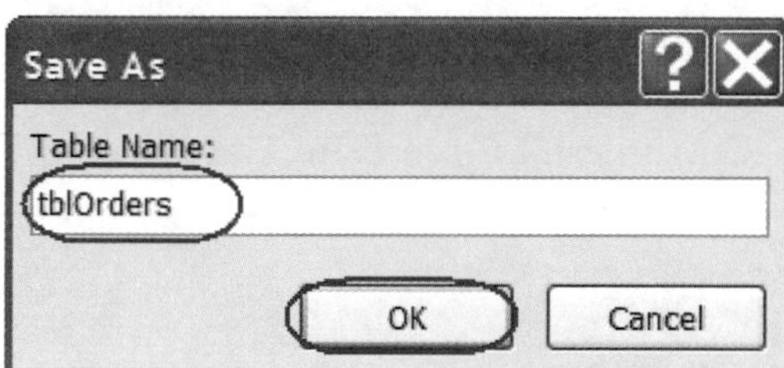

- Type: **tblOrders** in the Table Name box.

Before we can switch to Design view, we must first provide a name the new table.

- Click **OK**.

Saves the table and switches to Design view.

Field Name	Data Type	Description
OrderID	AutoNumber	
CustomerID	Number	
OrderDate	Date/Time	
DateShipped	Date/Time	
FreightCharge	Currency	
PaymentMethod	Text	

- Enter the information as shown in the screenshot for table tblOrders.
- Click the **Save** icon on the Quick Access Toolbar.

Saves our changes.

OrderID	CustomerID	OrderDate	DateShipped	FreightCharg	PaymentMethod	Add New Field
1	456	5/1/2002	5/7/2002	$5.95	MasterCard	
2	234	7/24/2002	7/29/2002	$6.00	Visa	
3	780	3/23/2000	3/24/2000	$5.50	American Express	
4	456	6/21/1999	6/23/1999	$5.50	Visa	
5	780	6/24/2003	6/27/2003	$5.50	Discover	
(New)						

- Click the **View** button on the ribbon.
- Press **Tab** key and type: **456**.

Notice OrderID is automatically entered. OrderID will be generated for all the records in the table.

- Press **Tab** key and type: **5/1/2002**.
- Press **Tab** key and type: **5/7/2002**.
- Press **Tab** key and type: **5.95** for FreightCharge.

The currency sign ($) will be added to the FreightCharge field when you tab the next field.

- Press **Tab** key and type: **MasterCard**.
- Enter rest of the information as shown in the screenshot for columns CustomerID, OrderDate, DateShipped, FreightCharge, and PaymentMethod.

- Click the **Save** icon on the Quick Access Toolbar.

Saves the changes.

- Click the **Close button** to close the tblOrders.
- Double click on **tblCustomers** under navigation panel.

Table opens in the datasheet view.

CustomerID	FirstName	LastName	Address	City	State	Zip	HomePhone
123	Florence	Bateman	4133 Redwood Ln.	Atlanta	GA	30303	(414) 234-4456
234	Sara	Beckman	343 Templeton Dr.	Racine	WI	52602	(414) 456-2342
345	Nicole	Travis	406 W. Pine St.	Glendale	VA	20123	(703) 435-5673
456	Jaime	Rickman	704 Clark St.	Fairfax	VA	20330	(703) 676-2314
780	Thomas	Henderson	98 Clinton Dr.	Orlando	FL	32825	(407) 555-8637
*							

- Enter the information as shown in the screenshot for table tblCustomers.
- Click the **Save** icon on the Quick Access Toolbar.

Saves our changes.

- Click the **Close button** to close the tblCustomers.

A Look at Relationships

In section, you will learn about database relationships.

The power of a relational database lies in its ability to relate records from one table to records in another table. You relate records between two tables by creating a **Relationship**. A relationship is a way of formally defining how two tables are related to each other by telling the database on which fields they are joined. Relationships allow you to bring data together from the related tables. A relationship works by matching data in **key fields**—usually, a field with the same name in both tables. These matching key fields consist of the **primary key** from the parent table, which provides that each record's value in that table must be unique, and the **foreign key** in the child table.

In the example below, we have a customers table and an orders table. The two tables are joined on the CustomerID field. The CustomerID field in the customers table is set as the primary key, which is joined to the CustomerID field in the Orders table (the foreign key). Now, records for a customer with a particular CustomerID number will be related to any records in the order table where the CustomerID number is the same.

Imagine we had a customer named Jane Smith whose CustomerID was 45. When entering any orders for Jane Smith in the orders table, Jane would be identified by her CustomerID number. We can then bring the data together, such as in a query. We might want to view a customer's order information. To see this, we would use data from the Customers and Orders table.

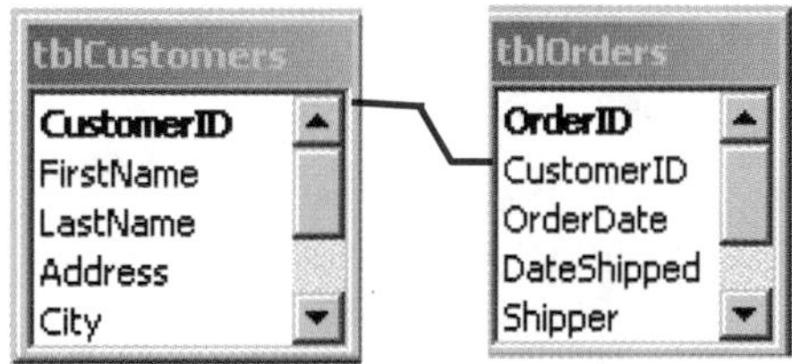

Database relationships fall into one of the three following categories:

- *One-to-one.* Each record has only one related record in the second table.
- *One-to-many.* Each record has one or more related records in the second table.

- **Many-to-many**. Each record in one table may have many related records in the second table, and those related records may in turn have related records in the first table.

  We will examine each relationship type in subsequent sections.

Creating Relationships

A **One-to-One Relationship** is a relationship where each record in the first table has one—and only one related record in the second table. This is not a very common type of relationship but does exist nonetheless. For example, we may have an employees table that is accessible by many people. We may not wish to have employee salary information easily available so we place it in a separate table with the Employee ID and Salary fields. We then create a one-to-one relationship between the two tables. By setting the EmployeeID field as a **primary key** in both tables, we have thus created a one-to-one relationship. Remember, a field that is designated as a primary key field will not allow any duplicates in that field.

Relationships are created in the **Relationships Window**. To display the Relationships Window, click the Database Tools tab on the Ribbon and then click the **Relationships button** on the Ribbon.

In the example below, we have a customers table and a credit card table. For security reasons, we have decided to create a separate table to hold a customer's default credit card information. As each customer will have only one default credit card on file, we create a one-to-one relationship.

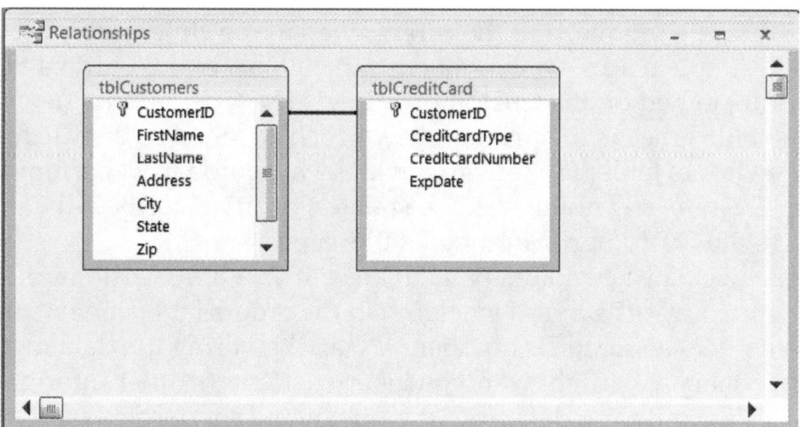

To Create a One-to-One Relationship

1. Click the **Database Tools** tab on the Ribbon.
2. Click the **Relationships button** on the Show/Hide group.
3. Click the **Tables** tab if necessary on the Show Table dialog box.
4. Select the first table to be added to the relationship.
5. Click **Add**.
6. Select the second table to be added to the relationship.
7. Click **Add**.
8. Click **Close** to close the Show Table dialog box.
9. Click the primary key field in the first table and then drag to the primary key in the second table.
10. Click **Create** in the Edit Relationship dialog box.

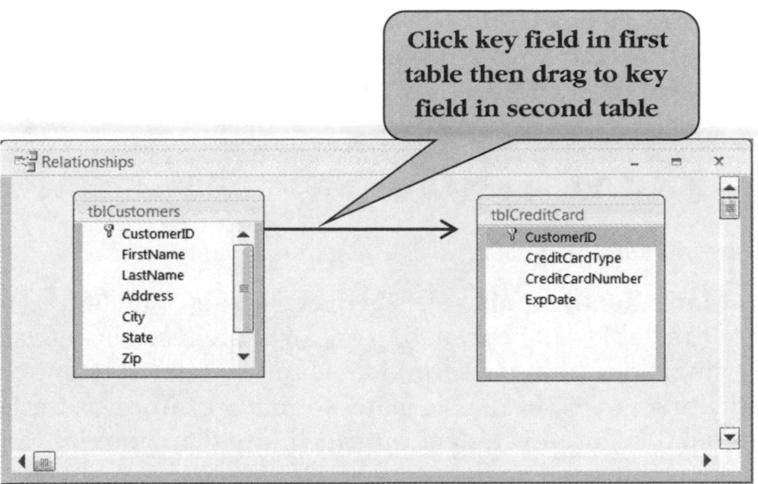

> **NOTE:** If a previous relationship has already been created, the "Show Table" dialog box will not appear. Click the **Show Table** on the Data Tools Ribbon to display the Show Table dialog box.

In section, you will learn how to create a one-to-many relationship.

A **One-to-Many Relationship** is a relationship where each record in the parent table has one or more related records in the child table. The one-to-many relationship is the most common type of relationship. A frequently used example is that of the Customer and Orders table. The Customer Table is the parent table and usually contains a Customer ID field which is set as a primary key. The Orders Table is the child table or the "many" side of the relationship. This table also contains a Customer ID field but it is not set as a primary key as a customer could place more than one order. This field is referred to as the **foreign key**.

In the example below, the tblCustomers table is the "one" table as each customer is listed only once. The tblOrders table is the "many" table as a customer could place more than one order.

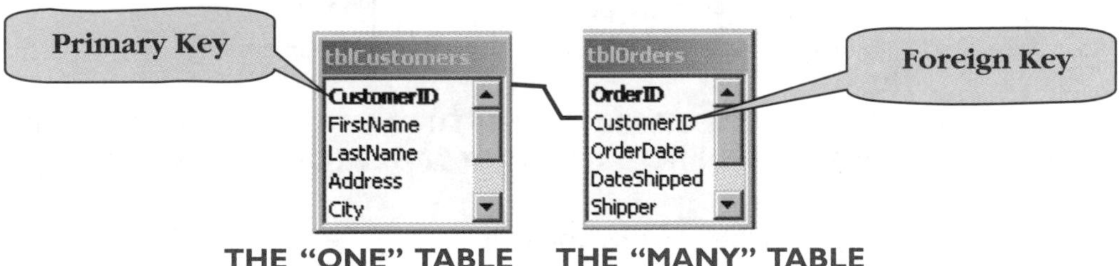

To Create a One-to-Many Relationship

1. Click the **Database Tools** tab on the Ribbon.
2. Click the **Relationships button** on the Show/Hide group.
3. Click the **Tables** tab if necessary on the Show Table dialog box.
4. Select the first table to be added to the relationship.
5. Click **Add**.
6. Select the second table to be added to the relationship.
7. Click **Add**.
8. Click **Close** to close the Show Table dialog box.

9. Click the **primary key** field in the parent table and then drag with your mouse to the **foreign key** in the child table.
10. Click **Create** in the Edit Relationship dialog box.

Creating a Many-to-Many Relationship

In section, you will learn how to create a many-to-many relationship.

A **Many-to-Many Relationship** exists between a pair of tables if a single record in the first table can be related to one or more records in the second table, and a single record in the second table can be related to one or more records in the first table. The classic many-to-many example is the Students and Classes relationship—a student can take more than one class and a class is usually taken by more than one student. However, if you linked the Students and Classes table directly, you would receive a large amount of redundant data in your resultset. Inserting, Updating and Deleting data in this type of relationship can also be a problem.

You solve the many-to-many relationship problem be creating an **intermediary table** (sometimes referred to as a junction table) that contains the primary keys from each of the two tables, thus creating a one-to-many relationship between each table and the intermediary table. For instance, in the Students and Classes example, we would create a linking table perhaps called StudentClasses, which would contain the **StudentID** field and the **ClassID** field as **foreign keys**. We would then create a one-to-many relationship between the Students table and StudentClasses table and another one-to-many relationship between the Classes table and the StudentClasses table.

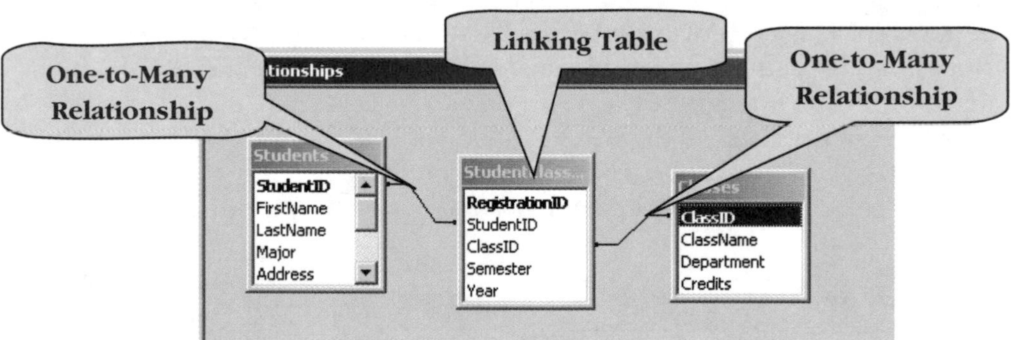

A MANY-TO-MANY RELATIONSHIP CONSISTING OF TWO ONE-TO-MANY RELATIONSHIPS WITH AN INTERMEDIARY TABLE (OR LINKING TABLE)

To Create a Many-to-Many Relationship

1. Click the **Database Tools** tab on the Ribbon.
2. Click the **Relationships button** on the Show/Hide group.
3. Click the **Tables** tab if necessary on the Show Table dialog box.
4. Select the **first** table to be added to the relationship.
5. Click **Add**.
6. Select the **second** table to be added to the relationship.
7. Click **Add**.
8. Select the **Linking table** (or intermediary table) to be added to the relationship (the linking table contains the primary key fields (as foreign keys) from the first and second tables).
9. Click **Close** to close the Show Table dialog box.

10. Click the **primary key** field in the first table and then drag with your mouse to the matching **foreign key** in the linking table.
11. Click **Create** in the Edit Relationship dialog box.
12. Click the **primary key** field in the second table and then drag with your mouse to the matching **foreign key** in the linking table.
13. Click **Create** in the Edit Relationships dialog box.

Let's Try It!

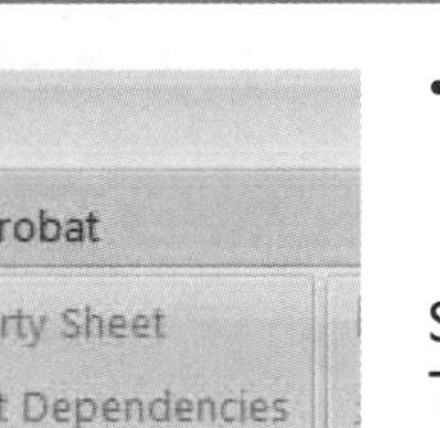

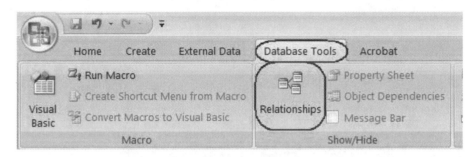

- Click the **Database Tools** tab on the Ribbon.

Switches to Database Tools commands and tools.

- Click the **Relationships button** on the Show/Hide group.

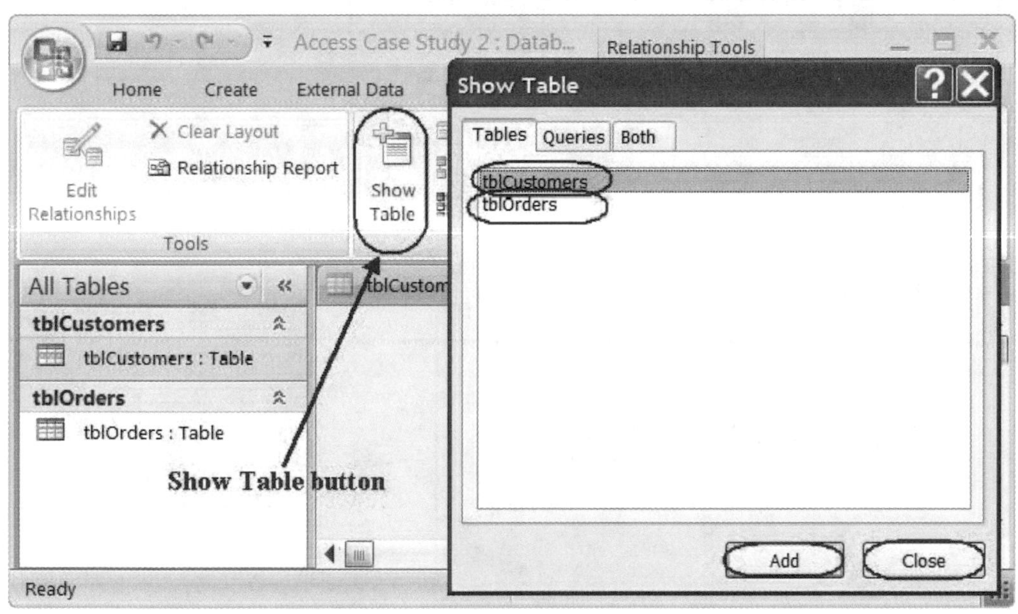

Displays the Relationships window.

- Click the **Show Table** button on the Relationships group if Show Table is not displayed.

Displays the Show Table dialog box.

- Select **tblCustomers**.

Selects the table we want to add to the Relationship window.

- Click **Add**.

Adds the selected table to the Relationships window.

- Select **tblOrders**.

Selects the linking table we want to add to the Relationship window.

- Click **Add**.

Adds the selected table to the Relationships window.

- Click **Close**.

Closes the Show Table dialog box.

- Click the **CustomerID** field in the **tblCustomers** table and then hold your mouse button down.

Selects the field in the Parent Table.

- Drag with your mouse button held down to the **CustomerID** field in the **tblOrders** table and then **release** the mouse button.

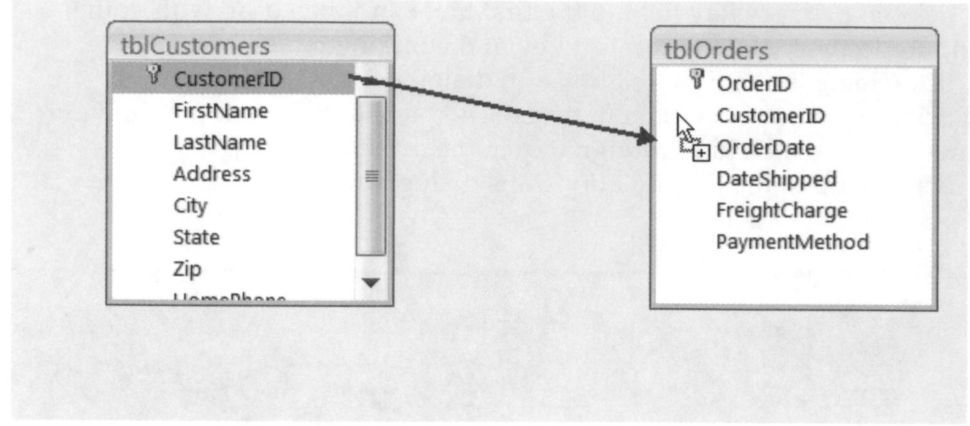

Displays the Edit Relationships dialog box.

- Click **Create**.

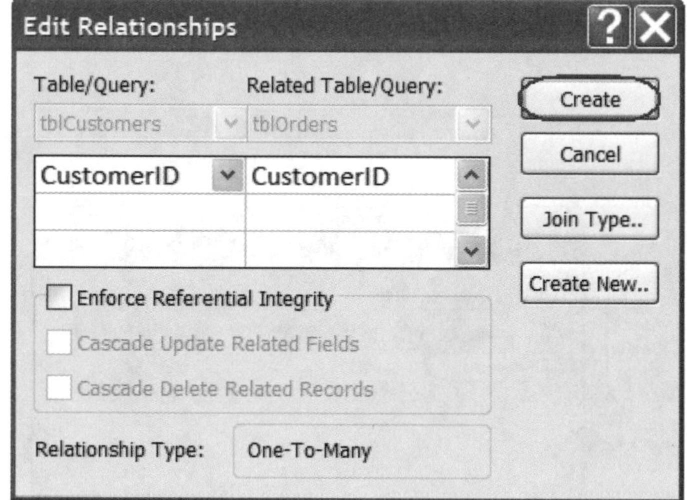

Creates a one-to-many relationship from tblCustomers (the "one" table) to tblOrders (the "many" table), linking both tables on the CustomerID field.

- Click the **Save button** on the Quick Access Toolbar.

Saves the design changes.

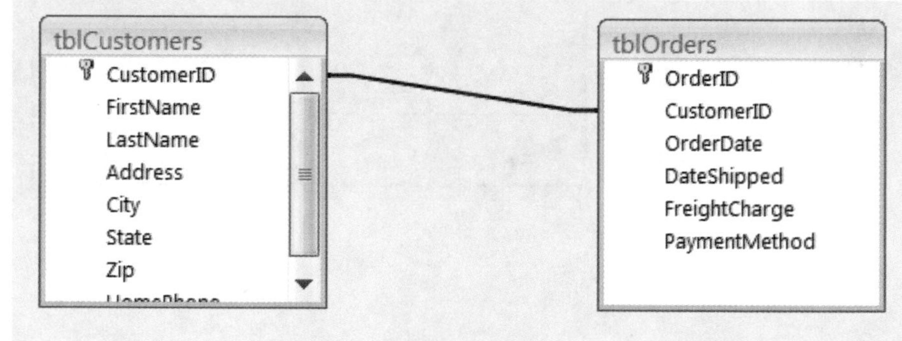

Enforcing Referential Integrity, Cascade Update Related Field, and Cascade Delete Related Records

In section, you will learn how to enforce referential integrity, cascade update and cascade delete related records in a relationship.

Referential Integrity is a system of rules that Access uses to ensure that relationships between records in related tables are valid, and that you don't accidentally delete or change data in one table and not the other. For example, referential integrity ensures that you cannot enter a record into the Orders table for a customer that does not exist in the Customers table.

Once you have chosen to enforce referential integrity in your tables, your data is protected in the following ways:

- You cannot enter a value in a foreign key field of a relationship if there is no matching value in the primary (or parent) table. For example, you cannot enter a record in the Orders table for a customer that does not exist in the Customers table.
- You cannot delete a record in the primary table if a related record exists in a matching table (unless you have checked the Cascade Delete Related Records option). For instance, you cannot delete a record for a customer in the Customers table if that customer has orders in the Orders table.
- You cannot change the value of the primary key field in the primary table if there are matching records in the related table (unless you have checked the Cascade Update Related Fields option).

However, before you can enforce referential integrity, there are certain conditions that must be met. These are:

- The matching field in the parent table must be a primary key or have a unique index.
- The related fields must have the same data type.
- The tables must reside in the same Access database.

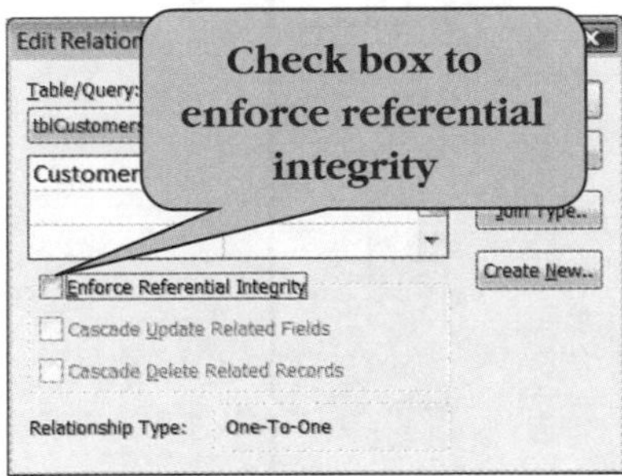

To Enforce Referential Integrity

1. After creating the relationship link, check **Enforce Referential Integrity** in the Edit Relationships dialog box.
2. If the relationship has already been created, **double-click** on the relationship link to display the Edit Relationships dialog box and then check the Enforce Referential Integrity check box.

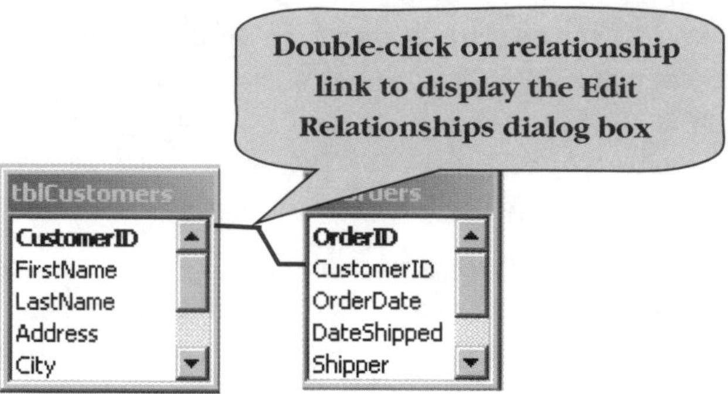

Let's Try It!

- Double-click the **link line** between tblCustomers and tblOrders as shown.

Displays the Edit Relationships dialog box for that relationship.

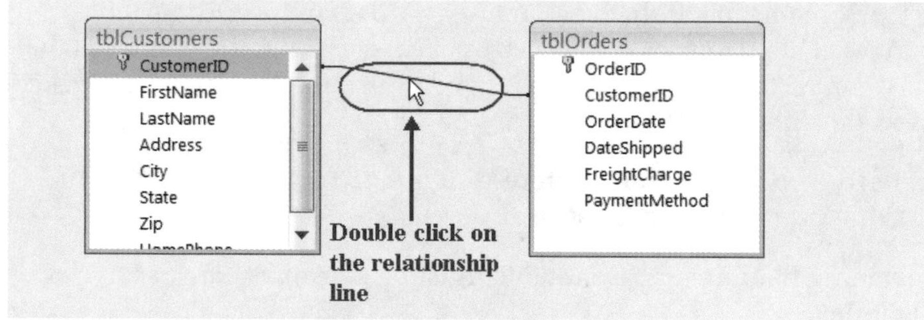

- Click the **Enforce Referential Integrity** check box.

Enforces referential integrity for the relationship.

- Click **OK**.

Closes the Edit Relationships dialog box.

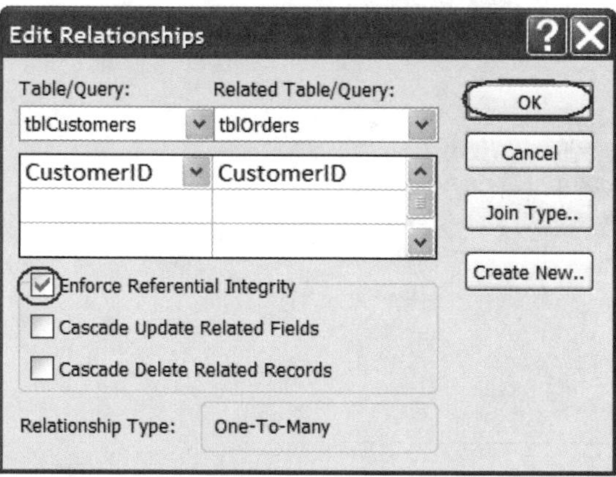

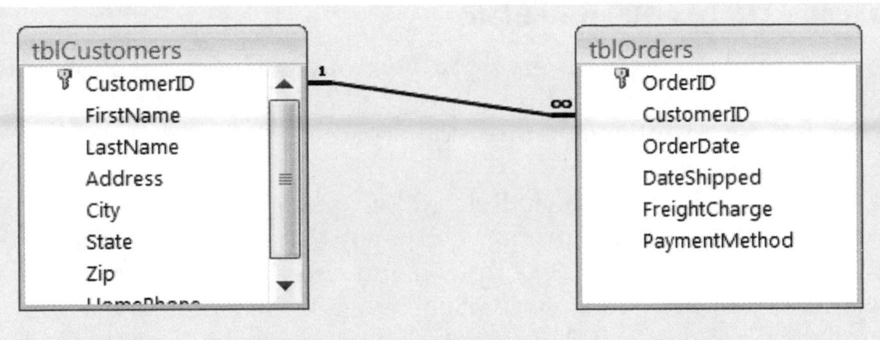

- Click the **Save button** on the Quick Access Toolbar.

Saves the design changes.

Cascade Update Related Fields

Once referential integrity is enforced, you may wish to set the **Cascade Update Related Fields** option in the Edit Relationships dialog box. With this option set, update options that would normally be prevented by referential integrity rules are allowed.

Setting the Cascade Update Related Fields option specifies that any time you change the primary key of a record in the primary (or parent) table, Access will automatically update the primary key to the new value in all related records. For example, if you change a customer's ID in the Customers table, the CustomerID field in the Orders table is automatically updated for every one of the customer's orders. This prevents the relationship from being broken and the creation of orphaned records.

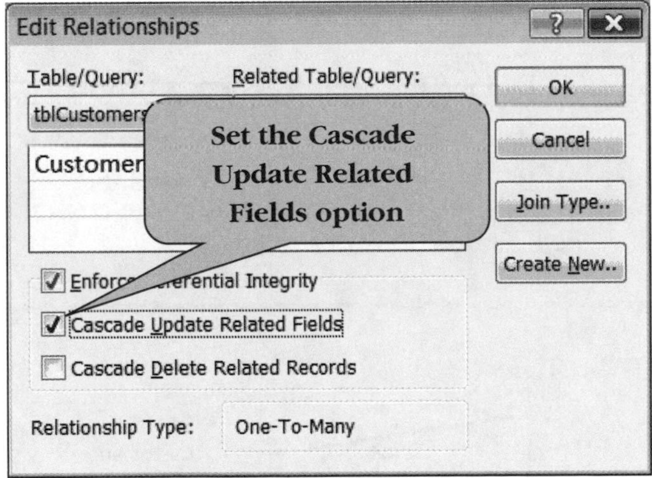

To Set the Cascade Update Related Fields Option

1. After creating the relationship link, check the **Cascade Update Related Fields** check box in the Edit Relationships dialog box.
2. If the relationship has already been created, **double-click** the relationship link to display the Edit Relationships dialog box.

Cascade Update Related Fields

Once referential integrity is enforced, you may wish to set the **Cascade Delete Related Records** option in the Edit Relationships dialog box. With this option set, delete options that would normally be prevented by referential integrity rules are allowed.

Setting the Cascade Delete Related Records option specifies that when you delete a record in the primary (or parent) table, all of the related records will be deleted as well. For example, if you delete a customer in the Customers table, all orders for that customer in the Orders table will automatically be deleted. This prevents the relationship from being broken and the creation of orphaned records.

If this option is not set and you wished to delete a customer along with his or her orders, you would first need to delete all records from the orders table before being able to delete the customer.

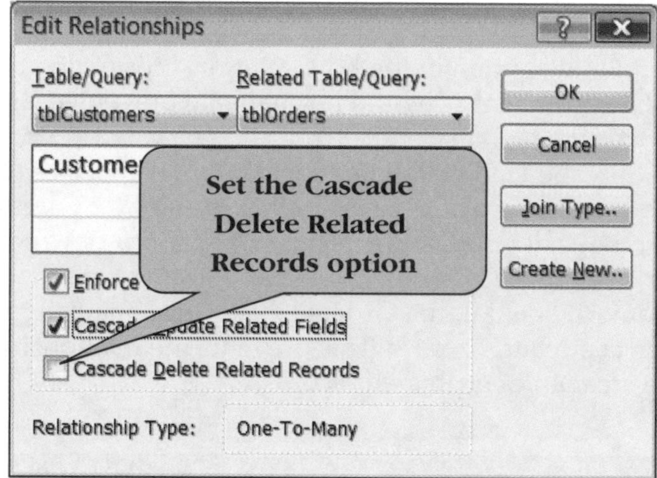

To Set the Cascade Delete Related Records Option

1. After creating the relationship link, check the **Cascade Delete Related Records** check box in the Edit Relationships dialog box.
2. If the relationship has already been created, **double-click** the relationship link to display the Edit Relationships dialog box.

Let's Try It!

- Double-click the **link line** between **tblCustomers** and **tblOrders**.

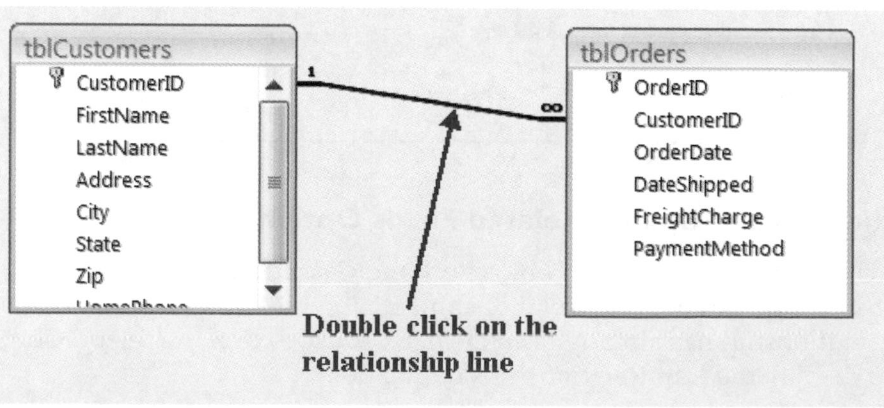

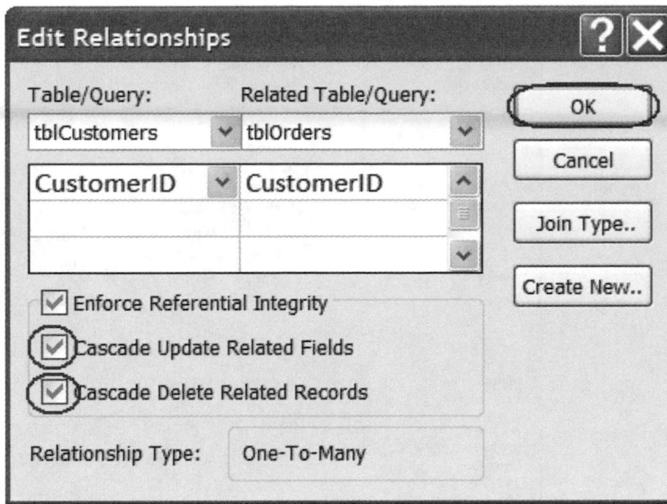

Displays the Edit Relationships dialog box for that relationship.

- Click the **Cascade Update Related Fields** check box and **Cascade Delete Related Records** check box.

Sets the option to Cascade Update Fields and Delete Related Records for the relationship.

- Click **OK**.

Closes the Edit Relationships dialog box.

- Click the **Save button** on the Quick Access Toolbar.

Saves the design changes.

- Click the **Close button** for the Relationship Window.

Setting Validation Rules

In this section, you will learn how to set validation rules for your data.

To ensure that users enter valid data in a field, you can set a **validation rule** for data entry. A validation rule is a property that defines valid input entries for a field in a table. For example, if you started your business on March 15, 1997, you could set a validation rule for the order date field to be >=3/15/1997. If the data entered does not meet the requirements of the validation rule, the user receives an error message. You can even customize the error message the user receives by typing in the desired error message in the **validation text** box in Table Design view.

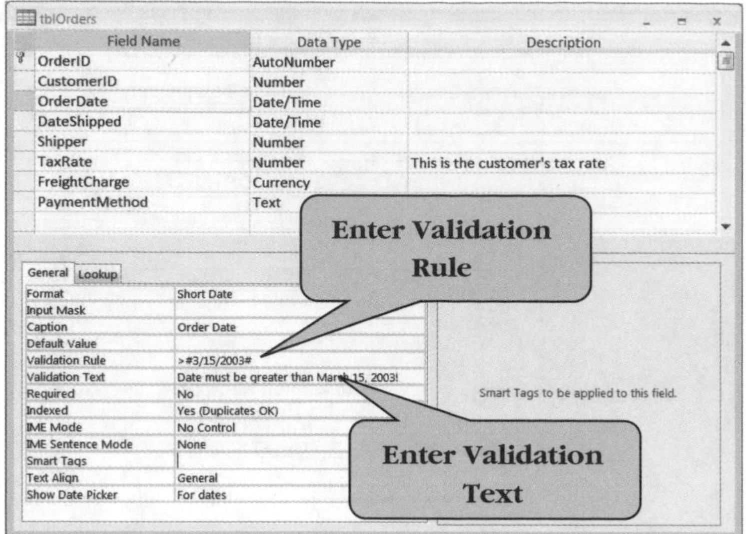

You can either type the validation rule directly in the Validation Rule box under field properties or click the build button to the right of the property. The build button launches the **expression builder**, an Access tool that allows you to create an expression by selecting common functions, constants and operators from the expression window.

To Set a Validation Rule

1. Open the table in Design View that contains the field you want to restrict.
2. Click anywhere in the row of the field for which you want to set a validation rule.
3. Type in the expression in the **Validation Rule** box under Field Properties.
4. If desired, type in a custom error message in the **Validation Text** box under Field Properties

VALIDATION RULE EXAMPLES

Validation Rule Expression	Description
>=50	Entry must be greater than or equal to 50
"MI" or "WI"	Enter must be either MI or WI
Between 5/1/2000 And 6/30/2003	Date must be between 5/1/2000 and 6/30/2003.
>5/1/2000	Date must be greater than 5/1/2000
=Date()	Entry must be today's date

Let's Try It!

- Right-click on **tblOrders** in the Navigation Pane and then click the **Design View**.

Displays tblOrders in Design view.

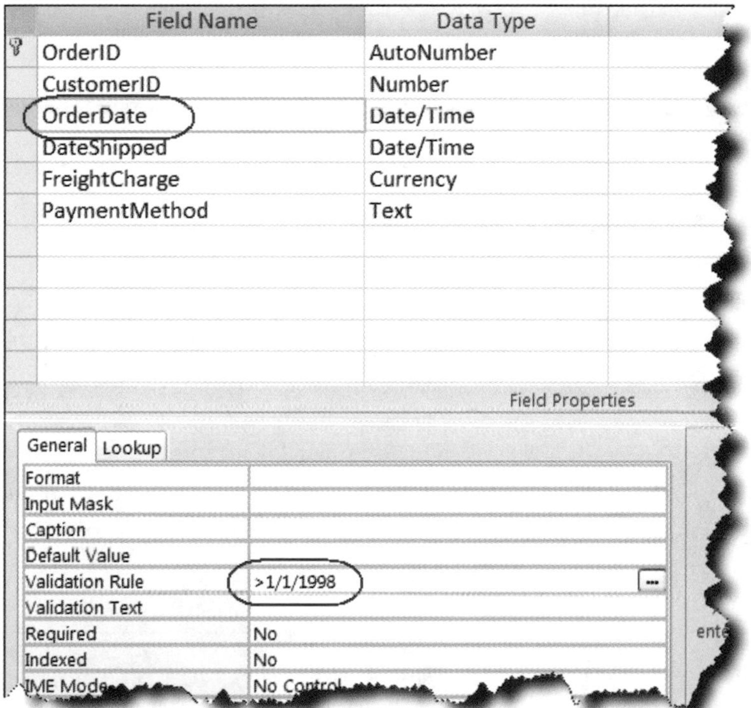

- Click in the Field Name column for the **OrderDate** field.

Selects the OrderDate Field.

- Under Field Properties, click in the **Validation Rule** box and then type: **>1/1/1998** as shown.

Sets a validation rule for the OrderDate field that the date must be greater than January 1, 1998.

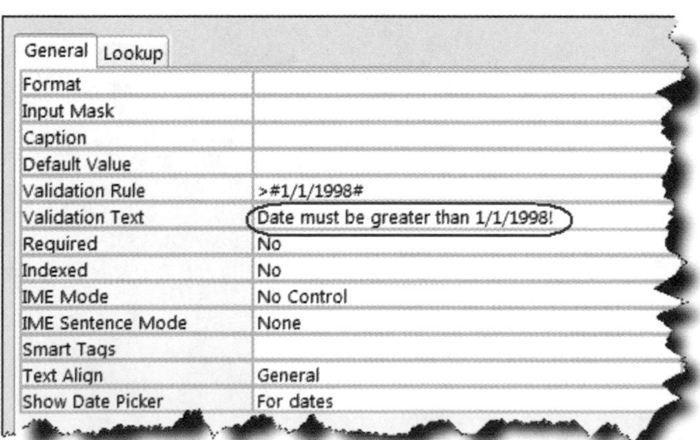

- In the **Validation Text** box, type: **Date must be greater than 1/1/1998!**

Enters a custom error message that the user receives if the validation rule is violated.

- Click the **Save** button on the Quick Access Toolbar.

Saves the design changes.

- Click **Yes** when the message box appears.

Access asks us if it should check to ensure that existing data in our table does not violate our new validation rule.

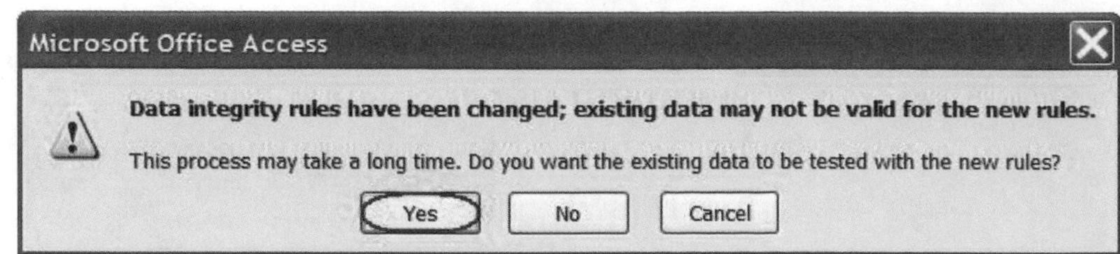
Microsoft Office Access
Data integrity rules have been changed; existing data may not be valid for the new rules.
This process may take a long time. Do you want the existing data to be tested with the new rules?
Yes
No
Cancel

- Click the **View** button on the Ribbon.

Switches to Datasheet view.

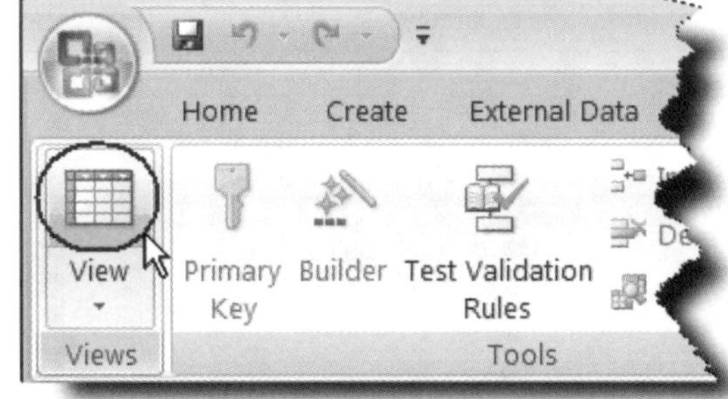
Home
Create
External Data
View
Primary Key
Builder
Test Validation Rules
Views
Tools

- Click in the new row under **CustomerID** and type: **123**.

Creates a new row and enters a value of 123 for the CustomerID.

- Press the **Tab** key.

Moves to the next field.

	OrderID	CustomerID	OrderDate	DateShipped	FreightCharg	PaymentMethod	Add Nev
	1	456	5/1/2002	5/7/2002	$5.95	MasterCard	
	2	234	7/24/2002	7/29/2002	$6.00	Visa	
	3	780	3/23/2000	3/24/2000	$5.50	American Express	
	4	456	6/21/1999	6/23/1999	$5.50	Visa	
	5	780	6/24/2003	6/27/2003	$5.50	Discover	
	6	123					
*	(New)						

- Type: **6/25/1997**

Enters a value for the OrderDate field.

	OrderID	CustomerID	OrderDate	DateShipped	FreightCharg	PaymentMethod	Add Nev
	1	456	5/1/2002	5/7/2002	$5.95	MasterCard	
	2	234	7/24/2002	7/29/2002	$6.00	Visa	
	3	780	3/23/2000	3/24/2000	$5.50	American Express	
	4	456	6/21/1999	6/23/1999	$5.50	Visa	
	5	780	6/24/2003	6/27/2003	$5.50	Discover	
	6	123	6/25/1997				
*	(New)						

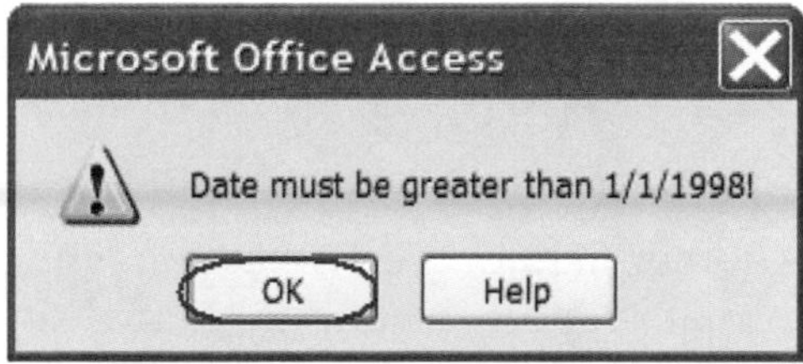

- Press **Tab**.

As the data we entered in the OrderDate field violates the validation rule we set, our custom error message is displayed.

- Click **OK**.

Closes the error message box and returns us to the OrderDate field so that we can enter valid data.

	OrderID	CustomerID	OrderDate	DateShipped	FreightCharg	PaymentMethod	Add Nev
	1	456	5/1/2002	5/7/2002	$5.95	MasterCard	
	2	234	7/24/2002	7/29/2002	$6.00	Visa	
	3	780	3/23/2000	3/24/2000	$5.50	American Express	
	4	456	6/21/1999	6/23/1999	$5.50	Visa	
	5	780	6/24/2003	6/27/2003	$5.50	Discover	
	6	123	6/25/2004				
*	(New)						

- Press the **Backspace** key four times and then type: **2004**.

Changes the year to 2004.

	OrderID	CustomerID	OrderDate	DateShipped	FreightCharg	PaymentMethod	Add Nev
	1	456	5/1/2002	5/7/2002	$5.95	MasterCard	
	2	234	7/24/2002	7/29/2002	$6.00	Visa	
	3	780	3/23/2000	3/24/2000	$5.50	American Express	
	4	456	6/21/1999	6/23/1999	$5.50	Visa	
	5	780	6/24/2003	6/27/2003	$5.50	Discover	
	6	123	6/25/2004	6/27/2004	$4.95	American Express	
*	(New)						

- Press **Tab**.

Moves to the next field. Our validation rule is no longer violated.

- Enter the rest of the data for the current record as shown. Press **Tab** to move from one field to the next.

DateShipped: 6/27/2004
FreightCharge: $4.95
PaymentMethod: American Express

Enters the data for the remaining fields of the current record.

Formatting Fields

In this section, you will learn how to modify the Format property of a field.

Another field property that you will find useful is the **Format** property. The format property is used to change how the data is displayed on your screen and in printed form. Access has several pre-defined formats that you can use to change the appearance of your data. Each data type in Access has its own set of format property settings. For example, you can format a date/time field so that it displays the date as Thursday, August 28, 2003 or as 8/28/2003.

There may be times when the pre-defined formats are not sufficient for your needs. Luckily, there are a wide variety of **custom formats** that you can use. Custom formats are formatting symbols that are entered manually in the format field rather than choosing a pre-defined format from a list. For instance, you may wish a date field to be displayed as Wed May 01. To accomplish this, you would enter: **ddd mmm dd** in the format field. Or to display your date in European format with the month preceding the date, enter: **dd/mm/yyyy**.

To Change the Formatting of Fields

1. Open the table in Design View that contains the field you wish to format.
2. Click anywhere in the row of the field to be formatted.
3. To use a pre-defined format, click in the **Format** box under Field Properties, click the arrow on the right of the box and then select a pre-defined format from the drop-down list.
4. To use a custom format, type the desired formatting characters directly into the Format box.

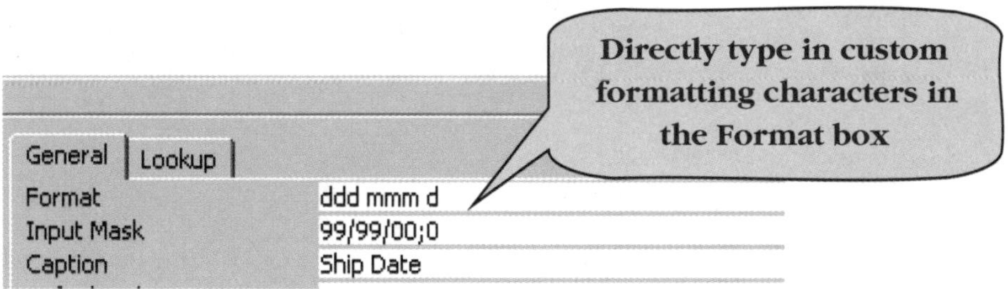

Let's Try It!

- Click the **View** button on the Ribbon.

Switches to Design View.

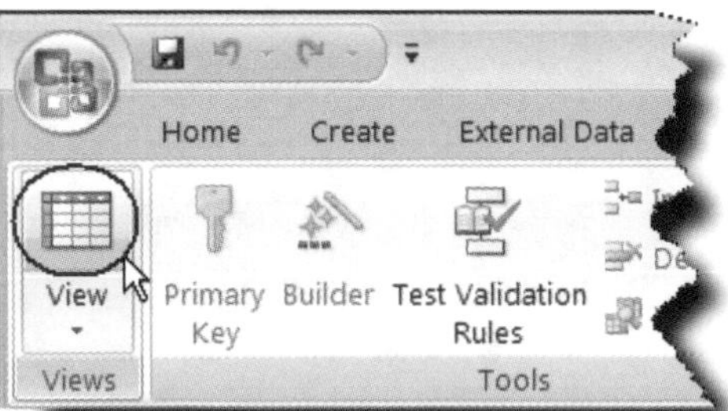

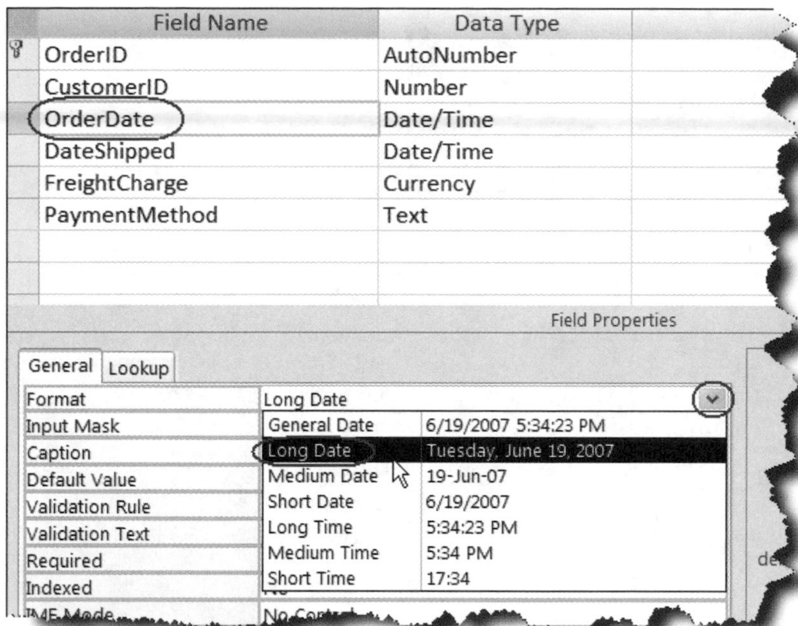

- Click in the Field Name column for the **OrderDate** field.

Displays the field properties for the OrderDate field.

- Under Field Properties, click in the **Format** box.

Activates the Format box for the OrderDate field.

- Click the arrow on the right of the Format box and then select **Long Date** from the drop-down list.

Changes the format of the OrderDate field to Long Date.

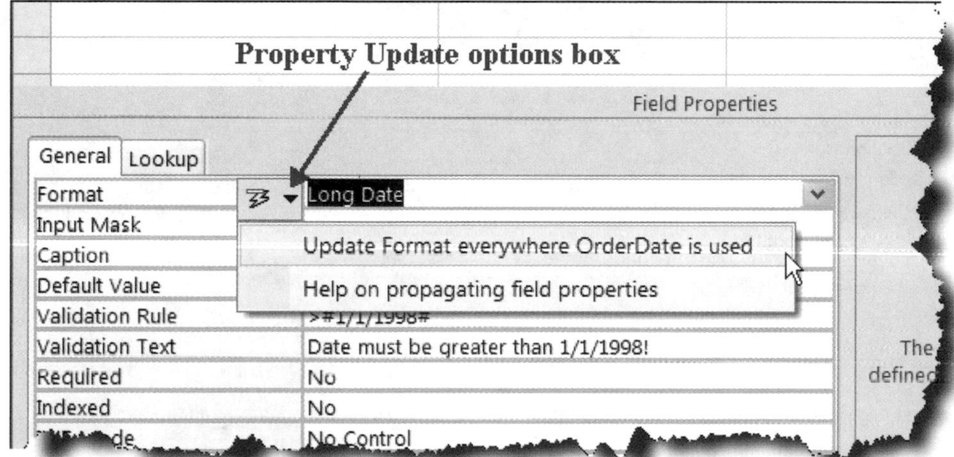

- Click the **Property Update Options box** and select "**Update Format everywhere OrderDate is used**".

The Property Update Options box allows you the option of automatically updating the properties of any controls in forms or reports that are bound to the field in a table when that field is updated in the table. This feature is known as "Propagating Field Properties." When a change is made to a field in a table, the Property Update Options Box is displayed.

- Click **OK**.

As there were no controls in any forms or reports bound to the OrderDate field, Access informs us that no fields needed to be updated.

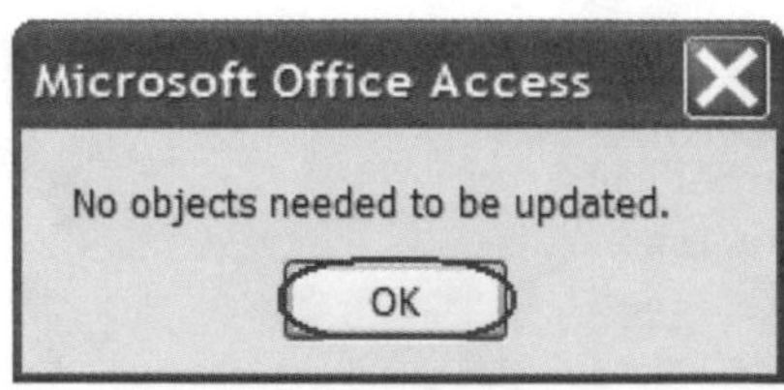

- Click in the Field Name column for the **DateShipped** field.

Displays the field properties for the DateShipped field.

- Under Field Properties, double-click in the **Format** box.

Selects the current format setting for the DateShipped field.

- Type: **dddd mmm dd**

Enters a custom date format.

- Click the **Save** button on the Quick Access Toolbar.

Saves the design changes.

Field Name	Data Type
OrderID	AutoNumber
CustomerID	Number
OrderDate	Date/Time
DateShipped	Date/Time
FreightCharge	Currency
PaymentMethod	Text

Field Properties

General | Lookup

Format	dddd mmm dd
Input Mask	
Caption	
Default Value	
Validation Rule	
Validation Text	
Required	No
Indexed	No

- Click the **View** button and then observe the OrderDate and DateShipped fields. Widen the columns if needed in order to view all of the data.

The formatting of our data has changed based on what we entered in the Format box.

- Click the **Close** button for tblOrders. **Save** changes if prompted.

Closes tblOrders.

OrderID	CustomerID	OrderDate	DateShipped	FreightCharge	PaymentMethod
1	456	Wednesday, May 01, 2002	Tuesday May 07	$5.95	MasterCard
2	234	Wednesday, July 24, 2002	Monday Jul 29	$6.00	Visa
3	780	Thursday, March 23, 2000	Friday Mar 24	$5.50	American Express
4	456	Monday, June 21, 1999	Wednesday Jun 23	$5.50	Visa
5	780	Tuesday, June 24, 2003	Friday Jun 27	$5.50	Discover
6	123	Friday, June 25, 2004	Sunday Jun 27	$4.95	American Express
(New)					

Requiring Data Entry

In this section, you will learn how to set the Required field property.

Another common field property is the **Required** property. You can use the Required property to specify whether a value is required in a particular field. If the property is set to **Yes**, the user must enter a value in a field. This is helpful to ensure that essential data is not left out of a record. For example, you might want to make sure that the Last Name field in a Customer Table is never left blank.

To Set the Required Property

1. Open the table in Design View that contains the field you wish to modify.
2. Click anywhere in the row of the field to be changed.
3. Under Field Properties, click in the **Required** box.
4. Click the drop-down arrow and then choose either **Yes** or **No**.

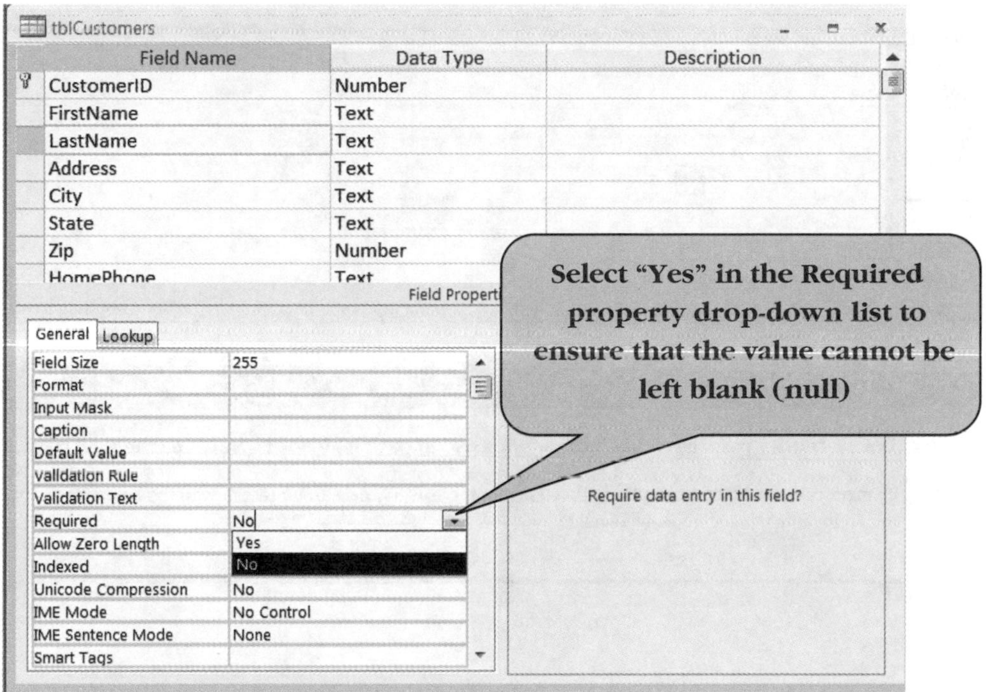

Let's Try It!

- Open **tblCustomers** table in a **Design** view.
- Click in the Field Name column for the **LastName** field.

Displays the field properties for the LastName field.

- Under Field Properties, click in the **Required** box.

Activates the Required field property box for the LastName field.

- Click the arrow in the Required box and select **Yes**.

Sets the property of the LastName field to require a value.

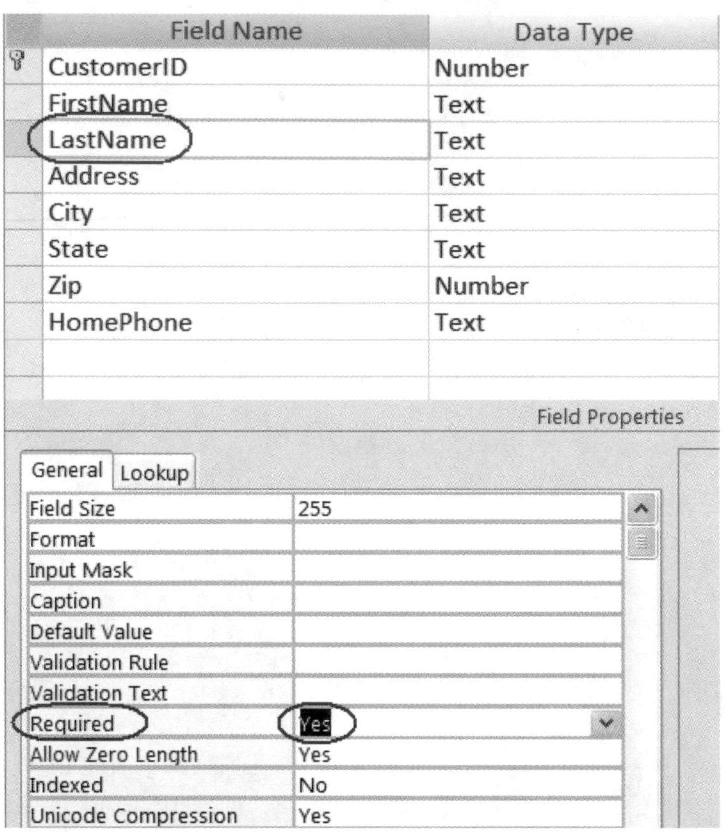

- Click the **Save** button.

A message box appears asking us if we wish to test the existing data with the new data integrity rules.

- Click **Yes**.

Tests the data integrity rules and saves our design changes.

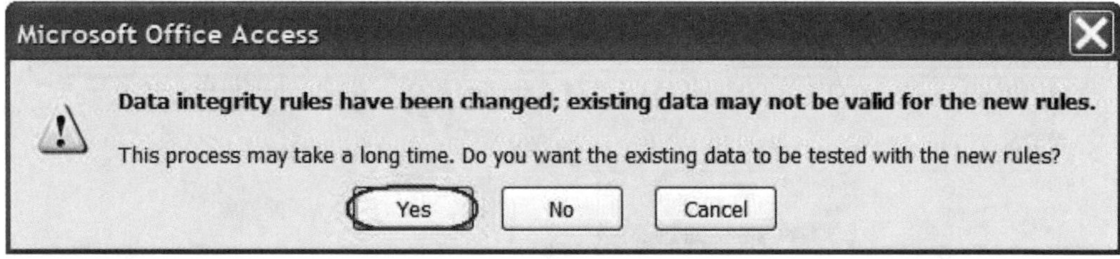

Creating an Input Mask

In this section, you will learn how to create an Input Mask for a field.

You can use the **Input Mask** property (for text or date/time data types only) to ensure that data gets entered in the correct format. For instance, you might want the phone number field to be in the format: **(000) 000-0000**. Using an input mask will not only ensure that the data is in a particular format, but it also saves you the trouble of typing certain characters, like parenthesis or hyphens. In the telephone number example, Access would not let you enter a number without an area code or would not let you save a record that did not contain the required number of characters.

For common types of entries such as phone numbers, social security numbers, dates, or zip codes, use the Input Mask Wizard by clicking on the Build button in the Input Mask property box and then choose one of the available pre-defined Input Masks.

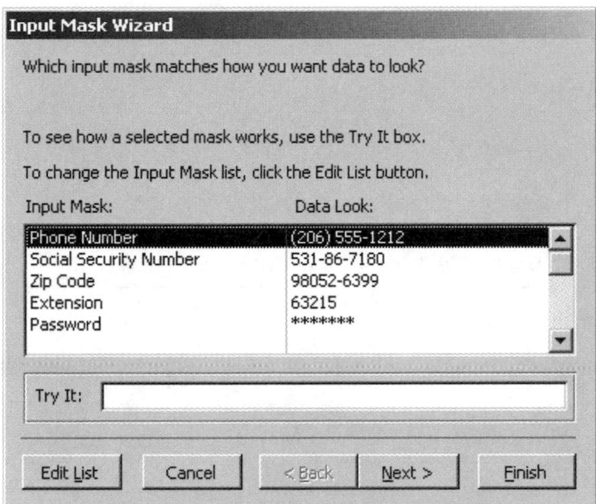

THE INPUT MASK WIZARD

For entries not supported by the Input Mask Wizard, you can create your own Input Mask manually. The Table below lists the characters available to create a **manual Input Mask**. The Input Mask contains 3 sections, each separate by a semicolon:

1. The mask characters listed in the table below.
2. Enter 1 if you want all literal placeholders to be saved with the data. Enter 0 (or leave blank) to save only the characters in the field.
3. Optional: Enter the placeholder that you want to appear on-screen as the user enters data.

For example, let's say we had an employee number in the following format: ######-##. The first 6 characters are required and must be numbers, and the two characters after the dash can be letters or numbers and are optional. We also want an underscore (_) as a placeholder. Thus, our manual Input Mask would be entered as 000000-aa;1;_. See the breakdown below.

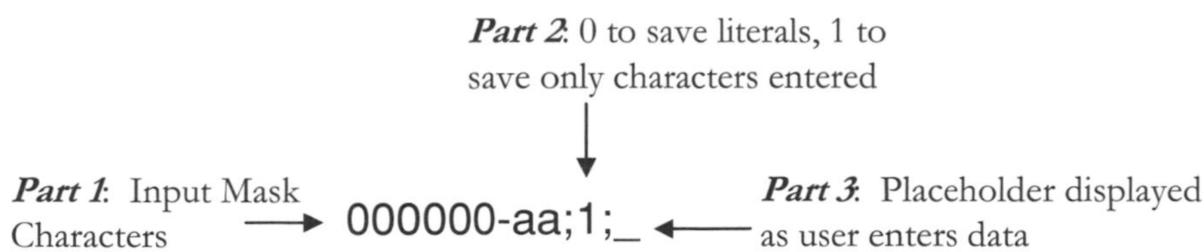

INPUT MASK CHARACTERS

Character	Description
0	Number (0 through 9, entry required; plus and minus signs are not allowed).
9	Number or space (entry optional; plus and minus signs not allowed).
#	Number or space (entry optional; plus and minus signs allowed).
L	Letter (A through Z, entry required).
?	Letter (A through Z, entry optional).
A	Letter or number (entry required).
a	Letter or number (entry optional).
&	Any character or a space (entry required).
C	Any character or a space (entry optional).
. , : ; - /	Decimal placeholder and thousands, date, and time separators.
<	Converts all characters that follow to lowercase.
>	Converts all characters that follow to uppercase.
!	Characters are displayed from right to left, rather than from left to right.
\	Causes the character that follows to be displayed as a literal character (for example, \A is displayed as just A).
Password	Creates a password entry text box. Any character typed in the text box is stored as the character but is displayed as an asterisk (*).

To Create an Input Mask

1. Select the table that contains the field for which you want to create an Input Mask.
2. Switch to **Design View**.
3. Click anywhere in the row of the field to receive the Input Mask.
4. To enter an Input Mask manually, type the desired characters in the Input Mask box in the Field Properties area.
5. To enter an Input Mask using the wizard:
   a. Click in the Input Mask box in the Field Properties area.
   b. Click the **Build button**.
   c. Chose the desired Input Mask from the list box.
   d. Click **Next**.
   e. Make any desired changes to the Input Mask characters or to the placeholder.
   f. Click **Next**.
   g. Select whether to store data with the literals or without the literals.
   h. Click **Finish**.

Let's Try It!

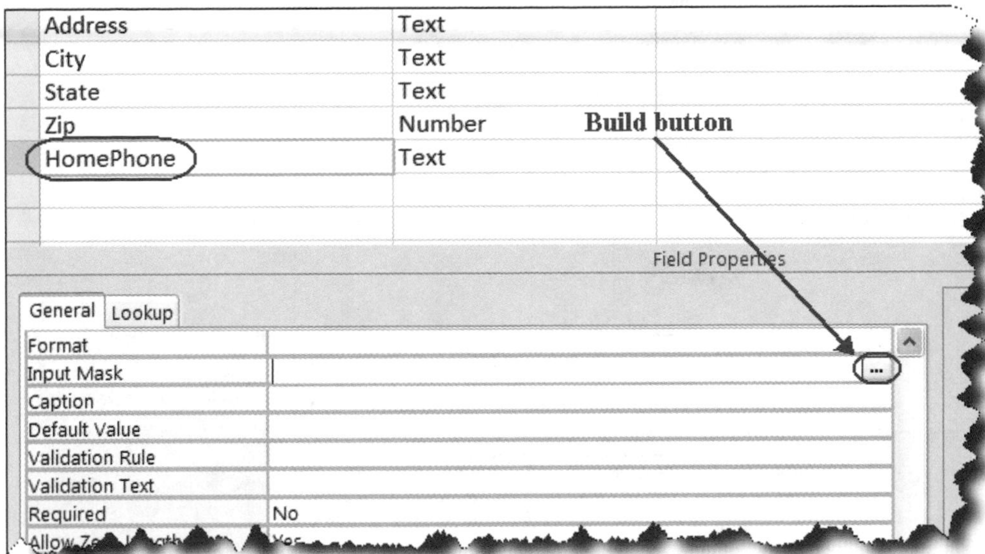

- Click in the Field Name column for the **HomePhone** field.

Displays the field properties for the HomePhone field.

- Under Field Properties, click in the **Input Mask** box.

Activates the Input Mask field property for the HomePhone field.

- Click the **Build button** on the right edge of the Input Mask box.

Launches the Input Mask Wizard.

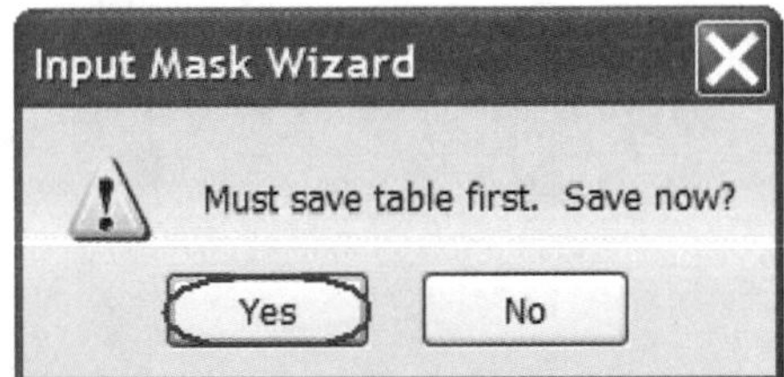

- Click **Yes** if asked to save the table.

Input Mask Wizard

Which input mask matches how you want data to look?

To see how a selected mask works, use the Try It box.

To change the Input Mask list, click the Edit List button.

Input Mask:	Data Look:
Phone Number	(206) 555-1212
Social Security Number	831-86-7180
Zip Code	98052-6399
Extension	63215
Password	*******
Long Time	1:12:00 PM

Try It:

Edit List | Cancel | < Back | Next > | Finish

- Select **Phone Number** from the Input Mask window as shown.

Selects the Input Mask to use.

- Click **Next**.

Moves to the next step of the Wizard.

- Click the **Placeholder Character** arrow and then select **#** from the drop-down list.

Selects the placeholder we want use in our Input Mask.

- Click **Next**.

Moves to the next step of the Wizard.

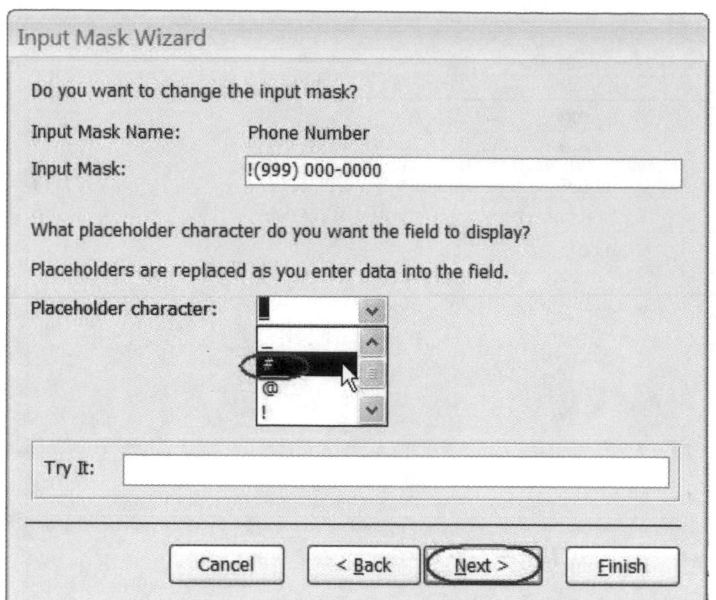

- Click **Finish**.

As we do not wish to save the literal characters with the data, we will accept the default value.

- Click the **Save** button on the Quick Access Toolbar.

Saves our design changes.

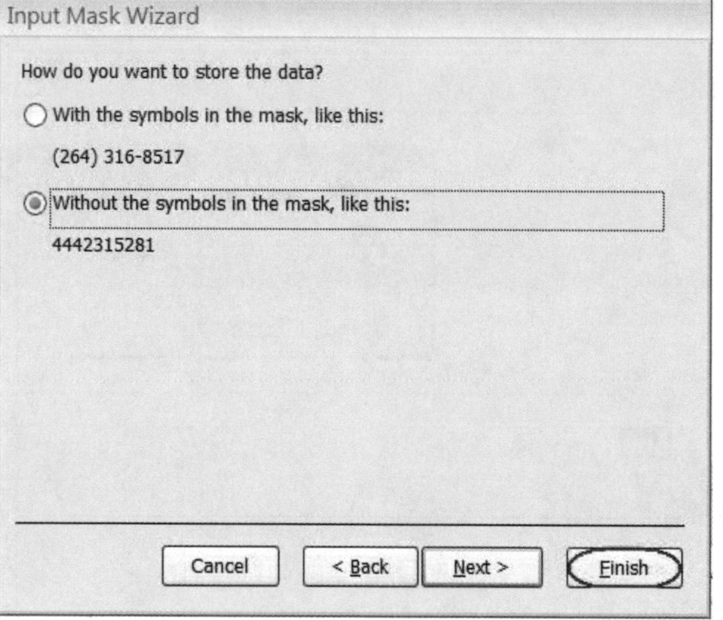

- Click the **View** button.

Switches to Datasheet View.

- Click in the **Zip** field for **Jaime Rickman**

Sets the focus in the Zip field.

- Press **Tab**.

Moves the focus to the HomePhone field.

CustomerID	FirstName	LastName	Address	City	State	Zip	HomePhone
123	Florence	Bateman	4133 Redwood Ln.	Atlanta	GA	30303	(414) 234-4456
234	Sara	Beckman	343 Templeton Dr.	Racine	WI	52602	(414) 456-2342
345	Nicole	Travis	406 W. Pine St.	Glendale	VA	20123	(703) 435-5673
456	Jaime	Rickman	704 Clark St.	Fairfax	VA	20330	(703) 676-2314
780	Thomas	Henderson	98 Clinton Dr.	Orlando	FL	32825	(407) 555-8637

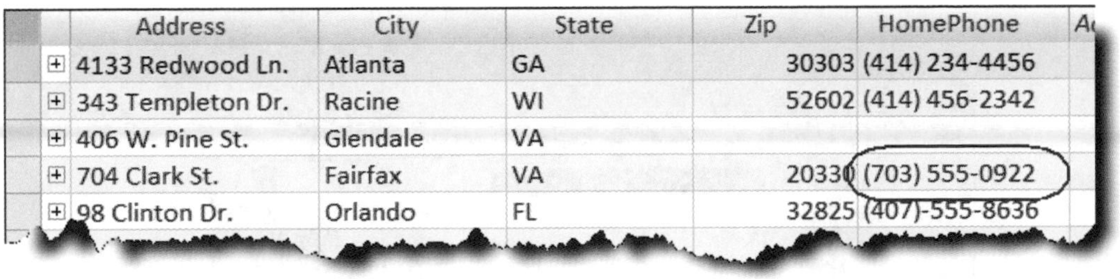

	Address	City	State	Zip	HomePhone	A
⊞	4133 Redwood Ln.	Atlanta	GA	30303	(414) 234-4456	
⊞	343 Templeton Dr.	Racine	WI	52602	(414) 456-2342	
⊞	406 W. Pine St.	Glendale	VA			
⊞	704 Clark St.	Fairfax	VA	2033[illegible]	(703) 555-0922	
⊞	98 Clinton Dr.	Orlando	FL	32825	(407)-555-8636	

- Type: **7035550922**

Enters the phone number without having to enter a parenthesis around the area code or any dashes.

- Click the **Close button** for tblCustomers.

Closes tblCusotmers.

- Open the tblCustomers in a datasheet view and notice the format of the phone number.
- Click the **Close button** for tblCustomers.

Closes tblCusotmers.

Creating a Lookup List and Value List

In this section, you will learn how to create a Lookup Field.

Lookup Fields allow you choose the data for a field from a list of values, usually from a query or from another table. Let's say you were entering customer orders. If you remember from the last section, only the Customer ID is entered in the Orders table, not the customer's name. So how do you know what Customer ID goes with a particular customer? That's where a lookup field comes in. Using a lookup field, you can get a list of all customer names from the Customers table, and then choose which customer to enter into the orders table. Even though the customer names are displayed in the list, you set up your lookup field so that the Customer ID is stored in the field (in the case of our Orders table, only the Customer ID **can** be stored).

The best thing about creating a Lookup Field is that **the Lookup Wizard** will step you through the process of creating a Lookup Field. The Lookup Wizard is the last option in the Data Type drop-down list. If you have already created relationships, you may have to delete them in order to change the Data Type to the Lookup Wizard. Thus, it is advisable to create the Lookup fields in your table before establishing your relationships.

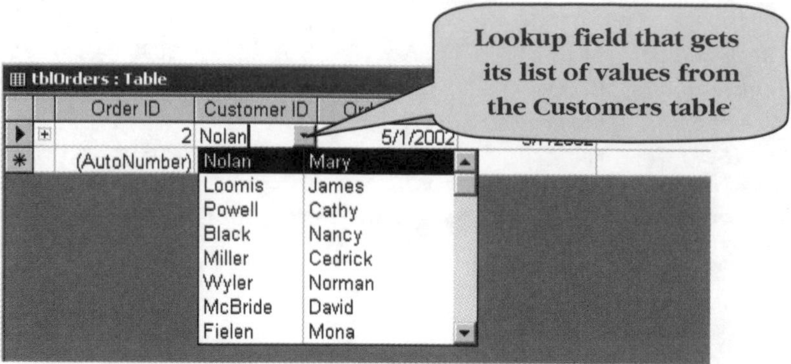

To Create a Lookup List

1. Select the table that contains the field to which you want to add a Lookup field.
2. Switch to **Design View**.
3. Click the **Data Type** arrow for the field to receive the Lookup list and then select **Lookup Wizard**.
4. Select the option that indicates you want the Lookup field to look up the values in a table or query.
5. Click **Next**.
6. Choose the table or query from where the lookup data will be retrieved.
7. Choose which field(s) are to be displayed in the Lookup List.
8. Adjust the columns to the desired width. Notice that the **Hide Key Column** is selected. Uncheck this box to display the Primary Key column (which will be the bound column).
9. Click **Next**.
10. Type the desired label for the Lookup column.
11. Click **Finish**.

A **Value List** is similar to a Lookup field except instead of looking up the values in another table, you type in the values you want to be displayed. If there are only a few items that need to be displayed in a drop-down list, using a Value List is preferable to creating an entire table to hold just a few values to serve as a Lookup List.

Use the Lookup Wizard to create a Value List just like we did in the last section. However, choose "**I will type in the values that I want**" in the first step of the Wizard, and then manually enter the items that are to appear in your list.

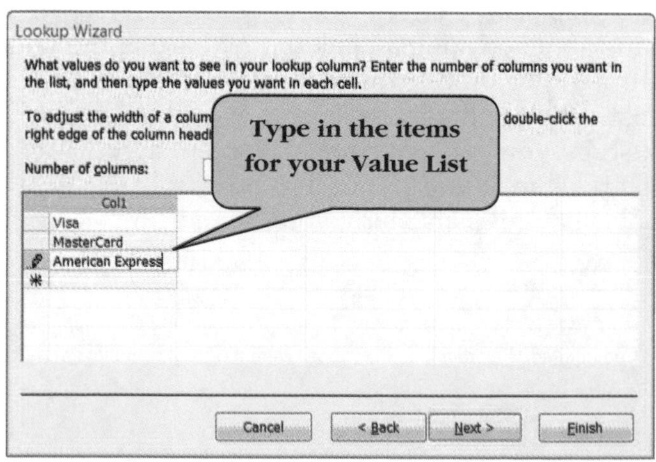

To Create a Value List

1. Select the table that contains the field to which you want to add a Value List.
2. Switch to **Design View**.
3. Click the **Data Type** arrow for the field to receive the Value list and then select **Lookup Wizard**.
4. Select the option "**I will type in the values that I want**".
5. Click **Next**.
6. Choose the number of columns that are to be displayed in the list.
7. Enter the data in the columns that should appear in your list.
8. Click **Next**.
9. Type the desired label for the Value List.
10. Click **Finish**.

Let's Try It!

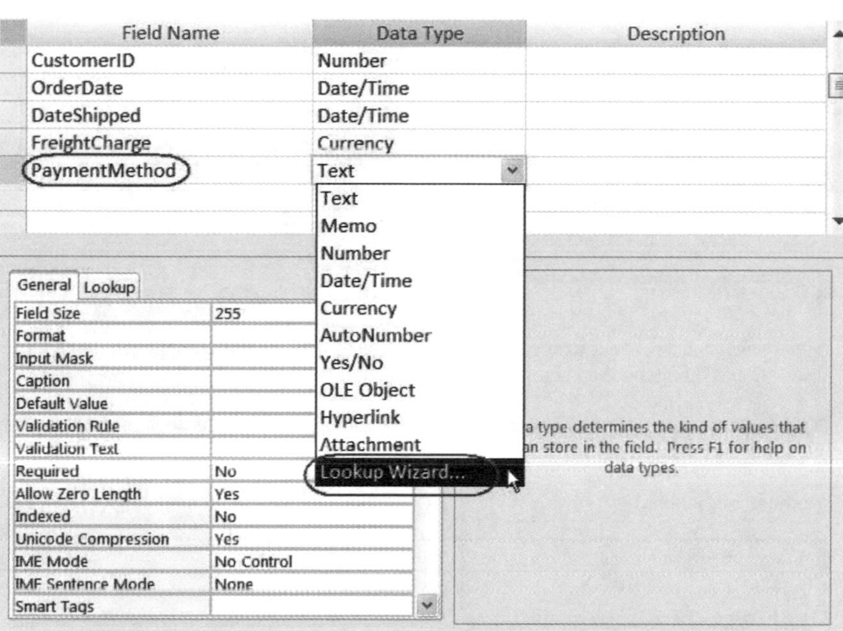

- Open **tblOrders** in a Design view.

Displays tblOrders in Design View.

- Click in the **Data Type** column for the **PaymentMethod** field.

Displays the Data Type arrow.

- Click the arrow and then select **Lookup Wizard** from the drop-down list.

Launches the Lookup Wizard.

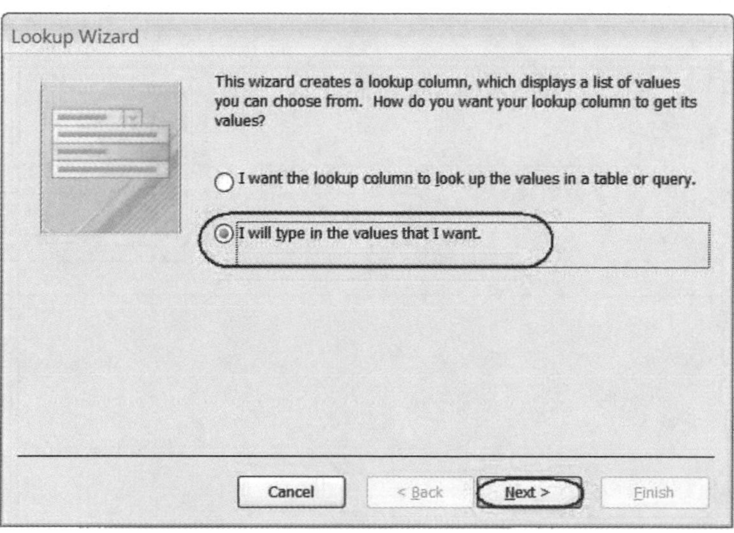

- Select the option "**I will type in the values that I want**".

Sets the option for the Lookup field to get its values from a manually typed list.

- Click **Next**.

Moves to the next step of the Wizard.

- Click in the first blank column and type: **Visa** as shown.

Enters the first value of our Value List.

- Press the **Tab** key.

Moves to a new row.

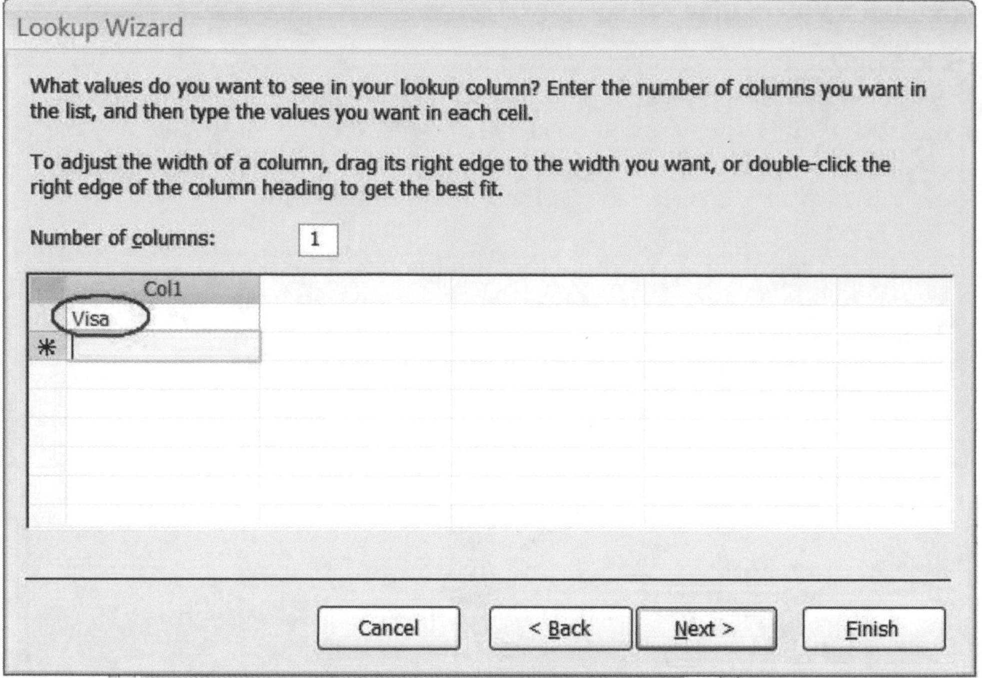

- Type: **MasterCard**

Enters the next value of our Value List.

- Press the **Tab** key.

Moves to a new row.

- Type: **American Express**.

Enters the next value of our Value List

- Click **Finish**.

Completes the Lookup Wizard.

- Click the **Save** button on the Quick Access Toolbar.

Saves our design changes.

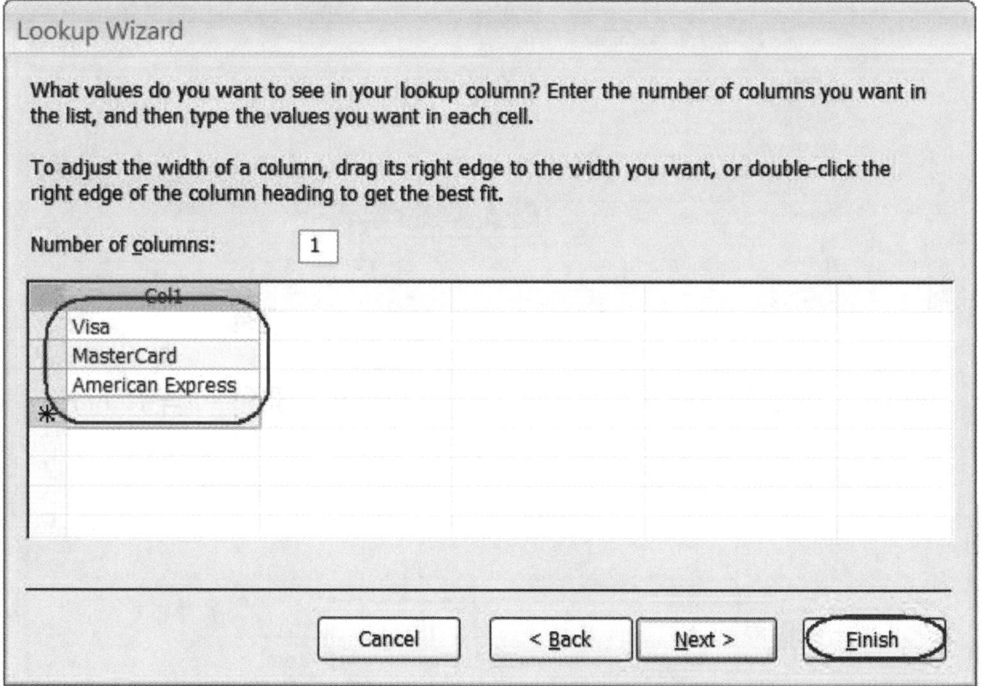

DateShipped	FreightCharge	PaymentMethod	Add New Field
Tuesday May 07	$5.95	MasterCard	
Monday Jul 29	$6.00	Visa	
Friday Mar 24	$5.50	American Express	
Wednesday Jun 23	$5.50	Visa	
Friday Jun 27	$5.50	Discover	
Sunday Jun 27	$4.95	American Express	
*			

- Click the **View** button on the Ribbon.

Switches to Datasheet View.

- Click in the **PaymentMethod** field for the first record.

Displays the arrow for the PaymentMethod field.

DateShipped	FreightCharge	PaymentMethod	Add New Field
Tuesday May 07	$5.95	MasterCard	
Monday Jul 29	$6.00	Visa	
Friday Mar 24	$5.50	MasterCard	
Wednesday Jun 23	$5.50	American Express	
Friday Jun 27	$5.50	Discover	
Sunday Jun 27	$4.95	American Express	
*			

- Click the arrow and then select **AmericanExpress** from the drop-down list.

Selects "AmericanExpress" from the Value List. This value will be stored in the PaymentMethod field.

- Click the **Save** button on the Quick Access Toolbar.

Saves the changes.

- Click the **Close button** for tblOrders.

Closes tblOrders.

Creating Multi-Table Queries

In this section, you will learn how to create a query using more than one table.

A **multi-table query** is a query that retrieves information from more than one related table. When adding tables to your query, Access automatically creates the joins between your tables, assuming that you have set up your relationships beforehand.

Once you have chosen the tables you want including in your query and the joins have been created, select which fields to add to the query grid and then specify any desired criteria.

To Create a Multi-Table Query in Design View

1. Click the **Create tab** on the Ribbon.
2. Click the **Query Design button** on the Other group of the Ribbon.
3. Click the **Tables** tab if necessary.
4. Select the first table upon which you want to base your query and then click the **Add** button.

5. Repeat step 4 until all desired tables have been added.
6. Click **Close** when finished.
7. Add the desired field to the query grid by:
   Double-clicking the field name in the field list box
   Or
   Clicking and dragging the field from the field list box to the design grid
   Or
   Clicking the field row and then choosing the desired field from the drop-down list.

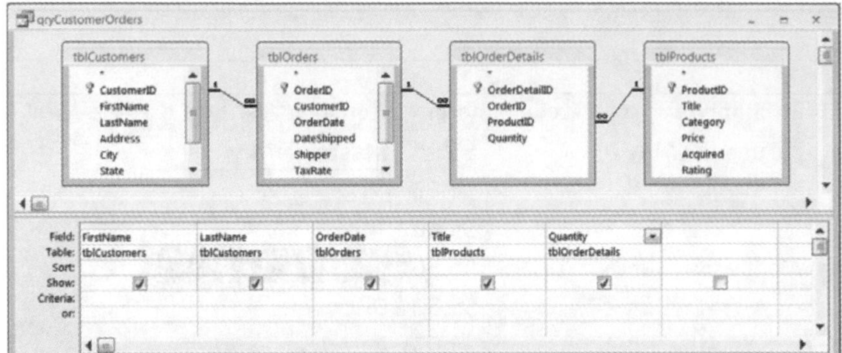

Let's Try It!

- Click the **Create tab** on the Ribbon.

Switches to Create commands and tools.

- Click the **Query Design button** on the Other tab of the Ribbon.

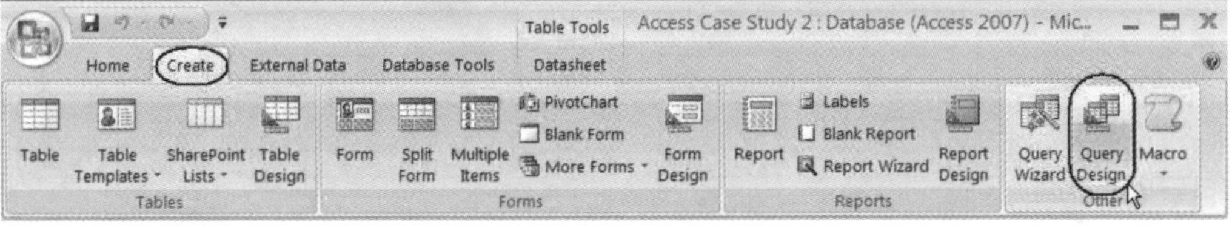

Displays the Show Table dialog box.

- Select **tblCustomers** and then click **Add**.

Adds tblCustomers to the query.

- Select **tblOrders** and then click **Add**.

Adds tblOrders to the query.

- Click the **Close** button.

Closes the Show Table dialog box.

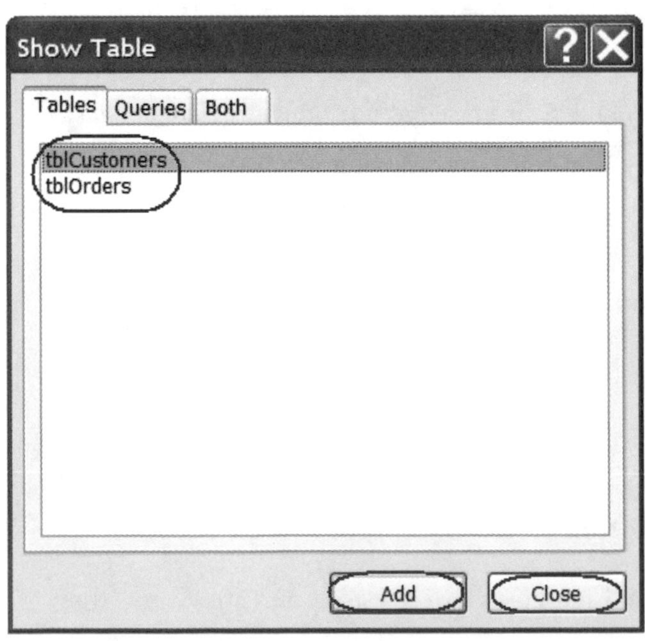

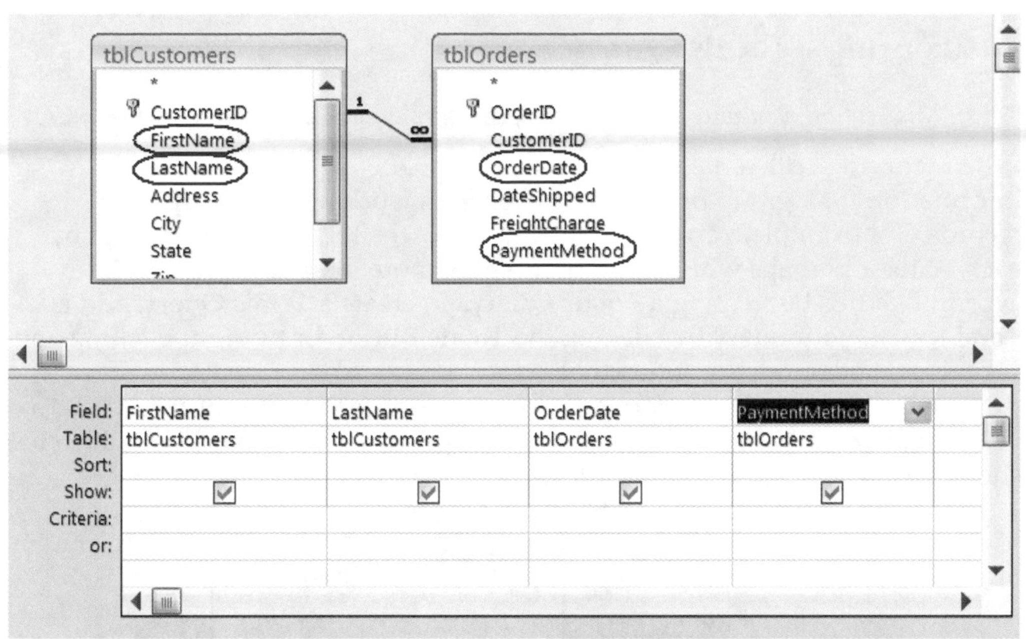

- Double-click the following fields to add them to the query grid:

FirstName (tblCustomers)
LastName (tblCustomers)
OrderDate (tblOrders)
PaymentMethod (tblOrders)

Adds the selected fields to the query grid.

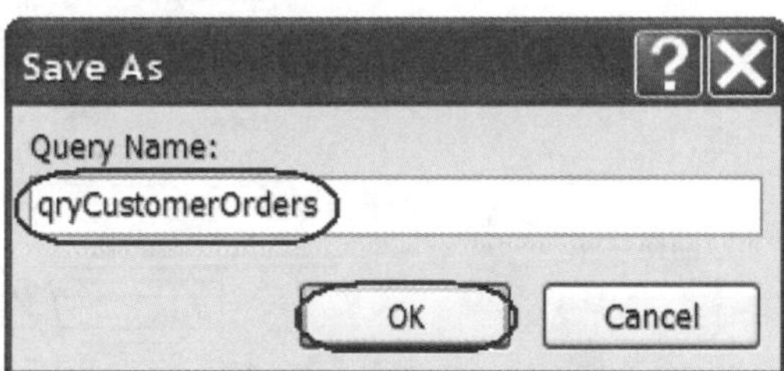

- Click the **Save** button on the Quick Access Toolbar and then type: **qryCustomerOrdes** in the Query Name box.

Provides a name for our query.

- Click **OK**.

Saves the query.

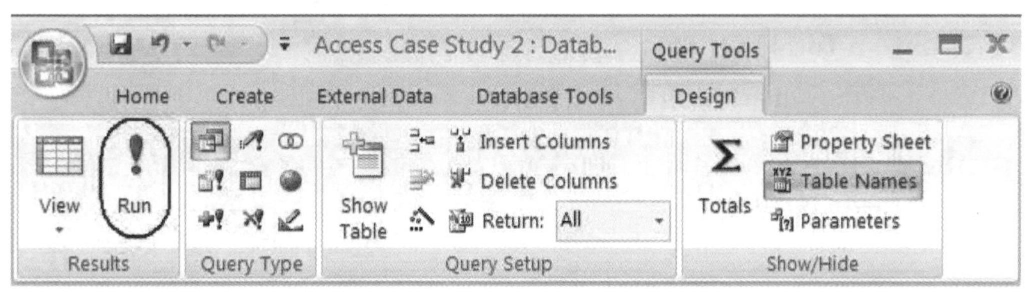

- Click the **Run button** on the Results group and observe the results.

FirstName	LastName	OrderDate	PaymentMethod
Florence	Bateman	Friday, June 25, 2004	American Express
Sara	Beckman	Wednesday, July 24, 2002	Visa
Jaime	Rickman	Wednesday, May 01, 2002	MasterCard
Jaime	Rickman	Monday, June 21, 1999	Visa
Thomas	Henderson	Thursday, March 23, 2000	American Express
Thomas	Henderson	Tuesday, June 24, 2003	Discover

Displays the results of our query.

Creating a Totals Query

In this section, you will learn how to perform calculations on groups of records.

When working with a database, you will inevitably need to summarize information for a group of records, rather than working with individual records. For example, you might need to know the total amount of sales by each state or perhaps which customers spent more than $200. You can accomplish this be creating a **Totals Query**. To create a Totals Query, add a **Total** row to your query by clicking the **Totals Button** or by right-clicking and selecting **Totals** from the contextual menu.

The Totals Row allows you to choose the way each group of records is to be summarized. Access provides several **Aggregate Functions** from which to choose. These are listed in the table below.

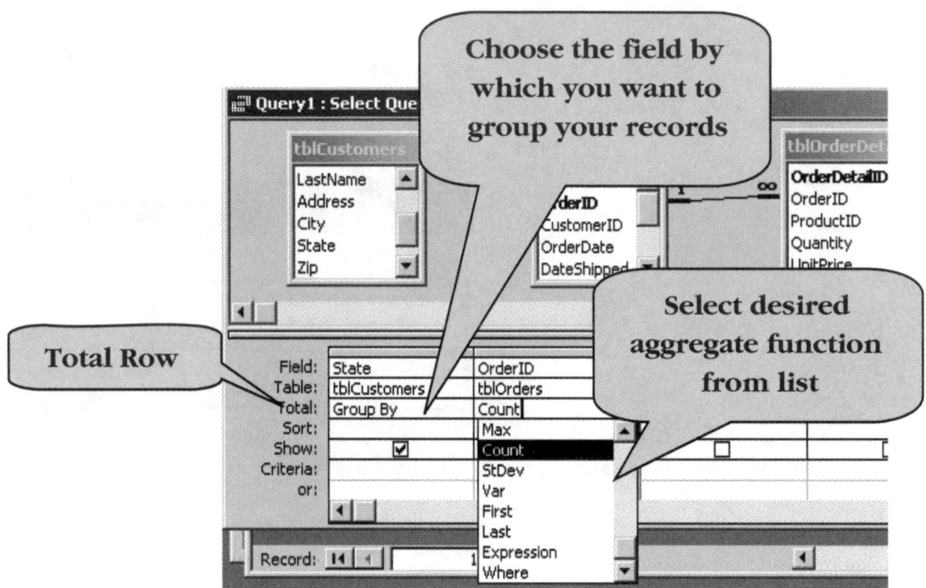

To Create a Totals Query

1. Create a new query in design view.
2. Add the field(s) by which you to group your records to the grid.
3. Add the field to which you want to apply an aggregate function (such as sum) to the grid.
4. Click the **Totals Button** on the Show/Hide group to display the Total row.

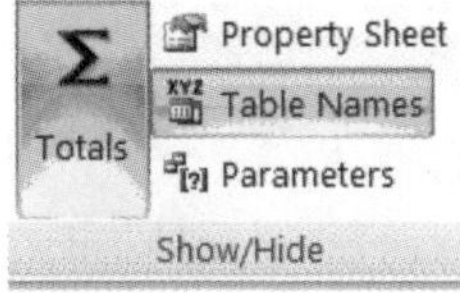

Or

Right-click and click **Totals** from the contextual menu.

5. Click in the **Total** row for the field you wish to calculate.
6. Select the desired aggregate function from the drop-down list.

AGGREGATE FUNCTIONS

Function	Description
Sum	Totals the values for each group.
Avg	Calculates the average value for each group.
Min	Returns the lowest value in each group.
Max	Returns the highest value in each group.
Count	Returns the number of items in each group, not including blank (Null) records.
StDev.	Returns the standard deviation for each group.
Var.	Returns the variance for each group.
First	Returns the first value in each group.
Last	Returns the last value in each group.
Expression	Create a calculated field that includes an aggregate function in its calculation.
Where	Specify criteria for a field you are using to define groupings.
Group By	Define the groups for which you want to perform the calculations. For example, to show total sales by Product, select Group By for the Product Name field.

Let's Try It!

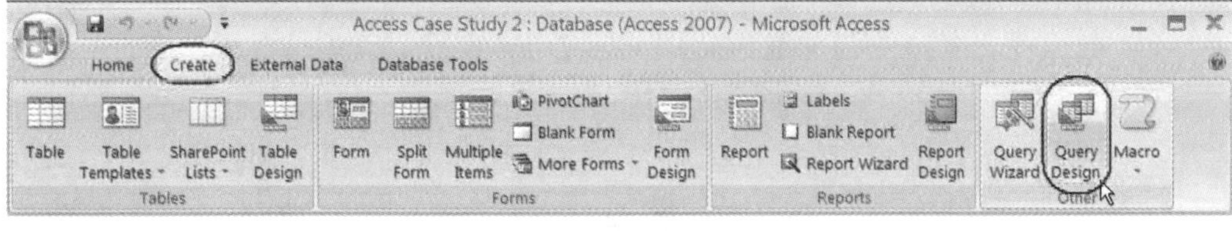

- Click the **Create tab** on the Ribbon.

Switches to Create commands and tools.

- Click the **Query Design button** on the Other tab of the Ribbon.

Displays the Show Table dialog box.

- Select **tblCustomers** and then click **Add**.

Adds tblOrders to the query.

- Select **tblOrders** and then click **Add**.

Adds tblOrders to the query.

- Click the **Close** button.

Closes the Show Table dialog box.

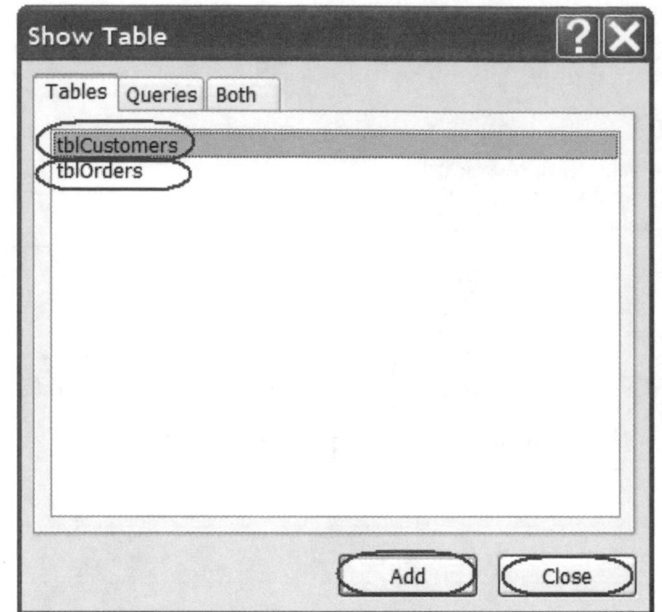

- Double-click the **State** field in tblCustomers.

Adds the State field to the query grid. This is the field by which we wish to group our records.

- Double-click the **OrderID** field in tblOrders.

Adds the OrderID field to the query grid. This is the field we wish to total.

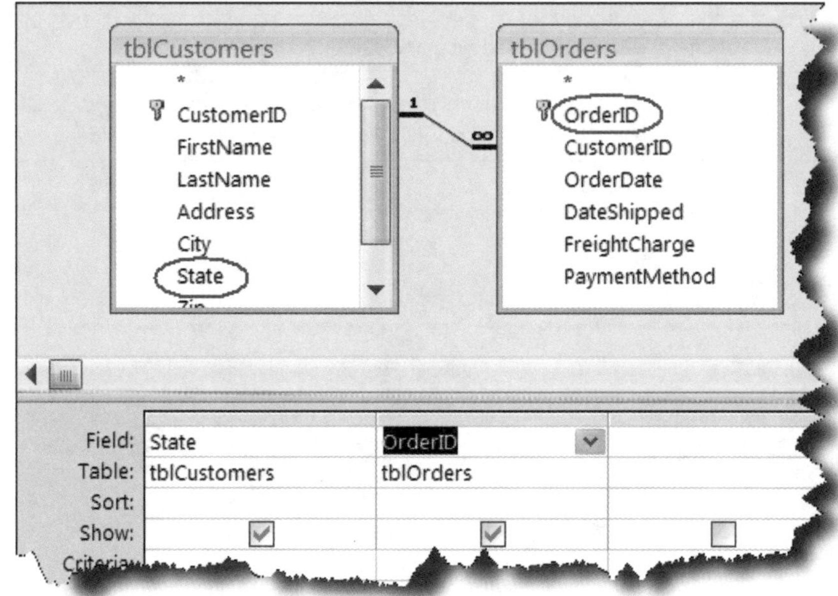

- Click the **Totals button** on the Show/Hide group on the Ribbon.

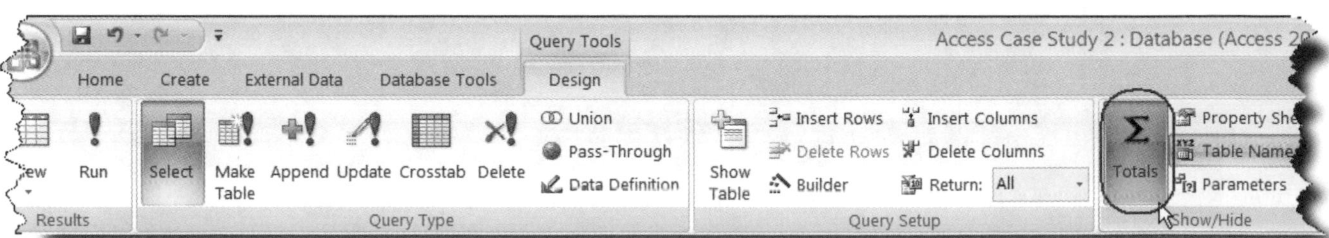

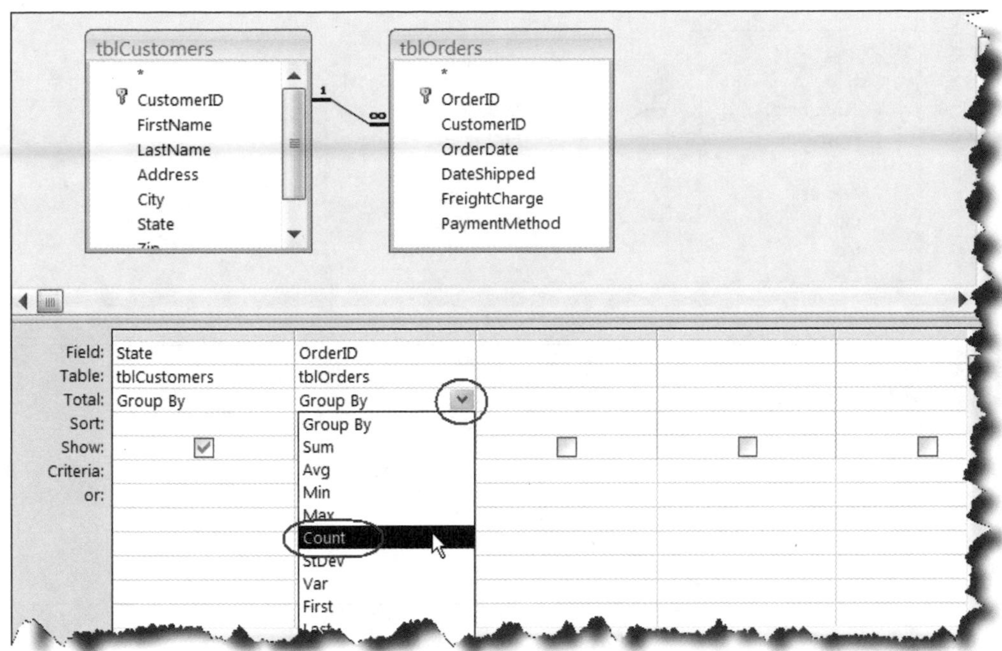

Displays the Totals row.

- Click in the **Total** row for the **OrderID** field.

Displays the drop-down arrow for the OrderID field.

- Click on the arrow and then select **Count** from the drop-down list.

Selects Count as the aggregate function for the OrderID field. This query will generate a total of orders (count of all of the orders) by each state.

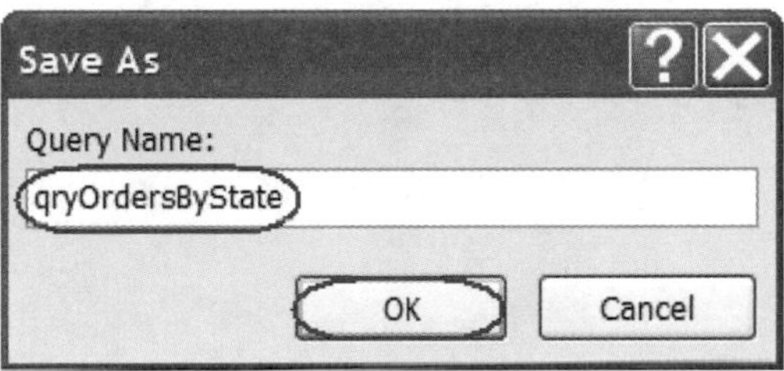

- Click the **Save** button and then type: **qryOrdersByState** in the Query Name box.

Provides a name for our query.

- Click **OK**.

Saves the query and then closes the Query Name box.

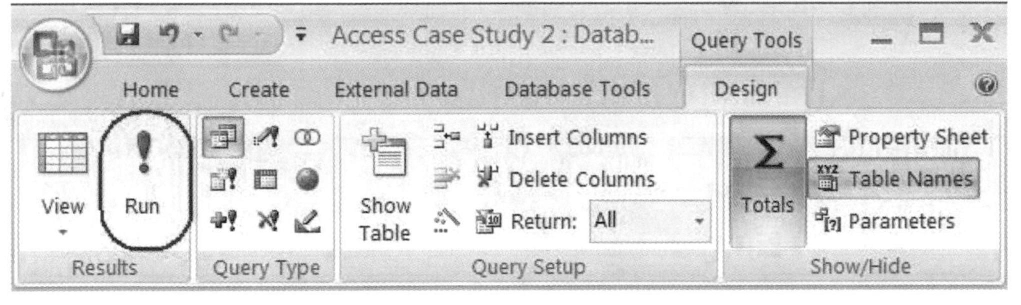

- Click the **Run** button.

State	CountOfOrderID
FL	2
GA	1
VA	2
WI	1

- Observe the results. The totals query displays the number of orders placed for each state. Note that the calculated field is automatically named: CountofOrderID

- Click the **View** button on the Ribbon.

Switches to Design View.

- Click in the **Field** row of the **OrderID** field.

Sets the insertion point in the first row of the OrderID field.

- Press the **Home** key on your keyboard.

Moves the insertion point to the beginning of the line.

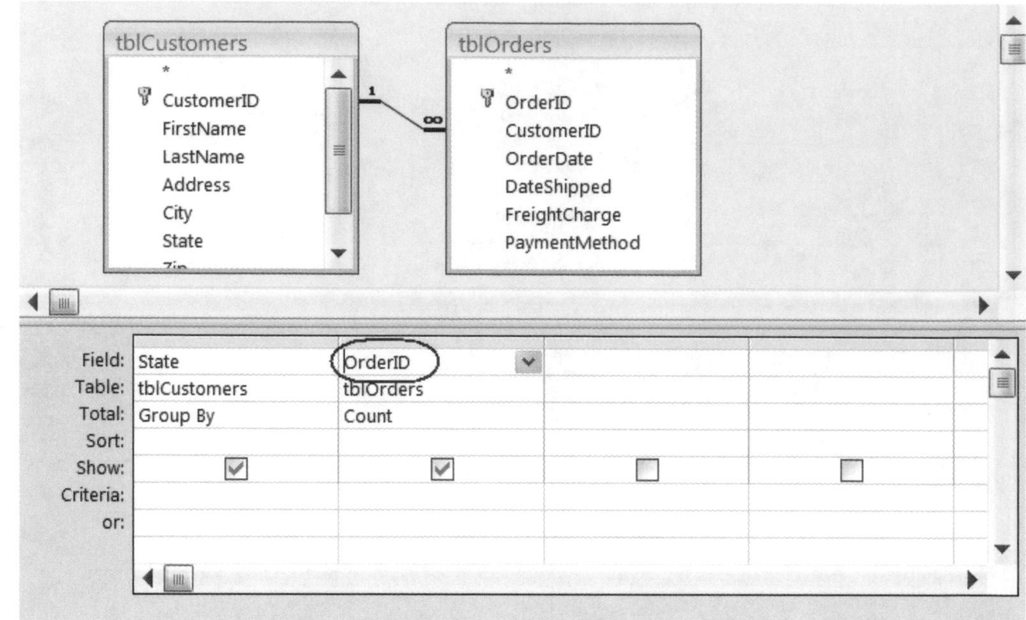

- Type: **Total Orders** and then press the **Spacebar** key.

Changes the name of the calculated field to Total Orders.

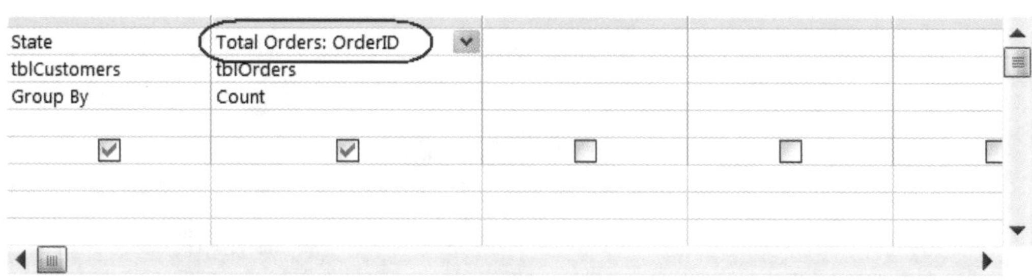

- Click the **Run** button.

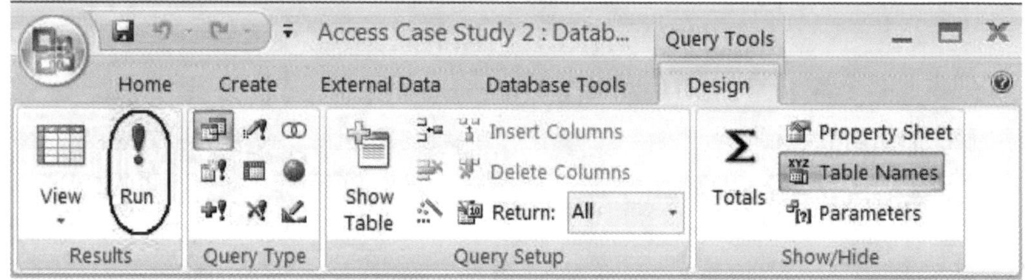

Returns the results. Notice the name of the calculated field.

State	Total Orders
FL	2
GA	1
VA	2
WI	1

Creating a Parameter Query

In this section, you will learn how to create a parameter query.

If you find yourself changing the criteria for the same query over and over, you may wish to convert your query into a **Parameter Query**. Instead of manually entering the criteria, a Parameter Query prompts the user for the criteria before the query is run. For example, you could create a Parameter Query to view orders for different states, rather than having to write a separate query for each state. When the query is run, the user receives a custom message, such as "Please Enter a State." The data the user enters is then applied as the query's criteria.

To create a Parameter Query, click in the Criteria cell of the desired query column and then **type the message, enclosed in brackets**, that you want the user to receive when the query is run. Access will then display to the user a parameter prompt that contains the text of the parameter expression that you entered in the Criteria row.

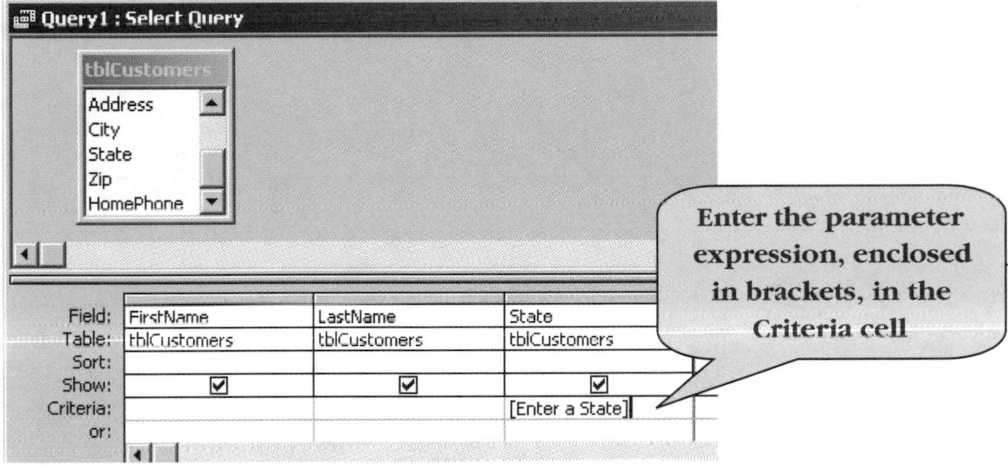

To Create a Parameter Query

1. Create a new query in design view.
2. Click in the Criteria row of the field to which you wish to add a parameter expression.
3. Type the message, enclosed in brackets, that you want to appear to the user.

Prompting for Dates

A common use of parameters is to prompt the user for a specific date range. For example, you might wish to see all orders for the past week. When you want to prompt user for a specific date range, use the **Between And** operators, combined with parameter expressions as shown below:

Between [Enter the Beginning Date] And [Enter the Ending Date]

In the above structure, the user will receive two prompts—"Enter the Beginning Date" for the first date in the time period and "Enter the Ending Date" for the last date in the time period.

TIP: To control the order of the parameters for multi-parameter queries or to control the data type, use the **Query Parameters** dialog box. Click the Parameters button on the Ribbon and enter your parameters on each row.

Let's Try It!

- Click the **View** button on the Ribbon.

Switches to Design View.

- Click in the **Criteria Row** for the **State** field.

Sets the insertion point in the Criteria row for the field for which we want to enter a parameter expression.

- Type: **[Enter a State]**

Enters the parameter expression.

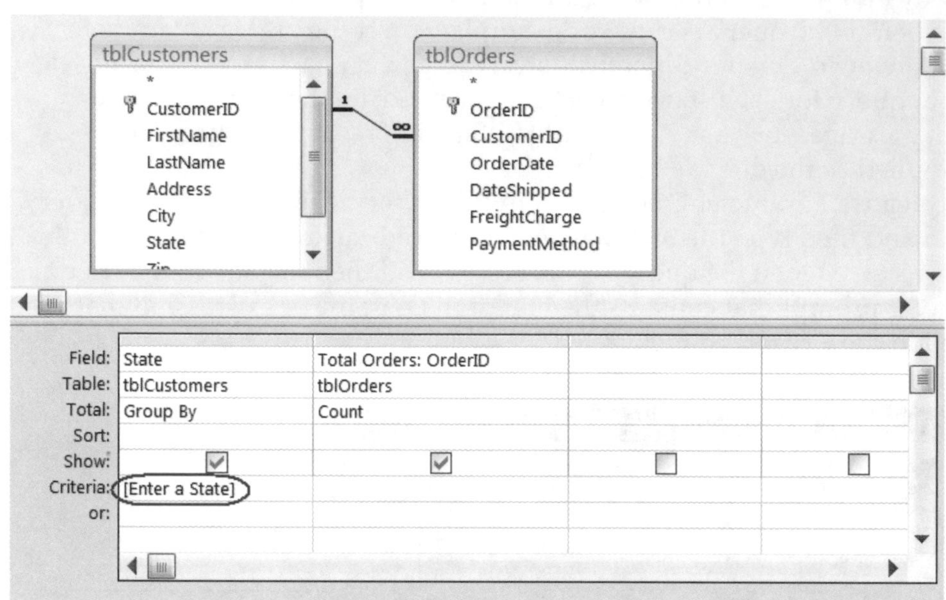

- Click the **Run** icon.

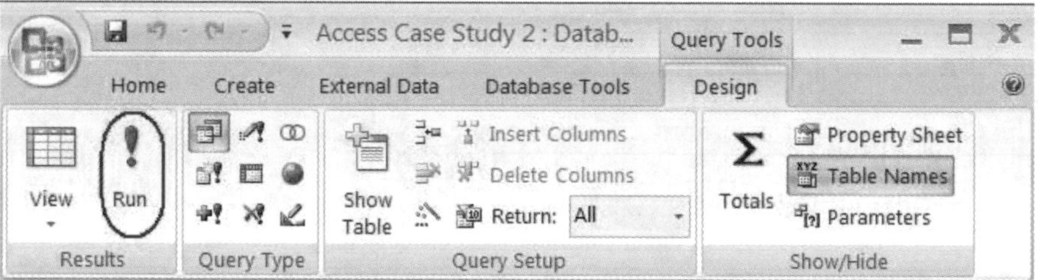

The Enter Parameter Value box appears.

- Type: **FL** in the box.

Enters the criteria for the query.

- Click **OK**.

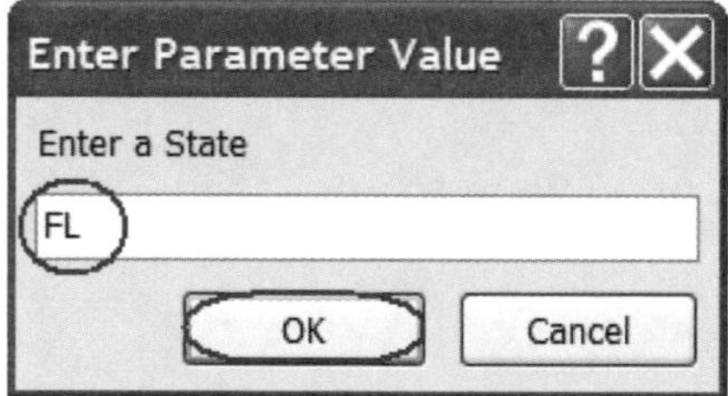

Runs the query, and applies the criteria of FL that you entered into the parameter value box.

State	Total Orders
FL	2

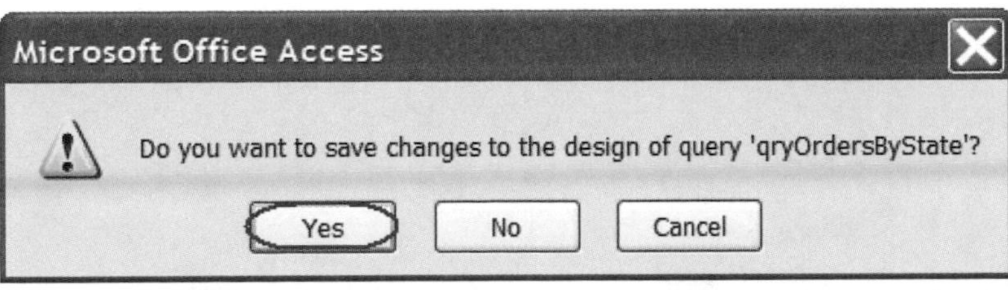

- Click the Close button on the Query window. **Save** your changes.

Saves and closes the query. We will now create a new query that prompts the user for a specific date range.

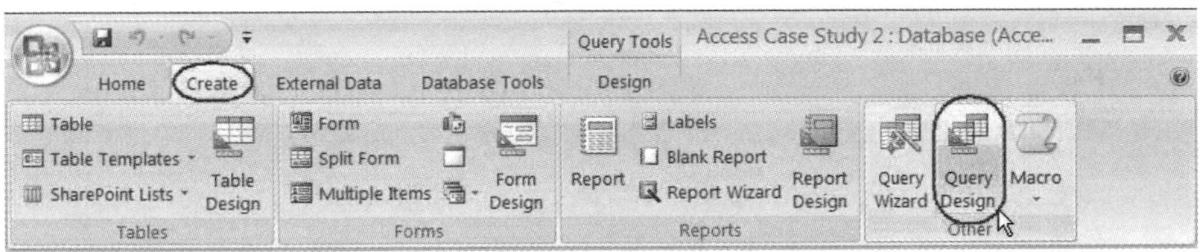

- Click the **Create tab** on the Ribbon and then click the **Query Design button.**

Displays the Show Table dialog box.

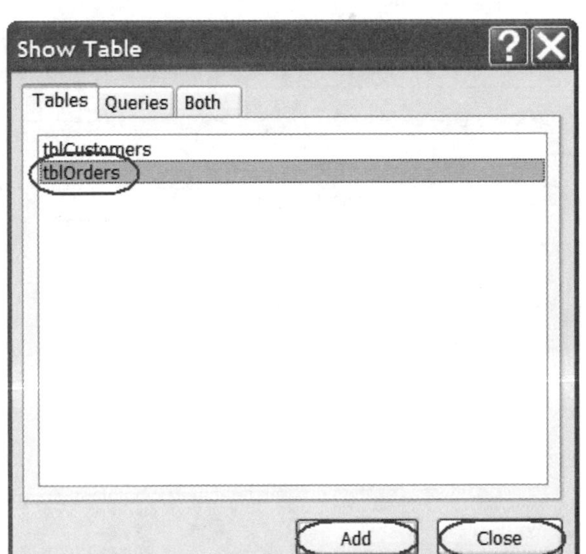

- Select **tblOrders** and then click **Add.**

Adds tblOrders to the query.

- Click the **Close** button.

Closes the Show Table dialog box.

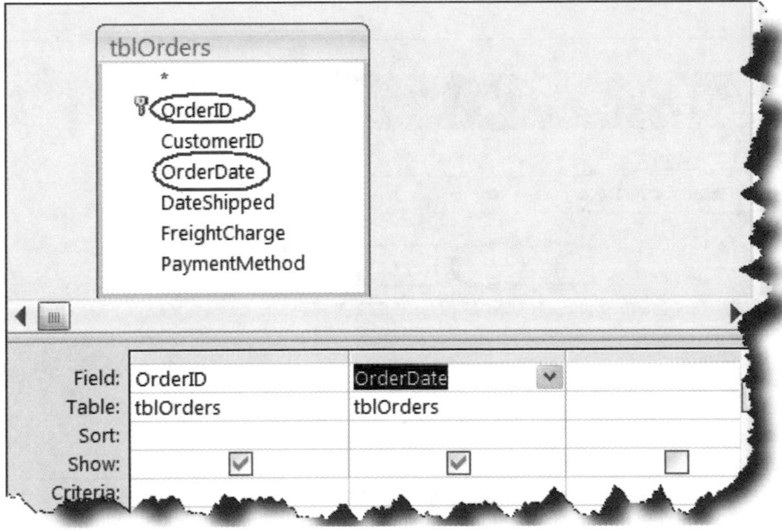

- Double-click **OrderID.**

Adds the OrderID field to the query.

- Double-click **OrderDate.**

Adds the OrderDate field to the query.

- Click in the **Criteria Row** for the **OrderDate** field.

Sets the insertion point in the Criteria row of the field for which we want to enter a parameter expression.

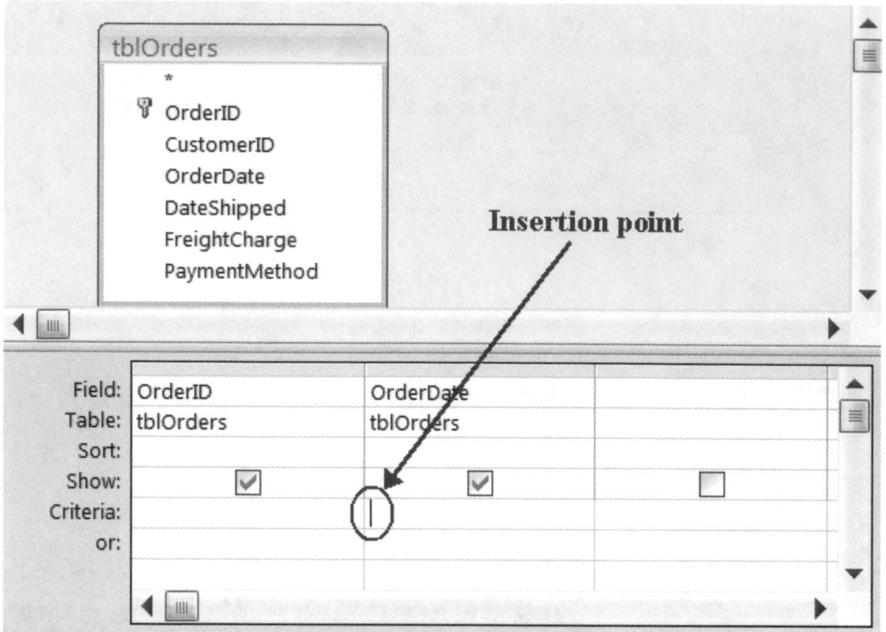

- Press the **Shift + F2** key combination.

Opens the Zoom window.

- Type: **Between [Enter the Beginning Date] And [Enter the Ending Date]** in the Zoom Window.

Enters the parameter expression for a specific time period.

- Click **OK**.

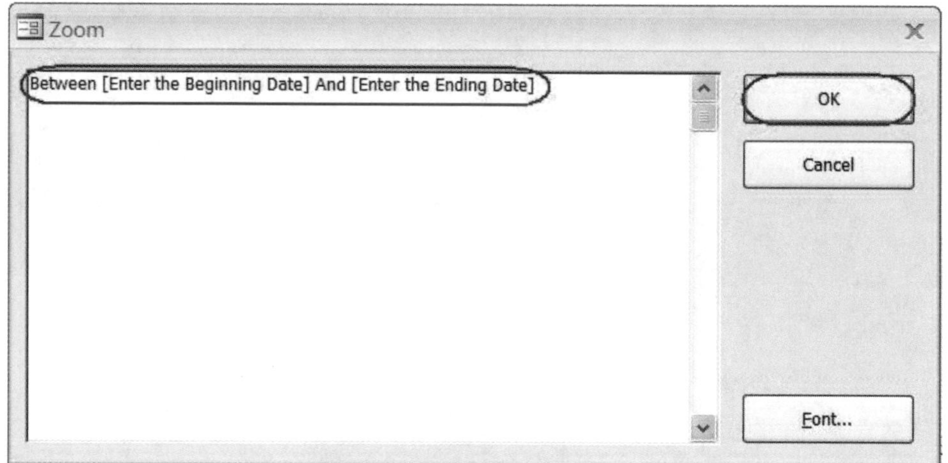

Closes the Zoom window.

- Click the **Save** button and then type: **qryParamOrderDate** in the Query Name box.

Provides a name for our query.

- Click **OK**.

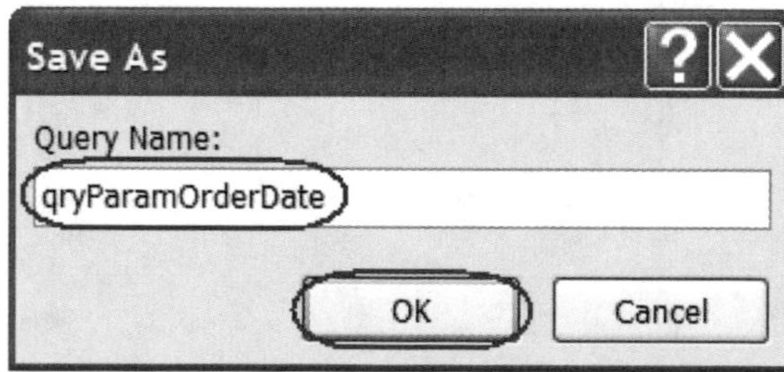

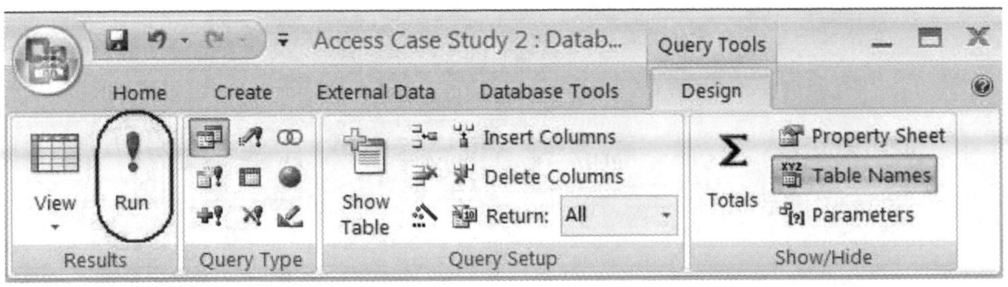

Saves the query and then closes the Query Name box.

- Click the **Run** icon.

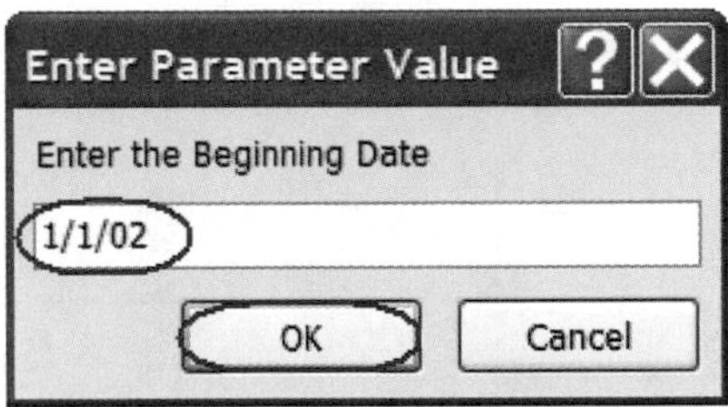

Displays the parameter box for the first time period date. In this case, we want to see all orders placed during 2002.

- Type: **1/1/02** and then click **OK**.

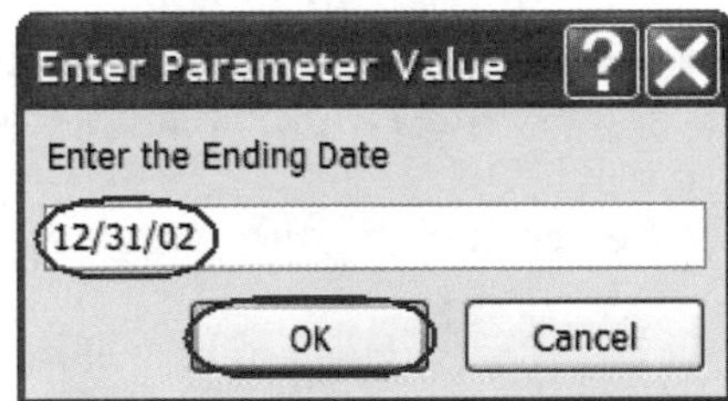

Enter the first parameter and then displays the parameter box for the last time period date.

- Type: **12/31/02** and then click **OK**.

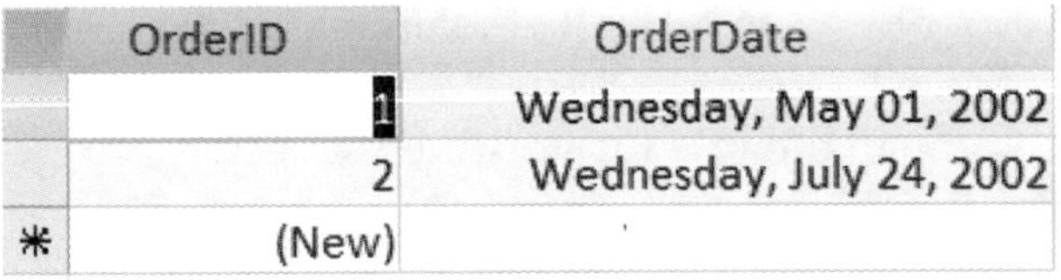

	OrderID	OrderDate
	1	Wednesday, May 01, 2002
	2	Wednesday, July 24, 2002
*	(New)	

Enter the second parameter and then displays the query results.

- Click the **Close** button on the Query window.

Closes the query.

Creating a Find Duplicates Query

In this section, you will learn how to create a query to find duplicate records.

Access provides a nice tool to help you quickly find duplicate records in a table. For instance, the same customer could have been entered into the Customers table more than once or perhaps an order was inadvertently entered in twice by different data entry persons. To quickly find duplicate records, use the **Find Duplicates Query Wizard**.

To launch the Find Duplicates Query Wizard, click the Query Wizard button on the Create Ribbon and then choose the Find Duplicates Query Wizard. The wizard will then step you though the process of finding duplicate records in your table.

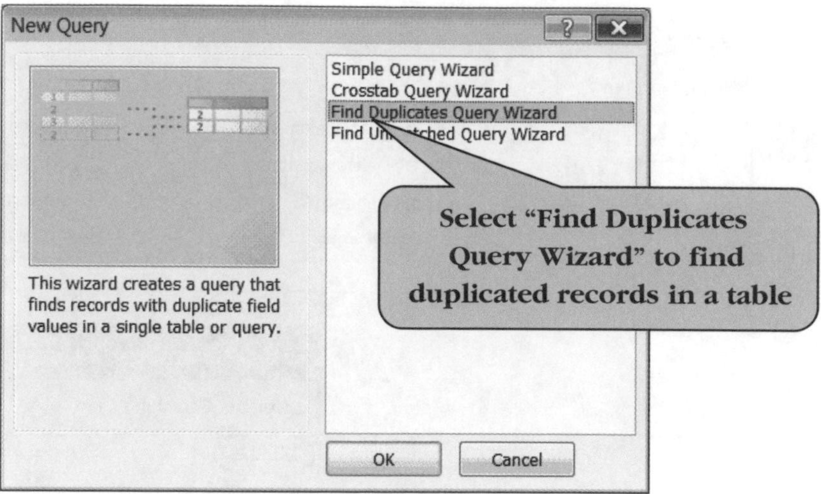

To Create a Find Duplicates Query

1. Click the **Create** tab on the Ribbon.
2. Click the **Query Wizard** on the Other group of the Ribbon.
3. Click **Find Duplicates Query Wizard**.
4. Click **OK**.
5. Select the table that you want to search for duplicate values.
6. Click **Next**.
7. Double-click the fields that you want to search for duplicate values.
8. Click **Next**.
9. Double-click any other fields you want to see in the results (or click the >> button to add all additional fields at once).
10. Click **Next**.
11. Type in a name for your new query.
12. Click **Finish**.

Let's Try It!

- Click the **Create** tab on the Ribbon.

Displays Create commands and tools.

- Click the **Query Wizard button** on the Other group on the Ribbon.

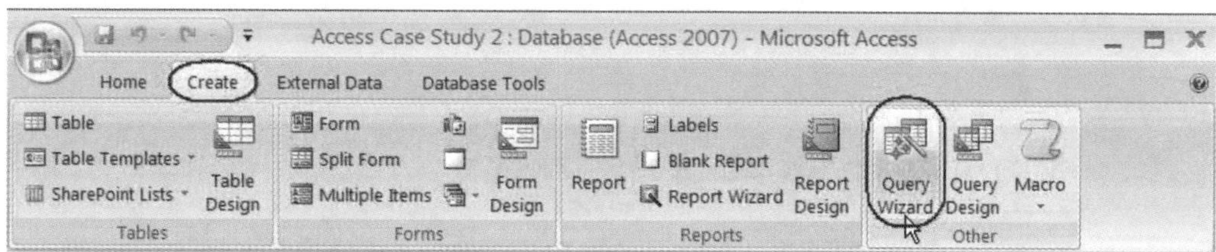

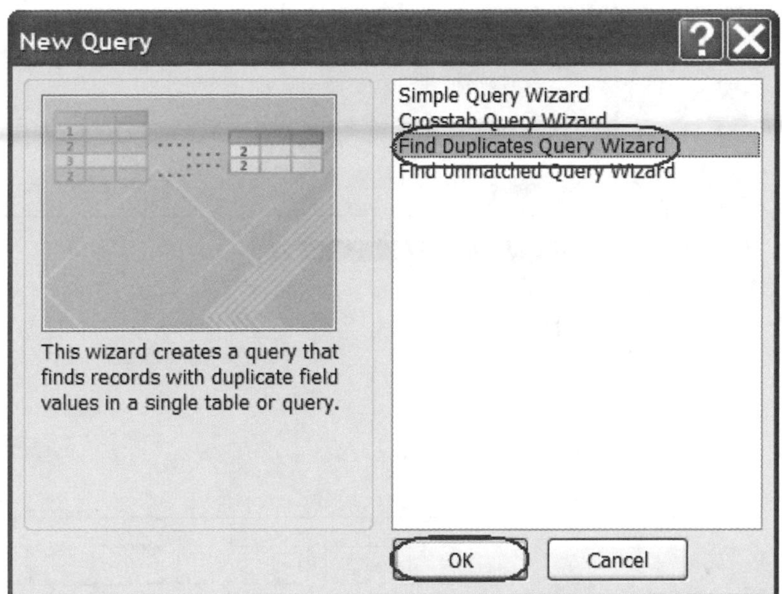

Launches the Query Wizard.

- Select **Find Duplicates Query Wizard** and then click **OK**.

Launches the Find Duplicates Query Wizard.

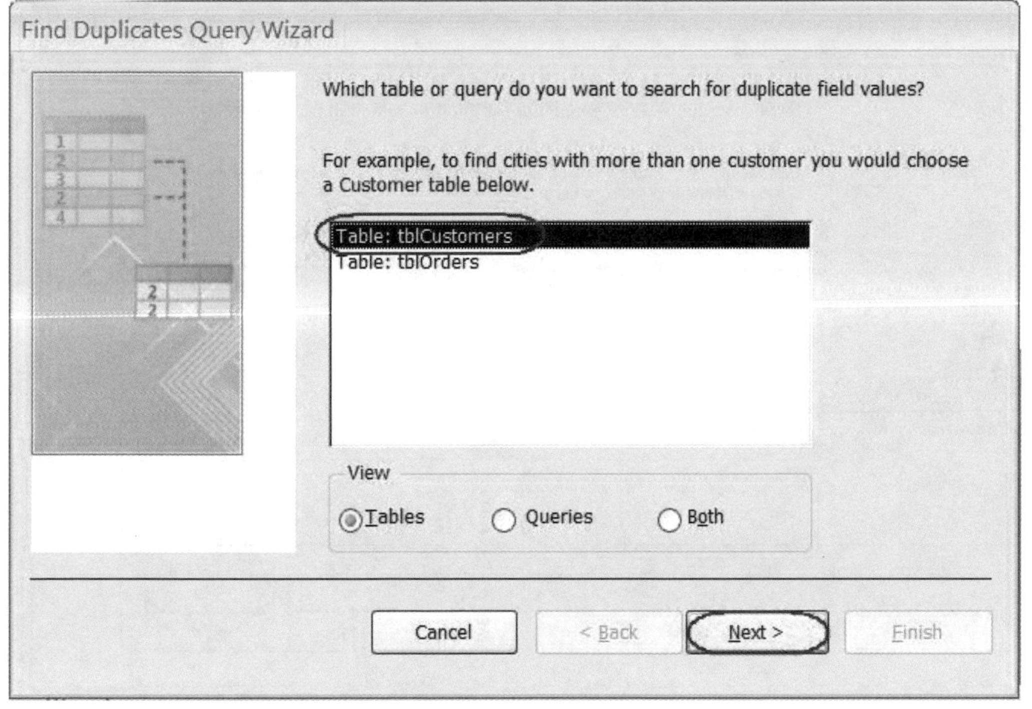

- Select **tblCustomers**.

Select the table in which we want to search for duplicates.

- Click **Next**.

Moves to the next step of the Wizard.

- In the available fields window, **double-click** the following fields:

FirstName

LastName

Select the fields that we want to search for duplicates. As several customers could have the last name, we will search for duplicates in the FirstName and LastName fields.

- Click **Next**.

Moves to the next step of the Wizard.

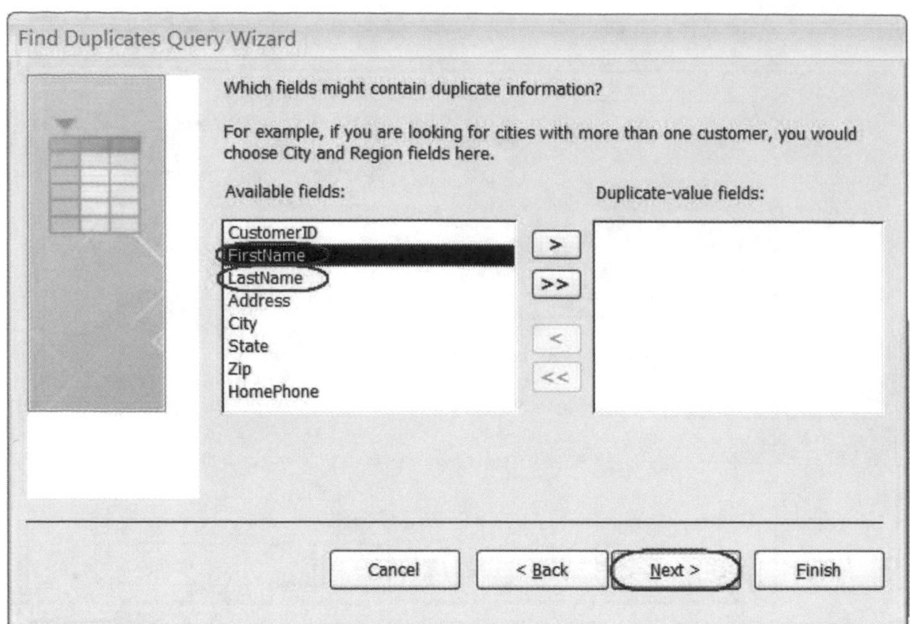

- Click the **>>** button.

Adds the rest of the fields to the query. This is optional - you could just include only the fields for which you want to find duplicates.

- Click **Finish**.

Completes the Wizard and runs the query.

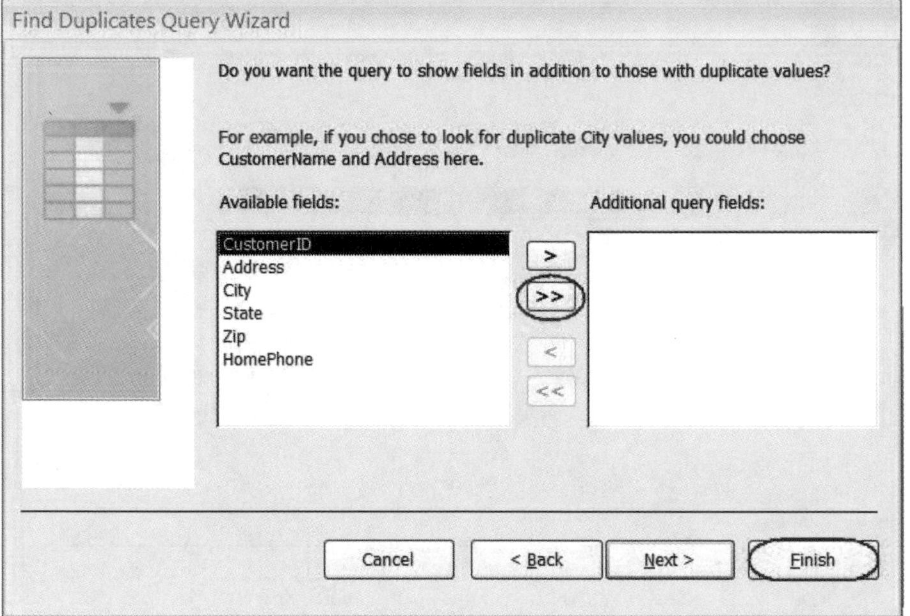

As we can see, we do not have any duplicate records but if there were any they had showed up in this query.

- Click the **Close button** for the query. Save any changes.

Closes the Find Duplicates query.

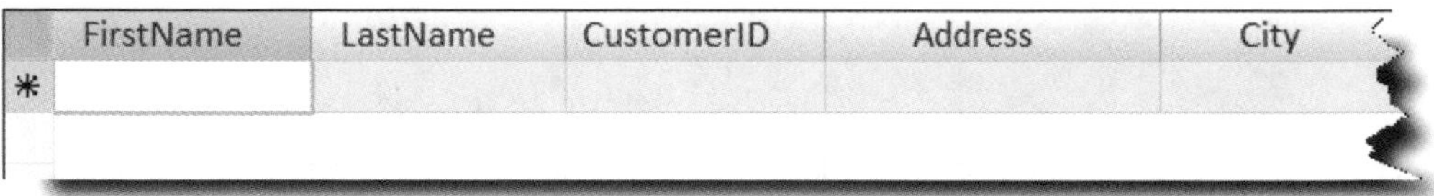

Creating a Find Unmatched Records Query

In this section, you will learn how to create a query to find unmatched records in two tables.

Another Query Wizard available is the **Find Unmatched Query Wizard**. This wizard builds a query that helps you find records in one table that do not have matching records in another table. A use for this query might be to find customers who have never placed an order. If this were the case, a record for a customer would exist in the Customers table but not in the Orders table.

Another use for the Find Unmatched Query Wizard may be to fix Referential Integrity Errors. Someone could have typed in incorrect customer number in the Orders table, thus creating an orphaned record, that is to say, a record in the child table that does not have a related record in the parent table. Of course, many of these types of problems can be avoided by setting Referential Integrity when creating your relationships.

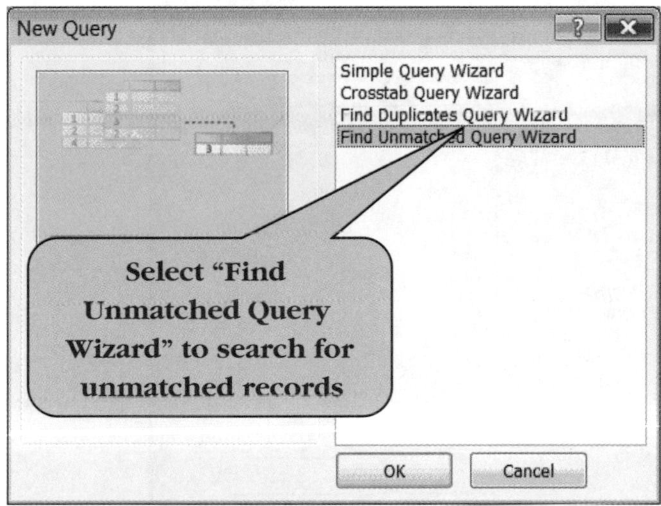

To Create a Find Duplicates Query

1. Click the **Create** tab on the Ribbon.
2. Click the **Query Wizard** on the Other group of the Ribbon.
3. Select **Find Unmatched Query Wizard** and then click **OK**.
4. Select the table for which you want to display the query results. For example, in a Customers → Orders scenario, this would be the Customers Table.
5. Click **Next**.
6. Select the table that contains the related records. For example, in a Customers → Orders scenario, this would be the Orders Table.
7. Click **Next**.
8. Select the matching field in both tables. For example, in a Customers → Orders scenario, this would most likely be the Customer ID field.
9. Click **Next**.
10. Double-click any fields that you want to appear in the query's results.
11. Click **Finish**.

Let's Try It!

- Click the **Create** tab on the Ribbon.

Displays Create commands and tools.

- Click the **Query Wizard button** on the Other group on the Ribbon.

Launches the Query Wizard.

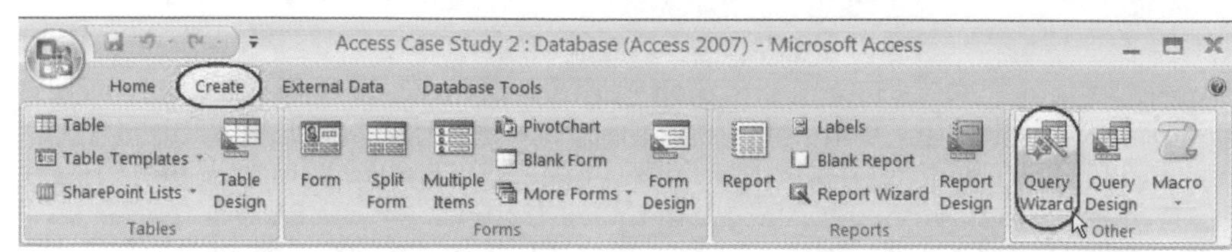

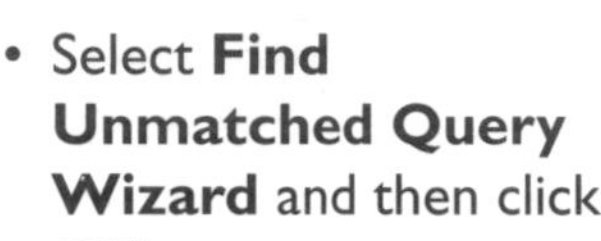

- Select **Find Unmatched Query Wizard** and then click **OK**.

Launches the Find Unmatched Query Wizard.

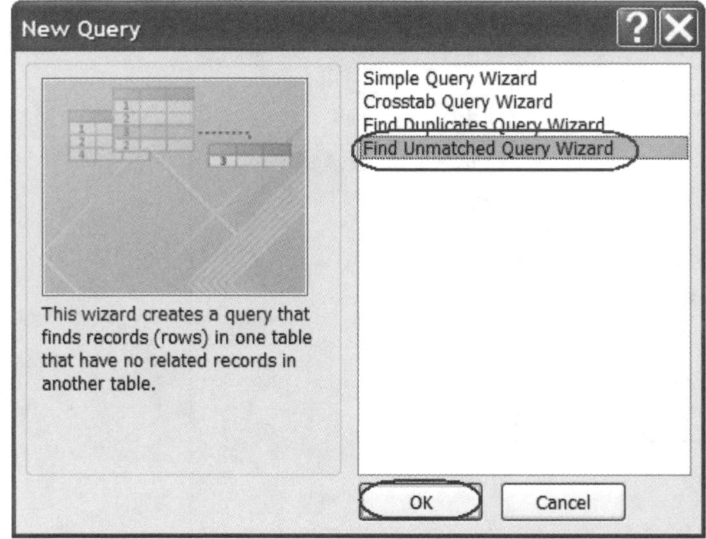

- Select **tblCustomers**.

Selects the table for which we want to see the query results. This would often be the parent table in a relationship.

- Click **Next**.

Moves to the next step of the Wizard.

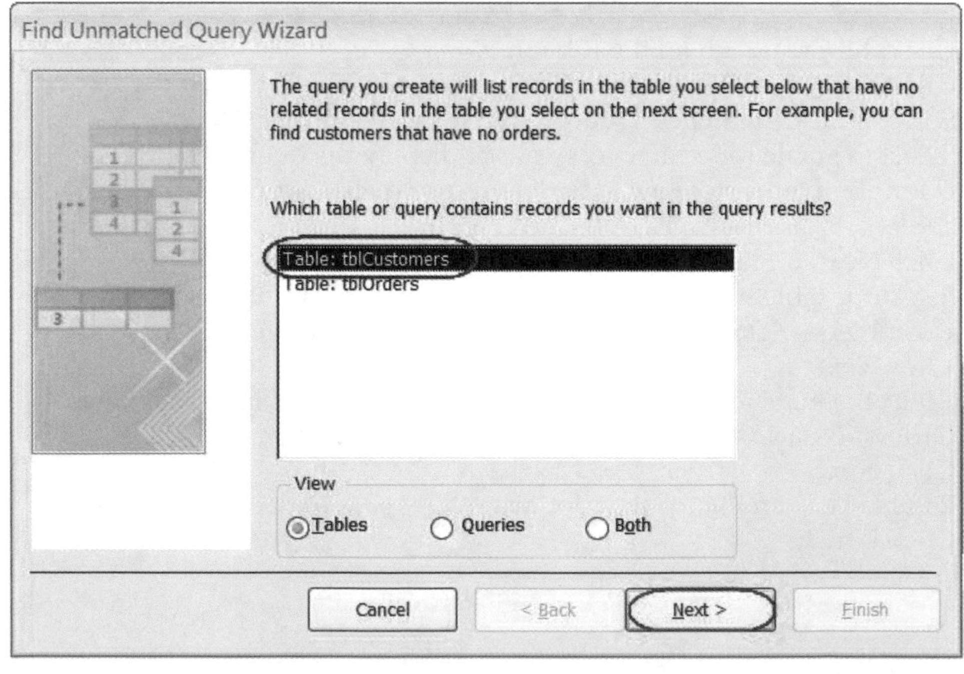

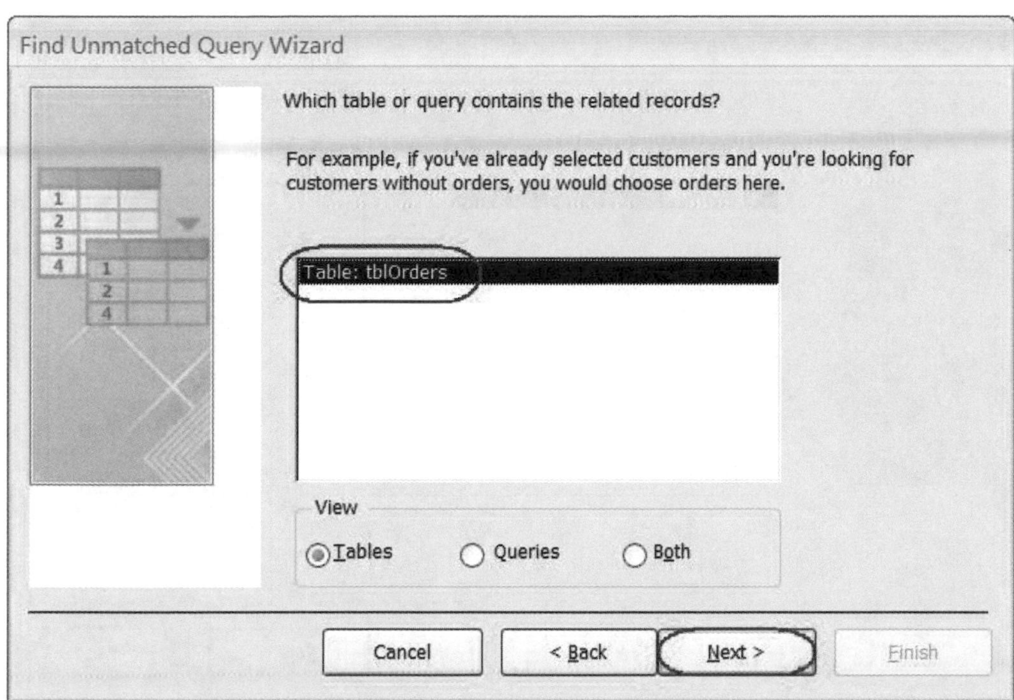

- Select **tblOrders**.

Selects the table that contains the related records. This would often be the child table in a relationship.

- Click **Next**.

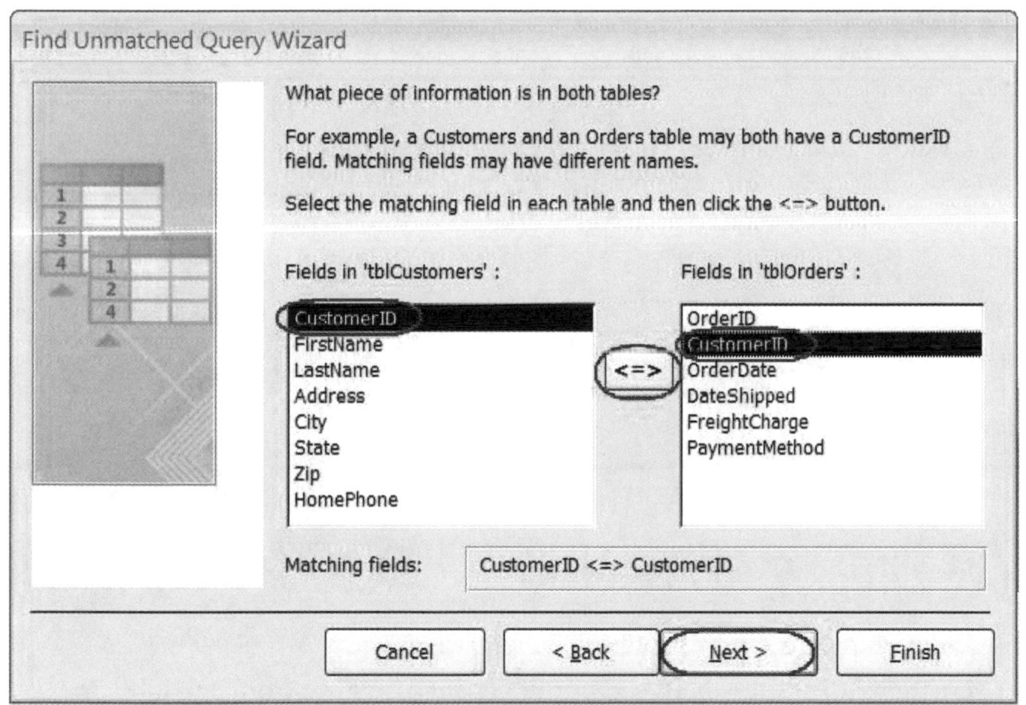

Moves to the next step of the Wizard.

- Select the **CustomerID field** in both the tblCustomers window and the tblOrders window and then click the **<=> button**.

Selects the matching field in the two tables.

- Click **Next**.

Moves to the next step of the Wizard.

- Click the **>>** button.

Adds the rest of the fields to the query.

- Click **Finish**.

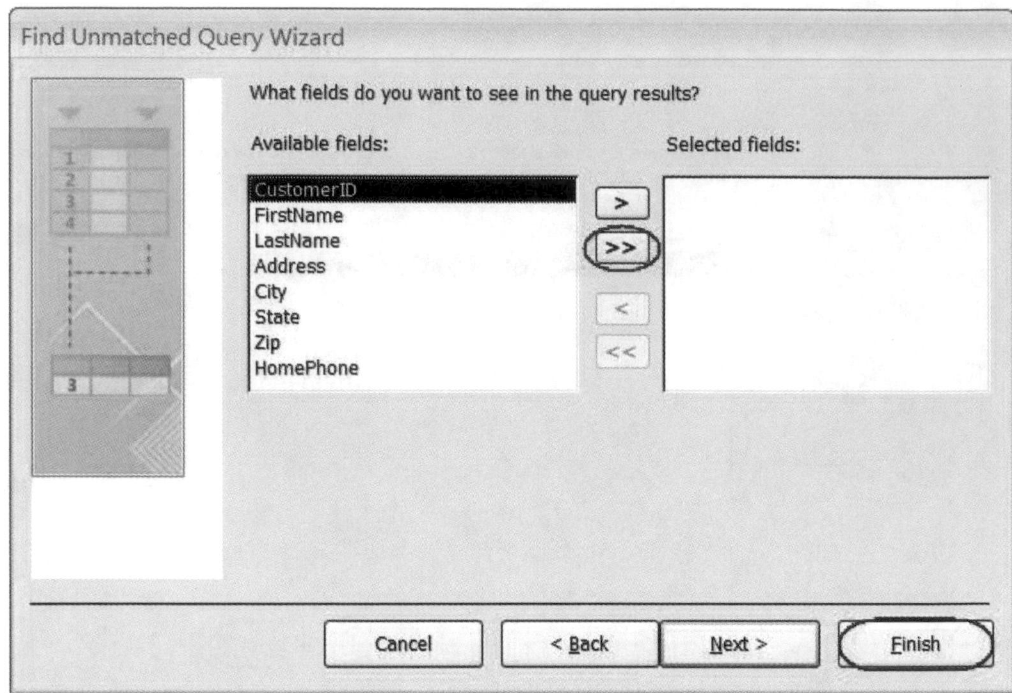

Completes the query and displays the results. In this case, we have one customer that has not placed an order, Nicole Travis.

	CustomerID	FirstName	LastName	Address	City	State
	345	Nicole	Travis	406 W. Pine St.	Glendale	VA
*						

- Click the **Close button** on the query window. Save any changes.

Closes the Find Unmatched query.

Modifying Query Joins

In this section, you will learn how to change the type of join in a query.

We create relationships between our tables by dragging from one table to another. This in turn creates a **join line**, which informs us that a relationship exists between two tables. The default join type is an **inner join**, which displays data only if there are matching values in both the join fields.

For example, in the last section, we discovered that there were some customers in the tblCustomers who did not place an order. Thus, there was no matching record for them in tblOrders. If we created a query than included tblCustomer and tblOrders, joining the two tables on CustomerID, the customers who had never ordered would not be displayed in the query results.

If you want the query to display all records from one table regardless of whether if has matching records in the other table, you can change the join type to an **outer join**. There are two types of outer joins: the **left outer join** and the **right outer join**. A left outer join displays all records from the table on the left side of the join and only matching records from the table on the right side of the join. Likewise, a right outer join displays all records from the table on the right side of the join and only matching records from the table on the left side of the join.

To change the join type of a relationship in a query, double-click the join line and then select number 1 for an inner join, number 2 for a left outer join or number 3 for a right outer join.

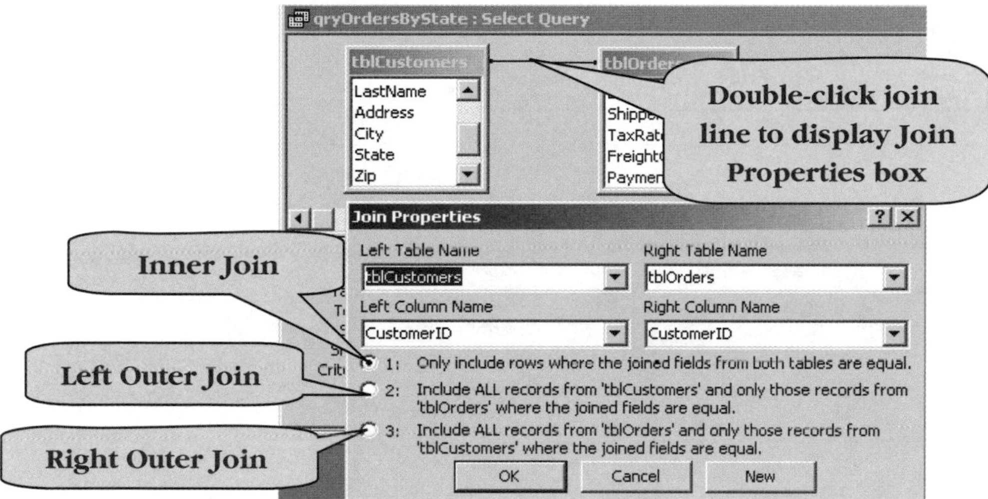

To Modify a Join Type in a Query

1. Select the query whose **join type** you want to change.
2. Click the **Design View** button.
3. Double-click the **join line** that you wish to modify.
4. In the Join Properties box:
   a. Select **1** to set the join type as an **inner join**.
   b. Select **2** to set the join type as a **left outer join**.
   c. Select **3** to set the join type as a **right outer join**.
5. Click **OK**.

Let's Try It!

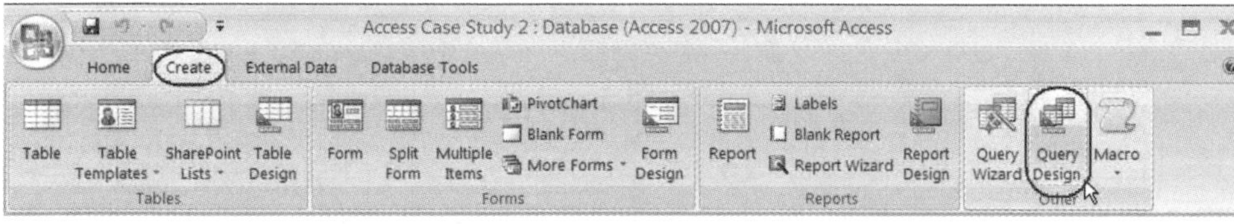

- Click the **Create** tab on the Ribbon.

Displays Create commands and tools.

- Click the **Query Design button** on the Other group on the Ribbon.

Displays the Show Table dialog box.

- Select **tblCustomers** and then click the **Add** button.

Adds tblCustomer to the query.

- Select **tblOrders** and then click the **Add** button.

Adds tblOrders to the query.

- Click the **Close** button.

Closes the Show Table box.

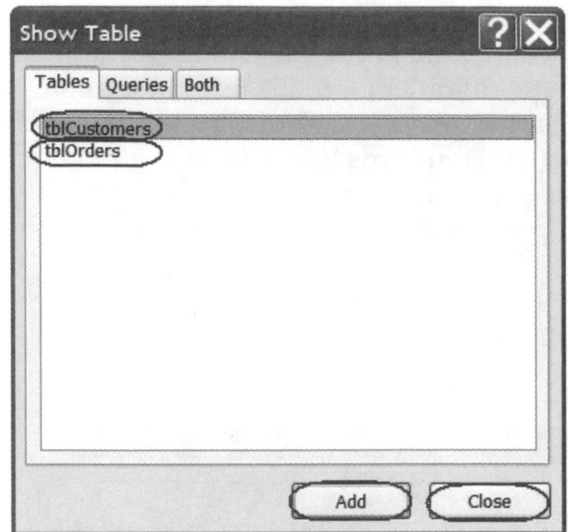

- Double-click the **LastName** field in the Field List for tblCustomers.

Adds the LastName field to the Query Grid.

- Double-click the **FirstName** field in the tblCustomers field list.

Adds the FirstName field to the Query Grid.

- Double-click the **OrderID** field in the tblOrders field list.

Adds the OrderID field to the Query Grid.

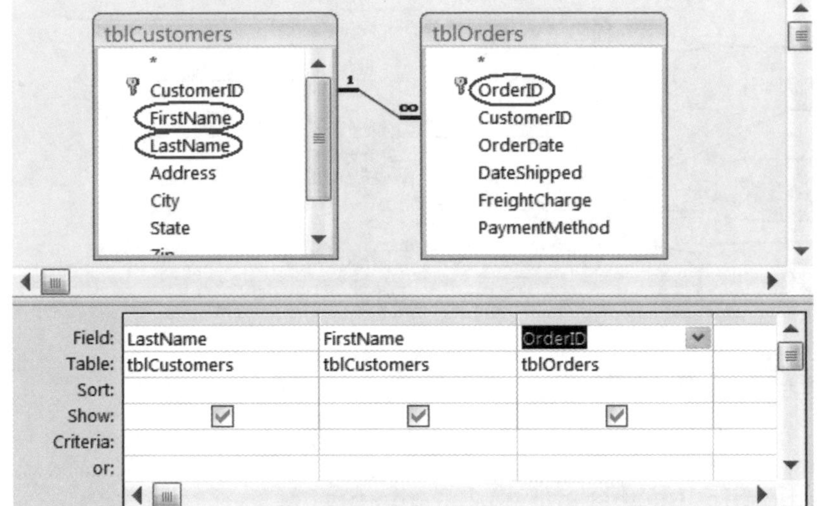

- Click in the **Sort** field for the LastName field and then chose **Ascending** by clicking on the arrow.

Sets the query to sort ascending by the LastName field.

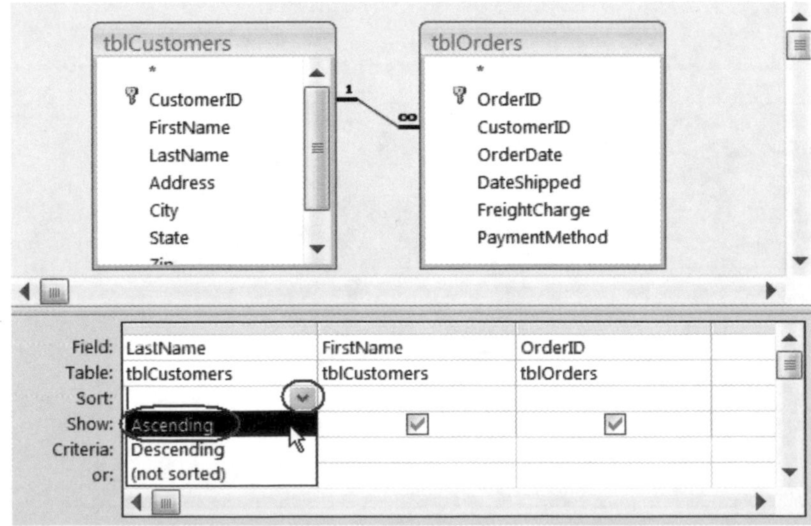

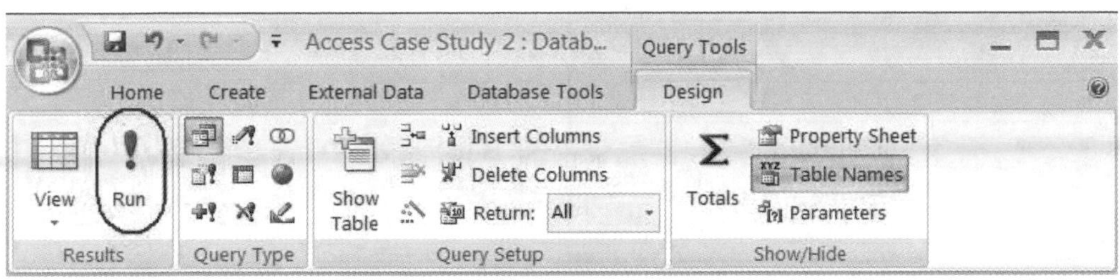

• Click the **Run** button.

LastName	FirstName	OrderID
Bateman	Florence	6
Beckman	Sara	2
Rickman	Jaime	1
Rickman	Jaime	4
Henderson	Thomas	3
Henderson	Thomas	5
*		(New)

Executes the query. Notice that one customer who did not place an order, Nicole Travis is not listed in the results. There are 6 records in the table.

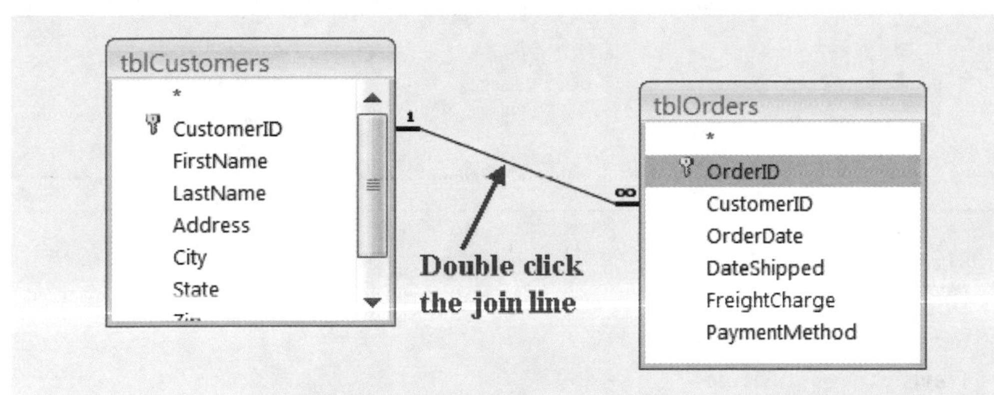

• Click the **View** button on the Ribbon.

Switches to Design View.

• **Double-click** the join line between tblCustomers and tblOrders.

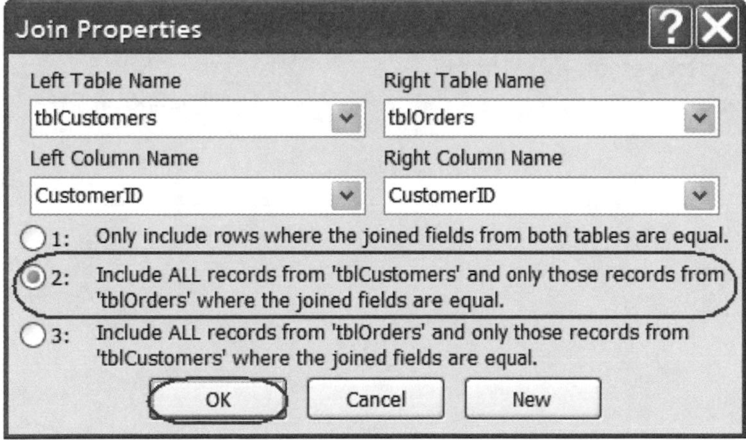

Displays the Join Properties box.

• Click the radio button to the left of the **2** option.

Sets the join type as a left outer join. This will display all records from tblCustomers and any matching records from tblOrders. All customers, regardless of whether or not they placed an order, will be displayed.

• Click **OK**.

Closes the Join Properties box.

- Click the **Save** button.

Opens the Save As dialog box, as we have not yet saved our query.

- Type: **qryCustomersWithoutOrders** in the Query Name box.

Provides a file name for our new query.

- Click **OK**.

Saves the query and closes the Query Name dialog box.

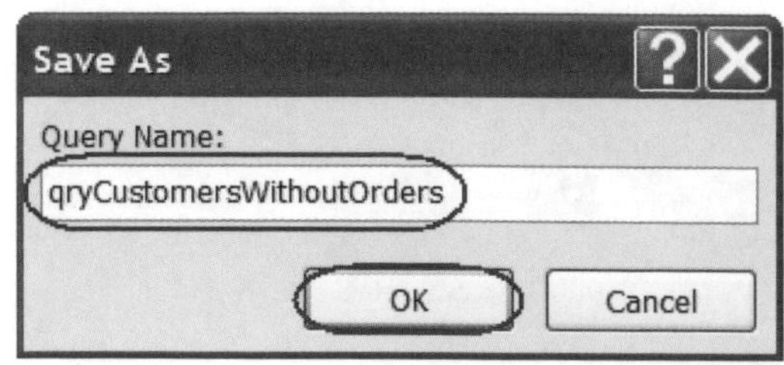

- Click the **Run Query** button.

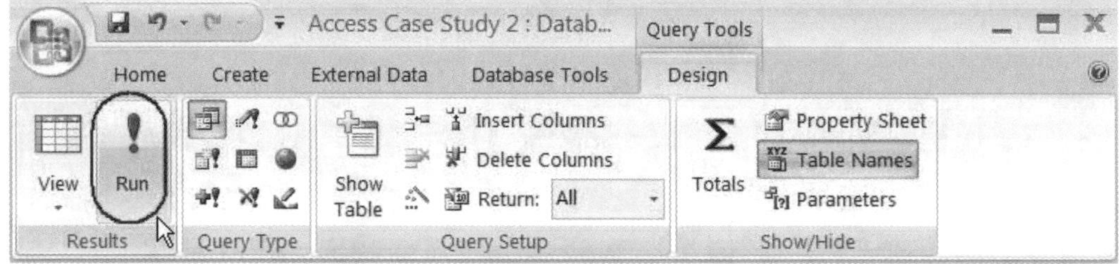

Executes the query. Notice that Travis Nicole is now included in the result. The OrderID field for this customer is blank however, as he had not placed any orders.

- Click the **Close button** on the query window.

Closes the query.

	LastName	FirstName	OrderID
	Bateman	Florence	6
	Beckman	Sara	2
	Travis	Nicole	
	Rickman	Jaime	1
	Rickman	Jaime	4
	Henderson	Thomas	3
	Henderson	Thomas	5
*			(New)

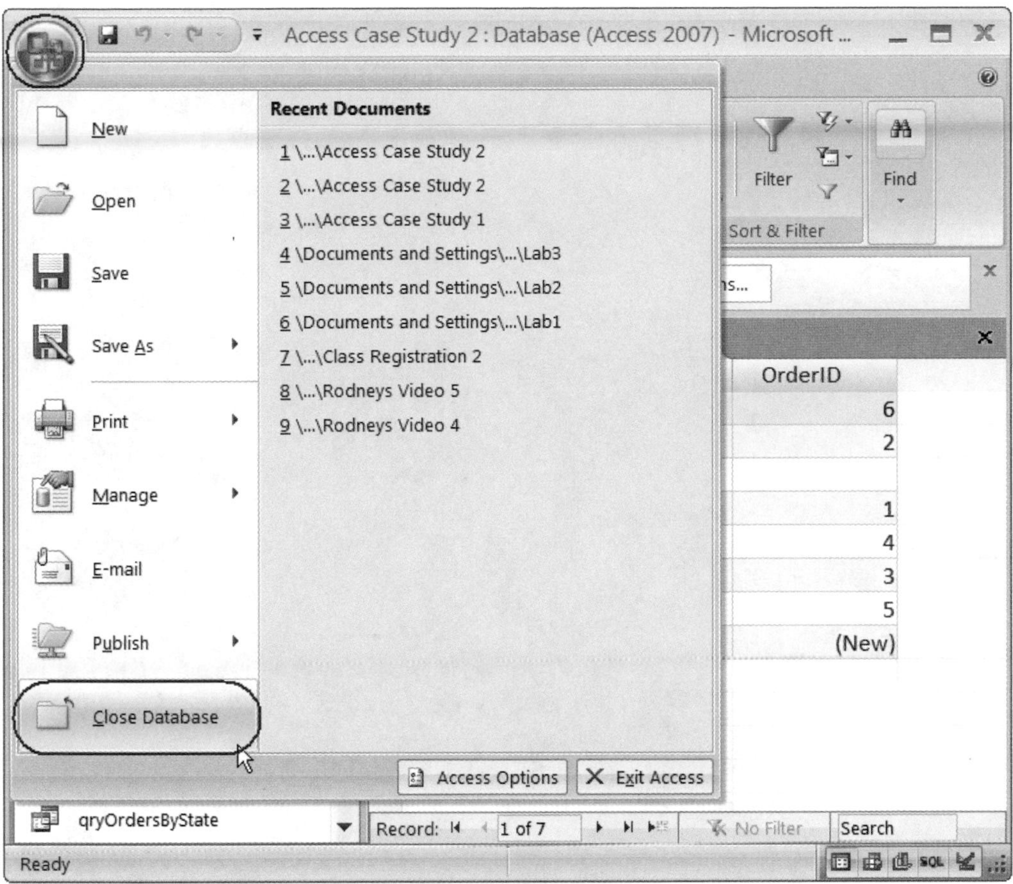

- Click the Microsoft Office button and click **Close Database** from the File Options menu.

Closes the database.

Conclusion

You have completed Access 2007—Case Study II. You are now ready to use several advanced MS Access skills that you have learned in this chapter. You are encouraged to experiment with all you have learned in this case study. To reinforce your understanding of these techniques, it is recommended that you read and work through it once again.

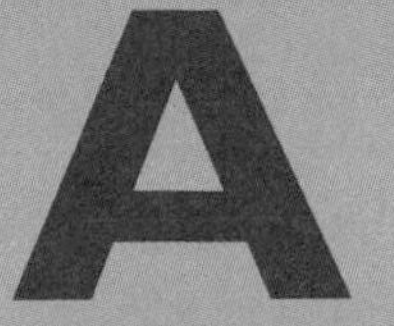

APPENDIX

A

What's New in Windows Vista?

What's New	Description of Feature
Ease of Access Center	The new Ease of Access Center, which replaces the Accessibility Options in earlier versions of Windows, comes with several improvements and new features, including centralized access to accessibility settings and a new questionnaire that you can use to get suggestions for accessibility features that you might find useful.
Games	Four new games added: Mahjong Titans, Chess Titans, Purble Place and InkBall.
Internet Explorer 7	IE now includes tabbed browsing, a phishing filter and RSS feeds.
Searching	The Search Box appears on the top of every folder window. When you type in the Search Box, Windows filters the view based on what you entered into the box. You can also search among your e-mail messages, saved instant messages, appointments, contacts, Internet favorites, and your Web page history.
Security	Features such as Windows Firewall and Windows Defender can help keep your computer more secure. From the Windows Security Center, you can check your computer's firewall, antivirus software and update status. The new User Account Control can help prevent unauthorized changes to your computer by requiring permission before performing actions that could potentially affect your computer's operation or that change settings that affect other users.
Streamlined Start Menu	New Start Menu design. All installed applications are now displayed in a pane. Items such as the Pictures, Documents, Music, Games, and Control Panel are displayed in the right pane of the Start Menu. A convenient Search Box is now located on the bottom of the Start Menu. Windows has also dropped the word "My" from the Documents, Pictures and Music folders.
Sync Center	The Sync Center helps you keep your devices such as MP3 players and mobile devices in sync.
Turning Off your Computer	When you click the Power button on the Start menu, Windows saves your work and programs just as they are, and then puts the computer into sleep mode.
Windows Aero	Windows Aero features translucent glass design with subtle window animations and new window colors.
Windows Backup and Restore Center	Helps you make backups of your files either manually or automatically scheduled.
Windows Defender	Helps protect your computer against spyware. If it detects suspicious activity, it alerts you to the potential threat.
Windows DVD Maker	Now you can create professional-looking DVD's.
Windows Easy Transfer	You can easily transfer: you user accounts, files and folders, program settings, Internet settings and favorites, e-mail settings, contacts, and messages from your old computer.
Windows Flip 3-D	Part of Windows Aero, Flip 3-D allows you to display your open windows in three-dimensional stacks. Taskbar buttons displayed thumbnail-sized window previews when moving your mouse pointer over them.
Windows Mail	Improved e-mail program with junk mail filters and malicious software detection.
Windows Media Center	Allows you to access all of your entertainment media from one menu system. You can even watch television from your PC and records shows to your hard drive.

What's New	Description of Feature
Windows Meeting Space	Allows you to collaborate with other people, share your desktop and share documents.
Windows Movie Maker	Windows Movie maker has improved graphics, new effects and new transitions.
Windows Photo Gallery	Allows you to view, organize, print and edit digital graphic files.
Windows Sidebar	Windows Sidebar, which displays on the right side of your screen, allows you to access and organize information quickly without cluttering your workspace. It's made up of "gadgets", which are customizable mini-programs that can display continuously updated headlines, a picture slide show, contacts, and more, without having to open a new window.

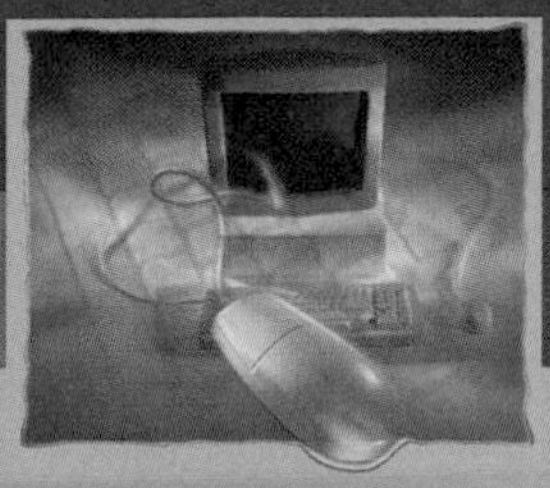

APPENDIX

B

What's New in Internet Explorer 7?

What's New	Description of Feature
Browsing History	Delete temporary Internet files, passwords, form data, cookies, and history, all from a single window.
Built-in Searching	Web searches using your favorite search provider can now be entered into a search box. You can choose a provider from the dropdown list or add more providers.
Favorites Center	New Favorites Center provides one place to access Favorites, Tab Groups, Browsing History, and RSS Feed subscriptions.
Information Bar	To help protect you from browsing with unsafe settings, Internet Explorer 7 warns you with an Information Bar when current security settings may put you at risk.
Phishing Filter	This filter warns you about and helps to protect you against potential or known fraudulent websites, and blocks the sites if appropriate.
Printing	Internet Explorer 7 scales Web pages for printing, so the entire webpage fits on the printed page. Print options also include adjustable margins, customizable page layouts, removable headers and footers, and an option to print only selected text.
Quick Tabs	Allows you to view and navigate through open tabs by displaying thumbnails of them all in a single window.
RSS Feeds	Internet Explorer 7 automatically detects RSS feeds on sites and lights up the RSS icon on the toolbar. A single click on the icon allows you to view and subscribe to the RSS feeds.
Tab Groups	Opened Tabs can be grouped together, so you can open multiple tabs with a single click. A Tab Group can also be set as the Home Page Group so the entire Tab Group opens every time Internet Explorer is launched or when the Home button Is clicked.
Tabbed Browsing	Tabbed Browsing allows you to open multiple sites In a single browser window. Easily switch from one site to another through tabs at the top of the browser windows.
Zooming	Enlarge Web pages, including both text and graphics.

APPENDIX

C

What's New in Word 2007?

What's New	Description of Feature
Building Blocks	Allows you to store and reuse text and graphics, saving the time of having to recreate them for each new document. Word 2007 also comes with an extensive gallery of built-in building blocks.
Calendar Button	You can click the new Calendar button to quickly choose dates.
Collecting Data by E-mail	You can now send forms by e-mail from Access to gather information. The form responses are then added to the appropriate table in your database when it arrives in your Inbox.
Dialog Launchers	Displays the traditional style dialog boxes by clicking on the dialog launcher in the lower-right hand corner of a command set.
Digital Signature	Word offers the ability to add a digital signature or signature line to your documents.
File Menu	The new Microsoft Office System logo button now indicates where the previous File menu resides.
Full Screen Reading View	You can view your document in a two-page format while hiding the Ribbon and scrollbars.
Galleries	When selecting a command with a downward pointing arrow, an options palette appears allowing you to see and change color combination, formatting, color scheme, etc.
Getting Started Window	Offers a library of pre-build database solutions that can get you to work quickly.
Key Tips	Allow you to toggle on the display of keyboard shortcuts using your keyboard. Previous keyboard shortcuts still work in Office 2007.
Live Preview	Allows you to temporarily preview an effect before you apply it.
Live Word Count	Word count appears by default on the lower-left corner of the Status Bar.
Professional Templates	Word includes a collection of professionally designed templates that you can use and modify for your own needs.
Quick Access Toolbar	Located to the right of the File menu, the Quick Access Toolbar allows you to add tools you use regularly. The default tools are Save, Undo, and Redo.
Quick Cover Pages	You can now quickly add a professionally designed cover page to your documents with just two clicks of your mouse.
Quick Styles	Allows you now to preview a number of styles before applying them to your document.
Redesigned Help System	Completely redesigned Help dialog box.
Remove Personal Information	The new Document Inspector can find and remove metadata and personal information your documents.
Smart Art Graphics	Allows you to create quick diagrams that illustrate hierarchies, cycles, relationships and data processes.
Spell Checker Enhancements	Many new spell checker enhancements, including global settings.

What's New	Description of Feature
Super Tooltips	Provides contextual help and provides more information than traditional tooltips for items that need additional explanation.
Themes	Allows you to apply preset formatting to text, tables and other Word elements.
User Interface	Completely redesigned user interface stretches across the top of the screen and includes command tabs, command sets and contextual commands.
View Controls	New View controls include commands formerly listed under the Windows or View menus.
XML Format	Default Word file format is now XML.

APPENDIX

D

What's New in Excel 2007?

What's New	Description of Feature
Calculated Columns	Uses a single formula that adjusts for each row. Now, you need to enter a formula once—no need to fill or copy.
Cell Styles	Predesigned cell formats now available from the Cell Styles command.
Charting Enhancements	Improved charting tools, galleries of predesigned formats, new 3-D options and contextual tools.
Color Palette	Now supports 16 million colors.
Column Headings	You can now rotate your headings with a click of a mouse.
Data Visualizations	New data visualizations that help illustrated trends and comparisons: Data Bars, Color Scales and Icon Sets.
Dialog Launchers	Displays the traditional style dialog boxes by clicking on the dialog launcher in the lower-right hand corner of a command set.
Faster Calculations	Faster calculations when working with huge, formula intensive worksheets.
File Menu	The new Microsoft Office System logo button now indicates where the previous File menu resides.
Function AutoComplete	AutoComplete helps you write functions with proper syntax.
Galleries	When selecting a command with a downward pointing arrow, an options palette appears allowing you to see and change color combination, formatting, color scheme, etc.
Headers and Footers	New click-and-type headers and footers from the Insert Ribbon.
Increased Rows and Columns Size	Excel now handles spreadsheets with up to 1 million rows and 16,000 columns.
Key Tips	Allow you to toggle on the display of keyboard shortcuts using your keyboard. Previous keyboard shortcuts still work in Office 2007.
Live Preview	Allows you to temporarily preview an effect before you apply it.
Named Ranges	The new Name Manager helps you organize and manage multiple named ranges.
New Office Shapes and WordArt	Improved and more accessible.
New Templates	Excel 2007 provides easy access to new templates.
Page Layout View	New view allows you to see how your worksheet will be distributed between pages before printing.
Pivot-Tables	Enhances PivotTables make them much easier to work with and understand.
Professional Templates	Excel includes a collection of professionally designed templates that you can use and modify for your own needs.
Quick Access Toolbar	Located to the right of the File menu, the Quick Access Toolbar allows you to add tools you use regularly. The default tools are Save, Undo, and Redo.

What's New	Description of Feature
Quick Styles	Allows you now to preview a number of styles before applying them to your document.
Redesigned Help System	Completely redesigned Help dialog box.
Remove Personal Information	The new Document Inspector can find and remove metadata and personal information your documents.
Resizable Formula Bar	Formula bar automatically resizes when entering long, complex formulas.
Rich Conditional Formatting	Major improvements on Conditional Formatting—now includes dynamic conditions, top/bottom rules and more.
Smart Art Graphics	Allows you to create quick diagrams that illustrate hierarchies, cycles, relationships and data processes.
Sorting and Filtering	Improved Sorting and Filtering—can now sort by color and up to 64 levels.
Spell Checker Enhancements	Many new spell checker enhancements, including global settings.
Structured References	You can now use table column header names in formulas instead of cell references.
Super Tooltips	Provides contextual help and provides more information than traditional tooltips for items that need additional explanation.
Table Header Rows	Table header rows can be turned on or off.
Table Tools	Improved table tools allows you to create a table with a single click.
Themes	Allows you to apply preset formatting to cells, tables and other Excel elements.
Unlimited Formatting	Excel now supports unlimited formatting in the same workbook (previously, was 4,000 format types).
User Interface	Completely redesigned user interface stretches across the top of the screen and includes command tabs, command sets and contextual commands.
XML Format	Default Excel file format is now XML.

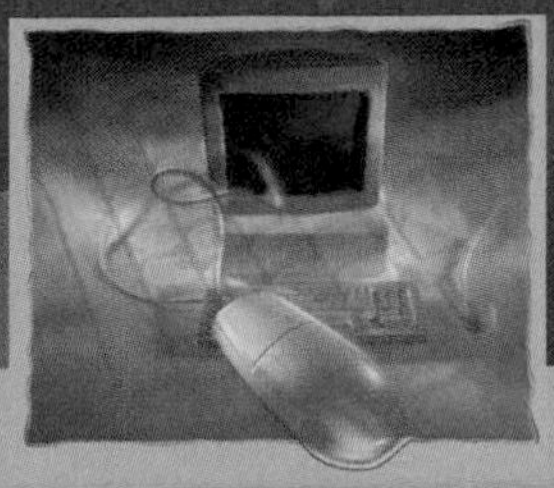

APPENDIX

E

What's New in PowerPoint 2007?

What's New	Description of Feature
Character Styles	New character styles include all caps, small caps, strikethrough, double-strikethrough, double underline and color underline. You can also add fills, lines, shadows, glow, kerning and 3-D effects to your text.
Color Schemes	New color schemes and accent colors to control the appearance of text and background.
Dialog Launchers	Displays the traditional style dialog boxes by clicking on the dialog launcher in the lower-right hand corner of a command set.
Effects	You can now add effects such as shadow, glow, soft edges, warp, bevel, 3-D rotation, etc to your PowerPoint objects.
File Menu	The new Microsoft Office System logo button now indicated where the previous File menu resides.
Galleries	When selecting a command with a downward pointing arrow, an options palette appears allowing you to see and change color combination, formatting, color scheme, etc.
Live Preview	Allows you to temporarily preview an effect before you apply it.
Multiple Slide Master Sets	You can now have multiple slide master sets with custom slide layouts for different slide topics.
Personal Information	You can now easily find and remove hidden metadata and personal information from your PowerPoint files.
Presenter View	New Presenter View allows you to run your presentation from one monitor while your audience views it on a second monitor.
Professional Templates	PowerPoint includes a collection of professionally designed templates that you can use and modify for your own needs.
Quick Access Toolbar	Located to the right of the File menu, the Quick Access Toolbar allows you to add tools you use regularly. The default tools are Save, Undo, and Redo.
Quick Styles	Allows you now to preview a number of styles before applying them to your document. Quick Styles also help you create professional looking tables and charts.
Redesigned Help System	Completely redesigned Help dialog box.
Security	New security features include hiding the author's name, ensuring that all comments have been deleted and restricting who can make changes to the presentation document.
Slide Themes	PowerPoint 2007 comes with a selection of predefined themes (20 in all) that you can apply to your slides with one click of the mouse.
Smart Art Graphics	Allows you to create quick diagrams that illustrate hierarchies, cycles, relationships and data processes.
Spell Checker Enhancements	Many new spell checker enhancements, including global settings.

What's New	Description of Feature
Super Tooltips	Provides contextual help and provides more information than traditional tooltips for items that need additional explanation.
Table & Chart Enhancements	Redesigned tables and charts make them much easier to work with and edit.
Text Options	New text formatting features include text wrapping within a shape, text in columns or running vertically down a slide and paragraph rulers. You can also now select discontinuous text.
User Interface	Completely redesigned user interface stretches across the top of the screen and includes command tabs, command sets and contextual commands.
View Controls	New View controls include commands formerly listed under the Windows or View menus.
XML Format	Default PowerPoint file format is now XML.

APPENDIX

What's New in Access 2007?

What's New	Description of Feature
Attachment Data Type	New attachment data type allows you to attach other types of files to your database fields.
Calendar Button	You can click the new Calendar button to quickly choose dates.
Collecting Data by E-mail	You can now send forms by e-mail from Access to gather information. The form responses are then added to the appropriate table in your database when it arrives in your Inbox.
Data Type	Automatic data type detection is added to Access 2007.
Dialog Launchers	Displays the traditional style dialog boxes by clicking on the dialog launcher in the lower-right hand corner of a command set.
Enhanced Filtering	Several new filtering tools make filtering data quick and easy.
Field Templates	Access now provides templates for individual fields in a table.
File Menu	The new Microsoft Office System logo button now indicated where the previous File menu resides.
Galleries	When selecting a command with a downward pointing arrow, an options palette appears allowing you to see and change color combination, formatting, color scheme, etc.
Getting Started Window	Offers a library of pre-build database solutions that can get you to work quickly.
Greenbar type rows	Access 2007 allows you to add alternating row color to your tables.
Home Window	Provides a summary of the data in your database.
Importing and Exporting	You can save frequently used import and export routines for reuse.
Improved Field Insertion	Now you can quickly insert fields by simply typing a new value in a column in the datasheet.
Key Tips	Allow you to toggle on the display of keyboard shortcuts using your keyboard. Previous keyboard shortcuts still work in Office 2007.
Live Preview	Allows you to temporarily preview an effect before you apply it.
Multivalued Fields	You can now create fields that hold multiple values.
Navigation Pane	Located on the left edge of the database window, the Navigation Pane gives you quick access to all of your database objects.
New Report and Form Views	The new Layout View makes creating forms and reports in Access 2007 much easier.
Professional Templates	Access includes a collection of professionally designed templates that you can use and modify for your own needs.
Quick Access Toolbar	Located to the right of the File menu, the Quick Access Toolbar allows you to add tools you use regularly. The default tools are Save, Undo, Redo and print.

What's New	Description of Feature
Redesigned Help System	Completely redesigned Help dialog box.
Report View	New Report View allows you to browse records without having to display in Print Preview view.
Rich Text in Memo Fields	Rich text in memo fields allows you to change formatting of memo fields such as font size, color and type, adding bullets or numbering, etc.
Security	A security warning will let you know if a database contains a macro, add-in or ActiveX control that was created by someone not on your Trusted Publishers list.
Split Form View	You can now view your form in single form view and datasheet view in the same window.
Super Tooltips	Provides contextual help and provides more information than traditional tooltips for items that need additional explanation.
Tabbed Windows	When you open a table, query, report or form, each item becomes a tabbed window in the display, allowing you to quickly move among opened items.
Themes	Access 2007 includes 25 new themes that you can add.
Total Row in Datasheet	You can now apply aggregate functions such as sum, count, average, minimum, standard deviation, or variance to your columns in datasheet view.
User Interface	Completely redesigned user interface stretches across the top of the screen and includes command tabs, command sets and contextual commands.
View Controls	New View controls include commands formerly listed under the Windows or View menus.
XML Format	Default Access database file format is now XML.

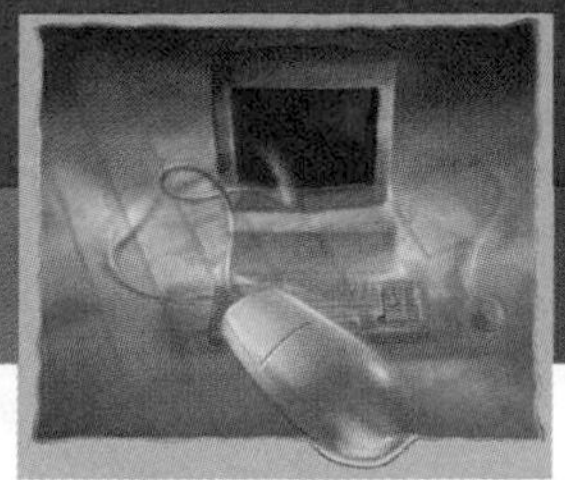

Index

C

D

E

T

Y

Z